914.304
GER
1-25

CRITICAL ACCLAIM FOR THE BERKELEY GUIDES

"[The Berkeley Guides are] brimming with useful information for the low-budget traveler — material delivered in a fresh, funny, and often irreverent way."
—The Philadelphia Inquirer

"...hip, blunt and lively...these Cal students boogie down and tell you where to sleep in a cowboy bunkhouse, get a tattoo and eat cheap meals cooked by aspiring chefs."
—Atlanta Journal Constitution

"...Harvard hasn't yet met 'On the Loose's' pledge to plant two trees in Costa Rica for every one felled to print its books — a promise that, given the true grit of these guides, might well mean a big new forest in Central America."
—Newsweek

"[The Berkeley Guides] offer straight dirt on everything from hostels to look for and beaches to avoid to museums least likely to attract your parents...they're fresher than Harvard's 'Let's Go' series."
—Seventeen

"The books are full of often-amusing tips written in a youth-tinged conversational style."
—The Orlando Sentinel

"So well-organized and well-written that I'm almost willing to forgive the recycled paper and soy-based ink."
—P.J. O'Rourke

"These guys go to great lengths to point out safe attractions and routes for women traveling alone, minorities and gays. If only this kind of caution weren't necessary. But I'm glad someone finally thought of it."
—Sassy

"The very-hip Berkeley Guides look like a sure-fire hit for students and adventurous travelers of all ages. This is real budget travel stuff, with the emphasis on meeting new places head on, up close and personal....this series is going to go places."
—The Hartford Courant

"The guides make for fun and enlightening reading."
—The Los Angeles Times

"The new On the Loose guides are more comprehensive, informative and witty than 'Let's Go'."
—Glamour

GW00502440

the BERKELEY guides

THE BUDGET TRAVELER'S HANDBOOK

GERMANY 1994

ON THE LOOSE

WRITTEN BY BERKELEY STUDENTS IN COOPERATION WITH THE ASSOCIATED STUDENTS OF THE UNIVERSITY OF CALIFORNIA

COPYRIGHT © 1993
BY FODOR'S TRAVEL PUBLICATIONS, INC.

The Berkeley Guides is a registered trademark of Fodor's Travel Publications, Inc.

All rights reserved under International and Pan-American Copyright Conventions. Published in the United States by Fodor's Travel Publications, Inc., a subsidiary of Random House, Inc., New York, and simultaneously in Canada by Random House of Canada Limited, Toronto. Distributed by Random House, Inc., New York.

No maps, illustrations, or other portions of this book may be reproduced in any form without written permission from the publisher.

ISBN 0-679-02443-3

First Edition

GERMANY ON THE LOOSE

Editor: Karyn Krause
Assistant Editors: Nina Goldschlager, Melanie Monteverde
Contributing Editors: Linda Cathryn-Everstz, Scott McNeely, Shelly Smith
Project Manager: David DeGusta
Production Editor: Linda K. Schmidt
Map Editors: Robert Blake, Marcy Pritchard
Executive Editor: Andrew Barbour
Creative Director: Fabrizio LaRocca
Cartographers: David Lindroth; Eureka Cartography
Text Design: Tigist Getachew
Cover Design and Illustration: Rico Lins

SPECIAL SALES

The Berkeley Guides and all Fodor's Travel Publications are available at special discounts for bulk purchases for sales promotions or premiums. Special editions, including personalized covers, excerpts of existing guides, and corporate imprints, can be created in large quantities for special needs. For more information, contact your local bookseller or write to Special Markets, Fodor's Travel Publications, 201 East 50th Street, New York, NY 10022. Inquiries from Canada should be directed to your local Canadian bookseller or sent to Random House of Canada, Ltd., Marketing Department, 1265 Aerowood Drive, Mississauga, Ontario L4W 1B9. Inquiries from the United Kingdom should be sent to Fodor's Travel Publications, 20 Vauxhall Bridge Road, London, England SW1V 2SA.

MANUFACTURED IN THE UNITED STATES OF AMERICA
10 9 8 7 6 5 4 3 2 1

Contents

What the Berkeley Guides Are All About

**Last year, a motley collection of Berkeley students launched *The Berkeley* ***Guides*, a new series of budget guidebooks. We wrote the books because, like thousands of travelers, we had grown tired of the outdated information served up unblinkingly each year in other budget guides. We began by covering Eastern Europe, Mexico, California, and the Pacific Northwest and Alaska. In researching the guides, our writers slept in whorehouses in Mexican border towns, landed bush planes above the Arctic Circle, and milked cows in Romania in exchange for precious food. This year was no different. While working on our new guides, gutsy student writers weathered guerrilla attacks in the Guatemalan Highlands, police shakedowns in Britain, and racist skinheads in Germany. The result is five new guidebooks, covering Central America, France, Germany, San Francisco, and Great Britain and Ireland, as well as complete updates of the first guides. And in every book, we're brutally honest about what we've found; if a place sucks, we say so and recommend somewhere else.

But most of all, these guides are for travelers who want to see more than just the main sights. We find out what the locals do for fun, where they go to eat, play, or just hang out. Most guidebooks lead you down the tourist trail, ignoring important local issues, events, and culture. In *The Berkeley Guides* we give you the information you need to understand what's going on around you, whether it's the rise of the neo-Nazi movement or the drastic economic situation in eastern Germany.

It's one of life's weird truisms that the more cheaply you travel, the more you usually experience. You're bound to experience a lot with *The Berkeley Guides*, because we believe in stretching a dollar a long, long way. You won't find much in our guides about the style of curtains in a hotel room or how a restaurant prepares its duck à l'orange; instead, we tell you if a place is cheap, clean (no bugs), and worth your money.

Many of us are Californians, so it's not surprising that we emphasize the outdoors in these guides, including lots of info about hiking and tips on protecting the environment. To further minimize our impact on the environment, we print our books on recycled paper using soy-based inks, and we plant two trees for every one we use. Coming from a community as diverse as Berkeley, we also wanted our books to be useful to *everyone*, so we tell you if a place is wheelchair-accessible; where people of color may encounter discrimination; provide resources for gay and lesbian travelers; and recognize the needs of women travelers.

We've done our best to make sure the information in *The Berkeley Guides* is accurate, but the world changes: Prices go up, places go out of business, and museums close for renovation. Call ahead when it's really important. These books are brand new, and we would really appreciate some feedback. Tell us about your latest find, a new scam, whatever—we want to hear about it. Write to the editors at 505 Eshleman Hall, University of California, Berkeley, CA 94720.

Thanks to You

Hundreds of people helped us put together *The Berkeley Guide to Germany*; some are listed below, but many others—whom our writers met briefly in Jugendherbergen, train stations, and beer halls—also pitched in. We'd like you to help us update this guide by giving us feedback from the road. Drop us a line—a postcard, a scrawled note on a piece of toilet paper, whatever—and we'll be happy to acknowledge your contribution. Our address is 505 Eshleman Hall, University of California, Berkeley, CA 94720.

Special thanks go to Silke Allroggen (Heidelberg); Professor Margaret Andersen (Berkeley, California); the Bagel Society (Ft. Collins, Colorado); Johnny "The Mad Hungarian" Balazs (Hungary); Antje, Horst and Claudia Böhmer (Hamburg); Dr. Michael Bernstein (Ann Arbor, Michigan); William "Will E." Bold (Washington, DC); Julia "B" Brasser (Oakland, California); Debbie Crowley (Berlin); Enno Dreppenstedt (Hamburg); Meka Dunivin (Saratoga, New York); Bruno Fleurquin (Paris); Hanna Godowa (Poznań, Poland); Michael "Piggy" Grishaver (Worms); Judith Heine (Hannover); Bjoern Hodler (Bisingen); Harold Lee Holden (New York, New York); Stefan Hornauer (Frankfurt); Herr and Frau Jungkunz (Mosbach); Angela Kalb (Bad Godesberg); Frau Kraus (Frankfurt); R. Kae Lesinski (Koblenz); Ian McLaughlin (Santa Rosa, California); Jefferey "Richard" Mercer (Dortmund); Professor Adrienne Miller (Berkeley, California); Dominador and Sarah Monteverde (Hillsborough, California); Bettina Mursch (Köln); Wolfgang Nadvornik (Waldkraiburg); Michael Nowak (Frankfurt); Steven "Grumpus" Olsen (San Francisco, California); David and Mabel Poon (Layfayette, California); Edouardo Raccah (Sao Paulo, Brazil); Frau and Herr Reimann (Wetzlar); Hugh G. Retshin (Düsseldorf); Herbie and Ellen Ruderman (Encino, California); Nicole Sakoun (Paris); Kregg Charles Strehorn (Poondorf); the Wilken family (Ft. Collins, Colorado, and Barbados); Jo Toomey and Mark Watkin (Dublin, Ireland); Jess Lawrence Weinstein (Brüderen); Thomas, Elizabeth, and Peter Zervas (Köln); and Zivi's at the Frankfurt youth hostel (Frankfurt).

Among the many organizations that lent a hand, we'd especially like to thank Herb Libbs at Deutsche Bundesbahn; Lisa Fahringer and Gerd Schmidt of the German National Tourist Office, Los Angeles, California; the Hannover French Club (Germany); the brewers of Kölsch beer; and the ever-helpful Joseph Zucker of Lufthansa (Los Angeles, California).

As students, we're familiar with low-budget travel. But when it came to cartography, page design, production, and assorted technobabble, we needed some help. Luckily, some real publishing pros at Fodor's in New York were there to give us a hand. For their time and effort, we'd like to thank Linda Schmidt, Ellen Browne, Bob Blake, David Low, Marcy Pritchard, and Kristen Perrault.

Berkeley Bios

The Writers

Behind every restaurant blurb, lodging review, and introduction in this book lurks a student writer. You might recognize the type—perpetually short on time, money, and clean underwear. Nine Berkeley students spent their summer traveling around Germany, researching and writing *The Berkeley Guide to Germany.* Back in Berkeley, a three-woman editorial team whipped the manuscript into shape.

Christy Camille Collins, better known as CiCi, had a blast cruising through Hessen—even though she ended up staying in certain places longer than expected. In Wetzlar, for example, she met Frau Reimann at the train station and ended up getting a guided tour of the city as well as lunch at her house, which turned out to be the historic Supreme Court building. In Frankfurt she made friends with some German guys doing their social-service work at the youth hostel. From them, she got all kinds of great information on Frankfurt and a home base to boot. Back in Berkeley, CiCi is finishing her majors in mass communications and French.

Armed with just enough German to order another beer, **Peter Edwards** landed in Berlin and immediately hooked up with a group of East Africans, who had mistaken him for a compatriot. As an African-American, Pete heard countless warnings about neo-Nazis and saw offensive graffiti everywhere. Still, he remarks, "I found the people very warm, though a little overcurious toward me. In Halle, a family opened their home for me to stay after just meeting me on the street. The father even apologized for the lack of tourist materials in English, saying that perhaps I was the first American in the town since 1945!" Before coming to U.C. Berkeley as a graduate student in English, Pete lived and worked in Poland for two years and often traveled to Berlin.

Les Kruger, a liberal Jewish vegetarian, often felt like the antithesis of the German Role Model. Hanging out in the Neckar Valley, with its natural beauty and ancient castles, cheered him up: "You just know those castles have all kinds of stories and history wrapped up in them." One German was puzzled by Les's fondness for historic buildings. "They're just a bunch of old stones," shrugged the modern fellow. A recent graduate in political science, Les is now updating *The Berkeley Guide to California.*

Ann McDevitt survived being locked into her train compartment by an overprotective station attendant to write the Franconia and Saxony chapters. Ann is currently working toward her master's degree in Slavic languages.

Scott McNeely, after covering the whole of Ireland, was prevailed upon to write the Thuringia chapter for the Germany book. Unwilling to leave his motorcycle behind, he drove from Ireland to Germany in one epic ride. He began to respect communist engineering just a little after getting passed on the Autobahn by junky little Trabants.

Geraldine Poon had a hellish introduction to travel writing, spending her first 29 hours on planes, trains, and automobiles to reach Ludwigslust in northern Germany. Upon arrival, she discovered all the hotels were way out of her budget, and ended up crashing on a patch of grass near the train station. Being the liberated woman she is, Geraldine started to cry. Before she drowned in self-pity, some young dudes offered her cigarettes and beer. She ended up going to a bar with them and was able to stay at their apartment for the evening. Geraldine had further misadventures in the course of her travels through Mecklenburg-Vorpommern, Schleswig-Holstein, and Hamburg—she got her ass fried on a nude beach, was picked up by a 14-year-old boy (pretending he was 17) who toyed with her emotions, and spent a very smelly night in a tiny barn with 20 other backpackers and about 20,000 empty beer cans. The trip was a homecoming of sorts for Geraldine, who had spent a year in Hamburg as an exchange student.

Adam Ruderman wrote the chapters on the Rhine and Mosel valleys and Bonn, Köln, and Düsseldorf. An avid soccer player, Adam found that the American style of play didn't fly with the Germans. "Surprisingly enough, they don't play as rough as we do. When I bumped some guy during a pickup game they thought I was trying to start a fight," he reported. Being Jewish, he says, added another dimension to the trip. "A lot of the young Germans I hung out with had never really known a Jew, and it was interesting to see how they reacted."

Linda Shing soon figured out how to deal with German intimidation. "Traveling in Germany was like going to New York without knowing its reputation as a get-out-of-my-face kind of place," she wrote. "But now when people are curt and rude, I don't just stand there gaping; I screw up my face and shout back. It really works. They like you more—one guy even smiled and was really nice after I chewed him out!" Despite getting in a fight with a nun (something about a curfew, American women, and morals), Linda did have fun covering Munich and Bavaria. "If you don't think small towns party, you haven't been to Mittenwald during its once-every-five-years celebration. Everyone was dressed up—even the little kids were clad from head to toe in Bavarian garb—and they were all dancing and drinking in the streets."

Oliver Wilken's travel-writing career began in a Berkeley café, where he met a stunningly beautiful woman who had written for *The Berkeley Guides* the previous year. All he could think of to string out the conversation was to ask her questions about her literary adventures. Long after he'd lost track of her, he still remembered the job, eventually signing on for a stint of his own. If he'd known that he would spend an entire summer tramping around France, in addition to writing the Lower Saxony chapter for the Germany book, perhaps he would have stayed in his café. Then again, he did find time to down large amounts of good European bread, cheese, coffee, and beer.

The Editors

Of all the editors at the Berkeley Guides, **Karyn Krause** had the snazziest computer (her very own Macintosh Powerbook) and one of the toughest assignments: Edit a guide to a country going through major changes. After finishing up her interdisciplinary-studies major, Karyn headed off to update the Hungary chapter of *The Berkeley Guide to Eastern Europe.*

Assistant Editor **Nina Goldschlager** jumped at the opportunity to put her English major to work as an editor. She is currently getting her master's degree in science journalism at Boston University, and plans to work as a science editor.

In between battles with the German language, Assistant Editor **Melanie Monteverde** established herself as the office Balderdash champion. She is an environmental-science major and recycles even when nobody is looking.

Linda-Catherine Everstz helped plan and edit the book before leaving to accept a fellowship at the Ford Foundation in New York. She lived in Germany for eight years and is now working toward her doctorate in education.

Introduction

By Herbert Grieshop

Every German can tell you where he or she was on the night of November 9, 1989, when the news spread that the Berlin Wall was open. I remember sitting in front of our TV with my friends, drinking champagne and watching speechless, stunned, and happy as young Berliners climbed up the wall and cheered to the crowd. It is one of those events that, like the assassination of John F. Kennedy, is permanently branded on the memory of a nation.

The euphoric mood that prevailed directly after the fall of the Berlin Wall, however, has vanished. Three years after the country was officially reunified, on October 3, 1990, emotions about unification, especially among Easterners, are mixed. Whereas the political and bureaucratic structures of West Germany were quickly introduced into the former East Germany, the economic and psychological gap has yet to be overcome. For the average West German, unification has meant an increased tax burden, as state resources are siphoned off to support and modernize eastern Germany. For East Germans, nearly every aspect of their lives has changed. People are still happy about their newly won political freedom, but there remains a lot of anger over the past. Moreover, unification has meant a huge surge in unemployment, and many East Germans, long used to a cradle-to-grave welfare system (where everyone was guaranteed a job), are struggling to cope with the demands of a free-market economy. The number of homeless in both East and West has increased considerably, and panhandlers are now a common sight in the bigger cities.

Herbert Grieshop is a doctoral student in comparative literature in Berlin. A German citizen, he recently spent some time doing research at U.C. Berkeley.

For travelers, unification means easy access to a part of Germany that is in many ways more "German" than the rest of the country. A trip to the East German countryside is not only a trip to the core of Prussia, the most powerful and important of the German states of the 19th century, but also a trip into Germany's past. Although many changes have taken place over the last three years, some of the smaller towns look as if time has stood still for the last 60 years: Cobbled streets are lined with lime trees, wrought-iron fences surround ramshackle buildings, and old-fashioned ads push products that no longer exist. Sadly, urban planners ruined the outskirts of many towns with high rises that look even uglier and shabbier than their Western counterparts. But most of the historic centers—if not destroyed by the war—remain untouched.

Traveling through Germany you will find that the people in the countryside still look very "German," whereas you will see lots of "foreign" faces in cities like Berlin, Frankfurt, and Munich. Whether they want to or not, Germans have to face the phenomenon of an increasingly multicultural population. "Foreigners" today comprise fully 8% of Germany's population of 78 million. Most of these were recruited from southern and southeastern Europe during the economic booms of the '60s and early '70s. In terms of Turkish population, Berlin is the third-largest city after Istanbul and Ankara.

As Germany's economy has soured and the social costs of reunification have soared, some Germans have become increasingly hostile to the presence of these minorities, whom they accuse of stealing jobs. Over the last two years, gangs of neo-Nazi skinheads have attacked foreign-worker hostels, Turkish families, and other minorities (for more information, *see* Chapter 1). This rising anti-immigrant sentiment has led the government to tighten the asylum laws, which had been the most liberal in Europe. Through the years, hundreds of thousands of immigrants have sought asylum in Germany, flooding in from Africa, the Middle East, and former Eastern-bloc countries. Critics of the government assert that, by changing the asylum laws, the government has caved in to the demands of the radical right while doing little to condemn the violence against minorities.

One issue that causes much concern among Easterners is the claims of homeowners whose property was confiscated by the state when they fled East Germany and who now want it back. Kleinmachow, a seemingly tranquil village near Berlin, is a good example of the upheaval resulting from unification: More than one third of its inhabitants face eviction from houses in which they've lived for decades.

Regardless of the desires of the rabid right, though, multiculturalism is here to stay. Nowadays, the fast food of choice in Germany is as likely to be a Döner Kebab (a Turkish dish of grilled lamb wrapped in flat bread) as a bratwurst, and in many towns travelers can take their pick from Chinese, Greek, and Italian restaurants. At the same time, Germany's traditional folk culture is on the wane; regional dresses have disappeared from daily life almost everywhere—Bavarian lederhosen and dirndl are among the few exceptions. The big cities still have their traditional funfairs like Hamburg's *Dom*, Stuttgart's *Cannstatter Wiesn*, and Munich's *Oktoberfest*, but to get an impression of less commercialized traditions you now have to go to the countryside. In Germany's rural villages you will still find an incredible variety of New Year's celebrations, Easter ceremonies, May feasts, and fairs featuring shooting matches (Schützenfeste). A simple, cheap, and delightful pleasure is the Easter fires ("Osterfeuer") held in villages all over Germany. Originally intended to chase the ghosts of winter away, these ceremonies were later turned into a Christian celebration of Easter. The village people gather around the huge fire, often a local band plays, and you have beer and bratwurst while staring into the flames. In hilly regions like Hessen, these fires are often lighted on top of a hill, so that you can see five or more fires simultaneously.

Increasingly, though, German folk traditions are becoming the domain of tourist villages and kitsch culture. Today, particularly in the big cities, there is a cultural backlash reminiscent of the heady days of the Weimar Republic. "When I stayed in Vienna I discovered culture," one friend told me. "In Berlin I discovered counter-culture." No other words can better sum up one of the most interesting phenomena of the last 20 years in Germany: the emergence of a broad and diverse "Alternativkultur," with Berlin as its undisputed capital. A quick look at one of the bigger cities' local magazines provides you with an idea of what this alternative culture is about: "WGs" (an abbreviation for *Wohngemeinschaften*, communities of people who share housing and living) look for politically correct roommates; environmental and left-wing political groups extend invitations to their meetings; drama-therapy groups offer healing through action; body therapists offer healing through massage; men's peer groups want to explore men's emotional lives; Zen-based meditations or aura readings promise to establish inner balance; and the "lonely hearts" pages list a huge number of gay ads and coming-out groups. We're talking California with a German accent.

Germans, who were famous for being workaholics, are now champions of leisure. The average German worker has a 38-hour week, six weeks of annual vacation, plus 12 national holidays. And the 35-hour week is already in sight.

Today, environmental thinking is probably more popular in Germany than in any other country and has been embraced by all the major political parties. No environmental cause has done more to raise awareness and prompt stricter laws than *Waldsterben*, literally "Forest Death"; more than one third of Germany's beloved forests are dying because of industrial pollution. The environmentally correct German—and there are lots of them—buys drinks only in returnable bottles, recycles everything, and brings his own backpack to the supermarket. (Often, you get plastic bags only on request and for an additional fee.)

The issue of pollution received even more attention after unification, when it became obvious that lax controls and the use of obsolete technology over the last 40 years had severely contaminated broad swaths of East Germany's industrial regions. Although many of the biggest polluters have been closed, the air quality in East German cities is still not great. In winter especially, the stench of burning brown coal fills your nose and mouth.

An area where many Germans are not prepared to make environmental sacrifices is the automobile. The German highways are notorious for their endless *Staus* (traffic jams) during the summer vacation, and there is no *Fahrvergnügen* at all if you are trapped in one of them for hours. The highways are even more (in)famous for speed maniacs who like to show that their cars can really drive more than 200 kilometers per hour. With lights on bright and nearly touching your bumper, they aggressively signal that they want to pass. Proposals to introduce a speed limit stir up emotions easily as intense as those aroused by environmental problems. When the Berlin senate tried to introduce a speed limit for part of its city highway, thousands of furious Berliners blocked the roads for hours.

Most of my American friends who have spent some time in Germany complain about German rudeness, whether behind the steering wheel, in shops, or in restaurants—almost any social setting, in fact. Germans display little of the outgoing friendliness of Americans, and, as a result, it can be difficult for visitors to make friends. Don't be surprised if you go to parties and nobody introduces him- or herself. You might talk to people for two hours and never find out their names. That is normal. It is also normal to be very critical. Don't praise the nice decoration, the great food, or the music too much—as an American, you will be automatically classified as superficially friendly. Be nasty instead and complain about everything. It sounds weird, but you will make friends easily that way.

BELGIUM
LUX.
FRANCE
SWITZERLAND
AUSTRIA
CZECH REPUBLIC
Aachen
Bonn
Koblenz
Rhine
Mosel
Trier
Marburg
Giessen
Alsfeld
Fulda
Bad Hersfeld
Eisenach
Meiningen
Suhl
Saalfeld
Zwickau
Chemnitz
Plauen
Coburg
Hof
Münchberg
Wiesbaden
Mainz
Bingen
Bad
Kreuznach
Frankfurt-am-Main
Darmstadt
Main
Würzburg
Bamberg
Bayreuth
Mannheim
Ludwigshafen
Heidelberg
Rothenburg-
o-d-Tauber
Fürth
Nürnberg
Speyer
Saarbrücken
Karlsruhe
Heilbronn
Stuttgart
Baden-Baden
Regensburg
Straubing
Deggendorf
Passau
Danube
Tübingen
Offenburg
Rhein
Ulm
Neu-Ulm
Augsburg
Isar
Munich
Inn
Biberach
Freiburg
Tuttlingen
Memmingen
Ravensburg
Wangen
Rheinfelden
Konstanz
Friedrichshafen
Garmisch-
Partenkirchen
Bad Reichenhall
Berchtesgaden

Germany

Germany

0 100 miles
0 150 km
Rail Lines
N
North Sea
Baltic Sea
DENMARK
HOLLAND
POLAND
FORMER BORDER BETWEEN EAST AND WEST GERMANY
Ems
Elbe
Oder
Neisse
Fehmarn
Rügen
Flensburg
Husum
Kiel
Neustadt
Rostock
Barth
Stralsund
Greifswald
Anklam
Wismar
Cuxhaven
Carolinensiel
Norden
Wilhelmshaven
Emden
Bremerhaven
Hamburg
Lübeck
Schwerin
Güstrow
Teterow
Neubrandenburg
Waren
Neustadt-Glewe
Ludwigslust
Pritzwalk
Neustrelitz
Bremen
Oldenburg
Perleberg
Wittenberge
Neuruppin
Oranienburg
Salzwedel
Meppen
Stendal
Berlin
Potsdam
Brandenburg
Wolfsburg
Hannover
Osnabrück
Rheine
Braunschweig
Frankfurt-an-der-Oder
Minden
Magdeburg
Bielefeld
Hildesheim
Münster
Halberstadt
Bernburg
Dessau
Wittenberg
Lübben
Cottbus
Bitterfeld
Essen
Dortmund
Hagen
Göttingen
Nordhausen
Halle
Leipzig
Görlitz

German Länder

German Länder

BASICS 1

By Les Kruger

If you've ever traveled with anyone before, you know the two types of people in the world: the planners and the nonplanners. You also know that travel brings out the very worst in both groups: Left to their own devices, the planners will have you ticking off sights on a cultural checklist, and the nonplanners will invariably miss the flight, the bus, and the point. One way or the other, you're going to end up wanting to bury a hatchet in the back of your companion's head. And that just won't do. This Basics chapter offers a middle ground, giving enough information to help you plan your trip without saddling you with an itinerary. From the minute you decide to take a trip, you're confronted with a seemingly endless series of choices: how to get there, where to stay, where to buy M&Ms. We don't want to make the choices for you, but we hope to provide you with the resources to help you make those all-important decisions yourself. If all else fails, we tell you where to buy the hatchet. Keep in mind that companies go out of business, prices inevitably go up, and, hey, we're only too human; as a Reagan official so eloquently said, "mistakes have been made."

Planning Your Trip

USEFUL ORGANIZATIONS

GOVERNMENT TOURIST OFFICES Aside from offering the usual glossy tourist brochures, state and local tourist offices can answer general questions about travel in their area or refer you to other organizations for more information. If writing for information, you may want to request brochures on specialized interests, such as boating, horseback riding, or bicycling, which may not be included in a generic information package.

➢ **IN THE UNITED STATES** • The **German National Tourist Office** (122 E. 42nd St., New York, NY 10168, tel. 212/661–7200; 11766 Wilshire Blvd., Suite 750, Los Angeles, CA 90025, tel. 310/575–9799; 104 S. Michigan Ave., Suite 600, Chicago, IL 60603–5978, tel. 312/332–3213) provides excellent maps and travel information.

➢ **IN CANADA** • The **German National Tourist Office** (175 Bloor St. E, N. Tower #604, Toronto, Ont. M4W 3R8, tel. 416/968–1570) has travel information and maps.

➢ **IN THE UNITED KINGDOM** • The **German National Tourist Office** (Nightingale House, 65 Curzon St., London W1Y 7PE, tel. 071/495–3990) can answer queries and provide maps and travel information.

BUDGET TRAVEL ORGANIZATIONS **Council on International Educational Exchange** (CIEE, 205 E. 42nd St., New York, NY 10017, tel. 212/661–1414) is a nonprofit organization dedicated to the pursuit of work, study, and travel abroad. Through its two subsidiaries, Council Travel and Council Charter, CIEE offers budget-travel services, including discounted airfares, rail passes, accommodations, and guidebooks. **Council Travel** is an international network of travel agencies that specialize in the diverse needs of students, youths, teachers, and indigent travelers. They also issue **Youth Hostel** cards, the **ISIC** (International Student Identity Card), the **IYC** (International Youth Card), and the **ITC** (International Teacher Card) (*see* Student I.D. Cards, *below*). At least 36 Council Travel offices serve the budget traveler in the United States (*see* box, *below*), and there are about a dozen overseas in Britain, France, Germany, and Japan. University travel centers may also carry CIEE's "Student Travel Catalog," a gold mine of travel tips (including work and study-abroad opportunities) that details CIEE's services and discounts. **Council Charter** (tel. 212/661–0311 or 800/223–7402) buys blocks of seats on commercial flights and sells them at a discount. Departure dates, rates, destinations, and seat availability change seasonally.

Educational Travel Center (ETC, 438 N. Francis St., Madison, WI 53703, tel. 608/256–5551) sells tickets to students and real people for low-cost flights (most departing from Chicago) within the continental United States and around the world.

Council Travel Offices

Arizona: Tempe, tel. 602/966–3544. California: Berkeley, tel. 510/848–8604; Davis, tel. 916/752–2285; La Jolla, tel. 619/452–0630; Long Beach, tel. 213/598–3338 or 714/527–7950; Los Angeles, tel. 310/208–3551; San Diego, tel. 619/270–6401; San Francisco, tel. 415/421–3473 or 415/566–6222; Sherman Oaks, tel. 818/905–5777. Colorado: Boulder, tel. 303/447–8101. Connecticut: New Haven, tel. 203/562–5335. District of Columbia: Washington, D.C., tel. 202/337–6464. Florida: Miami, tel. 305/670–9261. Georgia: Atlanta, tel. 404/377–9997. Illinois: Chicago, tel. 312/951-0585; Evanston, tel. 708/475–5070. Indiana: Bloomington, tel. 812/330–1600. Louisiana: New Orleans, tel. 504/866–1767. Massachusetts: Amherst, tel. 413/256–1261; Boston, tel. 617/266–1926 or 617/424–6665; Cambridge, tel. 617/497–1497 or 617/225–2555. Michigan: Ann Arbor, tel. 313/998–0200. Minnesota: Minneapolis, tel. 612/379–2323. New York: New York, tel. 212/661–1450, 212/666–4177, or 212/254–2525. North Carolina: Durham, tel. 919/286–4664. Ohio: Columbus, tel. 614/294–8696. Oregon: Portland, tel. 503/228–1900. Pennsylvania: Philadelphia, tel. 215/382–0343; Pittsburgh, tel. 412/683–1881. Rhode Island: Providence, tel. 401/331–5810. Texas: Austin, tel. 512/472-4931; Dallas, tel. 214/363–9941. Utah: Salt Lake City, tel. 801/582–5840. Washington: Seattle, tel. 206/632–2448 or 206/329–4567. Wisconsin: Milwaukee, tel. 414/332–4740. United Kingdom: London, tel. 071/437–7767. Germany: Düsseldorf, tel. 211/329–088.

ETC claims to beat student and charter fares. It also issues American Youth Hostel cards. For more details, request their free brochure, "Taking Off."

International Youth Hostel Federation (IYHF, 733 15th St. NW, Washington, DC 20005, tel. 202/783–6161) is the grandmammy of hostel associations, offering single-sex dorm-style beds ("couples" rooms and family accommodations are available at certain IYHF hostels) and kitchen facilities at more than 6,000 locations in 70 countries around the world. Membership in any national Youth Hostel Association (*see* Hostels, *below*) allows you to stay in any IYHF-affiliated hostel at member rates, which run about $7–$20 per night. Members also have priority if the hostel is full, and are eligible for discounts on rail and bus travel around the world. A one-year membership runs about $25 for adults (renewal $20) and $10 for those under 18. A one-night guest membership is about $3. Family memberships are $35, and a lifetime membership will set you back $250. Lightweight handbooks listing all current hostels, special offers, and opportunities (like budget cycling and hiking tours) are available from the national associations; Volume 1 covers Europe and the Mediterranean ($10.95).

Other associations aiding and abetting hostel goers include **American Youth Hostels** (AYH, 733 15th St. NW, Washington, DC 20005, tel. 202/783–6161), **Canadian Hostelling Association** (CHA, 1600 James Naismith Dr., Suite 608, Gloucester, Ontario K1B 5N4, tel. 613/748–5638), **Youth Hostel Association of England and Wales** (YHA, Trevelyan House, 8 St. Stephen's Hill, St. Albans, Herts. AL1 2DY, England, tel. 0727/55215), **Australian Youth Hostels Association** (YHA, Box 61, Strawberry Hills, Sydney 2012, New South Wales, tel. 02/212–1266), and **Youth Hostels Association of New Zealand** (YHA, Box 436, Christchurch 1, tel. 03-79–9970).

Student Travel Australia (STA) has 120 offices worldwide and offers low-price airfares to destinations around the globe. STA offers the **ISIC** and their own **STA Travel Card** (about $6) for recent graduates, which gets you some travel discounts (*see* Student I.D. Cards, *below*). Write or call one of the offices for a slew of free pamphlets on services and rates. North American West: 7204½ Melrose Ave., Los Angeles, CA 90046, tel. 213/937–5714. North American East: 17 E. 45th St., Suite 805, New York, NY 10017, tel. 212/986–9470 or 800/777–0112. Australia: 224 Faraday St., 1st floor, Carlton 3053, tel. 03-347–6911. New Zealand: 10 High St., Box 4156, Auckland, tel. 09-39–9723. United Kingdom: Priory House, 6 Wrights La., London W8 6TA, tel. 07-938–4711.

Travel CUTS (Canadian Universities Travel Service, Ltd., 187 College St., Toronto, Ontario M5T 1P7, tel. 416/979–2406) is a full-service travel agency that sells discount airline tickets to Canadian students, and issues the ISIC, IYC, and IYH cards. Their 25 offices are on or near college campuses. Call weekdays 9–5 for information and reservations.

HOW MUCH IT WILL COST

Let's face it, the days of Germany on $5, $10, and even $20 a day are a thing of the past. What you'll spend depends on how you want to travel and the level of comfort you require. If you get around by hitching, eat only food you buy at markets, and either camp or rough it every night, it's quite possible to travel in Germany on DM 35 ($25) a day. On the other hand if you use public transportation, take most of your meals in restaurants, and stay in hotel rooms with private showers, you can easily blow DM 90–DM 100 ($50–$55) a day. Compared to the cost of traveling in other European countries, Germany lies somewhere in the middle of the spectrum, leaning toward the expensive end. Traveling during the off season can save you a little money in resort towns and large cities, but otherwise prices in Germany stay nearly the same year-round.

LODGING The cheapest way to bed down in most German towns is to head directly to a youth hostel. Beds in hostel dorm rooms go for DM 14–DM 17 for those under 27 and DM 18.50–DM 22.50 if you're over 26. A significant step up in price, hotels and pensions offer more privacy and fewer rules. Cheap hotels run DM 25–DM 45 for singles and DM 50–DM 90 for doubles, depending on the size of the city and whether or not you want a private shower. For those who have come prepared, a cheaper option is to stay at one of the many campgrounds found in most rural towns and even in many big cities in Germany. A night's stay at a *Campingplatz* usually runs about DM 3.50–DM 6.50 per person, DM 3–DM 5 per tent, and DM 4–DM 6 per car. Rooms in *Privatzimmer* (private homes), most of which require a three-day minimum stay, will set you back DM 18–DM 45 per night, depending on the time of year and the size of the town. Student housing, when available, goes for DM 20–DM 40 a head.

FOOD One of the best ways to save money in Germany is to shop at local markets or grab a bite at one of the numerous wurst, *döner Kebab,* or schnitzel takeout joints; you'll blow about DM 5–DM 10, depending on whether you want a drink and some fries with that main course. Assembling a meal from various markets and shops is cheaper still. Bakery bread runs from DM 1.50 for a simple baguette to DM 4 for a hearty loaf of wheat bread, known as *Vollwertbrot,* packed with seeds, nuts, and other high-energy ingredients. Add to that 100 grams of cheap cheese, for about DM 2, and 100 grams of salami for DM 3.50. The going rate for a ½ liter of Coke is 80 pfennigs, a can of beer DM 1.20, and a cheap bottle of wine DM 3. A full meal in restaurants serving German fare, including a salad, entrée, and drink starts at DM 15. A better option is to seek out ethnic restaurants, especially Italian or Turkish, where you can eat a full meal for DM 10–DM 15. For better or worse—but probably the latter—you can also eat rather cheaply in American-style fast-food restaurants, most commonly McDonald's, for about DM 10.

TRANSPORT The cost of German public transportation varies widely. The quickest and most convenient option is, in most cases, train travel. Buses frequently cover only shorter routes, and taking the bus almost always means increasing the length of your trip (sometimes doubling your travel time); in most regions of the country, bus fares correspond with train fares, so you won't even save money for your troubles. Here are some sample one-way train fares: Berlin–Frankfurt, DM 125; Berlin–Munich, DM 133; Augsburg–Munich, DM 14.80; Leipzig–Frankfurt, DM 56. One of the best options for traveling cheaply in Germany is to utilize the ride-sharing offices known as *Mitfahrgelegenheit.* Located in most towns of any significance, these offices can hook you up with rides to many destinations in Germany (and sometimes around Europe) for your share of the fuel plus a small fee.

ENTERTAINMENT The cost of keeping yourself amused depends on your definition of entertainment. A 4/10-liter mug of beer in a local pub goes for DM 3–DM 4.50, although in big cities like Munich, prices of the sacred elixir may be higher. Most bars also serve wine for DM 3–DM 7 a glass, and some places offer mixed drinks, but at DM 7–DM 15 these will quickly eat up your cash reserves. Cover charges at clubs, discos, and live-music bars are DM 5–DM 15; drinks generally go for about the same price as they do in bars. Movies cost about DM 10. Theater prices vary; for example, tickets for a classical concert in a small town might start as low as DM 10, and an opera in Stuttgart's famous Staatstheater can cost DM 80 or more. To see big-name rock shows, usually held in huge open-air stadiums, you'll have to fork out DM 45–DM 65.

WHEN TO GO

The summer months bring crowds of *Ausländer* (foreigners) and local vacationers to Germany. Although school vacations are rotated in an attempt to quell the holiday crunch, this system is far from effective, and summer in Germany often means confronting long lines and harried tourist-information offices. Hostels, too, are inundated with school groups. Prices for food and especially lodging drop slightly during winter, but many places close for at least part of the season, and transportation in some areas, such as the Black Forest, becomes much more difficult. If you can, swing some free time in autumn or spring, the best seasons to explore Germany. In particular, traveling in May or October allows you to cash in on off-season prices while the weather is still decent and the streets are relatively free from camera-toting tourists.

CLIMATE The German climate defies generalization; the strength and length of the seasons vary widely across the country. Summers are usually dry and warm, bordering on uncomfortably hot in the south, but occasional cloudy and wet days should be expected. Nearly all of Germany sees snow in winter, but it's less common in the Harz mountains and southern Germany. Winters in northern Germany are infamously gray and dreary. The average daily highs and lows stack up as follows.

City	January High/Low	July High/Low
Berlin	36F/27F	76F/58F
	2C/-3C	24C/14C
Bonn	40F/32F	74F/57F
	4C/0C	23C/14C
Dresden	36F/25F	76F/56F
	2C/-4C	24C/13C
Frankfurt	39F/29F	77F/59F
	4C/-2C	25C/15C
Freiburg	40F/29F	76F/58F
	4C/-2C	24C/14C
Hamburg	36F/29F	72F/56F
	2C/-2C	22C/13C
Munich	35F/23F	74F/55F
	1C/-5C	23C/13C

PUBLIC HOLIDAYS To avoid being caught without money on bank holidays or without food when markets are closed, you should keep in mind the following national holidays, on which most businesses in Germany shut down: January 1 (New Year's Day), April 1 (Karfreitag, or Good Friday), April 3 (Oster Sonntag, or Easter Sunday), May 1 (Tag der Arbeit, or Worker's Day), May 12 (Himmelfahrt, or Ascension Day), May 22–23 (Pfingsten, or Whit Sunday and Monday), October 3 (Reunification Day), mid-November (Buß und Betentag, or Day of Repentance and Prayer), and December 25–26 (Christmas).

FESTIVALS Heaps of local festivals provide travelers with one of the most enjoyable ways to experience German culture. Outdoor theater festivals abound in town centers and castles in summer; wine festivals take place at the end of summer and beginning of autumn; and endless varieties of local fairs are held throughout the year. To find out more about these local festivals, contact the German National Tourist Office (*see* Useful Organizations, *above*) or see individual chapters in this book. What follows is a list of some of Germany's largest festivals:

January: Fasching, during which carnivals, parades, masked balls, street fairs, and other events take place, is one of the most important festivals in Germany. Lasting for up to three weeks in some areas and running through February, the often raucous activities reach a peak just before Ash Wednesday. The most colorful Fasching events take place in southwestern Germany, where participants from towns in the Black Forest and Swabian Jura dress in outrageous costumes and dance through the streets.

February: Internationale Filmfestspiele, featuring flicks from around the world in cinemas across the country, is Germany's Cannes.

March: Spring fairs in towns across Germany, including Münster, Hamburg, Nürnberg, Stuttgart, and Augsburg, welcome the arrival of spring.

July: A variety of **folk festivals** is held in and out of doors throughout the country in towns such as Krov, Wald-Michelbach, Waldshut-Tiengen, Würzburg, Geisenheim, Speyer, Lübeck, Karlsruhe, Düsseldorf, Oestrich-Winkel, and Paderhorn.

August: The **Heidelberger Schloßfestspiele** is the most renowned of the many open-air music-and-theater festivals that take place in Germany throughout the summer. Many of these festivals feature fireworks over the various castles at night. **Wine festivals,** where participants are encouraged to down more than their fair share of vino at DM 2–DM 5 per glass, take place throughout the Rhineland and much of southwest Germany.

September: Oktoberfest, Munich's world-famous beer-guzzling marathon, is easily the largest party of the year in Deutschland. In fact, along with internationally renowned ragers like Carnival in Brazil and Mardi Gras in New Orleans, Oktoberfest is one of the most happening parties anywhere on the planet, so plan ahead if you're up to the challenge.

November: St. Martin's Festival, with children's lantern processions, takes place throughout the Rhineland and Bavaria.

December: Christmas markets featuring local foods and handicrafts are held in many towns across the country. The most famous markets include those in Augsburg, Munich, Heidelberg, Hamburg, Nürnberg, Lübeck, Freiburg, Berlin, and Essen.

PASSPORTS AND VISAS

Visas are not required for U.S., Canadian, British, Australian, or New Zealand citizens for stays of up to three months. (For information on longer stays, *see* Working Abroad, *below*). However, all travelers need a passport. Hang onto your passport for dear life—you can't do anything (cross the border, check into accommodations, change money, etc.) without it.

OBTAINING A PASSPORT

➢ **U.S. CITIZENS** • First-time applicants, those whose passports were issued more than 12 years ago or before they were 16, those whose passports have been lost or stolen, and travelers between the ages of 13 and 17 (a parent must accompany them) must apply for a passport in person. Other renewals can be taken care of by mail. Apply at one of the 13 U.S. Passport Agency offices a minimum of five weeks ahead of your departure. For fastest processing, apply between August and December. It is possible to get a passport issued within five days of departure—if you manage to wade through a ton of red tape. Local county courthouses, many state and probate courts, and some post offices also accept passport applications.

The following items are required:

(1) A completed passport application (form DSP–11), available at courthouses, some post offices, and passport agencies.

(2) Proof of citizenship (certified copy of birth certificate, naturalization papers, or previous passport issued in the past 12 years).

(3) Proof of identity with your photograph and signature (for example, a valid driver's license, employee I.D. card, military I.D., student I.D.).

(4) Two recent, identical, 2"-square photographs (black-and-white or color head shot).

(5) A $55 application fee for a 10-year passport, $30 for those under 18 for a five-year passport. First-time applicants are also hit with a $10 surcharge. If you're paying cash, exact change is necessary; checks or money orders should be made out to Passport Services. For more information or an application, contact the Department of State

Office of Passport Services (tel. 202/647–0518), and dial your way through their message maze.

Those lucky enough to be able to renew their passports by mail must send to the nearest Passport Agency a completed Form DSP–82 (available from a Passport Agency); two recent, identical passport photos; their current passport (less than 12 years old); and a check or money order for $55 ($30 for those under 18). Renewals take three to four weeks.

➢ **CANADIAN CITIZENS** • Canadians should send a completed passport application (available at any post office or passport office) to the Bureau of Passports (Suite 215, W. Tower, Guy Favreau Complex, 200 René Lévesque Boulevard W., Montréal, Québec H2Z 1X4, tel. 514/283–2152). Include C$35; two recent, identical passport photographs; a guarantor (as specified on the application); and proof of Canadian citizenship (original birth certificate or other official document as specified). You can also apply in person at regional passport offices in many locations, including Edmonton, Halifax, Montréal, Toronto, Vancouver, and Winnipeg. Passports have a shelf life of five years and are not renewable. Processing takes about two weeks by mail and five working days for in-person applications.

➢ **U.K. CITIZENS** • Passport applications are available through travel agencies, main post offices, or one of six regional passport offices (in London, Liverpool, Peterborough, Belfast, Glasgow, and Newport). The application must be countersigned by your bank manager or a solicitor, barrister, doctor, clergyman, or justice of the peace who knows you personally. Send or drop off the completed form, two identical passport photos, and a £15 fee to a regional passport office (address is on the form). Passports are valid for 10 years (five years for those under 18) and take about four weeks to process.

➢ **AUSTRALIAN CITIZENS** • Australians must visit a post office or passport office to complete the passport-application process. A 10-year passport for those over 18 costs AUS$76, and the under-18 crowd can get a five-year passport for AUS$37. For more information, call toll-free in Australia 008/02–60–22 weekdays during working hours.

➢ **NEW ZEALAND CITIZENS** • You can pick up passport applications at any post office or consulate. Completed applications must be accompanied by proof of citizenship, two passport-size photos, and a letter from a friend confirming the applicant's identity. The fee is NZ$50 for a 10-year passport. Processing takes about three weeks.

LOST OR STOLEN PASSPORTS In case of mishap, report lost or stolen passports immediately to your nearest home embassy or consulate and to local police authorities. If you have a record of the information contained in your passport, the consular officer can probably cut some red tape and issue you a new one. As a precaution, make two photocopies of your passport identification page and leave one with a trusted person at home. Carry the other copy with you in a nook or cranny separate from your passport. The fee charged to replace a passport depends on your country of origin.

The U.S. embassy/consulate will issue a new passport only in emergencies. In nonemergency situations, the staff will affirm your affidavit swearing U.S. citizenship, and this paper will get you back to the United States. The British embassy or consulate requires a police report, any form of identification, and three passport-size photos. They will replace the passport in four working days. Canadian citizens face the same requirements as the Brits, but you must have a guarantor with you: someone who has known you for at least two years, lives within the jurisdiction of the consulate or embassy, and is a mayor, practicing lawyer, notary public, judge, magistrate, police officer, signing officer at a bank, medical doctor, or dentist. Since most travelers do not know anyone fitting this description, there is also the legal option of paying an officer of the consulate/embassy to be your guarantor—proving once again that throwing enough money at a problem usually makes it go away. A replacement passport usually takes five working days. New Zealand officials ask for two passport-size photos, and the Australians require three, but both can usually replace a passport in 24 hours.

STUDENT I.D. CARDS

Student identification cards are a must for the budget traveler in Germany. They provide access to discounts at museums, theaters, most tourist attractions, and even some restaurants and accommodations. I.D. from your local high school, college, or university will suffice in most situations, but the following cards may be useful, too. For details on ordering them, *see* Budget Travel Organizations, *above.*

The **International Student Identity Card (ISIC)** entitles students 12 years of age and over to special fares on local transportation, and discounts at museums, theaters, sports events, and many other attractions. If purchased in the United States, the $14 cost for the popular ISIC card also buys $3,000 in emergency medical coverage; limited hospital coverage; and access to a 24-hour international, toll-free hot line for assistance in medical, legal, and financial emergencies. In the United States, apply to CIEE or STA; in Canada, the ISIC is available for C$12 from Travel CUTS. In the United Kingdom, students with valid university I.D.s can purchase the ISIC at any student union or student-travel company. Applicants must submit a photo as well as proof of current full-time student status, age, and nationality.

The **STA Travel Card** is available to travelers age 35 and under for $6. With it, you'll gain access to discounted student fares and *Discount Counter,* a coupon book that offers dollars-off coupons for a limited number of subscribing businesses' services. Purchase the STA card *before* departing for Germany.

The **Youth International Educational Exchange Card (YIEE)** is issued to travelers (students and nonstudents) under age 26 by the Federation of International Youth Travel Organizations (FIYTO, 81 Islands Brugge, DK–2300 Copenhagen S, Denmark). It provides services and benefits similar to those given by the ISIC card, but travelers need not be students; they need only be under age 26. The card is available from CIEE or FIYTO.

MONEY

DEUTSCHE MARKS The German currency is the deutsche mark (DM), which is broken into 100 pfennigs. Around the time of reunification, new bills were printed and distributed, so you'll run into two kinds of DM 10, DM 20, DM 50, and DM 100 bills. The Germans also use plenty of coins, namely 1 pfennig, 2 pf., 5 pf., 10 pf., 50 pf., DM 1, DM 2, and DM 5 pieces. Be forewarned that there are two different DM 2 pieces, both the same size. Prices throughout this book are given in marks. At the time of publication, US$1 equalled DM 1.63; DM 1 equalled 63¢.

TRAVELING WITH MONEY Cash never goes out of style, but traveler's checks and a major credit card are usually the safest and most convenient way to pay for goods and services on the road. Depending on the length of your trip, strike a balance among these three forms of currency. Protect yourself by carrying cash in a money belt or "necklace" pouch (available at luggage or camping stores), and by keeping accurate records of traveler's checks' serial numbers, credit-card numbers, and an emergency number for reporting the cards' loss or theft. Carrying at least some cash (hard currency) is wise, since most budget establishments accept cash only, and changing traveler's checks outside urban areas can prove difficult. Bring about $100 (in as many single bills as possible) in cash; changing dollars will be easier, though more expensive, than cashing traveler's checks. Aside from panhandling, travelers may be able to replenish cash supplies at ATM machines (*see* Cash Machines, *below*), by cashing personal checks at an American Express office, or by having money sent to them while on the road (*see* Obtaining Money from Home, *below*).

TRAVELER'S CHECKS Traveler's checks may look like play money, but they work much better. They can be used for purchases in the same way as a personal check (always ask first), or they can be exchanged for cash at banks, some hotels, tourist offices, American Express offices, and currency-exchange offices. American Express checks are the most widely accepted; other brands are sometimes refused. Some banks and credit unions issue checks free to established customers, but most charge a 1%–2% commission. Members of the American Automobile Association (AAA) can purchase American Express traveler's checks from AAA commission-free.

By purchasing large denominations of traveler's checks ($100, for example) you will diminish the commissions most financial institutions in Germany charge for converting your checks into local currency. For example, post offices charge a DM 3 fee per check cashed. On the other hand, many establishments won't accept large-denomination checks, and, even when they do, breaking a large check for small purchases leaves you carrying too much cash.

American Express (tel. 800/221–7282) card members can order traveler's checks in U.S. dollars and deutsche marks by phone, free of charge (with a gold card) or for a 1% commission (with your basic green card). In three to five business days you'll receive your checks: Up to $1,000 can be ordered in a seven-day period. American Express also issues **Traveler's Cheques for Two**, which can be signed and used by you or your traveling companion. If you lose your checks or are ripped off, American Express can provide you with a speedy refund—often within 24 hours. At their Travel Services offices (about 1,500 around the world) you can usually buy and cash traveler's checks, write a personal check in exchange for traveler's checks, report lost or stolen checks, exchange foreign currency, and pick up mail. Ask for the "American Express Traveler's Companion," a handy directory of their offices, to find out more about services at different locations.

Citicorp (tel. 800/645–6556; outside U.S., 813/623–1709 collect) traveler's checks are available from Citibank and other banks worldwide in U.S. dollars and some foreign currencies. Plan ahead if you want checks in deutsche marks, since they must be special-ordered. For 45 days from date of check purchase, purchasers have access to the 24-hour International S.O.S. Assistance hot line, which provides referrals to English-speaking doctors, lawyers, and interpreters; assistance after loss or theft of travel documents; traveler's-check refund assistance; and an emergency message center.

MasterCard International (tel. 800/223–7373; outside U.S., 609/987–7300 collect; in Europe, 447/335–02–995 toll-free or 07/335–02–995 collect) traveler's checks, issued in U.S. dollars only, are offered through banks, credit unions, and foreign-exchange booths. Call for information about acceptance of their checks at your travel destination and for the local number to call in case of loss or theft.

The **Thomas Cook** brand of MasterCard traveler's check is available in U.S. dollars and deutsche marks. If purchased through a Thomas Cook Foreign Exchange office (formerly Deak International), there is no commission. For more info, contact MasterCard (*see above*).

Visa (tel. 800/227–6811 for refund-referral service; outside U.S., 415/574–7111 collect), as a sponsor of the '92 Olympics, boosted its name recognition and acceptance worldwide. When two giants in the traveler's-check universe (BankAmerica Corporation and Barclays) embarked on a joint venture, their baby was born as **Interpayment Visa Travelers Cheques,** which are imprinted with the name of the financial institution that sells the checks. Don't be fooled: You're getting Visa traveler's checks, widely accepted and available in at least 10 currencies.

➢ **LOST OR STOLEN CHECKS** • Unlike cash, traveler's checks, if lost or stolen, can be replaced or refunded *if* you keep the purchase agreement and a record of the checks' serial numbers. Common sense dictates that you keep the purchase agreement separate from your checks. Prudent travelers should give a copy of the purchase agreement and checks' serial numbers to their travel partner and/or someone back home. Most issuers of traveler's checks promise to refund or replace lost or stolen checks in 24 hours, but you can practically see them crossing their fingers behind their backs. If you are traveling in a remote area, expect the process to take longer. In a safe place—or several safe places—record the toll-free or collect telephone number to call in case of emergency (*see above*).

EXCHANGING MONEY Hunting down the best exchange rate can be time-consuming and, in the end, not all that profitable. Still, it's important to check the commission charge to avoid being gypped out of 8% of your capital. If you have traveler's checks, local offices of the issuer, such as American Express, often cash checks free of commission. Your next best bet, especially for cashing traveler's checks of large denominations, are local post offices, which charge DM 3 per check. Purchase some deutsche marks ($20–$50) from a bank at home before you go; you may not find an exchange office open when you arrive, or you may confront long lines at airport banks—particularly during peak times for international arrivals. Though their rates are usually not bad, most airport banks are open during daytime only.

OBTAINING MONEY FROM HOME Provided there is money at home to be had, there are at least five ways to get it:

(1) Have it sent through a large commercial bank that has a branch in the town where you're staying. Unless you have an account with that large bank, though, you'll have to go through your own bank, and the process will be slower and more expensive.

(2) If you're an American Express card holder, you can cash a personal check or a substitute counter check (as long as you know your personal bank-account details) at any American Express office in Germany for up to $1,000 ($2,500 for gold-card holders) every 21 days; the money is usually in traveler's checks rather than cash. There is a 1% commission on traveler's checks. An American Express MoneyGram can be a dream come true if you can convince someone back home to go to an **American Express Moneygram** agent (in American Express offices, bus stations, airports, and even some convenience stores), fill out the necessary forms, and transfer cash to replenish your empty wallet. Transactions must be made in increments of $50 and paid for with cash, MasterCard, Visa, or Optima. Fees vary according to the amount of money sent but average 8%–10%. You'll need to show I.D. when picking up the money, and you'll need to get the transaction reference number from your sender back home. Word is the money will be available in 15 minutes, but don't bet on it. For the American Express MoneyGram location nearest your home and the locations of offices in Germany, call 800/543–4080 (outside U.S., 303/980–3340 collect). **Visa** and **MasterCard** also give cash advances from many banks even in small towns. The commission for this handy-dandy service is a whopping 6½%.

(3) Have funds sent through **Western Union** (tel. 800/325–6000). Although this has a certain glamorous ring, it's prohibitively expensive. If you have MasterCard or Visa, you can have as much money sent as you have credit left on your card. Or have someone at home take cash, a certified cashier's check, or a healthy MasterCard or Visa to a Western Union office. The money will reach you in two business days but may not be available for several more hours or days, depending on the whim of the local authorities. Unlike money sent through American Express, Western Union transfers are available only in the local currency.

(4) In extreme emergencies (hospitalization, arrest, or something worse) there is one more way American citizens can receive money in Germany: by setting up a **Department of State Trust Fund** (this does not require adoption by the State Department). This service is available only in emergencies and involves a friend or family member

sending money to the Department of State, which then transfers the money to the U.S. embassy or consulate in the German city in which you're stranded. Once this account is established, you can send and receive money through Western Union, bank wire, or mail, all payable to the Department of State. For information, write to Overseas Citizens Services (CA/OCS/EMR, Room 4800, Department of State, 2201 C St. NW, Washington, DC 20520).

(5) Virtually all U.S. banks belong to a network of ATMs (automated-teller machines), which gobble up bank cards and spit out cash 24 hours a day in cities throughout the country and abroad. These bank substitutes are better in theory than practice; they may not always function or even exist outside big cities. To find out if there are any cash machines in a given city in Germany, call your bank's department of international banking. Since you pay a flat fee for each ATM transaction, you may want to withdraw a sizeable amount when you do the deed. If the transaction cannot be completed, chances are that the computer lines are busy (try to avoid Friday afternoon—rush hour for withdrawal action), and you'll just have to try again later.

To receive a card for an ATM system, you must apply at a bank and select a Personal Identification Number (PIN). A Visa or MasterCard can also be used to access cash through certain ATMs (provided you have a PIN for it), but the fees for this service are usually higher than bank-card fees. Also, a daily interest charge usually begins to accrue immediately on these credit-card "loans," even if monthly bills are paid up. Check with your bank for information on fees and on the daily limit for cash withdrawals.

Express Cash allows American Express card holders to withdraw up to $1,000 in a 21-day period from their personal checking accounts via ATMs worldwide. Gold-card holders can receive up to $2,500 in a 21-day period. Each transaction carries a 2% fee, with a minimum charge of $2 and a maximum of $6. Apply for a PIN and set up the linking of your accounts at least two weeks before departure. Call 800/CASH–NOW for an application.

CREDIT CARDS Visa and MasterCard (but not American Express) are commonly accepted at banks throughout Germany for withdrawing cash. Each bank seems to set its own limits on the amount of money you can withdraw and which cards it accepts; policies may even vary from branch to branch. Typically, the daily withdrawal limit is about $300. A small commission—no more than if you were exchanging traveler's checks—is charged. Expensive restaurants and hotels accept credit cards, most commonly Visa or MasterCard, as do car-rental agencies and ATMs—look for the card logo on windows. In short, credit cards are excellent backups and can be lifesavers in financial emergencies.

WHAT TO PACK

As little as possible. Besides the usual suspects—clothes, toiletries, camera, a Walkman, and your favorite pair of lederhosen—bring along a day pack or some type of smaller receptacle for stuff; it'll come in handy not only for day excursions but also for those towns where finding a place to sleep is a pain in the butt. You can check heavy, cumbersome bags at the train or bus station and just carry the essentials with you while you look for lodging. Germany gets plenty of rain all year round, so don't forget to bring something to protect yourself and your luggage. If you plan on traveling in winter, pack plenty of warm, fuzzy things to combat the often subfreezing temperatures and snow that inundate much of the country.

BEDDING If you're planning to stay primarily in hotels or pensions, you won't need to bring any bedding. Hostels require that you use a sleep sheet; you can bring your own or pay DM 4–DM 6 per night to rent one. Since some hostels strictly enforce the IYHF rule that guests use a sleep sheet and not a sleeping bag or regular sheet, it usually pays to invest in your own. Sleeping mats are essential for travelers thinking about roughing it on train-station floors or park benches. Sleeping bags usually take up a lot of luggage space, and you really won't need one if you plan to crash indoors; but if you're considering camping or roughing it you'll definitely want to bring one along. Prices for sleeping bags in Germany are about the same as those in the United States and the United Kingdom.

CLOTHING What clothes you bring really depends upon the time of year. In the summer, smart—and not terribly fashion-conscious—travelers will bring two outfits and learn to wash clothes by hand regularly. Keep in mind that artificial fabrics don't breathe and will make you hotter than you thought possible, so go with light cotton instead. Bring several T-shirts and one sweatshirt or sweater for cooler nights. The winter months get very cold, so you'll need several layers of clothes to keep warm, not just one bulky coat or sweater. A light wind- and water-resistant jacket over a warm sweater fend off most cool temperatures and take up less luggage space than heavy jackets. No matter what time of year you travel, socks and undies don't take up much room, so throw in a couple of extra pairs.

THE SLEEP SHEET DEFINED

Take a big sheet. Fold it down the middle the long way. Sew one short side and the long, open side. Turn inside out. Get inside. Sleep.

Shoes may be your best friend or worst foe: Packing a sturdy pair of walking shoes or hiking boots (break them in before your trip) and something more comfortable (probably sandals) you can slip into after a hard day of pounding the pavement allows you to switch off and give your tootsies a rest. Plastic sandals or thongs have the additional benefit of protecting feet on wet, frequently skanky hostel-shower floors and are also useful for camping and beach hopping.

In general, Germans don't frown on casual dress, and you can usually get away with jeans—even at the symphony. Remember that the clothes you bring will probably all be washed together with an unknown, strong detergent, so leave that new red underwear and white shirt at home.

TOILETRIES Toiletries are heavy and bulky, so leave as many of them at home as possible. What you do bring, seal tightly in a separate, waterproof bag; the pressure on airplanes can cause lids to pop off and create instant moisturizer slicks inside your luggage. Despite persistent rumors to the contrary, you'll find almost everything you need in Germany; however, portions of eastern Germany are a tad behind their western counterparts in modern-day toiletry technology, so if you are headed beyond the former Wall consider stocking up on essentials such as tampons. Bring some toilet paper with you, and have some in your pockets or day pack at all times. If you plan on doing any hiking or camping, bring insect repellent, sunscreen, and lip balm. Try Avon Skin so Soft bath oil—it repels bugs and attracts connoisseurs of cheap perfume. Another option is Green Ban's environmentally sound insect repellent: stinky, but good.

CONTRACEPTIVES Condoms *(Kondom or Präservativ)* are readily available throughout Germany. Avoid buying them from machines: They could be ancient or only for novelty use. *Apotheken* (pharmacies) and large grocery stores have the most reliable goods. Prescriptions for birth-control pills require a visit to the doctor.

LAUNDRY The last way you want to spend your long-awaited vacation is cleaning your soiled duds. With this in mind, consider taking along all the ingredients necessary to set up your very own launderette in any hotel or campground bathroom: a plastic bottle of liquid detergent or soap (powder doesn't break down as well), about 6 feet of clothesline (enough to tie to two stable objects), and some plastic clips (bobby pins or paper clips can substitute). In case of plugless sinks, stuff a sock or plastic bag in the drain. Be sure to bring an extra plastic bag or two for damp laundry and dirty clothes. If this just isn't your style, you can find a *Waschsalon* (laundromat) in most German towns. A load in a coin-op will cost DM 8–DM 10. Ten minutes in their dryers will set you back an additional DM 2–DM 3. Many laundromats require you to buy their soap, for another DM 2–DM 3.

MISCELLANEOUS Stuff you might not think to take but will be damn glad to have: (1) extra day pack (for valuables or short jaunts), (2) flashlight (good for electricity failures, and reading in the dark), (3) Walkman (entertainment for bus and train rides), (4) pocket knife (for cutting fruit, spreading cheese, removing splinters, and opening bottles), (5) fork and spoon (for meals on the road), (6) water bottle, (7) sunglasses, (8) several large zip-type plastic bags (for wet swimsuits, towels, leaky bottles, and stinky socks), (9) travel alarm clock (NOT!), (10) needle and small spool of thread (for extracting a little more life out of your tattered rags), (11) batteries, (12) string (for clotheslines and simple repairs), (13) a good book (one that you'll be able to trade with other travelers).

PROTECTING YOUR VALUABLES

Money belts may be dorky and bulky, but wouldn't you rather be embarrassed than broke? You'd be wise to carry all cash, traveler's checks, credit cards, plane tickets, and your passport in a pickpocket-proof place: front or inner pocket, a bag that fits underneath your clothes or even in your shoes. Neck pouches and money belts are sold in luggage and camping-supply stores. Fanny packs are safe if you keep the pack part in front of your body, safer still if your shirt or sweater hangs over the pack.

When is it safe to take your valuables off your body? Hostels and even hotel rooms are not necessarily safe; don't leave anything valuable out in the open. Keep what you cherish on your body even while you sleep. And it may go without saying, but we're gonna say it anyway: Never leave your pack unguarded, or with a total stranger, not even if you're planning to be gone only for a minute—it's not worth the risk. If you're carrying a bag with a strap (or a camera), sling it crosswise over your body, and try to keep your arm down over the bag in front of you. Back pockets are fine for maps, but don't keep a wallet there; more than your cheeks could get pinched.

CUSTOMS AND DUTIES

ARRIVING IN GERMANY Limitations on duty-free goods that can be brought into Germany include 2 liters of wine, 1 liter of hard alcohol, 200 cigarettes (if you're hassled, ask the customs official to count 'em individually), DM 70 worth of perfume, and gifts valued at no more than DM 115. Any goods that exceed these limits are subject to a tax of 4%–20% of their total value.

If you're bringing any foreign-made equipment with you from home, such as cameras or video gear, it's wise to carry the original receipt or to register it with customs before leaving home (in the United States, ask for U.S. Customs Form 4457). Otherwise, you may end up paying duty on your return. When going through German customs, looking composed and presentable expedites the process. To avoid hassles, don't even think about drugs. Being cited for drug possession is no joke, and even embassies and consulates can't do much to persuade country officials to release accused drug traffickers/users (*see* Crime and Punishment, *below*).

RETURNING HOME

➢ **U.S. CUSTOMS** • You won't have to pay duty unless you come home with more than $400 worth of foreign goods, including items bought in duty-free stores. Each member of the same family is entitled to the same exemption, regardless of age, and exemptions may be pooled. If you went crazy and maxed out all your credit cards on cuckoo clocks, lederhosen, and Birkenstocks, you'll have to pay 10% duty on the value of anything between $400 and $1,000. Duty-free allowances are as follows: 1 liter of alcohol or wine (you must be 21 or older), 100 non-Cuban cigars, 200 cigarettes, and one bottle of perfume. Anything above and beyond these limits will be taxed at the port of entry and may also be taxed in the traveler's home state. Gifts valued at less than $50 may be mailed duty-free to friends or relatives at home, but the limit is one package per day to a single addressee, and you may not send perfume, tobacco, or liquor. A free leaflet about customs regulations and illegal souvenirs, "Know Before You Go," is available from the U.S. Customs Service (1301 Constitution Ave., Washington, DC 20029, tel. 202/927–6724).

➢ **CANADIAN CUSTOMS** • Exemptions for returning Canadians range from $20 to $300, depending on how long you've been out of the country: For two days out, you're allowed to return with C$100 worth of goods; for one week out, you're allowed C$300 worth. Above these limits, you'll be taxed 20% (more for items shipped home). In any given year, you are allowed only one $300 exemption. Duty-free limits are: 50 cigars, 200 cigarettes, 2.2 pounds of tobacco, and 40 ounces of liquor—all must be declared in writing upon arrival at customs and must be with you or in your checked baggage. To mail back gifts, label the package: "Unsolicited Gift—Value under $40." For more dreary details, request a copy of the Canadian customs brochure "I Declare/Je Déclare" from Revenue Canada Customs and Excise Department (Connaught Bldg., MacKenzie Ave., Ottawa, Ont., K1A OL5, tel. 613/957–0275).

➢ **U.K. CUSTOMS** • Travelers age 17 or over who return to the United Kingdom may bring back the following duty-free goods: 200 cigarettes or 100 cigarillos or 50 cigars or 250 grams of tobacco; 1 liter of alcohol over 22% volume or 2 liters of alcohol under 22% volume, plus 2 liters of still table wine; 50 grams of perfume and 250 milliliters of toilet water; and other goods worth up to £32. If returning from Germany or another EC country, you can choose instead to bring in the following, provided they were not bought in a duty-free shop: 300 cigarettes or 150 cigarillos or 75 cigars or 400 grams of tobacco; 1.5 liters of alcohol over 22% volume or 3 liters of alcohol under 22% volume, plus 5 liters of still table wine; 75 grams of perfume and 375 milliliters of toilet water; and other goods worth up to £250.

➢ **AUSTRALIAN CUSTOMS** • Australian travelers 18 or over may bring back, duty free: 1 liter of alcohol; 250 grams of tobacco products (equivalent to 250 cigarettes or cigars); and other articles worth up to AUS$400. If you're under 18, your duty-free allowance is AUS$200. To avoid paying duty on goods you mail back to Australia, mark the package "Australian goods returned." For more rules and regulations, request the pamphlet "Customs Information for Travellers" from a local collector of customs (or write Collector of Customs, GPO Box 8, Sydney NSW 2001, tel. 02/226–5997).

➢ **NEW ZEALAND CUSTOMS** • Although greeted with a "Haere Mai" ("Welcome to New Zealand"), homeward-bound travelers face a number of restrictions. Travelers over age 17 are allowed, duty-free: 200 cigarettes or 250 grams of tobacco or 50 cigars or a combo of the three up to 250 grams; 4.5 liters of wine or beer and one 1,125-milliliter bottle of spirits; and goods with a combined value of up to NZ$700. If you want more details, ask for the pamphlet "Customs Guide for Travelers" at a New Zealand consulate.

STAYING HEALTHY

ACCIDENT OR ILLNESS The general police/help line in every German city is 110. To call an ambulance dial 112. These numbers do not require coins at pay phones. Stay calm, and ask for someone who speaks English. If you don't know your address, ask the operator if it is possible to pinpoint your location based on the telephone from which you are calling. Keep in mind that this system does not work as smoothly in the eastern part of the country. If the operator can't locate your phone, look for identifying landmarks or ask a passerby if he or she can describe your location to the operator for you.

FIRST-AID KIT Packing a few first-aid items could save you physical and financial pain during your travels. Prepackaged travel kits are available, but the rugged individualist should pack bandages, waterproof surgical tape and gauze pads, antiseptic, cortisone cream, tweezers, a thermometer in a sturdy case, an antacid such as Tums, something for diarrhea (Pepto Bismol or Immodium), and a pain reliever. If you're prone to motion sickness or are planning to use particularly rough modes of transportation during your travels, take some Dramamine. No matter what your skin tone, if you'll be exposed to sunlight for any length of time, pack sunscreen to protect against cancer-causing rays.

DOCTORS The majority of doctors in Germany speak at least passable English. In case of a medical emergency, ask for a referral at the nearest classy hotel; in most cases the front desk will be able to point you toward an English-speaking doctor. Hospital listings for specific cities can be found in individual chapters throughout this book.

Membership in the nonprofit **International Association for Medical Assistance to Travelers** (IAMAT, 417 Center St., Lewiston, NY 14092, tel. 716/754–4883; 40 Regal Rd., Guelph, Ont. N1K 1B5, Canada, tel. 519/836–0102; Box 5049, Christchurch 5, New Zealand) is free (donations are requested to keep it afloat) and entitles you to a worldwide directory of qualified English-speaking physicians who are on 24-hour call and who have agreed to a fixed-fee schedule.

HEALTH AND ACCIDENT INSURANCE Some general health-insurance plans cover health expenses incurred while traveling abroad, so review your existing heath policies (or a parent's policy, if you're a dependent) before leaving home. Most university health-insurance plans stop and start with the school year, so don't count on school spirit to pull you through. Canadian travelers should check with their provincial ministry of health to see if their resident health–insurance plan covers them on the road. Budget- and student–travel organizations, such as STA and CIEE, and credit–card conglomerates include health-and-accident coverage with the purchase of an I.D. or credit card. Several private companies offer coverage designed to supplement existing health insurance for travelers; travel agents often provide travel-insurance information and sell policies.

Carefree Travel Insurance (Box 310, 120 Mineola Blvd., Mineola, NY 11501, tel. 516/294–0220 or 800/323–3149) is actually quite serious about providing coverage for emergency medical evacuation and accidental death and dismemberment. It also offers 24-hour medical advice over the phone.

International SOS Assistance (Box 11568, Philadelphia, PA 19116, tel. 215/244–1500 or 800/523–8930) provides emergency evacuation services, worldwide medical referrals, and optional medical insurance.

Travel Guard (1145 Clark St., Stevens Point, WI 54481, tel. 715/345–0505 or 800/782–5151). The American Society of Travel Agents endorses the Travel Guard plan, an insurance package that includes coverage for sickness, injury (or untimely death), lost baggage, and trip cancellation.

PRESCRIPTIONS If you take prescription drugs, ask your doctor to type an extra prescription for you prior to your trip. Make sure he or she includes the following information: dosage, the drug's generic name, and the manufacturer's name. If you need to fill a prescription after regular business hours (9–6:30 in most cities), each German town has a system of rotating after-hours pharmacies. Every Apotheke posts the name, address, and telephone number of the night's late-night pharmacy on its front door.

RESOURCES FOR WOMEN

Women traveling in Germany should use common sense when it comes to safety, especially when traveling alone. Harassment may seem minimal, especially during the daytime or in public at night, but this doesn't mean the problem doesn't exist. Programs to increase awareness of rape have been sponsored by the police and other socially active groups, so it's no longer a foreign concept to anyone. If you're being hassled by a man, women will frequently come to your aid, more so in smaller villages towns than in larger cities. As always, keep your wits about you, and try not to get yourself into any sticky situations where you're alone with a man in a hotel room or train compartment. Be wary of travel partners you find along the way; although he may seem nice in the beginning, his true intentions may shine through after a couple of days.

ORGANIZATIONS **Pacific Harbor Travel** (519 Seabright Ave., Suite 201, Santa Cruz, CA 95062, tel. 408/425–5020) specializes in independent adventure travel with an emphasis on women's travel.

Woodswomen (25 W. Diamond Lake Rd., Minneapolis, MN 55419, tel. 612/822–3809 or 800/279–0555) specializes in adventure travel for women of all ages. This nonprofit group claims to be the largest and most extensive women's-travel organization in the world and organizes safe, educational, and environmental-conscious excursions for its members. Yearly membership donations start at $20.

RESOURCES FOR PEOPLE OF COLOR

Race relations in Germany have become increasingly tense since reunification (*see box*). As always, exercising common sense can usually keep you from encountering any dangerous situations. Larger cities tend to be more cosmopolitan and tolerant. With a little extra care, nothing should stop you from going where you want to go or doing whatever you want to do. If, however, a confrontation arises, make it understood that you are a tourist traveling through Germany; in most cases, you'll be left alone. If you're out after dark in unfamiliar areas, grab a cab if you can afford it; when taking public transportation, sit close to the driver.

GAY AND LESBIAN RESOURCES

Homophobia is no more rampant in Germany than anywhere else in the Western world. As could be expected, this is more true in western Germany than in eastern Germany, where views of gender roles are more "traditional." If confronted by homophobia, your best bet is simply to turn around and walk away. On a more positive note, gay nightclubs and other gathering spots can be found in most large cities in Germany. Refer to individual chapters in this book for specific listings. For further information, *Spartacus International Gay Guide* ($28 plus shipping) focuses specifically on gay male travel in Europe. This book is available at gay and lesbian bookstores or by mail through the Damron Company (Box 422458, San Francisco, CA 941403, tel. 415/255–0404).

ORGANIZATIONS **International Gay Travel Association** (IGTA) (Box 4974, Key West, FL 33041, tel. 800/448–8550) is a nonprofit organization of 387 members worldwide that provides listings of member agencies.

International Lesbian and Gay Association (ILGA) (81 Rue Marche au Charbon, 1000 Brussels 1, Belgium, tel. 32/2–502–2471) is a good source of info about conditions, resources, and hot spots in any given country.

RESOURCES FOR THE DISABLED

Accessibility may soon have an international symbol, if an initiative begun by the Society for the Advancement of Travel for the Handicapped (SATH) catches on. A bold, underlined, capital H is the symbol SATH is publicizing for hotels, restaurants, and tourist attractions to display in order to indicate accessible facilities. Although awareness of the needs of travelers with disabilities in Germany increases every year, budget opportunities are harder to find. Always ask if discounts are available, either for you or for a companion. In addition, plan your trip and make reservations far in advance; companies that provide services for people with disabilities go in and out of business regularly.

Neo-Nazi Movement Colors Any Trip to Germany

The rise of the neo-Nazi movement has dominated news coverage of Germany over the last two years. What began in Rostock in 1992 with riots against foreign-worker hostels has spread across the country. Minority workers and their families, especially the three-million-strong Turkish population, have been the target of increasing attacks by skinheads, who want "Germany for the Germans." It's not unusual to see graffiti saying "Foreigners Out" scrawled on building walls. Many people blame the violence on the poor state of the German economy, high unemployment, and the problems arising from reunification. Others point to Germany's recent history and see a more sinister national trait. Chancellor Kohl and the government have come under increasing criticism for their failure to act or even speak out against the racism and violence. In the spring of 1993, Chancellor Kohl declined to attend the funeral in Solingen of a family of five Turks burned to death by a skinhead, the second arson-murder of a Turkish family. At the other end of the spectrum, you read about the candlelight vigils attended by thousands of Germans protesting the violence, and about the anti-Nazi demonstrations staged all over the country. So what's the scoop? As with everything, the situation is not cut and dried, and it's difficult to gauge from newspaper reports how a non-white and/or non-Christian traveler will be treated in Germany. You might travel for six months and see nothing, or you could get beaten up your first night. The writers of this book spent 8–10 weeks each in Germany. Draw your own conclusions from their experiences:

- *Writer Linda Shing, an Asian American who traveled extensively in both Germany and Hungary, reported that she was stared at in both countries. The difference, she said, was that in Hungary people stared from curiosity, not hostility. In one incident, a German riding in a car pointed a gun at Linda and her black friend as they walked down a street.*
- *Writer Pete Edwards, an African American, stayed with some Sudanese men when he first arrived in Germany. In a letter from Berlin, he wrote: "They know all the nightspots where foreigners are and are not welcome. One man is healing from an encounter with a skinhead's knife, and they just heard tonight of another man from Sudan being beaten. They specifically say that the East is much worse than the West. Yes, I plan on being very careful!"*
- *Writer Oliver Wilken saw a hostel in Lower Saxony try to turn away a Jewish traveler, although there were several empty beds in the hostel. The man was only admitted when disgusted guests pointed out all the available beds.*

COMING AND GOING Flying is the easiest option for disabled travelers who wish to travel to Germany. Most major airlines are happy to help travelers with disabilities make flight arrangements, provided the airlines are notified 48 hours in advance.

Most public transportation in Germany is accessible to those with physical disabilities. All trains and most public buses in western Germany are outfitted to accommodate passengers in wheelchairs, and the transit system in the former East Germany is beginning to catch on to the needs of its disabled citizens. For more specific information, contact one of the groups listed below.

ACCOMMODATIONS Most youth hostels and some hotels and pensions are able to accommodate disabled travelers, but always phone ahead prior to your arrival. Whenever possible, reviews in this book will indicate whether rooms are disabled-accessible.

ORGANIZATIONS **Directions Unlimited** (720 N. Bedford Rd., Bedford Hills, NY 10507, tel. 914/241–1700 or 800/533–5343) sets up individual and group tours and cruises for any destination.

Mobility International USA (MIUSA, Box 3551, Eugene, OR 97403, voice and TDD tel. 503/343–1284) is an internationally affiliated nonprofit organization that coordinates exchange programs for disabled people around the world and offers information on accommodations and organized study programs to members. Membership ($20 annually) gives you discounts on publications, services, MIUSA travel and educational programs, and a quarterly newsletter. Nonmembers may subscribe to the newsletter for $10.

Moss Rehabilitation Hospital's Travel Information Service (1200 W. Tabor Rd., Philadelphia, PA 19141–3009, tel. 215/456–9603; TDD 215/456–9602) provides information on tourist sights, transportation, accommodations, and accessibility in destinations around the world. You can request information by state or country for a $5 postage and handling fee. They also provide airlines' toll-free numbers for the hearing-impaired.

In an Atmosphere of Intolerance, the Disabled Become Victims

Those neo-Nazi storm troopers who so bravely burn Turkish families in their homes have also begun picking on Germany's disabled. In a six-month period in 1993, there were more than 80 attacks against disabled people, according to the Kiel-based National Forum on Violence Against the Disabled. Like much of the violence sweeping Germany today, the attacks on the disabled have their roots in the policies of Hitler and the Nazis, who gassed many of Germany's disabled in the interests of "racial purity." Recent attacks on the disabled have ranged from threatening telephone calls to assaults and murder. The brutality of many of the attacks has been sickening: One man, who was slightly retarded and almost blind, was kicked to death by two teenage skinheads; in another case, a 13-year-old boy soaked a retarded man's shirt in gasoline, persuaded him to put it back on, and then set him on fire.

Society for the Advancement of Travel for the Handicapped (3475 5th Ave., Suite 610, New York, NY 10016, tel. 212/447-7284, fax 212/725-8253) is a nonprofit educational group that works to inform and educate people about travel for the disabled. Annual membership costs $45, or $25 for students and senior citizens, and entitles you to a quarterly newsletter that details new tours, tourism guides, resources, and late-breaking political advances for the disabled. Members can also request information about a specific destination; send $2 and a stamped, self-addressed envelope.

Travel Industry and Disabled Exchange (TIDE, 5435 Donna Ave., Tarzana, CA 91356, tel. 818/368-5648) publishes a quarterly newsletter and a directory of travel agencies and tours for disabled travelers. The annual membership fee is $15.

PUBLICATIONS ***Access to the World: A Travel Guide for the Handicapped,*** by Louise Weiss, is highly recommended for its worldwide coverage of travel boons and busts for the disabled. It's available from Henry Holt and Company (tel. 800/247-3912) for $12.95; the order number is 0805001417.

The Itinerary (Box 2012, Bayonne, NJ 07002, tel. 201/858-3400) is a bimonthly travel magazine for the disabled. It's not available in bookstores, but you can order a one-year subscription for $10.

Twin Peaks Press (Box 129, Vancouver, WA 98666, tel. 206/694-2462; orders only, 800/637-2256) publishes *Travel for the Disabled,* which offers helpful hints as well as a comprehensive list of guidebooks and facilities. The *Directory of Travel Agencies for the Disabled* lists more than 350 agencies throughout the world. Each is $19.95 plus $2 ($3 for both) shipping and handling. Twin Peaks also offers a "Traveling Nurse's Network," which puts disabled travelers in touch with registered nurses to aid and accompany them on their trip. Travelers fill out an application that Twin Peaks matches to nurses' applications in their files. The rest of the arrangements, such as the nurse's pay, is left to the traveler. An application is $10.

WORKING ABROAD

As the economic and financial hub of the new European Community, as well as the continent's leader in all things hi-tech, automotive, and pharmaceutical, Germany attracts many foreigners in search of work every year. Generally, you'll have the best chance of setting up a decent job if you have some specialized skill and a good contact in the area in which you wish to find employment. On the other hand, plenty of wandering souls simply arrive in Germany and stumble upon a job. If in the latter group, be sure to let everybody you meet know that you're in the job market, and ask around at local cafés, pubs, and restaurants.

Students interested in working or volunteering in Germany should contact **CIEE**'s Work Abroad and Voluntary Service departments (205 E. 42nd St., New York, NY 10017, tel. 212/661-1414, ext. 1130 and 1139 respectively). CIEE has work and study-abroad programs in Europe, Latin America, Asia, and Australia and publishes several resource books on work/travel opportunities, including *Work, Study, Travel Abroad: The Whole World Handbook* ($12.95 plus $1.50 book-rate postage or $3 first-class postage), *Volunteer! The Comprehensive Guide to Voluntary Service in the U.S. and Abroad* ($8.95 plus $1.50 book-rate postage or $3 first-class postage), and *The Teenager's Guide to Travel, Study, and Adventure Abroad* ($9.95 plus $1.50 book-rate postage or $3 first-class postage).

Those looking for either long-term employment in Germany (generally one year or longer) or for a summer job can contact *Zentralstelle für Arbeitsvermittlung* (Feuerbachstr. 42, 6000 Frankfurt/Main, Germany). In your letter to the agency, be sure to include the following: full name; complete home address; citizenship; age, family status, and number of dependents; educational history; level of proficiency in German language; previous occupation; kind and duration of employment you seek; part of Germany in which you prefer to settle.

LEGAL REQUIREMENTS If you're planning to work in Germany and wish to do so legally, you'll need to jump through some bureaucratic hoops. To obtain a work permit, which can be done before you leave home through your local German consulate or once in Germany through the local labor office, you must present proof of employment, preferably in the form of a letter from your prospective employer. You'll also need two passport photos and proof of citizenship. Work permits must be obtained *before* starting work and are officially required for any length of employment.

PAYING YOUR WAY Many footloose and fancy-free travelers hope to pay their way by picking up odd jobs as they travel. Adventurers considering such a plan should realize that this type of work is very difficult to obtain in most parts of Germany. However, chances do increase if you migrate toward the larger urban areas and if your German-language skills are strong. Ask around at cafés, restaurants, hotels, pensions, and hostels. Women, more than men, can also often find short-term employment taking care of children; look in the local newspapers or inquire at day-care centers.

STUDYING ABROAD

Studying in another country is the perfect way to scope out a foreign culture, to meet locals, and often to learn or improve language skills. Students thinking about spending some time studying in Germany are in luck: German universities generally reserve 8% of their available places for foreign students.

Interested students should start the process by speaking with an adviser at their school about the wealth of programs available to students of all levels in Germany. Another good option is to write to **Deutscher Akademischer Austauschdienst** (Kennedyallee 50, W-5300 Bonn 2, Germany). This organization can provide you with a comprehensive booklet that includes addresses of more than 80 universities throughout Germany that have foreign-student programs, the courses they offer, and general information about the German university system and its standards.

The information center at the **Institute of International Education** (IIE, 809 U.N. Plaza, New York, NY 10017, tel. 212/984–5413) has reference books, foreign-university catalogs, study-abroad brochures, and other materials that may be consulted free of charge if you're in the neighborhood. The center is open weekdays 10–4. The IIE also publishes a series of annual study-abroad guides, including *Academic Year Abroad* and *Vacation Study Abroad.* For teachers, there is *Teaching Abroad.* To get a list of IIE's current publications, complete with price and ordering information, write to Publications Service, care of IIE.

If you want to start your studies in the winter semester, the application is generally due by July 15 (January 15 for the summer semester). Year-long programs are also available; application deadlines depend on the specific university. The application usually consists of a statement of personal qualifications, focusing on language knowledge, and copies of your transcript from the academic institution you've attended most recently.

Those considering entering the world of German academia should realize that the cost of living in Germany is pretty high; for the year 1991 the German Academic Exchange Service estimated monthly expenses of DM 1,000 for students. Although German universities do not charge tuition, there are mandatory "contributions" to student organizations (DM 25–DM 65), compulsory health-insurance fees (DM 400 per semester), books and study materials to be purchased (DM 450–DM 600), and other small expenditures. Also, don't forget about renting a room, an enterprise that can cost DM 150–DM 400 per month, depending on the city in which you choose to study and the type of accommodation you seek (student hostel, private room, shared apartment, etc.). Foreign-student offices and other student-body organizations at the university can frequently help you in your quest for a place to call home.

Coming and Going

BY AIR

Flexibility is the key to getting a serious bargain on airfare. If you can play around with your departure date, destination, amount of luggage carried, and return date, you will probably save money. Options include charter flights, flying standby, student discounts, ticket consolidators, and courier flights. On your fateful departure day, remember that check-in time for international flights is a long two hours before the scheduled departure. For an in-depth study of tackling plane travel, consult *The Airline Traveler's Guerilla Handbook,* by George Albert Brown (Blake Publishing Group, 320 Metropolitan Sq., 15th St. NW, Washington, DC 20005; $14.95).

BUYING A TICKET The major airlines offer a range of tickets with wildly varying prices, depending on the date of purchase, the date of departure, the length of your stay, and the current position of Jupiter. As a rule, the farther in advance you book a seat, the less expensive the ticket but the greater the penalty (up to 100%) for cancellation. Keep in mind that "advance purchase" to an airline does not mean the week before departure; a month's lead time will probably net a significant savings.

When your travel plans are still in the fantasy stage, start studying the travel sections of major Sunday newspapers: Courier companies, charter airlines, and fare brokers often list incredibly cheap flights. Travel agents are another obvious resource, as they have access to computer networks that show the lowest fares before they're advertised. Budget travelers are the bane of travel agents, though; an agent's commission is based on the price of your ticket. Try travel agencies on or near college campuses; they often cater to this pariah class.

Hot tips when making reservations: Call every toll-free number you can find—it's free and can't hurt. Don't be shy about asking for the cheapest flight possible. If the reservation clerk tells you the least expensive seats are no longer available on a certain flight, ask to be put on a waiting list. If the airline doesn't keep waiting lists for the lowest fares, call them on subsequent mornings and ask about cancellations and last-minute openings—airlines trying to fill all their seats sometimes add cut-rate tickets at the last moment. When setting travel dates, remember that off-season fares can be much lower and that there will be fewer people vying for the inexpensive seats. Be sure to ask if you'll get a discount by flying on certain days.

➢ **CONSOLIDATORS AND BUCKET SHOPS** • Consolidator companies, also known as bucket shops, buy blocks of tickets at wholesale prices from airlines trying to fill flights, and sell them at reduced prices. Drawbacks: Consolidator tickets are often not refundable, and the flights to choose from often feature indirect routes, long layovers in connecting cities, and undesirable seat assignments. If your flight is delayed or canceled, you'll also have a tough time switching airlines. As with charter flights, you risk taking a huge loss if you change your travel plans, but at least you will be on a regularly scheduled flight with less risk of cancellation than on a charter. Once your reservation is made, call the airline to confirm it at least two days in advance of departure. You may also want to check the consolidator's reputation with the Better Business Bureau. Most are perfectly reliable, but it's best to be sure. If you can deal with these restrictions and minor risks, consolidators might offer the cheap flight of your dreams. Pay with a credit card, so that if your dream goes up in smoke and the ticket never arrives, you won't have to pay. Bucket shops generally advertise in newspapers—be sure to check restrictions, refund possibilities, and payment conditions. Read all the fine print.

Among the best-known consolidators are **UniTravel** (1177 N. Warson Rd., Box 12485, St. Louis, MO 63132, tel. 314/569–2501 or 800/325–2222), and **Up & Away Travel** (141 E. 44th St., Suite 403, New York, NY 10017, tel. 212/972–2345). Check travel sections of local papers for more listings.

If you're departing from the United States and can risk developing an ulcer, consider going through **Airhitch** (2790 Broadway, Suite 100, New York, NY 10025, tel. 212/864–2000), a service that informs you of flights to and from western Europe that *might* have empty seats. From the west coast, a one-way voucher costs $269; from the east coast, $169. For this price, Airhitch guarantees they'll find you a flight within seven days of your preferred departure date to a city as close as possible to your preferred destination. For all but those with nerves of steel, this can be a nail-biting ordeal, since you never know for sure when you'll get on a flight, where you'll leave from, or where you'll end up. Fly Airhitch only if you are trying to get to Germany cheaply at the last minute; otherwise, you can book charter flights or find other deals that may cost even less and won't turn your hair white.

➢ **STAND-BY AND THREE-DAY-ADVANCE-PURCHASE FARES** • Flying standby is almost a thing of the past. The idea is to purchase an open ticket and wait for a seat on the next flight to your chosen destination, but most airlines have dumped standby policies in favor of three-day-advance-purchase youth fares, which are open only to the under-25 market and (as the name states) only within three days of departure. Three-day-advance works best in the off season, when flights aren't as jampacked, and the savings are substantial.

There are a number of brokers that specialize in discount and last-minute sales, offering savings on unsold seats on commercial carriers and charter flights, as well as tour packages. If you're desperate to get to Germany by tommorrow, try **Last Minute Travel Club** (tel. 617/267–9800) or **Interworld Travel, Inc.** (tel. 305/443–4929); neither charges a membership fee.

➢ **CHARTER FLIGHTS** • "Charter flights" can have vastly different characteristics, depending on the company you're dealing with. Generally speaking, a charter company either buys a block of tickets on a regularly scheduled commercial flight and sells them at a discount (this is the most prevalent form in the United States), or they may lease the whole plane and then offer relatively cheap fares to the public (most common in the United Kingdom). Despite a few potential drawbacks (infrequent flights, restrictive return-date requirements, lickety-split payment demands, et cetera), a charter company may offer the cheapest ticket at the time you want to travel, especially during high season, when APEX fares are at their most expensive. Make sure you find out a company's policy on refunds should a flight be canceled by either yourself or the airline. Summer charter flights fill up fast and should be booked a couple of months in advance.

You're in much better shape when the company is offering tickets on a regular, commercial flight. After you've bought the ticket from the charter folks, you generally deal with the airline directly; essentially, you're treated like a normal, fare-paying customer. When a charter company has chartered the whole plane, things get a little sketchier: Bankrupt operators, long delays at check-in, overcrowding, and flight cancellation are fairly common. You can minimize risks by checking the company's reputation with the Better Business Bureau or a travel agency and taking out enough trip-cancellation insurance to cover the operator's potential failure.

The following list of companies isn't exhaustive, so check the travel sections of major newspapers: **Council Charter** (tel. 212/661–0311 or 800/223–7402), **DER Tours** (Box 1606, Des Plains, IL 60017, tel. 800/782–2424), **TRAVAC** (tel. 212/563–3303 or 800/872–8800), **Travel Charter** (1120 E. Long Lake Rd., Troy, MI 48098, tel. 313/528–3570 or 800/521–5267), and **Travel CUTS** (187 College St., Toronto, Ont. M5T 1P7, tel. 416/979–2406).

➢ **STUDENT DISCOUNTS** • Student discounts on airline tickets are offered through **CIEE,** the **Educational Travel Center, STA Travel,** and **Travel CUTS** (*see* Budget Travel Organizations, *above*). Keep in mind that in most cases you will *not* receive frequent-flyer mileage for discounted student, youth, or teacher tickets. For discount tickets based on your status as a student, youth, or teacher, have an I.D. when you check in that proves it: an International Student Identity Card, Youth Identity Card, or International Teacher Identity Card.

➢ **COURIER FLIGHTS** • A few restrictions and inconveniences are the price you'll pay for the colossal savings on airfare offered to air couriers—travelers who accompany letters and packages between designated points. Restrictions include luggage limitations (check-in luggage space is used for the freight you're transporting, so you take carryons only), limited stays of a week or two, and often a limit of one courier on any given flight.

Check newspaper travel sections for courier companies, look in the yellow pages of your phone directory, or send away for a telephone directory that lists companies by the cities to which they fly. Send a self-addressed, stamped envelope to **Pacific Data Sales Publishing** (2554 Lincoln Blvd., Suite 275–I, Marina Del Rey, CA 90291). *A Simple Guide to Courier Travel* also gives tips on flying as a courier. Send $17.95 (includes postage and handling) to Discount Travel (Box 331, Sandy, UT 97035, tel. 800/344–9375).

Now Voyager (74 Varick St., Suite 307, New York, NY 10013, tel. 212/431–1616) connects 18-and-over travelers scrounging for cheap airfares with companies looking for warm bodies to escort their packages overseas. Couriers are limited to one carryon bag and must be flexible about departure dates and destinations. Flights in summer and over school holidays are in high demand, so try to book two months in advance. Departures are from New York, Newark, or Houston. Most trips are one week in length, with round-trip fares from $150 up. A nonrefundable $50 registration fee, good for one year, is required. Call for current offerings.

➢ **APEX** • **Advanced Purchase Excursion** (APEX) fares offer the advantage of security: Barring acts of Mother Nature, you'll get to where you want to go and arrive when you planned because you'll have confirmed reservations. Disadvantages are that reservations must be made 21 days in advance; the length of your trip is usually limited to a seven-day to three-month period; and changes in travel plans—voluntary or not—result in a penalty of $50–$100. Even with a penalty, though, APEX fares are still less than fares you pay at the last minute.

Super Apex works along the same lines as Apex, with slightly tighter restrictions. Tickets must be purchased 30 days, rather than 21 days, in advance. Trips must be at least three days and no more than three months in length, and changes in itinerary still result in a $50–$100 penalty.

FROM NORTH AMERICA Thanks to the fact that the air routes between North America and Germany are heavily traveled, you'll have a choice of many airlines and fares. But remember, fares can change quickly, so always consult your travel agent before booking a flight. From New York, the flight to Frankfurt takes 7½ hours; from Chicago, 10 hours; from Los Angeles, 12 hours.

The U.S. airlines that serve Germany are **Northwest Airlines** (tel. 800/447–4747), which flies to Frankfurt, Munich, Stuttgart, and Nürnberg; **Delta** (tel. 800/241–4141), which flies to Frankfurt, Stuttgart, Hamburg, Berlin, and Munich; **TWA** (tel. 800/892–4141), which flies to Frankfurt, Stuttgart, Munich, and Berlin; and **American Airlines** (tel. 800/433–7300), which flies to Frankfurt, Berlin, Hamburg, Munich, Düsseldorf, and Nürnberg. **Lufthansa** (tel. 800/645–3880), the German national airline, flies direct to Düsseldorf, Frankfurt, Köln/Bonn, Hamburg, Munich, and Stuttgart. Another German carrier, **LTU International Airways** (tel. 800/888–0200), flies from New York, Miami, Orlando, Atlanta, San Francisco, and Los Angeles to Frankfurt, Munich, and Düsseldorf.

FROM THE UNITED KINGDOM **British Airways** (tel. 081/897–4000) and **Lufthansa** (tel. 081/897–4000) are the most important airlines to remember when flying from London to Germany. Between them, they serve nine German destinations—10 including Münster, to which Lufthansa's subsidiary airline, **DLT,** flies.

The main gateways to Germany by air are Düsseldorf, Köln, Frankfurt, Munich, and Berlin. British Airways and Lufthansa each have up to two flights a day into Köln, with a minimum round-trip fare of £90. British Airways has up to seven flights and Lufthansa six flights to Frankfurt from London, with a minimum fare of £95. Each airline has three flights to Munich, with a minimum fare of £135. British Airways has up to three nonstop and three one-stop flights to Berlin each day, with a minimum fare of £135. Lufthansa inaugurated flights to Berlin in late 1990. The airlines also fly to Bremen, Hannover, and Stuttgart, and Lufthansa has one flight daily to Nürnberg. Flying time from Britain is about one hour 40 minutes.

➢ **DISCOUNT FARES •** Substantial discount can be obtained if you deal with a travel agent instead of with the airlines. Fixed-date (APEX) fares booked two weeks ahead and including at least one Saturday spent in your destination are also discounted.

Commuter-style airline **Connectair** (tel. 0293/862971) flies twice a day from Gatwick to Düsseldorf, at £80 for the cheapest round-trip fare. **Air UK** (tel. 0345/666777) flies weekdays from London's third airport, Stansted, to Frankfurt (one hour 55 minutes' flying time), and DLT goes to Frankfurt from Gatwick.

Dan Air (tel. 071/229–2474) operates the cheapest regular charter flights (four or more days a week) from Gatwick to Berlin and Munich and two flights weekly to Hamburg, Hannover, Frankfurt, Düsseldorf, and Stuttgart.

FROM DOWN UNDER The only airline that offers direct flights from Sydney and Melbourne to Frankfurt is **Lufthansa.** In Sydney, call 02–367–3888. Otherwise, **Qantas** has flights from Sydney, Cairnes, Melbourne, and Brisbane to Frankfurt via Bangkok. In Sydney, call 02–957–0111. **British Airways** operates flights from Auckland, Sydney, Melbourne, and Perth to Frankfurt, Bonn, Berlin, Düsseldorf, Hamburg, Munich, and Stuttgart via London. In Sydney, call 02–258–3300; in Auckland, call 03–367–7500. Finally, **Cathay Pacific** has flights from Melbourne and Brisbane to Frankfurt via Hong Kong. For flight reservations and more information, call 02–131–7477 in Sydney.

Bikes in Flight

Most airlines will ship bikes as luggage, provided they are dismantled and packed in a special box. Call to see if your airline sells bike boxes (about $10) but sometimes you can get them free from bike shops. International travelers can substitute a bike for the second piece of checked luggage at no extra charge; otherwise, this service usually costs about $100. Domestic flights are less gracious and charge bike-toting travelers a $45 fee.

FROM THE U.K. BY BUS

If you're coming from the United Kingdom and have something against trains, consider hopping on a bus. The fastest service is by **Europabus,** which has up to three departures a day from London's Victoria coach station. The buses cross the Channel on Sealink's Dover–Zeebrugge ferry service and then drive via the Netherlands and Belgium to Köln (14½ hours), Frankfurt (17½ hours), Mannheim (18¾ hours), Stuttgart/Nürnberg (20½ hours), and Munich (22¾ hours). One-way and round-trip fares are: Köln (£38/£62), Frankfurt (£40/£69), Mannheim (£43/£74), Stuttgart/Nürnberg (£51/£81), and Munich (£55/£91). For a full schedule of international services connecting with German destinations contact Deutsche Touring (Am Römerhof 17, 6000 Frankfurt am Main 90, tel. 069/79030).

Bookings can also be made through **Transline** (tel. 0708/864911), which runs a service to 35 smaller towns in western Germany. There are up to four departures per week, also from Victoria, and the buses cross either via P&O European Ferries' Dover–Ostend or Sally Line's Ramsgate–Dunkerque services. Destinations include Hannover, Dortmund, Essen, and Düsseldorf as well as smaller towns. Fares range from £32 to £36 one-way and £59–£66 round-trip.

BY TRAIN

FROM THE UNITED KINGDOM Most people traveling from the British Isles to Germany will want to follow one of two major routes: either London–Hamburg or London–Köln. Unless you have a Eurailpass (*see* Getting Around, *below*), though, you're probably better off flying. To reach Hamburg, catch a train at Liverpool station in London to Harwich and cross the English Channel to Hoek van Holland. From there you can get a train to Amersfoot, where you can transfer to a train headed for Hengelo. From Hengelo either catch the direct train to Hamburg or change at Osnabrück. The entire tiresome journey takes somewhere in the neighborhood of 17 hours and will set you back about DM 263 (DM 201 for those under 26).

To get from London to Köln, start at Victoria Station and head to Dover Western Docks, where a ferry will carry you to Oostende. From Oostende regular trains run to Köln, where connections are available to Bonn, Frankfurt, Stuttgart, Munich, Düsseldorf, Hannover, and Berlin. The trip from London to Köln can take anywhere from 9 to 11 hours and runs about DM 172 (DM 130 for those under 26). Book through British Rail Travel Centers (tel. 0371–834–2345).

FROM WESTERN EUROPE There are as many different routes into Germany as there are travelers. What follows is a partial list of some of the quickest and cheapest ways to reach Germany from around Europe.

Direct trains from **Paris** run to Frankfurt and Köln. Though both journeys take 5½–7 hours, the ride to Köln from Paris Nord costs only DM 92.40 (DM 72 under 26), and the ride to Frankfurt from Paris Est runs DM 144 (DM 110 under 26). Trains running from **Copenhagen** to Hamburg via Puttgarden take approximately five hours and cost DM 91 (DM 81 under 26). It's also possible to travel from Copenhagen to Berlin via Warnemünde in eight hours for DM 117.20 (DM 110 under 26). Trains from **Oslo** and **Stockholm** to Berlin require transfers at Malmö. The 19- to 20-hour trek from Oslo costs DM 308 (DM 232 under 26), and the 15- to 17½-hour ride from Stockholm runs DM 260 (DM 215 under 26).

One of the best rail lines to know about if you're going to Germany from the East is one that runs from **Budapest** to Berlin via **Vienna** and **Prague**. The approximately 14-hour ride from Budapest will set you back DM 137 (DM 74 under 26); the 10- to 12-hour ride from Vienna goes for DM 112 (DM 94 under 26); and the relatively short five- to six-hour journey from Prague runs DM 51 (DM 42 under 26). To get from the east to southern Germany, you'll need to first travel to Munich. Eight- to nine-hour trains from Budapest run DM 125 (DM 97 under 26); five- to six-hour trains from Vienna run DM 90 (DM 71 under 26). On both routes changing trains in Salzburg is sometimes necessary. The seven- to nine-hour trip from Prague to Munich costs DM 82 (DM 73 under 26) and usually requires a transfer in Nürnberg. Direct trains from **Warsaw** to Berlin take 6½–9½ hours and cost DM 45 (DM 34 under 26)—easy on your wallet but infamously hard on your ass.

If you're coming north from Italy, the best way is to take a six-hour train from **Milan** to Basel, Switzerland, where connections can be made to most major German cities. The ride will set you back Sfr. 81 (Sfr. 62 under 26).

Staying in Germany

GETTING AROUND

The most important rule to remember when traveling in Germany is "Whenever you're in doubt, jump on a train." The rail system is nearly perfect: It's fast, convenient, clean, comfortable, notoriously punctual, and just as affordable as any other form of public transportation in the country. Though they often reach nooks and crannies that the rail lines do not, buses are generally much slower than trains and are just as expensive. If you borrow, buy, or rent a car, the *Autobahnen* are smooth, slick, and dangerous—and the absence of a speed limit makes them attractive to aspiring Grand Prix drivers. The best way to save money on travel in Germany is to hitchhike, a very feasible but always risky alternative. If you have some cash on hand but want to save a bit of time and money, think about getting in touch with the local Mitfahrgelegenheit office, a service that hooks up riders and drivers heading to the same destination for a small fee. For staunch travelers who want to see the country as they travel through it, hiking and biking are viable transportation options in many parts of Germany.

BY TRAIN Since reunification, mass transit in Germany has faltered a bit; Deutsche Bundesbahn (German Rail), which now serves the entire nation, consumed the *Reichsbahn* of the former East Germany, and the integration was not entirely smooth. Connections to and from East Germany are sometimes late—a shock to the nation's morale—and the rail lines and train cars are often dilapidated.

Still, train travel remains the most efficient means of transportation in Germany. Information in a variety of languages, including English, and user-friendly time charts can be found in most stations. Once you find the correct platform, letters hanging above the tracks let you know where the first- and second-class cars will stop. Reservations for long trips are a good idea, especially if you want to take an overnight train. For trips of less than four hours, seats are usually not a problem. Look above the seat you desire or on the door outside the *Kabine* (a small room with six seats), for the yellow or orange slip of paper that reveals the seat's status: free or reserved.

Tickets should be bought at the station before your trip but may be obtained on board (for a small additional fee). Expect to pay about DM 30 for a two-hour trip, but make sure you're not boarding an InterCity (IC) or, even worse, an InterCity Express (ICE) train, unless you don't mind tacking 10%–30% on to your fare. Most trains traveling less than six or seven hours don't have dining cars, and those that do serve only the most mediocre, overpriced food. The food carts that patrol the walkways are good for some candy or a Coke, but bringing your own supplies is always best. Personal security on German trains is simple: Take all valuables with you whenever you go to the bathroom.

➢ **RAIL PASSES** • If you're under 26, your best option is to get a **German Rail Junior Flexipass**, which is good for a limited number of travel days in a one-month period: In 1993, a five-day pass cost $130; a 10-day pass was $178; and a 15-day pass $218. The pass is good for 2nd-class travel on all trains, on most buses run by Europabus and Deutsche Touring (part of Deutsche Bundesbahn); and for KD Rhine-line ferries operating on segments of the Rhine, Mosel, and Main rivers. Travelers over 26 can buy a regular **Flexipass** for more money: $170 (five-day), $268 (10-day), and $348 (15-day). To buy a rail pass before you leave the United States, contact **DER Tours** (tel. 800/782–2424).

If Germany is just one stop on a much larger European tour, consider buying a **Eurailpass** instead. The Eurailpass is good for travel in 17 European countries: Austria, Belgium, Denmark, Finland, France, Germany, Greece, Hungary, Italy, Luxembourg, Netherlands, Norway, Portugal, Republic of Ireland, Spain, Sweden, and Switzerland. All passes are first-class, except the Youthpass, which is good for second-class travel and available to travelers under 26. In 1993, a Eurail Youthpass cost $508 (one month) and $698 (two months); a regular Eurailpass cost $728 (one month) and $998 (two months), but shorter segments are available. Unless you're going to live on the trains, you may prefer a Eurail Flexipass, which permits a limited number of travel days within a two-month period. In 1993, the Eurail Youth Flexipass cost $220 (five days of travel), $348 (10 days), and $474 (15 days); the regular Flexipass cost $298 (five days), $496 (10 days), and $676 (15 days). It's cheaper to buy your Eurailpass before you leave home—it's available through travel agents, Council Travel offices, and DER Tours (*see above*). It can be difficult (and more expensive) to procure a Eurailpass after you arrive in Europe.

BY BUS Buses are often a pain in the ass (literally) but are a necessary evil for travel to some suburbs and rural areas. Most medium- and larger-size cities have a central bus depot with an information booth, and train stations usually offer bus information and often function as bus terminals, as well. Some bus lines (Europabus) honor Eurail- and DB Rail passes (read the fine print on your pass), and most offer daily and monthly passes. Often bus lines are connected with subway and streetcar lines; this makes travel within city limits especially easy; you can purchase a ticket based on where you want to go, and, regardless of how many transfers—buses or subways—you must make, one ticket will suffice. Bus tickets can be bought on the bus or from machines found at bus stations and larger bus stops.

BY MITFAHRGELEGENHEIT Germany has an abundance of car-pool agencies, known as *Mitfahrgelegenheit*, which connect drivers and riders heading in the same direction. Ride shares are often the cheapest and quickest way to travel within Germany and even between Germany and other major European cities. As a rider, all you pay is a small commission to the agency that arranges the ride share (usually about DM 5) and your portion of fuel costs. To avoid being scammed, make sure to ask the Mitfahrgelegenheit agent the approximate cost of fuel to your destination. Some drivers take advantage of the fact that carpooling agencies don't ask how long the trip will take, or what other detours the driver plans. In other words, your driver may decide to go shopping in a junkyard, stop by a friend's house, or stop for a meal. The addresses and telephone numbers of local Mitfahrgelegenheit offices throughout Germany (also known as *Mitfahrzentrale*) can be found in the "Basics" section for each city in this book.

BY CAR If you want to drive, get an international driver's license before you leave home. Driving on the Autobahnen might cause extreme nervosa: It's not only the excessive speeds, it's the fact that, at those speeds, any distraction or hazard becomes 10,000 times more distracting and hazardous! Potholes, windshield grime, rain—all are treacherous. Most deadly, however, are the legendary fogs that roll in and cover the highways. At high speeds, drivers cannot see accidents ahead of them in time to avoid joining the party. Rumors of 200-car pileups are told by many a weary traveler after a summer on the Autobahnen. Americans should remember that gas, sold throughout the rest of the civilized world in liters, is about three times more expensive in Germany than in the United States. In Germany, you drive on the right, and seatbelts are mandatory for *all* passengers.

➢ **CAR RENTALS** • Budget travelers will run out of money in a hurry if they insist on tooling around Germany in a rental car. National car-rental firms charge about DM 60 a day or DM 415 a week for a small Volkswagen with unlimited mileage. You're much better off renting a car for one or two days to reach areas like the Harz Mountains that suffer from a lack of public transport. If you want to reserve a car before you leave, contact **Budget Rent-a-Car** (3350 Boyington St., Carrollton, TX 75006, tel. 800/527–0700), **Connex Travel International** (883 Main St., Peekskill, NY 10566, tel. 800/333–3949), and **Cortell International** (770 Lexington Ave., New York, NY 10021, tel. 800/223–6626, or, in NY, 800/442–4481). Other budget rental companies include **Europe by Car** (1 Rockefeller Plaza, New York, NY 10020, tel. 800/223–1516 or, in CA, 800/252–9401), **Auto Europe** (Box 1097, Sharps Wharf, Camden, ME 04843, tel. 800/223–5555; in ME 800/342–5202; in Canada, 800/237–2465) **Foremost Euro-Car** (5430 Van Nuys Blvd., Van Nuys, CA 91404, tel. 800/423–3111), and **Kemwel** (106 Calvert St., Harrison, NY 10528, tel. 800/678–0678).

HITCHHIKING Germany is a fantastic country for hitchhikers. People are incredibly easygoing about giving rides, and planning a trip to Germany with hitching as your mode of transport is not unreasonable—especially if you're on a tight budget. Naturally, Germany is not devoid of depraved humanity. But although there are nuts around, there is far less incidence of trouble on the hitch-ways in Germany than in the United States or most other European nations. Obviously, hitching alone and accepting rides from drooling drivers is unwise.

Besides accommodating the future Mario Andrettis of this world, Germany's Autobahnen make hitching easy. Find a map with Autobahn ramps indicated (or ask at the tourist office), pick your direction, and hold up a destination sign (McDonald's place mats are a good size). Don't attempt to hitch a ride while actually *on* the Autobahn; not only is it incredibly dangerous but the police are likely to come down on you pretty hard, too. Most Germans will understand what you want if you stand on the roadside with your thumb out, but locals signal drivers by waving their outstretched arm up and down. You may feel like a one-winged whooping crane, but it works. Learning the German name of your desired city is also a good idea; you're more likely to score a ride to "München" than to "Munich."

BY BIKE Germany is a virtual paradise for those looking to pedal themselves around town or between cities. Bikes abound in Germany, and in some cities, such as Münster, they outnumber cars. Almost all German cities have bike paths, and many of the larger intercity roads have bike lanes. Bikes are available for rent from most train stations; otherwise ask for the name of a local firm. You can usually find a bike for DM 8–DM 15 per day, or DM 30 per week. For selective cyclists, many German trains have space for bikes, so that you can travel by rail through the steep or mundane areas and hop right back on your bike for the scenic and more moderately sloped routes.

Many cyclists swear that the best bike tour in Germany is along the scenic Rhine river, especially between Köln and Mainz or Worms.

HIKING For good reason, Germany is very proud of the extensive network of *Wanderwege* (walking trails) that traverse much of the country's undeveloped lands. And thanks to this network, opportunities for those wishing to hoof it from one town to the next are nearly unlimited, especially in the western portion of the country. Almost without fail, these trails are wellmarked and maintained with a degree of care perhaps only the Swiss can match. Making the Wanderwege even more user-friendly, many of the trails are dotted with campgrounds and occasional overnight huts or *Naturfreund* (Nature's Friends) hostels, options that are easy on your wallet. For maps and more information on specific trails, your best bet is to get in touch with a local tourist office. If you really crave information before leaving home, contact the German National Tourist Office (*see* Government Tourist Offices, *above*). Detailed trail maps are also available from many local bookstores.

PHONES

Germany's phone system, though it has many nuances, is modern, efficient, and easy to use. Well, at least this is the case in the west. The system in eastern Germany is still a wee bit antiquated, and connections to and from the former communist areas are often poor. If you'll be making a lot of calls you should invest in a telephone card, which come in amounts of DM 12 and up and are available at post offices and many currency-exchange agencies. The card allows you to use the many phones that do not accept coins and can save you a good deal of time and frustration.

LOCAL CALLS Making a connection for a local phone call will run you 30 pfennigs. Most public phones take 10 pfennig and DM 1 coins. If you think you'll be talking for a while, take along a hefty supply of DM 1 coins—public phones seem to eat up your money. Most phone booths, including all of the new hi-tech digitalized varieties, have instructions in English. One of the more annoying nuances of the German phone system is that phones do not give change (unless no connection is made); also, there is no warning signal that informs callers that their money has run out; when this happens, your call is simply terminated. The best way to beat the system, other than carrying around a bucket of 10 pfennig coins, is to buy a phone card.

You can make collect calls as well as phone-card calls through AT&T (tel. 01300010) and Sprint (tel. 01300013).

INTERNATIONAL CALLS International calls can be made from phone booths marked with the silhouette of a receiver and the words *INLANDS UND AUSLANDSGESPRÄCHE*. International phones generally accept 10 pfennig, DM 1 and DM 5 coins. Although rates vary from city to city, DM 5 will give you about two minutes worth of conversation to the United States. To avoid the necessity of lugging around a bag o' coins, your best bet is to place calls from the local post office. Simply give the attendant the number you wish to dial, and pay when you complete your call.

OPERATORS AND INFORMATION Dial 1188 to reach an operator or 00118 for an international operator. Most operators speak English; if yours doesn't, he or she will transfer you to one who does.

MAIL

SENDING MAIL HOME The easiest way to send mail from Germany is the ol' time-tested method of dropping by the local *Postamt* (post office), handing your postcard, letter, or package to the (sometimes) friendly clerk, and letting them do their thing. If you're feeling confident, you can buy extra postage and mail your next batch from any postal box (found in front of all post offices as well as on urban street corners) all by yourself. Airmail letters to North America cost DM 1.40, and postcards require 90 pfennigs in postage stamps. Letters to the United Kingdom run DM 1; postcards cost 60 pfennigs.

➢ **TELEGRAMS AND FAXES** • Telegrams can be sent from any post office during normal business hours. Fax machines are available at many post offices as well as most larger hotels, but international rates are outrageous, so fax only in emergencies.

RECEIVING MAIL You can receive mail at any German post office free of charge. Simply have the letter marked with your name, the address of the post office (Postamt, city name, zip code), and the words "Postlagernd Briefe." Another option is to have your mail sent to any American Express office. Just make sure the sender writes the words "client mail" somewhere on the envelope. Packages are not accepted. This service is free for American Express card holders; just show the clerk your card or an American Express traveler's check and some sort of identification. Others pay DM 2 per collection.

BUSINESS HOURS

Business hours vary between large cities and smaller towns and between different regions, but **banks** are generally open weekdays from 8:30 or 9 to 3:30 or 4. Banks, as well as most other businesses in Germany, frequently shut their doors for 1–1½ hours between noon and 1. Banks in train stations and airports keep longer hours; some open as early as 6 and close as late 11:30. **Shops** are usually open weekdays 9–6:30; on Thursday many stay open until 8 or 8:30 and on Saturday until 2. On *langer Samstag*, the first Saturday of each month, larger shops don't close until 4 in summer, 6 in winter. **Museums** are generally open Tuesday–Sunday 9–6. Some close 1–1½ hours for lunch, and a few are open Monday.

TIPPING

Even though the bill you get at a restaurant includes tax and service, it is common to round up to the nearest mark or two. Instead of leaving it on the table (considered rude), tell your waiter or waitress how much you want back or hand them the tip. For hairdressers, taxi drivers, and the like, round up a couple of marks, or tack on about 5%.

WHERE TO SLEEP

Used to hordes of tourists invading every summer, Germany is well equipped with lodging options for both the rugged, pfennig-pinching traveler and the weary traveler seeking affordable comfort. If you have a small budget, you're best off spending your nights in youth hostels or campgrounds. If things get really tight, there's always the park bench or the train station. When you need a soft bed to rest your road-worn bones, splurge at a local pension. These tend to be nearly as comfy as low-end hotels but with a more personable, "homey" feeling. Or book a room in a private home for a few nights. Besides being affordable and cozy, this is a great way to meet local families.

In the summer months, hostels and cheap pensions are filled to the brim, so (especially when heading to a big city) be sure to make reservations. If all of the lodgings listed in a particular city in this book are full when you arrive, most local tourist offices have comprehensive lists of accommodations in their area. Do your feet a favor and always call ahead before walking to that pension. The price categories in this book typically refer to the cost of a double room plus tax.

HOTELS Hotel prices in Germany vary widely as you travel from big cities to smaller towns or rural villages. Although most hotel prices include breakfast, the primary factor affecting rates is whether or not the room has a shower. In the cities prices usually start at DM 35–DM 45 for singles and DM 65–DM 80 for doubles without a shower. But don't fret, most hotels with rooms ohne Douche have bathing facilities off the hallway. If you insist on a private bath, the price of a room will usually go up DM 5–DM 10 for singles and DM 10–DM 15 for doubles. In smaller towns not yet saturated with tourists, single rooms can start as low as DM 25, with doubles at DM 45; but usually the range is about DM 30–DM 35 for singles and DM 50–DM 60 for doubles. Again, another DM 5–DM 10 will get you a private shower in a single, and DM 10–DM 15 will do the trick in a double.

PENSIONS As far as the budget traveler is concerned, a pension is just a cheap hotel. Breakfasts tend to be a bit simpler—usually two pieces of bread, butter, jam, cheese, a slice of meat, and tea or coffee—and there are typically fewer rooms than in a hotel, but otherwise the differences are minimal to nonexistent. Prices are basically the same as low-end hotels, but sometimes you can find pensions for a few duetsche marks less than the rates listed above. In more popular destinations reservations are strongly recommended, especially during the high season.

JUGENDHERBERGEN With more than 700 locations around the country, the youth-hostel network in Germany is one of the most extensive in Europe. Almost without exception the hostels (known as *Jugendherbergen*) are affiliated with the IYHF, which means there is a shopping list of rules and regulations: single-sex dorm rooms, no smoking, no noise after 10, curfews that range from 10 to midnight depending on the specific hostel, and, officially, no sleeping on beds without sleep sheets or the hostel's own linen, which you can borrow for DM 5.50 per night.

One way to avoid being denied a room at a crowded youth hostel is to make a telefax reservation; ask a hostel clerk for details.

Hostels affiliated with IYHF also require that you have an IYHF membership card, which can be bought at student-travel agencies around the world (*see* Budget Travel Organizations, *above*). If you space out, you can get a card from the first hostel you visit. You'll then receive a stamp costing DM 5 each night you stay at an IYHF hostel, and once you collect six stamps you're an official IYHF member (congratulations!). All IYHF hostels provide you with a simple breakfast, and most serve lunch and dinner for DM 6–DM 8 by prior arrangement (let them know when you check in). Check-in time is usually about 4 or 5. Most hostels have a lockout between 9 and 10 AM until anywhere between noon and 5 PM so the hostel can be cleaned.

For putting up with all these rules and regulations you'll be rewarded with the cheapest beds in Germany. Prices range DM 14–DM 17 for those under 27 and DM 18.50–DM 22.50 for those whose best years are already behind them.

UNIVERSITY AND STUDENT HOUSING Unfortunately, student housing options in Germany are few and far between. Only a handful of larger German cities, such as Berlin, have universities willing to rent dorm rooms for short stays. When available, student housing generally means sharing a two- or four-bed dorm room with communal kitchens and bathrooms. Rates run about DM 35 per person.

PRIVATZIMMER If you're looking to save a little money and would like to meet a German family, renting a room in a private home is a great option. Prices for these rooms, often every bit as nice if not nicer than rooms in pensions or cheap hotels, run DM 18–DM 30 per person, usually including breakfast. Showers, on the other hand, are either in the hall or are unavailable, so be sure to ask. The only real drawback is that most of these rooms require minimum stays of two or three nights; if you're only looking for an overnight stay, try phoning anyway, as many families are flexible. Lists of rooms in private homes can be acquired from the local tourist office in most German cities.

CAMPING Germany offers campers a wide selection of choice spots to pup their tents and sleep cheap. A camping tour of Germany can be one of the best ways to see the country and meet locals and fellow travelers.

Beating Hostel Curfews

Although all IYHF hostels have pesky curfews, many as early as 10 PM, there is an easy way to get around them in most cases: It's a little-known but important fact that most German youth hostels have extra keys that they'll let you hang on to for a small deposit, usually in the neighborhood of DM 20. With keys in hand, you can go out and paint the town red, let yourself in at the end of the night, and still take advantage of the low, low rates.

➢ **CAMPGROUNDS** • Germany is loaded with campsites. Campgrounds around urban centers tend to be on the outskirts of town but are usually accessible by public transport. Unless you really go off the beaten path (*see* Off-Road Camping, *below*), you'll find that most campgrounds have modern facilities such as toilets, showers, running water, and even kitchens. Some sites, especially those around beaches, may also have shops, restaurants, and the occasional movie theater or mini-golf course. The trade-off is that these sites are often overcrowded with rowdy youth groups and RV-driving tourists, particularly in the warmer months.

Prices at most campgrounds are pretty steady throughout the country: about DM 6.50 per person per night and an additional DM 5 for each tent. If you're traveling with more than five or six people you may want to call ahead to make reservations. Local tourist offices will have all the necessary info.

The farmers around the Black Forest are especially well known for their hospitality toward backpackers. Asking permission to camp in a field will often result in an invitation to sleep in a warm bed or join the family for a traditional meal.

➢ **OFF-ROAD CAMPING** • Camping anywhere but at official campgrounds is frowned upon. Still, hard-core outdoors enthusiasts should not be deterred. If you're backpacking in the boonies and want to camp off-road, just make sure you're far enough off the trail to avoid detection. When closer to civilization, the primary goal is to avoid getting arrested; ask the local tourist office or police department about acceptable unofficial campsites and the laws of the region. Otherwise, make damn sure that no one will see you. If you find a farmhouse, chances are the owners will let you set up in a field if you ask politely, promising to keep the ruckus after dark to a minimum and to clean up before moving on. If there's nobody around to ask, try to avoid climbing fences, find the safest-looking place to set up camp, and realize you're taking a risk.

ROUGHING IT When your money starts to run dangerously low or your yen for adventure begins to grow dangerously high it might be time to consider roughing it—sleeping anywhere that will cost you nothing but a bit of nerve. The usual list of possible places to crash for free includes train stations, airports, park benches, and overgrown bushes; but for the imaginative, the possibilities are infinite. Desperate travelers have been known to sleep in dark alleys, stairwells, and even under parked cars. It all depends on where you draw the line between risky and ridiculous.

FOOD

If you care at all about your fat intake, your cholesterol level, or your budget, then eating traditional, robust German fare may not be for you. This is a pig-and-potato land that has as many words for cooking and referring to swine as America has for beef. Being a vegetarian in Germany is a bit like being a virgin at an orgy. Hypersaturated fats and heavy sauces are worshipped most fervently at beer halls and gardens, where the patrons are mostly well into their 50s and apparently unaware of the health craze beginning to creep into their country. However, you probably won't be able to afford many such meals—stick to the excellent beer rather than forking over big bucks for what, to the American palate, is fairly bland stuff.

If you want to have a decent sit-down meal, you're much better off looking for cheap ethnic restaurants. Italian, Greek, and Balkan restaurants are usually far less expensive than German restaurants. Chinese restaurants, too, tend to be cheap, and often offer cheap lunch specials. Budget travelers can save even more money by eating at street-side stands and butcher shops, or buying supplies at markets. You can find street stands, known as *Imbiss*, on almost every busy shopping street, in parking lots, train stations, and near markets. They serve *wurst* (sausage) and rolls filled with cheese, cold meat, or fish. Prices range from DM 3 to DM 6 per portion. Many Turks and Italians have migrated to Germany over the years, bringing their culinary habits with them. You won't need to look far for a stand selling *doner Kebabs*, a Turkish delicacy featuring meaty slabs of grilled lamb in pita bread with various vegetables and dressings. Also widely available, affordable, and greasy are the pizzas sold at stands and restaurants all over the country. No surprises here—pizza's pizza in Germany, too. Cafeterias at department stores like Hertie and Kaufhof serve cheap, mediocre food, and university **Mensas** (cafeterias) slop up edible meals for incredibly low prices.

Many *Metzgerei* (butcher shops) also serve hot food and meat sandwiches. The Vincenz-Murr chain in Bavaria serves good and reasonably priced food. Try *warmer Leberkäs mit Kartoffelsalat,* a Bavarian specialty that consists of baked meat loaf with sweet mustard and potato salad. In north Germany, try *Bouletten,* small hamburgers, or *Currywurst,* sausages in curry sauce.

Your last budget option is the dreaded McDonald's, which, although cheap and familiar, could mean the McTrauma of sitting in a sterile, plastic booth eating McGrub while the "true" Germany awaits beyond the golden arches—enough to bum your McHigh.

The price categories in this book are loosely based on the assumption that you are going to chow down a main course, a drink, and maybe a cup of coffee. Antacids are extra.

SPORTS AND OUTDOOR ACTIVITIES

The Germans are nothing if not sports crazy. The following is a list of some of the more popular participant sports. More detailed information can be found throughout this book. Details of important sporting events are published every month by regional and local tourist offices.

HIKING AND MOUNTAINEERING Germany's hill and mountain regions have thousands of kilometers of marked hiking and mountain-walking tracks. These Wanderwege are administered by regional hiking clubs and, where appropriate, mountaineering groups, all of which are affiliated with the *Verband Deutscher Gebirgs- und Wandervereine e.V.* (Reichsstr. 4, 6600 Saarbrücken 3). This hiking-and-mountaineering society can provide information on routes, hiking paths, overnight accommodations, and mountain huts in western Germany. The former East German state-run hiking organization has collapsed. Local tourist offices in eastern and western Germany can provide information about trails and regional hiking clubs.

For information on more serious backpacking and mountaineering options, contact the *Deutsche Alpenverein* (Praterinsel 5, D–8000 Munich 22). The club administers more than 50 mountain huts and about 15,000 kilometers (9,500) miles of Alpine paths. In addition, it provides courses in mountaineering and touring suggestions. Foreign members are admitted.

Various mountaineering schools offer week-long courses ranging from basic techniques for beginners to advanced mountaineering. Contact the *Verband Deutscher Ski und Bergführer* (Lindenstr. 16, D–8980 Oberstdorf).

SAILING Renting a sailboat for a day or longer is possible on many of Germany's larger bodies of water. Most North Sea and Baltic resorts and harbors have either sailing schools or sailboats for rent. Lake sailing is equally popular, particularly on the Chiemsee in Bavaria and on the Bodensee. For details, write *Verband Deutscher Segelschulen* (Graelstr. 45, 44 Münster). If you're planning on renting a sailboat, be sure to bring some type of sailing certification issued by the authorities in your home country.

SWIMMING Almost all larger towns and resorts have open-air and indoor pools, the former frequently heated, the latter often with wave or whirlpool machines. In addition, practically all coastal resorts have indoor saltwater pools, as well as good beaches, and German spas have thermal or mineral-water indoor pools. Bavaria's Alpine lakes and a large number of artificial lakes have swimming and sunbathing areas.

Note that swimming in rivers, especially the larger ones, is not recommended and in some cases is positively forbidden—either due to shipping, pollution, or both. Look for BADEN VERBOTEN signs.

Those with sharp vision will quickly notice that Germans are keen on nudism. Many pools have special days for nude bathing, and on certain beaches nude bathing is allowed. Signs that read FKK mean nudity is permitted.

WINDSURFING Windsurfing has become so popular in Germany, particularly on the Bavarian lakes, that it has had to be restricted on some beaches as a result of collisions between windsurfers and swimmers. Nonetheless, there are still many places where you can windsurf and where windsurfers can easily be rented. Lessons, at about DM 25 per hour, are also generally available. For further information, contact the German National Tourist Office (*see* Government Tourist Offices, *above*) or VDWS (Fasserstr. 30, 8120 Weilheim, Oberbayern).

WINTER SPORTS Southern Bavaria is Germany's big winter-sports region and Garmisch-Partenkirchen the best-known center. There are also winter-sports resorts in the Black Forest, the Harz region, the Bavarian Forest, the Rhön Mountains, the Fichtelgebirge, the Sauerland, and the Swabian Alps. The season generally runs from the middle of December to the end of March, but at higher altitudes, such as the Zugspitze (near Garmisch), you can usually ski from as early as the end of November to as late as the middle of May. Unless you're really serious, there's no need to bring skis with you—you can rent them on the spot.

For *Langlauf* (cross-country skiing), which is becoming increasingly popular in Germany, there are stretches of *Loipen* (prepared tracks) in the valleys and foothills of most winter-sports centers, as well as in the suburbs of larger towns in southern Bavaria. Many Wanderwege are used as cross-country ski trails in the winter.

Alpin (downhill) skiing is not very popular in Germany, but there are a few ski resorts in the Bavarian Alps and the Black Forest. In the Alps, runs and schools can be found at Bayrischzell, Berchtesgaden, Garmisch-Partenkirchen, Füssen, and Oberstdorf. There are ski resorts at Altglashütten, Bernau, and Feldberg in the Black Forest.

Ice rinks, many open all year, are everywhere.

FRANKFURT AND HESSEN

2

By Christy C. Collins

Although Hessen doesn't draw the masses like some of its more distinctive and famous neighbors, it still presents the perfect opportunity to see a slice of Germany that tourists often don't touch. Part industrial center, part rural landscape with ancient villages and castles, Hessen has both the ugliness of towns rebuilt after World War II, and the charm of towns virtually untouched for ages. Hessen also contains the practically unavoidable, ultramodern city of Frankfurt, which you might come to like if you get past its resemblance to other charmless financial centers you may know. In the north of Hessen lies the Lahn Valley, a small river valley dotted with villages and castles. Nature lovers should look south to the huge forest of Odenwald. Two ranges of hills roughly divide the region in half: the austere, volcanic Vogelsburg and the lusher Taunus, covered with orchards and natural springs. The southwest offers the Rheingau, a wine-producing region and ritzy resort area near the Rhine.

From the destruction of the Allied attacks on Hessen during World War II arose the modern cities of Darmstadt and Kassel; however, the university town of Marburg, the Baroque Fulda, and smaller villages like Gelnhausen or Michelstadt retain their ancient feeling, with beautiful old churches, exquisitely preserved city centers, and many examples of traditional German half-timbered houses.

Frankfurt

When you tell people you're going to Frankfurt, whose main claim to fame is its airport, they usually reply, "So where are you flying from there?" The second most popular response is, "Why?" Despite its reputation as a mere point of departure for more exciting destinations, the city is also a thriving metropolis. Locals call Frankfurt "Mainhattan," because it lies on both banks of the Main River and because it's so Americanized. About 250,000 people commute into the city every day to work in its modern skyscrapers.

Frankfurt was completely destroyed in World War II, and only a few historical buildings still stand. If you want to explore the past, you'll have to visit museums and the popular but rebuilt Goethehaus, where the literary genius Johann Wolfgang von Goethe was born and raised.

Frankfurt is definitely not the easiest city to befriend; it's primarily an industrial and commercial center, the drug and crime capital of Hessen, and the host of the American military headquarters in Germany. But if you decide to stay for a few days, it

Hessen

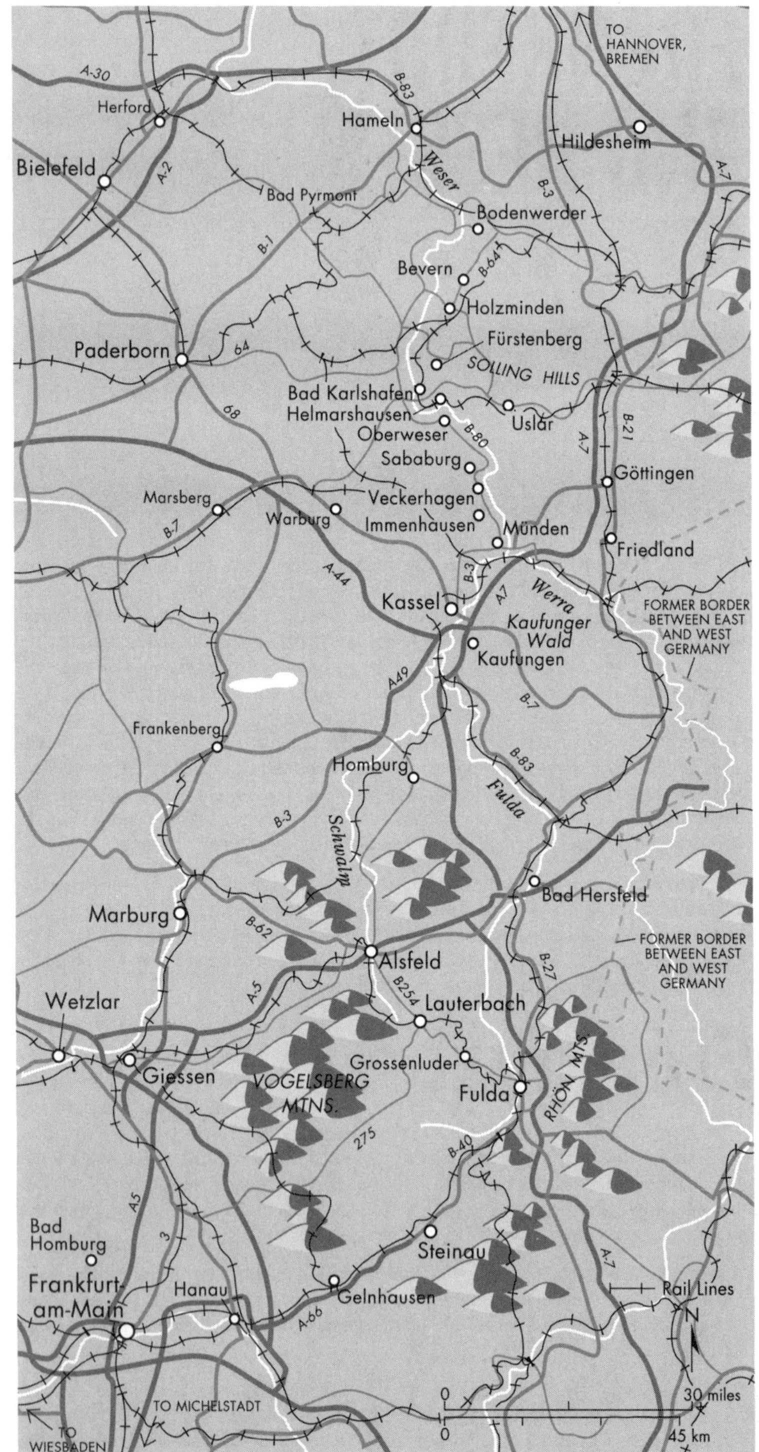
TO HANNOVER, BREMEN
A-30
Herford
B-83
Hameln
Hildesheim
Bielefeld
A-2
Weser
A-7
B-3
Bad Pyrmont
Bodenwerder
B-1
Bevern
B-64
Holzminden
Fürstenberg
Paderborn
64
SOLLING HILLS
Bad Karlshafen
Helmarshausen
Uslar
68
Oberweser
B-80
A-7
B-21
Sababurg
Göttingen
Marsberg
Veckerhagen
B-7
Warburg
Immenhausen
Münden
Friedland
A-44
B-3
Werra
Kassel
A7
FORMER BORDER BETWEEN EAST AND WEST GERMANY
Kaufunger Wald
Kaufungen
A49
B-7
Frankenberg
B-83
Homburg
Fulda
B-3
Schwalm
Bad Hersfeld
Marburg
B-62
FORMER BORDER BETWEEN EAST AND WEST GERMANY
Alsfeld
B-27
A-5
B254
Wetzlar
Lauterbach
Grossenluder
Giessen
VOGELSBERG MTNS.
Fulda
RHÖN MTS.
275
B-40
A5
3
Bad Homburg
Steinau
A-7
Frankfurt-am-Main
Hanau
Gelnhausen
Rail Lines
N
A-66
0
30 miles
TO MICHELSTADT
0
45 km
TO WIESBADEN

might just grow on you. Frankfurt claims an extremely diverse citizenship—from the junkie passed out with a syringe dangling from his limp hand to the rushed corporate banker to the teenage techno head to the student anarchist. The thing that makes this city so different from others is that it caters to the lifestyles of *all* of these crowds. You can find tons of lively, crowded pubs and *Apfelwein* (apple-wine) taverns in Sachsenhausen (the district on the south side of the Main) and cellars with good jazz bands almost anywhere. Frankfurt is *the* German center of techno music, and discos here are alive until 6 in the morning. If you're more interested in eyeing potential partners across a smoky room, or just hanging out with the people you're already with, Frankfurt has more than its fair share of small bars and cafés.

Frankfurt is like a job applicant whose resumé sucks but who dazzles you in the interview. It looks lousy on paper with its high drug and crime stats, but once you experience it, you're hooked.

BASICS

AMERICAN EXPRESS You can change money, change any kind of traveler's checks for free, or get a cash advance on your American Express card. *Kaiserstr. 8, tel. 069/720016. 24-hour refund assistance for traveler's checks: tel. 069/01303100. 10-min walk from Hauptbahnhof. Open weekdays 9:30–5:30, Sat. 9–noon.*

BUREAUX DE CHANGE Banks are your best bet, charging only a 1% commission to change traveler's checks. Post offices (*see* Mail, *below*) charge a DM 3 commission for each traveler's check. To change money in the evening, go to the airport or train station. The banks at the Hauptbahnhof charge DM 3 to change up to DM 100 and DM 7.50 to change DM 101–DM 750. *Airport: Departure Hall B, open daily 7 AM–9:30 PM; Arrival Hall B6, open daily 7:30 AM–9 PM; Arrival Hall BB, open daily 6:15 AM–9:30 PM. Hauptbahnhof: Deutsche Verkehrs Kredit Bank at s. entrance, open daily 6:30 AM–10 PM; in shopping passage, open daily 8–8.*

CONSULATES **United States.** *Siesmayerstr. 21, tel. 069/75350. Bus 35 from Konstablerwache to Palmgarten/Siesmayerstr.*
Great Britain. *Bockenheimer Landstr. 42, tel. 069/170–0020.*
Australia. *Gutleutstr. 85, tel. 069/273–9090. From Hauptbahnhof turn right on Baseler Str., left on Gutleutstr.*

LAUNDRY **Wasch Center.** For DM 6 you can wash a load, and for DM 1 you can dry it for 15 minutes. *Wallstr. 8, near hostel. Open daily 6 AM–10 PM.*

MAIL AND PHONES Post offices at the Hauptbahnhof and the airport are open 24 hours. The **main post office** near the city center has poste restante services (Windows 6 and 7) and a fax machine. Sending a fax (Window 60) to the United States costs DM 21 for the first page and DM 18 for each additional page. Picking up a fax (Windows 24–27) costs DM 5.50 for the first page, then DM 2.50 for each page after that. You can make international calls from the phones at the airport, Hauptbahnhof, and main post office. The area code for Frankfurt is 069. *Mailing address: Hauptpostlagernd/Zeil 110, 60313 Frankfurt, tel. 069/2111, fax 069/296884. U-Bahn Hauptwache. Open weekdays 8–6, Sat. 8–noon.*

MEDICAL AID The pharmacy in the Hauptbahnhof is open weekdays 6:30 AM–9 PM and weekends 8 AM–9 PM. Outside the door to the left is a list of all-night pharmacies; two pharmacies are open each night of the week. **Medical emergency:** tel. 069/19292.

VISITOR INFORMATION **Tourist Information Römer.** The friendly staff can provide you with information about the city and upcoming events. Watch out or you might walk out with five pounds of paper under your arm. *Römerberg 27, tel. 069/212–38708. Next to Römer in Römerberg Pl. Open Apr.–Oct., weekdays 9–7, weekends 9:30–6; Nov.–Mar., weekdays 9–6, weekends 9:30–6.*

Frankfurt

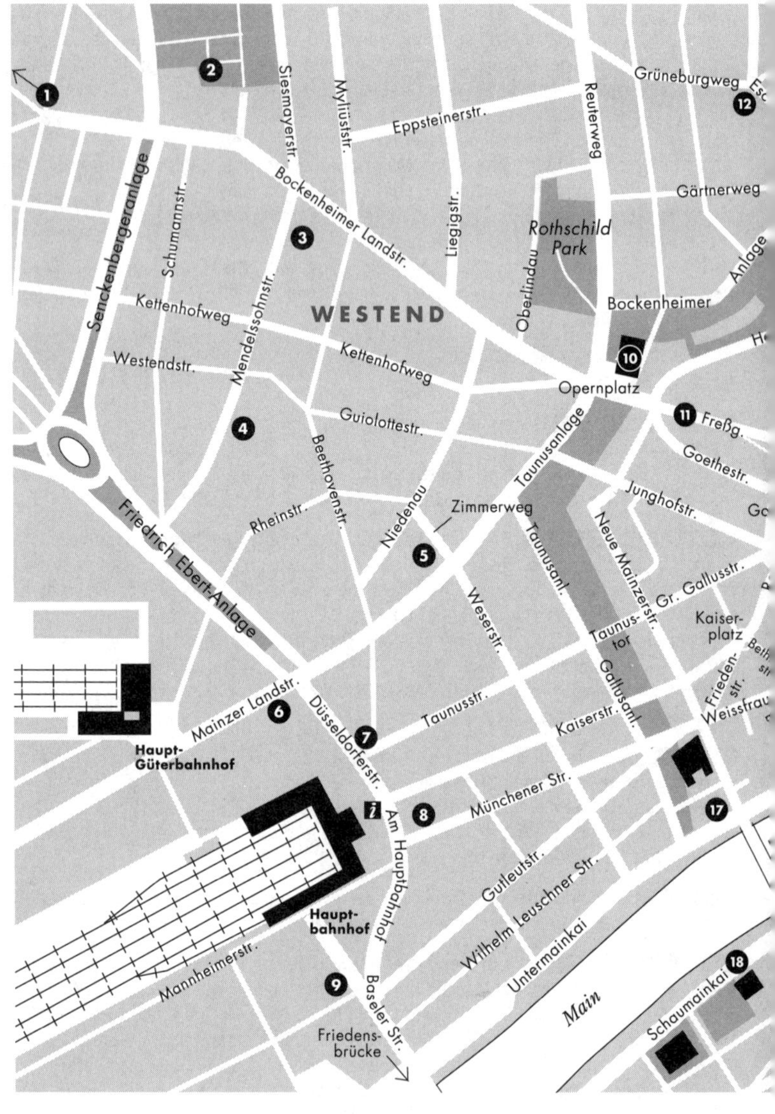

Sights
Alte Oper, **10**
Bockenheim, **1**
Dom St. Bartholomäus, **21**
Freßgasse, **11**
Goethehaus und Goethemuseum, **16**
Hauptwache, **14**
Jüdisches Museum, **17**
Katharinenkirche, **15**
Museumsufer, **18**
Palmengarten und Botanischer Garten, **2**
Römerberg, **20**
Sachsenhausen, **19**
Zoologischer Garten, **23**

Lodging
Haus der Jugend, **22**
Hotel Adler, **7**
Hotel Atlas, **5**
Hotel Münchner Hof, **8**
Nord-Hotel, **13**
Pension Aller, **9**
Pension Backer, **3**
Pension Bruns, **4**
Pension Fennischfuscher, **6**
Pension Uebe, **12**

Frankfurt

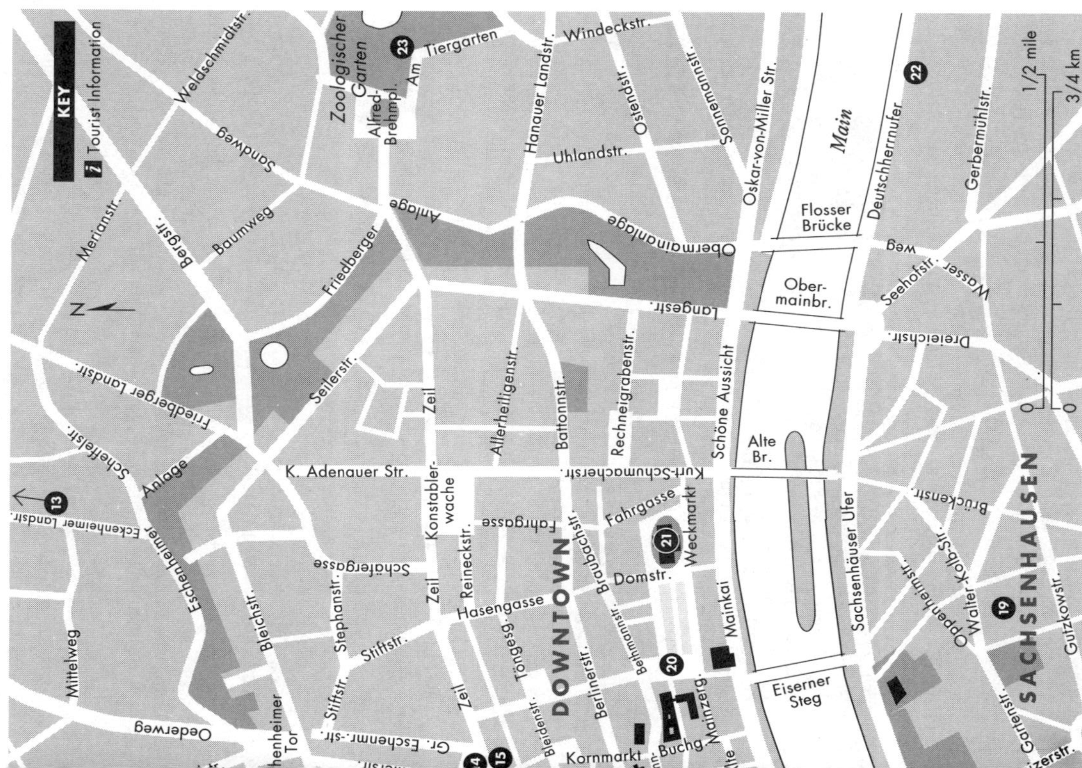
KEY
Tourist Information
N
Mittelweg
Eckenheimer Landstr.
Scheffelstr.
Friedberger Landstr.
Merianstr.
Oederweg
Eschenheimer
Anlage
Bergstr.
Weldschmidtstr.
Baumweg
Sandweg
Bleichstr.
henheimer
Tor
K. Adenauer Str.
Seilerstr.
Friedberger
Stiftstr.
Stephanstr.
Schäfergasse
Stiftstr.
Gr. Eschenmr.-str.
Zoologischer
Garten
Alfred-
Brehmpl.
Anlage
Am
Tiergarten
Zeil
Konstabler-
wache
Zeil
Zeil
Reineckstr.
Hasengasse
Töngesg.
Allerheiligenstr.
Fahrgasse
Bleidenstr.
DOWNTOWN
Battonnstr.
Hanauer Landstr.
Uhlandstr.
Windeckstr.
Kornmarkt
Berlinerstr.
Braubachstr.
Kurt-Schumacherstr.
Bethmannstr.
Domstr.
Fahrgasse
Rechneigrabenstr.
Langestr.
Obermainanlage
Ostendstr.
Weckmarkt
Mainzerg.
Mainkai
Schöne Aussicht
Sonnemannstr.
Oskar-von-Miller Str.
Alte
Br.
Eiserner
Steg
Ober-
mainbr.
Flosser
Brücke
Main
Sachsenhäuser Ufer
Deutschherrnufer
Oppenheimstr.
Walter-Kolb-Str.
Brückenstr.
Dreieichstr.
Seehofstr.
weg
Wasser
Gerbermühlstr.
Gartenstr.
SACHSENHAUSEN
Gutzkowstr.
0
1/2 mile
0
3/4 km
13
15
19
20
21
22
23

Tourist Information Hauptbahnhof. This office is a little busier than the Römer office, so it might take longer to get what you need. *Hauptbahnhof, opposite Track 23, tel. 069/212–38849. Open Apr.–Oct., Mon.–Sat. 8 AM–10 PM, Sun. 9:30–6; Nov.–Mar., Mon.–Sat. 8 AM–9 PM, Sun. 9:30–6.*

Lesben Informations und Beratungsstelle (LIBS). The "Lesbian Information and Advice" phone service can provide counseling, group support for coming out, information on lesbian activities in the city, and listings for lesbian roommates. The staff speaks a little English. *Tel. 069/499–0008. Phones open Thurs.–Fri. 5–7:30.*

Rosa Telefon Ffm. Rosa offers men's support groups and consultation and has general information about Frankfurt's gay community—gay bars, clubs, activities. *Tel. 069/730–6767. Phones open Sun. 6–10.*

COMING AND GOING

BY TRAIN The **Hauptbahnhof** is the main terminal of the Deutsche Bundesbahn (German Federal Railway), so you'll have no problems getting in and out of Frankfurt. EuroCity (EC) trains connect Frankfurt with big European cities; InterCity (IC) trains with German cities; InterCity Express (ICE) with most big western German cities. You can ride any of these trains free with a Eurailpass. For information, call **Deutsche Bundesbahn** (tel. 069/19479) or ask at the DB information office opposite Track 8 in the Hauptbahnhof. Frankfurt has connections to Berlin (6½ hours), Hamburg (3½ hours), Munich (3½ hours), and almost everywhere else in Europe. Frankfurt's Hauptbahnhof, about 1 kilometer (⅔ mile) west of downtown, has a bank, a 24-hour post office, a pharmacy, a tourist-information office, and luggage lockers.

BY BUS **Deutsche Touring** (Am Römerhof 17, tel. 069/79030), Germany's main bus company, is affiliated with Deutsche Bundesbahn and has lines going to 200 European cities. Buses arrive at and depart from the south side of the Hauptbahnhof, where the company has an office open weekdays 7:30–6 and weekends 7:30 AM–2 PM.

BY MITFAHRGELEGENHEIT Ride-share offices can match you with a driver going your way. **Mitfahrzentrale** has an extensive computer file of drivers' names, driver's-license numbers, and vehicle-registration numbers, so if something goes wrong you can report it easily. *Baseler Str. 7, tel. 069/236444 or 069/236445. 200 yds from Hauptbahnhof on Baseler Pl. Open weekdays 9–6:30, Sat. 8–noon.*

The listings at the **Interdrive Mitfahr-Zentrale** aren't as extensive, but you can try it if the main office doesn't meet your needs. *Homburger Str. 36, tel. 069/770211. U6 or U7 to Bockenheimer Warte. Open weekdays 8–7, Sat. 8–4.*

BY PLANE All major European cities and many U.S. cities have direct flights to **Flughafen Frankfurt,** Europe's second-busiest airport. The Köln-Munich Autobahn (A–3) links Frankfurt with the airport, 10 kilometers (6 miles) southwest of downtown. The airport has a bureau de change open from early morning to evening, a 24-hour post office, and phones from which you can make international calls.

➢ **AIRPORT TRANSPORT** • Two S-Bahn lines (suburban trains) run from the airport to downtown Frankfurt. S15 goes to the Hauptbahnhof every 10 minutes and S14 goes to Hauptwache Square (*see* Getting Around, *below*) every 20 minutes. Each trip takes about 15 minutes. Although taking the S-Bahn into the city is easiest, you can also catch city Bus 61, which makes the half-hour trip to the Südbahnhof in Sachsenhausen every 15 minutes. A taxi ride from the airport to the city center (about DM 35) takes 20–40 minutes, depending on traffic.

GETTING AROUND

There are four main districts of Frankfurt: downtown, Sachsenhausen, Westend, and Bockenheim. The downtown area is a pentagon-shaped region on the north bank of the Main River, between Untermain Brücke on the west and Obermainbrücke on the east. From downtown you can cross the Eiserner Steg, a pedestrian bridge, to the south side of the Main to reach Sachsenhausen, a mostly pedestrian neighborhood with pubs and cobblestone streets. The Westend, Frankfurt's financial district, is northwest of downtown and north of the Hauptbahnhof. Bockenheim, primarily a student and low-income area, is northwest of Westend.

Beware the streets in Frankfurt; their curves and abrupt name changes can make you feel like you've had a few beers even if you haven't. Much action takes place around the city's two main squares: Römerberg and Hauptwache. Römerberg is in the southern part, near the Main; Hauptwache is north of Römerberg and is the center of the downtown area. Both the U-Bahn and the S-Bahn stop at Hauptwache. Although Frankfurt doesn't have as many pedestrian zones as other German cities, the easiest way to explore the downtown area is on foot. Most of the walk-only areas are near Hauptwache and Römerberg squares, on Zeil and Freßgasse (*see* Worth Seeing, *below*), and in Sachsenhausen.

Frankfurt's public-transportation system is complex but efficient. The four modes of transport—U-Bahn (subway), S-Bahn (underground suburban railway), Straßenbahn (streetcar-tram), and bus—all use the same tickets. You can buy short-trip tickets, one-day tickets, and three-day tickets at blue machines labeled FAHRSCHEINE or from bus drivers. Short-trip tickets cost DM 2, DM 2.60 during rush hour (weekdays 6:30 AM–8:30 AM and 3:30 PM–6:30 PM); one-day tickets are DM 5; and three-day tickets run DM 12. You can also buy one-day and three-day tickets that include transportation to Frankfurt's suburbs (DM 16, DM 24). Eurailpasses are valid on the S-Bahn only. The U-Bahn and S-Bahn are your best bets for rapid transportation to all of Frankfurt's areas until the system closes, at about midnight. Some bus routes have night lines, but check their routes, which may differ from daytime operations. *U-Bahn, streetcar, bus information: Stadtwerke Frankfurt am Main, tel. 069/213–22236 or 069/213–22295. S-Bahn information: tel. 069/19419.*

BY TAXI Taxis (tel. 069/542003 or 069/250001) are expensive in Frankfurt, so use them sparingly. The initial pickup fee is DM 4, then it's DM 2.15 per kilometer until 11 PM and DM 2.35 per kilometer 11 PM–6 AM. The best places to hail a taxi are near the Hauptbahnhof and big hotels. Cabs charge an additional pickup fee (depending on the distance) when you request them by phone.

WHERE TO SLEEP

Frankfurt's various trade fairs and the wealthy businesspeople they attract make inexpensive accommodation an oxymoron. The **Haus der Jugend** (youth hostel) is the least expensive place to stay. If that's booked, try the **Campingplätze Niederräder** (Ufer 2, tel. 069/673846) or the cheap hotels in the red-light district near the Hauptbahnhof. If you can't find or afford anything in the city, try the suburb of Bad Homburg (*see* Near Frankfurt, *below*). Unless stated otherwise, rooms in the hotels and pensions reviewed below have private sinks and hallway showers and toilets. Call to reserve a spot before showing up at a hotel, because rooms fill quickly throughout the year.

➢ **UNDER DM 70 • Pension Backer.** Aside from the youth hostel, Backer is the best deal in town. On the same street as Pension Bruns (*see below*), it's a short walk to Palmengarten and around the corner from the U-Bahn Westend station. The neighborhood is nice, safe, and has some beautiful old homes. Some doubles are larger than others, but avoid the ones overlooking the street unless you enjoy noisy automotive serenades. Singles run DM 20–DM 40, doubles DM 60, triples DM 80. *Mendelssohnstr. 92, tel. 069/747992 or 069/747900. From Hauptbahnhof walk up*

Friedrich-Ebert-Anlage and turn right on Wilhelm Hauffstr., which turns into Mendelssohnstr. at Bettinapl.; or U6 or U7 to Westend, walk up Bockenheimer Landstr. and turn left on Mendelssohnstr. 35 rooms, none with bath. Showers DM 3, breakfast included.

➢ **UNDER DM 80 • Hotel Atlas.** Once you check in and have got past the scowling faces of the owners, you'll find clean, comfortable rooms. Speaking English doesn't cut it here, so bust out a little French or German if you can. Singles go for DM 54 and doubles for DM 74. *Zimmerweg 1, tel. 069/723946. Walk up Mainzer Landstr. and turn left on Zimmerweg. 12 rooms, none with bath. Showers DM 4, breakfast included.*

If you use the words "cheap lodging" and "Frankfurt" in the same sentence, locals will either laugh at you or look at you with that knowing smile that says, "A tourist, no doubt."

Pension Bruns. Located in a large old building, the pension's spacious, airy rooms have hardwood floors and comfortable beds. Since single rooms are not offered, solo travelers can share a room with other travelers (*see also* Roulette, Russian). Doubles cost DM 72, and triples are DM 96 (breakfast included). The upper echelons of Frankfurt's Jewish community lived in the surrounding neighborhood before World War II, and it's worth taking a walk just to check out the ritzy houses. *Mendelssohnstr. 42, tel. 069/748896. From Hauptbahnhof walk n. on Friedrich-Ebert-Anlage, turn right on Wilhelm Hauffstr., which turns into Mendelssohnstr. at Bettinapl.; or U6 or U7 to Westend, walk northwest on Bockenheimer Landstr., and turn left on Mendelssohnstr. 7 rooms, none with bath. Showers DM 2.*

➢ **UNDER DM 90 • Hotel Adler.** Clean sheets, available (but musty) rooms, and a location five minutes from the Hauptbahnhof are the redeeming qualities of this nondescript hotel. Singles are DM 60, doubles DM 90. Breakfast is DM 5, and an extra bed costs DM 30. *Nidda Str. 65, 4th floor, tel. 069/233455 or 069/231445. From Hauptbahnhof turn left on Düsseldorferstr., right on Nidda Str. 22 rooms, 7 with bath. Disabled accessible.*

Hotel Münchner Hof. Tourists and swashbuckling entrepreneurs attending Frankfurt's trade fairs make up the clientele at this seven-floor Hyattlike hotel. The rooms are small, but you can watch *Cheers* reruns in German on your color TV. Singles go for DM 70 (DM 90 with bath), doubles DM 90 (DM 110 with bath). The friendly management can answer any questions on Frankfurt. *Münchener Str. 46, across from Hauptbahnhof, tel. 069/230066 or 069/230067. 42 rooms, some with bath. Disabled accessible, luggage storage, breakfast included.*

Nord-Hotel. As the name indicates, this dim hotel is in the northern part of Frankfurt. It's close to Holzhausen Park but not much else. The café downstairs attracts old ladies and their dogs, but don't let that dissuade you from ordering a pastry and cup of coffee. Singles are DM 60, doubles DM 90. *Eckenheimer Landstr. 166, tel. 069/555518. From Hauptbahnhof U5 to Adickes-Nibelungenallee. 25 rooms, none with bath.*

Pension Fennischfuscher. These cramped rooms have clean sheets, but some of the sinks have a few random strands of hair around the drain. Most of the rooms overlook a main street, so if noisy cars threaten your slumber, go downstairs to the restaurant-pub and indulge in the country's best remedy for insomnia: a few German beers. Singles are DM 55, doubles DM 85, and triples DM 120. *Mainzer Landstr. 95, tel. 069/253855. 5-min walk from Hauptbahnhof, at Ottostr. and Mainzer Landstr., Pl. der Republik. 18 rooms, none with bath. Luggage storage.*

Pension Uebe. Those living on cheese and bread will find the rooms' small refrigerators key for survival. Uebe is a good place to meet locals (mostly businesspeople and apartment seekers) and to start your walk to Holzhausen Park (*see* Cheap Thrills, *below*) or the Palmengarten. Singles are DM 55–DM 80, doubles DM 90, and breakfast DM 9. *Grüneburgweg 3, tel. 069/591209. From Hauptbahnhof U4 to Theaterpl., transfer to U1, U2, or U3 to Grüneburgweg; or S15 to Hauptwache, and transfer to U1, U2, or U3 to Grüneburgweg. 18 rooms, some with bath. Showers DM 3.50, disabled accessible, luggage storage.*

➢ **UNDER DM 130 • Pension Aller.** Frau Kraus's lively wit and endless stories are enough to make you want to lay down your life savings to spend time with her. She was born in this beautiful home about 60 years ago. The rooms, with hardwood floors, look like they came out of *Architectural Digest.* Singles cost DM 85 and doubles DM 125, including a generous breakfast of bread, cheese, wurst, and coffee. Rooms for groups are available. If you're willing to splurge, this place is worth every pfennig. *Gutleutstr. 94, tel. 069/252596. 3-min walk from Hauptbahnhof, at Karlsruher Str. and Gutleutstr. Luggage storage, kitchen facilities, breakfast included.*

HOSTELS **Haus der Jugend (IYHF).** This cheap, clean, convenient youth hostel is the only true deal Frankfurt will offer you. It's on the south bank of the Main in Sachsenhausen, near the major sights and Apfelwein taverns. The two patios (one indoor, one outdoor) are perfect for reading, writing letters, or hanging out with other travelers. Theft is not a big problem here, as long as you put your stuff in the room lockers. Bring your own lock or buy one here. The midnight curfew is not strictly enforced, so don't worry if it takes you a little longer to stumble home than you expected. For DM 8 you can get lunch or dinner (wurst, french fries, salad, and dessert). Those under 20 pay DM 18.50, and those 20 or over pay DM 22.50. Four-bed rooms cost DM 27.50, two-bed rooms DM 32.50, and singles DM 40. There is a mandatory DM 10 deposit. *Deutschherrnufer 12, tel. 069/619058. From Hauptbahnhof Bus 46 to Frankensteiner Pl. 120 rooms (500 beds), none with bath. Disabled accessible, luggage storage, linen provided, pay phones, breakfast included. Rooms and reception desk (but not front door) closed daily 9 AM–1 PM.*

Avoid roughing it in Frankfurt—especially if you're a woman. You might go to bed with your backpack and chastity and wake up without either. The airport, the Hauptbahnhof, and Grüneburgpark are your safest bets. To get to Grüneburgpark take U1, U2, or U3 from Hauptwache to Holzhausenstraße.

FOOD

This city is the home of the frankfurter, a smoked sausage of beef or beef and pork. If meat makes you sick, however, don't fret. Vegetarians can get pasta in Italian restaurants or falafel at Turkish fast-food places. Head over to **Freßgasse** (*see* Worth Seeing, *below*) and take your pick of cafés, restaurants, and delis. To get inexpensive traditional German food and Apfelwein visit Sachsenhausen across the Main. Try the local specialty, *Grüne Soße* (green sauce), with eggs or potatoes. Ketchup with your fries may not pass muster after you try this.

UNDER DM 10 **Ali Baba.** The 40 thieves would think this place is a steal. The tiny Turkish food stand in Sachsenhausen serves hot dogs (DM 2.50), hamburgers (DM 3), and bratwurst (DM 3). *Kleine Rittergasse 7, Sachsenhausen. Disabled accessible.*

Pizza Pedro. If you're not in the mood for pizza, *get* in the mood. The portions are large, the prices are cheap, and the taste will have you coming back every day. Single pizzas cook in about six minutes in an original wood-burning stone oven. To experience a super-cheap thrill, look in the front window and watch your pizza bake. Cheese pizza is DM 5, pepperoni pizza DM 6, and spaghetti dishes about DM 8. For a falafel, go to **Kebab Haus** right next door. *Paradiesgasse 38, Sachsenhausen, tel. 069/626307. Bus 36 from Konstablerwache to Elisabethenstr.*

Saladin. Vegetarians, Saladin is your godsend. Escape Germany's pork-infested dining rooms and seek refuge in this vegetarian and fish restaurant. You can choose from more than 60 different salads or serve yourself at the salad bar (DM 2.50 for every 100 grams). Hot meals, such as tofu paprika goulash, cost DM 9–DM 10. *Adalbertstr. 6, Bockenheim, tel. 069/779005. From Hauptwache U6 or U7 to Bockenheimer Warte. Disabled accessible. No Sat. dinner. Closed Sun.*

UNDER DM 15 **Apfelwein Klaus.** On a small street off Freßgasse, this restaurant serves Frankfurt cuisine to travelers and businesspeople. On a sunny day, kick back at an outdoor table and order the popular Frankfurter salad (DM 12): hard-boiled eggs, ham, and green sauce. If the "Sam I Am" motif resonates too strongly for you, try the *Leiterchen*: spare ribs and sauerkraut with ham gravy and bread (DM 14). *Meisengasse 10, tel. 069/282864. U-Bahn or S-Bahn Hauptwache. Disabled accessible.*

Klaane Sachsenhäuser. Typical Frankfurters have been eating the typical Frankfurt cuisine served here since 1886. The large open-air beer garden, sheltered by an enormous tree, creates a mellow atmosphere on a warm night. The Salini Room inside is named after a famous local artist whose paintings of German life decorate the walls. You may start resembling the rosy-cheeked, beer-bellied men in the paintings if you stay here long enough. A couple of frankfurters (the meat, not the people) with potato salad will set you back DM 8.50, and pork with sauerkraut and bread goes for DM 6.50. Larger entrées cost up to DM 15. *Neuer Wall 11, Sachsenhausen, tel. 069/615983. Disabled accessible. No lunch. Closed Sun.*

Struwwelpeter. Named after the unruly character in the famous children's book by Heinrich Hoffmann, this restaurant has long wood tables that create a festive tavern-like atmosphere. Small pots of Apfelwein (seven glasses' worth) go for DM 14. The patrons are mostly locals, and the waiters are friendly—once you get their attention. *Handkäse mit Musik* served with bread and butter costs DM 4, and *Schnitzel Paniert* (breaded pork with fried potatoes) costs DM 14. Menus have English translations. *2 entrances: Neuer Wall 3, Am Affentorpl., and Kleine Rittergasse 39, Sachsenhausen, tel. 069/611297 or 069/621297.*

UNDER DM 20 **Das Wirsthaus.** Despite its fake candles and fake indoor tree, this medieval-style restaurant somehow avoids sinking into the depths of cheesiness. An iron chandelier lights the room and lanterns light the tables, but the place is still dark. Locals love Das Wirsthaus for its big servings and reasonable prices. Try the Wirsthaus salad tray (cheese, tuna, eggs, onions, shrimp) for DM 15 or the Nürnberger *Rostbratwürstchen* (grilled Nürnberg sausages with sauerkraut and mashed potatoes) for DM 12.50. *Freßgasse 29, tel. 069/284399. U-Bahn or S-Bahn Hauptwache.*

Marco Polo and Taberna Royal. Wander around this 300-year-old castle and picture Teutonic knights raising their steins to camaraderie and good fortune. Raise a stein of your own in the bar upstairs or on one of the outdoor patios. Spaghetti with tomato sauce costs DM 9.50; if you can afford to spend DM 18.50, get the scallops with onions, home-fried potatoes, and salad. Try not to get too hammered—it's easy to get lost in this place. *Paradiesgasse 15–17, Sachsenhausen, tel. 069/632663. No lunch.*

WORTH SEEING

Most of Frankfurt's attractions are on the north bank of the Main between the Untermain Brücke and the Alte Brücke, but to get to the **Museumsufer,** a row of the city's seven best museums, you have to cross one of the bridges to the south bank of the Main. The **tourist-information office** at the Römer (*see* Visitor Information, *above*) can provide you with a map and pamphlet called "On the Way," which details walking tours of Frankfurt's churches.

ALTE OPER Some rich guys agreed to fork out heaps of money for the construction of the Old Opera House in 1870, as long as they got the best seats in the house. The building, seats and all, was bombed in 1944, and no one sang here again until 1981, when the Alte Oper reopened. Although it was reconstructed in its original style (costing DM 200 million), the theater now hosts modern shows and concerts—like *The Phantom of the Opera* and Howard Jones—as well as classical operas and symphonies. *Opernpl., tel. 069/1340. U6 or U7 to Alte Oper, or walk from Konstablerwache.*

BOCKENHEIM You're most likely to see black-clad hipsters, revolutionary activists, and lower-income Frankfurters in this predominantly student area. Like many student communities, Bockenheim is an energetic place conducive to protests and an occasional riot. Graffiti such as "Nazis raus" ("chuck out the Nazis"), "police + government = fascism," and "L.A. riots" decorate the sides of buildings. For some local flavor, hang out in one of the many cafés. Try **Stattcafé** (Grempstr. 21) for an artsy atmosphere or **Café au Lait** (Am Weingarten 12, tel. 069/701039), where you can get breakfast until 5 PM. *U6 or U7 to Leipziger Str.*

DOM ST. BARTHOLOMAUS Although most of the cathedral's chambers are closed for restoration until 1994, you can still admire the 300-foot-high red sandstone tower. The Dom is Frankfurt's biggest church and was the coronation site for the Holy Roman emperors. It's got plenty of those standard Gothic-cathedral features, including frescoes, altars, and tombstones, but the tower is what really sets it apart. *E. end of Römerberg Pl. U4 from Hauptbahnhof to Römer. Selected chambers open Mon.–Thurs. 2–6.*

FREßGASSE Also known as Große Bockenheimer Straße, this pedestrian zone that leads from Hauptwache to the Alte Oper is a posh tree-lined street full of specialty cheese shops, bakeries, delicatessens, and outdoor cafés. Freßgasse (Gobble Lane) is more upscale than the neighboring shopping street Zeil, since most of the businesspeople and well-dressed yuppies from the city's financial center lunch here. *Große Bockenheimer Str. U1, U2, U3, U6, or U7 to Hauptwache.*

GOETHEHAUS UND GOETHEMUSEUM The birthplace and childhood home of Johann Wolfgang von Goethe, the famed writer, poet, and theorist and one of Germany's most highly esteemed writers, will mean a lot more to you if you're familiar with his work—he actually talks about the house in his autobiography, *Fact and Fiction.* The house was fully reconstructed after the original was obliterated in World War II. The museum annex contains portraits of people who influenced Goethe and original letters written to him by lovers and friends. *Großer Hirschgraben 23–25, tel. 069/282824. U-Bahn or S-Bahn Hauptwache. Admission: DM 3, DM 2 students. Open Apr.–Sept., Mon.–Sat. 9–6, Sun. 10–1; Oct.–Mar., Mon.–Sat. 9–4, Sun. 10–1.*

An Apple a Day Keeps Sobriety Away

Sachsenhausen is commonly known as the "apple-wine quarter" for good reason—almost every restaurant and pub in this area serves **Apfelwein** ***(or Ebbelwoi). Look for the pine wreaths above the door that indicate apple wine is on tap. When you're craving sweet wine, try*** **Süßer**, ***which is made with lemonade. If a more savory (even sour) taste is up your alley, drink Sauer, a sour wine mixed with water rather than lemonade. Blend in with the locals and order*** **Handkäse mit Musik** ***(a hunk of cheese served with onions, herbs, and a vinegar dressing) to go with this Hessian specialty.***

JUDISCHES MUSEUM This museum documents Jewish history in Germany from 1100 to 1950. Except for the religious artifacts, practically all of the explanatory boards are in German. On one of the walls is a list of Jews who were deported from Frankfurt, either to ghettos or concentration camps, and what finally became of them. *Untermainkai 14–15, near n.-bank entrance to Untermain Brücke, tel. 069/212–35000. U1, U2, U3, or U4 to Theaterpl. Admission free. Open Tues., Thurs.–Sun. 10–5; Wed. 10–8.*

KATHARINENKIRCHE This large, roomy church with many stained-glass windows was the first Protestant church in Germany and is the baptismal site of Goethe. In one of the windows is a clock reading 9:30 with Mar. 22, 1944, written on a slip of paper beneath it, a remembrance of the morning the church was bombed. *Katharinenpl., next to Hauptwache. Open weekdays 2–6.*

MUSEUMSUFER Locals call the string of museums on **Schaumainkai,** the street lining the southern side of the Main River, the Museumsufer. There's a museum for every taste, but one that's sure to please is the **Deutsches Filmmuseum** (Schaumainkai 41, tel. 069/212–38830). A theater (DM 6.50, DM 5 students) on the ground floor of this fun museum shows famous and not-so-famous films from all over (France, Argentina, United States). The permanent exhibit is set up to make you feel like you're walking in and out of little cinemas and includes many hands-on machines that display the use of light and depth in projection. The **Deutsches Postmuseum** (Schaumainkai 53, tel. 069/60600) colorfully exhibits the history of communications, postal uniforms, and mailboxes, as well as a large collection of stamps. Downstairs are postal bikes, carriages, and trucks interspersed with phone booths, TVs, and other gadgets. Even if you're not a philatelist, you'll have a good time. The **Museum für Völkerkunde** (Ethnological Museum, Schaumainkai 29, tel. 069/212–35391) compares different cultures, attempting to foster understanding among them through yearly exhibits. The **Museum für Kunsthandwerk** (Museum for Arts and Crafts, Schaumainkai 17, tel. 069/212–34037) displays ceramic, glass, metal, and wood works, as well as some ancient book illustrations and tapestries. Admission usually costs about DM 3 (DM 1.50 students). The **Deutsches Städelsches Kunstinstitut und Städtische Galerie** (a.k.a. **Städel,** Schaumainkai 63 and Halbeinstr. 1, tel. 069/605098) is a typical art museum with an impressive collection of paintings from the 14th to 20th centuries, sculptures from the 19th and 20th centuries, and drawings and prints from the 15th to 20th centuries, including works by Rembrandt, Monet, Braque, Picasso, and Matisse. The **Liebieshaus Museum** (Schaumainkai 71, tel. 069/212–38617) houses sculptures from various artistic movements (Middle Ages, Renaissance, Baroque) and civilizations (Egyptian, East Asian, Roman). Fees for special exhibits at the Städel and the Liebieshaus Museum vary. Unfortunately, most of the museums' description plaques are in German, and only the Deutsches Postmuseum has a free explanatory brochure in English. *Schaumainkai. U1, U2, or U3 to Schweizer Pl.; S15, S16, or S26 to Gartenstr.; or Bus 46 to Städel (for Liebieshaus or Städel), Untermainbrücke (for Postmuseum, Architekturmuseum, or Filmmuseum), or Eiserner Steg (for Kunsthandwerk or Völkerkunde).*

PALMENGARTEN UND BOTANISCHER GARTEN Although this tropical and subtropical garden is frequented by slow old ladies and screaming young kids, it's a great place to mellow out for a day before getting on the road again. The garden footpaths take you past ponds, small meadows, and more than 12,000 varieties of plants. To take a break from the sun, check out the cacti and orchids in the conservatories. During the year the garden hosts flower shows and outdoor concerts. *Siesmayerstr. 61, tel. 069/212–33939. U6 or U7 to Westend. Admission: DM 5, DM 2 students. Open Apr.–Sept., daily 9–6; Oct.–Mar., daily 9–dusk.*

ROMERBERG Most of what remains of Frankfurt's historical buildings lies in and around the Römerberg, the square that was the center of city life for centuries: The Gothic three-building Römer (city hall) has overlooked the markets and fairs held on the square since 1405. Newly coronated Holy Roman emperors celebrated in the

Kaisersaal (imperial banquet hall) in the upper story of the Römer. *Kaisersaal admission: DM 1, DM .50 students. Open Oct.–Mar., Mon.–Sat. 9–5, Sun. 10–4; Apr.–Sept., Mon.–Sat. 9–6, Sun. 10–4.*

ZOOLOGISCHER GARTEN Frankfurt's zoo is one of Europe's oldest (1858) and best. The open-air enclosures have nothing but a moat between you and the animals—it's hard to believe they can't just jump across. The museum is famous for its preservation of rare species, especially nocturnal mammals. The huge bat cage, with jillions of flying, hanging, screeching bats, may gross you out or just remind you of home. *Alfred-Brehmpl., tel. 069/212–33731. U6 or U7 to zoo. Admission: DM 9.50, DM 4.50 students. Open Oct. 1–15, daily 8–6; Oct. 16–Feb. 15, daily 8–5; Feb. 16–Mar. 15, daily 8–6; Mar. 16–Sept. 30, daily 8–7.*

CHEAP THRILLS

If you learn no other German while you're here, at least learn the word *frei.* It means "free" and will help you in your quest for inexpensive things to do. Tourist information at the Römer can give you pamphlets and advice about upcoming festivals and events. Check out the *"Eintritt Frei"* ("entrance" . . . and you already know the other word) column in their "Summertime Festival" brochure. During the summer months, hang around the Römerberg and Alte Oper for free jazz concerts, plays, and nighttime art showings. The monthly magazine *Prinz* (available at any kiosk for DM 3.50), has a column in the back called *"Freies Theater"* that tells where and when free comedy shows, dance performances, and plays will be held in Frankfurt and outlying areas.

The Frankfurt **flea market** is among the best in Germany, and once you see it you'll understand why. Tons of people crowd the streets looking through the new, used, or stolen stuff for sale, or for food stands that serve almost every cuisine imaginable. If you're in Frankfurt on a Saturday, it would be a shame to miss this animated scene on the Main. *Sachsenhäuser Ufer. From Hauptbahnhof Bus 46 to Eiserner Steg; from Hauptwache U1, U2, or U3 to Schweizer Pl. Open Sat. 8–2.*

FESTIVALS The *"Rhein Main Feste"* brochure (from the tourist office) is published every six months and tells you about festivals in Frankfurt, Wiesbaden, Darmstadt, and other nearby cities. *"Frankfurt Feiert"* is a small publication that lists the name, date, and location of every Frankfurt festival throughout the year. A local favorite is the **Wäldchestag,** a huge celebration in early June that comes with a portable amusement park. In late August, all of the museums on Schaumainkai set up special outdoor exhibition tents, and the theater puts on outdoor plays for the **Museumsuferfest.** Most special activities and outdoor festivals take place during the summer.

AFTER DARK

At night Sachsenhausen is transformed into Party Central. Its Apfelwein taverns, restaurants, and discos draw people from all over the city, especially tourists and American GIs—just whom you came to Germany to see. Some locals prefer the nightlife in the city center. *Prinz* magazine (DM 3.50), available at any kiosk, lists popular discos, gay bars, and cafés in the city center and outlying districts. Whether you go to a bar, pub, or café, you'll find that the action does not start until 11 or later. Discos get lively around midnight or 1, so you have plenty of time to bar hop beforehand.

GIs have reportedly come to the youth hostel (located in Sachsenhausen) asking how many American women are staying and where they hang out at night—so be wary.

BARS Sachsenhausen, on the south side of the Main river, has pub upon Apfelwein tavern upon pub. Women in Sachsenhausen at night should expect some hassles: a sex-starved stare here, a tactless "Hey baby, what's your name?" there. But not everyone is slimy. Fortunately,

Sachsenhausen is lively enough that when someone bugs you, there's always another full bar next door. Locals prefer cafés and bars in the downtown area to the Sachsenhausen mania. Beers usually cost DM 4–DM 5.

Blaubart. Give your eyes a few seconds to adjust, or you might fall down the steep staircase that leads into this candlelit cellar. Large oak tables make it almost impossible for you not to exchange a few words with your neighbor. Despite the dark surroundings, a cheery atmosphere prevails throughout the night, as this cave gets more and more packed with young Frankfurters. *Kaiserhofstr. 18, off Freßgasse, tel. 069/282229. U6 or U7 to Opernpl.*

Café im Hof. A chic, fashionable crowd hangs around this sparkling-clean, upscale café. Wear black and get ready to be checked out by artsy Frankfurters and disco goers. Espresso is DM 3.50, beer DM 4.50. *Kaiserhofstr. 20, off Freßgasse, tel. 069/289052. U6 or U7 to Opernpl.*

Club Voltaire. On weekdays from 3 to 6, students and young people manage this small joint. The graffiti-adorned entrance opens onto a small crowd of politically active intellectuals listening to loud music and hanging out together. After 6, the crowd gets slightly older and more eccentric-artistic and the concentration of black clothing increases. If you're looking to eavesdrop on an intense conversation you can probably do it here. The café serves salads (DM 9), quiche lorraine (DM 6), and chili con carne (DM 7). *Kleine Hochstr. 5, off Freßgasse, tel. 069/292408. U6 or U7 to Opernpl., or short walk from Hauptwache.*

Lilliput. This predominantly gay bar has a refreshing outdoor garden, and small, intimate tables for two on the patio. The patrons are into themselves, thus making the atmosphere pretty smug—a lot of looking and not a lot of talking. Straight people are welcome, too. *Sandhofpaßage, tel. 069/285727. From Hauptbahnhof U4 to Römer, walk w. on Weißfrauenstr., turn left on Kornmarkt, right on Battonnstr.; when you see Paulskirche on right, walk into shopping passage on left.*

CINEMAS Two cinemas (admission DM 10–DM 12) in Frankfurt show English-language films on a regular basis. **Turm 4** (Am Eschenheimer Turm, tel. 069/281787) has seven screens and plays recent films as well as some older classics like *The Rocky Horror Picture Show* and *Clockwork Orange.* The **Orfeo** (Hamburger Allee 45, tel. 069/702218), in Bockenheim, shows more obscure films.

DISCOS Frankfurt is the techno pop center of Germany and the tons of techno discos here prove it. The discos don't all play techno, however, and some play it only one or two nights a week. **Plastik** (Seilerstr. 34, tel. 069/285055) has gay night on Sunday. **Dorian Gray** (Airport C, Level 0, tel. 069/690–2212) is a four-club complex playing different styles of music and catering to different groups of people. Other techno clubs include **Negativ** (Walter-Kolb-Str. 1–7, tel. 069/628118) and **XS** (Theaterpl. L–3, tel. 069/232328).

Cooky's. The leather-clad, earring-bedecked bouncers really get off on the power trip of picking and choosing people to enter their hallowed ground. The ironic thing is that they let almost everyone in; that is, after they've made you grovel sufficiently. Depending on the night you go, you'll encounter different types of people. Live bands jam on Monday, and during the rest of the week, DJs play techno, rap, rockabilly, hip hop . . . you name it. No matter what the crowd is, the good vibes fly. *Am Salzhaus 4, tel. 069/287662. U1, U2, U3, U6, or U7 to Hauptwache, walk down Roßmarkt and turn left on Am Salzhaus. Cover: DM 10.*

The Omen. You've either got to dress as off-the-wall as possible or super expensively to walk even in the door of this techno club. Because the individuals who groove here are so stylish, you'll have fun just people-watching. Friday night attracts the most outlandish people and the best DJs. *Junghofstr. 14, off Goethepl., tel. 069/282233. U1, U2, U3, U6, or U7 to Hauptwache. Cover: DM 12. Closed Sun., Tues., Thurs.*

MUSIC You can hear live music, especially jazz, everywhere in Frankfurt. For the best jazz in town, head to Kleine Bockenheimer Straße, fondly called *Jazzgasse* (Jazz Alley). *Skyline* is a free monthly available at tourist offices, museums, and cafés. Look in the back for a calendar that lists live-band shows.

An Sibin. People are smiling and laughing all the time in this warm cellar—maybe they've had too much to drink. Come join the fun and enjoy the live bands (rock, blues, jazz) on Tuesday and Wednesday nights. On the first Thursday of every month, a bluegrass band plays. *Wallstr. 9, Sachsenhausen, no tel. From Konstablerwache Bus 36 to Elisabethenstr. Closed Sun.*

Irish Pub. Popular with the college-age tourist crowd, the Irish Pub has that American frat-party feel, which is great if you're in the mood to meet a lot of people with not a lot to say. Nightly live bands keep things upbeat. *Kleine Rittergasse 11, Sachsenhausen, tel. 069/615–9086.*

Jazzkeller. Jazz masters from all over the world (Brazil, the United States, Europe) come to Jazzkeller to play their stuff. Styles range from traditional jazz to Latino jazz-piano to funk jazz. The cellar is small and hits maximum capacity easily. Old folks, young folks, Germans, and foreigners congregate here. Beers are DM 5. *Kleine Bockenheimer Str. 18A, tel. 069/288537. U1, U2, U3, U6, or U7 to Hauptwache. Cover charges can go up to DM 20, depending on performers, so call in advance. Closed Sun.–Tues.*

Jazz Life. This spacious bar has tables, booths, and benches—and you can usually take your pick. It doesn't draw a crowd, which makes it a good place to duck into if the Sachsenhausen whirl starts getting to you. Generally, the bands that play here lack talent, but that adds to Jazz Life's charm. The better bands play on the weekends. *Kleine Rittergasse 22–26, Sachsenhausen, tel. 069/626346.*

Near Frankfurt

BAD HOMBURG

You'll see plenty of white hair, wheelchairs, and crutches in this 1,200-year-old spa town, but don't let your age dissuade you from visiting or even wallowing in one of the 11 mineral baths along with the old folks. Visit the **Schloß Homburg** (tel. 06172/26091), a 14th-century castle whose 172-foot **Weißer Turm** (White Tower) is all that's left of the original. Walk over to the low wall bordering the outdoor café for a great view of the Taunus. Unfortunately, you can't run around the castle by yourself, and they give English tours only if you prearrange them for a group of 25 or more. Don't feel stupid taking the German tour, because it's worth the DM 2 (DM 1 students)—if only to see how many bizarre closets got turned into bathrooms during the 19th-century renovations.

Even if all churches are starting to look alike to you, try to make it to the **Erlöserkirche** (Dorotheanstr., before entrance to Schloß), probably the only church in Germany that looks more like a New York City nightclub than a house of worship. In the early 20th century, Kaiser Wilhelm II used Byzantine and Romantic architectural models to build this eccentric, "nouveau" church. The ceiling in the entryway is navy blue with flowers painted on it, and the walls and ceiling of the chapel glimmer with tiny gold tiles (10,000 per square yard).

In the **Kurpark,** you can meander among the statues and columns that surround the many drinking fountains and little tubes with water bubbling in them—these, friends, are the famous spas. (Yep, the reality is a slight letdown). The **Spielbank** (Im Kurpark, tel. 06172/17010), the world's first casino, is probably the most popular of the park's attractions. The Blanc brothers opened it in 1841, only for it to be shut down with all the other casinos in Germany under the orders of Wilhelm I in 1872. The Spielbank was reopened in 1949 and named the "Mother of Monte Carlo," after the Blancs' successful second casino, the Monte Carlo. The atmosphere is predictably stuffy: You can't wear sports shoes in the casino, and guys have to wear a jacket and tie. So if you feel like playing a little blackjack or trying your luck at roulette, baccarat, or the slot machines, be sure to bring along the necessary wardrobe. The club has an admission of DM 5, and you must be at least 21 to enter. The park also has some random attractions, like the **Russian Chapel,** a gift from Czar Nicholas II, and the **Siamese Temple,** a groovy little hut with mystical-sounding wind chimes.

Bad Homburg, at the base of the Taunus mountains, is a 25-minute S-Bahn ride from Frankfurt (S5 from Hauptbahnhof, Hauptwache, or Konstablerwache stations). The **tourist-information office** is inside the **Kurhaus** (Louisenstr. 58, tel. 06172/121310). It doesn't have much information in English but does give some helpful maps. Bad Homburg's **Jugendherberge** (Meiereiberg 1, tel. 06172/23950) charges DM 17 for those under 27 and DM 20.50 for those over 26 and has an 11:30 PM curfew.

Since you're already in Bad Homburg, hop on Bus 5930, which leaves from the Kurhaus, and take the 10-minute bus ride to **Saalburg** (open daily 8–5). Admission to this reconstructed Roman fort, an accurate model of ancient strongholds, is DM 1.50. This is probably not a great place to go if you're fighting with your travel companion—the ancient Roman weapons inside could prove too tempting.

Do You Believe in Fairy Tales?

The Märchenstraße (Fairy-tale Road), a highway that runs from Hanau all the way to Bremen, "traces" the lives of Jacob and Wilhelm Grimm, who lived and studied and gathered fairy tales in this region and neighboring Lower Saxony. The brothers were born in Hanau, where the route begins; spent most of their childhood in Steinau, a small village with a medieval castle; studied at the university in Marburg; and worked as librarians in Kassel. They also spent years in Göttingen (see Chapter 12) lecturing and doing research at the university, as well as in Berlin. Although some of the towns on this route had their mythical qualities blown to smithereens in World War II, other, smaller villages remain well preserved and give you the feeling that you're either in a fairy tale or about to bump into someone who'll want to tell you one. That's pretty much how the Grimm boys got their info in the old days: word of mouth (although later they added their own embellishments). This countryside gave birth to Little Red Riding Hood, Sleeping Beauty, Snow White, Cinderella . . . some pretty high rollers in the fairy-tale world.

The larger cities of the Märchenstraße, such as Fulda and Kassel, have regular connections to and from other large German cities. You can reach most of the small villages by regional trains, although sometimes you'll have to transfer; the information offices at the train stations can help with transfers. Because the Märchenstraße isn't as popular as some of the other routes created especially for tourists (like the Romantische Straße and the Weinstraße), its towns and villages are not as commercialized yet.

MICHELSTADT

Michelstadt is known as the "Heart of the Odenwald," a hilly forested region south of Frankfurt. The city's Altstadt is a maze of cobblestone streets and historical half-timbered houses with sloping roofs. The town is a little touristy, but the few shops that sell Michelstadt key chains don't detract from the overall beauty of the place. The **tourist-information office** (Marktpl. 1, tel. 06061/74146) is next to the **Rathaus,** a steepled half-timbered structure with wood supports. At the office you can pick up a booklet with a map and list of hotels. Trains leave irregularly for Michelstadt from Darmstadt, so check the schedule at the station.

The **Schloß Fürstenau** is probably the most awesome castle in Hessen. It's a private residence now, so you can't go inside, but just looking at the exterior beats taking the tours at some of the other castles in the state. A large wooded courtyard and two tall stone towers connected by an enormous Roman archway greet you as you enter the castle gates. Because they can't go inside, very few tourists come here. Just wander around undisturbed and ponder what life used to be like here. To reach the Schloß from the train station make a right on Hulster Straße and another right on Kutschenweg. Just before you get to the big bend in the road, take the pathway to the right. When you reach the end, make a left over the bridge.

GELNHAUSEN

A half-hour's train ride east of Frankfurt is Gelnhausen, an amazingly well-preserved medieval city on the southern edge of the Vogelsberg Mountains. Early on the town acquired a nickname, Barbarossastadt (Red Beard City), due to the distinctive red beard of its founder, Frederic I of Hohenstaufen, who ruled the Occidental empire in the 12th century and founded Gelnhausen in 1170.

Gelnhausen was left unscathed by World War II, and it is delightful to wander among the half-timbered houses with their flower beds in front. The steeple of the Protestant **Marienkirche** juts above the rooftops. The huge ruined **Kaiserpfalz,** or Imperial Palace (Beschliesser Burgstr. 31, tel. 06051/3805), commonly called Barbarossaburg (Barbarossa Castle), sits on the Kinzig River and gives you a good idea of what was considered resplendent in the Middle Ages (not much).

Behold the immense dungeon on Barbarossastraße, the **Hexenturm** (Witch's Tower), where persecuted "witches" were tried in the 16th century. If you're into funky torture instruments and willing to pay to see them, call the tourist office (tel. 06051/820054) to arrange a tour of the dungeon for DM 20.

As a grand finale, check out the panoramic view of the city and surrounding scenery at the **Halbmond** (Half Moon), an ancient fortification.

VISITOR INFORMATION **Verkehrsamt.** The staff here is so friendly, you'd like to stay and have coffee with them. Most maps and information are in German. However, they do have one great map that marks all the major sights with brief historical references—in English! *Am Obermarkt, tel. 06051/820054. Open weekdays 8–noon, 12:30–5; Sat. 9–noon, 2–5; Sun. 2–5.*

WHERE TO SLEEP The hotels here are all extremely expensive. The dirty and weathered **Jugendherberge (IYHF)** is as far as you can get from the train station, but it's still less than 20 minutes away. The floors need to be swept and the covers of the sagging mattresses need some shaking out, but you can't beat the price. The hostess, Frau Huyk, is a talkative, friendly woman who will help you out as much as she can and, if you ask nicely, will keep an eye on your pack while you wander around. Getting a bed is no problem, since few travelers stop in Gelnhausen. Beds are DM 11, sheets DM 4, and a breakfast of rolls, jam, and coffee is DM 5. *Schützengraben 5, tel. 4424. 20-min walk from Hauptbahnhof. 80 beds. 10 PM curfew.*

FOOD **Krause's Fried-Chicken Schnellgaststätte.** Those dying for some good ol' American-style fried chicken have a haven around the corner from the hostel. Grab a chicken sandwich for DM 4.90, barbecued ribs for DM 8.50, or a piece of chicken, mashed potatoes with gravy, and fries or cole slaw for DM 6.50. Yep, you got it, Germany's substitute for KFC. *Röthergasse 14, tel. 06041/8461.*

Wiesbaden

You'll see hordes of wealthy people sporting expensive clothes and walking well-groomed, pedigreed dogs in this ritzy city, the capital of Hessen. Glitz and glamour aside, Wiesbaden is a beautiful city with well-preserved classical and Gothic buildings. The **Kurhaus** (Paulinenstr. 1, tel. 0611/729299), the old congress center, is open 24 hours and hosts conventions, meetings, and conferences. Check out the incredibly ornate interior, complete with marbled floors, walls, and columns. Plaster moldings and classical sculptures will make you feel you've died and gone to ancient Greece. If the people at the information desk don't look too busy, ask them to open some of the elaborately decorated concert and conference halls for you. The **Spielbank,** a casino in the Kurhaus, caters to people who don't carry budget guidebooks around; if you dress to kill, though, you can try your hand at roulette or blackjack. Admission is DM 5; the casino is open daily 3 PM–3 AM. The columned building nearby, the **Kurhaus Kolonnade,** houses a low-scale, cheesy casino, **Casino Kleines Spiel** (tel. 0611/729299). It only has slot machines, but there's no dress code and admission is cheap (DM 1). To the west of Kurhausplatz is the **Altstadt**. Cross Wilhelmstraße and walk until you hit the cobblestone streets lined with cafés and expensive boutiques.

The brilliant white **Greek Chapel** overlooks the city from a high hill. It has five golden domes, and the interior has an amazing array of old frescoes and gold-trimmed designs. To get to it, you have to ride a cable car up a wooded hill, where you have a great view of Wiesbaden and the Rhine River. From the Hauptbahnhof take Bus 1 to the last stop, Nerotal. Then hop on the Nerobergbahn (DM 1) for the ride to the top. Admission is DM 2, DM 1 for students. The chapel is open weekdays noon–4 and weekends 10–5. The last tram down from the chapel leaves at 7. The **tourist-information office** (tel. 0611/172–9780) in the Hauptbahnhof is open daily 8 AM–9 PM.

COMING AND GOING

Wiesbaden is connected to Frankfurt by the S1 (40 minutes) and the S14 (45 minutes). If you're traveling by car, take A66 from the west or east, A63 from the south, or A3 from the north.

Wiesbaden's bus system, which operates from the Hauptbahnhof, is efficient and covers a lot of ground. A one-way ride costs DM 2.50. You can get a 24-hour pass from a bus driver for DM 6. Use taxis only when absolutely necessary—they're a rip-off.

WHERE TO SLEEP AND EAT

Finding dirt-cheap accommodations is nearly impossible in Wiesbaden. As always, the **Jugendherberge** (Blücherstr. 66, tel. 0611/48657), a 15-minute walk west of the city center, is the best deal in town. One night will put you out DM 18.50 (DM 22 if you're over 26). Sheets cost DM 5, and breakfast is included in the price. The **Mainzer Hof** (Moritzstr. 34, tel. 0611/372028) has large, clean, comfortable rooms; doubles without shower are DM 69, with shower DM 80; singles without shower are DM 49, with shower DM 65. **Jägerhof** (Bahnhofstr. 6, tel. 0611/302797) has your typical, nondescript, cheap hotel rooms. All rooms are equipped with a shower and toilet. Doubles are DM 80, and singles are DM 60.

Kuddel Muddel (Mortizstr. 33, tel. 0611/309423) doles out large servings of great food at small prices in an airy, pleasant environment. Housewives decked out in dresses and pearls catch up on the latest gossip over dinner. A chef salad with ham, cheese, eggs, and onions costs DM 10, cheese bread with onion rings goes for DM 7, and rump steak with mushrooms and seasonings is DM 14. In the Altstadt you'll find **Der Eimer** (Wagemannstr. 9, tel. 0611/374821), a jovial family-run restaurant whose ceiling drips with trinkets from all over the world. Chef salad with cheese, egg, and ham is DM 12.50, and a beefsteak with onions, potatoes, and salad goes for DM 14.50.

AFTER DARK

The bars and cafés most popular with the under-30 set are in the Altstadt. **Daily** (Goldgasse 6, tel. 0611/306662) sees a constant crowd of people, day and night. The tattooed, pierced-eared, card-playing clientele gives the place an urban atmosphere—sort of like a Levis 501 ad. Beers cost DM 3.50, and caffeine-packed cappuccino costs DM 4. A few doors down, **Cargo** (Goldgasse 18, tel. 0611/303265) also caters to a fashion-conscious crowd. People kick back at the outdoor tables and drink beer (DM 3.50) or cola (DM 3.50) in a relaxed atmosphere where the waiters are even friendly. **Pupasch** (Bärenstr. 6, tel 0611/371914) is a dark bar with blinking Christmas lights. A mixed crowd winds its way through the maze of booths and tables. This bar is a "communications pub," so singles, especially women, can expect to have a few drinks bought for them.

Near Wiesbaden

A short train ride from Wiesbaden is the fertile, 25-kilometer-long (16-mile-long) stretch of land known as the **Rheingau,** famous for its wine production. Vineyards, the Rhine River, and small cities such as Rüdesheim make up this scenic area. For more information about the villages along this stretch of the Rhine, *see* Chapter 16.

RUDESHEIM

Trains leave from the Wiesbaden Hauptbahnhof every 30–45 minutes for the half-hour journey to Rüdesheim, a small, well-touristed city at the base of vineyard-covered hills. From the train windows you can see the Rhine River on the left and expansive, green vineyards everywhere. Make a right from the train station on to Rheinstraße and walk to the **tourist-information office** (Rheinstr. 16, tel. 06722/2962). The staff can load you down with heaps of information about the city, as well as a long list of wine cellars that offer tastings. If you're here during the summer, ask about Rüdesheim's wine festivals. Base yourself in the **Jugendherberge** (Am Kreuzberg, tel. 06722/2711) to explore the rest of the Rheingau. One night costs DM 16.50, DM 20 if you're over 26. Sheets are DM 6, and breakfast is included in the price.

Rüdesheim sees more than its fair share of tourists picking their way through shops selling "Made in Taiwan" trinkets for three bucks each, but even that can't detract from the festive atmosphere here. Music pours out of the restaurants and cafés lining the narrow, winding cobblestone streets, and everyone seems to be having a great time—can they all be drunk? The **Brömserburg**, an ancient stone fortress built about the year 1000, served as a customs check for visitors in the 12th century. Today it houses the **Wine Museum** (Rheinstr. 2, tel. 06722/2348). Old flasks, unusual wine bottles, and elaborate goblets are displayed within forbidding stone walls. Use your imagination as you travel through the museum's passageways, and you'll feel like you're a kid again in some "haunted" house. The museum charges DM 3, DM 2 for students. It's open mid-March–mid-November, daily 9–6. **Siegfried's Mechanisches Musikkabinett** (Oberstr. 29, tel. 06722/2711) will surprise you with its bizarre collection of self-playing musical instruments dating from 1780 to 1930—it's supposedly the largest collection of its kind in Germany. Every 15 minutes, 45-minute tours are conducted in whatever language is spoken by most of the group members. During the tour 15 of the instruments are played, some of which are pretty elaborate. Admission is DM 7, DM 3.50 for students; the museum is open mid-March–mid-November, daily 10–10.

Kassel

The Brothers Grimm lived here before the bombs made it sterile, working as librarians and using the town as a base to venture into the countryside and gather what would become world-famous tales. Later, 80% of Kassel was destroyed in World War II and then rebuilt in Early Industrial Ugly. In fact, some travelers have gone so far as to call it an "industrial hellhole," "boring," and "depressing." However, Kassel does contain the biggest mountain park in Europe, complete with two castles and an art gallery. And, to its credit, the city has taken some innovative steps in the rebuilding process, including closing off its downtown to cars and cultivating its green spaces along the banks of the Fulda River. For 100 days once every five years, Kassel really gets its chance to shine with its huge international art exhibition, **documenta,** which displays the best and brightest contemporary art in a variety of settings. The next one will be in 1997. The congenial English-speaking staff at the **tourist-information office** (Im Bahnhof Wilhelmshöhe, tel. 0561/34054) gives public-transportation maps, city maps, and English brochures reiterating how "fascinating" Kassel is. They also have a monthly booklet (in German) entitled "Kassel Live!" that tells you about concerts, art shows, and museums.

COMING AND GOING

The **Hauptbahnhof** and the **Bahnhof Wilhelmshöhe** are Kassel's two train stations. Trains to destinations in the north usually leave from the Hauptbahnhof, and Bahnhof Wilhelmshöhe handles service to cities in the south. The Hauptbahnhof has a **bus-information office** (open weekdays 7:15–4:45) that can provide you with information about bus schedules to smaller cities outside Kassel (*see* Near Kassel, *below*). Trains from Kassel run to Frankfurt (two hours), Hamburg (3½ hours), and Munich (3½ hours).

The city's public transportation, consisting of trams and buses, operates with a uniform ticket system. Public-transit maps and tickets are available from the tourist-information office (*see above*). You can also purchase transit tickets from drivers. Since the city is a huge sprawl, do the smart thing by buying a 24-hour ticket (DM 6.50) or a weekend ticket (DM 6.50), which allow unlimited travel within a given time frame, instead of the customary one-way ticket (DM 3). You can also buy a packet of five tickets in any Tabak/smoke shop or kiosk for DM 10. A seven-day ticket is available for DM 19, but with any luck you won't have to stay that long.

WHERE TO SLEEP

The tourist-information office has a list of hotels as well as a list of people offering private rooms. As always, your best budget option is the youth hostel.

Hotel Palmenbad. The management is incredibly friendly, and they'll talk your ear off even if you can understand only one of every 10 German words. This hotel has medium-size rooms and caters primarily to college-age travelers from everywhere, especially European countries. Wilhelmshöhe Park is a short walk away, and Bahnhof Wilhelmshöhe is five minutes away by tram. At the small bistro on the first floor you can chow down on a hearty German meal of schnitzel or wurst for about DM 12. Double rooms without bath are DM 76, doubles with bath DM 98, singles without bath DM 38. *Kurhausstr. 27, tel. 0561/32691. From Bahnhof Wilhelmshöhe Tram 3 or 4 to Brabanterstr. 21 rooms, some with bath. Extra beds available, breakfast included.*

Hotel Stock. This is a place to sleep—period. An older woman who seems extremely bored with life presides over this dark joint that caters to a sketchy crowd of older men. The hotel is on a busy street and offers little charm or personality. The bathtub may have a dirty ring, but the rooms are clean and spacious enough. Guests can get dinner for about DM 15. Doubles without bath are DM 84, with bath DM 104. *Harleshaüser Str. 60, tel. 0561/68912. From Hauptbahnhof Bus 10 to Riedelstr. 9 rooms, some with bath. Disabled accessible, breakfast included.*

HOSTEL **Jugendherberge (IYHF).** This clean, comfortable youth hostel has a café where you can hang out and read or drink espresso. Nearby trams can get you to Wilhelmshöhe Park (*see* Worth Seeing, *below*) on the western edge of town and to the museums in the eastern part of the city. Many art students who are trying to get into the city's University of Art stay here during the summer months, making for an interesting clientele of black-clad youth. You also get a good breakfast of unlimited bread, cheese, cold cuts, yogurt, and cereals. A bed is DM 19 if you're under 27 and DM 22.50 if you're over 26; sheets cost DM 5. *Schenkendorfstr. 18, tel. 0561/776455. From Hauptbahnhof Bus 10 toward Rasenallee to Achenbachstr., backtrack down Kölnische Str. and turn left on Schenkendorfstr. From Bahnhof Wilhelmshöhe Tram 4 toward Lindenberg or Tram 6 toward Wolfsanger to Annastr., backtrack on Friedrich-Ebert-Str. and turn right on Querallee, which becomes Schenkendorfstr. Reception open 8 AM–1 AM; if arriving after 1 AM, ring bell outside and someone will let you in.*

FOOD

Friedrich-Ebert-Straße has many cafés, bars, and small restaurants. **Restaurant Plaka** (Friedrich-Ebert-Str. 98, tel. 0561/776126), a two-story restaurant that serves Greek food in a German atmosphere, has an outdoor patio with colorful flowers and some trees that try to hide the busy street out front. Go to the fresh salad bar for Greek fare, or try the calamari salad (DM 9.50) or the veal with noodles, cheese, and salad (DM 19). If you crave pasta, head for **nudelnudel** (Friedrich-Ebert-Str. 55, tel. 0561/777110), a small fast-food place that offers all types of noodles (ravioli, tortellini, spaghetti, etc.) with your choice of nine different sauces. A healthy portion of noodles with vegetable or bolognese sauce costs DM 7.50; with tomato sauce, DM 7. The salad bar has only the basics (peppers, tomatoes, lettuce); small salads are DM 5, large ones are DM 8. **Zum Postillion** (Brüder Grimm Pl. 4, tel. 0561/17831) is an airy café near some of Kassel's less interesting museums. The café's quiet, tree-surrounded patio exudes an artsy atmosphere as people in their twenties smoke, talk, and read the newspaper over Apfelwein (DM 3) or pastries. Some older people trying to look young hang out and talk business. Try the creamed mushrooms with zucchini and garlic bread (DM 10.50) or the roasted potatoes with fish, mushrooms, and vegetables (DM 11.50).

WORTH SEEING

You can reach all of Kassel's scattered places of interest by taking Tram 1 or 3 from Bahnhof Wilhelmshöhe. Schloß Wilhelmshöhe, Löwenburg, the Herkules castle and monument, and the Great Fountain are all within the boundaries of Wilhelmshöhe Park, and the Brothers Grimm Museum and Neue Galerie are across the street from each other.

BROTHERS GRIMM MUSEUM The Brothers Grimm lived and worked as librarians in Kassel for most of their lives and got more than 30 of their fairy tales from a woman named Dorothea Viehmann who lived in Niederzwehren, a southern suburb of Kassel. The museum, in an old palace called **Bellvue Schlößchen**, documents the lives of Wilhelm and Jacob Grimm in German and displays some of their fairy tales in various languages, as well as furniture, manuscripts, letters, and other memorabilia. German speakers will get a lot more out of it than the German illiterate, but anybody interested in the fairy tales will appreciate it. *Schöne Aussicht 2, across from Neue Galerie, tel.*

0561/787–2033. From Bahnhof Wilhelmshöhe Tram 1 or 3 to Rathaus, turn left on Fünffensterstr., right on Frankfurter Str., walk through underground passage to cross hwy. Admission free. Open daily 10–5.

HERKULES The hike uphill from Schloß Wilhelmshöhe (*see below*) to the top of **Herkules,** an enormous octagonal castle that presides over the park, will take about 40 minutes. Be sure to climb to the top of the 230-foot tower for a great view of the entire park and the city. Hercules, the symbol of Kassel, stands on the very tip of the monument and looks down upon the head of the conquered giant Encelados. If you look hard enough you can find Encelados's head at the top of the 825-foot-long cascades that carry water to a lake, over a waterfall, under a bridge, and finally to the **Great Fountain** in the lower part of the park. The fountain shoots water high into the sky for all the little kids and retirees to enjoy. If you don't mind hordes of people—kids screaming in your face, toddling old ladies—you can follow the water through the park all the way from Herkules to the Great Fountain. *Hike through Wilhelmshöhe Park or take Tram 3 from Bahnhof Wilhelmshöhe to Drüseltal, then Bus 43 for 10-min ride to Schloß. Admission: DM 2, DM 1 students. Open Mar. 15–Nov. 15, Tues.–Sun. 10–5.*

MUSEUM FUR SEPULKRALKULTUR The most worthwhile museum in Kassel is the Museum für Sepulkralkultur, otherwise known as the Death Museum. It contains tombstones from the past and present, various painters' and sculptors' interpretations of death, and a few coffins. The display of rotting skulls might gross you out before you read that they're simulated—it might gross you out anyway. Special exhibitions, such as caricatures of famous dead people and one-frame cartoons dealing with death, come through every once in a while. *Weinbergstr. 25, tel. 0561/91893. From Bahnhof Wilhelmshöhe Tram 1 or 3 to Rathaus; 10-min walk through sts s. of Brüder Grimm Pl. Admission: DM 5, DM 3 students. Open Tues.–Wed., Fri.–Sun. 10–7; Thurs. 10–9.*

NEUE GALERIE The large Neue Galerie exhibits art from 1750 to the present. Pop Art, Minimal Art, Concept Art, and New Realism pieces from artists such as Andy Warhol and Walter Dahn are also housed here. *Schöne Aussicht 1, tel. 0561/15266. From Bahnhof Wilhelmshöhe Tram 1 or 3 to Rathaus, turn left on Fünffensterstr., right on Frankfurter Str., walk through underground passage to cross hwy., follow signs to Neue Galerie. Admission free. Open Tues.–Sun. 10–5.*

SCHLOß WILHELMSHOHE AND LOWENBURG On the western edge of the city is **Wilhelmshöhe Park,** the biggest forested city park in Europe. It covers almost 600 acres of mountainous land and contains two castles, **Schloß Wilhelmshöhe** and **Löwenburg.** The former is a large, simple castle built between 1786 and 1798 by Elector Wilhelm I. You can't enter the castle's **Schloßmuseum** without a guide, who conducts tours only in German. They provide you with an English handbook to follow along, but the tour is tedious, and the 60 minutes pass slowly. The rooms are unimpressive with their bright '70s wallpaper—it seems like the decorator had a momentary lapse of reason and forgot which era he was reproducing—and typical castle furnishings of wood tables, chairs, and dressers. *From Bahnhof Wilhelmshöhe Tram 1 to Wilhelmshöhe or Tram 4 to Kurhausstr. Admission: DM 2, DM 1 students. Open Mar.–Oct., Tues.–Sun. 10–5; Nov.–Feb., Tues.–Sun. 10–4.*

Löwenburg is an awesome stone castle built by Wilhelm I between 1793 and 1801. Because he was a huge romantic with a passion for the Middle Ages, he built Löwenburg to look like a medieval ruin. It has steeples and towers galore, some with large chunks missing for effect. The **Armory** has examples of full-body protection from the 16th and 17th centuries that put modern-day latex to shame. It's hard to believe that people could actually move in these things, let alone fight battles in them. The second floor gives a great view of Schloß Wilhelmshöhe and Kassel. The interesting 45-minute tours leave every hour from 10 to 2, and you can get English brochures to follow along. *Tram 1 to Wilhelmshöhe or Tram 4 to Kurhausstr. Admission: DM 2, DM 1 stu-*

dents. Open Mar.–Oct., Tues.–Sun. 10–4; Nov.–Feb., Tues.–Sun. 10–3. Additional tour Mar.–Oct., daily at 3.

Near Kassel

KAUFUNGEN Kaufungen is a modernized medieval city. Wide sandstone streets have replaced some of the winding cobblestone lanes, and many half-timbered houses have been restored at the expense of their former character. The **Stiftskirche Kaufungen,** a monstrous Gothic church dating to the year 1000, presides over the rooftops from a hill above the city. Aside from the short walk up to the church, the best way to explore Kaufungen is to wander through the crooked streets and check things out.

To get to Kaufungen, which is 12 kilometers (7 miles) south of Kassel, take a half-hour bus ride (DM 5) on Bus 5205 or 5220 from the Kassel Hauptbahnhof and get off at Bürgerhaus. The **tourist-information office** (Leipzigerstr. 463, tel. 05605/8020) is at the bus stop. They can give you a city map, but you won't need it since the church is the only real sight, and its location is obvious. The office is open 9–noon and 4–6 Monday, Tuesday, Thursday, and Friday.

WARBURG Trains leave every hour from the Kassel Hauptbahnhof for the 40-minute journey to this incredible medieval city. When you get off the train, hop on Bus 509 (DM 2) and ask the bus driver to announce the **Altstadt** stop. You'll probably think you're passing right through the Altstadt and that the driver has forgotten about you, but the narrow cobblestone streets and ancient buildings that you see are part of the present-day city. When you get off, you'll find yourself on a square with the Gothic **Altstadtkirche** looking over it and the **Evangelische Kirche** dominating the whole scene from its perch on a nearby hill. If you go around to the left of the Altstadtkirche, a huge stone structure built in 1200, you'll see a small dirt trail with a couple of gravestones at its head. Hike about 10 minutes up this switchback to the **Burg Graben,** a large wooded cemetery with flowers everywhere. From the cemetery hike up to the Evangelische Kirche through the winding cobblestone streets and check out the Altstadt below you and the wooded hills and meadows beyond.

Fulda

In the early 1980s, NATO thought World War III would begin in Fulda because the landscape on the town's eastern edge (the "Fulda gap") seemed like the perfect place for an East German–Soviet invasion. It's hard to imagine this Baroque city, beautifully set in the Fulda River valley, as the starting place for a war.

Fulda has long held a central place in the Catholic world. From 969 its abbot was the primate (head honcho) of all the Benedictines in France and Germany; 300 years later the abbot was promoted to prince-abbot, thus gaining him power in this world as well as the next. When the abbots were much later promoted to prince-bishops, they built themselves a castle in Fulda, and in the 18th century a university was founded here. The carefully restored Baroque quarter still has a strong 18th-century flavor.

The **Stadtschloß** (Schloßstr. 1) is the town's overblown castle; it runs the length of an entire street. It used to be a Renaissance castle, but between 1706 and 1721 the resident prince-abbot had it put in a Baroque dress to match the rest of the city. Today, it mainly houses municipal offices, but there's a **Schloßmuseum** (at castle entrance D-1) that includes some rooms decorated in the fashion of the 1700s, and the **Schloßturm**, a tower that dates to 1300. From the top of the tower, you have an amazing 360° view of Fulda and the surrounding areas. While roaming the museum's rooms, be sure not to miss the enormous **Fürstensaal** (Princes' Room), with seven huge chandeliers, ceiling frescoes, and extravagant gold and maroon wallpaper—it looks like it came straight out of "Cinderella."

The **Michaelskirche,** across the Pauluspromenade from the northern exit of the Schloßgarten, was built in the Middle Ages, before walls could support stained glass. The tiny windows gridded with iron bars, essential when it was constructed in the 9th century, make it look more like a stone prison than a church. An eerie circle of pillars delineate the pulpit area, and downstairs is a series of tiny crypts that will make claustrophobics queasy.

The airy **Dom** in the town center, with its dazzling white interior and incredibly high ceilings, will throw you for a loop. When you get to the altar, look up at the dome and spot four fat little cherub faces peeking over a wall at you. Downstairs you'll find the **Crypt of St. Boniface** and the entrance to the **Dommuseum,** which displays a bunch of crowns, goblets, figurines, and priests' robes. The museum (DM 3, DM 1.50 students) also contains what's left of St. Boniface's skull (his face got crushed when he was murdered in 754 by the Frisians) and the skull of the founder of Fulda—two lovely sights. It's closed in January.

Fulda celebrates its 250th anniversary in 1994. Check with the tourist office about special celebrations and festivities occurring throughout the year.

BASICS

MAIL AND PHONES The post office is next to the Stadtschloß's eastern end. At Counter 9, you can fax, cash traveler's checks (DM 3 commission per check), and pick up poste restante (Postlagernd, 6400 Fulda). You can also call abroad at Counter 9 and pay later to save yourself the pain of having to change all your bills into coins. Postal code: 6400. Area code: 0661. *Heinrich-von-Bibra-Pl. 5, tel. 0661/890. Open weekdays 8–6, Sat. 8–noon.*

VISITOR INFORMATION **Städtisches Verkehrsbüro.** Conveniently located in the Stadtschloß, this tourist office has maps, information in English, and an extremely friendly English-speaking staff. *Schloßstr. 1, tel. 0661/102345. Entrance D–2 of Stadtschloß. Open weekdays 8:30–noon, 2–4:30; Sat. 9:30–noon.*

Fremdenverkehrsverband. This information office deals solely with the Rhön area (home of the huge Rhön nature park) and its small towns and villages. Most handouts are in German. *Landratsamt, Entrance G, Room 338, tel. 0661/600–6305. Walk underneath train tracks at Heinrich-von-Bibra-Pl. to Magdeburger Str., turn left on Wörthstr. and look right, to Wörthstr. and Am Waldschlößchen. Open Mon.–Thurs. 8–3:30, Fri. 8–1.*

COMING AND GOING

You can easily reach Fulda by car or train. By car, follow B254 from the south or west, B27 from the north, or B458 from the east. Trains run regularly to Fulda from Frankfurt (1½ hours), Hamburg (three hours), and Munich (three hours). Trains leave from Fulda to these destinations every hour. Buses for outlying areas leave from the train station. Ask for a schedule at the information desk.

Once in Fulda, bust out your walking shoes; they're the best mode of transportation. All bus lines of the inner-city bus system begin and end at the **Omnibus Bahnhof,** on the corner of Rabanusstraße and Schloßstraße, about five blocks from the train station. The inner-city bus fare is DM 1.60.

WHERE TO SLEEP

Gaststätte "Gambrinushalle." Although the singles are tiny, the place has big doubles. All rooms have a table and chairs and are clean and cozy. A single without a shower is DM 30, a double without a shower is DM 60, and a double with full bath is DM 80.

Peterstor 14, tel. 0661/72862. 10-min walk from Hauptbahnhof: Walk down Bahnhofstr., turn left on Rabanusstr. then right on Peterstor. 10 rooms, some with bath.

Zum Kronhof. When you first walk in the front door of this homey hotel, you're greeted by tons of flowers and green plants and the smell of schnitzel wafting from the kitchen. The rooms are clean and comfortable, and breakfast is included in the price. Lunch and dinner are also available—if you like schnitzel (*Schweineschnitzel* DM 10, *Wienerschnitzel* DM 13, *Zigeunerschnitzel* DM 12, and the list goes on and on). Singles are DM 30 (DM 20 for an extra bed), and doubles go for DM 60. The hotel is within walking distance of all the sights in town. *Am Kronhof 2, tel. 0661/74147. From Hauptbahnhof walk on Bahnhofstr., make left on Rabanusstr., walk 2 blocks to central bus station, then Bus 10 to Am Kronhof. 23 rooms, none with bath.*

HOSTEL **Jugendherberge (IYHF).** This hostel has small, cramped rooms that need a cleaning. The pillows and mattresses look, smell, and feel like they've been there for decades. It's a 10-minute bus ride into town, and Bus 12 (the one you need) does not run often. The only good thing about this place is the breakfast—rolls, cheese, yogurt, fruit, cold cuts, cornflakes—it's huge and delicious. Bed and breakfast are DM 18 (under 27) and DM 21 (over 26); sheets cost DM 6. *Schirmannstr. 31, tel. 0661/73389. From central bus station Bus 12 (DM 1.60) to Stadion and walk uphill 3 min. 126 beds. 11:30 PM curfew, disabled accessible. Last bus for hostel leaves town weekdays 6:20 PM, Sat. 2:20 PM. No bus service to or from hostel on Sun.*

FOOD

Plenty of cafés, bakeries, and small restaurants are packed in the city center (the Baroque Quarter). A local favorite is **"Nordsee" Fischrestaurant** (Marktstr. 8, tel. 0661/22621), Germany's answer to healthy fast food. You can order a fish sandwich for DM 2 or a tuna salad complete with cucumbers, tomatoes, peppers, and dressing for DM 6.95. They also serve a variety of grilled fish dishes (DM 4.95 and up) and fish salads (DM 2.65 for 100 grams). In a large half-timbered house, **Roma** (Pfandhausstr. 1, tel. 0661/75922) looks like an old blacksmith's workshop. Try the mushroom omelet (DM 9), spaghetti with ham and onions (DM 9.50), or any one of the pizzas (each about DM 9). A great place for those with only a few pfennigs in their pockets is **Fraiche** (Bahnhofstr. 26, tel. 0661/74291), a buffet deal that has rolls for DM .70, three slices of salami for DM .60, and slices of cheese for DM .60, among other things. They also have a salad bar (DM 1.50 for 100 grams) and hot dishes (vegetarian soufflé with sauce, DM 7.95).

AFTER DARK

BARS Most of the lively bars are on Karlstraße, a pedestrian zone off Mittelstraße. The bars mentioned below are pretty much the most happenin' scene here. Most don't get started until 11 PM. Beers and sodas usually go for about DM 3.

Monte Carlo. This is a cool bistro with a 1920s flair: Fringed lamp shades, a wall mural that brings *The Great Gatsby* to mind, and a dark wood bar dominate the scene. Outdoor tables are provided. Call ahead—word has it this place may close. *Karlstr. 2, tel. 0661/75770.*

Schöppen. Outdoor tables and a cozy atmosphere make this place popular among young, old, preppy, and mellow locals. The cobblestone floor makes you feel like you never left the street. Knickknacks and 19th-century advertisements cover the walls. *Karlstr. 16, tel. 0661/79180.*

Zur Windmühle. This large beer hall is in a huge half-timbered house built in 1562. It looks like an enormous gingerbread house whose top leans so far over its base that it could fall over at any minute. *Karlstr. 17, tel. 0661/22272.*

MUSIC **Irish Folk Pub.** This roomy bar attracts young and old alike. Rock, blues, and folk bands get the place going Wednesday through Sunday nights. Take advantage of happy hour on Tuesday from 8:30 to 10:30, when pilsners and tequila shots are DM 2 each. *Gerbergasse 9, 2nd floor of Herküles shopping mall, tel. 0661/78381. From Hauptbahnhof walk down Bahnhofstr., turn left on Rabanusstr. and right on Peterstr., which turns into Ohmstr., which turns into Karlstr., which becomes Löherstr., then turn right on Gerbergasse.*

Musik-ecke. Complete with dart boards and a "beer garden" that overlooks the train station's bus park, this stucco bistro caters to different crowds every night, depending on the DJ (8 PM–1 AM) and drink special of the night. On Sunday night, women get a free glass of champagne just for walking in. On Wednesday night, tequila shots are DM 2, and hard German rock blares from the speakers. *Bahnhofstr. 26, next to Hauptbahnhof, above shopping mall, tel. 0661/77642.*

Near Fulda

Fulda is conveniently located between the **Rhön Nature Park** and the **Vogelsberg**. The nature park, which covers 750 square kilometers (290 square miles), contains a number of small villages, nature trails, and lots of beautiful landscapes. Use the nearby city of **Gersfeld** as your base; it's got a few attractions of its own, including a 120-acre deer park, walking trails, and a couple of castles. The **Waßerkuppe,** the Rhön's highest summit and an incredibly popular hang-gliding spot, is a short trip from Gersfeld. Visit Fremdenverkehrsverband (*see* Visitor Information, *above*) in Fulda to get information on the Rhön before you take off.

The Vogelsberg is a region west of Fulda characterized by low rolling hills, forests, meadows, and small villages. Two of these villages, **Lauterbach** and **Alsfeld**, are easy to reach from Fulda and make great day trips. Get an early start to explore both in one day.

STEINAU

The Grimm brothers spent most of their childhood in this tiny village southwest of Fulda among the hills of the Vogelsberg. Because it's small, you can easily explore it in a day. To reach the town center from the train station, walk down to Alte Bahnhofstraße, cross Leipziger Straße, and walk straight on Bahnhofstraße. Make a left at **Brüder-Grimm-Straße,** and voilà. The whole walk takes less than 20 minutes. The **Städtisches Verkehrsamt** (Brüder-Grimm-Str. 47, tel. 06663/560) is in the **Rathaus** and provides a map, list of hotels and restaurants, and a brochure in English that goes over some history and the sights. In front of the information office is the **Märchenbrunnen,** a fountain around a stone column with scenes from various fairy tales carved on it. On top of the column is a little castle with Rapunzel's golden locks flowing from one of its windows. The princess from "The Frog King" sits on the fountain's edge and impatiently looks at the frog in the fountain, who holds her gold ball.

The immense Renaissance **Schloß** is an enchanting stone fortress built between 1525 and 1558. Once you wander through the castle grounds, you can easily see how it sparked the imagination of the brothers. Nooks and crannies are as common as huge columns and locked doors—your imagination can have a heyday here. For DM 1 you have access to the **Brüder-Grimm-Museum,** the **Schloßräume** (a reconstructed kitchen and a room with changing art exhibits) and the 115-foot-high **Schloßturm,** with a great bird's-eye view of Steinau, the forested Spessart, and the Vogelsberg (ask to see the tower at the Schloßräume). The documentation of the entire Brüder-Grimm-Museum is in German. *Schloß, tel. 06663/6843. Admission: DM 2, DM 1 students. Open Mar.–Oct., Tues.–Sun. 10–11:30 and 1–4:30; Nov.–Feb., Tues.–Sun. 10–11:30 and 1–3:30.*

The Grimm family lived at the **Amtshaus,** also known as the "Fairy-tale Home of the German People," from 1791 to 1796, when Father Grimm served as judge. Today, the romantic half-timbered house holds the **Heimatmuseum,** which contains Grimm family belongings, an enlightening family tree, and historical artifacts from Steinau and the surrounding area. The Brüder-Grimm-Museum and the Heimatmuseum are very similar with respect to the Grimm family; the basic difference is that the Heimatmuseum also includes a bunch of ancient relics from Steinau. *Brüder-Grimm-Str. Admission: DM 2. Open Apr.–Oct., daily 2–5.*

Other sights include the **Marionettentheater** (Am Kumpen 4, tel. 06663/245), which puts on puppet shows of the Grimm tales as well as other works of fantasy (such as Saint-Exupéry's *The Little Prince*) throughout the year, and the **Puppentheater-Museum** (Brüder-Grimm-Str. 64, tel. 06663/245), which displays ancient puppets from all over the world.

COMING AND GOING Steinau is on the main rail line between Frankfurt and Fulda; trains leave both cities several times per day going in both directions. The trip takes about a half hour from Fulda and an hour from Frankfurt.

WHERE TO SLEEP **Weißes Roß.** The lively old lady who owns this Gästehaus claims that the Brothers Grimm used to stop at the 200-year-old house. She has a framed sketch of two men eating at a table and is convinced that it's Jacob and Wilhelm Grimm sitting in her breakfast room—where would we be without imagination? Whether they ever slept here or not is questionable, but the carpeted rooms are homey, and the hotel is only a minute from the major sights. Without a shower, a single runs DM 35 and a double is DM 70; with shower, singles are DM 40 and doubles are DM 80. All prices include breakfast—a hard-boiled egg, cheese, jam, bread, and coffee, tea, or hot chocolate. Call first because rooms fill quickly. *Brüder-Grimm-Str. 48, tel. 06663/5804. 8 rooms, some with bath.*

FOOD **Café der Ratsschänke.** Chiffon curtains, plants, and clean tables make this inexpensive restaurant a great place to take a load off and enjoy a home-cooked meal. Soups (onion, tomato, goulash) go for about DM 3, and schnitzels of all sorts are DM 8–DM 10, with half portions for about DM 6. Vollkorn ravioli (whole-grain ravioli, DM 9.50) and Vollreis risotto (DM 9.50) will please almost any vegetarian. *Brüder-Grimm-Str. 60, across from castle and Rathaus, tel. 06663/465.*

LAUTERBACH

Looking at the dizzying rows of half-timbered houses lining the streets of this town northwest of Fulda is enough to make you think someone dropped hallucinogens in your water. Don't miss the especially good-looking houses by the **Ankerturm** (Anchor Tower), the last remaining piece of the medieval town's defenses, across from the Rathaus. Check out Numbers 28–32 on Am Oberen Graben—they lean so far to the left that you may come away from viewing them more skewed than before. Don't miss the houses along the banks of the River Fulda, as well as the river itself.

This town is also the place where the Grimms' character Scalawag loses his sock. A fountain of Little Scalawag in front of the **Stadtmühle** (town mill, at Obergasse and Marktplatz) makes the most of this town's small claim to fame. The mill is an old stone structure with a fairy-tale quality. Its steeply sloping roof stands out among the half-timbered houses.

Almost every building here gropes for recognition. Many have a plaque denoting some historical significance—the town even marked the house of the guy who began gymnastic instruction in schools. One of the buildings that truly merits a plaque is the **Hohhaus** (Berlinerpl., tel. 06641/2402), the residence of the baron of Eisenbach between 1769 and 1773. It's a large, three-wing castle that houses the **Hohhausmuseum,** a maze of rooms with ancient furniture, clothing, artifacts, and a huge collection of pistols and rifles.

The **Verkehrsbüro** (Marktpl. 14, tel. 06641/18412), in the **Rathaus,** provides information about the town and bike rides through the Vogelsberg. The office also has information on the secluded **Schloß Eisenbach,** a beautiful castle surrounded by woods, about 5 kilometers (3 miles) out of Lauterbach. Although the fairy tale–perfect castle is closed to the public, you're free to wander through the chapel and grounds.

Trains leave Fulda every hour for the half-hour journey to this historic town. Get off at Lauterbach Nord. Walk along Bahnhofstraße for 15 minutes. Once on the cobblestone street, take the first left and then the first right, and you'll find yourself on the **Marktplatz.**

ALSFELD

In 1990 Alsfeld received Hessen's award for protection of historic monuments. The city's Altstadt, a tangle of half-timbered houses that slope in every direction, is exceptionally well preserved and has some interesting sights. The **Marktplatz** has colorfully painted thresholds, posts, and buttresses everywhere. The **Walpurgiskirche,** a massive stone church built in the 13th century, has an interior elaborately (if not tackily) painted in turquoise and orange. In the middle of the Marktplatz is the **Altes Rathaus,** one of Germany's best-known half-timbered guildhalls.

The **Städtisches Verkehrsbüro** (Rittergasse 3–5, tel. 06631/182165) offers a map and a list of hotels and restaurants. A tourist-information book in English (DM .50) is not a necessity but is good if you want a cheap souvenir. In the same building is the **Regionalmuseum** (tel. 06631/4300), four floors of historic artifacts, some dating to the days before Christ. The Baroque spiral staircase (1687) inside looks like Jack's beanstalk. Both the tourist-information office and museum are open weekdays 9–12:30 and 2–4:30, Saturday 9–noon and 1–4, Sunday 10–noon and 2–4:30.

Trains to Alsfeld leave Fulda every hour, and the ride takes 50 minutes. From Lauterbach the train ride is 20 minutes. When you get off the train, walk down Bahnhofstraße, which turns into Am Lieden, and make a left on Mainzer Tor to find the Altstadt.

Marburg

Since 1527, university students have been the driving force behind Marburg. Of course, they didn't always have tattoos and purple hair, but they've always added energy and life to the city. Jacob and Wilhelm Grimm even studied here between 1802 and 1805. The **Unterstadt** (lower city) is the oldest part of Marburg, containing the Elisabethkirche and a lot of new university-administration buildings. On the western bank of the Lahn River and on the side of a hill is the exceptionally well-preserved **Oberstadt** (upper town), which comprises the bulk of the city. This attractive mess of steep, winding cobblestone streets and passageways is lined with half-timbered houses and old buildings with painted posts and buttresses. It offers shops, pubs, and cafés. The long, narrow stairway of **Enge Gasse** connects the cobblestone **Wettergasse** in the Oberstadt with the smoothly paved **Pilgrimstein,** one of the city's main roads, below. Enge Gasse, however, hasn't always been called Enge Gasse and wasn't always the pleasant walkway it is today. It's original name meant "trash hole," and it used to be the spot from which the castle's sewage flowed into the valley.

You can make the winding, *steep* climb through the Oberstadt to the **Landgrafenschloß,** an enormous castle that overlooks the entire city. Or you can take Bus 16 (DM 1.60) from Marktplatz in the Oberstadt. Dating to the 14th century, this huge stone structure has domed and steepled towers and gabled facades. When you reach the Schloß you may find some locals offering a tour of the witch's tower and underground passages of the castle—*don't do it* unless you are extremely captivated by long lectures on obscure German history (in German) and long discussions about who was considered a witch and why. They make the tour sound fascinating, but for the casual tourist it may be too much. You're better off in the five floors of the castle's free **Museum of Cultural History** (tel. 06421/282355). The wooded grassy **Schloßpark** is great to kick back in before facing the busy Oberstadt again. Below the Oberstadt and to the north lies the oldest Gothic church in Germany, the **Elisabethkirche** (Elisabethstr. and Deutschhausstr.). Its two 265-foot steepled towers are probably the second sight, after the castle, that will catch your eye upon entering the city. The huge stone edifice contains coffins, altars, colorful stained-glass windows, and the jewel-bedecked, gold shrine that used to hold the remains of Saint Elisabeth, a countess who became a nun and opened an orphanage after her husband died; she was sainted soon after her death. Admission is DM 2 (DM 1 students); tours (German only) cost DM 3 (DM 2 students).

The amiable staff at the **tourist-information office** (Neue Kasseler Str. 1, tel. 06421/201249) outside the train station gladly answers all your questions and provides you with a map of the city, a list of hotels, and a brochure in English. You can also nab a free weekly called *Express* that tells about art exhibits, sporting events, and films in Marburg and surrounding cities.

COMING AND GOING

Marburg has direct train connections to Frankfurt (one hour), Heidelberg (two hours), Kassel (1¼ hours), and some smaller cities. The Hauptbahnhof is in the northern part of the city. B3 (north/south) is the only major automobile thoroughfare that runs through Marburg. The city has an easy-to-use bus system that charges DM 1.60 for a one-way trip.

WHERE TO SLEEP

Gästehaus Einsele. A five-minute walk from the Oberstadt, this small hotel is owned by a stout little man whose round face always wears a smile. He knows only two English words, "private" and "atmosphere," and constantly uses them to describe his hotel. The rooms are large and comfortable with that extra-special '70s plastic-wood motif. Singles are DM 45, and doubles are DM 90. *Frankfurter Str. 2A, tel. 06421/23410. From Hauptbahnhof Bus 4 to Pilgrimstein, walk straight on Pilgrimstein, which turns into Universitätsstr., turn left on Am Grün, which turns into Frankfurter Str. 7 beds without bath. Disabled accessible, breakfast included.*

Haus Müller. When you set foot in this beautiful house you'll think you've entered a museum of 18th-century furniture. It's on a street lined with amazing historic houses with steepled roofs and half-timbered and Baroque facades. Don't mind that old-house smell—it adds to the atmosphere. Singles are DM 65, and doubles are DM 90. You might want to call first, because it fills up fast. *Deutschhausstr. 29, tel. 06421/65659. From Hauptbahnhof Bus 1, 2, 3, 4, or 5 to Deutschhausstr. 7 rooms with bath. Breakfast included.*

HOSTEL **Jugendherberge.** For some unknown reason, the staff here cops an attitude. They'll answer your questions but not without a certain amount of contempt. However, for the traveler with few questions or a thick skin, the facilities are okay: The large rooms were recently renovated, so the mattresses are comfortable and relatively new. The great breakfast buffet of cereal, cheese, meat, and bread makes up for the DM 1 charged for a city map—get a free one at the tourist-information office instead. One night costs DM 19.50 (over 26, DM 23); sheets are an extra DM 6. *Jahnstr. 1, tel. 06421/23461. From Hauptbahnhof Bus 4 to Erlenring, walk straight, turn right on Erlenring, right on Sommerbadstr., right on Jahnstr. 158 beds.*

CAMPGROUND **Campingplatz Lahnaue.** This campground on the east bank of the Lahn River attracts some seedy characters, but it's cheap. For DM 4 you get a campsite, water spigots, and grimy showers. They don't rent tents, so either bring your own, or shack up with a friend. *An der B 3A, behind hostel, tel. 06421/21331.*

FOOD

Locals will often recommend that you try the **Terraßencafé Vetter** (Reitgasse 4, tel. 06421/25888), a two-story café serving pastries, coffee, and ice cream, with a view of Marburg and the forested hills beyond. Students come here to read and relax on the outdoor terrace. **Zur Krone** (Markt 11, tel. 06421/25390), a dark restaurant decorated with antlers and small trinkets, serves German cuisine to a very German clientele. All types of schnitzel go for about DM 12.50, and noodles with ham and a salad are DM 11.50. You might get a few stares as you walk in, because you'll probably be the only tourist. **Café Auflauf** (Steinweg 2, tel. 06421/681343) specializes in soufflés and vegetarian dishes. Broccoli soufflés are DM 9, and mincemeat soufflés cost DM 9.50.

Near Marburg

WETZLAR The Lahn River runs from northern Germany through Marburg to the southwest. Of the four main cities of the Lahn Valley—Gießen, Wetzlar, Weilburg, and Limburg—Wetzlar is exceptional for its well-preserved medieval Altstadt and impressive cathedral. Take special note of how the half-timbered houses curve with the street: This is medieval engineering at its finest. Trains for Wetzlar leave Gießen about every 15 minutes for the 10-minute ride. Wetzlar is also accessible from Marburg, but it's not listed on the departure schedules hanging in Marburg's Hauptbahnhof. Ask at the information office in the station for departure times.

The friendly staff at the **tourist-information office** (Dompl. 8, tel. 0641/405338) near the Dom can give you a map of the city and a brochure in English. The Dom, an enormous stone church and the focal point of the town, was bombed during World War II but was later restored to its original state. It is a combination of Gothic, Romanesque, and Baroque architectural styles and hosts Catholic and Protestant services on Sunday.

Wetzlar has seen its share of famous people—Goethe served as a law apprentice here in the summer of 1772. During this time he met and fell in love with Charlotte Buff (a daughter of the Teutonic Order's administrator), who inspired his novel *The Sorrows of Young Werther.* Goethe often visited Charlotte at the **Lottehaus** (Lottestr. 8–10, tel. 06441/405221), now a museum, where she lived with her family. No ropes separate you from the 18th-century furniture, so you feel like a visitor rather than a tourist. Next to the Lottehaus is the **Stadt und Industriemuseum** (Lottestr. 8–10, tel. 06441/405221), which has five floors of old cannonballs, metalwork, and furniture, as well as displays of cameras and radios.

The **Jugendherberge** (Richard-Shirrmann-Str. 3, tel. 06441/71068) in Wetzlar is clean and comfortable. It costs DM 21.50 per night, DM 24.50 if you're over 26; sheets cost DM 6, and breakfast is included. From the Hauptbahnhof take Bus 12 to Sturzkopf (DM 2).

HEIDELBERG AND BADEN-WURTTEMBERG 3

by Les Kruger

Created out of three smaller provinces in 1952, making it the youngest of the German *Länder* (states), Baden-Württemberg embraces such diverse landscapes as the Neckar Valley in the north; the Bodensee, in the south; the Black Forest in the east (*see* Chapter 4); and the underrated Schwäbische Alb in the heart of the *Land* (state). These regions comprise some of the most beautiful parts of the country. In stark contrast to these scenic splendors are such cities as Mannheim and Stuttgart, home to many of the cutting edge, high-technology firms that are at the center of the lean, mean, well-oiled German industrial machine. Striking a balance between these two environments are the two lively, riverside university towns of Tübingen, home of Germany's oldest institution of higher learning, and Heidelberg, world-renowned for its romantic atmosphere and enormous castle. Throughout the province, there is a variety of Romanesque, Renaissance, Gothic, and Baroque architecture, spared by the bombing raids that shook much of Baden-Württemberg during World War II.

Reaching Baden-Württemberg is easy. Frequent trains roll into Heidelberg, Ulm, Stuttgart, Heilbronn, Karlsruhe, and Lindau from all over the country. The region's largest airport is just outside Stuttgart. The Frankfurt airport, which accommodates many international flights, is only about an hour north of Heidelberg by train, and Munich's airport is about two hours east of Ulm. Within Baden-Württemberg, quick, efficient regular train service makes rail travel the best option. Buses, most of which connect only towns that are a short distance apart, but are vital in the few areas where rail lines are few and far between, notably in the Schwäbische Alb. You can hitchhike fairly easily, though, as always, you've got to be wary of taking rides going only part of the way to your destination, or you may get stuck in low-traffic areas where the hitching is more difficult. Rides between major destinations can be arranged through the *Mitfahrgelegenheit* (ride-share) offices found in every medium-size city in the region. Bikers will be glad to hear that Baden-Württemberg is pretty friendly territory for two-wheel transport. Many roads have bike lanes, and there are few large climbs.

Heidelberg

The natural beauty of Heidelberg, a city surrounded by mountains, forests, vineyards, and the Neckar River, has long been considered by travelers to embody the spirit of Germany. The city has been celebrated by virtually the entire German Romantic movement and by scores of poets, writers, and composers, including Goethe, Mark Twain, Sigmund Romberg (who set

Baden-Württemberg

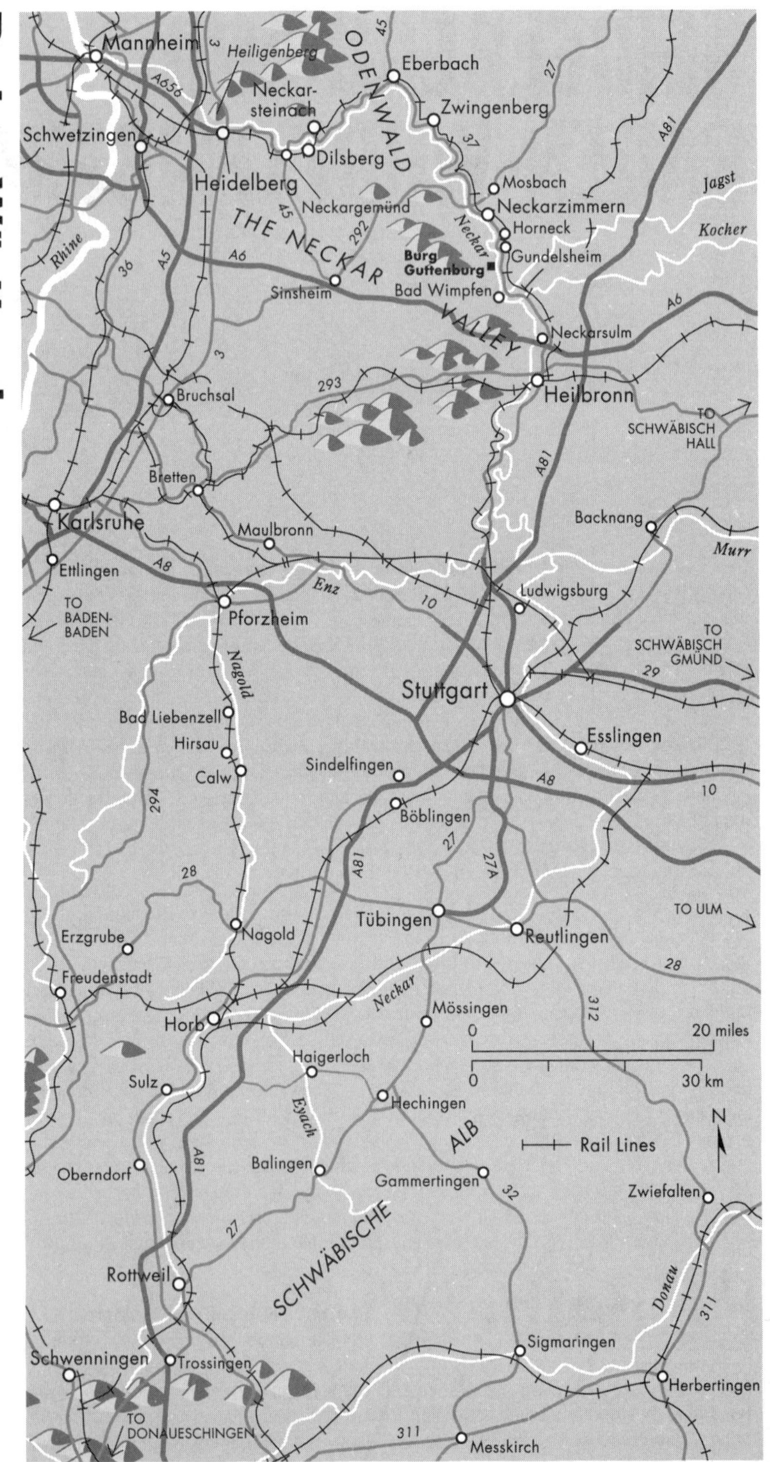

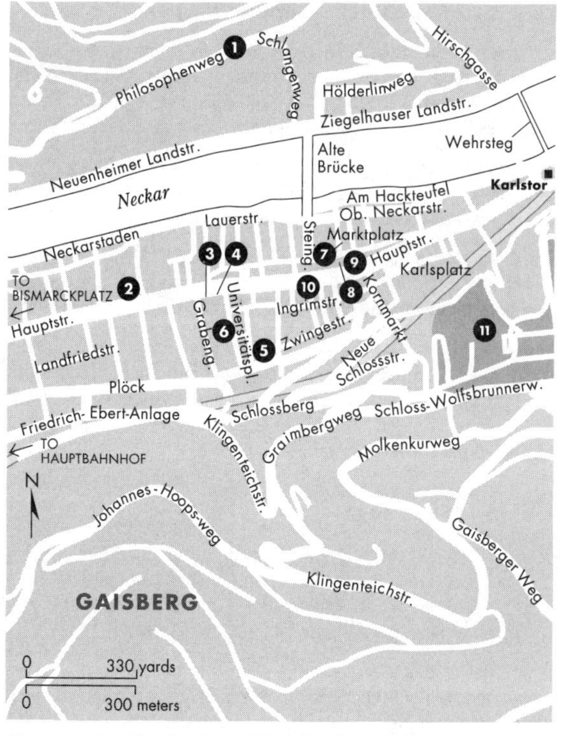

Heidelberg

Alte Universität, **3**
Haus zum Ritter, **10**
Heidelberger Schloß, **11**
Heiliggeistkirche, **7**
Hercule's Fountain, **8**
Kurpfälzisches Museum, **2**
New University, **5**
Philosphenweg, **1**
Rathaus, **9**
Studentenkarzer, **4**
Universitätsplatz, **6**

the operetta *The Student Prince* here), and Robert Schumann, who studied at the local university, the oldest in the country. That venerable academic institution, which gave impetus to the Romantic movement, today ensures the city's youthful atmosphere.

Heidelberg served as the Rhineland Palatinate's political center. When the Thirty Years War (1618–1648) ended, the elector Karl Ludwig married his daughter to the brother of Louis XIV in an attempt to foster peace in the region. When the elector's son passed away without an heir, however, Louis XIV used the alliance as an excuse to take over the political center. Heidelberg was ransacked in 1689 and again four years later. A Baroque town was constructed on Gothic foundations, and this old heart of the city remains intact, despite the influence of U.S. army barracks and industrial development that has extended into the suburbs. The city was also spared destruction during World War II. Today Heidelberg attracts more than 2.5 million visitors annually, with summer bringing record crowds. It's better to visit in late fall or early spring, when life here is more peaceful.

BASICS

AMERICAN EXPRESS This office changes American Express traveler's checks at no charge, holds clients' mail, and serves as a travel agency. *Friedrich-Ebert-Anlage 16, near Bismarckpl., 6900 Heidelberg 1, tel. 06221/91270. Open weekdays 9–5:30, Sat. 9–noon.*

BUCKET SHOPS **Reisservice Düsentrieb** (Kurfürstenanlage 57, tel. 06221/25458; open weekdays 9–1 and 2–6, Sat. 10–1), in the same office as the Mitfahrgelegenheit (*see* Coming and Going, *below*), offers student discounts on flights all over the world. **HS Reisebüro** also offers cheap flights for students. *Bismarckpl., tel. 06221/27151. S1 from Hauptbahnhof to Bismarckpl. Open weekdays 9–12:30, 2–6; Sat. 9–noon.*

EMERGENCIES **Police,** tel.110. **Fire,** tel. 112. **Ambulance,** tel. 13013.

MAIL AND PHONES The **main post office** (Belfort Str., tel. 06221/551; open weekdays 8–6, Sat. 8–noon), a big white building near the train station, handles *poste restante* and all regular postal services. The postal code for Heidelberg is 69115. Other post offices are at Sofienstraße 6–10, just off Bismarckplatz, and on Universitätsplatz.

To make international phone calls, go to any of the three branches of the post office, where you can either call collect or pay through the nose after you're through. *Main post office phone center open weekdays 8 AM–9 PM, weekends 7–3.*

MEDICAL AID To contact a **doctor,** call 06221/27171 or 06221/27172. Every pharmacy has a list of each day's late-night *Apotheke* on its door. Check the **Universitäts,** a pharmacy in the center of town. *Hauptstr. 114, 2 blocks w. of Universitätspl., tel. 06221/22514. Open daily 8:30–6:30.*

VISITOR INFORMATION The polite staff at the **tourist-information office** (Am Hauptbahnhof, tel. 06221/21341) in front of the train station finds rooms for DM 4 and answers questions. Another tourist office, **Verkehrsverein Heidelberg,** is at Friedrich-Ebert-Anlage 2 (tel. 06221/10821 or 06221/10823).

COMING AND GOING

BY TRAIN From Heidelberg you can reach any major city in Germany; frequent rail service goes to Frankfurt, Stuttgart, Mannheim, and Karlsruhe. The Hauptbahnhof (tel. 06221/27156 or 06221/525345) is about 3 kilometers (2 miles) west of the city center and has luggage storage, a bank, a small market, and a McDonald's.

BY BUS Buses to major cities in this area are no bargain; they take almost twice as long as the trains, and they aren't much cheaper. However, they are the best way to get to some of the smaller towns near Heidelberg. Buses to Schwetzingen (Bus 7007) and Neckargemünd (Bus 35) leave regularly from the Hauptbahnhof and Bismarckplatz. Buses leave for Dilsberg (Bus 7021) only four times a day, so you're better off picking up a bus to Dilsberg from Neckargemünd. Ask the tourist-information office (*see* Visitor Information, *above*) for details.

HITCHING AND MITFAHRGELEGENHEIT The best place to hitch a ride is at the Autobahn entrance at the western end of Bergheimer Straße. The **Mitfahrgelegenheit** (ride-share) office is about 1 kilometer (½ mile) straight ahead of the Hauptbahnhof. *Kurfürstenanlage 57, tel. 06221/19444. Open weekdays 9–6:30, Sat. 10–2, Sun. 11–2.*

GETTING AROUND

Navigating Heidelberg is quick and easy. To get from the Hauptbahnhof to Bismarckplatz (west of the Altstadt), hop on S1. To reach the other end of the Altstadt, pick up Bus 33 outside the side door of the station and get off at Kornmarkt. Single rides on any bus or S-Bahn (streetcar) within Heidelberg cost DM 2.40. If you plan to use public transportation a lot you can get a *Tageskarte* (day card, DM 7) from any driver or from a ticket machine at any major stop. Once you reach the Altstadt, it's easiest to walk. When your abused feet need a rest, call a **taxi** (tel. 06221/37676).

WHERE TO SLEEP

To put it bluntly, trying to find a cheap room in Heidelberg—especially during the summer—is a royal pain in the ass. Make reservations in advance if you can; otherwise, be sure to call ahead to see if there's room. Expect to pay DM 80 for a plain but clean double room in a hotel, or DM 100 if you want to splurge. If none of the accommodations listed below has any space, get a complete list of Heidelberg's hotels from the **tourist-information office** (*see* Visitor Information, *above*). Outside the office, you can call most of the hotels on this list for free using a computerized phone system. In dire straits, contact the **Mitwohnzentrale** (Zwingerstr. 14–16, 2 blocks s. of Marktpl., tel. 06221/166166), which may be able to find you a room in a hotel or private home. In summer, consider staying outside the city in Mannheim, whose youth hostel is generally less crowded and has easy access to public transportation (*see* Coming and Going, *above*), or in a nearby Neckar Valley town.

➢ **UNDER DM 25 • Hotel Jeske.** Surprisingly, the cheapest place in town is in the heart of the Altstadt, but it's usually full. No reservations are accepted, so call as soon as you get into town. If you're given the green light, be sure to look presentable—the sprightly, good-natured proprietor (Jeske) screens all prospective guests from a window above the front door. Beds in doubles, triples, or quads are DM 22 each. *Mittelbadgasse 2, off Marktpl., tel. 06221/23733. Bus 33 from Hauptbahnhof to Kornmarkt. 17 beds. Showers DM 2. Closed late Nov.–early Jan.*

➢ **UNDER DM 100 • Astoria.** Charging DM 100 (breakfast included) for a double room, this hotel might be a stretch for budget travelers, but the jovial proprietors and gorgeous ivy-covered building in a tranquil neighborhood make a stay here worthwhile. Across the river from the Altstadt, the lodging isn't far from the heart of the city. *Rahmengasse 30, between Ladenburger Str. and Schröderstr., tel. 06221/402929. S1 from Busbahnhof to 1st stop after Theodor-Heuss Brücke. 12 rooms, some with bath.*

Hotel Elite. This recently renovated hotel, about four blocks south of Bismarckplatz, offers beautiful and spacious rooms with two large double beds; the charge for each additional person is just DM 10, a good deal for groups of three or four. The reasonable price of DM 95 includes a generous breakfast that you can eat in the garden. *Bunsenstr. 15, tel. 06221/25734. Bus 21 from Hauptbahnhof to Hans-Böckler-Str., turn right on Bunsenstr. 14 rooms with bath.*

Hotel Garni Ballman. Just around the corner from the Elite, this three-building lodging has drab rooms, but they're clean. Prices seem to fluctuate with the number of tourists searching for a room, the mood of the staff at the front desk, and Jupiter's alignment with the sun. Try bargaining. Rates should be DM 40–DM 50 for singles and DM 80–DM 100 for doubles, including breakfast. Some rooms have televisions and refrigerators. *Rohrbacher Str. 28, s. of Kurfürstenanlage, tel. 06221/24287. Bus 21 from Hauptbahnhof to Hans-Böckler-Str. 50 rooms, some with bath.*

Hotel Weißer Bock. Its greenish-brown carpeting and yellowing walls bring one word to mind: ugly. Yet its location between the Universitätplatz and the Neckar River makes it a great base for exploring the Altstadt, and a double room costs only DM 80–DM 90 (breakfast and showers included). *Große Mantelgasse 24, tel. 06221/22231. Bus 10 or 12 from Hauptbahnhof to Universitätspl. 13 rooms, some with bath.*

HOSTELS **Heidelberg Jugendherberge.** Frequently inundated with schoolchildren from Germany and abroad, you'll need a lot of luck to find space here during the summer if you don't have a reservation. If you luck out, you'll get a clean, cheap room (DM 15.50 for those under 27, DM 18.50 over 26). This is one of the only hostels in Germany with a bar and disco. *Tiergarten Str. 5, tel. 06221/412066. Bus 33 from Hauptbahnhof to Sportszentrum Nord. After 8 PM on weekends, take S1 to Chirurgische Klinik, transfer to Bus 330 and get off at Sportzentrum Nord. 451 beds without bath. 11:30 PM curfew, lockout 9 AM–1 PM, reception open 7:30–9 and 3–11, 1st-floor is disabled accessible.*

CAMPGROUNDS **Camping Haide.** On the opposite side of the river from Camping Neckertal (*see below*), Haide offers similar accommodations. There are bathrooms, showers, and laundry facilities. *Between Ziegelhausen and Kleingemünd, tel. 06223/2111. Bus 35 from Bismarckpl. to orthopedic clinic, cross bridge and turn right. Disabled accessible. Closed Nov.–Mar.*

Camping Neckertal. Offering scenic views of Heidelberg and the Neckar Valley, this clean, safe campground on the banks of the Neckar River is about 5 kilometers (3 miles) east of the city center. If you don't mind being next to the road or sharing your campground with RVs and cars, you can sleep here for only DM 5 per person, DM 6 per tent, and DM 3 per car. There are bathrooms and showers on the premises. *Tel. 06221/802506. Bus 35 from Bismarckpl. to orthopedic clinic. Disabled accessible. Closed winter.*

FOOD

Biergärten (beer gardens) aren't the only eateries here, although they are good places to relax and have a brew and a snack. You can get almost any kind of food in Heidelberg—from German to Mexican to Greek. Hundreds of restaurants blanket the area on and around Hauptstraße, although finding dirt-cheap food may be tough. You'll probably end up paying at least DM 8–DM 10 for a decent meal; check the prices on the menus posted near the front doors. Be prepared for incredulous stares from meat-'n'-potatoes locals if you mention you're a vegetarian. For cheaper food, head for one of the many markets in Heidelberg—try **Nanz** (Hauptstr. 116) in the center of town. After dinner, treat yourself to an ice cream or coffee and cake at one of the local cafés.

UNDER DM 8 **Gino's Mexico Grill.** One of the first and only Mexican eateries in Germany, this cafeteria-style restaurant serves authentic Mexican dishes such as chili con queso (DM 4.50) and enchiladas (DM 6), along with a series of fried "stuffed tortillas" similar to burritos (DM 4). The eclectic wall decorations include a picture of Sammy Davis, Jr., and paraphernalia from U.S. fast-food restaurants. *Hauptstr. 113A, w. of Universitätspl., tel. 06221/28586. Disabled accessible.*

UNDER DM 15 **Da-Elio.** Students and yuppies frequent this Italian restaurant for its friendly service, outdoor seating next to the Stadtgarten (city park), and serious munchies. Da-Elio is also important to keep in mind after late-night drinking. You can get pizzas (about DM 10) and pasta dishes (DM 8–DM 14) until 3 AM. *Friedrich-Ebert-Anlage 2, at Sofienstr., s. of Bismarckpl., tel. 06221/12805. Disabled accessible.*

Goldener Stern. This no-frills Greek restaurant is a favorite among locals. The souvlaki (DM 12) and moussaka (DM 14) won't disappoint. *Lauerstr. 16, on Neckar River w. of Alte Brücke, tel. 06221/23937. No lunch.*

Zum Sepp'l. Having served the students of Heidelberg University for the past 300-plus years, this famous tavern has developed quite a bit of character. The wood walls and tables have been inscribed with the names of thousands of students—from Bismarck (yes, the "Iron Chancellor" who brought Germany together in the 19th century) to "Bubba." Long-dead frat brothers stare at you from pictures on the walls. Unfortunately, the Zum Sepp'l now caters more to tourists than to students. Traditional German dishes cost DM 8–DM 25; a huge plate of fries and a beer costs DM 11. (For another historic student tavern, try Roter Ochsen two doors down.) *Hauptstr. 217, e. of Karlspl., tel. 06221/23085. Disabled accessible.*

UNDER DM 20 **Indian Palace.** Excellently prepared traditional Indian dishes such as eggplant bharta (DM 17.50) and chicken masala (DM 19) are served in this elegant restaurant just off the main drag. The friendly service and relaxed atmosphere will help you forget you're a weary traveler. *Kettengasse 11, 2 blocks s. of Hauptstr. between Marktpl. and Universitätspl., tel. 06221/10710. Disabled accessible. Closed 2:30–6.*

Kowa's Vegetarischem Restaurant. Healthy, strictly vegetarian meals prepared with organic produce are served in a tranquil, no-smoking environment. The small but exquisite dishes include soups (DM 5), salads (DM 8–DM 14), and a host of daily specialties (DM 8–DM 20). *Kurfürstenanlage 9, near Landhauserstr., tel. 06221/22814. Behind building and upstairs, look for sign. No dinner.*

WORTH SEEING

Although Heidelberg stretches for many miles along both sides of the Neckar River, the area you will be most concerned with is the *Altstadt* (Old Town). The Altstadt is bisected by the 3-kilometer (2-mile) pedestrian walkway Hauptstraße, which runs from the Bismarckplatz in the west to Karlstor (Karl's Gate) in the east. Most of the major attractions—such as the Baroque Rathaus—as well as many restaurants, pubs, and shops, lie on or near Hauptstraße.

HAUS ZUM RITTER It's hard to ignore the elaborate facade of the Haus zum Ritter, the only Renaissance building in the city that was spared the attentions of the invading French in 1689 and 1693. This architectural triumph, built in 1592, contains five tiers of intricately carved decorations, columns, and gables, topped by a bust of St. George dressed as a *Ritter* (knight). The structure served as the town hall between 1695 and 1705; now it's an atmospheric hotel. *Hauptstr. 178, tel. 06221/24272.*

HEIDELBERGER SCHLOß Sitting on a ridge above Heidelberg, the grandiose, well-preserved ruins of the Heidelberger Schloß seem to dominate the rest of the city. Its oldest remains date from the late 15th century, though most of the complex was built in the Renaissance and Baroque styles of the 16th and 17th centuries, when the Palatinate electors were in power. The architectural variety of the building reflects changing tastes during the 400-year period (beginning about 1300) in which it was constructed and rebuilt. In the late 17th century, French troops attacked the Schloß, leaving it in a state of disrepair from which it never recovered. To reach the Schloß either walk up one of the two steep paths that begin south of the Kornmarkt, or ride up the Bergbahn Funicular (DM 4.50 round-trip). You can meander around outside to your heart's content, but to get inside you have to join a tour group, included in the admission price. Especially notable are the remains of the graceful, ornate Renaissance courtyard. *Tel. 06221/53840. Admission: DM 5, DM 3 under 20, DM 2.50 students. Open Apr.–Oct., daily 9–5; Nov.–Mar., daily 9–4.*

Included in the price of a tour is admission to the **Faß** (Great Vat), an enormous wine barrel made from 130 oak trees with a holding capacity of 55,000 gallons. In 1751 Elector Karl Theodor bet the ruler of Saxony that he could build a larger wine barrel. Guess who won. Wrong. The holding capacity of Saxony's barrel overshadowed that of Karl Theodor's by about 5,000 gallons. *Admission without tour: DM 1, DM .50 students.*

In the eastern-wing basement of the Schloß is the delightful **Deutsches Apothekenmuseum** (German Pharmaceutical Museum), which contains a set of instruments used by alchemists from the 16th to the 19th centuries, and a reconstruction of an 18th-century apothecary's shop. *Admission: DM 3, DM 1.50 students. Open mid-Mar.–Oct., daily 10–5; Nov.–mid-Mar., weekends and holidays 11–5.*

Faß-cinating Legends

Having been the world's largest functioning wine barrel, the Faß at the Heidelberger Schloß became the subject of some funky legends. The most popular story concerns a dwarf named Perkeo who was guardian of the Faß in the 18th century. Little Perkeo, a court jester with a big thirst for wine, drank 18 bottles a day for 50 years in an attempt to empty the great barrel. One day he substituted a glass of water for wine—and instantly died. Another legend has it that one of the prince electors secretly guzzled 30 liters of wine from the Faß each day while he was president of the German temperance society.

HEILIGGEISTKIRCHE Architecture buffs might be confused by the Heiliggeistkirche (Church of the Holy Ghost)—it looks like someone swiped a Baroque roof and steeple and plopped it down onto Gothic walls. The bottom half was built in the early 15th century, and the top half was reconstructed in the mid-16th century. The separation of church and state was foreign to the project's financiers; if you look up at the vaulted ceiling you'll find paintings of coats of arms and one vain aristocrat. The church once housed the Palatinate electors' family tombs, but today only the 15th-century tomb of Elector Ruprecht III and his wife remains. *W. end of Marktpl., no tel. Admission to tower: DM 1. Open Mon.–Sat. 10–5, Sun. 1–5.*

On the Marktplatz at the east end of Hauptstraße you'll find Hercule's Fountain. Although the fountain isn't impressive, its history is: Petty criminals were once caged and whirled around here in front of a taunting public. This practice was stopped in 1740, but since history tends to repeat itself, think twice before jaywalking.

KURPFALZISCHES MUSEUM Housed in a Baroque palace, Heidelberg's leading museum contains paintings, sculptures, furniture, and engravings that focus on the history of the city. The most famous piece on display is the Twelve Apostles altarpiece, the exquisitely detailed and technically sophisticated work of early Renaissance sculptor Tilman Reimenschneider. The recently renovated archaeology wing contains a plaster cast of the lower jawbone of *Homo Heidelbergensis,* the oldest human bone discovered in Europe. *Hauptstr. 97, tel. 06221/583402. Admission: DM 3, students free. Open Tues., Thurs.–Sun. 10–5; Wed. 10–9.*

PHILOSOPHENWEG This age-old path affords gorgeous views of the Schloß, the Neckar River, and the green hills that form the Neckar Valley east of Heidelberg. The thoroughfare has been trodden by the likes of Georg Hegel and Max Weber. If you take the path off the Philosophenweg that leads to the top of the hill, you'll find the ruins of **St. Michael's Basilica** and the **St. Stephen Cloister,** as well as a Nazi-era **amphitheater** no longer in use because of its blemished history. *Cross Alte Brücke to n. side of Neckar and climb Schlangenweg.*

UNIVERSITATSPLATZ On the north side of this historic square lies the unimpressive **Alte Universität,** once home of Germany's oldest university. Behind it stands the **Student-karzer,** the former students' prison, where between 1712 and 1914 university administrators incarcerated students for offenses ranging from public drunkenness to practical jokes. Naturally, most students felt the university experience was not complete without at least one trip to the slammer. You can look at graffiti on the walls of the cells, which are strikingly similar to modern college dorm rooms. *Augustinergasse 2, tel. 06221/542334. Bus 33 from Hauptbahnhof to Kornmarkt, walk w. on Haupstr. Admission: DM 1.50, DM 1 students. Open Apr.-Oct., Tues.-Sat. 10–noon, 2–5; Nov.–Mar., Sat. 10–1.*

On the south side of Universitätplatz is the hoof-shape **New University.** Incorporated into the modern (1931) building is the **Hexenturm** (Witches' Tower), a 14th-century stone structure that was used as a prison for alleged witches.

AFTER DARK

Once the sun goes down the "Romantic City" is transformed into a lively playground. Tourists and locals of all ages materialize at about 10 and don't disappear before 3 AM. On weekends the raucous nightlife reaches a peak unrivaled in Germany (though Müncheners and Berliners might disagree). Since bars catering to tourists are interspersed with local hangouts, you'll have to poke around to find your niche; but in general Heidelbergers head toward the rowdy establishments on **Unterestraße,** a small four-block street between the Neckar and the more touristy Hauptstraße.

BARS Right before the south entrance to the Alte Brücke is **Bistro zur Alten Brücke** (Obere Neckarstr. 2, tel. 06221/20201), described by one young *Frau* as a "German meat market." It has a Mexican–Southwest American theme, a bar, and a disco with music that packs in young locals. **Sonderbar** (Unterestr. 13, tel. 06221/25200, closed Sun.) is owned by a former top student of Heidelberg U. who thumbed his nose at the system; it's small, sweaty, smoky, and crowded with fans of heavy-duty rock-and-roll. Visit **Weinloch** (Unterestr. 19, tel. 06221/25093, closed Sun.) if you want to drink—not *sip*—wine with locals of all ages in a casual environment. In a converted warehouse near the Hauptbahnhof, **Zigarillo** (Bergheimer Str. 139, w. of Mittermaierstr., tel. 06221/160333, closed Sun.), Heidelberg's largest disco, plays nonstop hip-hop for a youngish crowd, and Wednesday's "oldies" night features dance music from the '60s to '80s (cover: DM 5).

MUSIC To find local live music, your best bet is to read the advertisements posted all over the city. Upcoming shows are also listed in *Voice,* a free magazine you can pick up at the Gloria (*see* Cinemas, *below*). To get tickets for bigger-name acts that occasionally play in or near Heidelberg, head to the tobacco shop **Zigarren Grimm** (tel. 06221/20909) on the east side of Bismarckplatz. Two clubs that regularly have live music are **Zieglerbräu** (Bergheimerstr. 1B, tel. 06221/25333), featuring R&B, and the **Schwimmbad Music Club** (Tiergartenstr. 13, near youth hostel, tel. 06221/470201), which hosts "underground" bands who play everything from funk to "subpop post-grunge."

CINEMAS The **Harmonie-Kino Center** (Hauptstr. 110, tel. 06221/22000) shows mostly American films with German subtitles. The hip but seedy **Gloria** (Hauptstr. 149, tel. 06221/25319) lets you swig beers and whiskey while you watch world-famous flicks.

Near Heidelberg

MANNHEIM

One of Germany's youngest cities (founded in 1606) and the second-largest European river port, Mannheim is an underrated destination just 15 kilometers (9 miles) north-west of Heidelberg. Most travelers are turned off by the vast industrial sprawl surrounding the city center, and they usually come here only to crash when Heidelberg's lodgings are full. But if you look beyond this city's concrete-block architecture, you might be pleasantly surprised by its elegant Altstadt, carefully reconstructed after wartime bombing. Historic buildings, museums, parks, fountains, and a Schloß await you—and they're not as crowded as those in Heidelberg.

The layout of Mannheim's city center is the embodiment of German logic and efficiency, built by Palatinate elector Friedrich IV. It consists of a series of squares designated by numbered and lettered coordinates rather than street names. The exception is Kurpfalzstraße, which divides the city into western and eastern halves. The squares to the west of Kurpfalzstraße are lettered A–K as you move from south to north; the streets to the east are lettered L–U from south to north. Each square is then assigned a number between 1 and 7 (except for the "L" series, which mysteriously stretches up to 15).

The **Hauptbahnhof** is at the southeast corner of the grid just off L15. Not far from the station's front doors is the **tourist office** (Kaiserring 10–16, tel. 0621/101011).

A few blocks north of the tourist office and east of N7 at Friedrichsplatz, **Städtische Kunsthalle** is the foremost of Mannheim's hidden treasures, a city-run art gallery in a building designed in the Jugendstil (Art Nouveau) style. The museum has an impressive collection of 19th- and 20th-century painting and sculpture; the big names, from Manet to Warhol, are all here. *Moltkestr. 9, tel. 0621/293–6413. Admission: DM 4, free Thurs. Open Tues., Wed., Fri.–Sun. 10–5; Thurs. 10–8.*

The **Reiss Museum** (C5 and D5, tel. 0621/293–2219, admission free Thurs. 1–8) houses two vastly different collections. One building offers an outstanding anthropological exhibit on African and Asian cultures. The boring **Zeughaus** (arsenal) contains art, handicrafts, and furniture from the 18th and 19th centuries.

"In Mannheim they make money, in Heidelberg they spend it," says a Mannheim schoolteacher who grew up in Heidelberg.

The **Jesuitenkirche** (Jesuit Church) on A4 is Germany's largest and most significant Baroque church, with a massive classical facade, domed spires resembling old German helmets, and an immense dome. Note the ornate wrought-iron entrance gates. Although the church was bombed during the war, its interior is still impressive; if you look up into the center of the dome you'll find an eye staring back at you.

The other grandiose Mannheim landmark is the **Residenzschloß** (just south of the grid between A4 and L3), the largest Baroque palace in Germany. The prince electors who authorized its construction between 1720 and 1760 seem to have put a premium on quantity rather than quality. Five architects produced an enormous symmetrical structure of more than 400 rooms and 2,000 windows; all this was reduced to ruins during World War II and rebuilt in the 1950s. Mannheim University now owns this rather unattractive edifice; the great hall and some state rooms are open to the public, but they're not exciting. More impressive is the view down Kurpfalzstraße from the main palace staircase. *Admission: DM 2. Open Apr.–Oct., Tues.–Sun. 10–noon and 3–5; Nov.–Mar., weekends 10–noon and 3–5.*

COMING AND GOING The buses in this region are much slower than the trains and only a little cheaper, so Mannheim is best reached by train. The **Hauptbahnhof,** just outside the southeast corner of the grid, has regular service to Frankfurt, Stuttgart, Hamburg, and Basel, Switzerland, as well as an hourly train to Heidelberg. The **Mitfahrzentrale** (L14, 6; tel. 0621/21846) helps travelers find rides to most major German cities and some destinations abroad (e.g., Paris). It's easier to find rides on weekends than during the week. Within Mannheim you can walk to every sight of interest, but there's also an extensive system of electric streetcars (S-Bahn) and buses that charge DM .60–DM 2.40, depending on the length of your journey. S30 goes from the train station to the center of town.

WHERE TO SLEEP Most of Mannheim's hotels are well out of the budget traveler's range. However, if you can brave the steep, winding stairwell, the centrally located **Arabella Pension** (M2,12; tel. 0621/23050) has clean rooms and showers at DM 30 for singles and DM 60 for doubles. The place is usually full, and it doesn't accept reservations, so call before showing up. Another long shot during high season is **Hotel Rosenstock** (N3, 5; tel. 0621/10037), whose combative management may grudgingly give you a single with shower (DM 40) or a double with shower (DM 60). The hotel is closed on Sunday, holidays, and July 20–August 11. For a complete listing of hotels in Mannheim, consult the **tourist office** (*see above*).

The cheapest option is the **Jugendherberge** (Rheinpromenade 21, tel. 0621/822718), whose beds in clean, ordinary dorm rooms cost DM 14 (under 27) and DM 18.50 (over 26) for card-carrying IYHF members under and over age 26, respectively. This price includes breakfast and communal showers. To get here, slip out the back entrance of the Hauptbahnhof and hang a right, your first left, and a left again just before you reach the water. Both of Mannheim's rivers have campgrounds. To the east of the city along the Neckar is **Neuostheim** (tel. 0621/412536). The campground south of the city on the Rhine is called **Neckaran** (tel. 0621/856240).

FOOD The area known as the *Fußgängerzone* (pedestrian zone) teems with restaurants serving traditional German fare and has several bars for late-night activity. For something a bit different try **Merhaba** (K1, 7; tel. 0621/291469), which offers an astounding variety of Turkish treats, belly dancing on Wednesday night, and live guitar music on Friday night. For vegetarians, there's **Heller's Vollwert-Restaurant und Café**

(N7, 13; tel. 0621/153525). The salad bar costs DM 2 per 100 grams, and hot items run anywhere from DM 4 to DM 10. To save money, try the natural-foods market **Alta Natura** (N7, 12; tel. 0621/152690), next door to Heller's, or the colorful open-air market at the **Marktplatz** (*see above*) on Tuesday, Thursday, and Saturday mornings.

SCHWETZINGEN

When Elector Karl Theodor of the Palatinate decided in the mid-18th century to spend his summers in Schwetzingen rather than in his regular residence at Mannheim, he thought it would be nice to build a small Baroque castle with a little yard he could veg out in. The result was the imposing, rose-color **Schwetzinger Schloß** and the unusual, sprawling grounds of the **Schloßgarten.** Today the Schloß houses the **Xylon Museum** (open Tues.–Fri. 10–4, weekends and holidays 9:30–4:30), whose exhibits catalog the castle's former inhabitants. Unless you have a Ph.D. in Palatinate history, stay away. Instead, head toward the **Schloßgarten** (open summer, daily 8–8; spring and fall, daily 9–6; winter, daily 9–5), which blends formal French and informal English styles; its monuments pay homage to distant and ancient civilizations. These include temples dedicated to Minerva, Apollo, and Mercury, "ruins" of an ancient Roman aqueduct, a Chinese bridge, and an elaborate Turkish mosque. The garden also contains dozens of statues and fountains and an ornate bathhouse. To see the spectacular **Rococo theater** on the Schloßgarten grounds you have to join one of the guided tours (DM 2), which leave at 11, 2, 3, and 3:30. Look up at the painting on the ceiling—the young boy playing piano is Wolfgang Amadeus Mozart. At the age of seven he performed in the theater with his older sister.

This theater continues to attract some of the world's best classical-music talents each year during the **Schwetzinger festival** (tel. 06202/4933), which runs from the end of April to the middle of June. The other annual music festival in Schwetzingen is the **Mozartfest,** which takes place in September.

Besides its garden and theater, Schwetzingen is also famous for high-quality *Spargel* (asparagus), which has been grown here since 1658. During asparagus season (April–June) you can munch on this vegetable—prepared in ways you never dreamed possible—in any of the overpriced restaurants on the **Schloßplatz**.

The advent of asparagus season is marked in and around Schwetzingen by numerous posters reading DER SPARGEL IST VERKOMMEN (THE ASPARAGUS IS COMING). *It's kind of like a German version of* Attack of the Killer Tomatoes.

COMING AND GOING To reach Schwetzingen from Heidelberg, take Bus 7007, which leaves every half hour from the Hauptbahnhof. The 30-minute ride costs DM 3.90 and deposits you on the Schloßplatz. Schwetzingen lies on a short rail line that connects it with Karlsruhe and Mannheim. To get to the castle and gardens from the Schwetzingen's Hauptbahnhof, head north on Bahnhofanlage to Karl-Theodor-Straße.

WHERE TO SLEEP Since you can see the whole town (i.e., the garden and theater) in three or four hours, you can visit on a day trip from Heidelberg. Otherwise, stay here during the music festivals or when Heidelberg's beds are full. You can get a list of local hotels from **tourist information** (Schloßpl. 2, tel. 06202/4933).

Pension Seitz (Zegherstr., tel. 06202/26077), just north of the castle entrance, offers clean, comfortable doubles with shower and breakfast for DM 80. **Parkhotel Mamma Rosa** (Dreikönigstr. 8, tel. 06202/4535) has renovated rooms for DM 50 per single and DM 100 per double.

The Neckar Valley

The Neckar Valley offers travelers a winding river, densely forested hills, and rustic villages with narrow cobblestone streets, and the **Burgenstraße** (Castle Road), a gorgeous area relatively untainted by tourists. This route of almost 50 medieval castles starts in Mannheim then runs through the Neckar Valley and east all the way to Nürnberg (*see* Chapter 7). Keep in mind that you can easily explore each of these towns or castles in half a day or less, so plan to visit more than one each day. You can also take day trips to the Neckar Valley from Heidelberg, at the north end of the valley, or Heilbronn, at the south end.

BASICS

➢ **VISITOR INFORMATION** • All of the towns worth visiting in the Neckar Valley have tourist offices. For information on the entire region, call, write to, or stop by the tourist-information office in Heidelberg (Am Hauptbahnhof, 6900 Heidelberg, tel. 06221/21341) or Heilbronn (Rathaus, Marktpl., 7100 Heilbronn, tel. 07131/562270).

➢ **GETTING AROUND** • A train running between Heidelberg and Heilbronn stops at all the important towns in the valley and runs, for the most part, right along the riverbank. Unless you're going to Dilsberg, avoid the buses—they're slow and not much cheaper than the train. Hitchhiking in the valley is unbelievably easy, especially for men traveling solo. The most pleasant way to travel between Neckargemünd and Eberbach is by boat. From June through September, ships regularly connect Heidelberg, Neckargemünd, Neckarsteinach, and Eberbach. For information call **Rhein-Neckar-Fahrgastschiffahrt GmbH** (Am Neckarlauer, tel. 06229/526) in Neckarsteinach.

➢ **WHERE TO SLEEP** • Break out your camping gear, because you can usually find space in one of the Neckar Valley's campgrounds (closed Nov.–Apr.). Most are dominated by cars and RVs, but the views of nearby castles make up for it. If you don't mind spending your nights and early mornings with swarms of schoolchildren, there are plenty of youth hostels in the region. Try to call ahead and make reservations, because the hostels are often booked solid, especially in the summertime. For a taste of true German culture, consider renting a room in a private home. Listings are available at most tourist-information offices, and most of them will book rooms.

➢ **FOOD** • Affordable restaurants in the Neckar Valley are scarce. To eat cheaply, your best bet is to hit the local markets and stock up on plenty of bread, cheese, and fruit, especially if you're a vegetarian. If you eat meat, munch at one of the wurst or *döner Kebab* (like a gyro) stands you'll find in any self-respecting Neckar Valley town.

➢ **OUTDOOR ACTIVITIES** • Since the Neckar River marks the southern boundary of the **Odenwald** (*see* Chapter 2), you can easily take day hikes into the forest from towns in the valley. Good places to start are Eberbach, Zwingenberg, Neckarsteinach, and Neckargemünd; you can get trail maps from their tourist-information offices. Biking along the riverbanks is popular among Germans, though a bit difficult to arrange for visitors; one option is to rent a bike from Heidelberg's Hauptbahnhof (*see* Heidelberg, *above*) and do a day trip to Neckargemünd or Neckarsteinach.

NECKARGEMUND

Neckargemünd, just 12 kilometers (8 miles) from Heidelberg at the western end of the valley, was described by Goethe as a "complaisant and lovely town." This is an uneventful spot, but because of its small size it's the perfect place to stroll or relax before moving on to your next stop. The town's narrow cobblestone streets are lined with 16th-century half-timbered houses, one of which is the **Haus zum Ritter** (tel. 06223/7035). Stretching from the waterfront to Hauptstraße, this excellently preserved house is now a hotel and restaurant.

To get to the center of town from the Hauptbahnhof, walk east on Bahnhofstraße until it turns into Hauptstraße, the main street. You can get a simple town map from the **tourist-information office** (Hauptstr. 25, tel. 06223/3553) in the **Altes Rathaus,** which also contains a tiny **museum** devoted to the town's history.

COMING AND GOING To reach this town from Heidelberg, take one of the many boats heading upstream or one of the hourly trains.

WHERE TO SLEEP If you want to stay overnight, get a list of hotels and rooms in private homes from the tourist-information office (*see above*). If it's closed, ask for details at the Hauptbahnhof. For camping, go to **Friedensbrücke** (tel. 06223/2178) on the west side of town. It's packed with car-camping types, but the view is nice, the bathrooms clean enough, and it only costs DM 5 per person and DM 5 per tent.

NECKARSTEINACH

Travelers come to Neckarsteinach to see its four **medieval castles.** To reach them from the Hauptbahnhof, walk west on Bahnhofstraße until it becomes Hauptstraße and look for the path on your right marked ZU DEM VIER BURGEN (TO THE FOUR CASTLES). On the way, you'll pass the **tourist-information office** (Hauptstr. 7, tel. 06229/313) in the **Altes Rathaus.** The castles were built between 1100 and 1230 by four members of the same family. Back then, the eldest son of an aristocrat inherited the lion's share of his father's fortune, including the castle, of course. A series of disgruntled sons farther down the line decided they'd just have to build their own humble abodes. The first two castles you'll reach on the 2-kilometer (1¼-mile) hike—**Vorderburg** and **Mittelburg**—are still inhabited today. The first is strictly off limits to visitors (unless you've been invited to dinner), but you can climb the tower of Mittelburg for a fabulous view of the valley. If you still have the energy, visit the ruins of the two westernmost castles, **Hinterburg** and **Schwallbennest.**

COMING AND GOING In addition to train and boats, Bus 2017 runs regularly from Heidelberg's Hauptstraße to Neckarsteinach.

WHERE TO SLEEP Neckarsteinach does not teem with hotels. Downhill from the Hauptbahnhof is the **Hotel Garni** (Bahnhofstr. 27A, tel. 06229/1224), which offers standard double rooms without bath for DM 72. Across the river from downtown is the campground **Unterm Dilsberg** (*see* Dilsberg, *below*), where you get a good view of three of the castles. A list of rooms in private homes is available from the tourist office.

DILSBERG

High on a hill above the Neckar Valley, the walled city of Dilsberg overlooks the twisting river and green countryside. In 1150 **Schloß Dilsberg** was built at this spot so its inhabitants could see approaching enemies. For hundreds of years the castle stood its ground against its besiegers. Unfortunately and ironically, it couldn't protect itself against its owners. In 1826 they deemed it worthless and decided to tear it down to build new houses. If the castle ruins don't amuse you, take in the panoramic view of the valley from the **city wall.**

COMING AND GOING To reach Dilsberg, catch Bus 7021 from Heidelberg or a more frequent bus (also numbered 7021) from Neckargemünd.

WHERE TO SLEEP Housed in one part of the old city wall, inside the **gate tower,** is the **Jugendherberge** (Unteregasse 1, tel. 06223/2133), with typical, clean rooms. If you're traveling with a significant other or a newly acquired, strictly temporary travel partner, consider splurging a bit (DM 100) and stay in the romantic **Schöne Aussicht** (Vor Dem Tor 2, tel. 06223/2132). Down the hill, you can camp at **Unterm Dilsberg** (tel. 06223/72585) for DM 5 per person, DM 5 per tent, and DM 2 per car.

ZWINGENBERG

The **castle** above the village of Zwingenberg is one of the best preserved along the Neckar. Unfortunately, it's open only part of the year, when you can get a tour that includes the frescoed 15th-century chapel, a room full of hunting trophies, and the interior of the castle itself. *Admission: DM 3. Open May–Sept., Tues., Fri., Sun. 2–4.*

When the castle is closed, you'll get to the end of the 2-kilometer (1¼-mile) hike from town and find yourself looking at a large stone wall and a pair of medieval towers that are better viewed from below—ideally from a boat on the Neckar. But don't be totally discouraged—the short hike is beautiful. Behind the castle is a ravine known as **Wolfsschlucht** (wolf's ravine). Legend has it that long ago the Devil, in the guise of a hunter, would give men seven magic bullets that could hit any target. The first six would do just what that low-down dog Satan promised, but the seventh would kill his poor stooge. *Der Freischütz,* an opera based on this tale, along with a host of other operas, is performed yearly in the castle at the end of August in the **Schloßfestspiele Zwingenberg** (tel. 06263/9120).

WHERE TO SLEEP Other than a couple of small hotels in town, the only place to crash here is at the **campground** on the opposite side of the Neckar. You can get there only by ferry.

EBERBACH

Eberbach lies on the edge of the Odenwald (*see* Chapter 2), where the Neckar River makes a sharp southeast turn. Once walled to protect itself from uninvited visitors, Eberbach now attracts guests who make use of its health facilities, including spas, saunas, and massage studios. After you've been bathed, baked, and kneaded, check out the Altstadt's narrow cobblestone streets and half-timbered houses. One of the most impressive of these is the 13th-century **Altes Badhaus** (Am Lindenpl. 1, tel. 06271/71057), which once served as a public bathhouse and health center and offered such popular healing techniques as bloodletting. On Oberen Badstraße is the **Krabbenstein,** an inn where locals have met to drink and eat since the 17th century. The **Hotel Karpfen** (Am Alten Markt 1, tel. 06271/71015) in the center of the Altstadt, is decorated with frescoes depicting some of the more important figures of Eberbach's history.

WHERE TO SLEEP For cheap accommodations, head over the bridge and turn right. On the right, along the Neckar is **Campingpark Eberbach** (Alter Pleutersbacher Str. 8, tel. 06271/1071), which has hot water and laundry and kitchen facilities for DM 7 per person, DM 8 per shelter. A bit farther along you'll come to the **Jugendherberge** (Richard-Shirrmann-Str. 6, tel. 06271/2593), with dorm-style rooms. Otherwise, go to the **tourist-information office** (Kellereiststr. 32–34, tel. 06271/4899), at the southwest corner of the Altstadt next to the old **clock tower,** for lodging advice.

MOSBACH

Mosbach, about 5 kilometers (3 miles) east of the Neckar River, may not be steeped in history, but it's one of the valley's mellowest towns. The only true "sights" lie on the **Marktplatz** in the center of the pedestrians-only **Altstadt.** You can't miss the **Palm'sche Haus,** an intricately designed half-timbered building. Look closely at the bottom of the corner jutting into the square and check out the striking young man holding up the house like a Renaissance Samson. Across the street from the Palm'sche Haus is the more modest **Rathaus,** a mid-16th-century stone building lined with brightly colored flower beds. Next to the Rathaus is a **tourist-information office** (tel. 06261/18333). On a third side of the square is the **Collegiate Church.** Built as a Catholic church in the 14th century, it was converted to a Protestant church when Lutheranism became the official state religion in the 16th century. In the 18th century the church was divided by a wall down the middle when an edict granted both religions equal rights. To this day, Catholics and Protestants share the church.

If you're here on a summer weekend, go to the tourist office for a list of featured events of the **Mosbacher Sommer.** During this festival you can see puppet shows, opera, and world-beat concerts.

COMING AND GOING Mosbach is easily reached by train from Heidelberg, Heilbronn, and most of the smaller towns in the Neckar Valley.

WHERE TO SLEEP The cheapest beds in town are in the sparse rooms of the **Jugendherberge** (Am Sonnerain 60, tel. 06261/2940). Walk west on Eisenbahnstraße, behind the Hauptbahnhof, and follow signs from the flight of stairs you'll spot at the first turn of the road. If the hostel is full, get a list of the city's hotels and pensions from the tourist office (*see above*). The cheapest are **Gasthof Schrekhof** (Schrekhof 12, tel. 06261/2590) and **Gasthof zum Hirsch** (Martin-Luther-Str. 1, tel. 06261/7293), both of which charge DM 50 for doubles.

FOOD For cheap grub, head for any of the gyro and wurst takeout stands throughout town. To chow down on local specialties at reasonable prices try the **Goldener Hirsch** (Hauptstr. 13, tel. 06261/17037), on the main drag south of Marktplatz. If you're in Mosbach on a Wednesday or Saturday morning go to the open-air food market in the Marktplatz.

BURG GUTTENBURG

During the Middle Ages countless battles were fought in the Neckar Valley, yet somehow Burg Guttenburg (tel. 06266/228) escaped unscathed. The castle overlooks two valleys, the Neckar and the Mühlbach, so its inhabitants knew when attackers were coming; and its only vulnerable side is fortified by a pair of enormous walls. Spread out over four floors of the castle tower is an excellent **museum** filled with old documents, weapons, suits of armor, and items depicting the everyday life of the castle's inhabitants. At one end of the museum, if the day is clear, you get a superb view of the two valleys and the ruins of a few nearby castles. *Admission: DM 3. Open daily 9:30–5.*

The Burg is also the home of the German wildlife preserve for endangered birds of prey, which are bred and trained here then released into the wilderness. About half of these birds—including falcons, owls, eagles, and vultures—are on display in an aviary on the castle grounds. Twice every day world-renowned ornithologist Claus Fentzloff takes some of the hawks and vultures out of their cages and demonstrates the skills he's taught them. Watching these graceful creatures swoop amazingly close to your head and glide over the valley is a spectacular experience. *Tel. 06266/388. Admission, including bird show: DM 6. Open daily 9–6. Bird show at 11 and 3.*

COMING AND GOING To reach Burg Guttenburg, catch a train to the town of Gundelsheim, cross the bridge, and hike up the hill in front of you.

HEILBRONN

Because Heilbronn was flattened late one winter night in 1944 by a U.S. Air Force bombing raid, only a few old buildings stand today. Miraculously, the Gothic **Kilianskirche** (Church of St. Kilian) survived devastation. The exterior of the building is dominated by an enormous, exquisitely adorned belfry, and the church's interior contains an equally intricate carved-wood altarpiece. Across the street you'll find the **Marktplatz,** with a friendly **tourist-information office** (tel. 07131/562270). On the north side of the Marktplatz is the 15th-century **Rathaus,** notable for its 16th-century **ornamental clock.** This complex and beautifully decorated timepiece is actually three clocks—an astronomical clock, a time clock, and a moon-phase clock—enclosed in a single frame. Try to catch the noises and movements the clock's adornments make every hour; a bell is struck alternately by two angels on either side of it. The **Städtische Museum** (Deutschofstr. 6–8, tel. 07131/562295), south of Kilianskirche, is easily one of the best local-history and art museums in Württemberg (and admission is free).

Although Heilbronn is one of the big wine-production centers in Germany, you don't really feel it while you're here. The industry is more a part of the city's economics than a part of its culture. Nevertheless, through the tourist-information office (*see above*), you can find out about wine tasting, wine lectures, and wine walks through the vineyards. For nine days every September a "Wine Village" is set up near the Rathaus, where you can sample hundreds of wines at the various booths.

COMING AND GOING If you prefer cars to trains, call **Mitfahrzentrale** (tel. 07131/627662). Otherwise take one of the regular trains from Heidelberg (and other Neckar Valley towns) or Stuttgart. To reach the Marktplatz from the Hauptbahnhof, walk on Bahnhofstraße and cross Friedrich-Ebert-Brücke to Kaiserstraße; the Marktplatz will be on your left. The pedestrian zone stretches northeast on Sulmerstraße to Berliner Platz and southwest on Fleiner Straße to the Fleinertor fountain.

WHERE TO SLEEP Although its slime-green walls surround the cheapest beds in town, the **Jugendherberge** (Schirrmannstr. 9, tel. 07131/72961) might make you believe you've died and gone to hostel hell. Besides the combat-ready couple who run the place, the worst aspects of the nightmarish, conventlike institution include a 9–5:30 lockout, 9:45 curfew, and strict enforcement of a usually ignored IYHF rule that only certain types of sheets can be used—i.e., no sleeping bags—on sacred hostel beds. To reach this place, you'll have to take a long ride on Bus 1 from the Hauptbahnhof, get off at the Trappansee stop, and walk 100 yards up a steep hill then turn left. To sleep more comfortably without spending a pfennig, get off Bus 1 at the same stop and walk downhill to the long, skinny park on your right.

The cheapest hotel in town is the **Hotel Armida** (Frankfurter Str. 14, tel. 07131/80013) down the street from the Hauptbahnhof before you reach the Neckar. A clean double room complete with color TV runs DM 70, including breakfast and a shower in the hall. **Hotel Schlachthof** (Frankfurter Str. 83, tel. 07131/81413) charges similar rates for slightly less attractive rooms. For more lodging advice, go to the tourist-information office on Marktplatz (*see above*).

FOOD The culinary choices in Heilbronn, especially for those on a budget, are limited. Your best bet is to try one of the fast-food restaurants around the pedestrian zone. Wurst fans can choose from a variety of greasy dishes at **Wurstbraterei Silzer** (Grosse Bahngasse and Fleiner Str.). Those preferring seafood should head for **Restaurant Nordsee** (Fleiner Str. and Deutschhofstr.). The local market is held on the Marktplatz on Tuesday, Thursday, and Saturday 7–1. The cheapest supermarket in town is **Norma** (Sulmerstr. and Schellengasse, tel. 06281/8128) on the north side of the pedestrian zone.

Stuttgart

It's fitting that one of the first things you see when you get to this hypermodern city is the famous three-pointed Mercedes-Benz symbol high above the train station. Stuttgart's star began to rise when Gottlieb Daimler invented the gas-powered engine in a nearby suburb in 1883. The Industrial Revolution pushed the city into the machine age, only to be leveled in World War II. Since then, Stuttgart has once again become one of Germany's top industrial and technological centers, but it is almost entirely lacking in historical interest. Nevertheless, the capital of Baden-Württemberg has used its wealth to become a center of the graphic and performing arts. What Stuttgart lacks in historical monuments it compensates for with a host of excellent museums, galleries, and theaters.

BASICS

AMERICAN EXPRESS American Express changes money, holds mail, and serves as a travel agency. It's in front of the Hauptbahnhof. *Lautenschlagerstr. 3, tel. 0711/208-9128. Open weekdays 9–5:30, Sat. 9–noon.*

BUCKET SHOPS Students and young travelers can get discount airline tickets at **Asta,** not far from Charlottenplatz. *Weberstr. 86, tel. 0711/242968. Open weekdays 10–1, 2–5:30.*

BUREAUX DE CHANGE **Deutsche Verkehrsbank** at the Hauptbahnhof (tel. 0711/19419) has long hours: Monday–Saturday 8–8:30 and Sunday 9–8. You can get better rates, though, at **American Express** (*see* American Express, *above*), especially if you're cashing their traveler's checks.

MEDICAL AID Check the listing at any pharmacy in town for the location of the one open late that night. **Apotheke am Eugensplatz** (Haußmannstr. 1, tel. 0711/240575) is near the youth hostel on Eugensplatz. The most centrally located hospital in town is **Bürgerhospital** (Hohenheimerstr. 21, tel. 0711/21561). The **Women's Center** (Kernerstr. 31, tel. 0711/296356 or 0711/296432) handles health problems.

MAIL AND PHONES The main branch of the post office performs all postal services, holds *poste restante* mail, has international phone facilities, and changes money. The postal code for Stuttgart is 70173; the area code is 0711. *Bolzstr. 3, at Lautenschlagerstr., w. of Schloßpl., tel. 0711/206-7264. Open weekdays 8–6, Sat. 8:30–12:30, Sun. 11–noon.*

The Hauptbahnhof post office offers all postal services, has international phone facilities, and changes money. *Open Mon.–Sat. 6 AM–11 PM, Sun. 7 AM–10 PM.*

VISITOR INFORMATION Stuttgart's **tourist-information office**, in front of the Hauptbahnhof in the underground Arnulf-Klett-Passage, is one of the most efficient tourist offices in Germany. The staff provides useful sightseeing tips, books rooms for free, and sells theater tickets. Go to the *Jugendinformation* (Information for Youth) desk to get tips on cheap places to eat and sleep and the scoop on cool clubs. *Königstr. 1A, tel. 0711/222-8240. Open May–Oct., Mon.–Sat. 8:30–10, Sun. and holidays 11–6; Nov.–Apr., Mon.–Sat. 8:30–9, Sun. and holidays 1–6.*

COMING AND GOING

Stuttgart is one of Germany's main rail hubs and has regular train connections to every major city in the country. The most frequent service runs to Frankfurt (3½ hours), Munich (two to three hours), and Ulm (1¼ hours). The **Hauptbahnhof** (tel. 0711/19419), in the city center, has exchange facilities, markets, shops, and restaurants. The **Busbahnhof** (bus station), beside the Hauptbahnhof, has service to small nearby towns only. Hitchhiking out of Stuttgart is notoriously difficult. A better bet is to arrange a ride through **Mitfahrzentrale** (Lerchenstr. 65, tel. 0711/636-8036). Stuttgart also has a large airport (tel. 0711/790-1388), with service to every major German city as well as international flights to London (Heathrow), New York, and Los Angeles. Buses connect the airport to the Hauptbahnhof every 20 minutes 5 AM–11:30 PM. The fare is DM 6.

GETTING AROUND

When you come out of the underground passage of the Hauptbahnhof you'll find yourself nearly in Stuttgart's center. Ahead of you and on your right, to the west, lies the city's thriving business-and-financial district. Ahead of you and on your left, to the east, lies the commercial center whose main artery, **Königstraße,** runs into the city's main square, the **Schloßplatz.** Directly behind you, the bulk of the long, skinny **Schloßgarten** stretches northeast, blossoming into the city's largest full-blown park,

Rosensteinpark. In the low-lying hills around you are the 'burbs, most of which contain Stuttgart's various high-tech industrial facilities. Many of the sights are scattered around the city, so you're bound to become intimate with the public-transportation system. Luckily, the system is more or less user-friendly. The inner city is crisscrossed by an extensive network of S-Bahn trains (streetcars), U-Bahn trains (subways), buses, and trams, which all use the same tickets. You can buy tickets from orange machines at most bus stops; when there is no machine, buy your ticket from a bus driver. Rides within the city center cost DM 2.30. Tickets good for four rides cost DM 8.10. If you plan to cover a lot of ground in a day, buy a *Tageskarte,* good for 24 hours of unlimited travel on any of the city's public transportation (cost: DM 13). The S-Bahn, the easiest and most popular option, runs to the suburbs as well as within the city center. You can ride it free with a Eurailpass. For information on Stuttgart's public transportation, call 0711/660–6200. For a **taxi,** dial 0711/566061.

WHERE TO SLEEP

Aside from the youth hostel, cheap lodgings in the center of Stuttgart simply don't exist, so be prepared to travel a little. Also keep in mind that if you want to delve into the city's nightlife, you should try to find a hotel, since things don't get shaking until about 11, a half hour before the hostel's curfew. If all of the places below are booked, you can get a list of budget accommodations from Jugendinformation at the tourist office. You can usually get a space at the hostel in Esslingen (*see* Near Stuttgart, *below*), but it won't be convenient.

➢ **UNDER DM 70 • Gästehaus Garni Eckel.** The rooms are not aesthetically appealing, but they are clean and adequate. Singles and doubles run DM 35 and DM 70 (breakfast included). *Vorsteigstr. 10, tel. 0711/290995. Bus 40 to Hölderlinpl., walk up Zeppelinstr. and turn at 2nd left onto Vorsteigstr. 15 rooms, some with bath.*

Hotel-Restaurant Lamm. It isn't attractive, but it's cheap, clean, and nicely located (near a U-Bahn station and Rosensteinpark). Singles start at DM 35, and doubles run DM 60 (breakfast included). The management is a bit lackadaisical, so if they don't answer the phone on your first try, don't give up. *Karl-Schurz-Str. 7, tel. 0711/267328. U14 to Mineralbäder and follow path to Karl-Schurz-Str. 15 rooms without bath.*

Jugendgästehaus Stuttgart. The impeccable rooms, pleasant atmosphere, and unbeatably convenient location next to a U-Bahn stop make this the best budget lodging in Stuttgart. Singles go for DM 35; doubles go for DM 60. Probably because many young people doing internships in Stuttgart make this their home for several months, the Gästehaus feels more like a home than a hotel. The members of the International Association for Social Work, who run the place, are amazingly friendly. A washer and refrigerator are available. *Richard-Wagner-Str. 2, tel. 0711/241132. U15 or U16 toward Heumaden to Bubenbad; hotel on corner in front of bus stop. 50 rooms, some with bath. Partially disabled accessible.*

➢ **UNDER DM 100 • Schwarzwaldheim.** This hotel-above-a-restaurant number is the closest thing you'll find to budget accommodations in Stuttgart's center. The hotel may be small, but the rooms aren't. Clean, recently renovated doubles go for DM 80 (breakfast included), but space is limited, so call ahead. *Fritz-Elsas-Str. 20, at Theodor-Heuss-Str., tel. 0711/296988. S1 or S6 to Stadtmitte, across from S-Bahn stop. 5 rooms without bath.*

Museum-Stube. This small hotel around the corner from the Schloßplatz is one of the best values in town. The amiable proprietors can set you up in a clean, simply decorated double for DM 98 (breakfast included). *Hospitalstr. 9, tel. 0711/296810. From Hauptbahnhof walk up Lautenschlagerstr. to Theodor-Heuss-Str., turn right on Büchsenstr. and left on Hospitalstr. 11 rooms, some with bath.*

HOSTELS **Jugendherberge.** The hostel in the hills to the east of the city is utterly characterless, but it also has guests other than schoolchildren. Beds in various-size dorm rooms go for DM 17.50, DM 22.50 if you're a senior citizen in the hostel world. The jovial breakfast chef is always ready with a "Guten Morgen" and a smile. It's possible to walk to the hostel, but it's a pretty good hike—ask for directions at tourist information (*see* Visitor Information, *above*). *Haußmannstr. 27, tel. 0711/241583. U15 or U16 to Eugenspl., walk down Haußmannstr. and up stairs on right. 220 beds without bath. Curfew 11:30, lockout 9–noon, check-in noon–2:45 and 3:15–11, sheets DM 5.50.*

CAMPGROUNDS **Cannstatter Wasen.** The closest real campground is along the Neckar River in the suburb of Bad-Cannstatt, about 15 minutes east of the city center. This is definitely city camping—you'll share space with loads of RVs and pushy people. The charge is DM 5.50 per person, DM 5.50 per tent, and DM 4 per car. *Mercedesstr. 40, tel. 0711/556696. From Hauptbahnhof, U9 to Staatsgalerie then S2 or U1 to Mercedesstr.; walk e. Showers DM 3, telephones, cooking facilities.*

Stuttgart Camp International. The brainchild of Stuttgart's tourist board, this canopied campground-shelter is meant to help young travelers from around the world meet each other in a positive environment. Presently it's in the suburb of Feuerbach near the sports stadium, but the tourist board was planning to change the location at press time. Ask for specifics at the tourist-information office. A spot on the floor with an insulated pad and a blanket costs DM 7 per person. There are cooking facilities, a cafeteria, and showers. *Wiener Str., tel. 0711/817–7476. U6 or S16 toward Gerlingen to Sportpark Feuerbach. Check-in 9–5, 3-night maximum. Closed fall–spring.*

FOOD

Stuttgart's culinary scene offers everything from run-of-the-mill wurst stands to excellent (and expensive) international cuisine. If you're looking for something quick and cheap go to **Schulstraße,** which runs between Königstraße and the Marktplatz. Here you'll find wurst, schnitzel, burgers, sandwiches, pasta, and seafood in a smattering of fast-food restaurants. Be sure to try *Maultaschen* (ravioli-like pasta filled with meat and spinach) and *Käsespätzle* (thick egg noodles), which are traditional Schwäbische dishes. If you're going the bread-and-cheese route, head for the shops on the Marktplatz.

➢ **UNDER DM 8** • **Le Buffet Restaurant.** This cafeteria-style restaurant serves local specialties in the basement of the Hertie department store. The food may taste institutional, but it's cheap (about DM 7). *Königstr. at Schulstr., no tel. Disabled accessible. Closed Sun., Mon.*

➢ **UNDER DM 15** • **Bohnenviertele.** Come to this local Weinstube for good local fare in a comfortable environment. If you don't want to be scoffed at, make sure to order a glass (DM 4.50–DM 6.50) or a bottle of vino with your meal. *Esslingerstr. 18, tel. 0711/233778. From Charlottenpl. walk s. on Esslingerstr. Closed weekends.*

Iden. Vegetarians shouldn't miss this excellent cafeteria-style eatery. Choose from an honest-to-goodness salad bar (DM 2 per 100 grams), vegetarian soups (DM 4), hot vegetarian dishes (DM 6–DM 12), and fresh juices (DM 3). *Eberhardstr. 1, in Schwäben-Zentrum, e. of Rathaus, tel. 0711/235989. Disabled accessible. No Sat. dinner. Closed Sun.*

Litfass bei Ali. You can grab Schwäbische or Turkish dishes while relaxing to the incessant reggae beat at this student hangout. Try the Käsespätzle with green salad for DM 11. Food is served until 4 AM, but after 11 PM most of the patrons drink rather than eat. On weekends local bands play everything from reggae to funk to blues. *Eberhardstr. 37, tel. 0711/243031. Walk s. on Königstr., turn left on Schulstr., cross Marktpl. to Marktstr., turn right on Eberhardstr., walk down stairs on right.*

➢ **UNDER DM 20 • Saigon.** If you're sick of wurst and schnitzel, try the Vietnamese dishes at this upscale restaurant. Beef with lemongrass, pork chop-suey, and roasted tofu cost DM 16 each. *Eberhardstr. 6A, tel. 0711/247271. Walk up Königstr., turn left on Eberhardstr. No Sun. lunch. Closed daily 2:30–6.*

CAFES Stuttgart has more cafés than an average American city has Burger Kings. As usual, your best bet is to wander around until something strikes your fancy. To mingle with Stuttgart's ultrahip yuppie crowd try the chic **Osho's** (Eberhardstr. 31, tel. 0711/241789). To do the P.C.-multicultural thing head for **Café Merlin** (Augustenstr. 72, tel. 0711/61854), which features vegetarian snacks and occasional live bands.

WORTH SEEING

ALTES SCHLOß AND SCHLOßPLATZ The center of the city's action is the spacious **Schloßplatz** (Castle Square) in the middle of the bustling commercial district. On the east side is the enormous Baroque **Neue Schloß,** home to government offices, and on the west side is the **Königsbau,** whose imposing neoclassical columns enclose a shopping arcade. South of the Schloßplatz, the **Altes Schloß** (Old Castle) has a drab exterior compared to the more famous castles in Bavaria or along the Neckar and Rhine valleys. However, it does contain the **Landesmuseum** and a beautiful courtyard where classical-music concerts are held in summer. The third floor offers unusual displays of astronomical and timekeeping devices, musical instruments, and beautifully restored furniture. The tower off the second floor contains some of the old aristocracy's crown jewels. *Admission free. Open Tues. and Thurs.– Sun. 10–5, Wed. 10–7.*

HEGEL-HAUS This museum tracing the life of Stuttgart's most famous native philosopher through letters, manuscripts, and pictures is strictly for German-speaking Hegelian cultists. *Eberhardstr. 53, near Rathaus, tel. 0711/216–6733. Admission free.*

SCHILLERPLATZ This square has a somber statue of the poet-dramatist-philosopher Friedrich Schiller, who was born in the nearby suburb of Marbach. Behind Schillerplatz is **Stiftskirche,** a late-Gothic church (1433–1531) whose otherwise bland interior is blessed with a fabulous Renaissance sculpture depicting 11 of the dukes and counts of Württemberg.

STAATSGALERI Don't miss this impressive art museum, one of Germany's finest, housed in two connected buildings. The old edifice contains paintings from the Middle Ages to the 19th century, including works by Rembrandt, Cézanne, and Manet. The new building, completed in 1984, is a work of art in itself. The exterior's lavender, blue, and green metallic structures and the interior's green plastic floor will make you feel like you're in a Lego fantasy world. The postmodern gallery houses 20th-century creations by such artists as Dalí, Dix, Kandinsky, Klee, Mondrian, and Picasso. *Konrad-Adenauer-Str. 30–32, tel. 0711/212–5050. Admission free. Open Wed., Fri.-Sun. 10–5; Tues., Thurs. 10–8.*

IN THE SUBURBS East of the city center is the spacious **Mercedes-Benz Museum,** which traces the history of the automobile line as well as the development of the engine for ships and planes. You'll probably enjoy the plethora of gorgeous Benz classics in this museum, but be forewarned that the telephone-like "walking sticks," which are meant to provide audible commentary on displays, are not up to par. *Mercedesstr. 136, tel. 0711/172–2578. S1 toward Plochingen to Neckarstadion and follow signs. Admission free. Open Tues.–Sun. 9–5.*

The **Porsche Museum** is a one-room affair containing a single example of each of the company's models, about a dozen race cars, and a few engines. Only hard-core Porsche enthusiasts need bother. However, you can arrange a tour of Porsche's production facilities by phoning two to three months in advance. *Porschestr. 42, tel.*

0711/827–5685. S6 toward Weil der Stadt to Neuwirtshaus. Admission free. Open Tues.–Sun. 10:30–5:30.

If you prefer drinking to driving, hit the **Schwäbisches Brauereimuseum.** It traces the history of beer from Mesopotamian times to the present and the production of beer from the hop-and-malt harvest to the bottling process. There's even an exhibit on the religious aspects of beer. *Robert-Koch-Str. 12, tel. 0711/737–0201. U1, U3, U6, S1, S2, or S3 to Vaihingen; walk down Vollmoellerstr. and turn right on Robert-Koch-Str. Admission free. Open Tues.–Sun. 10:30–5:30.*

AFTER DARK

Equally as famous as the Staatsgalerie (*see* Worth Seeing, *above*) across the street is Stuttgart's **Staatstheater** (Oberer Schloßgarten, tel. 0711/221795), a complex of theaters that host ballet, opera, and plays. Listings and tickets are available at the tourist-information office (*see* Visitor Information, *above*), where you can also get information about the city's smaller theaters. Stuttgart's bars, clubs, and discos are spread all over the city, but many of the more interesting places are near the south end of Königstraße. If you're out on the town and things seem a bit dull, be patient. The action in Stuttgart generally doesn't start until 11 or midnight, but once it gets rolling it can really rock. Don't worry about staggering home late at night—the streets of Stuttgart are pretty safe.

Cinderella (Tübingerstr. 17, tel. 01711/640–6000, closed Mon. and Wed.) has blaring funk and hip-hop guaranteed to make your body bump and grind all night long; Fridays feature music by black artists. The lively **King's Club** (Calwer Str. 21, at Lange Str., tel. 0711/226–1607) plays technopop hits from the glorious '80s for a predominantly gay clientele; Sundays are for women only. At **Rockpalast** (Rotebühlpl. 4, tel. 0711/224412) loud hard rock and heavy metal fill a smoky room made to look like a cave. If live jazz is your thing, go to a **Roger's Kiste** (Hauptstätterstr. 35, tel. 0711/233148).

Der Bräu in Tü 8 (Tübingerstr. 8–10, tel. 0711/295949) Stuttgart's only microbrewery serves homemade Pils (DM 3) and Weizener (DM 4.50) to a young, lively crowd.

Near Stuttgart

ESSLINGEN

Despite the fact that its rich history dates to Roman times and that until the late 19th century it rivaled Stuttgart as an industrial powerhouse, modern-day Esslingen has been swallowed up by the industrial sprawl of Stuttgart. Luckily, Esslingen's historic **Altstadt** is bordered by steep, vineyard-carpeted hills that block out the high-tech production facilities that surround it, making it a medieval oasis in the middle of the metropolitan desert.

From the Hauptbahnhof head northeast on Bahnhofstraße, cross the Neckar River via the Agnesbrücke, and veer right to get to the **Marktplatz,** a large square lined with historic buildings. For an explanation of the history of each of these buildings and a map of Esslingen, head to the **tourist-information office** (Marktpl. 16, tel. 0711/351–2441) to your left. Dominating the square is the **Stadtkirche St. Dionys,** built in Romanesque style but completed with an unmistakable Gothic flair. Its two towers are connected because the church also served as a lookout during turbulent times. On the square adjacent to the Marktplatz is the **Altes Rathaus,** whose peach-color Renaissance facade is adorned with an astronomical clock and a glockenspiel. Try to be here at the top of the hour, when the glockenspiel plays a groovy tune from its large repertoire. A small alley on the east side of the Altes Rathaus leads to the

Hafenmarkt, whose most infamous building is a medieval brothel known as the **Gelbes Haus** (Yellow House), closed since 1701.

North of the Marktplatz across Augustinerstraße is the Gothic **Frauenkirche,** whose extravagant tower is topped by a lofty openwork spire. The church contains some beautiful 14th-century stained-glass windows, but even more impressive are the two intricately carved wood portals depicting the Last Judgment and the life of the Virgin. East of the church a covered pathway leads up to the ruins of the **Burg,** which once served as part of Esslingen's defenses. The only standing (or squatting) structure, the half-timbered **Dicker Turm** (Fat Tower), was restored in the 19th century and today houses an expensive restaurant. So little is left of the former fortress that you may wonder if you're in the right place, but the view of the town, the Neckar Valley, and the Swabian Jura in the background make the steep climb worthwhile. For even more fantastic views you can walk the **Höhenweg,** which runs through terraced vineyards. To get to the path, follow the signs from town or ask for directions at the tourist-information office.

COMING AND GOING Esslingen is on the rail line between Ulm and Stuttgart; you can easily reach Stuttgart by catching the S1 from its Hauptbahnhof.

WHERE TO SLEEP The **Jugendherberge** (Neuffenstr. 65, tel. 0711/381848) offers clean rooms and nice views of the town below, but it's pretty far from the city center. Take Bus 118 to Zollernplatz, turn around and head up Zollernstraße, and turn left onto Neuffenstraße. **Gasthof Falken** (Bahnhofstr. 4, tel. 0711/357288) is more conveniently located (near the Hauptbahnhof) but more expensive. Basic doubles cost DM 50; singles, DM 30.

FOOD Head for the Weinstuben, which serve light meals and local wines. Try the dark, cozy **Weinstube Einhorn** (Heugasse 17, tel. 0711/353590) east of the Altes Rathaus.

Tübingen

This town on a stretch of the Neckar River lined with weeping willows was spared by Allied bombers during World War II and has enough beautiful old buildings to make you feel like you've been transported back in time. But the feeling won't last long; the city is immersed in the life of the university, and the dress and speech of the liberal students who crowd the winding, often steep cobblestone streets will jolt you back to the 20th century. Add a thriving nightlife and a great setting for outdoor adventures to this enticing mixture of historic buildings and young inhabitants (they account for a third of Tübingen's population of 75,000), and you've got the perfect recipe for one of the most inviting university towns in Germany.

BASICS

BUCKET SHOPS Visit **Campus Reisebüro** (Wilhelmstr. 13, in Mensa bldg., tel. 07071/25028) to get good deals on travel arrangements.

MAIL The main **post office** (Europapl. 2, tel. 07071/101) around the corner from the train station holds *poste restante* mail, changes money, has international telephone facilities, and performs the usual postal services. The postal code is 7400; the telephone code is 07071.

VISITOR INFORMATION On the south side of the bridge between the train station and the Altstadt, the **tourist-information office** offers maps, exchanges money, and books rooms. *An der Neckarbrücke, tel. 07071/35011. Open fall–spring, weekdays 8:30–6:30, Sat. 8:30–12:30; summer, weekdays 8:30–6:30, Sat. 8:30–12:30, Sun. 2–5.*

COMING AND GOING

Regular trains connect Tübingen with Stuttgart (one hour), with the Nagold Valley through the town of Horb (25 minutes), and with most other Black Forest destinations. Buses to Stuttgart, the Nagold Valley, the Black Forest, and the Bodensee depart from the **Busbahnhof** in front of the train station. Bus tickets cost about the same as rail tickets, but the rides take longer. Stand on Wilhelmstraße, north of the university, to easily **hitchhike** to Stuttgart or any of the smaller towns to the north, like Böblingen or Sindelfingen. The **Mitfahrzentrale** (Münzgasse 12, tel. 07071/26789) is in a copy shop about five blocks west of the Marktplatz.

From the **Hauptbahnhof** (tel. 07071/19419), walk to the right to Karlstraße, and head left across the bridge. To your left is the old section of town, where most of the action is, and 2 kilometers (1¼ miles) ahead of you are the university buildings, where you can sit in on a few classes, if the school of life isn't doing it for you.

WHERE TO SLEEP

Alongside the Neckar and a five-minute walk from the Altstadt, the **Jugendherberge** (Gartenstr. 2212, tel. 07071/23002) has creaky beds for DM 16.50 (DM 21 over 26) along with lockers and laundry facilities downstairs. (Members only). From the station, cross the bridge and take your first right, or catch Bus 11 (DM 2.20) to the Jugendherberge stop for door-to-door service. **Hotel Am Schloß** (Burgsteige 18, tel. 07071/21077) has clean, plain-vanilla singles for DM 45 and doubles for DM 95. The only other affordable hotel is **Kürner** (Weizsückerstr. 1, tel. 07071/22735), with doubles for DM 90. To get there, take Bus 1 or 7 from the station to the Mohlstraße stop. On the north bank of the river, west of the Altstadt, is a **campground** (Rappenberghalde 61, tel. 07071/43145) that charges DM 7 per person, DM 6 per tent. For a list of rooms in private homes at prices ranging from DM 20 to DM 50, ask at the tourist-information office, or let them book a room for a DM 3 service charge.

FOOD

To satisfy a warped craving for institutional cuisine, head straight to the university's cafeteria, or **Mensa** (Wilhelmstr. 13), where you can get a four-course meal for DM 2.70 or help yourself at the pay-according-to-size salad buffet. From the bridge, walk up the hill and veer right on Wilhelmstraße. Also outside the Altstadt is the student-run **Marquadtei** (Herrenberger Str. 34, tel. 07071/43386), where the music is loud and the staff smokes, but the food—pizzas (DM 7.50–DM 12.80) and a wide array of dishes for carnivores and herbivores—is good. Very popular with the 30-something crowd is **Wurstküche** (Am Lastnauer Tor, tel. 07071/51333), which serves typical Schwäbisch dishes like Maultaschen (DM 10.90) and Käsespätzle (DM 12.80) until 1 AM. Middle Eastern–food connoisseurs will be in heaven at **Die Kicher Erbse** (Metzgergasse 2, tel. 07071/52171), downhill from Holzmarkt, whose falafel (DM 5) and other vegetarian plates are the best you'll find this side of Jerusalem.

WORTH SEEING

Tübingen's most interesting attraction, the exceedingly well-preserved **Bebenhausen Kloister** is set in the rolling green hills of Naturpark Schönbuch, about 5 kilometers (3 miles) north of the city center. With your imagination as your guide, you'll get a good idea of what life was like for the silent order of monks who lived in this abbey. *Tel. 07071/200–2664. From Hauptbahnhof, Bus 7955 or 7600 to Waldhorn. Admission: DM 3.50, DM 2 students. Tour of abbey and adjoining castle: DM 6.*

On the eastern end of the Altstadt, Holzmarkt is dominated by the late-Gothic **Stiftskirche** (Collegiate Church). Inside you can browse around the choir (DM 1, DM .50 students), which is decorated with stone statues of the rulers of Württemberg in full armor and some of their wives in stately costume. Climb the tower (DM 1, DM .50 students) for a view of the city's red-tile roofs and the murky brown waters of the Neckar. The **Hölderlinterum,** on the bank of the river behind Holzmarkt, was home to local poet Friedrich Hölderlin for his last 36 years, during which his mental illness became incurable. The building now houses a museum containing memorabilia associated with this 18th-century poet.

Connected to Holzmarkt by Kirchegasse, Tübingen's **Marktplatz** is filled with half-timbered buildings and anchored by a **fountain of Neptune.** The four nymphs below the god of the sea represent the four seasons. The real eye-catcher on Marktplatz, though, is the gabled **Rathaus,** built in 1435 but periodically reconstructed since then. The building is decorated with late-19th-century murals depicting allegorical figures: University founder Duke Eberhard is the large, bearded figure off center on the third story. From behind the Rathaus you can follow signs marked SCHLOß to the 16th-century **Schloß Hohentübingen,** whose buildings are now used by the university. You can get a good view down the Neckar in both directions and check out the outstanding (but grimy) lower gate and the rest of the exterior.

North of Marktplatz on a street of the same name is the giant half-timbered **Kornhaus,** home to the **Stadtmuseum,** which features a pictorial history of the town concentrating on the rise of the Nazis and the student uprisings in the late 1960s. *Open Tues.–Sat. 3–6; Sun. 11–1, 3–6.*

AFTER DARK

Tubingen's nightlife will certainly satisfy your yen to party. Locals distinguish the endless number of bars in town on the basis of types of beer served. Tubingen's A. K. C. (Average Keg Consumption, per student per year) breaks the scales. The Most Popular Bar in Town award goes to **Marktschenke** (Am Markt 11, tel. 07071/22035), where the noisy crowds spill onto the Marktplatz. Always rocking, **Tangente-Night** (Pfleghof 10, tel. 07071/23007) pours Schwäben Brau pilseners and potent Klosterbrau Weizens until 3 AM every day. Tübingen's premier disco, **Zentrum Zoo** (Schleifmühleweg 86, tel. 07071/45003), plays a variety of danceable tunes and has regular theme nights featuring African, Brazilian, and "modern classics" (i.e., '80s technopop).

OUTDOOR ACTIVITIES

On sunny days students gather in the grassy park, once a botanical garden, between the Altstadt and the university to while away the hours reading, studying (yeah, right!), chatting, picnicking, downing beer, and working on their tans. Rent a bike from the train station (DM 12 per day, DM 8 with rail pass), and ride east along the bike path on the south side of the Neckar to Lake Kirchentellinsfurt, about 10 kilometers (6 miles) downstream. You can also rent a rowboat from a booth marked BOOTSVERMIETUNG (DM 9 per day for 3 people, DM 3 each additional person) next to the tourist office. (On Saturday you can join a regularly scheduled punting trip for DM 6 from the dock beside the Hölderlinturm.) For a scenic hike, head for the soft, rolling hills of the **Naturpark Schönbuch,** north of town; the tourist office has maps of the many well-marked trails.

Schwäbische Alb

East of the Black Forest and north of the Bodensee lies the vast, sparsely populated region known as the Schwäbische Alb (Swabian Jura). Characterized by forested limestone plateaus and grassy flatlands, the region is frequently denigrated as aesthetically inferior to other, much more heavily touristed regions nearby. But the placid, small towns and pleasant walking trails in the region, along with the lack of tourists, make for a mellow, off-the-beaten-track adventure. The main drawback to visiting the region is the lack of transportation. Major rail lines connecting Stuttgart to Konstanz and Friedrichshafen run along the border of the Schwäbische Alb, but only a few smaller lines run through the heart of the region, making train travel time-consuming. Regular buses improve the situation but transfers add to a trip's length. If you've got the time and energy, you can explore the Schwäbische Alb on foot. Grab a trail map at most decent-size book shops or at the tourist-information office in Rottweil or Donaueschingen (*see below*).

SCHWABISCH GMUND

Schwäbisch Gmünd, 50 kilometers (31 miles) east of Stuttgart, marks the northern boundary of the Schwäbische Alb and is known for its architectural triumphs, which date to the 12th century. The most impressive of these is the early 14th-century **Heilig-Kreuz-Münster,** which lacks a tower. The Münster's exterior is ringed by elaborate pinnacles and sculptures of tortured creatures who look like they're trying to jump out of the building. The inside of the church, illuminated by innumerable stained-glass windows, features carved wood choir stalls, a vaulted ceiling, and rows of stone statues. The exterior of the 13th-century **Johanniskirche,** a stone's throw northeast of the Münster, contains statues of wild-eyed figures meant to ward off evil spirits. In front of the church is the long, Baroque-style **Marktplatz,** lined with impressive buildings. Note the giant half-timbered **Amtshaus Spital,** built in the late 15th century, at the northern end of the rectangular "square." At the south end of the Marktplatz is the **Kornhaus,** which houses the **tourist-information office** (Im Kornhaus, tel. 07171/603415).

COMING AND GOING Schwäbisch Gmünd is connected by rail to Nürnberg (DM 26, 1½ hours) and Stuttgart (DM 13, 40 minutes). From the Hauptbahnhof walk south on Bahnhofstraße and turn left on Ledergasse, which will bring you to the Amtshaus Spital at the north end of the Marktplatz.

WHERE TO SLEEP The cheapest hotel, located on the west end of town, is the **Gasthof Weißer Ochsen** (Parlerstr. 47, tel. 07171/2812), which has get-what-you-pay-for singles for DM 27 and one double for DM 46. On the east side, **Gasthof Goldener Stern** (Vordere Schmiedgasse 41, tel. 07171/66337) has much nicer singles for DM 32 and doubles for DM 60. To get to the **Jugendherberge** (Taubentalstr. 46/1, tel. 07171/2260) from the Hauptbahnhof, turn left under the tracks and follow Taubentalstraße. When it turns into a footpath, veer right. Beds are DM 16.50 (DM 21 if you're over 26).

SCHWABISCH HALL

Hall means "place of salt" in German, a fitting description of the town that dominated southern Germany's salt trade for about 700 years. That's how the residents of Schwäbisch Hall (the locals call it "Hall") acquired the money that enabled them to erect the beautiful buildings that attract visitors today. The town has regular train connections to Stuttgart and Heilbronn.

From the Hauptbahnhof head down the steps of the path marked FUßGANGER ZUR INNENSTADT to Bahnhofstraße, cross the two bridges (Theatersteg and Epinalsteg) over the Kocher River, and walk north toward the **Marktplatz.** You're on the right track as long as you're heading toward the clock tower that dominates the skyline. On the north side of the square, the **tourist-information office** (Am Marktpl. 9, tel. 0791/751246) sells a highly detailed city map (DM 1) that tells you more than you'll ever need to know about the town.

The Marktplatz is full of pre-19th-century buildings. Overlooking the square is the late-Gothic **St. Michael's Church,** a mammoth structure whose interior decorator appears to have been fixated on Jesus's crucifixion. The event is depicted more than a dozen times inside the church, most vividly by the centerpiece—one of those excessively lifelike jobs complete with veins and rib cage practically popping out of Jesus's skin. For DM 1 you can climb the 173 steps of the tower, but the view is not spectacular. Across the square from St. Michael's is the 18th-century Baroque, palace-like **Rathaus,** which was restored after World War II. Another impressive historical building, the gargantuan half-timbered inn **Goldener Adler** (Am Markt 11, tel. 0791/6168), has been frequented by locals since the 16th century.

On the square you'll find the painstakingly crafted **Marktbrunnen** (Market Fountain), depicting St. Michael, St. George, and Samson. Walking south on Pfarrgasse brings you to the bottom of the **Neubau** (tel. 0791/751212), built in the 16th century as a granary but now used as an events center. From here you get a good look at the walls and dry moat, which were built to delineate the town's Altstadt boundaries rather than to protect it.

Running parallel to Pfarrgasse are Obere Herrngasse and Untere Herrngasse, both lined with more old buildings. West of Untere Herrngasse is Keckenhof, at the end of which sits yet another monster of a building, the eight-story **Keckenburg,** home of the Hällisch-Fränkisches local-history museum (tel. 0791/751360). Beginning at the **Säumarkt** (Pig Market) north of Marktplatz is **Gelbinger Gasse,** another road with more interesting architecture. In the middle of the Kocher River's rich brown waters, under the Theatersteg, are two grassy islets connected to each other and to both banks by a series of small wood-and-stone bridges. If you cross the Epinalsteg to the east side of the river and follow the path south for 3 kilometers (2 miles), you'll be rewarded not only by a walk in lovely surroundings but by an excellent view of the imposing **Klosterburg Gross Komburg.** You can climb to this fortress-monastery via a statue-lined trail starting in the town of Limpurg, at the south end of the river path. When you explore the largely Romanesque grounds, be sure to catch the **Klosterkirche,** which houses an enormous chandelier.

The Marktplatz is transformed into an open-air theater from May through August for the **Freilichtspiele,** a three-play festival. To get tickets (not cheap) head to the tourist-information office. Each Pentecost weekend, the town celebrates the **Feast of Cakes and Fountains,** featuring traditional music and dancing.

WHERE TO SLEEP The **Hotel Kronprinz** (Bahnhofstr. 17, tel. 0791/6212) has peeling paint, chipped walls, and old wallpaper, but the rooms are clean, the English-speaking management chipper, and the location unbeatable. Singles go for DM 33, doubles DM 55. If it's full, **Gasthof Krone** (Klosterstr. 1, tel. 0791/6022) behind the St. Michael's Church has similar conditions at slightly higher prices. In the hills above town, the spotlessly clean **Jugendherberge** (Langenfelder Weg 5, tel. 0791/41050) charges DM 16.50, DM 21 if you're over 26. It's a bit of a hike from the Hauptbahnhof, so be sure to call ahead. From behind the Marktplatz turn right up Crailsheimer Straße, left on Ziegeleiweg, and left again on Langenfelder Weg.

Located beside a lake in the shadow of Komburg is a pleasant **campground** (Steinbacher See, tel. 0791/2984). Open April–October, it charges DM 6 per person, DM 8 per tent, and DM 1 per shower.

SWABIAN-FRANCONIAN FOREST

Two peaceful forests that have been combined into a single **Naturpark** occupy most of the space between Heilbronn, Schwäbisch Hall, Schwäbisch Gmünd, and Stuttgart. The northern part is the Schwäbischer Wald (Swabian Forest); the southern part, the Fränkischer Wald (Franconian Forest). The forest's deciduous fir and pine trees, rolling hills, valleys, and green meadows are crisscrossed by marked trails and intermittently dotted with campgrounds. This territory provides welcome relief for the traveler tired of frenzied sightseeing in the surrounding cities.

The town of **Murrhardt,** in the middle of the two forests, makes a convenient base for exploring the park; it's also the park's only town with a youth hostel. Murrhardt has rail and bus connections to Stuttgart and Schwäbisch Hall–Hessental (one stop east of Schwäbisch Hall proper). The **Jugendherberge** (Karnsberger Str. 1, tel. 07192/7501) sits in the hills on the north side of town. You'll find the **Waldsee campground** (tel. 07192/6436) on a lake in the village of **Fornsbach,** about 3 kilometers (2 miles) east of Murrhardt. To get there take a bus from Murrhardt's Hauptbahnhof. You can get a complete list of reasonably priced hotels and rooms in private homes from the **tourist-information office** (Marktpl. 10, tel. 07192/213124) in the center of town. The staff can also sell you a map of the forest (DM 12) that indicates all trails and campgrounds.

If you need more information on the park, go to the nearby **Naturpark information office** (Marktpl. 5, tel. 07192/213128). If you'd like to go biking or skiing through the area try Murrhardt's **Bike and Snow** (Hauptstr. 2–4, tel. 07192/20547). Technically they only sell equipment, but you may be able to convince them to rent you a bike or cross-country skis if you're nice. Ask for Martin.

HAIGERLOCH

Amid a sea of green hills in southwest Germany, the tranquil town of Haigerloch sits on and around a gently rising ridge beside the Eyach River, 15 kilometers (9 miles) west of Hechingen. The topography of the region gives the town a unique layout: The valley is known as the Unterstadt (lower city), and the Oberstadt (upper city) lies on the sloping ridge.

Take the staircase leading up from the Marktplatz to the **Schloß,** which stands on a massive rock in the Unterstadt. The Schloß now houses a hotel, a restaurant, and several art galleries. On the way up you'll pass the **Schloßkirche,** whose typically gaudy Rococo interior is drowned in brightly colored murals and lime-green plasterwork. The courtyard of the Schloß gives a view of Haigerloch and its sparsely populated surroundings. (For an even better perspective of the town, follow signs to the **Kapf,** a jagged rock adorned with a large wood cross overlooking the center of town.) The **Atom-Keller Museum** (tel. 07474/1800), in a small, cavelike room hewn out of the Schloß's bedrock, depicts the history of a group of German scientists who studied the possibilities of generating atomic energy during World War II, until a special force of American soldiers stopped their activities in 1945.

Spanning the Oberstadt is Oberstadtstraße, whose most eye-catching monument is the redbrick Romanesque **Römerturm,** which accepts visitors only April–October, weekends and holidays 10–6. **Café Charlott** (Oberstadtstr. 44, tel. 07474/2568), across the street from the Römerturm, has a deck where you can sip a drink or have a light snack while enjoying a view of the Schloß and the rest of the Unterstadt. The **Evangelische Kirche,** within spitting distance of the Römerturm, contains a convincing reproduction of Leonardo da Vinci's *Last Supper.* Signs from the courtyard in front of the church point the way through the old Jewish ghetto to the **Jüdischer Friedhof** (Jewish Cemetery). The 18th-century pilgrimage **church of St. Anna,** near the top of Oberstadtstraße, has an interior that rivals the Schloßkirche in terms of Rococo audacity.

COMING AND GOING Although there is no rail service to Hagerloch, regular but infrequent buses run to and from Horb (with connections to the Black Forest), Balingen (with connections to most other towns in the Schwäbische Alb, including Hechingen and Rottweil), and Rottenburg (with connections to Tübingen). Buses leave from the Marktplatz, Schulzentrum Unterstadt, and several stops on the Oberstadtstraße.

WHERE TO SLEEP Tastefully decorated, immaculate rooms make **Gasthof Krone** (Oberstadtstr. 47, tel. 07474/411) the kind of place you could confidently send your parents; you'll pay DM 68 for a double with a private shower and an excellent breakfast.

ROTTWEIL

One of the Schwäbische Alb's most important towns since Roman times, Rottweil has a distinguished history that is reflected in its impressive buildings and monuments designed in a variety of styles. As a gesture toward modernization, Rottweil has paved its cobblestone streets. Still, it is this very modernity that makes Rottweil the most accessible town in the Schwäbische Alb.

To reach town from the **Hauptbahnhof** (tel. 0741/12838), gather your strength, trudge up the long, steep Eisenbahnstraße, turn right, and cross the 12th-century **Hochbrücke** (High Bridge). You'll find yourself on Rottweil's main east-west thoroughfare, Hochbrücktorstraße, which forms a "T" with Hauptstraße, the major north-south road. Late Renaissance and Baroque houses, marked by their oriels, colorful carvings, and occasional murals, cram both streets. The carvings are mostly of familial coats of arms and guild insignia, and the murals depict symbols of importance to former Rottweilers. On the corner of Hochbrücktorstraße and Hauptstraße is the red sandstone **Marktbrunnen,** a Renaissance-style fountain with five tiers and crowned by a figure also displayed on the Swiss *Vennerbrunnen,* symbolizing the links between Rottweil and the confederation of Switzerland. The Gothic **Kapellenkirche,** behind the Marktbrunnen, was meant to provide the Altstadt with a central monument, but the results were less than impressive, largely because plans to heighten the tower were never realized.

As you might suspect, the infamous canines known as Rottweilers have their origins in Rottweil. When the Romans came to the area in the 1st century, they brought dogs and bred them with the local hounds. The ferocious, love-'em-or-hate-'em crossbreed was subsequently named after its city of origin. The hometown of the Rottweiler, however, no longer contains an abnormally large population of the short, stocky dogs.

For a look at the carvings that once adorned the Kapellenkirche's tower, as well as other stone statues and Renaissance fountains, head down Hauptstraße and turn left on Lorenzgasse to the **Lorenzkapelle** (Lorenzgasse 17, tel. 0741/494298; admission: DM 2, DM 1 students). The **Dominikaner Museum** (Am Kriegsdamm, tel. 0741/494330), directly up the hill from the **Pulverturm,** beside the Lorenzkapelle, holds the rest of the town's ancient treasures. The highlight of the latter is a colorful mosaic consisting of 570,000 stone fragments. Rottweil's **Stadtmuseum** (Hauptstr. 20, tel. 0741/94256), housed in the Baroque **Herder'sches Haus** on the upper half of Hauptstraße, is worth a look for a model of the city in all its glory in 1560 and a room containing samples of the outlandish masks that locals wear every year during the carnival season known as **Fastnet** (usually late February or early March). In a 600-year-old tradition meant to scare away the winter snows and bring on spring showers, more than 2,000 participants each year don these wild wood masks and parade through town.

The 16th-century **Altes Rathaus** houses your friendly neighborhood **tourist-information office** (tel. 0741/494280). Behind the Altes Rathaus is the **Heilig-Kreuz-Münster** (Cathedral of the Holy Cross), a patchwork quilt of a basilica. Constructed in Romanesque style, it received Gothic additions in the 15th century, a Baroque rebuilding after the Thirty Years War, and a neo-Gothic face-lift between 1840 and 1843. Standing guard over Rottweil is the bulky **Schwarzes Tor** (Black Tower) at the top of Hauptstraße, from whose base you can get a good view of town. For an even better view, ascend the 177-foot **Hochturm** (High Tower), built in the 13th century as a watchtower and dungeon. Get a tower key from the tourist office.

COMING AND GOING As a stop on the rail line between Stuttgart (1½ hours) and Konstanz (1¼ hours), Rottweil has frequent service to both towns; regular trains to Horb (30 minutes), Neustadt (1¼ hours), and Villingen (25 minutes), allow easy access to the Black Forest. Bus 7440 (45 minutes) travels from the train station to Balingen for connections to Schwäbische Alb towns like Hechingen and Haigerloch.

WHERE TO SLEEP The cheapest hotels in town are **Gasthof Goldenes Rad** (Hauptstr. 38, tel. 0741/7412), with singles for DM 35 and doubles for DM 65, and **Gasthof Löwen** (Hauptstr. 66, tel. 0741/7640), with comfortable, spacious singles for DM 35 and similar doubles for DM 70. Rottweil's **Jugendherberge** (Lorenzgasse 8, tel. 0741/7664) has DM 12 beds for IYHF members only. Optional breakfasts run another DM 5. It's stone's throw from the Lorenzkapelle, and, despite its address, it's entered from an unnamed alley off Lorenzgasse two blocks from Hauptstraße.

FOOD For the usual variety of low-cost schnitzels and wursts, head to **Quisiana-Imbiß** (Friedrichspl. 14, tel. 0741/6704), one block east of the Marktbrunnen. **Mandarin Garden** (Hauptstr. 18, tel. 0741/8809) serves tasty Chinese dishes, most for less than DM 15.

DONAUESCHINGEN

Sitting on a sparsely vegetated plateau between the Black Forest and the Schwäbische Alb, Donaueschingen may just send you into paroxysms of sleepiness. Many hikers and bikers stop here, however, on their way to the Black Forest, Schwäbische Alb, or along the Danube. It's known mainly for the spring that is officially recognized as the source of the 3,840-kilometer-long (2,380-mile-long) Danube River. Although the river it feeds is the second-longest in Europe, running through seven countries before spilling into the Black Sea, the spring itself is less than awe-inspiring, and the 19th-century stone monument built around it, the **Donaquelle,** adds little zest. The Baroque **Schloß** beside the Donaquelle rivals the spring in provoking that feeling of "okay, what next?" The castle, which has been transformed into a museum and can be seen only by guided tour (Mon., Wed.–Fri. 9–noon, 2–5), holds the furniture, paintings, jewelry, weapons, and other relics of the Fürstenberg family, members of the German nobility who built the castle in the early 18th century and inhabited it until World War II. You can get a tour in English if you show up early and no German-speaking tourists are in line. Many book stores in town, including **Mary's Holfbuchhandlung** (Karlstr. 25, tel. 0771/2530 or 0771/2545) carry trail maps of the region.

Donaueschingen is home to the Fürstenberg brewery, producer of one of Germany's most beloved pilseners for more than 700 years. Nearly every bar and restaurant in town serves the locally produced beer, so don't miss your chance to have a fresh stein—or two, or three.

COMING AND GOING Donaueschingen lies on the rail line between Karlsruhe (1½ hours) and Konstanz (one hour) and is connected by regular trains to the Black Forest towns of Neustadt (45 minutes) and Villingen (10 minutes), as well as Rottweil (45 minutes) in the Schwäbische Alb. Josefstraße runs from the train station to Karlstraße, Donaueschingen's main drag.

WHERE TO SLEEP Not far from the train station is the **Southern Cross Independent Hostel** (Josefstr. 8–13, tel. 0771/3327 or 0771/12911), purportedly the first and thus far only independent hostel in Germany. Southern Cross, with beds for DM 15, comes complete with kitchen and laundry facilities, a bar serving beer and snacks from around the world, an adjoining travel agency specializing in discount flights and rail tickets, and a stress-free environment. The **Hotel Bären** (Josefstr. 7–9, tel. 0771/2518) next door has comfortable doubles for DM 80, including breakfast. A list of rooms in private homes (DM 18–DM 35) is available at the **tourist-information office** (Kurlstr. 58, tel. 0771/857221).

Lakeside camping is available 8 kilometers (5 miles) east of town at **Riedsee-Camping** (tel. 0771/5511) for DM 8 per tent and DM 5 per person. For the low price, the campground provides a tennis court, a sauna, and a restaurant. Take Bus 7282 (DM 3) toward Immendingen from the train station, and get off at Pfohren Riedsee.

FOOD **Ristorante Gran Sasso** (Karlstr. 63, opposite Johanneskirche, tel. 0771/7421) serves tasty Italian food, including pizza (DM 7.50–DM 12) and 27 pasta dishes (DM 8–DM 15).

Karlsruhe

When margrave of Baden-Durlach Karl Wilhelm decided that his wife's repeated complaints concerning his mistresses were unbearable, he did what any self-respecting aristocratic playboy would do—he built a castle away from home where he could conduct his affairs with a little privacy. Around the castle retreat, begun in 1715, Wilhelm designed a fan-shape city that became known as Karlsruhe, or "Karl's rest." After becoming capital of the state of Baden in 1771, Karlsruhe prospered and grew into one of the largest cities in southwest Germany. With the formation of the Land of Baden-Württemberg after World War II, Karlsruhe lost its designation as a capital city but received the consolation prize of Germany's two most important courts: the federal supreme court and the federal constitutional court. Today travelers visiting this modern, upper-class city can choose from a wide selection of excellent museums, all of which are free.

BASICS

BUREAUX DE CHANGE Change cash and traveler's checks at the post office next to the train station or at the main branch on Europaplatz in the town center (*see* Mail and Phones, *below*). You can also change money at the **Deutsche Verkehrsbank** in the train station. *Tel. 0721/32651. Open weekdays 8–7, Sat. 8–5, Sun. 9–1.*

MAIL AND PHONES Take care of all your postal errands, place international phone calls, pick up *poste restante* mail, and change money at the **main post office** (Kaiserstr. 217, tel. 0721/350–1464; open weekdays 8:30–6, Sat. 8:30–noon), on Europaplatz. There is another post office next to the Hauptbahnhof (Poststr. 1, tel. 0721/350333; open weekdays 7:30 AM–10 PM, Sat. 7:30–6, Sun. 10–6). The postal code is W–7500. The telephone code is 0721.

MEDICAL AID Check at **Stadt-Apotheke** (Karlstr. 19, tel. 0721/23577) off Europaplatz or any other Apotheke for a schedule of late-night pharmacies in town. Dial 110 for the **police** and 112 in **fire** emergencies.

VISITOR INFORMATION Across the street from the Hauptbahnhof, the **tourist-information office** (Bahnhofpl. 6, tel. 0721/35530; open weekdays 8–7, Sat. 8–1) will book a room for you free of charge. In the center of town, **Stadtinformation** also provides tourist advice and sells tickets for local events. *Karl-Friedrich-Str. 22, 1 block s. of Marktpl., tel. 0721/355320. Open weekdays 8:30–6:30, Sat. 8:30–12:30.*

COMING AND GOING

As one of southwestern Germany's transportation hubs, Karlsruhe is readily accessible by rail. Regular trains run to all major German cities and many destinations around Europe. The most frequent service runs to Baden-Baden (30 minutes), Frankfurt (3½ hours), Heidelberg (50 minutes), Konstanz (four hours), and Stuttgart (1½ hours). The **Busbahnhof** (tel. 0721/30905) is adjacent to the **Hauptbahnhof** (tel. 0721/19419) and has service to nearby towns, including Rastatt, Ettlingen, and Weingarten. Arrange cheap rides through the **Mitfahrzentrale** (Rankestr. 14, tel. 0721/33666).

To reach the city center from the train station, which lies about 2 kilometers (1 mile) to the south, catch the S4 west to Europaplatz or S3 or S6 east to Marktplatz. Once in the center, bipedal transportation is all you need, but buses are also available. Single rides on local buses or the S-Bahn cost DM 2.50. The 24-hour ticket is a steal at DM 5.

WHERE TO SLEEP AND EAT

Pension am Zoo (Ettlinger Str. 33, tel. 0721/33678) charges DM 90 for spacious doubles, complete with your very own television and breakfast. Less attractive but almost a sure bet is **Kolpinghaus** (Karlstr. 115, on Kolpingpl., tel. 0721/31434), which has 142 beds for DM 40 per person. Conveniently located north of Europaplatz, the **Jugendherberge** (Moltkestr. 26, tel. 0721/28248) is easily the best deal in town, with its clean rooms, buffet breakfast, liberal 11:30 PM curfew, and beds for DM 16 (DM 21 over age 26). To get there from Europaplatz, walk up Karlstraße, turn left on Stephanienstraße, right on Seminarstraße, and left on Moltkestraße.

The nearest campground is **Campingplatz Turmbergblick** (Tiengerer Str. 40, tel. 0721/44060), in the neighboring village of Durlach. The cost is DM 6.50 per person and DM 8 per campsite. From the station take the S3 to Durlacher Tor and transfer to the S1 or S2 to Durlach. If times are tough, a worn-out traveler can curl up and catch some shut-eye undetected in one of the nooks in the Schloßgarten.

Karlsruhe abounds with cheap restaurants. For traditional German fare, choose from the multitude of eateries on Ludwigplatz, southeast of Europaplatz, including the buffet-style **Marché** (Waldstr. 57, tel. 0721/25187). For Middle Eastern food with a twist, try **Ararat Imbiß** (Akademiestr. 43, tel. 0721/24801), north of Europaplatz, which offers excellent Kurdish specialties. East of Europlatz is **Afrika** (Kaiserpassage 16, tel. 0721/21632), with an array of African cuisine. West of Europaplatz, **Alta Natura** (Kaiserstr. 229, tel. 0721/25571) is a natural-foods store that doubles as a vegetarian café at lunchtime.

WORTH SEEING

At the axis of the fan-shape plan sits the yellow **Schloß,** an uninspired piece of Baroque architecture. The interior underwent renovation after a serious pummeling in World War II and today houses the **Badisches Landesmuseum** (Im Schloß, tel. 0721/135–6542). The prized display of an otherwise mediocre collection of ancient objets d'art and Baroque decorative arts is the *Türkenbeute* (Turkish booty), an array of 17th-century Turkish goodies, including military equipment and rugs, brought to Germany by a victorious local margrave who battled the Turks between 1683 and 1692. Around the perimeter of the Schloß is the impressive **Kunsthalle** (Hans-Thoma-Str. 2, tel. 0721/135– 3355), with a collection of paintings by European artists from the 15th to 19th centuries. Its adjunct, the **Kunsthalle Orangerie** (Hans-Thoma-Str. 6, tel. 0721/135–3355) has a smaller but equally impressive collection of 20th-century art by famous names ranging from Braque and Delacroix to Marc, Beckmann, and Miró. The **Prinz Max Palais** (Karlstr. 10, tel. 0721/133–3670) houses the **Städtische Galerie,** with two floors of surprisingly good modern-art exhibits.

The heavily fortified **Bundesverfassungericht** (Federal Constitutional Court), known worldwide for its trials of World War II war criminals, sits next to the Schloßgarten's botanical garden at the intersection of Ritterstraße and Kriegsstraße. Today leaders of German political parties vying for power must come here to pledge allegiance to the democratic process, a safeguard against the rise of another Nazilike totalitarian regime.

Karlsruhe's two most important squares, Marktplatz and Europaplatz, lie along Kaiserstraße, the city's commercial lifeline. The **Marktplatz** is adorned with a series of structures by Friedrich Weinbrenner, frequently praised as the architect who gave Karlsruhe its appearance. On the north side of the square is a red sandstone **pyramid** that commemorates the tomb of city founder Karl Wilhelm. The western side is home to the pink, neoclassical **Rathaus.** The simple but stunning **Church of St. Bernhard** sits at the east end of Kaiserstraße. Four blocks southwest of the Marktplatz is the **Museum am Friedrichsplatz** (Erbprinzenstr. 13, tel. 0721/175111), a decent natural-history museum containing a vivarium, an aquarium, plenty of old rocks, and a herd of stuffed animals.

AFTER DARK

The nightlife in Karlsruhe is slow. Most of the action takes place on the many side streets off Kaiserstraße between Europaplatz and Marktplatz. The most popular spot is Ludwigplatz's **Krokodil** (Wuldstr. 63, tel. 0721/27331), a café-restaurant with a beer garden in back and tables on the square out front, good for people-watching. Down the street in the Kaiserpassage, a rocking bar called **Mad House** (Kaiserpassage, tel. 0721/22462) occasionally features live bands. For more highbrow entertainment—like musicals, operas, and ballets—there's the **Stadtstheater** (Baumeisterstr., tel. 0721/373163), in the southeast corner of town.

Ulm

If you're "Jeopardy!" contestant material, two facts about Ulm should immediately pop into your mind. First, it's the site of the world's tallest church spire (523 feet). Second, it's the birthplace of noted genius, scientist, and Nobel prizewinner Albert Einstein. Less well known but equally important to Ulm's history is Napoléon's declaration that the Danube River would mark the administrative boundary between Bavaria and Württemberg, splitting the city into western and eastern halves. The older and more interesting part of the city, on the Württemberg side of the river, retained the name Ulm. The younger section, officially in the Land of Bavaria, took the name of Neu-Ulm. During World War II Ulm suffered severe damage from a crushing air raid, but enough of the historical structures were spared or rebuilt to enable Ulm to retain the prewar architectural charm that so excited author Hermann Hesse. If you're looking for a happening club scene, go somewhere else. But if you're into churches and historic buildings, the extravagant Münster, the old Fisherman's and Tanner's Quarter, and the many half-timbered houses should keep you satisfied.

BASICS

BUREAUX DE CHANGE For the smallest charges and longest hours, go to the post office adjacent to the Hauptbahnhof (*see* Mail and Phones, *below*). If you're in the center of town you can change money at **Ulmer Volksbank.** *Hirschstr. 2, off Münsterpl., at Pfauengasse, tel. 0731/183259. Open Mon.–Wed., Fri. 8–4; Thurs. 8–5:30.*

MEDICAL AID For information on **medical services** during nonbusiness hours, call 0731/65003 or 0731/65004. To find out the location of the 24-hour **pharmacy** on a particular night, check the listing at any Apotheke.

MAIL AND PHONES The **post office** adjacent to the Hauptbahnhof holds mail, changes money, has international phone booths, and performs all standard postal services. Ulm's postal code is 7900; its phone code is 0731. *Bahnhofpl. 2, tel. 0731/1001. Open weekdays 8–6, Sat. 8–1, Sun. 11–noon.*

VISITOR INFORMATION The tourist-information office will provide travel tips and book a room for you for DM 5. At press time, the office was located on Münsterplatz in a rectangular building marked MUNSTER BASAR, but there are plans to move to the new **Stadtbau,** also on Münsterplatz, by early 1994. *Münsterpl. 5, tel. 0731/64161. Open weekdays 9–6, Sat. 9–12:30.*

COMING AND GOING

One of the transportation hubs of southwest Germany, Ulm lies almost directly between and has frequent train service to Munich (1¼ hours) and Stuttgart (1¼ hours). Regular service also runs to Augsburg (1½ hours), Hamburg (six hours), and

Karlsruhe (two hours). For rail information, call 0731/19419. Buses leaving from the south side of the Hauptbahnhof travel to all sorts of rinky-dink towns around Ulm but to no major cities. The **Mitfahrzentrale** (König-Wilhelm-Str. 28, tel. 0731/28024) is open weekdays 10–1 and 3–7 and Saturday 10–1.

All of Ulm's sights, as well as most of the hotels, restaurants, and measly nightlife, are near the city center. From the Hauptbahnhof, cross under Friedrich-Ebert-Straße to the main drag, first called Bahnhofstraße and then Hirschstraße, which leads to the Münsterplatz, the heart of Ulm. City buses and S-Bahn trains, both costing DM 2, crisscross the city, but you can get around easily on foot.

WHERE TO SLEEP

The **Ulmer Stuben** (Zinglerstr. 11, tel. 0731/67041) is decorated in about 18 shades of brown, but the rooms, which go for DM 72 per double, are clean and spacious. Follow Friedrich-Ebert-Straße south from the station for about five minutes, and you'll run into Zinglerstraße. **Gasthaus Rose** (Kasernstr. 42A, tel. 0731/77803), on the other side of the Danube in Neu Ulm, has doubles for DM 65, including breakfast. Take Bus 7 to Maximilianstraße. The characterless but clean **Geschwister-Scholl-Jugendherberge** (Grimmelfinger Weg 45, tel. 0731/384455) has the cheapest beds in town (DM 16.50, DM 21 for those over 26), but it's up on a hill and not easy to reach. Take the S1 from the Hauptbahnhof to Ehinger Tor, transfer to Bus 4 or 9, and get off at Königstraße. From here, cross the street, head back down Königstraße, turn right on the footpath through the gardens, right at the end of the path, and left on Grimmelfinger Weg.

FOOD

Dozens of places in the city center serve local and international food. For the quick, cheap, greasy stuff, head to Hirschstraße, the main drag, which is lined with fast-food places serving Spätzle, wurst, döner Kebabs, and burgers. For outstanding local cuisine at affordable prices, hit **Eulenspiegel** (Kornhaus Pl. 2, tel. 0731/66708). Three blocks northeast of the Münster (*see* Worth Seeing, *below*), this cozy restaurant affords vegetarians a rare chance to try Maultaschen (DM 12). For tasty Italian grub, try **Ristorante La Riviera** (Marktpl. 5, tel. 0731/619470), where you can choose from the regular array of personal-size pizzas (DM 8–DM 12) and pasta dishes (DM 8–DM 16). If you crave Chinese food, head to **Panda** (Bahnhofpl. 6, tel. 0731/65669), across from the Hauptbahnhof. Open-air markets are held on Wednesday and Saturday mornings on the Münsterplatz.

WORTH SEEING

Undoubtedly the most gripping sight in Ulm is the mighty **Münster,** whose construction began in 1377 but wasn't finished until 1890. The spire is not only the tallest in the world but also one of the most intricately carved and beautifully adorned. If you're into churches, definitely go into this one—it contains meticulously carved choir stalls, a colorful fresco above the pulpit, and hundreds of panels of 15th-century stained glass. You can climb the 768 steps of the steeple to get a view of the town, and on a clear day you can see all the way to the Alps. South of the Münster, the **Rathaus** (1420) features dull orange walls decorated with brightly colored frescoes depicting scenes from the Bible, medieval battles, and allegorical tales. The eastern facade has a 16th-century astronomical clock. The **Ulmer Museum** (Marktpl. 9, tel. 0731/161–4300) exhibits art ranging from prehistoric to modern times, but concentrates on Gothic and Baroque art from Ulm and Upper Swabia.

The **Metzgerturm,** a brick tower with a multicolor tile roof, lies south of the Marktplatz. Although it has been dubbed the "Leaning Tower of Ulm," the tilt is hardly discernible unless you've had a few drinks. Beyond the tower, a stretch of grass along the Danube allows a good view of some of the remnants of the **old city wall.** A couple of windy streets west of the Rathaus, you'll find the dainty pink-and-yellow facade of the **Schwörhaus,** where part of the Schwörmontag festivities take place (*see* Festivals, *below*). On the other side of the Blau River, a small tributary of the Danube, is the **Fisherman's and Tanner's Quarter,** whose crooked half-timbered houses, miniature stone-and-wood bridges, and cobblestone squares are a perfect place to stroll. A few blocks northwest of the Münster you'll find the **Deutsches Brotmuseum,** detailing the history of bread. It's an interesting museum—honest!—and displays are labeled in English. *Salzstadelgasse 10, tel. 0731/69955. Admission: DM 4, DM 3 students.*

The Bodensee

Spanning some 80 kilometers (50 miles) in length and 13 kilometers (8 miles) in width, the Bodensee (Lake Konstanz) is the largest lake in the German-speaking world; it was formed thousands of years ago by a glacier that rolled through the area and left a gaping hole. The hole soon filled with water from the Rhine, creating the lake you see today. Forming a natural border between Germany, Austria, and Switzerland, the lake offers warm weather, cool waters, busy resorts, and ancient cities encircled by gentle hills. On the rare occasion when every last bit of haze burns off, you can see as far south as the Alps. Even when this spectacular backdrop teasingly stays behind the clouds, the Bodensee beckons you to spend much of your time in the great outdoors. You can swim, boat, windsurf, water-ski, or scuba dive in the lake or hike and bike around it. For weary travelers looking for a break, there's plenty of grass on which to lie back, relax, and bask in the sun. But don't get the impression that all of this comes without a price tag. A fair number of youth hostels and loads of campgrounds provide the cheapest places to crash, but during the high season, from about mid-June until August, these fill up quickly, so do yourself a favor and call ahead. Otherwise, be prepared to spend a lot of cash at expensive hotels.

Ships are the most pleasant way to travel around the lake. The **Weiß Flotte** (White Fleet, tel. 07531/281389) has regular service between all of the worthwhile towns on the lake; if you flash a Eurail- or InterRail pass, you get 50% off the regular ticket price. Otherwise, you can pick up a rail line from the island of Lindau on the eastern end of the Bodensee to Rodolfzell, where a second line completes the route around the German section of the lake. Regular buses fill the gaps between trains.

Lindau

The cobblestone streets of Lindau's Altstadt are packed with centuries-old gabled and half-timbered houses. Dreamy promenades encircle the 2½-kilometer-long, 1-kilometer-wide (1½-mile-long, ½-mile-wide) island in the eastern end of the Bodensee. On clear days, you can see past the green hills along its shore to the Austrian and Swiss Alps. The town's harbor is marked by three monuments. Standing guard over the island is a massive marble **statue of a seated lion,** the symbol of Bavaria. Opposite the statue is the **Neuer Leuchtturm** (New Lighthouse), which you can ascend for DM 1 (DM .50 students). The **Alter Leuchtturm** (Old Lighthouse), standing on the ruins of Lindau's 13th-century city walls in the inner harbor, has a colorfully tiled roof that looks woven.

From the harbor, plunge into the Altstadt, whose maze of streets seems to lead to the 15th-century **Altes Rathaus,** behind the harbor on Maximillianstraße. This fine building, with its vibrant murals, covered stairwell, and gaily adorned, steeped gables, was constructed between 1422 and 1436 and received a Renaissance overhaul 150 years

Bodensee

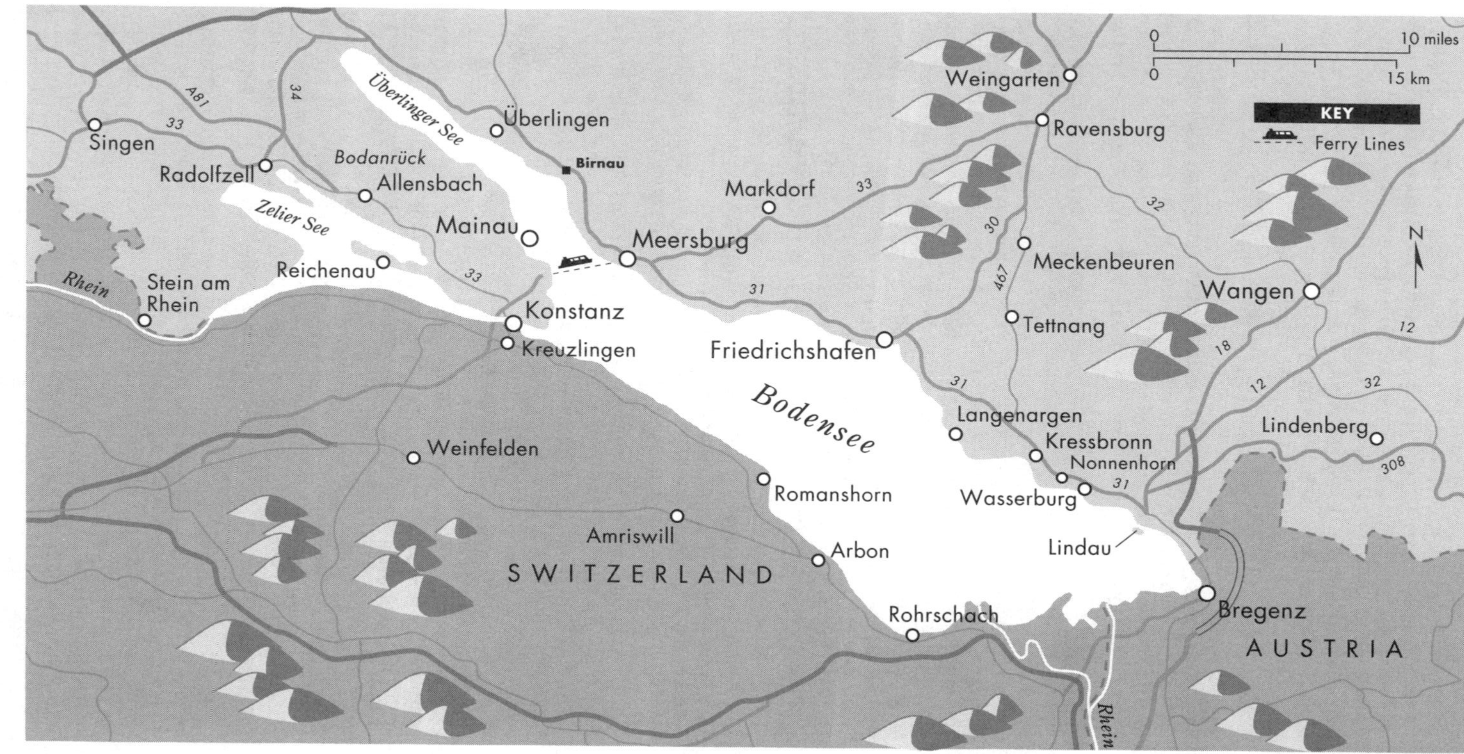
Singen
Radolfzell
Stein am Rhein
Rhein
Zelier See
Reichenau
Bodanrück
Allensbach
Überlinger See
Überlingen
Birnau
Mainau
Konstanz
Kreuzlingen
Meersburg
Markdorf
Friedrichshafen
Bodensee
Weinfelden
Amriswill
SWITZERLAND
Romanshorn
Arbon
Rohrschach
Langenargen
Kressbronn
Nonnenhorn
Wasserburg
Lindau
Bregenz
AUSTRIA
Weingarten
Ravensburg
Meckenbeuren
Tettnang
Wangen
Lindenberg
A81
33
34
31
30
467
32
18
12
308
0
10 miles
0
15 km
KEY
Ferry Lines
N

later. The bulky Romanesque **St. Peters Kirche,** two blocks northwest of the Altes Rathaus, dates to the 10th century, making it one of the Bodensee's oldest buildings. Used today as a war-memorial chapel, it contains murals by Hans Holbein the Elder. Some depict scenes from the life of St. Peter, patron saint of fishermen; fishing was crucial to Lindau's economy before the advent of commercial tourism. A number of old buildings enclose the **Marktplatz,** which lies between the Altes Rathaus and the bridge connecting Lindau to the mainland.

BASICS You can pick up *poste restante* mail, make international phone calls, and change money at the **post office** (Maximilianstr. 52, tel. 08382/27770). The postal code is 8990. Across the street from the train station, the **tourist-information office** (Am Bahnhofpl., tel. 08382/26000) provides a map and brochures. They also book rooms for a DM 3 service charge.

COMING AND GOING Lindau is a transfer point for international trains running to Austria through the border town of Breganz (10 minutes) and Swiss cities such as Bern (3¼ hours) and Zürich (two hours). Rail lines link Lindau to nearly every major German city, with the most frequent trains running to Munich (2¾ hours) and Ulm (1¾ hours). You can get connections to the rest of the lake towns through the rail line that circles the Bodensee, with trains running through Wasserburg to Friedrichshafen. The **Busbahnhof** (tel. 08382/22077), up the road from the train station, has service to neighboring towns, including Friedrichshafen (Bus 7587), Wasserburg (Bus 7587), and Wangen (Bus 9723). Ships travel between Lindau and Bregenz, Wasserburg, Friedrichshafen, and Meersburg and less frequently to Mainau and Konstanz.

The train station and dock are within walking distance of each other, so whether you travel by train, bus, or ship you'll end up in the southwest corner of Lindau's Altstadt. The post office marks one end of Lindau's pedestrian street, Maximilianstraße, which snakes to the left, changes its name to Cramergasse, and spills into the Marktplatz. A 200-yard causeway attaches Lindau to the mainland.

WHERE TO SLEEP Catering to German, Swiss, and Austrian families who flock to Lindau in the summer, Lindau's hotels, pensions, and *Gasthofen* (guest houses) are clean and comfortable but rarely cheap or easy to find space in. Reservations during the high season from mid-June to August are strongly recommended. With singles from DM 32 and doubles from DM 64, including breakfast, **Gästehaus Limmer** (In der Grub 16, tel. 08382/5877) is the cheapest place to stay on the island. From the station, walk down Bahnhofstraße, right on Maximilianstraße, left on Schafgasse, and right to In der Grub. You can do much better by walking off the island to **Pension Haus Inselblick** (Hasenweidweg 31, tel. 08382/5779), where doubles cost only DM 46. Walk along the railroad tracks across the mainland, continue for several minutes, and look to your right. A list of Lindau's accommodations is available from the tourist-information office (*see* Basics, *above*).

Bus 6 from Lindau's train station takes you to **Campingplatz Lindau-Zech** (Fraunhoferstr. 20, tel. 08382/72236), along the lake, 4 kilometers (2½ miles) east of town, which has kitchen facilities, showers, a general store, and a cafeteria. The campground operates April–October; spots cost DM 9.70 per person, DM 3.50 per tent, and DM 11 per car.

FOOD Sample an unusually wide range of Schwäbisch specialties like strudel (DM 13.50–DM 15.50) and several Maultaschen (DM 13.50–DM 14.50) and Spätzle (DM 9.50–DM 12.50) in the quiet, cozy **Gastätte am Raichlebeck** (Linggstr. 14, tel. 08382/28759). Eat good Italian at **Il Mulino** (In der Grub 30, tel. 08382/6704), where you can choose from pizzas, pasta, fish and meat dishes. From the Rathaus, walk up Schneeberggasse and turn right on In der Grub. If you turn left on In der Grub you'll come to **Taverna** (Paradiespl. 14–16, tel. 08382/23702), where you can get scrumptious gyros and other Greek treats at reasonable prices. Lindau's many grassy areas beg for picnickers. Stock up on groceries at **Plus** (Marktpl. 5, tel. 08382/5288) on the bottom floor of the Heka department store. On Tuesday and Saturday mornings, the Marktplatz hosts small produce markets.

OUTDOOR ACTIVITIES Rent **bikes** at the train station for DM 12 (DM 8 with rail pass). You can get maps of bike trails from the tourist-information office (*see* Basics, *above*). **Bootsvermietung** (tel. 08382/5514), on the small dock beside the bridge, can handle your waterskiing needs and rent you a boat. Hour-long **cruises** (DM 9) that sail around the eastern side of the Bodensee leave from the harbor regularly during the summer. You can either dive into the lake from the seawall along the eastern end of the island or pay DM 4 (DM 2.80 students) for the privilege of swimming at **Strandbad Eichwald** (Eichwaldstr. 16, tel. 08382/5539), about 2 kilometers (1 mile) east of town; rent windsurfers here for DM 10–DM 20.

NEAR LINDAU

WASSERBURG Occupying a short, stumpy peninsula 4 kilometers (2½ miles) west of Lindau, tiny Wasserburg is a 1,200-year-old medieval port town with the atmosphere of an island resort. This unusual combination lures tourists seeking relaxation and a chance to go swimming, boating, windsurfing, hiking, or biking in the blue waters and green hills surrounding the ancient town. Encircled by a small cemetery, the **Pfarrkirche St. Georg** is marked by its onion-shape tower, and the bright interior contains ceiling murals, stucco work, and an elaborate altar, all typical of the Baroque period. The stone plaques on the columns indicate the years of the *Seegfrörnen,* when the Bodensee was completely frozen. The peninsula's other dominating structure, the **Schloß,** houses an upscale hotel and restaurant (Hauptstr., tel. 08382/5692).

From the **Bootsverleih** office (tel. 08382/3799 or 08382/8583) in the pint-size harbor you can rent sailboats, paddleboats, rowboats, electric boats, and motorboats. At the **Freizeitzentrum** (tel. 08382/25187), reached by following Unterstraße east along the shoreline, you can catch some rays and go swimming in the lake or pool for DM 3.50 (DM 2.50 for students). Windsurfers are available for DM 15 an hour. Hiking and biking trails radiate from Wasserburg in every direction. You can pick up trail maps at the **tourist-information office** (Im Rathaus, tel. 08382/5582) in the **Rathaus**, a five-minute walk north of the peninsula along Hauptstraße. Renting a bike from the train station, one block north, at the Rathaus, will set you back DM 12 (DM 8 with rail pass).

➢ **COMING AND GOING** • Wasserburg is on the rail line between Lindau and Friedrichshafen. Buses leaving from the train station cover the same route to fill the often long gaps between trains. Wasserburg is also a stop for ships running between Konstanz and Bregenz.

➢ **WHERE TO SLEEP** • Cheap accommodations are scarce during the summer, so make reservations early. **Hotel-Pension Walser** (Nonnenhorner Str. 15, tel. 08382/89085, closed Nov.–Mar.) has clean doubles for DM 72, including breakfast. Stop by the tourist-information office in the Rathaus to obtain a list of accommodations, including rooms in private homes (starting at DM 20 per person). **Campingplatz Boger** (Höhenstr. 1B, tel. 08382/887951) is on a grassy field halfway between the Rathaus and the water. Follow signs from the Rathaus along Höhenstraße.

Meersburg

Built on a steep hillside surrounded by vineyards across the lake from Konstanz, the 1,000-year-old town of Meersburg is packed with half-timbered houses and other medieval buildings decorated with murals, gables, and oriels. Unfortunately, most of these contain cheesy souvenir shops and overpriced restaurants catering to summer tourists. On a bluff overlooking the lake, the 7th-century **Altes Schloß** is the oldest inhabited castle in Germany; its massive central tower has walls 10 feet thick. The maze-like **Burgmuseum** (tel. 07532/6441), inside the Schloß, contains 28 rooms with furnishings, artworks, and weapons. The pink Baroque **Neues Schloß,** built next door in the 18th century, when a prince-bishop decided the old castle just wasn't stylish enough, houses a gallery for contemporary local art, the municipal art collection, and the **Dorniermuseum** (tel. 07532/82385). This small museum features photographs and models of seaplanes designed by local aviator Claude Dornier. To find out about the history of local wine production head to the **Weinbaumuseum** (Vorburggasse 11, tel. 07532/82383), in the square behind the two castles. In the center of the **Oberstadt** (upper city) is the **Marktplatz,** surrounded by vine-clad Renaissance houses. From here, Steigstraße, a steep street lined by half-timbered houses, leads down to the lake and the **Unterstadt** (lower city).

COMING AND GOING A few **ships** run daily from the harbor to Friedrichshafen (one hour), Konstanz (30 minutes), Lindau (2½ hours), Mainau (30 minutes), Uberlingen (one hour), and Wasserburg (1¼ hours). Much more frequent **ferries** (30 minutes) run from a dock on the west side of the Unterstadt to Konstanz. Across the street from the ferry dock you can catch a **bus** to Uberlingen (30 minutes) or Friedrichshafen (35 minutes).

WHERE TO SLEEP The centrally located **Gästehaus am Hafen** (Spitalgasse 3–4, tel. 07532/7069) has tiny, clean doubles starting at DM 60. From the harbor, walk along Unterstadtstraße toward the center of town, and take the first left. For a list of accommodations, go to the **tourist office** (Kirchstr., tel. 07532/82382) west of the Marktplatz.

OUTDOOR ACTIVITIES In the harbor, you can rent rowboats, paddle boats, electric boats, and motorboats from the kiosk marked BOOTSVERLEIH. The **Beheiztes Freibad** (tel. 07532/82387), past the harbor, has lots of grass, a little sand beside the lake, three pools, and a volleyball court. A bit farther east along the promenade, **Kolja's** (Uferpromenade 37, tel. 07532/5330) rents windsurfers and in-line skates. Beginners and certified divers can scuba dive in the lake at **Tauchschule Meersburg** (Von Laßbergerstr. 1, tel. 097532/9277). Biking enthusiasts should head to **s'Sport Lädele** (Am Sentenhart 2, tel. 07532/6786).

NEAR MEERSBURG

UBERLINGEN This medium-size resort town near the western end of the Bodensee draws crowds of tourists, many of them budget travelers, with its range of sporting opportunities and its well-preserved Altstadt. The late-16th-century Gothic **St.-Nikolaus-Münster** in the center of town contains a lofty, stone, vaulted ceiling and a massive Renaissance carved-wood High Altar with 23 life-size figures arranged in four tiers. Beside the Münster is the gabled **Rathaus,** whose otherwise bland exterior is adorned with a 20th-century mosaic showing Emperor Charles V. Inside the Rathaus is the Baroque **Rathaussaal,** an ornate town-meeting hall with a timbered ceiling and a carved frieze whose 41 statuettes represent guild members from the time when the town was part of the Holy Roman Empire.

Uberlingen is a two-station town, but Bahnhof West (tel. 07551/61082) on the west side of the Altstadt is where all trains stop. From here regular trains run to Friedrichshafen (30 minutes), Lindau (one hour) and Rudolfzell (20 minutes), where you can connect to major cities like Karlsruhe, Heidelberg, Frankfurt, and Stuttgart. The bus trip from Bahnhof West to Meersburg takes 30 minutes. Ships sail from the harbor for Konstanz (1¾ hours), Mainau (40 minutes), and Meersburg (one hour). For a good map of the Altstadt and help finding a room head to the **tourist office** (Landungspl. 14, tel. 70551/4041) on the promenade in front of the Rathaus.

With an indoor swimming pool, laundry facilities, and a bathroom for each two dorm rooms, the best place to shack up in Uberlingen is the ultramodern **Jugendherberge Martin Buber** (Alte Nußdorfer Str. 26, tel. 07551/4204), about 2 kilometers (1 mile) from the town center, where a bed and breakfast run DM 16.50 (DM 21 for those over

26). To get there from Bahnhof West, take the bus toward Friedrichshafen to the Jugendherberge/Außchut stop and follow the signs up the hill. Uberlingen has three campgrounds, all of which lie along the lake not far from major roads and teem with RVs. **Camping-Park Uberlingen** (tel. 07551/64583) is five minutes west of Bahnhof West; **Nell** (tel. 07551/4254) and **Denz** (tel. 07551/4379) are side by side, about five minutes east of the youth hostel.

Beach bums can choose between **Strandbad-West** and **Strandbad-Ost** on either end of the lengthy promenade. For windsurfing, head straight for Strandbad-West. Fourteen-foot sailboats can be rented for DM 16 per hour from **Segelschul Uberlingen** (tel. 07551/4718 or 07551/3218) at the dock next door. Landlubbers can rent bicycles for DM 12 per day (DM 8 with a rail pass) from Bahnhof West and can pick up trail maps at the tourist office.

BIRNAU The **Birnau monastery,** in an otherwise deserted stretch of vineyard-clad shoreline between Meersburg and Uberlingen, is widely considered the most fascinating church in the Bodensee area. Built between 1746 and 1750, the Rococo building contains a stunning ceiling covered with murals, a gold-and-white cherub beside the altar dedicated to St. Bernard of Clairvaux, gilt dripping from the walls, and swooning, swaying statues. The tower holds four clocks, as well as a statue of the Madonna holding a lily, symbol of purity. English-language guides provided here explain the abundant symbolism in the basilica's decorations. Buses run regularly to Birnau from Meersburg and Uberlingen.

Friedrichshafen

Friedrichshafen earned a place in history with the first successful flight of a hydrogen-filled zeppelin on July 2, 1900. During World War II, Allied bombers leveled 70% of Friedrichshafen's buildings in hopes of thwarting the city's thriving aviation industry. Today Friedrichshafen is a popular lakeside resort despite the fact that it is more urban than most other Bodensee towns. Housed in the Rathaus on the eastern end of the lakeside promenade is the **Zeppelin-Museum** (Adenauerpl. 1, tel. 07541/203307), which details the history of the overgrown balloons through photographs, design plans, and nine models, including a large, detailed replica of the infamous *Hindenburg* complete with moveable parts. Also in the Rathaus, you'll find an above-average municipal art collection, featuring a room full of characteristically warped paintings by the Bodensee-born and -bred Otto Dix. The **Graf-Zeppelin-Haus** at the western end of the promenade is a hypermodern arts-and-convention center.

COMING AND GOING Regular trains run from the station in the center of town to Lindau (25 minutes), Radolfzell (one hour), Ravensburg (15 minutes), and Ulm (1¼ hours). From Radolfzell, you can take the train into Konstanz (1½ hours), but you'll save time and money by riding the bus (55 minutes) from the train station. You can also hop aboard a ship bound for Konstanz or another Bodensee town.

WHERE TO SLEEP The **Jugendherberge Graf Zeppelin** (Lindauerstr. 3, tel. 07541/72404), about 3 kilometers (2 miles) from town is a typical German youth hostel, except it offers a choice of two breakfasts. Ride the Lindau bus from the train station to the Jugendherberge stop. **Camping Dimmler** (tel. 07541/73421), open from Easter to October 1, stretches along the lake and offers campsites for DM 7 per person, DM 4 per tent, and DM 6 per car. The next best option is to get a list of rooms in private homes from the **tourist office** (Friedrichstr. 18, tel. 07541/21729) in front of the train station. The friendly staff here also books rooms in private homes for a DM 4 fee and rents bikes for DM 10.

Konstanz

Divided by the Rhine as it exits the western end of the Bodensee, the city of Konstanz is divided into two parts: the large medieval Altstadt, on the otherwise Swiss shore of the lake, and a number of scenic grassy beaches on the long, narrow peninsula opposite. Spared during World War II by Allied bombers afraid of accidentally nailing neutral Switzerland, this university city is now the lake's most popular vacation destination. Konstanz's central monument, the **Münster,** is on the north side of the Altstadt and is topped by a spire that affords excellent views of the city and the Bodensee area. The 11th-century cathedral's Romanesque core and airy, elegant Gothic side-chapels contain decorations representing more than 400 years of artistry, including complex Renaissance nave vaulting, 15th-century choir stalls, and a late-17th-century silver High Altar.

The Romanesque **Stephanskirche,** a block south of the Münster, received a late-Gothic face-lift in the 15th century and contains a Rococo choir and a series of early 20th-century paintings depicting the 14 stations of the cross. The colorful 19th-century frescoes adorning the facade at the front of the **Rathaus,** a few doors from the Obermarkt in the center of the Altstadt, depict scenes from the city's history. If you walk through the arched entrance below the murals, you'll find a dainty courtyard. Between the main bridge connecting the two sides of town and the small harbor of the Konstanzer Yacht Club runs **Seestraße,** a romantic promenade lined by Renaissance mansions on one side and clear views down the Bodensee on the other.

BASICS You can change money, place international calls, and pick up *poste restante* mail at the **post office** (Bahnhofpl. 2, tel. 07531/7750) across the street from the tourist-information office (*see below*). The postal code is W–7750, and the telephone code is 07531. For **police** or **ambulance,** dial 110; in case of **fire,** dial 112. The centrally located pharmacy, **Hofapotheke zum Malhaus** (Am Obermarkt, tel. 07531/25289), is a few doors from the Rathaus. If you're in need of a pharmacy after normal business hours, check here or at any other Apotheke for the name, address, and phone number of the rotating late-night pharmacy. The **tourist-information office** (Konzilstr. 5, tel. 07531/284376), beside the Hauptbahnhof, books rooms.

COMING AND GOING Ships from the Weiß Flotte (Hafenstr. 6, tel. 07531/281398) run from the harbor behind the train station to Bregenz, Austria (3½ hours), Friedrichshafen (1½ hours), Lindau (3¼ hours), Mainau (10 minutes), Meersburg (35 minutes), and Uberlingen (1–1½ hours). If you're headed to Meersburg it's usually quicker to take the ferry (30 minutes). Take Bus 1 from the stop in front of the post office to the ferry dock. Considering that Konstanz is a decent-size city on an international border, rail traffic here is rather slow, but a few trains run each day to Frankfurt (four–five hours), Karlsruhe (3¾ hours), Rudolfzell (25 minutes), and Stuttgart (three hours), where you can connect to the other towns on the German side of the lake. In the other direction, fairly regular rail service connects Konstanz to most major cities in Switzerland. To hitch up with a car headed in your direction, contact the **Mitfahrzentrale** (Münzgasse 22, tel. 07531/21444). From the Hauptbahnhof walk up Konzilstraße past the tourist office and take the second left.

Despite the fact that most of Konstanz lies on the peninsula north of the Rhine, the heart of the city is the Altstadt on the south side of the river. To get there from the station, walk past the post office and the tourist office and turn left on Marktstätte. A few blocks farther is Obermarkt, which divides the Altstadt's main drag. To the south it is called Hussenstraße, and to the north, where you'll find the Münster, it's called Wessenberg Straße.

WHERE TO SLEEP You'll find Konstanz's cheapest beds in the **Jugendherberge Otto-Moericke-Turm** (Allmanshohe 18, tel. 07531/32260), housed in a decaying 10-story tower whose top-floor common room has an unbeatable view of the city and Bodensee. To reach the hostel, which charges DM 15.50 including breakfast (DM

20.50 for those over 26), take Bus 4 from Bahnhofstraße, ahead of the train station, to the Jugendherberge stop. By putting down a DM 20 deposit you can get a key to the front door, which allows you to avoid the 10 PM curfew. If you prefer something quieter, a bit cleaner, and closer to the beach and don't mind commuting 20 minutes from the city center, head south to the **Jugendherberge Kreuzlingen** (Promenadestr. 7, tel. 0041/72/752663; in Switzerland, 072/752663) in the Swiss town bordering Konstanz. Take Bus 8 from the stop in front of the post office to the first stop after the border, Helvetiaplatz; continue a half block down Hauptstraße, turn left on Hafenstraße and left again on Promenadestraße after about 10 minutes. A bed and breakfast run DM 18 regardless of your age. **Campingplatz Bruderhofer** (Fohrenbühlweg 50, tel. 07531/31388) has 180 tightly packed sites north of Freibad Horn (*see* Outdoor Activities, *below*) that go for DM 5.50 per person, DM 6 per tent, and DM 4 per car. Take Bus 5 to Falk along the pedestrian path up the shoreline. If you don't call ahead and all of these spots are filled up—not during the summer—head to the tourist-information office to see if rooms (DM 22) are open in private homes.

FOOD If you're longing for down-home cafeteria cuisine, hit the **University Mensa,** where lunch goes for DM 2.50. To get there, take Bus 9 to the university. For tasty pizza slices (DM 3) or döner Kebabs (DM 4.50) head to **Hussen-Stuble** (Hussenstr. 48), a takeout stand 2 blocks south of Obermarkt. Below the Deutscher Haus hotel, between the post office and Obermarkt, is **Casablanca** (Marktstätte 15, tel. 07531/16652), offering pizza (DM 8–DM 12), pasta dishes (DM 8–DM 15), and people-watching from sidewalk tables. Or assemble a picnic at **Hensler** (Wessenbergstr. 2), just off Obermarkt.

OUTDOOR ACTIVITIES The largest and most popular beach in Konstanz, **Freibad Horn,** is at the tip of the peninsula. To reach the beach, which has a section for those who want to tan *all* of their body parts, take Bus 5 from the front of the post office (*see* Basics, *above*) to the last stop. Rent windsurfers for DM 10 per hour or DM 35 per day from a shack north of the beach. A younger crowd of scantily clad sun worshippers perform their pagan rituals at a smaller, quieter beach on the university campus. Take Bus 4 from Bahnhofstraße to Egg, follow the path downhill, and cut between the Limnologisches Institut and the Sportshalle. All kinds of boats can be rented by the hour or half hour in the harbor. Also in the harbor, **Wilfried Giess Personnenschiffahrt** (tel. 07531/2177) runs 45-minute cruises around the lake for DM 6 and hourly boats to Freibad Horn (DM 2). For longer cruises around the entire lake, check out the schedules at the dockside office of the Weiß Flotte (Hafenstr. 6, tel. 07531/281398). If you can afford to fork out DM 29 (DM 23.60 for students) consider the three-hour cruise down the Rhine to Schaffhausen, Switzerland, from which you can walk another 4 kilometers (2½ miles) to the Rheinfall, Europe's tallest waterfall. Or rent a bike from the train station (DM 12, DM 8 with rail pass), and ride along the coast toward the island of Mainau or in the gentle hills around the university.

AFTER DARK Konstanz's nightlife is spread all over the Altstadt. If you head for the jumble of winding alleys between the Münster and the Rhine and stand on the Münsterplatz and face the river, the alley at your far right is Brückengasse; here you'll find **Aladin** (Brückengasse 1, tel. 07531/18215), a popular café where beer (DM 2.20–DM 4), wine (DM 3.50–DM 6), and mixed drinks (DM 5–DM 6) are served on an outdoor terrace. Following the Brückengasse for a few minutes more brings you to **Brauhaus Joh. Albrecht** (Konradigasse 2, tel. 07531/25045), a microbrewery with tasty beer (DM 4.40). There's a bunch of crowded bars and alcohol-serving cafés on Konzilstraße, across the street from the Stadtgarten, beside the harbor.

THE BLACK FOREST 4

By Les Kruger

Looking like something out of J. R. R. Tolkien's *The Lord of the Rings*, the Schwarzwald (Black Forest) is an enchanting region of steep hills and deep valleys blanketed with fir and oak. Tourists and locals flock to the forest for its superlative hiking and skiing opportunities, and the many villages and towns offer the kind of gemütlich Germany that travel agencies like to flog. And why not? The residents of the Black Forest are some of the friendliest and most colorful characters in Germany: They speak a dialect even fellow Germans have difficulty understanding, and many of them still live in the sloping, thatched homes characteristic of the region. These are also the folks who gave the world cuckoo clocks, some of the wackiest traditional clothing on the planet, and many of the fairy tales made famous by the Brothers Grimm. Like Bavaria, though, much of the Black Forest has gone full-tilt oompah, particularly in the central Black Forest, where Teutonic kitsch translates into major tourist dollars.

More than one traveler, driven mad by the din of thousands of cheap cuckoo clocks, has broken down and bought a wood carving of Hansel and Gretel.

The Black Forest stretches some 165 kilometers (102 miles) from Karlsruhe, in the north, to the Swiss border and is flanked by the Rhine to the west. Until the 20th century the Black Forest was largely inaccessible to the outside world. Today getting around is a snap. Trains from all over Germany stop in Karlsruhe; from here another rail line heads to Baden-Baden in the northern Black Forest and to Freiburg in the southern Black Forest (also known as the Hochschwarzwald, or High Black Forest). If you're coming from the east, trains regularly make the trip from Stuttgart to Donaueschingen, one of the area's main transport hubs. Traveling by train through the Black Forest is spectacular, but many towns aren't served by rail. Fortunately, buses pick up the slack, although service to some of the more remote destinations can be slow and infrequent, especially during the winter.

More than 20,000 marked trails make hiking and biking in the warmer months and cross-country skiing in winter the best ways to see the forest. The tourist offices in Pforzheim in the north and Freiburg in the south provide the most comprehensive information about the region, including detailed trail maps. Even the dinkiest towns, though, have tourist offices with local maps and information.

The Black Forest

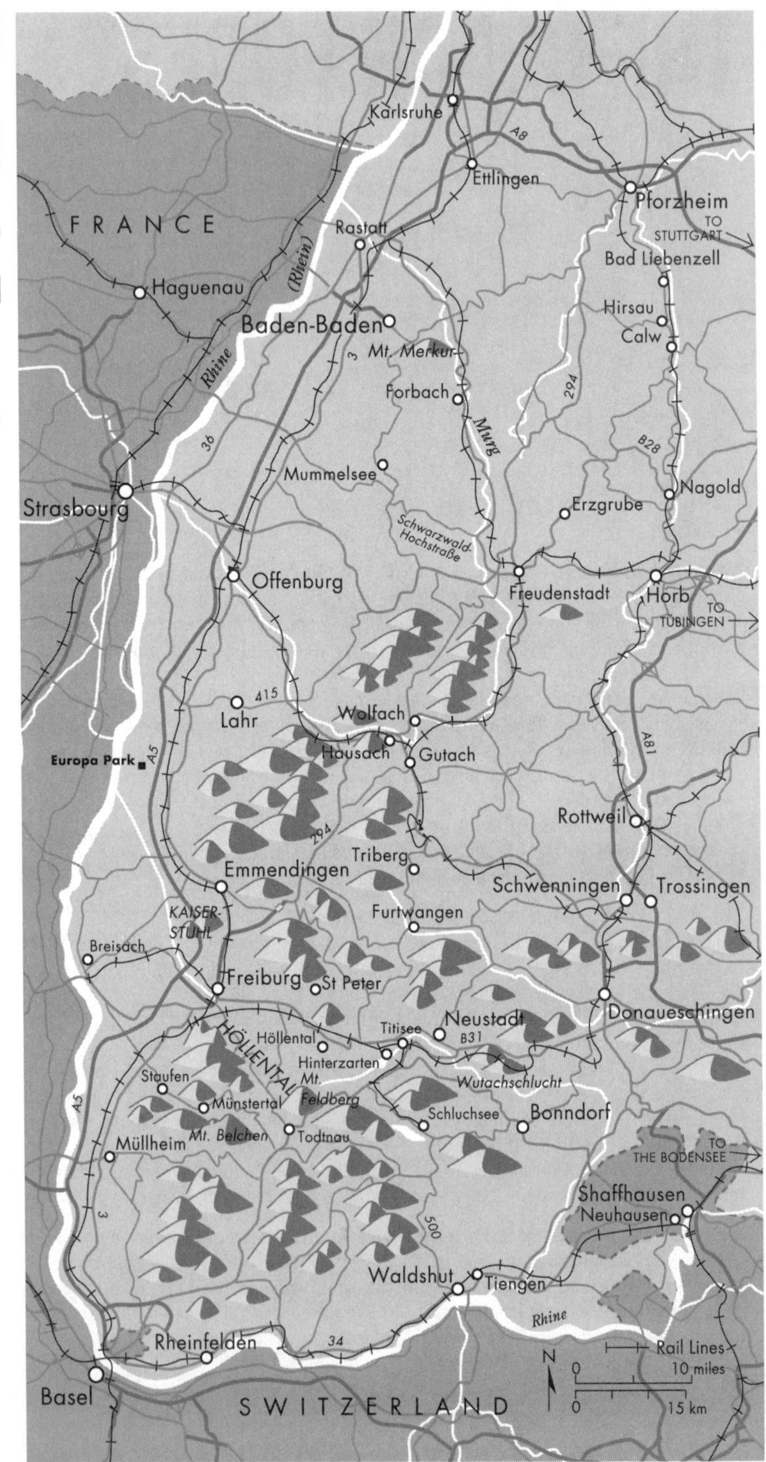

Freiburg im Breisgau

The largest and most accessible city in the southern Black Forest, Freiburg makes a perfect base for exploring the villages and hills of the High Black Forest. The city was blown to bits in a World War II bombing raid but has reconstructed many of its most impressive buildings, preserving the historical atmosphere of the Altstadt (Old City). Freiburg draws much of its identity from the surrounding forest and the centuries-old university in its center. The town teems with young, blond, blue-eyed types who all look as if they run up mountains before breakfast. However, they seem to find plenty of time to sit in the city's many cafés sipping coffee and discussing art, politics, and the meaning of life. By German standards the streets are remarkably lively, packed with extraordinarily talented street musicians, many of whom attend the local music school.

BASICS

BUREAUX DE CHANGE You can grab cash in the train station at **Deutsche Verkehrs Bank,** but you'll get a better rate if you walk two blocks to the post office (*see* Mail and Phones, *below*). *Im Hauptbahnhof, tel. 0761/33891. Open weekdays 7:30–7, Sat. 8–5, Sun. 9–1.*

EMERGENCIES **Police** and **ambulance,** tel. 110; **fire,** tel. 112; **emergency medical service,** tel. 85085.

LAUNDRY To clean your soiled threads head to **Miele,** which has washers for DM 7 and 10-minute dryers for DM 2. *Adelhauser Str. 24 at Marienstr., across from Museum für Neue Kunst, tel. 0761/356560. Open weekdays 7 AM–8 PM, Sat. 7–5.*

MAIL AND PHONES You can make international phone calls, pick up posterestante mail, and change money at the main **post office,** located between the train station and the tourist-information office. The postal code is W–7800. *Eisenbahnstr. 58–62, tel. 0761/27610. Open weekdays 8–6, Sat. 8–noon, Sun. 9–10 AM.*

MEDICAL AID Take care of all your pharmaceutical needs at **Berthold-Apotheke,** just behind the Martinstor. After normal business hours check the list on the door here or at any other pharmacy to find out which pharmacy is slated to stay open late. *Kaiser-Joseph-Str. 258, tel. 0761/36981. Open weekdays 8:30–6, Sat. 8:30–1.*

VISITOR INFORMATION The **tourist office,** two long blocks from the train station, gives out city maps, helps find rooms free of charge, sells tickets for upcoming cultural events, and can provide a wealth of information on Freiburg and the entire region. An adjoining travel agency offers special youth fares on trains and flights. *Rotteckring 14, tel. 0761/368900. Open May–Oct., Mon.–Sat. 9 AM–9:30 PM, Sun. 10–2; Nov.–Apr., weekdays 9–6, Sat. 9–3, Sun. 10–noon.*

COMING AND GOING

Freiburg lies on the major rail line between Basel and Karlsruhe, from which you can connect to most major cities in Germany. Some sample fares: Karlsruhe (DM 37, 1¼ hours), Basel (DM 14.80, 45 minutes), Frankfurt (DM 64, 2¼ hours), and Hamburg (DM 195, 11–12 hours). Buses to most of the little towns in the Black Forest leave from the **Omnibusbahnhof** (tel. 0761/19419), next to the train station. The local **Mitfahrzentrale** (Bertholdstr. 47, tel. 0761/36774), in the center of town, can help find you a ride to most major German cities and occasionally to destinations around Europe.

Freiburg

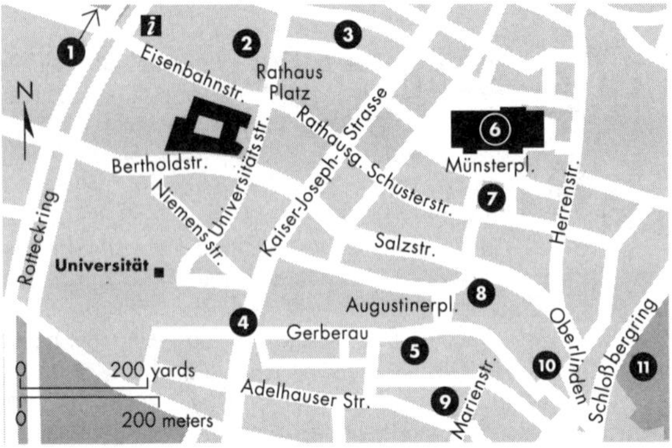

Augustiner Museum, **8**
Colombi Palace, **1**
Haus Zum Walfisch, **3**
Kaufhaus, **7**
Martinstor, **4**
Münster, **6**
Museum für Naturkunde/ Bölderkunde, **5**
Museum für Neue Kunst, **9**
Neues Rathaus, **2**
Schloßberg, **11**
Schwabentor, **10**

To reach the center of town from the train station, walk two blocks up **Eisenbahnstraße,** Freiburg's major east–west boulevard, to its intersection with **Kaiser-Joseph-Straße,** the largest north–south street. Getting your bearings in the small Old City takes no time at all, and you can see almost everything on foot. If you need to take longer journeys, use the extensive **bus** and **S-Bahn** (streetcar) systems. Rides to most parts of the city cost DM 2.50. Public transportation stops running about 1 AM; if you need a **taxi** call 0761/37777.

WHERE TO SLEEP

Aside from the hostel, the cheapest option is to take a room in a private house for DM 20–DM 30 per person. Unfortunately, a lot of places require a three-night minimum stay, but you might be able to find someone who will make an exception. The tourist office (*see* Visitor Information in Basics, *above*) can provide you with a list of private rooms and other lodging options.

Hotel Hirshen-Dionysos. In a beautiful neighborhood south of the city center, this hotel has clean, adequate doubles for DM 70. *Hirschstr. 2, tel. 0761/29353. S-Bahn 4 from overpass beside train station to Klosterpl., then double back 1 block.*

Hotel Löwen. Right in the center of town, this more upscale hotel has spring-fresh, dainty doubles for DM 90, including breakfast. *Herrenstr. 47, tel. 0761/33161. From station, walk up Eisenbahnstr., Rathausgaße, and Schusterstr., then turn right on Herrenstr.*

Hotel Schemmer. This small hotel near the station has simple, clean doubles (DM 66), some with decks perfect for catching early morning rays. The price includes breakfast. *Eschholzstr. 63, tel. 0761/272424. From station take overpass across tracks, walk straight ahead past big church, then take first left.*

HOSTEL With 400 beds in a characterless modern building on the outskirts of town, Freiburg's **Jugendherberge** (IYHF youth hostel) epitomizes institutional hostel living. For DM 17 (DM 22.50 for those over 26) you get the cheapest bed in town, including breakfast. The 11:30 PM curfew is a real pain, though. During summer this place fills up quickly, so call ahead. *Kartäuserstr. 151, tel. 0761/67656. S-Bahn 1 toward Littenweiler to Römerhof, double back ½ block, take first right on Fritz-Geiges-Str., cross small river, then turn right.*

CAMPGROUNDS Pick up a list of the four campgrounds in town at the tourist office. The most convenient of them all is **Camping Hirzberg,** which charges DM 3.50 per tent, DM 6 per person, and DM 5 per car. *Kartäuserstr. 99, tel. 0761/35054. S-Bahn 1 toward Littenweiler to Messpl., turn left on Heimatstr., turn right along river, then cross bridge.*

FOOD

Like most college towns, Freiburg has plenty of places serving cheap grub. Just outside the Martinstor, in the **Freiburger Markthalle** (open only until 6:30), more than a dozen food stands serve Chinese, Indian, Italian, Greek, and even Afghan food, usually for less than DM 10. The salad bar at the Greek stand is absolutely orgasmic—vegetarians may never want to leave. **Ristorante Roma** (Kaiser-Joseph-Str. 225, tel. 0761/33157), on the other side of the Martinstor, serves good pizzas (DM 7–DM 17) and pastas (DM 9–DM 13.50) in an elegant but down-to-earth courtyard. For traditional German fare like schnitzel (DM 11) and *Maultaschen* (a kind of ravioli, DM 10.50), try **Schwabentörle** (Oberlinden 23, tel. 0761/34041), beside the Schwabentor.

WORTH SEEING

A series of narrow streams, known as **Bächle,** runs through the city's cobblestone streets. Used for watering cattle and as protection against fire in medieval times, they now help keep the air cool and provide a perfect place for uninhibited travelers to wash their feet.

The **Münster** (cathedral), dominated by a 380-foot tower on its west end, has been Freiburg's main landmark for more than 700 years. For a view over the city and—better yet—a close-up of the cathedral's intricately fashioned, perforated spire, grit your teeth and climb the tower's 329 steps. Besides a butt-load of tourists, the dark interior of the cathedral contains marvelously bright stained-glass windows, some dating to the 13th century, and 10 richly decorated side chapels arranged in a semicircle around the high altar.

On **Münsterplatz** surrounding the cathedral, a daily outdoor **market** offers the best in fresh produce, Black Forest meats and cheeses, flowers, and local handicrafts; the market is widely regarded as the finest in southwestern Germany. The maroon **Kaufhaus** on the south side of the square is the old market hall, decorated with coats of arms and statues of the Habsburgs, who ruled Freiburg for more than 400 years.

Guarding the southeast corner of the city, the 13th-century **Schwabentor** gate houses Freiburg's smallest and quirkiest museum, the **Zinnfigurenklause,** or Tin Figure Collection (tel. 0761/24321), basically a moderately interesting, free way to spend a half hour. From the Schwabentor you can cross the overpass and walk up the **Schloßberg,** a small hill with excellent views of the Münster tower, the city, and the long valley that runs out of the city. Three blocks west of the Schwabentor on Kaiser-Joseph-Straße is **Martinstor,** a medieval tower whose encounter with the 20th century has left it scarred by an advertisement for McDonald's.

Between the tourist office and the Münster sits the **Neues Rathaus** (Town Hall), constructed in the 20th century from a pair of Renaissance buildings. Be sure to peek through the arched doors at the picturesque, green inner courtyard. From the square in front of the Rathaus, Franziskanerstraße leads to the **Haus zum Walfisch** (House of the Whale), a beautiful gold-trimmed building reconstructed shortly after World War II. The scholar Erasmus of Rotterdam lived here for two years following the Reformation.

MUSEUMS Freiburg's numerous city-run museums are all free. Housed in an old Baroque monastery between the Schwabentor and the Martinstor, the mediocre **Augustiner Museum** (Augustinerpl., tel. 0761/216–3300) has a collection of 14th- to 20th-century paintings, sculpture, glassware, and furniture, mostly by artists from the upper Rhine region. The most impressive room holds a number of original statues from the Münster. Across the street from Augustinerplatz are the **Museum für Naturkunde** (Natural History Museum, Gerberau 32, tel. 0761/216–3325) and the **Museum für Bölderkunde** (Museum of Ethnology, tel. 0761/216–3343). The ethnology museum contains an excellent collection focusing on the cultures of eastern Asia and the indigenous peoples of South, Central, and North America. The natural history museum, with a small collection of rocks and dried plants, is decidedly less interesting. The **Museum für Neue Kunst** (Museum of Modern Art, Marienstr. 10A, tel. 0761/216–3671) has some good examples of the type of art that's best described as "interesting." From Augustinerplatz walk east on Gerberau toward the Schwabentor, and cross the stream to Marienstraße. The **Museum für Ur- und Frühgeschichte** (Museum of Prehistory and Early History, Rotteckring 5, tel. 0761/216–3311) has a mediocre collection of archaeological artifacts from the area, but its location in the gorgeous neo-Gothic **Colombi Palace** makes it worth a visit.

FESTIVALS Freiburgers will use any excuse to party. Starting in mid- to late June, the two-week **Zeltmusikfestival** (Tent Music Festival) brings world-class classical, jazz, and rock musicians to Freiburg. Check at the tourist office for schedules and tickets. May and October mean two other 10-day fairs, the **Frühjahrsmesse** and **Herbstmesse,** featuring lots of amusement-park rides. During the four-day **Weintagen** (Wine Days), in the last weekend of June, you are encouraged to "sip" wines and not "consume in quantity," but that doesn't stop young foreigners from wandering around town completely shit-faced. The same goes for the **Weinkost** (Wine Tasting), a similar event in mid-August that features wines produced within the city limits.

AFTER DARK

A number of bars, discos, and cafés grace the streets of the university quarter in the southwest corner of the Old City. Freiburg also has loads of theaters and classical-music venues; pick up a copy of *Aktuell* at the tourist office for current listings.

Circus is Freiburg's newest hip disco if you're in the mood to shake them bones. *Kaiser-Joseph-Str. 248, tel. 0761/36536. Cover: DM 5–DM 10. Open weekdays until 3 AM, weekends until 4 AM.*

Domino (Konwiktstr. 21, tel. 0761/35060), two blocks east of the Münster, is a good place to go for a relaxing evening. Sit outside and sip Irish coffee (DM 6.70), herbal tea (DM 7.20), a milk shake (DM 5), or a host of other hot and cold drinks.

Drifter's Club (Schwenlinstr. 3, tel. 0761/383234), just down the street from the Freiburger Jazzhaus (*see below*), is a hard-core "disco" where you're more likely to see a thrash pit than a strobe light.

Freiburger Jazzhaus has been graced in the past by performers as diverse as the late Miles Davis and Kool and the Gang. It features a wide selection of live blues, folk, Latin, rock, and jazz nearly every night of the week. Get listings and buy tickets at the tourist office. *Schwenlinstr., tel. 0761/34973. Cover: DM 10–DM 40. From train station, walk 1 block along tracks past Omnibusbahnhof.*

Schlappen (Löwenstr. 2, tel. 0761/33494) is the most popular bar among students. Right around the corner from the Martinstor, it's where heavyweight beer-drinkers can prove their prowess by downing a 2-liter *Stiefel* (DM 15), a.k.a. "the boot," preferably in one chug.

Near Freiburg

BREISACH Breisach sits on the banks of the Rhine on the border between France and Germany. Not surprisingly, the town has had the stuffing kicked out of it on numerous occasions during the many wars between the two countries. The oldest part of town, strategically placed on a small hill beside the river and surrounded by tiered defensive walls, testifies to this violent history. Two bulky towers, the **Gutgesellentor** and the **Hagenbachtor,** guard the south side of the hill. The Baroque **Rheintor** sits at the northwestern entrance to the city, and the gabled **Kapftor,** which dates to the year 1200, stands at the top of the hill.

On the brow of the hill is **St. Stephans Münster,** the town's pride and joy. This cathedral, which combines Romanesque and Gothic architecture, brims with late-15th- and early 16th–century artwork. On the western wall of the church, a powerful but fading fresco depicts the Last Judgment. The real eye-catcher, though, is the extravagant carved-birchwood altar. If you're wondering why the top of the altar curves forward, legend has it that the sculptor bet the town's mayor that he could build an altar higher than the ceiling, a feat accomplished with the curve. For this bit of cleverness the wily architect won the hand of the mayor's daughter in marriage.

Breisach has regular train service from Freiburg (DM 6.40, about 30 minutes). From the station walk left along Neutorplatz and then Rheinstraße to Marktplatz, where you'll find the rather worthless **tourist office** (Werd 9, tel. 07667/83227). On the opposite side of the square is the office of **Breisacher Fahrgast-Schiffahr** (Werd 16, tel. 07667/7947), which runs two-hour cruises up the Rhine from April to October (DM 12).

➢ **WHERE TO SLEEP** • The friendly **Jugendherberge** (Rheinuferstr. 12, tel. 07667/7665), along the Rhine about 1 kilometer (⅔ mile) south of the town center, provides comfy beds and an impeccable environment. Beds cost DM 17 (DM 22.50 for those over 26), including breakfast. To get here from Marktplatz, continue up the main drag, turn left at the cheesiest souvenir stand in southern Germany, and follow Rheinuferstraße along the river for about 10 minutes. You can camp at **Campingplatz Münsterblick** (tel. 07667/93930), 2 kilometers (1¼ mile) southeast of town, in Breisach-Hochstetten. To get here from behind the station, follow Inringer Landstraße for about 15 minutes, and hang a right on Hochstetten Straße.

The hills around Breisach are famous for their wines, including the rich Sylvaner and the tremendously sweet Gewürztraminer dessert wine. Gewürztraminer is made by leaving the grapes on the vine until after the regular harvest, allowing a fungus known as the "noble rot" to set in. The fungus softens the skin of the grapes and lets the juice evaporate, leaving behind an intensely flavored and sweet concentrate.

EUROPA PARK Europa Park, some 30 kilometers (19 miles) north of Freiburg, offers the standard array of amusement-park roller coasters, water rides, and variety shows. A series of artificially reproduced European "theme areas" is designed to whisk you to places like Italy, France, Switzerland, the Netherlands, and Scandinavia. The park shamelessly imitates the Disney model, with such attractions as a geodesic dome, needle tower, monorail system, and even a mascot named **Euro-Maus,** a thinly disguised Euro version of Mickey. *Tel. 07822/7720. Admission: DM 25. Open Easter–late Oct. daily 9–6. Buses make 1-hr trip from Freiburg twice each morning and make return trip just before and just after 6 PM.*

KAISERSTUHL Immediately northeast of Breisach sits a vineyard-covered mound of volcanic dirt known as the **Kaiserstuhl,** or Emperor's Seat. The name derives from a legend that Emperor Frederick Barbarossa, who died here in the 12th century, is patiently resting in these hills until the time is ripe for him to arise and rule Germany once again. The Kaiserstuhl is circled by a rail line, with service from Breisach a few times a day during weekdays in summer. Rail line or no, you'll really see the area only by hiking. You can get trail maps at tourist-information offices in Breisach and Freiburg.

MT. BELCHEN Shaped more like an overgrown molehill than a mountain, Mt. Belchen is nevertheless the second-highest peak (4,623 feet) in the southern Black Forest. What makes it such a popular attraction for visitors, though, are the tiny villages and deep valleys that surround it, as well as the views stretching to the Bodensee, the Rhine Valley, and even the Swiss Alps. The easiest way to get to Belchen, about 17 kilometers (11 miles) south of Freiburg, is via the small village of

Münstertal, which has regular train connections to Freiburg (DM 8.40, about 40 minutes). From the Untermünstertal train station, it takes two to three hours of walking along a well-marked trail to cover the 10 kilometers (6 miles) to the top of Mt. Belchen. If you can't hack the trek, or the trek leaves you hacking, take one of the two buses a day that make the trip from the train station to the top of the hill.

ST. PETER The Benedictine Kloster of St. Peter, some 20 kilometers (12 miles) east of Freiburg, was founded in 1093, but only in the 17th century did the village of St. Peter achieve fame, with the construction of a Baroque church designed by architect Peter Thumb. Its pair of imposing towers and red sandstone exterior contrast strikingly with the green hills around the small village, making the church a popular subject for photographers. Inside are a series of colorful frescoes, but the real highlight is the **Rococo library,** elaborately decorated with white stucco. You can view the library only on a guided tour, given Tuesday and Thursday at 2:30; otherwise, you'll have to content yourself with a postcard. Buses make the scenic one-hour trip between Freiburg and St. Peter regularly.

The Black Forest Is Dying of Industrial Disease

Just as the Black Death once ran amok through the human population of Europe, so today a deadly disease is attacking the trees of Germany's Black Forest. The disease, termed Waldsterben, *or Forest Death, has highly visible symptoms, including premature loss of leaves, undersize trunks, death of young saplings, dropping boughs, and yellowing needles on pine trees. The causes of the illness, reported to affect two-thirds of the trees in the forest, are less clear. When inhabitants first noticed the disease in 1976, many assumed it was the result of acid rain blown over from industrial regions of Germany and elsewhere. Today, scientists studying the disease are less certain. Although most experts fault some type of air pollution, some believe the real villain is nitrogen oxide emitted by cars traveling through the forest. Such fears have led to a growing number of signs along Black Forest roads reading* AUTOS TOTEN WALDER *(CARS ARE KILLING FORESTS)*

Worse than the uncertainty over the disease's origins is the fact that no cure has yet been found. So far 1 out of every 50 trees in the Black Forest is dead or beyond hope of recovery. The only thing scientists agree on is that the forest's air must be cleaned up one way or another. The Green Party, a strong and rising power in German politics, leads the battle to save the region on a national level, while various local environmental-activist groups, many based in Freiburg, are also pushing for a solution. With luck, something can be done before the forest suffers the fate of so many of Eastern Europe's once-grand forests.

Titisee and Schluchsee

A small lake sealed off from the rest of the world by a series of pine-covered hills, Titisee possesses the type of almost mystical natural beauty that lures you into a dreamy never-never land. Unfortunately, never-never land has a problem with tourists. Whenever the sun is shining, swarms of tourists descend on the little town beside the lake and indulge in a souvenir-grubbing feeding frenzy of frightening proportions. **Seestraße,** the main promenade, is tourist ground-zero. If you want to join the madding crowd, rent a paddleboat or rowboat from one of the innumerable stands along the shore, or jump on a ship for a short cruise around the lake. But if you prefer to get away from it all, follow one of the several excellent hiking and biking trails that circle the Titisee; you can obtain trail maps at the **tourist-information office** (Seestr. and Strandbadstr., tel. 07651/810104) in the Kurhaus (the big building with all the flags). You can rent three-speed clunkers from the train station for DM 12 per day (DM 8 with rail pass). More serious cyclists can rent mountain bikes from the **Sporthaus** (tel. 07651/8816 or 07651/7494), located down the stairs to the lakeside Boothaus, about 55 yards farther down Strandbadstraße from the tourist office; rates are DM 15 for three hours, DM 25 per day.

You can jump in the lake from along the southern and eastern shores, but if you want a pool and a grassy beach hit **Beheiztes Freibad** (tel. 07651/8272), about 550 yards west of the Kurhaus, on Strandbadstraße. For the privilege of sharing these facilities with hundreds of others, you have to shell out DM 4 (DM 2 students).

About 10 kilometers (6 miles) south on the rail line is **Schluchsee,** a larger lake with a smaller town, far fewer tourists, and the same magical beauty as Titisee. Plenty of narrow beaches line the shores. **Acqua Fun** (tel. 07656/7738) charges DM 5 (DM 3.50 students) for access to its pool, water slide, and swaths of grass.

COMING AND GOING

Trains travel twice per hour to Titisee from Freiburg (DM 8.40). The 40-minute ride passes through **Höllental,** or Hell's Valley. Despite the satanic name, the ride to Titisee from Freiburg is one of the most beautiful in Germany—the train climbs more than 2,000 feet through a gorge, passing along the way a station called Himmelsreich (Kingdom of Heaven).

WHERE TO SLEEP

You can get a list of campgrounds and other accommodations, including rooms in private homes (about DM 18), at the tourist office in Titisee (*see above*).

SCHLUCHSEE **Campingplatz Wolfsgrund.** This campground has modern luxuries like hot running water, laundry facilities, and a good old W.C. Rates are DM 6 per person, DM 5 per tent, and DM 3 per car. *Tel. 07656/7739. Walk past entrance to Schluchsee-Wolfsgrund hostel* (see below) *to lake, then along shore for about 800 yds.*

Jugendherberge Schluchsee-Seebrugg. At the very end of the lake and the rail line is Seebrugg, which consists of little more than the hostel and the train station. You would think Seebrugg's isolation would make it ideal, but a well-traveled road and the DM 4 admission to the beach somehow manage to spoil the place. Beds here are only DM 15.50 (DM 20.50 for those over 26). *Seebrugg 9, tel. 07656/494.*

Jugendherberge Schluchsee-Wolfsgrund. This hostel is so much better than the Schluchsee-Seebrugg. A stairway leads from this hostel to one of the nicest beaches on the lake. The DM 16.50 fee (DM 21.50 for those over 26) includes breakfast.

Wolfsgrund 28, tel. 07656/329. With your back to water, walk left from station along rd., turn left onto dirt trail, and cross 2 bridges.

TITISEE **Gästehaus Wald und See.** This centrally located guest house has the cheapest rooms in town. Singles and doubles start at DM 28 per head. *Alte Poststr. 14, tel. 07651/8389. From Kurhaus walk west on Strandbadstr., then right on Alte Poststr.*

Jugendherberge Veltishof. In an idyllic setting just two minutes from the lake, this hostel is worth the long trek out here. Comfy beds in spotless rooms go for DM 16 (DM 21 for those over 26) including breakfast, which you can eat outside at picnic tables. *Brunderhalde 27, tel. 07652/238. Take one of the infrequent buses from station toward Todtnau to Feuerwehrheim, or walk about 3 km (2 mi) along shore past Beheiztes Freibad.*

Naturcamping Weiherhof. This campground between the hostel *(see below)* and the lake charges DM 7 per person, DM 5.50 per tent, and DM 3 per car, but loads of people camp out for free in the pine grove right above the campground. *Tel. 07652/1468.*

FOOD

In Titisee avoid paying the grossly inflated rates of most of the tourist-trap sidewalk restaurants. You can assemble a picnic at **Gutscher** market (Seestr. and Strandbadstr.), which features a variety of Black Forest meats and cheeses, as well as a take-out salad bar. You might want to buy some goods here before heading to Schluchsee; the tiny town has precious few restaurants and an even smaller number of grocery stores.

Near Titisee and Schluchsee

MT. FELDBERG At 4,882 feet, Mt. Feldberg is the Black Forest's tallest peak. Unfortunately, its rounded top received a serious crew cut in the 18th and 19th centuries from a group of farmers determined to turn the forested mountain into pastureland. To add insult to injury, the 20th century brought the addition of a TV tower and numerous radio dishes. Despite all this, the Feldberg is still a center for outdoors enthusiasts. In summer, hiking and biking dominate the scene, and in winter the mountain turns into the Black Forest's most popular downhill ski area. If you intend to hike or ski, your best option is to base yourself at the mountain's only youth hostel, the **Jugendherberge Hebelhof** (Passhöhe 14, tel. 07676/221). It lies within walking distance of the ski lifts (DM 5) and of many trails, including an ugly gravel path to the top of the mountain. The hostel charges DM 16 (DM 21 for those over 26). To get here, hop on a bus from Titisee toward Todtnau and get off at Hebelhof, or catch a train to Feldberg-Bärrental, the highest train station in Germany, and then get a bus to Hebelhof. Feldberg-Bärrental lies on the Titisee–Schluchsee line.

WUTACHSCHLUCHT The Wutachschlucht, on the eastern fringes of the Black Forest, is a fine example of the type of deep, dark gorge for which the Black Forest is named. Cut by a narrow, swift river, most of the 25-kilometer (16-mile) gorge is protected as a nature reserve. A marked trail, characterized by steep drops and many tiny wood bridges, runs the length of the gorge.

Bonndorf is the town closest to the gorge's dramatic eastern end. You can get to Bonndorf by bus from Schluchsee-Seebrugg (25 minutes), Donaueschingen (45 minutes), and Neustadt (45 minutes). The bus stop in front of the post office is within spitting distance of the **Tourist-Informations-Zentrum** (Schloßstr. 1, tel. 07703/7607), which can outfit you with a map of the gorge. From the post office walk up Martinstraße and follow the signs to the right to Philosophenweg, a dirt hiking path that leads 4 kilometers (2½ miles) through the one-tractor towns of Boll and Tiefental to the Wutachschlucht. From here you can walk as far as you like in either direction and double back when you run out of steam; or take the highly recommended hike to the town of Schattenmühle, at the eastern end of the Schlucht, from which you can catch a bus back to Bonndorf.

At the **Jugendherberge Bonndorf** (Waldallee 19, tel. 07703/359) you can cool off in the indoor pool before catching some Zs. Rates run DM 16 (DM 21 for those over 26), including breakfast. To get here from the tourist office, walk down Schloßstraße and Mühlenstraße, turn left on Rothausstraße, right on Waldallee, and trek straight ahead for about 10 minutes.

Triberg

Deep, thickly forested valleys surround the town of Triberg, offering some of the best hiking and biking in southwest Germany. Built on a steep hillside, the town itself offers enough attractions to draw busloads of camera-toting tourists. Be prepared, though, for a sickening overdose of German kitsch—it's a cottage industry here. The biggest draw is Germany's highest **waterfall,** which drops 540 feet in seven rocky steps. Spectacular as it is, the waterfall loses much of its appeal because of the huge swarms of tourists, who must pay DM 2 (DM 1 students) to view the cascade. You can reach the waterfall via a path at the top of the main drag, Hauptstraße. The **tourist office** (Lusienstr. 10, tel. 07722/81230) is in the Kurhaus, two blocks from the entrance to the waterfall; you can pick up maps of the town and the surrounding hiking trails here.

The **Schwarzwaldmuseum**, one block from the waterfall, possesses one of the quirkiest and most interesting collections of Black Forest culture. The museum contains hundreds of cuckoo clocks, models of traditional artisans' workshops, and a room designed to look like a mining shaft, full of minerals from the surrounding hills. Best of all, though, are the heaps of player pianos and other carnivallike mechanical instruments that you can activate for a few marks. *Wallfahrtstr. 4, off Hauptstr., tel. 07722/4434. Admission: DM 4, DM 2 students. Open daily 9–6.*

To reach the Baroque **Wallfahrtskirche,** walk past the museum and trudge up the hill on Clemens-Maria-Hofbauer-Straße. *The Virgin of the Pines,* an image of the Virgin Mary embedded in the wood of the altar, is reputed to have been involved in a couple of miracles and has been a popular destination for pilgrims since the 17th century. Triberg also lies in the heart of cuckoo-clock territory. Although the cuckoo clock does constitute a legitimate part of Black Forest culture, it's difficult to take this town's cuckoo mania too seriously. Shops with names like House of 1,000 Clocks and Big Ben proliferate, creating a sort of Disneyland-Germany effect. Hard-core cuckoo-clock aficionados or connoisseurs of serious kitsch should not miss the **world's largest cuckoo clock.** Walk, hitch, or take a bus about 3 kilometers (2 miles) up the main road, toward Furtwangen. On the outskirts of the town of Schonach you'll find a small house with a clock face and swinging doors, through which a really big cuckoo appears at the top of every hour. You need to be seriously giddy or popping some colorful pills to appreciate this place fully.

COMING AND GOING

You can reach Triberg by rail from Hausach (DM 6.40, 20 minutes) and Donaueschingen (DM 10.80, 40 minutes). To reach the town center from the station, cross the overpass, go down the stairs, and walk left, up the hill and past the post office, for about 15 minutes. Otherwise, hop on the bus, which drops you at the top of the hill in the center of town.

WHERE TO SLEEP AND EAT

Offering impressive views of the area, Triberg's **Jugendherberge** (Rohrbacher Str. 35, tel. 07722/4110) is a steep 20-minute hike up Friedrichstraße. Prices are par for the course, at DM 16.50 (DM 21 for those over 26), including breakfast. **Krone** (Schulstr. 37, tel. 07722/4524), in the center of town, has DM 56 doubles with creaky but comfortable beds and a restaurant serving hearty Black Forest meals. To get here from the waterfall, walk two blocks down Hauptstraße and turn right on Schulstraße. For tasty pizzas (DM 8–DM 12) or pasta (DM 8–DM 15), head to **Pinnochio** (Hauptstr. 64, tel. 07722/4424), also near the top of the hill.

Near Triberg

FURTWANGEN Furtwangen, about 15 kilometers (9 miles) south of Triberg, attracts visitors solely because of its **Deutsches Uhrenmuseum** (German Clock Museum, Gerwigstr. 11, tel. 07723/656117), which has a collection of more than 1,000 timepieces from every corner of the planet. German-speakers can take advantage of guided tours and detailed explanations of the history and technical aspects of clock production; everybody else has to content themselves with looking at loads of display cases full of everything from simple wristwatches to enormous, beautiful grandfather clocks. Regular buses make the scenic 45-minute journey from Triberg's train station to Furtwangen. To get to the museum, get off at the Friedrichstraße stop, walk ahead one block, cross the street, and continue on Gerwigstraße. Admission is DM 3 (DM 1 students), and the museum is open May–October, daily 9–5 and November–April, weekdays 9–noon and 2–4. For a list of places to crash and a map of local trails, pop into the **tourist office** (Marktpl. 4, tel. 07723/61400), in the Rathaus between the bus stop and the museum.

Pom-pom–laden Bollenhütte carry real significance for women in Gutach. The color of your balls, it seems, tells all. Red balls mean that you're unmarried, whereas black balls mean you're settled down. Freud would have had a ball with this one.

GUTACH Sitting in a wide valley 13 kilometers (8 miles) north of Triberg, the village of Gutach boldly asserts itself as the true home of *Bollenhütte,* women's hats decorated with bright red or black fuzzy balls. As much a part of the culture as they are, Bollenhütte still look pretty damned goofy.

On the outskirts of town, the **Schwarzwälder Freilichtmuseum** (Black Forest Open-Air Museum) provides a glimpse of the everyday life of the region's colorful inhabitants. This is an excellent museum—maybe the best in the Black Forest. Housed in a number of traditional dwellings, most of which were brought to Gutach from other areas of the Black Forest, the museum features live demonstrations of crafts that have been practiced in the region for hundreds of years. Catch Bus 7160 in front of Triberg's post office to the Vogtsbauernhof stop. Only three to five buses make the trip each day, and the last returns between 3 and 5:30, so plan ahead if you don't want to hitch or hike back to Triberg. *Tel. 07831/230. Open April–Oct., daily 8–6.*

Freudenstadt

Freudenstadt was bombed silly by the French in World War II and is consequently rather modern and sterile. Most visitors come only because of its proximity to the surrounding forest. Making matters worse, the town is popular among the Europe-through-the-window-of-a-bus crowd, whose wardens probably stop here because it's the only place to get fuel and meals for 40 people between Freiburg and Baden-Baden. You'll find most of these types roaming the arcade-lined Marktplatz, one of the largest in Germany. It owes its size to the unfulfilled plans of Duke Friedrich I of Württemburg, who wanted to build a Schloß on the site. The **Stadtkirche,** in the square's southwest corner, was built in the shape of an "L," with men seated on one side and women on the other so the congregation couldn't check one another out during services. Enclosed in a glass case next to the altar is an impressive 12th-century Romanesque **lectern,** adorned with images of the Four Evangelists. From Marktplatz Loßburgerstraße leads to **Promenadeplatz,** where you'll find the Kurhaus. Inside is the **tourist office** (Promenadepl. 1, tel. 07441/8640), which performs all the usual services and sells trail maps of the surrounding area.

COMING AND GOING

Freudenstadt sits on the rail line that runs between Karlsruhe (DM 19, two hours) and the Black Forest junction town of Hausach (DM 8.40, 45 minutes). All trains stop at the **Hauptbahnhof,** from which it's about a 20-minute uphill climb via Bahnhofstraße and Turnhallestraße to Promenadeplatz. Much more convenient is the **Stadtbahnhof** (City Rail Station), next to the city's bus station. Most trains go from the Hauptbahnhof to the Stadtbahnhof, but if yours doesn't, hop the next train through. From here it's only a two-minute walk on Martin-Luther-Straße to Marktplatz.

WHERE TO SLEEP

The most exciting thing about the **Jugendherberge** (Eugen-Näegle-Str. 69, tel. 07441/7720) is the washing machine downstairs. A bed costs DM 16 (DM 21 for those over 26), including breakfast. To get here from the Stadtbahnhof, turn left on Ringstraße, left on Ludwig-Jahn-Straße, and right on Gottlieb-Daimler-Straße. **Gästehaus Benedik** (Kolpingstr. 2, tel. 07441/81122) has spacious doubles in a quiet residential neighborhood near the tourist office for DM 56. To get here from Promenadeplatz walk one block down Lauterbadstraße, turn right on Eugen-King-Straße and left on Kolpingstraße. If you want to camp, take Bus 12 from either train station to **Langenwald** (tel. 07441/2862), about 3 kilometers (2 miles) west of town.

FOOD

Two good grub spots lie between the Stadtbahnhof and Marktplatz. Restaurant **See** (Forststr. 15–17, tel. 07441/1527) serves dirt-cheap German cuisine like *Käsespätzle* (thick egg noodles with cheese, DM 7.50), and *Wurstsalat* (sausage salad, DM 8). For a little more money you can try heavenly Greek treats at **Poseidon** (Martin-Luther-Str. 3, tel. 07441/6016), one block west.

Near Freudenstadt

FORBACH Sprinkled with half-timbered houses and red sandstone fountains, Forbach lies in the pristine Murg River valley, which remains largely ignored by tourists. The striking **St. Johanneskirche (St. John's Church)** sits on a small hill overlooking the center of town, flanked by a pair of thin towers. The colorfully painted interior looks more like an Arab mosque than a church, except for the large sculpture of Christ's crucifixion hanging from the vaulted ceiling. The 16th-century **Alte Holzbrücke,** the largest single-span covered wood bridge in Europe, traverses the Murg on the north side of town. The **tourist office** (Striedstr., tel. 07228/2340), in the Kurhaus just north of the bridge, can outfit you with a map of trails and campgrounds in the area.

Forbach lies on the scenic Murgtalbahn rail line, which covers the 60 kilometers (37 miles) between Freudenstadt (DM 6.40, 45 minutes away) and Rastatt (DM 6.40, 40 minutes away) and continues to Karlsruhe (DM 10.80, 1¼ hours).

➢ **WHERE TO SLEEP • Naturfreundhaus Holderbronn** (Klammstr. 27, tel. 07228/728), a five-minute walk up Hauptstraße and Klammstraße from the bridge, offers lodging in a downright friendly environment for DM 9. If that's full, a **Jugendherberge** (Birket 1, tel. 07228/2427) in the hills above town charges DM 15.50 (DM

20.50 for those over 26), including breakfast. To reach it from the station, cross the bridge, turn right on Friedrichstraße, bear left on Hauptstraße, and follow the signs up Braidstraße for about 2 kilometers (1¼ miles).

SCHWARZWALD-HOCHSTRAßE Covering 57 kilometers (35 miles) between Freudenstadt and Baden-Baden, the Schwarzwald-Hochstraße (Black Forest Highway) runs along a series of ridges, offering outstanding views of the Rhine Valley and the Vosges Mountains in France. Two or three buses make the trip daily from Freudenstadt to **Mummelsee** (DM 6.80, 45 minutes), halfway to Baden-Baden. This small lake is sadly infected by a hotel, a large parking lot, and a number of tacky souvenir shops. Sitting at the base of the **Hornigsgrinde,** the highest peak in the northern Black Forest, the lake is reputed to be haunted by a king who was forced by an evil sorceress to live there for 1,000 years beyond his natural life. Too bad he hasn't scared away the bus-loads of tourists yet. Two or three buses a day cover the remaining 28 kilometers (17 miles) to Baden-Baden; the one-hour trip costs DM 7 (free with rail pass). If you've got the time, you can better see the area by hiking all or part of the **Westweg,** a trail that runs parallel to the road.

➢ **WHERE TO SLEEP • Jugendherberge Zuflucht.** Conveniently located about halfway between Freudenstadt and the Mummelsee, this large hostel sits practically right on the Westweg and is also a stop on the Freudenstadt–Baden-Baden bus line. It makes an excellent base for biking in summer and skiing in winter, and you can rent equipment for both sports for DM 7 per day. A bed in the hostel's comfy rooms sets you back DM 17 (DM 21.50 for those over 26), including breakfast. *Tel. 07804/611.*

Naturfreundehaus Baden-Höhe. This cheap lodging option is about 2 kilometers (1¼ miles) east of the Westweg and the Sand bus stop, between Baden-Baden and the Mummelsee. Beds go for DM 14, including breakfast. *Tel. 07226/238. Closed Tues.*

Baden-Baden

After visiting this elegant spa town some 115 years ago, Mark Twain remarked: "Baden-Baden sits in the lap of the hills, and the natural and artificial beauties of the surroundings are combined effectively and charmingly. . . . It is an inane town, filled with sham, and petty fraud, and snobbery, but the baths are good." Other than the fact that Euro-yuppies, tourists, and hypochondriacs taking advantage of Germany's liberal health-care system have replaced the aristocrats with whom Twain rubbed elbows, not much has changed. As it was in 1878, the **Friedrichsbad** (Römerpl. 1, tel. 07221/275920) is the most luxurious bath complex in town. Here you can get a 15-step "Roman Irish Bath" in the nude for DM 38 (DM 32 if you bring a stamp proving you're staying in the town's youth hostel.) Disrespecting its ancestors, the Friedrichsbad has built a parking lot practically on top of the ruins of the **Roman baths,** where soldiers used to get gussied up after a hard day of conquering. The **Caracalla-Therme** (Römerpl. 11, tel. 07221/275940), a more modern bathhouse down the street, caters to those with more modesty and less money; three hours in the thermal baths here—bathing attire required—costs DM 18 (DM 14.60 with a stamp from the youth hostel).

The Gothic **Stiftskirche,** on the opposite side of the Friedrichsbad from the Caracalla-Therme, features an impressive 15th-century sculpture of Christ's crucifixion. From here stairs lead up to the **Neue Schloß** (New Castle), a jumble of Renaissance and Baroque buildings. Tours of the castle start at 3 on weekdays. Inside you'll find a small **local-history museum** (tel. 07221/278381), whose most interesting display features a number of dolls and dollhouses from the turn of the century. The terrace of the castle offers the best view of town, but for incredible panoramas of the Rhine Valley and Vosges Mountains head to the **Merkur,** the area's tallest peak. To get here, take Bus 5 (toward Merkurwald) from **Augustaplatz,** in the center of town, to the last stop. From there you can hike the rest of the steep hill or take the funicular (DM 5 round-trip) to the top.

Baden-Baden's ultra-elegant **casino** leans more toward Monte Carlo than Las Vegas; in other words, hoi polloi are not encouraged to schlep in with bags of quarters to play the slots. Unless you're 21, dressed to kill, and not a student, your only chance of seeing the inside is during one of the tours (DM 3) that leave every half hour between 9:30 AM and 11:30 AM. If you want to play, minimum stakes are DM 5, but high rollers can slap down as much as DM 50,000.

The **Trinkhalle,** a columned 19th-century building next to the casino, has a striking entryway with 14 frescoes depicting scenes from local legends. Stretching south from the casino is **Lichtentaler Allee,** a pleasant promenade lined with rare and exotic trees; here you'll find the **Kunsthalle** (Hall of Art, Lichtentaler Allee 8A, tel. 07221/23250), a museum that features rotating exhibitions of art from around the world. The **tourist office** (Augustapl. 8, tel. 07221/275200), two blocks south of Leopoldsplatz, gives out shoddy city maps, sells much better ones for DM 1, and has lists of the city's accommodations.

COMING AND GOING

On the rail line between Karlsruhe (DM 8.40, 20 minutes) and Konstanz (DM 5, 3½ hours), Baden-Baden offers rail connections to nearly every major city in Germany and many around Europe. The train station is about 3 kilometers (2 miles) northwest of the town center. Bus 1 runs from the station to **Leopoldsplatz,** the town's central square, which lies directly between the clutch of sights centered around the Friedrichsbad and those near the casino.

WHERE TO SLEEP AND EAT

You'll pay a pretty penny for most accommodations in this town. **Hotel Löhr** (Alderstr. 2, tel. 07221/26204), in the center of town, has comfy doubles for DM 65, which isn't a bad deal. The hotel's reception desk is at Café Lohr, on Augustaplatz. The spotless, modern **Jugendherberge Werner Dietz** (Hardbergstr. 34, tel. 07221/52223) has the cheapest beds in town, up in the hills between the train station and the city center. A bed here costs DM 17 (DM 22.50 for those over 26), including breakfast. To get to the hostel, take Bus 1 from the station to Große-Dollen-Straße, cross the street, and follow the signs uphill.

During the day, **Hatip's** (Gernsbacherstr. 18, tel. 07221/22364) serves doner kebabs (similar to gyros, DM 5) and a host of excellent Middle Eastern vegetarian dishes. At night, though, you'll find more people drinking beer (DM 3) than munching a pita sandwich.

Pforzheim

The modern city of Pforzheim, in the northeastern corner of the Black Forest, bears little or no relation to the rest of the densely forested region. Most of the city was leveled in World War II and now holds little attraction for budget travelers except as a starting point for three major hikes (*see* Outdoor Activities, *below*). Pforzheim is most famous for its jewelry, which explains the town's other moniker, *Goldstadt* (City of Gold). In the **Reuchlinhaus** (Jahnstr. 42, tel. 07231/392126) you can see a collection of jewelry spanning the period from the 3rd century BC to the present day. Smile and wave at the cameras in the corners. To get here from the train station walk down Schloßbergstraße, cross the bridge, take a right on either of two footpaths between the two rivers, and turn right again where the paths end.

Across the street from the Reuchlinhaus, the **Edelsteinausstellung Schütt** displays more than the recommended daily allowance of minerals, gems, and precious stones in the showroom of one of Pforzheim's largest jewelry dealers. Don't miss the gorgeous

17th-century Burmese tapestry generously studded with semiprecious stones. If you just can't get enough, hit the **Technisches Museum** (Bleichstr. 81, tel. 07231/392869), open only Wednesday 9–noon and 3–5 and on the second and fourth Sundays of each month 10–noon and 2–5. Located three blocks west of the Reuchlinhaus, it has an exhaustive collection of machinery detailing the production of jewelry and timepieces in Pforzheim. The bulky Gothic **Schloßkirche St. Michael** is one of the few old structures left undamaged by the air raids of World War II; it still looks sturdy enough to get the better of any encounters with incoming bombs.

Pforzheim has rail connections to most major German cities, with frequent service to Karlsruhe (DM 8.50, 20 minutes), Stuttgart (DM 12.60, 30 minutes), Heidelberg (DM 19, one hour), and Konstanz (DM 48, 3¾ hours). The **tourist-information office** (Marktpl. 1, tel. 07231/392190) in the center of town is staffed by a friendly bunch, who can set you up with maps and all kinds of trail info.

WHERE TO SLEEP

Perhaps the nicest thing about Pforzheim is the **Jugendherberge** (Kräheneckstr. 4, tel. 07231/72604), outside town in the neighboring village of Dillweißenstein. Housed in the ruins of an old castle, the hostel sits in a beautiful wooded area next to the Nagold River. Beds cost DM 16 (DM 21 for those over 26). To reach the hostel, take Bus 3 from the station to Papierfabrik, then walk until you reach the bridge, cross the river, continue one block, and turn right.

OUTDOOR ACTIVITIES

In addition to promoting itself as the Goldstadt, Pforzheim also fancies itself as the gateway to the Black Forest, since three long-distance trails through the region start here. The most challenging, the 280-kilometer (174-mile) **Westweg,** runs to Basel via Forbach, the Mummelsee, and the Titisee; it's recommended as a 12-day hike. The 220-kilometer (136-mile) **Mittelweg** is a nine-day hike that runs to Waldshut via Wildbad, Freudenstadt, and Titisee. Also pegged as a nine-day hike is the 240-kilometer (149-mile) **Ostweg,** which runs to Schaffhausen in Switzerland via the Nagold Valley, Freudenstadt, Alpirsbach, and Villingen. To get descriptions of each hike (in German only), including places to stay along the trails, detailed trail maps, and lists of people who will transport your baggage from one destination to the next, talk to the friendly people at the tourist-information office (*see above*).

Nagold Valley

The serene waters of the Nagold River flow through a narrow, densely forested valley in the northern Black Forest. The tiny towns in this enchanting valley are almost completely devoid of tourists.

Worn-out, tired clichés aside, the true gem of the valley is undoubtedly the Altstadt of **Calw** (sounds like "calve"). In the center of town is the cobblestone **Marktplatz,** a small square lined with half-timbered houses, which features a local produce market on Wednesday and Saturday mornings. One of Calw's most famous sons, writer Hermann Hesse, was born in one of these half-timbered houses.

The **Hermann Hesse Museum,** on the far end of Marktplatz, details the novelist and poet's life through original manuscripts, documents, and photographs. In the same building, and included in the DM 3 entrance fee (DM 2 students), is the small **Galerie der Stadt Calw,** which features works by a handful of local artists. *Marktpl. 30, tel. 07051/7522. Both museums open Tues.–Sat. 2–5, Sun. 11–5.*

Calw is a medieval textile town that was largely destroyed by fire in the 17th century. To learn a little more about the town's history, visit the **Museum der Stadt Calw** (Bischofstr. 48, tel. 07051/167260), open Wednesday 2–4 and Sunday 10–noon. About 110 yards south of Marktplatz sits the early 15th-century **Nikolausbrücke,** an itty-bitty stone bridge with a teeny-weeny votive chapel in the middle. You'll easily spot the austere red sandstone **Stadtkirche Peter und Paul,** towering above Calw.

Consider bringing along a loaf of bread, a hunk of cheese, and a bottle of wine when you visit the ruins in Hirsau. The soft grass that now grows where the Kloster's buildings once stood and the stunning natural beauty of the surrounding valley make a perfect setting for a picnic.

A five-minute train ride or a pleasant 40-minute walk brings you to the smaller village of **Hirsau.** Hirsau is home to the Benedictine **Kloster,** once one of the most influential monasteries in Germany. Built in the 9th century and added to intermittently over the centuries, the cloister stands in ruins today, with two notable exceptions: the 12th-century **Eulenturm** (Owl Tower) and the beautifully restored 16th-century **Marienkappelle.** In the **Klostermuseum** (Aureliuspl. 10, tel. 07051/5671) you can view the remains of the cloister's decorations and learn the history of the monastery, which launched a reform movement to transfer control of religious institutions from secular rulers to the pope.

The town of **Nagold** lies south of Calw, where the valley widens into a small plain. The largest town in the valley, Nagold has an unattractive modern demeanor except for its Altstadt, which retains many medieval buildings. You'll find the giant late-17th-century **Hotel Post,** the early 18th-century **Alte Schulhaus,** and an unnamed crooked affair at Marktstraße 15. You can't miss the two tallest structures in town: the early 15th-century **Alter Turm,** once part of the town's defenses, and the handsome red sandstone **Stadtkirche,** built between 1870 and 1874. On a hill above town you can see the meager ruins of a 17th-century **Burg** and score a good view of Nagold and the river valley. To get to the ruins, cross the river behind the **Rathaus,** on Marktstraße, walk across the park, and follow one of the many paths up the hill.

COMING AND GOING

A **rail line** runs along the Nagold River from Pforzheim in the north to Horb in the south, connecting all the small towns in the valley. You can also catch this line from Freudenstadt, Tübingen (through Horb), and Stuttgart (through Pforzheim). A narrow road beside the river carries enough traffic to make **hitchhiking** an option. The best way to see the valley, though, is to get off your ass and walk through it. The area has loads of marked trails and paved paths, with maps readily available at the tourist offices in Pforzheim (*see* Pforzheim, *above*) and Tübingen (*see* Tübingen in Chapter 3) and in many bookstores in the valley's towns.

WHERE TO SLEEP AND EAT

The **Jugendherberge** (Im Zwinger 4, tel. 07051/12614) in a green half-timbered house in the center of Nagold makes the best base for exploring the valley. A comfortable bed and standard hostel breakfast run DM 16 (DM 20.50 for those over 26). Of the affordably priced hotels, the **Hotel Garni Alte Post** (Bahnhofstr. 1, tel. 07051/2196) in Calw charges DM 24 per person, and the **Gasthof Schwarzwald** (Hohenberger Str. 50, tel. 07452/2976), south of Nagold's Altstadt, starts at DM 32 per person. You can sleep under the stars at numerous **campgrounds,** including sites in Calw (tel. 07051/12845), Nagold (tel. 07452/2608), and Bad Liebenzell (tel.

07052/40460), about 7 kilometers (4 miles) north of Calw. For a complete list of campgrounds in the Nagold Valley and the entire northern Black Forest, ask at the tourist-information offices in Pforzheim (*see* Pforzheim, *above*) or Tübingen (*see* Tübingen in Chapter 3).

While in Calw, chow down on excellent Swabian or Italian food for less than DM 15 at **Peters Pilsstube** (Im Calwer Markt, tel. 07051/40933), between Marktplatz and the bridge to the train station.

MUNICH

5

By Linda Shing

As a big city—the third largest in Germany—situated in the middle of predominantly Catholic and ultraconservative Bavaria, Munich presents the visitor with all kinds of weird contradictions and surprising juxtapositions, which the tourist office tries to present as well-roundedness. Not only does the city offer a huge array of high-quality culture, including opera, ballet, four symphony orchestras, and the world's most comprehensive museums of science and technology, but it also tosses one of the wildest and most indulgent parties anywhere, the 16-day Oktoberfest. The city remains home to plenty of stereotypical Bavarians clad in their form-fitting, beer belly–hugging lederhosen, but a stroll through the sophisticated district of Schwabing will reveal a chic, self-conscious crowd that totally disdains the Bavarian tradition of oompah bands and unrestrained friendliness. Munich will adequately cater to your simpler needs (like beer for breakfast, the need to lie in the sun without any clothes on, cheap picnic supplies, and beer for lunch), but if you suddenly come upon a huge amount of money, you can spend that here, too; just witness the consumer heaven of Maximilianstraße, or take a gander at statistics citing Munich as the wealthiest city in Germany.

Munich has been a center of political and economic activity since its founding, in 1158, after greedy Duke Henry the Lion redirected the profitable salt trade by destroying a strategic bridge and replacing it with a new one near Munich. The art-loving Wittelsbachs, who ruled Bavaria for almost 750 years, generously funded art museums, classical musicians, and literary academies, creating a cultural legacy that lives today: The city still draws an inordinate number of artists, musicians, and students, both German and foreign, to its ancient streets and hallowed halls. And when you get sick of it all, you can take off to some of the most beautiful countryside anywhere; the city lies an hour away from the Bavarian Alps and lake getaways like the Starnberger See and Ammersee.

The city has six major breweries and a huge industry entirely devoted to the consumption of beer, including beer gardens, beer halls, beer-stein shops, beer-brewing monasteries, and enormous beerfests. In Munich, the subject of beer demands a seriousness one normally associates with death and taxes (in fact Müncheners have nicknamed beer "liquid bread"). The brewing process stems from a long tradition ensuring high quality and pure ingredients.

Like all big cities, Munich has its share of skeletons in its closet: Just ask anyone who's tried to look for affordable housing, or one of the growing number of people who can't afford *any* housing and make their homes in the streets. Munich's past has also left the city's reputation somewhat tarnished and some tourists wary; Hitler's first attempt to seize power (known as the Beer Hall Putsch), in 1923, was quickly crushed, but he later regained his standing, thanks to reactionary Munich, which he called "the capital of the movement."

Basics

AMERICAN EXPRESS This office holds mail for cardholders and will give you a bad exchange rate (somewhat offset by the fact that they charge no commission) for your American Express traveler's checks. *Promenadepl. 6, tel. 089/21990. Open weekdays 9–5:30, Sat. 9–noon.*

BUCKET SHOPS **Studiosus Studienreisen** offers discount plane tickets to those under 26 flying to the United States or within Europe. To buy an International Student (ISIC) card or youth-hostel (IYHF) card, go downstairs with a picture, dated proof of student status, and DM 10. You can also get tickets to mainstream plays at the office on Amalienstraße; both cards and theater tickets are available in the morning only. *Amalienstr. 73, tel. 089/500–60542; cards and theater tickets, tel. 089/280768. Open weekdays 9:30–noon. Luisenstr. 43, tel. 089/500602. Open weekdays 9:30–6, Sat. 9:30–12:30.*

Oktoberfest

The world's largest folkfest started as a wedding celebration in 1810, when Crown Prince Ludwig (later King Ludwig I) married Princess Therese of Saxe-Hildburghausen. They named the fields where the party was held Theresienwiese (Therese's Meadow), after the princess, and added horse races, an agricultural show, an amusement park, and seven huge, out-of-control tents. Most of these features have now disappeared or been eclipsed by the big theme of this party: beer. Go to Oktoberfest today, and you'll still find the seven tents, or rather seven international pickup halls full of bloated people drowning in beer and thumping on tabletops to the tune of traditional oompah music. Sounds fun, doesn't it?

Traditionally, the mayor taps the first keg on opening day, always a Saturday, at noon. During the 16-day celebration, which starts in late September and ends on the first Sunday of October, the tents open at noon on weekdays, 10:30 on weekends. Everything except a few restaurants shuts down by 11:30 PM, but, if you're still conscious, slosh on over to one of the beer halls (see ***Bars and Beer Halls in After Dark***, below) ***with the diehards. On the last day, thousands of people from around Europe take part in a parade with traditional costumes and bands.***

BUREAUX DE CHANGE The best hours and deal for changing money are at the **Deutsche Verkehrsbank** (Bahnhofpl. 2, tel. 089/551–0837), in the main train station, open daily 6 AM–11:30 PM. You can change as many traveler's checks as you want for a flat DM 3.75 commission if you flash a copy of Eur-Aide's monthly publication *Inside Track* (*see* Visitor Information, *below*); otherwise, they take a steep DM 7.50. You can also get credit-card advances here. Big banks, nice hotels, and exchange services also change money. Most banks are open weekdays 8:30 or 9 to 3:30 or 4 (Thursday until 6), mostly closing for lunch between 12:30 and 1:30. Often they charge a commission for each traveler's check, so traveling with smaller denominations can get expensive. Go to a smaller exchange service if you are changing only one check. Try **Schmidts Wechselstube** (Bahnhofpl. 5, enter at Dachauerstr., tel. 089/557870), which charges DM 2 per check, or **Wechselstube Schwarz** (Schillerstr. 3A, tel. 089/598236). An **automatic exchange machine** at the end of Tal (near Marienplatz) spits out DMs for hard cash in other currencies.

CONSULATES

United States. *Königinstr. 5, tel. 089/28881. Open weekdays 8 AM–11:30 PM.*

Canada. *Tal 29, tel. 089/222661. Open Mon.–Thurs. 9–noon, 2–5; Fri. 9–1:30.*

United Kingdom. *Amalienstr. 62, tel. 089/211090.*

Ireland. *Mauerkircherstr. 1A, tel. 089/985723. Open weekdays 9–noon, 2–4.*

EMERGENCIES **Ambulance,** tel. 089/19222. **Police,** tel. 089/110. **Fire,** tel. 089/112. **Medical-emergency service,** tel. 089/558661. **Pharmacy-emergency service,** tel. 089/594475. **Rape hot line,** tel. 089/763737. **Lost and found** on street, U-Bahn, bus, or tram, tel. 089/2331; on German Federal Railways, tel. 089/128–6664; on all S-Bahns except S6, tel. 089/128–84409.

ENGLISH BOOKS AND NEWSPAPERS **Anglia English Bookshop** is jammed with new and used books published in Great Britain and the United States, but don't expect any bargains. *Schellingstr. 3, tel. 089/283642. Open weekdays 9–6:30, Sat. 10–2.*

Sussmann's International Press is a newsstand in the Hauptbahnhof that sells all sorts of foreign-language books, magazines, and newspapers, including *USA Today* and the monthly English-language publication *Munich Found. Tel. 089/551–1717. Open daily 7 AM–10:45 PM.*

LUGGAGE STORAGE The **Hauptbahnhof**'s lockers, opposite track 26, upstairs, and near the front entrance to the station by the erotic movie theater, are open 5 AM–midnight. Normal-size lockers go for DM 2, large ones DM 4, per day.

MAIL The **main post office** is Postamt 32, across from the Hauptbahnhof. You can buy stamps at counters 1–11, pick up faxes at 1–12, send faxes at 14–17, change traveler's checks at 1–17 (DM 3 charge per check), buy telephone cards at 18 and 18A, and pick up mail addressed to you poste restante at counters 16 and 17 between 7 AM and 10 PM. Regular services are available 7 AM–10:30 PM, but all night long you can buy stamps and phone cards or change money at the night counter. Mail sent anywhere outside Munich goes in the boxes marked ANDERE ORTE. *Bahnhofpl. 1, tel. 089/538–82732 or 089/538–82733. Poste restante: your name, Post Office Munich 32, Poste Restante.*

Other post offices are located at the **Hauptbahnhof** (main train station, 2nd floor, tel. 089/538–82720; open weekdays 7 AM–9 PM, Sat. 8–8), on **Residenzstraße** (tel. 089/538–82510; open weekdays 8–6, Sat. 8–1), and at the **Flughafen** (airport, tel. 089/970–1460; open Mon.–Sat. 7 AM–9 PM, Sun. and holidays 10–1 and 2–7:30). **Eur-Aide** also has a message service called Overseas Access (*see* Visitor Information, *below*).

MEDICAL AID There are **pharmacies** on Schleißheimerstraße 201 (tel. 089/308-6731), Neuhauserstraße 8 (tel. 089/260–3021), and Schützenstraße 5/Bayerstraße 4 (tel. 089/557661). If you need an English-speaking **doctor** or **dentist,** the American consulate (Königinstr. 5, tel. 089/28881) and the British consulate (Amalienstr. 62, tel. 089/211090) can make recommendations.

PHONES You can dial anywhere in Germany and to more than 180 countries without operator assistance. If you do need help, you can reach a local operator at 1188 or 01188 and an international operator at 00118. **Telefonkarten,** sold at the Hauptbahnhof's bank and post office, give you DM 60 worth of calls for DM 50. If you don't have a calling card from home, these phone cards can make calling long distance a lot simpler.

Local calls from a phone booth cost DM .30 for the first three minutes. Each three-minute unit thereafter is also DM .30. If you wish to make more than one call and have money left in the telephone, don't hang up after the first call; tap the hang-up button, and dial again when you hear the dial tone.

VISITOR INFORMATION At the **Fremdenverkehrsamt,** in the train station, you can pick up a free city map, make room reservations (DM 5 charge), and purchase helpful publications like the *Monatsprogramm* (*Monthly Program,* DM 2), which lists everything from hotels, restaurants, and post offices to concerts, sports, and art exhibits. Although the listings are in German, English translations of the headings are given, so you at least know what you're looking at. You can also get a list of accommodations (DM .50), the "Young People's Guide to Munich" (DM 1), a booklet with pictures of Munich and interesting highlights (DM 1), or one on museums and galleries (DM 1). The office provides no train information. *Opposite track 11 in Hauptbahnhof, tel. 089/239–1256. Open Mon.–Sat. 8 AM–10 PM, Sun. 11–7.*

For train information, try **Reisezentrum** (*see* Coming and Going by Train, *below*) or the efficient office of **Eur-Aide,** which performs a variety of services. American owner Alan Wissenburg and his English-fluent employees make room reservations (DM 6 charge), organize trips to Dachau and castles, and operate a convenient message-and-mail service. *Along wall by track 11 in Hauptbahnhof, tel. 089/593889. Open May, daily 7:30–11:30, 1–4:30; June–Oktoberfest, daily 7:30–11:30, 1–6.*

Other tourist offices, not all of which make room reservations, include the **Zentral Fremdenverkehrsamt** (Sendlinger Str. 1, tel. 089/23911), around the corner from Marienplatz; an airport booth (tel. 089/975–92815); and one at **Rindermarkt/Pettenbeckstrabe** (tel. 089/239–1272).

For information on the Bavarian mountain region south of Munich, contact the **Fremdenverkehrsband München-Oberbayern** (Upper Bavarian Regional Tourist Office, Sonnenstr. 10, tel. 089/597347). Finally, you can get 24-hour information in English about museums and galleries by calling 089/239162; for info on palaces and other sights, call 089/239172.

COMING AND GOING

BY PLANE Munich is well served by a huge new airport, the **Franz Josef Strauss Flughafen,** 28 kilometers (17 miles) northeast of the city. Many major airlines, including **Lufthansa** (tel. 089/977–2544), serve the airport; for all other general flight information call 089/975–21313. The airport also has a **tourist-information office** (tel. 089/975–92815, open Mon.–Sat. 8:30 AM–10 PM, Sun. 1–10), which will book rooms for DM 5; a **bank** that exchanges money and traveler's checks for a charge of DM 5; and 24-hour **luggage lockers** cost DM 3–DM 6, depending on size.

➢ **AIRPORT TRANSPORT** • S-Bahn line 8 links the airport with the Hauptbahnhof, in the center of Munich. Trains run about every 20 minutes 3:15 AM–12:15 AM; single fare to the airport is DM 10 (for discount tickets, *see* Getting Around by Public

Transportation, *below*). The trip into town takes about 40 minutes. If you want to take a **taxi,** set aside about DM 90.

BY TRAIN The **Hauptbahnhof,** Munich's main train station, is dirty and chaotic, albeit laden with fast-food joints. It handles most domestic and international train traffic into and out of Munich. The **Ostbahnhof** (East Train Station) sometimes serves as a departure point, but it's mainly just a U-Bahn and S-Bahn stop. The S-Bahn stop **Pasing** is a connecting point for some destinations.

Beware of line-cutting Bavarian-style—they're experts at squeezing people to the side, especially unsuspecting tourists.

A post office, a DVB bank, lockers, and tourist offices are conveniently located in the Hauptbahnhof, *the* center of public transportation: U-Bahn lines 1, 2, 4, and 5 and S-Bahn lines 1–8 run underneath the station, and you can also get Trams 19, 20, 25, and 27 and Bus 58 from here. The station lies east of the city center; from the main entrance, at Bahnhofplatz outside the DVB Bank, you can cross the street onto Schützenstraße, which becomes the main pedestrian zone and leads to Marienplatz, the main city square (a 10- to 15-minute walk, or two stops on the S-Bahn).

Some destinations and one-way sample fares from Munich include: Vienna (9 trains per day, DM 83), Paris (8 per day, DM 171), Prague (8 per day, DM 94), London (9 per day, DM 320), Copenhagen (10 per day, DM 277), Budapest (8 per day, DM 126), Amsterdam (18 per day, DM 205), Oberammergau (14 per day, DM 21), Berlin (30 per day), Frankfurt (34 per day). For train information and reservations, try the chaotic **Reisezentrum** office across from track 26. You can find out times and prices for specific destinations by picking up the schedules printed on scraps of paper under **Städteverbindungen Inland,** for domestic routes, or **Städteverbindungen Ausland,** for international connections. Save yourself time and frustration by calling 089/554141 (for fare information), or 089/19419 (for other information); the staff speaks English.

BY BUS **Europabus,** which also operates under the name of **Touring,** offers service to destinations throughout Europe, including Greece, Scandinavia, and Turkey, although none to Austria or Switzerland. Traveling by bus usually costs less and takes longer than train travel, and some destinations aren't accessible from Munich—you have to change buses in another city, like Frankfurt, first. The best deal is for those who have a Eurailpass or a German DB Rail pass; you can join Europabus's Romantic Road trip for free. The trip begins in Füssen and ends in Frankfurt, but you can hop on board at Munich, the midpoint. It's about an 11-hour tour, passing through a variety of landscapes and historic towns. A similar bus route, the Castle Road, runs from Munich to Heidelberg or Mannheim and is also free for certain pass holders and discounted for students under 26. InterRail pass holders get a 50% reduction on both tours. Call **Deutsche Touring** (tel. 089/591–82425) for more information on these tours and other destinations. One-way ticket prices are as follows: Berlin, DM 66; Paris, DM 100; Frankfurt, DM 92; Budapest, DM 105. For tickets and information, you can also visit the bus-line office in the Hauptbahnhof (Arnulfstr. 3). It's open weekdays 8–7, Saturday 8:30–7, and Sunday and holidays 4:30–6:30.

HITCHHIKING You can hitch at the entrance to the Autobahns, but don't stand beyond the blue signs with the picture of the road or white car. If you're heading for Salzburg, Vienna, or Italy, you can get to Autobahn A–8 by taking the U1 or U2 to Karl-Preis-Platz. To get to Stuttgart, Karlsruhe, France, or England, you can get to A–8 heading west by taking the U1 to Rotkreuzplatz, Tram 12 to Amalienburgstraße, then Bus 73 or 75 to Blulenburgstraße; or catch the S2 to Obermenzing and hop on one of those same buses. If you're traveling north (to Nürnberg, for example), you can get to Autobahn A–9 by taking the U6 to Studentenstadt, then walking 500 yards to the entrance of the Frankfurter Ring (Outer Ring) Autobahn. To get to Autobahn 96 toward Lindau, Lake Constance, and Switzerland, take the U4 or U5 to Heimeranplatz, then Bus 33 to Siegenburgerstraße. For Füssen and Garmisch-Partenkirchen, you can get to

Autobahn A-95 by taking the U6 to Westpark, then Bus 33 to Luise-Kiesselbach-Platz.

BY MITFAHRGELEGENHEIT Ride-share destinations and fares from Munich include: Berlin, DM 52; Frankfurt, DM 39; Hamburg, DM 63; Leipzig, DM 44; Amsterdam, DM 71; Barcelona, DM 110; Florence, DM 59; Paris, DM 76; Prague, DM 39; Vienna, DM 42; Salzburg, DM 21. Call two to seven days in advance for information about possible rides. There are a number of agencies you can try.

Mitfahrzentrale. *Lämmerstraße 4, tel. 089/594561. Exit Hauptbahnhof at Arnulfstraße, cross street and walk down Pfefferstraße, turn left on Hirtenstraße and right on Lämmerstraße. Open daily 8–7.*

Känguruh. *Amalienstraße 87, tel. 089/19444. U3 or U6 to Universität, exit to Schellingstraße, turn right on Amalienstraße and left on Amalienpassage. Open weekdays 8:30–7, Sat. 9–3, Sun. and holidays 10–3.*

Frauenmitfahrzentrale. This agency matches women drivers and passengers. *Klenzestr. 57B, tel. 089/201–6510. U1 or U2 to Fraunhoferstr. Open weekdays 9–1, 3–7.*

GETTING AROUND

Since downtown Munich is only a mile square, it's easy to explore on foot. Pedestrian streets link Karlsplatz, by the Hauptbahnhof, to Marienplatz and the Viktualienmarkt, extending north around the Frauenkirche and up to Odeonsplatz. Sights outside the city center can easily be reached on Munich's excellent transportation system. Public transport in Munich includes the **U-Bahn** (the underground subway), **S-Bahn** (suburban rail system), **Straßenbahn** (trams), and buses. Together, the U-Bahn and S-Bahn cover the inner city well, and the S-Bahn outlying places like the airport, Dachau, Starnberger See, and Herrsching. Trams and buses are less efficient, since they can get stuck in traffic, but they do serve more stops.

BY PUBLIC TRANSPORTATION Despite the apparent lack of law enforcement on the U-Bahn and S-Bahn, you really should invest in a valid ticket, because plainclothes checkers do make the rounds, and the dumb-tourist look doesn't always fly (they all speak English, as well). In general, anyone caught riding without a valid ticket is fined DM 60 on the spot, and if you don't pay, your next free ride may be to a German jail. Eurailpass, InterRail pass, and certain German DB Rail pass holders may ride the S-Bahn (but not the U-Bahn, trams, or buses) free.

Munich's public transport uses a fare system based on zones: The *Innenraum* (inner zone), indicated on the transport map by a blue ring, and the *Außenraum* (outer zone), anything outside the blue ring. Your ticket options begin with the *Einzelfahrkarte* (DM 2.50), good for one journey on all modes of transport as long as you're traveling in one direction, within a two-hour period, and within one zone. If you take a *Kurzstrecke* (short trip), defined as a maximum of four stops (only two of which can be on the U-Bahn or S-Bahn) within one hour, a ticket costs DM 1.30. For example, a trip from Marienplatz to the Hauptbahnhof or to Universität is considered a short trip.

If you think you'll be making a number of trips or you're traveling with another person (or your whole family), a *Tageskarte* (day ticket) is a much better deal, costing DM 8 for either the inner zone or the outer zone. For DM 16 per day, you can get the *Gesamttarifgebiet*, covering the inner city and outer regions. A one-day ticket covers two adults, three children, and a dog (no kidding) and is valid weekdays beginning at 9 AM and all day on weekends and holidays.

Your third option is to buy *Mehrfahrtenkarten* (strip tickets) that cost DM 10 for 10 strips. These are more worthwhile if you're traveling alone or not using public transportation that often. The number of strips canceled depends on how many zones you cross. If you're making a short trip, you only need to cancel one strip (equivalent to

Munich Public Transit System

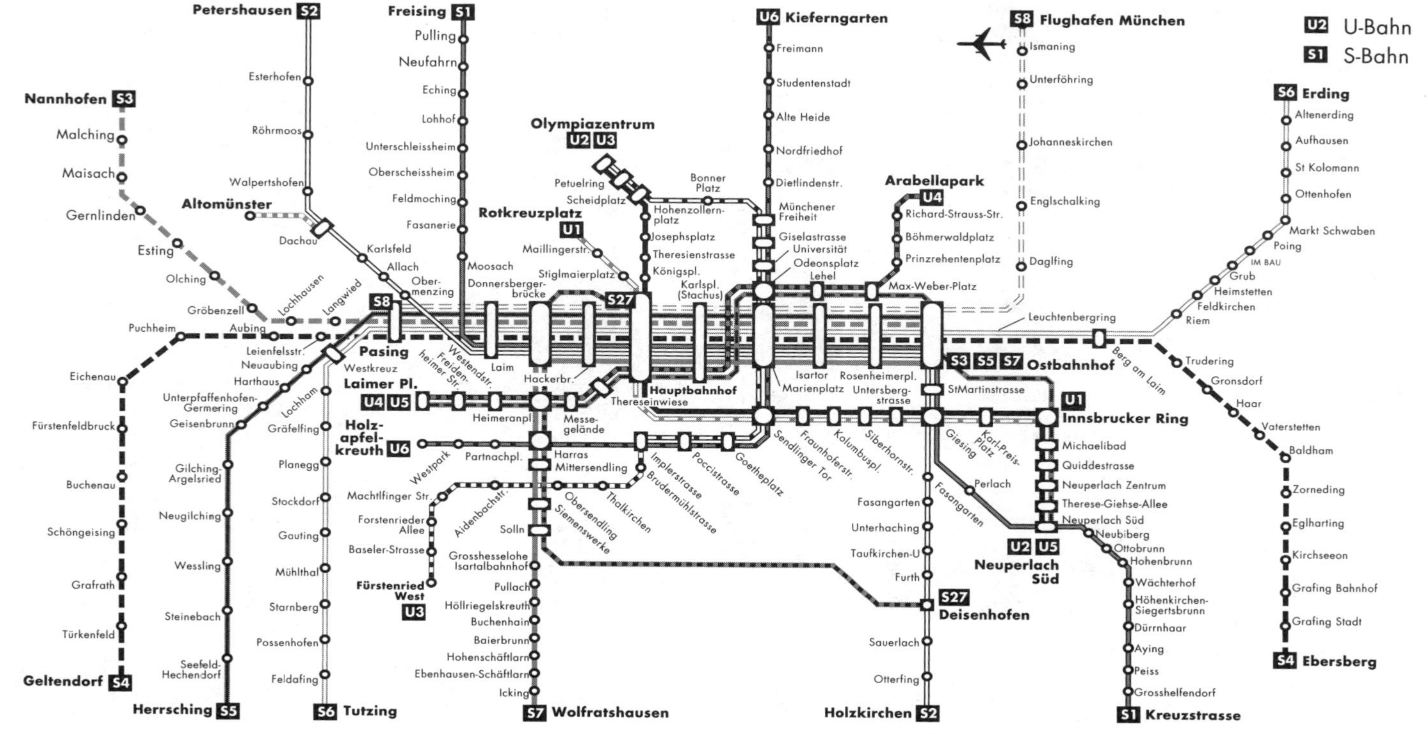

DM 1); otherwise, traveling in each zone uses two strips. To cancel a ticket or strip, punch it in the blue machines marked E, located by U-Bahn and S-Bahn stops and at platforms for trams and buses.

Finally, if you plan to stay in Munich for a longer period of time, the *Grüne Karte* (green ticket), a monthly pass, works out to be really cheap. It also covers three children and a dog and is valid weekdays beginning at 9 AM and all day on weekends and holidays. Prices range from DM 44 to DM 65, depending on the number of zones you want to travel.

Day, single, and strip tickets are sold from vending machines, by tram and bus drivers, at some tourist offices, and at kiosks with a white K on the window. Grüne Karte are available at all MVV ticket sales points. Don't forget to cancel all tickets before using them. If you're still confused, pick up a copy of "Rendezvous mit München" at the tourist-information center.

BY TAXI Taxis are not cheap, but they may be your only option if you're out after public transportation stops running, at about 1 AM. You can find the cream-color Mercedes cabs in front of the Hauptbahnhof or in front of large hotels or just hail them from the street. Fares start at DM 3.90, with an additional DM 2.10 per kilometer (⅔ mile), regardless of how many people share the ride. There is an additional charge if you call for a cab (tel. 089/21610).

BY BICYCLE The environmentally conscious city of Munich has tons of bike paths; a number of major streets, such as Leopoldstraße, have narrowed the lanes available for automobile traffic in favor of more bike lanes. The bike traffic is chaotic for people not used to it, but cycling is probably the best way to explore Munich and can be the most efficient way to get around. Pick up a copy of "Radl-Touren," a booklet with suggested biking tours, at the tourist office. It's in German, but the routes are clearly mapped out and easy to follow.

You can rent bikes for DM 4 per hour, or DM 20 per day, from **Radius Touristik** (Arnulfstr. 3, tel. 089/596113, open daily 9–6:30). at the Hauptbahnhof, or at the **Englischer Garten** (entrance at Veterinärstr. and Königinstr., tel. 089/566113, open daily 10:30–6 in good weather). You can also rent bikes at many **S-Bahn stations,** including Dachau, Herrsching, and Starnberg.

Another option is to join a three-hour guided cycling tour called "Munich by Bicycle." Tours, including bike rental, cost DM 28 and leave at 10:30 from the Radius Touristik office in the main train station. You can book a space through Eur-Aide (*see* Visitor Information in Basics, *above*) or by calling 089/596113.

Where to Sleep

Munich offers a variety of budget lodging options, but you may have a rough time finding a cheap place to stay during peak season if you fail to make reservations. Youth hostels and campgrounds are always the cheapest, but rooms in pensions and in some cheaper hotels are often worth the extra marks if you don't want to stress about your stuff getting ripped off or if you prefer some privacy and freedom (no curfew or lockouts, later checkout times). Some pensions charge an extra DM 2–DM 3.50 for a shower and DM 5–DM 6 for breakfast, or tack on a few marks for a laundry fee if you stay only one night. If you plan to stay in a pension, try to reserve at least a day in advance; otherwise, you'll waste time and money calling around or end up paying DM 5–DM 6 for the tourist offices to find you a room. Don't flake, because hotels will give your room away if you don't show by the stipulated time. Expect to pay at least DM 40–DM 50 for a single, DM 75–DM 100 for a double, and DM 35–DM 45 per person in triples and quads.

If those prices are beyond your modest means, camping is the way to go. The **Jugendlager am Kapuziner Hözl,** otherwise known as "the Tent," opens in late June and charges only DM 6 per night. Hostels are also an excellent deal if you're under 27, have a youth-hostel card, and don't mind curfews and hordes of young student groups. You can make reservations for most hostels by writing in advance, and Munich's hostels also accept fax reservations. Munich also has two youth hotels without age restrictions that are a step up from hostels in comfort and in price.

The area around the **Hauptbahnhof**—an amalgam of sex shops, electronics stores, and hotels—is a convenient base for exploring the city and has a large concentration of inexpensive pensions, but it is also one of the seediest parts of town. Both **Schwabing** and the **university district** are great neighborhoods for young people and for nightlife; those staying in the **city center** *(Stadtzentrum)* have easy access to some of the city's top attractions.

NEAR THE HAUPTBAHNHOF

UNDER DM 70 **Pension Augsburg.** Reception's on the third floor, and there's no elevator, but this plain pension is cheap and only three minutes from the station. What the place lacks in character it makes up for in price: Rooms without showers cost about DM 42 for singles, DM 64 for doubles, and DM 90 for triples. To use hall showers, you pay an additional DM 3.50. For rooms with an attached shower, add DM 10–DM 15. Breakfast is an extra DM 6. *Schillerstr. 18, tel. 089/597673. 26 rooms, some with bath. Reception open 7 AM–9 PM.*

Pension Schiller. Operated by a pleasant woman, this small pension is only a three-minute walk from the train station. Rooms are clean and spacious. Including hall showers, singles are DM 43, doubles range from DM 63 to DM 66, and triples cost DM 90. Add DM 2 per person if you're staying only one night. Breakfast in bed is yours for DM 6. *Schillerstr. 11, tel. 089/592435. 10 rooms, none with bath.*

UNDER DM 100 **Hotel-Pension Erika.** This popular pension has more to offer than most places in this price range. The management may be curt, but most of the rooms are huge, nicely decorated, and an excellent value. Without showers, singles are DM 50, doubles DM 80, and triples DM 115. Add DM 10 for rooms with showers, even more for rooms with full bath. Reservations are advised. *Landwehrstr. 8, tel. 089/554327. Exit train station from front (by DVB bank), turn right on Schillerstr., then left on Landwehrstr. 30 rooms, some with bath. Closed Dec. 20–Jan. 7.*

Pension Hungaria. Located in an unintimidating neighborhood north of the train station, this pension has sunny rooms at reasonable rates. Including breakfast, singles are DM 52, doubles DM 80–DM 85, triples DM 105, and quads DM 125. Use of the hall shower costs DM 3. Checkout is at 11:30, and reception is open 7:30 AM–10 PM. *Brienner Str. 42, near Augustenstr., tel. 089/521558. U1 to Stiglmaierpl. (1 stop from Hauptbahnhof), exit to Brienner Str.; or exit Hauptbahnhof to Dachauerstr., turn right on Augustenstr. 20 rooms, none with bath.*

Pension Luna. The little Finnish guy at the reception speaks a little bit of every language (meaning neither his English nor his German is very good), and he loves to practice the phrases he learns from travelers passing through. The large rooms have carpets and polished wood furniture. Prices include breakfast and hall showers. Singles go for DM 50, doubles DM 90. *Landwehrstr. 5, tel. 089/597833. Exit front of main train station (by DVB Bank), turn right on Schillerstr., then left on Landwehrstr. 16 rooms, some with bath.*

Pension Marie-Luise. Rooms here range from basic to lavish. The cheapest singles (DM 45) are bird cages, whereas some doubles (DM 118) have full bath, Oriental carpets, and a sofa. Rooms are generally tiny, especially the cheaper doubles. This pension isn't the best value, so use it when others are booked. The friendly management

Munich Lodging

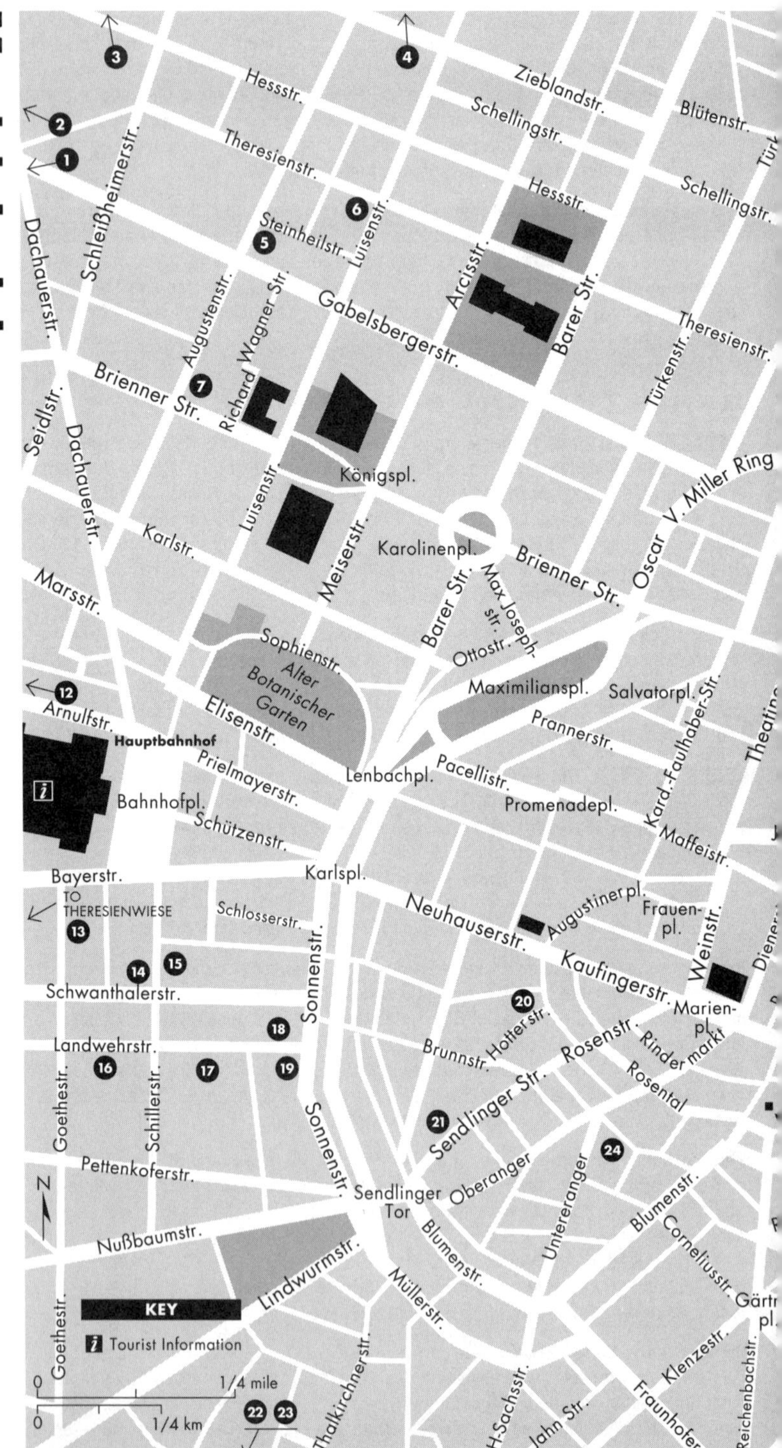

Munich Lodging

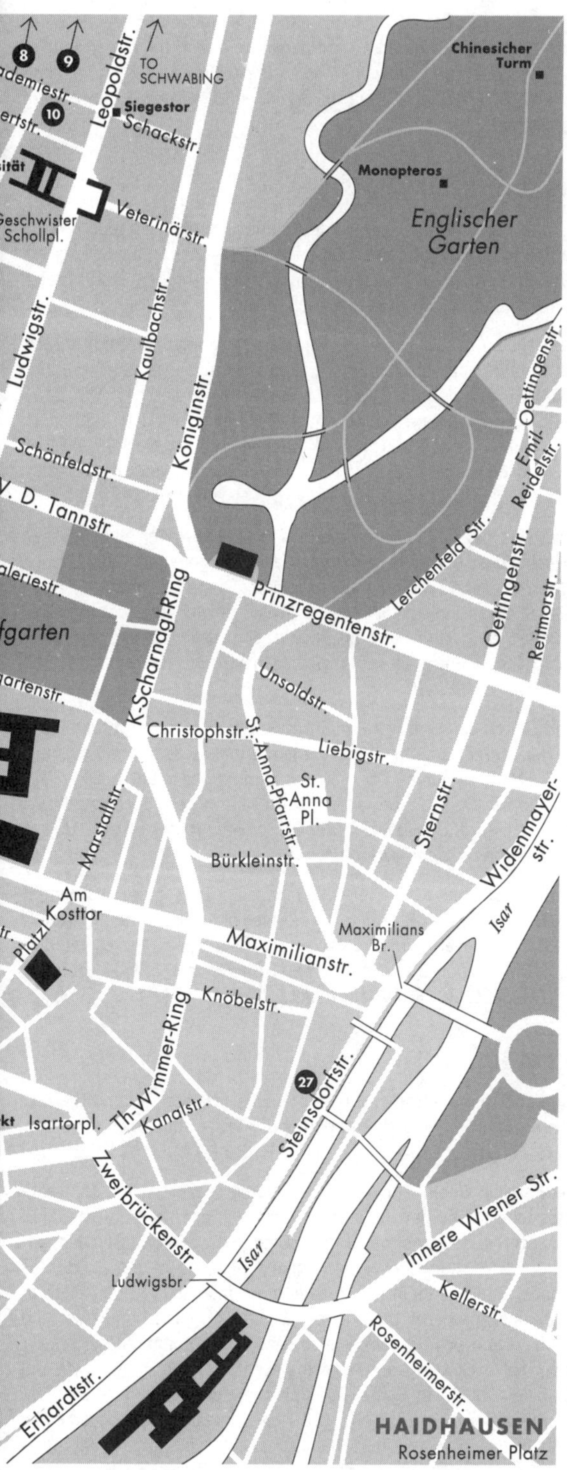

Camping München-Thalkirchen, **23**
Campingplatz München-Obermenzing, **12**
CVJM Jugendgästehaus, **17**
DJH Jugendherberge, **1**
Haus International, **3**
Hotel Atlanta, **21**
Hotel Blauer Bock, **24**
Hotel-Pension am Markt, **25**
Hotel-Pension am Siegestor, **10**
Hotel-Pension Beck, **27**
Hotel-Pension Erika, **18**
Jugendherberge Pullach, **26**
Jugendlageran Kapuziner Hözl ("The Tent"), **2**
Marienherberge, **13**
Pension am Kaiserplatz, **8**
Pension Augsburg, **14**
Pension Diana, **20**
Pension Doria, **9**
Pension Frank, **11**
Pension Geiger, **5**
Pension Hungaria, **7**
Pension Luna, **19**
Pension Marie-Luise, **16**
Pension Scheel, **4**
Pension Schiller, **15**
Pension Theresia, **6**
Youth Hostel Thalkirchen, **22**

speaks fluent English. Singles run DM 45–DM 55, and doubles without private bath run DM 83–DM 90. You'll pay DM 30 to add a third person to one of the larger double rooms. *Landwehrstr. 37 (reception at Landwehrstr. 33), tel. 089/596067. From front of main train station (by DVB Bank), turn right on Schillerstr., right on Landwehrstr. Refundable DM 10 key deposit.*

SCHWABING

About 1 kilometer (⅔ mile) north of the city center is the upscale neighborhood of Schwabing, formerly inhabited by artists and musicians. Today the area provides all kinds of entertainment for the crowds of students, Schicki-Mickis (Munich's odd breed of yuppies), and tourists who nightly converge in search of fun.

UNDER DM 80 **Hotel-Pension am Siegestor.** This pension near the southern end of Leopoldstraße has comfortable, carpeted rooms and competitive prices. Excluding breakfast, singles are DM 55 and doubles DM 80, and the few triples cost DM 110. Add DM 5 per person for breakfast and DM 2 to use the hall shower. Reception is open 7 AM–10 PM, and checkout is at 10:30 AM. *Akademiestr. 5, tel. 089/399550 or 089/399551. U3 or U6 to Universität, exit at Prof.-Huberpl., turn left by Siegestor onto Akademiestr. 20 rooms, none with bath.*

Pension am Kaiserplatz. This pension is recommended by everyone for good reason; not only is it one of the cheapest places to stay, but it also has gorgeous rooms decorated in Baroque, Art-Nouveau, and modern styles. Including breakfast and one shower, singles cost DM 39–DM 55, doubles DM 75, and triples DM 95. It's just a matter of good timing and luck to get a room here; advance phone reservations are usually not accepted, but call in the morning to see if people have left. *Kaiserpl. 12, tel. 089/349190. 10 rooms, some with bath.*

Pension Doria. This seven-room pension in the heart of Schwabing is a bit dilapidated but has great prices, if you can get a room. Breakfast is not included, but hall showers are. Singles run DM 45–DM 55, doubles DM 75, and a three-bed room is DM 100. *Hohenstaufenstr. 12, tel. 089/333872. U3 or U6 to Gieselastr., exit to Georgenstr., turn right on Friedrichstr., then left on Hohenstaufenstr.; or walk through Leopold Park after exiting at Gieselastr. 7 rooms, none with bath.*

UNDER DM 100 **Pension Scheel.** This overlooked pension in a quiet residential neighborhood is polished and modern yet retains an old-fashioned flair. The huge well-furnished double rooms that convert into triples are the best deals. Prices include breakfast, but there is a DM 2 charge for hall showers. Singles are DM 50, doubles DM 90. *Isabellastr. 31, tel. 089/271–3611. U2 to Josephspl. 10–15 beds.*

CITY CENTER

Close to the train station and many of the city's major sights, the area around the city center tends to be more expensive than neighborhoods farther out and is usually booked during high season.

UNDER DM 80 **Hotel-Pension Beck.** Although the building is more than 100 years old, the pension's rooms look totally new, and most come equipped with phones and TVs. Everyone who comes through seems to love this place, not only for its nicer-than-average rooms, but for its prime location within walking distance of the Deutsches Museum, the Hofbräuhaus, and Haidhausen. To save more moolah, you can cook in the kitchen, and Frau Beck emphasizes that her prices, which include breakfast and hall showers (if you don't have a private one), are somewhat negotiable and are never jacked up during Oktoberfest and other crowd-drawing events. Singles range from DM 48 to DM 58, doubles from DM 78 to DM 120. Triples, quads, and quints cost DM 40–DM 42 per person. Reception is open 7 AM–10:30 PM; checkout is supposed to be about 10:30 AM, but exceptions are sometimes made for guests who had a rough night at the Hofbräuhaus or Oktoberfest. *Thierschstr. 36, tel. 089/225768 or 089/220708. U4 or U5 to Lehel, exit toward Maxmonument, walk left from underground, cross intersection with Maxmonument; pension is on left. Tram 19, 20, or 27 to Maxmonument (on Maximilianstr.) or S-Bahn to Isartor. 44 rooms (100 beds), some with bath.*

Pension Frank. You'll have to compete with fashion models, student groups, and backpackers to get a room here, but if you get lucky you'll find yourself with a cheap room in a lively part of town. Without breakfast but including showers, doubles are DM 75, and three- to five-person rooms always go for DM 35 per head. This is one of the few pensions that will add a single traveler to a room with other people for a DM 35 charge. Add DM 5 per person if you want breakfast. *Schellingstr. 24, tel. 089/281451. U3 or U6 to Universität, exit on Schellingstr. 18 rooms, none with bath.*

Pension Theresia. This pension around the corner from Pension Geiger (*see below*) offers simple rooms with telephones and is an especially good choice if you intend to stay for more than one night. For two or more nights, including breakfast, singles range from DM 43 to DM 54 per night, doubles from DM 76 to DM 86, triples DM 110, and quads DM 122. Add DM 3 per person for one-night stays. The more expensive rooms have private showers; hall showers are an extra DM 3. Reception is open 6:30 AM–10 PM. Checkout is at 11 AM. *Luisenstr. 51, tel. 089/521250. U2 to Theresienstr., exit at SO (southeast) Augustenstr., walk straight, then turn right on Luisenstr. 25 rooms, some with bath.*

UNDER DM 100 **Hotel Atlanta.** Reopened in April 1992, after extensive remodeling, this excellent hotel has new management that actually appreciates the energy and liveliness of backpackers. The hotel is centrally located, every room has its own shower, and an all-you-can-eat breakfast buffet is included in the price. There are no single rooms. Doubles cost DM 80–DM 120; triples, quads, and quints are usually DM 40 per person. Checkout is at 11 AM, and reception is open 7 AM–midnight. *Sendlinger Str. 50, tel. 089/263605. U1 or U2 to Sendlinger Tor, exit at Sendlinger Str., pass through old arch. 20 rooms with bath.*

Hotel Blauer Bock. Rooms here aren't anything special, but the location—between the Viktualienmarkt and the Stadtmuseum, 300 yards south of Marienplatz—is prime. The prices, which include breakfast and hall showers, aren't bad, especially for doubles (rooms with a private bath are a different story). Singles without bath run DM 65–DM 105, doubles DM 90–DM 100, and triples (all with private bath) are DM 160–DM 175. Reception is open 24 hours; checkout is between 11 AM and noon. *Sebastianpl. 9 at Prälat-Zistl-Str., tel. 089/231780. 75 rooms, some with bath.*

Hotel-Pension am Markt. It's amazing that this busy hotel is so cheap. Right next to the Viktualienmarkt, it has a beautiful, old-fashioned breakfast area and clean medium-size rooms. A number of the celebrity faces whose pictures adorn the walls in the reception area actually stayed here. Singles are DM 56, doubles DM 98–DM 104 (without shower) to DM 130–DM 140 (with shower). Triples are DM 142 without shower, DM 170 with shower. Breakfast is included in the room rates. Call ahead for reservations. *Heiliggeiststr. 6, tel. 089/226844. 32 rooms, most with bath. Closed over Christmas.*

Pension Diana. This newly renovated pension off the main pedestrian zone is smack in the middle of the city center. Doubles are DM 90, triples DM 120, and quads DM 160, with showers and breakfast included. Reception is open 7 AM–10 PM, and checkout is by noon. *Altheimer Eck 15, tel. 089/260–3107. From main station or Karlsplatz, turn right off Neuhauserstr. (pedestrian st.) onto Eisenmannstr., then left on Altheimer Eck. 17 rooms.*

Pension Geiger. Within walking distance of the Alte and Neue Pinakotheks, Pension Geiger has modest but comfortable rooms. Prices include breakfast, but hall showers are an extra DM 2 if you don't have your own. Singles run DM 38–DM 49, doubles DM 78–DM 89. Triples are DM 120 and have a shower. *Steinheilstr. 1, tel. 089/521556.*

U2 to Theresienstr., from corner of Augustenstr. and Theresienstr. walk down Augustenstr. and turn left at Steinheilstr. 17 rooms, some with bath.

HOSTELS

CVJM (YMCA) Jugendgästehaus. Reservations are a good idea here, since this newly renovated hostel is popular with youth groups and backpackers alike. Each of the clean rooms comes with a large sink area, and showers and toilets are down the hall. Singles are DM 43, doubles DM 38 per person, and triples DM 35 per person. For stays of more than three nights, the price is a few marks lower. Breakfast is included and served in the adjoining restaurant, which also opens for dinner Monday–Saturday 6–11. There is a 12:30 AM curfew, hostel cards are not required, and a 14% tax is charged for those over 26. *Landwehrstr. 13, tel. 089/552–1410. Leave train station from front exit (by DVB bank), turn right on Schillerstr., then left on Landwehrstr. 80 beds.*

DJH Jugendherberge. Within easy reach of the main train station and close to a grocery store, bank, and 24-hour Laundromat, this hostel is convenient if you don't mind lots of people, noise, and a 7 AM wake-up call over loudspeakers. Don't come here craving a good night's sleep: With beds for more than 500 young people and lockout from 8:30 AM–noon, this place can unnerve a weary traveler. If you've got some energy, however, it's extremely easy to meet people here. Stay in Building A if you can; not only is it newer, roomier, and more comfortable than Buildings B and C, but the showers are on the same floor as the rooms, not in the basement. Lock your valuables in the safety boxes (refundable DM 50 deposit), since this place has a huge problem with theft. Only reservations made one month in advance or by fax are accepted. You must have a youth-hostel card (or buy one here for DM 30), and you cannot stay more than three nights, although exceptions are sometimes made. Prices, including sheets, breakfast, and locker for luggage storage, are DM 18.80 for a bed in the all-male, 40-person dorm room, or DM 20 for a bed in a four- to six-person room. There's a 1 AM curfew. You can use the pay phones and purchase snacks, lunch, and dinner here, too. Check-in begins at 10 AM, checkout by 8:30 AM. *Wendl-Dietrich-Str. 20, tel. 089/131156. 523 beds, none with bath.*

Haus International. For the price, this place is an expensive drag: curt service, bland rooms, and hordes of teenyboppers shrieking down the halls. Even the bathrooms attached to the dorm rooms turn out to be a pain in the ass, because the water-saving showers turn off every few seconds, so to keep them on, you have to back your behind against the knob (sounds inviting, doesn't it?). Besides a boppin' disco and swimming pool, the only redeeming quality about this place is the international crowd. The per-person rate for singles (including a shower and breakfast) is DM 69, doubles DM 59, triples DM 40, and quads DM 37. Without bathrooms, singles are DM 46 and doubles DM 44 per person. *Elisabeth Str. 87, tel. 089/120060. U6 to Münchener Freiheit, then Bus 33 to Barbara Str. 250 beds, some with bath.*

Jugendherberge Pullach (Burg Schwaneck). This castle–turned–youth hostel is worth a try if you can't get into one of the more central hostels and happen to adore hyperactive kids running up and down the halls. Per-person rates are DM 16.50 including breakfast; sheets cost DM 4.50 extra. There's an 11:30 PM curfew, and you must have a youth-hostel card and be under 27 to stay here. Reception is open 5 PM–11 PM. *Burgweg 4–6, tel. 089/793–0643. S7 to Pullach, then climb 10 min. to castle.*

Jugendherberge Thalkirchen. With the exception of the newly remodeled 15-bed dorms (which are also the only ones with lockers; DM 5 charge each time you open a locker), rooms here look much older than they are. You can leave your stuff in the storage room, but it's best to lock your valuables in the safety-deposit boxes (no charge). Although this hostel isn't centrally located, it does have singles, and you can make reservations by phone, by fax, or by writing in advance. Prices are per person rather than per room and include a breakfast buffet and hall showers. Coveted singles go for

DM 30, doubles DM 26, triples and quads DM 24, and six- to 15- person dorms are DM 22 per person. You can buy dinner for DM 8, and checkout is at 9 AM. *Miesingstr. 4, tel. 089/723–6550. From train station, U1 or U2 to Sendlinger Tor, then U3 toward Forstenrieder Allee to Thalkirchen. 344 beds.*

Marienherberge. You wouldn't expect to find a Catholic nun–run hostel around the train station, but it's here—only a minute's walk from the station and a few doors down from such attractions as Sexyland and a variety of erotic toy stores. Despite its location, in a sleazy, sex-infested part of town, this women-only hostel is actually safe, clean, and cheap. Singles are DM 31, doubles and triples are DM 27 per person, and a bed in a six-person room costs DM 25. Prices include breakfast, which ends at 8 AM sharp. Reception opens weekdays at 6 AM, weekends and public holidays at 7 AM. Check out by 9 AM. There's a midnight curfew. *Goethestr. 9, tel. 089/555891. Exit main train station at Bayerstr. 25 beds (55 between Aug. 1 and Sept. 10), none with bath.*

CAMPGROUNDS

Camping München-Thalkirchen. Munich's most centrally located (and most crowded) campground is 4 kilometers (2½ miles) from the city center. Sites cost DM 5.50 per adult, DM 2 per child, and DM 5.50 per tent. *Zentralländstr. 49, tel. 089/723–1707. U3 toward Forstenrieder Allee, get off at Thalkirchen (Tierpark), then Bus 57 to last stop. Closed Nov.–early Mar.*

Campingplatz München-Obermenzing. This campsite is situated in a huge park some 900 yards from the beginning of the Autobahn toward Stuttgart. Adults pay DM 6 per night; children ages 2 to 12 stay for DM 3.50. *Lochhausener Str. 59, tel. 089/811–2235. Closed Nov.–early Mar.*

Jugendlager am Kapuziner Hözl. This oversize circus tent, which enthusiasts call "Germany's Biggest Slumber Party," is open from late June through August. A camping spot, with blankets, mats, and a hot shower, costs only DM 6 per night. Lock your stuff up at the train station, but bring your passport with you. Reception opens at 5 PM. *Franz-Schrank-Str., tel. 089/141–4300. U1 to Rotkreuzpl., then Tram 12 to Botanischer Garten. 420 spaces.*

ROUGHING IT

If you're hard up for money or if you pop in on an extra-congested weekend, you can try camping along the Isar; some stragglers pitch tents and barbecue on the grassy bank in front of the Volksbad (Public Baths) by the Ludwigsbrücke (Ludwig's Bridge). You can also try the southern stretch around Thalkirchen and the zoo (take Bus 57 from Sendlinger Tor to Thalkirchen or Bus 52 from Marienplatz to Alemannenstraße) or the more northern banks toward Hirschau and Studentenstadt. Other desperate adventurers have slept in the Englischer Garten (*see* Parks and Gardens in Exploring Munich, *below*), but it's not a good idea to try any of these stunts on your own, if at all. Patrols do cruise around, although it's more likely that you'll get a slap on the wrist than a hefty fine. If you have a train ticket, you can spend the night in the train station without being hassled. During Oktoberfest the station's packed and totally chaotic; lock up your valuables.

Food

For the cheapest grub in Munich, stop at an *Imbiß* or *Steh-café*, stand-up snack bars where you can feed on cheap Bavarian specialties like wurst and *Leberkäs* (*see* box, *below*). Imbißes cluster in the Viktualienmarkt (*see* Worth Seeing in Exploring Munich, *below*), which also has tons of fruit-and-vegetable stalls. **Danmark,** in the Karlsplatz underground shopping center, has everything from pizza (DM 3.50) and cheeseburgers (DM 3.20) to chop suey (DM 7) and all-natural fruit drinks (DM 3). Butcher shops are an excellent budget option, selling an array of cheeses, breads, and pre-made sandwiches (DM 3–DM 5.50); some have salad bars, as well. Otherwise, scarf with students at one of the ***Mensen,*** or university cafeterias (Leopoldstr. 13, U3 or U6 to Gieselastr.; Arcisstr. 17, by the Pinakotheks), and pay DM 2.70–DM 4 for a meal, including entrée and

How to Eat Like a Bavarian

Typical Bavarian Brotzeit *(snacks), meals, and desserts include:*

- Bratwurst: *grilled or fried pork sausages.*
- Hax'n: *juicy, roasted* Schweinshaxe *(leg of pork) or* Kalbshaxe *(leg of veal), served with dumplings and sauerkraut.*
- Knödel *(dumplings) come in different forms:* Leberknödel *are liver dumplings (the soup* Leberknödelsuppe *is very popular),* Kartoffelknödel *are made of potatoes, and* Semmelknödel *are made of white bread, egg, and parsley and are eaten with lots of hearty Bavarian meat dishes.*
- Leberkäs: *warm slabs of ground beef, bacon, and pork served with sweet* Senf *(mustard).*
- Obatzta: *cheese mixed with chopped onions, egg yolk, paprika, and other spices.*
- Radi: *thinly sliced white radish, dipped in salt and often eaten as a snack in a beer garden.*
- Sauere Züngerl: *pickled lung.*
- Sauerkraut: *salty, shredded white cabbage.*
- Schweinebraten: *roasted pork.*
- Schweinswürste: *small, fried pork sausages, ordered by the pair and eaten with mustard and sauerkraut.*
- Tellerfleisch: *boiled beef, sliced and served with horseradish and boiled potatoes.*
- Weißwürste: *sausages made of veal, lemon, and parsley. These traditionally are eaten before noon, but they're served throughout the day on most menus. Dip them in Senf and have a* Brezel *(pretzel) and some* Weißbier *(light beer made of wheat) on the side.*
- Wollwürste, *or* G'schwollene: *fried veal sausages.*
- Auszogne, *or* Schmalznudel: *flat, deep-fried, greasy doughnuts.*
- Dampfnudeln: *sweet dumplings in vanilla sauce.*
- Krapfen: *doughnuts filled with marmalade.*

side dishes. Both are open November–July, weekdays 11 AM–1:45 PM. In the quarters just south of the train station, takeout Turkish Döner Kebabs will cost you about DM 5. Of the numerous cuisines available around town, Italian is the cheapest and Bavarian the liveliest. The area around the university has lots of smoky, relatively cheap, student restaurant-pubs. The best is **Gaststätte Engelsburg** (Türkenstr. 51), with pizzas and Bavarian food for DM 9–DM 15, but **Atzinger** (Schellingstr. 9) and **Türkenhof** (Türkenstr. 78) are good, too. All are open daily 10 AM–1 AM. **Da Enzo Trattoria** (Wendl-Dietrich-Str. 4, by Rotkreuzpl.), outside the city center, will sell you a big pizza to go for DM 6. A provisional note to the following restaurant reviews: The price range at a lot of restaurants can vary hugely, from a few marks for the standard wursts that appear on almost all menus, to items you'll never be able to afford.

CITY CENTER

If you're looking to try some hearty Bavarian fare, you'll find Munich's most popular Bavarian locales clustered around the city center, especially in and around the pedestrian zone.

UNDER DM 15 **Augustiner Bierhalle.** Although it's a pleasure year-round, sipping a beer here is best in summer, when you can kick back outside with a plate of *Abgeröstete Kartoffel und Semmelknödel* (DM 9.50), something like a ham-and-potato omelet, while you watch people stroll the main pedestrian zone. With good timing, you'll even get free, bizarre entertainment from street performers. The restaurant next door is more expensive, so make sure you're at the right place. *Neuhauserstr. 16, between Karlspl. and Marienpl., tel. 089/551–99257. Closed Sun.*

Buxs. The soup, salad, dessert, and juice selection in this self-service restaurant-café changes daily, but it's always huge. It costs DM 2.40–DM 2.70 per 100 grams, roughly DM 10–DM 15 for an average-size meal. *Frauenstr. 9, by Viktualienmarkt, tel. 089/229482. Closed Sun.*

Fraunhofer. Named after a famous German scientist, this lively *Gaststätte* (guest house) with a beer-hall feel is frequented by earthy intellectuals socializing and drinking over a hearty meal. You won't rub elbows with tourists in this joint. Try the *Zwei Paar Schweinswürste* (pork sausages), for something affordable and typically Bavarian (DM 8.80). Vegetarian dishes are also available, and most entrées cost between DM 9 and DM 18. If you don't feel like forking over the marks for dinner, drop in for a mug of Optimator, a dark, strong beer (DM 5 for ½ quart) that lives up to its cool name. *Fraunhoferstr. 9, tel. 089/266460. No lunch.*

Nürnberger Bratwurst Glöckl am Dom. Located by the Frauenkirche cathedral, this restaurant is a great pit stop for a beer or pair of Weißwürste (DM 5.40), or a bigger meal, any time of day. Entrées cost DM 12–DM 20. *Frauenpl. 9, tel. 089/220385. Closed Sun.*

UNDER DM 20 **Weisses Bräuhaus.** You won't find lederhosen or oompah bands here, but you will get a glimpse of where real Müncheners go. Large, crowded, and energetic, with the typical wood tables and deer antlers on the wall, this long-standing Bavarian restaurant is worth a stop, even though entrées may be a bit pricey for many budget travelers. The specialties, hidden behind less-than-savory names, are filling and delicious. Some local favorites include ½ *Kalbskopf gebräunt mit Ochsenauge und Kartoffelsalat* (half head of veal with a fried egg and potato salad, DM 16.50) and *Kalbsherz vom Rost* (grilled heart of veal, DM 19). Try the *Bayerischer Bauernschmaus* (DM 18.50) for a medley of traditional Bavarian food. For the less daring, familiar dishes such as omelets and spaghetti Bolognese (DM 10.50) are available. If you're up for a drink (or two or three), try the *Schneider Weisse*, a dark white beer. *Im Tal 10, between Marienpl. and Isartorpl., tel. 089/299875.*

Zum Franziskaner. This is one of Munich's fancier Bavarian restaurants, and it's got the prices to prove it. The food is excellent—try the delicate and delicious Weißwürste. Pastas and vegetarian dishes range from DM 12 to DM 16, wursts start at DM 6, and entrées cost from DM 13 (Leberkäs with salad) to DM 28 (Kalbshaxe, or leg of veal). *Residenzstr. 9/Perusastr. 5, tel. 089/231–8120.*

HAIDHAUSEN

You'll find few tourist-oriented restaurants and many more ethnically diverse ones on the streets of Haidhausen, although prices aren't particularly cheap. Besides serving food, the places listed below also provide a lively atmosphere for hanging out and drinking.

UNDER DM 15 **El Español.** The food in this Spanish restaurant-bar is excellent, whether you want to splurge a bit (try one of the fish dishes, DM 19–DM 32) or just snack on *tapas* (Spanish hors d'oeuvres, starting at DM .50 per piece). Come when live performers serenade the tables, usually a few times a week between 9 and 10; call for an exact schedule. *Pariser Str. 46, tel. 089/488496. No lunch.*

Haidhausen Augustiner. This restaurant-bar has a huge menu with awesome daily specials and tons of salads, pastas, and meaty dishes. *Wörthstr. 34, tel. 089/480–2594.*

Kytaro. Munich's best-known Greek restaurant isn't cheap, but it's always packed, especially on the back terrace during summer. Lots of smoke and the music of occasional live bands will accompany your meal. Try one of the lamb dishes (DM 14.50–DM 19.50). *Innere Wiener Str. 36, tel. 089/480–1176. No lunch.*

Lissabon Café/Bar. Musicians and an international crowd frequent this Portuguese bar-café, and a couple of times a week you'll find live Latin and jazz music, too, for no cover. Try a large glass of *galao*, a creamy Portuguese coffee drink, or the delicious and filling *caldo verde* soup, another traditional specialty. Vegetarian dishes (DM 13–DM 14), salads (DM 7–DM 15), and meatier plates (DM 16–DM 28) are also served. A half quart of beer starts at DM 4.50. *Breisacherstr. 22, tel. 089/448–2274. No lunch.*

CAFES

Many of Munich's cafés double as bars and evening hangouts, especially on Leopoldstraße (*see* After Dark, *below*).

Baader Café. It gets pretty kickin' in here at night, and you can't go wrong with cheap beer and food and a diverse clientele. This may be the only place in Munich where you can get a BLT (DM 7). Come on Sunday morning for a great buffet (small, DM 8.50; large, DM 14). *Baaderstr. 47, tel. 089/202–1481. U1 or U2 to Fraunhoferstr.*

Café Größenwahn. You can walk in here alone, do whatever you damn well please, and not feel like a total dolt. You can't do that in the cafe's in Schwabing. This place is relatively cheap (coffee, DM 3; Brie sandwiches, DM 6; cereal with fresh fruit and yogurt, DM 6), has an intellectual atmosphere, and plays great tunes. Dress in black, and have that sixth espresso, you displaced Bohemian, you. Supposedly, the Communists who took power in Munich for a few short weeks in the 1920s hung out here. *Lothringerstr. 11, tel. 089/448–5035.*

Café im Stadtmuseum. This café attracts lots of students and artsy types, and really comes alive in the evening. The *Milchkaffee* (DM 3.50) is extra big, and beer runs about DM 4.10 for ½ quart. Menu options range from salads to soup to sandwiches and will run you DM 5–DM 13. *St.-Jakobspl. 1, in Stadtmuseum, tel. 089/266949. No Mon. lunch.*

Chain Restaurants Can Help Rein in Your Budget

One way to keep costs down in Munich, one of the most expensive cities in Germany, is to eat at one of its numerous chain restaurants. The term might inspire ugly visions of Burger Kings, but these places actually have some cheap, decent food to offer.

- Bella Italia. *The food is awesome and the prices just as good. Plus, this chain is located in all the right spots—on the main strip of Leopoldstraße across the street from U-Bahn stop Giselastraße, by the university (Türkenstraße 50), near Marienplatz (Sendlingerstraße 66), and in Haidhausen (Weissenburgerstraße). Pizzas start at about DM 6 and pastas at DM 5.50. Beer is cheap, too; a ½-quart Radler (beer with lemon soda) is DM 3. To finish, have a little slice of heaven—rich* tiramisù *(mascarpone and sponge cake)—for DM 5.*
- Café Richart. *These seem to crop up everywhere, offering slightly different menu options at different locations; the one in the main pedestrian zone (Neuhauserstr. 53) sells sumptuous, affordable pastries. Give in to the strawberry-caramel cake (DM 3.40), or have a snack at the cheap Steh-café, which also serves your basic German breakfast (rolls, jam, and coffee) for a hard-to-beat DM 4.50.*
- Münchner Suppenküche. *This cheap, health-conscious chain, whose name means "Munich Soup Kitchens," offers filling soups and sandwiches for prices almost unheard of in Munich, and you even get to sit down. Soups vary daily, but some selections include minestrone (DM 6.70), Leberknödelsuppe (DM 4.90),* Tomatencremesuppe *(cream-of-tomato soup, DM 5.90), and* Sauerkrautsuppe *(sauerkraut soup, DM 6.30). Sandwiches cost DM 3.90–DM 4.50, and you can fill your own salad dishes (small, DM 5; large, DM 7.50). A really good deal is the* Schmankerl, *a pair of Weißwürste, Brez'n, and a Weißbier for DM 7.50. The branch at Schellingstraße 24 (tel. 089/765857), by the university, cuts students a special deal. On weekdays you can order a* Studententopf, *the soup of the day plus bread, for DM 5. They also sell their sandwiches for half price between 6 PM and 7 PM. Other branches at Feilitzschstraße 7 (by Münchener Freiheit), Kreuzstraße (by Sendlinger Tor), and Viktualienmarkt.* Closed Sun. No Sat. dinner.
- Wienerwald. *Wienerwalds are a classier Bavarian version of Denny's, but the food is actually tasty and a relative bargain. Half a grilled chicken is DM 9.30. At Steinsdorfstraße, fix yourself a salad (small, DM 5.20; large, DM 8.20) or inhale a schnitzel or burger (DM 4.50–DM 7) in the adjoining Imbiß. Look in the phone book for many other locations.*

Café Schmalznudel. After a big night on the town, come here for a sobering coffee and *Schmalznudel* (Bavarian doughnut) before you go to bed. *Prälat-Zistl Str. 8, off Viktualienmarkt. Closed Sun. No dinner.*

Café Stöpsel. This small café in Haidhausen is a laid-back hangout for the down-to-earth. Go for a shot of ouzo or to write in your journal. Nicaraguan coffee (DM 3.10 and up) is the big hit here. *Preysingstr. 18, tel. 089/448–6559. S-Bahn to Rosenheimerpl. Closed Mon.*

BEER GARDENS

To keep their kegs cool during hot summers, brewers used to store them under shady chestnut trees. This practice evolved into the beer garden, where you share long tables with everybody else in the city and lap up liters during those long, hot summer days. At most beer gardens, you can bring your own snacks or buy your meal there. When weather permits, gardens stay open from 9 or 10 in the morning to 10 or 11 at night. One indispensable bit of beer-garden vocabulary is *eine Maß*: This is the standard measure (about 1 quart) of beer in Bavaria and presents an excellent opportunity to build up your tolerance, or at least gain a few pounds.

For Bavarians, Beer Is Good for What Ales You

*In Bavaria, the beer-drinking and -producing capital of the world, you'll find quite a different approach to beer: It's cheaper than water, it's respected as "liquid bread," it's consumed by the liter, and it's brewed by monks and nuns. It is also protected by the world's most ancient food law, which hasn't changed since 1516. According to the decree, which was issued by Duke Wilhelm IV and first put to use in Bavaria, only the purest ingredients—water, hops, yeast, and barley—are acceptable for the fine art of beer brewing. The only exception is made for the delicious, light Weißbier, in which wheat is substituted for barley. Weißbier is served in a tall, slim glass (instead of a large stein) and comes in variations of light, dark, or yeasty-cloudy (*Weizenbier*). When making a toast, clink glasses at the base instead of the rim and hit the table with your beer before sipping. When ordering the standard pale beer, ask for a* Helles*; for dark beer,* Dunkles*. And don't forget to try the tasty beer-and-lemonade concoction called a* Radler *while you're here.*

Most beer halls and pubs reserve tables for regulars; you're not supposed to sit in these areas, marked STAMMTISCH*, and don't ring the bell unless you want to buy the whole table of old-timers a round. For a get-ripped-quick drinking game, buy an extra Maß among your buddies and take turns sipping from it and passing it in a circle. You can drink as much as you want when it's your turn, but it has to be a continuous gulp. Whoever polishes off the last drop of this public Maß wins; the person who would have been next to drink has to finish his or her own Maß, and the winner starts off the next round.*

Chinesischer Turm. Along with Seehaus (*see below*), this smaller garden is located in the Englischer Garten and sees a lot of tourists taking pictures of one another with their enormous beer steins; on weekends a brass band plays from inside the tower. A Maß starts at DM 8.

Hirschgarten. Since it's so close to Schloß Nymphenburg, Munich's largest beer garden (it seats 8,000) is touristy and expensive but it's a great pit stop if you're in the neighborhood. *Hirschgarten 1, tel. 089/172591. S-Bahn to Laim.*

Hofbräukeller. This small garden in Haidhausen sees mostly regulars and young people having their recommended daily allowance of liquid bread. It's a refreshing break from the touristy, more centrally located gardens. A Maß starts at DM 7.60. *Innere Wiener Str. 19, tel. 089/489489.*

Max Emanuel Brauerei. You can't bring your own food to this beer garden in the university district, but meals start at about DM 8.50, and they have the hottest, freshest, plumpest pretzels around (DM 4.50). A beer is DM 7.80, and inside is a restaurant-club. *Adalbertstr. 33, tel. 089/395028.*

Seehaus. Munich's most lively and gorgeous beer garden sits along the Kleinhesseloher See in the middle of the Englischer Garten and is a Schicki-Micki favorite. It makes an excellent substitute for a restaurant, as it's totally packed on warm nights and perfect during sunsets. Make your own salad (DM 8.50) or try some Bavarian wursts. A Maß costs DM 8.50–DM 9.

Viktualienmarkt Biergarten. Squeeze in with the locals at this cheap garden in the center of the Viktualienmarkt. A Maß is DM 7.20.

Waldwirtschaft Großhesselohe. Although farther from the city center and more expensive than most beer gardens (DM 9.50 per Maß), this place features live jazz (daily noon–9:45) and is beautifully situated on the bank of the Isar. *George-Kalb-Str. 3, tel. 089/795088. S7 to Großhesselohe/Isartalbahnhof, turn right at Kreuzeckstr. and follow curve of rd. to left.*

Exploring Munich

The Hauptbahnhof (main train station) sits on the western border of the city center, facing the beginning of the main pedestrian zone, which changes names three times: from Schützenstraße to Neuhauserstraße to Kaufingerstraße. This crowded shopping venue and all-purpose hangout leads to the busy Karlsplatz (also known as Stachus) and Marienplatz, the heart of the city. Most of Munich's major tourist attractions are concentrated in this area and within walking distance of one another. North of the city center are the university district and lively Schwabing, once a flourishing artists' and musicians' quarter and now full of yuppies, outdoor cafés, and nighttime fun. The main strip cutting through the area is Ludwigstraße, which turns into the main Schwabing artery, Leopoldstraße, past the university. Cross the River Isar at Ludwigsbrücke (or take the S-Bahn to Rosenheimerplatz) to reach the heart of Haidhausen, where more international and alternative restaurants, cafés, and bars lie undiscovered by tourists. The River Isar cuts through the city, lined with campgrounds, picnic grounds, and nude-sunbathing areas.

WORTH SEEING

ALTE PINAKOTHEK Ranking among the top six picture galleries in the world, the Alte Pinakothek houses some 800 works from the dominant European schools of the 14th–18th centuries. It is particularly respected for its Flemish Baroque collection—more than 80 Rubenses and 40 Van Eycks—and is unsurpassed in its collection of Early German masterpieces, which include Matthias Grünewald's *Sts. Erasmus and*

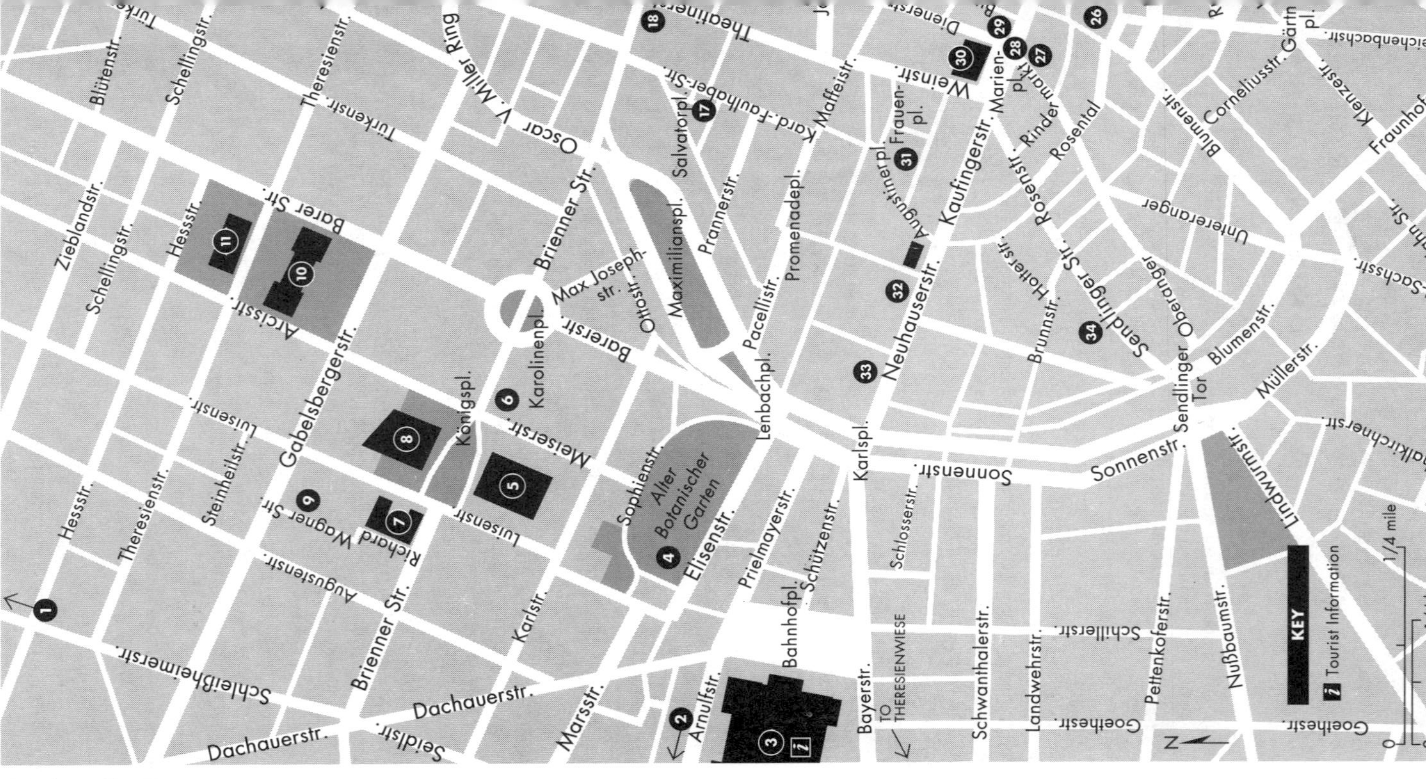
Blütenstr.
Schellingstr.
Theresienstr.
Oscar V. Miller Ring
Theatinerstr.
Dienerstr.
Türkenstr.
Zieblandstr.
Schellingstr.
Hessstr.
Barer Str.
Arcisstr.
Brienner Str.
Max Joseph-str.
Ottostr.
Maximilianspl.
Salvatorpl.
Kard.-Faulhaber-Str.
Prannerstr.
Promenadepl.
Maffeistr.
Pacellistr.
Frauen-pl.
Augustinerpl.
Weinstr.
Kaufingerstr.
Marien-pl.
Rindermarkt
Rosenstr.
Rosental
Blumenstr.
Corneliusstr.
Gärtnpl.
Reichenbachstr.
Klenzestr.
Fraunhofer
Unteranger
Jahn Str.
H-Sachsstr.
Neuhauserstr.
Hotterstr.
Brunnstr.
Sendlinger Str.
Oberanger
Blumenstr.
Müllerstr.
Sendlinger Tor
Karolinenpl.
Barerstr.
Königspl.
Meiserstr.
Gabelsbergerstr.
Luisenstr.
Steinheilstr.
Hesstr.
Theresienstr.
Richard Wagner Str.
Luisenstr.
Augustenstr.
Sophienstr.
Alter Botanischer Garten
Elisenstr.
Lenbachpl.
Karlspl.
Prielmayerstr.
Schützenstr.
Sonnenstr.
Sonnenstr.
Thalkirchnerstr.
Lindwurmstr.
Schlosserstr.
Bahnhofpl.
Karlstr.
Brienner Str.
Schleißheimerstr.
Dachauerstr.
Dachauerstr.
Seidlstr.
Marsstr.
Arnulfstr.
Bayerstr.
TO THERESIENWIESE
Schwanthalerstr.
Landwehrstr.
Schillerstr.
Pettenkoferstr.
Nußbaumstr.
Goethestr.
Goethestr.
KEY
Tourist Information
1/4 mile
1/4 km
0
0
N

Munich

Munich

Alte Pinakothek, **10**
Alter Botanischer Garten, **4**
Altes Rathaus, **29**
Antikensammlungen, **5**
Asamkirche, **34**
Bayerisches Nationalmuseum, **16**
BMW Museum, **1**
Bürgersaal, **33**
Deutsches Museum, **24**
Feldherrnhalle, **21**
Frauenkirche, **31**
Glyptothek, **8**
Graphische Sammlung, **6**
Hauptbahnhof, **3**
Jüdisches Museum, **22**
Ludwigskirche, **13**
Marienplatz, **28**
Michaelskirche, **32**
Nationaltheater, **21**
Neue Pinakothek, **11**
Neues Rathaus, **30**
Paläontologisches Museum, **9**
Peterskirche, **27**
Prähistorische Staatssammlung, **15**
Residenz, **20**
Salvatorkirche, **17**
Schloß Nymphenburg, **2**
Siegestor, **12**
Staatsgalerie Moderner Kunst/ Haus der Kunst, **14**
Städtische Galerie im Lenbachhaus, **7**
Theatinerkirche, **18**
Tierpark Hellabrunn, **25**
Viktualienmarkt, **26**
Z.A.M., **23**

Maurice; the painstakingly detailed *Battle of Alexander the Great,* by Albrecht Altdorfer; and Albrecht Dürer's *Four Apostles* and *Self-Portrait*, among many others. At the entrance you can buy a short guide covering the highlights of the museum. Most of the first floor is dedicated to paintings with religious themes (many of them formerly belonged to churches). The collection of Flemish paintings of the 16th and 17th centuries is most notably represented by Jan Brueghel and Pieter Brueghel the Elder.

King Ludwig II commissioned the public art gallery as a place to display the art collected by his family, the royal Wittelsbachs, for more than three centuries. The richness of the museum's collection is due both to the aggressive acquisitions of the Wittelsbachs (Maximilian I, who ruled from 1597 to 1651, was an avid Dürer fan, for example) and to the process of secularization, under which an enormous amount of church property was transferred to the state in the early 19th century. For detailed English explanations of the paintings and masters, take advantage of the plastic-covered leaflets available in almost every room. These are excerpts from a larger book that covers the entire Pinakothek. Note that if you plan to visit both Pinakotheks (*see* Neue Pinakothek, *below*) and don't have a student card, you can purchase a ticket to both museums for DM 7. *Barerstr. 27, tel. 089/238–05215. U2 to Königspl., Tram 18 to Pinakothek, or Bus 53 to Schellingstr. Admission: DM 4, DM 1 students. Open Wed., Fri., weekends 9:15–4:30; Tues., Thurs. 9:15–4:30, 7–9.*

ASAMKIRCHE Formally named St.-Johann-Nepomuk-Kirche, this extravagant 18th-century church is better known as the Asamkirche because of the two Asam brothers, Cosmas Damian and Egid Quirin, who built it. It's so modest on the outside that you can easily overlook it, but open the door and you enter a Baroque vision of paradise on earth—complete with an overwhelming combination of intricate stucco work, swirling frescoes, and a ton of gilding. Above the entrance is the figure of St. Nepomuk, a 14th-century Bohemian monk who drowned in the Danube. He is immortalized in wax in a glass shrine on the high altar. The younger Asam brother, Egid Quirin, paid for the church's construction and wanted to make it a private place of worship, but local citizens had a fit and forced him to make it public. Maybe he wanted to keep it private to cut down on the crowds tromping in and out, since he and his brother lived next door. *Sendlinger Str. 62. Walk from Marienpl., or take U1, U2, U3, or U6 to Sendlinger Tor.*

BAYERISCHES NATIONALMUSEUM This gigantic, three-story museum covers in detail the history of Bavarian culture and the influence of the region's European neighbors. More than 25,000 items from the Middle Ages to the 19th century are on display, including medieval and Renaissance wood carvings, tapestries, arms and armor, religious artifacts, and pottery. The ground floor focuses on arts and crafts, the basement shows folk art (with furniture and rooms of peasant houses, traditional costumes, and a collection of cribs), and the first floor houses specific collections like ivory sculpture, glass painting, clocks, and porcelain, to name only a few.

The architect Gabriel von Seidl designed each part of the building in a different architectural style, so different genres of art appear in rooms that reflect their period and style. Most of the captions are in German, but you can buy an English guide at the entrance. Some parts of the museum are being renovated; find out which halls are closed at the entrance. *Prinzregentenstr. 3, tel. 089/21681. U4 or U5 to Lehel. Admission: DM 3, DM 1 students, free Sun. and holidays. Open Tues.–Sun. 9:30–5.*

DEUTSCHES MUSEUM Whether you're into astronomy, musical instruments, mining, locomotives, ships, aeronautics, physics, telecommunications, brick making, glassblowing, or anything remotely related to science and technology, you can marvel and tinker away in this 13-acre, six-story playground. One of Munich's most popular attractions, this museum of science and technology is the largest of its kind in the world. A thorough visit would take days, if not weeks, so plan which exhibits you'd like to see most. Among the 16,000 items on display are the first Mercedes-Benz, the original airplanes of the Wright brothers, and tons of hands-on gadgets. Since not all exhibitions have English explanations, visitors planning to stay awhile should invest in the 288-page *Guide through the Collections* (DM 10), sold in the museum store (open daily 9–5:30) and at the information desk in the entrance hall. For a list of demonstrations (available only in German) and a map of the exhibitions, pick up an "Information for Your Visit" leaflet (DM .30) after entering the museum. Check the information desk to see if the planetarium on the sixth floor has scheduled English tours. If aeronautics is your thing, swing by the Deutsches Museum's **Flugwerft Schleißheim** (Effrierstr. 18, tel. 089/21791). It's located on Germany's oldest airfield, about 13 kilometers (8 miles) from Munich's center. *Museuminsel 1, tel. 089/21791. S-Bahn to Isartor, then walk or take Tram 18 to Deutsches Museum. Admission: DM 8 adults (16 and over), DM 2.50 students with I.D., DM 4 disabled (assistance is available), DM 2 extra for planetarium. Open daily 9–5.*

At the Deutsches Museum engineers will go into paroxysms of joy at the mere sight of such a scientific extravaganza, but those who've dreaded the word "science" since elementary school might feel overwhelmed.

FELDHERRNHALLE The Generals' Hall, facing Odeonsplatz, is a copy of the Loggia dei Lanzi in Florence. Hitler and his followers marched here in 1923 in their first attempt to seize power; the hall became a key Nazi shrine in the 30s and 40s. A bronze statue of the Bavarian commander of the Thirty Years War, Count Tilly, now stands on the left. On the right is Prince Wrede, who fought against the French in 1814. In the center is the Bavarian Army Memorial, which commemorates the Franco-Prussian War.

FRAUENKIRCHE In preparation for April 1994, the 500th anniversary of its consecration, Munich's most famous cathedral, the Frauenkirche (Church of Our Lady), has undergone renovation and is scheduled to reopen in early 1994. Construction of the late Gothic brick church took only 20 years (1468–1488): We're talking quick for those days. The cathedral has already undergone one 10-year restoration, after being severely damaged by wartime bombing; workers significantly changed the original design to create a simpler, modern interior, which sharply contrasts with the weathered and war-scarred brick exterior. Inside on the stone floor is the large, dark footprint known as the *Teufelstritt*, or Devil's Footprint. According to legend, the Devil, hoping to chalk up another soul on his bedpost, challenged architect Jörg von Halspach to build a nave without windows. The architect managed to design 66-foot-high windows that are entirely invisible to anyone standing in a certain area. The Devil was led to the spot and, unable to see the source of all the light, stamped his foot in a fury, leaving the famous mark.

Even if you don't get inside, you can't miss the two bulb-topped towers, 327 feet and 330 feet high, added almost 75 years after the cathedral was complete. The view from the top is definitely worth the effort it takes to get up there and will give you an excuse to treat yourself to a beer when you get back down. *Frauenpl. Admission: DM 4, DM 2 students. Open Apr.–Oct., Mon.–Sat. 10–5. Closed holidays.*

HAIDHAUSEN On the right bank of the Isar, where tourists rarely venture, lies the district of Haidhausen. Originally full of cheap housing and workers it metamorphosed first into a haven for hippies and artists and then into a more developed area that replaced Schwabing for a while as the chic place to hang out. Now Haidhausen has a healthy mix of contrasting personalities, including Müeslis (European granolas), people in black, and Schicki-Mickis, making it a great place to explore and even make some new friends. Aside from its wealth of intimate, alternative cafés, this peaceful and uncongested quarter has a number of small, pretty squares within easy walking distance of one another, including Weißenburger Platz, Pariser Platz, and Bordeaux Platz. *S-Bahn to Rosenheimerstr. or Ostbahnhof.*

MARIENPLATZ Originally a marketplace for farmers and traders, Marienplatz has been Munich's main square since the city was founded, in 1158. Today all of Munich wanders through at various times, including tourists, street musicians and performers, and real Bavarians going about their everyday business. Many transportation lines converge here, and several of the city's big historical attractions lie within walking distance; a variety of shops, restaurants, and cafés will meet your more secular needs.

The square got its name from the Mariensäule, the gilded statue of the Virgin Mary and Child that stands in the square's center. The 16th-century statue was originally part of the Frauenkirche's (*see above*) high altar, but Maximilian I hoisted Mary onto the red marble column after Munich survived the Thirty Years War; golden mother and child have been perched in the square since 1638.

Bordering Marienplatz on the north is the **Neues Rathaus** (New Town Hall), a neo-Gothic building constructed between 1867 and 1908. It's probably best known for the **Glockenspiel,** Europe's fourth-largest carillon, in its tower. Every day at 11 AM and noon (also at 5, May–October) tourists flock to the square to see and even videotape the mechanical figures spinning around to folk-music chimes. Although many are enchanted by it, you'll probably kick yourself if you go too far out of your way to see this. The upper level commemorates a Bavarian knight's victory in a jousting match held at Marienplatz, where he won his bride in 1568. The lower level depicts the first Schäfflertanz (Dance of the Coopers) in 1517, a dance by Munich's barrel makers meant to cheer people up after the ravages of the plague, although some were undoubtedly more cheered by what was *in* the barrels than by the dance itself. For DM 2, tower enthusiasts can make the 281-foot climb up the carillon.

The **Altes Rathaus** (Old Town Hall) sits in the eastern corner of the square. Destroyed in World War II, it was reconstructed according to the original 15th-century Gothic design. In its tower is the **Spielzeugmuseum** (Toy Museum), exhibiting 200 years of European and American toys; too bad you can't play with any of them. *Tel. 089/294001. Admission: DM 4. Open Mon.–Sat. 10–5:30; Sun., holidays 10–6.*

NEUE PINAKOTHEK Just across the street from the Alte Pinakothek (*see above*), this complementary gallery, opened in 1853, features European art from the 19th and 20th centuries. Like the Alte Pinakothek, the Neue Pinakothek was started by King Ludwig I and was severely damaged during the Second World War. The new building, designed by Munich architect Alexander von Branca, opened in 1981 and is hailed for its ingenious design and use of natural lighting.

You can pick up a brief but informative guide to the museum at the entrance. The gallery traces the development of international art from about 1800 (including works by Jacques-Louis David, Thomas Gainsborough, Francisco José de Goya, and Joseph Mallord William Turner, among others) and covers the development of 19th-century German schools extensively. Other highlights include the collection of French Impressionism, with works by Edouard Manet, Claude Monet, Pierre-Auguste Renoir, and Edgar Degas; the room dedicated to Paul Cézanne, Vincent van Gogh, and Paul Gauguin; the rooms for social realism and German Impressionism, including works by Max Liebermann; and the international collections of symbolism and Art Nouveau. *Barerstr. 29, entrance on Theresienstr., tel. 089/238–05195. U2 to Theresienstr., Tram 18 to Pinakothek, or Bus 53 to Schellingstr. Admission: DM 4, DM 1 students, free Sun. and national holidays. Open Wed.–Sun. 9:15–4:30; Tues. 9:15– 4:30, 7–9.*

RESIDENZ Construction of the royal residence began in the late 14th century, when the Wittelsbach family decided their place at the Alter Hof (Old Court) was too small and vulnerable to attack. For more than six centuries the Residenz served as the royal palace. Two years after Ludwig III, the last Bavarian king, abdicated, in 1918, the palace was transformed into a museum. Like many of Munich's treasures, it was heavily damaged during the Second World War and was restored in the 1960s.

Over the centuries the complex went through a number of construction phases, resulting in the mix of architectural styles you see today. Catch one of the two tours of the palace—one in the morning and one in the afternoon—or guide yourself. The "Residenz Guidebook" is available at the entrance.

Although the **Neuveste,** or New Fortress, the oldest part of the palace, burned down in 1750, one of its finest rooms—the **Antiquarium**—survived. This is the largest Renaissance room north of the Alps, and it houses Duke Albrecht V's collection of classical statues and busts. The Rococo **Ahnengalerie** (Gallery of Ancestors) has portraits of 121 Wittelsbachs, although some of those portrayed, like Charlemagne, are genealogically questionable. Other rooms worth a look are the Rococo **Reiche Zimmer** (Rich Room), designed by François de Cuvilliés; the **Silberkammer** (Silver Chamber), which contains all 3,500 pieces of the Wittelsbachs' silverware; and the suitably named **Reiche Kapelle** (Rich Chapel).

You need to buy a separate ticket to see the Wittelsbach treasures displayed in the **Schatzkammer** (Treasury), which holds a blinding collection of jewel-studded crowns, swords, house altars, icons, and more. Its most famous possession is the **Statuette des Ritters St. Georg**; this small Renaissance statue of St. George riding a horse is studded with 2,291 diamonds, 209 pearls, and 406 rubies. When the figure of St. George is removed, the horse becomes possibly the most opulent drinking cup in the world. Hard-core museum visitors might also visit the **Staatliche Sammlung Ägyptischer Kunst** (State Collection of Egyptian Art, *see* Museums and Galleries, *below*) and the **Münzhof** (State Collection of Coins), which is also housed in this huge palace.

North of the Residenz is the Italian-style **Hofgarten,** the former royal garden. On its east side, the bombed ruin of the **Armeemuseum** (Bavarian Army Museum) is slowly turning into the controversial **State Chancellery Bavarian,** which some people oppose on the grounds that it will detract from the garden and its historic surroundings. In front of the Armeemuseum, the **Kriegerdenkmal** (Tomb of the Unknown Soldier) leads visitors down to a sunken crypt that contains the remains of a German soldier from World War I. Residenz: *Enter Residenzmuseum at Max-Joseph-Pl. 3, tel. 089/290671. Admission: DM 4, DM 2.50 students. Open Tues.–Sun. 10–4:30. Enter Cuvilliés's Theater at Residenzstr. 1, tel. 089/290671. Admission: DM 2.50 adults, DM 1.50 students. Open Mon.–Sat. 2–5, Sun. 10–5. U3, U4, U5, or U6 to Odeonspl., or walk north on Dienerstr. from Marienpl.*

SCHLOß NYMPHENBURG The Schloß was originally a small summer villa constructed in 1663 by Prince Ferdinand Maria to placate his homesick Italian wife, Henriette. The enormous and opulent group of aristocratic digs you see today, which includes the biggest Baroque palace in Germany, is the product of more than 200 years of additional construction. Some of the features of the complex, including the canals that wind through the palace grounds and which were meant to recall Venice for poor Henriette, date all the way to the 17th century. Most of the complex sprang up later, the work of several enterprising architects who met the needs of several increasingly greedy kings. As the Wittelsbachs' summer palace, Nymphenburg was used only eight weeks of the year. Notable features of this monstrosity, which stretches $\frac{4}{5}$ kilometer ($\frac{1}{2}$ mile) from one wing to the other, include the ceiling of the **Steinerner Saal** (Great Hall), which contains the fresco *Nymphs Paying Homage to the Goddess Flora,* for which the palace was named.

Also check out Ludwig I's **Schönheiten Galerie** (Gallery of Beauties), which has 36 portraits, all painted by Joseph Stieler between 1827 and 1850, of the king's pick of Munich's most beautiful women. The unusual part about this particular portrait gallery is that it includes paintings of women from all different social classes. **Helene Sedlmayr** (bottom right of the north wall) was supposedly the king's favorite; the 17-year-old shoemaker's daughter was selling toys when she caught his eye. Also part of this collection is the infamous **Lola Montez** (bottom left of the west wall), the beautiful dancer and former mistress of Franz Liszt and Alexandre Dumas; her alleged affair with the king was partly responsible for a revolt in 1848 and the king's forced abdication.

King Ludwig II, also known as the Fairy-Tale King because of his fascination with building extravagant castles, was born in the bedroom next to the **Blue Salon** in 1845. In those days, ministers watched the royal births to ensure that the baby wasn't switched with another. Later on, when Ludwig started liberally sprinkling his fantasy castles across the countryside to the severe detriment of the national budget, much of his family probably wished they *had* exchanged him while they had the chance.

You could spend the whole day wandering around the beautiful 500-acre **Nymphenburg Park,** lined with classically French gravel paths and low, excessively trimmed hedges. On the grounds you'll also find three pavilions and a miniature palace, built as king after king expanded Nymphenburg according to his tastes. The **Amalienburg,** an 18th-century hunting lodge designed by Cuvilliés, is one of the finest examples of the Rococo style. The pastel-color, opulent stucco lodge was created for Maria Amalia, who confined her hunting activities to the rooftop: Palace peons drove game along below her, and she shot the animals from overhead. How's that for sportsmanship? Intricate carvings depicting more typical hunting scenes decorate the wall panels and ceiling; don't miss the kennels, a prime example of living in luxury, doggie-style.

Also within the park is the two-story **Pagodenburg,** with its French exterior and Oriental interior, used for royal tea parties. The **Badenburg,** Max Emanuel's bathing pavilion, was Europe's first indoor pool. The **Magdalenenklause,** or Hermitage, served as a refuge for the royal family when they got tired of all that *opulence.* Built by Josef Effner as a meditation-and-prayer retreat for Max Emanuel, the grottolike chapel was designed with the cracks on the outside to make it look old.

You can also visit the former royal stables in the southern wing of the palace, now the **Marstallmuseum** (Museum of Royal Carriages). Lavish coaches, riding equipment, and sleighs belonging to the Wittelsbachs are on display, including a coach built for King Ludwig II's wedding, which never happened. Upstairs you'll find a **collection of porcelain** produced at Nymphenburg between 1747 and 1920. *Schloß Nymphenburg 1, tel. 089/179080. U1 to Rotkreuzpl. and Tram 12 toward Amalienburg Str. to Schloß Nymphenburg. Admission: combination ticket to palace, Amalienburg, Marstallmuseum, DM 4.50, DM 3 students. Palace open Apr.–Sept., Tues.–Sun. 9–12:30, 1:30–5; Oct.–Mar., Tues.–Sun. 10–12:30, 1:30–4. Amalienburg also open Mon. Badenburg, Pagodenburg, and Magdalenenklause open summer, daily 10–12:30, 1:30–5. Marstallmuseum and porcelain exhibit, open Apr.–Sept., Tues.–Sun. 9–noon, 1–5.*

SCHWABING This legendary artists' quarter, north of the city center and university district, centers around the café-lined Leopoldstraße, which begins at the Siegestor arch. You can still find some artists setting up their easels on the boulevard, but for the most part it's the tons of bars, cabarets, restaurants, and outdoor cafés on Leopoldstraße and its smaller side streets that make Schwabing a favorite nighttime hangout, especially for Schicki-Mickis. At night it gets so packed it's hard to walk, but any time of day you'll find a lively area full of young locals and tourists trying to decide which café to hit. To reach the quarter, take U3 or U6 to Gieselastraße or Münchener Freiheit.

STAATSGALERIE MODERNER KUNST The pillared, neoclassical **Haus der Kunst** (House of Art), designed in the 1930s monumental style favored by Hitler's regime, houses the State Gallery of Modern Art in its west wing. The museum now displays 450 works representing all the major art movements of the 20th century and is ranked among the top 10 modern-art galleries in the world. You can see entire rooms devoted to fauvism and expressionism, cubism, the Blaue Reiter (Blue Rider) movement, surrealism, Bauhaus and constructivism, abstract art of the 1940s–1960s, Italian plastic arts, abstract expressionism, pop art, minimal art, and chromatic painting, as well as the work of Pablo Picasso, Paul Klee, and Joseph Beuys, among many others. The museum is currently closed for renovation, but some works are on display at the Alte Pinakothek, Neue Pinakothek (*see above*), and Schack-Galerie (*see* Museums and Galleries, *below*). *Prinzregentenstraße 1, tel. 089/292710. U4 or U5 to Lehel. Admission: DM 3.50, free Sun. and holidays. Open Tues.–Sun. 9–4:30, Thurs. also 7–9.*

THEATINERKIRCHE King Ferdinand Maria also commissioned the building of Theatinerkirche (as well as Schloß Nymphenburg) to honor the birth of his and Henriette's long-awaited son and heir. Italian architect Agostini Barelli began construction of the Court Church and Theatine monastery in 1662 but was later dismissed and succeeded by Enrico Zuccalli. The church, which is modeled after the Roman St. Andrea della Valle, ignited a fascination with the Baroque style and became a model for this elaborate kind of architecture. However, the facade wasn't finished until almost a century later, by Cuvilliés. Under the high altar there's a burial vault containing more Wittelsbachs, including Ferdinand Maria, Max Emanuel, and King Maximilian I. *Theatinerstr. 22, U3, U4, U5, or U6 to Odeonspl. or walk north from Marienpl.*

TIERPARK HELLABRUNN Extending over 90 acres, Munich's world-famous zoo has grouped animals together according to their continents of origin. The zoo strives to reproduce natural environments and has enjoyed tremendous success in breeding endangered species. If the romping chimpanzees make you homesick for family, you can wail out your sorrows along with the squawking birds in the *Groß Voliere,* an amazing, junglelike, net-covered aviary in which birds fly freely all around you. The polarium features different species of penguins and sea lions, and the aquarium provides an opportunity to sit quietly and meditate on the fish. *Siebenbrunnerstr. 6. Admission: DM 6. Open Apr.–Sept., daily 8–6; Oct.–Mar., daily 9–5. U3 to Thalkirchen, or take Bus 31, 52, or 57.*

VIKTUALIENMARKT The colorful Viktualienmarkt, Munich's best-known open-air food market, is held on the square where public executions took place during the Middle Ages. Six fountain-statues of the most popular folk singers and comedians of the city's past dot the market grounds; the statue of Karl Valentin, Munich's best-loved comedian, receives fresh flowers from the market women every morning. The many stands sell high-quality and slightly expensive fresh fruits, vegetables, flowers, meat, and fish—everything you could possibly need for a picnic on the river. Try a Bavarian dish at one of the many crowded food joints here, or, better yet, join the locals for a Maß (DM 7.20) at the packed beer garden in the center of the market. The Viktualienmarkt opens Monday–Saturday at about 7 AM and is particularly vibrant on Saturday morning, when the whole world comes out to shop and socialize. The market is closed Saturday afternoon and Sunday. Bordering the market on the north is the **Heiliggeistkirche.**

CHURCHES AND CHAPELS

Many of Munich's churches suffered severe damage during the Second World War, but most have been reconstructed. The most famous churches—the Frauenkirche, Asamkirche, and Theatinerkirche—lie near the city center, and the first three are covered in Worth Seeing, *above.* Michaelskirche and the Bürgersaal sit close to each other on the main pedestrian zone, so it doesn't take much effort to check them out on your way to other sights.

Bürgersaal. Initially an assembly hall when it was built in 1710, the two-story Bürgersaal has been used as a church since 1778. It managed to keep its original facade, although the rest of it was restored after the war. Compared to the richly decorated Baroque upper level, the ground floor is barren, but it does hold the tomb of Rupert Mayer, a famous Jesuit priest and opponent of the Hitler regime. *Neuhauserstr. 48.*

Ludwigskirche. This curious neo-Byzantine/early Renaissance–style parish church's claim to fame is its 60-foot-by-37-foot fresco of the Last Judgment, second in size only to Michelangelo's version in the Sistine Chapel in Rome. *Ludwigstr. 22.*

Michaelskirche. When the tower of St. Michael's Church collapsed in 1590, only seven years after the building's completion, Duke Wilhelm V interpreted the disaster as a sign from heaven that the church wasn't big enough. During the seven-year reconstruction a great deal of square-footage was added, minus a tower: They learned their lesson about building too close to heaven. Now the Michaelskirche is not only the largest Renaissance church north of the Alps but also has the biggest barrel-vault roof in the world. The duke rests in peace in the crypt, along with 40 members of the Wit-

The White Rose Society

A large number of students and professors had already joined the Nazi party by 1934, the year the University of Munich came entirely under Nazi control. At the same time, however, five students and one professor formed the White Rose Society, an underground resistance movement that secretly printed six leaflets attacking the Nazi regime and calling for passive resistance. The small circle of friends met often to discuss literature, philosophy, and the many authors they were reading, and the ideas they found in works by Goethe, Lao-Tzu, and Aristotle became an integral part of the pamphlets. On February 18, 1943, Hans and Sophie Scholl dropped the last copies of their sixth leaflet from the balcony of the university, but a janitor saw them and locked all the doors. The Scholls were subsequently arrested, tried, and sentenced to death. Copies of the last pamphlet reached England and were then reprinted and dropped over Germany, but the Scholls were executed by guillotine, as were the other members of the White Rose. Today the White Rose is a widely respected and treasured aberrration in Munich's Nazi past. Explains Franz Joseph Müller, one of the nine survivors who participated in the underground movement, "civil disobedience is the best thing you can do to avoid dictatorship." Sixty-seven-year-old Müller, who was 18 when he was arrested, believes he was spared the guillotine because the Nazis did not want to risk public outrage by executing too many young students. Müller formed the White Rose Foundation in memory of the original members who lost their lives and in celebration of one of Germany's "biggest and most important uprisings." Discussions conducted in German schools, two feature-length films, and numerous TV and radio interviews are all part of the foundation's way of keeping alive the spirit of the original society. Today angry protesters still wave banners calling people to action in the name of the White Rose, dozens of squares and streets all over Europe are named in honor of the secret society, and an exhibition featuring photographs, documents, and the history of the White Rose and the Nazi era travels to major cities all over the world.

The university now has a monument to the White Rose; it's located between the entrance, at Geschwister-Scholl Platz, and the fountain standing in front. On the ground you'll find reproductions of the original pamphlets and pictures of the Munich members.

telsbach family. The most infamous of them, mad, fanciful King Ludwig II, the castle-building nut, also lies here. *Neuhauserstr. 52. Crypt admission: DM 1. Open weekdays 10–1, 2–4:30; Sat. 10–3.*

Peterskirche. Excavations in 1952 revealed that St. Peter's Church, affectionately and appropriately nicknamed "Alter Peter" ("Old Peter"), was preceded by another church that stood on the site before Munich was founded in 1158. Over the centuries Old Pete has been restored in a variety of architectural styles. Today it has a Baroque interior with a late Gothic high altar. Labor up the 300 stairs in the 303-foot tower for a view of the city that extends as far as the Alps on a clear day. *Rindermarkt. Admission: DM 2, DM 1 students. Open Mon.–Sat. 9–6; Sun., holidays 10–6.*

Salvatorkirche. St. Salvator's, a late Gothic brick church built in 1494 by Lukas Rottaler (who succeeded Jörg von Halspach, creator of the Frauenkirche, as city architect), is now the main Greek Orthodox Church of Munich. The architect Cuvilliés is buried in its yard. *Salvatorpl. 17, near Odeonspl.*

MUSEUMS AND GALLERIES

Munich's got so many public and private museums and odd collections that it's hard to keep them straight, much less decide which ones to visit. A number of eccentric, eye-opening, amusing exhibitions vie with the city's world-famous museums for your attention. Many of the museums are closed Monday but open late one or two nights each week, and most offer student discounts with the ISIC card. Few exhibits provide English translations, but you can often buy extensive guides at the entrance if you're really interested. Check your map before you go; a number of museums are clustered together, so you can sometimes plot a convenient museum-hopping route and see things you wouldn't normally seek out. Of the biggies, the Alte Pinakothek, Neue Pinakothek, Deutsches Museum, Residenz and Schatzkammer, and Bayerisches Nationalmuseum are discussed in Worth Seeing, *above.*

Exploring Munich's offbeat museums, you may discover you're not the only one harboring a secret fascination with chamber pots, sewing machines, corkscrews, erotica, or puppets.

BMW Museum. This ultracool, high-tech museum uses videos, slides, and its gorgeous collection of cars, engines, and cycles to chronicle the technical development, social history, and future plans of the Bayerisches Motoren Werke (Bavarian Motor Works). What's more, everything you want to know is translated into English, as well as French and Spanish. If you still can't get enough, book a tour of the BMW factory, and watch the workers guzzle beer as they put cars together Bavaria-style. Two-hour tours, given weekdays at 9:30 and 1:15, start at the museum's front counter and are free but extremely popular, so book a few days ahead (tel. 089/389–53306). *Petuelring 130, tel. 089/389–53307. U2 or U3 to Olympiazentrum. Admission: DM 4.50 adults, DM 3 students. Open daily 9–5, last entry at 4.*

Glyptothek. Together the Glyptothek and the Staatliche Antikensammlungen (*see below*) comprise Germany's largest collection of classical art. The neoclassical building was commissioned by Ludwig I, who had a fascination with classical Greece, and it appropriately houses Greek and Roman sculpture. Don't miss the *Aeginates,* sculptures dating to the 5th century BC, from the pediments of the Temple of Aphaia in Aegina, Greece; they depict the conflict between the Greeks and Trojans. *Königspl. 3, tel. 089/286100. U2 to Königspl. Admission: DM 3.50, DM 1 students, free Sun. and holidays. Combination ticket with Staatliche Sammburgen: DM 6. Open Tues., Wed., Fri.–Sun. 10–4:30; Thurs. noon–8:30.*

Jüdisches Museum München. The tiny, private Munich Jewish Museum has a wall detailing the search for Raoul Wallenberg, the Swedish diplomat who saved hundreds of Jews during World War II; some of the articles are in English. Also on display are photographs and the yellow stars that Jews were forced to wear in Nazi Germany. The owner and founder of the museum is happy to translate or explain anything that interests you. *Maximilianstr. 36, tel. 089/297453. Admission free. Open Tues., Wed. 2–6; Thurs. 2–9.*

Paläontologisches Museum. A 10-million-year-old skeleton of a mammoth tries to steal center stage of this paleontological and geological collection, but don't let it eclipse your visit to the impressive remains of a giant tortoise, cave bears, saber-toothed tigers, and pterodactyls. *Richard-Wagner-Str. 10, tel. 089/520–3361. U2 to Königspl. Admission free. Open Mon.–Thurs. 8–4, Fri. 8–2.*

Prähistorische Staatssammlung. Archaeologists and those with a penchant for unusual embalming techniques will appreciate the State Prehistorical Collection, which traces the development of Bavaria from the Early Stone Age to the early Middle Ages and the founding of Munich. An especially spine-chilling exhibit features the perfectly preserved body of a young girl who was ritually sacrificed, to be recovered centuries later from a peat bog. *Lerchenfeld Str. 2, next to Bayerisches Nationalmuseum, tel. 089/293911. U4 or U5 to Lehel, or Bus 53. Admission: DM 2.50, DM 1 students, free Sun. and holidays. Open Tues., Wed., Fri.–Sun. 9–4; Thurs. 9–8.*

Staatliche Antikensammlungen. The State Collection of Antiquities, an impressive collection of Greek, Roman, and Etruscan art, came about thanks to King Ludwig I, who commissioned it and collected a number of the ancient Greek vases on display. Also featured are small bronzes, Greek and Etruscan gold jewelry, and pottery from Crete and Mycenae. *Königspl. 1, tel. 089/598359. U2 to Königspl. Admission: DM 3.50; DM 1 students; free Sun. and holidays; combination ticket with Glyptothek, DM 6 adults. Open Tues., Thurs.–Sun. 10–4:30; Wed. noon–8:30.*

Staatliche Graphische Sammlung. The State Graphic Collection is one of the few museums in Munich that's open Monday and doesn't charge admission. Its 300,000 Western drawings and graphics from the 14th through 20th centuries include works by Dürer and Rembrandt, as well as a lot of stuff by artists you've never heard of before. *Studiensaal Meiserstr. 10, tel. 089/559–1490. U2 to Königspl., or Tram 18. Admission free. Open Mon.–Wed. 10–1, 2–4:30; Thurs. 10–1, 2–6; Fri. 10–12:30.*

Städtische Galerie im Lenbachhaus. Most famous for its collection of works by members of the Blaue Reiter movement (which includes paintings by Wassily Kandinsky, Paul Klee, Franz Marc, August Macke, and Alexey von Jawlensky), the City Gallery, in the Lenbach House, displays primarily the work of modern Munich painters. The house is an Italian villa and former residence of the painter Lenbach, one of Munich's important late-19th-century artists. The rooms containing the Blaue Reiter works are painted in different colors, giving the exhibit a fun and funky atmosphere. *Luisenstr. 33, tel. 089/521041. U2 to Königspl. Admission: DM 5, DM 2.50 students, free Sun. and holidays. Open Tues.–Sun. 10–6.*

Zentrum für Außergewöhnliche Museen (ZAM). If you're a little quirky, you'll love this place. The Center for Unusual Museums includes the world's first museums devoted to the pedal car, the chamber pot, the corkscrew, the lock, and the Easter Bunny. The **Sissi Museum** collection is a mishmash of bibelots gathered in memory of Empress Elisabeth of Austria. Other wacky historical and cultural exhibits come and go; call to inquire about the latest irrational preoccupation on display. *Westenriderstr. 26, tel. 089/290–4121. S-Bahn to Isartor. Admission: DM 8, DM 5 students. Open daily 10–6.*

PARKS AND GARDENS

All the beautiful spots of green within Munich's city limits may make you forget you're in Germany's third-largest city; what's even more disconcerting, they may make you want to take off all of your clothes and drink a lot of beer. If you're a less hedonistic traveler you may just want to walk or bike around and watch everyone else taking off all of their clothes and drinking beer.

Alter Botanischer Garten. Once a botanic garden, this site became a public park in 1937. Its green expanses provide a restful place to wait for a train out of town. *Elisenstr., within walking distance of Karlspl. and main train station.*

Botanischer Garten. With 14,000 plants, including orchids, cycads, alpine flowers, and rhododendrons, and steamy greenhouses full of cacti and exotic greens, Munich's Botanical Garden is one of the best in all of Europe. The variety of landscapes makes it a great place for a peaceful, fragrant stroll. *Nymphenburg, Menzinger Str. 63, tel. 089/178–2310. Admission: DM 3 adults, DM 1.50 students. Open Nov.–Jan., daily 9–4:30; Feb., Mar., Oct., daily 9–5; Apr., Sept., daily 9–6; May–Aug., daily 9–7. Greenhouses open summer, daily 9–11:45, 1–6:30; winter, daily 9–11:45, 1–4.*

Englischer Garten. More than 200 years old, the Englischer Garten (English Garden) is the world's largest and oldest recreational city park. Named after the rolling parklands popular with the English aristocracy during the 18th century, Englischer Garten runs along the Isar River for 5 kilometers (3 miles) and is almost 2 kilometers (about 1 mile) wide. On sunny days the park teems with baseball, soccer, and Frisbee games; picnics; cyclists; music groups; and a disconcerting or delightful (depending on your point of view) number of nude sunbathers letting it all hang out. (If you want to ogle or strip, go toward the **Eisbach,** a tributary of the Isar.) The park has four beer gardens, a Japanese tea garden, a lake with ducks and swans, and open space great for naps or playing.

Walk up a small hill to reach **Monopteros,** a Greek pavilion in the southern part of the park. North of here grab a huge pretzel (DM 4.50) and a Maß (DM 8.50) at the **Chinesischer Turm** (Chinese Tower), a world-famous beer garden that serves a fair number of tourists and locals. On weekends a traditional brass band plays from inside the tower. Farther north you'll find the **Seehaus,** a chic beer garden beautifully situated by the **Kleinhesseloher See,** a man-made lake perfect for admiring sunsets. If you like this beer-garden thing, walk northeast of Seehaus to **Hirschau,** a local hangout, or toward the northern border of the park, to **Aumeister.** Rent a bike to see the park most thoroughly or to terrorize innocent strollers (*see* Outdoor Activities, *below*).

Hirschgarten. This former wildlife preserve near Nymphenburg still has wild buck and roe deer in enclosures. The park also features children's playgrounds, and Munich's largest beer garden, serving as many as 8,000 happy customers at a time. *Any westbound S-Bahn line to Laim.*

In More than One Way, the Statue of Bavaria Rings Hollow

Overlooking Theresienwiese from the west is the hollow statue of Bavaria; standing more than 100 feet tall, she reigns as the largest bronze figure ever cast. You can climb 126 awkward steps to get a view from her eyes. Right behind the statue is the **Ruhmeshalle** ***(Hall of Fame). This open hall has Doric columns and honors 80 famous Bavarians, none of them women. The statue and Ruhmeshalle were commissioned by King Ludwig I and designed by Leo von Klenze.*** **Theresienhöhe 16. U5 to Theresienwiese. Admission: DM 1.50, DM 1 students. Statue open Tues.–Sun. 10–noon, 2–5:30; winter, Tues.–Sun. 10–noon, 2–4.**

West Park. Laid out for the 1983 International Horticulture Exhibition, this park, situated in the southwest part of Munich, is one of the city's most popular. It was designed to resemble the hilly, green landscape of upper Bavaria, and within its grounds you'll find restaurants, cafés, two beer gardens, an open-air theater, and a concert arena. *U3 or U6 to West Park or Renlandstr.*

CHEAP THRILLS

On a sunny day the **Englischer Garten** provides a glorious haven for broke budget travelers—come to sunbathe, picnic, stroll, or relax on the huge grassy grounds. Bands often set up and play there on weekends, as well. The **Theatron,** in Olympiapark (*see* Outdoor Activities, *below*), features free rock concerts periodically throughout the summer. You can also catch live music, puppet shows, mimes, and other entertaining street performers in the **pedestrian zone,** particularly at Marienplatz and by the Feldherrnhalle monument in Odeonsplatz. Many **breweries,** such as the Löwenbräukeller (Nymphenburgerstr. 2, tel. 089/520–0496 or 089/526021), offer free guided tours that end with free beer samples and, at times, some bread thrown in for good measure. On the last Wednesday of every month, get into **clubs** such as the Schwabinger Brette, Rattlesnake Saloon, Schwabinger Podium, Allotria, and Unterfahrt for free. State-run **museums,** such as the Alte Pinakothek, Neue Pinakothek, and Deutsches Museum, are free on Sunday.

FESTIVALS

➢ **JANUARY AND FEBRUARY** • To prepare for the ascetic period of Lent, Munich indulges in an orgy of masquerades, elegant balls, and wild partying during the four to six weeks of **Fasching** (carnival), from January 7 until Ash Wednesday. Almost every society, corporation, and club throws a ball during these weeks, but the hard-core street partying begins on Fasching Sunday (the Sunday before Ash Wednesday), when a huge public festival rips through the city center. On the morning of Fasching Tuesday (Shrove Tuesday), you can see those hefty women of the Viktualienmarkt doing a traditional jig and transvestites showing their stuff in sexy attire. The rest of the day is one big rager, officially ending at midnight at the onset of Ash Wednesday and the fasting period. Most people here don't observe Lent too strictly, but it's a great excuse to cut loose, regardless of religious convictions or the lack thereof; besides, by the time Fasching's over, just the thought of drinking will make your tongue curl. During the carnival, check out the Löwenbräu Brewery and Max Emanuel's; both feature some wild theme parties. Once every seven years, the Schäfflertane (*see* Marienplatz in Worth Seeing, *above*) is performed on Marienplatz (the next scheduled time is for 1998). For more information, check the tourist offices, and grab a copy of the monthly program.

➢ **MARCH** • **Starkbierzeit,** the strong-beer season, marks the coming of spring with (how'd you guess?) dark, strong beer, originally brewed to nourish monks during Lent. This stuff hits a lot harder than you'd expect, and all the major breweries have their own version, identifiable by the *-ator* suffix (Animator, Optimator, and the most famous, Salvator, are just a few). The season runs for two weeks, beginning the third Friday after Ash Wednesday. Places to try include the Salvatorkeller (Hochstr. 77) and Löwenbräukeller (*see above*).

➢ **APRIL AND MAY** • **Auer Dult** (April Fair), a traditional, eight-day Bavarian fair, is held three times each year on Mariahilfplatz (in the Au district) and is known for its antiques and junk markets. The first fair, **Maidult** (May Fair), begins at the end of April, on the last Saturday of the month, and runs into the first week of May. (For information on the other two Auer Dult festivals, *see below.*) The **Frühlingsfest,** or Spring Festival, is a small version of Oktoberfest that also takes place at the end of April, at Theresienwiese. Around the end of April is the first testing of the light, strong *Maibock* (May beer), which brings the Starkbierzeit to a close. Also, on **Corpus Christi,** the second Thursday after Whitsunday, there's a huge procession throughout Munich.

➢ **JUNE** • **Castle concerts** and musical events are held in several Munich castles; try the Schleissheim Palace, which usually has weekend concerts in June and July. **Filmfest München** (Munich Film Festival), at the end of June, has been held annually since 1984; the Gasteig (Rosenheimer Pl.) has information as well as tickets. June is also the month of the **Tollwood** festival, started by left-wing environmentalists, which features diverse, international music performances in the Olympiapark (*see* Outdoor Activities, *below*).

➢ **JULY AND AUGUST** • The summer Auer Dult (*see above*), called **Jakobidult** (St. James's Fair), starts in the last week of July and is held at Mariahilfplatz. The traditional **Magdalenenfest** (Magdalene Fair) takes place in the Hirschgarten in June. The **Sommerfest** (Summer Festival), which includes concerts in Schloß Nymphenburg and at the Brunnenhof in the Residenz, ballet recitals, and other performances, takes place in July and August.

➢ **SEPTEMBER AND OCTOBER** • From the middle of September to the first week of October, Munich's world-famous **Oktoberfest** rages for 15 days. Then, in mid-October, the year's last Auer Dult (*see above*), called the **Herbst Dult** (Autumn Fair) takes place.

➢ **DECEMBER** • During the three weeks before Christmas, the **Christkindlmarkt** (Christmas Markets) teem with people and offer all sorts of goods; the main spot to find them is Marienplatz, but you can also try the square in front of the Frauenkirche, at Münchener Freiheit, Rotkreuzplatz, and Weißenburgerplatz (in Haidhausen).

After Dark

In the Schwabing district alone, you could visit a new café, club, cabaret, or bar every night for a year without seeing them all. Munich's got tons of films, concerts, clubs, and live-music venues, but enjoying them will cost you tons of bucks. Look in the monthly *Monatsprogramm* for detailed listings, and pick up a free copy of *In Munich* at the ticket kiosk under Marienplatz. You can stretch your mark much farther in bars and cafés than in clubs or live-music venues. Stroll through the cliquish scene on the main strip **Leopoldstraße,** crowded with outdoor cafés, exclusive clubs, and schickie-mickies. Of the Leopoldstraße cafés, most of which manage to blend the best elements of an ice-cream parlor and a trendy bar, **Roxy** (Leopoldstr. 48) is the schickiest and **Café Servus** the most mellow.

BARS AND BEER HALLS Cruise the very cool and somewhat expensive strip **Occamstraße,** in Schwabing if you want to find a really good bar or beer hall. **Tomate** (Siegesstr. 19) and **Schwabinger Podium** (Wagner Str. 1), catercorner from each other, pack in a mishmash of Germans and Americans; beers start at about DM 5.50.

Gorki Park. Study a fresco of Lenin in this red bar while pounding down some Russian beer (DM 4.33) or Soviet cocktails (DM 4–DM 7). *Breisacherstr. 19.*

Haus der 111 Biere. Kick off your night at the House of 111 Beers with the Aku Kulminator (DM 6), the strongest beer in the world. This Schwabing bar even has expensive French beer (DM 20). *Franzstr. 3, tel. 089/331248.*

Hofbräuhaus. Just as tourists feel obliged to pass through the Louvre while in Paris, so they pay homage to the enormous Hofbräuhaus while in Munich. Come to bow to its 400-year-old beer-brewing tradition, to marvel that Hitler used to hang out here in the early days, and then split. The atmosphere of the place has slowly degenerated ever since 8 million Americans came home from their summer vacation and told all their friends they'd found the perfect German beer hall. The result: the largest fraternity party outside American borders. Served by a crew that appears to hate its job, the beer is reputed to be watered down: You be the judge. Upstairs you'll find a less hectic, more German restaurant. *Am Platzl 9, tel. 089/221676. From Marienpl., head e. past*

Roderick's Pick of Munich's Finest Gay Bars

More than five years ago, Roderick bought a one-way ticket from California to Munich and landed in his new hometown with $100 to his name. He took a shine to Munich and professes to be a pretty good source of information on gay life in the city. These are his picks for Munich's best gay hangouts. Regardless of your sexual orientation, you should get at least a glimpse of the city's bustling gay nightlife; it's one of the most happening and fun scenes when the sun goes down. A large number of the bars, cafés, and clubs are concentrated between Isartor and Sendlingertor, particularly around Gärtnerplatz and on Hans-Sachs-Straße. If you're in town during Oktoberfest, be sure to hit the gay tent on the second day of the fest (it's called Bräu-Rösl).

- *Alcatraz. Friday and Saturday nights are gay. Show up after 11:30. During the week the joint has theme nights ('70s, subterranean, etc.) and is 99% straight.* Thalkirchnerstr. 2, tel. 089/260–8403.
- *Club New York. This club admits men only and has "the best dance music and decor." It's open daily 11 PM–5 AM (don't bother showing up before 1), and the cover is DM 13.* Sonnenstr. 25, tel. 089/591056.
- *Florida. This small club plays funky dance music for a mixed gay and lesbian crowd; the later it gets, the trippier the crowd. It's just around the corner from Together* (see below).
- *Moritz. Rodney sez, "Total lounge scene with a lot of extremely well-dressed, extremely good-looking Schicki-Micki men." You heard it here.* Klenzestr. 43, tel. 089/201–6776.
- *Mutti Bräu im Lehel. This mixed restaurant-bar has really good food for higher-than-average prices. It's a good place for a splurge.* Thierschstr. 14, near Isartorpl., tel. 089/298266.
- *Nümfe. This women-only café is a good resource for lesbians; as usual, the lesbian scene has fewer resources than the gay men's scene. Good food for good prices.* Nymphenburgerstr. 182. No lunch. Closed Mon.
- *Ochsengarten. Your basic leather scene, on the mild side. A good place to stand around in leather and jeans and have a beer before going elsewhere.* Müllerstr. 47, tel. 089/266446.
- *Together. This is "your typical Californian gay bar." It's laid-back and is frequented by men and women, gay and straight. The cover is DM 10 and includes a drink.* Hans-Sachs-Str. 17, tel. 089/263469.

Other suggested clubs and bars are Karotte (Reichenbachstr. 37, tel. 089/201–4294), a small meeting place–restaurant for women; Mrs. Henderson's (Mullerstr. 1, tel. 089/260–4323), which usually features drag shows and is mainly for men; and Nil (Hans-Sachs-Str. 2), a crowded, Schicki-Micki gay bar, open daily until 3 AM.

Altes Rathaus to Im Tal, take 1st left onto Sparkassenstr., turn right on Ledererstr., left on Orlandostr.

Mathäser Bierstadt. Don't let the wasted-off-their-ass regulars stumbling in and out the door intimidate you; once inside, you'll find a raucous, jovial, international crowd. This wild and rowdy joint stakes claims to be the largest beer hall in the world and is a less insidious alternative to the Hofbräuhaus. Waiters don't bat an eye when sloshed tourists wearing gray triangular Bavarian hats clamber onto tabletops. When tents close shop during Oktoberfest, the party continues here. A fairly diverse crowd frequents the Mathäser Bierstadt; on a good night you can witness (or join) inebriated Japanese tourists doing the wave. *Bayerstr. 5, tel. 089/592896. Between main train station and Karlspl. Maß: DM 8.50. Open daily 10 AM–midnight.*

MOVIE THEATERS **Cinema** (Nymphenburger Straße 31, tel. 089/555255. U1 to Stiglmaierpl.) shows some English films. On Monday and Thursday all films are DM 5.90; regular tickets cost DM 8–DM 10. Look for the designations "OF" and "OmU," which mean "original language" and "original language with subtitles," respectively. **Türkerdolch** (Türkenstr. 74, tel. 089/271–8844), **Neues Arena Filmtheater** (Hans-Sachs-Str. 7, tel. 089/260–3265), **Museum Lichtspiele** (Lihenstr. 2, tel. 089/482403), and **Atlantik** (Schwanthalerstr. 2–6, tel. 089/555670) also show films with their original sound track. The annual week-long **film festival** takes place at the end of June (*see* Cheap Thrills in Worth Seeing, *above*).

MUSIC AND DANCING Pick up a free copy of *München Life*, available at many hotels, for comprehensive listings of theater, music, and film venues. Burly bouncers decorate the entrances of many nightclubs, and getting in depends a lot on their mood. They'll tell you that you have to know a regular to be picked, which is really just a cover for a very elitist door policy. Many spots are less selective on weekdays, when crowds are thinner; arriving unfashionably early—10 or so—might work, or if you pose a lot and look bored, they might decide you're sufficiently blasé to be a nice addition to the scene. Expect clubs to be unventilated and smoky, with pounding techno. If you're feeling especially fashionable and elitist, try the discos **Babalu** (Leopoldstr. 19) or **Park-Café** (Sophienstr. 7), both open daily 10 PM–4 AM; **P-1** (Prinzregentenstr. 1), the most famous, pretentious, and expensive club in Munich; or the immensely popular late-night café and jazz bar **Nachtcafé** (Maximilianspl. 5), open daily 7 PM–5 AM. Cover charges range from DM 8 to DM 15, but a number of clubs are free on the last Wednesday of the month.

To buy tickets for big classical or pop concerts, hit **Hieber Max** (Liebfrauenstr. 1, tel. 089/226571) or the **two kiosks under Marienplatz** (tel. 089/229556). For tickets to concerts in Olympiapark (*see* Outdoor Activities, *below*), go to the **Eissportstadion** at Olympiapark or to the third floor of the **Kaufhof** in Marienplatz (tel. 089/260–3249). **Studiosus-Studienreisen** (Amalienstr. 73, tel. 089/280768) sells discounted theater and concert tickets to students.

➢ **CLASSICAL** • Consult the *Monatsprogramm* for detailed listings of all concerts and theater. Students can get some incredible deals on first-rate operas, ballets, and symphonies; get in line an hour before the show, and whip out that student I.D. card. When they're available, standing-room tickets are also extra cheap; try at the Nationaltheater (*see below*) and Staatstheater am Gärtnerplatz (*see below*). Many major performance halls are closed for vacation late July–September. The Nationaltheater is especially packed in June and July, when the annual Opera Festival is on. The **Schloßkonzerte** (Palace Concert Series), held in Nymphenburg, Schleißheim, Dachau, and Blutenburg, as well as in the Brunnenhof of the Residenz, also take place in summer. Organ concerts are common, too.

The **Bayerische Staatsoper/Nationaltheater** (Max-Joseph-Pl., tel. 089/221316) features ballet and opera; the **Staatstheater am Gärtnerplatz** (Gärtnerpl. 3, tel. 089/201–6767) offers opera, as well as musicals and operettas. Ballet and musicals play at the **Deutsches Theater** (Schwanthalerstr. 13, tel. 089/514–4360). Concerts by

Munich's fine philharmonic and other classical concerts take place in one of three halls in the **Gasteig Cultural Center** (Rosenheimerstr. 5, tel. 089/480980), at the **Herkulessaal** of the Residenz (Odeonspl., enter through Hofgarten, tel. 089/290–67263), at **Bayerischer Rundfunk** (Rundfunkpl. 1, tel. 089/558080), and in the **Kongressaal,** in the Deutsches Museum (Museuminsel 1, tel. 089/21791). Students at the **Hochschule für Musik** (Arcisstr. 12, tel. 089/559101) often give free concerts, too. The gorgeous, Rococo **Altes Residenztheater** (Residenzstr. 1, tel. 089/221316), also known as the **Cuvilliés Theater,** stages folk pieces, operas, and chamber music.

➢ **DANCE CLUBS** • **Far Out.** The crowd may be a little young at times, but this club still caters to people who'd rather dance than pose. The bouncers aren't picky, either. *Am Karlstor 2, no tel.*

Max Emanuel Brauerei. The Latin dance parties and the Irish theme parties at this restaurant–beer garden–club get packed with a really international crowd. It's a blast on all nights. The DM 8 cover includes a drink. *Adalbertstr. 33, no tel.*

➢ **LIVE ROCK AND JAZZ** • The rock and jazz scenes are big here and usually expensive, but **Shamrock** (Trautenwolfstr. 6, tel. 089/331081), which opens at 9, and **The Dubliner** (Candidpl. 9, tel. 089/655676), open daily 11 PM–3 AM, pack 'em in with live music—usually Irish bands—for free.

Allotria. Come to this intimate Munich favorite to hear great jazz and funky fusion bands. The cover varies but is at least DM 8. *Oskar-von-Miller-Ring 3 at Gabelsberger, tel. 089/285858. Closed Mon.*

Crash. The name pretty much sums it up. Bang your head with other hard rockers until 1 AM Monday–Friday, 3 AM Saturday and Sunday. *Lindwurmstr. 88, tel. 089/773272.*

Novak's Schwabinger Brettl. This small, intimate club features great blues bands for a DM 5 cover. Shows begin at 9. *Occaamstr. 11, tel. 089/347289.*

Oklahoma-Country Saloon. Country bands from Germany and abroad jam here Wednesday through Friday beginning at 8:30, Saturday at 8. *Schäftlarnstr. 156, tel. 089/723–4327. U3 to Thalkirchen, exit at Zennerstr. Cover depends on band; free last Wed. of month.*

Unterfahrt. If you're a jazz junkie, you'll dig this hot Haidhausen club. The best deal is the jam session every Sunday at 9 PM for DM 5. Otherwise, the cover will run you DM 10–DM 15. *Kirschenstr. 96, tel. 089/448-2794. Closed Mon.*

THEATER If your German is pretty good, Munich's got tons of theaters and cabarets. The favorite place to see a variety of theater productions is the **Münchner Kammerspiele-Schauspielhaus** (Maximilianstr. 26, tel. 089/237–21268). Its other branch, the **Werkraum,** stages experimental pieces (Hildegardstr. 1, tel. 089/237–21328). Similarly, the well-established **Residenztheater** (Max-Joseph-Pl. 1, tel. 089/225754) also stages experimental operas and dramas at the **Theater im Marstall** (Marstallpl., tel. 089/225754).

Near Munich

STARNBERGERSEE

Once a favorite summer destination for the Wittelsbach rulers, the Starnbergersee was rediscovered by tourists in the middle of the 19th century, when a new S-Bahn connection made transportation to and from Munich easy and quick. Halfway between the Bavarian capital and the Alps, the gorgeous 19-kilometer-long (12-mile-long) lake is a popular weekend getaway for sunbathers, sailors, windsurfers, swimmers, and hikers. In 1886, King Ludwig II drowned in this lake, along with his doctor, after he was deposed and confined to the castle at **Berg,** a small village on the shores of the lake.

Boat rides to Berg (DM 8.50 round-trip) depart from the lakeside promenade outside the S-Bahn station mid-April–late October and take 12 minutes. (You can also cruise farther around the lake to Leoni, Possenhofen, or Seeshaupt; the full cruise takes about two hours. Check at the Starnberg stop in front of the S-Bahn for details.) Stroll through the **Schloßpark** (Castle Park) to reach the **Votivkapelle,** a memorial chapel built high above the point where the king's body was discovered; a cross marks the spot. Ludwig's favorite cousin, Sissi, lived in a castle across the lake, in **Possenhofen.** Some theorize that the king drowned trying to swim the mile to her home. For a perfect finish to a day at Starnbergersee, catch Bus 951 from the Starnberg S-Bahn to the Herrsching S-Bahn (trains don't run frequently; the last departure on weekdays is at 5:36, on Saturday at 5:15) and haul over to the Andechs monastery, where you can chug a few liters of their famous brew before hopping on the S-Bahn back to Munich (*see* Ammersee and Andechs, *below.*)

COMING AND GOING To get to the Starnbergersee, hop on the S6 toward Tutzing and disembark at Starnberg. The trip takes less than 40 minutes and is free with a valid Eurailpass or InterRail pass; otherwise, it requires four strips of a strip ticket. Only those day passes valid for both inner and outer zones are accepted.

OUTDOOR ACTIVITIES From the train station, face the lake and walk left along the promenade if you feel like **catching some rays** or **swimming.** You'll find both secluded and packed stretches of grassy beachfront (cross the two wood bridges). From the station, head to your right to rent **motorboats** (DM 20 per hour), **pedal boats** (starting at DM 6 per half hour), or **rowboats** (starting at DM 8 per hour). For **sailing,** go to Bootshaus 3 train station (weekdays only). Take windsurfing lessons (or just rent the equipment) from the **Windsurfingschule** (Bahnhofstr. 7, tel. 08151/16161). For more information, visit the **tourist-information office** (Wittelsbacherstr. 9, tel. 08151/13008). From the S-Bahn station, walk five minutes away from the lake on Wittelsbacherstraße. If you're interested in **hiking,** request information about the 13-kilometer (8-mile) trail to the **Ludwig Weg** (King Ludwig Way), a 120-kilometer (74-mile) path that stretches from Starnberg and to Füssen. Many long hiking routes run past Starnbergersee; if you want, buses will carry your luggage while you walk.

DACHAU CONCENTRATION CAMP

Although the 1,200-year-old town of Dachau attracted hordes of painters and artists from the mid-19th century until the First World War, most people remember it as the site of Germany's first concentration camp. Opened in 1933, the camp's **Jourhaus,** the front gate, greeted more than 206,000 political dissidents, Jews, clergy, and other "enemies" of the Nazis with the promise that ARBEIT MACHT FREI (WORK BRINGS FREEDOM). The camp's watchtowers and walls remain, and the **gas chambers,** disguised as showers, are also original. For some reason the chambers were never actually used, yet more than 32,000 prisoners died here before American soldiers stormed the camp in 1945; even after the liberation, many former prisoners perished from disease and the effects of prolonged starvation. Through photographs, letters, and official documents, the **museum** (open Tues.–Sun. 9–5) chronicles the rise of the Third Reich and the cruel working and living conditions endured by the camp's prisoners (brief English captions accompany most exhibits). A 22-minute film is shown in English at 11:30 and 3:30 and is sometimes repeated between these two showings.

In the center of town and upstairs from the **tourist-information center** (Konrad-Adenauer-Str. 3, tel. 08131/84566) is a **picture gallery.** The remaining wing of a **palace,** built for Wittelsbach ruler Max Emanuel in 1715, and its tree-lined grounds are a short distance from here, up a hill. The palace's hall, which hosts classical concerts in summer, has a pretty, carved 16th-century ceiling.

COMING AND GOING Take S2 toward Petershausen (about 20 minutes) to Dachau. To get to the former concentration camp from the station, take Bus 722 to Gedenkstätte (Memorial). If you're using a strip ticket, cancel four strips. If you're using a rail pass you only have to pay for the bus (DM 1.50), and, if you have a day pass, both the train and bus rides are already paid for. To get to Dachau's city center, take Bus 710 or 722 to Rathaus.

AMMERSEE AND ANDECHS

Smaller and less visited than the Starnbergersee, the Ammersee and the nearby monastery at Andechs make another excellent getaway for water-sport enthusiasts, hikers, and beer connoisseurs. The S-Bahn stop at Herrsching is only minutes from the lake promenade, where you can stop to take in the beauty of the gently stirring water or catch a 40-minute ferry ride (DM 12.50) to other lakeside towns like **Diessen,** which is full of fishermen and artists and is known for its pottery and a splendid Baroque church. The famous court architect Cuvilliés designed the high altar of the **Marienkirche** (St. Mary's Church, open 10:30–noon and 2–6). Facing the lake promenade by Herrsching, veer right to a romantic **villa** built for the artist Ludwig Scheuermann. The villa is now used as a cultural center and summer concert hall. For **boat** rentals, rocky **beaches,** and expensive lakeside **restaurants,** wander to your left from the promenade.

Ward off that beer belly by undertaking the scenic 3-kilometer (2-mile) trek up **Heiliger Berg** (Holy Mountain) and the Benedictine monastery-brewery of Andechs. The walk takes about an hour. People visit now mainly to taste the monks' own special brew, either in the beer garden (open daily 9:45–8:45), overlooking rolling farmland, or in the hall. Before you get too hammered to remember it, check out the 15th-century pilgrimage church, which was originally Gothic but was lavishly redecorated in the Rococo style during the 18th century. The church closes at 7. If you didn't pack your own picnic, do the typical rolls or pretzel thing, and try the home-made cheese (DM 3); it may stink but it's pretty tasty. A Maß of the monks' special brew costs only DM 6.20.

COMING AND GOING From Munich take S5 to the last stop, Herrsching. The trip takes less than an hour. Cancel six strips on a strip ticket. You don't need to pay if you have a valid rail pass, but only those day passes covering both the inner and outer city are valid. To get to Andechs by bus, catch the 956 from the Herrsching S-Bahn station.

CHIEMSEE AND SCHLOß HERRENCHIEMSEE

Nicknamed the "Bavarian Sea," the enormous, pure Chiemsee (Lake Chiem) is a water-sport paradise. Its shores are dotted with resorts where you can go rafting, horseback riding, cycling, hiking, and mountaineering. You can also hang glide in nearby **Übersee** or paraglide in **Aschau** (13 kilometers, or 8 miles, south of Chiemsee).

There are three islands in the lake: **Fraueninsel** (Ladies' Island), **Herreninsel** (Men's Island), and tiny **Krautinsel** (Herb Island). Traffic-free Fraueninsel is a lovely old fishing village. Although its artist-colony days have passed, you can still find summer **art galleries** and the tombstones of some famous artists in the cemetery of the **Benediktiner Kloster** (Benedictine convent). Next to the Baroque church is an arch-domed **Glockenturm** (clock tower) and the nuns' colorful **Krautgarten** (herb garden).

On Herreninsel sprawls the unfinished palace **Herrenchiemsee,** a Versailles look-alike commissioned by infamous King Ludwig II, the one with the castle fetish. A devoted fan of the Sun King, Louis XIV, with whom he shared a name, Ludwig wanted to command the same respect and power as his French idol. Of the 20 rooms open to the public, the spectacular **Spiegelsaal** (Hall of Mirrors) and Ludwig's sumptuous, Midas-touched **bedroom** are the most impressive. Stroll through the fine gardens, too, and find the **old castle,** once the Augustinian monastery and the site where Germany's constitution was written in 1948. *Admission: DM 7, DM 5 students. Palace open Apr.–Sept., daily 9–5; Oct.–Mar., daily 10–4. Guided tours only.*

COMING AND GOING From Munich you can get a bargain excursion ticket that includes the one-hour train ride to and from the lakeside town of **Prien,** a bus or steam-train trip to the village of **Stock,** and the round-trip ferry ride from Stock to **Herreninsel** and **Fraueninsel** (DM 38, tickets usually available May–Sept., Tues.–Sun.).

LANDSHUT

About 75 kilometers (47 miles) northeast of Munich is Landshut, a beautifully preserved 15th-century town still unknown to most tourists. Lined with unevenly shaped, pastel-color Baroque facades, the cobblestone street **Altstadt** definitely deserves its reputation as one of Germany's prettiest, along with its sister, **Neustadt,** a similar but less bustling avenue. That strange-looking missile-shape thing in the center of town is the 436-foot tower of **St. Martin's Church,** the largest brick tower in the world. Inside is a famous late Gothic (16th-century) carving of the Madonna, designed to please the eye from all angles. Don't miss the unusual stained-glass windows, which juxtapose the crimes of Hitler and other Nazi leaders with the martyrdom of St. Kastulus.

A short walk from here is the castle **Burg Trausnitz,** a 13th-century medieval relic sprawled atop a hill overlooking the town; it was home to the Wittelsbach dukes until 1503. Labor your way up the hill to the castle for fantastic views of the town's striking red roofs, and take a 45-minute tour (tel. 089/226138; DM 2 adults, DM 1.50 students; tours given daily 9–5) of the castle's innards.

Also on Altstadt is the 16th-century **Stadtresidenz,** which succeeded Burg Trausnitz as home of the Wittelsbachs. It was the first Italian Renaissance palace north of the Alps, and it houses the **city museum** and a **picture gallery** (tel. 0871/3484).

COMING AND GOING Trains from Munich make the 45- to 60-minute trip to Landshut at least hourly. Landshut is also a convenient and worthwhile stop if you're on your way to Passau (shove your stuff in a locker at the station).

GETTING AROUND From the train station, hop one of the many city buses that will take you to the Altstadt, in the city center (15 minutes, DM 1.50 adults, DM .90 students). You can walk to all major sights from here.

WHERE TO SLEEP AND EAT For a cheap lunch, try one of the many **Metzgerei** (butcher shops); the one at Neustadt 529 sells a respectable sandwich for DM 3. Pick up some food for the road or for a picnic along the Isar at **H. L. Markt,** on Dreifältigkeitplatz.

The **Jugendherberge** (Richard-Schirrmann Weg 6, tel. 0871/23449), which provides beds for DM 10.50–DM 13, is centrally located by Burg Trausnitz. Camp at **Campingplatz der Stadt Landshut** (tel. 0871/53366, closed Oct.–Mar.), in Mitterwöhr along the Isar. Pension and hotel rooms start at DM 30 per person, although rooms in the city center cost bucks. Try **Hotel Park Café** (Papiererstr. 36, tel. 0871/69339), which isn't too far out in location or price; beds start at DM 36 per person. Ask at the station's information office or at the tourist office (tel. 0871/23031) for a listing of more hotels and prices. While you're at it, grab the pamphlet "Kunst, Kultur, *und* Sport," for festivals, theater, and sports info.

BAVARIA 6

By Linda Shing

Bavaria draws hordes of tourists every year to its soothing lakes, Alpine peaks, medieval cities, and pristine nature preserves. Sprawled across some 70,200 square kilometers (27,000 square miles), Bavaria's romantic landscape beckons outdoorsy folks, history freaks, lovers, and those who still believe in fairy tales. Its four main cities—Nürnberg (in the northern region known as Franconia, *see* Chapter 7), Augsburg (in the western region of Bavarian Swabia), Regensburg (in East Bavaria), and Munich (in Upper Bavaria, *see* Chapter 5)—are historic and cultural giants, making a trip to Bavaria potentially a very, very long one. Deeply Catholic and conservative, Bavaria is also Germany's largest, most well-known, and most distinctive state.

Bavaria was ruled by the royal Wittelsbach dynasty for seven centuries, beginning in 1180 as a duchy presented to Otto von Wittelsbach by Emperor Barbarossa, and ending in the turbulent post–World War I period with the forced abdication of the last Wittelsbach monarch, King Ludwig III. Although the Prussian military and political strategist Otto von Bismarck yanked the land from Ludwig II, incorporating it into his Confederation of Northern German States, Bavaria held steadfastly to its distinct traditions, dialect, and its name: To this day Bavarians call it the Free State of Bavaria.

Bavaria's contradictions make it the ideal place to look for all that you expect, hope for, and dread from Germany: It's got the scenery, the castles, the lingering legacy of Nazism, the Alps, the beer (boy, does it have the beer), and the history in every town square and edifice.

If you visit elsewhere in Germany you'll undoubtedly notice, and probably have long, drunken discussions about, the differences between Bavarians and the so-called Prussians of the north. Northerners consider the Bavarians less refined, too provincial, and loud, whereas Bavarians describe the northerners as stuffy, highfalutin, and boring. Perhaps it's fairest to say that the stereotypes of Bavarians as brash, rude, and conservative contain some truth, but so do the others characterizing them as boisterously friendly and hospitable. The one thing northerners and southerners *can* agree on, though, is that Bavaria is unlike any other region in the country.

Northerners will sternly remind you that you can't *really* say you've visited *Germany* if you've only spent time in Bavaria; nonetheless, the most common images of the country—lederhosen, brass bands, beer gardens, castles, and Oktoberfest—actually originated in this southern state.

Augsburg

History in Augsburg is alive; you can get a taste of it on any of the worthwhile tours offered by the tourist office, or just by wandering around its cobbled streets. Augsburg was founded in 15 BC by Drusus and Tiberius, stepsons of the Roman emperor Augustus, and is today the oldest and third-largest city in Bavaria. During the 16th century its ambitious merchant families sought out markets as far away as South America. The most famous of these well-to-do clans were the Fuggers, under whose patronage Augsburg really flourished. The Fuggers were to Renaissance Augsburg what the Medicis were to Florence: Many of Augsburg's historic monuments owe their existence to the Fugger treasury, and much of the city's appeal lies in the fact that so much of the Altstadt (Old Town) was built around the same time, in the same lavish style, by the same flamboyant people.

Augsburg also saw a lot of the key action of the Protestant Reformation. Martin Luther stayed for a time after being called here to meet with Catholic Church fat cats, eventually leading his incensed followers to revolt against the church and demand reforms. In 1555, the influential Augsburg Religious Peace, a settlement supporting religious tolerance in Germany and of great significance for all of Europe, was concluded here. Augsburg remained a free imperial city from the 13th century until 1806, when Napoléon annexed it to Bavaria.

Today a healthy student population and a variety of cultural events keep Augsburg young. Despite its business and industrial districts, the Altstadt manages to preserve an honest Renaissance flavor that earns the town a place on the Romantic Road tour (*see* Chapter 7), a popular tourist trail that starts far to the north in the Franconian town of Würzburg.

BASICS

BUCKET SHOPS **A & S Reisebüro** sells ISIC and FIYTO cards and also offers student discounts on some flights. *Maximilianstr. 14, tel. 0821/502–7010. Open weekdays 9–6, Sat. 9–noon.*

LUGGAGE STORAGE Pay DM 2 per day for a small locker (big enough for most backpacks) in the train station, DM 4 for a big one.

For some reason, urban Augsburg has long been a mecca for heroin addicts, and throughout the city center you'll see constant reminders that not all in Augsburg is as "romantic" as the tourist board would like you to think.

PHONES AND MAIL The main post office, right next to the train station, has the longest hours of any currency-exchange desk in town; they take a fairly standard commission of DM 3 per traveler's check. You can also make long-distance calls and purchase phone cards here. *Jakobspl. 16, by Fuggerei, tel. 0821/33319. Open weekdays 8 AM–10 PM, weekends 8–8.*

VISITOR INFORMATION The main tourist office, **Verkehrsverein,** sits 300 yards from the train station on the west side of the Altstadt. The office stocks all the usual maps and lodging information, and can book you into a private room for a DM 3 fee. *Bahnhofpl. 7, tel. 0821/502070. Open weekdays 9–7.*

The **information office** across from the town hall at Rathausplatz dishes out more tourist literature and is open on weekends, too. The office will also make room reservations (DM 3). This is the only place to get the *Radwegskarte,* a map of bicycle routes, and the indispensable English-language pamphlet "See and Enjoy," which lists all sights and opening hours, and maps out a number of walking tours. The tours take you to such places as a tannery, a bakery, and a goldsmith, and around the city's medieval walls. You'll see color-coded signs all over town corresponding to the different routes.

Augsburg

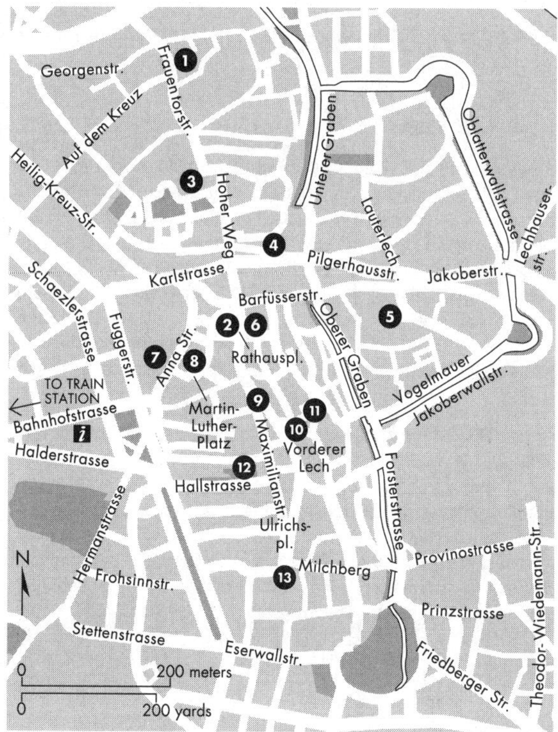

Brechthaus, **4**
Deutsche Barockgalerie (Schaezler Palace), **12**
Dom St. Maria, **3**
Fuggerei, **5**
Holbeinhaus, **11**
Maximilian Museum, **8**
Mercury Fountain, **9**
Mozarthaus, **1**
Perlachturm, **2**
Rathaus, **6**
Römisches Museum, **10**
St. Annakirche, **7**
Sts. Ulrich and Afra, **13**

You can also hook up with a guided German/English bus tour of the city that leaves from outside the town hall at 10:30 AM (May–Oct. only, DM 12, DM 5 students). The tourist brochure "*Augsburger Kulturnachrichten*" has complete listings of current exhibits and cultural events. *Tel. 0821/502–0724. Open Mon.–Wed. 7:30–4:30, Thurs. 7:30–5:30, Fri. 7:30–noon, Sat. 9–6, Sun. 10–2.*

A guided **walking tour** in German and English leaves from outside the town hall at 2 daily during the summer, and at 2 every Saturday from November to April. Tickets cost DM 7, DM 4 for students. Buy tickets from your guide.

COMING AND GOING

Get information, make reservations, and buy tickets for train and bus connections at the **Reisezentrum** (travel center) in the train station (tel. 0821/19419); it's open Monday through Saturday 5:30 AM–9:30 PM and Sunday 5:30 AM–10 PM.

Trains to Munich leave four or five times every hour (40 minutes, DM 14.80 one-way). Connections to Regensburg (2½ hours, DM 46 one-way) and other German cities are frequent. You can also get from here to the Bavarian Alps, Amsterdam, Basel, and Rome. To reach the city center from the depot, head east down Bahnhofstraße and veer left onto Anna Straße. If you want to peddle around town, the Hauptbahnhof rents **bikes** for DM 8 per day.

From the **Busbahnhof,** opposite the train station, there's daily service to Munich (DM 8) and Stuttgart (DM 20). Between April 10 and September 26, Augsburg is also serviced by Deutsche Bahn's Romantic Road Bus, with scheduled stops in Füssen, Munich, Nördlingen, Dinkelsbühl, Rothenburg, Würzburg, and Frankfurt.

Hook up with a carpool to other German and European cities through the ride-share agency **Mitfahrzentrale Augsburg** (Branderstr. 36, tel. 0821/414655 or 0821/418529).

WHERE TO SLEEP

The tourist office books private rooms (DM 25–DM 35) in the Altstadt for a DM 3 fee. Rooms in decently located hotels, pensions, and guest houses generally start at DM 35 for a single and DM 65 for a double. Try **Jakoberhof** (Jakoberstr. 39–41, tel. 0821/510030), a simple but cozy guest house near the Fuggerei, about a 10-minute walk from the center of town. It has singles for DM 38, doubles for DM 65–DM 125. **Lenzhalde** (Theilottstr. 2, tel. 0821/520745), conveniently located behind the train station, has singles for DM 39–DM 45, doubles for DM 72. At **Hotel-Pension Georgsrast** (Georgenstr. 39, tel. 0821/502610), past the Dom at the northern end of the city center, singles run DM 52, doubles DM 72–DM 96. All prices include breakfast.

Upscale options include the **Dom Hotel** (Frauentorstr. 8, tel. 0821/153031), across the street from the cathedral. The Dom is large (43 rooms) but comfortable. All rooms come equipped with bath or shower and radios, and rooms on the top floor have tiptop views of the city. Doubles start at DM 110 and peak at DM 130. Around the corner is the **Augsburger Hof** (Auf dem Kreuz 2, tel. 0821/314083), a 40-room guest house set in an elegant mansion with a stunning Renaissance facade. The Dom is a few blocks away, the city center a five-minute saunter. Facilities at the Augsburger Hof include a restaurant, garden, and sauna; doubles start at DM 90 and peak at DM 120.

Jugendherberge Augsburg, in the center of downtown and only a three-minute walk from the Dom, is by far the cheapest and most convenient place to crash. Only hostellers under 27 are accommodated; space in one of its 153 beds costs DM 15 per night, including breakfast. *Beim Pfaffenkeller 3, tel. 0821/33909. From train station, Tram 2 toward Kriegshaber to Stadtwerke, walk toward Dom, and turn right on Inneres Pfaffengäßchen (30 min.). Closed Dec. 20–Jan. 20.*

Campers should head for **Campingplatz Augusta** (tel. 0821/714121), in the direction of Neuburg at Autobahnsee, or **Campingplatz Ludwigshof** (tel. 08207/1077, closed Nov.–Mar.), toward the district of Mühlhausen.

FOOD

Augsburg has the usual setup: Street stands and Imbisses line both the main market square, Rathausplatz, and nearby Maximilianstraße. Of the nicer restaurants here try the **Fuggerkeller** (Maximilianstr. 40, tel. 0821/510031), a traditional Franconian restaurant housed in the cellars of the former Fugger family home. A full dinner will set you back at least DM 25, but the lunch menu has a few selections priced under DM 15. For fresh produce, meats, and cheeses, check out the **Stadtmarkt** (city market), open weekdays 7–6, Saturday 7–noon. Enter the market from Fuggerstraße, Anna Straße, or Ernst-Reuter-Platz.

Caruso. This classy Italian restaurant features a jumbo menu, good grub, and quite reasonable prices—a better bet than Nuova Italia (*see below*) if you're looking for a sit-down meal. The *penne ai broccoli* is a steal at DM 10; pizzas start at DM 7.50. *Karlstr. 9, enter at Karlpassage, tel. 0821/155240. Closed Wed. and daily 2:30–5:30.*

König von Flandern. This spot brews its own tasty beer, *Drei-Heller-Bier* (DM 3.20 per ⅓ liter). It also serves fresh homemade bread—for free—with your drinks or meal. The menu's small but the price is decidedly friendly. Go for the generous, colorful salad plate (DM 8.90), the typical Bavarian-food sampler *Bauernteller* (DM 12.60), or the classic *Schweinshaxe* (pig knuckles, DM 9). Ramble down the road (turn left out of the restaurant) if you want to join Augsburg's night café scene afterward. *Karolinenstr. 12, tel. 0821/158050. Under Bücher Pustel bookstore.*

Nuova Italia. This Italian joint has cheap food and a student clientele. Grab a slice of pizza on the run for DM 3; otherwise, pizzas begin at DM 6.10, pastas at DM 6.50. *Maximilianstr. 17, tel. 0821/152881.*

WORTH SEEING

Augsburg may be a large city, but its historic Altstadt is reasonably compact and easily covered on foot. The tourist office sells three color-coded, self-guided tours (DM 3 apiece) that outline one- to two-hour rambles through the old town. The office also organizes a bevy of guided walking and bus tours. If you'd rather strike out on your own, head east along Bahnhofstraße from the tourist office and veer left onto Anna Straße. Keep straight and you'll soon pass the 14th-century **St. Annakirche,** Augsburg's most important Protestant church (in 1518 Martin Luther stayed in the church, in Room 5, during his meetings with Cardinal Cajetanus, the papal legate sent from Rome to convince Luther of his reformist errors).

Hang a right at the northern end of Anna Straße and you'll soon stumble upon **Rathausplatz,** which marks the historic heart of Augsburg. The square is dominated by the 258-foot-tall **Perlachturm** tower (admission DM 2; open Apr.–Oct., daily 10–6), worth climbing for a good view of the city center. Adjacent to the tower is the massive **Rathaus** itself, considered one of the finest Renaissance structures north of the Alps. Unfortunately, like so many historic buildings in Germany, the Rathaus you see today is only a detailed reconstruction; the original was mostly destroyed at the end of World War II.

DOM ST. MARIA From Rathausplatz head north along Karolinenstraße and Hoher Weg—two popular shopping streets—to reach Dom St. Maria, Augsburg's largest and most dominating cathedral. (If you're lost, scan the skyline for its hard-to-miss Gothic towers.) The western part of the cathedral comprises a Romanesque basilica originally built in the 11th century (the inner walls in this part of the church are red and white); the Gothic eastern end (with the pure white walls) is a relative baby in cathedral years, constructed only in the 14th century. Considering that half of Augsburg was flattened in the Second World War, it's incredible that the church escaped unscathed. By the western entrance is a column topped by a pinecone (Augsburg's symbol), erected in gratitude for this miracle.

The Dom's real draw, however, is the art it holds within. Besides the five fantastic altarpieces by Hans Holbein the Elder, there's an equally stunning cycle of stained-glass on the church's south side that dates from the 11th century, making it the oldest stained-glass work in central Europe. *Open Mon.–Sat. 9–6, Sun. noon–6.*

Access to the Fuggerei is controlled by guarded gates that are locked from 10 PM to 6 AM, severely curtailing the social lives of the occupants; if they come in after midnight, residents are fined the equivalent of seven months' rent—a whopping DM 1.

FUGGEREI The Fuggerei, a 10-minute walk east of the city center, is the world's oldest social-housing scheme. This tranquil complex was originally built in 1519 by the Fuggers to accommodate the city's poor. Believe it or not, the 147 homes still serve the same purpose: As long as you're a native of Augsburg, Catholic, and destitute through no fault of your own (i.e., no heroin fiends)—and as long as you agree to pray for the Fuggers on a daily basis—one of these simple but comfortable homes can be yours for the low price of "one Rheinisch Guilder," or roughly DM 1.72 annually. That's right, little more than $1 per year.

The Fuggerei is located at the foot of Vorderer Lech, just off Barfußerstraße. You can walk the grounds, but none of the lived-in homes is open for public viewing. However, you can see how people lived during the Fuggers' time in the **Fuggerei Museum,** an original apartment. Next door is the former apartment of the poor mason Franz Mozart, Wolfgang's great-grandfather. Be sure to check out the old bellpulls (the ancestors of doorbells), which are all shaped differently; back in the old days, residents could identify their houses in the dark streets by the feel of their bellpull.

MAXIMILIANSTRAßE Maximilianstraße, which lies a few blocks south of Rathausplatz, is Augsburg's busiest shopping street. This lantern-lined avenue contains dozens of shops and cafés, as well as a good collection of 15th- and 16th-century half-timbered homes. At its northern foot, the **Mercury Fountain,** finished in 1599 by the Dutch artist Adrian de Vries, shows Mercury in his traditional pose. Continue south along Maximilianstraße and you'll soon pass another de Vries fountain, this one depicting Hercules battling the Hydra.

Farther along the street is the 18th-century **Schaezler Palace.** This squat palace was paid for and built by the von Liebenhofen family. At the time the place was built, property tax was levied according to the size of street frontage. To beat the tax man the von Liebenhofens designed their palace to be deep and narrow, running far back from Maximilianstraße. Descendants of the von Liebenhofens donated the palace to the city after World War II. Today it contains the **Deutsche Barockgalerie** (German Baroque Gallery), with its large holding of 17th- and 18th-century works. Among the paintings look for Dürer's portrait of one of the Fuggers. *Maximilianstr. 46. Admission free. Open May–Sept., Tues.–Sun. 10–5; Oct.–Apr., Tues.–Sun. 10–4.*

The adjacent churches **St. Ulrich** and **St. Afra,** set on Ulrichsplatz at the southern foot of Maximilianstraße, mark the site where St. Afra was buried in AD 304. In the saint's honor a late-Gothic church was begun in 1467, and after the adjoining St. Ulrich was completed in 1710, St. Afra's tomb was moved into the churches' joint crypt, where you'll also find the tomb of St. Ulrich himself, a 10th-century bishop. The two churches are worth a gander for their Baroque wrought iron and woodworking.

MUSEUMS Augsburg has a wealth of small, unique museums: The descriptions of exhibits are usually in German, but at some you can buy an English guidebook at the entrance. In addition to those listed here, you can also visit museums on glass painting, balloon flights, aviation, Jewish history and culture, natural science, and modern art, although some of these sit quite far from the city center; get more information at one of the tourist offices. Unless otherwise noted, the following museums are open May to September, Tuesday–Sunday 10–5; October–April 10–4.

➢ **BRECHTHAUS** • This modest house marks the birthplace of playwright Bertolt Brecht, a dramatic genius who grew up in Augsburg before moving first to Munich and then, after the Nazis took power, to New York and Los Angeles. Brecht is best remembered as the author of the plays *Mother Courage* and *The Threepenny Opera*, and as the director of East Berlin's Berliner Ensemble following World War II. Inside the Brecht family home are exhibits dedicated to Brecht and his work. *Auf dem Rain 7, 3 blocks n. of Rathauspl. Admission: DM 2, DM 1 students.*

➢ **HOLBEINHAUS** • Near the Fuggerei on Vorderer Lech you'll find the reconstructed home of Hans Holbein the Elder, one of Germany's most famous 16th-century painters (and a native son of Augsburg). There's not much to remind visitors that Hans once lived here; instead, the house has been transformed into the city art gallery, with a regularly changing program of exhibits. You can see some of his renowned altar paintings in Augsburg's Dom. *Vorderer Lech 20. Admission: DM 2, DM 1 students.*

➢ **MAXIMILIAN MUSEUM** • Housed in the former residence of the Welsers, this small civic museum traces Augsburg's cultural and architectural history and also displays local arts and crafts. *Phillippine-Welser-Str. 24.*

➢ **MOZARTHAUS** • In the Mozart family, it was Wolfgang Amadeus who enjoyed the greatest musical reputation. However, his father, Leopold Mozart, was an accomplished composer and performer in his own right. And more to the point, Leopold Mozart was born in this small Augsburg house in 1719. These days the Mozart family house serves as memorial and museum, documenting Leopold's stint as court violinist at Salzburg, the birth of Wolfgang (who supposedly was weaned on water, not milk), and Leopold's subsequent involvement in the development of his son's musical career. *Frauentorstr. 50, 3 blocks n. of Dom St. Maria. Admission: DM 2, DM 1 students. Open Mon., Wed., Thurs. 10–noon and 2–5; Fri. 10–noon and 1–4; weekends 10–noon.*

➢ **ROMISCHES MUSEUM** • This former monastery displays artifacts found in the Augsburg region from the prehistoric, Roman, and early Middle Ages. This is an interesting minor diversion and will give you a clearer sense of the historical richness of Augsburg. *Dominikanergasse 15. Admission: DM 2, DM 1 students.*

AFTER DARK

Once the sun sets, cruise down **Maximilianstraße** for a taste of Augsburg's lively café scene. **Café Max** (Maximilianstr. 67, tel. 0821/154700) and **Peaches** (Maximilianstr. 73, tel. 0821/312258) are especially popular meeting spots, or bring your own bottle of vino to one of the street fountains that draw people on summer evenings. Augsburg's **student pubs** are concentrated around the alleys and streets behind the Rathaus. **Heilig-Kreuz-Straße** is another good place to check out; here you'll find the **Thorbräukeller** (Wertabheruckertorstr. 9, tel. 0821/36561), a beer garden favored by locals, and **Bodega** (Heilig-Kreuz-Str. 18, tel. 0821/37115), a fun Spanish bar west of the Dom.

Ingolstadt

Most tourists have never heard of Ingolstadt, but this walled Bavarian town offers an intriguing blend of culture, including one of the most bizarre collections of museums you'll find in any small Bavarian town; college life, which spices up the nightlife considerably; and modern industry (Audi produces its fine road machines here). To see Ingolstadt at its prettiest and most historic, wander around the tiny **Altstadt** (Old Town), which has an impressive collection of preserved buildings.

Frequent trains whiz between Munich and Ingolstadt, and Eichstätt and the Altmühl valley are less than an hour's ride from here; one-way fare to Eichstätt will run you DM 8.40. To get to the center of town from the train station, take Bus 10 (DM 1.50) to Rathausplatz; it's about a 10-minute ride. The **tourist office** (Rathauspl. 4, tel. 0841/305417) is efficient and comprehensive.

WHERE TO SLEEP

The tourist office (*see above*) will help you find a room, but if you come late, try the information board in the Rathausplatz; it lists hotels and pensions with their phone numbers and prices. You'll find that lodging in Ingolstadt is a bit pricey unless you're willing to stay quite far from the center. Try **Gaststätte City-Pub** (Kupferstr. 6, tel. 0841/910128), which has simple rooms above a bar. At DM 40 for singles and DM 80 for doubles, it's as cheap as you'll find in the city center. Campers should head for **Campingplatz Auwaldsee** (tel. 0841/68911), about a one-hour ride from town; to get there, take Bus 10 from the main train station to the Omnibus depot. Transfer to Bus 50 to Auwaldsee; the campground sits right by the lake. It's open from April 1 through September 30.

Jugendherberge. Wise travelers will head straight for this well-located establishment in the western part of town near the Kreuztor and a great café and bar area. The many cyclists passing through in the summer are *early* risers and the hostel's halls echo like mad, so don't expect to sleep late. With breakfast, a night here costs DM 15.50, DM 4.50 for sheets. *Friedhofstr. 4¼, tel. 0841/34177. From Hauptbahnhof, Bus 10 to Omnibusbahnhof, then change to Bus 50, 53, or 60 to Kreuztor; from city center, walk from Theresienstr. or Ludwigstr. w. past Kreuztor. 11:15 PM curfew, reception closed 9 AM–3 PM, wheelchair accessible. Closed mid-Dec.–Jan. 6 and every 2nd and 4th weekend Nov.–mid-Dec. and Feb.–mid-Mar.*

FOOD

The café-restaurant **Nuova Italia** (Milchstr. 1, tel. 0841/35273) has gyros (DM 5), hamburgers (DM 3.50), and other cheap fare, and best of all, they're open till midnight, 1 AM on weekends. For authentic, inexpensive Bavarian fare, head for **Weißbierbrauer Kuchlbauer** (Schäffbräustr. 11A, tel. 0841/35512), where people sometimes get up and groove to the live folk music in the beer garden. A half liter starts at DM 3.80; entrées start at DM 8, but the Schweinshaxe are definitely worth the DM 14. For the best budget Italian fare in town go to **Osteria Italiana** (Dollstr. 13, tel. 0841/33300), and for the tastiest Greek food try **Poseidon** (Am Stein 1, tel. 0841/34967). All of these establishments stay open until at least midnight.

WORTH SEEING

Ingolstadt has a wide array of surprising and unusual museums, all of which cost DM 3.50 (students DM 1) and are free on Sundays and holidays. Standard museum hours are 9–noon and 2–5; all are closed Monday.

History buffs will dig the 39-room **Stadtmuseum** (City Museum, in Kavalier Hepp at Auf der Schanz 45, tel. 0841/305130), a collection of historical artifacts, including paintings, models, and tools, which chronicles the development of Ingolstadt. Those with an abiding admiration for Rambo types can commando their way through the **Bayerische Armee Museum** (Bavarian Army Museum, Neues Schloß, Paradepl. 4, tel. 0841/35067), home to Germany's oldest and most famous collection of military history, started by King Ludwig II himself. If you want to indulge in a bit of art talk with your beer, speculate on the philosophy behind "concrete art" in the eyebrow-raising **Museum für Konkrete Kunst** (Museum of Concrete Art, Tränktorstr. 6–8, tel. 0841/305728). Notice the use of the primary colors blue, red, and yellow, the repetition of simple shapes and angles, and the manipulation of proportions and mathematics in the works displayed here.

Probably the most intriguing collection, however, is in the **Deutsches Medizinihistorisches Museum** (Anatomiestr. 18–20, tel. 0841/305493), which documents the development of lay medicine, folk medicine, the different practices of ethnic groups and early advanced civilizations, hygiene, orthopedics, radiology, and so on. Different displays that could enter your dream life for weeks to come include: chairs that look like plush, old-fashioned toilets with convenient handles that are actually 19th-century contraptions designed to help women give birth, 16th-century iron saws used for amputations, and other instruments that will have you eating your apple a day and giving thanks to the gods of modern medicine. The English guidebook (DM 10) is really worth it if you're interested in this kind of stuff; otherwise, everything's in German only and you'll have to rely on a vivid imagination to figure out what you're looking at.

Of the city's churches, don't miss the **Maria-de-Victoria-Kirche** (Neubaustr. 1½, tel. 0841/17518, admission DM 1, open 9–5). The Asam brothers, who tripped through Bavaria redecorating churches left and right, designed the sublime Rococo interior in the 18th century. To appreciate Cosmas Damian's ceiling masterpiece, find the faded circle on the ground a few steps in front of you when you enter the church. From this point, the ceiling fresco takes on a three-dimensional perspective; you'll feel it even more as you walk away from this spot—the pictures seem to get flat. Other churches to check out include the 14th-century **Kreuztor** and the 15th century late Gothic **Liebfrauenmünster,** one of the largest hall churches (the type with no windows near the ceiling since the nave and arches are the same height) in Bavaria.

AFTER DARK

The beer garden **Glocke am Kreuztor** (Oberer Graben 1, tel. 0841/34990) is the busiest and best in town. Supplement your *Maß* (DM 7.50) with light Bavarian snacks (DM 5.50–DM 12.50). It's also the perfect gateway to the young and vigorous café-bar scene that starts right pass the Kreuztor on **Theresienstraße.** The area is known as the Bermuda Triangle, but looks more like the Bermuda Octagon: Confusing if you've had more than a couple of beers.

You can find jazz, organ, and classical concerts in Ingolstadt all year round, but especially during the summer. Jazz greats drop into town in late-October and early November for the annual **Jazz Festival.** Swing by the tourist office (*see above*) for details.

Near Ingolstadt

EICHSTATT AND THE ALTMUHL

Eichstätt is a serene, green, and totally pristine little university town tucked between verdant hills and majestic cliffs in a valley of the **Altmühl River.** As the heart of the **Naturpark Altmühl,** Germany's largest natural park, the town makes the best base for exploring this untouched and untouristy region. Nature lovers, cyclists, hikers, and yes, even paleontologists will love it here.

Cross the Altmühl River from the train station to reach Eichstätt's main town and sights. The unique **national-park information center** is located in the former Baroque church of **Notre Dame** (Notre Dame 1, tel. 08241/6733) and has an unbelievable wealth of information. There's a great exhibit on the park's topography and a hands-on, play-while-you-learn center on the first floor. You can get maps of the region's castles and museums, and information on hiking, cycling, boating, climbing, and even fossil-collecting here. Both this regional information office and the **Eichstätt tourist office** next door (Karl-Preysing-Pl. 14, tel. 08241/7977) will help you find a place to stay. To reach the offices from the train station, cross the bridge Spitalbrücke, cut through Residenzplatz to Leonrodplatz, and pass the Schutzengelkirche.

The **Dom** (Dompl. 10, tel. 08241/501), just across Spitalbrücke on Domplatz, dates to the 8th century and is now an amalgam of Romanesque (the spires), Gothic (the nave, main body, and mortuary), and Baroque (the western facade) styles. Don't miss the stone-carved **Pappenheim Altar,** an emotionally charged depiction of the Crucifixion and the grieving masses gathered at the base of the cross. Light penetrates the stained-glass windows designed by Hans Holbein the Elder to brighten the **Mortuarium** (mortuary). A row of pillars, dominated by the exquisitely carved **Schöne Säule** (beautiful column), divides this Gothic hall into two aisles.

On the palace-lined Residenzplatz is the **Residenz,** which boasts a fancy Rococo staircase and a richly decorated **Hall of Mirrors** (Residenzpl. 1, tel. 08241/701). Once the residence of bishops, today the building houses administrative offices. To see the interior, you must join one of the **tours** available Monday through Thursday at 10, 11, 2, and 3; Friday at 10 and 11; weekends and holidays every half hour from 10 to 11:30 and 2 to 3:30.

The **Mariensäule** statue (Column of the Virgin), rises from a fountain in the Residenzplatz. East of the Residenz, on Leonrodplatz, the pink **Schutzengelkirche** (Church of the Guardian Angel), a Baroque treasure completed in the 18th century, boasts a distinctive pulpit and altarpiece. A block from here down Ostenstraße sits the **Sommerresidenz,** where Eichstätt's prince-bishops once spent the warmer months. Unless you really miss university administration offices, there's not much to see inside. Still farther east on Gottesackergasse, the **Kapuzinerkirche** (Church of the Capuchins) lays claim to the world's oldest replica of the Holy Sepulchre in Jerusalem, dating back to the 12th century. North of the Residenz sits the cobblestone **Marktplatz** (market square), with its numerous markets and shops. Of the many Italian Baroque facades in the colorful square, the **Altes Rathaus** (old town hall) has the finest. In the front of it stands the **Willibaldsbrunnen,** a fountain with a statue of Willibald, who founded the town of Eichstätt as a bishopric in the 8th century. Farther north, off Westenstraße, the **Abbey of St. Walburg** contains the tomb and relics of Willibald's sister, St. Walburga for centuries it was the object of pilgrimages.

The fascinating **Jura Museum** (tel. 08241/2956), isolated from the rest of Eichstätt's sights—it's behind the railroad station and up a hill overlooking the town—is housed in the **Willibaldsburg Castle,** built by bishops in the 14th century. This natural history museum displays an extensive collection of fossils—from insects to a crocodile—embedded in limestone found in this region. It also has one of the world's five known specimens of the *Archaeopteryx,* the oldest of prehistoric birds and a vital developmental link between dinosaurs and birds. Prepare to be disappointed by this display; for all the hype *Archaeopteryx* was still pretty damn tiny. Be sure not to miss the collection of (live) brightly colored and nerdy-looking fish. Also in the castle, you'll find the **Historisches Museum,** which complements its neighbor with the standard array of findings from prehistoric, Roman, and Celtic times.

Those with a hankering to get on the river should paddle or pedal down the swampy Altmühl. Rent canoes (DM 6 per hour) or pedal boats (DM 8 per hour) by the Herzogsteg bridge near Ritter-von-Hofer Weg (Herzoggasse 7, tel. 08241/3142).

COMING AND GOING The train ride from Ingolstadt to Eichstätt's center (Eichstätt Stadt) takes about a half hour and costs DM 13.50 one-way. You will have to change trains at Eichstätt Bahnhof (the main train station) since it's 5 kilometers (3 miles) out of town; connections are frequent.

WHERE TO SLEEP AND EAT Choose from a number of inexpensive *Metzgerei* (butcher shops) in Marktplatz or try one of the many restaurants on adjoining Westenstraße. The **university cafeteria** (Ostenstr. 28, tel. 08241/20461) serves up institutional grub for next to nothing.

Rooms in **private homes** are a reasonable lodging option, starting at DM 23 per person, but houses usually have only two or three rooms. The information offices have lists with prices. Otherwise, try a larger bed-and-breakfast guest house like **Gasthof zum Griechen** (Westenstr. 17, tel. 08421/3500); conveniently located just north of Marktplatz, it offers rates ranging from DM 39 to DM 48 per person.

To reach the excellent **Jugendherberge,** go behind the train station and walk halfway up the hill to *Willibaldsburg.* For a bed and a breakfast, one night here costs DM 16.50, DM 4.50 for sheets. *Reichenaustr. 15. tel. 08241/4427. 112 beds. 10 PM curfew, walk-in registration after 5 PM. Closed mid-Dec.–Jan.*

Regensburg

Although it's actually on the Danube, Regensburg gets its name from the smaller River Regen, which feeds into the larger and more well-known river. The Romans first established a fortress here in AD 179; in subsequent centuries it became the first capital of Bavaria, a center of Christianity, a free imperial city, the seat of the Imperial Diets, and a major hub of trade. As a result, the city boasts a spectacular collection of historical artifacts. Mostly spared from wartime bombings, Regensburg has managed to preserve no less

Regensburg

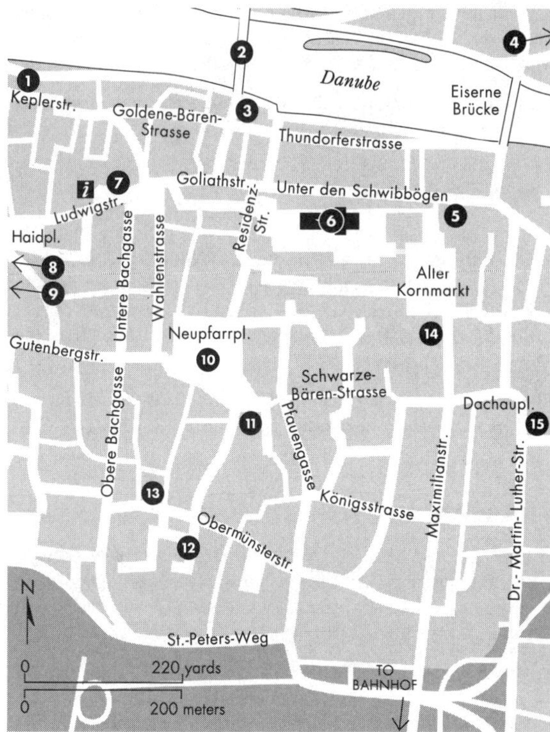

Alte Kapelle, **14**
Altes Rathaus, **7**
Brückturm, **3**
Dom St. Peter, **6**
Jugendherberge, **4**
Kepler-Gedächtnishaus, **1**
Museum der Stadt Regensburg, **15**
Museum Ostdeutsche Galerie, **9**
Neupfarrkirche, **10**
Porta Praetoria, **5**
St. Emmeram Basilica and Crypts, **13**
St. Kassian, **11**
Schloss Thurn-und-Taxis, **12**
Schottenkirche St. Jakob, **8**
Steinerne Brücke, **2**

than 1,400 historical monuments, making a walk around the city a delightful, visceral plunge into history. If you only have a day here, take a long walk and skip the museums entirely, and don't miss the stunning views of the Danube from the city's bridges.

The center of the city is pretty compact and features some of Regensburg's finest and oldest relics: its alleys. Don't miss **Untere Bachgasse,** one of its oldest streets. When you're wandering around, notice all the **patrician houses** with towers of varying heights; high towers were the status symbols of rich traders, just as flashy cars and portable telecommunications devices are today's status symbols. For detailed coverage of the city's sights, pick up the English pamphlet "Where History Is Fun" from the tourist office.

BASICS

BUREAUX DE CHANGE AND MAIL Most **banks** are generally open weekdays 8:30–4, with a long lunch hour between noon and 2, and charge a heftier commission than post offices for changing traveler's checks. Most banks take MasterCard for cash advances; go to **Citibank** (Maximilianstr. 15, tel. 0941/55075) if you carry Visa.

The main **post office** by the train station (Bahnhofstr. 16, tel. 0941/5050) charges DM 3 per check, as does another branch across from the Dom. *Both branches open Mon.–Wed. and Fri. 8–6, Thurs. 8–7:30, Sat. 8–noon; train station branch open Sun. 11–noon.*

EMERGENCIES Dial 110 for the **police,** 112 for **fire**, 19222 for an **ambulance,** or 502000 for the **Women's Clinic.**

VISITOR INFORMATION The friendly **tourist information** office has maps, English pamphlets, a list of hotels and pensions, and also sells tickets for concerts, the Reichstagsmuseum, and two-hour English walking tours from May to September, Wednesday and Saturday at 3. Pick up the pamphlet "Where History Is Fun" for detailed walks. The **lost and found** (tel. 0941/507–2105) is here, too. *Altes Rathaus, tel. 0941/507–3417. Open weekdays 8:30–6, Sat. 9–4, Sun. 9–noon.*

For information on the region of East Bavaria, call or visit the **Fremdenverkehrsband Ostbayern** (Landshuterstr. 13, tel. 0941/57186).

COMING AND GOING

Trains to and from Munich depart hourly and sometimes go through Landshut (1½ hours, DM 32 one-way). There are also frequent connections to Nürnberg (DM 23 one-way) and Passau (DM 27 one-way). Inquire about the cheap day-trip excursion fares to these cities, valid only on Thursdays and weekends. The station is south of the city center; to reach it, take Bus 17 or walk 10–15 minutes up Maximilianstraße from the station.

The **Reisezentrum** in the station sells train tickets, makes reservations, and gives information. *Tel. 0941/19419. Open weekdays 7:30–7, Sat. 7:30–6:10, Sun. 7:30–7:10.*

WHERE TO SLEEP

The few cheap beds in town are very busy, so try to call ahead. Strangely enough, some hotel reception desks are closed on Sundays or the whole weekend; you can't check in on those days, although you can stay through the weekend if you checked in during the week.

Diözesanzentrum Obermünster. With plain but large, immaculate rooms, this centrally located former monastery near the St. Emmeramus Basilica and Thurn und Taxis Palace is an excellent alternative to the hostel. Singles start at DM 32, doubles at DM 54. Add DM 3 per person if you stay only one night. Breakfast is not included. *Obermünsterpl. 7, tel. 0941/56810. 74 rooms. Reception open Oct.–July, weekdays 7–6; Aug.–Sept., Mon.–Thurs. 7–4:30, Fri. 7–4.*

Hotel-Restaurant Peterhof. On first glance this establishment seems a bit old, dark, and seedy, but the rooms are in decent shape, the adjoining restaurant is good and cheap, and it sits conveniently between the train station and city center. Singles start at DM 38, doubles at DM 68. *Fröhliche-Turken-Str. 12, tel. 0941/57514 or 0941/58874. 70 rooms.*

Stadlerbräu. Rooms in this old restaurant–guest house are bare and showerless, so if you have a single (DM 27), be prepared to smell bad while gloating about all the money you're not spending. Doubles (DM 54) have private showers. *Stadtamhof 15, tel. 0941/85682. From city center, cross Steinerne Brücke to Stadtamhof. Reception closed Sun.*

HOSTEL **Jugendherberge Regensburg.** Often full of youths going through their tragic teen years, Regensburg's hostel sits on an island in the Danube between the bridges Eiserne Brücke and Nibelungen Brücke. It's a short bus ride or a half-hour walk from the train station. *Wöhrdstr. 60, tel. 0941/57402. Take Bus 17 across the street from the train station in the direction Keilberg-Grünthal, and get off at Eisstadion. To walk, go down Maximilianstr. until you hit the Danube, cross at Eisernebrücke, turn right at Werftstr., left at Am Wiriterhafen, and right on Wöhrdstr. 243 beds. 11:30 PM curfew. Laundry, bike rentals DM 5 per day.*

CAMPGROUND **Campingplatz.** The imaginatively named "camping place" charges DM 5 per person, DM 3 kids, DM 6.50 for car and tent, or DM 3.50 for tent only. *Weinweg 40, tel. 0941/26839. Bus 6 out of town to Hans-Sachs-Str., get off and head right on Hans-Sachs-Str., which turns into Weinweg. (30-min. walk). Closed Nov.–Mar. 15.*

FOOD

You'll get the best deal on fruits and veggies at the **Donaumarkt** (Danube Market, near Hunnenpl.) on Saturday morning from 6 to noon. Morning people can catch the **Alter Kornmarkt,** in a plaza by the same name near the cathedral (*see box*), which has an equally rich selection of fruits and vegetables, open daily 5 AM–8 AM in summer, 6 AM–9 AM in winter. If you're sick of greasy slabs of meat and the like, head for **Antagon** (Rote-Hahnen-Gasse 2, tel. 0941/54661), a vegetarian bar-restaurant that stays open until 1 AM.

Bischofshof. This beer garden–hotel–restaurant was the residence of Regensburg's bishops until the state confiscated and sold church property in the early 19th century. If you've got a big appetite and a few extra marks to spare (the average dish is about DM 13), drop in. It's right next to the Dom. *Krautermarkt 3, tel. 0941/59080.*

Glöckl. The stand-up Imbiß in this large butcher shop has a wide selection of cheap soups, sandwiches, and full meals (DM 1.80–DM 9). *Corner of Maximilianstr. and Dreikrönengasse. No Sat. dinner. Closed Sun.*

Historische Wurstküche. This beer garden–restaurant, which has been in the same prime spot by the Steinerne Brücke on the Danube for 850 years, serves up beers—and not much else—to a lively crowd of tourists and locals. Foodwise, you have one option: juicy *Schweinbratenwürste* (small pork sausages), which cost DM 5 for four and come with sauerkraut; ½ liter of brew costs DM 4.10. *Thundorferstr. 3, tel. 0941/59098.*

Hofbräuhaus. Order an inexpensive snack (like a wurst, DM 5) or stuff your face with a heavy Bavarian dish (around DM 9.50–DM 13.50), but don't forget the beer (starts at DM 3 per ½ liter). *Rathauspl., tel. 0941/51280. Closed Sun. mid-May–mid-Sept.*

WORTH SEEING

ALTES RATHAUS Visit the interior of the old town hall on a guided tour of the **Reichstag Museum.** You'll see the Imperial Hall, where the country's decision-makers congregated up until 1506, and some appropriately gruesome but creative torture devices in the original interrogation room and prison cells. *Admission: DM 3, DM 1.50 students. English tours May–Sept., Mon.–Sat. 3:15. German tours Mon.–Sat. every ½ hr. 9:30–noon and 2–4, Sun. and holidays every ½ hr. 10–noon.*

DOM ST. PETER St. Peter's Cathedral is considered Bavaria's most outstanding example of Gothic architecture. Built over a period of six centuries, the cathedral chronicles the development of Gothic architecture. To start, compare the two towers rising from its western end. The older, south tower (to your right as you face the towers) is much simpler than its northern counterpart, which features the characteristic late Gothic double arches and fancier designs. The top third of this tower becomes much simpler again, not due to architectural whimsy, but rather to the state's lack of cash. The towers were finally completed in 1869, when King Ludwig I forked over the money. He was a fan of the Gothic style, which he considered very German, although it actually originated in France.

The stained-glass windows and thin pillars that dominate the dark, immense interior were designed to achieve a mystical effect and to draw your gaze upward. Although the church was gussied up in Baroque dress in the 18th century, Ludwig I, or "Mister Gothic," undressed it again. The precious silver and gilded-copper **high altar** is one of the only Baroque remnants. If you look toward the apse, you'll see the cathedral's two most famous sculptures facing each other across the aisle. On the right, the **Laughing Angel,** Gabriel, tells **Mary** that she's going to be pregnant. On the left, Mary concentrates on the Bible, showing that she not only accepts the news but expected it.

On the south wall you'll see a Christ figure, complete with real human hair. On the west wall, the figures of **St. Martin** and **St. George** protect the church from the darkness outside. On either side of the entrance lurk two less hopeful figures: On the left is the **Devil's grandmother,** wearing a shawl on her head, while on the right sits old **Mr. Evil Incarnate** himself. The two together serve as a little preview of the evil that awaits you just outside the doors.

If you take a tour of the cathedral, you can also visit the cloisters, **Allerheiligen kapelle** (All Saints' Chapel), and **St. Stephanskapelle** (St. Stephen's chapel). **The Domspatzen,** the famous boys' choir, performs during mass every Sunday morning at 9. *Admission: DM 2.50, students DM 1.50. Tours May–Oct., weekdays at 10, 11, 2; Sun. and holidays, noon and 2; Nov.–Apr., weekdays 11 AM, Sun. and holidays at noon.*

HAIDPLATZ Romans used this square for tournaments and it's possible that it was also a center of slave trade in medieval times. Historic negotiations between Catholics, Protestants, and Holy Roman Emperor Charles took place in the **Neue Waag** house (the red building) in 1541. Kings, emperors, and other high rollers stayed in the hotel **Zur Goldenen Kreuz** (the gray building). Here, Emperor Charles V had a little rendezvous with 18-year-old Barbara Blomberg, which produced Don Juan of Austria. He led the decisive victory against Turkish fleets in 1571 and is thus credited with saving the West from the Turks.

PORTA PRAETORIA The original northern gate of the Roman fortress, built in AD 179, is still standing, so you can get an idea of what things looked like more than 1,500 years ago. It's on the street Unter den Schwibbögen.

ST. EMMERAMUS BASILICA AND CRYPTS Next to the palace is the 8th-century basilica of St. Emmeram, which the Asam brothers converted into Baroque style in 1730. The crypts of St. Emmeram, Abbot Ramwold, and St. Wolfgang are here. If you're into dead bishops and/or tombs, 19 of Regensburg's first 21 bishops are also buried here, as well as assorted dukes and historical figures you've probably never heard of. In case you didn't know, the huge 17th-century clock is one of the heaviest in the world. *Emmeramspl. Basilica and crypts open Mon.–Sat. 10–4:30, Sun. noon–4:30.*

SCHLOß DER FURSTEN VON THURN UND TAXIS Formerly the cloister of St. Emmeram (*see above*), this converted palace became the home of the Thurn and Taxis princes, a family (currently believed to be the richest in Germany) that came to Regensburg in the 16th century and has exerted a profound influence on the local economy ever since. They still own this palace, only parts of which are open to the public. You can also visit the **Meios Museum** (or Marstallmuseum) for a look at one of Europe's largest collections of sleds, coaches, and harnesses. Check at the palace or tourist office for admission charges and times of guided tours.

STEINERNE BRUCKE Built from 1135 to 1146 after Roman designs, Germany's oldest bridge was an engineering miracle for its time. As the first and only bridge across the Danube for years, it made Regensburg a vital trading hub; bloody feuds over control of the strategic bridge raged for years between bishops, dukes, and traders. Go up the adjoining **Brückturm** (Bridge Tower) for a splendid view.

CHURCHES The interior of the modest-looking, 9th-century **Alte Kapelle** (Old Chapel), redone 1,000 years later in Rococo style, is extravagant but not as excessive as most Bavarian Baroque churches. The 13th-century statue of the Madonna in the Grace Chapel is one of the oldest in Germany. *Alter Kornmarkt.*

Neupfarrkirche, Regensburg's first Protestant church, stands in stark and somber contrast to the flashy, heavily decorated Catholic ones. *Neupfarrpl.*

Like the Alte Kapelle, **St. Kassian** (Regensburg's oldest church) was given a Rococo interior during the 18th century with stucco work in the famous Weßobrunn style—a Baroque style made famous by the Asams. It's most noted for its carved altar and the 16th-century *Schöne Maria* (Beautiful Madonna). *S. side of Neupfarrpl.*

The **Schottenkirche St. Jakob** ("Scots" Church of St. Jacob), despite its name, was founded by Irish monks in the 11th century. It has a gorgeous coffered ceiling, and many consider the portal, with hard-to-decipher reliefs, a masterpiece. *W. of city center, off Bismarckpl.*

MUSEUMS Unless otherwise noted, the following museums charge DM 2.50 admission, DM 1 for students. Check the brochure "*Kultur*," available at the tourist office, for additional exhibits.

Kepler-Gedächtnishaus. Kepler, the astronomer, mathematician, and man behind the laws of planetary motion, died here in 1630 without ever getting the money the state owed him; he lived a few doors down at No. 2. In the Kepler Memorial House, original furniture, instruments, and sketches document his life and work. *Keplerstr. 5, tel. 0941/507–2957. Guided tours Tues.–Sat. 10, 11, 2, 3; Sun. 10, 11.*

You can find everything you ever wanted to know about Regensburg and East Bavaria within the 100 rooms of the **Museum der Stadt Regensburg** (Municipal Museum), whether you're into the morbid (death rituals and tombs), art (lots of Albrecht Altdorfer, stained glass, and sculptures), or old Roman settlements. While you're here, check out the original stone tablet that proclaimed the foundation of the Roman fort Castra Regina in AD 179. *Dachaupl. 2–4, tel. 0941/507–2944. Open Tues.–Sat. 10–4, Sun. and holidays 10–1.*

Museum Ostdeutsche Galerie (East German Gallery) has a unique collection of 19th- and 20th-century East German art, plus changing exhibits. Don't miss the hall that features Lovis Corinth canvasses and other modern art. The museum is located in the Stadtpark (City Park) in the western part of town. *Dr.-Johann-Maier-Str. 5, tel. 0941/22031. Admission: DM 2.50, DM 1 students. Open Tues.–Sat. 10–4, Sun. 10–1.*

AFTER DARK

Start your night at a beer garden like **Kneitinger Keller** (Galgenbergstr. 18, tel. 0941/76680), Regensburg's largest, or the **Spitalgarten** (Katharinenpl. 1, tel. 0941/84774), which overlooks the Danube from across the Steinerne Brücke. The chic discos **Scala** (Gesandtenstr. 6, tel. 0941/52293), which is only open Wednesday and Saturday and has a DM 3–DM 7 cover—and **Sudhaus** (Untere Bachgasse 8, tel. 0941/51933), which usually has gay night on Thursdays, are by far the most popular. The crowded pub **Irish Harp** (Brückstr. 1, tel. 0941/57268) has live music; also try **Keplerstraße** for some sturdy bars.

Passau

With its Italian-influenced architecture and sub-lime location at the confluence of three major rivers, Passau far exceeds the typical quaintness of Bavarian towns—you might even call it beautiful. Although the town is small enough to see in a day, you may find yourself overcome with the desire to hang out a lot longer. Take advantage of it: Passau is one of the few towns in Bavaria with the appeal of a Venice or Budapest. The forest-green **Danube,** flowing from the Black Forest; the milky-green **Inn,** flowing down from the Swiss Alps; and the murky **Ilz,** descending from the Bavarian Forest, gave Passau its nickname as **Dreiflussestadt,** Three River City.

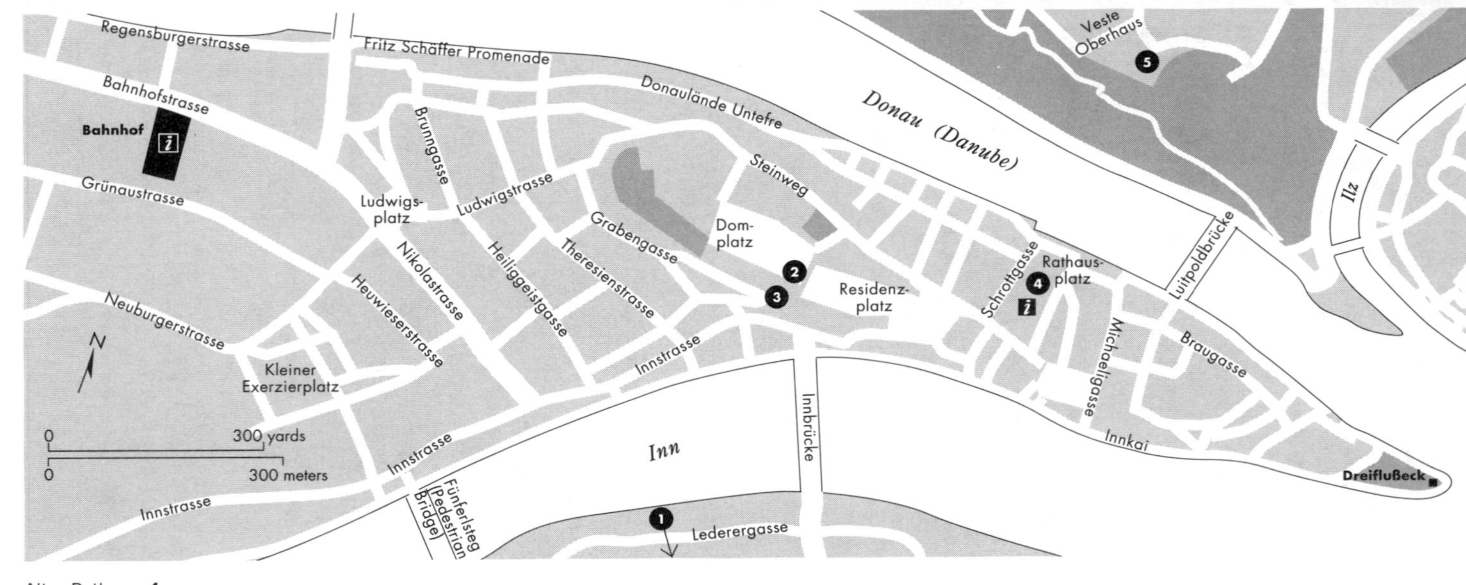

Altes Rathaus, **4**
Residenz, **3**
Römermuseum
Castell Boiotro, **1**
Stephansdom, **2**
Veste Oberhaus, **5**

Passau

BASICS

BUREAUX DE CHANGE The **post office** (tel. 0851/5050) by the station charges DM 3 per traveler's check (instead of the DM 10 that banks usually skim off). It's open weekdays 8:30–12:30 and 2–5:30, Saturday 8–noon.

EMERGENCIES Dial 110 for the **police,** 112 in case of **fire,** and 19222 for **pharmacy** information. The police office is at Nibelungenstraße 17 (tel. 0851/5030).

VISITOR INFORMATION To find the **information office** by the train station (open weekdays 9–5, weekends 10–1), head toward Track 1A. In addition to the usual brochures, they have info on the Bavarian Forest and tons of cycling routes, six of which pass through Passau. Pick up a copy of the orange pamphlet entitled "Information" for concert, theater, festival, exhibit, and sports listings. The main **tourist office** at Rathausplatz 3 (open Apr.–Oct., weekdays 8:30–6, weekends and holidays 10–2; Nov.–Mar., weekdays 8:30–5) makes room reservations (DM 1.50) and also has maps and general information, including Danube cruise schedules.

COMING AND GOING

Passau has frequent train and bus connections to Munich, Regensburg, and the Bavarian Forest. For **train information,** call 0851/55001. You can cruise to a number of cities in Austria from Passau as well; a trip to Linz, Austria, will run you DM 30 round-trip. Check for schedules, destinations, and prices at the tourist office or at kiosks along the Danube. The station has **luggage lockers** for DM 2–DM 4. The **Dreiflüsse-Rundfahrt,** a 45-minute cruise around the peninsula on the Wurm and Köck cruise line, makes a great visual introduction to the city; if you speak German you'll get a historical overview from the tour guide as well (May–Oct. departs every half hr., DM 7).

WHERE TO SLEEP

You may have a hard time finding budget accommodations near Passau's center. The tourist office and information booth at the train station have booklets with lodging options nearby and on the city's outskirts; they'll also book you a room for a DM 1.50 charge. One option is to snag a room at the cheap and central guest house **Gasthof Zum Hirschen** (Im Ort 6, tel. 0851/3623812). With breakfast, singles are DM 30, doubles DM 55. Overlooking the Danube, the **Gasthof Blauer Bock** (Fritz-Schäffer-Promenade, tel. 0851/34637) has tidy rooms for DM 70 for two.

Passau's **Jugendherberge** (DM 15 per person, with breakfast), which occupies part of a 13th-century castle on top of a hill, is a pain to reach, but at least you get a great view from the top. To get here, catch Bus 1, 2, or 3 from Ludwigsplatz (Schanzl) to IlzBrücke and walk 10 minutes; or take the Dendelbus from Rathausplatz to the hostel: From mid-April to October, it leaves every half hour from 11:30 to 5 and costs DM 3 one-way, DM 4 round-trip. If you arrive after 5, when the buses stop and the shortest path up the hill is closed, you might want to stash your stuff in a locker at the station for the hike. Head east toward the center of town (from the station, face the Danube, and follow it to the right); cross the Danube at LuitpoldBrücke and you'll see the first of many steps up (about a 20-minute climb). At night, you've got the stars and St. Stephan (the lit-up cathedral) to keep you on the trail. *Veste Oberhaus 125, tel. 0851/41351. 173 beds. 11:30 curfew, sheets DM 4.50.*

FOOD

Passau's the kind of place that inspires you to dangle your legs over the Danube with a buddy as you pass a cheap bottle of wine, munch on sandwiches, and talk. Try **Kleine Passauer Markthalle** on Ludwigstraße for all your picnic needs, or drop in for a cheap meal (about DM 7) in the *Stehimbiß* (stand-up snack bar).

Otherwise, **Pizzeria Angelina** (Brunngasse 2, off Ludwigstr., tel. 0851/33203) offers students and other cashless souls hefty, delicious pizzas and pasta dishes for DM 6–DM 7 until 11:30 PM. Order from the menu's *Studentenkarte* section; you're supposed to have a Passau University I.D. card, but they don't usually check. Overlooking the Inn River, **Café Innsteg** (Innstr. 15, tel. 0851/51257, open daily 10 AM–1 AM) doubles as a student pub at night and is ideal for an inexpensive meal, or just a beer, by the Fünferlsteg Brücke to Innstadt.

WORTH SEEING

ALTES RATHAUS The Gothic town hall was a private house until locals usurped it during an uprising in 1298. One giant fresco in the great hall show scenes from the *Nibelungenlied*, a famous 13th-century epic believed to have been written in Passau. In the building's tower, Bavaria's largest **glockenspiel** chimes daily at 10:30, 2, 7:25, and 9. It plays an extended concert every Saturday at 3:30 for hard-core glockenspiel fans. *Admission: DM 1. Open Easter–Oct., weekdays 10–noon and 1:30–4, weekends and holidays 10–4.*

ROMERMUSEUM CASTELL BOIOTRO When the Romans booted out the Celts (the original settlers of Passau around 300 BC), they fortified the town so heavily that it held out against Germanic tribes longer than any other city in the region. In 1974, construction workers preparing to build a kindergarten discovered the remains of the Roman fort Boiotro; you can see its original walls and other archaeological treasures at its museum (Roman Museum of Fort Boiotro), located across the Inn River in Innstadt. *Lederergasse 43, tel. 0851/34769. Admission: DM 2, DM 1 students. Open Mar.–Nov., Tues.–Sun. 10–noon and 2–4; June–Aug., Tues.–Sun. 1–4.*

STEPHANSDOM Originally a church built in the 8th century and later converted to a Gothic cathedral, St. Stephan's was rebuilt in its present Baroque style after two huge fires razed the city in the 17th century. Inside looms a 231-register, 17,388-pipe organ, the largest in the world. Attend one of the cathedral-trembling concerts (admission: DM 3, DM 1 students) weekdays at noon from May through October. Lines are usually long by 11:30. Concerts are also given every Thursday until mid-November at 7:30 PM for DM 6–DM 10. Otherwise, hear the organ played for free and get a chance to atone during Sunday morning mass at 9:30 and 11, when the choirboys also perform. The cathedral is closed during organ concerts. The **Cathedral and Diocese Treasure Museum** is housed in the great hall of the **Residenz** (where the prince-bishop used to live), behind the cathedral. *Tel. 0851/393374. Open May–Oct., Mon.–Sat. 10–4. Admission: DM 2, DM 1 students.*

VESTE OBERHAUS Once a 13th-century castle that sheltered the bishops from enraged citizens, the Veste Oberhaus now houses Passau's minor-league **Museum of History and Art,** as well as the youth hostel and a weather station. *Tel. 0851/396312. Admission: DM 3, DM 1.50 students, free Sun. Open Mar.–Jan., Tues.–Sun. 9–5.*

AFTER DARK

During the university's summer vacation (except for the month of September), and during Christmas and Easter breaks, the **Katholische Studenten Gemeinde** (Catholic Student Association, Kleiner Exerzierpl. 159) provides a philanthropic service for all poor students: a half liter of beer for DM 2–DM 2.50. Also check out the outdoor cafés on **Theresienstraße,** or **Café Rialto** (Rindermarkt 16, tel. 0851/2771), which has a tempting menu with savory pictures of every kind of sundae imaginable.

Near Passau

BAVARIAN FOREST NATIONAL PARK

You need to travel north from Passau to reach the pristine but touristy Bavarian Forest National Park, which covers an area of 120 square kilometers (46 square miles), 25 kilometers (16 miles) of which border the Czech Republic's Bohemian Forest. The two together form one of Europe's largest forested areas.

Bavarian Forest

Hardly any non-German tourists, other than Austrians and Czechs, even make it to East Bavaria, much less to the Bavarian Forest. However, nature lovers looking for clean air (the cleanest in Germany, supposedly), surprisingly low prices, excellent skiing and hiking opportunities, and few fellow visitors will find the forest a great getaway. Its small, sparsely populated towns are separated by rolling hills and linked by infrequent bus connections, so expect transportation to be something of a drag unless you have a car. Trains most commonly enter the forest via Platting, Deggendorf, and Zwiesel. If you're coming from Passau or Regensburg, buses run to various towns in the forest a few times a day. In addition to the popular Bavarian Forest National Park near Grafenau, consider visiting one of the many glashütte *(glass-making factories), where you can watch local glassblowers do their part in making this region the largest glass producer in Europe. Glass museums in Frauenau, Zwiesel, and Passau have displays chronicling the development of this craft over the last 700 years. You'll find glass factories all over the forest, particularly in Bayerisch-Eisenstein, Riedlhütte, and Zwiesel; the Joska Waldglashütte in Bodenmais (Arberseestr. 4–6, tel. 09924/1842) is everyone's favorite.*

Bodenmais also sees tourists because of its location near the lake Arbersee, at the foot of Mt. Arber, the most imposing peak of the Bavarian Forest. This is also the site of Germany's highest (4,389 feet) youth hostel (Chamberhütte 1, tel. 09924/281), which you can reach only by hiking for two hours from Bodenmais; by catching the Arbersessellift *(Arber chair lift) to Bergstation and hiking for 45–60 minutes; or by skiing there from the chair lift in winter. You can cross-country or downhill ski from early December through April in this area, but the youth hostel is closed from April 20 until May 20 and November through December. From certain towns, like Bayerisch-Eisenstein, you can cross the Czech border if you bring your passport. Many towns also offer day-trips to Prague.*

Hiking and skiing—both downhill and cross-country—are big draws for tourists. The ski season generally runs from November through May. Stop by the tourist offices in Grafenau or Neuschönau for hiking, skiing, and other information.

Hikers can choose from some 200 kilometers (122 miles) of trails, some of which head all the way to the top of both Mt. Rachel and Mt. Lusen, the two highest peaks in the park. Although the sight of other visitors may be the closest you get to spotting wildlife, with good timing you may catch some critters doing their thing in the **Tierfreigelände**—a big chunk of forest divided into natural enclosures for different animals. Tours and other special theme hikes are arranged through the huge information center/office/library/exhibition hall called the Hans-Eisenmann-Haus, located in Neuschönau (Bohmstr. 35, tel. 08558/1300); the office is open daily from 9 to 5 and closed from November to mid-December.

COMING AND GOING Getting around the Bavarian Forest can be a hassle without a car since buses run infrequently, so check out schedules ahead of time. To reach the national park, catch one of the infrequent RVO (Regional Bus Ostbayern) buses that depart from the bus depot next to Passau's main train station for Grafenau (1½ hours, DM 9 one-way, free with valid rail pass). From Grafenau's train station, transfer to a bus that travels the 11 kilometers (7 miles) to the park (three per day, last one leaves at 1:15 PM, 20 minutes, DM 3 one-way). Grafenau also has trains and buses to Deggendorf, Zwiesel, Bodenmais, and Mt. Arber. Again, connections are infrequent and the train station (tel. 08552/1313), which is in the middle of nowhere and has no lockers, is open only weekdays 8–noon and 1:15–4:30.

WHERE TO SLEEP A room in a private guest house or pension can cost as little as DM 15 per night. Call the tourist office in **Neuschönau** (Kaiserstr. 13, tel. 0558/1850) for information about room vacancies near the park, or about the possibility of staying in a farmhouse.

Unless you have a car, staying at hostels can also be a transportation ordeal; once again, make a note of the bus schedules before heading off to any backwoods hostels. The hostel closest to the park, **Jugendherberge Waldhäuser** (Herbergsweg 2, tel. 08553/300), with beds for DM 16 per night including breakfast, is a two-hour hike away if you miss the last bus leaving the park at 5 PM. Modern and spacious, it's also quite empty in the summer, except for the ubiquitous kiddie groups. Maybe it's the 10:30 PM curfew. Its 120 beds are usually packed during ski season. To get there from Grafenau, take the bus going toward Waldhäuser; tell the driver to let you off at the youth hostel (DM 4.80 one-way).

If that one's booked, try **Jugendherberge Mauth** (Jugendherbergestr. 11, Mauth, tel. 08857/289) for DM 16.50 per night, including breakfast; sheets cost DM 4.50. Buses connecting this hostel and the national park sometimes run only once or twice a day, and it's a 4½-hour hike if you miss it. The hostel is closed November through December.

Bavarian Alps

Stretching from the Bodensee (Lake Constance) in the west to Berchtesgaden in the east, the Bavarian Alps encompass famous castles, lakes, and mountains galore. Pictures of this area have graced the covers of many a tourist brochure, spreading pastoral Alpine scenes and country kitsch worldwide. And the covers don't lie: You really will see milkmaids and meadows and church steeples set against snowy peaks. After a while, though, the excessive quaintness of the villages may grow tiresome and prompt you to want to take a hike. You're in the right place. With a few major exceptions (in particular, Berchtesgaden), sightseeing takes a backseat to general recreation like hiking, swimming, and skiing. Spring through fall, few non-German tourists hang out here, and the cozy towns are much cheaper, friendlier, and relaxing than nearby

The Bavarian Alps

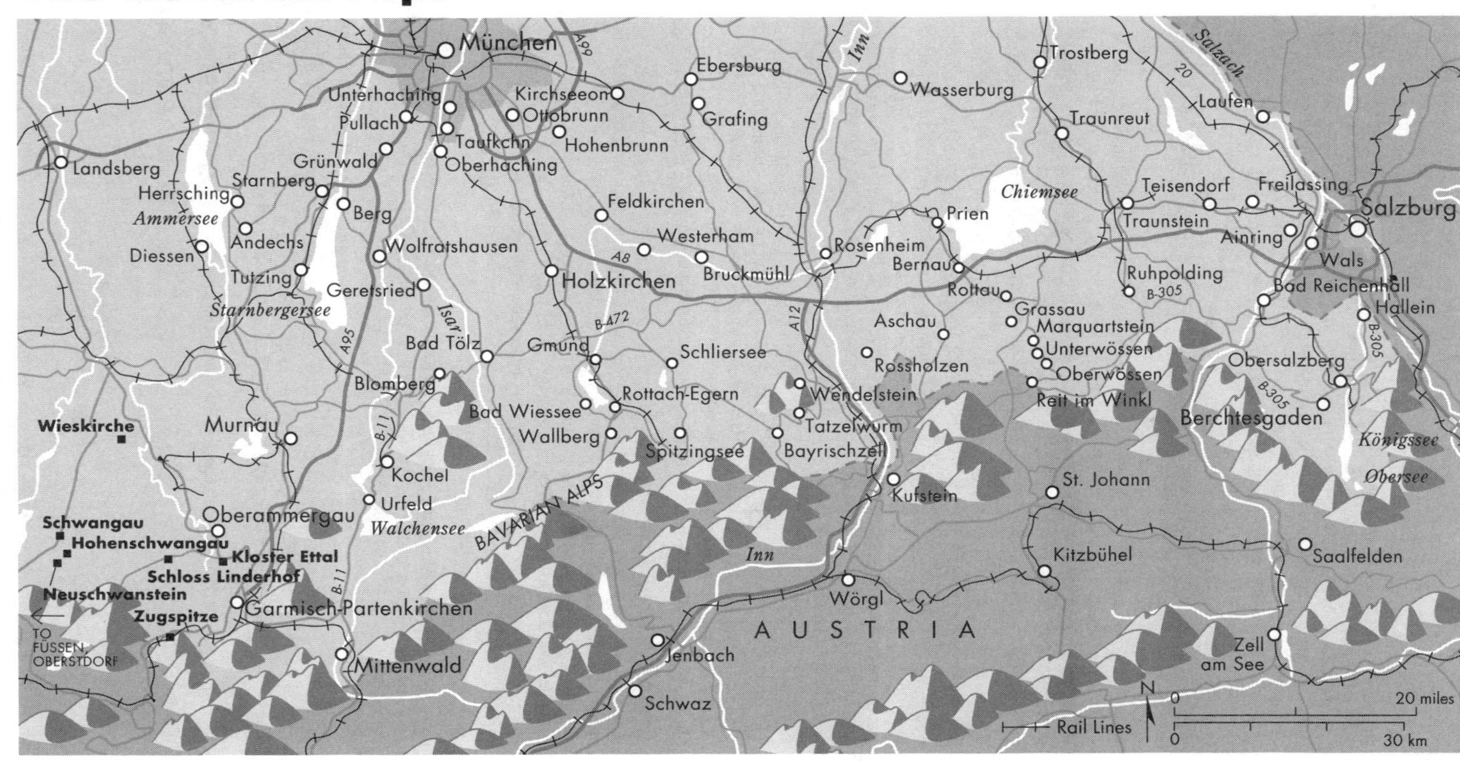

Munich; the trip from the big city is worth it, even for one day. Many of the small towns are also climatic health resorts (i.e., health spas for old people). Be warned that the weather is totally unpredictable; on a single hike you may encounter sun and fog and rain and perhaps some other meteorological aberration.

BASICS

VISITOR INFORMATION The **Kurverwaltung** or **Verkehrsamt** (tourist offices) in each town give lodging suggestions, but they don't make formal reservations. Some offer guided hikes, and all give you trail maps. Get a free **Kurkarte** (visitors card) from wherever you're staying, or ask for one at the tourist office. These helpful passes often get you free or reduced admission fees, or even free local bus transportation.

WHEN TO GO The Bavarian Alps are gorgeous and adventure-packed during every season. Fall is an especially good time to visit since crowds go home and the leaves begin their colorful metamorphoses, further enhancing the spectacular views. The off seasons (cheapest seasons) are January 9 to 31, April and May, and mid-October to mid-December.

COMING AND GOING Trains from Munich can get you to most of the main Alpine towns, but if you want to travel between towns (between Garmisch-Partenkirchen and Berchtesgaden, for example), you can take only the **RVO buses,** or *Regional Verkehrs Oberbayern.* Buses are relatively cheap and efficient, and since they're run by the Deutsche Bundesbahn, they accept Eurail and German rail passes; InterRail pass holders get a 50% discount. The main RVO bus depot is usually at the train station or the main post office; cough up DM .20 for a regional schedule, available from drivers.

GETTING AROUND Most villages have an old town center that's both the hub of village life and a helpful starting point for orienting yourself. The train stations, usually set at the edge of town, often have tourist offices. You can usually get around on foot, or rent bikes from the stations. Ask at the tourist offices if you're interested in renting a mountain bike. Local or RVO buses shuttle you to more removed sights and to the depots for mountain cable cars. Call a taxi only if you're desperate.

WHERE TO SLEEP Relive the obnoxiousness of childhood at one of the youth hostels, or crash in a more peaceful room in a private guest house for DM 20–DM 30 per night. Many places discourage short stays and charge DM 3–DM 5 more if you don't stick around for three nights. Still, with generally clean, cozy rooms, and breakfast included, they make better budget sense than the more expensive pensions and hotels. Campgrounds are easy to find and cheap, but are often packed.

FOOD You'll see authentic Italian restaurants and pizzerias all over the place; these generally offer the best deals. The **Wienerwald** chain provides basic Bavarian food throughout the Alps. Look for *Selbst-Bedienung* (self-service) spots for bottom-of-the-budget meals, or stop in at a *Metzgerei* (butcher shop) or a stand-up Imbiß for a selection of cheap soups and sandwiches.

Füssen

Füssen, a small Alpine town at the base of the Alps near the German-Austrian border, has a handful of monasteries and an impressive late-Gothic castle. It's also surrounded by some incredibly lush countryside. Yet Füssen's greatest appeal is its proximity to the castles cum palaces at **Neuschwanstein** and **Hohenschwangau** (*see* Near Füssen, *below*), two sights that you should really make an effort to see. Neither castle is connected to the German rail network, and since only Füssen has a youth hostel, most budget travelers use Füssen as a base from which to explore the two nearby sites.

If you're sick to death of half-timbered mansions and fairy-tale castles, of Romantic Road hype and tourist hordes, Füssen lies near some pleasant Alpine and lakeside hikes; **Forggensee,** a large teardrop-shape lake, is only ½ kilometer (⅓ mile) to the northeast. Another option is to take Bus 9713 from Füssen's Bahnhof to **Tegelberg-bahn.** From here you can catch the cable car up to the top of **Mt. Tegelberg,** where the view will reaffirm your faith in life. The ride costs DM 20 round-trip, but a student discount is available. The cable car runs daily 8:30–5 in summer, daily 9–4:30 in winter.

Füssen itself also has a few worthwhile sights. **Hohes Schloß** (Magnuspl. 10; admission DM 4), Füssen's imposing castle, is situated just above the city. It was built on the site of a Roman fortress designed to guard this section of the Via Claudia, an important trading route that once connected Rome with the Danube. After the Romans were vanquished by the barbarian horde, the site lay mostly abandoned until a new castle was begun by Bavarian princes in the early 13th century. However, when Bavarian emperor Heinrich VII was strapped for money, he mortgaged Hohes Schloß to the bishop of Augsburg for a meager 400 pieces of silver. The mortgage was never redeemed, and the castle remained under church control until it was annexed by the government in the early 19th century. Besides the walk to the castle itself, the highlight is the 16th-century **Rittersaal** (Knights' Hall), with its finely carved ceiling and ornate period furniture.

Füssen's **Rathaus** was originally built in the 9th century as a Benedictine abbey. A Romanesque crypt in the basement preserves a 10th-century fresco, the oldest in Bavaria. During the summer, concerts are sometimes held in the Rathaus's Fürstensaal (Princes' Hall). The **tourist office** (Augsburger Torpl. 1, tel. 08362/7077) is located in the center of Füssen's small, walkable old town.

COMING AND GOING Daily trains connect Füssen with Augsburg (DM 19) and Munich (via Buchloe or Kaufbeuren, DM 17). All year round, regional buses connect Füssen with Hohenschwangau (DM 2) and Schwangau (DM 2.50). Between April 10 and September 26, Füssen is the southern hub for Deutsche Bundesbahn's **Romantische Straße** (*see* Chapter 7) bus. These leave daily from Füssen's Bahnhof at 9 AM and 10:45 AM and stop in Augsburg, Nördlingen, Dinkelsbühl, Rothenburg-ob-der-Tauber, Würzburg, and Frankfurt. The ride is free with a Eurail or InterRail pass; otherwise tickets cost DM 104 each way between Frankfurt and Füssen.

WHERE TO SLEEP The tourist office has information on private rooms (DM 25–DM 35) in both Füssen and Schwangau, bookable for a DM 4 fee. The only cheaper option is Füssen's youth hostel, **Jugendherberge Füssen** (Mariahilferstr. 15, tel. 08362/7754; closed Nov. 1–Dec. 15), an easy 10-minute walk from the train station (follow the tracks west). Like most hostels in Franconia and Bavaria, this one will only house people under 27. Each of its 147 beds costs DM 15 per night, including breakfast. If you can afford it, the **Fürstenhof** (Kemptenerstr. 23, tel. 08362/7006; closed Nov.–late Dec.) is a comfortable guest house nestled on the edge of the forest, only a five-minute walk from the train depot. The 15 double rooms, all with bath, start at DM 90 and peak around DM 110. In the same price range is **Hotel Sonne** (Reichenstr. 37, tel. 08362/6061), a modern-looking hotel that tries a bit too hard to create that "traditional Bavarian" feeling. All of its 32 rooms have a bath or shower, and there's a small café downstairs. A better bargain is the budget-priced **Haus Schwansee** (Parkstr. 9, tel. 08362/8353), a quiet pension near the castles. Each double room comes equipped with a shower; they start at DM 40 per person.

FOOD **Gasthaus zum Schwanen** (Brotmarkt 4, tel. 08362/6174, no Sun. dinner, closed Mon.) is one of the better budget restaurants in town. It's a modest, no-frills sort of place where good, cheap food makes up for any atmospheric deficiencies. The homemade *Maultaschen*, the local version of ravioli, is particularly good. The **Roma-Citta** (Bahnhofstr. 6, tel. 08362/5444), a family-run pizzeria, serves filling Italian meals for under DM 10. Perched on the mountainside just outside Füssen, the **Alpen-Schlößle** (Alatseestr. 28, tel. 08362/4017, closed Tues. and Nov.–mid-Dec.) serves tasty Franconian dishes for under DM 25—not a budget choice, but a good place for a splurge.

NEAR FUSSEN

Füssen is a short hop from two impressive Romantisches Straße sights, the castles of Hohenschwangau and Neuschwanstein. Both are within 5 kilometers (3 miles) of Füssen, and when the weather's good you might consider tackling them by foot. Otherwise, from Füssen there's a daily bus to Garmisch-Partenkirchen that stops in Hohenschwangau, and another to Peiting that stops at the lakeside resort of Schwangau, 1½ kilometers (1 mile) from the two castles. Cars and buses are barred from the approach roads, but if you're footsore there's a bus that goes from Schwangau to Aussichtpunkt Jugend, a 10-minute walk from Neuschwanstein. From Füssen you can also catch the hourly RVO buses from the train station to Königschlößer, which stops a short distance from Neuschwanstein. If you catch the one at 8:15 AM, you arrive at Neuschwanstein just in time to be near the front of the line; although tours start at 9, doors open for line formation by 8:30. The castles themselves are only a kilometer (⅔ mile) apart, an easy walk.

Keep in mind that roughly 1 million people pass through the two castles every year. During summer you can wait in line upward of two hours before gaining entry, so try to visit as early as possible. Of the two castles, Neuschwanstein is by far the most popular and most crowded. It's a good idea to tackle it, rather than Hohenschwangau, in the wee hours of the morning.

HOHENSCHWANGAU The Hohenschwangau palace is where Bavaria's famous king Ludwig II spent most of his childhood. And it's said that the palace's neo-Gothic atmosphere dictated the tone and look of Ludwig's wildly romantic Neuschwanstein castle. Hohenschwangau itself was built by the knights of Schwangau in the 12th century, in a heavy Romanesque style. In 1832, the castle was renovated

Madness, or Just a Fairy Tale?

Although the so-called mad or fairy-tale King Ludwig II was deposed for almost bankrupting the state more than a century ago, his extravagant castles Linderhof, Neuschwanstein, and Herrenchiemsee sure rake in the bucks today. Ludwig II's parents, the Wittelsbach King Maximilian II and Queen Mary, were normal enough, but Ludwig somehow acquired a few unique fetishes. He was born in Munich's Nymphenburg Palace but grew up at Hohenschwangau, where he fell in love with the serene landscape. It was here he first met the composer Richard Wagner, who would later milk the king's fascination with him for all it was worth—the king obsessively commissioned the painting of frescoes and the construction of grottos that featured themes from Wagnerian operas. He didn't exactly conceal his other two passions—swans and Louis XIV—either. By 1886, the state had about as much money as a backpacker, so Ludwig was confined to a castle at Lake Starnberg where he no longer had access to the royal funds. A few days after being sent there, he and his doctor were found drowned. Some say he was murdered, some speculate he got into a brawl with his medical adviser, and still others claim he tried to swim across the lake. It may have just been an accident, but who'll ever know for sure?

by Ludwig's father, Maximilian, King of Bavaria. Under his direction the castle was transformed from a fortress into an elegant palace, one that attracted the notice of composer Richard Wagner. Wagner spent a few summers here, during which he became acquainted with the young Ludwig. Their friendship deepened Ludwig's already keen interest in music, theater, and mythology, although it's unlikely Wagner saw Ludwig as anything more than a wealthy patron from whom he could squeeze a few gold pieces. The castle's interior is worth a quick look, particularly Maximilian's elegant bedroom. But if you want to be really dazzled, head across the valley to Neuschwanstein. *Admission: DM 8, DM 5 students. Open Apr.–Oct., daily 8:30–5:30; Nov.–Mar., daily 10–4.*

NEUSCHWANSTEIN Walk 20 minutes northeast from Hohenschwangau and it's impossible to miss King Ludwig's so-called Fairy-Tale Castle, Neuschwanstein. Set atop a hill in the middle of a small forest, Neuschwanstein looks like something straight out of a story book. It has towers and gates and battlements and courtyards and gables and spires and lookouts and spiral stairways and just about everything a proper castle should have.

Neuschwanstein isn't simply a castle, it's the *castle; Walt Disney himself used Neuschwanstein as a model for the castle in Sleeping Beauty, and later as a model for the Disneyland castle you find in Walt's theme parks.*

Inside Neuschwanstein you'll find flamboyant parlors and elaborately decorated apartments. On the somber side is Ludwig's tomblike bedroom, dominated by a massive Gothic-style bed. The real pleasure at Neuschwanstein, however, is walking from room to room, eyes wide and mouth open, simply trying to process the incredible atmosphere of the place. In September, chamber music concerts are sometimes held in the ornate Minstrel's Hall, a definite highlight. Another outstanding feature is the castle grounds. Spend some time rambling through the surrounding forest, and be sure to make the crossing on **Marien Brücke** (Mary's Bridge), a giddy span that covers a deep, narrow gorge. From this vantage point, there are mind-numbing views of the castle and the Upper Bavarian plain beyond. *Admission: DM 8, DM 5 students. Open Apr.–Sept., daily 8:30–5:30; Oct.–Mar., daily 10–4.*

Oberstdorf

The small, cute mountain town of Oberstdorf (population 12,000), as far south as you can get in Germany, is home to a diverse range of attractions, including the world's longest ski jump *and* the world's largest shoe. Its numerous health resorts attract wrinkled and arthritic folk, especially in the summer. You won't encounter many English-speaking tourists, so either get used to trading pleasantries in German about such scintillating topics as rheumatism and varicose veins or hit the uncrowded hiking paths, accessible only via gondola. **Mt. Nebelhorn** is a hot spot for mountaineers and hikers. The gondola (tel. 08322/1095) to the peak costs DM 34 round-trip, and less if you get off at one of the intermediary stations (open 8:45–5, last ascent 4:30). **Mt. Fellhorn** (tel. 08322/3035 for information) is a less strenuous alternative, but opt for **Söllereck** (tel. 08322/5757) if you want a fairly easy hike. All three of these peaks offer excellent skiing in winter. You can also get to **Kleinwalsertal,** which is actually on the Austrian side, either from Söllereck or via the **Breitachklamm gorge** (open daily 8–4, tel. 08322/4887). The huge shoe, among other articles chronicling the riveting history of the town, are housed in the 35-room **Heimatmuseum** (Oststr. 13, tel. 08322/5470).

VISITOR INFORMATION The train station, about a 10-minute walk from the city center, has a basic **information booth,** open weekdays from 9:25 to 1 and 2 to 5:15. Across the street from the station is the **Amtl. Zimmer-Vermittlung** office, which will help you find rooms without charging for the service. You can pick up a **Kurkarte** here, and scope out the concert information posted outside. The **tourist office** at Marktplatz (tel. 08322/7000) has sports information and also helps with accommodations (for no charge), which usually run DM 25–DM 35 per person in a guest house.

COMING AND GOING Oberstdorf is a two-hour bus ride from Füssen or four hours from Garmisch-Partenkirchen; tickets cost DM 21.80 unless you have a Eurailpass. Trains from Munich take about 2½ hours and require a transfer at Immenstadt, Buchloe, or Kempten. One-way tickets cost DM 40.

WHERE TO SLEEP You shouldn't have a problem finding a cheap, centrally located room here; the tourist office can help you find a room for DM 25–DM 35. Some cheap guest houses include **Buchenberg** (Lorettostr. 6, tel. 08322/2315), with tiny rooms with shower for DM 29 per person, or the **Alpenglühn** (Wittelsbacherstr. 4, tel. 08322/4692), with singles for DM 29 and doubles for DM 35–DM 40 per person. Otherwise, the sharp-looking **Jugendherberge** (Kornau 8, tel. 08322/2225), with beds for DM 16.50 and DM 4.50 for sheets, is surprisingly quiet in the summer and has yummy granola and yogurt for breakfast, as well as laundry facilities. To get here, take the bus marked KLEINWALSERTAL from the train station, and get off at Reutte. If you plan to go bar-hopping in this town, skip the hostel and instead get a room at a guest house; the hostel, 5 kilometers (3 miles) away in Kornau, is a 45-minute walk away, and buses stop running about 8 PM.

FOOD For cheap eats, you'll find a **Vinzenz Murr,** one of a big Bavarian chain of butcher shops, on Hauptstraße in the city center, and a bakery with a Steh-Café (stand-up café) next door. On Nebelhornstraße next to the bank is **Knaus,** another butcher shop/Imbiß place. Slurp soup for DM 3, scarf down half a chicken for DM 4.50, or masticate some noodles with salad for DM 6. All these places are open weekdays from 7:30 or 8 until about 6, Saturdays until about 1 PM. **Pfarrstraße** has a number of cheap restaurants, as well as bars for those who seek nightlife.

Garmisch-Partenkirchen

Since the two separate towns of Garmisch and Partenkirchen merged for the 1936 Winter Olympics, tourism has exploded and recreational facilities of all kinds, including five casinos, compete for your DMs. Part of a larger region known as Werdenfelser Land, Garmisch-Partenkirchen sits at the foot of the craggy Wetterstein Mountains and at the confluence of the Partnach and Loisach rivers. The biggest high around here, in both price and altitude, is **Zugspitze,** Germany's tallest mountain (9,781 feet). Dropping DM 60 for a ride to the top of Zugspitze on a dreary day is an experience with all the rewards of tossing a huge wad of currency into a fog bank, but on a clear day, the view of the surrounding peaks and lowlands is priceless. You can make the ascent on a 75-minute cogwheel train, or by a 10-minute cable car leaving from pretty **Lake Eibsee.** During the winter, the round-trip ride costs only DM 48 and includes a lift ticket. Other cable cars are cheaper and give access to heavenly hiking trails (ski runs in winter), like the **Alpspitze,** which drops you off at the 6,765-foot **Osterfelderkopf** for DM 30; the **Wankbahn,** taking you 5,874 feet for DM 22; the **Kreuzeckbahn,** lifting you 4,451 feet for DM 23; or the **Eckbauerbahn,** getting you 4,079 feet high for DM 15. Tourist information gives lift hours and trip descriptions.

If heights freak you out, perhaps you'd feel more secure *surrounded* by tons of rock and ice instead. Wander through the cave-like passageways of the **Partnachklamm gorge,** carved over thousands of years by the Partnach River. In the winter, ice formations dangle from the gorge's walls. The best way to get there is via the local bus to the **Olympic ski stadium,** built for the 1936 Olympics and now the site of a New Year's ski-jumping contest. From the stadium it's about a 35-minute hike to the gorge (admission: DM 2). You need at least half a day for the equally fabulous **Höllentalklamm gorge** (closed in winter), accessible from Hammersbach or the Kreuzeck mountain.

BASICS The main **post office,** located by the train station, stays open longer than those in other villages: weekdays from 8 to 7, Saturdays from 8 to 1, and Sunday and holidays from 10 AM to 11 AM. The office also changes money. For **police,** call 08821/50021; for **ambulance** call 770; in case of **fire,** in Garmisch call 3220, in Partenkirchen call 2640.

Both the **main tourist office** (Richard-Strauss-Pl., tel. 08821/1806; open Mon.–Sat. 8–6, Sun. and holidays 10–noon) and the information booth at the train station (open daily 4–7:30) book rooms for free and provide general information. The main branch also leads hikes, and can point you in the direction of whatever sport you desire. For a weather report, dial 797979.

COMING AND GOING Hourly **trains** (information, tel. 08821/52521) connect Garmisch-Partenkirchen with Munich (1½ hours, DM 30 round-trip), and Mittenwald (20 minutes, DM 5). If you're coming from Munich or Augsburg, inquire at the train station about a special round-trip train ticket to Garmisch-Partenkirchen that includes the Zugspitze cable car for DM 77. **RVO buses** (tel. 08821/51822), cheaper and slower than trains, also run the first two routes, and connect Garmisch-Partenkirchen to other Alpine villages, such as Oberammergau (16 per day, 40 minutes, DM 8.20 one-way), Füssen (three per day, DM 22 one-way), Oberstdorf (one per day, four hours, DM 38 one-way), and Linderhof (seven per day, 1¼ hours, DM 10.40 one-way).

The train station acts as a dividing line between the two parts of town. On the western side is **Marienplatz,** the heart of Garmisch; attractions are to the north, in the old town, around Frühlingstraße, Loisach Straße, and Kreutzstraße. On the east side of the tracks is **Ludwigstraße,** Partenkirchen's main strip, although Sonnenbergstraße and Ballergasse are also key places to find restaurants and shops. Since the two halves together comprise an extra-large Alpine town, and the sights are spread out, you should use the **Ortsbus** (local bus) to get around. The Kurkarte gets you on free; bus maps are available at the tourist information office.

WHERE TO SLEEP If you're skipping the hostel, the best way to find a room is through tourist information. If the tourist office and information booth are closed by the time you arrive, 24-hour screens outside the tourist office and above the travel agency in the train station display telephone numbers, addresses, and prices of accommodations. After hours you can also call 08821/19412 for listings. A room in a private guest house fluctuates between DM 20 and DM 35 per person. Some centrally located, classically Bavarian guest houses include **Gästehaus Hohenzollern** (Alpspitzstr. 6, tel. 08821/2950), with cute little rooms and breakfast for around DM 35 per person (call ahead; the place may be closing), and **Gästehaus Kornmüller** (Höllentalstr. 36, tel. 08821/3557), on the outskirts of town.

To get to the **Jugendherberge** (Jochstr. 10, tel. 08821/2980), 4 kilometers (2½ miles) out of town, hop Bus 5, 6, or 7 from the train station to Burgrain. Reception is open from 7 AM to 9 AM and 5 to 10 PM. With breakfast, a night costs DM 15, plus DM 4.50 for sheets if you're female, DM 3 if you're male (you may complain about sexist policies but the girl sheets are nicer). They have 270 beds, laundry facilities, and an 11:30 PM curfew.

For a cheap bed on the western edge of Partenkirchen—and rude service—try the hostel-like **Naturfreundeheim** (Schalmeiweg 21, tel. 08821/4322). It's only DM 11 per night if you have a sleeping bag, DM 13.50 if you don't. **Campingplatz Zugspitze** (Bundestr. 24, tel. 08821/3180) is a year-round campground at the foot of the Zugspitze, between Grainau and Garmisch-Partenkirchen; it costs DM 7 per person, DM 10 per site.

FOOD AND AFTER DARK For quick, inexpensive meals, stop by **Bavaria-Grill** (Bahnhofstr. 77A, closed Sun. and Mon.), **Grill-Shop** (Ludwigstr. 66, closed Sat.), or the **Cafeteria** (Griesstr. 1). Otherwise, feast on a delicious plate of *Käsespätzle* (cheese noodles) for DM 7.90, one of the mongo salads (around DM 12), or something more

Bavarian like *Schweinebraten* (roasted pork), for DM 13, at **Sebastians Stub'n** (Ludwigstr. 93, tel. 08221/78889). Pasta freaks will love **Charivari** (Sonnenbergstr. 17), which serves sandwiches and salads, too. It's also a cool place to have a few beers before you head off to the disco **Surprise** (Klammstr. 47, in Alpspitze Wellenbad center), which starts up late and doesn't close until early morning.

Oberammergau

Sometime during the 16th century, the inhabitants of this region concluded that perhaps the arctic winters here weren't conducive to agriculture. Enlightened, they decided to utilize the nearby forests and turned to handicrafts; Oberammergau has since become a world-renowned center of wood carving, and the first thing you'll notice are the wood-crammed shops *everywhere.* Here's the brain teaser of the day: How do these carvers make any money when there are thousands of seemingly identical shops selling seemingly identical figures for seemingly identical (steep) prices?

Regardless of the profit margin, the work of the craftspeople is universally flawless. For DM 2.50, travelers can view an impressive collection of wood-carved crafts at the local history museum, **Heimatmuseum** (Dorfstr. 8, tel. 08822/32256), which also displays wax works, glass paintings, and an incredibly extensive crib collection. In the summer you can watch wood-carvers tediously chipping figures in the workshop of the **Pilatushaus,** located on Verlegergasse, open weekdays 2–6 and Saturday 10–2. The most famous *Lüftlmaler* (*see* box, *below*), Franz Seraph Zwirick, painted the house's facade; on the southern side, the fresco depicts Christ with Pilate.

Still more distinguished than wood carving is Oberammergau's **passion play,** which was first performed in 1634 and has been staged once a decade since 1680. When the Black Plague struck Oberammergau during the Thirty Years War, citizens tried to save themselves by vowing to act out the suffering and death of Christ every 10 years. The 16-act, 5½-hour play features 1,500 locals, but won't run again until the summer of the year 2000 (reserve at least two years ahead). In the meantime you can check out the open-air **Passionspielhaus** (Passion Play Theater) on Passionweise, with its intriguing backstage museum (descriptions in English). Admission is DM 4, DM 2.50 for students.

BASICS The **post office** is across from the train station at Rottenbucher Straße 36 (tel 08822/3061). Call the **police** (Otmar-Weiß-Straße) at 6081, and an **ambulance** at 19222. **Pharmacies** are located at Dorfstraße 5 (tel. 540) and Ettaler Straße 12 (tel. 08822/6664).

Lüftlmalerei

The fancy frescoes adorning so many Alpine house facades in Oberammergau first appeared in the 18th century. At first, residents just dressed up the windows or added mock columns to the house. Religious themes became the fad during the Counter-Reformation, and in this century, creative exterior decorators have added a new motif: fairy tales. On Ettaler Straße in Oberammergau, you can see facades depicting the stories of Hänsel und Gretel and Little Red Riding Hood. The Lüftlmalerei originator, Franz Seraph Zwinck (1748–92) of Oberammergau, is the most celebrated of the painters and his work on the Pilatushaus the most renowned.

Oberammergau's **tourist office** (Zugen-Papst Str. 9A, tel. 08822/1021 or 08822/4771 is a few minutes' walk from the train station. Exit the train station onto Bahnhofstraße, cross the Ammer canal, and turn right onto Zugen-Papst-Straße. The staff will help you find rooms (usually a DM 1 charge, but often flexible) and shower you with brochures.

COMING AND GOING **Trains** between Oberammergau and Munich take less than two hours (14 per day, DM 21 one-way), but you'll have to change at Murnau. **Bus 9606** to and from Garmisch-Partenkirchen departs hourly until 6 PM or 7 PM (45 minutes, DM 8.20 one-way), passing through Kloster Ettal (*see* Near Oberammergau, *below*). You can also travel three times a day between here and Füssen by bus. It's a 1½-hour trip on Bus 1084 (DM 17.60 one-way).

WHERE TO SLEEP AND EAT There's a super cheap *Metzgerei* at Dorfstraße 26, with standing room to eat your *Leberkäse* (meatloaf; DM 1.70 per slice) or half of a grilled chicken (DM 6). For a sit-down meal, try the **Alte Post** (Dorfstr. 19, tel. 08822/1091), a 350-year-old inn with a beer garden that serves traditional Bavarian specialties. Entrées run between DM 10 and DM 15.

Although a bit far from the city center, the **Jugendherberge** (Malensteinweg 10, tel. 08822/4141) has beds for DM 14.50 with breakfast. From the train station take Raisachweg south along the Ammer River, hang a right at König-Ludwig-Straße, then a left on Malensteinweg; it's about a 30-minute walk. A more soothing option is to get a **private room** (DM 25–DM 30 per person) through the tourist office.

OUTDOOR ACTIVITIES Summer hikers and winter ski enthusiasts should head for **Mt. Laber** (5,610 feet), accessible by cable car, or **Mt. Kolben,** accessible by chair lift, both of which are within walking distance of town.

NEAR OBERAMMERGAU

KLOSTER ETTAL This church, originally built by Emperor Ludwig the Bavarian in 1330, underwent reconstruction in 1774 after a fire gutted it. By then, Gothic was out and Baroque was in, so today brilliant stucco work and gilding dominate the abbey walls. The dome rises an impressive 235 feet and an enormous fresco depicts the Benedictine Order in the glory of heaven. Supposedly, the abbey's liqueur (speaking of the glory of heaven) was invented for, um, medicinal purposes, but if a beer's all you need to feel good, try the monks' other brew across the street.

Bus 9606 from Oberammergau deposits you at the monastery's front door (get off at Ettal, Klostergasthof) and runs once or twice hourly (15 minutes, DM 4.20 one-way). From Garmisch-Partenkirchen (on the same bus line), the trip takes a half hour and costs DM 7.20.

SCHLOß LINDERHOF If you don't have the time to go castle-hopping through Bavaria, snap a few shots of Neuschwanstein and then explore the stunning Rococo interior of Schloß Linderhof. King Ludwig spent the most time here, at his smallest castle, and it's the only one that was finished during his lifetime. Modeled after the Petit Trianon at Versailles, Linderhof was built in 1874–78, on the former site of a hunting lodge owned by Ludwig's father. The magnificent master bedroom has an 8½-foot bed covered in blue velvet, and a chandelier that could have a very successful career as a mass-murder weapon. The immaculate English- and French-style **park** features an intense **grotto** constructed for Wagner's operas. Don't miss the **Moorish Kiosk,** with its stained-glass windows and chandeliers. Originally built for the Second World Expo in Paris, it was moved to the castle grounds, giving Ludwig II the opportunity to parade around in exotic costume. This decadent affair is open April–September, daily 9–12:15 and 12:45–4. The admission price, DM 8 and DM 5 for students, includes guided tours of palace, grotto, and kiosk. RVO Bus 9622 runs the 15 kilometers (9 miles) from Oberammergau to Linderhof seven times daily (30 minutes, DM 7.20 one-way). Don't miss the last return at 5:35 PM.

Mittenwald

If you have only a day or two to kick around in the Bavarian Alps, spend it in Mittenwald. Sandwiched between the Karwendel and Wetterstein mountains, this romantic, charming town epitomizes every Alpine village cliché you've ever heard—it's got everything from snowcapped peaks to breathtaking views to lederhosen-clad villagers. Despite such an awe-inspiring setting, cheery locals, and authentic small-town feel, Mittenwald is often overlooked because of its more famous neighbor, Garmisch-Partenkirchen, only 20 kilometers (12 miles) away.

BASICS To change money try the post office or one of the several banks on **Obermarkt** or **Bahnhofstraße** in the center of town. The **post office** (tel. 08823/1002), across from the train station, is open weekdays from 8 to noon and 2 to 6, Saturday 8 to noon, and Sunday 9:30 to 10:30, but it won't change money on Sunday. For **police** (Phnz-Zugen-Str. 5–7) call 1047; for an **ambulance** call 19222. You can find **pharmacies** at Obermarkt 11 (tel. 08823/8468) and Bahnhofstraße 18 (tel. 08823/1348).

The **Kurverwaltung** (tourist office) at Dammkarstraße 3 will help you find a place to stay for no charge and offers excellent hiking maps and other sport and sightseeing information. If you arrive late, the 24-hour computer screen by the entrance lists available lodging options. Tel. 08823/33981. Open weekdays 9–noon and 2–5, Sat. 10–noon).

COMING AND GOING Mittenwald is less than two hours from Munich by **train** (hourly trains, DM 27 one-way) and an hour from Innsbruck (hourly trains, DM 65 one-way). Frequent trains also run between Garmisch-Partenkirchen and Mittenwald (20 minutes, DM 7). Stop by the train station (tel. 08823/1333) for time schedules. RVO **buses** also run from Garmisch-Partenkirchen's train station to Mittenwald's but take a little longer and aren't as frequent (30 minutes, DM 8.20 one-way). The station is in the center of town.

WHERE TO SLEEP AND EAT Mittenwald has plenty of regular *Gäststätte* (restaurants), but if you're counting pennies, go for the decent gyros for DM 5.50 and schnitzel with fries for DM 7 at the nameless fast-food joint at Hochstraße 11. Otherwise, look for the Metzgerei all around town. Yummy schnitzels (DM 10–DM 14) and other Bavarian fare dominate the menu at **Gasthof Horsteiner** (Schwibbacherweg 2, tel. 08823/1382), which also offers excellent views of the town and the surrounding mountains.

Like most Alpine villages, Mittenwald has a number of private guest houses that offer singles and doubles for DM 20–DM 35 per person. Since the 120-bed **Jugendherberge** (Buckelwiesen 7, tel. 08823/1701) is inaccessible by bus and a one-hour hike (on the Tonihof-Buckelwiesen trail), private rooms are the less masochistic choice. Call to see if any of the eight rooms are available at the centrally located **Haus Antonia** (In der Haßerwiese 14, tel. 08823/5749); it's an incredible deal, with singles for DM 20–DM 27.50, and doubles for DM 55, including breakfast. Otherwise, get tips from the tourist office. The family-owned **Gasthof Horsteiner** (Schwibbacherweg 2, tel. 08823/1382), about a 15-minute walk from town, offers cheery rooms for about DM 35 per person, some with fantastic views of the mountains. The nearest year-round **campground** is at Isarhorn (tel. 08823/5216), 3 kilometers (2 miles) north of Mittenwald.

WORTH SEEING The **Geigenbau und Heimatmuseum mit Schauwerkstatt** (Ballenhausgasse 3, tel. 08823/2511) displays violins by some of the best violin makers, and you can see them on weekends from 10 to 11:45. You'll see violin-making in action at the museum's **workshop** (open weekdays until 11:45 AM). Next to the museum sits the 18th-century church of **Sts. Peter and Paul,** famous for its Baroque tower decorated with frescoes. Outside the church is a **bronze statue** dedicated to the violin-maker Klotz. West of the church extends the oldest part of town, **Im Gries,** which is delightful walking territory, as is **Obermarkt,** one of the main streets, lined with fruit stands and other markets. Awesome views and hiking opportunities abound; you can reach the **Karwendel summit** (7,867 feet)—boasting Germany's longest downhill ski run (6 kilometers, or 4 miles)—via the cable car that leaves from Alpenkorpstraße 1 (tel 08832/8480, DM 25 round-trip), or take the chair lift up **Kranzberg** (tel. 08823/1553) for only DM 6.50. Hikes to **Leutaschklamm gorge** and **waterfall** or to the tiny **Lautersee** aren't too strenuous. Check with the tourist office for other outdoor activities.

Berchtesgaden

It's not just the famed **Königssee**, Germany's cleanest and arguably most beautiful lake, or towering **Mt. Watzmann** (second only to the Zugspitze) that sucks tourists in: Berchtesgaden has some of the most unique sights anywhere, and it's virtually next door to popular Salzburg. Historically, Berchtesgaden is a former salt-mining center and infamous for its connection to Hitler (it was his favorite resort); two of its major attractions revolve around these themes. If you want to avoid the trampled track, inquire at the tourist office for more information about **Hintersee** in the neighboring village of Ramsau, or the three-hour hike to the **Schellenberg ice cave,** Germany's largest. Neither is exactly remote, but they're a lot mellower than the Eagle's Nest or salt mines (*see* Worth Seeing, *below*).

BASICS Change money at **banks,** the **post office** (tel. 08652/6011), or the **Reisebüro ABR** (tel. 08652/5081) in the train station. Because you're so close to the border, many places accept Austrian schillings as well. Call for the **police** at 61034, an **ambulance** at 2222, and the **hospital** at 571.

The **tourist office** (Königseerstr. 15, tel. 08652/5011) is opposite the main train station; it's open in the summer weekdays 8–6, Saturday 8–5, and Sunday 9–3, and during the off-season on weekdays 8–5 and Saturday 9–noon. They'll help you find midprice rooms (count on at least DM 30–DM 35 per person) and give students a 10% discount on a guided tour of Berchtesgaden's major sights. The 24-hour computer screen outside the office lists expensive pensions and hotels. The **Nationalpark Haus** on Franziskanerplatz (tel. 08652/64343) offers guided hikes and information about the national park. The **national-park information office** (tel. 08652/62222) by the Königssee offers similar services and is open from mid-May to mid-October.

COMING AND GOING There are **trains** (tel. 08652/5473) to and from Salzburg, but the **bus** is both faster and cheaper (50 minutes, DM 5.50 one-way). Trains between Berchtesgaden and Salzburg run hourly, and take less than an hour (DM 10.80 one-way). You must change at Freilaßing if you come by train from Munich; trains depart hourly and the ride takes 2½–3 hours (DM 41 one-way).

WHERE TO SLEEP The closest **Jugendherberge** is in nearby Strub (Gebirgsjägerstr. 52, tel. 08652/2190), and offers 400 luxurious beds usually dominated by 14- to 16-year-olds. Take Bus 9539 (DM 2) to Jugendherberge or to Strub Kaserne (a farther but more frequently serviced stop). It's DM 15 per night with breakfast, and another DM 4.50 for sheets. Reception is open from 7 to noon and 5 to 7, and there's a 10 PM curfew, which they'll extend to 11:30 PM if you ask nicely. The hostel is closed November and December. At the private, pretty lakeside **Königssee-Betriebe Hostel** (Seestr. 29, a five-minute walk from the Königssee bus stop; tel. 08652/5473), pay a worthwhile DM 27–DM 30 for a bed. The **Hotel zum Türken** (8240 Obersalzberg-Berchtesgaden, tel. 08652/2428), located at the foot of the road that leads up to Eagle's Nest, has beds for about DM 35 per person and adjoins some of the Nazis' wartime bunkers, to boot! It's about a 10-minute walk from the city center.

Camp by Königssee either at **Camping Mühlleiten** (tel. 08652/4584), 3 kilometers (2 miles) from Berchtesgaden, for DM 7 per adult and DM 7 per site; or at **Camping Grafenlehen** (tel. 08652/4140), for DM 7 per adult and DM 7.50 per site. **Camping Allweglehen** (tel. 08652/2396) is 3½ kilometers (2 miles) from Berchtesgaden in the direction of Salzburg. Adults pay DM 6.60 per night; tents are DM 8.50 per night. You can make reservations here and all three campsites are open year-round.

FOOD For fast food, try **Bernds Grillstüberl** (Marktpl. 24), **Brotzeitstüberl** (Schloßpl. 3), or **Expressgrill** (Maximilianstr. 8), all centrally located and open daily 9–6; for a more solid, yet inexpensive, Bavarian meal, try **Schwabenswert,** across from the train station.

WORTH SEEING Berchtesgaden's top attractions draw thick crowds and aren't cheap, but they're pretty damn distinctive!

➢ **KEHLSTEINHAUS** • King Ludwig II doesn't seem wacked at all after you see Kehlsteinhaus (Eagle's Nest), a Nazi retreat perched atop a 6,052-foot mountain. Its architects basically gored out a huge shaft in the center of the mountain, occupied by a brass elevator that carries you 407 feet to the top. This, combined with the super-harrowing, windy roads carved into the mountainside, makes for a crazier experience than Ludwig could have even dreamed of. The Nazi party presented the extraordinary site to Hitler for his 50th birthday. Today the rocky steps have been worn down by the hooves of many a tourist, but the panorama remains unforgettable. Buses leave every 30–45 minutes from the Berchtesgaden train station for Obersalzberg-Hintereck (DM 5.50 round-trip), from where you ride another 20 minutes up a steep, coiling road in a super-brake-equipped bus (DM 18, every half hour) to the parking lot; you're then blasted up the elevator shaft to the peak for another DM 5.

➢ **KONIGLICHES SCHLOß** • Tons of Wittelsbach treasures, including an impressive collection of fine wood carvings, are displayed in the Renaissance rooms of the Königliches Schloß, another Wittelsbach palace, in the center of town. Walk through the original 13th-century dormitory and cool cloisters while you're here. *Tel. 08652/2085. Admission: DM 5, DM 3 students. Open Oct.–Easter, weekdays 10–1 (last tour at noon) and 2–5 (last tour at 4); Easter–Sept., weekdays 10–1, 2–5. Closed holidays.*

➢ **OBERSALZBERG** • Far below the Eagle's Nest lie the former southern headquarters of the Nazi party, where you should check out the remains of the **Berghof,** the bunkers where Hitler schmoozed with gullible foreign dignitaries such as British prime minister Neville Chamberlain and convinced them to let him do just about anything he damn well pleased. You enter the bunkers, which also served as underground air-raid shelters, through Hotel zum Türken (*see* Where to Sleep, *above*).

➢ **SALZBERGWERK BERCHTESGADEN** • Although the costumes they give you to wear at this one-of-a-kind tourist extravaganza are supposed to make you look like a miner, you look more like a karate kid or a little tyke whose jammies are too big. You'll be carried around through the saltworks by four distinct modes of transportation, making you feel like you've landed in a game of Chutes and Ladders or Willy Wonka's chocolate factory, minus the chocolate. Go—it's fun, it's informative, and you'll enjoy it more if the exact details remain a surprise. *Bergwerkstr. 83, tel. 08652/60020. 2 km (1¼ mi) from Hauptbahnhof; take Bus 9540 from station or walk 15 min. from town center. Admission: DM 16, DM 14 students. Open May–Oct. 15 daily and on Easter 8:30–5; Oct. 16–Apr., weekdays 12:30–5:30.*

NURNBERG AND FRANCONIA

7

By Ann McDevitt

M

Mainly a rural region, Franconia is dominated by quiet farm villages and large swaths of thinly populated forest. The region's real charm, however, lies more in its architecture and history. Franconia was at one time the unrivaled power in southern Germany. Even after it was integrated into medieval Germany's patchwork of feudal kingdoms, Franconia continued to prosper under the kind leadership of the Holy Roman Empire. Generations of flamboyant Holy Roman rulers sought dreamy retreats where they might enjoy the perks of absolute power. And in Franconia they found sylvan valleys and rugged mountaintops that screamed "Build your castle here, stupid," which they did. Vast luxurious palaces, too, not to mention a sprawling network of monasteries, abbeys, and churches.

At the same time, rural farm villages grew into thriving trading centers, each of which hosted a legion of wealthy merchants who lavished their towns with elegant half-timbered mansions and colorful market squares. Prosperity also brought a flowering of the arts. Albrecht Dürer, the first indisputable genius of the German Renaissance, was born and worked in Franconia. Germany's great composer Richard Wagner also lived and wrote many of his great operas in the Franconian town of Bayreuth. Franconia is also known for its generous royal patrons—people like Heinrich II, Ludwig II, and the Saxe-Coburg nobles, men and women largely responsible for preserving Franconia as a center of art, music, and all sorts of highbrow culture.

At the heart of modern Franconia lies Nürnberg, the second-largest city in Bavaria (just so you know: Franconia is a region within the larger *Land,* or state, of Bavaria). Nürnberg has a sordid association with Hitler and the post–World War II war trials. But it's really the 12th-century old town that draws the bulk of visitors. Nürnberg's Kaiserburg castle is another popular stop—definitely worth a gander if you don't have time to explore the bevy of fortresses that stud the length of the nearby Romantische Straße (Romantic Road).

North of Nürnberg, the cities of Bamberg and Bayreuth both fall into the "well-preserved medieval town" category. Each is peppered with museums and dazzling churches (and, in Bayreuth's case, with a lavish opera house designed by Richard Wagner himself). Bamberg and Bayreuth are also within a short hop of both Kulmbach, Germany's self-acclaimed "Beer City," and Coburg, the seat of the Saxe-Coburg royal family (and the childhood home of Prince Albert, Queen Victoria's husband).

Franconia

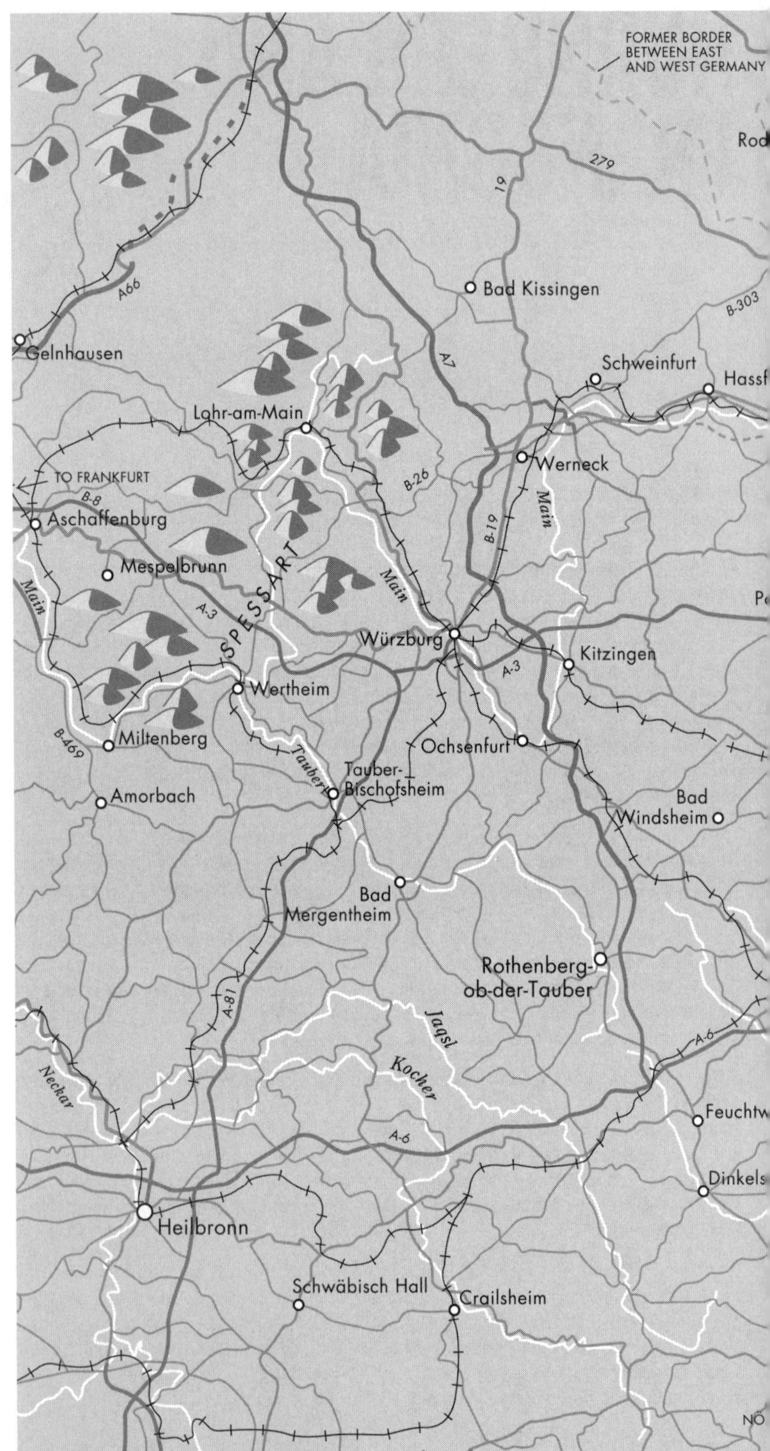
FORMER BORDER
BETWEEN EAST
AND WEST GERMANY
279
19
Bad Kissingen
B-303
A66
Gelnhausen
A7
Schweinfurt
Lohr-am-Main
Werneck
TO FRANKFURT
B-26
Main
B-8
Aschaffenburg
B-19
Mespelbrunn
SPESSART
Main
Main
A-3
Würzburg
Kitzingen
A-3
Wertheim
B-469
Miltenberg
Ochsenfurt
Tauber
Tauber-
Bischofsheim
Amorbach
Bad
Windsheim
Bad
Mergentheim
Rothenberg-
ob-der-Tauber
A-81
Jagst
Kocher
A-6
Neckar
A-6
Heilbronn
Schwäbisch Hall
Crailsheim

Franconia

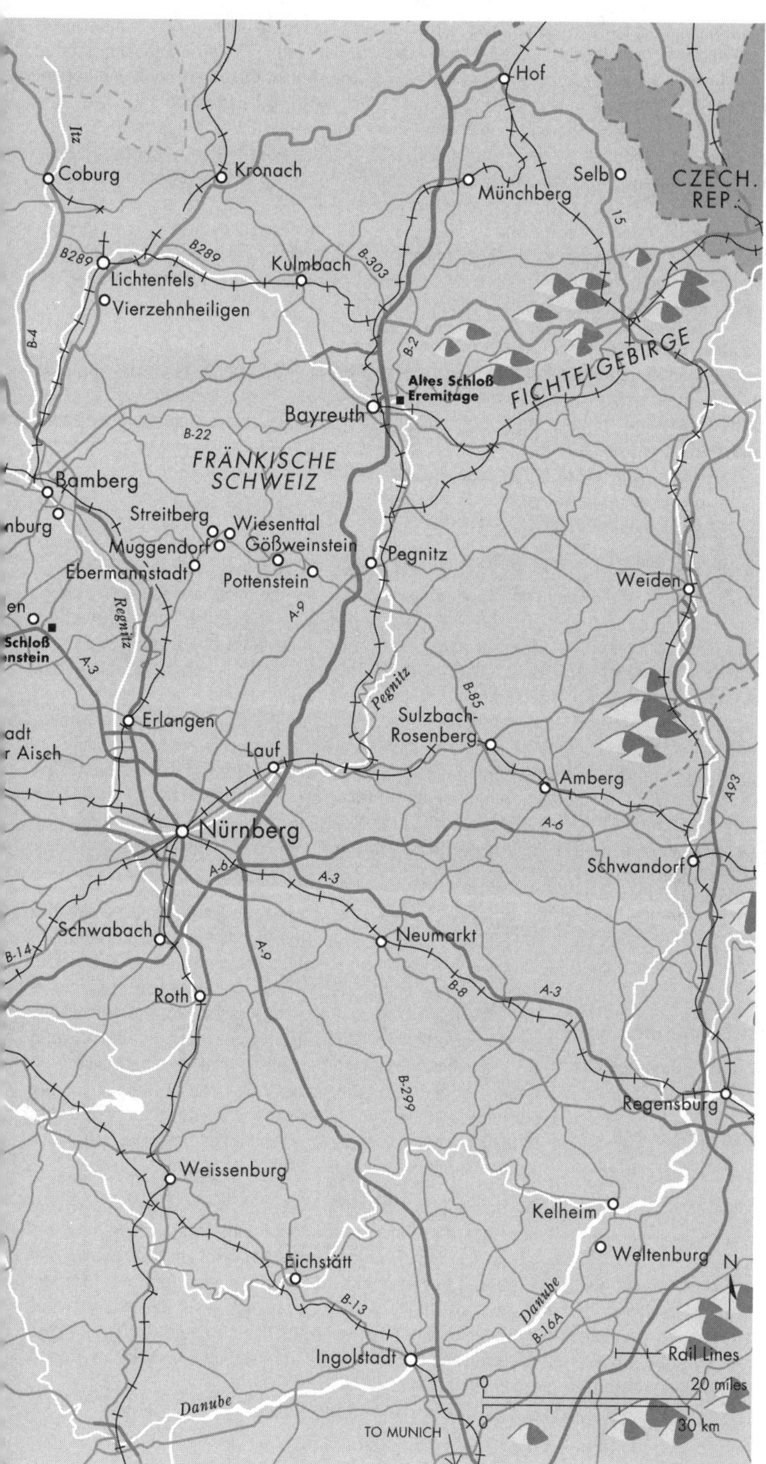
Hof
Coburg
Itz
Kronach
Selb
CZECH. REP.
Münchberg
15
B289
B289
Kulmbach
B-303
Lichtenfels
Vierzehnheiligen
B-4
B-2
Altes Schloß
Eremitage
FICHTELGEBIRGE
Bayreuth
B-22
FRÄNKISCHE SCHWEIZ
Bamberg
Streitberg
Wiesenttal
Muggendorf
Gößweinstein
Pegnitz
Ebermannstadt
Pottenstein
Weiden
A-9
Regnitz
Schloß
A-3
Pegnitz
B-85
Sulzbach-Rosenberg
Erlangen
Lauf
Amberg
A93
A-6
Nürnberg
Schwandorf
A-6
A-3
Schwabach
Neumarkt
B-14
A-9
B-8
A-3
Roth
B-299
Regensburg
Weissenburg
Kelheim
Weltenburg
N
Eichstätt
Danube
B-13
B-16A
Rail Lines
Ingolstadt
0
20 miles
0
30 km
Danube
TO MUNICH

Another of Franconia's "don't miss" attractions is the Romantische Straße, the most rewarding of Germany's specially designated tourist trails. The Romantische Straße runs primarily from Würzburg in the north to Nördlingen in the south (with the option of continuing through Bavaria all the way to the German-Austrian border). Like the Fairy-Tale Road, the Romantische Straße provides a thematic link to towns that might otherwise go unnoticed by the tourist horde. In this case the theme is hilltop castles, medieval citadels, and stoically ruined churches, all set against a rugged rural backdrop. Rothenberg-ob-der-Tauber, which has one of Europe's best-preserved medieval Altstädte, is a Romantische Straße town that's definitely worth visiting. And so long as you don't mind sharing its cobbled streets with a pride of camera-wielding tourists, medieval Würzburg makes a good day-trip from Nürnberg and a convenient base for longer excursions along the Romantische Straße.

Because Franconia is nearly overrun with castles and medieval towns, crowds can be a serious problem during summer. There's no real way around this, so just get used to it; in Franconia, video cameras and retirees are simply a part of the landscape. Another thing to keep in mind is that youth hostels in Franconia only accommodate people under 27. Everyone else should plan to plunk down a few extra deutsche marks for a private room or hotel. In either case, during summer it's a good idea to reserve a bed as far in advance as possible.

Nürnberg

Nürnberg is the largest city in Franconia, and by far the most interesting. The core of the Altstadt, through which the winding Pegnitz River flows, dates from at least 1040, making it one of the oldest in southern Germany. Nürnberg still has its 14th-century city walls, and peppered throughout the old town are restored half-timbered homes and lavish, flamboyantly embellished facades—reminders of the city's prosperity during the Middle Ages, when Nürnberg sat at the meeting point of a dozen important trade routes. Kaiserburg castle—a sprawling complex of towers and walled-in fortresses that define the city's imposing northern skyline—is another reminder of Nürnberg's past glories. Parts of the castle date from the city's founding, but its most impressive ruins were built and financed by the Holy Roman Empire (Nürnberg hosted the first diet, or meeting, of nearly every Holy Roman Emperor).

Such patronage helped to transform Renaissance-era Nürnberg into a center for the arts and sciences. Albrecht Dürer—Germany's genius woodcarver, artist, and all-around brilliant Renaissance guy—was born here in 1471, and he returned in 1509 to spend the rest of his life working in a still-existent studio in the old town. Other Renaissance-era Nürnberger artists include wood-carver Michael Wolgemut and sculptors Adam Kraft and Peter Vischer. Be advised that Nürnberg also gave birth to some astounding inventions—the pocket watch, the clarinet, and the globe (after deciding that the world was indeed round, some clever Nürnberger pasted a map to a sphere, thus creating the world's first geographic globe).

The Altstadt's outstanding looks—a mix of centuries-old apartments and shops, stone bridges and riverside walkways, cobbled streets—are what really merit a visit to Nürnberg.

On the gloomy side, Hitler orchestrated some of the largest pro-Nazi rallies ever held in Nürnberg. In fact, Nürnberg was one of the few Bavarian towns that strongly supported Hitler and the Nazi program; the 1936 Laws of Nürnberg made it illegal for Jews to marry gentiles, and also deprived Jews of their German citizenship. This partially explains why the city was chosen by the Allies to host war trials (which came to be known as the Nuremberg War Trials). During the trials, hundreds of Nazi officials were tried (and generally convicted) of "crimes against humanity."

Nürnberg

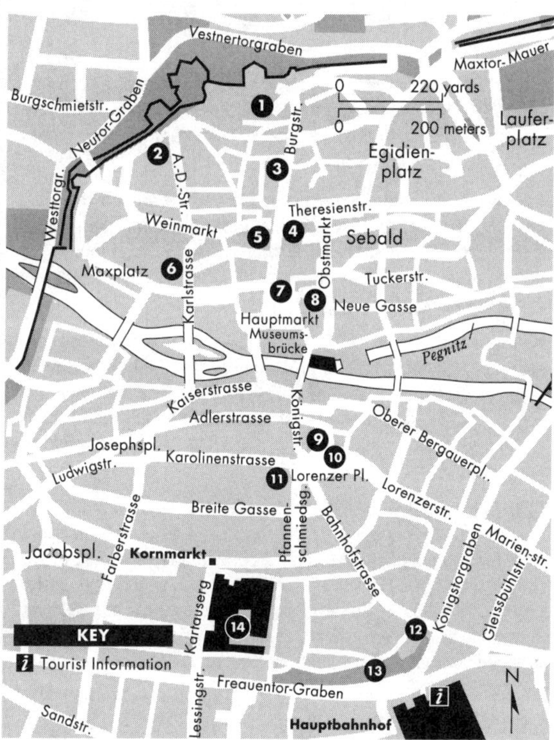

Albrecht-Dürer Haus, **2**
Alt-Stadt-Museum, **3**
Altes Rathaus, **4**
Frauenkirche, **8**
Germanisches National-museum, **14**
Handwerkerhof, **13**
Kaiserburg, **1**
Königstor, **12**
Nassauer House, **11**
St. Lorenz-kirche, **10**
St. Sebaldus-kirche, **5**
Schöner Brunnen, **7**
Spielzeug-museum, **6**
Tugendbrunnen, **9**

During summer, Nürnberg's Hauptmarkt overflows with street vendors and musicians; in winter, it hosts all kinds of events associated with **Christkindlmarkt,** an enormous pre-Christmas fair that runs from November 27 through Christmas Eve. During the fair the whole city is transformed into a bustling winter wonderland. If you're in the neighborhood, consider visiting on December 10, when Nürnberg hosts its annual candlelight Christmas march through the old town.

BASICS

AMERICAN EXPRESS AmEx customers' mail is held in this Altstadt office for one month. You'll need an AmEx card and a photo I.D. to pick it up. Other services include issuing/cashing traveler's checks (no commission) and currency exchange (2% commission). *Adlerstr. 2, tel. 0911/232397. Open weekdays 9–5:30, Sat. 9:30–12:30.*

BUCKET SHOPS **Schüler und Studentenreisen** specializes in cheap, last-minute flights and package deals for students. They happily serve nonstudents, too, but you may not get the same bargain prices. Wake up early and join the line of students often waiting impatiently outside. *Beckschlagergasse 6, tel. 0911/533091. From Rathauspl. walk e. on Theresienstr. to Innere Laufer Gasse. Open weekdays 10–6, Sat. 11–1.*

BUREAUX DE CHANGE In the Hauptbahnhof the **Deutsche Verkehrs-Bank** is open Monday–Saturday 7:45–7:45, Sunday 9:15–12:30. It charges a hefty DM 7.50 fee for cashing traveler's checks, so if you got 'em, head to the AmEx office. The bank's ATM accepts both Visa and American Express cards. **Citibank**'s two branches (Hallpl. 23 and Ludwigstr. 65–69) each have a 24-hour ATM, but these only accept Visa.

CONSULATES **British Consulate.** This consulate is only honorary—more like a tourist office than a real embassy—so messy problems will be referred to the Consulate General in Munich. Still, there's an English-language reading room, and English speakers are welcome to call for advice on Nürnberg. *Maxfeldstr. 10, tel. 0911/3609522.*

LAUNDRY Bring your dirty clothes to **Pritzl** Laundromat in the Altstadt. Use of a washer (including soap) costs DM 5, a 10-minute dry DM 1. For DM 11 Pritzl will dry-clean that rumpled suit or dress hiding in your backpack. *Obstmarkt 6. Open weekdays 7:30–6.*

LUGGAGE STORAGE Lockers in the **Hauptbahnhof** are accessible around the clock and cost DM 2 (small) and DM 4 (large) per day. There's a four-piece maximum, after which you'll have to pay in person and get someone to open the locker for you (call tel. 0911/2192021). If you'll be gone for several days use the train station's attended luggage service for DM 2 per piece, per day.

MAIL AND PHONES At the main post office, **Postamt 1,** located opposite the train station, you can send telegrams, buy stamps and phone cards (in DM 12 and DM 50 denominations), and exchange currency. The staff will help you place a standard or collect call abroad, or you can dial direct from one of the international booths (most require a phone card). Nürnberg's postal code is 8500. *Bahnhofpl. 1. Open weekdays 8–6, Sat. 8–noon, Sun. 11–noon.*

VISITOR INFORMATION The tourist information office in the **Hauptbahnhof** (tel. 0911/233632, open Mon.–Sat. 9–7) has a wall of city and Land (regional) brochures that cost anywhere from a few pfennigs to DM 1. A second tourist office is on the **Hauptmarkt** (Am Hauptmarkt, tel. 0911/233635, open Mon.–Sat. 9–6). It suffers from long, long, very long lines, especially around noon when everyone's at the square to watch the Männleinlaufen clock display. In any case, both offices stock city maps and, for a DM 3 fee, will book you into a private room or pension.

COMING AND GOING

BY TRAIN The **Hauptbahnhof** (Bahnhofspl., tel. 0911/19419 or 0911/204801) is conveniently located at the Altstadt's southeast corner; to reach the old town take the underground passage to Königstraße and continue northwest. Inside the depot there's a bank, luggage lockers, and a tourist-information office, not to mention trains running around the clock to all parts of Germany. Principal destinations from Nürnberg include Bayreuth (DM 21), Würzburg (DM 24), Bamberg (DM 14.80), Coburg (DM 27), Munich (DM 46), Frankfurt (DM 54), and Berlin Hauptbahnhof (DM 81). Trains for each of the above leave hourly. Nürnberg's train depot is also the main hub for local public transport (trams, local buses, and the U-Bahn).

BY BUS The central bus station, **ZOB** (Marienpl. 10, tel. 0911/226992 or 0911/2440162), is a short hop northeast of the Hauptbahnhof. Buses leave daily for Bayreuth (six per day, DM 18), Lichtenfels (two per day, DM 21), Bamberg (five per day, DM 10), and Coburg (six per day, DM 19).

If you're planning a trip to Rothenburg-ob-der-Tauber along the *Burgenstraße* (Castle Road) or the Romantische Straße, the DM 10 ticket (DM 18 round-trip), bought on the bus, lets you stop three times along the way and is valid for five days. The bus runs daily from May 31 to September 27, leaving from Nürnberg ZOB at 8:45 AM.

HITCHING If you're heading northeast to Berlin, take Tram 13 from the Hauptbahnhof to Nordostbahnhof/Leipziger Platz and work your way toward Außere-Bayreuther-Straße—as good a place as any to stick your thumb out. Westbound travelers should take Tram 9 from the Hauptbahnhof to its end in Thon. Thon's Erlanger Straße is a good place to hitch for Würzburg, Frankfurt, and the Northwest. For Munich, take U-Bahn 11 from the Hauptbahnhof to Messezentrum and then flag down your ride from Münchener Straße.

BY MITFAHRGELENGEHEIT **Citynetz Mitfahr-Zentrale** efficiently gets you almost everywhere in Europe. You can try to score a ride on the day you call, but your chances are better if you ring ahead. The most popular destinations include Heidelberg (DM 22), Hamburg (DM 53), Prague (DM 25), and Paris (DM 52). *Strauchstr. 1, tel. 0911/19444. Walk e. from Hauptbahnhof through Allersberger Unterführung (tunnel), then s. on Allersberger Str. to Strauchstr. Open weekdays 9–6, Sat. 8:30–1, Sun. and holidays 11–2.*

GETTING AROUND

You shouldn't need to bother with public transportation if you keep within the moats, towers, and gates of the Altstadt. To orient yourself remember that the train station is perched on the Altstadt's southeast corner, Kaiserburg castle and the youth hostel on the northwest corner. Königstraße, accessed via an underground passage from the train station, essentially runs the entire north–south length of the old town (and passes all the main sights). Snaking its way west–east through the old town is the **River Pegnitz,** another good landmark. Its main crossing point is the pedestrianized **Museumsbrücke** (Museum Bridge), which connects the **Hauptmarkt** in the north with **Lorenzer Platz** in the south.

If you have the urge to ride a tram or bus, buy a ticket (DM 3) on board or from any street-side *Automaten* (ticket machine). These DM 3 tickets are identical to the *Einzelfahrkarte* (DM 3), which is available from any ticket machine and is valid for 90 minutes of unlimited bus, tram, and subway transport. A 24-hour pass costs DM 6.50 and is valid any weekday until 1 AM, and from Friday night until Sunday night. The neighboring Hauptbahnhof and ZOB station are the best places to catch a bus, tram, or U-Bahn. In Nürnberg, all public transportation stops running daily at 1 AM.

BY U-BAHN Three underground lines (U1, U2, U11) service Nürnberg's Altstadt. From the U-Bahn stop on Bahnhofsplatz you can reach Ludwigsplatz, Lorenzer Platz, and Richard-Wagner-Platz. You won't find any ticket machines in the underground stations, so purchase tickets (DM 3) in advance from a street-side *Automaten.* Trains run every 7–10 minutes until 1 AM nightly.

BY BUS Unlike the U-Bahn, local buses service every nook and cranny in the Altstadt. The most useful are Buses 46, 47, and 36. The first two start at Heilig-Geist-Spital (i.e., the almshouse one block east of Museumsbrücke) and then meander north through the old town. Bus 36, which stops at the Hauptmarkt, travels east–west across town and is convenient for short hops between the Altstadt's "midtown" sights. Buses use the same ticket system as the trams and subway; drivers sell the 90-minute *Einzelfahrkarte* (DM 3) on board.

BY TAXI Taxis cluster around the Hauptbahnhof and the Hauptmarkt. The meter starts at DM 4.50. Standard fare from the Hauptbahnhof to Kaiserburg castle and the youth hostel is DM 12–DM 15; to the Hauptmarkt DM 8–DM 12. German-speakers can order a taxi by calling 0911/19410.

WHERE TO SLEEP

Nürnberg has an excellent youth hostel and two very respectable pensions. Unfortunately, that's about all for budget-minded wanderers. If the hostel is full (as it often is during summer), head to either tourist office and book yourself into a private room for a DM 3 fee. The rooms themselves, many of which are located in the Altstadt, typically cost DM 25–DM 35 per person, per night.

➢ **UNDER DM 90 • Burg-Hotel Kleines Haus.** If you can afford the DM 90 price tag, this 22-room "little house" ain't a bad choice. First of all, it has an indoor pool. Secondly, there's a sauna. Last but not least, it's only a stone's throw from Kaiserburg castle and the Hauptmarkt. What are you waiting for? *Schildgasse 16, tel.*

0911/203040. Head n. from Hauptmarkt along Burgstr., past Fembohaus, and turn right on Schildgasse.

Hotelgarni Pfälzer Hof. Don't bother unless it's late and you're desperate. The owners get away with charging DM 80–DM 95 per double only because they're near the Hauptbahnhof. The patroness lacks German promptness and perfectionism, so clogged sinks and burned-out lights tend to stay that way. Lone and women travelers also note: This isn't the safest neighborhood. In fact, it's practically the red-light district. On the plus side the Pfälzer does have an indoor sauna. *Am Gräslein 10, off Jakobstr., tel. 0911/221411. From Hauptbahnhof head w. on Frauentorgraben, turn right on Kartäusergasse, left on Kornmarkt, and left on Am Gräslein.*

➢ **UNDER DM 120 • Steichele.** This 52-room pension is housed in a converted wine tavern. The rooms are warm and fuzzy and possessed of something guidebooks like to call an "Old World air." If you're in the mood to splurge, you could do a lot worse. Doubles start at DM 110 and peak around DM 150. The downstairs restaurant is open daily except Monday. The pension is located in the Altstadt, a short walk from Ludwigsplatz and the train station. *Knorrstr. 2, tel. 0911/204377.*

HOSTELS **Jugendgästehaus Nürnberg.** The only youth hostel in town is inside the 500-year-old Kaiserburg castle, towering high above the city (the views alone are worth the trip). The rooms were converted from the former castle stables, and for DM 23 per person you get a bunk with red-checkered sheets and a 7–8:45 AM breakfast; dinner costs an additional DM 4–DM 7. Doubles and small singles are available but often book up fast in summer. Reserve in advance if possible. At the very least call from the train station to avoid a fruitless journey. *Burg 2, tel. 0911/221024. Reception closed 1 AM–7 AM. 1 AM curfew; 10 PM "Silent Time." Luggage storage, wheelchair access.*

FOOD

The pedestrianized streets around Lorenzer Platz, and the streets intersecting the Hauptmarkt, boast the thickest concentration of "Ye Olde German" eateries and elegant (i.e., expensive) riverfront cafés. If you're pressed for cash, head instead for the university district, nestled on the River Pegnitz's southern bank a few blocks east of Museumsbrücke. Street stands and hole-in-the-wall Imbiß-style joints are the norm here—the sort of places where you can fill up for less than DM 10. This is also where you'll find a good selection of student-ish bars. That said, one of the most popular bars in town, the **Irish Castle Pub** (Schlehengasse 31, off Spittlertormauer, tel. 0911/224878), is on the other side of town by Ludwigsplatz. Stop in for a pub grub meal—sandwiches, soups, shepherd's pie, and Irish stew, all under DM 10—or for a pint of stout and a dram of whiskey. From Ludwigsplatz walk west on Schlotfegergasse and turn right at Spittlertormauer.

Bakeries all over town sell Nürnberg's famous Lebkuchen, *a sweet-smelling, delicious gingerbread cake. Stands on the Hauptmarkt sometimes offer piping hot squares of Lebkuchen for as little as DM 4.*

Königshof (Zirkelschmiedsgasse 28, tel. 0911/227678, closed Mon.) is one of the oldest wine taverns in Franconia, dating from 1560. At DM 15–DM 25 per person, dinner here is not even close to cheap, but the reasonably priced three-course lunch menu saves it from the trash heap. A better bargain is **Bratwurstglöcken** (Handwerkerhof, tel. 0911/227625, closed Sun. and Christmas–Feb. 28), located in the touristy craft village opposite the train station. Its main courses are priced under DM 12.50, and during summer you can sit in the pleasant beer garden outside. In the same vein is **Zur Schranke** (Beim Tiergärtnertor 3, tel. 0911/225474, closed Sun. and Oct.), an ancient beer tavern that probably has the cheapest menu—mainly wieners and cabbage—in all Nürnberg. It's located beside the Altstadt wall near Kaiserburg. If you need more "ambience" try the ever-popular **Helig-Geist-Spital** (Spitalgasse 16, tel. 091/221761), by the river just east of the Hauptmarkt. This authentic wine tavern packs in tourist hordes with its dark wood decor and expansive wine list. A full meal costs under DM 20. Visit in the afternoon before the crowds arrive.

WORTH SEEING

Nürnberg is a compact city, and all of its sights are within easy walking distance of one another. Since there's little to see outside the Altstadt, start with a quick tour of Nürnberg's city walls, the last of which was built in 1452. Large sections were seriously damaged during World War II, but they've since been lovingly restored, complete with their attendant network of moats, gateways, and watchtowers. **Königstor** (Royal Gate), opposite the train station, is a typical example of the wall's sturdy, centuries-old fortifications. **Handwerkerhof** (open Mar. 20–Dec. 23, Mon.–Sat. 10–6:30), nestled behind the gate, is meant to be a medieval artisans' courtyard, a place where (at least according to tourist brochures) "charming little gadgets are offered on view and, of course, also for sale." In other words, glassblowers, weavers, potters, candle makers, and silversmiths dress up in costume and perform craft demonstrations, all the while trying to hawk their handmade goods at a heady price. Worth a quick peek, but don't lose any sleep over it.

ALBRECHT-DURER-HAUS This stunning late-medieval house, located opposite the Tiergärtner Gate just west of Kaiserburg castle, was formerly home to Albrecht Dürer, one of Germany's most talented painters and wood-carvers. Dürer lived here from 1509 until his death in 1528, and his three-story pad is one of the best-preserved medieval relics in all Nürnberg. Though you'll have to visit Dresden, Leipzig, and Berlin to see the bulk of Dürer's original work, many of the intricate woodcut prints displayed here are authentic. *Albrecht-Dürer-Str. 39, tel. 0911/231–2271. Admission: DM 3, DM 1.50 students. Open Mar.–Oct., Tues.–Sun. 10–5, Wed. until 9 PM; Nov.–Feb., Tues.–Fri. 1–5, Wed. until 9 PM, weekends 10–5.*

ALT-STADT-MUSEUM This small museum, housed inside one of the city's most lavish Renaissance-era mansions, is dedicated to one thing and one thing only—the glorious history of Nürnberg. Every aspect of Nürnberg is dealt with in almost painful detail, from its founding all the way through World War II and beyond. Non-German speakers should probably steer clear. *Burgstr. at Theresienstr., 1 block n. of Rathauspl. Admission: DM 3. Open Tues.–Fri. and Sun. 10–5, Sat. 10–1.*

GERMANISCHES NATIONALMUSEUM The sprawling Germanic National Museum is dedicated to all aspects of German culture and history, from Stone Age Nürnbergers to Nazi-era war criminals, from why Germans wear lederhosen to why they eat salted cabbage and pretzels. The collection here is heralded as one of the largest and most comprehensive in all Germany, and it's certainly one of the best arranged. Highlights

A Museum Devoted to Playtime

Ninja turtles may placate some imaginations. But if you like toys with a bit more "oomph" don't miss the impressive Spielzeugmuseum. Nürnberg claims to be the toy capital of the world, and this museum—dedicated exclusively to toys and amusing doohickeys—documents the evolution of all sorts of imaginative diversions. Original Renaissance doodads and Baroque whirligigs compete with 19th-century fandangles and 20th-century widgets. **Sigmundstr. 220, 1 block from Albrecht-Dürer-Haus. Admission: DM 3. Open Tues.–Sun. 10–5, Wed. 10–9.**

include the German Renaissance exhibit (heavy with works by Dürer and Cranach), the medieval pieces (manuscripts, altarpieces, stained glass, suits of armor), and the exhibit of antique and modern toys. *Kornmarkt. From Lorenzer Pl. walk s. down Pfannenschmiedsgasse and turn right on Kornmarkt. Admission: DM 3. Open Tues., Wed., and Fri.–Sun. 9–5, Thurs. 8 AM–9:30 PM. Sun. and Thurs. evening free.*

HAUPTMARKT The Hauptmarkt is Nürnberg's central open-air market, the always busy and colorful meeting place of old men, brawny fruit sellers, and video camera tourists. In the center of the square look for **Schöner Brunnen,** an elegant, 60-foot-high fountain carved around AD 1400. It's adorned with more than 30 carved figures that include Biblical prophets, local noblemen, Julius Caesar, and Alexander the Great. **Frauenkirche,** directly behind the fountain, is the square's other main attraction. This church was built in 1350 on the site of a razed synagogue (most of the Hauptmarkt was built atop the city's former Jewish quarter). There's not a lot to bother with inside Frauenkirche. Instead, most are attracted by its 16th-century **Männleinlaufen,** the grand clock that adorns the church's facade. Every day at noon crowds gather, eagerly anticipating the stroke of 12 that brings a parade of Holy Roman electors who glide and dance and spin and then bow to Emperor Charles IV. In other words, more fodder for package-tour groups bristling with video cameras. If you've ever seen a glockenspiel demonstration, then you'll know to evacuate the Hauptmarkt by 11:45 or so.

KAISERBURG Kaiserburg castle is definitely one of Nürnberg's highlights. It towers over the city at the northern end of Burgstraße, an immense cluster of buildings that looks more than a little imposing as you climb the cobbled streets to reach it. The castle complex comprises three separate groups of buildings. To the east is **Kaiserstallung** (Imperial Stables), the 15th-century stables that now house the local youth hostel (*see* Where to Sleep, *above*). The real focus of the site, however, is the castle itself, which occupies the westernmost part of the fortress. Take a quick walk around the perimeter and then make a beeline for the **Doppelkapelle** (Double Chapel). The lower part of the chapel was used by court minions and thus has little decoration. The upper half, the part used by royalty and their keepers, is much larger and more ornate. The castle's *Kaisersaal* (throne room) and *Rittersaal* (Knight's Hall) are also worth a look for their mural-laden ceilings and creaky oak interiors. If you want a good view of the site, on your way down the hill climb to the top of the **Sinwellturm,** a rugged round tower built right into the rock. The Kaiserburg complex is free to enter and open around the clock, but if you want to visit the castle itself you'll have to pay DM 4.

LORENZER PLATZ This historic square, located a few blocks south of the Hauptmarkt and the River Pegnitz, is dominated by the medieval **St. Lorenzkirche,** lauded as Nürnberg's most beautiful church. Two brawny towers flank the church, and its arched entranceway is covered floor to ceiling with ornate carvings, a tribute to the artistic richness of medieval Nürnberg. Inside, notice the stone sculptures by Adam Kraft and Veit Stoss. Kraft did the stone tabernacle to the left of the altar; Stoss the *Annunciation* at the nave's east end. Back on the square, the **Tugendbrunnen** (Fountain of Virtues) is a popular spot for a summer's day water fight. Nürnberg's oldest dwelling house, the lavish **Nassauer Haus** (Lorenzer Pl. 6), is on the square's west side.

ALTES RATHAUS Nürnberg's Old Town Hall was bombed into oblivion during World War II. The structure you see today is a painstaking reconstruction of the 14th-century original. It looks nice enough from the outside, but the highlight is the underground dungeon, hacked from damp rock and decked out with some fascinating medieval relics. Attached to the rear of the Rathaus is the 13th-century **St. Sebalduskirche,** a lavish Gothic creation, tall, elegant, and utterly peaceful. *Rathauspl. Admission: DM 2. Open May–Sept., weekdays 10–4, weekends 10-1.*

Würzburg

Würzburg, one of the Romantische Straße main attractions, is set on the banks of the Main River roughly 90 kilometers (56 miles) northwest of Nürnberg. The river passes through the town center and is crossed by three stoically weathered stone bridges—Ludwigsbrücke, Alte Mainbrücke, and Friedensbrücke. Many a town would be grateful for Würzburg's dreamy riverside setting, or for its inviting network of bridges and narrow lanes. But in many ways these pale in comparison with Würzburg's two main sights, Festung Marienberg (Marienberg Fortress) and the Baroque Residenz palace. The former sits atop a small hill on the western edge of town, absolutely dominating Würzburg's steeple-pricked skyline. The Residenz, a short walk away on the eastern edge of the old town, was the rulers' actual residence and is considered one of Europe's most impressive architectural monuments. Though it is less visible than the hilltop fortress, it certainly is no less stunning.

The Romantic Road

The Romantische Straße is the most rewarding of Germany's specially designated tourist routes. It runs from Würzburg, 90 kilometers (56 miles) northwest of Nürnberg, to Nördlingen, about 80 kilometers (50 miles) southwest of Nürnberg.

It was meant to capture Germany at its most romantic. The surprising part is, the idea worked. The countryside itself is less dramatic than it is simply rural. But the towns and castles clustered along the route are, in general, incredibly bewitching. Without exception they all have a true and tangible medieval feel; within the massive gates of these once-besieged villages, cobbled lanes meander across wistful open-air squares before disappearing into a colorful labyrinth of Baroque mansions and gabled apartments.

The Romantische Straße is definitely not limited to Würzburg and Rothenburg-ob-der-Tauber. However, without your own transportation, the remaining sights can be difficult to reach. If renting a car is out of the question, your only option may be the Romantische Straße bus, created by Deutsche Bahn (DB), the German rail conglomerate, to encourage tourism along the route. The bus is free to all Eurail and InterRail pass holders, and to anyone with a DB rail pass. Service runs only between April 10 and September 26, during which time there are two buses daily in each direction between Frankfurt and Füssen (Füssen is southwest of Munich on the German-Austrian border) and Frankfurt and Munich. Along the way, both services have scheduled stops in Romantische Straße destinations like Würzburg, Rothenburg-ob-der-Tauber, Dinkelsbühl, Nördlingen, and, on the Bavarian section of the Romantische Straße, Augsburg and Füssen.

Tourist brochures boast that Würzburg is serviced by 159 long-distance trains daily, so coming and going is definitely not a problem. However, crowds are, especially during June's **Mozart Festival** (held on the grounds of the Residenz; contact the tourist office for details). During the summer season hotels are sometimes booked weeks in advance, and restaurants have been known to jack up the prices of their already dear tourist menus. Würzburg does have a youth hostel, but since it's one of the few budget options available for miles, it, too, books up fast. The moral of the story: Reservations are in order between June and August.

BASICS

Head to the main post office, **Postamt 1** (Bahnhofspl. 2, tel. 0931/330), across from the train station, to buy stamps or exchange money at competitive rates. It's open Monday through Friday from 6 AM to 9 PM, Saturday until 8 PM, and Sunday 9 AM–8 PM. Other old town banks include **Commerzbank** (Domstr. 38, tel. 0931/30940) and **Deutsche Bank** (Juliuspromenade 66, tel. 0931/30890).

There are three tourist offices in town: the main **tourist information** (Pavilion am Hauptbahnhof, tel. 0931/36436, open Mon.–Sat. 8–8), which is located just outside the train station; a second **tourist information** (Haus zum Falken, Am Markt, tel. 0931/37398, open weekdays 9–6, Sat. until 2 PM), which is on the central market square; and a smaller office, **Fremdenverkehrsamt** (Am Congress Centrum, tel. 0931/37335, open Mon.–Thur. 9–6, Fri. until 2 PM), which sits overlooking the Main River near Friedensbrücke. They all stock city maps and English-language walking guides. They also organize guided city tours and book private rooms (DM 30–DM 45) for a fee of DM 4.

COMING AND GOING

Würzburg is one of the Romantische Straße's major hubs. It's extremely easy to reach by train and, if you're headed to other nearby Romantische Straße villages, a main starting point for regional buses. Another option is ride sharing. The local **Mitwohnzentrale** (Zeller Str. 23–25, tel. 0931/416832), near Alte Mainbrücke on the Main's west bank, arranges rides throughout Franconia and beyond.

BY TRAIN The train station, or **Hauptbahnhof** (Bahnhofpl., tel. 0931/19419), is on the north edge of the Altstadt, a 15-minute walk from Am Markt and a 30-minute walk from the youth hostel. To reach Am Markt and the adjacent Schönbornstraße, Würzburg's pedestrian-only shopping avenue, walk out of the station and past the

The New Old Würzburg

Würzburg was all but decimated by an Allied saturation bombing raid on March 16, 1945, a scant seven weeks prior to Germany's surrender. In the space of 20 minutes, nearly 90% of the city simply disappeared; at least 4,000 buildings were destroyed, and at least that many people were killed. Following the war, residents and government contractors began to rebuild the once elegant Altstadt. Years of painstaking restoration went into the project, and by most accounts it was a success. In many cases stones and beams from the original bombed-out structures were used, which helped recreate the prewar Altstadt in exact detail. The only structural alteration was the transformation of Schönbornstraße into a pedestrian-only zone.

fountain, head south down Kaiserstraße, and hang a right on Juliuspromenade. Schönbornstraße is a few blocks farther on the left; the River Main a few hundred yards ahead. Würzburg is extremely well served by rail, particularly from Nürnberg (hourly, DM 34) and Frankfurt (hourly, DM 36).

BY BUS The bus station is directly in front of the rail depot on Pavillon am Hauptbahnhof. All year round, Würzburg is connected twice daily by bus with Nürnberg (DM 11) and Frankfurt (DM 13). Between April 10 and September 26, Würzburg is also serviced by **Deutsche Bahn's Romantische Straße bus.** One of these departs daily at 9 AM and stops in Rothenburg-ob-der-Tauber, Dinkelsbühl, Nördlingen, Augsburg, and Füssen. Another departs daily at 10:15 AM and stops in Rothenburg-ob-der-Tauber, Dinkelsbühl, Augsburg, and Munich. In the opposite direction, the Romantische Straße bus also runs twice daily between Würzburg and Frankfurt.

WHERE TO SLEEP AND EAT

Any of the tourist offices can, for a DM 4 fee, book you into a private room (DM 30–DM 45). During summer these become scarce, so either book in advance or make a beeline to the youth hostel, **Jugendgästehaus Würzburg** (Burkaderstr. 44, tel. 0931/42590). Besides its excellent location, nestled below Festung Marienberg on the River Main's west bank, it's also one of the few youth hostels to attract a more upscale clientele. That's because there just ain't that many beds in town, and certainly not many priced under DM 100. That said, the hostel is still not cheap: space in one of its 223 beds costs DM 30 per night, including breakfast. From the train station, take Tram 5 in the direction of Heuchelhof and alight at Ludwigsbrücke, the first stop once you cross over the Main. From here head north along the Main (keep the river on your right) and follow the signs.

In a pinch try either **Franziskaner** (Franziskanerpl. 2, tel. 0931/15001) or **Greifenstein** (Häfnergasse 1 am Marienpl., tel. 0931/51665). Neither guest house does well in the "cozy" or "atmospheric" categories. Sadder still, at DM 120 per double room they are two of the cheapest guest houses around.

To pitch a tent in the great outdoors, head to one of two nearby campgrounds: **Campingplatz Kalte Quell** (Winterhäuser Str. 160, tel. 0931/65598) or **Campingplatz Estenfeld** (Maidbronner Str. 38, Estenfeld, tel. 09305/228). The former is located in the suburbs about 6 kilometers (4 miles) south of Würzburg; the latter, also in the suburbs, 5 kilometers (3 miles) north. Both charge roughly DM 8 per tent and DM 2 per person. During summer there are buses that run 1–3 times daily to both sites; inquire at the train station's tourist office for current schedules.

Würzbrug's central market, Am Markt, and the adjacent streets boast the usual high concentration of Imbiß stands, cafés, and tourist-geared beer halls. There's another cluster of cheapish food stands and greasy hole-in-the-walls around the train station, and in the maze of streets around Sanderstraße and Münzstraße. At the opposite end of the spectrum is **Backofele** (Ursulinergasse 2, tel. 0931/59059), a historic tavern that features Franconian specialties priced mostly under DM 20. Nicer still is **Juliusspital Weinstuben** (Juliuspromenade 19, tel. 0931/54080, closed Wed. and Feb.), a popular wine tavern that also serves mostly Franconian specialties and—more to the point—wines from its own vineyard. Another popular drinking hall is **Bürgerspital** (Theaterstr., tel. 0931/53887), where liters of sweet white Franconian wine cost roughly DM 5—a mere pittance for this excellent, locally grown elixir.

WORTH SEEING

Festung Marienberg and the Residenz palace, situated on opposite sides of the Main River, are Würzburg's two main tourist sights. However, peppered in between them are no less than 16 churches, 5 historic mansions, and a solid handful of galleries. Of the latter, don't miss the **Municipal Art Gallery** (Hofstr. 3, tel. 0931/54534, open

Tues.–Fri. 10–5, weekends until 1 PM), which displays 19th- and 20th-century Franconian art and sculpture. It's located between the *Dom* (cathedral) and Residenzplatz, on the same street as **Otto-Richter-Halle** (Hofstr. 11, tel. 0931/51552, open Tues.–Fri. 10–1 and 2–5, weekends 9–noon), which presents rotating collections of international modern art.

The only way to conquer Würzburg's gaggle of sights is with the excellent English-language walking map (free) available from any of the three tourist offices. Between May 5 and October 31, another good option is a guided **walking tour.** These leave Tuesday through Saturday at 11 AM from outside the Am Markt tourist office. The two-hour tour encompasses nearly every major and minor site in the city. Tickets, which include free entrance to the Residenz palace, cost DM 6 for students, DM 9 for everyone else.

AM MARKT AND SCHONBORNSTRABE Würzburg's central marketplace, Am Markt, is where people come to sit and soak up the sun on a steamy summer's day. It's also where motley street sellers gather most days to hawk fresh fruit and tourist trinkets. The square itself isn't much to look at, but it is surrounded by an inspired collection of Baroque-era relics. First and foremost is **Haus zum Falken,** hailed as Würzburg's finest Baroque mansion (it also houses a tourist office). Although it was one of the many structures restored following Würzburg's virtual destruction at the end of World War II, the lavish Rococo facade dates from 1752 and is original. The late Gothic church **Marienkapelle,** also on the square, was completed in 1481 and then rebuilt in 1946. Facing the square from the church portal is the tombstone of Balthasar Neumann, the architect responsible for Residenz palace and countless other Würzburg monuments.

Schönbornstraße, Würzburg's pedestrian-only shopping avenue, runs north–south. At the southern end of Schönbornstraße it's nearly impossible to miss the towering **Dom,** an 11th-century Romanesque church. Like so much in Würzburg, it, too, was destroyed in 1945, then completely rebuilt, almost seamlessly. Inside, notice the ornate stucco ceilings and the row of imposing tombstones, one of which belongs to Prince-Bishop von Schönborn, who first commissioned the Residenz. **Neumünster,** built alongside the Dom, holds the tomb of the Irish martyr and missionary St. Killian. He is credited with first bringing the Word of God to Würzburg, a crime for which he was murdered in 689. In the churchyard, look for the grave of Walther von der Vogelweide, Germany's most famous minstrel. The Baroque **Augustinerkirche,** which lies at Schönbornstraße's northern end, is another distinctive example of Balthasar Neumann's work. The original structure dates from the 13th century; Neumann added the aisle and portal in 1741.

All About Walt and Tilly

As you caper along the Romantische Straße it's quite impossible to avoid two names: Walther von der Vogelweide and Tilman Riemenschneider. Walt was a 13th-century **Minnesänger,** ***or bard, a poet-musician who wrote dandy songs about chivalrous deeds. He died in Würzburg in 1230, not before gaining a reputation as one of medieval Germany's wittiest lyricists. Tilman, on the other hand, was a 16th-century sculptor who received little recognition during his lifetime (except as mayor of Würzburg). Nowadays Tilman is considered one of Germany's greatest sculptors.***

FESTUNG MARIENBERG From Am Markt, head west along any street and you'll soon dead-end into the Main River. From the statue-lined Alte Mainbrücke (Old Main Bridge), which dates from 1473, there's a photo-worthy view of Festung Marienberg, an imposing complex set atop an equally imposing hill. The fortress dates from 1200 and, at least until the Residenz was completed in 1744, was home to generations of Würzburg prince-bishops. The focal point of the fortress is **Marienkirche,** a religious chapel that was begun in the early 8th century, making it one of the oldest in Germany. The nearby **Well House,** built above a truly deep well (343 feet), is also worth a quick look for its ragged stone walls hewn straight from the rock. The structure was built around 1640, roughly the same time Gustav Adolf of Sweden besieged and conquered the fortress. Once control of Marienberg was returned to the Würzburg princes, they embarked on a massive fortifying campaign. A major addition was the Armory, now home to the **Mainfränkisches Museum** (Main-Franconian Museum). Its collection includes a hodgepodge of Marienberg treasures—weapons and armor to faded maps and historical documents—and a vast gallery dedicated to Würzburg-born Tilman Riemenschneider, Germany's most famous Renaissance-era sculptor. Also on display are works by Tiepolo and Cranach the Elder; a healthy helping of sundry Greek and Roman art; and an exhibit on wine making that includes a mammoth antique winepress.

Marienberg Fortress can be reached by following the signposted trails from the foot of Alte Mainbrücke—a steep, 20-minute proposition. Another option is to take a bus (DM 2) from the western foot of Alte Mainbrücke. This departs every 30 minutes, daily, starting at 9:45 AM. Once on the hilltop there are scenic walking paths that give good views of the town below. *Fortress admission free. Open Apr.–Sept., Tues.–Sun. 9–noon and 1–5; Oct.–Mar., Tues.–Sun. 10–noon and 1–5. Mainfränkisches Museum admission: DM 3. Open Apr.–Oct., Tues.–Sun. 10–5; Nov.–Mar., Tues.–Sun. 10–4.*

RESIDENZ The sprawling and sumptuous Residenz palace was first conceived by Prince-Bishop Johann Phillip Franz von Schönborn around 1715. He envisioned an elegant residential palace that might balance secular Baroque embellishment with a proper respect for God (Johann, after all, was a bishop, even if only in name). To bring his vision to life, Schönborn commissioned a trio of craftsmen: Germany's finest Baroque architect, Balthasar Neumann; the highly regarded Italian stuccoist, Antonio Bossi; and the Venetian painter Giovanni Battista Tiepolo. Work began in 1719 and was completed in 1744.

The palace has many highlights. Some, like the lavish Baroque apartments and salons, are intentional. Others, however, are simply impromptu—sunlight striking a Volkswagen-size chandelier in just the right way, or maybe the soulful cadence of chamber music emanating from the courtyard during the occasional (and free) summertime recital. Of the "official" sort, the most dazzling is probably **Treppenhaus,** the largest Baroque staircase in the country. As this ornately carved and painted passage lumbers toward the second floor it suddenly splits in two and peels away to the left and right at 180-degree angles. Whichever way you climb it you're still greeted by Tiepolo's massive fresco, *The Four Continents* (only four were known at the time), a typically Baroque explosion of color and texture.

On the second floor, **Kaisersaal** (Throne Room) is another Baroque-Rococo fantasy gone utterly to extremes. Architecture melts into stucco, stucco invades the frescoes, and the blue and pink and vermilion plasterwork seems actually to move and live within the very walls. Much the same is true of **Hofkirche,** the palace chapel, which offers some proof that being a bishop didn't require an austere sense of aesthetics. The small chapel is nearly suffocated by rich marble and heavy stucco work, just the way Würzburg's ostentatious prince-bishops liked it. Next to the chapel is the entrance to **Hofgarten,** the palace's formal outdoor garden. *Residenzpl. From Am Markt walk e. to Theaterstr. and turn right. Admission (including guided tour): DM 4.50, DM 3.50 students. Open Apr.–Sept., Tues.–Sun. 9–5; Oct.–Mar., Tues.–Sun. 10–4.*

Rothenburg-ob-der-Tauber

Rothenburg is rightly considered the most evocative Romantische Straße destination—an almost Disneyland-like jumble of gingerbread architecture and cobbled hillside streets set against a backdrop of towers and turrets and staunch medieval walls. Rothenburg-ob-der-Tauber, which literally means "the red castle on the Tauber," is best known for its compact and walled-in old town, nestled along the eastern bank of the Tauber River. Preserved inside the stout city wall is simply the most impressive medieval citadel anywhere. Honest. There's not one modern building in the walled old town. And the fact that the area is mostly closed to vehicular traffic has helped sustain the town's authentic medieval look.

After the Thirty Years War (1618–48) wreaked serious havoc on the region's economic base, Rothenburg foundered for centuries, impoverished and forgotten. In the late 19th century it was "rediscovered" by tourism, and crowds are an inevitable part of the Rothenburg Experience, and it's hard to deny that the city does sometimes feel like a superficial tourist trap—beware the esurient army of souvenir shops.

In case the tourist horde proves too overwhelming, spend the day rambling in the countryside and return to Rothenburg around dusk, when most day-trippers have returned to their lairs. Sunrise is another prime time for lonesome, pensive exploring.

Yet none of this really matters as you wander aimlessly through Rothenburg's narrow lanes, lingering in one of its dazzling, flower-infested courtyards. The most popular time to visit Rothenburg is summer, when the flowers adorning balconies and doorways are in full bloom, and little kids swim and splash in the Tauber. Yet even in the dead of a freezing cold winter, when thick blankets of snow droop from tightly packed rows of colorful red-tile roofs, Rothenburg is equally charming (and a lot less crowded).

The **tourist office** (Marktpl., tel. 09861/40492, open weekdays 9–noon and 1–6, Sat. 9–noon), located in the center of the walled-in Altstadt, stocks city maps and walking guides. Particularly useful is the English-language exploring guide, *Rothenburg: Worth Seeing, Worth Knowing.* For a fee of DM 4 the office can also arrange private rooms in the DM 25–DM 35 range. From Marktplatz the main **post office** (Hafengasse 20, open Mon.–Sat. 8–6) is a short stroll east.

COMING AND GOING

The train station, or **Hauptbahnhof** (Bahnhofstr.), is a 15-minute walk from the old town. Turn left out of the station, right on Ansbacher Straße, and keep straight on Rödergasse; Marktplatz is a few hundred yards ahead. Rail destinations from Rothenburg-ob-der-Tauber include Nürnberg (via Steinach, 8 per day, DM 14) and Würzburg (via Steinach, 3 per day, DM 12.60). Destinations served by regional **buses,** which depart from the rail depot, include Feuchtwangen (DM 7) and Nürnberg (depart 4:30 PM, DM 11). Between April 10 and September 26, Rothenburg is also serviced by **Deutsche Bahn's Romantische Straße Bus,** which has daily scheduled stops in Dinkelsbühl, Nördlingen, Augsburg (with connections to Munich), and Füssen, heading south; Würzburg and Frankfurt, heading north.

WHERE TO SLEEP AND EAT

The cheapest options are private rooms (DM 25–DM 35), which are bookable through the tourist office, and the youth hostel, **Jugendherberge Rothenburg** (Mühlacker 1, tel. 09861/4510, DM 16.50 per person, closed Dec. 15–Jan. 2). The youth hostel is

Rothenburg-ob-der-Tauber

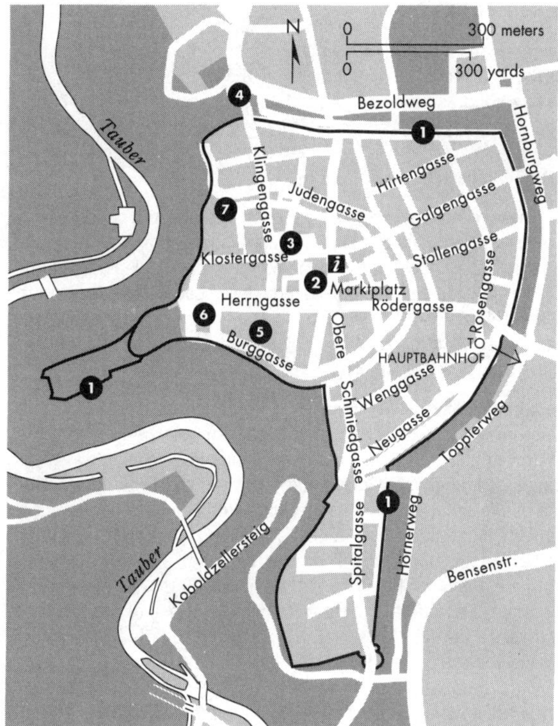

City Walls, **1**
Mittelalterliches Kriminalmuseum, **5**
Puppen und Spielzeugmuseum, **6**
Rathaus, **2**
Reichsstadt-museum, **7**
St. Wolfgang's, **4**
Stadtpfarrkirche St. Jakob, **3**

divided into two distinct sections, the 93-bed Rossmühle house, and the more spartan 90-bed Spitalhof annex. They're located around the corner from one another at the southern end of the old town. From Marktplatz walk due south along Obere Schmiedgasse and turn right into the large courtyard just before passing through the city wall.

Upscale options include **Altes Brauhaus** (Wengasse 24, tel. 09861/6774), an old inn tucked away on a peaceful medieval lane halfway between Roeder Gate and Unter Schmiedgasse. Doubles cost roughly DM 110, and most of its 34 rooms come equipped with baths. Downstairs there's a restaurant and garden terrace.

Campers should head straight for Detwang, a small historic village located 1¼ kilometers (¾ mile) northwest of Rothenburg. In Detwang, both **Tauber-Romantik** (tel. 09861/33226) and **Tauber-Idyll** (tel. 09861/33256) charge DM 5 per tent and DM 2 per camper. To reach either by foot, cross the Tauber and follow the road signs.

The Altstadt contains the best selection of cafés and restaurants, but nothing in "Historic Rothenburg" is particularly cheap. Try your luck at any streetside food stand, or at one of the few Imbiss shops that line the streets near Marktplatz. On the square itself, **Goldenes Lamm** (Marktpl. 2, tel. 09861/3488, closed Christmas–mid-Mar.) does schnitzels and stews for under DM 20. Although the food is respectable, what you're really paying for is the Lamm's central location and undeniable historic flavor; this steeply gabled hostelry has been in business since the 16th century. For a real splurge try **Baumeisterhaus** (Obere Schmiedgasse 3, tel. 09861/3404), just south of Marktplatz, a lavish inn set in a stunning medieval courtyard. A rotating menu has Bavarian and Franconian dishes that generally cost DM 20–DM 30, slightly less for lunch.

WORTH SEEING

Rothenburg's most obvious feature is the city wall, which stretches for nearly a mile around the perfectly preserved medieval citadel. Inside the old town, viewing platforms are spaced every few hundred yards and give photogenic views of Rothenburg's spire-tangled skyline and the rolling countryside beyond. If you plan on circumscribing the wall, a 90-minute endeavor, remember that the western stretch which overlooks the Tauber River is by far the nicest.

If you want an insightful overview of the city, join a guided walking tour sponsored by the tourist office. Between April and October only, German-language tours leave daily from Marktplatz at 11 AM and 2 PM. During the same months, English-language tours leave daily at 1:30 PM from outside Hotel Riemenschneider, located one block north and one block east of Marktplatz. Even if your German stinks, join the 9 PM German-language evening tour (meet at Marktplatz). It's led by a night watchman who hobbles through town with a bag of stories and a lantern.

MARKTPLATZ The **Rathaus** (Town Hall) dominates Rothenburg's pedestrian-only market square. The structure was originally built in a heavy Gothic style in 1240. But when a fire in 1501 destroyed half the Rathaus, a new Renaissance-inspired wing was built (hence the building's seemingly split personality). Inside, the **Historiengewölbe** museum, housed in the vaults below the building, charts Rothenburg's development during the Thirty Years War. Much ado is made of the *Meistertrunk,* or Master Drink. According to legend, when Protestant Rothenburg was captured by Catholic troops during the war, the conquering general found he could not down a six-pint tankard of wine, a town tradition. The general offered to spare Rothenburg if any of the captured town councilors could manage the feat. The mayor stepped up, quaffed his tankard (which is on display in the Reichsstadtmuseum, *see below*), and so saved the town. On the square's north side there's a daily, mechanical reenactment of the Meistertrunk every hour on the hour 11 AM–3 PM and 8–10 PM. *Admission: DM 3. Rathaus and museum open mid-Mar.–Oct., daily 9–6.*

MITTELALTERLICHES KRIMINALMUSEUM This museum is dedicated to medieval legal procedures and—the real reason it's so popular—the ways and means of medieval criminal punishment (in other words, torture). There's an impressive array of torture instruments here, from shackles and iron manacles to Gumby-esque stretch-tables and funky, multipointed pikes meant to fix, spit, transfix, and skewer thewless scofflaws. The museum is not to be missed, if only because every display is labeled and explained in English. *Burggasse 3. 2 blocks s. of Marktpl., off Obere Schmiedgasse. Admission: DM 4 adults, DM 2 students. Open Apr.–Oct., daily 9:30–6; Nov.–Feb., daily 2–4; Mar., daily 10–4.*

Up the street from the criminal museum look for the **Puppen und Spielzeugmuseum,** with an excellent collection of antique dolls and toys. Many of the delicate dolls are made of wood, clay, and sometimes even wax, and all date from 1780 to 1900. *Hofronnengasse 13. Admission: DM 3.50. Open Mar.–Dec., daily 10–5; Nov.–Mar., daily 1–4.*

REICHSSTADTMUSEUM The Imperial City Museum displays an eclectic mix of Rothenburg relics, from ancient coins and maps to city charters and courtly pronouncements. Also on exhibit is the *Pokal,* the tankard supposedly used in the great Meistertrunk. If you're sick of museums, this one is worth a look for its setting. It's housed in a 13th-century convent, and the original cloister, kitchens, and dormitories are still visible. *Hofronnengasse 13. 3 blocks w. and 1 block n. of Marktpl. Admission: DM 3.50. Open Apr.–Oct., daily 10–5; Nov.–Mar., daily 1–4.*

STADTPFARRKIRCHE ST. JAKOB Northwest of Marktplatz, the parish church of St. James looms large on the horizon with its massive Gothic body and towering cross-topped spires. It's certainly the largest church in Rothenburg, and also its most famous. Construction began in 1311, and throughout the Middle Ages it became a point of pilgrimage for holy ones seeking to prostrate themselves before the church's Holy Blood reliquary. Of particular note are the Heiliges Blut (Holy Blood) altar, by Tilman Riemenschneider, and, above the altar, a crystal capsule said to contain an actual drop of Christ's blood (yeah right). *Klingengasse. Admission free. Open Easter–Oct., daily 9–5; Nov.–Easter, daily 10–noon and 2–4.*

ST. WOLFGANG'S This brawny, 15th-century Gothic church was built right into the town wall. Inside there's not much to gawk at except the underground vault. It contains casement windows and a 16th-century platform that leads to the town wall via a "secret" passage. Outside St. Wolfgang's notice the Klingentor Gate and its 15th-century tower. *Klingentorpl., off Klingengasse. Admission free. Open Mar.–Oct., daily 9–5; Nov.–Apr., daily 10–2.*

Near Rothenburg-ob-der-Tauber

FEUCHTWANGEN AND DINKELSBUHL

The small village of **Feuchtwangen,** which lies far off the main highway nearly 30 kilometers (19 miles) south of Rothenburg-ob-der-Tauber, is a worthwhile stop only if you're traveling by car or bike. Although it can be reached by bus from Rothenburg, tiny Feuchtwangen will likely disappoint after the snail-paced bus ride. There's not much in terms of official sights. And you'll probably be forced to sleep here unless you take an early bus and do your sightseeing in under two hours.

Besides its rural setting, Feuchtwangen's main attraction is the central marketplace, overshadowed by a dreamy Baroque fountain and an outstanding collection of colorful half-timbered houses (not to mention a few cafés and beer halls). From mid-June to early August, open-air concerts are sometimes held in the graceful cloisters next to **Stiftskirche,** or collegiate church, located nearby in the village's sub-tiny center. Inside the church is a 15th-century altar carved by Albrecht Dürer's mentor, Michael Wolgemut.

Dinkelsbühl, 11 kilometers (7 miles) farther south, is another beautifully preserved medieval town that seems fully stuck somewhere in the 16th century. Its Romantische Straße location ensures a sturdy influx of wealthy tourists year-round, yet this hasn't marred the town's honestly rural tone. Dinkelsbühl main draw is the late Gothic **Stadtpfarrkirche St. Georg,** on the Marktplatz. The church is large (235 feet long) and voluminous, and it quite literally looms over the cafés and shops that line Marktplatz. The adjacent 200-foot tower can be climbed, and it offers stunning views of the village's spire-spiked skyline. The rest of Dinkelsbühl, from Altrathausplatz and Seringerstraße to Bahnhofstraße, harbors no "official" sights. But anyway, the real pleasure here is to walk from street to street, all the while savoring the sumptuous mix of Gothic facades, Baroque fountains, and medieval alleyways. The **tourist office** (Marktplatz, tel. 09851/2331) sells an excellent walking guide that's ideal for aimless rambles through the old town. For a DM 4 fee it also arranges private rooms.

The one time this quiet burg gets remotely bacchanal is during July's **Children's Pageant,** a 10-day event held usually at the beginning of the month. This festival celebrates the sparing of the town during the Thirty Years War. (According to local legend, when Dinkelsbühl was under siege by Swedish troops, a young woman led the town's children to the enemy general, Colonel Klaus Dietrich von Sperreuth. She implored Sperreuth to spare the children and their town, which was on the verge of destruction. And so he did.) Open-air concerts and costumed children capering along the streets are typical of the pageant; so, too, are crowds and NO VACANCY signs.

COMING AND GOING Feuchtwangen is accessible by bus, year-round, from either Dinkelsbühl (DM 2) or Rothenburg-ob-der-Tauber (DM 7). On the other hand, between April 10 and September 26 Dinkelsbühl is serviced by **Deutsche Bahn's Romantische Straße bus.** This travels twice daily between Frankfurt, Würzburg, Rothenburg,

Nördlingen, Augsburg (with connections to Munich), and Füssen. Dinkelsbühl has a train depot, but it's exclusively serviced by a slowpoke, historic steam engine that runs only on Sundays from Nördlingen (DM 6.40).

WHERE TO SLEEP Both villages are well stocked with elegant pensions and luxury hotels. A quick stroll around either's Marktplatz should suffice if you have an urge to spend big bucks. For a DM 4 fee, Dinkelsbühl's tourist office, on Marktplatz, books private rooms in the DM 30–DM 40 range. A better bet are the two village's respective youth hostels. **Jugendherberge Feuchtwangen** (Dr.-Günthlein-Weg 1, tel. 09852/842, closed Nov.–Feb.) charges DM 14.50 for one of its 102 beds, **Jugendherberge Dinkelsbühl** (Koppengasse 10, tel. 09851/9509, closed Oct. 30–Mar. 1) the same price for one of its 148 beds. Both only house hostelers under 27 years of age, but they're flexible when the crowds die down.

NORDLINGEN

The midsize town of Nördlingen sits nearly halfway between Rothenburg-ob-der-Tauber and Augsburg. Like most Romantische Straße destinations it has its share of half-timbered houses, cobbled squares, and spire-capped churches. Yet the real attraction is the 3-kilometer-long (2-mile-long) city wall, one of the best preserved in all Germany. Nördlingen's ground plan is like two concentric circles. The inner ring of streets marks the earliest boundary of the medieval town. A few hundred yards beyond is the second ring, this time in the form of the massive wall built to protect the expanding town. The wall is fortified with 11 towers and punctuated with five strapping gates.

Every night you can hear the night watchman's cry, *So G'sell so* (All's well). The town employs sentries who make a quick inspection along the wall and then climb to the top of **Georgenkirche**'s 300-foot-high tower—which marks the exact center of town—to give the all clear. They do this nightly at half-hour intervals between 10 PM and midnight. The tradition goes all the way back to the Thirty Years War, when a band of Swedes attempted to overrun Nördlingen one night but were detected by an alert townsperson. On a clear day the view from the tip of Georgenkirche's tower (open 8 AM–dusk) is top rate, just so long as you don't mind a 365-step climb.

The **tourist office** (Marktpl. 4, tel. 09081/84338) stocks the standard collection of maps and city guides, and can book private rooms (DM 20–DM 30) for a DM 3 fee. If you're under 26, cheaper accommodations can be found at the local youth hostel, **Jugendherberge Nördlingen** (Kaiserwiese 1, tel. 09081/84109, closed Nov.–Feb.). It's located just outside the city wall, and space in one of its 80 beds costs DM 14.50 per night. From Nördlingen's rail station there are daily connections to Stuttgart (via Aalen, DM 25), Nürnberg (via Donauwörth, DM 25), and Augsburg (via Donauwörth, DM 14). Between April 10 and September 26, Nördlingen is also serviced twice daily by the Romantische Straße Bus. Heading north from Nördlingen, this bus stops in Dinkelsbühl, Rothenburg, Würzburg, and Frankfurt. Heading south, it stops in Augsburg (with connections to Munich) and Füssen.

Bayreuth

If you're not into crowds sporting formal wear, or, more importantly, if you don't like Richard Wagner's music, don't come to Bayreuth during July or August. Repeat: DO NOT COME. Depending on your perspective, Bayreuth is blessed or plagued with a yearly Richard Wagner festival—the first of which was held in 1876—because Wagner settled in Bayreuth after years of wandering through Europe. During this hoity-toity summer festival, the town's abuzz with 19th-century-opera junkies who reserved their expensive tickets (up to DM 230) literally years in advance. The influx of high-culture fiends means hotel and private room space become impossible to find while restaurants become filled to overflowing. At the same time, prices on just about everything jump far beyond the reach of a haggard backpacker.

Likewise, if opera gives you the willies you'll find little else in Bayreuth to divert you. Bayreuth is not what you'd call a "pretty" town, and there's little here that's not somehow connected even tangentially with Wagner and his music. A few museums and historic homes break up the monotony, but locals are more excited about their sports teams, the city's 5,000-student university (opened in 1971), and the Maisel Brewery, which cooks up Germany's leading diabetic beer (yuck).

BASICS

BUREAUX DE CHANGE Outside the train station, Bahnhofstraße and Luitpoldplatz are loaded with banks. **Schmidt Bank** (Luitpoldpl. 15) has the best hours: It's open Tuesday through Friday 8:30–5:30 and Saturday 8:30–12:30. Sadly, it charges a whopping DM 8 for cashing traveler's checks. Other banks on Bahnhofstraße and Luitpoldplatz—Stadtsparkasse, Deutsche Bank, Commerzbank—keep standard banking hours and cash traveler's checks for a similar commission. Visa card holders can suck cash out of a 24-hour ATM outside **Citibank** (Opernstr. 2, tel. 0921/66099).

LAUNDRY There's a Laundromat, **Wäscherei Badewitz** (St. Georgen 30, tel. 0921/26644, open weekdays 8–noon and 2–6), on the other side of the tracks from the Altstadt; take Bus 1 from the Markt to St. Georgen. It's not designed to be self-serve, but no one will stop you from putting your own load through the washer and dryer for DM 15. It costs another DM 4.50 for staff to do it; you pick it up two hours later.

LUGGAGE STORAGE The **Hauptbahnhof** has small lockers (DM 2 per day) and large lockers (DM 4 per day). Reisegepäck, the station's left-luggage desk (DM 4 per day), is open daily 8:15–4:45.

What's So Great About Wagner?

If you've ever seen a picture of Richard Wagner (1813–83), you probably think he looks like a real jerk. Learning more about him won't change your mind. He was stubborn, a womanizer, childish and selfish, temperamental and demanding... you name it. Lucky for Wagner, King Ludwig II of Bavaria—known as the young and impressionable "dream king"—took a liking to Wagner's music and so provided much of his financial backing. Ludwig II also financed the development of Festspielhaus, the Bayreuth opera house that was custom-made to suit Wagner's theatrically spectacular works.

So what's so terrific about this guy? Well, he revolutionized opera, creating what he called a Gesamtkunstwerk *(total art form). Rather than making music the dominating performance element, Wagner interwove musical motifs with words and actions, shaping the dramatic form of opera that still prevails today. Wagner may have had little formal musical training, but he created an opera of word, drama, and song that back then seemed remarkably novel and today seems so absurdly simple and obvious. And that's why they call him a genius.*

MAIL AND PHONES From the main post office, **Postamt** (Burgerreuther Str. 1), located across the street from the train station, you can buy stamps, send a telegram, and make an international call from any of its pay phones. The office is open weekdays until 6, Saturdays until 1 PM.

VISITOR INFORMATION The **Gästedienst des Fremdenverkehrsvereins** doubles as a travel agency and tourist-information center. Staffers at the information desk provide city maps and brochures, and can make private room reservations for a DM 3 fee. The latter also offer useful tips on how to crash music performances and Wagner festival events. They do not, however, sell any festival tickets. *Luitpoldpl. 9, tel. 0921/88588. From Hauptbahnhof turn left on Bahnhofstr. and walk straight until it becomes Luitpoldpl. Open weekdays 9–6, Sat. 9–noon.*

COMING AND GOING

Bayreuth's **train station** is a 10-minute walk from the old town. From the depot turn left onto Bahnhofstraße (which turns into Luitpoldplatz) and left again when it deadends at Opernstraße. Bayreuth is well connected to the German rail network, and from here you can reach Nürnberg (hourly, DM 12), Bamberg (hourly, DM 12), Coburg (hourly, DM 10.60), Munich (hourly, DM 40), and Berlin Hauptbahnhof/Zoo Garten (six trains per day, DM 80).

Regional buses depart from outside the Hauptbahnhof, and there's a ride-share service, **Mitfahrzentrale** (Von-Römer Str. 9, tel. 0921/53658, open weekdays noon–6, Sat. 10 AM–1 PM), that will try to get you out of town in someone else's vehicle.

WHERE TO SLEEP

Don't bother in July or August unless you've booked months in advance. The rest of the year, Bayreuth's hostel and even a few pensions are fairly priced and located within a reasonable walk of the Altstadt. The travel agency–cum–tourist desk books private rooms (DM 30–DM 35) for a DM 3 fee, probably the best bet if you want semi-private accommodations within a stone's throw of the old town's bars and restaurants. During summer the youth hostel sometimes opens its backyard to tent campers, but you'll have to negotiate for price and use of indoor facilities.

Gasthof Kropf. Wagner's Festspielhaus is just around the corner, which means you're a 20-minute walk from the Altstadt. Even so, this quiet guest house is wonderfully peaceful, surrounded by a lush garden and well kept. Doubles start at DM 64 and peak at DM 74. If you're not up for the walk into the old town, have a meal and beer at the restaurant here. *Tristranstr. 8, tel. 0921/26298. From Hauptbahnhof turn right and walk n. on Bürgerreuther Str., turn right on Gravenreuther Str. and left on Tristanstr. 9 rooms, some with bath.*

Gasthof Vogel. This guest house is smack dab in the center of the Altstadt, so you can hit the town at night or linger in its beer garden and watch all Bayreuth pass by. The manager is gruff, but if you pay the DM 60 for a double (single DM 30) he'll leave you be. The rooms are clean and reasonably large, as are the communal bathrooms. *Friedrichstr. 13, tel. 0921/68268. From tourist office walk left (e.) down Opernstr., cross Richard-Wagner-Str., and turn right on Friedrichstr. 7 rooms, none with bath.*

Gasthof Zum Brandenburger. It's far from the main sights, but this 16-room guest house has cheap and well-kept rooms (DM 60 per double, DM 80 with bath) and is a short bus ride from the train depot. It's also across from a Laundromat (*see* Laundry in Basics, *above*). *St. Georgen 9, tel. 0921/20570. 16 rooms, some with bath.*

HOSTELS **Jugendherberge Bayreuth.** Like all Bavarian youth hostels, the Jugendherberge Bayreuth takes in only those under 27, and "the younger the better" could be its motto. Luckily, an older crowd is not far away: The hostel is within walking distance of the old city, close to the university, and next door to the huge pool and sports complex, Kreuzsteinbad. For DM 11 you get a bed in a quadruple and a footlocker. Bring your own breakfast; the one served here is meager and way overpriced at DM 6. *Universitätsstr. 28, tel. 0921/25262. From tourist office (30 min. total): Turn left on Opernstr. and walk straight to Friedrichstr., turn left and left again at Wittelsbacherring (which turns into Universitätsstr.). 160 beds. Kitchen, small lockers. Lockout 9 AM–noon, curfew 10 PM or DM 20 deposit for night key if you're registered for more than 1 night.*

FOOD

Bayreuth has dozens of street stands and fast-food possibilities in the Altstadt, especially on Maximilian-Straße and Richard-Wagner-Straße. For espresso and ice cream in the old town head for **Capri Eisdiele** (Am Sternpl., tel. 0921/64808) or **Venezia Eissalon** (Maximilian-Str. 49, tel. 0921/65246).

UNDER DM 10 **Café Florian.** It's on the edge of the old town and virtually unknown to the tourist horde. In fact, most of the people in this quiet café are local students. Feel free to stay as long as you like, pondering the newspaper, playing backgammon (boards available), or lounging in the outdoor seating area. For sustenance there's meat-'n'-bread plates, sandwiches, and salads. *Dammallee 12A, 3 blocks s. (and parallel to) Maximilian-Str., tel. 0921/56757. Wheelchair access.*

Herzogkeller. At sunset almost everyone under 40 begins the pilgrimage up the path to this massive beer garden. Large tankers of Maisel beer fetch DM 3.50, snacks like pretzels and paprika–cheese balls DM 3–DM 5, and full-blown meals of wieners and cabbage DM 8–DM 12. *Hindenburgstr., tel. 0921/43419. Walk northwest on Maximilian-Str., cross Hohenzollernring, and walk straight on Hindenburgstr. Closed Nov.-Mar.*

UNDER DM 15 **Miamiam-Glouglou.** This intimate and candlelit French restaurant, tucked away in an alley in the Altstadt, serves excellent food at surprisingly reasonable rates. The huge *salade niçoise,* with tuna, rice, and egg, is well worth the DM 8 price, and the quiche lorraine is a steal at DM 5. For a splurge try one of the delicate meat or fish entrées; the salmon (DM 21.50) is tops. *Von-Römer-Str. 28, tel. 0921/65666. From northwest end of Maximilian-Str., walk 1 block s. and turn left on Von-Römer-Str. Wheelchair access.*

Brauereischänke am Markt. This top-rate eatery is located in the heart of the Altstadt, a short walk from the Rathaus and Stadtkirche. In terms of food it's really the German equivalent of a Sunday brunch place, with young waiters whisking about serving big glasses of OJ and *Bratkartoffelpfanne* (panfried potatoes, ham, and veggies; DM 12). The other favorite is *Nudelauflauf* (DM 12), a noodle dish with lots of cheese and vegetables. *Maximilian-Str. 56, tel. 0921/64919. Wheelchair access.*

WORTH SEEING

Bayreuth's Altstadt is compact, and all the sights are within easy walking distance of one another. For a quick overview, turn right from the tourist office and left onto Opernstraße. This passes the opera house and curves to meet Richard-Wagner-Straße on your left (east) and Maximilian-Straße on your right (west). The former becomes briefly pedestrianized, leads past some snazzy shops and the Richard Wagner museum, and then meanders toward suburban Bayreuth; the latter leads toward the Rathaus, Altes Schloß, and the pedestrianized alleyways around Spitalkirche.

FESTSPIELHAUS Wagner designed and largely financed this vast and austere opera house, which presented its first public performance in 1876. The Spartan look is partly due to Wagner's grim financial state (Wagner was nearly always on the verge of bankruptcy) and partly due to his desire to achieve perfect acoustics. The walls are thus bare and the wooden seats free of upholstery. The stage itself is vast, capable of accommodating a hundred actors without seeming crowded. Nowadays the theater stands alone on a hill, the temple to which Wagner worshipers promenade in their finest finery every July and August. During the festival, which is run by grandson Wolfgang Wagner, nearly 2,000 tough-bunned fans (no padding on those wood seats) sit through 30 performances of various Wagner operas. If you haven't bought tickets literally 1–2 years in advance, don't even dream of catching a summer show. The odds are better in winter and spring; stop by the tourist or ticket office for current schedules. *Auf dem Grünen Hügel, tel. 0921/20221. From Hauptbahnhof turn right and walk straight for 6 blocks. From Am Markt, Bus 7 to Festspielhaus stop. Admission: DM 2. Required tour in German every 45 minutes. Open Apr.–Sept., Tues.–Sun. 10–11:30 and 2:15–4:30; Oct. and Dec.–Mar., Tues.–Sun. 10–11:30 and 2:15–3:45.*

HAUS WAHNFRIED Wagner only owned one house in his entire life, Bayreuth's Wahnfried House, which nowadays contains the **Richard Wagner Museum.** The house is a simple and squat neoclassical creation, graced by a surrounding green and tree-lined walkway. The house was originally built by Wagner himself in 1874; the name *Wahnfried* means "Peace from Delusion," but during construction he thought *Argersheim* (Home of Annoyance) more appropriate. Wagner lived here with his wife, Cosima, the daughter of composer Franz Liszt. In a sense they're both still here—look for their graves (and the grave of their dog) in the backyard. Other famous guests include Ludwig II of Bavaria, the "dream king," and Adolf Hitler, who actually slept here once as a guest of the near-senile Cosima. *Richard-Wagner-Str. 48, tel. 0921/25404. Admission: DM 2.50 (DM 3.50 in July and Aug.), DM 1 students. Open daily 9–5.*

HOFGARTEN Keep straight on Opernstraße and you'll funnel onto Ludwigstraße. This is where you'll find the Neues Schloß and, directly behind, the Hofgarten, a prim park that occupies most of the Altstadt's southeastern corner. The Hofgarten is pleasant for lazy afternoon strolls, and on its grounds are two medium-interest museums. The **Jean-Paul-Museum** (Wahnfriedstr. 1, tel. 0921/25351, open July–Sept., daily 9–noon and 2–5; Oct.–June, weekdays 9–noon and 2–5, Sat. 10–1), a few doors down from Haus Wahnfried, is dedicated to the 19th-century romantic poet, Jean-Paul. On the other side of Haus Wahnfried, the **Deutsches Freimaurermuseum** (Im Hofgarten 1, tel. 0921/ 69824, open weekdays 10–noon and 2–6, Sat. 10–noon) is all about Freemasonry. There's a voluminous library and more than a few displays about the history of Germany's Freemason movement (a movement imported from Great Britain in the 1600s).

MAXIMILIAN-STRAßE Maximilian-Straße runs from Hohenzollernring in the northwest to the intersection of Opernstraße and Richard-Wagner-Straße in the southeast. It's mostly pedestrianized and lined with a dense jumble of shops, cafés, and restaurants—making it the liveliest and busiest street in the old town. The **Stadtmuseum** (Kanzleistr. 1, tel. 0921/25527, open Tues.–Sun. 10–5), just off Maximilian-Straße near Opernstraße, has a small collection of firearms and Baroque furniture. Across the street you can't help but gawk at the **Stadtkirche,** a massive Gothic creation that inside has a standard collection of religious relics and priests going contemplatively about their business. Between the church and the northern end of Maximilian-Straße are dozens of pedestrian-only lanes—Sophienstraße and Von-Römer-Straße being the largest—each teeming with smart-looking shops and shoppers.

NEUES SCHLOß The Neues Schloß, or New Palace, originally dates from the 16th century. But in the 18th century, after a fire destroyed large sections, it was rebuilt by Margravine Wilhelmina, sister of Frederick the Great of Bavaria and wife of the margrave (marquis) of Brandenburg. She had an eye for detail and a very serious love of Rococo embellishment. In renovating the structure—a project that nearly bankrupted the town—she created a wildly ornate palace that takes the already elaborate Rococo aesthetic one step beyond. Prepare yourself for puffy paneling, a cacophony of color, gilded molding, and frankly gaudy furniture littered throughout. The **Staatsgalerie** (State Art Gallery), with its collection of mainly Bavarian 19th-century paintings, is also housed inside the palace. *Ludwigstr. 21. Admission: DM 3, DM 1.50 students.*

Required tour in German. Open Apr.–Sept., Tues.–Sun. 10–11:30 and 1:20–4:30; Oct.–Mar., Tues.–Sun. 10–11:30 and 1:30–3.

MARKGRAFLICHES OPERNHAUS Standing in front of the Neues Schloß you can't help but see Wilhelmina's other great architectural legacy, the Margrave Opera House. She had it built in 1748 in a lush Rococo style (Wilhelmina's favorite); every nook and cranny is packed with gilded work, ravishing frescoes, and ornate Rococo baubles. Apollo and the nine Muses frolic across the hand-painted ceiling. This 500-seat theater originally drew Wagner to Bayreuth. He felt its sumptuous design and large stage would suit his epic works. Wagner worked in the Margrave until his self-designed (and near acoustically perfect) performance space, Festspielhaus, was built in 1876. Try hard to catch a performance at Margrave; tickets are sold at the tourist office and box office. Otherwise, take a gander at the flamboyant interior. *Opernstr. Admission: DM 2, DM 1.50 students. Open Apr.–Sept., Tues.–Sun. 9–11:30 and 1:20–4:30; Oct.–Mar., Tues.–Sun. 10–11:30 and 1:30–3.*

CHEAP THRILLS

The cheapest thrill is hanging out at one of Bayreuth's **fountains.** Young high school punks frequent the one on Am Markt, but if that's not your scene, scope out one of the many others scattered in and around town—try the ones at Eremitage (*see* Near Bayreuth, *below*) or the ones in the Hofgarten.

FESTIVALS Unfortunately, the words "cheap" and "festival" do not walk hand in hand in Bayreuth. The **Wagner Festival,** held every year in July and August, costs big bucks: A "good" seat can fetch as much as DM 300, a cruddy nosebleed seat as much as DM 150. Diehard Wagner fans should write to **Theaterkaße** (Luitpoldpl. 9, Bayreuth 8580, tel. 0921/20221) months before the November 15 deadline. Don't be surprised, however, if they write back only to say that all seats were sold out a year ago. The **Bayreuther Volksfest,** held yearly in early June, features street markets and live music in venues throughout town.

AFTER DARK

Bayreuth caters to highbrow concert goers with its snazzy Altstadt bars, and to lowbrow students with its handful of clubs and discos. **PI Disco** (Sophienstr. 26, tel. 0921/64209), just off Maximilian-Straße, is a popular late-night dance club. At **Disco Crazy Elephant** (Maximilian-Str. 30, tel. 0921/66430) you can dance with students and lowlife until the wee hours. If you hate dancing but enjoy the company of students, **Odeon Day and Night Café** (Alexanderstr. 7, tel. 0921/12601) serves cheapish food and alcoholic drinks, all the while bathing the sitting area with American oldies on a tape deck. **Funzel** (Richard-Wagner-Str. 8, tel. 0921/54554) is where the beautiful people go. It's most crowded between 1 and 3 AM, after which the hardcore partyers all head for **Mohrenstuben Cocktailbar** (Mittelstr. 2, tel. 0921/27604).

During the Wagner Festival season, the **Hof-Theatre im Steingraeber-Palais** (Friedrichstr. 1) does its own version of Wagner opera. Get your tickets for the nightly 8 PM performance at the box office. Shakespeare goes German at the open-air **Römische Theater** in the Eremitage (*see* Near Bayreuth, *below*). You can buy tickets, which cost DM 15 and go on sale a few hours prior to the 8:30 PM performance, only at the box office.

Near Bayreuth

ALTES SCHLOß EREMITAGE

The Altes Schloß Eremitage, not to be confused with the princely Altes Schloß (Old Castle) on Bayreuth's Maximilian-Straße, is a cozy little castle set 5 kilometers (3 miles) north of Bayreuth. It was built in the early 18th century as a summer retreat for local nobility. But in 1740 the Margravine Wilhelmina got her artsy hands on the place and completely remodeled it. From the outside the castle looks dully bland. Inside, however, it's sumptuously Rococo, lavished with gilded panels and fluffy, puffy furniture. Unfortunately, the tour guides who blab at you in German for 25 minutes lack her vibrant touch, yawn. The surrounding garden and park (and the fountains that spout every hour on the hour) are alone worth the trip. During summer, the on-site **Römische Theater** presents Shakespeare (in German) most nights at 8:30 PM. Tickets, which go on sale the night of the show, cost DM 15 and can be purchased only at the box office.

To reach the Altes Schloß take Bus 2 from Bayreuth's Am Markt to the Eremitage stop, a 25-minute proposition. Admission to the castle costs DM 2, which includes the mandatory German-language guided tour. The castle is open April to September, Tuesday through Sunday 9–noon and 1–5; October to March, Tuesday through Sunday 10–noon and 1–3.

COBURG

Coburg, which lies 85 kilometers (53 miles) northwest of Bayreuth, is a smart-looking town nestled along the banks of the River Itz. Historically speaking, Coburg was home to the royal Herzogs of Saxe-Coburg-Gotha until 1918, when Herzog Carl Edvard abdicated on account of the war. Until then, the Saxe-Coburg-Gotha line had made a point of marrying well and moving up the European social ladder; Prince Albert of Saxe-Coburg-Gotha aimed quite high and snared Queen Victoria for his wife in 1840. She visited the Herzog home here in Coburg and had the honor of using Germany's first flush toilet—still visible next to her guest bed in the **Residenzschloß Ehrenburg** (Castle of Honor, Schloßpl., admission DM 3, DM 2 students), located in the center of town just east of Marktplatz. The castle, where Prince Albert spent much of his childhood, was built in the mid-16th century. Following an early 19th-century fire it was renovated in a heavy Gothic style—dark, stiff, and sober. The throne room, Hall of Giants (named for its wall-size frescoes), and a small Baroque chapel can still be visited; the rest of the castle is occupied by the present duke.

Coburg's main attraction, **Veste Coburg** (Coburg Fortress), is a 30-minute walk from Marktplatz (you can also take Bus 8 from Marktplatz to the site). By foot, follow the signs for the Hofgarten (Palace Gardens), which contains a natural history museum, **Naturmuseum** (Im Hofgarten, admission DM 2, open Apr.–Sept., daily 9–6; Oct.–Mar, daily 9–5), said to be the largest of its kind in Germany. The stuffed animals on dis-

How Long Is Your Wiener?

Coburg's Marktplatz is lined with elegant Renaissance and Baroque buildings, the most noticeable of which is the ornately gabled, 16th-century Rathaus. Outside the Rathaus look for the statue of Bratwurstmännla; his staff is claimed to be the "official" and proper length of a Coburg bratwurst sausage. Buy a wiener from one of a dozen nearby street vendors and see how they measure up.

play aren't anything unusual, but the minerals, meteors, crystals, and fossils in the basement are pretty cool.

From the nature museum it's a short walk to Veste Coburg, set on a small hill overlooking town. The first brawny buildings date from 1055, but most of what you see today dates from the Gothic and Renaissance eras. Protected by the fortress's thick walls are three top-rate museums. The first, **Fürstenbau** (Palace of Princes), sheltered Martin Luther for six months during 1530; nowadays it shelters jewels, worn manuscripts, and a few paintings by the Renaissance-era painter Lucas Cranach. The **Kunstsammlungen,** the fortress's art museum, has an eclectic mix of guns, armor, torture instruments (and how-to pictures), as well as paintings by Albrecht Dürer, Rembrandt, and (again) Lucas Cranach. Last and least is **Herzoginbau,** a museum that displays 18th-century carriages and snow sleds. *Admission to Fürstenbau and Herzoginbau: DM 3.50, DM 2 students. Admission to Kunstsammlungen: DM 3. Castle complex and museums open Apr.–Oct., Tues.–Sun. 9:30–noon and 2–4; Nov.–Mar., Tues.–Sun. 2–5.*

Coburg is a cultural place. It annually celebrates its "adopted" son, composer Johann Strauss, with a festival and music competition held in early July. The principal venue is **Landestheater Coburg** (Rückertstr., tel. 09561/92742), located a few hundred yards north of Ehrenburg castle. Tickets cost anywhere from DM 15 to DM 30. The rest of the year the theater presents a mixed bag of opera and ballet.

COMING AND GOING Coburg's **train station** is a 15-minute walk from Marktplatz and the town center. From the depot walk east along Mohenstraße and turn right on Spitalgasse, which forms Marktplatz's western border. Trains make the 90-minute chug to Bayreuth (DM 16.50) hourly until 6 PM; until 8 PM if you're coming from Bayreuth. Trains run roughly six times daily from Coburg to Bamberg (DM 10.80). On either trip you go through Lichtenfels, the "basket-making" town.

WHERE TO SLEEP Coburg turned Schloß Ketschendorf, a 20-minute walk south from the old town, into a big and fairly luxurious **Jugendherberge** (Parkstr. 2, tel. 09561/14330, closed Dec. 1–Jan. 31), set in the middle of a beautiful park. A modern sleeping facility has been added to the redbrick castle, but this hasn't diminished its charm (the common room still has short chandeliers and dark oak paneling). The hostel is chock full of kids during the week but generally quiet on the weekends. You must be under 27 to stay. Beds cost DM 16.50 (including breakfast) and, sadly, there's a 10 PM curfew. From the train station take Bus 1 to the Ketschendorf stop.

The **Goldenes Kreuz** (Herrngasse 1 at Am Markt, tel. 09561/90473) is a cute 45-bed guest house located right in the thick of things. Singles run DM 35–DM 45, doubles DM 60–DM 80. If that's full, the guest houses **Juliusturm** (Pilgrimsroth 45, tel. 09561/29968) and **Goldene Sonne** (Creidlitzer Str. 93, tel. 09561/29097) are similarly priced though a bit farther out. From the train station take Bus 4 (direction: Lobelstein) to Danziger Straße for the former; Bus 1 to Creidlitz for the latter.

FOOD On and around Marktplatz you'll find wieners and cabbage galore courtesy of a battalion of street stands and hearty German-style restaurants. Those tired of wieners and wurst should consider **Del Passatore** (Oberer Bürglass, tel. 09561/92993), which does Italian pasta every which way for about DM 10. **Café-Bistro "Hallo Dolly"** (Rückerstr. 2, tel. 09561/90709), near Ehrenburg castle, serves hot and cold sandwiches on family-size baguettes for around DM 7. And if you're hungry after your tour of the Veste fortress, hurry over to the **Burgschänke** (Veste Coburg 1B, tel. 09561/75153), which serves light meals and beer until 6 PM daily—the beer garden overlooks the forests and hills below and beyond. For evening debauchery there's the popular pub **Humpen** (Am Markt 11, tel. 0956192719), open weekdays until 1 AM and weekends until 3 AM. For dessert and/or a romantic evening with a loved one, the candlelit wine cellar **Künstlerklause** (Theaterpl. 4A, tel. 09561/75261) serves luscious cakes and pastries. It also has an expansive wine list.

KULMBACH

Serious beer drinkers will want to make a pilgrimage to Kulmbach, home to no fewer than five breweries. The best time to visit is during the 9-day-long **Kulmbach Beer Week** (funny how time slips by when there's a beer in your hand), which begins the last Saturday in July. Its main festival site, a village-size tent, is known as *Festspulhaus* (Festival Swallowing House), a subtle insult to Bayreuth and its Festspielhaus, the opera house where Wagnerphiles yearly gather to celebrate in their own high-cultured way.

In Kulmbach, the thick and heavy aroma of hops assaults your nostrils the moment you step off the train.

Kulmbach pumps out more beer per person than any other town in Germany (9,000 pints for every man, woman, and kinder). It also makes the country's strongest elixir: Doppelbock Kulminator 28 (at 22 proof, it sits in your gut like lead). Hardly surprising, the best way to experience Kulmbach is on a tour of its three most popular breweries: **Erste Kulmbacher Actienbrauerei AG** (EKU-Str. 1, tel. 09221/882283), **Mönchshof-Bräu GmbH** (Hofer Str. 20, tel. 09221/80535), and **Kulmbacher Reichelbräu AG** (Lichtenfelser Str., tel. 09221/705228). Tours run Monday through Thursday and cost DM 5 for students, DM 6–DM 12 for everyone else. You should call at least one day in advance to ensure a spot on the sometimes crowded guided tours.

Kulmbach's other main draw is the 16th-century **Plassenburg,** a huge hilltop castle that looms high above the city center. It's considered one of the most important Renaissance complexes in Germany. But you don't sense its true grandeur until you trek up the hill and breach its thick redbrick walls. Once inside, notice the airy and column-lined central courtyard. It's offset by four dome-crowned towers, and enclosed by three levels of apartments that each present an intricately carved arch and balcony to the square. This marble-lined court is the real highlight of the castle proper, a real gem of Renaissance craftsmanship. It also makes a fine setting for the free summertime concerts sometimes held in the courtyard; ask at the tourist office for current schedules. The castle's circular terrace, located just outside the brawny walls, is also worth a gander. On a sunny day the hilltop terrace gives tremendous views of the city. To reach Plassenburg from Marktplatz, head southeast down Obere Stadt and turn left at the fountain; the subsequent alleyway meanders through a warren of narrow streets and then rises to meet Festungsberg, Plassenburg's kilometer-long (⅔-mile-long) driveway, of sorts.

The very modern-looking tourist office, **Fremdenverkehrsbüro** (Stadthalle Sutte 2, tel. 09221/802216), can supply English-speaking guides (DM 20–DM 30), book private rooms (DM 1 fee), and fill your pockets with city maps. Kulmbach's **train station** is a 15-minute walk from the old town; head south from the depot, cross the Main River, and you'll eventually funnel onto Marktplatz. From Kulmbach there are daily train connections to Bayreuth (DM 6.40), Bamberg (DM 12.60), and Lichtenfels (DM 8.40).

You can usually find a bare-bones double for under DM 70 at either **Gasthof Reichenbächer** (Weihrer Str. 23, tel. 09221/74318) or **Wirtshaus zum Gründla** (Am Gründlein 5, tel. 09221/2438). Cheaper still is the local youth hostel, **Jugendherberge Kulmbach** (Mangersreuther Str. 43, tel. 09221/7243, closed Dec. 10–Jan. 10), a 90-bed complex located 3 kilometers (2 miles) from the city center. From the train station hop on Bus 2 and alight at Mangersreuther Straße.

Bamberg

Bamberg is absolutely stunning. What started as a minor farming village in the late 2nd century AD was transformed into an elegant seat of power under the guidance of native son Heinrich II, an 11th-century Holy Roman emperor. He's responsible for Bamberg's impressive Dom, or cathedral, considered one of the most important medieval relics in all Germany. Nowadays the cathedral and surrounding Domplatz, with its two lavish Baroque-era palaces, give Bamberg a wonderfully refined, centuries-old air. Even if you're sick of churches and museums, Bamberg's old town, on an island in the River Pegnitz, looks like it just stepped from the pages of some medieval chronicle. Cobbled lanes meander in and out of narrow alleyways, past colorful and rickety half-timbered houses. Seen from afar, Bamberg's skyline is a hazy jumble of red-tile roofs, gables, and church towers (Bamberg has 10)—itself worth the trip to Bamberg.

Bamberg seems like it was created just so impoverished backpackers could enjoy long, pensive walks along the river and dangle their feet from medieval bridges on lonesome summer afternoons.

There are enough "official" sights to keep you occupied for at least a day. But during summer consider sticking around for the night. Bamberg's handful of bars and beer halls grow respectably bacchanal during the semi-touristy summer season, and there are always plenty of nooks along the river where you can pass the time with a friend and a bottle. If you've exhausted Bamberg's museums and churches, spend some time gawking at the merchants and shoppers along the Grüner Markt, Bamberg's pedestrian-only commercial avenue. Or make an easy day-trip to Schloß Weissenstein (*see* Near Bamberg, *below*), a lavish Baroque palace that (like Bamberg's Dom) is considered one of the best examples of its kind in Germany.

BASICS

BUCKET SHOPS **Terraplan Reiseagentur.** This budget travel shop is on a small Altstadt side street. It's also near the university, and is usually full of students planning for their breaks, so come early. This is your best bet for cheap and/or last-minute flights. *Hasengasse 2, tel. 0951/202031. From Grüner Markt walk northwest on Jesuitenstr. to Austr.; Hasengasse is 1 block s. Open weekdays 9:30–6, Thurs. 9:30–8, Sat. 10–1.*

BUREAUX DE CHANGE Plan on a uniform DM 10 charge for exchanging up to $100 worth of traveler's checks. The **Dresdner Bank** (Willy-Lessing Str. 20, tel. 0951/86890), **Bayerische Vereinsbank** (Lange Str. 48, tel. 0951/86020), and **Volksbank** (Grüner Markt 16, tel. 0951/86070) are all conveniently located in the city center and stay open until 4 PM on weekdays, until 5:30 PM on Thursday. The 24-hour ATM outside **Citibank** (Hainstr. 2–4, tel. 0951/28344) gives Visa cash advances.

LAUNDRY The self-service machines at **SB Atrium Waschsalon** cost DM 6 per wash (including soap), and DM 1 for every 10 minutes in the dryer. *Ludwigstr. 2, tel. 0951/38495. From Hauptbahnhof turn left. Open Mon.– Sat. 7 AM–10 PM.*

Follow the bubbly signs to **Bamberger Waschsalon,** stuck in a back alley between the train station and old town. Self-service laundry costs DM 6.50 per wash, DM 4 for 15 minutes of dryer time. For a few extra marks they'll do your laundry for you. *Untere Königstr. 32, tel. 0951/21517. Follow Luitpoldstr. southwest from Bahnhof and turn right on Obere Königstr. Open weekdays 10–7, Sat. 8–2.*

LUGGAGE STORAGE The **Hauptbahnhof** has large (DM 4) and small (DM 2) luggage lockers, both available on a 24-hour basis. The train station has a luggage storage desk (tel. 0951/832352) that charges DM 4 per 12 hours. It's open weekdays 8–noon and 1–5, weekends 8–3. **ZOB** (Zentral Omnibus Bahnhof) has really narrow, not-quite-backpack-size lockers that cost DM. 50 per 12 hours.

MAIL AND PHONES The **main post office** is the place to call home or pick up letters sent by Postlagernd. Bamberg's postal code is 8600. *Ludwigstr. 25, tel. 0951/836281. Across from Hauptbahnhof. Open weekdays 8–6, Sat. 8–noon, and Sun. 11– noon.*

VISITOR INFORMATION **Tourist information** has glossy brochures on the parks in Franconia, as well as other Bavarian towns, for about DM .30 a pop. The staff also arranges bus tours to nearby areas, and books city hotels and guest houses (but NOT private rooms, which don't exist in Bamberg). If you'd rather hunt down your own food and lodging, the office publishes a very useful city map, *Herzlich Willkommen in Bamberg* (free), that lists all the town's pensions, restaurants, and pubs. *Geyerwörthstr. 3, tel. 0951/871161. From Maxplatz walk s. on Grüner Markt and, before crossing Regnitz, turn left on Am Kanal. Geyerwörthstr. is accessed via small bridge about 165 ft. ahead. Open Apr.–Sept., weekdays 9–7, Sat. 9–5; Oct.–Mar., weekdays 9–6, Sat. 9–2.*

COMING AND GOING

BY TRAIN Bamberg's **Hauptbahnhof** (Ludwigstr. 6, tel. 0951/19419) is roughly 1 kilometer (⅔ mile) northeast of the old town. To reach the Altstadt walk straight out the station and go straight (direction: southwest) on Luitpoldstraße. Cross the Main–Danube Canal and, two blocks farther, turn right onto Franz-Ludwig-Straße; Maxplatz and Grüner Markt are one block ahead. Rail destinations from Bamberg include Bayreuth (hourly, DM 19), Berlin Hauptbahnhof/Zoo Garten (six per day, DM 85), Berlin Lichtenberg (five per day, DM 85), Coburg (hourly, DM 10.80), Frankfurt (hourly, DM 55), Kulmbach (hourly, DM 12.60), Lichtenfels (hourly, DM 6.40), Munich (hourly, DM 60), and Nürnberg (hourly, DM 12.60).

BY BUS Zentral Omnibus Bahnhof, a.k.a. **ZOB** (tel. 0951/19419), has two departure points in Bamberg: one outside the train station, and one on Promenadestraße, opposite Maxplatz in the old town. Either way, buses leave up to five times daily for Bayreuth (first at 7 AM, last at 7:20 PM, DM 12), Coburg (first at 9 AM, last at 9:45 PM, DM 5), and Pommersfelden (depart 11 AM and 1:30 PM, return 4 PM, DM 5.90).

GETTING AROUND

Nearly everything of interest in Bamberg is located within the easily navigated Altstadt. This is divided into three sections: **Burghers' Town,** which contains the train station and comprises everything north and east of the Main–Danube Canal; **Bishops' Town** (sometimes called Cathedral City), which comprises everything west of the Regnitz River; and the historic core of Bamberg itself, which stretches for ½ kilometer (⅓ mile) between the Regnitz and the Main–Danube Canal. It sounds confusing, but just remember that the two rivers flow parallel, and that Bamberg's warren of historic lanes and squares—including the open-air **Maxplatz** (a.k.a. Maximilianplatz) and the pedestrianized **Grüner Markt**—are squashed in between.

WHERE TO SLEEP

For some inexplicable reason, private rooms do not exist in Bamberg. To make up for this deficiency guest houses and pensions abound, and most are priced under DM 90 for a double. Bamberg's two youth hostels are both 3 kilometers (2 miles) from the Altstadt, and both rent rooms only to people under 27. The tourist office (*see* Visitor Information in Basics, *above*) books pensions and hotels for free.

➢ **UNDER DM 75 • Hotel Garni Graupner.** The Graupner is a great deal. It's cheap—doubles start at DM 70, singles at DM 40. It's clean—you almost trip over the army of housekeepers bustling between rooms. And it's well located—smack dab in the middle of the old town, a short walk from Grüner Markt and the Regnitz River. If street noise isn't your idea of a lullaby ask for a room that doesn't face Lange Straße.

The staff are friendly, speak English, and will hold your luggage until 10 PM on the day you check out. Reservations are advised, especially on summer weekends. *Lange Str. 5, off Grüner Markt, tel. 0951/980400. 20 rooms, some with bath. Luggage storage.*

Hotel Lieb. If the kids are making too much noise at the Jugendherberge Wolfsschlucht, the peaceful Hotel Lieb is just down the road, right on the water where the Regnitz's two branches rejoin. You can enjoy a moonlit walk along the shore, but make sure you're back for the 10 PM curfew. Also note that the Lieb is often closed on Friday; call in advance to confirm. The rooms are big and clean and comfy. Doubles start at DM 65 (if you don't mind your bathroom in the hallway) and peak at DM 95. The city center is 3½ kilometers (2 miles) northwest; buses makes the 15-minute trek frequently throughout the day, but after 8 PM they don't come this far out. To soften the blow the Lieb has an on-site beer garden. *Am Regnitzufer 23, tel. 0951/56078. 14 rooms, some with bath. 10 PM curfew.*

Zum Gabelman. In a word, cheap. Really and truly very cheap, with doubles starting at DM 45, singles at DM 25, neither price including breakfast. Best of all you're only a 5-minute walk from Grüner Markt and the old town's pubs and eateries. The rooms are neither overly large nor overly clean, but you won't find anything cheaper or better located. Reservations are a good idea on summer weekends. *Keßlerstr. 14, off Grüner Markt, tel. 0951/26676. 8 rooms, none with bath.*

➢ **UNDER DM 100 • Beim Dominikaner.** This 8-room guest house is right in the heart of the old town, set overlooking the Regnitz River. The clean rooms all come with radios, and some have good views of the busy Altstadt street scene below. Doubles start at DM 90, singles at DM 50. *Dominikanerstr. 3, tel. 0951/58080. From Maxpl. walk southwest down Grüner Markt, cross Regnitz and immediately turn right; Dominikanerstr. is ahead. 8 rooms, some with bath.*

Fässla. The Fässla is best known for its beer tavern, where home-brewed, deep amber beer is tapped from kegs with a big wooden hammer. It isn't near any major sights but is a convenient three-block walk from the train station. Doubles cost DM 90, singles DM 50, and most come equipped with a shower, television, and radio. Even if you already have a place to sleep, stop in for a pint and a snack. If the Fässla is full, **Gasthof Spezial** (Obere Königstr. 10, tel. 0951/24307), across the street, is a similar tavern–cum–guest house with rooms priced under DM 80. *Obere Königstr. 21, tel. 0951/22998 or 0951/126516. From Hauptbahnhof walk straight (southwest) down Luitpoldstr. and, 3 blocks ahead, turn right on Obere Königstr. 21 rooms, all with bath. Closed Sun.*

If you're short on cash, things get real woodsy around both hostels, with lots of dark corners to crawl into for a few sleepy hours. Take Bus 2 to the stadium or Bus 18 to Am Regnitzufer and scout out a leafy hideaway.

HOSTELS **Jugendherberge Stadion.** Yuck. If the Stadion's daytime lockout disturbs you, be advised that there's no place to lounge around inside this cramped hostel anyway. The rooms are just big enough for the bunks, and only the dining room and balcony are left as common space. It costs DM 15 for a bed and breakfast, and you have to help clean up after the meal. Pay another DM 4.50 for linen. The hostel, which lies a good 3 kilometers (2 miles) from the old town, only houses people under 27, which unfortunately means there's often a gaggle of giggly preteens capering in the hallways. The one plus: next door there's a large outdoor swimming pool (DM 3, DM 1.50 students). Call ahead: This place may close. *Pödeldorferstr. 178, tel. 0951/12377. From Hauptbahnhof, Bus 2 to Stadium. 70 beds. Curfew 10 PM, hostel lockout 9 AM–5 PM. Closed Oct.–Apr.*

Jugendherberge Wolfsschlucht. The Wolfsschlucht is set in a large mansion within a stone's throw of the River Regnitz. Down the street there's a miniature golf course, and across the footbridge there's a park and boat rental stand. The hostel is roughly 3 kilometers (2 miles) from the old town. Buses are frequent during the day but stop servicing the hostel around 8 PM. Plan on at least one DM 6–DM 10 taxi ride. Bed space costs DM 15 (including breakfast), sheets an additional DM 4.50. *Oberer Leinritt 70, tel. 0951/56002. From ZOB's Promenadestr. depot, Bus 18 to Am Regnitzufer and walk n. on Oberer Leinritt. 94 beds. Curfew 10 PM. Closed Dec. 15–Jan. 31.*

Bamberg is associated with a few culinary oddities. One is Rauchbier, *or smoked beer, a deep amber brew whose unique smoky taste comes from being filtered through charred beechwood logs. Another local specialty is* Leberkäs, *a spiced liver sandwich that—even if you detest liver—tastes surprisingly good. Also try* Bierbrauervesper, *a mixed plate of smoked meat, sour-milk cheese, and black bread.*

CAMPGROUNDS **Campingplatz Insel.** The Insel is roughly 5 kilometers (3 miles) south of the city center. It's a beautiful and popular spot, stretched along the Regnitz River, with showers in clean bathrooms to boot! If you have a tent it's DM 4 to stake it plus an additional DM 5 per person. The camp's cantina is stocked with all kinds of food supplies. Slurp down a cheap meal—like ravioli for DM 5.50—as you watch the Regnitz creep peacefully along. The Insel is open year-round. *Karl-May Str., Bamberg-Bug, tel. 0951/56320. From ZOB's Promenadestr. depot, Bus 18 to Bug, then walk s. on Hauptstr., which becomes Karl-May-Str.*

FOOD

Bamberg's Altstadt is littered with cheap Imbiß stands and snazzy tourist-oriented *Gaststätten* (restaurants). For the former concentrate on Maxplatz and the streets immediately south and east; the dirt-cheap **Fischer** (Franz-Ludwig-Str. 5B), a small Imbiß that's popular with locals, ain't a bad choice at all. For home-brewed beer and light snacks head to **Fässla** or **Gasthof Spezial** (*see* Where to Sleep, *above*), two top-rate taverns that double as guest houses.

➢ **UNDER DM 15 • Calimero's Cantina.** Calimero's goes all out with the Mexican theme: Snoozing hombres are enshrined on the hand-painted walls, and the music is definitely of the Mexican radio variety. A big plate of not-so-authentic but passable enchiladas, tacos, or burritos—choice of meat or vegetarian—fetches a reasonable DM 10.50. They also serve up Italian pastas and, for DM 7.50, good ol' American hamburgers. *Lange Str., off Grüner Markt.*

Greifenklau. This small wiener-and-cabbage inn is pretty as a postcard and perched slightly above the old town. You can savor local ale and a good view at the same time, ponder a plate of Franconian pork and dumplings (DM 12), and then head back into town along the kilometer-long (⅔-mile-long) Kaulberg road. If you're looking to escape the bustle of the city center, this is an excellent choice. *Laurenpl. 20, tel. 0951/53219. From Dompl. walk s. to Unter Kaulberg (which turns into Laurenpl.) and turn right. No Sun. dinner.*

Ni Hao. Bland but respectable Chinese food inside a bland restaurant inside a bland shopping mall that could be Anytown, USA. Lunch specials—usually noodle-and-rice dishes with soup or a spring roll—go for DM 10–DM 15. Full entrées like almond chicken and myriad sweet and sours cost around DM 15. You can eat while doing your laundry at the nearby Atrium Waschsalon (*see* Laundry in Basics, *above*). *Ludwigstr. 2, Atrium Mall, 2nd floor, tel. 0951/25885. Wheelchair access.*

Schlenkerla Brauereigaststätte. The Schlenkerla is the place to go for real Bamberg cuisine. It brews its own *Rauchbier,* or smoked beer (DM 2.80 per ½ liter), and serves up a damn fine mushroom omelet (DM 10.80). Also try the Bamberg ham and salad plate (DM 11.50). Grab a chair at a long table and mingle with the middle-aged German crowd in one of the restaurant's several small dining rooms. *Dominikanerstr. 6, tel. 0951/56060. Cross Untere Brücke from Lange Str. onto Dominikanerstr. Closed Tues.*

CAFES **Café im Rosengarten.** Grab a *Kännchen* (pot) of steaming coffee at this intimate café, located in the middle of the Neue Residenz rose garden. It's difficult to tell what kind of torte you're getting by the menu listings, but you can't go wrong with coffee cake (DM 3) and ice cream (DM 4.50). Sit outside for a good view of old Bamberg and Kloster Michaelsberg. *Neue Residenz, Dompl. 8.*

Galeria Café and Bistro. By day the Galeria is a quiet place filled with people who want nothing more than to sip coffee and ponder the Regnitz's slow-moving waters. Light meals—try the tomato, mozzarella, and pesto plate (DM 7.50)—are complemented with a large menu of coffee and beer. Come nightfall the place is utterly transformed: Orange-red lights replace subdued white; the bar, tall tables, and upper level fill up; and the servers move a lot faster to keep glasses filled. *Untere Sandstr. 16, tel. 0951/55873. From Dompl. walk n. on Elisabethstr. and turn right on Untere Sandstr.*

Rather than tackling Bamberg sight by sight, concentrate on one quarter at a time—or simply get as lost as possible.

WORTH SEEING

Klein Venedig (Little Venice), the quarter huddled along both banks of the Regnitz just north of the Old Rathaus, is typical of Bamberg's sights. This riverfront collection of red-roofed and brightly colored homes has no "official" attractions. It's simply damn pleasant to wander through, especially when the odd fishing skiff glides lazily by around dusk. The same holds true for **Maxplatz,** Bamberg's "other" square, and **Grüner Markt,** the pedestrian-only shopping avenue. You could do worse than spend a few hours just staring at the squat **Altes Rathaus** (Old Town Hall), which sits straddling the Regnitz on a centuries-old stone bridge, the Obere Brücke (actually, this colorful and rickety Gothic creation is best seen from the adjacent bridge upstream).

DOMPLATZ Domplatz lies in the heart of Bishops' Town only a few hundred yards west of the Regnitz River and the Altes Rathaus (look for four closely grouped towers on the skyline; that's Domplatz). Its most impressive landmark is the 13th-century **Dom,** also known as the Imperial Cathedral. The original structure was built in 1003 by Heinrich II, and it was in this partially complete cathedral that he was crowned Holy Roman Emperor in 1012. In the early 13th century the Dom was largely destroyed by fire, after which work on the present structure was begun. The Dom's trademark features are the four symmetric towers that anchor each corner.

Heading inside the dark, almost somber nave you'll stumble upon one of the most outrageous art collections of any European church. First and foremost is the *Bamberger Reiter (Bamberg Rider),* an equestrian statue that dates from 1230. The artist is unknown, but it's an easy guess he or she was an impassioned genius possessed of unprecedented skill. Across from the stoic Bamberger horseman there's an elaborate cycle of carved figures huddled in the dark recesses above the church doorway. In the center of the nave is another striking work of sculpture, the tomb of Heinrich II and his wife, Kunigunde.

Diözesanmuseum (Cathedral Museum), next door to the Dom, houses an eclectic mix of church relics, random pieces of silver and jewels, and line drawings of the Dom floor plan. It also contains a fleck of wood and the *Heilige Nagel* (Holy Nail), both reputedly taken from the one and true cross of Jesus (sure). Also on display are the well-preserved skulls of Heinrich and Kunigunde, a popular attraction. *Dompl. 5. Admission: DM 2.50. Open Apr.–Sept., daily 9–noon and 1:30–5; Oct.–Mar., daily 9–noon and 1:30–4.*

Admission to the Cathedral Museum buys free entrance to the adjoining Neue Residenz, a sprawling Baroque palace that was once home to princes and electors of the Holy Roman Empire. Tour the typically lavish interior—the Throne Room and its flamboyant ceiling frescoes are definitely worth a peek—then head for the palace's **Staatsbibliothek** (State Library). What started as a small personal collection by Heinrich II has grown into a vastly impressive (and somewhat dusty) holding of rare handwritten and illuminated manuscripts. Highlights include a 5th-century copy of a manuscript by the 1st-century Roman historian Livy, and manuscripts written by painters Cranach and Dürer. Afterward, head outside into the stately, pollen-filled rose garden. *Dompl. 8. Admission free with Cathedral Museum ticket, otherwise DM 2.50. Neue Residenz open Apr.–Sept., daily 9—noon and 1:30–5; Oct.–Mar., daily 9–noon and 1:30–4. Staatsbibliothek open weekdays 9–5, Sat. 9–noon.*

Domplatz's final attraction is Alte Hofaltung, a tired-looking, half-timbered Gothic palace. Inside you'll find a history museum with a dull collection of maps and German-language placards that document the development of Bamberg. Ho hum. The only time you should go out of your way to visit is during June and July, when open-air concerts occasionally liven up the place. Call 0951/25256 for advance tickets, generally priced between DM 6 and DM 15. *Dompl. 7. Admission: DM 2. Open Dec.–Apr., Tues.–Fri. 9–1, weekends 9–4:30; May.–Oct., Tues.–Sun. 9–5.*

HOFFMANN-HAUS Ernest Theodore Hoffmann, the Romantic writer and composer, lived in this small Baroque house between 1809 and 1813. If you've never heard of Hoffmann, have no fear—he's less famous for his corpus vitae than for the opera written about him by Jacques Offenbach, *The Tales Of Hoffmann.* Even so, Hoffmann's house is a good example of late Baroque craftsmanship and worth a quick look. Reams of personal papers are preserved inside, along with personal belongings and—the most popular attraction—the hole in his study floor through which he spoke with his wife below. Odds are good they didn't have the best of marriages. *Schillerpl. 26. From Altes Rathaus cross to Regnitz's w. bank and turn right on Am Kanal, left at Nonnenbrücke. Admission: DM 1. Open May–Oct., Tues.–Fri. 9:30–5:30, weekends 9:30–1.*

AFTER DARK

The **Hoffmann Theater** (Schillerpl. 5, tel. 0951/87498) hosts opera and chamber music on a regular basis, September to May. During summer it hosts the occasional play and opera, but much more irregularly. The **Bamberg Symphony Orchestra** gives regular concerts in the Dom; during June and July they also sometimes play in Alte Hofaltung. Call 0951/25256 for ticket information, or inquire at the tourist office.

More festive diversions are offered at **Pelikan** (Untere Sandstr. 45, tel. 0951/62110), the **Jazz-Klub** (Obere Sandstr. 18, tel. 0951/53740), and **Strandcafe** (Memmelsdorfer Str. 82, tel. 0951/32366). These three music pubs cater to a younger crowd, and some nights the music is actually decent. In any case, they're a good bet for late-night conversations with slightly giddy locals.

Near Bamberg

SCHLOß WEIßENSTEIN

Schloß Weißenstein (tel. 09548/203) was built between 1711 and 1718 by Lothar Franz von Schoenborn, elector and archbishop of the Holy Roman Empire. This position (plus the cache of money that went with it) enabled Lothar to realize his lifelong desire—his own lush summer palace that might perfectly integrate the many artistic ideals of the Baroque age. Lothar and his architects didn't do such a bad job, for nowadays Castle Weissenstein is considered the finest of its kind in northern Bavaria. Particularly stunning is the exquisite Baroque staircase—hailed in tourist brochures as *the* finest staircase in all Germany—and the seemingly endless procession of plastered, carved, frescoed ceilings. Room after elegant room opens onto statue-lined hallways that meander through a labyrinth of frescoed salons and marble-bathed galleries. Add a 700-piece collection of 16th- to 18th-century European art (which includes original works by Dürer, Titian, and Rubens) and you're left with a really, truly, and fully realized Baroque fantasy.

The castle is open April 1 through October 31, daily except Monday. Hour-long guided tours (mandatory) are given every hour on the hour from 9–11 AM and 2–4 PM. At 11:30 and 4:30 a shorter 30-minute version of the tour is offered. The tours are all in German and cost under DM 5 per person. A bland, English-language mini-pamphlet is available free at the door.

Inside the castle's elegant dining room, the Schloßgaststätte-Dorn (tel. 09548/224) serves pheasant and wild game dinners in the DM 15–DM 25 range. On a sunny afternoon you also can sip drinks (DM 5–DM 10) leisurely on its outdoor terrace.

COMING AND GOING Pommersfelden, the small village next to which the castle is located, is accessible only by infrequent bus. These leave Bamberg's train station daily at 7:38 AM and arrive 45 minutes later. The one-way trip costs DM 5.90. As there are no buses that leave from Pommersfelden, returning to Bamberg entails a 2-kilometer (1¼-mile) walk to the village of Steppach, where a bus then departs daily for Bamberg at 3:51 PM and 4:27 PM. Also note: If you can't make the 7:38 AM bus, at 11:10 AM and 1:30 PM buses leave Bamberg train station for Steppach.

WHERE TO SLEEP If you miss the last bus, don't despair. The adjacent **Schloßhotel Pommersfelden** (tel. 09548/680 or 09548/388) has elegant doubles, equipped with televisions and radios, that start at DM 75. This also buys access to the hotel's pool and sauna, but not the breakfast buffet (an additional DM 12). The **Stirnweiß** (Schönbornstr. 13, tel. 09548/385, check-in after 5 PM), located one block from the castle, rents cheaper, more modest rooms for about DM 20 per person.

FRANKISCHE SCHWEIZ

The *Fränkische Schweiz* (Franconian Switzerland) region is shaped like an upside-down triangle, with Nürnberg forming the tip, Bayreuth and Bamberg the base. There's nothing particularly "Swiss" about the area except, perhaps, the range of low-lying hills that might, after a few dozen steins, look vaguely like the mile-high Alps. More likely, the region's "Swiss-ness" stems from the age-old German perception that Switzerland is a land where rugged people like to do rugged outdoor things in the rugged countryside. Fränkische Schweiz is hardly rugged (nor is it anywhere near as scenic as Switzerland itself). But in relation to much of Bavaria this region of cliff-faced hills and uncut forest, scant with towns but interwoven with hiking trails, is still Franconia at its rural best. During winter there's often a thick blanket of snow on the ground, which keeps crowds to a minimum. After the spring thaw mainly German tourists descend on the area to hike, bike, fish, canoe, kayak, and horseback ride—just about any activity that is best done in a sylvan and mountainous, unpopulated setting. The region is littered with ruined castles perched high atop long-abandoned hills, so you can also temper outdoor pursuits with some historical sightseeing.

We're not quite sure how Fränkische Schweiz got its name. The fact is, there ain't a Swiss-looking Alp for miles. No fondue-eating yodelers. No signs of Heidi or of clandestine watch factories. Nothing at all having remotely to do with Switzerland. Go figure.

Fränkische Schweiz is not well connected with the German rail network. Only those who won't mind hitching, cycling, or busing between the area's tiny dorfs and burgs should consider a prolonged stay. Day-trippers, however, can visit Ebermannstadt and Gößweinstein conveniently by train. **Ebermannstadt,** which lies roughly 25 kilometers (16 miles) southeast of Bamberg, is home to the Fränkische Schweiz regional tourist office, **Tourismuszentrale** (Oberes Tor 1, Ebermannstadt, tel. 09194/8101), which stocks hiking and topographic maps, and can fill you in on the area's lodging and dining scene. The tourist office can also help outfit a fishing or biking expedition (they publish a useful listing of local sport shops).

Hikers and spelunkers should head for **Streitberg, Muggendorf,** or **Wiesenttal,** three small villages that are often lumped together under the woefully unoriginal name of Muggendorf–Streitberg–Wiesenttal. All are located just east of Ebermannstadt and within a short 2-kilometer (1¼ mile) walk of one another. Streitberg, in particular, has an amazing underground labyrinth of caves that are open mid-March through October, daily 8–noon and 1–5; November through early March call 09196/340 for the haphazard opening times. Also in Streitberg, the **Schwimmbad** (tel. 09196/298) rents canoes and rowboats (both mid-May–mid-September only) for use on one of a dozen small, nearby rivers. Full-day rentals generally cost under DM 25. At Streitberg's **Schottersmühle** (tel. 09196/1503) you can find kayaks priced under DM 40 per day. Rent bikes at Schauertal No. 2 (tel. 09196/256) for under DM 15 per day.

Gößweinstein is a good-looking market town that's been around since the Middle Ages. Visit its Baroque basilica, go fly-fishing, or spend the day biking in the hills. Fishing permits cost DM 20–DM 25 and are available from **Karl-Heinz Schmitt** (Behringersmühle 43, tel. 09242/357) or **Gasthof "Frankenhöhe"** (Hühnerloh 1, tel. 09242/347). These latter also rent bikes (DM 10 per day) and sometimes stock regional hiking maps. Heading east from Gößweinstein, flat-topped peaks slowly fade into the rolling, low-lying hills that surround **Pottenstein,** a quiet market town that's overshadowed by the looming ruins of a medieval castle and cathedral. In Pottenstein, **Stadt Verkehrsbüro** (Im Gästezentrum, tel. 09243/833) stocks hiking and exploring maps, and rents bikes at DM 12 per day.

COMING AND GOING Trains from Bamberg leave daily for Ebermannstadt (DM 5), Streitberg (DM 6), Muggendorf (DM 6), and Gößweinstein (DM 7). From Bayreuth Bus 8448 stops in Gößweinstein on the way to Bamberg and Nürnberg. A weekend bus pass, which costs DM 25 and is valid Friday night through Sunday, buys unlimited travel on the region's buses; procure them from any driver. In Bamberg, **Reisebüro Brand** (Markuspl. 12, tel. 0951/63549) offers a five-town bus tour of Fränkische Schweiz. You need at least five people (at DM 40 per person) and a free afternoon.

WHERE TO SLEEP There are three DJH youth hostels in the region, all priced under DM 16 per person (including breakfast): **Jugendherberge Gößweinstein** (Etzdorfer Str. 6, tel. 09242/259, closed Jan. 11–Feb. 28), **Jugendherberge Pottenstein** (Jugendherbergstr. 20, tel. 09243/1224, closed Jan. 11–Feb. 28), and **Jugendherberge Streitberg** (Am Gailing 6, tel. 09196/288). Within 2 kilometers (1¼ miles) of Pottenstein's city center you'll also find two campgrounds. **Bepürenschlucht** (Weidmanns Gesees 12, Pottenstein, tel. 09243/206) is quite large and open year-round. **Campingplatz "Fränkische Schweiz"** (Tüchersfeld 57, Pottenstein, tel. 09242/440 or 09242/1788 during summer) is prettier, but only open Easter through October.

Also try the **Gasthaus-Pension Sponsel** (Oberfellendorf 2, Wiesenttal, tel. 09196/269), a small guest house run by the Sponsel family. The rooms are all clean and comfy, and happily priced at DM 18–DM 22 per person for a double. **Pension "Zur Schönen Aussicht"** (Behringersmühle 22, Gößweinstein, tel. 09242/294) has a beautiful view from its hilltop location. A double with bath fetches a low DM 52. In Ebermannstadt, the centrally located **Gasthof-Pension "Zur Post"** (Am Marktpl. 3, tel. 09194/201) has doubles for DM 66–DM 74.

BERLIN

8

By Peter Edwards, with Scott McNeely

When you speak of Berlin you're really speaking of two very different cities. On one hand there's West Berlin, once the lone bastion of capitalism in communist Eastern Europe. For years it was an isolated stump of a city, surrounded by Russian soldiers, a fine setting for spy stories and daring escapes. Particularly after the erection of the Wall in 1961, West Berlin was portrayed as a city quite literally on the edge. Its 2 million inhabitants lived in relative prosperity, but there was always something slightly schizophrenic about this walled-in fortress of nude bars and neon-lit cafés. Something odd about its people and their darkly cynical wit, about its mix of wealthy bankers, immigrant factory workers, and unemployed bohemians.

Even during the worst of the Cold War, West Berlin still nurtured all types of culture, both high and low. It was helped by a steady influx of Western capital, and by a desire in Bonn to keep Berlin from the Communists. Berlin's special status meant that residents were exempt from military service (which was mandatory for all other German males), and any family or business that relocated here was rewarded with a hefty tax break. The Bonn government was equally generous in issuing grants for artists and musicians who came to work in Berlin.

Berlin became a magnet for adventure seekers, slackers, and working-class immigrants (hence the joke that Berlin is Turkey's fifth-largest city). Some were drawn by cheap rents, some by the city's thriving cultural and night life, and some by an almost tangible sense of urgency that was missing in other German cities. Berliners knew that at any moment Cold War politics might thrust their city into the middle of World War III. And if West Berlin was considered slightly absurd and superficial, that's because in many ways it was. What else could you expect from a walled-in city that was most often viewed as an issue rather than a place?

East Berlin weathered the Cold War quite differently from its western counterpart. Under the communists East Berlin was vigorously industrialized. Where World War II bombing had left gaping holes in the street, the GDR stepped in and built yet another high-rise apartment block. Where the Soviets had dismantled the city's factories for shipment back to the motherland, East Berlin was forced to erect new ones as cheaply and quickly as possible. East Berlin's Unter den Linden, once an elegant and tree-lined promenade, turned ragged after years of neglect. So did the once-stylish Alexanderplatz and the congested maze of working-class suburbs that now make up East Berlin's gloomy skyline.

The real irony is that while East Berlin was often perceived as a cultureless wasteland, it actually contained the bulk of Berlin's historic districts and the best of its museums. Berlin's first great ruler, Prince Friedrich Wilhelm, built his palace on East Berlin's Marx-Engels-Platz. Until World War II nearly all the city's governmental offices were on the east side. So, too, were Berlin's principal university and all the wildest nightclubs, bars, and cabarets. Historically speaking, East Berlin was the Berlin that mattered.

It was often said that East rather than West Berlin was the "occupied" city. Yet this simply wasn't true. The Soviet-backed GDR may have been less than subtle in its efforts to maintain control—the Berlin Wall was certainly not the work of a "sensitive" government. But even as East Berlin was slowly overcome by the communist cement-and-steel aesthetic, West Berlin, too, was conquered and occupied—not by industry and working-class slums but by neon boutiques, swank cafés, and all the trappings of a Westernized (i.e., Americanized) megacity. And while each half of Berlin claimed title to the city's name, they could easily have been called anything else—Lin Vegas and Berleningrad, perhaps. Both cities tried to preserve their splintered cultural traditions, yet both sides were thwarted by one obvious fact: The Berlin of old was dead.

Needless to say, all this changed on the night of Friday, November 10, 1989. As the world watched, East Germans began smashing through the Wall, unhindered and in vast numbers. By November 14 there were more than 20 official crossing points, with the promise of more to come. The effect on the city was overwhelming. East Germans packed a lifetime into their sputtery, two-cycle Trabants and headed west. At the border each person was greeted with a cheer and DM 100 in cash. In West Berlin, the Opera House presented free performances of Mozart; tickets and inspectors were officially banned on the U-Bahn, the city's underground rail system; and beer and food stalls appeared at Brandenburg Gate to cater to around-the-clock celebrants. For the first time in 30 years all Berlin was free to mingle along a now-defunct border. And for a few weeks, at least, Berlin was the biggest party around.

And then came the questions. Can we West Berliners afford to be so generous? Can we reasonably support 1.2 million East Berlin immigrants? Who will pay for the new housing and new schools, for new trams and subways and buses? For all Berliners, the

The Berlin Wall

Throughout the 1950s the German Democratic Republic (GDR) grew increasingly embarrassed that nearly 20,000 East Germans were crossing into West Berlin every month, never to return. To stem the flow, the government decided to seal the border completely. So at 1 AM on August 13, 1961, more than 25,000 GDR workmen wiped the sleep from their eyes and set about raising a wire-and-mortar barrier—the Berlin Wall—along the entire length of the border, demolishing houses and dissecting streets whenever necessary. The "civilized" world was predictably outraged, but short of a war there was very little they could do. Berliners, on the other hand, felt an acute and lasting shock. Berliners had survived the horrors of World War II, and in the ensuing years they had accepted the fact that their city was bitterly divided between two irreconcilable ideologies. But now they were forced to confront their division in glaringly public terms. The Iron Curtain may have marked an ideological boundary, but the Berlin Wall was a very real, very tangible reminder of the city's seemingly irreparable split.

demise of the Wall was confusing and thrilling and vaguely troubling all at once. And while West Berliners were thrilled to see so many Easterners in their half of the city, they weren't quite sure what to do with them all. Let them browse and gawk at the wonders of the West, but aren't they going home soon?

After 30 years of division, two distinct kinds of Berliners had evolved—one brash and cynical and completely comfortable sipping $5 espressos in a swank Kurfürstendamm café, one sullen and docile and accustomed to standing in long lines. On top of this there were the purely practical complaints. West Berliners had jobs, snazzy cars, and plenty of money. Most East Berliners didn't. They could afford West Berlin's lifestyle in small doses only. And if that was to change, West Berliners soon realized, they would have to sacrifice more than just a little.

In unified Berlin you can still sense a gaping divide between highbrow and lowbrow, between rich and poor. To put it bluntly—as many Berliners are apt to do—there's still a divisive distinction between the Ossies (Easterners) and Wessies (Westerners).

Few Berliners expected their city to be rejoined seamlessly overnight. Yet today there's a growing sense of annoyance as both halves of Berlin continue to struggle with their long-awaited reunification. The Wall is largely invisible but still emotionally perceptible, and no matter how you slice it Berlin remains tangibly divided between cement apartment buildings and prim shopping avenues—by 45 years of distinct and generally incompatible development. The German Bundestag's June 1991 decision to move the capital from Bonn to Berlin will certainly help homogenize the two halves. But lawmakers have given the government until 2003 to complete the move, so it will take at least a decade before Berlin once again becomes the political and cultural focus of a united Germany; perhaps a generation or two before the words "East" and "West" become unnecessary as prefaces to the word "Berliner."

In the meantime, all Berliners must learn to cope with the most obvious effect of reunification—the fact that unified Berlin is simply an overwhelming city. The city familiar to Western visitors was already massive before reunification, but Berlin has now become really and truly enormous. The revamped city center now stretches for miles in every direction—a vast patchwork of parkland, forest, shops, cement, and suburbs. All told, unified Berlin measures nearly 900 square kilometers (346 square miles), which makes it larger than some European countries.

1920s Berlin: A Heady Hedonism

During the short-lived Weimar Republic (1919–33), Berlin was briefly the most tolerant and progressive (some would say libertine) city in all Europe. This was a time of scandalous nightclubs, seedy jazz, and bourgeois coffeehouse culture. Repelled by the horrors of World War I, 1920s Berlin sought a new identity based on everything from individualism and excess to socialism, anarchism, and communism. Along the way it attracted the likes of playwrights Bertolt Brecht and Erwin Piscator, moviemaker Fritz Lang, architect Walter Gropius and his Bauhaus school, singer Marlene Dietrich, and painters Otto Dix and Vasily Kandinsky. While Berlin's Schöneberg district harbored the largest and most open community of gays and lesbians in all Europe, East Berlin's Unter den Linden became world famous for its nude dance clubs and all-night cabarets. In this Golden Age of 20th-century Berlin, morality was relative, sex a coffee-table subject, and cocaine and opium free for the asking.

For the traveler, just getting around the city is a challenge; to see all the "sights" is almost impossible. Berlin has some of the very best museums and monuments in Europe. You may not have heard of the Dahlem or Schloß Charlottenburg museums, but if you've ever taken an art history course you'll probably recognize the better part of their holdings (remember the bust of Queen Nefertiti? Donatello's *Madonna and Child*?) Add East Berlin's three lavish opera houses and dozen world-class museums, and you're left with a city of impressive cultural dimensions. In fact, you could spend weeks hopping from sight to sight without exhausting all the possibilities.

What really give Berlin its unmistakable character, though, are its many diverse districts. The Kurfürstendamm—Berlin's most famous shopping avenue, universally known as the Ku'damm—and prim suburbs like Wilmersdorf represent the city's refined side, places where every second car is a BMW, every third a Mercedes. Other districts, like Kreuzberg, Schöneberg, and East Berlin's Prenzlauer Berg, reveal Berlin at its wildest, a city where artists and punks huddle in vacant lots and cement tenements by day, in cafés and basement dive bars by night; where immigrant factory workers, Turkish bazaars, and sputtering Trabant cars form a unique urban vignette. Depending on what you're looking for, Berlin can be as refined or as grungy as you want it to be.

Basics

AMERICAN EXPRESS Bring your passport to exchange money, cash traveler's checks, and, for American Express cardholders only, to pick up mail from home. *Kurfürstendamm 11, 2nd floor, across from Kaiser-Wilhelm Memorial Church, tel. 030/882–7575. Open weekdays 9–5:30, Sat. 9–noon. Friedrichstr. 172, near Frankreichstr., tel. 030/238–4102. Open weekdays 9–5:30.*

BUCKET SHOPS **Reisebüro Rose** has a friendly, English-speaking staff who will find budget deals on domestic and international travel. *Leibnizstr. 36, tel. 030/312838. Walk s. from intersection of Kantstr. and Leibnizstr. Open weekdays 9–6:30, Sat. 10–1.*

Reisebüro-Hochhaus are eastern Germany specialists, so stop by if you're planning a trip through the former GDR. They have oodles of tourist literature and can help arrange budget air, rail, and bus excursions. *Alexanderpl. 5, tel. 030/215–4161. U- or S-Bahn to Alexanderpl. Open weekdays 8–8, weekends 9–6.*

BUREAUX DE CHANGE If you can avoid changing money in Berlin, do so. Not one exchange place stays open 24 hours and, as a general rule, all charge heavy commissions (3%–5%). If you're desperate, most luxury hotels have bureaux de change in their lobbies. These, too, impose hefty commissions and have a smarmy attitude to boot.

For convenience try an American Express office (*see above*) or the nearby **Berliner Bank** (Ku'damm 24, open weekdays 9:30–6:30, Sat. 9:30–1:30). Berliner Bank charges a flat rate of DM 10 *per exchange*, so pool your money with a friend. Another group of banks lies along **Joachimstalerstraße,** south of Zoo Station. Particularly useful is **Wechselstube** (Joachimstalerstr. 26, open Mon.–Sat. 8 AM–9 pm, Sun. 10–6), one of the few open on weekends.

EMBASSIES Now that Berlin has been named the capital of the unified Germany, many embassies are expected to relocate here from Bonn. In the meantime, the foreign consulates listed below can deal with the most delicate of problems, even if you're calling from a Berlin jail. No less appreciated are their reading rooms, stocked with reasonably current newspapers, travel bulletins, and medical information.

United States. *Western Berlin: Clayallee 170, 1000 Berlin 33, tel. 030/832–4087. Eastern Berlin: Neustädtische Kirchstr. 4–5, O–1080 Berlin, tel. 030/220–2741.*

Canada. *Europa Center, 12th floor, 1000 Berlin 30, tel. 030/261–1161.*

United Kingdom. *Eastern Berlin: Unter den Linden 32–34, O–1080 Berlin, tel. 030/220–2431.*

Australia. *Wilhelm-Külz-Str. 46, O–1080 Berlin, tel. 030/2410.*

ENGLISH BOOKS AND NEWSPAPERS Along with the consulates (*see above*), bookstores in the city center stock a small selection of English books and newspapers. Expect weeks-old copies of *USA Today*, the *New York Times*, and *The Times* (United Kingdom) for about DM 10. The only up-to-date newspaper is the *International Herald Tribune* (DM 4–DM 7), but it's harder to find. Search the newsstands at Tegel Airport and Zoo Station, or try **Amerika Haus** (Hardenbergstr. 22–24, tel. 030/819–7661). The latter is located one block due west of Zoo Station and has a good selection of English books. **Books in Berlin** (Goethestr. 69, off Steinpl., tel. 030/316233) also stocks a wide selection of English reading material, including maps and comic books. Also try **Das Internationale Buch** (Spandauerstr. 34, tel. 030/45532), open daily 10–6.

A free pamphlet, "Berlin for Young People," is the only readily available English-language guide to what's up in Berlin. It lists art, music, theater, and cinema events, complete with addresses, dates, and times. Pick up a copy at the Informationszentrum (*see below*).

LUGGAGE STORAGE Berlin's larger train stations all have luggage lockers for around DM 2–DM 3 per half-day. Zoo Station, in particular, has row upon row of backpack-size lockers, which cost DM 2 per 12 hours. It's easier to find empty lockers in the early morning. Also inside is a **left-luggage desk** (open daily 7 AM–9 PM), where you can deposit your bags for DM 5 per day. The advantage here is that you're allowed repeated access to your stored bags without any surcharge.

MAIL Berlin's main **post office** is inside Bahnhof Zoologischer Garten (tel. 030/313–9799). Open 24 hours, it's the place to come for stamps, and to send mail, a telegram, or even a fax. It's also the place to pick up mail from home. This service costs DM 3 per letter; proper I.D.—preferably a passport—is required. Letters should be addressed: Poste Restante, Postamt Bahnhof Zoo, D–1000 Berlin 12. Also inside are dozens of international phone boxes, some even of the "Call Back" variety (*see below*). Ancillary post offices are spread throughout Berlin, both East and West. You'll have no problem finding one.

MEDICAL AID *Apotheke* (pharmacies) are usually open weekdays 9–6:30 and Saturdays 9–2. Posted on every pharmacy's door is the address of the nearest all-night pharmacy. In West Berlin, **Europa Apotheke** (Tauentzienstr. 9, near Europa Center, tel. 030/261–4142) stays open every day until 9 PM. In East Berlin, try **Apotheke am Alexanderplatz** (Heinz-Beimler Str. 71–72, tel. 030/212–5766, open daily 9 AM–8 PM). If your German is good, dial 1141 from West Berlin or 160 from East Berlin for a recorded list of late-night pharmacies.

Both **Deutsche AIDS-Hilfe** (tel. 030/323–6027) and **Bundeszentrale für gesundheitliche Aufklärung** (tel. 0221/892031) provide over-the-phone AIDS counseling.

PHONES The reunification of Berlin's phone system is nearly complete, although service in East Berlin is still sometimes poor. The new phone code for all parts of Berlin is 030 (drop the first 0 if calling from abroad). Also note: Don't be confused if one phone number has seven digits while another has six or eight—that's just the way it is in Berlin.

➢ **LOCAL CALLS** • Coin-operated phones are everywhere in the city. All accept 10-pfennig, DM 1, and DM 5 coins. A standard local call costs DM .30, meaning three 10-pfennig coins. This buys you five minutes, after which you'll hear a series of beeps that signals you have 10 seconds to insert more money before the line goes dead. Invest in a **telephone card** if you plan on making lots of calls. These are available at most post offices and newsstands in DM 5, DM 10, and DM 20 denominations. To reach a local operator dial 1188 free from any pay phone.

➢ **LONG-DISTANCE CALLS** • You can make international calls from any phone box labeled INLANDS UND AUSLANDSGESPRÄCHE. They're generally colored red instead of white or yellow. Newer phone boxes are sometimes labeled "International." All accept direct-dial and collect calls. A standard four-minute call to the United States costs around DM 18, so bring plenty of change. To place a collect call, dial an international operator at 00118.

Another thing to watch for are "Call Back" boxes, identified by the silhouette of a ringing phone. For around DM 5 you can place a direct-dial call, quickly give someone back home the phone number, and then wait for him or her to ring you back. Another option is the post office. Go to Window 9 at the Zoo Station post office and ask for a collect call form. There's no charge for this service, but expect a 10- to 15-minute wait before you're connected.

VISITOR INFORMATION Although they're in German, the magazines *Zitty, Tip, Berlin Programm*, and *Stadtbuch 4,* each priced around DM 4, list all the major happenings in Berlin—and it doesn't take a genius to decipher dates, times, and addresses. Look for them at the tourist office or your local newsstand.

Berlin's most useful information service is the state-run **Verkehrsamt Berlin** (Berlin Tourist Information). All offices stock tourist literature, maps, and bus/train information. For a DM 5 fee they also book rooms in hotels, pensions, hostels, private homes, and universities—the easiest way to find a place in sprawling Berlin. Even better, they're generally staffed by fluent English-speakers. Look for them at West Berlin's **Tegel Airport** (tel. 030/410–13145), at **Zoo Station** (tel. 030/313–9063, closed Sun.), and East Berlin's **Hauptbahnhof** (tel. 030/279–5009, open daily 8–8). The main office is located in West Berlin's very central **Europa Center** (Breitscheidpl., off the Ku'damm, tel. 030/262–6031). Unless noted otherwise, all are open Monday–Saturday 8 AM–10:30 PM, Sunday 9–9.

Berlin Gay Association has complete listings of gay/lesbian events. This East Berlin office can also tell you which clubs are popular gay hangouts and which should be avoided. *Friedrichstr. 14A, tel. 030/872–9001 or 030/324–3277. Take U-Bahn to Friedrichstr. Open weekdays 9–4.*

Jewish Community Center offers information and advice to Jewish visitors. They'll also update you on any religious or special events in Berlin. Even if you're not Jewish, stop by for one of the center's excellent kosher meals (*see* Food, *below*). *Fasanenstr. 79, tel. 030/884–2030. Walk w. on Ku'damm to Fasanenstr. Open Mon.–Sat. 10–5.*

Informationszentrum stocks city maps and English-language walking guides. Particularly useful is the English-language pamphlet "Berlin for Young People," a free monthly that lists music and art events. For a DM 4 fee, this office will book you into a hotel, hostel, or private room. Call ahead; the office may close soon. *Hardenbergstr. 20, 2nd floor, tel. 030/310040. Open Mon.–Sat. 9–7.*

COMING AND GOING

BY PLANE Unified Berlin has two major airports, West Berlin's **Flughafen Tegel** (tel. 030/411011) and East Berlin's **Flughafen Schönefeld** (tel. 030/678–74031). Although it's generally cheaper to fly into Frankfurt, Tegel has started to compete more aggressively for commercial business, so check prices before you leave. Currently, the only American carrier with direct flights to Berlin is **Delta** (tel. 800/241–4141), connecting Tegel and New York once daily. The national German airline, **Lufthansa** (tel. 800/645–3880), offers flights to Tegel from the States and the United Kingdom with a short stopover, usually in Frankfurt. Schönefeld is used mainly by East European and Russian airlines. The former military base at **Tempelhof** (tel. 030/662893) is increasingly used for some domestic flights, but it's unlikely you'll end up here.

➢ **AIRPORT TRANSPORT** • Tegel Airport is 6 kilometers (4 miles) north of the city center. Don't be fooled into thinking that the U6 subway (confusingly marked "Tegel") goes to the airport—it doesn't. If you're coming from the city center you have two options. Blue airport buses Numbers 9 and 109 zip between Zoo Station and Tegel Airport every half hour daily from 5 AM until 11:30 PM. The ride takes 35 minutes and costs DM 5 each way. By subway from Zoo Station, take the U1 to Bismarckstraße and transfer to the U7 heading toward Rathaus Spandau. Alight at Jakob-Kaiser-Platz and catch Bus 9 or 109. A taxi from the center costs around DM 25.

If you're traveling by taxi from the airports, agree on a fare—or at least get a ballpark figure—before leaving. Airport taxis are notorious for charging too much or driving in circles to jack up the rate.

Schönefeld Airport is 24 kilometers (15 miles) south of East Berlin's center. Fortunately, both the S9 and S10 make the trip every 30 minutes or so from Alexanderplatz, toward Flughafen Schönefeld. A taxi from East Berlin costs upward of DM 50.

BY TRAIN Berlin has four major train stations. If you're coming from western Germany, odds are you'll end up at the central Zoo Station, the city's busiest hub. From points east you're likely to end up in East Berlin's Friedrichstraße Station. All stations are served by Berlin's extensive subway network, so don't worry about making a connection or finding the city center. To avoid a large "I've missed my train" headache, pick up a timetable (DM 3) at any ticket window. Since unification, East Germany's Deutsche Reichsbahn (DR) and West Germany's Deutsche Bundesbahn (DB) train networks have been roughly integrated. This means that InterRail passes and Eurailpasses are now accepted throughout unified Germany, and that stations on either side of the former border sell tickets for any and all destinations. The only lingering difference, at least for the moment, is that only West Berlin stations sell the 10-day Berlin Saver Ticket, good for a 33% reduction on all fares. For German-language information, dial 030/19419 daily between 8 AM and 7 PM.

➢ **BAHNHOF ZOOLOGISCHER GARTEN (ZOO STATION)** • Zoo Station (Hardenbergpl., tel. 030/19419) is Berlin's principal train station, handling the bulk of trains to Western European cities. Destinations include: Bonn (two trains per day, DM 130), Dresden (three per day, DM 50), Frankfurt (two per day, DM 125), Hamburg (three per day, DM 67), Leipzig (three per day, DM 42), and Munich (four per day, DM 133). International destinations include: Amsterdam (two per day), Moscow (one per day), Prague (three per day), and Warsaw (two per day).

Zoo Station marks the center of Berlin and is within easy walking distance of some major tourist sights. Moreover, it's also a main hub for the U- and S-Bahn, the city's subway and commuter rail systems. The bottom line: If you're confused or lost, head for Zoo Station and regroup. Inside is a tourist desk (*see* Visitor Information, *above*), a bureau de change, a 24-hour post office with international phones, a luggage desk, and a late-night cafeteria. To reach the city center exit onto Hardenbergplatz (by Track 1) and head left. Within five minutes you'll stumble into Europa Center, Breitscheidplatz, and the Ku'damm.

➢ **BAHNHOF FRIEDRICHSTRAßE STATION** • Until the Hauptbahnhof is renovated, Bahnhof Friedrichstraße (Friedrichstr., tel. 030/94533) is East Berlin's principal train terminal. (Check train information carefully. At press time, renovation of the Hauptbahnhof was nearly complete.) Destinations from Friedrichstraße Station include: Dortmund (two trains per day, DM 165), Dresden (three per day, DM 50), Hannover (three per day, DM 65), Kassel (three per day, DM 86), Köln (two per day, DM 134), and Moscow (one per day). The station overlooks the River Spree, a few blocks north of Unter den Linden, East Berlin's main drag. It's also close to Oranienburgerstraße, where you'll find a few good bars and pensions. Inside the station are a tourist desk, a cafeteria, newsdealers, and a luggage counter. By Track 2 there's an S-Bahn and U-Bahn stop.

➢ **HAUPTBAHNHOF** • Formerly East Berlin's principal station, the Hauptbahnhof (Bahnhofsvorpl., tel. 030/312–5647) is presently undergoing serious renovations, although the tourist desk, bureau de change, cafeteria (daily until 9 PM), and ticket windows are still open. You can catch the S-Bahn near Tracks 9 and 10. Destinations from the Hauptbahnhof include: Frankfurt (two trains per day, DM 125), Hannover (three per day, DM 64), Leipzig (five per day, DM 42), Moscow (one per day), Prague (four per day), and Vienna (two per day).

➢ **LICHTENBERG** • Located in East Berlin, Lichtenberg (Bahnhofstr., tel. 030/871–2334) handles the bulk of traffic to the former GDR as well as destinations in many Eastern European countries. Destinations from Lichtenberg include: Bucharest (one train per day), Budapest (two per day), Chemnitz (four per day, DM 70), Copenhagen (two per day), Cottbus (three per day, DM 15), Dresden (three per day, DM 50), Eisenach (three per day, DM 80), Erfurt (three per day, DM 70), Leipzig (five per day, DM 42), and Prague (two per day). Inside this small, decrepit station you'll find a cafeteria, newsdealers, and a luggage desk. The station is a long haul from most anywhere you'll want to be, so hop on the S- or U-Bahn and head for the city center.

BY BUS The **Zentralen Omnibus-Bahnhof** (ZOB), Berlin's main bus depot, is a grimy pit infested with drunks and junkies—strongly *not* recommended. If you must persist, the ZOB offers service to most major German cities, including those in the former GDR. Fares cost about 10% less than for a train, but take roughly twice the time. All Verkehrsamt tourist offices (*see* Visitor Information, *above*) carry timetables and price information, or contact the ZOB directly. *Masurenallee at Meßedamm, tel. 030/301–8028 or 030/302–5294. Bus 149 from Zoo Station to Meßedamm.*

HITCHING Hitching from Berlin is quite easy, though you'll face stiff competition from locals during summer. Heading west or south toward Hannover, Frankfurt, and Munich, hop on the S1 or S3, alight at Wannsee Station, and follow the signs to Drei Linden. Within a kilometer (⅔ mile) you'll come across Autobahn A–115. For northern destinations like Hamburg and Kiel take the U6 to Tegel Station and follow the signs to Route E–26. For southeastern destinations, take the S-Bahn to Potsdam Stadt Station and, for Leipzig and Chemnitz, follow the A–9/A–10 signs; for Dresden and Prague, the A–10/A–13 signs.

BY MITFAHRZENTRALE Ride-sharing is a cheap way to get around. If you're in Berlin for a few days, stop in early at this office and see who's offering rides to where, when, and for how much. The service itself is free, but typically you'll be asked by the driver to split the cost of gas. Occasionally you may find some lonely soul offering a free ride. Destinations offered vary from week to week. Sometimes you'll find rides as far as Paris or Prague; sometimes to Leipzig or Munich. *Ku'damm Eck, Kurfürstendamm 227, 3rd floor, tel. 030/882–7604. Open Mon.–Sat. 9–5.*

GETTING AROUND

The Berlin subway system is a complex group of arteries that course through all major sections of the city. The city's 150 bus routes serve as capillaries to the subway and can put you within walking distance of virtually any point in town. One ticket costs DM 3 and gives unlimited access to every bus and subway for two hours. A pack of four tickets costs DM 10.40. A better deal is the **Berlin Ticket** (DM 12), valid for 24 hours of unlimited bus and subway travel. Better yet is the six-day **Berlin Pass** (DM 28), good for unlimited travel between Monday and Saturday. Purchase tickets from a bus driver or from machines at subway stations. The Berlin Ticket and Pass, however, can be purchased only at the main offices of **Berliner Verkehrsbetriebe (BVG),** which manages Berlin's subway and bus network. *Kleistpark U-Bahn station, tel. 030/871–*

8999. Open Mon.–Sat. 9–6. Hardenbergpl., in front of Zoo Station, tel. 030/216–5088. Open Mon.–Sat. 9–6, Sun. 10–4.

In general, the transportation system is prompt, clean, and safe. Maps are posted at every stop and station and on all trains. Except for night buses, waits greater than 10 minutes are uncommon. Late at night, shady figures often lurk around dark subway tunnels and remote bus stops, especially in East Berlin. Stay alert, look mean as hell, then think about hailing a taxi. **Trolley cars** still operate in East Berlin, but BVG hopes to eliminate them by 1994—the trolley system is simply too old and decrepit. In the meantime, they accept all the above tickets and operate daily between 6 AM and midnight, less frequently on Sunday. Inquire at a BVG or tourist office for route maps and the latest details.

BY SUBWAY Berlin has two types of subway—the underground **U-Bahn** and the aboveground **S-Bahn.** Both accept the same tickets, and operate during the same hours (4 AM–1 AM). On weekends, however, the U1 (Zoo Station–Schöneberg—Kreuzberg) and U9 (Wilmersdorf–Ku'damm–Zoo Station) operate all night.

Friedrichstraße Station, Alexanderplatz, and Berlin Hauptbahnhof handle the largest amount of subway traffic. However, the **Bahnhof Zoologischer Garten** (Zoo Station) is usually considered the center of the center. It's not only within easy walking distance of the Tiergarten, the Ku'damm, and Schöneberg, but it also handles six different U- and S-Bahn lines. If you're confused or lost, head straight here. Outside on Hardenbergplatz, a subway information booth stocks maps, sells tickets, and consoles overwhelmed travelers.

BY BUS Berlin has over 150 different bus lines. At some point, most West Berlin routes run past Zoo Station. In East Berlin, the busiest bus hub is Alexanderplatz. Standard operating hours are 6 AM–1 AM daily. Buses marked with an "N" are so-called night owls and run all night. "N" bus stops are recognizable by the green and yellow tabs atop the streetside stands. Pick up a comprehensive route map from one of BVG's offices. From Zoo Station the most useful lines are: 146 (Kantstraße–Savignyplatz–Wilmersdorf), 119 (Ku'damm–Charlottenburg), and 129 (Joachimstalerstrabe–Rathaus Schöneberg).

BY TAXI BMW and Mercedes taxis—only in Germany. The standard fare is DM 3.50 plus an additional DM 1.70 per kilometer (2/3 mile), DM 2.50 after midnight. Add DM .50 for each bag you plunk in the trunk. Expect to pay around DM 20 to travel from East Berlin's Alexanderplatz to Zoo Station; DM 25 from Tegel Airport to the city center; and DM 15 from Zoo Station to Kreuzberg. Cabs line up outside the airports, major train stations, and in front of many luxury hotels. If you're having trouble hailing a taxi, try phoning for one (tel. 030/6902, 030/21660, 030/261026, or 030/3646).

BY BICYCLE Because many locals commute on bikes, paths are everywhere and many street corners have signal lights especially for cyclists. Streets in the center of town are a bit dangerous for people on two wheels, so look out for the redbrick strips

Riding Without a Ticket?

When you board a bus in Berlin, the driver stamps the time on the blank space of your ticket. U- and S-Bahn stations have little four-foot red boxes that do the stamping. Don't think you can just waltz on a train, ignore those boxes, and save yourself some beer money. You may never cross paths with one of Berliner Verkehrsbetriebe's (BVG) humorless controllers, but if you do you'll pay a DM 40 fine on the spot if you don't have a stamped ticket. Pleading ignorance or poverty only makes them mad.

Berlin Public Transit System

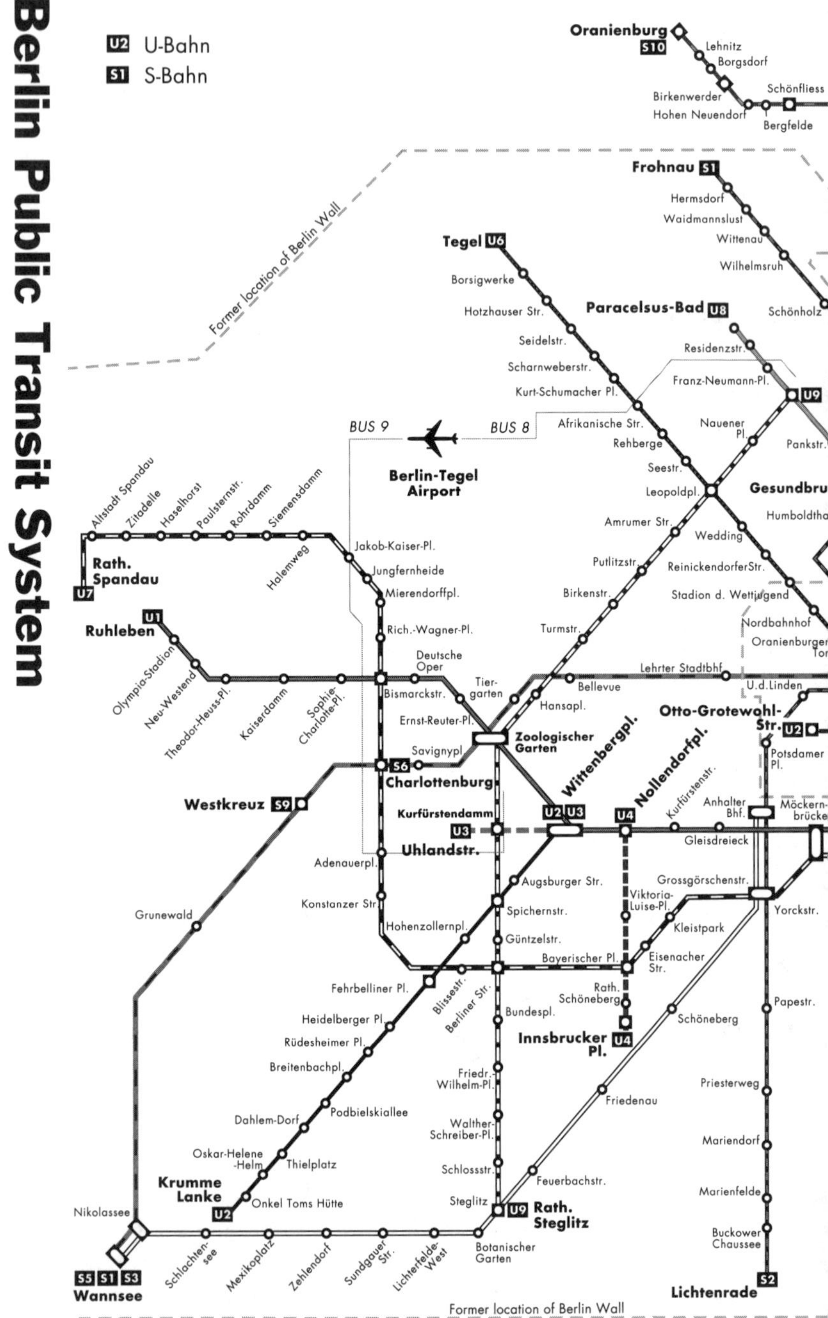

Berlin Public Transit System

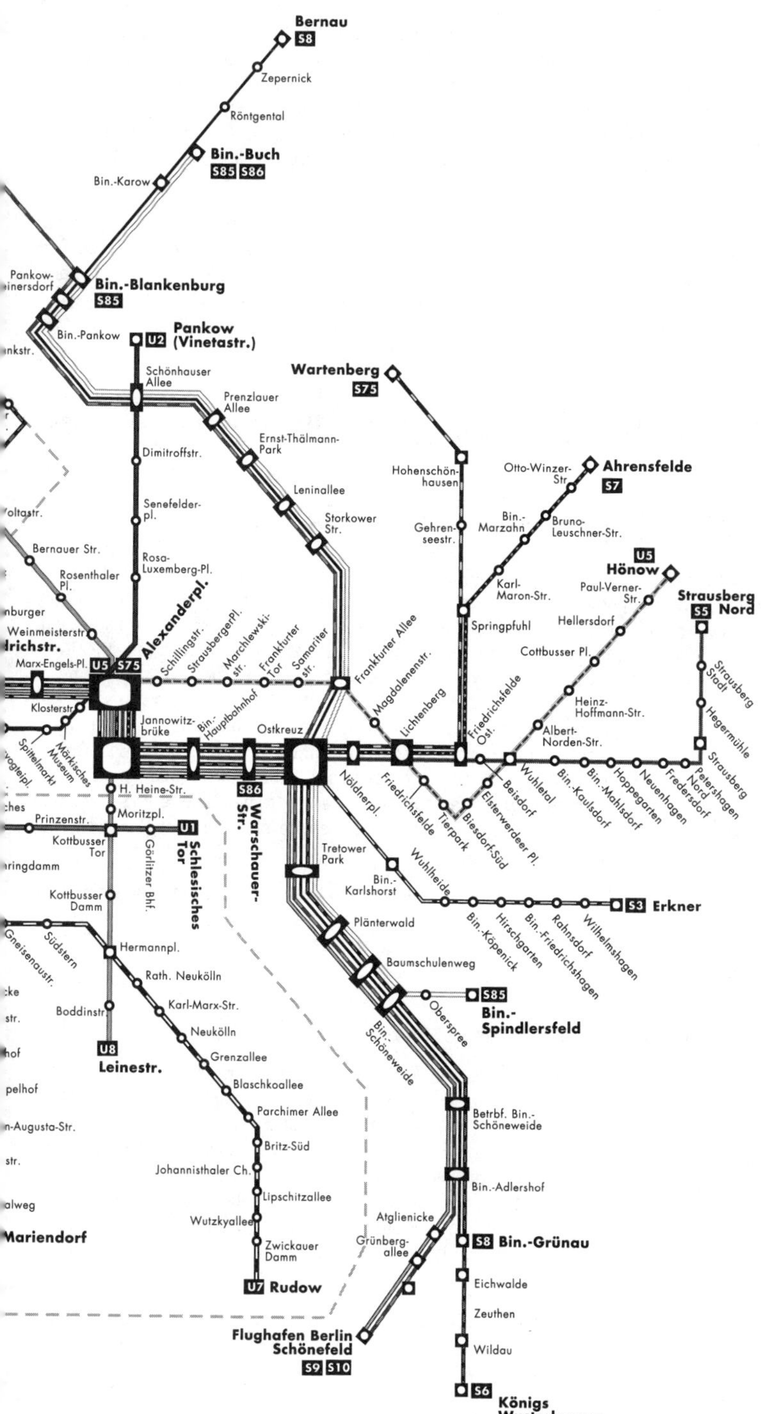

on the sidewalk. These mean cyclists can legally ride among pedestrians. If you don't see red, you belong in the street. Bicycling is best, however, in the suburbs or in one of Berlin's vast public parks. Both the Tiergarten and Grunewald (*see* Parks and Gardens, *below*) have bike-only paths that meander through the trees. Other scenic paths are listed in the *Berlin Bike Atlas* (DM 3–DM 6), an English-language guide that details the city's most popular routes. It's available at the tourist office and most bike shops. To bring your bike on the subway you must first purchase a DM 2 bike pass from a BVG office.

Fahrradbüro (Hauptstr. 146, s. of Kleist Park, tel. 030/784–5562) rents 10- and 18-speed bicycles for DM 12 per day, DM 50 per week. You have to show your passport and leave a DM 50 deposit. The **Räderwerk** (Körtestr. 14, by U-Bahn station Südstern, tel. 030/691–8590) offers similarly priced rentals. If you're headed for Grunewald, there's a rental stand (tel. 030/811–5829) in the Grunewald S-Bahn station; 18-speeds fetch DM 13 per day.

Where to Sleep

As a rule, Berlin's hotels cost between DM 110 and DM 150 per person per night—well beyond the reach of most budget travelers. A better bet are Berlin's pensions and hostels, most of which are priced between DM 30 and DM 45 per person. Unfortunately, these are often scattered in the suburbs rather than in the city center, which makes it difficult to strike a balance between budget price and prime location. Witness **Wilmersdorf,** a middle-class enclave situated 15 minutes from the center by subway. It has a few moderately priced (DM 70–DM 80) pensions, but you'll end up spending a good deal of time on the U-Bahn. Instead, try the lively **Kreuzberg** district, bordered by what remains of the Wall on the eastern extreme of West Berlin. It, too, is 15–20 minutes from the city center by subway, yet it's the sort of self-contained neighborhood that's popular with punks, drunks, and poets—an ideal spot if raucous nightlife is more important than proximity to Berlin's museums. Another option is **Charlottenburg,** located within walking distance of Zoo Station and the Ku'damm. For some reason, pensions and hostels are extremely scarce in **Schöneberg** and **East Berlin.** The only thing you'll find in either are private rooms, lots of them, bookable through any tourist office.

If you're confused or arrive late, your best bet is to head for the **Bahnhofsmission** (*see* Hostels, *below*), or one of Berlin's tourist offices. For a DM 3–DM 5 fee, these offices can arrange accommodation in a pension, hostel, or private room for DM 30–DM 50 per night.

CHARLOTTENBURG

Charlottenburg encompasses most of West Berlin's major attractions and is within walking distance of the city's museums, gardens, and fashionable shopping avenues. On the downside, there's not a lot of alternative nightlife here, only neon cafés (popular with wealthy Berliners) and seedy bars (popular with crackheads and heroin addicts). To get here, take the subway to either Zoologischer Garten (a.k.a. Zoo Station), the Ku'damm, or the S-Bahn station at Savignyplatz. A large number of pensions are located on Kantstraße near Savignyplatz.

Charlottenburg is convenient to the major train stations, is well served by S- and U-Bahn, and has the best selection of budget accommodation in the city.

UNDER DM 65 **Centrum Pension Berlin.** Most guests keep to themselves and the family that runs this pension strictly enforces a 10 PM rule of silence. However, they don't mind if you come home late so long as you tiptoe in quietly. Competitive rates and prime location on Kantstraße, two blocks north of Ku'damm, make reservations a must. Doubles go for DM 62, singles DM 45. Breakfast is an additional DM 7.50. *Kantstr. 31, tel. 030/316153. 6 rooms, some with bath.*

Hotelpension Bialas. This place is top-rate—a surprisingly elegant pension that charges under DM 65 for a grand double room. Most rooms have large bay windows and plush red-velvet furniture. Some have sinks, though clean communal bathrooms are spread throughout. *Carmerstr. 16, tel. 030/312–5025. From Zoo Station, walk w. down Hardenbergstr. and turn left on Steinpl. 26 rooms, some with bath.*

UNDER DM 85 **Hotel Charlottenburger Hof.** This friendly pension is in the heart of Charlottenburg, just around the corner from bus and subway lines at Bahnhof Charlottenburg (S3 and U7). All rooms have a private bath and cable television, along with comfortable beds and a good view of the street. The surrounding blocks offer a wide selection of shops, eateries, and dive bars. Doubles start at DM 80. Add DM 5 for breakfast. *Stuttgarter Pl. 14, tel. 030/324–4819. 45 rooms, all with bath.*

Pension Alexis. This quiet, family-oriented place is only 10 minutes by foot from Zoo Station. The spacious rooms are comfortable, if a bit grandmotherly (i.e., furniture that seems too nice to sit on). Doubles start at DM 85. *Carmerstr. 15, tel. 030/312–5144. From Zoo Station walk w. down Hardenbergstr. and turn left at Steinpl. 4 rooms.*

UNDER DM 100 **Hotel-Pension Majesty.** The rooms are small but comfortable, and most come with a phone and a safe. Good restaurants abound in this quiet neighborhood, and Zoo Station is a 15-minute walk away. Doubles cost DM 75–DM 145 depending on the season (more in summer) and whether you want a good view. *Mommsenstr. 55, tel. 030/323–2061. Walk or take Bus 149 from Zoo Station to Leibnizstr. and turn left. 55 beds, some with bath. Wheelchair access.*

Hotel-Pension Stadt Tilsit. This 65-bed pension is a meeting ground for travelers, with clean rooms and comfy beds. Location is its best asset, just a few steps from the Wilmersdorferstraße U-Bahn station. There are a couple of strip bars nearby, but the streets are well lit and relatively safe. A semistrict 11 PM curfew means you may have to warn or haggle with the management to stay out late. Doubles start at DM 100 and peak at DM 115. *Stuttgarter Pl. 9, tel. 030/323–1027. 27 rooms, some with bath.*

Pension Knesebeck. This family-run pension sits in a quiet middle-class neighborhood, only 10 minutes by foot from Zoo Station. Rooms are spacious, and the friendly staff has been known to give price breaks to poor travelers. Doubles, including breakfast, start at DM 100. *Knesebeckstr. 86, tel. 030/317255. 12 rooms, some with bath.*

Pension Viola Nova. This pension is very modern by Berlin standards—the sort of place you'd go with your parents. The sunny, spotless rooms contrast sharply with the building's tired-looking exterior. Double rooms cost DM 100 per night, and all have comfortable beds and writing desks. Breakfast is an additional DM 9.50. Check in before 7 PM. *Kantstr. 146, tel. 030/316457. 9 rooms, none with bath.*

KREUZBERG

The Kreuzberg district is an alluring option, mostly because it has a reputation for being an offbeat quarter filled with all sorts of cultural oddities. It's also a low-income working neighborhood, as evidenced by the number of faceless apartment buildings. You should probably stay elsewhere if you're conservative at heart, a woman traveling alone, or someone who doesn't feel comfortable among large crowds of drunken teens. Otherwise, the Kreuzberg is a good place to soak up the seedy side of Berlin. Unfortunately, pensions and hotels are scarce. Your best strategy is to head for a tourist office and request a private room, thankfully something this district does not lack.

Berlin Lodging

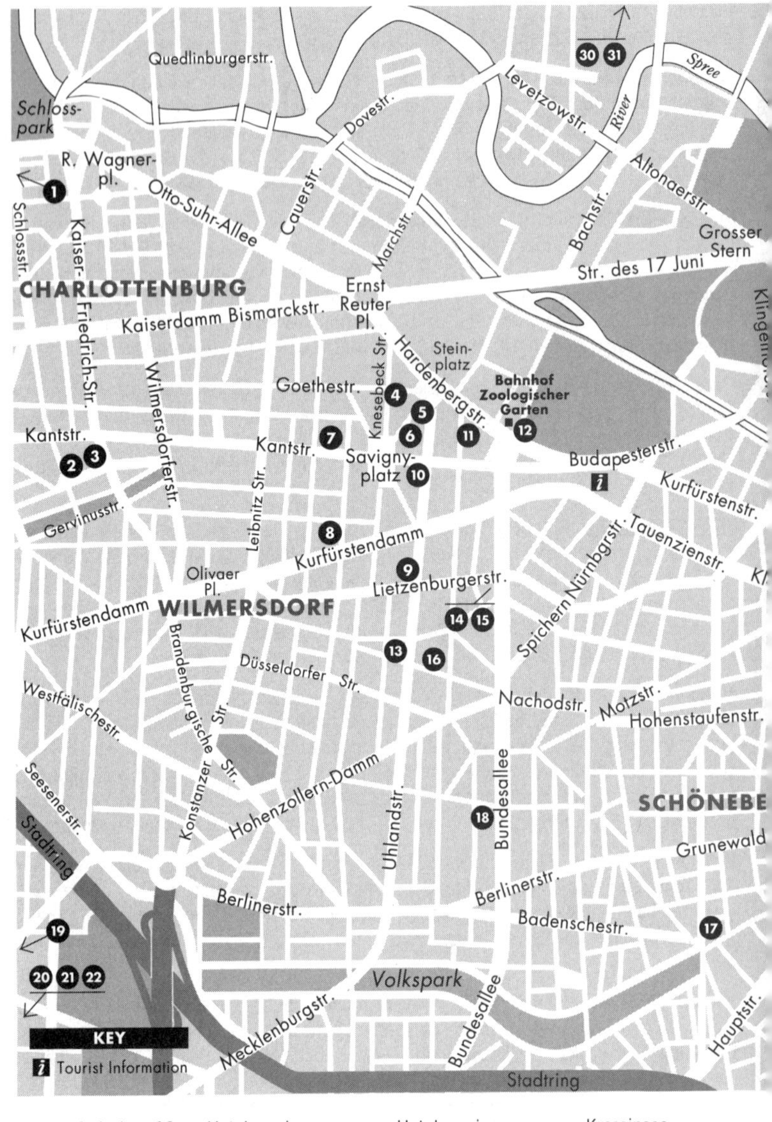

Bahnhofmission, **12**

Campsite Haselhorst, **1**

Centrum Pension Berlin, **7**

Dreilinden, **21**

Gästehaus der Fürst-Donnersmarck-Stiftung, **30**

Hotel Charlottenburger Hof, **3**

Hotel Transit, **26**

Hotelpension Bialas, **5**

Hotelpension Elton, **16**

Hotel-Pension Majesty, **8**

Hotelpension München, **18**

Hotel Pension Pariser Eck, **13**

Hotel-Pension Stadt Tilsit, **2**

Hotelpension Uhlietz, **14**

Hotelpension von Oertzen, **15**

Jugendgästhaus am Wannsee, **20**

Jugendgästhaus am Zoo, **11**

Jugendgästhaus Berlin, **23**

Jugendherberge Ernst Reuter, **31**

Jugendhotel am Tierpark, **29**

Kladow Camping, **22**

Krossinsee International Camping, **28**

Pension Alexis, **6**

Pension am Elsterplatz, **19**

Pension Iris, **9**

Pension Knesebeck, **4**

Pension Kreuzberg, **25**

Pension Süd-West, **24**

Berlin Lodging

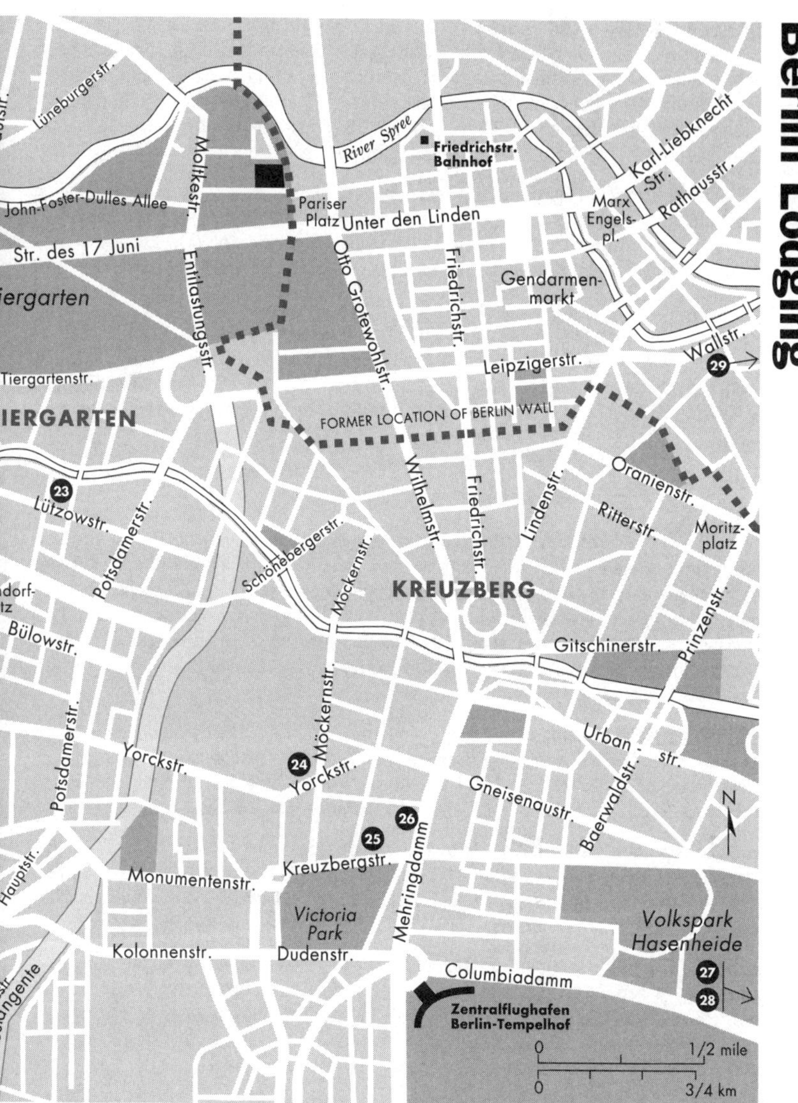

Pension Viola Nova, **10**

Studentenhotel Berlin, **17**

Touristenhaus Grünau, **27**

UNDER DM 100 **Hotel Transit.** This large, surprisingly upscale pension near Kreuzberg Hill and Viktoriapark offers comfortable doubles that each come equipped with a television and a small safe for valuables. You can do laundry in the pension's washers for DM 8 per load. The clientele is an odd mix of German families, foreign backpackers, and students. Doubles cost DM 95, breakfast included. *Hagelbergerstr. 53–54, tel. 030/785–5051. U7 to Yorckstr. 50 rooms, some with bath.*

Pension Kreuzberg. This pension offers the best of both worlds: It's close to some great clubs, but also sits on a quiet, tree-lined street. Even better, each spacious double room (from DM 85) has its own bath. *Großebeerenstr. 64, tel. 030/251–1362. U6 or U7 to Mehringdamm; walk w. on Yorckstr. to Großebeerenstr. 13 rooms, all with bath.*

Pension Süd-West. This pleasantly run-down pension lies in the heart of West Kreuzberg within reach of the district's many bars and cafés. Typical of Kreuzberg, the rooms are small and a bit damp. Doubles start at DM 75. *Yorckstr. 80A, tel. 030/785–8033. U7 to Mehringdamm and walk w. on Yorckstr. 8 rooms, none with bath.*

WILMERSDORF

Wilmersdorf is one of West Berlin's refined neighborhoods—a very quiet, very residential quarter bordered by the Ku'damm in the north and Schöneberg in the east. There aren't many official sights here, nor much nightlife, but it's a good escape from the noisy grind of the city center. Another plus is the number of reasonably priced pensions in the area, incentive enough to put up with the 20-minute subway ride to Berlin's livelier sections. To reach Wilmersdorf from Zoo Station, take the U9 south toward Berlinerstraße.

UNDER DM 80 **Hotelpension Elton.** This family-run hostel sits on a quiet side street away from the noise of the city. Rooms are well kept, but the communal bathroom has seen better days. Doubles cost DM 80. Add DM 5 for breakfast. *Pariser Str. 9, tel. 030/883–6155. From Zoo Station, Bus 249 to Pariser Str. 14 beds, none with bath.*

Hotelpension von Oertzen. This is one of the cheapest pensions in Berlin. Doubles start at DM 70 and singles at DM 50; breakfast is DM 8. It's located on a noisy street, however, so bring earplugs. *Lietzenburgerstr. 76, tel. 030/883–3964. From Zoo Station, Bus 249 to Lietzenburgerstr. 30 rooms, some with bath.*

UNDER DM 100 **Hotelpension München.** You won't find many budget travelers here, only a handful of German families on holiday. Needless to say, it's quiet and refined, with doubles fetching DM 70–DM 115, depending on whether you want a view and/or a private bathroom. Add DM 8 if you want breakfast. *Güntzelstr. 62, tel. 030/854–2226. U9 to Güntzelstr. 17 rooms, some with bath.*

Hotelpension Pariser Eck. The Eck's best feature is its location, on a safe and quiet side street only a few minutes south from the Ku'damm. All rooms come with a television and view of the street below. Some are quite large. Doubles cost DM 95, breakfast included. *Pariserstr. 19, tel. 030/881–2145. From Zoo Station, Bus 249 to Pariserstr. 30 rooms, some with bath.*

Hotelpension Uhlietz. This 92-bed pension is popular with all sorts of travelers, mostly because it receives numerous referrals from the tourist office. If you're put off by its semi-institutional look or the price—doubles start at DM 98—head next door to the cheaper Hotelpension von Oertzen *(see above). Lietzenburgerstr. 77, tel. 030/883–6177. From Zoo Station, Bus 249 to Lietzenburgerstr. 45 rooms, some with bath.*

Pension am Elsterplatz. To make up for its poor location—it's a 20- to 30-minute bus ride from the Ku'damm—this pension provides laundry facilities (DM 8 per load), a television in every room, and a helpful, friendly staff. Doubles start at DM 85, but breakfast costs an outrageous DM 20, so provide your own. *Plönerstr. 25, tel. 030/826–2880. From Gedächtniskirche, Bus 129 e. to Joachimpl., then walk southeast down Berkaerstr. 18 rooms, some with bath.*

Pension Iris. This medium-size pension is about five minutes from Zoo Station at the northernmost tip of Wilmersdorf. A friendly staff presides over the large, comfy rooms. Doubles go for DM 95, breakfast not included. *Uhlandstr. 33, tel. 030/881–5770. Take U9 s. to Uhlandstr. 30 beds, some rooms with bath.*

HOSTELS

Despite curfews and daytime lockouts, Berlin's many youth hostels fill up fast during the summer. This makes sense when you realize that they charge a mere DM 15–DM 25 per bed, about half what you'll pay for a pension. Another plus is the people—mostly backpackers and students looking for a friendly conversation with like-minded travelers. On the downside, many of Berlin's youth hostels are old and worn, so expect a minimum of comfort and sometimes dismal facilities, not to mention the occasional horde of prepubescent school kids who make much too much noise. Another problem is that most hostels require an IYHF or DJH (Deutsche Jugendherbergen) membership card. You can buy these in your home country for around $25, or from **Deutsche Jugendherbergswerke's** head office (Tempelhofer Ufer 32, tel. 030/262–3024; U6 to Bismarckstr.), or sometimes from the hostel itself for around DM 30.

Bahnhofmission. The purpose of this nonaffiliated hostel is to provide a bed for travelers whose trains arrive too late to arrange proper accommodation. As the hostel gets more crowded, the staff may ask for your train ticket to ensure that you've indeed just arrived. The front desk is open all night, checkout is around 6 AM, and the maximum stay is one night. Space in a windowless, four-bed dorm runs DM 15, which includes a meager breakfast. *Zoo Station, tel. 030/313–8088. 20 beds. Wheelchair access.*

Gästehaus der Fürst-Donnersmarck-Stiftung. This hostel is a 45-minute subway ride from the city center, yet it's also one of the few that cater to the disabled. Features include ramps, wheelchair-accessible bathrooms, dorms, and eating facilities. In other respects the hostel is like most others: semi-institutional and packed with school groups during summer. It costs DM 25 per person. *Wildkanzelweg 28, tel. 030/402021. From either Tegel Station (U6) or Frohnau Station (S1), Bus 125 to Am Pilz, then walk northeast to Wildkanzelweg. Reservations advised in summer. Disabled access.*

Jugendgästhaus am Wannsee (DJH). This large hostel lies on the outskirts of Berlin near Wannsee. The surroundings are perfect for picnics and strolls, but it's a 20-minute bus or subway ride into town. The facilities are clean and basic, with space in a sprawling dorm room fetching DM 25 (including breakfast). Because it caters to youth groups, reservations are imperative during summer. *Badeweg 1, tel. 030/803–2034. S3 or S5 to Nikolassee and walk w. on Spanische Allee. 300 beds. Midnight curfew. Check-in after 3 PM. DM 20 key deposit.*

Jugendgästhaus am Zoo. This is one of Berlin's best nonaffiliated hostels, located in the heart of the city only five minutes by foot from Zoo Station. For DM 25 you get a comfortable bed in a spacious four- to six-bunk dorm room. Another bonus is the people—mostly backpackers and other young vagabonds, not giddy preteens. *Hardenbergstr. 9A, tel. 030/312–9410. Midnight curfew.*

Jugendgästhaus Berlin (DJH). Due to its prime location in the middle of town near Tiergarten, this hostel fills up quickly. Reservations are an imperative. The hostel itself is your basic no-frills block, with typically institutional though clean dorm rooms. Beds cost DM 25. *Kluckstr. 3, tel. 030/261–1097. Bus 129 from Ku'damm's Gedächtniskirche to Kluckstr. 365 beds. Closed 9 AM–noon, midnight curfew, luggage storage. DM 20 key deposit. To book more than 2 weeks in advance, call 030/262–3024.*

Jugendherberge Ernst Reuter (DJH). This hostel has a helpful staff and clean, comfy facilities, but it's far from the town center—about 5 kilometers (3 miles) north of Tegel Airport. Rooms vary in size, and the price is DM 18 for everyone under 25, DM 21 for older folk. Breakfast is included. Nature-lovers take note: Tegel Forest is across the road. *Hermsdorfer Damm 48, tel. 030/404–1610. From Tegel Station (U6), Bus 125 to Hermsdorfer Damm and Dohnensteig. 110 beds. Flexible 11 PM curfew, check-in after 3 PM. DM 20 key deposit.*

STUDENT HOUSING

Along with the youth hostels, student housing is one of the cheapest options in Berlin. Accommodation generally entails a two- to four-bed dorm room with communal cooking and bathroom facilities, and, if you're lucky, a writing desk and wardrobe. A plus is the fact that most high-rise dorms are located in the middle of student quarters, with access to cheap pubs, restaurants, and grocery stores. The three student hotels listed below all charge DM 36 per person in a double, DM 34 per person for a quad. All require a DM 20 key deposit. The dorms are open year-round, which means you'll be housed with German students during the school year and with visiting foreigners during summer. For general information and availability, contact the student hotels directly or try Verkehrsamt Berlin (*see* Visitor Information in Basics, *above*).

Student I.D.s are generally unnecessary to stay in a university dorm. The staff may ask for one if you're balding or traveling with spouse and child, but otherwise they don't seem to care.

Jugendhotel am Tierpark. This student hotel has standard four- to six-bed dorm rooms and typically weathered facilities—good in a pinch, but hardly anyone's first choice. It's in East Berlin near the Tierpark in Lichtenberg, a 25-minute ride from the city center. *Franz-Mett Str. 7, tel. 030/510–0114. U5 to Tierpark Station; walk n. on Am Tierpark, then turn left onto Franz-Mett Str. 150 beds.*

Studentenhotel Berlin. This is the most centrally located student hotel, one block from John F. Kennedy Platz and a 10-minute walk from the Ku'damm. The 165-bed hostel has standard dorm rooms and reasonably clean bathrooms, along with a communal self-service kitchen. *Meiningerstr. 10, tel. 030/784–6720. 165 beds. From Zoo Station, Bus 146 to Rathaus Schöneberg.*

Touristenhaus Grünau. This 130-bed hotel in East Berlin offers dorm-style lodging close to Schönefeld Airport, about an hour from the city center. Not surprisingly, its bare-bones rooms rarely fill up, even during summer. Surrounding the Touristenhaus are restaurants and a few student bars. *Dahmestr. 6, tel. 030/681–4422. 130 beds. S8 to Grünau, then Streetcar 86 toward Köpenick for 2 stops.*

MITWOHNZENTRALE

If you plan to stay in Berlin for an extended amount of time, contact one of the city's **Mitwohnzentrale** (apartment-share offices). These privately owned agencies arrange long-term accommodation in all sorts of places—from apartments and family homes to defunct warehouses and student dorms. Obviously, the price varies according to what you want. A typical city center apartment fetches DM 500–DM 800 per month, while a one-room studio in a warehouse can go for as little as DM 400 per month. Shop around first since commissions vary wildly from one agency to the next (anywhere from 10% to 50% of your first month's rent). Even if you're staying for less than a month, the Mitwohnzentrale can sometimes arrange rentals on a weekly basis, especially if you're traveling in a group of three or more.

Erste Mitwohnzentrale. *Sybelstr. 53, tel. 030/324–3031, fax 030/324–9977. Bus 149 from Zoo Station to Leibnizstr., then walk s. to Sybelstr. Open weekdays 10–7, weekends 11–4.*

Mitwohnzentrale. *Ku'damm Eck, 3rd floor, Kurfürstendamm 227–228, tel. 030/883051. Open weekdays 10–7, weekends 11–3.*

Mitwohnzentrale. *Holsteinischestr. 55, tel. 030/861–8222. U2 to Hohenzollernpl. Open weekdays 10–7, Sat. 10–11, Sun. 1–2.*

Mitwohnzentrale Kreuzberg. *Mehringdamm 72, tel. 030/786–6002. U6 or U7 to Mehringdamm. Open weekdays 10–7, weekends 1–2.*

CAMPGROUNDS

Berlin has four main campgrounds, all of which are far from the city center and offer undeveloped sites in reasonably rural settings. As a rule, campground bathrooms are extremely clean, the showers (DM .50) hot, and the campgrounds quiet. During summer expect to meet families, youth groups, and other vagabond travelers. Unfortunately, summer also draws the largest crowds. To ensure a spot contact the **Deutscher Camping Club** (Geisbergstr. 11, W–1000 Berlin 30, tel. 030/218–6071, fax 030/213–4416). This organization will book you into any of the campgrounds for a DM 3 fee (so will any tourist office). All campsites cost DM 5 per night plus DM 6.50 per person over the age of 16 (DM 2 per person 16 and under).

Campsite Haselhorst. It's not as picturesque as the other campgrounds (note the plethora of RVs and portable televisions), but it can't be beat for location—near Spandau Citadel and only a stone's throw from the Haselhorst U-Bahn station. The on-site restaurant and bar give campers a place other than their tents to mix and mingle. *Pulvermühlenweg, tel. 030/334–5955. U7 to Haselhorst, then walk n. on Daumstr. to Pulvermühlenweg. 80 sites. Showers (DM .50). Wheelchair access. Flush toilets.*

Drei Linden (Albrechts-Teerofen). Although the campsite is woodsy, Drei Linden is a tedious 90 minutes by bus from the city center, plus an additional 2-kilometer (1¼-mile) walk. Consider staying here only if you're sick of crowds or devoted to nature. Facilities include showers (DM .50), flush toilets, and an on-site restaurant. *Kremnitz-Ufer, tel. 030/805–1201. U2 to Oskar-Helene-Heim, then Bus 118 to Kohlhasenbrück, then walk 2 km (1¼ mi) east on Kremnitz-Ufer. 100 sites. Closed mid-Oct.–Mar.*

Kladow Camping. This 300-site campground sits in a forest by a small lake, about 50 minutes by bus from the city center. Kladow is the most rural and peaceful of Berlin's four campgrounds, though it's also the largest and best known. Expect considerable summertime crowds. Its best features may be the on-site bar, restaurant, and food shop. *Krampnitzer Weg 111, tel. 030/365–2797. From Zoo Station take Bus 149 to Wilhelmstr. and Heerstr., switch to Bus 135 and disembark at Krampnitzer Weg. 300 sites. Showers (DM .50). Wheelchair access. Flush toilets.*

Krossinsee International Camping. This East Berlin campsite lies in a beautiful wooded valley on the edge of Krossin Lake. The only problem is that it's 90 minutes from the city center. All of the camp's 100 sites are shaded and out of earshot of one another, and all have access to showers and toilets. A 15-minute walk away is the sleepy village of Schöchkwitz, where you'll find grocery stores and a beer hall. *Wernsdorferstr., tel. 030/685–8687. S8 to Grünau and transfer to Streetcar 86 (eastbound); at end of line walk 2 km (1¼ mi) e. on Wernsdorferstr. 100 sites. Wheelchair access.*

ROUGHING IT

Sad to say, Berlin is not a good city for roughing it. Junkies and prostitutes often camp out on the Ku'damm, and there are always a few drunks passed out in Kreuzberg alleyways. If you're looking for something a bit safer, the only reasonable option is **Zoo Station.** This stays open until 2 AM, after which you can head across the street to **McDonald's,** to chain-smoke until the doors close at 4 AM. You're basically forced onto the street for the next hour, but Zoo Station reopens at 5 AM, when you can once again crash on a stiff wooden bench. All in all, it's a grim way to pass the night.

Another option is to take a late-night bus tour of the city. Night-owl buses operate all night, and one ticket buys you a round-trip journey—good for at least 90 minutes of bumpy sleep (sit close to the driver, and leave your bags locked somewhere else). Sleeping in the Tiergarten is a bad, bad idea, especially if you don't like being mauled by homeless heroin addicts. If you're penniless and desperate, try begging for mercy at the Bahnhofmission (*see* Hostels, *above*) inside Zoo Station. Beds run DM 15 per night, but you may get a free cot with some calculated pleading.

Food

Berlin is a haven for cheap eating. This is less true of an area like the Ku'damm, but otherwise it takes little effort to find a reasonable and wholesome place to eat. Every district in Berlin is littered with streetside Imbiß stands, and most offer sausages and fries or ethnic specialties like curry and falafel for under DM 10. The only way to eat more cheaply is to buy it yourself, either from a local grocer or an open-air market. Markets are less common in East Berlin, but in the western half look for weekend produce markets near Viktoriapark in Kreuzberg, near Kleistpark in Schöneberg, and sometimes in the Tiergarten.

You'll find Berlin's best selection of restaurants in Charlottenburg, which boasts hundreds of cheap student dives and a good selection of more upscale eateries. If you're in the mood to follow your nose rather than a guidebook, take the U9 to Savignyplatz, with its host of ethnic Imbisses, beer halls, and cafés. Schöneberg is another good district for ethnic eateries, particularly Indian, and for upscale restaurants with names like Chez Roland and Café Continental. You get a totally different experience in the Kreuzberg, a district famed for its Turkish street stands and offbeat cafés. Despite unification, you'll be dependent on East Berlin's rather bland and characterless tourist restaurants, a legacy of communism that may not be exorcised for a few more years.

CHARLOTTENBURG

Charlottenburg offers the widest variety of eating places in Berlin. Most everything along the Ku'damm is overpriced and geared for tourists, so head instead to **Savignyplatz** and the streets that border it, particularly **Grolmanstraße** and **Knesebeckstraße.** These are littered with cheap Imbisses, usually Indian or Middle Eastern. A good choice is **Ashoka-Imbiß** (Grolmanstr. 51, open daily 11 AM–midnight), a tiny Indian dive five minutes southeast of Savignyplatz. Even though the floors are covered with a thick layer of muck, the curry dishes (DM 7) and vegetarian *soja kurmma* (DM 6) are dependably good. Also check out some of the more refined restaurants along Kantstraße and Kaiserdamm. Typical of this category is **Cour Carrée** (Savignypl. 12, tel. 030/443-6552, open daily until 10 PM), a candle-lit French restaurant decorated in Louis XIV style. A full meal runs DM 30 per person, not including wine (DM 20–DM 100).

UNDER DM 10 **Einhorn.** This mainly vegetarian Imbiß serves everything from broccoli quiche (DM 9) to vegetarian lasagna (DM 7.40). The portions aren't huge but the food is tasty and the grease content low. Most people order to go, since there is only a handful of tables inside. Note the early 6:30 PM closing. *Mommsenstr. 2. S-Bahn to Savignypl. and walk s. on Bleibtreustr.*

Taj Mahal. The food in this small Indian restaurant is top-rate, ranging from curried vegetables (DM 8) to lamb *saag* (lamb with spinach; DM 10). Unfortunately, the Spartan dining room is uncomfortably cramped. *Grolmanstr. 12. From Savignypl. walk southeast on Grolmanstr.*

UNDER DM 15 **Bella Italia.** This Italian café serves large portions of food at ultralow prices. You can often hear the Italian family that runs the place singing, yelling, and laughing in the kitchen. As you'd expect, pizza (DM 5–DM 17) and pasta (DM 7–DM 10) dominate the menu. Also try one of the salads—Caesar, chef, and standard green—which are chock-full of good stuff and priced under DM 12. *Pestalozzistr. 84, tel. 030/312–3549. From Savignypl. walk w. down Kantstr., turn right on Bleibtreustr., left on Pestalozzistr. Open daily 1–11 PM.*

La Piazza. One of several indoor/outdoor cafés surrounding Savignyplatz, La Piazza serves Italian and German meals at bargain prices. Sit under the shade of huge umbrellas and sip coffee (DM 3), or feast on a salami, mushroom, and green pepper pizza (DM 8), the house specialty. *Savignypl. 13, tel. 030/312–3990.*

Time Square. This place falls somewhere between Taco Bell and Chuck E. Cheese—a bastion of Americana in the middle of Berlin. The friendly staff speaks fluent English, and the menus read like most family restaurants back in the States—hot dogs, burgers, pizza, burritos, Budweiser, and even margaritas. A standard meal runs DM 10–DM 15, plus DM 5 per beer. *Kurfürstendamm 203–205, tel. 030/881–3091.*

UNDER DM 20 **Fromme Helene.** This is a friendly, lively restaurant with a wonderfully eclectic menu. Besides traditional German fare there's a good sampling of Indonesian and Egyptian dishes. Highly recommended is the house specialty, *Trinkkeller* (DM 13.50), a mix of stir-fried meat basted in Egyptian spices. Vegetarians should try the Thai-spiced tofu lasagna (DM 9.50). *Bleibtreustr. 51, tel. 030/313–3278. Wheelchair access. No lunch.*

La Batea. This restaurant serves first-rate Latin American cuisine. Try the *carne asada* (grilled steak, DM 16), an enchilada salad (DM 12), or a meal-size empanada (DM 9), all of which are excellent by German standards. Because La Batea doubles as an art gallery it's popular with yuppies and local bohemians. *Krummestr. 42, tel. 030/317068. U1 to Wilmersdorferstr. No weekday lunch.*

Jewish Community Center. The center not only offers services for Jewish visitors, but also well-prepared kosher meals. Particularly good are the matzo brei, chicken soup, and brisket, all priced under DM 15. The place is clean and friendly, and the staff treats everyone like prodigal children who have returned home. *Fasanenstr. 79, tel. 030/884–2030. Wheelchair access. Closed Sunday.*

Restaurant Novo Skopje. You simply can't lose here, with menus in English, a wide variety of German and Macedonian dishes, and a prime location on the Ku'damm. Its specialty, a Macedonian mixed grill, allows you to sample six or seven different meats, each in a different homemade sauce, for DM 17.50. The rump steak (DM 18) is a favorite among meat eaters; the leafy Macedonian salad (DM 7.20) among vegetarians. *Kurfürstendamm 23, tel. 030/883–8549.*

EAST BERLIN

East Berlin is just starting to upgrade the quality and variety of its restaurants. You won't be served inedible slop, but the standards tend to be lower than in the western half of the city. As a rule, expect to find sausage-and-potato street stands and cement-block tourist restaurants, many of which still specialize in Eastern European cuisine (Hungarian, Polish, and Bulgarian). On the plus side, East Berlin is still relatively cheap compared with West Berlin, so it's possible to eat a full meal for DM 6–DM 10. Another plus is alcohol. East Berlin may not be leading the culinary revolution, but its beer and wine are cheaply priced and eminently drinkable.

For the moment, eating in East Berlin is more of a novelty than a recommended pursuit, especially if quality and taste are important considerations.

Most East Berlin restaurants are grouped either along **Unter den Linden,** around **Marx-Engels-Platz,** or around **Alexanderplatz.** To get here, walk through the Brandenburg Gate and continue east along Unter den Linden. From Zoo Station take the S7 east to Friedrichstraße, then any eastbound train toward Marx-Engels-Platz or Alexanderplatz.

UNDER DM 15 **City Café.** Near Brandenburg Gate, this café is typical of new eateries in postcommunist East Berlin. It's decked out with beveled mirrors and Art Deco furniture in imitation of the Ku'damm's trendiest eateries. Choose from an appealing menu of omelets, sandwiches, and salads for around DM 7. The outdoor tables are a good place to sit and watch all Berlin pass by. In the very back is a pool table. *Otto Grotewohlstr. 20, tel. 030/22198.*

Haus Budapest. Although this ancient Hungarian restaurant looks great, decorated with plush red velvet and antique oak furniture, the food borders on the bland. House specialties include meat paprikas (from DM 10) and goulash-type soups (DM 6–DM 10). *Karl-Marx-Allee 90–91, tel. 030/212–8744. From Alexanderpl. walk e. on Karl-Marx-Allee.*

UNDER DM 20 **Telecafé.** Eat in a motorized, sputnik-looking ball atop East Berlin's 365-meter-high (1,198-foot-high) Fernsehturm television and radio tower. The outer ring of tables rotates 360° every 30 minutes. Lunch in this 100-table restaurant ranges from omelets (DM 7) and sandwiches (DM 9) to cheese plates (DM 11) and fresh fruit. Dinner includes traditional German standards, mainly sausage-and-potato combinations from DM 15. Dinner reservations are a must during summer. There's a DM 5 fee to enter the tower even if you're having a meal. *Alexanderpl., Fernsehturm, top floor, tel. 030/242–3333.*

Zur Letzen Instanz. Established in 1525, this is Berlin's oldest restaurant. Its dark, old-fashioned interior contrasts nicely with East Berlin's look-alike cement districts, and the food is excellent. Try the beer-batter knockwurst for DM 12, or any one of its goulash-style soups for around DM 15. Reservations are a must during summer. *Waisenstr. 14–16, off Stralauerstr., tel. 030/212–5528. U2 to Klosterstr. and walk w. on Stralauerstr.*

UNDER DM 30 **Arkade.** One of East Berlin's more elegant restaurants, Arkade has a small indoor-outdoor café in front and an open-grill dining room in back. People often stop just for coffee and dessert on their way to the nearby Komische Oper (Comic Opera). Choose steak or grilled poultry from DM 20; soup and salads from DM 15. *Französische Str. 25, tel. 030/208–0273. From Marx-Engels-Pl. walk 1 block w. on Französische Str. Closed Sun.*

KREUZBERG

Because of the fly-by-night nature of many Kreuzberg restaurants, don't be surprised if some of the places listed below have been nailed shut by the time you arrive. On the up side, there's always something new opening here, so snoop around for the latest hot spot. A good place to start is **Oranienstraße,** Kreuzberg's unofficial main drag, lined with cafés, bars, and thrift stores. Intersecting Oranienstraße are **Moritzplatz** and **Alexandrinen Straße,** where you'll find a large number of student-run cafés. Another good area is **Viktoriapark** and, one block northeast, **Gneisenaustraße,** each boasting countless cafés and ethnic street stands. Kreuzberg is too large to walk around comfortably, so head either for Kotbusser Tor Station (U1) and Oranienstraße, or Gneisenaustraße Station (U7) and Viktoriapark.

UNDER DM 10 **Café am Ufer.** This trashy alternative bar doubles as a co-op café, which means it has a limited selection of easily prepared foods (sandwiches, soups, salads, and desserts) priced under DM 10. On weekends it does tremendous brunches—eggs, cereal, cheese, and fruit—for around DM 12 per person. *Paul-Lincke-Ufer 43–44, no tel.*

Ristorante-Pizzeria Diomira. This is one of Berlin's best Italian restaurants—ample justification for a trip to Kreuzberg. Sit outside at a sidewalk table or indoors in its dark, smoky, soothing dining room. Either way, try the spaghetti carbonara (with parmesan and bacon; DM 8) or spaghetti *amatriciana* (with spicy tomatoes and garlic; DM 8.50). There's a large selection of chocolate pastries and truffles for dessert, all priced between DM 4 and DM 8. *Stresemannstr. 60, tel. 030/262–3183. S-Bahn to Anhalter Bahnhof and exit onto Stresemannstr. Wheelchair access.*

Kreuzberg eateries come and go at a dizzying pace, mostly because they're operated on a shoestring budget or housed—sometimes illegally—in the remnants of a burned-out shop or crumbling warehouse.

Spots. Soups and salads for under DM 8 make this a great spot if you're poor or in the mood for a nongreasy meal. Most of the time its small eating area (carved from what remains of a piano factory) is bombarded with distorted guitar music, which makes conversation nearly impossible. Most patrons, however, seem content to commune privately with a mug of beer (DM 4). *Prinzenstr. 50, tel. 030/445–8781. U1 to Kotbusser Tor and walk w. on Gitschinerstr. No lunch.*

Türnagel. This small, friendly café serves a good selection of mostly vegetarian meals, from tofu omelets (DM 8) to vegetable stir-fries (from DM 10). You won't find many tourists here, only a handful of devoted locals and students. *Gneisenaustr. 56, tel. 030/334–5437. U7 to Gneisenaustr. Closed Sun.*

SCHONEBERG

The best place to get a sense of what's going on is around **Nollendorfplatz** and **Winterfeldplatz,** two open-air squares at the Ku'damm's eastern extreme. Lining these squares are dozens of Middle Eastern and Turkish eateries serving up some of the best falafel in Berlin. The area's nightlife affects both the atmosphere and hours of its restaurants; people eat out to be seen, and tiny stand-up places stay open late for hungry partyers. Schöneberg is an easy walk from the city center. From the Ku'damm's Gedächtniskirche, simply head east past Europa Center; the street becomes Kleiststraße, and Nollendorfplatz is 1 kilometer (⅔ mile) ahead. Otherwise, take the U4 directly to Nollendorfplatz or the U7 to Kleist park.

UNDER DM 10 **Café Strada.** Typical coffeehouse decor (subdued lights, marble-top tables, and literary knickknacks) complements a small menu of sandwiches and soups. Nothing here is exceptional, but it's a good place to relax and read the newspaper. Potent coffee starts at DM 3. *Potsdamer Str. 129, tel. 030/223–9004.*

Habibi. On Winterfeldplatz, this is the place to come for falafel. It stays open as late as possible to catch the last bar-hoppers and serves a wide variety of falafel from DM 5. All food is served to go. *Goltzstr. 24. U4 to Nollendorfpl.*

Rani Indischer Imbiß. This Winterfeldplatz Imbiß is popular with just about everyone. Try the chicken *sabzi* (DM 9.50) or the Indian vegetarian plate (DM 6.50), both cooked fresh and served in large portions. Like most Imbisses, the Indischer has no sit-down seating. *Goltzstr. 34. U1 or U4 to Nollendorfpl.*

UNDER DM 20 **Café Einstein.** Part coffeehouse and part French restaurant, the Einstein offers a semipricey selection of all your Gallic favorites, from roast duck (DM 20) and lamb (from DM 16) to coq au vin (from DM 18). Grab a coffee if you're not hungry and sit outdoors in the small garden. *Kurfürstenstr. 58–59, tel. 030/556–7811.*

Maharadscha. More formal than a stand-up Imbiß, this place is still relatively inexpensive for the Winterfeldplatz area. German food—mostly sausage and potatoes—is available, but stick with the Indian dishes: biryani (DM 15), lamb tandoori (DM 16), and curried vegetables (DM 8). *Fuggerstr. 21, tel. 030/216–2360. Bus 146 from Zoo Station to Fuggerstr.*

Cafés and Coffeehouses

During the 1920s and '30s, Berlin was awash with coffeehouses and cafés. These were the city's social and artistic crucibles, the meeting places for ideologues and poets, politicians and philosophers. After World War II, however, many of the city's most elegant cafés were closed and converted into public housing. Today you can still find unique coffee and dessert houses in Berlin, but the majority are covered in neon and devoted exclusively to tourism, a problem that's particularly acute along the Ku'damm. That said, Kreuzberg and Schöneberg have seen an intense proliferation of offbeat cafés since 1989. You won't find too many centuries-old hideaways, only irreverent, co-op–style spots that cater to Berlin's alternative crowd—places with thrift-shop decor and tattoo-covered servers. A more generic option is **Eduscho,** a coffee chain that sells potent espresso for under DM 2. You'll find one in the city center at Tauentzienstraße and Rahnstraße. Other branches are peppered throughout Berlin, both East and West. **Mövenpick** restaurants are also common in Berlin: They sell delicious ice cream and sweets at low prices; a cup of coffee and cake run about DM 3.

Café Bleibtreu. A seedy lowbrow café with the clientele to match, Café Bleibtreu is one of Charlottenburg's most pleasantly grimy hangouts. Most of the people here are friendly students or under-30 dropouts, so don't let the anti-American graffiti scare you away. Coffee starts at DM 3, pastries and snacks from DM 5. *Bleibtreustr. 45–46, tel. 030/212–5904. S-Bahn to Savignypl.*

Café Elephant. This Kreuzberg spot is exactly what a café should be: dark, smoky, and full of serious-looking idealists engaged in heated dialogues. Potent coffee costs DM 3.50, soups and sandwiches around DM 5. *Oranienstr. 12, no tel. U1 to Kotbusser Tor Station.*

Café Hardenberg. Flooded with light and decorated with odd-shaped tables and lamps, this subdued Charlottenburg café is a popular student hangout. Odds are good that someone here will speak fluent English. Coffee starts at DM 3, pastries and snacks from DM 4. *Hardenbergstr. 10, tel. 030/312–3330.*

Café Lure. Come here for phenomenal breakfasts (around DM 7) and thick, strong coffee. It's located in the middle of Schöneberg, just a few steps from Kleistpark and Winterfeldplatz. *Kyffhäuserstr. at Barbarossastr., tel. 030/215–7567. U-Bahn to Nollendorfpl.*

Extra Dry. This café serves women only and is a good place to come for information on Berlin's women-oriented events. The café serves only nonalcoholic drinks and easy-to-prepare snacks like sandwiches and soups. *Mommsenstr. 34., no tel. Bus 149 from Zoo Station to Wilmersdorferstr. then walk s.to Mommsenstr.*

Kleisther. A large, busy Schöneberg café that caters mostly to students. Card-playing and gossiping are the norm here. Coffee starts at DM 3. *Hauptstr. 62, tel. 030/889–4431. U-Bahn to Nollendorfpl.*

Kranzler. This is one of the most popular dessert spots along the Ku'damm. Unfortunately, it's also one of the most expensive. Kranzler's best feature is its outdoor tables, where you can sit back and watch wealthy Berliners studiously avoiding the Ku'damm junkies. *Kurfürstendamm 18–19, tel. 030/882–7578.*

Schoko-Cafe. Like Extra Dry (*see above*), this café is for women only. Set in an old, pleasantly run-down warehouse, it is quickly becoming one of Berlin's "in" spots. From September to May it operates a Turkish bathhouse (women only) next door. *Mariannenstr. 6 at Heinrichpl., tel. 030/652999.*

Exploring Berlin

Even before reunification, West Berlin was a confusing, sprawling city that took some getting used to. Rejoined with its eastern half, Berlin has now become the largest city in Europe, so prepare to be overwhelmed. Unified Berlin changes its street names like most people change their underwear, so you'll also need a detailed map, preferably the easy-to-fold *Falk Plan* (DM 6–DM 8), available at tourist offices and newsstands.

Because of Berlin's size and the sheer number of sights, your best strategy is to target a particular district rather than hopping from one "don't miss" attraction to the next. Of course, this strategy may not work if you're short on time, so consult the following section (*see* Worth Seeing, *below*) for a list of Berlin's most renowned attractions. Otherwise, depending on your energy level, you can comfortably cover one or two districts per day. For a good overview also consider a guided tour. One of the most popular is offered by **Bus-Verkehr-Berlin** (Kurfürstendamm 225, tel. 030/882–6847). Tours leave daily (weekends only in winter) from its Ku'damm office and last two to three hours; the price is DM 30 per person. Another option is one of **Kultur Kontor**'s (Savignypl. 9–10, tel. 030/310888) cultural/historical walking tours. These last three to four hours and cost DM 25 per person. Trips include "Berlin Becoming Berlin," which offers a look at the city's architectural and social development; "Berlin 1933–1945"; and "The Roaring '20s." **Wanderkreis Berlin** (Marschnerstr. 12, tel. 030/834–9977 also offers guided walking tours that emphasize the city's cultural and political heritage.

Worth Seeing

BRANDENBURGER TOR Those who watched the Berlin Wall crumble in 1989 will certainly recognize Brandenburger Tor (Brandenburg Gate), perhaps the most vivid symbol of German reunification. When the Wall was built in 1961, ostensibly as an "antifascist protection barrier," West Berliners watched in horror as their beloved city was divided and this historic gate was hidden behind a 10-foot-tall barrier (until 1989, West Berliners had to climb atop a wooden platform just to see the gate). Ironically, even though the gate belonged to the former GDR, East Berliners couldn't go anywhere near it either. It was set in no-man's-land, a narrow strip that was vigilantly patroled lest anyone try to escape to the West. On November 10, 1989, after thousands of East Germans began smashing the Wall, the Brandenburg Gate was swamped with celebrants. For weeks, East and West Berliners gathered underneath its arch to witness the collapse of communism. Television crews from around the world converged on the gate and its surrounding plaza, convinced that what they saw—Germans from both sides joined together, galvanized by a common hope—was the most potent image of change. Yet change is an unwieldy and often sobering force, which explains why some Berliners still regard Brandenburg Gate with unease. Since 1989, the gate and plaza have been transformed into an open-air flea market, a place where East Berliners come to peddle postcards. Though this plays well with foreigners, it evokes a certain bitterness among Germans.

Brandenburg Gate was built in 1791 for King Friedrich Wilhelm II, part of an original group of 14 gates that once encircled the city center. Designed by architect Carl Gotthard Langhans, it was loosely modeled on the Propylae in Athens, with massive marble columns supporting a majestically carved pediment. Its most famous decoration is the quadriga, a chariot drawn by four horses and driven by the goddess of

Berlin

Alexanderplatz, **35**
Alte Bibliothek, **22**
Altes Museum, **29**
Berliner Dom, **30**
Bebelplatz, **24**
Bertolt Brecht House and Museum, **21**
Brandenburger Tor, **18**
Breitscheidplatz, **8**
Checkpoint Charlie, **39**
Dahlem Museum Complex, **43**
Deutsche Staatsoper, **25**
Europa-Center, **9**
Hardenbergstraße, **3**
Humboldt University, **23**
Kaiser Wilhelm Gedächtniskirche, **7**
KaDeWe, **10**
Kleistpark, **12**
Kulturforum, **15**
Kurfürstendamm, **5**
Luftbrücken-denkmal, **41**
Marienkirche, **34**
Martin-Gropius-Bau, **20**
Moritzplatz, **37**
Museum für Deutsche Geschichte, **27**
Museumsinsel, **28**
Nikolaiviertel, **33**
Nollendorfplatz, **13**
Oranienstraße, **38**
Palast der Republik, **31**
Platz der Akademie, **32**
Potsdamerplatz, **19**
Prenzlauer Berg, **36**
Rathaus Schöneberg, **42**
Reichstag, **17**
St. Hedwig's Cathedral, **26**

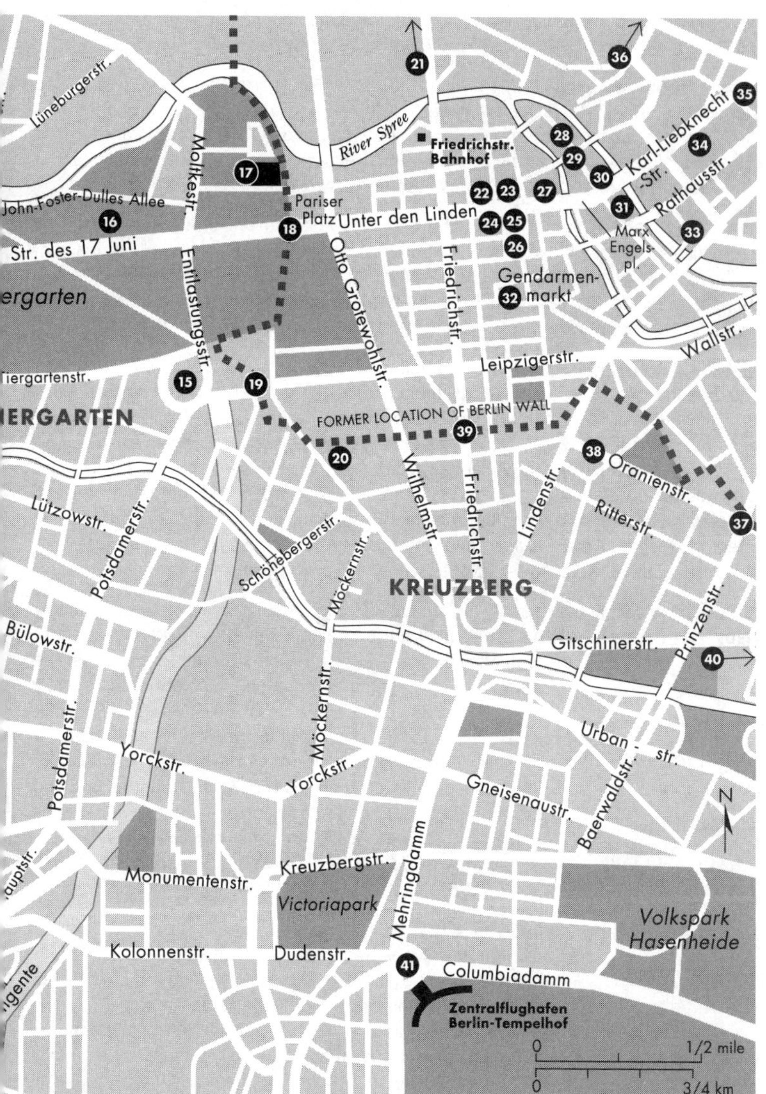

Savignyplatz, **4**
Schlesisches Tor, **40**
Schloß Charlottenburg, **2**
Siegessäule, **14**
Soviet Victory Memorial, **16**
Spandau, **1**
Zoologischer Garten, **11**
Zoo Station (Bahnhof Zoologischer Garten, **6**

peace. The sculpture was destroyed during World War II, but the original molds were rediscovered in West Berlin in 1957 and a new quadriga was cast.

Getting to Brandenburg Gate is difficult on public transportation. It's located on the Tiergarten's (*see* Districts, *below*) eastern extreme, just inside the former GDR's border. The most spectacular approach is from **Straße des 17 Juni,** a 2-kilometer-long (1¼-mile-long) avenue that cuts through the Tiergarten's center. *Str. des 17 Juni at Otto-Grotewohl-Str. Nearest S-Bahn is East Berlin's Bahnhof Friedrichstr.*

Immediately west of Brandenburg Gate you'll find what remains of the **Berlin Wall.** It's been hacked to death by souvenir hunters, but it's still an ominous reminder of Berlin's divisive history. Bring a chisel and collect your own piece of the one true wall (the police may arrest you, though) or walk its perimeter in search of the best graffiti. Highlights include: "Warning: Wet Paint" and "Last one out, turn off the lights."

CHECKPOINT CHARLIE Between 1961 and 1990, Checkpoint Charlie (Kochstr. and Friedrichstr.) was the most (in)famous crossing point between East and West Berlin. The checkpoint, one of a dozen that once broached the heavily guarded Wall, was under American control. During the Cold War, a nearby sign had this simple warning: "You are now leaving the American sector." The checkpoint itself, a wooden guard hut, was removed shortly after the Wall came down in 1989. Remaining are a grim, skeletal watchtower and a somber memorial slab dedicated to those killed in escape attempts. Also remaining is a red-and-white cement barrier used to guard against vehicles rushing the checkpoint—a favorite scenario in Hollywood spy movies.

Although the checkpoint has been dismantled, you can trace its history at the nearby **Haus am Checkpoint Charlie.** This small museum has hundreds of Cold War–era photographs and a fascinating exhibit on some ingenious escape attempts. Look for the miniature submarine that safely brought one East German across the River Spree, a hollowed-out surfboard used to smuggle another, and photos of tunnels dug under the Wall during the 1970s. Also look for short biographies of some of the 75 East Germans killed during escape attempts. The museum's gift desk sells numerous books about the wall, many in English. *Friedrichstr. 44, tel. 030/251–1031. U-Bahn to Friedrichstr. Admission: DM 5. Open daily 9 AM–10 PM.*

Behind the barrier at Checkpoint Charlie is the famous Café Adler, a lonely outpost of Western hospitality during the Cold War. Tradition held that any escaped East Berliner was entitled to a free beer at Café Adler, courtesy of an American soldier.

DAHLEM MUSEUMS The West Berlin suburb of Dahlem, 15 minutes by subway from the city center, is a quiet enclave of tree-lined streets and sleepy pubs. It's worth the trip just to escape the grimy bustle of Berlin proper, yet the suburb is best known for the **Dahlem Museum Complex,** considered one of the best in all Europe. Housed inside this gigantic gallery are eight world-class museums, each with a dizzying collection of Western art. It would take at least two full days to see everything, so concentrate instead on the main galleries: the **Gemäldegalerie** (Picture Gallery), the **Kupferstichkabinett** (Drawing and Print Collection), the **Museum fur Völkerkunde** (Ethnographic Museum), and the **Skulpturengalerie** (Sculpture Garden). All are free and open Tuesday–Friday between 9 AM and 5 PM; weekends from 10 AM. To reach the complex, take U1 from Zoo Station to Wittenbergplatz, switch to the U2 and alight at Dahlem-dorf Station. Walk south on Fabeckstraße, and enter at either Arnimallee 23–27 or Lansstraße 8.

The **Gemäldegalerie** (Arnimallee 23–27, tel. 030/83011) is Germany's foremost picture gallery, with an extensive collection of European painting from the 13th through 18th centuries. On the first floor are rooms dedicated to Dürer, Cranach, and Holbein, each organized chronologically to show the painter's development. The rooms are also organized by region: Next to the German masters gallery is the Italian masters room, with a solid collection of works by Botticelli, Titian, Giotto, and Raphael. If that's not enough, the Dutch room displays works by van Eyck, Bosch, Brueghel, and van Dyck.

On the second floor is the world's second-largest collection of Rembrandt oil canvases. More works by Rembrandt are exhibited next door in the adjacent **Kupferstichkabinett** (Arnimallee 23–27, tel. 030/83011), which features engravings and woodcuts from the 15th through 18th centuries. Along with the pen-and-ink studies by Dürer, the gallery's best feature is a series of 150 charcoal sketches by Rembrandt.

Nearby, the **Museum fur Völkerkunde** (Lansstr. 8, tel. 030/83011) is famous for its ethnographic holdings, including large sections on Asia, Africa, and North America. The museum pales in comparison with the picture gallery, although its scale-model re-creations are worth a quick look. Occupying the same building is the **Skulpturengalerie** (Sculpture Garden), which houses Byzantine and European sculpture from the 3rd through 18th centuries. Its best pieces are those from Italy, including Donatello's *Madonna and Child*, sculpted in 1422.

KULTURFORUM Berlin's art world has been forced to cope with some complex questions since unification: how to display collections that were split up in 1945; which museums should be closed; and which galleries should be renovated or expanded. The result is something akin to chaos. To solve the problem, the government has opted to shuffle much of Berlin's vast art collection into the already impressive Kulturforum, located near the Tiergarten on Kemperplatz. Prior to 1989, this large complex contained four excellent museums. With recent and scheduled additions (a fifth museum will be added by 1996), the Kulturforum will certainly rival the Dahlem and Schloß Charlottenburg collections. In the meantime, the Kulturforum is still one of Berlin's major art attractions—definitely worth a full day's exploration. Take the U2 to East Berlin's Potsdamer Platz, walk west, and cross into West Berlin (look for a hole in the Wall and climb through). The museums are straight ahead. Another option is to walk west from Brandenburg Gate along Straße des 17 Juni, turning left onto Moltkestraße.

The Kultorforum's finest attraction is the **Neue Nationalgalerie.** It's a delicate glass and steel structure, designed by Mies van der Rohe in 1966. The upper floor houses rotating exhibits of mostly contemporary art. The ground-floor gallery is dedicated to 19th- and 20th-century European and American work. The permanent collection leans heavily toward the Impressionists, from Manet and Monet to Renoir and Pissarro. Also well represented are German branches of the realist, surrealist, and Bauhaus movements. Look for lots of Courbet, Feurbach, Gropius, Grosz, and Dix, supplemented in an adjoining gallery by a hodgepodge of Paul Klee, Francis Bacon, Jasper Johns, and Salvador Dali. *Potsdamerstr. 50, tel. 030/266–2666. Admission free. Open Tues.–Fri. 9–5, weekends 10–5.*

Directly across from the Neue Nationalgalerie is the **Staatsbibliothek** (National Library). This is one of the largest libraries in Europe, with more than 4 million volumes in its cavernous vault. The building itself was designed by Berlin architect Hans Scharoun; if it looks familiar, you may have seen it in Wim Wenders's film *Wings of Desire*, which used the facade as a frequent backdrop. Inside is a small concert hall (check the notice board for performance schedules), a peaceful reading room stocked with English-language newspapers, and a tea shop. *Potsdamerstr. 33, tel. 030/2661. Admission free. Open weekdays 9–9, Sat. 9–5.*

A short walk north is the impressive **Kunstgewerbemuseum,** which houses Berlin's best collection of European arts and crafts (it may sound a bit dull, but it's not). Start on the first floor for a look at the development of medieval crafts. Exhibits range from the technical (the innards of antique clocks) to the purely decorative (handcrafted jewelry). In the basement there's a good collection of Art Deco and Bauhaus pieces. *Tiergartenstr. 6, tel. 030/266–2911. Admission free. Open Tues.–Fri. 9–5, weekends 10–5.*

For the moment, the Kulturforum's final offering is the **Musikinstrumenten-Museum.** On display are antique musical instruments ranging from a 17th-century lute to an 18th-century pneumatic organ. Even if you don't speak German, try to make the once-weekly guided tour (Saturday at 11, DM 3). The German-language tour may bore you to tears, but it's followed by a live demonstration of various instruments—perhaps the only chance you'll ever have to hear a 17th-century clavichord played live. The museum itself is housed in the Philharmonic, Berlin's dully modern concert hall. *Tiergartenstr. 1, tel. 030/254810. Admission free. Open Tues.–Fri. 9–5, weekends 10–5.*

KURFURSTENDAMM The Kurfürstendamm (or "Ku'damm") is West Berlin's most famous thoroughfare. Built during the 16th century by Elector Joachim II of Brandenburg, Kurfürstendamm means "Elector's Causeway." It originally connected Joachim's Berlin palace with his hunting lodge in Grunewald (*see* Parks and Gardens, *below*). In the 19th century, Chancellor Bismarck had it widened to 55 yards across, mostly because he felt Berlin needed a stately avenue befitting Germany's growing power, something akin to Paris's Champs Elysée. During World War II, nearly half of the Ku'damm's Baroque and Bismarck-era buildings were flattened by Allied bombs. This paved the way for the gaudy cafés and high-rises you see today, perhaps the images most commonly associated with the present street.

In its entirety, the Ku'damm stretches for 3½ kilometers (2 miles). Its liveliest section is just south of Zoo Station and the Tiergarten, near Europa Center. Here you'll find a sample of everything Berlin has to offer, from upscale boutiques to seedy sex shops. On **Breitscheidplatz,** immediately opposite Europa Center, you can find people carousing and browsing at all hours of the day—a crowd evenly divided between wealthy Berliners and junkies looking to score. This is probably the most unseemly section of the Ku'damm. Head in either direction to get a sense of the street's unique style—an eclectic mix of Baroque and fin-de-siècle elegance, and communist-era cement, all interspersed with neon signs and shopping malls.

The Ku'damm's most famous landmark is **Kaiser Wilhelm Gedächtniskirche,** opposite Europa Center on Breitscheidplatz. The church (1895) was all but destroyed during World War II, and it has been left in a war-scarred state to serve as a memorial. On one side of the neo-Romanesque bell tower stands a new, very stark chapel, designed by Egar Eierman. Inside this hexagonal structure, an exhibit of pre- and postwar photos document the church's history. *Breitscheidpl. Admission free. Open Tues.–Sat. 10–6, Sun. 11–6.*

REICHSTAG Just north of Brandenburg Gate, the imposing Reichstag (Imperial Parliament) looms into view. This bulky Renaissance-style structure was built in 1891 to house the Prussian Parliament, and performed the same function for the short-lived Weimar Republic (1919–33) following the chaos of World War I. Most people, however, associate the Reichstag with Hitler and the Nazis. On February 28, 1933, as Germany struggled with a broken economy and the Weimar Republic's warring ideologues, the Reichstag burned down under mysterious circumstances. No one's sure who actually set the fire, but the the Nazis swiftly and vociferously blamed the communists. The Nazis then overthrew the confused government, suspended the constitution, and outlawed all opposition parties. This paved the way for Hitler's Third Reich and marked the beginning of Germany's ill-fated experiment with fascism.

Sometime soon, the Reichstag will once again house the Bundestag (German Parliament), though it will take some time to move everything from Bonn to Berlin. Currently the Reichstag's west wing is home to a fascinating exhibit entitled "Questions on German History." Almost everything is labeled in German, but the Third Reich–era photographs offer an insider's look at Hitler and the Nazis. Afterward, head outside onto the large lawn that surrounds the building; odds are it will disappear soon only to be replaced with dull government buildings, so enjoy it while you can. *Pl. der Republik, no tel. From Zoo Station, Bus 100 to front steps. Nearest S-Bahn is East Berlin's Bahnhof Friedrichstr. Admission free. Open Tues.–Sun. 10–5.*

SCHLOß CHARLOTTENBURG Prior to its incorporation into Greater Berlin in 1920, Charlottenburg was one of Prussia's wealthiest principalities. This was due to King Friedrich I, the flamboyant Prussian monarch who took up residence here at the end of the 17th century. In 1695, at the request of his future queen, Sophie Charlotte, he renamed the area Charlottenburg (it was previously known as Lützenburg) and embarked on a massive building campaign. The end result was Schloß Charlottenburg, a lavish country palace graced by gardens and lakes. Though it was originally intended for the exclusive use of King Friedrich and Sophie, the palace became the city residence for all Prussian rulers. Friedrich II (a.k.a. Frederick the Great) was so enamored of the site that he commissioned a number of stately additions, including the gold-plated dome and Rococo wings.

Over the centuries, the complex continued to evolve under the direction of each new ruler. As such, Schloß Charlottenburg is representative of nearly every major stylistic trend in Germany, including Baroque, Rococo, and even Bauhaus. Entering the grounds on foot, you'll first notice the prim **Court of Honor,** dominated by an equestrian statue of Elector Joachim of Brandenburg, and the 156-foot domed tower that marks the palace's main entrance. Much of the complex was destroyed during World War II, but almost everything has been painstakingly restored. Inside, on the first floor, are the chambers of Friedrich and Sophie, decorated in lavish period style. Other highlights include the ground-floor **Oak Gallery,** with a solid collection of 18th- and 19th-century landscape paintings. Next door in the **New Wing** there's a permanent collection of works by Dürer and the 19th-century master Caspar David Friedrich, considered the founder of Germany's romantic movement.

Unfortunately, the only way to see the palace is on a guided tour (included in the DM 8 admission). These leave every hour, on the hour, between 9 and 4. Afterward, spend some time exploring the palace's grounds. They're quite large and easily worth an afternoon, especially when the weather is good. Along with the lake and shaded walking paths, check out the 18th-century **Belvedere House,** overlooking the River. Today it contains a reasonably priced tea shop. Just beyond this is **Schinkel Pavillion,** which houses paintings by Caspar David Friedrich, and some fin-de-siècle furniture. Slightly farther on is the **Charlottenburg Mausoleum,** which contains the tombs of King Wilhelm II and his wife, Queen Louise. *Schloß Charlottenburg: Luisenpl., tel. 030/320911. U-Bahn to Sophie-Charlotte-Pl. or Bus 109 from Zoo Station to Spandauer Damm. Admission: DM 8, palace grounds free. Open Tues., Wed., Fri.–Sun. 10–5, Thurs. 10–8; grounds open daily sunrise–sunset.*

Districts

Twenty-three distinct *Bezirks* (districts) make up the city of Berlin. Twelve lie in the western half of the city, 11 in the eastern half, and each has its own town hall and district government. The most intriguing districts—and those worth the majority of your time—are all within a short subway ride of Zoo Station.

As you might guess, trying to incorporate East and West Berlin into a single, homogeneous entity is a difficult task—a process that some Berliners liken to mixing oil with vinegar.

Considering Berlin's overwhelming size, it's a good idea to explore one district completely before moving on. This saves the hassle of hopping from one big-name attraction to the next—a process that is confusing and time-consuming. Plan on spending at least one day in each district, although you might be able to squeeze two districts into a single day if you're tenacious. Generally, the S- and U-Bahn are useful only for getting from one district to another, not for transport from sight to sight. In other words, plan on lots and lots of walking.

CHARLOTTENBURG

Charlottenburg is a huge and disparate quarter, stretching all the way from Schloß Charlottenburg in the north to Zoo Station and the Tiergarten in the east, and to the Ku'damm in the extreme south. As such, it's nearly impossible to explore the quarter comfortably on foot. Instead, spend one day at the sprawling Schloß and its adjacent museums (*see* Worth Seeing, *above*), then concentrate on its more accessible southern sites.

HARDENBERGSTRAßE Hardenbergstraße connects Zoo Station, Steinplatz, and Ernst Reuter Straße. There aren't any "don't miss" sights here, only a collection of Baroque apartments, some lazy cafés, and a large group of cheap restaurants. Steinplatz itself is rather dull, noted for its overgrown lawn and uncomfortable cement benches. Concentrate instead on **Goethestraße,** which runs due west from Steinplatz. Both streets have a fair share of clothing and souvenir stores, and prices are much cheaper here than on the Ku'damm. The same holds true for the bars and restaurants, which makes Hardenbergstraße a good place to start a night's carousing. To reach the area from Savignyplatz, walk northeast along Carmerstraße; from Zoo Station, simply walk northwest along Hardenbergstraße.

SAVIGNYPLATZ In many ways, the open-air Savignyplatz is central Berlin's response to the Kreuzberg. Although Savignyplatz tends to attract a more affluent crowd, it's nevertheless surrounded by cafés and dozens of cheap dive bars. It's very lively, especially when the club scene gets going after nightfall. The area is noted for its large immigrant populations (mostly Turkish and Indian), which means it's also a good place to come for cheap street-stand food; try one of the bargain-priced Imbiß stands that border the square. During the day Savignyplatz itself can be rather quiet, the sort of place where old men gather to play chess and gossip. If this sounds dull, explore some of the streets around the square. **Kantstraße,** which runs east–west through Savignyplatz, is home to upscale clothing shops and offbeat thrift stores. **Knesebeckstraße,** which runs north–south through the square, and **Grolmanstraße,** which runs southeast, both feature a large number of bars and restaurants. The same holds true for **Bleibtreustraße,** located one block west. Although the area's bars are liveliest after dark, you'll find students and unemployed slackers hanging around at all hours.

EAST BERLIN

Until recently, East Berlin was regarded with a mix of dread and awe. Much of this was due to the Berlin Wall, which effectively insulated the city from the West. Visas were not difficult to obtain, but it took a bit of courage to penetrate what was, after all, a dark and gloomy bastion of communism; back then, there seemed little reason to explore a city famed for shortages and cement. Because of this, East Berlin developed a reputation as a cultural and aesthetic zero. In many ways, however, nothing could be farther from the truth. Prior to World War II, in fact, Berlin's center was in the east, not the west. Berlin in the 1920s was on the cutting edge of just about everything. Jazz and cabaret dominated the club scene, while Erwin Piscator and Bertolt Brecht made their mark in theater. East Berlin also had the city's largest university, staffed in the 1920s by the likes of Albert Einstein.

Although East Berlin will only slowly regain its former stature after 45 years of oppressive rule, it remains a graceful, fascinating city. Already, the sweeping changes wrought by unification have given East Berlin a certain urgency.

You could easily spend weeks exploring the many districts that comprise East Berlin. The easiest way to do this is on the U- and S-Bahn, which serve most of East Berlin's major landmarks. Now that the Wall has crumbled, you can enter East Berlin on foot. The most popular crossing is at Brandenburg Gate, situated at the eastern end of Straße des 17 Juni. From here it's an easy walk to Unter den Linden and the sprawling Marx-Engels-Platz. If you're coming from Kreuzberg, Checkpoint Charlie is a good jumping-off point for Friedrichstraße.

ALEXANDERPLATZ Whether you love it or hate it, Alexanderplatz, named after Russian Czar Alexander I, is one of East Berlin's landmarks. If you despise it, blame the very tall, very ugly **Fernsehturm** TV tower, rising nearly 1,200 feet above the square. The tower is a good reference point if you get lost, but, aesthetically speaking, it's an absolute zero—a blend of cement, gaudy gold-plating, and poor taste. Set atop the concrete pylon, like a golf ball waiting to be thwacked, is the "command center," which houses the Telecafé restaurant (*see* Food, *above*). It costs DM 5 to ride the elevator, even if you plan on eating at the restaurant. From the top-floor **observation deck** (open daily 9 AM–midnight) you get a striking 360° view of Berlin. On a clear day you can see for miles.

Back on earth, the rest of Alexanderplatz is dominated by ugly high rises, fast-food stands, and the disheveled Centrum department store. This used to be East Berlin's premier shopping spot, but rumor has it that competition from the West will soon force its closure. In the meantime, head inside for unbeatable deals on out-of-date clothing and polka records. On the opposite side of the square are two stylish prewar buildings, **Alexander-Haus** and **Berolina-Haus.** They were built in the 1930s by Peter Behrens, an early modernist who employed the young Walter Gropius and Mies van der Rohe, founders of the Bauhaus movement. While everything else was flattened on Alexanderplatz during World War II, these two buildings survived somehow; today they house governmental offices and a library. At the opposite end of the square, near Karl-Liebknecht-Straße, look for the **Berliner Markthalle,** an informal produce market that's often stocked with boxes of fresh cherries and strawberries. Just south of this, **Das Internationale Buch** (Spendauerstr. 34, tel. 030/45532) has an extensive collection of English books and maps; head here for the latest copies of *Time* and the *International Herald Tribune.* Along the way you'll pass the 13th-century **Marienkirche** (Karl-Liebknecht-Str., open daily 8 AM–4 PM), one of the oldest churches in Berlin. The modest brick structure houses several treasures, including a beautifully carved 18th-century pulpit and the impressive 15th-century Totentanz fresco, a gruesome depiction of a "dance of death." Free guided tours are offered at 1 daily. *To get to Alexanderpl. take U5 or S75 to Alexanderpl. station; from Marx-Engels-Pl., walk northeast on Karl-Liebknecht-Str.*

FRIEDRICHSTRAßE Friedrichstraße stretches all the way from Checkpoint Charlie, in the south, to the Brecht Haus, 2 kilometers (1¼ miles) north. Along the way it crosses both Unter den Linden and the River Spree, passing close by Brandenburg Gate and Marx-Engels-Platz. Friedrichstraße is one of East Berlin's major commercial thoroughfares, though even unification hasn't brightened its noticeably "Eastern" look. Rickety Trabants still choke the street, while worn streetcars thunder by, filled with the sullen faces of factory workers and the unemployed. Other signs that you've crossed into East Berlin are boarded-up shops and the ever-present graffiti (highlights include "F— Yeu Amerika" and "This is democracy?"). More telling still are the crum-

For a Night Out in East Berlin, Skinheads Sometimes Catch a Foreign Act

Since 1989, East Berlin has seen a tremendous influx of Western tourists, many attracted by the area's cheap and sordid nightlife. Be warned, though, that some locals harbor a lot of anger toward foreigners, and beatings are not uncommon. East Berlin has been hit hard economically, and unemployment is generally two to three times worse than it is on the other side of the former border. If you're Jewish, a person of color, or simply unlucky, skinheads can pose a problem, especially in the city's working-class districts. East Berlin is hardly a war zone, but stay alert, avoid wandering alone at night, and don't be afraid to play up the stupid tourist routine if you sense trouble.

bling cement apartments and thick, sulfurous air—two communist-era legacies that will take years to clean up.

Friedrichstraße has pockets of 1920s architecture intermixed with the cement and steel of the communist era, and a few stylish bars have opened since 1989. Concentrate your energy, however, on its more scenic southern leg. Here you'll find one of the finest squares in all Europe, the **Platz der Akademie** (Johannes-Dieckmann-Str., 1 block w. of Friedrichstr.). While most of Berlin was flattened during World War II, the square and its Baroque architecture survived relatively intact. Note the rows of tightly packed apartment buildings, each with its own unique and brightly painted facade. The square's main feature, however, is the 18th-century **Deutscher Dom** (admission free, open daily 9–5), recognized by its broad steps and massive cupola. Inside is a plaque dedicated to the church's Lutheran founders, and a small but colorful cycle of stained glass. On the opposite side of the square, beyond the statue of Friedrich von Schiller, is the neoclassic **Schauspielhaus,** one of the greatest works by Berlin architect Karl Schinkel. Nowadays it's home to the Berlin Symphony Orchestra (*see* Music in After Dark, *below*). Completing this trio of stately prewar buildings is the **Französischer Dom,** one block north. It was built in 1708 by French Huguenots, and its design is based on the Huguenots' original cathedral in Charenton, France. This cupola-capped church is best seen from the outside, especially now that it's been painstakingly restored. Inside is a Huguenot museum and the Turmstuben café, housed inside the 70-foot-tall dome. The pricey food is mediocre, but it's a good place for beer (DM 4) and coffee (DM 3.50). If you keep walking straight up Friedrichstraße from the square, you'll end up at the Bahnhof Friedrichstraße (S7 and U5), overlooking the River Spree.

MARX-ENGELS-PLATZ This wide, barren square marks the historic heart of Berlin. Prior to World War II it housed the 15th-century Berliner Schloß, a lavish Baroque palace and imperial residence. Allied bombing, however, reduced the complex to rubble. Rather than rebuild it, the postwar government decided to wreck what little remained, thus clearing space for the gruesomely modern **Palast der Republik,** which dominates the square today. This once housed the GDR's parliament, the Volkskammer; today it contains government offices, a smarmy restaurant, and some useless clothing boutiques. You can walk its halls any time of day for free, but the best view of this bulky monster is definitely from the outside. Aesthetically speaking, the square is redeemed only by the remnants of Berliner Schloß's original Baroque portal, which is preserved outside the adjacent Staatsrat, an otherwise dull government building.

Marx-Engels-Platz (part of which has been renamed Lustgarten) is a convenient landmark, and well served by subway, but it's not what you'd call a "major" sight. Rather, the area surrounding the square is what draws the largest crowds. Here, in the dense network of lanes and canals that buffer the square, you'll find dozens of museums and centuries-old churches—remarkable considering the devastation caused during World War II. A stone's throw north of the Palast der Republik is the 19th-century **Berliner Dom** (tel. 030/242–4277; open Mon.–Sat. 10–5, Sun. 11:15–5), without a doubt one of Berlin's most impressive cathedrals. Part of the structure was destroyed in the war, but recent renovations have left it in pristine condition, particularly the vaulted nave and mosaic-covered dome. To get a better view of these, climb up to the second-story balcony via a set of ornately carved stairs. Admission is free and a visit is highly recommended. At the square's west end, the **Karl-Liebknecht-Brücke** leads west across the River Spree. The bridge was designed by Schinkel and is lined with classical statues, many of which sported spray-painted mustaches and pubic hair following the winter of 1989. Just beyond is the impressive **Museum für Deutsche Geschichte** (Unter den Linden 2; open Mon.–Thurs. 9–6, weekends 10–5), with fascinating displays on all aspects of German history. Particularly good are the sections on Hitler and the Nazis, and the former GDR. Exhibits include Napoléon's Waterloo hat and Bismarck's cane. Admission is DM 3. Next door is **Neue Wach,** the very first of Schinkel's Berlin creations. It's a modest, simple structure, built in 1818 in the style of a Roman temple. Prior to World War II it was used as a military arsenal, though it later became one of East Berlin's most famous war memorials. An eternal flame burns inside its intimate, pillared hallway, which also houses the tomb of an unknown soldier, killed during World War II.

MUSEUMINSEL Four major museums are located a short walk north of Marx-Engels-Platz. Bordered by the River Spree on either side, this area is known as Museumsinsel (Museum Island), and marks the site of one of Berlin's original settlements, Cölln, dating from AD 1237. The first museum you see as you walk north from the Palast der Republik is the **Altes Museum.** Its main feature is a vast collection of postwar East German art. The artists are generally obscure, yet their work is surprisingly satirical (and sometimes blatantly critical) of the former GDR, the artists' ostensible patron. Another exhibit includes etchings by Dürer, Cranach, and Rembrandt. *Lustgarten, tel. 030/456223. Admission: DM 5. Open Wed.–Sun. 10–6.*

One block farther north, the **Nationalgalerie** contains Berlin's largest collection of 18th-, 19th-, and 20th-century paintings. The 19th-century collection is a bit dull, anchored by repetitive landscape and portrait work. Better represented are a wide range of 20th-century masters, from Degas and Cézanne to the sculptor Rodin and the photographer John Heartfield. Also of note are the gallery's Bauhaus, Der Blaue Reiter, and Die Brücke holdings. *Bodestr., tel. 030/667–9033. Admission: DM 5. Open Wed.–Sun. 10–6.*

To the west is a museum that falls into the don't-miss category. The **Pergamonmuseum** has one of the world's best collections of Hellenic, Egyptian, and Middle Eastern art. The museum is named for its principal display, the Pergamon Altar, which should be familiar to anyone who's ever taken an art history course. This dazzling 2nd-century BC Greek temple was moved block by block from a mountaintop in Turkey; today it stands as a monument to those 19th-century German archaeologists who ceaselessly roamed the world, plundering as they went. The frieze depicts Zeus and Athena locked in battle against the giants, a remarkable feat of Greek sculpting. Equally remarkable is the Babylonian Processional Highway and, in the Asia Minor section, the Ishtar Gate, both of which date from the 6th-century BC reign of Nebuchadnezzar II. *Am Kupfergraben. Admission: DM 5. Open daily 10–6.*

Located in the same complex is the **Bodemuseum,** which houses a hodgepodge of Byzantine, Egyptian, and European relics. It pales in comparison with the Pergamonmuseum, yet the Bodemuseum's coin and sculpture gallery is worth a quick look. Also check out the massive Sphinx of Hatshepsut from 1500 BC, and the museum's vast papyrus collection. *Monbijourbrücke. Admission: DM 5. Open daily 10–6.*

NIKOLAIVIERTEL The Nikolaiviertel quarter is bordered by Alexanderplatz to the north and the River Spree to the south. Because of its location and old-style look, it's often called the historic "heart" of Berlin, but in reality it's only a detailed replica. Much of this district was reduced to rubble during World War II. Rather than build the standard cement-and-steel blocks, the GDR attempted to re-create an entire prewar neighborhood, including exact copies of the quarter's famous historical buildings. Fortunately, they were mostly successful. Today's Nikolaiviertel does indeed feel pleasantly old and refined, dominated by fin-de-siècle facades and ornate Baroque-style apartments (over 2,000 people live in the area). You can often see through the deception (e.g., columns are made of cement rather than marble), but, for the most part, the quarter really does look as if it's stuck in the 19th century. For a good overview, walk south from Alexanderplatz down Rathausstraße. Nikolaiviertel officially starts at Spendauerstraße, which is lined with tourist shops and a few swank, very modern restaurants. From here you're within easy reach of the district's four main alleys, each packed with dozens of taverns, cafés, and sidewalk food stands. By subway, take the U2 to Spittelmarkt and cross the River Spree on Mühlendamm.

The district is visually dominated by **Nikolaikirche.** The original late Romanesque church was erected in 1240, though what you see today is mostly a reconstruction, built in the aftermath of World War II. Even so, the church's Gothic interior looks impressively old, noted for its vaulted ceilings and arched, ornate windows. *Admission: DM 2. Open Tues.–Fri. 9–5, weekends 9–6.*

Opposite the church is **Knoblauchhaus,** a detailed replica of a 17th-century merchant house. A museum inside traces the life of Christian Knoblauch, a wealthy silk merchant who once lived on this site. Also inside is the Historische Weinstube, an expensive tavern popular with camera-wielding tourists. *Tel. 030/334–9092. Admission: DM 3. Open Tues.–Sun. 9–6.*

A stone's throw south is Berlin's most lavish Rococo house, the **Ephraim Palace.** It was originally built in 1766 for Veitel Ephraim, court jeweler to Friedrich II. Veitel was Jewish, so in 1933 the Nazis razed the structure and plundered its collection of rare stones. Fortunately, pieces of the original Rococo facade were discovered in West Berlin following the war. These were incorporated into the reconstruction you see today, commissioned by the GDR in 1987. Inside is a privately owned art gallery and a small, very posh restaurant. *Mühlendamm, tel. 030/767–0002. Open Tues.–Fri. 9–5, weekends 10–6.*

Across the road, the **Handwerkmuseum** (admission DM2, open Tues.–Sun. 9–5) displays all sorts of handmade crafts from medieval Berlin. If you're hungry, a handful of upscale cafés sit overlooking the River Spree on Spreeufer, one block west of Nikolaikirche. Another good bet, albeit an expensive one, is Zum Nußbaum, across from Nikolaikirche at the corner of Probststraße. A re-creation of Berlin's oldest inn, it still serves a hearty tanker of beer (DM 5) along with pricier traditional German meals.

PRENZLAUER BERG Prenzlauer Berg, which lies roughly a kilometer (2/3 mile) northeast of Alexanderplatz, is a drab working-class quarter, filled with apartment buildings. In many ways, though, it's also the social hub of East Berlin, a twin to West Berlin's Kreuzberg district. Like the latter, Prenzlauer Berg nurtures a large gay and lesbian community as well as a fairly wild club scene. None of its clubs has the swank art-deco feel you find elsewhere in the city, but that's because Prenzlauer Berg has yet to become chic or hip. Things are slowly beginning to change, so don't be surprised by the occasional high-priced clothing boutique. More common by far, though, are basement bars and underground discos, bacchanalian places with notoriously short life spans. Also common are student-run cafés and cheap food stands, intermixed with boarded-up buildings and poorly stocked shops—reminders that you're still in East Berlin.

Toward the end of the war the Nazis vandalized the Jewish graves at Jüdischer Friedhof, toppling and smashing many of the markers. Subsequent caretakers have left the disheveled burial ground as is—a symbolic memorial to hatred.

The best way to reach Prenzlauer Berg is via the subway. Take the U2 to Senefelderplatz or Dimitroffstraße. They both empty onto **Schönhauser Allee,** the district's main artery. It's a quiet shopping street lined with old-fashioned prewar buildings—remarkable considering the maze of cement-and-steel tenements to the east. Just north of Senefelderplatz Station is **Jüdischer Friedhof** (Schönhauser Allee 23, open Mon.–Thurs. 8–4), wherein lie the haunting, ivy-covered graves of some 20,000 Jews. Prior to World War II this was the principal burial spot for Berlin's large community of Jews. It's also the final resting place of artist Max Liebermann and composer Giacomo Meyerbeer.

Continue north on Schönhauser Allee to Wörtherstraße, then turn right. Two blocks ahead is the graceful **Käthe-Kollwitz-Platz,** named in honor of the famous German artist (she was born only a few blocks away, though her house was destroyed in World War II). The square is centered around a prim, Parisian-style park; in the middle stands Kollwitz's sculpture *Die Mutter* (*The Mother*). Leading north from the square is one of East Berlin's most remarkable streets, **Husemannstraße.** During the 1930s this narrow avenue was lined with colorful Baroque buildings. Following the war, poverty forced many residents to neglect their once stately homes, sometimes even to abandon them to the government. In 1986 the GDR decided it was time to beautify. They commissioned a troop of workers to repaint and restore the buildings, creating a glorious street scene from turn-of-the-century Berlin. At No. 4 is the local tobacco shop, bathed in dark oak and the sweet aroma of exotic cigars. At No. 19 is the Budike Bar, an old-style pub that serves hearty tankers of local beer. At No. 23 is Café-Stube, a smoky, Bismarck-era place where men sport spectacles and chat in hushed tones. The "old Berlin" atmosphere is heightened by wrought-iron street lamps and an occasional phaeton (hailable at DM 50 per 30 minutes) clopping down the street.

Husemannstraße also contains two excellent museums. The first is the odd **Friseurmuseum** (Husemannstr. 8, tel. 030/32459), ostensibly the world's first and only hairdressing museum. Inside are scale-model replicas of 1900s-era barber shops, a display of early safety razors, and snippets of hair from Goethe and Chancellor Bismarck. Admission is free, and a visit is strongly recommended. Two doors down is the free **Museum Berliner Arbeiterleben um 1900** (tel. 030/430–9872), which documents working-class Berlin at the turn of the century. Exhibits include period furniture and clothing, along with all sorts of faded advertisements and magazines.

UNTER DEN LINDEN Like the Ku'damm, the 1½-kilometer-long (1-mile-long) **Unter den Linden** is a sweeping, shop-lined thoroughfare that's almost impossible to avoid. It stretches all the way from Brandenburg Gate in the west to Marx-Engels-Platz in the east. On it you'll find fin-de-siècle mansions and numerous historic buildings—the sort of imperial architecture that gives East Berlin a surprisingly stately, almost majestic feel. Even the shops that compete for ground-floor space are, at least by East German standards, uncharacteristically well kept.

Until her death in 1945, artist Käthe Kollwitz was one of the few women associated with Germany's social realist school, a movement that grew out of expressionism. Like Otto Dix and George Grosz, Kollwitz was most concerned with the sufferings of the underprivileged, a concern reflected in her blunt and often gruesomely satirical sculptures.

Under the direction of Prince Wilhelm Friedrich, Unter den Linden was expanded from a footpath to a carriageway in 1647. At that time it connected the Tiergarten woodland with his Berlin Castle, a lush Baroque palace that stood on what's now Marx-Engels-Platz. Over time royal houses began to appear on the edge of Prince Friedrich's forested promenade, and in the 1760s Friedrich II decided to build an opera house, a library, and a second palace nearby, thus ensuring Unter den Linden's central role in the continuing development of Berlin. Friedrich II also ordered the planting of Linden (lime) trees along the avenue, which gave the street its name. By the turn of the century Unter den Linden had become Berlin's most famous thoroughfare, with all the best clubs and dance halls, and all the best cafés and whorehouses. It was the city's social and cultural focus, embodying the best of Weimar Germany. Sadly, wartime bombing devastated large sections of the historic street. This paved the way for the cement-and-steel replacements you see today. Despite these modern eyesores, this street is like a measuring stick, charting the ups and downs of style, history, and culture.

The best way to appreciate Unter den Linden is on foot, roughly a two-hour undertaking. The traditional starting point is **Pariser Platz,** just east of Brandenburg Gate. Continuing east, you'll pass a collection of bulky, worn buildings that once housed GDR ministries. The most forbidding is the former Soviet embassy, recognizable by the bust of Lenin and the Russian flag. Since reunification it's become a diplomatic mission, but it's not open to visitors. Farther east is the **Alte Palais,** former palace of Emperor Wilhelm I. It, too, is closed to the public, although its staunch facade is definitely photo-worthy. Across from the palace, in the middle of the street, is an equestrian sculpture (1851) of Friedrich II. The sculptor, Rauch, took a few liberties by incorporating the heads of Gotthold Lessing and Immanuel Kant, two of the emperor's harshest critics, on the horse's rear end, right below the tail. Across from this is the 18th-century **Humboldt University,** recognizable by the statues of Wilhelm and Alexander von Humboldt, the university's founders. During the school year, the front steps are filled with students, many of whom would love to practice their English (and might even show you around campus). Famous former students and staff have included Marx, Engels, Hegel, Einstein, Jakob and Wilhelm Grimm (a.k.a. the Brothers Grimm), and Max Planck.

The area just southeast of the university is known as **Bebelplatz,** a pleasant square bordered by lime trees. Bebelplatz marks the site of the 1933 *Büchverbrennung* (book burning), a propaganda event orchestrated by Hitler. Thrown into the fire were works considered too "dangerous" for public consumption; banned authors included Thomas Mann, Hegel, Benjamin Franklin, and Dostoevsky. Flanking the square is the elegant facade of the **Alte Bibliothek** (Royal Library). Also known as the Kommode (chest of drawers) because of its peculiar shape, it once housed the GDR's official state library, although the entire collection has been stored in the suburbs since unification. Nowadays it's used by university students in search of peace and quiet. Next door is Berlin's main opera house, the **Deutsche Staatsoper** (Unter den Linden 7, tel. 030/200–4762, box office open weekdays noon–5:45). The original Rococo structure was built in 1741 by Georg von Knobelsdorff, making it one of the world's first purpose-built opera houses. Unfortunately, it burned down in 1843 and was subsequently rebuilt in a blander neoclassic style by Karl Langhans. Even so, the lush interior is famed for its period decor and ceiling murals and is definitely worth a look. If you can't convince someone to let you in during the day (a smile and an obvious camera may help), tickets for its frequent performances can be had for less than DM 30. Immediately behind the opera house stands the circular **St. Hedwig's Cathedral.** No one's quite sure whether it's supposed to look like the Pantheon in Rome, but the similarities are undeniable. Inside is a dull collection of religious relics, hardly worth your time.

KREUZBERG

Kreuzberg is one of Berlin's liveliest quarters, home to an odd mix of progressive youth, Turkish immigrants, and factory workers. Few people come to Kreuzberg just for its looks. Instead, people are attracted by its "alternative" reputation. It's also *the* place for cheap dive bars and basement cafés. The district is divided into two distinct sections: semi-conservative West Kreuzberg, the area around Viktoriapark; and the wilder East Kreuzberg, the area around Kottbußer Tor and Skalitzerstraße. For the former take U7 or U6 to Mehringdamm Station; for the latter take U1 or U8 to Kottbußer Tor Station.

Kreuzberg has the largest population of Turks outside Turkey, so it has an exotic flair that's sometimes hard to reconcile with its gritty cement-and-steel look.

EAST KREUZBERG East Kreuzberg has always harbored the so-called dregs of Berlin. These include the Turkish immigrants who moved here en masse during the 1950s and '60s in search of factory work. It also includes the dropouts and hippies who were able to live cheaply in squat apartments. It's hard to tell whether historically low rents attracted the district's odd mix of characters, or whether an influx of "undesirables" forced local landlords to give up any hope of ever turning a profit. Either way, East Kreuzberg has evolved into one of Berlin's most offbeat (some would say downtrodden) quarters, which makes it the place to come for an alternative take on the city.

East Kreuzberg has few official tourist sights, and in many ways it's quite ugly. Years of neglect have turned its apartment buildings into shoddy-looking tenements, while civic "beautification" has often meant nothing more than a fresh coat of graffiti. Even so, it does boast the city's best nightlife. From Kottbußer Tor make your way north on any of the small side streets. Eventually you'll stumble upon **Oranienstraße,** the district's main drag. This is where you'll find the largest concentration of bars and cafés. Along the way you also pass **Moritzplatz,** a barren square lined with dozens of popular no-name hangouts that open and close on a monthly basis. Another popular starting point is **Schlesisches Tor** (U1), which provides access to Skalitzerstraße and Köpenickerstraße. Perhaps because it lies in the shadow of the old Berlin Wall, this part of town is less developed than Oranienstraße. You'll find a handful of unpublicized dive bars on Köpenickerstraße, but expect mostly working-class pubs and row after row of block housing.

WEST KREUZBERG While East Kreuzberg has the best clubs and dive bars, and the best streets for rambling walks, West Kreuzberg has the majority of restaurants and cafés. If you're traveling on foot, it's also more accessible from East Berlin and the Tiergarten. Unlike working-class East Kreuzberg, West Kreuzberg is a haven for yuppies and their well-maintained apartments. Prewar apartments frame many of its tree-lined streets, while quiet squares offer haven for old men and their chessboards.

West Kreuzberg runs from Checkpoint Charlie in the north to Viktoriapark and Tempelhof Airport in the south. As a general rule, avoid the area immediately surrounding the River Spree: It's filled with tenements and uninspired cafés. Instead, concentrate on Viktoriapark or the southern leg of Friedrichstraße, just below Checkpoint Charlie. Near the latter, look for the impressive **Martin-Gropius-Bau** (Stresemannstr. 110, tel. 030/254–8600), built in 1822 by Martin Gropius, uncle to Bauhaus founder Walter Gropius. It houses a rotating collection of international art, most of which is for sale.

Kreuzberg is named after Kreuzberg hill, which nowadays is enveloped by the peaceful **Viktoriapark.** This shady green is bordered by cafés and a few reasonably priced restaurants, so it's a good place to come on a sunny afternoon. The iron cross in the park's center was built by Schinkel in 1821, a monument to those who died in the 1813–15 Wars of Liberation, against Napoléon. The view from up here is superb, offering a unique panorama of East Berlin and **Tempelhof Airport.** At the height of the Berlin Airlift (1948–49), cargo planes landed every minute at Tempelhof airport, providing much-needed supplies to the city after the Soviets imposed a strict land blockade. **Mehringdamm,** which forms the park's eastern border, is the sort of well-kept shopping street that typifies West Kreuzberg. Where it touches the park's southern edge, the **Luftbrückendenkmal** commemorates the 81 people—mostly pilots and ground crew—who died during the Berlin Airlift. **Gneisenaustraße,** to the north, is another lively avenue filled with cafés and thrift shops. Look for the Mehringhof U-Bahn station where it crosses Mehringdamm.

SCHONEBERG

Schöneberg, which lies directly south of the Tiergarten, has a reputation for wild nightlife. To get to Schöneberg from the city center, walk east down the Ku'damm until you dead-end into Nollendorfplatz. From Kreuzberg simply walk west from Viktoriapark and turn right onto Hauptstraße, which passes Kleist Park on the way to Bülowstraße. By subway, take the U4 straight to Nollendorfplatz.

At the heart of Schöneberg lies **Nollendorfplatz,** the focus of the quarter's gay and lesbian scene. The square is lined with all sorts of bars and food stands popular with local immigrants (mostly Turkish and Indian) and an older, almost yuppie crowd. If the Kreuzberg seems a bit too wild, odds are you'll find a more middle-of-the-road option for boozing and dancing here. By day, head east from the square down Bülowstraße. In the defunct U-Bahn station look for the **Nollendorf Market,** offering an odd mix of fresh produce, electronic goods, and high-quality "junk," from candle holders and pepper shakers to records and communist-era posters. The market operates Thursday through Monday from sunrise to sunset. Farther west is the **Bülowstraße Bazar,** where you'll find an equally bizarre mix of track suits and bootleg music.

Stylish **Kleistpark** lies south of Bülowstraße. Fronting the park is the **Königskolonaden,** a stately colonnade erected in 1785 in honor of Prince Wilhelm I. It's a popular meeting point for local drunks and, after dark, the district's audacious prostitutes. Also inside the park is the **Kamergerichtsgebäude,** a former courthouse used by the Nazis. Until unification it was occupied by the American military. There's a rumor that its elegant courtroom may soon open to the public; contact the tourist office for details. Leave the park heading west on Grunewaldstraße and turn left onto Martin Luther Straße. A few blocks farther on stands the imperial **Rathaus Schöneberg,** built by the district government in 1914. It housed the West Berlin Senate until 1989, though it's most often associated with John F. Kennedy, who visited the site on June 26, 1963. He came to present West Berlin with a document supporting the city's struggle for freedom, signed by more than 17 million Americans. (At the end of his famous speech against communism, Kennedy concluded: "All free men, wherever they live, are citizens of Berlin. And, therefore, as a free man, I take pride in the words 'Ich bin ein Berliner.'" Unfortunately, no one had told Kennedy that *ein Berliner* actually refers to a jelly-filled doughnut.) Inside the Rathaus's 237-foot-tall tower is a replica of the American Liberty Bell, which rings daily at noon. The bell tower (admission free, open Wed. and Sun. 10–4) offers good views of the city from its top-floor balcony.

Speaking in German, President Kennedy told a crowd in Berlin: "I am a jelly doughnut."

SPANDAU

Spandau, 12 kilometers (7 miles) northwest of the city center, is the oldest established district in Berlin. It was first settled in the early 13th century by a hodgepodge of merchants and well-to-do princes. Over the centuries, Spandau grew into a prosperous village, never fully integrating itself with Berlin proper. This fact, along with its lack of heavy industry, probably saved Spandau from wartime bombing and unsightly postwar development. As a result, Spandau remains a beautiful Baroque village, dominated by crooked lanes and lavish turn-of-the-century architecture. You can easily spend a day wandering from café to café in its cobbled alleys, though its principal attraction is the 13th-century **Zitadelle.** This moated, heavily fortified complex once protected Spandau from marauding bands of Ottoman and Bulgarian treasure seekers. Today it's been turned into a "living history" exhibit, with costumed workers doing their best to re-create a typically medieval street scene. Inside, besides the inevitable tourist shops and Banquet Hall (where "medieval feasts" are served nightly during summer; DM 40 per person), a small museum documents the citadel's turbulent history. A serene park surrounds the complex, and a pleasant walking path follows the banks of the Rivers Spree and Havel. *U7 to Zitadelle. Admission: DM 3, DM 1.50 students. Open Tues.–Fri. 9–5, weekends 10–6.*

Spandau's other claim to fame is Spandau Prison, formerly on Wilhelmstraße 23 but now destroyed. Its most infamous inmate was Rudolf Hess, onetime leader of the Nazi party and one of Hitler's most trusted aides (Hitler and Hess became close friends when they were held together in Landsberg Prison following the Munich Putsch of 1923. To pass the time, Hess copied down what would later become Hitler's autobiographical manifesto *Mein Kampf.*) Hess flew to Scotland in 1941 and, following a failed attempt to ally England with Germany, was imprisoned for the duration of the war. He was later convicted at the Nürnberg trials. He served his life sentence in Spandau, and was the prison's only inmate during the 1980s. Hess committed suicide in 1987, after which the prison was destroyed.

TIERGARTEN

The Tiergarten district runs from Brandenburg Gate in the east to Zoo Station in the west—a peaceful expanse of forest and lake in the otherwise urban city center. Its main feature is the sprawling 1½-kilometer-long (1-mile-long) Straße des 17 Juni, which connects West Berlin's Bismarckstraße with East Berlin's stately Unter den Linden. Much of the Tiergarten, especially along the central section of Straße des 17 Juni, is undeveloped and attracts few tourists. Notable along this dull expanse is the **Siegessäule,** or Winged Victory column, visible from most points in the city center. This 226-foot-tall monument, built in 1873 to celebrate Prussia's military might, has an impressive observation deck (admission DM 2; open Mon. 3–6, Tues.–Sun. 9–6), reached after a long 285-step climb. It's worth a quick look, but don't go out of your way to get here. Instead, concentrate on either the Tiergarten's zoo, the **Zoologischer Garten** (*see* Parks and Gardens, *below*), or the area surrounding Brandenburg Gate. Here you'll find lots of street-sellers and a sizable open-air flea market. On Straße des 17 Juni, just west of Brandenburg Gate, you'll also find the **Soviet Victory Memorial,** built in the immediate aftermath of World War II. For some reason, the Soviets decided to erect their monument in what had already become the American-controlled sector. The semicircular structure depicts a Soviet soldier flanked by two very real tanks, supposedly two of the first to enter Berlin at the close of the war. During the Cold War, the monument's location caused more than a few problems: At first, the Soviets wanted it relocated; then they wanted (and were eventually allowed) to guard it with a troop of Red Army soldiers. Since unification the Soviets have forsaken this somewhat out-of-place monument, although the tanks, Soviet soldier, and Red Star remain—along with some pro-communist graffiti.

If you follow what remains of the Berlin Wall south, you trace the southeastern edge of the Tiergarten before funneling onto **Potsdamer Platz,** recognizable by its newly renovated U-Bahn station. Along with Unter den Linden, this barren square was the social heart of prewar Berlin. Following World War II, it marked the convergence of the British, American, and Russian sectors, as evidenced by the molested remains of the Wall, which cuts through the center of the square. Despite recent construction—an attempt to breathe life into this once beautiful square—the whole area remains bleak and run-down, a sad reminder of Berlin's divisive history. To view the entire square you have to either climb atop the Wall or cross over into East Berlin, which contains the other half of Potsdamer Platz.

On the East Berlin side of Potsdamer Platz, look for a small knoll just north of the square. This marks the site of **Hitler's bunker,** where the Führer spent the last days of World War II. On April 30, 1945, as Soviet tanks swept in from the east, Hitler finally recognized that his Third Reich was crumbling. Ringed by a small band of advisers, Hitler married his mistress, Eva Braun, and then wrote his will. Shortly after, Hitler encouraged Eva to poison herself and then put a gun to his own head. Their bodies were burned lest they be molested by vengeful Soviet troops, and the bunker was sealed shut. During the Cold War the GDR saw little reason to publicize the site; everyone knew of its existence, but no one was overly anxious to dig it up and make it presentable. Since reunification there's been talk of turning it into a museum, but for the moment it remains buried and ignored.

Parks and Gardens

Berlin has dozens of parkland escapes. In fact, over 30% of Berlin is covered by woodland and public parks. The most accessible is the centrally located **Tiergarten,** particularly the tree-lined area just east of Zoo Station, which contains Berlin's zoo and dozens of lakeside hiking trails. On the western edge of town is the vast **Grunewald,** complemented in East Berlin by the state forest surrounding **Großer Mußelsee.** A visit to these last two parks may require advance planning because of their semi-isolation.

GRUNEWALD This is West Berlin's most popular weekend retreat, a 32-square-kilometer (12-square-mile) expanse of horse trails, bike paths, beaches, and trees, trees, trees. The Havel River and **Großer Wannsee** lake entice thousands of swimmers and sun worshipers on warm days. Großer Wannsee is especially popular for its long stretch of powdery beach. If you're in the mood to walk, follow the signs to **Jagdschloß**

Grunewald (Am Grunewaldsee, tel. 030/813–3597), a 16th-century royal hunting lodge that now houses a privately owned art gallery. Another popular excursion is to **Pfaueninsel** (Peacock Island), set in a wide arm of the Havel River. The island is noted for its lush gardens—home to hundreds of wild peacocks—and its white marble **castle** (Zehlendorf, tel. 030/805–3042, admission DM 3.50). The latter occupies the island's southern tip and was built by King Friedrich Wilhelm II in 1795. Inside, a small museum features displays on the castle's history. If nothing else, the island is about the only place in Berlin that doesn't allow cars, dogs, or smoking. Between March and November an hourly ferry (DM 4 round-trip) connects Peacock Island with Blockhaus Nikolskoe, an elegant but pricey restaurant overlooking the water on the opposite shore.

The park is too large to cover in a single day. If you want nothing more than beach and water, take S1, S3, or S5 to Nikolaisee Station and follow the signs to Großer Wannsee; it's about a 20-minute walk. A more traditional starting point is Wannsee Station (S-Bahn), a 5-minute walk from some striking hiking trails; one in particular leads to the Peacock Island ferry and is well signposted. Either way, both S-Bahn stations afford access only to the park's southern tip. To reach the equally scenic northern section, take Bus 216 or 316 from Wannsee Station; both travel through the park's center, passing by the Jagdschloß Grunewald before terminating in Spandau.

VOLKSPARK KLEIN-GLIENICKE This is one of Berlin's finest parks, overlooking Havel River between Wannsee and Potsdam. The park was laid out by Karl Schinkel, who also designed the park's elegant palace. The palace is closed to the public, so spend your time meandering the forested riverbanks. Also check out the nearby **Glienicker Brücke,** a striking cast-iron bridge that connects Berlin with the suburb of Potsdam. The former border between the GDR and West Berlin ran down the center of the bridge. During the Cold War it was an established point for exchanging spies. *Koningstr. U-Bahn to Wannsee, then Bus 189 s. for 6 stops. Open daily sunrise–sunset.*

ZOOLOGISCHER GARTEN Berlin's zoo is located at the southwest corner of the Tiergarten, a 15-minute walk from Zoo Station. Founded in 1841, the zoo boasts the world's largest variety of animals—over 11,000 cuddly, noisy, slimy creatures representing some 1,600 different species. The fact that World War II left fewer than 100 animals alive makes the zoo's accomplishments even more amazing. You'll need at least three to four hours for a brief "Yup, that's a monkey" inspection, a full day to cover things in more detail. It's also worth the extra money to check out the massive aquarium complex. Most signs are in German, so pick up a copy of the free English-language guidebook when you enter. *Entrances at Hardenbergpl. and Budapester Str., tel. 030/254010. U- and S-Bahn Zoologischer Garten. Zoo admission: DM 7.50, DM 4 students. Combined aquarium and zoo admission: DM 12.50, DM 6 students. Open daily 9–dusk.*

The zoo gets crowded in nice weather, and school days bring enough kids to make you wonder who belongs behind bars.

Cheap Thrills

Like all great cities, Berlin offers a smorgasbord of activities for the chronically poor. Topping the list is street entertainment, a definite fixture of Berlin life. Whether you go for mimes and jugglers or the guy who plays the harmonica-guitar-drum-thing, the best place to head is the Ku'damm's **Breitscheidplatz, Tauentzienstraße,** or the large square surrounding **Brandenburg Gate.** Near the latter you'll find a daily open-air flea market where East Berliners gather to hawk junky antiques and tacky postcards. Another option is East Berlin's **Oranienburger Straße,** which is quickly becoming Berlin's hippest new hangout. In the squat tenements that line the street you'll find impromptu art galleries, no-name bars, and artsy dropouts looking for a remedy to urbana. None of the so-called galleries charges admission, but that's mainly because these venues—and most of the "art"—have grown out of what used to be vacant, trash-filled lots. On weekends it's common to find jazz and blues musicians holding informal gigs along the avenue. From Brandenburg Gate, walk east down Unter den Linden, turn left on Friedrichstraße (you'll pass Friedrichstraße. U-Bahn station) and right on Oranienburger Straße; it's 40 minutes by foot.

FESTIVALS

A complete list of Berlin festivals would fill a book larger than the one you're holding. Berlin is the political, cultural, and social capital of Germany (at least according to locals), so it's only natural that the city hosts a dizzying array of events year-round. The best source of information is the tourist office in Europa Center (*see* Visitor Information in Basics, *above*). Periodicals like *Zitty, Tip,* and *Berlin Programm* also have major festival listings, so pick up a copy at your local newsstand.

JANUARY **New Year's Eve** is celebrated throughout Berlin, with the largest crowds at Brandenburg Gate, along the Ku'damm, and on Kreuzberg's Oranienstraße. At the end of the month a small **Opera Festival** is held in venues throughout the city center.

FEBRUARY **Internationale Filmfestspiele,** Berlin's International Film Festival, rivals those in Cannes and Venice. It features new works from international filmmakers as well as remastered classics. Cinemas all over Berlin are co-opted for the event, and admission runs anywhere from DM 6 to DM 50. For tickets and more information, contact Filmfestspiele Berlin (Budapesterstr. 50, tel. 030/254890).

MAY **Berlin Drama Festival** is Berlin's largest theater extravaganza, featuring mostly German plays in a variety of venues. Many performances are of the puppet/experimental/music type, so fluent German isn't always a prerequisite. Prices vary according to the performance, but expect to pay around DM 15.

JUNE **Jazz in the Garten** brings local and international talent to the Neue Nationalgalerie for four consecutive Fridays in June. The music is first-rate and, best of all, free. Weather permitting, many of the sessions are held outside in the gallery's lush gardens. This festival is passionately recommended. Because of the influx of musicians, Berlin's jazz clubs are particularly lively in June.

JULY In recent years **Jazz in Juli** has become Berlin's premier jazz event, attracting big-name stars from the States and Britain. It's sponsored by the Quasimodo Club (Kantstr. 12A, tel. 030/312–8086), which is the festival's main venue. Tickets, generally priced between DM 10 and DM 25, should be purchased well in advance.

Berliner Bachtage (Bach Days) celebrate the music of J. S. Bach. It's usually held in the second week of the month, in venues (mostly churches) throughout Berlin. Contact the tourist office for a listing of free events; otherwise, expect to pay around DM 20 per performance.

AUGUST **Deutsch-Amerikanisches Volksfest** is a big late-August shindig at Truman Plaza, celebrating the "bonds of friendship" between Germany and America. Bring money for gambling in the casinos and phone numbers of your friends back home. At the front end of a massive line there's a "friendship phone" for free minute-long calls to the United States.

Berlin Festival Weeks, which runs August through October, combines a wide range of music, opera, ballet, and theater in venues throughout the city. The tourist office has complete listings, or write Festspiele GmbH (Kartenbüro, Budapesterstr. 50, 1000 Berlin 30) for schedules and ticket information. Festival passes cost around DM 110, good for entrance to all major events.

SEPTEMBER **Kreuzberger Festliche Tage,** Kreuzberg's largest festival, includes street musicians, open-air markets, and lots of beer. Come here for good deals on local art and offbeat antiques. The festival usually falls on the last weekend of September, though exact dates change from year to year.

The **Berlin Marathon** is held on the third Sunday of September. If you're in town it's hard to miss the large gang of spectators gathered along Straße des 17 Juni and the Ku'damm, the race's respective starting and finishing points. For entry information, write SCM Berlin (Alt-Moabit 29, 1000 Berlin 15, tel. 030/392–1102). All applications are due one month prior to the race.

OCTOBER Toward the end of October, Berlin holds a small **Oktoberfest** in beer halls throughout the city. Featured events include oompah bands and beer-induced singalongs. For the moment there's no official venue, but the city is trying to organize a beer-and-wienie tent near Brandenburg Gate; contact the tourist office for details.

DECEMBER Berlin celebrates Christmas with its annual **Christmas Bazaar,** an outdoor market held on the Ku'damm's Breitscheidplatz. Besides mobile food and drink stalls, look for handcrafted jewelry and clothing along with the obligatory overpriced stocking stuffers.

After Dark

With unification, Berlin has regained some of its former diversity, intermixing the Ku'damm's stylish cafés with East Berlin's seedy dive bars. More than ever, Berlin is an exciting city caught in the midst of overwhelming change. No one's quite sure what postunification Berlin will be like, but in the meantime there's an exciting buzz on the streets, a sense that Berlin is once again becoming a city that caters to all tastes at all times. On the downside, Berlin's size makes it unwieldy. Each district has its own after-hours personality, so there's no place to go for a comprehensive overview unless you're willing to take a **nighttime bus tour** (*see* Exploring Berlin, *above*). These cost DM 20–DM 50 and often include free entrance and drinks at some of Berlin's better jazz and cabaret clubs.

For a detailed listing of events check the biweekly magazines *Tip* or *Zitty*, available at newsstands for around DM 4. Another excellent periodical is the monthly *Berlin Programm* (DM 3.90), available at the tourist office. They're all in German, but it's easy to decipher dates, times, and addresses.

BARS Berlin supposedly has more bars per square kilometer than any other city in the world, and that's not including cafés, beer gardens, and liquor shops. The list below contains some of the city's best, but it is by no means exhaustive. Berlin's bars are notoriously short-lived, especially those in Kreuzberg and Prenzlauer Berg. To avoid disappointment, you should probably target an area rather than a name. Bars within a particular district are generally of the same type and style, and one grungy dive bar is a lot like the next. Most bars draw a good mix of people, though several cater specifically to gays and lesbians. Either way, all bars usually open around 6 or 7 at the latest and close by 2. Some stay open later if customers linger, and police don't mind people drinking on the streets.

The main strip in Kreuzberg is **Oranienstraße,** noted for its Turkish bars and offbeat cafés. German yuppies tend to gather at Charlottenburg's **Savignyplatz,** while **Martin-LutherStraße** in Schöneberg attracts an odd mix of artists, long-haired dropouts, and well-dressed business types. The main drag in Prenzlauer Berg is **Schönhauser Allee** and the adjacent **Kollwitzplatz,** frequented by the artsy and chic of former East Berlin.

Anderes Ufer. Artistic types enjoy Anderes Ufer's quiet atmosphere. The crowd is predominantly gay/lesbian, but straights are welcome. Some nights feature live folk and blues, usually free of charge. Beer and wine start at DM 8. *Hauptstr. 157. U7 to Kleistpark.*

Die Zwei. This women-only (but not necessarily lesbian-only) bar plays varied music to its immensely diverse crowd. Women should at least pop their heads in to check out the scene. Beer starts at DM 6; sandwiches and pastries at DM 5. *At Martin-Luther Str. and Motzstr. U4 to Viktoria-Luise-Pl., then walk northeast on Motzstr.*

Flip-Flop. Tourists as well as locals stop to drink and socialize at one of Berlin's best-known gay bars. It's a friendly, relaxed place open to both gays and straights, though gawking is not appreciated. Beers fetch DM 5–DM 8; mixed drinks around DM 8. *Kulmerstr. 20A. S1 to Göschenstr., then walk w. to Kulmerstr.*

Hafen. If this gay men's cruising spot is packed, go next door to Tom's Bar for more of the same. Both usually stay open long past 2. *Motzstr. 19. U4 to Viktoria-Luise-Pl. and walk w. on Hohenstaufenstr.*

Irish Pub. An Irish pub with Guinness, Murphy's, and a tourist-cum-yuppie crowd. At night expect live music and large, friendly crowds. *Europa Center, ground floor, tel. 030/262–1634.*

Kant Billiard-Café. This local hangout has more flair than the big pool halls along the Ku'damm. Six pool tables and a large-screen television attract a predominantly male crowd. Beers fetch DM 4–DM 7, a game of pool DM 2. *Kantstr. 38, no tel.*

Klo. Klo is slang for bathroom, and this theme is carried all the way: large beers (DM 11) come in bedpans instead of steins, flush noises blast over the sound system, and scrub brushes dangle from the ceiling. A strictly enforced "no drunks" policy keeps people from getting out of hand, which makes Klo popular with Germans of all ages. A small food menu has wieners and sandwiches priced under DM 10. Don't leave without visiting the bathrooms—they're unique. *Leibniz Str. 57, no tel. Take 149 from Zoo Station to Leibniz Str.*

Loretta im Garten. This lively, smoky beer hall is decidedly untouristy. An oompah band sometimes plays for free on weekend nights, though the biggest draw is an adjacent Ferris wheel (DM 3). Excellent traditional meals, mostly wursts and stews, are served daily until 8 PM; a full meal runs DM 9–DM 15. *Lietzenburgerstr. 89. From Zoo Station, Bus 219 to Lietzenburgerstr.*

Luisen-Bräu. This microbrewery serves homemade ales, pilsners, and lagers for around DM 8. The drinking area overlooks vats and a hopper; the front door overlooks Schloß Charlottenburg. Warning: If you don't cover your empty glass with a coaster, you'll soon get a full-price refill. *Luisenpl. 1, tel. 030/341–9388. U-Bahn to Sophie-Charlotte-Pl., or Bus 109 from Zoo Station to Spandauer Damm.*

Max und Moritz. This Kreuzberg hangout has good food as well as a full bar. Neither grimy nor seedy, it's a mellow place to drink and play cards. *Oranienstr. 168. U8 to Moritzpl.*

Nachtbar Moskau. Stop in this highbrow watering hole to get a taste of East Berlin's swank nightlife—something unheard of prior to 1989. Cheap beer (DM 5) makes up for the pretentious crowd. *Karl-Marx-Allee 34, tel. 030/279–2869. U5 to Schillingstr.*

Restauration 1900. This Kollwitzplatz spot attracts a young, artsy crowd and makes a good starting point for exploring other Prenzlauer Berg hangouts. Local artists display their work on the walls. Beers run DM 4–DM 5. *Husemannstr. and Wörtherstr. U2 to Senefelderpl. and walk n. on Kollwitzstr.*

Rost. Just south of Savignyplatz, the Rost attracts the local theater crowd and has recently become *the* place to be seen. The atmosphere is surprisingly relaxed, and the beers (DM 5) don't cost as much as at other spots nearby. *Knesebeckstr. 29, tel. 030/881–9501.*

CLUBS Many clubs outside the flashy Ku'damm have free admission or charge less than DM 10 cover. Beers inside cost around DM 7, so you may want to drink elsewhere first. Clubs are often grouped together, so you can easily club-hop. Many places aren't strict about closing hours; they'll stay open until the beer's gone or the last patron has left.

Abraxas. Where Charlottenburg locals come for Latin, Caribbean funk, and jazz music. The crowd is young and friendly and very much into dancing—no scamfest or meat market here. Cover charge and drinks cost around DM 5. *134 Kantstr., tel. 030/312–9493.*

Cha-Cha. One of Berlin's more style-conscious dance clubs, this is the sort of place where people doll up, strike poses, and try their best to look very, very cool. A DJ spins Top 40 and hip-hop records until the wee hours of the morning. Drinks fetch DM 6–DM 8. *Nürnberger Str. 50, tel. 030/214–2976. From Breitscheidpl. walk e. on Tauentzienstr. and turn right at Nürnberger Str. Cover: DM 5. Closed Mon.*

Dschungel. The patrons and music here are almost identical to Cha-Cha's next door. The only difference: Dschungel is free on Mondays. *Nürnberger Str. 53, tel. 030/246698. U2 to Augsburger Str. Cover: DM 10, free Mon. Closed Tues.*

Madow. One of Berlin's busiest dance clubs, Madow is popular with all types and ages. The music is eclectic, but always very danceable. Drinks fetch DM 4–DM 7. *Pariser Str. 23. Bus 249 from Zoo Station to Pariser Str. Closed Mon., Tues.*

Trash. Black walls, black lights, and a stylish rock crowd typify this Kreuzberg dance club. Music includes New Wave favorites (Cure to Soft Cell) and some rap. Beer is expensive at DM 9, so do the bulk of your drinking elsewhere. *Oranienstr. 40–41, no tel. U8 to Moritzpl. Closed Mon.*

Wu-Wu. This nightclub for gay males in Schöneberg plays an assorted mix of tunes. Drinks start at DM 4. *Kleiststr. 4, tel. 030/213–6392. From Europa Center walk e. on the Ku'damm until it turns into Kleistr. Cover: DM 4.*

MOVIE THEATERS You can enjoy mainstream movies in Berlin even if you don't speak German. Check the listings carefully and look for one of the following symbols: "OmU" for original language with subtitles, "OF" for original language. Otherwise, the film will be dubbed in German. Tickets in large theaters cost DM 12–DM 16, except Wednesdays when they're DM 6. Small theaters usually charge less than DM 10.

The **Odeon** (Hauptstr. 116, tel. 030/781–5657) shows second-run Hollywood films in English, the sort that were hits in the late 1980s. The **Eiszeit** (Zeushofstr. 20, tel. 030/611–6016) shows experimental and alternative films, sometimes in English. **Cinema** (Bundegallee 111, tel. 030/852–3004) makes a point of showing films produced or directed by women. **Amerika Haus** (Hardenbergstr. 22–24, tel. 030/819–7661) shows oldies from the States; next door, the **British Council Film Club** (Hardenbergstr. 20, tel. 030/310716) shows classics made in the United Kingdom. Both are English-language cinemas. East Berlin's most popular art house is the **Babylon** (Rosa-Luxemburg-Str. 40, tel. 030/242–5076), which features American and European classics in their original languages.

MUSIC Berlin's live music scene is good but not great. You'll find lots of first-rate jazz clubs, but there are surprisingly few music-only venues for rock. Instead, the majority of gigs happen in cafés, bars, and unmarked basements throughout Berlin. Look for fliers and posters, or flip through the magazines *Tip* and *Zitty* for up-to-date listings. Otherwise, wander around Kreuzberg or on East Berlin's Oranienburger Straße and keep your ears open.

➢ **CLASSICAL • Deutsche Oper Berlin.** West Berlin's German Opera hosts a wide range of ballet and music year-round. Best of all, student tickets start around DM 15; regular tickets at DM 25. *Bismarckstr. 34–37, tel. 030/341–0249. U-Bahn to Deutsche Oper.*

Deutsche Staatsoper. East Berlin's German State Opera offers classical concerts throughout the year. *Unter den Linden 5–7, tel. 030/203540. S-Bahn to Unter den Linden.*

Komische Oper. East Berlin's main venue for opera, operettas, and dance. *Behrenstr. 55–57, tel. 030/229–2555. From Marx-Engels-Pl. walk w. on Behrenstr.*

Konzertsaal der Hochschule der Künste. Part of the Academy of Fine Arts, this concert hall hosts a wide range of opera, ballet, and classical concerts year round. *Hardenbergstr. 23, tel. 030/318–2367.*

Metropol Theater. A popular East Berlin venue for opera and dance, Metropol is known for its comical, offbeat productions—nothing stuffy or sleepy here. *Friedrichstr. 101, tel. 030/208–2715.*

Philharmonic. Home to the world-famous Berlin Philharmonic and the lesser-known Berlin Radio Symphony Orchestra, the concert hall was recently renovated, so the acoustics are superb. Tickets are expensive (DM 20–DM 60) and often difficult to come by; stop by the box office or a ticket agency as soon as possible. *Matthäikirchstr. 1, tel. 030/805–1418. S1 or S2 to Potsdamerpl., then walk northwest on Bellevue Str.*

Schauspielhaus. One of East Berlin's top concert halls is located opposite the Deutsche Dom, south of Unter den Linden. *Pl. der Akademie, tel. 030/227–2156. From Marx-Engels-Pl. walk w. on Behrenstr. and turn left on Charlottenstr.*

Theater des Westerns. This city center concert hall features comic opera and musicals, mainly from the West. Past productions include *South Pacific* and *West Side Story. Kantstr. 12, tel. 030/319–03193.*

Berlin has three English-language theater companies: BELT (Berlin English-Language Theater, tel. 030/801–3467), Berlin Play Actors (tel. 030/784–7362), and Out to Lunch (tel. 030/891–3725). Lacking permanent homes, these companies co-opt theaters throughout Berlin. The most interesting of the three is probably Out to Lunch, founded in 1989 by American Joy Cutler.

Urania. A forum for smaller orchestras and chamber groups, Urania also has the cheapest seats in town, priced from DM 10 for students. *An der Urania 17, tel. 030/249091. From Gedächtniskirche, Bus 129 e. to An der Urania.*

➢ **JAZZ** • Berlin's jazz scene is second to none. Jazz performances usually start around 9 and often continue until 3 or later. Crowds are generally middle-aged, but by no means dull. Cover charges vary from DM 2 to DM 8. Tickets for major events can be purchased at the door or, for a DM 3 fee, at West Berlin's massive **KaDeWe** (Tauentzienstr. 21, tel. 030/882–7360) or at **Berlin-Jazz** (Ku'damm 26, tel. 030/677–9902). In June and July, Berlin hosts two world-class jazz festivals (*see* Festivals in Exploring Berlin, *above*). The tourist office sells passes to these for around DM 80, good for entrance to all major festival events.

Blues Café. Seedy and intimate, Blues Café features local talent and the occasional big-name act. It's the place to come if you enjoy the dive jazz scene but aren't necessarily interested in flawless music. *Körnerstr. 11A, off Potsdamerpl., tel. 030/862–0911.*

Flöz. It looks the way a blues joint ought to—dark and smoky. Local and big-name bands play pre-1950s jazz, Dixieland, and swing. Very bohemian. *Nassauische Str. 37, tel. 030/861–1000. U2 to Hohenzollernpl.*

Jazz for Fun. Hear lots of new, local jazz talent or bring your own instrument for Thursday night's open jam session. The name says it all. Admission is free most nights. *Kurfürsten Str. 10. tel. 030/262–4556. U-Bahn to Kurfürstenstr. Cover: DM 5–DM 8.*

Quartier Latin. A popular rock and jazz club in Schöneberg, this is not the place to come on a whim (cover charges range from DM 10 to DM 15), but it's a hot spot for big-name international acts. *Potsdamerstr. 96, tel. 030/262–9016.*

Quasimodo. Largely responsible for Berlin's recent jazz renaissance, Quasimodo brings in the biggest international names and hosts segments of Jazz in July (*see* Festivals in Exploring Berlin, *above*). Even though Quasimodo is world famous, it's also surprisingly untouristy—warmly and highly recommended. Covers vary from DM 5 to DM 20. *Kantstr. 12A, tel. 030/312–8086.*

➢ **ROCK • Club 29.** East Berlin's premiere rock club features all sorts of alternative, independent, and downright strange local bands. *Rosa-Luxemburg-Str. 29, tel. 030/871–1654. From Alexanderpl. walk n. on Karl-Liebknecht-Str. and turn left on Belvederestr.*

Ef Klub. This small Kreuzberg club features a good mix of punk, indie, and '70s rock. Except for the occasional American and British band, the "talent" is mostly local. Typical cover charge is DM 5. *Oranienstr. 48. U8 to Moritzpl.*

Franz-Club. Popular with a university-age crowd, this relaxed, unpretentious bar has live jazz and rock most nights, free of charge. It's in East Berlin's Prenzlauer Berg, within easy reach of the district's other bars. If it's too smoky or the band is dreadful, there's a little patio outside. *Schönhauser Allee 36–39, tel. 030/448–5393. U-Bahn to Schönhauser Allee.*

Fritz-Haus. A grimy, sweaty place in the heart of Schöneberg, Fritz-Haus offers a variety of local punk and thrash bands. *Potsdamer Str. 146, tel. 030/788–6541.*

Metropol. Indie-rock and speed metal upstairs, top 40 and Winger-type rock downstairs. Needless to say, the crowd at this Schöneberg hangout is very eclectic. Covers range from DM 4 to DM 10. *Nollendorfpl. 5–7, tel. 030/212–8966.*

Nikki. A popular rock-punk-thrash hideout in the middle of Kreuzberg. Tattoos, Doc Martens, and long hair are the norm here. Covers range from free to DM 10, depending on who's playing. *Reichenbergerstr. 121. U1 or U8 to Kottbußer Tor and walk e. on Skalitzerstr.*

Near Berlin

POTSDAM

No matter how short your stay in Berlin, make time for a quick visit to Potsdam, the capital of Brandenburg. The town's historic quarters are intensely beautiful and give a good sense of what Berlin might have looked like, but for World War II. On the plush side there's Friedrich the Great's palace, Sanssouci (French for "without a care"). It's an appropriate name for this elegant summer residence. The palaces and parks of the Neuer Garten are another big attraction; this is where Truman, Attlee, and Stalin signed the 1945 Potsdam Agreement divvying up Germany. Potsdam literally drips with history, both ancient and modern, so don't come expecting another typical Berlin suburb.

Potsdam's proximity to Berlin is a double-edged sword. On the up side, it's only 30 minutes by subway from Berlin's Zoo Station. On the downside, Berlin's industrial complex has encroached, infesting the town with too many bleak, modern blocks. This shouldn't bother you if you stick to **Friedrich-Ebertstraße, Brandenburgerstraße,** and **Platz der Einheit,** the city's social and historic focal points. You can easily walk around Potsdam in four hours, although it has an excellent youth hostel if you get stuck.

VISITOR INFORMATION Potsdam's **tourist office** provides guidebooks and maps and, after 1, can book you into a private room (DM 25–DM 35) for a DM 3 fee. They also distribute the *Potsdam Programm* (DM 1), a monthly magazine that lists local film, theater, and sports events. *Friedrich-Ebertstr. 5, tel. 0331/21100. From Potsdam Stadt S-Bahn, walk northwest across Lange Brücke and turn left on Friedrich-EbertStr. Open daily 8–6 (closed Wed. noon–1).*

Female visitors may want to check out the local women's center, **Frauenzentrum** (Zeppelinstr. 189, tel. 0331/22383). On Friday and Saturday it runs a small café. To learn more about the gay scene, contact **Homosexuellen-Integrations-Projekt** (Berlinerstr. 49, tel. 0331/22065).

COMING AND GOING The quickest way to reach Potsdam is by subway. From Berlin's Zoo Station, take the S-Bahn to Potsdam Stadt Station. The 30-minute ride costs DM 3, and you'll end up a stone's throw from Potsdam's small city center; to get there walk northwest across Lange Brücke and turn left onto Friedrich-Ebert-Straße. A more enjoyable option is the ferry. Both **Wannsee ferry** (tel. 030/803–8750) and **Potsdam ferry** (tel. 0331/42241) make the 90-minute journey to Potsdam from the dock adjacent to the Wannsee S-Bahn station. Their open-deck ferries leave hourly year-round, between 10 AM and 5 PM. The trip costs DM 6 each way.

WHERE TO SLEEP **Jugendherberge Potsdam.** This hostel has cozy four- to five-person rooms and a self-service kitchen. Beds cost DM 15 per person; add DM 5 for breakfast and DM 7 for dinner. *Eisenhardt Str. 5, tel. 0331/225125. Take Buses 604, 609, or 650 from Potsdam Hauptbahnhof n. to Eisenhardt Str.*

FOOD Potsdam's Brandenburgerstraße has a good selection of cafés and cheap restaurants. Try **Am Stadttor** (Brandenburgerstr. 1–3, tel. 0331/21729), which serves a variety of traditional German dishes for under DM 15. A more elegant option is **Minsk-Nationalitätengaststätte** (Max-Plank Str. 10, tel. 0331/23490), overlooking the River Havel near Potsdam's S-Bahn station. The view of the city is superb, as are the ethnic Russian dishes (around DM 20).

WORTH SEEING Spend some time exploring Potsdam's smart historic districts. From Platz der Einheit, near the tourist office, the pedestrian-only Brandenburgerstraße meanders north through the **Baroque Quarter,** noted for its colorful facades. Avoid the touristy "market" streets and head instead for the network of lanes that fan outward from the larger shopping avenues. These run through quiet residential areas, passing a few tree-lined parks on the way. On **Alter Markt,** Potsdam's central market square, check out the Baroque **Nikolaikirche** (1724) and the colorful facade of the former city hall, or **Rathaus** (1755), recognizable by the gilded figure of Atlas atop the tower. Three blocks north of Alter Markt is **Holländisches Viertel,** the Dutch Quarter. It was designed in 1732 by Friedrich Wilhelm I, who hoped to induce Dutch artisans to settle in the city. Few Dutch ever came, but the quarter's gabled, redbrick homes give the district a distinctive, very un-German feel. Continue north past **Nauener Tor,** an 18th-century city gate, to the **Alexandrowka** district, with its dense jumble of wood houses built in 19th-century Russian style. The Russian church **Kapelle des Heiligen Alexander** sits on top of the hill.

➢ **NEUER GARTEN** • Bordering Sanssouci Park, Neuer Garten (New Garden) is a sprawling, tree-lined park with some excellent lakeside walking trails. Inside the park stands **Schloß Cecilienhof** (admission DM 4, open daily 9–4:15), a half-timbered manor house that hosted the 1945 Potsdam Conference. This is where President Truman, British prime minister Churchill (and then Attlee), and Stalin met to decide the fate of postwar Germany. Inside you can see the conference room—adorned with historical memorabilia—and the participants' personal studies. Nowadays the Schloß is a luxury hotel. Nearby stands the two-story **Marmorpalais** (Marble Palace), built by Friedrich Wilhelm II in 1792. Once home to a military museum, it's now closed for renovation until 1999 or so. *Admission free. Park and gardens open daily sunrise–sunset.*

➢ **SANSSOUCI PARK** • If you walk north along Brandenburgerstraße past the city gate, you'll eventually stumble upon the sprawling Sanssouci Park. Its main attraction is Friedrich the Great's 18th-century **Sanssouci palace,** built in a flamboyant Rococo style that leaves no part of the facade unadorned. Friedrich was an extravagant ruler, so it's hardly surprising that his palace would be extravagant, too. You sense this in his cedar-paneled bedroom, in his gilded and heavily carved study, and in the circular central library, where Friedrich was tutored by the philosopher Voltaire. Another highlight is the palace's music chamber, considered one of Germany's finest Rococo interiors. Here, Friedrich and J. S. Bach, a frequent visitor to the palace, would sometimes play duets on the harpsichord. Unfortunately, the only way to view the palace interior is on a guided tour. These leave every 30 minutes and are included in the price of admission. On the ground floor, the Sanssouci Park information center (tel. 0331/22051) stocks maps and walking tours of the park. *Admission: DM 7. Open Mar., daily 9–4; Apr.–mid-Oct., daily 9–5; late Oct., daily 9–3.*

West of the palace, the 18th-century **Neue Kammern** (New Chambers) once housed guests of the king in enviable style. Nowadays it displays period furniture and a handful of 19th-century portraits. *Admission: DM 4. Open Sat.–Thurs. 9–5. Guided tours only.*

On the east side of the palace stands the Renaissance-style **Orangerie,** recognizable by its colonnade and two companion towers. Climb up the towers (free) for a good view of the surrounding park. Farther east, the **Picture Gallery** displays Friedrich's impressive collection of 17th-century Italian, Flemish, and Dutch paintings. Friedrich made history when he opened this gallery to the public in 1785, creating Germany's first-ever public museum. *Admission: DM 4. Open mid-May–mid-Oct., daily 9–5.*

If you continue along the broad avenue that cuts through the park, you'll stumble on Friedrich's second palace, the **Neues Palais.** Friedrich built it after the Seven Years War to prove that his treasury was not empty—a typically extravagant maneuver. Highlights include a collection of antique musical instruments on the second floor, and paintings by 17th-century Italian masters in the Upper Gallery. German-language tours (DM 2) are given whenever there's enough interest. *Admission: DM 5. Open Apr.–mid-Oct., daily 9–5; mid-Oct.–Jan. daily 9–3; Feb. and Mar., daily 9–4.*

Following Friedrich the Great's death in 1786, another Prussian king, Friedrich Wilhelm III, started adding his own additions to Sanssouci Park. The most famous is **Schloß Charlottenhof,** designed in a severe classical style by Karl Schinkel. The exterior is dully Spartan, but inside Schinkel went a bit wild. Notice the "tent room," decorated after a Roman tent, with canvas hanging from the walls and ceiling. *Admission: DM 5. Open mid-May–mid-Oct., daily 9–5. Guided tours only.*

BRANDENBURG AND SAXONY-ANHALT 9

By Peter Edwards

Brandenburg and Saxony-Anhalt cut a large swath through unified Germany's eastern extreme. In fact, prior to reunification, these two regions constituted the bulk of the former German Democratic Republic (GDR). Brandenburg, which encompasses everything around Berlin, is extraordinarily rural, typified by lazy *Burgs* and *Dorfs* (equivalent to towns and villages) set among rolling pastureland. Brandenburg supports large populations of Poles, Serbs, and Czechs, mostly because it sits on Germany's eastern border and, at least during the communist era, actively encouraged the immigration of skilled East European workers. Saxony-Anhalt, on the other hand, is more insulated. Its western border once marked the division between East and West Germany, so for the last 50 years a large chunk of Saxony-Anhalt was a sort of no-go zone, an economically depressed stretch on the fringe of a crumbling empire.

Because Brandenburg and Saxony-Anhalt lie in what used to be East Germany, both regions bare the scars of their decades-long tenure under the Red Army, and both are still plagued by the foul legacy that has come to define Cold War–era communism—industry and cement. As you wander through some of these cities it will become clear why the tourist board wants to focus on the glories of the past rather than the present. Much of these two regions still suffers from damage wrought by World War II, and reconstruction during the communist era only added insult to injury. Since reunification some effort has been made to beautify or at least demolish and rebuild the most painful reminders of the past. Yet reunification itself has brought its own Pandora's box of troubles. As former East Germans struggle with their new economy, unemployment in Brandenburg and Saxony-Anhalt remains despairingly high. You will also find evidence of skinheads and neo-Nazis who want to keep Germany for the Germans; Fascist graffiti appears on many a wall, as do swastikas and anti-Semitic slights. To appreciate these regions you need to prepare for the troublesome dichotomy of modern Germany; of beautiful unspoiled parks tempered by thinning forests dying from acid rain; of industry and pollution balanced against farmland and nature.

Despite Brandenburg's and Saxony-Anhalt's sometimes depressing edge, traveling through these regions is not all doom and gloom. In some sense, Brandenburg and Saxony-Anhalt are all the more fascinating because they represent a way of life that will soon fade into oblivion; with reunification and the drive toward westernization, it's only a matter of time before these areas become a mirror of the West. In the meantime, the pace of rural life remains wonderfully slow.

Brandenburg and Saxony-Anhalt

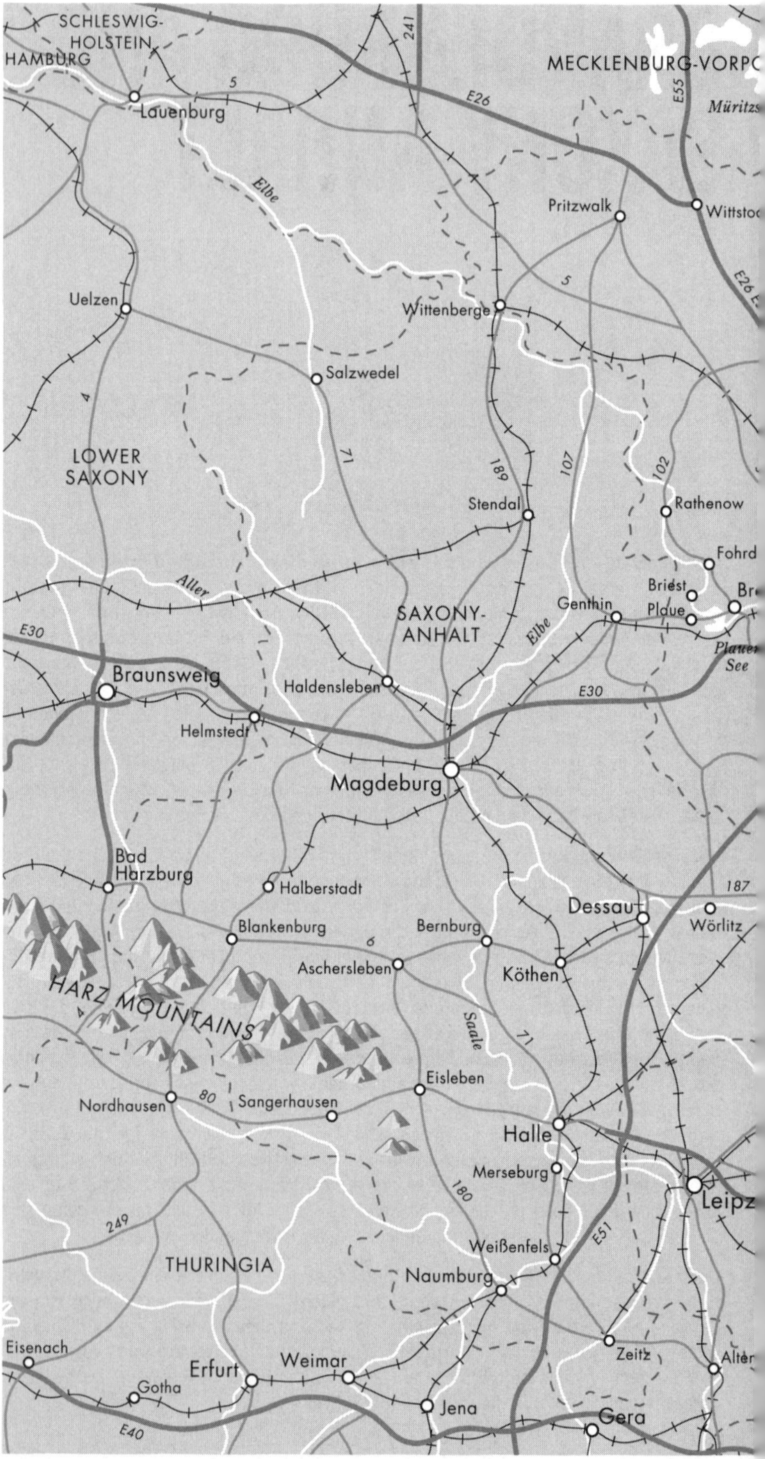

SCHLESWIG-HOLSTEIN
HAMBURG
MECKLENBURG-VORPO
Müritzs
Lauenburg
Elbe
Pritzwalk
Wittstoc
Uelzen
Wittenberge
Salzwedel
LOWER SAXONY
Stendal
Rathenow
Fohrd
Briest
Plaue
Genthin
Aller
SAXONY-ANHALT
Elbe
Plauer See
Braunsweig
Haldensleben
Helmstedt
Magdeburg
Bad Harzburg
Halberstadt
Dessau
Wörlitz
Blankenburg
Bernburg
Aschersleben
Köthen
HARZ MOUNTAINS
Saale
Eisleben
Nordhausen
Sangerhausen
Halle
Merseburg
Leipz
Weißenfels
THURINGIA
Naumburg
Zeitz
Alter
Eisenach
Erfurt
Weimar
Gotha
Jena
Gera
5
241
E26
E55
E26
5
4
71
189
107
102
E30
E30
187
6
71
80
180
249
E51
E40

Brandenburg and Saxony-Anhalt

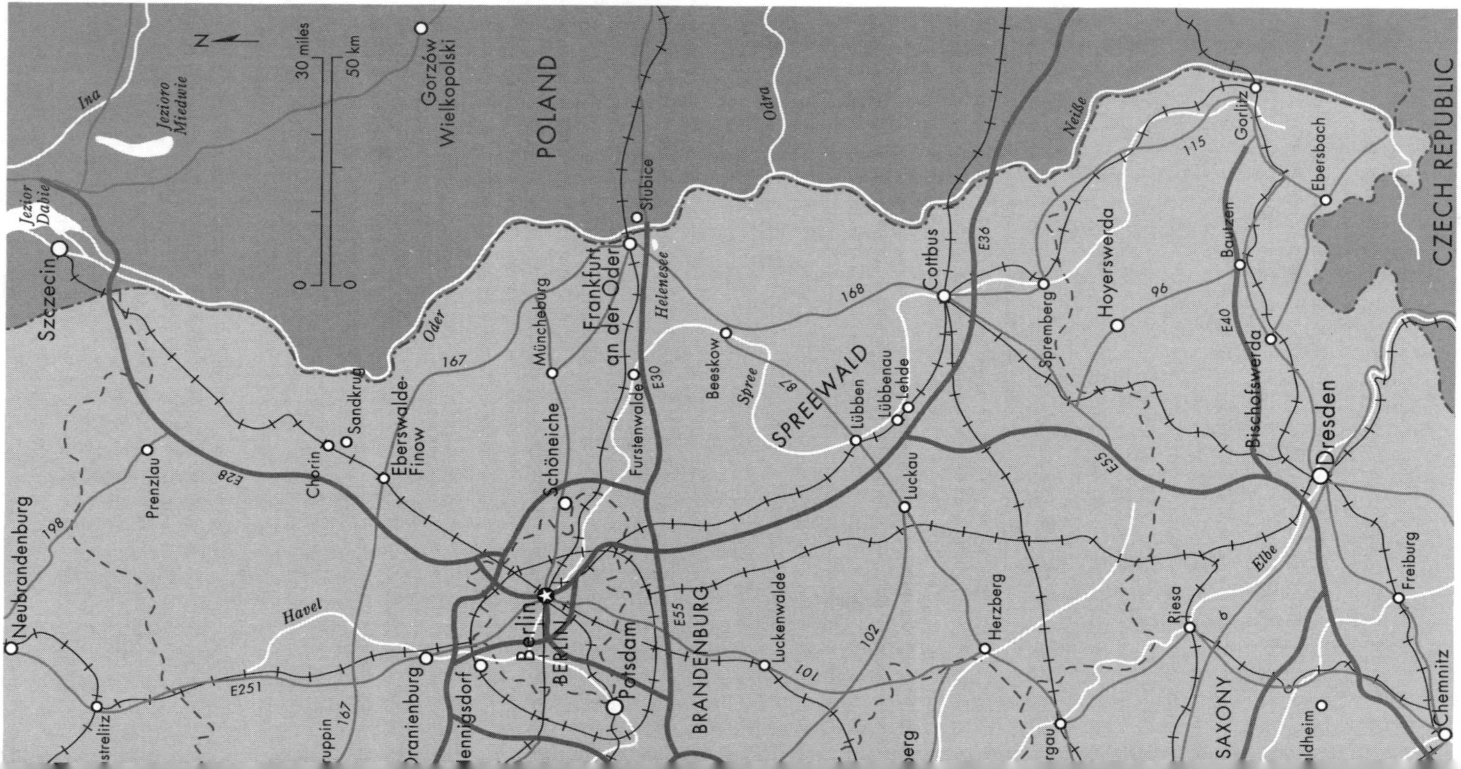

Neubrandenburg
198
Szczecin
Jezior Dabie
Ina
strelitz
Prenzlau
Jezioro Miedwie
N
E28
E251
Havel
0
30 miles
0
50 km
Chorin
uppin
167
Sandkrug
Eberswalde-Finow
Oranienburg
Oder
167
Gorzów Wielkopolski
ennigsdorf
Berlin
BERLIN
Schöneiche
Müncheburg
POLAND
Frankfurt an der Oder
Potsdam
Fürstenwalde
Słubice
E30
Helenesee
E55
BRANDENBURG
Beeskow
Spree
Odra
Luckenwalde
SPREEWALD
87
101
Lübben
168
102
Lübbenau
Lehde
erg
Luckau
Cottbus
E36
Herzberg
Spremberg
rgau
Neiße
E55
Hoyerswerda
96
Riesa
115
SAXONY
9
E40
Bautzen
Gorlitz
Elbe
Bischofswerda
ldheim
Dresden
Ebersbach
Freiburg
Chemnitz
CZECH REPUBLIC

To make the most of Brandenburg and Saxony-Anhalt, consider a brief trip to Frankfurt an der Oder—a small but historic town near the Polish border—only if it's convenient. In other words, only if you have some time to burn while staying in Berlin. A more worthwhile stop is the Spreewald, a vast river and wetland that's noted for its old-growth forests and farm villages. Major towns in the Spreewald include Cottbus and Lübben, each of which offers the chance to savor a canal ride in a punt, the regional version of a gondola—highly recommended. Another interesting stop is Dessau, home to Walter Gropius's Bauhaus School of Design. Dessau itself is rather ugly (aside from its Bauhaus sights), but it makes a good base for exploring the nearby towns of Wittenburg, where Martin Luther posted his 95 Theses and thus started the Protestant revolution; Köthen, where J. S. Bach wrote his celebrated *Brandenburg* concerti; and Halle, a large town that's rightly famous for its stunning marketplace and impressive late Baroque cathedral. Farther north, the riverfront city of Magdeburg, the largest and most developed town for miles, breaks the monotony of an endless farmland in northern Saxony-Anhalt.

Cows and sheep still outnumber people by about five to one, and in many towns, the chiming of a church bell or the passing of a train is still the day's most exciting event.

Brandenburg and Saxony-Anhalt are well connected with the German rail network. Halle, Magdeburg, and Cottbus are the regions' principal hubs. Each offers frequent connections to Berlin, Leipzig, Hamburg, Hannover, and destinations throughout Thuringia. Cyclists can have a ball in these areas because the distances are not great and because the scenery—at least once you escape into the countryside—falls somewhere between rural idyllic and sylvan nirvana. If you want to take your bike on a train, be sure to purchase a special pass (DM 10–DM 15) *before* getting on a train. Less appealing are the regions' buses—sputtery old things that lumber from dorf to dorf at a snail's pace.

Brandenburg

Since reunification Brandenburg has become a popular day-trip for Berliners, and not just because of the newly upgraded train line that connects the two cities in under an hour. In terms of scenery and historic grace, Brandenburg is one of the region's finest Baroque cities. Modern industry blankets a large section of its working-class suburbs, but within the confines of its historic city center you'll find a pleasant mix of half-timbered houses, old-style shop fronts, and relaxed, open-air squares. Brandenburg is nearly cut in half by the winding **Havel River,** so much of Brandenburg is given over to bridges, canals, and riverside walking paths (not to mention a handful of public gardens that make for excellent afternoon napping).

Brandenburg may be one of the region's better-preserved Baroque towns, but it did suffer serious damage during World War II. This can be blamed both on the Allies, who dropped over 1,000 tons of bombs on Brandenburg, and on the Nazis, who established a concentration camp and an armament factory within the city limits. These were destroyed long ago, but their impact, and the impact of the war, can still be felt in some districts. Look for bullet holes and tank blasts on city-center facades and for areas where cement apartment blocks have strangled all life. In central Brandenburg, the latter mark areas that were completely flattened by aerial bombardment.

BASICS The **tourist office** (Plauer Str. 4, tel. 03381/23743, open weekdays 9–5, Sat. 9–1) is located near the Markt in the Neustadt. From the train station or market square simply follow the signs. The office does not exchange money (try any of the banks on the Markt or along Hauptstraße; they're generally open weekdays 9–noon and 1–3:30). But they do book private rooms for a DM 3 fee. They also provide maps and bus/train information.

COMING AND GOING Trains run every two hours between Brandenburg and Berlin. The jaunt takes only an hour and costs less than DM 15. Brandenburg's train station, or **Hauptbahnhof** (tel. 03381/88325), is located 1½ kilometers (1 mile) from the Neustadt. You can walk between the two (follow the signs marked HAUPTBAHNHOF) or take Trams 1, 2, or 9 (DM 1, payable on board). Trams connect the station with the Neustadt and Markt every 10 minutes or so. Also note: The train station rents bikes for DM 10 per day. You'll need to leave your passport and a DM 50 deposit. The main bus station, or **Busbahnhof** (tel. 03381/27543), is adjacent to the train depot. If you're driving, hitching, or ride sharing you'll use Highway 1, which connects Brandenburg with Berlin, Potsdam, and Magdeburg. To reach Highway 1 from the city center, follow the many posted road signs.

WHERE TO SLEEP Brandenburg has no reasonably priced hotels—not one. The cheapest you'll find costs at least DM 90 per room in winter and from around DM 110 in summer. Luckily the tourist office can book you into a comfortable private room for DM 20–DM 25 per person (plus a DM 3 fee). Most are scattered in the Neustadt, only a short crawl from the nearest beer hall or wiener stand. The **Jugendherberge Brandenburg** (Hevellerstr. 7, tel. 03381/521040, midnight curfew, check-in after 3 PM) has rooms for under DM 15 but fills up quickly during the summer season. Reservations are advised. The hostel itself is typically large and informal, boasting single-sex rooms, communal showers, and a standard 8 AM breakfast (included).

FOOD The food here is nothing to jump and cheer about. Wander along the pedestrianized Hauptstraße for decent cafés and bargain-priced street stands. Locals like to eat at the town's **Ratskeller** (Altstädtischer Mark 10, tel. 03381/24051), a semi-pricey option when you consider that a standard beer and wiener fetches at least DM 10. Health nuts will enjoy Brandenburg's youth club, the **Jugendklubhaus Philipp Müller** (Steinstr. 42, no tel., no Sat. lunch, closed Sun.) which doubles as a vegetarian café. Food isn't always available—and it's not always good—but it's cheap (under DM 10), and often you'll meet up with some interesting locals, many of whom can speak English.

WORTH SEEING Brandenburg is divided into the Altstadt and Neustadt, but these are only relative terms. The old city, which hugs the banks of the Havel on the western edge of town, was founded by German merchants in the 10th century. The so-called new city, which lies to the south, was first settled as late as 1250, which explains Brandenburg's tangible historic flavor. **Dominsel** (Cathedral Island), which marks the spot of Brandenburg's original 10th-century settlement, is neither in the old or new section of town but rather nestled in between, so it makes a good navigating tool when exploring Brandenburg by foot. Dominsel's most recognizable sight is the 12th-century **Cathedral of Saint Peter and Saint Paul** (open Mon.–Sat. 9–6). It's a refined Gothic work that looms heavily over the river and its adjacent shopping streets. Inside, take a look at the unusual relief of the fox in monk's clothing. Oddly enough, he's spreading the Word to a congregation of geese. Also of interest is the cathedral's collection of 13th-century stained glass, particularly the ornate cycle that crowns the altar. Don't

No Bach Here

Classical music fans may expect Brandenburg to echo something of its rich musical past. After all, J. S. Bach's* Brandenburg *concerti were named in honor of the city. The connection, however, is illusory: Bach wrote the concerti in Köthen in 1716, and they were thus named only because they were dedicated to Prince Ludwig of Brandenburg. Bach himself perceived the concerti as minor works, and it's quite likely they were never performed during his lifetime.

bother with the cathedral's very dull **Brandenburg Museum** (admission free), which chronicles—in German—the town's history from the Middle Ages to the present.

From Dominsel, walk south along **Mühlendamm,** one of the city's more atmospheric shopping avenues. At the southern end of Mühlendamm is the Neustadt's **Markt,** lined with butchers and bakers, druggists, and the occasional street merchant. The first sight that jumps out at you is the Gothic **St. Katharinenkirche** (St. Catherine's Church, open daily 10 AM–4 PM, admission free), noted for its red-brick facade and its towering, ornately decorated spire. Also of note are the cathedral's stained-glass windows. Although much of the structure was badly damaged during World War II, the windows were thankfully hidden by church priests and thus preserved. Many of St. Catherine's windows originally stood in the now ruined **Klosterkirche,** a 12th-century monastery whose decayed skeleton can still be seen on nearby Paulikirchplatz. The Neustadt doesn't have much else in terms of official sights, but spend some time exploring the streets that crisscross the marketplace. On the whole they boast a solid collection of Baroque half-timbered houses and pleasant, less touristy shops.

From the Neustadt's Markt, walk west along **Hauptstraße,** Brandenburg's pedestrianized shopping avenue. Along the way you'll pass a horde of cafés, bakeries, restaurants, and even a few smart-looking bars that have sprouted up since reunification. Continue west and you'll cross over the Havel River. This marks the unofficial entrance to the Altstadt. Immediately you'll notice yet another late Gothic monument, the 15th-century **Altstädter Rathaus** (Old Town Hall, closed to the public). Made of weathered brick and surrounded by a handful of half-timbered buildings, the town hall looks impressively old—a bulky but respectable outcast in an otherwise impeccably Baroque district. North of the Rathaus is **St. Gotthartkirche** (Church of St. Gotthart, 23 Kirchestr., admission free, open Mon.–Sat. 9–5:30), another embellished Gothic creation that contrasts nicely with the nearby remnants of Brandenburg's 12th-century city wall. Also nearby are the ruins of four guard towers. They're closed to the public, but hopping the fence for a brief ramble is not unheard of.

A Break from Baroque

If you can't bear the thought of exploring yet another Baroque or Gothic monument, rent a bike at Brandenburg's train station and strike out along the Havel River. The old city provides a nice backdrop for a bike ride, but the cobblestones are murder on your bum. Another option is Highway 1, which leads west toward Plaue and Genthin. After it escapes the congested city center, it then passes through rural farmland and, near Plaue, along the banks of the Plauer See lake. An even more scenic detour starts from Highway 1 about 10 kilometers (6 miles) east of Plaue; take the rough-paved, two-lane road marked "Briest/Fohrde" north and you'll quickly find yourself in a wonderfully peaceful valley surrounded by farmland to the east and by an arm of Plauer See to the west. At Fohrde you can join Highway 102 and return, 13 kilometers (8 miles) later, to Brandenburg.

Frankfurt an der Oder

The "other" Frankfurt sits on the far eastern side of Germany, about 90 kilometers (56 miles) east of Berlin and quite literally just a short walk over the **Oder River** from Poland. The Poles, in fact, have played a significant role in the development of this once elegant riverfront town. In May 1945, after the Third Reich had already surrendered, a company of disconsolate Nazi soldiers remained in the city. They were awaiting the arrival of the victorious Soviet army, but, before the Nazis were disarmed, they were provoked by a rag-tag troop of Poles from across the river. Until then, Frankfurt an der Oder had escaped the devastation of World War II relatively intact. The clash between the Nazis and Poles, however, quickly degenerated into house-to-house warfare. This sparked a ferocious fire that consumed 90% of the town within days.

Today, Frankfurters still feel resentment toward the Poles, even more so since Germany's unification and Poland's free-market reforms have forced some measure of economic cooperation. Frankfurt an der Oder is hardly a hotbed of ethnic tension, but you will notice the subtle signs of racism—Poles and Germans sitting apart in cafés, occasional street brawls, and the curt treatment of Polish merchants who, at least according to the Germans, are taking jobs away from the locals.

The city center lies on the banks of the Oder. If time is short, hit the Altstadt near Rosa Luxembourg Straße. Its most impressive feature is **Marktplatz,** an expansive open-air square located a hundred yards west of the Oder. Marktplatz is lined with the town's few remaining Gothic and Baroque buildings, so it's easy to spot. Its most imposing monument is also its oldest, the 14th-century city hall, notable for its late Baroque towers. The facade dates from the 17th century and is adorned with a bent iron grille—the symbol of the 15th-century Hanseatic League, of which Frankfurt was once a member. Inside is a small modern art gallery, the **Galerie an der Oder** (tel. 0335/22763, open Tues.–Sun. 10–5). Behind the city hall, on the banks of the Oder, you'll find the world's only museum dedicated to Heinrich von Kleist, one of Germany's great writers. The **Kleist Museum** (Fährstr. 7, tel. 0335/24520, open Tues.–Fri. 10–noon and 2–4, weekends 2–5) is housed in a restored Baroque palace that dates from 1777, the year of the dramatist's birth. Kleist lived only 34 years (he shot himself in Berlin in 1811), but Goethe and Thomas Mann each claimed Kleist's work as a source of deep inspiration. On display in the museum are original manuscripts, personal items, and some contextual material.

Three times a week in summer, open-air classical concerts are held in the ruins of **St. Marienkirche** (St. Mary's Church, Große Scharrnstr., tel. 0335/22442), a former Franciscan monastery that's wonderfully dark and gloomy. The **Carl Philipp Emanuel Bach Concert Hall** (Lebuser Mauerstr., tel. 0335/22452), beside the Oder River, also attracts classical music lovers. Tickets for both venues can be purchased at the tourist office (*see* Basics, *below*), which publishes a free schedule of events. Ticket prices vary between DM 12 and DM 20.

Poland for a Day

Since visas are no longer required to visit Poland, Frankfurt an der Oder is a convenient hub for catching a train to Warsaw and makes a good base for quick jaunts across the border. Walk down Rosa Luxembourg Straße until it ends at the Oder, then across the bridge into Poland. With only the flash of a passport you can spend an afternoon wandering the Polish city of Slubice, a short walk from the Oder River bridge. Slubice isn't overly scenic, but then again, it's not every day you can lunch in Germany and dine in Poland.

BASICS The **tourist office** (Wilhelm-Pieck-Str. 8, tel. 0335/325216 or 0335/22565, open Mon.–Sat. 10–4) stocks maps and glossy brochures, books private rooms for a DM 3 fee, and publishes a free list of food and lodging options. The **Deutsche Bank,** on Marktplatz, exchanges money at competitive rates. It's open weekdays 9–3, until 5 PM on Thursdays.

COMING AND GOING Trains for Frankfurt an der Oder depart every two hours from eastern Berlin's Hauptbahnhof. The trip takes 90 minutes and costs DM 12.60 each way. Other trains depart hourly from Cottbus, twice daily from Magdeburg, and five times daily from both Dresden and Leipzig. There are also three trains daily to Warsaw, Poland; this trip takes six hours and costs around DM 60. Frankfurt's train station is located within a 15-minute walk of Marktplatz; walk straight out the depot, turn right, and continue until you intersect the Oder River. From the Busbahnhof, adjacent to the train depot, buses depart every few hours for Berlin, Cottbus, and Dresden.

WHERE TO SLEEP The tourist office books private rooms that cost around DM 20 per person, not including the DM 3 booking fee. A better bet is the **Jugendgästehaus** (Spartakusring 23, tel. 0335/45716), a 72-bed circular complex set on a hill overlooking town. Beds fetch DM 22 (under 27) and DM 32 (everyone else) per night, including breakfast. From the train station walk through the Bahnhofstraße tunnel, then turn south on Große Müllroserstraße. During summer the **Freizeit und Campingpark Helensee** (tel. 0335/42623, closed Oct. 15–Apr. 15) is transformed into a hip waterside resort. Vacationing families come to this vast, 2,000-site campground for the numerous water sports available on the adjacent lake (including skinny-dipping) and for long walks in the woods. A bed in one of the 50 or so bungalows costs anywhere from DM 20, for a bare-bones bed in a communal room, to DM 90 for the prime, private rooms. If you have a tent, get a spot under the trees for DM 6–DM 10. Call ahead to ensure yourself a place. From the train station take Bus H to Helensee (DM 6), then walk south toward the water. Along the way you'll pass signs for the campground.

FOOD The **Ratskeller** (Wilhelm-Pieck-Str. 31, tel. 0335/327005), in the City Hall's basement, serves regional dishes—mainly wieners, things with cabbage, and *Klösse* (potato dumplings)—in the DM 15 range. At night there's sometimes live traditional music. **Cultur-Café Calliope** (Oderallee 5, tel. 0335/325259) serves pizza and pasta in its Haus der Künste (House of Art). Mix and mingle with the local artisans who make a habit of sipping beer at one of the café's outdoor tables. Street stands in the city center offer a variety of wursts for under DM 5.

NEAR FRANKFURT AN DER ODER

EBERSWALDE-FINOW Tired of look-alike industrial cities? In the mood to watch wild boars roaming in one of the most beautiful forestlands in Europe? Well, the tiny town of Eberswalde-Finow, less than an hour from Berlin, is the place to go. The hyphenated name came about when the towns of Eberswalde and Finow brawled over rights to a nearby river. In an ingenious maneuver, someone suggested the two towns merge so as to avoid rather than confront the problem. So merge they did, in 1971. Today, Finow keeps afloat on industry while Eberswalde draws tourists with its natural beauty. Some local rivalry still exists, but don't believe people who tell you there is nothing to see in their neighbor city. The **Eberswalde-Finow information office** (Pavillon am Markt, tel. 03334/23168, open weekdays 10–6) does a good job selling both cities. If you've come to Eberswalde-Finow for nightlife, better go back to where you came from. Traffic lights stop working around 8 PM, and the streets empty soon after. Very few restaurants stay open past 9 PM on weeknights, and even the beer halls shut early (midnight-ish) on weekends.

The two towns are connected via Wilhelm-Pieck-Straße, a large street that's impossible to miss (it's the busiest avenue for miles). In Eberswalde itself, check out indigenous plants and animals in both the **Forstbotanischer Garten** (Botanical Garden,

Alfred-Möller-Str., tel. 03334/22193, admission free) and the **Tierpark Zoo** (Zoostr., tel. 03334/23332, admission DM 5). Recently the zoo has acquired some monkeys, tigers, and other endangered species from around the world. Still, its plump, short-legged wild boars are the prime attraction. Both the garden and zoo are open daily 10–6, until 8 PM or so in summer. Eberswalde residents proudly display their history in the **Kreis Heimat Museum** (Kirchstr. 8, tel. 03334/244365), which houses locally excavated treasures from the 13th century—mostly old coins, copper and iron tools, and some jewelry. The Gothic **Stadtkirche Maria Magdalena** (Church of Maria Magdalene) in the town center on Kirchplatz, also exhibits local artwork. Yet to best appreciate Eberswalde you need to get outside of it. Try striking out along the riverbank. The farther west you go, the greener and nicer it gets. In the forest's deeper regions you may also find the oft-heralded wild boar. They're tricky little buggers, known for their nasty temper and jagged teeth.

Asked about good nighttime hangouts in Eberswalde-Finow, one local replied, "Berlin!"

In **Finow,** a short walk from Eberswalde, a 211-foot-tall water tower looks down on the city as a symbol of its industrial heritage. This isn't a good omen for Finow, which is why most visitors prefer to wander the canals and lakes outside of town. Adventurous sorts should consider the 10-kilometer (6-mile) walk to the ruined **church** near **Sandkrug,** a small village north of Finow. Follow signs for Sandkrug, then signs marked KLOSTERRUINE. The road itself meanders through lush forested countryside. Another good hike, also 10 kilometers (6 miles), is to the ruined monastery at Chorin, the 14th-century **Kloster Chorin.** An English-language pamphlet (available at the site, DM 2) guides you through the grounds room by room. During the warmer months try to come on a Tuesday night at 8 PM, when the monastery hosts free open-air classical music concerts. The excellent acoustics, coupled with the beauty of the building, make it easy to forget what century you're in. If you don't relish the idea of walking, a cab from the Eberswalde train station to Chorin should cost no more than DM 10 each way. Do negotiate the price before leaving, however, as wily cabdrivers often charge extortionate rates.

➢ **COMING AND GOING** • To reach Eberswalde-Finow from Berlin's Bahnhof Zoo station—the only large hub that serves the area—take the S5 train toward Strausberg Nord and get off at the Lichtenberg station. Here you can catch a train to Eberswalde Hauptbahnhof, located in Eberswalde on Wilhelm-Pieck-Straße. The trip takes 90 minutes total and costs around DM 7. Traveling between Finow and Eberswalde is simple: Either walk along Wilhelm-Pieck-Straße (a 15-minute proposition), or take a cab for DM 4.

➢ **WHERE TO SLEEP AND EAT** • If you caught the late train into town and are starving, try Hotelrestaurant Eberswalde (Wilhelm-Pieck-Str. 62, tel. 03334/22160), one of the few places that stay open late. Two people can eat traditional German fare for less than DM 30. As for accommodations, the tourist office books private rooms. The general rate here is DM 35 per single, DM 60 per double. Campers can get off the train at nearby Finowfurt—12 kilometers (7 miles) west of Eberswalde-Finow—and pitch a tent at Zwischer Udersee und Oder-Havel-Kanal (tel. 03335/218, closed Oct.–Mar.). Sites in this forested campground, which has access to a small lake, cost DM 15 per night.

Spreewald

If you follow the Spree River southeast from Berlin, about 100 kilometers (62 miles) later you'll notice the formerly smooth and tame river fragment into countless small tributaries. The change is subtle at first: The river separates and encircles a lonely farm, then splits again as it meanders under a canopy of thick forest. Soon, however, in the heart of the Spreewald, one river fork branches into the next at a quicker pace until you're surrounded only by marshy farmland, dense forest, and a chaotic fan of undistinguishable waterways. Thousands of years ago, the last Ice Age–formed glaciers crashed through the area and carved out the hundreds of canals that, fed by the Spree, created and maintain this rich marshland.

The beer-swilling, strong-armed, and quick-witted women and men who steer you around on your private punt make a trip to the scenic Spreewald well worth the time.

In the Upper Spreewald, near Frankfurt an der Oder, the watery landscape is peppered with pastureland and lazy farm towns. In the Lower Spreewald, near Lübbenau and Cottbus, marsh is replaced by incredibly thick—and sometimes impassable—forest, to the extent that whole sections of the Spreewald have been left virtually untouched for centuries. In these areas you may still run across the occasional Serb community. The Slavic Serbs wandered into this marshland in the 5th century AD and have since remained in isolated pockets, preserving their ethnic identity even though more than one German ruler has vehemently sought their extinction. In the Spreewald you'll notice many street signs in both German and Serbian. In fact, if you plan a boat trip through the Spreewald, odds are good that your oarsman may be Serbian.

In the Spreewald, the preferred way of getting around is by boat, usually on a one- to three-day tour that starts in Lübbenau. This is the best way to commune with the Spreewald's tree-lined rivers, but, unfortunately, it's also quite expensive. Instead consider a half- or full-day tour on a **punt,** the local version of a gondola. The whole economy of the region seems to center around these little boats. You can sightsee on them, eat and drink on them, have your picture taken with one, and even do a little shopping from a punt listing with a load of sneakers and T-shirts. The season for punt tours extends from late April through late September. A three- to four-hour trip generally costs around DM 50, but that's not so bad split between two or three people. And depending on your ability to bargain, it's possible to scam a (very) short ride for as little as DM 10. Punts and other riverboats are found in nearly any town that borders even the sorriest excuse for water.

The Spreewald has always been a popular stop with Germans and, at least since reunification, some foreign tourists. Each year it's estimated that 1 million people pass through the Spreewald, though only about half linger for more than a few days. Several large and small towns in the Spreewald provide lodging, eating, and some sightseeing opportunities, but the towns are more or less all copies from the same mold. Most have a semi-industrialized shell, a shop-filled center (beer halls, pricey clothing boutiques, tourist restaurants), a handful of very luxurious and expensive hotels, and lots and lots of water. **Lübben** and **Lübbenau** are the region's most accessible towns, so that's where the tourists tend to congregate. The smaller **Lehde** is a typical example of a very quiet Serbian village. **Cottbus,** on the other hand, is a dully industrial city that's easily forgotten (and probably best avoided).

BASICS There are three tourist offices in the region. One is in **Cottbus** (Altmarkt 29, tel. 0355/223897), located on the town's main square. The **Strand Café tourist office** (Heinrich-Heine-Str., tel. 03546/2490), in Lübben, deals mostly with boating trips and private room reservations. And the **Lübbenau tourist office** (Hafen ders Freundschaft, tel. 03542/2225) books private rooms and punting excursions. None are well stocked with maps or English-language brochures, so stop by tourist offices in Berlin or Leipzig before coming. Oddly enough, the latter often have the best information on the Spreewald.

COMING AND GOING From Berlin Hauptbahnhof, trains leave daily every three hours for Cottbus (DM 23) and Lübbenau (DM 14.80). From Leipzig, Dresden, and Chemnitz there is direct service only to Cottbus, where you can then catch one of six daily connections to both Lübbenau (DM 10) and Lübben (DM 12.80). Or join a guided bus tour from Berlin, including a two-hour punting trip, with **Berliner Stadtrundfahrt** (Kurfürstendamm 216, Berlin, tel. 030/883–1015). These convenient package tours run about DM 50 per person. Hitchhikers and those lucky dogs with their own transportation should head for either Autobahn 13 (coming from Berlin or Dresden) or Highway 87 (coming from Leipzig).

WHERE TO SLEEP Finding accommodations in the Spreewald area can be a royal pain in the bum, so consider coming on a day-trip from Berlin. With the already huge and ever-growing number of tourists that visit the area every year, most lodging options are geared for the big spender. In the summer it's also a good idea to book a bed far in advance: Private rooms have become more numerous recently, but intense competition means you may be stuck in the cold if you fail to make a reservation. Any tourist office in Berlin can do this for you, as can the three regional tourist offices. At DM 20–DM 25 per night, a private room certainly is your best option. Other possibilities include the **Spreeblick** (Gübbener Str. 53, Lübben, tel. 03546/3278), a comfortable pension with doubles starting at DM 40. Less expensive is the **Jugendherberge Lübben** (Zum Wendenfürsten 8, tel. 03546/3046 or 03546/2669, 11:30 PM curfew, check-in after 3 PM). Beds in this large but friendly hostel, situated within a 10-minute walk of Lübben's train station, cost DM 15 per person (including an 8 AM breakfast). In Lübbenau book a private room at the tourist office or try **Pension Deutsches Haus** (Ehm-Welk-Str. 38–39, tel. 03542/2435). This is a popular stop with backpackers and young couples, and rooms start at DM 25 per person. The **Cottbus youth hostel** (Klosterpl. 2–3, tel. 0355/22558, 11 PM curfew, check-in after 3:15 PM) is the only reasonable choice in Cottbus. It's located in the heart of town, only a short walk from the Altmarkt and train station. Beds in sex-segregated rooms cost DM 16 per person.

For campers, the Spreewald is like a vast open-air campground. Unsupervised camping is illegal in most areas, but during summer the forests and riverbanks bristle with tents. A legal alternative is Lübbenau's **Am Schloßpark Camping** (tel. 03542/3533, DM 8 per site, closed Oct.–Mar.). Outside Lübben try **Am Burglehn** (tel. 03546/7135, DM 6 per site, closed Oct.–Mar.). Both cater to car campers and large families, but both give good access to scenic Spreewald hiking trails.

EXPLORING THE SPREEWALD

➢ **COTTBUS** • Cottbus, which lies 31 kilometers (19 miles) south of Lübbenau and 110 kilometers (68 miles) southeast of Berlin, is the kind of place you stop in to use the rest room and not a whole lot else. World War II and the following decades did not smile on Cottbus, so if you do end up here, make a beeline for the Altstadt. Its main feature is the **Altmarkt,** a pleasant open-air square lined with a handful of Baroque half-timbered facades. The square and nearby streets are flooded with Imbiß stands, beer halls, and snazzier tourist restaurants. A few blocks east of the Altmarkt is the brick-faced **Oberkirche** (open Mon.–Sat. 10–6, Sun. noon–5, admission free), a squat 17th-century church that looks out of place among the disheveled apartments that line the adjacent streets. Inside the church notice the stunning altar and the stained glass that illuminates the Oberkirche's musty interior. If you're tired of art and architecture head instead toward **Schillerplatz,** another of Cottbus's open-air squares. Facing it are a few cafés, beer hall–ish restaurants, and the **Stadttheater** (tel. 0355/223596), seasonal home to opera, dance, and drama. The main season runs February through June. Tickets can cost as little as DM 8 with student identification.

Cottbus is neither pretty nor exciting. Since it is well connected with the German rail network its main draw is strictly practical. (The train station itself is located a short walk from the town center; head straight out the depot and follow the signs marked ZENTRUM.) Cottbus is nestled along the banks of the River Spree, so another good place for mindless walking is along the waterfront. Here you'll find dull industry punctuated with the occasional riverside café. This is also the place to come if you're looking for a punt ride. The boats lie anchored in clumps all along the shore. If you look even vaguely interested someone will inevitably approach you with a proposition. In general, expect to pay DM 20–DM 30 for a short ride, upward of DM 50 for anything over an hour. Try inquiring at the tourist office if you're having a hard time finding an interested punter.

➢ **LUBBEN** • Lübben, 10 kilometers (6 miles) north of Lübbenau, marks the dividing line between two major sections of the region: the **Unterspreewald** to the north and **Oberspreewald** to the south. The latter area has a more complex canal system and attracts more tourists. Yet since Lübben straddles this amorphous border, it provides a good balance between tree-lined rivers and swampy forest, and it's hardly ever packed with tourists. From the central **Markt,** a small square lined with the usual shops and eateries, head toward the Spree River, about 1 kilometer (⅔ mile) east. There are dozens of marked walking trails here, along with the usual punters awaiting their next fare.

➢ **LUBBENAU** • Of all the towns in the Spreewald, Lübbenau is by far the most rewarding. It not only has a pleasant harbor and riverfront promenade, but it also marks the trailhead of some excellent forested hiking routes. One of the best starts at the harbor and meanders north along the Spree River toward Lübben. Another leads east toward the small Serbian town of **Lehde,** where there's a **Jugendherberge** (Weg zur Jugendherberge 220, tel. 035603/225) and, in the village's minute center, the **Frienlandmuseum** (tel. 035603/209, admission DM 3.50), an open-air museum with full-scale replicas of traditional Spreewald dwellings. Another good walk starts from the harbor and follows a well-marked footpath into the surrounding river forest. Touring by punt is another popular option. At Lübbenau's **Hafen ders Freundschaft** (Friendship Harbor, tel. 03546/2225) you can arrange all kinds of excursions, from romantic two-person day-trips to raucous dinner outings with tables set up right on the punts. Prices vary substantially, but in Lübbenau expect to pay at least DM 25 per hour per person; a bit less if you're with a group.

Lübbenau is quite large, boasting a population of 25,000. Confine yourself to the smaller and more easily navigated *Zentrum,* or center. Start along Waldstraße, Lübbenau's main shopping avenue. There's little of historical interest here, only a pleasant collection of bakeries, food stands, trinket shops, and beer halls. At the end of Waldstraße is the Hauptmarkt, a quiet square with an adjoining gate house. Nearby you'll find the **Spreewaldmuseum** (tel. 03546/2399, open May–Sept., daily 10–4; Oct.–Apr., weekends 11–3), located in a simple late Baroque palace that once housed Lübbenau's town council. The museum has displays on the Spreewald's unique ecology and on some of the ethnic groups who have settled in the region.

Halle

Your first glance of Halle might convince you to make it the last. But don't turn around so fast. If you are a true believer in "beauty-on-the-inside," look past the ugly shell of its cement-block architecture and grim look-alike working-class ghettos. Halle is certainly one of the worst examples of Communist urban planning, but its rich cultural tradition does a lot to soften the blow. And Halle is a university town, hip and cool in its own way, capable of maintaining a relatively offbeat nightlife. Considering the relative dearth of nightlife in eastern Germany (except in Berlin and Leipzig, of course), Halle's numerous student clubs and bars are reason enough for a visit.

Even so, avoid the grim Neustadt whenever possible. This example of Soviet-style "redecorating" gives a new and unwanted meaning to the word *wasteland,* and, if you're not careful, it can be dangerous. Halle is a strangely schizophrenic town, one of those places where the university and its attendant intellectuals don't mesh well with an impoverished working class. Unfortunately, reunification has only made the problem worse, resulting in a not-so-subtle racism and the occasional spurt of violence. Crime and neo-Nazi attacks are on the rise in the Neustadt. Don't be frightened away—just be careful.

Start on Halle's well-preserved marketplace, the **Markt.** Here you'll find four Gothic-style, sharp-steepled towers rising high above the square. They're connected (two via a catwalk bridge) to **Marienkirche** (St. Mary's Church), completed in 1529, where Martin Luther once preached. These towers, along with the adjacent **Roten Turm** (Red Tower), make up the five towers of Halle, the city's symbol. The Red Tower, built between 1418 and 1506, houses a bell carillon. The whole structure looks a bit out of place against the backdrop of modern Halle, but the chimes sound darn pretty on a sunny afternoon. Nestled between the Red Tower and Marienkirche is the **Marktschlössen,** a late Renaissance creation that now houses an art gallery (open Tues.–Sun. 10–5). Continuing the centuries-old tradition, this area comes alive with street vendors and curious gawkers on weekends.

North of the Markt is the imposing **Moritzburg** (Friedmann-Bach-Pl. 5, admission DM 2, open Wed.–Sun. 10–1 and 2–6, Tues. 2–9), a castle built in the late 15th century by the archbishop of Magdeburg. The castle is supremely peaceful, with four sturdy round towers buttressed by weathered stone walls and a dry moat. Bring some wine and bread and have lunch in the interior courtyard, where old men like to sit and gossip and sleep. Inside the castle is a small but impressive art museum, displaying some outstanding 19th- and 20th-century works, including Rodin's famous sculpture *The Kiss.* Less than 660 feet due south of the Moritzburg is Halle's "other" cathedral, the early Gothic **Dom,** a smaller and less imposing structure than the Marienkirche. With its striking glasswork, however, the Dom (and its 11 AM Sunday service) is worth a brief visit. Also notable is the surrounding Domplatz, where merchants and lovers like to gather on weekends. Just south of the Dom stands Halle's popular **Neue Residenz** (tel. 0345/5523, admission DM 3, open Tues.–Sun. 9:30–4), which houses a world-famous collection of fossils excavated from the nearby Geiseltal Valley.

Halle is very much a college town: Students carrying reams of books hurry to class down the main street, or, more often, descend en masse on a local watering hole to "discuss a lecture" over beer. The **University of Halle** and the city's secondary academic institution, the **Franckeschen Stiftungen** (Francke Foundation), together support a student population of 15,000. In the city center, university buildings are not grouped together but instead are spread out. This gives the entire town an intellectual air, but it also means there's no one place to mingle with college-age types. Try either the central Markt or, a hundred yards south, the **Alter Markt.** The latter is notable for its attendant student eateries and, on its eastern side, for a 19th-century statue that depicts a young boy walking his donkey.

Halle is also the birthplace of composer George Frideric Handel, and Halle residents continue their cultural traditions with an active theater and music scene. Don't miss the **Handelhaus** (Große Nikolaistr. 5–6, admission DM 2.50), located about 300 feet

Life in the Salt Mines

Halle came into existence because of salt. As early as AD 900, Halle attracted people seeking their fortunes in the depths of its nearby salt mines. If you've never mined for salt, know that it's a smelly, strenuous, and very desiccating experience. In the old days, workers were required to drink at least ½ gallon of water every two hours lest they sweat themselves into oblivion. Learn everything you want (and don't want) to know about salt at the **Salinemuseum,** ***or Saline Museum (Mansfelderstr. 52, admission DM 2). It's located on the west side of the Saale River; from Domplatz walk one block south, turn right on Mansfelderstraße, and cross the river.***

east of Domplatz (it's tucked away on a quiet corner, however, so look carefully). Handel was born in this house cum museum. Inside there's a piano used by the composer himself and dozens of original scores. The neighboring building serves as a musicology research center and sometimes stages informal musical performances. The strong, developing theater troupes at the **Neuen Theater** (New Theater, Große Ulrichstr.) and **Das Landestheater** (National Theater, Leipziger Str.) also deserve attention. Stop by the tourist office (*see* Basics, *below*) for performance and ticket information.

BASICS The **Fremdenverkehrsamt,** or tourist office (tel. 0354/23340, open weekdays 9–6, Sat. 9–1), is in the center of the Markt at the foot of the Red Tower. Besides offering the usual maps and tourist brochures, they can book you into a private room for a DM 5 fee. Buy youth-hostel cards, valid for one year, at **Landesverband Sachsen-Anhalt/Halle** (Große Nikolaistr. 6, tel. 0354/29875) for DM 30. Store your goods at the **24-hour lockers** in the train station (*see* Coming and Going, *below*) for DM 2. For **currency exchange,** head to one of the banks on the Markt or along Mansfelderstraße.

COMING AND GOING Calle's train station is located near Thälmannplatz, a 10-minute walk from the central Markt. Walk out of the depot and head northwest up Leipzigerstraße, a pedestrianized street lined with shops, cafés, and restaurants. Destinations from Halle include Berlin Lichtenberg and Berlin Schönefeld (five trains per day from each, DM 35), Dessau (four per day, DM 12.60), Köthen and Magdeburg (nine per day each, DM 8.40 and DM 21, respectively), Leipzig (six per day, DM 10.80) and, in the Harz Mountains, Wernigerode (four per day, DM 30). In town, taxis can transport you anywhere within the city center for under DM 10.

WHERE TO SLEEP AND EAT At DM 9.50 per person (add DM 5 for breakfast), the **Jugendherberge Halle** (August-Bebeltr. 48A, tel. 0354/24716, flexible midnight curfew, check-in after 3 PM) is your cheapest option. The rooms and showers in this city-center complex are quite clean. During summer, reservations are recommended. From the train station, take Leipzigerstraße to Hansering, then head north until you hit August-Bebel Straße at Curieplatz. At DM 20–DM 25 per person, a private room is the next best option. The tourist office reserves these for a DM 5 fee. If you're calling to make a private room reservation, ring the office's lodging hot line (tel. 0354/28371).

As for food, walk along the pedestrianized Leipzigerstraße, the main business strip, for tourist traps and cheap fast-food spots. Other good areas for cheap street food are Domplatz and the Markt, each of which is lined with cafés and Ratskeller-type eateries. Halle's only outstanding budget options are **Franckeklub** (Franckepl. 1, tel. 0354/28201), a student club that serves soups and sandwiches, and the youth hostel (*see above*), which offers full meals for under DM 8.

AFTER DARK Because of the large number of students, Halle's nightlife is never dull (except during finals). Spontaneous street parties are not uncommon in summer, although after-hours excitement is generally centered in clubs and bars. **Steintor-Varieté** (Am Steintor 10, tel. 0354/26360 or 38056), an offbeat grunge bar with cheap beer (DM 4), often has live music on weekends. During the summer, students pack the outdoor terrace at **Kaffeeschuppen** (Kleine Ulrichstr. 11, north of Dompl., tel. 0354/25249), an authentic Irish pub complete with heavy wooden tables and reasonable pints of Guinness. Artists, actors, and aspiring rock stars congregate at **Café NT** (Große Ulrichstr. 51), a short walk north of the Markt. The "NT" stands for New Theater, its next-door neighbor. Squatter cafés pop up here and there like short-lived spring flowers, so keep your eyes open for Halle's transient no-name clubs.

NEAR HALLE

NAUMBURG The tiny town of Naumburg sits overlooking the Saale River about 40 kilometers (25 miles) south of Halle. Its main claim to fame is the 238-foot-tall tower, the **Wenzelsturm Naumburg,** which offers a fantastic view of the town and surrounding woodland. The other big feature of the city is the **Naumburg Dom,** an imposing cathedral dedicated to St. Peter and St. Paul. It's a huge creation, built in a combination Romanesque and early Gothic style, which means it's simultaneously austere *and* flamboyant (notice the engraved gables and lavish exterior stonework). The Dom is also notable for the lifelike statues of its 12 13th-century founders. If you wander through town in June, you will notice cherries everywhere. These are the focus of the **Kirschenfest** (Cherry Festival), generally held in the first week of the month. The festival stems from a legend that dates to a time when children were sweet, naive, and ignorant. Threatened by an attacking army, the townspeople sent them to make peace with the enemy, and somehow they convinced the army to pillage and plunder elsewhere. As a reward the children were bombarded with cherries, now the symbol in Naumburg of love, peace, and friendship.

Naumburg-Information (Lindenring 36, tel. 03445/2514) books private rooms (DM 22–DM 25 per person) and stocks city maps. The lone youth hotel **Werner Lamberz** (Am Tennispl. 9, tel. 03445/5316) charges DM 15 per person. From Naumburg's unstaffed rail depot there are daily connections to Leipzig (DM 12.60) and Halle (DM 11).

Dessau

Dessau is typical of many eastern German towns. It has an impressive cultural heritage, but since World War II it has degenerated into a gruesome cement wasteland. You'll have trouble finding the historic Altstadt because so many concrete blocks have taken the place of Dessau's once elegant prewar buildings. In the industrial suburbs that surround modern Dessau, poverty and unemployment are the norm, while crumbling facades and rubble-filled vacant lots are the simple facts of life. Dessau's ugly exterior is particularly ironic when you consider that it nurtured one of the world's most ambitiously idealistic architectural movements, Walter Gropius's **Bauhaus.** After relocating from Weimar, Gropius set up his Bauhaus School of Design in Dessau in 1926. Check out the 316 Bauhaus-inspired villas in the **Törten** section of town, south of the city center. Törten is where Gropius tried to infuse Bauhaus ideas into the design of very functional things like warehouses, steel factories, and workers' dormitories. Also check out his most impressive work, the world-famous **Bauhaus building** (Gropiusallee 38, tel. 0340/5308). Its design is based on interchangeable interior cubes connected via long rectangular walkways, all encased within a vast facade of glass. The Bauhaus School of Design was forced to close in 1933 because of Nazi criticisms. They considered Gropius's idealism subversive and totally useless for a Germany preparing for war. Following a long dormancy—during which the building was used for office space—the design school was reopened in 1976. Today it boasts hundreds of students and a growing worldwide reputation. The building can be toured weekdays between 10 and 5, weekends from 10 to 12:30 and 2 to 5. The school and its immediate surroundings seem a world away from the rest of Dessau—as if Bauhaus fed on all the beauty, leaving the town a starved carcass.

Gropius's Bauhaus concept was to simplify design to allow mechanized construction of utilitarian pieces. That's not to say that Bauhaus pieces are bereft of decoration, because they're not. Instead, Bauhaus design reduced things to a simple base and then reconstructed them according to their purpose.

Along with its Bauhaus treasures, Dessau's proximity to Wörlitz and Köthen (*see* Near Dessau, *below*) is reason enough to visit. Another reason is the exquisite **Schloß Mosigkau**. This 18th-century palace lies 9 kilometers (6 miles) southwest of Dessau, accessed by bus from in front of the train station (take any bus marked MOSIGKAU). Prince Leopold commissioned the palace to be built for his favorite daughter, Anna Wilhelmine. She lived in this vast tree-lined palace by herself, a lonely spinster, and when she died she left the property to an order of nuns. Today, the Schloß has been restored in its original Baroque style—an expensive task that has left the current custodians a bit paranoid. They'll ask you to put on slippers before touring its rooms, and ask you to never, never, never ever TOUCH ANYTHING. Only about a third of its rooms can be visited. These include the impressive Baroque picture gallery, adorned with a swirling Rococo ceiling. *Tel. 0340/831139. Admission: DM 3. Open May–Oct., daily 9–6; Nov.–Apr. by appointment only.*

BASICS The **Dessau information office** (Friedrich-Naumannstr. 12, tel. 0340/474661, open weekdays 9–5, Sat. 9–1) stocks a standard collection of city maps and brochures. No surprise, they also book private rooms (DM 20–DM 30) in Dessau for a DM 4 fee. This office sometimes arranges guided tours of Schloß Mosigkau and Wörlitz, and also of Dessau's Bauhaus sites. When available, these tours cost roughly DM 25 per person. However, they're almost always conducted in German.

COMING AND GOING Dessau's **Hauptbahnhof** sits almost in the middle of town, only a short walk from Dessau's best sights. To reach the city center, walk two blocks north from the depot until you cross Antoinetterstraße, Dessau's main road. This curves south toward the center of town and the Bauhaus school. Destinations from Dessau include Berlin Friedrichstraße and Berlin Hauptbahnhof (five trains per day each, DM 25), Halle (four per day, DM 12.60), Leipzig (two per day, DM 14.80) and Magdeburg (eight per day, DM 12). The bus station is located adjacent to the train depot.

WHERE TO SLEEP AND EAT Besides private rooms, bookable via the tourist office, Dessau's only other budget option is the **Jugendherberge Dessau** (Waldkaterweg 11, tel. 0340/473312, check-in after 3:15 PM). Beds in this large city-center complex cost DM 16 per person. Campers can claim a spot at **Adria** (Dessau Mildensee, tel. 0354/7881, closed Nov.–Mar.), set on a beautiful little lake to the east of the city. Tent sites in this 200-space campground cost DM 8 per night, with an additional DM 1 per person. Take Bus 4 (or any marked MILDENSEE) from the Busbahnhof and ask to be let off near the campground. The **Ratskeller** (Am Markt, tel. 0340/44692) serves good, typical German cuisine at reasonable prices. Expect to pay DM 15 or so for a plate of wieners, dumplings, and cabbage. Otherwise, peruse the many Imbiß stands and cafés along Antoinetterstraße, Dessau's main drag.

AFTER DARK After dark, the best thing to do in Dessau is sleep. Or get intimate with a bottle of cheap red wine. If you decide to trudge through Dessau's grimy downtown, consider stopping by the **Der Klub im Bauhaus** (Gropiusallee 38, tel. 0340/4052), within a stone's throw of the Bauhaus school. Typically you'll find art students and the like hanging out, swilling beer and playing cards to the best in eastern German grunge rock. The club is open haphazardly, sometimes nightly between 8 PM and 1 AM, sometimes not. Believe it or not, Dessau does have a reasonably active cultural life. Contact the tourist office or **Theaterkasse** (Großes Haus am Fritz-Hesse-Pl., tel. 0340/ 757333) for current listings. Typical diversions include drama, classical music, and puppet theater. For the latest in offbeat possibilities (including all sorts of local live music), check out the most recent issue of *Franz* (DM 3), available at most newsstands.

NEAR DESSAU

WORLITZ The small village of Wörlitz softens the ugly industrial blow of Dessau. In the 18th century Prince Franz von Anhalt-Dessau and his architect friend Friedrich Wilhelm von Erdmannsdorff traveled extensively through Europe and Great Britain. When they returned they decided to create a garden complex like the ones they had seen in "civilized" Europe. They chose the old hunting park of Wörlitz for the site of their new creation; they dug lakes and canals, planted trees and flowers, and created what's now known as "Venice of Anhalt." Most of the park is covered by forest and gardens, but at the center is a vast lake, the Wörlitzer See. Branching off from the lake is a dense network of canals that feed smaller nearby lakes—all in all, a stunning place.

The **Wörlitz information office** (Angergasse 131, tel. 034905/95216), located in Wörlitz by the train depot, arranges guided walking tours and canal trips. The latter are great ways to experience the serene beauty of Wörlitzer Park. The typical boat trip lasts two hours and costs around DM 30 per person. The walking tours, which generally cost DM 10–DM 15 per person, take in the gardens and both **Schloß Wörlitz** and the Gothic **Gotisches Haus.** These historic monuments are situated in the center of the park; the first contains a dull collection of porcelain and china ware, the latter a handful of obscure 19th-century paintings. Both sites can be reached either by gondola or by foot. Trains to Wörlitz leave Dessau, 10 kilometers (6 miles) west, only at 9:40 AM and 4 PM. They return daily at 11 AM or 7 PM, so plan your day beforehand. The trip takes 20 minutes and costs DM 4. To reach the park from Wörlitz train station, walk out of the depot and follow the SEE, PARK, or ROSENINSEL signs.

KOTHEN Köthen sits 30 kilometers (19 miles) southwest of Dessau. Its claim to fame is Johann Sebastian Bach, the renowned composer, who lived in Köthen for six years. During his residency Bach composed some of his greatest works, including the *Brandenburg* concerti. Every November a Bach festival brings the master's inspiring Baroque tunes to local concert halls. Contact the Köthen **tourist office** (Am Markt 9A, tel. 03496/2378) or the tourist office in Halle (*see* Halle, *above*) for ticket and venue information. During the rest of the year, Köthen's marketplace and its narrow, medieval streets make a pleasant afternoon's diversion. Trains for Köthen depart five times daily from Dessau (DM 6) and nine times daily from Halle (DM 8.40).

WITTENBERG Martin Luther fans rejoice, but be forewarned. Wittenberg is the place where the great reformer posted his 95 Theses—thus splitting the Christian world in two—but this important historical event is the only thing of value left in an otherwise bleak place. Because the **Wittenberg Door** has become something of a shrine for Lutherans and other protestants, the Aldstadt has been reasonably maintained for tourists. However, a couple of museums can't mask the fact that the surrounding area was irrevocably damaged by World War II and 40 years of communism.

All of the worthwhile sights are conveniently clumped together in the **Altstadt,** officially known as the Lutherstadt-Wittenberg. On the far eastern corner of this small, grimy quarter is **Lutherhalle** (Collegien Str. 54, open Tues.–Sun. 9–6), the building where Martin Luther once lived and worked. Today it's been converted into a museum. For DM 5 you can see original documents from Luther's own hand, including drafts of his 95 Theses attacking the practice of indulgence—selling pardons that, for a few gold coins, would excuse even the worst of sins—by the Catholic church. Be sure to pick up the compact English-language guidebook (DM 2) at the front desk. It tells you everything you could want to know about Luther and Wittenberg. On the opposite end of the old town is the **Schloßkirche,** or palace church, where Luther actually nailed his 95 theses to a door. Said door is now cast in bronze, gleaming, a sort of holy marker that attracts an unbelievable number of pilgrims. Inside the palace is a dull museum of ethnology, a restaurant, and the **Jugendherberge Wittenberg** (Wittenberg Schloß, tel. 03491/3255), a clean and friendly, 104-bed complex. Space in its sex-segregated rooms costs DM 14 per person, including an 8 AM breakfast.

The Altstadt's other main attraction is the central marketplace, or **Markt.** Standing in the center of this wide open-air square are two statues, one of Martin Luther, the other of Professor Melanchton, the famous humanist and one of Luther's staunchest compatriots. The Rathaus and **Stadtkirche** (city church) also overlook the Markt, where merchants still vociferously hawk their goods as they have done for 700 years. East of the market, in the direction of Lutherhalle, stands the **Melanchtonhaus** (Melanchstr., admission free, open Tues.–Sat. 10–5), where the professor lived. The ivy-covered Renaissance facade faces away from the street, so keep your eyes peeled for it. Inside you'll find originals and copies of the great educator's manuscripts, along with displays explaining (in German) the town's history.

Wittenberg's **Hauptbahnhof** is only a short walk from the Altstadt: Walk south down Am Bahnhof Straße, then head west on Dresdenstraße. Along Dresdenstraße you'll pass Lutherhalle and soon hit the market square. You can rent bicycles at the train station (DM 20 full day, DM 12 half day) to speed up sightseeing, but everything is within walking distance. The **Wittenberg tourist-information office** (Collegienstr. 29, tel. 03491/2239, open weekdays 10–5, Sat. 10–3) is within a stone's throw of Lutherhalle. Train destinations from Wittenberg include Berlin Lichtenberg (four trains per day, DM 21), Magdeburg (via Rosslau, six per day, DM 19), and Dessau (three per day, DM 8.40).

Magdeburg

Like so many other cities in the area, Magdeburg, the capital city of Saxony-Anhalt, has really suffered since the end of World War II. Wartime bombing left whole districts flattened, while postwar famine and disease decimated the already thin population. If this weren't enough, Magdeburg's subsequent tenure under the Communists left the city and its people deeply scarred. Even today, cement tenements fester in outlying suburbs, and industry continues to encroach on once-elegant historic quarters. Despite all this, since reunification the city has done a good job of rebuilding. In the Altstadt decaying buildings are under reconstruction and throughout the city gardens and parks have been replanted. Artwork, usually in the form of sculpture, dots many a narrow street. And once-condemned shops have now been transformed into reasonably bustling bakeries, cafés, and beer halls.

Luther to the Pope: Drop Dead

Martin Luther came to Wittenberg in 1508. At the time he was a practicing Augustinian monk who had come to teach theology and philosophy at Wittenberg University. Yet he quickly found himself in the middle of a maelstrom. Luther was disillusioned with the Catholic church, particularly with its habit of granting absolution to wealthy slimeballs whose only redeeming quality was a bulging coffer. So, to show his annoyance, Luther wrote down a list of personal gripes. When his list reached 95—God knows why 95—he nailed it to the Schloßkirche's door. The date was October 31, 1517. Needless to say, Rome was none to happy with recreant Martin Luther. They saw his 95 Theses as a kick in the eye, which they were. To make matters worse, Luther was gaining support among the peasants, who always enjoyed a good scandal, and among the region's princes, who were darn sick of sending their hard-stolen cash straight to Rome. In 1520 the Pope thus issued a papal bull condemning "the errors of Martin Luther." Like a hippie with a draft card, Luther burned the bull and kept on preaching his new brand of religion. In 1521 Luther was excommunicated from the Catholic church, which only helped to spread his message and fame.

Magdeburg's most notable feature is its 1,200-year-old **Dom** (Dompl., off Breiter Weg, admission free), a Gothic creation dedicated to St. Maurice and St. Catherine. This cathedral is the oldest in Germany, and definitely worth the trip to Magdeburg. Construction was begun in 1209, and although the work wasn't finished until 1520, its monumental facade and twin towers represent the best in late-medieval Germanic religious architecture. The founder of the Holy Roman Empire, Otto I, lies buried beneath the choir, his tomb enclosed by graceful marble columns and stone carvings that depict a troop of Christian martyrs. In the nave look for the anti-war sculpture by Expressionist artist Ernst Barlach. It was removed by the Nazis in 1933 but reinstalled following the war. Adding to the church's stunning looks is its location, perched on Domplatz overlooking the Elbe River. If you walk north from the Dom, toward the Altstadt, you'll soon pass Magdeburg's "other" church, the 11th-century **Unser Lieben Frauen** (Regierungstr. 4–6). This Romanesque monastery and church now contains a concert hall and art gallery, displaying the best of medieval and modern Germany side by side. The dark, musty gloom of the church makes an excellent atmosphere for brooding classical concerts; consult the tourist office (*see* Basics, *below*) or call 0391/33741 for current performance schedules.

Continue north from Unser Lieben Frauen and you'll soon stumble upon Magdeburg's historic central square, the **Alter Markt.** Its west side is completely dominated by the 17th-century **Rathaus,** one of the town's few remaining Baroque buildings. Directly in front notice the equestrian statue; it's a bronze copy of the **Magdeburger Reiter,** Germany's oldest-known equestrian work. The original sandstone piece (completed by an unknown master in 1240) is currently on display in the **Kulturhistorisches Museum** (Otto-von-Güricke-Str. 68–73, admission DM 3, open Tues.–Sun. 10–6), located three blocks west of Domplatz. Also on display in the museum is the original equipment used by the 17th-century scientist Otto von Güricke to prove the power of a vacuum. The device consisted of two hollowed cups joined together and then drained of air by a pump. Güricke next attached the contraption to two teams of eight horses, gambling that the animals could not overpower the bond caused by the vacuum. As history records, Güricke was right.

BASICS The **Magdeburg information office** (Wilhelm-Pieck-Allee 14, tel. 0391/35352 or 0391/316667, open weekdays 10–5, Sat. 10–1) is near the main railway station. Stop in for city maps, English-language walking guides (when available), and to book a private room or pension. There's a handful of **banks** on Ernst-Reuter-Allee, the main commercial street, that exchange money at competitive rates. All are open without exception weekdays 10–1 and 2–4.

The Romanesque Road

Germans have an affinity for cutesy tourist trails. Already there's the Märchen Straße (Fairy-tale Road) and the Romantisches Straße (Romantic Road). Soon the world will be blessed with yet another "evocative" tourist trail, the Romanesque Road. The idea is to create an easy-to-follow route that hits Saxony-Anhalt's 10th- to 13th-century hot spots. Historic Magdeburg will definitely be a prime attraction, as will the banner of small towns that lie hidden in the nearby mountains. The tourist office has already printed some brochures and detailed a circular 35-city drive, but the whole thing is still in its infancy. In any case, stop by the Magdeburg tourist office for the latest news.

COMING AND GOING Magdeburg is well connected by train with most major German cities. Its **Hauptbahnhof** is at the western end of Ernst-Reuter-Allee; to reach the city center, walk east down this street in the direction of the Elbe River. Four blocks from the depot, the Alter Markt will be one block to your left and Domplatz will be two blocks to your right. Primary destinations from Magdeburg include Berlin (nine trains per day, DM 20), Dessau (eight per day, DM 12), Hamburg (six per day, DM 45), Hannover (six per day, DM 30), and Leipzig (five per day, DM 25). Other destinations include Erfurt, Halle, Brandenburg, and Frankfurt an der Oder. The bus station is adjacent to the train depot. Bus destinations from Magdeburg include Dessau (two per day, DM 10) and Halle (two per day, DM 18).

WHERE TO SLEEP AND EAT The tourist office can book you into a private room or luxury hotel for a DM 5 fee. The former costs around DM 20 per person, the latter around DM 80. There's no youth hostel in town. The cheapest pension is **JTH Magdeburg** (Leiterstr. 5, tel. 0391/3381). Rooms, which are clean and generally equipped with a sink, start at DM 50. As for food, **Haus des Handwerks** (Garaisstr. 10, tel. 0391/ 51422) serves up good traditional German meals for under DM 20 per person. Another high-priced option is the **Stadt Prag** (Ernst-Reuter-Allee 10, tel. 0391/ 51162), popular with German tourists and visiting business types; try the Viennese chicken, the Hungarian goulash, or a plate of Saxony dumplings. Expect to pay at least DM 25 per person. For cheap eats you'll have to make do with the cafés and street stands around the Alter Markt.

AFTER DARK You can actually find a wee bit of nightlife in Magdeburg. German-speakers should consider an evening of theater or cabaret. The tourist office has current performance information, as does **Theaterkasse** (tel. 0391/53510), which also sells tickets. The most popular youth-oriented club is **Diskothek Wolfsklause** (Süll-durfer Str. 5, tel. 0391/46440), a jazzy-looking place that entertains dancers with a smattering of Top-40 hits.

SAXONY 10

By Ann McDevitt and Scott McNeely

Throughout history Saxony has played a significant role in shaping the political and intellectual climate of Europe. In centuries past, the region had a big say in who would be elected ruler of the Holy Roman Empire. And even as the power of that empire waned, Saxony continued to be a major contributor to the cultural life of eastern Germany; Berlin and Weimar may have gotten all the political glory, but it was the Saxon towns of Leipzig and Dresden that often led the way in music and the arts. Composer Robert Schumann was born in Zwickau, near Chemnitz, and Richard Wagner and Richard Strauss opened several of their operas at Dresden's Semperoper (Semper Opera House). Johann Wolfgang von Goethe, Gotthold Lessing, and Friedrich Nietzsche studied at Leipzig University, and Johann Sebastian Bach played the organ at Leipzig's St. Thomas's Church, where he was the choir director for 27 years. Although you could argue that neighboring Thuringia has a better-preserved collection of historic homes and monuments (Saxony was particularly hard hit by World War II), Saxony's cultural heritage is potent by any standard.

With a population of approximately 5 million people, Saxony was the largest of the five former East German states. During the German Democratic Republic (GDR) years, Saxony produced almost 30% of the communist regime's gross national product. And, like many regions in the former GDR, Saxony bears the gross scars of industry and environmental exploitation. Coal pits infest the outskirts of Leipzig, chemical plants form a grim landscape around Chemnitz, and south of Dresden you'll see miles of gutted, seemingly lifeless land—places where mile after mile of tree stumps mock the region's former natural beauty.

Most towns in Saxony have well-preserved Altstädte (old towns), but behind their facades is the crumbling plaster of buildings that have foundered under 40 years of communist mismanagement.

Despite reunification, the differences between east and west are still quite apparent in Saxony. The region's phone system can be temperamental, and roads and bridges often lie abandoned or severely neglected. Saxony certainly is working to outgrow its communist past and catch up to the West. Streets have reverted to their old names, once again honoring figures other than Karl Marx, Friedrich Engels, and Vladimir Lenin. But sadly for Saxony, competition in Western markets has spelled the end for many local factories, once the lifeblood of the region.

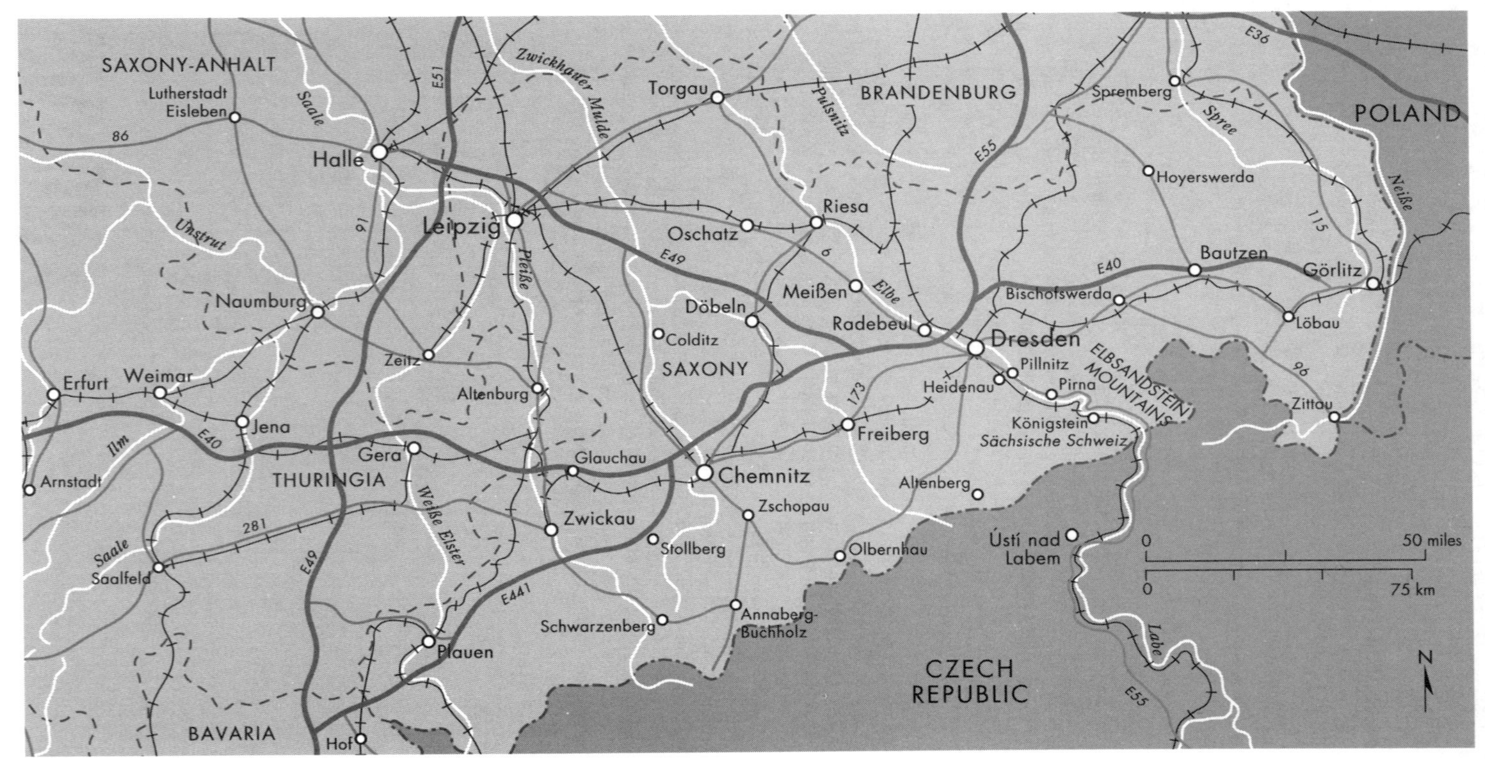
SAXONY-ANHALT
BRANDENBURG
POLAND
SAXONY
THURINGIA
BAVARIA
CZECH REPUBLIC
Lutherstadt Eisleben
Halle
Leipzig
Torgau
Riesa
Oschatz
Meißen
Döbeln
Colditz
Radebeul
Dresden
Pillnitz
Pirna
Heidenau
Königstein
Sächsische Schweiz
ELBSANDSTEIN MOUNTAINS
Spremberg
Hoyerswerda
Bautzen
Görlitz
Bischofswerda
Löbau
Zittau
Naumburg
Zeitz
Altenburg
Erfurt
Weimar
Jena
Gera
Glauchau
Chemnitz
Zwickau
Freiberg
Altenberg
Zschopau
Stollberg
Olbernhau
Annaberg-Buchholz
Schwarzenberg
Plauen
Hof
Arnstadt
Saalfeld
Ústí nad Labem
Saale
Unstrut
Ilm
Pleiße
Zwickauer Mulde
Pulsnitz
Elbe
Spree
Neiße
Weiße Elster
Labe
E36
E40
E49
E51
E55
E441
86
91
6
173
281
115
96
0
50 miles
0
75 km
N

Saxony

Does any of this matter to the average tourist just passing through? Not really, because Saxony offers a diverse mixture of sights. Leipzig and Dresden, Saxony's principal cities, each have scads of concert halls and museums. And in the few years since reunification each also has a solid—and growing—collection of bars, cafés, and hotels. Of course, Saxony may one day become as overdeveloped and commercialized as parts of western Germany, but in the meantime it sustains a fascinating balance between the old and the modern. In fact, part of the allure of a visit to Saxony is the ease with which you can alternate between urban and rural pursuits.

For lots of reasons—mainly the prevailing impression that eastern Germany is a grim armpit of industry—most foreign travelers make it only as far as Leipzig or Dresden. These towns certainly fall into the don't-miss category, but consider lingering a bit longer before moving on. Dresden is a base for some impressive day trips and excursions into Sächsische Schweiz, the striking range of mountains that hug the Elbe River on its winding journey into the Czech Republic. And in small towns like Pirna, Bautzen, or Colditz you'll have the chance to appreciate and make peace with nature.

Dresden

Dresdeners claim they live in the most beautiful city in Germany. This might seem a bold statement when you consider that much of the city was gutted by brutal Allied firebombing on February 13–14, 1945; and that for nearly 45 years the city was bleakly rebuilt with factories and cement-block housing courtesy of the GDR government. Since reunification, however, money from the richer western German Länder has flowed in to help this bastion of culture clean up and catch up. Today nearly as many cranes as spires crowd the old town's skyline. Twenty new hotels are being built to accommodate travelers, and throughout the city monuments and historic squares are getting a face-lift.

Dresden has long been the region's political and economic focus. Throughout the Middle Ages its only political rivals were Erfurt (in neighboring Thuringia) and Leipzig. These powerful principalities could do little to undermine Dresden's substantial trade-based economy, which benefited from Dresden's proximity to trading centers like Berlin and Prague and its location on the Elbe River, an important trading channel that flows to Hamburg and the North Sea. Even the gruesome Thirty Years War had little long-term effect on Dresden's development—a remarkable feat, when you consider how badly the war devastated the rest of Saxony.

For a fascinating (some would add "wacked-out") retelling of Dresden's destruction at the end of World War II, flip through Kurt Vonnegut, Jr.'s Slaughterhouse-Five.

In the 15th century Dresden became the capital of Saxony, but it wasn't until the 18th century that Dresden experienced its cultural golden age. For a host of complicated historical reasons the king of Poland, August II, came to rule Dresden in 1694. He and his son, Friedrich August II, brought leading Bavarian and Italian architects to the city to carry out a massive building campaign. Dresden's impressive palace, the Zwinger, and the Baroque Frauenkirche date from this period, as do a number of elegant mansions throughout the restored old town. These royal patrons pushed Dresden to become a center for art and music. They built opera houses and renovated theaters, improvements that would later entice a trio of brilliant composers: Carl Weber in the 1820s, Richard Wagner in the 1840s, and Richard Strauss at the turn of the century.

Despite its bleak reputation, Dresden is still incredibly cultured—the old town is littered with monuments and respected museums, while operas, ballets, and orchestral concerts fill the city's many venues on balmy summer nights. Dresden's Semperoper, which has had more reconstructive work than Michael Jackson, will impress you with its lavish crimson, gold, and white interior even if you're not into music. And if you're sick of museums and churches, there are at least a few bars and beer halls to keep you occupied in the old town, not to mention some picture-perfect riverside walks. The

Dresden

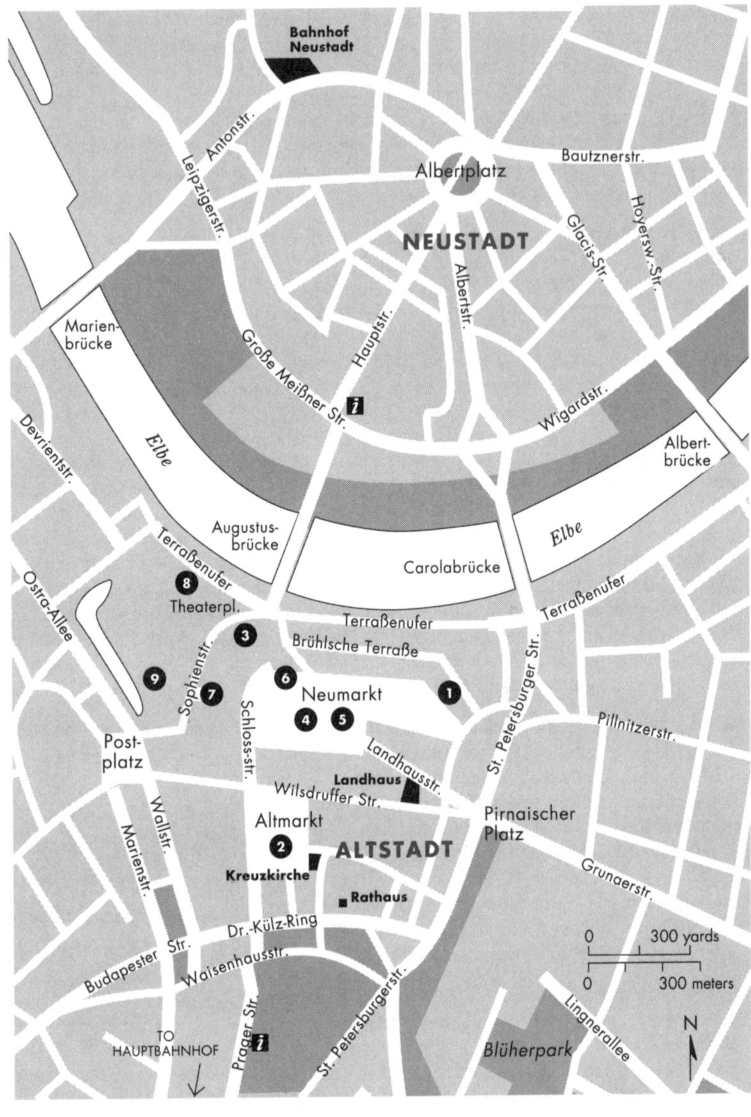

Albertinum, **1**
Altmarkt, **2**
Frauenkirche, **5**
Johanneum, **6**
Katholische Hofkirche, **3**
Neumarkt, **4**
Residenzschloß, **7**
Semperoper, **8**
Zwinger, **9**

moral of the story: You've a screw loose if you're within a couple of hundred kilometers of Dresden and don't visit.

BASICS

AMERICAN EXPRESS About the only taste a hard-up traveler will get of the ultra-chic, ultra-expensive Hotel Bellevue is the **American Express Travel Service.** The office issues and cashes traveler's checks, arranges Moneygrams, holds customer mail for a month, and has an ATM machine. *Große Meißner Str. 15, tel. 0351/566–2865. Tram 4 from Theaterpl. or Tram 5 from Hauptbahnhof to Neustädter Markt. Open weekdays 9–5:30, Sat. 9–noon.*

BUREAUX DE CHANGE An ATM inside the **Hauptbahnhof** accepts Visa and American Express if you have a PIN number. The adjacent **Deutsche Verkehrs-Bank** (open weekdays 7:30–8, Sat. 8–4, Sun. 9–1) exchanges traveler's checks but does not deal with plastic. Walking from the train station into the Altstadt you'll find two other banks that handle foreign exchange: **Deutsche Bank** (tel. 0351/495–1081) and **Commerzbank** (tel. 0351/495–3003), both near the intersection of Waisenhausstraße and the pedestrian-only Prager Straße.

LAUNDRY The **Waschsalon** (Bärensteiner Str. 10) is the best bet for self-service laundry. A wash *and* dry cost DM 4 per load, and you can iron those pesky wrinkles out of your sheets for DM 1. It's open till 9 on weekdays, until 4 on weekends.

Waschservice charges according to how much hot water you need—DM 2.50 for a 90° load, DM 2 for cooler settings. When you get tired of watching your clothes get agitated, check out the adjacent café. *Louisenstr. 48, at rear of bldg., tel. 0351/30250. Open Mon., Tues., Thurs. 8–7; Wed., Fri. 8–4.*

LUGGAGE STORAGE The train stations are the only places to store your stuff. The **Dresden Hauptbahnhof** and the **Bahnhof Dresden Neustadt** are convenient and have reasonably priced (DM 2 per 24 hours) lockers. You can also leave your stuff at the left-luggage desk for DM 3.

VISITOR INFORMATION **Tourist Information–Prager Straße,** the main office, sells theater tickets, arranges accommodations, and offers an overwhelming amount of info on things to do and places to see. *Prager Str. 10–11, tel. 0351/495–5025. From Hauptbahnhof walk up Prager Str. Open Apr.–Sept., Mon.–Sat. 9–8, Sun. 9–1; Oct.–Mar., weekdays 9–8, Sat. 9–2, Sun. 9–1.*

Dobro Pozhalovat v Dresden (Welcome to Dresden)

In the frenzy of reconstruction, memorials to Lenin and Marx have virtually disappeared. But vestiges of Soviet influence remain. Dresden is set up to deal with Russian-speaking visitors as well as English-speaking ones. A few Russian street signs remain, and in the tourist office and most large hotels you'll find Russian-language city guides, not to mention Russian-speaking tour guides who lament the recent drop in business. If you want to practice your Russian, look for a soldier of the old Red Army—troops are still stationed on the north side of Dresden—or join a service at the Russian Orthodox church on Juri-Gagarin-Straße.

Tourist Information–Neustädter Markt doesn't deal with hotels or theaters but sells tickets for trams and other public transportation. The friendly staff also offers brochures and sightseeing suggestions. If you can't get a copy of the monthly magazine *Dresdener* here (a German publication, so keep your dictionary handy), pick one up at a newsstand for lists of places to eat, drink, and be merry. *Fußgängertunnel, tel. 0351/53539. Between Augustusbrücke and Neustädter Markt (look for golden horseman), in pedestrian tunnel under Köpckestr. Open weekdays 9–6, weekends 9–4.*

COMING AND GOING

BY TRAIN Dresden has two train stations: the **Dresden Hauptbahnhof** (Wienerpl. at Prager Str.), on the southern fringe of the Altstadt, and the newer **Bahnhof Dresden Neustadt** (Friedrich-Wolf Pl.), at the opposite (northern) end of town. The Hauptbahnhof serves just about every place you're likely to go in Germany and beyond. Trains leave every hour or so for Berlin (DM 25), Chemnitz (DM 10.60), Erfurt (DM 30), and Leipzig (DM 15). The Hauptbahnhof has luggage-storage facilities (*see* Luggage Storage in Basics, *above*) and a bank with an ATM machine. From here it's only a short walk north, up Prager Straße, to the tourist office and Altstadt. The Bahnhof Dresden Neustadt is used mostly for local and industrial service, so it's unlikely you'll set foot in the place. If somehow you do, trains leave every 20 minutes for the Hauptbahnhof; for a longer ride try Tram 3 or 11.

BY BUS The main **Busbahnhof** is at the Hauptbahnhof. There are unstaffed pickup points in the city at Pirnascher Platz, Albertplatz, and the Neustadt station. The tourist offices stock bus schedules and will help you decide whether a destination is better served by train or bus; nine times out of 10 the train is a better bet. From the Busbahnhof there's frequent daily service to Bautzen (DM 22), Freiberg (DM 12), Görlitz (DM 18), and Leipzig (DM 11).

HITCHING The best way to hitch a ride out of Dresden is to head for the Autobahn and stake out a spot along any *Einfahrt* (entrance). For Berlin (accessed via Rte. E55) or Görlitz (accessed via Hwy. E40) take Bus 81 to Radeberger Straße; the Autobahn is a short walk from the bus stop.

BY MITFAHRZENTRALE Dresden has three ride-share services. Call as early as possible to arrange low-cost rides throughout Germany with businesspeople in BMWs and families in sputtery Trabants. Try these agencies: **Studentische Mitfahrzentrale** (Student Ride-Share Central, Nürnberger Str. 57, tel. 0351/463–6060), open weekdays 8–6, Saturday 8–2; **Reisezentrum** (Friedrich-Engels Str. 10, tel. 0351/51216), open weekdays 9–7, Saturday 9–2; and **Christophorus** (Robert-Blum-Str. 3, tel. 0351/55493), open weekdays 8–5.

GETTING AROUND

The Altstadt, where you'll find the most important sights, is easy to spot by the jumble of towers and spires. The Hauptbahnhof and its network of tracks form the southern border of the city center; outside the train station, the pedestrian-only Prager Straße leads straight to the open-air Altmarkt (Old Market). The Neumarkt (New Market), another elegant square, is a few hundred yards north. Farther north is the Elbe River, which divides the old town from the new. If you cross the river on Augustusbrücke you'll end up on Hauptstraße (near a tourist office) and eventually on Albertplatz—about as far north as you want to go in Dresden unless you like working-class ghettos and cement-block architecture.

BY S-BAHN Dresden's S-Bahn network is comprehensive, but unless you're a worker commuting from the suburbs it's unlikely you'll need it. The S-Bahn does connect the city's train stations, and from the Hauptbahnhof you can take one of a dozen S-

Bahn trains to the smart-looking neighborhoods along the Elbe. Trains run until 11 PM and pick up again at some ungodly hour like 4 AM.

BY TRAM AND BUS Trams and buses are efficient for short hops in the city. Information offices and newspaper stands sell tickets, and on a good day the driver might sell you one at a stop. The best deal is the DM 4 *Tageskarte* (Day Card), valid for one day of free bus and tram travel. If you'll be making lots of short trips, the DM 6 *Streifenkarte* (Strip Card) buys 11 10-minute trips. Just bend the ticket to the appropriate number and time, then validate it on board (this will make sense when you see the card). From the Hauptbahnhof, Tram 3 (toward Wilder Mann) stops at the Altmarkt and Rathenauplatz before crossing the Elbe. Also from the Hauptbahnhof, Tram 11 (toward Bühlau) stops at Postplatz, south of Theaterplatz, then crosses the Elbe on its way to Bahnhof Neustadt.

BY TAXI No haggling over taxi prices in this town; it costs DM 3.60 to pull the door shut and about DM 1.50 per kilometer (⅝ mile). As in restaurants, you don't have to tip, although you can keep things simple by rounding up to the nearest mark. The main taxi stands are at the Hauptbahnhof and on Dr.-Külz-Ring.

BY BIKE The Hauptbahnhof rents wobbly bikes at a reasonable DM 8 per day. But **Radsportshop Päperor** (Ana Körnerpl., tel. 0351/377945) has cornered the Dresden mountain-bike market. These sturdy machines go for DM 12 per day. To reach the shop take Tram 1 or 6 to Schillerplatz and cross the Loschwitzer Brücke. Hours are weekdays 9–1 and 3–6, Saturday 9–1.

WHERE TO SLEEP

The tourist office on Prager Straße (*see* Visitor Information in Basics, *above*) distributes a free list of hotels and pensions (with phone numbers and addresses). For an extra DM 5 the staff can book you a private room in a family home, at DM 20–DM 30 per night. The Rudi-Arndt (*see below*) is the only hostel in town, so if you don't get a spot here you'll most likely end up in a pension. Anything less than DM 50 per person is bound to be far, far, far from the city center.

There are only two vaguely affordable options in the city center, and both are in not-so-nice areas (be careful walking alone at night). The first is **Hotel Rothenburger Hof** (Rothenburger Str. 17, tel. 0351/502–3434), at the north end of the Neustadt. Space in this modern, 23-room hotel costs DM 65 for a single, DM 110 for a double. From the Hauptbahnhof take the S-Bahn to Bahnhof Neustadt, walk east along Antonstraße past Albertplatz, then turn left onto Rothenburger Straße (from the Hauptbahnhof you can also take Tram 3 to Albertplatz). The **Hotel Stadt Rendsburg** (Kamenzer Str. 1, tel. 0351/51551), a clean and comfortable 19-room hotel, is only a few blocks away. With breakfast included, singles cost DM 55, doubles DM 95. Because rooms here are so cheap, owner Harald Knofël, who speaks some English (a rare find in this town), recommends reserving a good two weeks in advance.

If you don't mind a 35-minute tram ride, the 78-bed **Pension Magvas** (Gondelweg 3, tel. 0351/223–6084) ain't a bad choice at all. It's by far the cheapest pension in Dresden, with singles priced DM 45–DM 50, doubles DM 70–DM 75. Take Tram 14 from the Altmarkt or Tram 9 from the Hauptbahnhof (both toward Kleinzschachwitz) to Meußlitzer Straße, the second-to-last stop. Walk three blocks south on Meußlitzer Straße and turn left onto Putiatinstraße, which turns into Gondelweg in a few blocks.

HOSTELS **Jugendherberge Oberloschwitz.** This hostel is in the classy Loschwitz residential area, a long haul from downtown. Call before you make the trek—they could be full or be closed for the weekend. Beds cost DM 13.50 (including breakfast) plus DM 6 if you don't have a sheet. The hostel is perched atop a steep hill. If you're too tired to walk, the *Schwebeseilbahn* (generally called the *Schwebebahn*), a gondola that shuttles to and from the hostel, costs DM 2.50 each way. *Sierksstr. 33, tel.*

0351/36672. From Bahnhof Neustadt, Tram 6 toward Bahnhof Niedersedlitz to Schillerpl.; walk 1 block northeast and cross Elbe to Körnerpl.; follow signs for hostel and Schwebebahn stop. 51 beds.

Jugendherberge Rudi-Arndt. This hostel is in a safe and quiet neighborhood, which is surprising, considering how close it is to the Hauptbahnhof. Another plus is the big and hearty breakfast. On the downside, the hostel is nearly always full, so book well in advance, and call before making the trip from the train station. The staff promises that showers will be installed within the year; for the moment there are only small sinks in the communal dorm rooms. Beds cost DM 15 for those under 27, DM 18 for everyone else. *Hübnerstr. 11, tel. 0351/471–0667. Walk s. from Hauptbahnhof on Winkelmann Str. and turn right on Schnorrstr., which becomes Hübnerstr. 75 beds. 1 AM curfew.*

CAMPGROUND **Wostra Strandbad.** You'll have to travel 10 kilometers (6 miles) from the city center to get to this unscenic but cheap camping spot. Get back to nature at the nude swimming area next door (DM 1 for students), or rent a volleyball for a game in the buff. The campground charges DM 8–DM 10 per site, DM 11.50 if you need a tent. You can rent a comfortable bungalow for DM 20 a night plus DM 10 per person. The bathrooms are clean, almost luxurious by most campers' standards. *Wilhelm-Weitling-Str., tel. 0351/223–1903. From Hauptbahnhof, Tram 9 toward Kleinzschachwitz to last stop; walk 2 blocks; just before Elbe, turn right onto Wilhelm-Weitling-Str. 70 sites. Last check-in 8 PM, gates closed 10 PM–6 AM.*

FOOD

Prager Straße, the Altmarkt, and the narrow streets along the riverfront are spiked with cafés, ice-cream shops, bakeries, and tourist-oriented restaurants; head to the Neustadt if you want something cheaper. During spring and summer almost every restaurant lines its sidewalk with tables and umbrellas. It's nearly impossible to pass a colorful shopping street like Münzgasse—next to the Hilton between the Neumarkt and Brühlsche Terraße—without being drawn to a table. Try **Kleppereck** (Münzgasse at Terassengasse) for its top-rate, topping-heavy pizzas; the veggie pie is a steal at DM 7.50. Across the way join the beer-swigging, bratwurst-chomping (DM 8.50) crowd living it up at the outdoor beer garden.

UNDER DM 10 **Pizza & Pasta.** This is a no-frills Italian joint with good food and low prices. There are only seven or eight tables in the characterless dining room, one of which is reserved for staff. Don't be shy about getting the waiter's attention: He or she will eventually set aside the newspaper to get you another drink. The baker tops pizzas with salami, pineapple, cheese, or mushrooms; one-person pies run DM 3–DM 6. A leafy green chef salad costs DM 8.20. *Bautzner Str. 9, tel. 0351/55870. 1 block e. of Alaunstr. and Albertpl. Closed Sun.*

Sleeping in the Suburbs

Radebeul, a small suburb 10 kilometers (6 miles) northeast of Dresden, has three things going for it: easy access by S-Bahn (Radebeul-Weintraube station), hills covered with villas and vineyards, and a pleasant youth hostel, Jugendherberge Radebeul (Weinstraubenstr. 12, tel. 0351/74786). The midnight curfew is actually a good thing; it keeps the preteens from running wild in the hallways all night. Beds cost DM 13.50 for those under 27 and DM 16 for those 27 and over, including breakfast. From the Radebeul-Weintraube station follow the exit path onto Weintraubenstraße.

UNDER DM 15 **Erich Kästner Café.** Budding poets and writers smoke ravenously, drink coffee, and wait for divine inspiration from the café's namesake: a 20th-century writer who grew up in the Neustadt area. The menu includes hearty breakfasts (DM 5–DM 9), every shape and flavor of ice cream (DM 3–DM 7), and fruity shakes (DM 3.60). There are the requisite selections of wieners, potatoes, and *Schweineschnitzel* (breaded pork steak, DM 14). *Alaunstr. 1, tel. 0351/570445. 1 block n. of Albertpl. Open daily 11–10. Wheelchair access.*

UNDER DM 30 **Kügelchen-Haus.** This multifaceted place contains a grill, coffee bar, restaurant, and historic beer cellar. The food ranges from traditional German (meat, stew, cabbage) to steak, burgers, and salads, all priced between DM 15 and DM 25. It's a popular spot, so arrive as early as possible. If there is a wait you can sit in the coffee bar and get wired on caffeine. *Hauptstr. 11–13, tel. 0351/52791. Closed Mon.*

Erich Kästner's humorous children's books are staples of German literature. His works often featured critters rather than people, which allowed him to work in some poignant, subtle social criticism. For a sample check out Kästner's classic Emil and the Detectives.

WORTH SEEING

If you only have one day in Dresden, focus on the old town's main attractions—the Altmarkt, Neumarkt, Zwinger palace, and Semperoper. Pick up a copy of the *"Dresden Stadtplan mit Informationen"* ("Dresden City Plan with Information") for a list of major sights and opening hours. It's free and available at the tourist offices. For an overview of Dresden, consider one of the hour-long tram or bus tours (DM 5) that meander through the Altstadt and Neustadt. During summer they're sometimes packed, so arrive a few minutes early. The tram version of the tour leaves from Postplatz (west of Altmarkt) Tuesday–Sunday at 9, 11, and 1:30. Buses leave from Dr.-Külz-Ring (between Altmarkt and Prager Straße) at 11 AM on Tuesday, Wednesday, and Thursday. For more information call 0351/495–5025.

ALBERTINUM Dresden's excellent art museum, the Albertinum, is named after Saxon king Albert, who between 1884 and 1887 converted a royal stable into an art gallery. The upper story of the Albertinum—entered from Brühlsche Terraße—houses the **Gemäldegalerie Alte und Neue Meister** (Gallery of Old and Modern Masters), temporarily displaying the Sempergalerie's (*see* Zwinger, *below*) highlights while that building is being renovated. The top-floor gallery contains Raphael's *Sistine Madonna,* standing on her heavenly perch and effortlessly holding a big baby Jesus, and Caspar David Friedrich's *Das Kreuz im Gebirge* (*The Cross in the Mountains*), among other jaw-droppers. The gallery also has a good collection of Flemish and Dutch art, works by German Renaissance genius Dürer, and impressionist and expressionist paintings.

Although it's technically part of the Albertinum, you have to leave the main gallery and reenter the building from Georg-Treu-Platz to reach the **Grüne Gewölbe** (Green Vault). Come here to see the amber, silver, and ivory treasures of the rich and famous. Look for necklaces made of precious gems, the world's largest green diamond (41 carats), and the gold coffee mug of August the Strong. Admission to the Grüne Gewölbe and Gemäldegalerie runs DM 5 each (DM 2.50 students). *Am Neumarkt, tel. 0351/953056 or 0351/484–0119. Open Fri.–Tues. 9– 5, Wed. 9–6.*

ALTMARKT Despite the best efforts of Allied bombers and communist city planners, the colonnaded Altmarkt retains much of its elegant pre–World War II grace. Okay, okay—the adjacent parking lot does seem more than a little out of place, as do the snazzy shops that have sprouted here since reunification, but the open-air square is a pleasant place to while away a languid afternoon. As for sightseeing, the church on the square's east side, **Kreuzkirche,** is a lush Baroque creation dating from 1764. If you're in the neighborhood on Saturday morning, stop in Kreuzkirche to hear the regionally famous Kreuzchor Boys' Choir. The newly rebuilt **Rathaus** (town hall) is just beyond the church, as is the 18th-century **Landhaus,** which houses the rather bland

Museum für Geschichte der Stadt Dresden (City Historical Museum). *Museum: Wilsdruffer Str. 2. Admission: DM 2. Open Mon.–Thurs., Sat. 10–6; Sun. 10–4.*

KATHOLISCHE HOFKIRCHE You can't miss the Katholische Hofkirche, also known as the Cathedral of St. Trinitas. It's the largest church in Saxony, and it dominates Dresden's old-town skyline. Commissioned by Friedrich August II in 1744, it was a Catholic oddity in this very Lutheran citadel. Legend has it Friedrich had the cathedral built secretly and presented it to the town only when completed—yeah, right. This place is a little too big to hide. Inside, look for the 250-year-old organ, said to be one of the finest to come from the Silbermann family's mountain workshops. Come for a concert at 4 on Saturday between April and October. *Theaterpl. Admission free. Open daily 8–6.*

NEUMARKT A stone's throw north of the Altmarkt is Dresden's other popular square, the Neumarkt. Despite its name, the Neumarkt is the heart of historic Dresden, and spire-capped buildings loom over the square. What really stands out are the burned-out ruins of **Frauenkirche,** once considered Germany's greatest Baroque cathedral. The structure survived the air raid on February 13, 1945 that leveled most of Dresden, but was ravaged by the subsequent fire storm, which consumed everything except the ragged walls. Like the Gedächtniskirche in Berlin, the Frauenkirche has been left in ruins as a war memorial.

At the northwest corner of Neumarkt stands the 16th-century **Johanneum,** which once housed the royal stables. Nowadays it is home to the **Verkehrsmuseum,** a collection of historical and vintage vehicles. Spanning the length of this 336-foot-long wall is a giant jigsaw puzzle made of 25,000 hand-painted tiles. The work was done in 1904–1907 by Wilhelm Walther and depicts more than 100 members of the royal Saxon house of Wettin. It's hard to study detail because the cycle is at least 10 feet off the ground, but the effect is dazzling, nonetheless. *Museum admission: DM 4. Open Tues. 9–6, Wed.–Sun. 9–5.*

SEMPEROPER The Semperoper bears the name of its creator, architect Gottfried Semper, even though the original opera house (built in 1841) burned down shortly after its completion. In the 1945 firebombing its replacement came down, too. What you're left with today is the Semperoper's third incarnation—a building that, because all of the prewar photos were black-and-white, may or may not match in color and detail its progenitor. Even so, the Semperoper is justifiably one of Germany's best-known theaters. Here Richard Wagner premiered his operas *Der Fliegende Holländer* and *Tannhäuser;* Richard Strauss his *Salome* and *Elektra.* Since the rebuilt theater opened in 1985, it's become incredibly popular with Germany's cultural elite, so obtaining tickets can be a nightmare even months in advance. Student and rush tickets can sometimes be bought on the night of a performance. If you miss out on tickets, you can still check out the lavish interior on the mandatory German-language guided tour (DM 5, DM 2.50 students). *Theaterpl. 2, box office tel. 0351/484–2491, tour information tel. 0351/484–2363. From Postpl. walk n. on Sophienstr. to Theaterpl.*

ZWINGER On the south side of Theaterplatz stands the Zwinger palace complex, one of the finest Baroque masterpieces in the world. It was designed by architect Matthaus Pöppelmann under the direction of King Friedrich Augustus I. Friedrich's idea was to build an elegant palace befitting his high (self-estimated) worth, as well as a showplace to display the many treasures he had commissioned or simply pillaged. Pöppelmann started with five linked pavilions built onto a section of the *Zwinger,* the name for Dresden's centuries-old fortifications. Had the Zwinger complex stopped there it would still have provoked awe in the brain dead. Yet a century later the famous architect Gottfried Semper made a few worthy additions, including a sixth pavilion and a serene central courtyard.

The wing next to the pond, the **Sempergalerie,** usually holds the **Gemäldegalerie Alte Meister** (Gallery of Old Masters). The collection has been temporarily moved to the Albertinum (*see above*) until restoration work here is complete. Still, there are several other museums to keep you busy in the Zwinger: You'd have to visit Turkey to find a porcelain collection larger than that in **Porzellansammlung,** one of the complex's elaborate pavilions; the **Mathematisch-Physikalischer Salon** has more microscopes, telescopes, and globes than you ever saw in school; and the **Glockenspielpavillon** is littered with clocks and carillons. There are two entrances to the Zwinger complex, one on Sophienstraße and one—the **Kronentor** (Crown Gate)—off Ostra-Allee, which leads northwest from Postplatz. The latter passes over a tree-lined arm of the Elbe and by itself makes the trip to the Zwinger worthwhile. *Theaterpl., tel. 0351/48420 or 0351/484–0119. Porzellansammlung admission: DM 5, DM 2 students. Open Sat.–Thurs. 9–5. Mathematisch-Physikalischer Salon admission: DM 3, DM 1.50 students. Open Fri.–Wed. 9–4. Glockenspielpavillon admission free. Open daily Fri.–Wed. 9–4.*

AFTER DARK

Dresden is the cultural heart of Saxony—maybe of all eastern Germany except for Berlin—and is as attractive to the club goer as to the opera and ballet lover. The Altstadt is for nose-in-the-air cultural events; the Neustadt is for nightlife. The tourist offices publish free events guides year-round. And the free weekly paper *Dresdner Woche* sometimes lists club and music schedules.

CLUBS AND BARS If you're not in the mood for Wagner or Mozart, there's always jazz at **Tonne** (Tzschirnerpl. 3, tel. 0351/495–1354 or 0351/496–0211), where the bands vary as widely as the cover charge (DM 5–DM 12). For dancing, local hipsters recommend **Sachs Music Hall** (Stephensonstr. 6, tel. 0351/229–2555). If you want to nurse a ½-liter stein among natives check out **Die 100** (Alaunstr. 100, off Albertpl.), a so-called alternative bar. More brooding and intellectual is **Raskolnikoff** (Böhmische Str. 36), a café and beer bar one block north of Hotel Rothenburger Hof (*see* Where to Sleep, *above*). Raskolnikoff is closed Monday–Wednesday. A short walk away is **Planwirtschaft** (Louisenstr. 20). After 1 AM you'll have to ring the bell to get in—the café will be closed but not the cellar tavern.

MUSIC AND THEATER Music festivals run throughout the summer; get tickets (DM 10–DM 60) at the Kaße (cashier) in the **Schauspielhaus** (Ostra Allee), across from the Zwinger. The **Schinkelwache** (Sofienstr., tel. 0351/484–2352 or 0351/484–2353) sells tickets for seasonal events throughout the city. For a shot at last-minute tickets, ask the folks at the Sofienstraße box office for an Ermäßigung (reduced ticket) or Stehplatz (standing-room ticket, DM 5). A night at the elegant and famous **Semperoper** is the ultimate goal here.

Near Dresden

Under no condition should you visit Dresden without making at least one day trip. Unique out-of-the-way places, especially for outdoorsy types, abound. The sights listed below are easy to reach from Dresden, and each can be covered in a single—albeit long—day.

PILLNITZ

By far the easiest day trip from Dresden is Pillnitz, a village on the east bank of the Elbe, opposite Dresden's Pension Magvas and the Wostra Strandbad campground (*see* Where to Sleep, *above*). Take Tram 9 from the Hauptbahnhof or Tram 14 from the Altmarkt toward Kleinzschachwitz, and get off at the last stop. Continue walking east (you'll be on Berthold-Haupt-Straße) until you reach the Elbe. A small ferry shuttles pedestrians across the river for DM .60 every 30 minutes or so. On the other side of the river is Pillnitz's tiny riverfront center. Smells of hops and seafood waft from **Der Pillnitzer Elbblick** (Söbrigener Str., tel. 0351/398206), luring tourists and sailors to its umbrella-shaded tables. Cash-strapped travelers will need a lot of willpower to be content with tomato soup or a tossed salad (DM 5) as the party at the next table feasts on fresh sole with mushrooms, mussels, and shrimp (DM 24.50). Next door, Weiße Flotte sells tickets for boat rides on the Elbe; you can start an adventure to Pirna (*see* Sächsische Schweiz, *below*) right here in Pillnitz.

From the docks stroll the riverbank, through a labyrinth of hedges and gardens, to **Schloß Pillnitz** (open daily 9–6), a few hundred yards south of the ferry port. It costs DM 3, DM 1.50 for students, to tour the elegant, well-kept grounds of this Baroque palace complex, plus an additional DM 2 to go inside any of the three orange-and-gold pavilions built by King August the Strong. There's not much to look at inside besides period furniture and portraits of long-forgotten dukes and counts, so spend your time wandering the gravel paths that lead across fountain-lined lawns. On Sunday afternoons between May and August, free orchestral performances are often given in front of the main pavilion.

SACHSISCHE SCHWEIZ

Just south of Dresden lies Sächsische Schweiz, Saxony's "Little Switzerland." The low-lying Elbsandstein Mountains extend from the outskirts of Dresden to the Czech Republic border, some 40 kilometers (25 miles) southeast. The area is threaded with highways and rural roads and is well served by train and ferry; but unless you're content to spend all—repeat, all—your time scurrying about in nature, there's little to do except sit in a beer hall waiting for the next train. The lure is the incredible topography, from plains to riverside canyons bristling with stubby rock formations and clumps of old-growth forest. You'll love the region if you appreciate kilometer-wide panoramas of the summer sky, but don't expect much in the way of tourist facilities. Most people arrive in cars and have enough cash to stay in the region's scattered luxury hotels.

Don't fret about lack of oxygen in the Elbsandstein Mountains. The highest point is only 1,713 feet.

For those who want just a taste of the area, the small village of **Pirna,** 18 kilometers (11 miles) southeast of Dresden, is a happy compromise. Near Pirna the banks of the Elbe rise sharply as the river begins its winding journey through the Elbsandstein Mountains. Pirna isn't overly scenic, but it does have lots of breweries, each marked by a distinctive white sign. (The breweries are the domain of seasoned male drinkers; those who don't fit the mold should be prepared for curious glances.) If you want to spend the night in town, try the **Jugendherberge Weltfrieden** (Birkwitzer Str. 51, tel. 03501/2388), which charges DM 13.50 for those under 27 and DM 16 for everyone else, including breakfast.

The preferred way to travel between Pirna and Dresden is by ferry. In fact, it's probably the best way to experience the rugged splendor of this region with minimum hassle. However, it's not until after Pirna that the banks of the Elbe begin to rise, marking the real beginning of the Elbsandstein Mountains. The cliffs continue to grow rapidly as you go upstream. Ragged outcroppings rise from the steep slopes of the riverbanks, and the sandstone cliffs, carved by erosion, assume bizarre shapes and colors. The dramatic scenery continues to the rather dull town of **Königstein,** roughly 15 kilometers (9 miles) downriver from Pirna and the next stop on the Weiße Flotte ferry. Sadly, the only place worth a go in Königstein is **Schrägers Gasthaus** (Kirchgasse, tel. 035021/352), a popular beer hall, restaurant, and guest house on a cobbled alley by the impossible-to-miss church. You can crash in a room above the restaurant for DM 25. Otherwise try the 156-bed **Jugendherberge Königstein** (Halbestadt 13, tel.

035021/2432), which charges DM 13.50 for those under 27 and DM 16 for those 27 and over for one of its 156 beds.

COMING AND GOING Between Dresden and Pirna you can travel by S-Bahn (DM 4) or ferry. The S-Bahn goes at a leisurely pace along the Elbe, but on the ferry you can watch the mountains pass slowly by from the open-air deck. During summer, ferries leave daily from Dresden's Terraßenufer, the part of the harbor directly below Brühlsche Terraße. The most popular carrier is **Weiße Flotte** (tel. 0351/502–2611). The trip to Pirna takes 2½ hours and costs DM 11 each way. From Pirna, Weiße Flotte ferries continue to Königstein; the two-hour trip costs an additional DM 9 each way.

BAUTZEN

Bautzen is strategically located on a granite bluff overlooking the Spree River—a romantic setting that gives this small village its character. The huge **St.-Petri-Dom** (Cathedral of St. Peter), on the open-air Fleischmarkt, houses two churches, one Catholic and one Protestant. The **Rathaus** (town hall) presides over the **Hauptmarkt,** the main outdoor market, which is full of food, clothing, and beer stands in summer. The stone **Friedensbrücke** (Bridge of Peace) looks out over the Spree Valley and a panorama of rolling farmland. Otherwise, Bautzen's main draws are its Serbian-influenced restaurants (for complicated historical reasons, Bautzen has a largish community of Serbs) and its super-cheap lodging options.

As for food, **Hosćenic Vojewik** (Kornstr. and An der Petrikirche, closed Sun.) serves Serbian-style stuffed peppers and grilled meats in a cavernous hall. **Serbsa Kofejownja** (Postpl.), a café and restaurant with a huge menu, serves Serbian onion soup (DM 2.90) and paprika-spiced meats (about DM 10). Vegetarians can feast on potato pancakes with applesauce (DM 5.90) or a mushroom omelet (DM 4.90). The lamplit courtyard is a relaxing place for wine or coffee. If you want to crash in Bautzen there's **Jugendherberge Am Zwinger** (Am Zwinger 1, tel. 03591/44045), in a former castle near St.-Petri-Dom. For DM 11.50 you get a bastion room with a view. The **tourist office** (Fleischmarkt 2–4, tel. 03591/42016) has a list of private rooms and pensions and will reserve a spot for a DM 4 fee. One of the best deals in town is **Detlef Pohl** (Unterm Schloß 15, tel. 03591/47070), which has rooms under the castle (hence the street name) for DM 15, including breakfast.

COMING AND GOING Bautzen is roughly 50 kilometers (31 miles) east of Dresden. From Bautzen's **Hauptbahnhof** (Bahnhofstr., tel. 03591/44643) there are daily connections to Cottbus (DM 9.20), Dresden (DM 6.40), and Görlitz (DM 3.60). To reach the city center from the depot, follow Ernst-Thälmann-Straße past Postplatz and onto Karl-Marx-Straße; the old town is dead ahead.

White Gold

No one has been able to make gold from hay since Rumpelstiltskin, but that hasn't stopped people from trying. King Friedrich Augustus was short on cash because of his building projects in Dresden, so naturally he set his alchemists to the task. They never came up with a recipe for the yellow shiny stuff, but in 1708 they developed their own white gold—porcelain. August was so happy that he shelled out more bucks for a castle to house porcelain manufacturing—the Albrechtsburg in Meißen. A tip for shoppers: Make sure the bottom of each porcelain piece is stamped with a pair of blue swords, the sign of real Meißen porcelain.

MEIßEN

Porcelain is to Meißen what stone and mortar are to other towns. Ever since alchemists in Meißen cooked up the recipe for porcelain, the village's civic buildings have been drenched in the stuff. Check out the bells of the **Frauenkirche** (Marktpl.), for instance, or the decorative figures in **Nikolaikirche** (Stadtpark), all of which are made of this coveted material. The main reason for coming here is to tour Meißen's porcelain factories. An obvious choice is the hilltop **Albrechtsburg** (Dompl., open Tues.–Sun. 10–5), the spire-tipped castle in the middle of town. It certainly looks impressive, but it's really just an aggrandized factory built by King August to house his profitable porcelain works. The workshops were closed ages ago, but the castle tour (DM 4) does a good job of explaining the manufacture of porcelain. To see porcelain makers in action, go back down the hill and across town to the **Staatliche Porzellan-Manufaktur** (Talstr. 9, open Tues.–Sun. 10–4), which has a work station and a good museum.

Once you've toured the porcelain factories, you've done all there is to do in Meißen. Hop on the next train, or, if you've missed that, stop by **Weinschänke Vincenz Richter** (An der Frauenkirche, tel. 03521/3285, closed Mon.), a pleasantly run-down wine tavern. If an afternoon in the pub somehow becomes a groggy evening in the pub, stop at Meißen's **Jugendherberge** (Wilsdruffer Str. 58, tel. 03521/453065), in the old town at the top of a steep hill, off Poststraße. The hostel is as cheap as they come in Saxony: DM 7 (under 27) and DM 9 (27 and over) per bed, including breakfast. Private-room seekers should head for the **Mitropa-Hotel** (Großenhainer Str. 2, tel. 03521/558), connected to the Bahnhof. Singles here cost DM 55, doubles DM 95.

COMING AND GOING From Dresden take the S-Bahn (DM 9) or the train (DM 11) to Meißen. The train from Dresden runs about every half hour and takes 30–40 minutes. Leipzig is another 80 kilometers (49 miles) farther on the same line. You know you've arrived in Meißen when you see porcelain-tile buildings on either side of the tracks. To reach the old town, walk out of the depot, cross the bridge, and walk straight.

Leipzig

Leipzig is the second-largest city in eastern Germany. Berlin undoubtedly has more museums and better nightlife, but Leipzig has its own worthwhile sights, and because of its 15,000-student university, which reopened in the 1970s after a long hiatus, it also has a lively bar scene. Like Berlin, Leipzig has long cultivated a progressive, almost libertine identity. Even during the GDR era, Leipzig's students were vociferous critics of the communist government, and more than once the army had to be called in to quell student-led riots. Throughout the 1970s and '80s this screw-you attitude drew thousands of disillusioned artists and dropouts to Leipzig, people who craved a cutting-edge life in a country known for its dull industry. Even now that Germany is unified, Leipzig produces a bevy of grunge and metal bands, and its café society—at least in the student quarters—echoes what you'll find in Berlin's Kreuzberg and Prenzlauer Berg districts. In Leipzig it's still cool to sport bright red mohawks and nipple rings.

For those who find Berlin overwhelming, Leipzig offers many of the same diversions without the suburban sprawl.

Leipzig's prominence as a center of culture and the arts was engendered in the 12th century, when the town was an important trading hub for merchants and soldiers on their way to the Baltic Sea. Since 1481 Leipzig has also been a publishing center (which explains its nickname, the City of Books). Of course, the fact that Goethe and Schiller lived here may have something to do with Leipzig's literary reputation. For 27 years J. S. Bach was the organist and choir director at the Thomaskirche, and Wagner was born here in 1813. Nowadays Leipzig's renowned orchestra celebrates the music of these composers with year-round concerts and summer festivals.

Leipzig

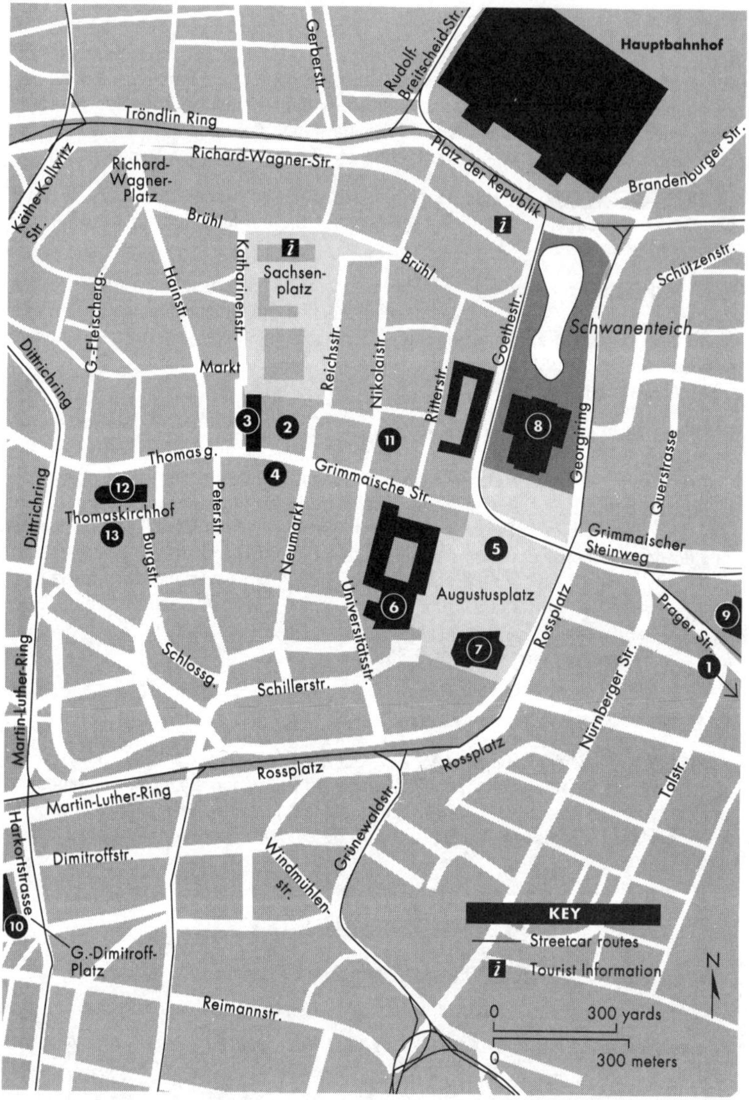

Altes Rathaus, **3**
Am Markt, **2**
Augustusplatz, **5**
Bosehaus, **13**
Grassimuseum, **9**
Leipzig University Tower, **6**
Mädlerpassage, **4**
Museum der Bildenden Künste, **10**
Neues Gewandhaus, **7**
Nikolaikirche, **11**
Opernhaus, **8**
Thomaskirche, **12**
Völkerschlachtdenkmal, **1**

BASICS

BUREAUX DE CHANGE There's only one ATM in town, inside the **Hauptbahnhof.** The machine accepts Visa and American Express (PIN number required) and is open 24 hours a day. The adjacent **Deutsche Verkehrs Bank** exchanges cash and traveler's checks at competitive rates and is open weekdays 8–6, Saturday 9–1. In the city center there's a clutch of banks along Katherinenstraße and around the Markt.

LUGGAGE STORAGE The Hauptbahnhof has rows of backpack-size lockers for DM 2 per day. Or leave your stuff with the attendant at the left-luggage desk for DM 2 per 12 hours.

MEDICAL AID There's always at least one pharmacy in town open past 9 PM. Check the paper or dial 01141—no coins needed—to find out which pharmacy is on late-night duty; many post a list prominently. When in tooth trouble, give the med students and staff a try at the **Stomatologische Klinik der Universität** (Nürnberger Str. 57, tel. 0341/71640). For a **doctor,** call 01141.

VISITOR INFORMATION **Leipzig-Information** is so big it has an information desk to help direct you to the proper information desk. Maps and city brochures crowd the front annex; pick one of a dozen weekly and monthly newspapers listing music and nightlife options. Swing over to the *Zimmervermittlung* (lodging-service counter) and book a private room for a DM 5 fee. Expect to pay a whopping DM 40–DM 50 for private accommodations. Bummer. During summer the office organizes guided bus tours of the city. Sometimes the staff also arranges guided city walks in German and English. *Sachsenpl. 1, tel. 0341/79590. Walk straight out of Hauptbahnhof, cross Pl. der Republik, and, a few blocks ahead, turn right onto Brühl; office is 1 block farther, on left. Open weekdays 9–8, weekends 9:30–2.*

COMING AND GOING

BY TRAIN Leipzig's **Hauptbahnhof** (Pl. der Republik, tel. 0341/311654) is the largest in Europe and one of the most elegant. Its 26 platforms can cause confusion, especially now that sections of this fin-de-siècle terminal are undergoing renovation to accommodate the substantial increase in traffic since reunification. The present gar-

Vive les Revolutions

Leipzig is often referred to as **Heldenstadt,** *the City of Heroes, because in 1813, backed by an army of Austrians, Prussians, Russians, and Swedes, the citizens of Leipzig fought a gruesome battle against Napoléon on the outskirts of town. This skirmish, known as the* **Völkerschlacht** *(the People's Battle), saved the city from ransacking by Napoléon's troops and reportedly paved the way for his defeat at Waterloo in 1815. More recently, in what have come to be known as the "Monday Meetings," thousands of Leipzigers gathered in the city center in the waning months of 1989 to demonstrate against communist rule in East Germany. On October 2, 1989, more than 15,000 marched through the streets, calling for freedom. A week later, on October 9, Leipzigers and other Saxons successfully withstood a brutal attack by East German security troops. Their revolt was documented in a videotape that was smuggled into West Berlin. Aired the same night on West German television, the video was one of the first glimpses the outside world had of East Germany's simmering revolution.*

gantuan structure is equipped with all the fixin's—luggage lockers, a bank and ATM, phones, newsstands, sweetshops, cafeterias, and bars. To reach the city center, walk out of the depot, cross the traffic-filled Platz der Republik, and go straight. The university and Augustusplatz are a few blocks south (straight); Sachsenplatz and the tourist office are a few blocks west (right). From Leipzig there are hourly trains to Berlin (DM 25), Dresden (DM 15), Erfurt (DM 20), and Halle (DM 3.60). Other destinations include Chemnitz (nine per day, DM 16), Dessau (five per day, DM 11), Frankfurt (five per day, DM 56), Magdeburg (six per day, DM 16), and Nürnberg (six per day, DM 40).

BY BUS From the main bus terminal, on the Hauptbahnhof's east corner, there are daily connections to Chemnitz (DM 11), Dessau (DM 8), Dresden (DM 11), and Halle (DM 3). There's no staffed information desk, so head to the tourist office or a Hauptbahnhof counter for advice on regional buses.

HITCHING If you're hitching to Berlin, take Tram 16 from the Hauptbahnhof (toward Wiederitzsch) to the last stop. From here it's a short signposted walk to Autobahn 14, which funnels into the Berlin-bound Autobahn 9. If you're heading toward Munich or Nürnberg, take Tram 3, 12, or 15 from the Hauptbahnhof to Saalfelder Straße (toward Miltitz), 12 stops from the train station. From here, walk or hitch along the main road until you hit Highway 181, which intersects Autobahn 9, 13 kilometers (8 miles) outside Leipzig.

BY MITFAHRZENTRALE Leipzig's ride-share programs are brand-new, so they're not as organized as those in western German cities. **Mitfahr-und Wohnzentrale** (Rudolf-Breitscheid-Str. 39, tel. 0341/211–4222, open daily 9–8) arranges rides throughout the country. The office is around the corner from the Hauptbahnhof; exit on the west side of the depot, and turn right on Rudolf-Breitscheid-Straße. A similar service is offered by the student-run **Mitfahrzentrale** (Augustuspl. 9, tel. 0341/719–2097), at the university.

GETTING AROUND

Nearly all of Leipzig's sights are concentrated in its extremely small center. This is bordered by the Hauptbahnhof to the north, the opera house to the east, the university and Augustusplatz to the south, and Thomaskirche to the west—an area no larger than 1 square kilometer. In the city center, stuff your tram tickets into a pocket and explore the sights on foot. If you get lost, scan the skyline for Leipzig's not-so-pretty church spires. One marks Thomaskirche, the other Nikolaikirche, halfway between Augustusplatz and Sachsenplatz. If it's late and/or you don't want to walk alone, Leipzig's taxis start their meters at DM 3.50 and add DM 1.50 per kilometer. Catch one outside the Hauptbahnhof or call 0341/7411 or 0341/594171.

BY TRAM AND BUS There's no need to use public transportation in the tiny city center, but if you're headed for an out-of-the-way pension or private room, be assured that even suburban Leipzig is only a short tram or bus ride from the downtown sights (and from the bars around the university). The Hauptbahnhof is the main hub, and maps and charts are available in its annex. Outside, look for the STRASSENBAHN and STADTBUS signs that locate the tram and bus stops, respectively. Single-ride tickets cost DM 1 and are available at blue *Fahrkartenautomaten* (ticket machines). These also sell full-day passes (DM 6). Trams and buses generally operate between 5:30 AM and 11 PM, but there are exceptions. Pick up a schedule at the tourist office.

WHERE TO SLEEP

Sleeping in Leipzig sure ain't cheap. In fact, unless you can squeeze into the always-crowded hostels, Leipzig can be downright expensive. Private rooms—bookable at the tourist-information center for a DM 5 fee—cost DM 40–DM 50 per night. Hotels and pensions are no better, at an average DM 80 per person, per night. Even if you hate camping, you may not have a choice in Leipzig.

If you can afford to splurge, try the **Parkhotel** (Richard-Wagner-Str. 7, tel. 0341/7821), across the street from the train station. It's nothing fancy—few of the Spartan rooms have baths—and the din of traffic may keep you up late, but with doubles priced at DM 115 it is one of the cheapest hotels in central Leipzig. **Hotel Corum** (Rudolf-Breitscheid-Str., tel. 0341/12510) is a modern, cement-block hotel that's surprisingly cheerful inside. All rooms have a bath; there's a restaurant downstairs; and you're only a five-minute walk from the Hauptbahnhof. Double rooms here start at DM 120 and peak at DM 150.

HOSTELS **Jugendherberge am Auensee.** This 40-bed hostel is a 30-minute tram ride from the Hauptbahnhof, so you'll have to finish your nightclubbing before the last tram leaves the city center, at about 11. On the plus side, the hostel is within a short walk of Auensee, a great place for afternoon strolls along a tree-lined lake. The hostel is pretty typical—rooms hold four to eight bunk beds, and the bathrooms are clean, if a bit bare. Beds cost DM 13.50 for those under 27 and DM 15.50 for those 27 and over, including breakfast. During summer the place is packed, and reservations are advised. *Gustav-Esche-Str. 4, tel. 0341/57189. From Hauptbahnhof take Tram 10 or 28 toward Wahren to Rathaus Wahren; walk to Linkelstr. and turn left on Am Hirtenhaus.*

Jugendherberge Leipzig-Großdeuben. Another hostel deep in the suburbs—this time in Großdeuben, 10 kilometers (6 miles) south of the city center. Considering how packed Leipzig can get in summer, this hostel may be your only budget choice. Call in advance to make sure it isn't already booked. Its 149 beds cost DM 14.50 (under 27) and DM 17.50 (over 26). There's a flexible midnight curfew, and check-in is after 3 PM. *Hauptstr. 23, tel. 034299/484 or 034299/651. From Hauptbahnhof, S-Bahn to Bahnhof Gaschwitz, then follow signs (15 min. on foot).*

Jugendherberge Leipzig-Zentrum. If you're sitting in an easy chair planning a trip to Leipzig, make a reservation for this hostel RIGHT NOW. It's the only reasonably priced option in Leipzig and only a 15- to 20-minute walk west of the city center. This homey place has a TV room, lounge areas, and a dining room with bay windows overlooking the backyard. Beds cost DM 14 (under 27) and DM 17 (over 26) per night, including breakfast. Young Germans—people who make reservations in advance—fill the place during summer, but you will occasionally find a haggard American or Aussie who's finagled a bed. *Käthe-Kollwitz-Str. 62–66, tel. 0341/470530. From Hauptbahnhof, Tram 1 toward Lausen or Tram 2 toward Plagwitz to Käthe-Kollwitz-Str. 143 beds. 1 AM curfew; check-in with reservations 2:30–6, otherwise after 4.*

CAMPGROUND **Campingplatz am Auensee** is on the other side of the lake from the Jugendherberge am Auensee. The campground was closed in '92 for electrical work, and it's now in top form and open year-round. The camp rents lean-to tents—little A-frame numbers—for DM 3, trailers for DM 7, and bungalows for DM 20 (plus DM 4 per person). Hot water is plentiful. *Gustav-Esche-Str. 5, tel. 0341/212–3031. From Hauptbahnhof, Tram 10 or 28 toward Wahren to Rathaus Wahren; walk to Linkelstr., turn right on Rittergutstr. and follow curves.*

FOOD

On Thomaskirchhof, **Bachstübl** and **Cafe Concerto** have potent espresso and a cornucopia of tourist brochures and souvenirs. A few blocks north of the church, **Zum Cafe Baum** (Kleine Fleischergasse 4, off Klostergasse) has served coffee to the likes of August the Strong, Goethe, and Wagner. Nowadays you can get a frothy mocha for a reasonable DM 5. The **Antiquitätencafé Galerie Kleinol** (Käthe-Kollwitz-Str. 71, tel. 0341/471555), near the Leipzig-Zentrum hostel, combines gallery and café traditions in an elegant, librarylike atmosphere. The **Winrestaurant Csárda** (Schulstr. 2, tel.

0341/281420), also near the Leipzig-Zentrum hostel, serves all kinds of veggie platters at DM 3 a pop and has a reasonably priced selection of wine. Back in the city center, just off Am Markt, **Leo's Calypso Pub 111** (Arthur-Hoffman-Str. 111) serves greasy but yummy kebabs and gyros for less than DM 6.

UNDER DM 15 **Paulaner.** This small, intimate tavern offers hearty servings of simple, satisfying food. You won't find many tourists here, only a handful of locals enjoying a quiet meal and a beer. Most meals cost DM 10–DM 15, although there's a menu of filling appetizers priced at less than DM 10. *Klostergasse 3, tel. 0341/281985. Closed Mon.*

UNDER DM 30 **Auerbach Keller.** This historic restaurant, built in 1530, was a favorite of Goethe's and made an appearance in his *Faust.* Centuries later the Auerbach keeps the Faustian thing alive with Faust-named entrées and a jacket-and-tie rule that keeps all but the most highbrow away. You don't really have to wear a tie—clean jeans and a nice sweater will do. But expect to pay upward of DM 20 for regional Saxon dishes—veal fricassee for DM 19, schnitzel DM 22—and more than DM 40 for ¾ liter of wine. *Grimmaische Str. 2–4, off Mädlerpassage, tel. 0341/211-6034. Dinner reservations required.*

Stadtpfeiffer. Because it's on Augustusplatz across from the opera house, the Stadtpfeiffer attracts concert goers for dinner and dessert. You can go the salad route (small, DM 4.90; large, DM 9.80) and save room for the apple strudel à la mode (DM 4.50), or go all out with grilled pepper steak (DM 15) or a fish platter (DM 24). Backpackers are generally seated on the outdoor patio, with its AstroTurf carpet and a view of buildings only a Communist could love. Well-dressed types get a shot at the elegant dining room. *Augustuspl. 8, tel. 0341/209113. Closed daily 3:30–5:30 and Sun. Wheelchair access.*

WORTH SEEING

Leipzig's city center is small and walkable. Most of your time will probably be spent around Augustusplatz and the university and around the pleasant shopping streets that extend outward from Am Markt and Sachsenplatz (where you'll find the tourist office). During summer the tourist office arranges 90-minute guided **bus tours** of Leipzig for DM 6 per person. These leave from the Sachsenplatz office daily at 10, 1:30, and 4 (mid-October–April there's no 4 o'clock departure).

AM MARKT One block south of Sachsenplatz and the tourist office is Am Markt, Leipzig's stunning central market square. Parts of it were severely damaged during World War II, but thanks to a detailed restoration the square retains its centuries-old look. One side is taken up by the 16th-century **Altes Rathaus** (Old City Hall), which is best known for its off-center tower and brilliant blue clock. The tower houses the **Stadtgeschichtliches Museum** (Markt 1, tel. 0341/70921; open Tues.–Fri. 10–6, weekends 10–4), the municipal museum. Fanning out from all sides of the square are small side streets that attest to Leipzig's rich trading past. Tucked in these narrow lanes are dozens of glass-roof shopping arcades, places of honest elegance that haven't changed much in 100 or so years. Check out the turn-of-the-century pharmacy at Hainstraße 9 or one of the antique-book shops on nearby Neumarkt Passage. On Grimmaische Straße is Leipzig's finest arcade, the **Mädlerpassage.** Goethe set a scene of *Faust* in its Auerbach Keller restaurant (Nos. 2–4). A few yards farther on, check out the red-and-black coffee shop **Mephisto.**

AUGUSTUSPLATZ Towering over Nikolaikirche and everything else around Augustusplatz is the 470-foot-tall **Leipzig University Tower,** a round stone structure capped with a puffy blue dome. Inside are administrative offices and lecture rooms and, on the top floor, an observation deck (free) that you can reach via a long climb up a spiral staircase. Bordered by the university and student dormitories, Augustusplatz is the place to go to rub elbows with the city's 15,000 students; on sunny afternoons they sit in large groups smoking cigarettes on the plaza, planning the night's diversions. Street performers are also common here, especially on summer weekends when there's substantial money to be made from the passing horde of tourists. Across the square is the glass-and-concrete **Neues Gewandhaus** (Augustuspl. 8, tel. 0341/71320), home to Leipzig's symphony orchestra. The statue of Beethoven at the front entrance won first prize for sculptor Max Klinger at the World Art Exhibition in Vienna in 1912. Tickets for symphony performances cost DM 5 (student rush tickets) to DM 50 (special events) and can be bought at the adjacent box office and sometimes at the tourist office. Failing that, try to catch a performance at the **Opernhaus** (Augustuspl. 12, tel. 0341/71680), on the square's north side. The opera house isn't much to look at—in fact, it has the dubious distinction of being the first postwar theater built in communist East Germany.

GRASSIMUSEUM The Grassimuseum complex houses three semi-interesting museums. The least interesting of the bunch is the **Museum of Arts and Crafts** (open Tues.–Fri. 9:30–6, Sat. 10–4, Sun. 9–1), with displays of local crafts, some of which date from the 17th century. Slightly more intriguing is the **Geographical Museum** (open Tues.–Fri. 10–3, Sun. 9–1), where you'll find lots of maps and models of Saxony, most of which answer questions like "What is a rock?" The **Musical Instrument Museum** (enter from Taübchenweg 2; open Tues.–Thurs. 3–6, Fri. and Sun. 10–1, Sat. 10–3), the best of the bunch, has antique violins, cellos, flutes, clavichords, and even a few music boxes. Also on display are original scores by J. S. Bach and Wagner. One ticket buys admission to all three museums and allows visitors to bypass the really boring stuff without feeling too guilty. *Johannespl. 5. Admission: DM 3.05, DM 1.55 students.*

MUSEUM DER BILDENDEN KUNSTE Don't think you'll slip away from Leipzig without going to the Museum of Plastic Arts. This is one of Leipzig's best, with an extensive collection of works by Old German and Dutch painters and a sizable holding of 20th-century sculpture. The museum's collection occupies the ground floor of the former Reichsgericht, the court where the Nazis held a propaganda trial for Georgi Dimitroff, the Bulgarian Communist accused of masterminding the Reichstag fire in Berlin in 1933. *Georgi-Dimitroff-Pl. 1, tel. 0341/313102. Admission: DM 3, DM 1.50 students. Open Tues., Thurs.–Sun. 9–5; Wed. 1–9:30.*

NIKOLAIKIRCHE In the last months of 1989 thousands of East Germans gathered every Monday outside the inauspicious Nikolaikirche to jeer, chant, and protest for political reform. Their peaceful pressure helped pull down the Iron Curtain. Now the most exciting thing that happens here is an occasional evening organ performance; outside the main entrance is a schedule. In the church interior, infinitely more impressive than the bland outside would suggest, is a spacious Gothic nave and choir. Luther is said to have preached from the church's 16th-century pulpit. *Nikolaikirchhof 3, tel. 0341/200952. Open weekdays 10–6; Sun. services at 9:30, 11, and 5.*

THOMASKIRCHE J. S. Bach was choirmaster of Thomaskirche for nearly 27 years, during which he wrote dozens of cantatas for the church's famous boys' choir, the **Thomasknabenchor** (tel. 0341/47561 or 0341/470334). They give concerts every Friday at 6 and Sunday at 1:30. Tickets cost DM 6–DM 15 and can be purchased inside the church. Ironically, even though the choir thrives on Bach's reputation, Bach himself was sorely underappreciated during his lifetime. When he died in Leipzig, he was given only a simple grave without a headstone in what was then a disreputable public cemetery. After people started feeling guilty about the whole thing, his coffin was moved to Johanniskirche in 1849. In 1945, after Johanniskirche was destroyed by Allied bombs, Bach found his final, fitting resting place in the basement vault of Thomaskirche, a church for which he had deep feelings. One of his friends lived across the street in what is now the **Bosehaus** (Thomaskirchhof 16, tel.

Thomaskirche has been a Protestant church ever since Martin Luther convinced the congregation—and Leipzig—to join the Reformation in 1539.

0341/7866, admission DM 2, open Tues.–Sun. 9–5), a Bach museum with an excellent display of period musical instruments. *Thomaskirchhof 18, tel. 0341/281703. Admission free. Open weekdays 8–1, 2–4; Wed. 8–1, 2–6.*

AFTER DARK

Because of the university, Leipzig's nightlife is pretty darn good. The club-and-bar scene doesn't have the diversity or temper of its counterpart in Berlin, but there are places in town where you can drink your fill among metal heads and punks, poets, and prophets. Since many clubs are run—generally illegally—by student co-ops, the "hip" watering holes come and go like the seasons. Your best bet is to scout the streets south of Augustusplatz and west of Nürnberger Straße. This student quarter has the largest concentration of no-name dives and weekend dance clubs. Also try **Moritzbastei** (Universitätstr. 9, tel. 0341/29232), a basement hangout south of the university. A crowd of mostly students does its drinking and dancing in the Moritzbastei's dungeonlike vaults (Moritzbastei translates as "Moritz Bastion"). Visit the two music stages, take a seat at one of the heavy wood tables, or set off down the brick halls in search of the café. Covers range from DM 2 to DM 8, depending upon who—if anyone—is playing. Another option is the **Casino Club** (Neumarkt 21–27, tel. 0341/281068), a low-key, predominantly male gay bar (straights, however, will not feel out of place). From Augustusplatz walk west on Grimmaische Straße and turn left on Neumarkt. Call first, though: This spot may close.

If you're a culture vulture, listening to the orchestra at the **Neues Gewandhaus** (Augustuspl. 8, tel. 0341/71320) is the thing to do. Performance schedules vary from year to year, with the main season running September to April. During summer the Neues Gewandhaus hosts music and drama festivals. The box office sometimes retains a number of reduced-rate tickets for sale on the night of a performance. If you can't get in, cross the square to the **Opernhaus** (Augustuspl. 12, tel. 0341/71680), which also hosts a year-round smorgasbord of events.

Near Leipzig

CHEMNITZ

Travel brochures are right to hype Chemnitz as a gateway rather than as a worthwhile sight in itself. You see, Chemnitz is ugly, the sad victim of communist urban planning. Unlike Dresden or Leipzig, Chemnitz doesn't have a historic city center interwoven with stately merchant mansions and elegant civic buildings. Although Chemnitz does have a few centuries-old monuments, mostly you'll find bland high rises and tedious shopping malls.

Orienting yourself in Chemnitz is pretty easy, mostly because urban planners had the good sense to keep the limited attractions fairly close together. All you have to do is get on **Straße der Nationen,** which parallels the Hauptbahnhof train tracks, and walk straight. **Theaterplatz,** the historic *Stadtanger* (city common or green), is a few blocks ahead. Although Theaterplatz is hardly green, it is the town's cultural hot spot. In addition to the obligatory **Opernhaus** (opera house) are two buildings housing the **Städtisches Museum** (Theaterpl. 1, tel. 0371/62275). Its **Kunstsammlungen** exhibits human-made art, and the **Naturkundemuseum** shows the organic stuff, like rock specimens and pinned insects. In front of the museum is the **Versteinerter Wald** (Petrified Forest), a group of 250-million-year-old tree stumps. They're not exactly beautiful, but what is at that age?

A few blocks farther on you'll funnel onto Chemnitz's central square, **Am Markt.** The high points here are the **Altes Rathaus** (Old Town Hall) and nearby **Rote Turm** (Red Tower). The Rathaus was the focus of town politics during the Middle Ages, but it has passed on the burden to the adjacent **Neues Rathaus** (New Town Hall), a gray (i.e., covered with pollution) Gothic structure built early in this century. Inside the Neues Rathaus is a cycle of ceiling murals by Max Klinger; inside the Altes Rathaus is the way-overpriced **Ratskeller,** serving bland traditional meals at a staggering DM 20–DM 30 per dish.

Unless you enjoy tedium, your sole experience in Chemnitz may be sitting in a beer hall waiting for the next train to whisk you away. If you're unconvinced, know that the name Chemnitz comes from an old German word for "stone" merged with the Slavic word for "chimney."

Chemnitz's final attraction is the **Schloßberg** (Schloßpl., tel. 0371/89563), a former Benedictine monastery that now houses a Protestant church. It doesn't have regular visiting hours, but rattle the door and someone might open it. If the gods are smiling on you, you might even arrive just in time for an evening organ or music concert, generally held Tuesday or Saturday at about 6. Inquire at the tourist office for performance schedules. To reach Schloßberg, walk down Georgstraße from the train station, past the Busbahnhof, turn right on Brühl-Boulevard, then left at Müllerstraße; it takes about 20 minutes on foot.

BASICS The **tourist office** (Str. der Nationen 3, tel. 0371/62051; open weekdays 9–6, Sat. 9–2), opposite the Altes Rathaus, stocks city maps, reserves rooms for a DM 6 fee, and organizes walking tours in summer. It also has free copies of *Chemnitzer Blick,* a weekly newspaper that lists the town's so-called cultural events.

There's no bank at the train station, although the nearby **Deutsche Bank** (Str. der Nationen at Carolastr.) has a bureau de change. The **CC-Bank** (Str. der Nationen 37) has a 24-hour ATM that accepts Visa cards. **Rats-Apotheke** (Rathausstr. 10, tel. 0371/61951) stocks all sorts of ointments and painkillers. It's open weekdays until 6, Saturday until 1 PM. The main **post office** (Str. der Nationen 33) is across from the tourist-information office. Here there are dozens of pay phones for national and international calls, direct-dial and collect.

COMING AND GOING Chemnitz is an important industrial town, so it's well connected with Germany's main rail routes. From the **Hauptbahnhof** (Bahnhofstr. at Str. der Nationen) there are hourly connections to Dresden (DM 9.20) and Leipzig (DM 16), and frequent service to Berlin (eight trains per day, DM 34), Weimar (nine per day, DM 21), and Zwickau (eight per day, DM 3.60). Chemnitz's **Busbahnhof** (Bahnhofstr. at Annaberger Str.) is a few blocks south of the Hauptbahnhof. There are two **Mitfahrzentralen** for ride-sharing: one at Ziethenstraße 40 (tel. 0371/414785) and one at Pornitzstraße 3A (tel. 0371/367–6204).

WHERE TO SLEEP Finding a place to stay in Chemnitz is more difficult and expensive than you might expect in this dud of a city. The tourist office can book a private room (DM 6 fee) for DM 20–DM 30, or try the creatively named **Jugendherberge Chemnitz I** (Augustusburger Str. 369, tel. 0371/71331), about 8 kilometers (5 miles)

In Chemnitz, Marx Is Now Just Another Blockhead

Prior to reunification Chemnitz was officially known as Karl-Marx-Stadt. Although locals voted in 1990 to revert to the town's original pre-1945 name, a huge sculpture of Karl Marx's head still gazes ominously over the central square—over the cement flower beds and broken fountains that infest the downtown. Look for the inscription WORKING MEN OF ALL COUNTRIES, UNITE! It's printed in English, French, German, and Russian.

outside of town. The youth hostel has 90 beds and charges DM 13 per night for those under 27, DM 15 for those 27 and over. From the bus station take any bus marked ZSCHOPAU and alight at Wilhelm-Kuppel-Straße, or take Tram 1 or 6 from the train station to Pappelhain, after which it's a 20-minute, signposted walk. The other youth hostel, **Jugendherberge Chemnitz II** (Kleinolbersdorfer Str. 61, tel. 0371/643027), is also a long haul from the city center. On the plus side, it has clean and comfy double rooms for DM 40 as well as standard dorm-style bunk beds for DM 9.50. There's also a restaurant, gym, and sauna on the premises. From the bus station hop on Bus 33 toward Adelsberg and get off at Georgistraße, which intersects with Kleinolbersdorfer Straße right where the bus lets you off.

FOOD Am Markt and Straße der Nationen offer a handful of beer halls and Imbiß-style eateries, so they're the places to come for cheap eats. Another good bet is **Café Schillerplatz** (Obere Aktienstr. 2, tel. 0371/411932), a snazzy café and restaurant in the center of town. Café Schillerplatz draws equal numbers of business types and students from the nearby Technische Universität who like to play pool in the billiard room. Beer costs a reasonable DM 4 per ½ liter. If you're hungry, the chef salad with roast beef and tuna (DM 16) is a huge masterpiece. Spaghetti Schillerplatz (DM 9.50) is also noteworthy. The **Bier Akademie** (Rosenhof 2, tel. 0371/6116) tries to live up to its name, educating its drinkers with a color photo of each of its 25 types of beer. The latter are priced DM 3–DM 5 per potent ½ liter.

If you spend much time in eastern Germany, it's nearly impossible to avoid the two-cylinder Trabant automobile, a throaty lawn mower with seats.

NEAR CHEMNITZ **Zwickau** is another dull industrial town within spitting distance of Chemnitz (okay, about 30 kilometers, or 18 miles). Zwickau's main claims to fame are composer Robert Schumann, who was born here in 1810, and the infamous Trabant car, which was first produced in a Zwickau factory in 1957. There's no tribute in Zwickau to the Trabant. However, there is a memorial to Schumann—the **Robert-Schumann-Haus** (Hauptmarkt 5, tel. 0375/5269, admission DM 1.50, open Tues.–Sun. 10–4). Schumann was born in this small, unassuming house on June 8, 1810. Nowadays it serves as a museum and archive, with lots of personal memorabilia on display. Each year in early June the town celebrates his birth with the **Robert Schumann Music Days and Competition,** which features music performances in venues throughout the city. Inquire at the tourist office for the latest scoop.

Zwickau is hardly the sort of place you go out of your way for. It's 50 minutes by train from Chemnitz, and the only reason most people visit is that they've been to—and disliked—Chemnitz and want a nearby alternative where they can sleep cheaply. There's no hostel in town, but **Tourist Information Zwickau** (Hauptstr. 6, tel. 0375/26007; open weekdays 9–5, Sat. 9–noon) books private rooms for DM 25–DM 40 per night. The **Bahnhof** (train station) is a 20-minute walk from the city center; walk straight out of the station and onto Bahnhofstraße, or hop on any bus outside the depot marked ZENTRUM. Rail destinations from Zwickau include Chemnitz (nine trains per day, DM 3.60), Glauchau (eight per day, DM 1.20), and Leipzig (five per day, DM 9.20).

THURINGIA

11

By Scott McNeely and Ann McDevitt

Thuringia can be quite a surprise if you're expecting eastern Germany to be all cement, steel, and gloom. Although formerly part of the German Democratic Republic (GDR), it remains one of the most scenic regions in Germany, with a dizzying array of rolling pastureland, lazy farm villages, forested mountains, forbidding castles, and flamboyantly Baroque palaces. Much of Thuringia's appeal stems from its history before World War II, when its two principal cities, Weimar and Erfurt, made it the cultural and political heart of Germany. From the Middle Ages until Soviet occupation in 1945, these two cities determined the shape and tone of countless movements in art, science, politics, and popular culture: Weimar alone can claim Johann Wolfgang von Goethe, Friedrich von Schiller, Friedrich Nietzsche, Johann Sebastian Bach, and Franz Liszt as former residents, in addition to having nurtured artist Paul Klee and architects Ludwig Mies van der Rohe and Walter Gropius, who founded his Bauhaus school in Weimar in 1919. Following World War I Weimar's progressivism seemed a solid model for country-wide government. In 1919 the German National Assembly met in Weimar to declare the founding of Germany's first-ever republic—the short-lived but dynamic Weimar Republic (1919–33).

Like Weimar, the sprawling city of Erfurt is steeped in history and culture. It was once home to Martin Luther, Georg Friedrich Handel, and even, for a few months, Emperor Napoléon Bonaparte. Best of all, it's got a lovely, vast *Altstadt* (Old Town), dominated by half-timbered houses and row after row of ornate Baroque facades. Even a small city like Eisenach, which lies 41 kilometers (25 miles) west of Erfurt, can lay claim to an impressive cultural heritage: J. S. Bach was born and raised here, as was Martin Luther, Germany's most revered heretic cum saint. Eisenach's fame also stems from nearby Wartburg, an imposing castle perched above the town. To many Germans, including Adolf Hitler, the Wartburg is a textbook example of how to build a *real* castle. Anyone familiar with the sputtery Wartburg automobile, the GDR's infamous shoe box–size death trap, will also appreciate a pilgrimage to the now-defunct factory—lovingly transformed into a museum to preserve the Wartburg's perilous claim that it is the "car of tomorrow."

Thuringia also bears the scars of its sometimes gruesome history. The most obvious example is Buchenwald, a Nazi-era concentration camp near Weimar. Between 1937 and 1945 at least 56,000 men, women, and children were murdered here. It's impossible to come away from Buchenwald without feeling utterly disgusted, which is exactly what makes it one of the most important monuments in the country.

Thuringia

Helmstedt
E30
Magdeburg
A39
A395
LOWER
SAXONY
SAXONY-
ANHALT
187
Elbe
A7
Bad
Harzburg
Halberstadt
71
Dessau
Wernigerode
Blankenburg
6
Bernburg
Aschersleben
Köthen
Northeim
Saale
Herzberg
Eisleben
Nordhausen
80
Sangerhausen
180
Halle
4
Sonderhausen
Unstrut
Ebeleben
249
E51
Mühlhausen
Werra
Naumburg
Bad
Langensalza
Sömmerda
Zeitz
THURINGIA
Buchenwald
Apolda
E40
Eisenach
Waldbahn
Rail Line
Erfurt
Weimar
Eisenberg
Dornburg
Wartburg
Gotha
Belvedere
Hernsdorf
Jena
Gera
Bad
Salzungen
Walterhausen
Tabarz
Wandersleben
Ilm
E40
Friedrich-
roda
Wachsenburg
Bad
Liebenstein
Brotterode
Rennsteig
Arnstadt
85
Schnellbach
Rudolstadt
Neustadt
Elster
Schmalkalden
Oberhof
Ilmenau
281
Großer
Inselsberg
Werra
Zella-Mehlis
Kickelhahn
Pössneck
Suhl
Saalfeld
Meiningen
Großer
Beerberg
Saale
Schleiz
THÜRINGER
WALD
Lauscha
Plauen
Eisfeld
E441
SAXONY
Bad
Neustadt
Sonneberg
Hof
Kronach
CZECH
REP.
Münchberg
Coburg
4
Main
Schweinfurt
A70
Main
N
A70
Bayreuth
Bamberg
A9
BAVARIA
Regnitz
A73
A3
A93
Weiden
A7
0
30 miles
0
50 km
Erlangen

Fortunately there is one place that's been left wholly untouched by the 20th century—the massive and pristine Thüringer Wald (Thuringian Forest). This old-growth forest blankets mountains and valleys from Eisenach to the Czech border, making it a popular stop for hikers. The core of the forest is difficult to penetrate, yet cities like Ilmenau, Meiningen, and Arnstadt, which lie on its fringe, still exude an Alpine tranquillity unparalleled in eastern Germany.

Erfurt

Although it's one of the most visited towns in eastern Germany, Erfurt is not your typical tourist trap. Despite the fact that its streets are crammed with luxury hotels and expensive restaurants, Erfurt still looks and feels like a thriving medieval market town, from its winding cobblestone alleys to the many spires that populate its skyline. To soak it all in, wander around the 2-kilometer-wide (1¼-mile-wide) Altstadt, a mostly pedestrian quarter that overflows with Gothic cathedrals and colorful Baroque shopfronts. This is the historic heart of Erfurt, dominated by three open-air squares: Anger Platz, the Fischmarkt, and the Domplatz. Anger Platz and Fischmarkt would constitute major don't-miss attractions in any other city, but it's the hillside Domplatz and its two Gothic cathedrals that draw the largest crowds in Erfurt. The city's other principal attraction is the Krämerbrücke (Merchant's Bridge), a 14th-century span lined with stately Renaissance- and Baroque-era facades—possibly the most beautiful shopping avenue in the world.

If you bypass the newly renovated shops and walk through the Altstadt's residential streets, you'll see Erfurt's dark side—its high concentration of crumbling plaster, fallen shingles, and dilapidated, abandoned buildings. This legacy of East German socialism is proof that the city has yet to become fully integrated—economically and aesthetically—with western Germany. Erfurt was heavily industrialized in the 1960s and is just now coming to grips with its sprawling working-class ghettos.

Despite its problems, Erfurt was—and in many ways still is—the cultural and political heart of Thuringia. In 1989 it was crowned capital of the newly created Freistaat Thüringen (Free State of Thuringia), a tribute to Erfurt's former political might. In 1993 its famous university is scheduled to reopen after a 177-year hiatus. This will undoubtedly swell the already substantial summertime crowds and help transform Erfurt into a progressive—rather than just historic—city along the lines of Leipzig and Hamburg.

More Ham Hocks, Please

In Thuringia there's a folk saying that goes: "Ess und Trink, und wächst das Ding." *This roughly translates as "Eat and drink and your thing will grow." Needless to say, native Thuringians take their eating very seriously, so try some of the local dishes. Particularly good is* Thüringen Bratwurst *(pork sausages). These are traditionally wrapped in pig intestines and cooked on a grill over beech-wood coals. Another specialty is* Thüringer Klöße, *potato dumplings made from cooked and raw potato shreds, then boiled with a crouton in the center to absorb moisture. Rounding out the list is* Schweinsfüße, *or ham hocks, which are at their best when crisply fried and doused in* Apfelrotkohl *(a sort of applesauce) or sauerkraut.*

BASICS

Erfurt has two **tourist offices.** The largest and most convenient is two blocks north of the Hauptbahnhof, at the intersection of the busy Juri-Gagarin-Ring; to get there walk straight ahead out of the station for 150 yards or so. The second is in the city center, on the famous bridge Krämerbrücke. Both book private rooms and stock free *Stadtpläne* (city maps), train and bus schedules, and tourist information, some of which is in English. *Bahnhofstr. 37, tel. 0361/23436. Open weekdays 9–6, Sat. 10–3. Krämerbrücke 3, tel. 0361/23436. Open weekdays 9–12:30 and 1–5, weekends 10–4.*

Neither office has a bureau de change, but the **Deutsche Bank,** opposite the Bahnhofstraße branch, changes money for a reasonable commission under the window marked AUSLÄNDISCHE WAHRUNGEN. It's open Monday, Wednesday, and Friday 8–4 and Tuesday and Thursday 8–5:30.

At the Hauptbahnhof, **luggage storage** is available in backpack-size lockers for DM 2 per 24 hours. There's a post office (Am Hauptbahnhof, tel. 0361/533421), open weekdays 9–4:30, outside and immediately left of the station, with an international telephone annex open until 6 PM. The main **post office** (66 Anger Pl., tel. 0361/542380), open Monday–Saturday 9–5, is in the city center, and also has an international **phone annex.**

COMING AND GOING

BY TRAIN The **Hauptbahnhof** is not the best introduction to Erfurt. Drunks frequent the plaza outside night and day, and the only nearby attraction is a long block of worn, communist-era apartments. To reach the historic city center, head straight down Bahnhofstraße, cross Juri-Gagarin-Ring, and walk straight. About 200 yards ahead is the Anger Platz, the southernmost of Erfurt's three pedestrian squares. Inside the station you'll find an information desk, cafeteria, and a handful of newsdealers. It's possible to sleep here, but keep a close eye on your bags. Destinations from Erfurt include Berlin (via Leipzig, three trains per day, DM 68), Dresden (eight per day, DM 54), Eisenach (10 per day, DM 12.60), Frankfurt (eight per day, DM 59), Gera (two per day, DM 21), Gotha (10 per day, DM 6), Leipzig (10 per day, DM 12.60), Nordhausen (three per day, DM 12.60), Northeim (three per day, DM 34), and Weimar

A Brief History

Erfurt was founded in AD 741. Soon thereafter it was integrated by Charlemagne into his Frankish empire. Erfurt occupied a pivotal spot on the **Via Regia** ***(King's Road), once the most important trade route between western Europe and the Slavic east. Erfurt became central Europe's largest producer of woad, a blue dye that brought the city 6 tons of gold per year in revenue. This lucrative trade cemented Erfurt's power, and by 1392 it boasted the second-largest university in Europe, which attracted such figures as Martin Luther (who lived and studied here between 1501 and 1505), Goethe, Schiller, Bach, and Handel. For the next 300 years Erfurt was the region's political and cultural center. In 1802 the city was conquered by Napoléon Bonaparte. The university was closed in 1816, and Erfurt soon faded into obscurity, overshadowed by the more powerful cities of Weimar and Leipzig.***

(five per day, DM 6.40). *Am Hauptbahnhof, tel. 0361/552343. Information desk open daily 8–6.*

BY BUS The **Busbahnhof** is about 50 yards north of the train depot; turn right from the depot, then turn left immediately on Wagner Straße. There's no office or staffed desk here, only a long rank of ragged buses. Head to the tourist office for information and timetables. Principal destinations from Erfurt include Dresden (three buses per day, DM 50), Eisenach (three per day, DM 11), Gotha (three per day, DM 5.50), and Weimar (four per day, DM 6).

BY MITFAHRZENTRALE Erfurt's ride-share board can be reached at 0361/25048. Call a few days in advance to arrange rides to almost any city in Germany for the price—negotiable with the driver—of gas. This often costs as much as the train, so think twice before agreeing to be squashed into somebody's backseat for a few hours. You also need to give the Mitfahrzentrale a phone number where you can be reached—another problem for budget travelers.

GETTING AROUND

Erfurt is definitely a walker's town. Nearly everything of interest is concentrated in the Altstadt, 1 kilometer (2/3 mile) north of the train station. Erfurt's historic section is interwoven with narrow, meandering lanes guaranteed to get you lost at least once. The town's three truly superlative attractions, its pedestrian squares—the Anger Platz, the Fischmarkt, and Domplatz—lie on a straight line, the first two connected by Schlösser Straße, the latter two by Marktstraße. One block east of Fischmarkt is the Altstadt's other main feature, the Krämerbrücke, a historic bridge that straddles the River Breitstrom. If you get confused, simply follow the largest street in view; it will inevitably bring you to one of the three squares.

Since the Altstadt is quite compact, buses and streetcars are useful only for getting to the youth hostel. Tickets cost DM 1 for 15 minutes of travel. They're available from dispensing machines at major stops—look for the word "bus" or a picture of a trolley car—or pay the driver as you board.

WHERE TO SLEEP

Erfurt's luxury hotels charge upward of DM 150 per night, which makes sleeping in the city center an economically unsound proposition. Besides the youth hostel, private rooms are the only budget option. Singles cost roughly DM 35, doubles DM 50–DM 60. An extra DM 5 will get you breakfast. Both tourist offices have comprehensive listings and will reserve your space for a DM 5 commission. Late in the day, locals often gather at the train station to hawk their private rooms. Be sure to agree on a price before accepting any offer, and don't be afraid to bargain. In a pinch, try the **Hotel Bürgerhof** (Bahnhofstr. 35, tel. 0361/642–1307), which charges DM 70 for comfortable doubles (call ahead; it may close). Slightly cheaper (DM 60–DM 75) is the nearby **Hotel Am Ring** (Juri-Gagarin-Ring 148, tel. 0361/646–5520). It's possible to sleep in the Hauptbahnhof with the drunks, but there's no guarantee the police—or some freak—won't disturb you.

HOSTEL **Jugendherberge Erfurt.** Three kilometers (2 miles) east of the city center, this hostel is housed in a turn-of-the-century mansion, but the ornamented ceilings and exterior plasterwork are little compensation for decrepit showers and uncomfortable bunk beds. A bed in a sex-segregated dorm room costs DM 18.50, which includes an 8 AM breakfast. Bed-linen rental is DM 6.50, and towels are an additional DM 1. *Hochheimerstr. 12, tel. 0361/26705 or 0361/5082. From northwest corner of Bahnhofstr. and Juri-Gagarin-Ring, take Bus 5 toward Steiger Str. to last stop. 80 beds. Midnight curfew, reception desk open 3–8, bedroom lockout 9–3.*

FOOD

Erfurt's Altstadt is moderately stocked with *Imbisses* (snack shops) and cheapish cafés. **Café Baldus** (Schlösserstr. 32, tel. 0361/23542) is a good choice for coffee (DM 2) and homemade pastries (DM 2–DM 4). It overlooks a small river on Walkstrom halfway between Anger Platz and the Fischmarkt. For cheap fried foods and morning coffee, try **Das Café** (Bahnhofstr. 45, tel. 0361/642–2384), one block north of the train depot; it's closed Sunday.

UNDER DM 10 **Café zur Krämerbrücke.** This Altstadt café, on the Krämerbrücke in a stately 14th-century house, serves traditional Thüringer cuisine in a romantic atmosphere. Homemade *Blech Kuchen* (pastries) go for DM 2–DM 3, sausage-and-kraut plates for DM 7.50. *Krämerbrücke 17, tel. 0361/24630.*

Feuerkugel. This traditional restaurant does an excellent job of balancing beer-hall ambience with hearty, filling meals. It's no secret, however, so expect a 10- to 15-minute wait come nightfall. Some of its best offerings include *Gulaschsuppe* (Hungarian-style stew, DM 4.90) and a schnitzel platter (DM 8.50). *Michaelisstr. 4, at Krämerbrücke's western foot, tel. 0361/63554. Closed Sun.*

Nordsee Meeres-Buffet. This fast-food stand serves fish sandwiches from a walk-up window. Salty *Matjesfilet,* a kind of German sushi on a roll with onions, costs DM 3.25. A milder *Seelachsschnitzel,* an ersatz lox, costs DM 2. A strip of Rheinischer herring in cream sauce goes for DM 6. *Anger Pl. 58, across from Anger museum.*

UNDER DM 20 **Museum für Thüringer Volkskunde.** Attached to the museum are eateries that will satisfy all tastes from the crude to the refined. The outdoor **Museum Garten** (no lunch) serves genuine Thüringer bratwurst (fried sausage, DM 2) and *Rostbratel* (pork marinated in beer, DM 4), both cooked on beechwood coals. Taxi drivers line up late at night for them. The adjacent and more upscale **Museum Gastätte** (closed Sun., no lunch Mon. and Tues.) serves full-course Thüringer meals with real Thüringer Klöße (potato dumplings). Try the *Wildschweinbraten mit Rahmsoße und Apfelrotkohl* (wild boar with apples, red cabbage, and cranberries), for DM 15.50, or the *Wurstsuppe* (sausage soup), for DM 3.50. *Juri-Gagarin-Ring 140A, tel. 0361/26641. From Bahnhofstr. tourist office, turn right on Juri-Gagarin-Ring and walk 1 km (⅔ mi).*

WORTH SEEING

Erfurt has more than 30 surviving Catholic and Evangelical churches, nearly 100 historic houses and colorful facades, and an endless supply of bridges, lanes, and walkways. The Krämerbrücke tourist office organizes guided city tours (DM 3) at noon on weekdays, June–August. Otherwise, pick up an English-language walking guide (available at a tourist office or from one of the Domplatz's street vendors) and do it yourself.

ANGER PLATZ AND MUSEUM Once the center of Erfurt's wool, wheat, and dye trade, the pedestrianized Anger Platz is now considered the least aesthetically pleasing of Erfurt's three squares. Despite this, the 17th-century **Grüne Aue und Kardinal Haus,** at No. 6, is a good example of Baroque craftsmanship, as is the **Zum Schwarzen Löwen Haus** (No. 11), built in 1577. At the plaza's northern end you'll see a dull statue of Martin Luther. Behind this is the **Kaufmannskirche** (Anger Pl. 18), an 11th-century Friesian church famed for its lush Renaissance interior. It's also the place where the parents of J. S. Bach were married. Directly behind the plaza's 19th-century fountain you'll find the closed Staathalterei (Governor's Palace), built in 1711, which has one of Erfurt's finest Baroque facades. Goethe and Emperor Napoléon Bonaparte met for the first time inside the palace's vast concert hall: Napoléon is reported to have said, "*Voilà un homme!*" ("Now there is a man!")

On the plaza's southern side is the **Angermuseum,** which houses a first-rate collection of medieval relics—coins, tools, jewelry, and a huge 14th-century crossbow—along with a hodgepodge display of 19th- and 20th-century landscape paintings. The building was erected in 1705 and served as the town's custom house. Notice its wrought-iron fixtures and detailed plasterwork. *Anger Pl. 18 at Bahnhofstr., tel. 0361/23311. Admission: DM 3, DM 2.10 students. Open Tues. and Thurs.–Sun. 10–5, Wed. 10–8.*

AUGUSTINERKLOSTER This Augustinian monastery was built in 1277. Although it sustained serious damage during World War II, it was rebuilt in 1952 and retains much of its medieval look. In this case, however, that's unfortunate, because the monks responsible for its construction adhered to a strict code of austerity both in their lives and in their architecture. The monastery's only flamboyant details are its original 14th-century stained-glass windows, worthy rivals of the glasswork found in the Domplatz's St. Marienkirche. Augustinerkloster's other claim to fame is that Martin Luther was a monk here between 1505 and 1511, and inside you'll find a small exhibition dedicated to his residence in Erfurt. Since this is still a working monastery there are no walk-in visitors, only guided tours (in German). *Augustinerstr. 10, tel. 0361/23603. From w. end of Krämerbrücke head n. (right) up Michaelisstr. and turn right on Augustinerstr. Admission: DM 4.50, DM 3 students. Open Apr.–Oct., Tues.–Sat. 10–4; Nov.–Mar., Tues.–Sat. 10–noon. Tours depart hourly on the hour; Sun. tours year-round at 10:30.*

DOMPLATZ AND DOMHUGEL The words *Domhügel* (Church Hill) and Domplatz once denoted different things, but nowadays they're synonymous for the vast plaza and its two adjacent churches on the western fringe of town at the end of Marktstraße. The plaza is unique only for its street vendors—split evenly between locals and immigrants hawking everything from bootleg cassettes to blue jeans—and for its views of Erfurt's landmark churches, Marienkirche and Severikirche. **Marienkirche** on the left (south), was founded in AD 752, although its triangular portal and flight of 70 hillside steps weren't added until 1324. Inside the cathedral you'll find an awe-inspiring cycle of 14th-century stained glass, a series of 13 panels that each measures almost 60 feet in length. Don't miss the "Wolfram" bronze candelabra, dating from 1161, and the huge 15th-century "Gloriosa" bell hanging from St. Mary's central spire. *Dompl., no tel. Admission free. Open May–Oct., weekdays 9–11:30 and 12:30–5, Sat. 9–11:30 and 12:30–4:30; Nov.–Apr., Mon.–Sat. 10–11:30 and 12:30–4.*

Across the courtyard the 13th-century **Severikirche** (Church of St. Severus), whose five equal-height naves make it architecturally unique. St. Severus's most impressive features are its carved-stone portal and, inside, the sarcophagus of St. Severus. This depicts the saint standing between his wife and daughter. And since saints and women weren't supposed to be too compatible, the two were forced into a nunnery after St. Severus received his calling. *Open May–Oct., weekdays 9–12:30 and 1:30–5; Nov.–Apr., weekdays 10–12:30 and 1:30–4.*

After touring the cathedrals, follow the narrow road that meanders down the hill from Severikirche. This leads to Lauentorstraße, which in turn veers left and climbs toward **Petersberg Citadel.** This marks the site of St. Peter's Monastery, built in 1103 and destroyed by an Austrian army in 1813. Of the original church and scriptorium only a ruin remains, but the views of Church Hill and the Erfurt skyline are spectacular. It's a perfect picnic spot.

FISCHMARKT Leading east from Domplatz is Marktstraße, a busy shopping avenue that eventually funnels onto Fischmarkt, another of Erfurt's pedestrian squares. Its Baroque-era houses have been meticulously restored since they were bombed by the United States during World War II. Of particular note is the Fischmarkt's 16th-century **Zum Roten Ochsen Haus** (Fischmarkt 7, tel. 0361/22188), which houses an excellent modern-art gallery; it's open Wednesday and Friday–Sunday 10–6 and Thursday 10–10. Across the square is the **Zum Breiten Herd Haus** (Fischmarkt 2), which has a 1584 exterior frieze depicting the five senses.

KRAMERBRUCKE The Krämerbrücke, built in 1325, is walled with half-timbered shops and an incredible collection of Baroque-era houses, making it one of the most beautiful shopping streets in the world. This is doubly true at dusk, when the cramped, cobbled street is empty of people, and the facades make you feel like you've somehow been transported into the 14th century. Of course, the Krämerbrücke is a big tourist attraction during the day; to avoid the crowds, walk instead along the shallow creek below the bridge. From here you get an undistracted view of the Krämerbrücke and its ornate buildings. *Between Futterstr. and Marktstr., 1 block e. of Fischmarkt. From Anger Pl., walk n. on Johannesstr., then turn left on Futterstr.*

MUSEUM FUR THURINGER VOLKSKUNDE The Thuringian Folklore Museum portrays the history of Thuringia's impoverished masses. Tours are in German, but the guides will communicate with *Händer und Füßen* (their hands and feet) in their exuberant efforts to show you how Thuringia's regular folks lived and died. Special exhibits include wreaths woven from the hair of maidens who died young, and animal-shape lead baubles that were melted and thrown into water to predict the future. The museum also displays such household objects as mangles and labor-intensive irons that were used to goad women and slaves into working more efficiently. *Juri-Gagarin-Ring 140A, tel. 0361/21765. From Hauptbahnhof, head straight on Bahnhofstr., turn right and continue on Juri-Gagarin-Ring for 1½ km (1 mi). Admission: DM 2.10, DM 1.05 students. Wheelchair access. Open Wed.–Sun. 10–6.*

AFTER DARK

There are few bars in Erfurt and only a handful of beer halls. None has much ambience, and all are rather expensive. For budget drinking, try one of the bars by the hostel or buy in advance at a supermarket. The only reasonable city-center option is **Feuerkugel** (*see* Food, *above*), a beer-hall-style restaurant that's often too packed and subdued to be any fun. The free pamphlet *"Erfurt Magazin,"* available at the tourist office, has listings in German of dozens of art, music, drama, and alternative happenings.

DANCE AND MUSIC **Disco Circus.** If you're feeling adventurous, take a taxi (it's the only way to get here) to Disco Circus, which claims to be the largest disco in eastern Germany. It occupies a large tent on the outskirts of town and contains four reflective disco balls, about eight bars, a stuffed bear and gorilla, a terrace (ringed with barbed wire), real amusement-park games, and a comparatively small dance floor. On Sunday you might see a magic show, a ballet, or a striptease. Womanhood gains you free admission and two free drinks on Thursday. From the city center, typical cab fare runs DM 12 each way. *Veranstalt, no tel. Cover: DM 4–DM 5, but it goes toward drinks. Closed Mon., Tues.*

Disco Circus is not safe for single women and people of color. According to club patrons, brainless skinheads of the Nazi variety are frequent guests.

Museumskeller. Hidden underneath the Museum für Thüringen Volkskunde, this club oscillates between being a German hip-hop dance hall and a live-rock venue. The latter happens every Sunday, Wednesday, and Friday at 10. Either way, the cover is DM 5–DM 10, depending upon who or what's playing. The Keller stays open until the last beer is downed, generally about 1 AM. *Juri-Gagarin-Ring 140A, tel. 0361/24994.*

OPERA AND THEATER For German-speakers, Erfurt's **Klostergang Theater** (Klostergang, off Karl-Marx-Pl., tel. 0361/646–4030) offers a year-round program of international and national drama. Classical-music fans should consider a night at the **Stadtoper** (Dalbergsweg 2, off Karl-Marx-Pl., tel. 0361/24314), which features a year-round program of opera and chamber music. Tickets for either venue range from DM 10 to DM 50, and both are located 1½ kilometers (1 mile) southwest of the city center. From Anger Platz, take Bus K or Tram 1 or 2 to Karl-Marx-Platz, a refined plaza with dozens of cafés and late-night restaurants. You can also walk from Domplatz:

Head south on An den Graden, cross both arms of the river and walk straight until you dead-end at Neuwerkstraße. Turn right, and Karl-Marx-Platz is about 200 yards ahead.

Eisenach

Eisenach is a small, very provincial town that's most famous for its hillside castle, the 12th-century Wartburg (*see* Near Eisenach, *below*). Although the Wartburg is the main tourist attraction, Eisenach has other appealing features, too: After all, this little burg counts J. S. Bach and physicist Ernst Abbe (founder of the Zeiss factories) among its native sons. Eisenach was also the childhood home of Martin Luther and the adopted home of Goethe and Schiller, each of whom spent many summers in Wartburg castle. Fittingly, Eisenach's city center has its share of museums and historic houses, the Bachhaus and Lutherhaus (*see* Worth Seeing, *below*) being among the best. It also has a stately collection of Gothic cathedrals and churches.

Historically Eisenach has never been a major political or cultural center. The looming Wartburg has been a constant draw throughout the centuries, but until reunification Eisenach was an industrialized outcast most noted for its now-defunct Wartburg automobile factory. Things have certainly changed since 1989, both in terms of the town's appeal and in the number of tourists who visit. Yet Eisenach is still a sleepy working-class town whose sights can be easily covered in a day or two—a good introduction to Thuringia but probably not the highlight. In practical terms, Eisenach's strongest appeal is its proximity to Erfurt and Weimar, only a few hours away by train.

BASICS

The **tourist office** (Bahnhofstr. 3–5, tel. 03691/732289 or 03691/69040, open Mon. 10–6, Tues.–Fri. 9–6, Sat. 9–3) stocks free city maps and English-language walking guides. It can also book private rooms for a DM 5 fee. The office is one block west of the Hauptbahnhof; turn right out of the station and walk straight. There's a smaller, souvenir-filled **tourist office** at the Wartburg (Am Schloßberg 2, tel. 03691/77072). It's open weekdays 9–1 and 1:45–5, weekends 10–3.

The best time to visit Eisenach is during the mid-August Bach Festival, a week-long event that features live renditions of Bach and much, much beer.

You can change money at the **Deutsche Bank** on Karlsplatz, one block west of the main tourist office. You'll get slightly better rates at the main post office, **Hauptpostamt** (Markt 16, tel. 03691/56331), open weekdays 8–6 and Saturday 8–noon; it also has an international telephone annex. There's a small **post office and telephone exchange** inside the train station, open weekdays 8–6. **Luggage storage** is available inside the Hauptbahnhof. Small lockers cost DM 2 per 24 hours; double-size lockers DM 3. The Hauptbahnhof also rents **bikes.** Train passengers pay DM 6 per day for a single-speed machine and DM 8 per day for multigear cruisers. Nonpassengers pay DM 10 and DM 12, respectively.

Eisenach is well stocked with *Apotheken* (pharmacies). Most are open until 8 on weekdays and until 6 on Saturday. For a list of late-night and weekend pharmacies (there's always one open, rotated on a weekly basis), check outside **Ost-Apotheke** (Bahnhofstr. 29, tel. 03961/3242), a few buildings down from the Hauptbahnhof.

COMING AND GOING

BY TRAIN Eisenach's **Hauptbahnhof** (Bahnhofstr., tel. 03691/4895) is one block east of the tourist office and three blocks east of the city center. To reach either, turn right out of the station and walk straight. Inside the depot is a staffed information desk, open Monday–Saturday 8–6 (English generally not spoken). The depot is fairly grimy and, because of its population of festering drunks, a place to avoid at night if you're female and/or traveling alone. Principal rail destinations from Eisenach include Berlin (two trains per day via Erfurt, DM 67), Dresden (five per day, DM 64), Erfurt (six per day, DM 12.60), Leipzig (six per day, DM 25), and Weimar (four per day, DM 14.80).

BY BUS The **Busbahnhof** (tel. 03691/77421) is to the right of the train depot. There's no information desk here, only a row of worn ticket windows where English is emphatically not spoken. Consult the nearby tourist office for bus timetables. Principal destinations include Bad Liebenstein (four buses per day, DM 30), Erfurt (three per day, DM 11), and Mülhausen (three per day, DM 10.50).

WHERE TO SLEEP

Eisenach's only youth hostel is a long 3½-kilometer (2-mile) walk from the train station. Take a taxi for about DM 6 if you're arriving late, or head to the nearby tourist office and book a *privat Zimmer* (private room). These generally cost DM 25–DM 30 per person, not including the DM 5 reservation fee or breakfast (DM 3–DM 5 extra). Private rooms are a good idea if you want to carouse in Eisenach's bars and cafés, as the hostel has a 10 PM curfew. In a pinch you can always rely on one of the following pensions to have at least a few beds free, mostly because they're too expensive to appeal to the general masses. Try **Haus Eisenach** (Marienstr. 60, tel. 03691/732619), which has beds for DM 50 per person and lies ½ kilometer (⅓ mile) due south of Frauenplan. Slightly farther out is **Villa Elisabeth** (Reuterweg 1, tel. 03691/732722), which has beds for DM 55 per person. It's possible to rough it in the train station, but mind your bags and money.

HOSTEL Eisenach's lone youth hostel is near Wartburg Castle, 3½ kilometers (2 miles) southwest of the train depot. It's worth the trip, however, as the hostel is perched on a forested hill on the fringe of town, making a stay here perfectly quiet and peaceful. Inside this three-story mansion are dozens of four- to eight-bed, sex-segregated dorm rooms. Showers and kitchen are communal. Beds cost DM 18.50 each, including an excellent but early breakfast (8 AM). From the Busbahnhof take Bus 3 to Mariental (ask the driver), and walk the remaining 50 yards to the hostel's door. A taxi from the train station costs less than DM 6. *Mariental 24, tel. 03691/3613. 105 beds. 10 PM curfew, reception desk open 3 PM.*

CAMPGROUND The **Altenburger See Camping Platz** is 9 kilometers (6 miles) south of Eisenach off the B19 highway. There's no public transportation to the site, so you'll need a car or bicycle. From the city center follow signs to the Wartburg (off the B19), then continue straight for 6 kilometers (4 miles). There's a sign for the campground just outside the village of Etterwinder; turn right and keep going. Campsites are DM 15 per person. On-site facilities include bungalows (DM 12 per person), showers, toilets, telephones, a snack bar, a lake, and heaps of family-owned motor homes. *Eckardtshausen, tel. 034467/74136 or 034467/ 74137. 60 sites.*

FOOD

The majority of Eisenach's restaurants are high-priced and touristy, so stick with the small food stalls and wurst shops throughout the city center. These stock bread and all sorts of sandwich supplies. Many also offer cheap take-out meals. The **Bäckerei Liebefrau** (Lutherstr. 7) has excellent Thüringer pastries for only DM .70. Try the tangy rhubarb muffins, traditional poppyseed cake, or your favorite flavor of *Quark,* a kind of German cream cheese. For a hot meal for less than DM 6, stop by **Wiener Feinbäcker,** a self-serve stand by the train station on Bahnhofstraße. Be sure to look closely at the display before ordering, however, or you're liable to end up with pig parts du jour.

UNDER DM 10 **Alte Nürnberg.** This restaurant is stylish and cultured, typical of eastern Germany's new breed of posh eateries. You'll find few locals here, only a handful of tourists and business types. It does, however, provide an opportunity to try *Hirsch* (venison) with cranberries or hand-stuffed Thüringer sausages, both priced at less than DM 9. *Marienstr. 7, tel. 03691/72177. Closed Wed.*

Gaststätte Zum Schwan. This joint restaurant and beer hall is full of smoking locals even at breakfast. Eisenacher and Erfurter beer on tap go for DM 1.30–DM 3. All meats originate from swine, processed into various incarnations. Have an *Eisbein* (hog shank) with sauerkraut and potatoes for DM 5.50, or the *Krautrolade* (cabbage rolls) and potatoes for DM 5. Vegetarians have to get up early to catch the egg breakfast (DM 7), served 8–10. *Bahnhofstr. 19, tel. 03691/4753.*

UNDER DM 15 **Café Lackner.** This is another post-unification restaurant, which means it's pastel colored and loaded with furniture that looks like it came directly from the Sprockets' living room. Fortunately, the food is superb: You can get seafood pastas from DM 9 or broiled lamb and veal from DM 12, all cooked fresh and in large quantities. Beer (DM 4–DM 6) and espresso drinks (DM 5) are available for those who'd rather sit and gawk at the Lackner's young, style-conscious crowd. Call ahead—the café may be closing. Johannispl.

WORTH SEEING

Most of Eisenach's sights are concentrated inside the cobbled, kilometer-long city center, between the tourist office and Karlsplatz in the east, Frauenplan in the south, and Am Markt plaza in the north. For a good overview, start at Karlsplatz and head south. Immediately you'll stumble upon **Karlstraße** and **Querstraße,** Eisenach's pedestrian shopping avenues. Head west (turn right) down Karlstraße for Am Markt and the

Johann Sebastian Bach

J. S. Bach was born in Eisenach on March 21, 1685. His father, the city's official piper, was commissioned to play and compose entertainments for Eisenach's civic and courtly celebrations. J. S. Bach probably learned the rudiments of music from his father, but, following the death of his parents in 1695, he moved to Ohrdruf to live with his brother. Fortunately, J. Cristoph Bach was an accomplished musician himself and helped foster his brother's burgeoning talent. In 1703 J. S. became a violinist at the Weimar court, followed by brief residences in Arnstadt and Lübeck. For four years Bach struggled to eke out a decent living, oscillating between composing music and tutoring the well-to-do children of aristocrats. In 1707 he moved to Mülhausen and married Maria Barbara, after which his career and reputation began to blossom. In 1708 he returned to Weimar and was appointed court organist. Following a few critical but underpublicized successes, Bach moved to Köthen in 1717 and was appointed court music director. Fame and fortune quickly followed. In 1721 he completed the **Brandenburg** ***Concerti and in 1722 premiered a series of organ and piano fugues dedicated to his second wife, Anna Magdalena. In 1723 Bach relocated to Leipzig, where he composed the Mass in B-flat Minor, considered by many to be his greatest work. J. S. Bach died in Leipzig on July 28, 1750.***

Rathaus, or continue south for Johannisplatz and Frauenplan. The latter two squares give a good sense of Eisenach's Baroque heritage and provide access to the nearby Bachhaus. On Am Markt look for the 16th-century **Georgenkirche,** a stunning Baroque monument that anchors this vast pedestrian plaza. J. S. Bach was baptized here, and inside you'll find a lush cycle of 14th-century stained glass.

AUTOMOBILE MUSEUM Housed in what's left of Eisenach's former auto plant, this museum offers an insightful glimpse at the GDR's most ridiculed creation, the Wartburg, named after the nearby castle. The Wartburg is one of those love-hate phenomena, a closet-size coffin whose engine sounds like a glorified lawn mower caught on a sprinkler. Inside the museum you'll find exhibits on the Wartburg's production, some heroic 1960s-era propaganda ("the Wartburg 1.3, a proud achievement of People's engineering"), and a few pristine showroom models. Don't miss it. *Wartburgallee, 1 block s. and e. of Frauenplan, tel. 03691/59809. Admission: DM 2.50, DM 1 students. Open Mon.–Sat. 9–4.*

BACHHAUS This museum is a must for Bach fans. Although Johann himself probably never set foot in this 16th-century flat, everything here is meant to re-create his life and times in exacting detail. This includes 17th-century period furniture, original handwritten scores, and various old instruments, many of which were actually used by Bach during his residence in Eisenach and Weimar. For non-German-speakers the German-only displays will detract only slightly from the overall experience: Every half hour there's a live, 10- to 15- minute concert featuring a musician who adroitly handles the museum's original 18th-century instruments. *Frauenplan 21, tel. 03691/3714. Admission: DM 5, DM 4 students. Open Mon. 2–5:45; Tues.–Sat., holidays 10–5:45.*

LUTHERHAUS During his schoolboy years (1498–1501), Martin Luther did live in the Lutherhaus, so it's a bit more authentic than the nearby Bachhaus. Yet Martin Luther spent most of his adult life elsewhere, and most significant historical records are on permanent display in the Wartburg (*see* Near Eisenach, *below*). As a result, this small museum sheds little light on Germany's most revered heretic. Inside are 16th-century, period-decorated rooms and a meager exhibit of personal letters. Ask to view the English-language video, which documents Luther's accomplishments and briefly recounts the history of Lutherhaus. *Lutherpl. 8, tel. 03691/4983. Admission: DM 3, DM 1.50 students. Open Oct.–Apr. Mon.–Sat. 9–11 and 2–5, Sun. 2–5; May–Sept., daily 9–1, 2–5.*

REUTER-WAGNER MUSEUM This museum is housed in a tree-shaded villa once owned by Fritz Reuter, a minor northern German poet and illustrator. A few of Reuter's manuscripts and ink drawings are on hand, but it's the Wagner exhibit that draws the (rare) crowds. Even though there's no historical reason for a Wagner museum in Eisenach, the curators have compiled the second-largest Wagner library in Germany, mostly comprised of voluminous biographies and obtuse critical studies. *Reuterweg 2, tel. 03691/3971. Walk s. from Frauenplan on Marienstr. and turn right onto Reuterweg. Admission: DM 3. Open Tues.–Sun. 10–5.*

AFTER DARK

The **Landestheater** (Theaterpl. 4, tel. 03691/6860), at the northern end of the Querstraße, provides one of the most bizarre ways to pass the night. Inside its black-box theater you'll discover a diverse, obscure, sometimes painful range of drama, from puppet to political, from Poulenc to Cocteau and Brecht. Many productions rely heavily on montage and mime, so fluent German is not generally a prerequisite. Stop by the theater's Querstraße box office, at No. 34, for schedules and ticket prices.

Another popular option is **Karlsplatz 10** (tel. 03691/3338), a three-story club, bar, and disco, one block west of the tourist office. **Café Swing** (no cover), on the bottom floor, is a mellow, smoky bistro with sandwiches and tap beer. On the second floor you can dance at **Haus der Jugend,** a grungy student hangout. The cover ranges from DM 3 to DM 6, with dancing every Wednesday and Saturday 6–midnight. There's also live rock 'n' roll (Metallica meets Winger) most Thursdays and Fridays at 8. The **Karlsplatz Café** is on the third floor; it's closed Monday–Thursday. Its slogan is "We're here when nothing else is going on, OK!" and the motley crowd sports leather, black eyes, and dreadlocks. Drinks are DM 2–DM 3. Occasionally there's a DM 4 cover. Otherwise, check out the **Jugendklub am Kuhgehänge** (Stregdaer Allee, tel. 03691/71437), a late-night student dance club. Because it's 4 kilometers (2½ miles) from the city center (take a taxi for DM 7) you won't find many tourists here—only a devoted handful of hip-hop-lovin' youth who don't speak much English. The standard cover is DM 8.

Near Eisenach

WARTBURG

Wartburg castle (tel. 03691/77072), Thuringia's main attraction, sits at the edge of a mountainside forest overlooking Eisenach. Although no one agrees when the Wartburg was built, the first reference to it is in the late 12th century, at the time when Eisenach received its first charter. Since then the Wartburg has been built and rebuilt by generations of German kings, who were attracted by the castle's strategic location and the nearby supplies of sturdy, old-growth timber, which was used in building the all-wood stronghold.

Despite the numerous changes in the Wartburg's structure and design (in the 15th century whole walls were removed to take advantage of the morning sun), it's still considered a textbook example of German castle architecture—the most German of all German castles, in fact. Prominent features include its plastered, half-timbered facades and the squat towers that guard its asymmetrical corners.

The Wartburg's best exhibits are those dedicated to Martin Luther. In 1521–22 Martin Luther holed up in the castle to hide from the pope and the German emperor, neither of whom was pleased with him for tacking his 95 revisionist theses onto a church door in Wittenburg. To pass time, Luther translated the Bible into German, giving common people direct access to theology. After you take a brief tour of the castle's small museum, loaded with torture-chamber instruments and Lutheran artifacts, the next stop is his study, **Lutherstube.** Here Luther would allegedly do battle with the devil on a semi-regular basis, throwing anything at hand to keep the beast at bay. During one spirited encounter Luther even hurled an inkwell at Satan, leaving an unsightly ink spot on the wall. This myth probably stems from a metaphor Luther once used in a letter, where he said he was "fighting the devil with ink," meaning with the power of words. Faithful pilgrims, however, took it a bit too literally, and over the centuries they chiseled away at the "ink-stained" wall to get souvenirs, leaving a large hole. Also in this room is Luther's footstool, sculpted from dinosaur vertebrae.

It costs DM 1 to enter the castle courtyard and climb the **Südturm,** where you can look down on Eisenach. You'll need to pay an additional DM 2 to get inside the half-timbered castle, where you'll find the museum and Luther's study. A German-language tour that includes the museum, study, and a boring English pamphlet is DM 6 and DM 3 for students. Permission to take photos is another DM 2. From April to October, tours go on from 8:30 until 4:30, and you can wander around the courtyard until 6; arrive early if you want to miss the biggest crowds. From November to March things mellow out a bit, but tours run only from 9 to 3:30, and the courtyard closes at 5.

COMING AND GOING The hillside castle is only 3 kilometers (2 miles) from the city center, yet it takes some effort to reach the summit. If you're in the mood to hike and don't mind a steep, sometimes muddy, 90-minute climb, try the **Reuterweg** or **Fahrweg zur Wartburg.** These two streets intersect the southern foot of Marienstraße (which is connected to Eisenach's Frauenplan). At the end of each you'll find posted hiking trails that lead to the Wartburg. Another option is the **Wartburg Trolley** (DM 3), a motorized "train" (a.k.a. bus), which leaves every 20 minutes from its Mariental Straße depot. From the city center simply follow the WARTBURG signs until you see the bus parking lot. From the Hauptbahnhof you can also take Bus 3 to Wartburg. This leaves daily every 30 minutes 9–6, and costs DM 2 each way.

GOTHA

During the 17th and 18th centuries, Thuringia's princes used the small village of Gotha as their unofficial summer resort, a rural retreat from the courtly bustle of Erfurt and Leipzig. Today Gotha's impressive Baroque architecture contrasts starkly with its suburban, communist-era ghettos and with the smokestacks that encroach upon the city's north side. Despite these eyesores, Gotha's vast and attractive **Hauptmarkt** allows the city to retain some of its former charm. Dominating this Renaissance-era market square is the bright-red **Rathaus** (town hall), which dates from 1577. At the Hauptmarkt's other end is an exquisite marble fountain, a lush Baroque fantasy that invites you to sit in its shadow, preferably with a bottle of cheap red wine. The fountain sits above the square on a gentle hill, and it's flanked by Gotha's best collection of color-washed, Baroque-era houses. Also worth checking out is the **Margaretenkirche,** an 18th-century cathedral that anchors the **Neumarkt,** Gotha's other open-air square. The Neumarkt is one block east of the Hauptmarkt; apart from the church, it has little of the Hauptmarkt's elegant air.

Gotha's main attraction is the **Schloß Friedenstein** (Am Friedenstein, tel. 03621/53036), a Baroque castle built in 1654 to commemorate the end of the Thirty Years War. It houses several museums that exhibit antique instruments, Egyptian mummies, and an unbeatable collection of 17th-century maps and navigational charts. The palace's most interesting sights are probably its well-preserved galleries, built in styles ranging from Baroque to Rococo and classical. Also inside, you'll find a 17th-century theater—eastern Germany's oldest active playhouse—with its original stage and ornamented ceiling. Schloß Friedenstein is about 200 yards south of the Hauptmarkt's fountain, and its three museums are open daily 9–5. Visitors can catch them all for DM 5 or select one for DM 3. Students get a break at DM 2.50 for all and DM 1.50 for one.

Gotha isn't the most exciting village in Thuringia, but it offers the art and architecture of a city with the peacefulness of a small town. And because Gotha is well connected by train to Eisenach and Erfurt, it can be a convenient day-trip or an overnight stop.

If you're planning a day-trip to the Thuringian Forest (*see* Thüringer Wald, *below*), Gotha is also the main terminus for the superconvenient ***Waldbahn,*** a special forest train that travels three times daily to Walterhausen and Friedrichroda, two small outposts on the forest's northeastern edge.

VISITOR INFORMATION Gotha has two information desks, one official and one privately owned. The official one used to be at Hauptmarkt 2, but it's in the process of being relocated. Check the billboard outside No. 2 for its new address, or try the private **Gotha Information** (Blumenbachstr. 3, off Hauptmarkt, tel. 03621/54036), which books private rooms (DM 3 fee) weekdays 9–5 and Saturday 9–noon. It also provides free city maps.

COMING AND GOING Gotha's **train station** is a 10-minute walk from the city center. Walk straight out of the depot for four longish blocks and turn left down any of the narrow, shop-filled side streets; these funnel directly into the Hauptmarkt. The station is connected with Walterhausen and Friedrichroda (three trains per day to each, DM 3) via the Waldbahn, and with Frankfurt (four per day, DM 53), Weimar (four per day, DM 10.80), Erfurt (four per day, DM 6.40), and Leipzig (three per day, DM 27) by standard passenger train.

WHERE TO SLEEP AND EAT Gotha's **Jugendherberge** (Mozartstr. 1, tel. 03621/54008) is a 10-minute walk from the Hauptbahnhof. Turn left from the station and left again on Mozartstraße. Official check-in is after 3, but if someone's around they'll most likely let you in. Its 30 beds (DM 13.50, DM 18 with breakfast) fill up on summer days, so arrive early or book in advance.

The **Carnaby Music Pub** (18 März Str.) is a popular place with young locals, serving onion soup and pizza slices for DM 4 and DM 6. It also has a large selection of juices and schnapps. On the Hauptmarkt the **Gockel Grill** (Hauptmarkt 7) serves Hungarian paprikas (DM 7) and traditional German wieners for less than DM 5. It's closed Sunday.

Weimar

In many ways Weimar is the highlight of a trip through Thuringia. Although Erfurt may be the historic heart of Thuringia and the region's largest and most visited city, Weimar has always been the seat of literature and the arts. This is less true of modern Weimar, but over the years the city was home to the likes of Goethe, Schiller, Nietzsche, Bach, and Liszt. Real power, however, was wielded by princes in Leipzig and Erfurt, so Weimar naturally developed a more liberal, even cynical, approach to politics and government. This helped turn Weimar into a progressive city peopled with thinkers, artists, and the radical fringe. Following World War I, in particular, Weimar, like Berlin, seemed to have many answers for a country wracked by runaway inflation and pervasive despair. Weimar also nurtured one of the most exciting artistic scenes anywhere in post–World War I Europe. Gropius formed his Bauhaus school of art and design here in 1919, and on any given day you could find people like Mies van der Rohe wandering its streets. Partially as tribute to Weimar's newfound identity, the German National Assembly met here in 1919 to declare the founding of Germany's first-ever republic—the short-lived Weimar Republic (1919–33). This constitutionally based government, which drew its support from a coalition of socialists, Communists, and capitalists (and anyone else who could produce a manifesto) did little to stem the rise of fascism and Hitler's Nazis. During its short tenure, however, it nurtured a progressive, dynamic culture that many consider the golden age of 20th-century Germany.

Modern Weimar makes no bones about the ironic contrast between its intellectual heritage and its Nazi legacy. Its tourist literature admits this duality, and road signs all over town point the way to the Buchenwald memorial.

Weimar bears the unmistakable imprint of history, apparent in its cobblestoned, tree-lined streets fronted with Baroque houses and dazzling Rococo palaces; in the colorful homes of Goethe, Schiller, and Liszt; and in the occasional Nazi- and communist-era monuments that recall a more immediate past. A particularly glaring reminder is Buchenwald (*see* Near Weimar, *below*), the infamous concentration camp 5 kilometers (3 miles) north of Weimar.

Despite its formidable history, Weimar is surprisingly small. Its historic center is much less dense and, at first glance, not nearly as stunning as Erfurt's vast Altstadt. Still, Weimar has all of Erfurt's historic appeal plus the small-town charms of a city like Eisenach. Best of all, Weimar is easily reached by train from almost anywhere in Germany, particularly Erfurt (30 minutes), Leipzig (one hour), and Berlin (four hours).

BASICS

Weimar has three tourist-information offices. All have city maps and English-language walking guides, and all offices can book private rooms for a DM 3–DM 5 fee. The largest and most useful is **Touristbüro** (Marktstr. 4, tel. 03643/202173), near the Rathaus, just north of the pedestrian-only Am Markt. It's open weekdays 10–1 and

2–4, Saturday 10–1. To get there from the train station, take Bus 3, 5, or 6 to Theaterplatz; turn left on Schillerstraße then right on Am Markt. A smaller Touristbüro (tel. 03643/3449) is at Jakobstraße 11A, four blocks north of the Marktstraße branch. You'll find another inside the Hilton Hotel (Belvederer Allee 25, tel. 03643/59037), 1 kilometer (⅔ mile) south of the city center. Only the latter office will change money (at a very mediocre rate), so head instead to the **Deutsche Bank** (Am Markt 10, tel. 03643/62811) or **Commerzbank** (Schillerstr., tel. 03643/64302). Both are open Monday–Thursday 8–noon and 1:30–4:30 and Friday 8–1. **Luggage** stored at the Hauptbahnhof, either in lockers or at the luggage counter, costs DM 3 per 12 hours. The main **post office** (Goethepl. 7–8, tel. 03643/7600) is one block north of Theaterplatz. It's open weekdays 9–5, Saturday 9–4.

COMING AND GOING

Weimar is simple to reach from most parts of Germany, so there's no excuse not to stop for at least a few hours on your way to Erfurt or Berlin. Weimar's **Hauptbahnhof** (Baudert Pl. and Carl-August-Allee, tel. 03643/3330 or 03643/2344) is 1½ kilometers (1 mile) north of the city center, which you can reach by taking Bus 3, 5, or 6 or Tram 4, 5, or 8 from outside the station to Theaterplatz or Goetheplatz. Otherwise, it's a 20- to 30-minute walk; walk straight out of the station and turn left after passing the Goetheplatz post office. Inside the Hauptbahnhof is a grocery store, cafeteria (open daily 8–6), and information desk (open weekdays 9–5, Sat. 9–3). Destinations from Weimar include Berlin (three trains per day via Leipzig, DM 64), Dresden (four per day, DM 19), Eisenach (nine per day, DM 14.80), Erfurt (nine per day, DM 5), Frankfurt (three per day, DM 64), and Leipzig (five per day, DM 19).

The **bus depot** (tel. 03643/3322) is adjacent to the train station. It's undergoing renovation, so for the time being it's utter chaos here. Head to the tourist office for timetables and prices. Bus destinations from Weimar include Erfurt (three per day, DM 7), Eisenach (two per day, DM 14), and Leipzig (one per day, DM 16.50).

WHERE TO SLEEP

The nearest campground is 25 kilometers (16 miles) away, so besides Weimar's three youth hostels, the cheapest option is a private room in a family house. These cost DM 25–DM 30 per person and can be booked through any tourist office for a DM 3–DM 5 fee. Among the cushier options is the **Hotel Elephant** (Am Markt 19, tel. 03643/61471), in a class by itself. It has sheltered the likes of Wagner, Gropius, Napoléon, and even Hitler. A 1960s-era renovation sterilized much of the once-elegant interior, but this is still the poshest hotel for miles. The price: DM 100–DM 220 per person, per night. More accessible is the **Hotel Liszt** (Lisztstr. 3, tel. 03643/54080), ½ kilometer (⅓ mile) southwest of the city center. It's a small, family-run hotel with eight comfortable rooms, all decorated in a loose Baroque style. Singles start at DM 50, doubles at DM 90. To get here from Goetheplatz, walk south down Heinrich-Heine-Straße, turn left at Sophienstifts Platz, right on Gropiusstraße, right on Steubenstraße, and left on Lisztstraße; total walking time is 15 minutes. If you arrive late there's a cheapish hotel, the **Thüringen** (Brennerstr. 42, tel. 03643/3675), near the Hauptbahnhof. Turn left out of the station and right on Brennerstraße; the hotel is about 200 yards ahead. Singles here start at DM 50, doubles at DM 92.

HOSTELS Along with the two hostels listed below, there's an independent 80-bed hostel only 10 minutes by foot from the city center. It's known as the **Jugendherberge Am Poseckschen Garten** (Humboldtstr. 17, tel. 03643/4021), and its dorm-style beds cost DM 15.50 per person, including breakfast. Take Bus 6 to the street Am Poseckschen Garten from the Hauptbahnhof.

Jugendherberge Germania. This convenient hostel is two blocks south of the Hauptbahnhof; walk out the station's doors and continue straight (south) on Carl-August-Allee. The hostel is clean and efficient but also large (72 beds) and somewhat noisy. Down the street is an excellent late-night restaurant, the Café Scenario (*see* Food, *below*). Singles fetch DM 18.50, including breakfast. Sheets cost DM 6.50. *Carl-August-Allee 13, tel. 03643/202076. 11 PM curfew, reception desk open 3 PM.*

Jugendherberge Maxim Gorki. Despite the urge to suppress all things reminiscent of the communist era, this hostel will retain its Russian name because of Gorki's contributions and writings for youth. (Gorki once wrote: "Our goal is that youth live and believe in life.") In any case, the hostel's best features are its three washing machines, a rare find in eastern Germany, and the beautiful graveyard nearby. On the down side, be prepared for visiting student and youth groups who watch television late into the night. The hostel is a 15-minute tram ride from the city center. From Goetheplatz or the Hauptbahnhof, take Tram 5 or 8 to Am Wilden Graben, then follow signs. The 52 beds run DM 18 per person, breakfast included. *Windmühlenstr., Am Wilden Graben 12, tel. 03643/3471. Flexible 11:30 PM curfew, reception desk open 3 PM, sheets DM 6.50.*

FOOD

Restaurants and cafés are packed into Weimar's dense city center; you'll find the largest concentration on Schillerstraße between Theaterplatz and Am Markt and near the Baroque castle on Burgplatz. Many of these are pseudo-German eateries geared to tourists, so try the area near Herderplatz, also. Here you'll find a handful of quiet, smoky beer halls that serve cheap pub grub, mostly wieners and fries. A good example is **Probierstube** (Eisfeld 4, tel. 03643/2131), one block west of Herderplatz. It serves traditional Thuringian sausage-and-potato meals (DM 8), and a large selection of Thuringian beer. Another budget option is **C-Keller-Galerie** (Am Markt), a joint art gallery and café where students do the cooking. Try one of its rotating vegetarian specials (DM 5–DM 9) and homemade desserts (DM 3–DM 5). South of Burgplatz in Weimarhallenpark Park you'll find **Lesecafe Gratis** (Asbachstr. 1, tel. 03643/61984), a hip, smoky spot where an arty crowd hangs out for poetry readings and occasional live-music evenings. Ice cream with liquor is about DM 5, beer DM 2.50. Close to the Am Poseckschen Garten youth hostel is the quiet beer hall **Felsenkeller** (Humboldtstr. 37, tel. 03643/61941), which serves wursts and soups.

UNDER DM 10 **Café Scenario.** The café is near the Hauptbahnhof, only two doors from the Germania youth hostel, and rates as one of the best restaurants in Weimar. It's a joint bar and Italian café, offering top-rate pizza from DM 7, vegetable-and-seafood pastas from DM 6, and garlic-basted *Gnoche* (potato dumplings) from DM 5. There's an outdoor patio for coffee and beer (DM 2.50–DM 4) and, inside, a stylish dining area dominated by a wall-length bar. The music ranges from Tom Waits to Bach to John Coltrane, the crowd from business types to students. *Carl-August-Allee, tel. 03643/419640. Closed Sun.*

UNDER DM 15 **Big Ben.** This restaurant is typical of those opened since reunification—arty, pastel-colored, and decorated with "modern" furniture straight out of a bad sci-fi movie. Even so, it's popular with Weimar's health-conscious, under-30 crowd, mostly because of its *Großer Vegetarischer* (DM 9), a huge tuna salad garnished with pineapples and grapes. The tempura-style *Champignons* (mushrooms) are also very tasty at DM 9. Have a sweet version of *Rote Grütze* (DM 3.50), a red fruit compote, for dessert. *Röhrstr. 16, tel. 03643/65600. No lunch.*

Ratskeller. As a rule, Ratskellers offer expensive, pseudo-German dishes in a characterless, almost lonely atmosphere. This one, however, is noteworthy for its vegetarian and tofu menu. Order the *Buchweizer-tofu-taler mit Bunten Gemüse* (DM 12) for a tofu patty simmered in beer and served with veggies. Meat eaters should try one of the

Chinese dishes, ranging from curried shrimp (DM 13) to pork fried rice (DM 9). *Am Markt 10, tel. 03643/4142. Closed Sun., Mon.*

WORTH SEEING

Weimar's sights are conveniently spread between its four main squares: Theaterplatz in the west, Am Markt and Burgplatz in the east, and Herderplatz in the north. All are within ½ kilometer (⅓ mile) of each other and are connected by mostly pedestrian lanes, so getting around isn't a problem. For a good overview, start at the Marktstraße tourist office and walk in a counterclockwise direction, your first stop being Am Markt; the second being the Schloß on Burgplatz. A map is handy, but even without one it's hard to get lost in Weimar's compact center. From the Marktstraße tourist office, hour-long **guided tours** (DM 2 per person) depart at noon on most summer days.

AM MARKT Weimar's market square dates from 1400, the year the city received its first charter. For 200 years the square was open on three sides and used mostly for knightly tournaments and the occasional bazaar. In 1774 the **Neptun Fontäne** (Neptune Fountain), by Martin Klauer, was added, as was the neo-Gothic Rathaus (now a decent restaurant). On the east side of Am Markt is the **Lucas Cranach Haus** (closed to the public), a Renaissance-style building with an exquisitely sculpted facade; a few doors down from that is the impressive **Hotel Elephant,** the first mention of which appears in 1561. It has hosted the likes of Goethe, Napoléon, and Hitler and was used by Thomas Mann as the location for his story "Lotte in Weimar." A fruit-and-vegetable market occupies the plaza every Tuesday and Saturday in summer. On Marktstraße, one block north, is the main tourist office.

BURGPLATZ Burgplatz, by the River Ilm on the east end of town, is Weimar's most impressive square. Built in the 16th century, its cobblestone walkways are lined with a notable collection of Baroque- and Renaissance-era houses, many of which are still occupied. Burgplatz's most famous attraction, the vast **Schloß Weimar** (tel. 0621/61831), has sections that date from the 10th century; it's open Tuesday–Sunday 10–6; admission is DM 5, DM 3 students. Inside the castle you'll find two top-rate museums. The **Kunstsammlungen** has a collection of 20,000 paintings, sculptures, and drawings by Albrecht Dürer, Lucas Cranach, Matthias Grünewald, various impressionist and expressionist masters, and members of Gropius's Bauhaus school. In the same wing is the small **Museum Schloß,** with a collection of artifacts, maps, and illustrations that document the castle's evolution. A short walk from the castle is the equally stunning **Zentralbibliothek** (Central Library, Burgpl., tel. 03643/65433), a Renaissance-era building that was later transformed into a masterpiece of Rococo design. Don't miss the library's central hall (open Mon.–Sat. 10–4), an oval-shape, three-story reading room decorated with oak banisters, carved plaster ceilings, and gilded molding—the epitome of Rococo embellishment.

GOETHEHAUS Goethe, one of Germany's most renowned poets and thinkers, lived in this three-story Baroque house from 1782 until his death in 1832. Inside you'll find his study, personal library, and period rooms containing his collection of classical art. Even for those who've never heard of Goethe, the monument's interior decor—from the oak-carved furniture to the pewter gaslights and wood cutlery—gives a good idea of Baroque-era Germany. Also inside is a small café, which closes 30 minutes before the museum does. *Am Frauenplan, tel. 03643/62041. From Am Markt, walk 1 block s. on Frauentorstr. Admission: DM 5, DM 3 students. Open Tues.–Sun. 9–5.*

HERDERPLATZ This quiet, cobblestone square houses the 18th-century **Stadtkirche** (open daily 10–4), a wonderfully Baroque cathedral visited by Martin Luther in 1518. Inside is Lucas Cranach's *Winged Altar* triptych, a painting familiar to anyone who's ever taken an art-history course. The church is typically German: gilded, flooded with light, and impeccably clean; for another view, take a quick tour of the basement vault, where you'll find the 16th-century tombs of various Ernestine kings. Opposite the Stadtkirche is the **Sächsischer Hof** (tel. 03643/5925), an inn first mentioned in historical documents in 1429. Its Renaissance gable is considered the finest in Weimar. Goethe lived here briefly in 1775, but in 1850 its private rooms were converted into the large, dark, and musty beer hall (closed Fri.) that remains today. On many summer weekends Herderplatz is the site of a craft bazaar and barbecue. Look for hand-made pottery, top-rate wieners, and wandering musicians playing to rapt crowds of tourists.

LISZTHAUS The pianist and composer Franz Liszt lived in this tree-ringed mansion from 1869 until his death in 1886. The house itself, set on the fringe of Ilm Park, is attractive, but inside you'll find only a weary collection of German-language exhibits and documents. Non-German-speakers will still appreciate Liszt's living room and study, which have been preserved and furnished in their original style. *Marienstr. From Am Markt walk s. past Goethehaus; at Wieland Pl., veer left onto Marienstr. Admission: DM 2.50, DM 1 students. Open Tues.–Sun. 9–noon, 1–5.*

SCHILLERHAUS Schiller lived in this squat Baroque mansion from 1802 until his death in 1805. The mansion displays a number of personal artifacts, from Schiller's writing desk to his top hat and coat. Also on exhibit in this dully renovated, sterile building are period furniture and costumes. Those familiar with the writer may appreciate the autographed first-edition folios, but most will just be annoyed by the large crowds. *Schillerstr., 2 blocks e. of Theaterpl., tel. 03643/62041. Admission: DM 5, DM 3 students. Open Wed.–Mon., 9–5.*

THEATERPLATZ Next to Am Markt, the cobblestone Theaterplatz is the largest square in Weimar. On its west side is the neoclassical **Deutsches Nationaltheater** (tel. 03643/755322); built in 1798, it was inaugurated with a performance of Schiller's *Wallenstein's Camp.* Goethe, who was the theater's director at the time, helped rebuild the structure after it burned in 1825. In 1945 it was once again destroyed, this time by American bombers. It reopened in its present form in 1948 with a production of Goethe's *Faust.* Opposite the theater is the impressive classical facade of the **Kunsthalle** (tel. 03643/61831), open Saturday–Thursday 10–6, Friday 10–8. Today it houses art and literary exhibits, most of which are dedicated to some aspect of Weimar's heritage (in other words, lots of Bauhaus and Gropius shows). The statue in the square's center, depicting Goethe and Schiller surveying the city they helped make famous, is the work of Ernst Rietschel and dates from 1857. An identical cast was given to the city of San Francisco in 1910, where it stands today in Golden Gate Park.

AFTER DARK

The German-language pamphlet *"Weimar Aktuell,"* available free from any tourist office, has a comprehensive listing of evening events. If you're in the mood for a no-frills stein in a seedy beer hall, check out the **Sächsischer Hof** (Herderpl., Eisfeld 12, closed Fri.) or, near the Am Poseckschen Garten hostel, **Sommer's** (Humboldtstr. 2). Another option is Weimar's top-rate **Deutsches Nationaltheater** (Theaterpl., tel. 03643/755321), which stages an international array of works, from Goethe, Schiller, and Shakespeare to Bertolt Brecht, Samuel Beckett, and Henrik Ibsen. If your German isn't up to it, you may want to consider an evening of music instead; the opera season runs October through February, supplemented by year-round chamber and symphony music. Tickets cost DM 7–DM 35 for premier events, DM 5–DM 15 for matinees and lesser-known titles. Students receive a 50% discount. Stop by the Theaterplatz box office (open Mon.–Sat. 10–noon, 4–6) or a tourist office for current schedules.

CLUBS Weimar has a large network of student clubs, such as **Studentklub Jakobsplan** (Am Jakobsplan 1, tel. 03643/737265) and the nearby **Jugendclub Nordlicht** (Stauffenbergstr. 20A, tel. 03643/777354). Both hold frequent dance nights year-round, usually on Friday and Saturday at 8. Covers are DM 3–DM 7. Call for current schedules, or look for fliers plastered around the city center.

Jugendzentrum Mon Ami. This youth club has regular avant-garde movie nights, usually showing American and French titles dubbed into German. On other nights, most people sit playing cards and gossiping, so it's a great place to practice your rusty German. Generous steins of beer fetch DM 2–DM 3 in the smoky bar, and there's a selection of alcohol-free drinks (DM 1–DM 2) in the adjacent café. *Goethepl. 11, tel. 03643/2319. Closed Sun.*

Studentenclub Kaßeturm. Student crowds have partied in this medieval tower for 30 years. The bottom floor is a stone-walled beer and wine cellar; the second floor, used for live bands, is domed and painted with murals. Above is a quieter bar. Covers range from DM 3 (no live band) to DM 15 (live music). However, Monday, Tuesday, and Thursday are "beer nights," which means there's no cover charge. Doors open at 8, and the last drunkard usually stumbles home at about 1 or 2. *Goethepl., tel. 03643/73623. Closed Sun.*

Near Weimar

BUCHENWALD

Whether you call Buchenwald a death camp, a processing depot, or a detention center, the fact of the matter is that at least 56,000 human beings were killed here between 1937 and 1945: men, women, and children from 35 nations whose only "crime" was a religious belief, a pigment of the skin, or an "unacceptable" political ideology. In Hitler's Germany, the labels "Jew" and "Gypsy" connoted second-rate breeds that, like laboratory animals, could be used for experiment and cheap labor, then ruthlessly murdered.

The whole point of Buchenwald's continued existence can be summed up in two words: Never forget. Buchenwald may have been created by Hitler and the Nazis, but the hatred it was built upon has yet to be eradicated. And although it may be a grim place, its greatest power lies in forcing people to confront the gruesome effects of hatred firsthand. Following the camp's liberation in 1945, the American army had the same idea: Only days after taking control, the army ordered that all the women and children of Weimar take a mandatory tour of Buchenwald. Some of the footage—grandly dressed women carrying parasols and fans, some fainting, some vomiting, some too shocked to move—can be seen in a 30-minute film at the tourist center.

After leaving the tourist center, you'll see a long path that leads to the camp's front gate. Its heavy iron door, once guarded by elite SS and Wehrmacht regiments, is intact. Although it's unlocked during visiting hours, it still feels strange to willingly open the only gate to Buchenwald. Inside, very little has been altered since the camp was liberated. The barbed wire remains, as do the gun posts and administrative buildings. The only things missing are the prisoner cell blocks, which once stretched for ½ kilometer (⅓ mile) in every direction; today only their charred foundations remain. At the north end of the compound you'll find a small **museum,** with multilingual displays and a fascinating collection of scale-model re-creations. These include the prisoner living quarters, furnished with letters, drawings, and a sad collection of personal belongings—worn-out shoes, spectacles, diaries, and frayed photos of anonymous loved ones. About 100 yards south of the museum is another exhibit, housed in what remains of the camp's original "medical research" facilities. These eventually lead into the **oven chambers,** where the majority of Buchenwald's victims were incinerated. Unlike many concentration camps, Buchenwald did not use gaseous showers to exterminate its victims (where people were herded into a room under the pretense of getting a hot-water shower and clean

Buchenwald's camp clock has read 3:15 since April 11, 1945. This is in commemoration of the camp's liberation, orchestrated by a brigade of inmates four days before the arrival of the American army.

clothes, only to be suffocated with poisonous gases); instead, victims here were most often worked to the point of exhaustion, tortured, or shot. Afterward, their bodies were burned, in order to save the effort of a mass burial.

Back at the tourist center there's a book shop and art gallery, both of which stock large collections of Buchenwald-related material, some of it in English. A movie theater adjacent to the book shop shows an excellent 30-minute **film** (free) about the camp. Screenings generally start every hour on the hour, with an English-language version presented three or four times per day. Tours of the camp in German (free) leave the tourist complex every hour or so. Although most people have little appetite after touring Buchenwald, there's a wholesome, inexpensive cafeteria opposite the book shop. *Tel. 0621/3345 or 0621/2173. Admission free. Memorial, book shop, cafeteria open May–Sept., Tues.–Sun. 9:30–5:45; Oct.–Apr., Tues.–Sun. 8:45–4:45.*

Before returning to Weimar, consider making the kilometer-long (⅔-mile) hike to the **Buchenwald Bell Tower,** on the southern slope of Ettersberg hill. The 165-foot-tall tower was built in 1954 on the site of a mass grave and, according to a plaque, is meant to "warn against the reestablishment of fascism in any form." There's a good view of Ettersberg hill and Buchenwald from the top, and in the crypt are the ashes of unknown inmates, brought from concentration camps throughout Europe. The sculpture at the tower's foot, portraying 11 waiflike prisoners gazing defiantly toward the camp, was created by Fritz Cremer. To reach the bell tower, walk south from Buchenwald and follow signs marked GEDENKSTÄTTE. *Admission free. Open Tues.–Sun. 9–4.*

COMING AND GOING Buchenwald lies 3 kilometers (2 miles) north of Weimar and is easily reached by bus (DM 6). Buses marked BUCHENWALD or ETTERSBERG leave daily from Goetheplatz (opposite the main post office) and the Hauptbahnhof Monday–Saturday, every hour on the hour 8–5 (less frequently on Sunday). Although the road to Buchenwald is not particularly stunning, the camp is an easy hour-long walk from the city center. Simply follow any sign marked BUCHENWALD from Goetheplatz or the Hauptbahnhof. Depending on demand, guided tours are sometimes organized by the Weimar tourist office. A typical price for these full-day excursions is DM 20 per person, but call for current schedules.

GERA

The city of Gera, 56 kilometers (35 miles) east of Weimar, is famous for two things: cement apartment buildings and the **Marktplatz,** a stunning Renaissance-era square. The former arose as a result of Gera's destruction during World War II, after which the Communists rebuilt the city. Everywhere you turn are rows of seedy housing, occasionally interrupted by shoddy shopping malls and rubble-filled lots—all in all, a depressing panorama.

Yet in the midst of all this is the remarkable Marktplatz, one of the few quarters spared by World War II. Its focal point, the 15th-century **Rathaus** (town hall), has an ornate entryway and an impressive 180-foot-high tower. Adjacent to the Rathaus, you'll see a 17th-century hospital and apothecary complex (closed to the public) and some of Thuringia's most beautiful Renaissance- and Baroque-era houses. Gera's other main attraction is the 16th-century **Orangerie** (Küchengarten, Dimitroffallee 4), an imposing palace that now houses the city art gallery. Look for works by Rembrandt, Cranach, Willi Sitte, and Dürer. A separate collection contains the work of Otto Dix (1891–1969), a native of Gera. Before his suppression by the Nazis in 1934, Dix was one of Germany's most renowned expressionists. Many of his canvases "disappeared" by order of Hitler; many of the surviving works are on permanent display in this semicircular Baroque pavilion. Unfortunately, you'll have to take a bus to get here. From the Hauptbahnhof, hop on any bus marked UNTERM HAUS or KUCHENGARTEN and ask to be let off at the Orangerie, 3 kilometers (2 miles) from the city center. *Admission: DM 2. Open Mon.–Thurs. 10–5, weekends 11–6.*

It's probably not worth traveling to Gera just to see the Marktplatz and Orangerie, yet the town is a convenient stopover for those headed north toward Leipzig or west toward Weimar and Erfurt.

BASICS The **Hauptbahnhof** (Bahnhofstr., tel. 0365/54326) is an easy 10-minute walk from town; simply follow signs reading ZENTRUM. Destinations from her include Chemnitz (three trains per day, DM 19), Erfurt (3 per day, DM 21), Leipzig (two per day via Zeitz, DM 15), and Weimar (four per day, DM 14.80). For city maps or to book a private room stop by the **tourist office** (Breitscheidstr. 1, tel. 0365/26432; open weekdays 10–6, Sat. 9–noon) or the **Information desk** 0365/24436, open weekdays noon–7). The town doesn't have a hostel. In a pinch, the **Stadt Gera Hotel** (Franz Petrich Str., tel 0365/26335) rents comfortable doubles from DM 70 per person. The nearest campground is **Campingplatz Weida** (tel. 0365/2561), 9 kilometers (6 miles) south of the city center. Standard tent spaces cost DM 9 per night, with access to hot showers and a snack shop. Public transportation doesn't make it here, so hitch or hike south on Route B92 toward Aumatalsperre. As for food, the **Comma Clubzentrum** (Heinrichstr. 47, tel. 0365/52180) has a soup-and-salad café where most meals are less than DM 6. Another option is the **Theaterrestaurant** (Küchengartenallee, tel. 0365/53444), a snazzy eatery near the Orangerie.

DORNBURG

Since its founding in the 10th century, this idyllic mountainside village has hosted an endless succession of German princes and kings, each of whom left his peculiar mark. Its principal monument is the **Dornburger Schlösser** (tel. 036427/55473), a complex of three Baroque- and Rococo-era castles built onto the side of the mountain. The southernmost, the **Renaissance House,** is a posh mansion with an elongated gravel drive and prim garden. Inside is a room devoted to antique clocks, a room of old maps and manuscripts, and a good collection of handcrafted Renaissance furniture.

Next door is the **Rococo House,** built by King Karl August for one of his many mistresses. The interior is fairly dull, but the hillside garden and patio give excellent views of the Saale River valley. The third and most impressive castle is closed for renovation until late 1995. Entrance to the grounds of Dornburger Schlösser is free, but to go inside costs DM 2 per castle, and then you'll be under the strict supervision of a German-speaking guide. *Open summer, Tues.–Sun. 9–noon, 1–5; winter, Tues.–Sun. 9–noon, 1–4.*

Dornburg makes an ideal setting for such high-minded luxury. The village sits in a forest high above the Saale River valley, and on a clear day you can see the outline of a dozen church steeples in the tiny villages that dot the valley floor. Unfortunately, Dornburg's rural setting means it's somewhat difficult to reach. From Weimar, you first have to catch one of eight daily trains (DM 6.40) to Jena's Bahnhof West. Unfortunately, the train from Jena to Dornburg leaves from Jena Paradies (Kahlaischestr., tel. 03641/24553), a small ancillary depot ¾ kilometer (½ mile) northeast of Bahnhof West (head down Hohestraße and follow signs). Six daily trains, costing less than DM 5 each way, run from this station to Dornburg's unstaffed depot. To reach Dornburg village and its castles, head out of the station and make the steep 45-minute climb to the top of the hill, or try to hitch a ride. Once you reach the block-long village, continue south for 100 yards to the castles. There's no youth hostel or tourist office here; for a hearty traditional Thuringian meal for about DM 15, head for the **Ratskeller** (Am Markt, closed Mon.). If you're in the area in late June, consider sticking around for the week-long **Dornburg Rose Festival,** which commemorates the birthday of King Karl August. The festival is known for its raucous drinking sessions and the open-air flea market held in the main square.

Thüringer Wald

The Thuringian Forest, with its tranquil woods, rugged trails, and sleepy Alpine villages, is one of eastern Germany's most treasured retreats. Sickly cement-and-steel towns encircle the forest, yet once you breach its border there's nothing but trees, lakes, and spiny peaks—an ideal place for an extended hike. The forest stretches from the outskirts of Eisenach to the Czech border, nearly 150 kilometers (93 miles) southeast. The region's largest cities, Arnstadt, Ilmenau, and Meiningen, lie on the forest's edge. It's possible to do one- or two-day hikes into the woods from any of these hubs, but if you want unblemished woodland you'll have to forge into the forest's undeveloped heart, which has only a handful of remote villages, some of which lack hostels, hotels, restaurants, and—gasp—even beer halls.

Outlying towns like Ilmenau and Meiningen are well connected by train with Erfurt, but almost everything else is served by infrequent bus on an irregular basis—a sure recipe for a splitting travel headache. For this reason you may want to stick with a larger town. Although few towns are interesting in their own right, they at least provide access to scenic day hikes. One super-convenient way of getting a quick taste of the Thüringer Wald is the aptly named **Waldbahn** (Forest Road), a special train that runs from Gotha (*see* Near Eisenach, *above*) to Friedrichroda and Walterhausen, penetrating the forest's northernmost corner with a minimum of hassle. On the Waldbahn it takes 30 minutes to reach Walterhausen and about 45 minutes to reach Friedrichroda from Gotha. This will give you a full day to explore the tiny center of either village, grab a quick lunch, then head into the nearby mountains for an afternoon hike. Both towns offer access to a bunch of scenic, posted trails. Neither town, however, has a tourist desk, and only Friedrichroda has a youth hostel.

As for supplies, long-term hikers will need lots of food, bad-weather gear, and a serious sense of adventure. A good topographic map is also imperative. The tourist offices in Eisenach and Erfurt stock the most comprehensive selection of maps, glossy brochures, and lists of hotels and restaurants within the forest proper. Meiningen and Ilmenau have tourist desks, but these often stock information on the immediate area only, not the forest as a whole, and they rarely have detailed hiking guides.

Serious hikers should consider the 168-kilometer-long (104-mile-long) **Rennsteig** (Border Way), a mountaintop trail that extends from Eisenach through Bavaria, all the way to Budapest, Hungary. The Rennsteig was mostly inaccessible for 40 years because it passed along the former GDR–West German border. The Rennsteig is the forest's principal trail, and nowadays it can be accessed from Eisenach, Friedrichroda, and Oberhof. The Erfurt–Ilmenau–Arnstadt train also stops at an unstaffed depot named Rennsteig, high in the mountains in the middle of nowhere. From here follow signs ¼ kilometer (⅒ mile) to the trail. Nonhikers will want to sleep indoors, yet it's not hard to sneak off the trail and crash in the woods—just don't light a campfire or sing drunkenly into the wee hours of the morning. Be warned, however, that hordes of articulate European birds will rouse you at about 4 AM. More accommodating are the youth hostels along the route: in Brotterode (tel. 03675/2544), 12 hilly kilometers (7 miles) east of Bad Liebenstein, and Schnellbach (tel. 03675/7462), 15 kilometers (9 miles) southeast of Brotterode. Since unification the trail has been reopened and remarked with a white "R" (painted on tree trunks); prior to 1989, people were always getting lost.

Walterhausen

The small village of Walterhausen, 17 kilometers (11 miles) southwest of Gotha, is your typical Thüringer Wald outpost. It's relaxed and walkable, especially the streets surrounding the **Marktplatz,** which is lined with bakeries, butcher shops, and upbeat beer halls. The nearby **Stadtkirche,** a 17th-century cathedral, has an ornate facade and a dazzling painted ceiling. Walterhausen's best asset, however, is its proximity to several scenic trails ideal for day hikes. The most popular leads from Marktplatz (follow DEYSINGSLUST signs) to **Schloß Tenneburg,** 3 kilometers (2 miles) away. Built in 1168, the castle houses an interesting puppet museum (Walterhausen used to be the largest producer of puppets in Thuringia), a peasant museum that documents everyday life from 1800 to the present, and a semipricey restaurant. The Deysingslust trail meanders through a serene valley and patches of dense forest before reaching the castle. Plan on an hour's walk each way. If you want to extend your hike, Friedrichroda is only 4 kilometers (2½ miles) south.

Walterhausen's unstaffed **train depot** is ½ kilometer (⅓ mile) from the city center; leave the station and scan the horizon for the Stadtkirche's spire, which marks the center of town. The easiest way to get here is on the Waldbahn from Gotha. There are three trains daily in each direction and tickets cost DM 3. The best place to stay nearby is the youth hostel in Friedrichroda (*see below*).

Friedrichroda

Friedrichroda, 6 kilometers (4 miles) south of Walterhausen, is a modern-looking resort town. It caters to middle-aged tourists with its luxury hotels and swank clothing boutiques. Grab a quick lunch from a street stand or at an outdoor beer hall, then head straight for the forest. Near the Waldbahn stop you'll find trailheads for three two- to three-hour circular hikes. The most popular heads toward **Marienglashöhle** (An der Marienglashöhle, tel. 03623/4853), an underground cavern that claims to have the largest crystal grotto in Europe. It was worked as a gypsum mine from 1775 to 1903. Nowadays you can take a guided tour for DM 5, DM 3 students. The white quartz walls are a chilly 46°F. It's open daily 9–4. Another popular hike (again, follow signs) leads to an overgrown ruin, **Schauenburg Friedrichroda,** on the cusp of a forested hill. Formerly home to a cell of Benedictine monks, this 17th-century ruin now makes an ideal picnic spot. On the same trail are signs for the Rennsteig, which runs within 3 kilometers (2 miles) of Friedrichroda.

Friedrichroda's unstaffed **train depot** is a stone's throw from its central square. From the platform, head straight, toward the cluster of shops. Via the Waldbahn, Friedrichroda is connected three times daily with Gotha (DM 3) and Walterhausen (DM 2). The unstaffed **Busbahnhof** is adjacent to the train station. Buses leave daily for Arnstadt (two buses per day), Bad Liebenstein (two per day), and Schmalkalden (one per day). Unless you have DM 80-DM 120 to spend in a luxury hotel, head for the youth hostel, **Jugendherberge Friedrichroda** (Waldstr. 24, tel. 03622/4410, check-in after 6 PM). It has no showers, just a room full of sinks and toilets complemented by an equally Spartan bunk-bed dormitory. Beds cost DM 14.50 per night. Head uphill from the Friedrichroda *Waldbahn* stop and follow signs.

Bad Liebenstein

Bad Liebenstein, 25 kilometers (16 miles) south of Eisenach, is another sleepy, Alpine village. Since there's absolutely nothing to see here—no museums, no quaint half-timbered houses or historic squares—you should come only if you want to hike. The trails that skirt the River Grumbach are particularly scenic. The river crosses under Herzog Georg Straße, the village's main drag, and flows southward into the network of low-lying hills that envelop Bad Liebenstein. Follow the river 1 kilometer (⅔ mile) south, and you'll see signs for Stilles Tal, a mountaintop trail that veers east toward Aschenberg summit (1,500 feet). Another hike leads to Bergruine Liebenstein (1,535 feet), a forested bluff overlooking the village. From the tourist office walk north through Kulturpark and start your ascent. Give yourself at least 90 minutes each way.

There's no train station in town, only the unstaffed **Busbahnhof** (Bahnhofstr. and Herzog Georg Str.), ½ kilometer (⅓ mile) northwest of the center. Destinations from here include Eisenach (two buses per day), Friedrichroda (two per day), Schmalkalden (two per day), and Walterhausen (two per day). Turn left out of the station and follow the main road past a jumble of butcher shops and bakeries. Within five minutes you'll see the **tourist office** (Kulturhaus, Ruhlaerstr. and Herzog Georg Str., tel. 036961/2733; open weekdays 9–5, Sat. 9–noon and 1–4), housed in a dully modern brown-and-tan building. Although Bad Liebenstein lacks a youth hostel, the tourist office can book you into a private room (DM 20–DM 30) for a DM 3 fee.

Meiningen

Meiningen is at the Thüringer Wald's southwestern edge, so it's not a good starting point for excursions into the woods. It is, however, a comfortably large city with lots of cafés, beer halls, and, for once, a few museums. With daily service to Erfurt, Arnstadt, Oberhof, and Gotha, Meiningen makes a convenient stopover for those headed into the forest by rail. And even if you're only window shopping, the smart-looking stores that line **Georgstraße** and the adjacent **Am Markt** are good places to prepare for or recuperate from a week in the dense wilderness.

The town's most notable feature is the **Elisabethenburg** (Burggasse, off Georgstr., tel. 03693/3641), a Baroque castle built in 1692 by the duke of Thuringia. In a small wood four blocks northwest of Am Markt, the castle dominates the skyline with its ornate spires and facade. Inside are an art gallery devoted to Italian and Dutch masters, lavish period rooms, and an exhibit on the history of theater in Meiningen (admission DM 3, open Tues.–Sun. 10–6). Meiningen used to be the cultural capital of lower Thuringia. Under the direction of George II, known fondly as the Theater Duke, Meiningen's theater scene was once respected throughout Europe. Past theater directors included Richard Strauss (1884–86), Max Reger (1911–14), and even Schiller on an informal basis. In **Schloßkirche,** the castle's church cum concert hall, there are weekly recitals and seasonal concerts. Contact the tourist office for schedules. Tickets generally cost DM 10–DM 25.

A Medieval Detour

Schmalkalden, only 20 kilometers (12 miles) north of Meiningen, is one of the best places in Thuringia to pretend you're living in the Middle Ages. The walkable Altstadt, much of which is still surrounded by the old city wall, has a fine array of colorful half-timbered houses, and fruit and fish sellers still push their carts down Schmalkalden's narrow cobblestone streets. Inside Schloß Wilhelmsburg (Treuenstr., admission DM 2.50, open daily 10–6), a well-preserved Renaissance-era palace, you'll see strange artifacts, from an all-wood organ to trick-lock treasure chests, cases of old coins, and gruesome 14th-century weapons. The tourist office (Mohrengasse 2; open weekdays 10–1 and 2–5, Sat. 11–2) has city maps and German-language walking guides, and can book you into a private room for DM 2. From Meiningen hop on a train to Zella-Mehlis; from there catch one of 11 daily connections to Schmalkalden. The trip takes 90 minutes and costs about DM 12 each way.

Adjacent to the castle is the **Baumbachhaus** (Burggasse, tel. 03693/3643), an 18th-century half-timbered house that contains a small literature museum, as well as exhibits on Schiller, Ernst Wagner, and Carl Gottlob Cramer, each of whom spent at least one summer working and living in Meiningen.

Meiningen's **tourist office** (Bahnhof, tel. 03693/3522; open weekdays 9–5, Sat. noon–3) stocks town maps and German-language walking guides. Since Meiningen doesn't have a hostel or cheap hotel, come here to book a private room (DM 20–DM 30). Destinations from Meiningen's train station include Arnstadt (four trains per day, DM 14.80), Erfurt (four per day, DM 19), Gotha (via Arnstadt or Gräfenroda, two per day, DM 16.80), Oberhof (two per day, DM 8.40), and Zella-Mehlis (15 per day, DM 6.40). To reach the town center, walk left out of the depot, turn right on Marienstraße and left on Georgstraße; Am Markt is five blocks ahead.

Ilmenau

Of all the towns in the area surrounding the Thüringer Wald, don't miss Ilmenau, 29 kilometers (18 miles) south of Arnstadt. Not only is it well connected by train with Erfurt, Arnstadt, and Meiningen, but Ilmenau also has a youth hostel and dozens of cafés and restaurants. Best of all for hikers, it's within easy reach of Thüringer Wald hiking trails.

Ilmenau's fame stems from its association with the poet Goethe, who spent many summers writing and doing scientific work in the surrounding mountains. In the town center is the **Goethe-Gedenkstätte im Amtshaus** (Am Markt, tel. 03677/2667), where Goethe lived for a few years; the only original pieces in his re-created living room and study are his diary and some personal letters. More interesting is **Jagdhaus Gabelbach** (Gabelstr., tel. 03677/2626), formerly the duke of Weimar's private hunting lodge. Goethe was a frequent guest at the lodge and did much of his scientific work in the restored library, which now houses a small museum. On display are Goethe's spectacles, notes from his research, and lots of period memorabilia. A few blocks farther is **Goethehäschen auf dem Kickelhahn,** where Goethe penned one of his most famous poems, "The Wayfarer's Night Song II." The house is closed until 1994, when it will reopen with a small museum. In the meantime, it marks the trailhead for various three- to four-hour hikes.

The poet's most lasting legacy in Ilmenau is the **Goethe-Wanderweg,** also known as **Auf Goethes Spuren** (In the Footsteps of Goethe). This rigorous trail, which is 18 kilometers (11 miles) long, follows the path established by Goethe during his many summer ramblings. It covers the poet's favorite haunts, and is a great way to experience the Thüringer Wald without having to rough it under the stars in a soggy sleeping bag. The entire circuit takes seven hours at a medium pace, and it's posted every 300 yards or so with a wood marker bearing the letter "G." You'll find the trailhead on Waldstraße, 100 yards south of the tourist office on the far side of the train tracks. Along the route, you can recover at the expensive **Schöffenhaus** restaurant (no lunch) and the medium-price **Gasthaus Auerhahn** (closed Mon.). Pick up a map from the tourist office, which also lists other Ilmenau-based hikes.

BASICS Ilmenau's train station, **Ilmenau Bad** (Am Bahnhof, tel. 03677/2245), has regular service to Arnstadt (three trains per day, DM 6.40), Erfurt (three per day, DM 10.80), and Meiningen (via Plaue, two per day, DM 19). To get to the city center (about a 10-minute walk), walk west up Bahnhofstraße, cross Wetzlarer Platz, and continue west on Friedrich-Hoffmann-Straße. Turn right on Marktstraße to get to Am Markt or left on Lindenstraße for the **tourist office** (Lindenstr. 12, tel. 03643/762342; open weekdays 9–6, Sat. 9–noon), which stocks city maps and hiking guides. For a DM 3 fee the staff books private rooms (DM 20–DM 30). Besides selling stamps, the post office, **Hauptpost** (Poststr., 1 block n. of Wetzlarer Pl., tel. 03677/2544), has an international telephone annex and a competitive bureau de change. It's open Monday–Saturday 9–5.

WHERE TO SLEEP Although Ilmenau has a good youth hostel, the city's two luxurious pensions are both priced at about DM 30 per person. **Zum Elephant** (Marktstr. 16, tel. 03677/2441) is modern and centrally located. Each of its five rooms has fluffy comforters and a sink. Near the youth hostel is **Villa Silvana** (Waldstr. 14, tel. 03677/4881), which rents four rooms. There's an outdoor terrace, a sauna (about DM 5 extra), and an informal downstairs bar—a budget traveler's dream. The youth hostel, **Jugendherberge Ilmenau** (Waldstr. 22, tel. 03677/2413, check-in after 3 PM), has space for 66 and is in an old, worn building. Beds cost DM 14.50 per night, which includes an 8 o'clock breakfast. To get there, turn right from the tourist office, cross the train tracks, and veer right onto Waldstraße, where you'll also find the Goethe-Wanderweg trailhead.

Daredevils should try Ilmenau's skiing/roller-skating slope, where you can fly at uncontrollable speed down a 12°, 1,320-foot-long track. It's open May–October and is located on nearby Kickelhahn Mountain. The youth hostel organizes trips for about DM 20 whenever there's enough interest; contact them for details.

FOOD Marktstraße and Lindenstraße have a host of cafés, restaurants, and bargain-price Imbiß stands. The neighboring **Zum Schwan** (Marktstr. 15) and **Zum Elephant** (Marktstr. 16) serve traditional Thuringian fare—from sausages and stews to potato cakes and local beer—for less than DM 15 per person. **Zur Post** (Am Mühltor 6, 1 block s. of Wetzlarer Pl.), populated by leathery locals, serves similar dishes for slightly less in a smoky, informal atmosphere. For coffee and desserts try the **Milchbar** (Lindenstr. 26) or **Café Schindler** (Weimarer Str. 2, 1 block e. of Am Markt, closed Mon.).

Oberhof

Oberhof, halfway between Meiningen and Arnstadt, is popular for two reasons. First, it's connected by rail to Erfurt, Arnstadt, and Meiningen, making it one of the few remote mountain villages that's easy to reach. Second, the Rennsteig trail passes within 1 kilometer (⅔ mile) of town, bringing a steady flow of backpackers through the village in summer. Oberhof's appeal ends there, however, as it's otherwise just an ugly resort dominated by luxury hotels and boring housing projects. Wealthy German families have transformed this Alpine village into a smarmy tourist trap. Take your cue from other backpackers and head straight for the Rennsteig; follow white "R" signs from the town center.

Oberhof's unstaffed **train station** is at the bottom of a steep hill, 1 kilometer (⅔ mile) south of town. Take any bus marked ZENTRUM for DM .50, or huff and puff your way to the top. Destinations from here include Arnstadt (two trains per day, DM 6.40), Erfurt (three per day, DM 12.60), Meiningen (two per day, DM 8.40), and Suhl (three per day, DM 3). The town doesn't have a tourist desk, so try at one of the luxury hotels for maps and hiking information. The **Panorama Hotel** (Steinstr., tel. 036842/5679) sometimes has English-language walking guides, although you might have to haggle a bit if you're not a registered guest. As for sleeping, Oberhof has neither a hostel nor a cheap pension. If you have a tent, sleep under the stars on the Rennsteig trail. Otherwise, pull out your Visa card. The cheapest hotel in town starts at DM 120 per night.

Arnstadt

Arnstadt, 29 kilometers (18 miles) north of Ilmenau, is a surprisingly cheerful town with lots to offer. Activity Number 1 is hiking: Arnstadt is perched on the northern cusp of the Thüringer Wald, encircled by thick forest and mountains. Try the flat, six-hour hike to **Die Drei Gleichen,** where three ruined castles sit side by side in a landscape of rolling wheat fields and lazy farm villages. The castles' name, *Gleichen,* means "the same" in English: One explanation for this is that all three were bombed on the same day during World War II. Nowadays no one occupies or administers the skeletal ruins, although you'll sometimes find kids scrambling through the grounds. All are within view of one another about 8 kilometers (5 miles) northwest of town: Two are just south and one just north of Autobahn 4. Either hike from Arnstadt (the tourist office has free route maps) or take a train to the village of Wandersleben, which saves two hours of walking along the not-so-scenic Mühlberg Highway. **Familie Binneberg** (tel. 03628/723), in Wandersleben, rents horses (from DM 20 per hour) for the one-hour trot to Die Dreie Gleichen.

The town of Arnstadt is best known for its association with J. S. Bach. Between 1703 and 1707 he was the organist at the stately 16th-century **Bachkirche** (Am Kirche, tel. 03628/8822, museum open daily 9–4), the town's most impressive church. It's impossible to miss; simply look up and walk toward the spire. Inside you'll find typical church stuff, along with Bach's organ and some personal memorabilia. A better bet for Bach fans is the **Stadtgeschichte Museum** (Jenastr., tel. 03628/667, admission DM 2, open Tues.–Sun. 10–6), with exhibits on Bach's musical legacy and on his residence in town. The room-size museum is one block from **Am Markt,** where you'll also find a statue (1986) of young Bach. Overlooking it all is the **Markt Café** (Am Markt 12, no dinner), which serves tasty Thüringer meats and beers for less than DM 15 per person. Arnstadt's well-preserved shopping avenues, which balance modern boutiques with Baroque-era timbered houses, radiate outward from Am Markt.

Follow Schloßstraße north, and you'll dead-end at the **Schloßmuseum,** a 16th-century castle that's been converted into an arts-and-crafts museum. Yes, it sounds woefully dull, but don't miss the intriguing "Mon Plaisir" ("My Pleasure") exhibit—the largest collection of handmade dolls in Thuringia, commissioned in about 1700 by Princess Augusta Dorothea von Schwarzburg-Arnstadt. *Schloßpl. 1, tel. 03628/2932. Admission: DM 2. Open summer, Tues.–Sun. 8:30–noon and 1–4; winter, Tues.–Sun. 8:30–noon and 1–4:30.*

BASICS The helpful **tourist office** (Am Markt 3, tel. 03628/2049; open weekdays 9–noon and 12:30–6, Sat. 9–noon) has acquired the wonderful habit of handing out fresh strawberries with its maps and hiking guides. For a DM 3 fee the staff will book private rooms that typically cost DM 25 per person—your best bet, considering the dearth of cheap lodging in Arnstadt. A **Deutsche Bank** will soon open on Am Markt for currency exchange. Until then, head to the main post office, **Hauptpost** (Ritterstr., tel. 03628/9902; open weekdays 9–5, Sat. 9–2), which also has an international telephone annex.

COMING AND GOING **Arnstadt Hauptbahnhof** (Bahnhofstr., tel. 03628/2231), the main train station, is a 15-minute walk north of the city center. Head out of the station and aim for the cluster of steeples to the south. Inside the station there's an occasionally staffed information desk and a food stand of sorts—try the unidentified meat (?) balls at your risk. Destinations include Erfurt (seven trains per day, DM 6.40), Ilmenau (five per day, DM 6.40), Meiningen (five per day, DM 14.80), Plaue (four per day, DM 3), and Suhl (five per day, DM 8.40).

The **Busbahnhof** is adjacent to the train depot and most frequently populated not by travelers but by drunks. There's no information desk or amenities of any sort, only a worn placard with half-legible departure times. Stop by the tourist office for advice. Destinations include Ilmenau (two buses per day, DM 5), Erfurt (three per day, DM 5.50), and Suhl (two per day, DM 7).

LOWER SAXONY 12

By Oliver Wilken

Lower Saxony draws plenty of vacationing Germans, but lacks the glitz and sparkle to lure many foreigners. If you have the time, though, the region will handsomely repay your patience. The beautiful Weser River starts at Hannoversch Münden and flows though the heart of Lower Saxony's gentle landscapes. The river gives its name to the 16th-century Weser Renaissance style of architecture so typical of the region, particularly in the south. As part of this exuberant style, the facades of half-timbered houses are carved, painted, and gilded into rollicking visual circuses. Weser-style houses compose the sole attraction of several towns in Lower Saxony, but often they are worth the trip alone. Though many *Altstädte* (old towns) cashed in their chips in '45, Hannoversch-Münden, Duderstadt, and Hameln, among others, survived with their medieval cores intact or rebuilt them entirely.

Lower Saxony is the least densely populated Land in Germany and harbors plenty of natural enclaves and parks: The low Harz Mountains provide hilly hiking terrain (skiing in winter); the rolling heaths of Lüneburg Heide bloom purple in August; and East Frisia's marshy bogs support thousands of specially adapted critters. The East Frisian

A Roll in the Hay

Lower Saxony's most unlikely sleeping innovation is the Heu-Hotel, a barn or farm outbuilding where, for DM 14, you can spread your sleeping bag out on a pile of fresh hay. It's damned comfortable, but definitely not for the squeamish: Your sleeping bag will smell strongly of hay, mice are common bed partners, there's no heating, and most barns are mixed—everybody rolls in the same hay. In return, you get astounding hospitality, cheaper lodging than in the hostels, and huge, delicious breakfasts, often made with fresh produce from the farm. Most Heu-Hotels lie in the countryside, especially near Lüneburg, Celle, and Hameln; get a full list from a tourist office in any of these towns.

Lower Saxony

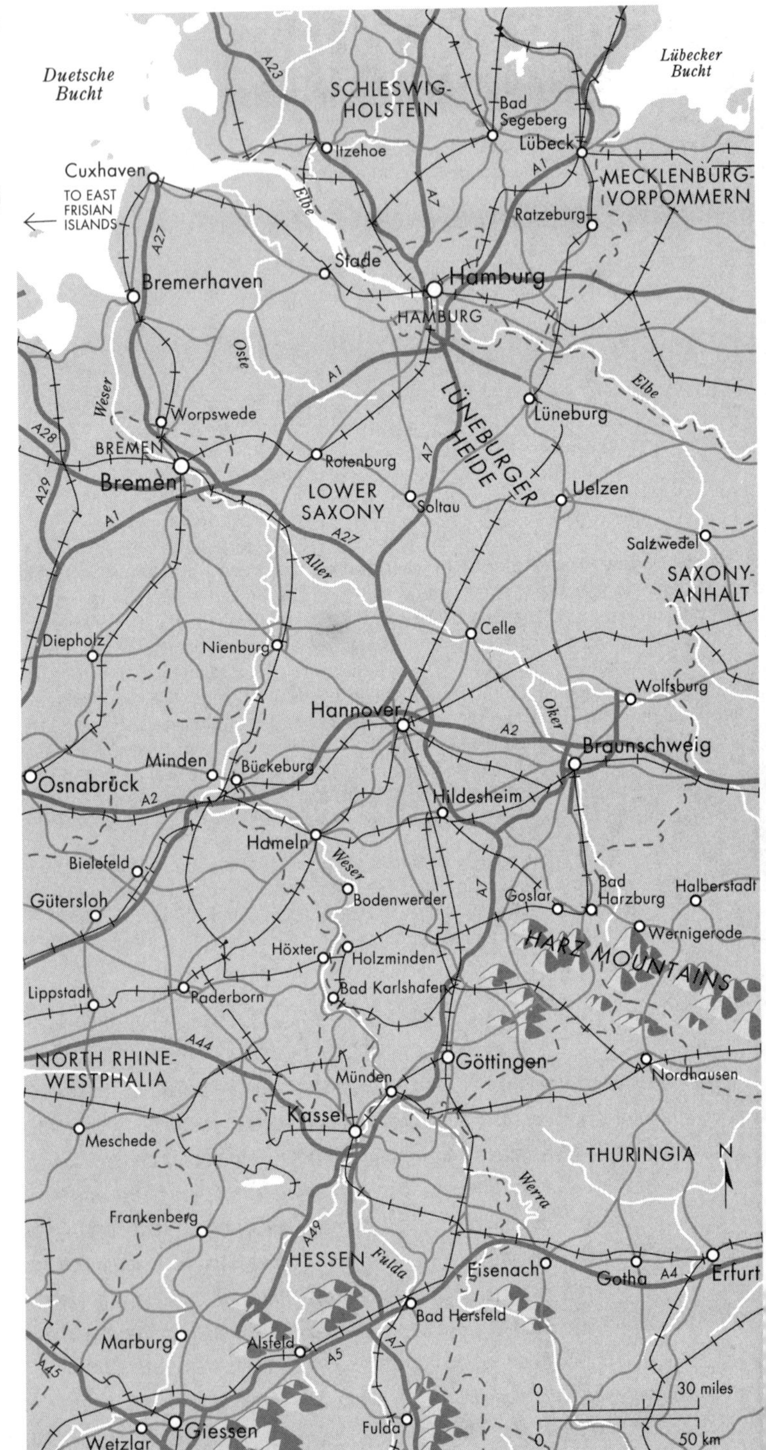

Islands, just off the North Sea coast, draw huge crowds to their chilly beaches and wind-raked dunes, but you can still find solitude, even at high season.

Travel in Lower Saxony invariably ends up as an exploration of local culture rather than a connect-the-dots tour of palaces and museums.

Several university towns, most prominently Göttingen and Bremen (actually a separate Land), nurture rich cultural scenes as well as rowdy nightlife. It's fun to come here, after frolicking in the countryside, to sit in the cafés, wear black, and act like Dieter in "Saturday Night Live." Lower Saxony's scarcity of foreign tourists rarely translates into lower prices, but it does mean that fewer locals speak English, and in smaller towns even tourist office staff occasionally struggle with rusty language skills. Foreigners always spark interest, though, and folks often shower you with attention and questions.

Hannover

If you have a lot of time, Hannover (anglicized to "Hanover") provides an entertaining stop, but its incredibly expensive lodging scene, combined with a noticeable lack of flair, means the hurried traveler probably shouldn't pause for long. Hannover was bombed back to the Stone Age during World War II, and the residents made a bit of a hash of the reconstruction. The city is big and modern, suffering from charmless commercial streets, a sobering crime rate, and an icy big-city mentality. The main reason to visit is the museums, all of which are free, and the tremendous gardens: Hannover has probably the best-preserved Baroque garden in the world. In addition, the city's large pedestrian zone hosts frequent and energetic festivals.

BASICS

AMERICAN EXPRESS Your friendly **American Express Travel Service** lurks just down the street from the Opera House. *Georgestr. 54, tel. 0511/363428. Open weekdays 9–5:30, Sat. 10–1.*

BUCKET SHOPS Most travel agencies sell the German rail system's special ticket deals. **RDS Reisedienst** (Asterstr. 34, tel. 0511/702454) specializes in last-minute and student flights, as does **Reisebüro im Ihme-zentrum** (Ihmepassage 7, tel. 0511/444057).

BUREAUX DE CHANGE The **American Express Office** (*see above*) has good rates and no commission, and they'll change any brand of traveler's checks. If you have a Visa card, drop by the 24-hour **Citicorp** ATM on Karmarschstraße at Kröpcke, or the cash machine in the train station, for withdrawals up to DM 500. Other than that, the **Deutsche Verkehrs Bank** inside the train station has acceptable rates and a DM 1 commission on cash, or a DM 3 commission on traveler's checks, up to DM 100 (DM 7.50 above DM 100). It's open weekdays 7:30 AM–8 PM, Saturday 7:30–5, and Sunday 10–5.

LUGGAGE STORAGE The central **Hauptbahnhof** (main train station) has thousands of small lockers for DM 2 and larger ones for DM 4; you can leave your bags in the lockers for 24 hours. Small bright-green lockers at the entrance to the Kröpcke U-Bahn (subway) station are DM 2 per 24 hours, with a 72-hour maximum stay.

MAIL AND PHONES The **main post office** sits right next to the train station. Harried employees staff a poste restante counter (Hannover's postal code is 3000), a currency exchange with the same rates as the train station's bank (see Bureaux de Change, above), and a fax service ("Telefax"). During extended hours, weekdays 6 AM–10 PM and weekends 7 AM–10 PM, you can buy stamps and make phone calls only. *Ernst-August-Pl. 2. Full service weekdays 8–6, Sat. 8–1, Sun. 11 AM–noon.*

VISITOR INFORMATION The efficient **Verkehrsbüro Hannover** (Ernst-August-Pl. 8, tel. 0511/1682319), across the platz from the station, charges DM 5 to find a room; be forewarned that the cheapest hotels start at DM 40. If you have to find your way to a youth hostel, make sure you take their larger city map, which appears in the "Hotels" brochure. Bus tours in English offer a touristy look at Hannover; the 2½-hour tours cost DM 17 (students DM 8.50) and leave Monday through Saturday at 1:30 (May–Sept.), Wednesday and Saturday at 1:30 the rest of the year.

COMING AND GOING

BY TRAIN Punctual, frequent trains leave the **Hauptbahnhof** (tel. 0511/19419 for information) for Berlin (four hours, DM 59–DM 66, depending on route), Bremen (1½ hours, DM 29), Frankfurt (two–four hours, DM 82), Göttingen (one hour, DM 25), Hamburg (two hours, DM 41), and Köln (three–four hours, DM 71). The train station is in the center of town, and features luggage lockers, pay toilets, innumerable snack stands, and access to the Passerelle, an underground mall (*see* Shopping, *below*). The station is so big that it has its own police force, but it's still dangerous at night.

BY BUS Buses leave from right behind the train station, but they travel only to nearby, uninteresting destinations. The exception is Bus 349, which runs four to six times daily except Sunday to Hildesheim (45 minutes, DM 6.30).

HITCHING As in any big city, it can be hell getting a ride unless you're incredibly persistent. It makes sense to catch a bus or U-Bahn as far out of town as possible before sticking out your thumb. Take U-Bahn 8 (direction Langenhagen) to Wiesenau for the on-ramps to the east–west A2 autobahn, or take line 5 to its "Kirchrode" terminus, then Bus 37 to "Ahlten" for the north–south A7 autobahn.

BY PLANE **Flughafen Hannover** (tel. 0511/977–1223 for information), 15 kilometers (10 miles) north of town, has service to most major European airports. Bus 60 (DM 4.90) runs from the airport to the rear of the train station every 20–30 minutes.

BY MITFAHRZENTRALE **Citynetz Mitfahr-Zentrale** (Weißekreuzstr. 18, tel. 0511/19444) can hook you up with long-distance rides; the staff estimates fees of DM 16 to Hamburg, DM 28 to Berlin, and DM 164 to Thessaloniki, Greece. To get to the office, pass under the train station and cross the plaza with the fountain in it.

Wanted: Protestant Monarch for Britain. No English Required.

It's always been difficult to get good help. In 1701 the British Parliament, trying to find a Protestant monarch for the throne, eventually chose Queen Sophia of Hannover, a distant member of England's House of Stuart. At birth she had been 54th in line to the throne, but by 1701 the other 53 were all either dead or Catholic. So began the five-generation reign of the House of Hannover over both Hannover and England. Hannoverian monarchs included George I, who ruled England for 13 years without ever learning English, and George III, notable for having lost control of several small colonies across the Atlantic. The German wives of these kings introduced to the English-speaking world what had until then been a uniquely German tradition—the Christmas tree. Because of different laws of succession, the union between Britain and Hannover died with William IV in 1837.

GETTING AROUND

Huge and sprawling, Hannover is a nightmare to negotiate on foot. The center of Hannover life *and* public transit is **Kröpcke,** a large plaza 600 feet in front of the train station; the freestanding clock here has been a traditional meeting spot for centuries. About a five-minute walk southwest of the Kröpcke lies the reconstructed **Altstadt,** where you'll find most museums and sites of historical interest; further north sits a modern shopping district.

The bus and U-Bahn (subway) network covers an immense area, and some lines run as late as 2:30 AM. However, the DM 2.90 tickets, which are good for one hour and for all forms of public transit, quickly add up. If you plan to stay more than a night, it makes sense to get a special discount ticket. Drop by the **Ustra** (entrance to the Kröpcke U-Bahn station) for a strip of six tickets (DM 12.30), a 24-hour ticket (DM 6.50), or a students-only week-long ticket (DM 11.50 and a photo), as well as a map of the public transit network. You can purchase bus tickets as you board, but you must buy U-Bahn tickets in advance at one of the stations; ticket dispensers are located right by the turnstiles.

For a ride, call **Taxi** (tel. 0511/2143) or **Hallo Taxi** (tel. 0511/8484); given the price of mass-transit tickets, taxis are actually cheaper for groups of three or four within central Hannover.

WHERE TO SLEEP

A complete absence of cheap hotels makes Hannover's youth hostels the only really affordable place to spend the night. All the hostels are distant, but right on the edge of large parks.

Hospiz am Bahnhof. This hotel's proximity to the train station, its TV common room, and its firm beds manage to offset the nauseating '60s green and beige furniture; bone up on your Deutsch with the trilingual Gideon's Bibles. Singles range from DM 46 (no shower) to DM 81 (with shower); doubles, which come with king-size beds, top out at DM 108. *Joachimstr. 2, tel. 0511/324397. Turn left out of Hauptbahnhof. 36 rooms. Breakfast included, shower down hall. Reservations strongly advised.*

Hotel Flora. Hannover's cheapest hotel has plain, cramped rooms that are frequently booked weeks in advance. Still, the owner is nice, and the hotel is only a 10-minute walk from the station. Singles run DM 40 (no shower) or DM 50–DM 60 (with shower), while small doubles go for DM 80 (no shower), DM 90 (with shower), and DM 100 (with shower and toilet). *Heinrichstr. 36, tel. 0511/342334. Turn left out of Hauptbahnhof down Joachimstr., left under tracks at Thielenplatz onto Königstr., then follow park to Heinrichstr. 23 rooms. Breakfast included, shower down the hall. Reservations strongly advised.*

Hotel Gildehof. The rooms are drab and often full, and the peremptory receptionist has little patience with non German-speakers, but it's the only other hotel in Hannover with beds under DM 50 per person. Singles start at DM 55, but doubles without shower are DM 95, DM 115 with bath and toilet. *Joachimstr. 6, tel. 0511/363680. Turn left out of Hauptbahnhof, and walk 2 min. 43 rooms. Breakfast included, showers on each floor.*

HOSTELS **Jugendgästehaus.** This luxurious hostel accepts guests of all ages, but you can usually expect lots of school groups. Rooms are immaculate, with views of the neighboring river and trees. DM 29 gets you a bed in a second-floor double, triple, or quadruple; DM 40 gets a third-story double; and DM 50 a single. For DM 6 extra, you can have a crack at the sauna and small swimming pool. Unfortunately, the trip from the train station can take an hour. *Wilkenburgerstr. 40, tel. 9511/864440. U1 toward Sarstedt or U2 toward Rethen to Am Brabrinke, then follow tracks for 20 min. back to Wilkenburgerstr. on left. 65 beds. Breakfast included. Reservations strongly advised.*

Jugendherberge Hannover. A sullen, unhelpful staff manages to make an otherwise typical hostel a distasteful stopover. Nevertheless, getting here requires the least hassle of any of the hostels (the trip from town takes about a half hour), and the canalside location makes for great sunsets. Beds in small eight-bed rooms are DM 17; a limited number of camping spots are available out back for DM 6 per person, DM 8 for those over 26. IYHF cards are required, but they sell them for DM 30. *Ferdinand-Wilhelm-Fricke Weg 1, tel. 0511/131–7674. U3 or U7 toward Mühlenberg to Fischerhof/Fachhochschule, backtrack 10 yds to intersection, follow signs right and across bridge, then turn right; or Bus 24 toward Stadionbrücke straight from Hauptbahnhof (Mon.–Sat. 4–8 only, once per hr). 219 beds. 11:30 PM curfew, reception open sporadically 7:30 AM–11:30 PM, sheets DM 5, washer DM 4.50, dryer DM 4.50, breakfast included. Reservations advised.*

"Late one night during my stay at Jugendherberge Hannover, the staff turned away a Jewish man, saying the hostel was full. When it was pointed out there were free beds in several rooms, they scanned their register, admitted him, and quickly changed the subject. This happened during the Rostock neo-Nazi anti-immigration riots, and left the hostellers who witnessed it shaken and disgusted." — Oliver Wilken

Naturfreundhaus Misburg. Squeezed in between a lake and a dense forest, this small hostel is tranquil to the point of being comatose. It caters mainly to adults and families. The trip from the train station takes well over an hour by public transport. Spots in six-bed rooms run DM 20, and breakfast is an extra DM 7.50. *Am Fahrhorstfelde 50, tel. 0511/580537. U3 to Lahe terminus, then Bus 32 to Meyers-Garten, transfer to Bus 31 to Waldriedhof, then walk down Am Fahrhorstfelde and through parking lots at end. Reception open 1–6 PM, but hrs vary. Closed Mon.*

Naturfreundhaus Stadtheim. This large, distant, and secluded hostel offers misanthropes and lovebirds the cheapest singles (DM 35) and doubles (DM 24 per person, nonmembers DM 28) available. At the other end of the spectrum, DM 20 gets you a spot in a 10-bed dorm. The trip from town takes about 40 minutes. *Hermann-Bahlsen-Allee 8, tel. 0511/691493. U3 toward Lahe or U7 toward Fasanenkrug to Spannhagengarten, backtrack to intersection, turn left down Hermann-Bahlsen-Allee; look for sign on right after about 10 min. 76 beds. Reception open 8 AM–10 PM; breakfast and sheets included. Reservations advised.*

CAMPGROUNDS Hannover's campgrounds, though generally beautiful, lie hopelessly far from the city's center. The nearest, **Campingplatz Birkensee** (3014 Laatzen 3, tel. 0511/529962), is only accessible via a DM 30 taxi ride. Spend the money on a youth hostel card and camp under the trees behind the Jugendherberge Hannover (*see above*) for DM 6–DM 8. Lock that tent flap during daytime sorties.

FOOD

For a list of restaurants in Hannover, complete with price estimates, shell out DM 6.80 at the tourist office for *Extra*, the comprehensive guide to fun in Hannover. For the same amount of money, though, you could buy two slices of **pizza,** the city's favorite grease-on-the-go option, at any of the million stands near Kröpcke. Below Kröpcke (in the Passarelle), a **co-op supermarket** has reasonably priced groceries. The markets in the train station are the only ones open Sunday.

Several vegetarian and semivegetarian places dot the map: **Flambee** (Jakobistr. 43, tel. 0511/623914) and **Bei Hiller** (Blumenstr. 3, near the Hauptbahnhof, tel. 0511/321288) have organic slants, while **Schmelz** (Karmarschstr. 16, up the street from Kröpcke, tel. 0511/320976) serves lunch to dieters and salad-nibblers. **Café Aleuron** (Königstr. 46, behind the Hauptbahnhof near Berliner Allee, tel. 0511/311112) doles out dainty but delicious dishes, many meatless, for about DM 10.

➢ **UNDER DM 5 • Hauptmensa.** This noisy, colorful university cafeteria serves standard cafeteria meals—bland but nutritionally balanced, and large enough to torpedo any hunger. Any student card works, but nonstudents can't get a thing. DM 1.90 buys you an unappetizing "one-pot" meal; three-course glop-on-a-tray meals are DM 2.40; and nicer pasta or fish meals are DM 3. In the basement, the **Labor** pub (open daily 3 PM–2 AM) draws students like flies. *Jägerstr. 3–5. U4 or U5 toward Stöcken to Schneiderberg/Wilhelm-Busch-Museum; it's the big green building on left down Schneiderberg. No dinner. Closed weekends.*

Markthalle. Locals throng to this fun, raucous indoor market, where scores of small stands dish out quality produce and cheap stand-up meals. A sizable portion of aromatic lasagna, tortellini, or ravioli costs DM 5 at the popular **Amorosa,** while at the **Fleischerei Horst-Nagel** you can get servings of goulash with noodles for DM 2.75. A half-dozen places have great coffee for around DM 1.50; the best is the DM 1.20 espresso at the **Caffe Segafredo.** *Leinestr. and Karmarschstr. Follow Karmarschstr. south from Kröpcke. No weekend dinners.*

➢ **UNDER DM 10 • Gaststätte Klickmühle.** Tirelessly friendly waitresses serve beer after beer to the boisterous crowd of locals (mostly male) who frequent this small pub. Laughter, singing, and good humor are the order of the day, particularly after a few glasses (DM 2) of the local Herrenhäuser beer. The menu changes constantly, and the fare is creative and good: beef goulash or spaghetti will set you back about DM 9.50, and a tureen of lentil soup costs about DM 7. *Leinestr. 25, opposite Markthalle, tel. 0511/18972. Follow Karmarschstr. from Kröpcke away from Hauptbahnhof. Closed Sun.*

Shiva. Indian tandoori dishes fill the air with the scents of cumin and curry at this wide-open, saffron-colored restaurant. Dinner dishes and the fixed lunch menu of soup, rice, salad, lamb, chicken, and ice cream cost about DM 19, but individual lunch dishes are easier on the wallet. Lamb in saffron-curry sauce costs DM 8.90, including rice and salad; vegetables in curry sauce with rice and salad run DM 7. *Lavesstr. 11, tel. 0511/329682. Turn left out of Hauptbahnhof down Joachimstr., which turns into Lavesstr.*

➢ **UNDER DM 20 • Broyhan Haus.** Cord Broyhan, the famous 16th-century beer brewer, lived in this medieval timber-frame house. It's now the jewel of the Altstadt, and a damned fine pub to boot. The terrace is a favorite venue for street musicians. The German-English menu includes grilled swordfish with butter sauce, baked potatoes, and salad for DM 20.50, and turkey with spinach and pepper rice for DM 19. Drinks and snacks are available as well; salads run DM 11.50–DM 14.50. *Kramerstr. 24, in front of Markt Kirche, tel. 0511/323919. No Sun. lunch.*

COFFEEHOUSES Although cafés litter the old city, it's worth trekking down to Limmer Straße (U-Bahn 10 to "Küchengarten"), with its maze of great little nooks and niches, where the style is casual, folks are friendly, and the coffee is cheap and often superb. The leftist **Café Klatsch** (Limmer Str. 58, near Linausstraße, tel. 0511/455231), an artsy breakfast-and-lunch café, serves lethal DM 2 espressos and grainy loaves from the Kollectiv Koppelkorn bakery. Veggie lunches here run DM 6–DM 8.50.

WORTH SEEING

Allied bombs left precious little of historical or architectural worth in Hannover. A red line painted on the sidewalk leads tourists from one city sight to the next as part of a 4-kilometer (2½-mile) loop, but this self-guided tour is pathetic. Life is too short for such boondoggles, especially with the truly magnificent Herrenhausen Gardens and invigorating Sprengel Museum nearby. With the exception of the Wilhelm-Busch Museum, all of Hannover's museums are free (and all are closed on Monday).

ALTSTADT AND RATHAUS Hannover's miniscule, largely rebuilt Altstadt huddles around **Ballhofstraße, Knochenhauerstraße,** and **Kramerstraße** and includes two medieval brick churches, a handful of half-timbered buildings, and the 17th-century **Ballhof** theater, which was originally a gymnasium. The 14th-century **Marktkirche** (the city's unofficial emblem) and the 15th-century brick **Altes Rathaus** (Old Townhall) face each other across Marktplatz. On nearby Holtzmarkt, directly behind a fountain, is the reconstructed facade of **Gottfried Wilhelm Leibniz**'s Renaissance home. Leibniz (1646–1716) was something of a Renaissance man himself, an authority on subjects ranging from history to philosophy and mathematics.

On Trammplatz, the elaborate **Rathaus** (Friedrichswall) has been rebuilt to look exactly as it did at the turn of the century. It's topped with an enormous dome visible from all over town; for DM 2 (students DM 1), an elevator hoists you to the top of the dome for a great view of the city. The best view of the Rathaus itself is probably from across the Maschteich, a small lake behind the building. Inside the Rathaus, four fascinating dioramas replicate the Hannover of 1689, 1939, 1945, and today.

ROYAL GARDENS OF HERRENHAUSEN If you do nothing else in Hannover, make the trip out to these gardens northwest of the city. Of the three main gardens, laid out between 1666 and 1720, the **Großer Garten** (Great Garden) is the most famous, and typifies the Baroque era's conception of nature and beauty; it also doubles as a splendid picnic spot. Giant swaths of flowers curve in precise mathematical swirls around elaborate fountains, while rape scenes and licentious nymphs—standard 17th-century images of life in Eden—constitute three-quarters of the statues. Activities here are practically endless: Get dizzy in the hedge maze, arrange a romantic tryst in the shrub gardens, or ogle the stupefying Great Fountain. From May through September, the fountains shoot water high into the air on weekdays 11–noon and 3–5, and on weekends 11–1 and 3–6; for DM 4 you can also see the fountains lit up at dusk (Wed.–Sun.). The tourist office has an invaluable map of the whole layout, plus a list of classical concerts that take place in the **Orangerie** and **Galerie** (decorated with tremendous frescoes) and plays staged in the beguiling **Gartentheater** (Garden Theater); ticket prices range from DM 12 to DM 40. *U4 or U5 to Herrenhausen-Garten. Admission free. Open May–Sept., daily 8–8; Oct.–Apr., daily 8–4:30.*

Across Herrenhäuser Straße from the Großer Garten, the **Berggarten** displays more exotic greenhouse flora, including rare orchids, as well as a riotous rhododendron stand. At the far end of the garden is the Neoclassical **mausoleum** of the House of Hannover.

The 2-kilometer (1¼-mile) **Herrenhaüser Allee,** lined by more than 1,300 lime trees, runs smack through the **Georgengarten,** which flanks the Großer Garten. Laid out in the best English style, the garden features plenty of meandering paths and lakes. It's worth getting off the U-Bahn two or three stops early, at Universität or Schneiderberg, to amble through. Within the Georgengarten, in the Neoclassical **Georgenpalais,** is the popular **Wilhelm-Busch Museum,** which features permanent and temporary exhibitions by a variety of famous cartoonists; some cartoonists delve into the realm of social commentary, while others are more artistically inclined. *Tel. 0511/714076. U4 or U5 to Universität or Schneiderberg. Admission: DM 3, DM 1.50 students. Open Tues.–Sun. 10–5.*

SPRENGEL MUSEUM A new wing opened in 1992, permitting this superb modern-art museum to show even more of its collection of works by Beckmann, Ernst, Klee, Nolde, Picasso, and a gaggle of other artists. Go early to avoid a long line for the James Turrell room, a playground for your eyeballs near the museum entrance. Hannover's homegrown hero Kurt Schwitters gets several rooms for his lively efforts at making art (in the form of pictures and even entire houses) out of discarded scraps. *Kurt-Schwitters-Pl., northern tip of Maschsee, tel. 0511/168–3875. Admission free. Open Tues. 10–10, Wed.–Sun. 10–6.*

MISCELLANEOUS MUSEUMS Just up the street from the Sprengel Museum, the **Landesmuseum** houses large collections of medieval and 17th-century art, an archaeological breakdown of the area's ancient history (including a body found preserved in a peat bog), a natural-history section, and, in the basement, an aquarium. *Am Maschpark 5, tel. 0511/883051. Admission free. Open Tues.–Sun. 10–5, Thurs. 10–7.*

Highlights of the amusing **Historisches Museum** include several horse-drawn coaches of the House of Hannover and a 1928 two-seat prototype car dubbed the "*Kommissbrot*" (army loaf). *Between Am Hohen Ufer and Burgstr. in Altstadt, tel. 0511/168–3052. Admission free. Open Tues. 10–8, Wed.–Fri. 10–4, weekends 10–6.*

Next to the Rathaus, the **Kestner Museum** displays masterpieces of sculpture, pottery, and other decorative arts from a range of cultures. *Trammpl. 3, tel. 0511/168–2120. Admission free. Open Tues., Thurs., Fri. 10–4, Wed. 10–8, weekends 10–6.*

FESTIVALS

The tourist office has a list of all the great parties that Hannover throws. Most notable are the Rabelaisian **Schützenfest,** a 10-day shooting festival with floats and fireworks in early July; the **Maschseefest,** two weeks of lakeside merriment in early August; and the **Altstadtfest,** a weekend of music and madness at the end of August. A popular party game at the Schützenfest is downing a *Lüttje Lager*, a shot glass of schnapps sitting in a glass of beer; you're supposed to chug the whole thing.

On a dozen spring and autumn Sundays, thousands of people stroll the shopping district for **Schorsenbummel,** a street fair with origins in the 18th century. You'll find jazz music (a relatively recent addition) around the **Opera House** (Georgstr., off Am Steintor), street vendors, and a variety of culinary delights, most of which revolve around the wurst.

AFTER DARK

Nights in Hannover are surprisingly sedate. The best hunting grounds for bars are the Altstadt's Kramerstraße, Knochenhauerstraße, and Ballhofstraße. The rowdy crowd at the always-packed **Irish Pub** (Brüderstr. 4 at Odeonstr., tel. 0511/14589) has been known to break into song on good nights; two of the owners are rumored to be cousins of Shane McGowan of the Pogues. Half liters of pugnacious Irish beer run DM 5.

Summer weather brings out the beer gardens; two of the best, **Backöfle** (Mittelstr. 11, tel. 0511/18524) and **Waterloo-Biergarten** (Waterloopl. 1, next to Waterloo U-Bahn stop, tel. 0511/15643), are within convenient staggering distance of the Jugendherberge Hannover. The Waterloo serves the local Broyhan beer.

CINEMAS Across from the Bahnhof, **Filmfestspielhaus Venedig** shows undubbed English first-run films. The **Künstlerhaus** (Sophienstr. 2, tel. 0511/168–4732) screens classics and arty flicks and also serves as a venue for experimental dance and theater.

MUSIC Nothing escapes the comprehensive ***MagaScene*** monthly, an invaluable guide to the region's music, especially rock, as well as film and theater events. The monthly ***Hannover Aktuell*** booklet lists some local concerts, though it omits addresses and prices. Classical strains sweeten the air at the **Opera House** (Georgstr., off Am Steintor) and at the Herrenhausen Gardens' **Galerie** (*see* Worth Seeing, *above*); tickets cost from DM 15 to DM 20. The **Music Hall** (Göttingerstr. 14, tel. 0511/453035) and **Raschplatz,** right behind the train station, host frequent rock concerts. You can buy tickets to all these events at the tourist office. Of course, the street musicians in the Altstadt offer the cheapest, most hassle-free harmonies around.

NIGHTCLUBS The ingenious ***Extra*** magazine, available at the tourist office for DM 6.80, has a list of all local discos, including breakdowns of their clientele, with such concise stats as "20% Club-Kids, 80% Disco Lilies."

Capitol. An older set gets around to Top 40 tunes in this converted movie house; cartoons play continuously on a screen. *Schwarzer Bär 2, tel. 0511/444066. Cover: DM 5. Closed Sun.–Thurs.*

Men's Factory. This techno gay club opens its doors to straight folk as well on Friday nights. *Engelbosteler Damm 7. Cover: DM 10. Closed Sun.–Thurs.*

Osho-Disco. Right next to Palo Palo, this joint is more of a generic dance hall. *Raschpl. 7, tel. 0511/342217. Cover: DM 8. Closed Mon., Tues.*

Palo Palo. Spins "ethnic" grooves in its "multi-Kulti-Basement" for an alternative crowd. *Raschpl. 8A, behind Hauptbahnhof, tel. 0511/331073. Cover: DM 5.*

Sub. Hiphop is the scene here. *Raschpl. 6, tel. 0511/314859. Cover: DM 5. Closed Mon., Tues.*

Near Hannover

HAMELN

Along with Hannoversch-Münden and Duderstadt, Hameln is one of the best places to scope out the intricately carved facades of Weser Renaissance houses. Hameln's collection is smaller, but includes some of the most energetically whimsical work around. You can find the best examples of these houses on the wide pedestrian streets Osterstraße and Bäckerstraße, as well as cramped Wendenstraße off Bäckerstraße; most houses now double as overpriced cafés or restaurants.

If he were to return today, Hameln's pied piper would probably make a fortune. Many is the hosteler who would pay him to rid Germany's youth hostels of the summer infestation of school groups, screaming kids, and ghastly teenagers.

Of course, Hameln (anglicized as Hamelin) is most famous as the site of the *Rattenfänger* (Pied Piper) fairy tale. According to the legend, a mysterious musician rid the town of a rat infestation by luring the dance-happy rodents out of town with his pipe playing. When the town honchos refused to pay the DJ as they had agreed, he used his pipe to similar effect on their children (no doubt playing a mix of hiphop and house industrial), who were never seen again. The local tourist industry drives the story into the ground; *Bäckerei* sell rat-shape pastries, rodenty tourist knickknacks abound, and Sundays at noon a reenactment in front of the stone *Hochzeitshaus* plays to huge crowds. Support a kitsch-free Germany—don't spend a *pfennig* on any of it.

The **Verkehrsbüro** (Diesterallee next to Bürgergarten, tel. 05151/202617) charges DM 2 to find rooms and has a wide range of brochures in English.

COMING AND GOING Trains run to Hameln from Hannover (one hour, DM 10.80) and Hildesheim (50 minutes, DM 10.80) once or twice an hour. The train station is out in the boonies; to get into town proper, walk straight out of the train station, take the second right, and then turn left on Diesterallee. The tourist office is on the right after a 15-minute walk; before continuing, orient yourself using the map outside the office.

WHERE TO SLEEP AND EAT **Private rooms** are the cheapest option, with singles as low as DM 25 and doubles twice that; the tourist office has a complete list. Expect to pay double these prices in one of Hameln's hotels.

It's a long trek out to the **Jugendherberge** (Fischbeckerstr. 33, tel. 05151/3425), but at least the hostel lies on the edge of the tranquil Weser River. The crusty management accepts new guests between 5 PM and 10 PM; beds in dorm rooms are DM 16.50 (DM 20 for over 26), breakfast included, and sheets are DM 4. The hostel closes in November. To get here, take Bus 11 to Lachsgrund, then walk toward the river. **Campingplatz "zum Fährhaus"** (Uferstr. 80, tel. 05151/61167), across the river from the hostel, charges DM 4.50 per person, DM 2 per car, and DM 7 for a tent site in a fenced-off enclosure.

Get cozy in the **Kaffee-Stube Pfannkuchen** (Hummenstr. 12, tel. 05151/ 41378). At night the subdued, candlelit interior is perfect for long discussions over one of their pancake dishes. A pancake with mushrooms and cheese goes for DM 8; with chili con carne, DM 11. Whole-grain flour pancakes are DM 1 extra. **Markets** brighten up the square at Kastanienwall and Sedanstraße Wednesday and Saturday until 1 PM.

Hildesheim

Hildesheim, 30 kilometers (18 miles) southeast of Hannover, almost managed to survive World War II intact, until a 20-minute bombing raid a month before the German surrender left 80% of the town in cinders. Sterile, modern pedestrian streets and enormous department stores now form most of the town's center, but an ambitious reconstruction effort has rebuilt large sections of Hildesheim's cultural treasures. Several churches are worth attention for their quirky features, particularly the Dom (cathedral), with its thousand-year-old rosebush and massive bronze castings, and St. Michael's, with its delightful Romanesque painted ceiling. Most impressive of all, though, is the town's gracious Marktplatz, as spellbinding a collection of old buildings as you're likely to find.

BASICS

LAUNDRY Wash about 7 pounds' worth of grunge for DM 6 at the **Wasch Salon.** DM 1 buys 15 minutes of drying time. *Bahnhofsallee 10. Open weekdays 6 AM–11 PM; last wash at 10 PM.*

MAIL AND PHONES The **post office** holds *poste restante* mail (postal code 3200), changes money at average rates, and slaps a DM 3 commission on traveler's checks. Phone booths outside take both cards and coins. *Outside Hauptbahnhof. Open weekdays 8–6, Sat. 9–noon.*

VISITOR INFORMATION The **Verkehrsverein,** the only tourist office in town, has various maps of Hildesheim and a room-finding service for DM 5. To get here from the station, walk up Bernwardstraße (which changes into Almstraße), turn left on Rathausstraße, and then right onto Am Ratsbauhof (it's a 15-minute walk); otherwise, take Bus 1 to the Schuhstraße stop. *Am Ratsbauhof 1C, tel. 05121/159956. Open weekdays 9–6, Sat. 9–1.*

COMING AND GOING

BY TRAIN AND BUS Frequent **trains** link Hildesheim's Hauptbahnhof to Braunschweig (30 minutes, DM 10.80), Göttingen (1½ hours, DM 21), Hameln (50 minutes, DM 10.80), and Hannover (30 minutes, DM 8.40). **Buses** leave from right outside the train station for nearby rinky-dink towns, but they take twice as long and cost just as much money as trains. You'll find a handful of small (DM 2) and medium-size (DM 4) lockers near the station entrance. The train station is in the northern part of the city; to get to the town center, take Bernwardstraße, which becomes Almstraße.

BY MITFAHRZENTRALE Hildesheim's **Mitfahrzentrale** (Annenstr. 15, tel. 05121/ 39051) can hook you up with long-distance rides; the staff estimates DM 15 to Hamburg, DM 23 to Berlin, and DM 72 to Paris. They also book cheap last-minute seats on international flights. To get here from the Rathaus, walk east up Rathausstraße, hook a right on Gartenstraße, a right on Braunschweiger Straße, and then a left onto Annenstraße.

BY BIKE Hildesheim has plenty of great places to bike, including the wooded Kehrwiederwall just south and the Hildesheimer Wald to the west. You can rent bikes at the **train station** for DM 10 per day (DM 12 for a three-speed); there's a DM 4 rebate if you have a train ticket.

WHERE TO SLEEP

Most of the cheap hotels in Hildesheim lie frustratingly far from the town center and require a bus ride; if you don't have reservations, call first from the station. Those intent on roughing it might try the **Hildesheimer Wald** (forest); take Bus 3, 13, 23, 33, or 43 (toward Hildesheimer Wald) to the end of the line; skirt around the huge Bosch-Blaupunkt factory to reach the forest.

Hotel-Gastätte Meyer. More impersonal than its neighbor (Hotel Marheineke across the street), this place is nevertheless clean and pleasant. Ten singles run DM 37–DM 45, six doubles go for DM 74, two doubles with showers for DM 100, and two triples for DM 111 and DM 120. Reservations are held until 6 PM, and more rooms are often available on weekends. *Peiner Landstr. 185, tel. 05121/53179. Bus 1 from Hauptbahnhof toward Drispenstedt to Alt Drispenstedt, cross under hwy.*

Hotel Marheineke-Gastätte. This pristine pension is run by a shy family that takes a genuine interest in foreigners. Rooms are airy, and beds have down comforters. Downstairs, a pub-like restaurant doles out typical wurst and schnitzel dishes. Two singles are DM 40 each, the seven doubles are DM 75, and one double with shower goes for DM 85; breakfast is included. *Peiner Landstr. 189, tel. 05121/52667. Check in until 10 PM. Reservations advised.*

Pension Kurth. A cagey, standoffish Hausfrau offers clean, light-filled rooms down the hall from the hotel's sole shower and toilet. Hole up in the feather beds or make friends with fellow travelers in the cozy hallway. Five singles with sinks go for DM 35, two doubles are DM 70, and one double with shower and bath runs DM 100. Breakfast is included. *Küsthardstr. 4, tel. 05121/32817. From Hauptbahnhof, walk down Bernwardstr., keeping to pedestrian zone; turn right on Schuhstr., right on Zingel, left on Braunschweiger Str., and immediately left on Küsthardstr.; doorbell is under Gast zum Post sign. Reservations required.*

HOSTEL **Jugendherberge.** This '60s youth hostel perches on the edge of the Hildesheim Forest, overlooking the town. Unfortunately, it's a long haul to get up here. Check-in is between 5 and 10 PM, but it's worth trying to get a bed before 2; the 10 PM curfew is negotiable, too. Those 26 and under pay DM 16.50, over 26 DM 20; sheets are DM 4 extra. Breakfast is included in the rate, but after three days you have to pay DM 26.50 for full board. The hostel management is supposed to change in 1994—showers will be renovated and bathrooms may even be cleaned. At the moment, the toilets look clean but smell bad. *Schirrmannweg 4, tel. 05121/42717. Bus 1 to Am Dammtor, then Bus 4 to Triftstraße, cross street, turn left, follow the sign up long slope for 15 min; trip takes about 45 min. 10 beds in doubles, 71 beds in dorm rooms. Sometimes closed Dec. and/or Jan.*

CAMPGROUND **Campingplatz am Müggelsee.** Few RVs make it to this spacious lawn despite its location right next to the B–494 Autobahn. The spot's not exactly secluded, but it's pleasant enough and has its own swimming lake. The owners will even rent you a leaky rowboat. They charge DM 5 per person for camping. *Am Müggelsee 4, tel. 05121/53131. Turn left out of Hauptbahnhof down Butterborn, go under then across bridge, and walk north (25 min). Reception open intermittently 9:30–7.*

FOOD

Hildesheim has plenty of traditional German restaurants where entrées cost around DM 15. As usual, pizzerias serve the cheapest meals; **Pizzeria La Gondola** (Bahnhofsallee 11, tel. 05121/133282) is one of the cheapest, with pizzas for DM 9–DM 10.50. The pedestrian-zone eateries are okay for quickie wursts, but they don't have much atmosphere. Hildesheim's large student population supports a galaxy of good café-bars. Several popular bars cluster around Hindenburgplatz; **Cafe Trödel** and its sidekick **Trödelchen** cater to a yuppie crowd, while **Cafe Brazil** on nearby Friesenstraße has a cooler clientele. A couple of other student spots worth trying are **Penguin Café** (on Wallstr. at Almsstr.) for breakfast muesli and fresh fruit (DM 6.50), and **Schluckspecht** (Goschenstr. 29, tel. 05121/33142) for lunch, dinner, or drinks.

Gastwirtschaft Café Schärling. Under the slogan "Zeitgeist der Welt," this is where the intellectual crowd hangs out to chew the fat. Greek salads are DM 10, a hunk of baked Camembert DM 6.50, and ground-meat stew DM 6; beer and tea start at DM 2.50. *Burgstr. 2, opposite Roemer-und Pelizaeus-Museum, tel. 05121/134494.*

Schlegels Wein-Stuben. Beamed ceilings, walls lined with wine bottles, and rough old-fashioned windowpanes conspire to make this *the* place for that romantic evening. Restoration workers recently uncovered a deep, mossy 16th-century well here; it's been covered with a glass top, and you can have it as a table if you reserve in advance. The specialty is wine, especially German wine; dry Badische Riesling is DM 6.50–DM 8 per glass, sweet Rhein Hessen wines are DM 5 per glass, and bottles go for DM 16–DM 38. *Eintöpfe* (soups and stews) cost up to DM 7.50, entrées run from DM 12.50 up to DM 32, and pumpernickel ice cream costs DM 6. Count on a stiff DM 30 minimum for a full meal. *Am Steine 4–6, opposite Roemer-und Pelizaeus-Museum, tel. 05121/33133. No lunch.*

Seestern. Just down the street from the tourist office, this stand-up seafood place offers several pricey meals (for example, a DM 13 fish fillet), but for DM 4.50 you can scarf a bowl of delicious fish or oxtail soup. Greasy fries are DM 2.50. *Am Ratsbauhof 9, tel. 05121/05063. No dinner.*

WORTH SEEING

Hildesheim's sights lie within easy walking distance of one another. White roses spray-painted on the sidewalks delineate a 5-kilometer (3-mile) circuit that leads past all the biggies. Get a map at the tourist office to orient yourself; the tourist staff also hawk a 50-page accompanying brochure, filled with interesting trivia, for DM 2. If a 15th-century edifice looks surprisingly new, it probably is; most attractions had to be rebuilt from the ground up after World War II.

HILDESHEIMER DOM The cathedral itself is unspectacular; what makes it worth visiting are its quirky accessories. The Dom checklist includes the giant main doors and the imposing Christ Pillar, both bronze castings made under the ambitious 12th-century Bishop Bernward; the crypt and its gold shrine; and an enormous wheel-shaped chandelier. If you're prepared to fork over 50 pfennig (30 pfennig for students), you can check out the **Tausendjährigen Rosenstock** (1,000-Year-Old Rosebush) in the secluded cloister. As legend has it, the 9th-century Emperor Ludwig the Pious hung his personal relics on this same rosebush while hunting, and found them frozen there the next morning; of course he had to build a chapel to honor this clearly divine message. The small white blooms appear for two weeks only, in early June. *Open weekdays 9:30–5, Sat. 9:30–2:30; Rosenstock and cloister also open April–Oct. weekends noon–5.*

Next door, the **Domschatz/Diözesan Museum** (Am Dom, tel. 05121/168950) exhibits the church's glittering treasures, including some 11th-century Bibles and an intricate *Scheibenkreuz* (disk cross). *Admission: DM 4, DM 1.50 students. Open Tues.–Sat. 10–5, Sun. noon–5.*

MARIENBURG CASTLE Some 12 kilometers (7 miles) west of Hildesheim, this stately fairy-tale castle dominates the valley from its position atop a forested ridge. You'll pass it if you're traveling west by train, and you'll wish you were stopping. Guided tours (DM 5) amble through the richly crafted interior of this 19th-century abode Monday–Saturday 8–noon and 2–6, and Sunday 8–6. Take the train to Nordstemmen (one per hour, seven minutes, DM 4.20), then make the half-hour trek uphill to the castle.

MARKTPLATZ Give yourself a good half hour to drink in all the captivating details of this recently restored square. The magnificent **Knochenhaueramtshaus** (Butchers' Guildhouse), a massive 16th-century half-timbered building, looms in the northwest corner of the square. Leveled in World War II and replaced by a hotel, it was reconstructed in 1987 using traditional techniques—the structure is held together only with wood pegs, no nails. The **Bäckeramtshaus** (Bakers' Guildhouse) next door forms the other half of a masterful half-timber duet. Continuing counterclockwise around the square, you come across reconstructions of the 14th-century **Rolandhaus,** the **Lüntzelhaus,** and the rollicking sculpted oak facade of the **Wedekindhaus.** A crusader's memories of Middle Eastern architecture inspired the bizarre 15th-century **Tempelhaus** next door. The **Rathaus** (Town Hall), rebuilt in a hurry after the war, makes a mockery of its former self. More pleasing are (from right to left) the **Wollenwebergildehaus** (Weavers' Guildhouse), the daintily pink **Rokokohaus,** and the **Stadtschänke,** along the square's north side. Many of the buildings now serve as pricey restaurants, cafés, and hotels; delightfully, the Bakers' Guildhouse still contains a bakery.

Housed in the upper five stories of the Knochenhaueramtshaus, the **Stadtmuseum** displays tankards, halberds, and other shards from Hildesheim's past. Willi Bergmann, one of the museum staff, specializes in making visitors laugh with his attempts at English. *Tel. 05121/301163. Admission: DM 3, DM 1 students. Open Tues., Thurs.–Sun. 10–6, Wed. 10–9.*

ROEMER-UND PELIZAEUS-MUSEUM Take a break from Western Europe at this expensive but excellent collection on ancient civilizations. The museum's strong suit is its Egypt section, though Chinese porcelain and a Peruvian exhibit deserve some time as well. Temporary exhibitions, often fantastic, pass through regularly. *Am Steine 1–2, tel. 05121/93690. Follow white roses from front of Dom. Admission: DM 10, DM 5 students. Open Tues., Thurs.–Sun. 10–6, Wed. 10–9, hrs change frequently.*

ST. ANDREAS After its demise in March 1945, this Gothic beast was restored without its former gaudy accoutrements. The unpainted stonework gives the vast interior an unadorned appeal unusual among Germany's colorful churches. If you can wangle your way in when the monstrous pipe organ is thundering, you won't regret it. To get here from the tourist office, head south on Amratsbauhof and then turn right on Schuhstraße.

ST. MICHAEL'S Originally a Benedictine monastery, St. Michael's is probably the most important building in Hildesheim from an architectural standpoint. It was started by Bishop Bernward, who from 993 to 1022 presided over all matters religious in the town. The design of the church indicates a clear abandonment of the multicolumned look of the Roman basilicas in favor of square pillars interspersed with fewer columns (a style that came to be known as Lower Saxon). Many architects ascribe the church's sense of harmony to the fact that the height of the ceiling is double the length of each bay of the nave. The mathematical harmonies, however, take a back seat to the startling colors of the painted wood ceiling, showing various biblical scenes involving trees (the church's relic was a fragment of the true cross). When the church turned Protestant with the Reformation, the crypt remained Catholic, since it contained the remains of Bishop Bernward. To get to the church, follow Michaelisstraße almost a kilometer (½ mile) west from the Marktplatz.

AFTER DARK

The **Hildesheimer Volkshochschule** (Wollenweberstr. 68, tel. 05121/93610) shows a great lineup of films in its "Kellerkino" on Tuesday nights; a lot of Latin American films play, plus subtitled films by auteurs like Ingmar Bergman, Stanley Kubrick, and Peter Greenaway. Showtimes are 6 and 8:30; a ticket costs DM 7.

BeBop. For hard rock and occasional live music by local punksters, zip through the tunnel under the train station to this joint. *Steuerwalder Str. 60, tel. 05121/515153. Closed Sun.–Thurs.*

Thav. In a big garage set back from the street, this sleek bar and dance floor with DJ is as lefty as Hildesheim gets, according to the management: Political groups often meet here. Beer goes for DM 3.50–DM 4, or try a *Heiße Zitrone* (very sour hot lemon water) for DM 2. Salads are around DM 7, and various soups run DM 4–DM 6. *Güntherstr. 21, tel. 05121/132829. From Hindenburgplatz, walk past post office down Zingel, turn left on Braunschweiger Str., right on Annenstr., and right on Günterstr.*

Vier Linden. A few times a week, this local cultural center stages live music, ranging from pop to jazz to reggae, plus frequent theater (in German). Tickets are DM 20–DM 25 for concerts, DM 15–DM 20 for theater; student tickets usually cost DM 4 or less. Dancing draws an alternative crowd after 10 PM on Monday, Wednesday, and Friday. *Alfelder Str. 55B, tel. 05121/23255. Bus 1 to Dammtor, then Bus 5 toward Ochtersum 2 stops to Vier Linden (last bus around 10:30–11 PM).*

Near Hildesheim

WOLFENBUTTEL

If you're looking for cute, come here rather than Braunschweig. Unscarred by World War II, placid Wolfenbüttel has scads of half-timbered homes gathered around picturesque little squares and canals. Otherwise, the big draw is a giant library, the **Herzog August Bibliothek** (behind the castle, tel. 05331/8080), where 135,000 works collected by a scholarly 17th-century duke jam shelf after shelf. The entire collection, handbound by the duke himself in bone-colored covers, is on display, and includes 16th-century tomes, illuminated manuscripts, psalm books covered with Martin Luther's margin notes, and old globes. The philosopher Gottfried Leibniz and the dramatist Gotthold Lessing both spent time as librarians here, and Casanova left his carnal pursuits to come here for a week of reading. Pay the DM 5 entry and pick up the excellent English brochure. The library is open daily from 10 until 5.

The same admission fee also gives you access to the nearby **Lessinghaus,** interesting for fans of Gotthold Lessing, who spent the last 11 years of his life here. Exhibits cover various periods in Lessing's life. The pink, barnlike **Zeughaus,** on the north side of Schloßplatz, is a former armory that now houses book-related exhibits.

Inside the **Schloß,** now a free museum, you can get a feel for 18th-century aristocratic life. *Schloßpl., tel. 05331/5713. Open Tues.–Sun. 10–1, Wed., Fri., and Sat. also 3–5.*

If culture is giving you a headache, cruise south down Lange Straße to **Stadtbad,** which features an Olympic-size pool, a two-story diving board, and a dizzying water tube. *Admission: DM 3. Open daily 6 AM–7:30 PM.*

COMING AND GOING It's easiest to get to Wolfenbüttel from Braunschweig—take a train (two per hour, 12 minutes, DM 4.20) or Bus 20 (one–three per hour, 30 minutes, DM 2.40). From Wolfenbüttel's train station, go left down Bahnhofstraße and through the passageway to the Stadtmarkt and the super-friendly **Tourist Information** (Stadtmarkt 9, tel. 05331/86487).

WHERE TO SLEEP AND EAT Confront the indifferent woman at the **Gästehaus "Kaltes Tal"** (Goslarche Str. 56, tel. 05331/43828) for clean but noisy rooms right next to an intersection. Singles are DM 50, doubles DM 80, and breakfast is DM 5 extra per person. The **Jugendgästehaus** (Jägerstr. 17, tel. 05331/27189) looks like a hostel, but isn't—you don't need an IYHF card, and you can stay here longer than at a hostel. Beds in four-bed rooms are DM 30 (DM 22 for those under 21), breakfast included. The idyllic **Campingplatz** (next to the Stadtbad, tel. 05331/2538), with trees, a canal, and its own swimming pool, costs DM 6.50 per person, DM 6.50 for a tent spot, and DM 3.50 per car.

On the corner in front of the train station, **Döner-Kebap** sells snack-size portions of such Turkish fare as stuffed bell peppers for DM 3–DM 5. Cheap food of all types changes hands at the Wednesday and Saturday morning markets on the Altstadtmarkt.

Göttingen

Ask any German what is most important about Göttingen and he or she will talk about the university, built in 1734 by Kurfürst Georg-August of Hannover. By 1777 the Georg-August Universität had become the biggest in Germany, with over 30,000 students, and the numbers have held steady over the years. The Brothers Grimm carried on much of their work on German philology here, and these streets have seen no fewer than 30 Nobel Prize winners. Physicists Friedrich Gauss and Wilhelm Weber, Nobel recipients who pioneered the study of electromagnetism, have been immortalized in statues scattered throughout the city.

The city owes much of its character and spunkiness to its large student population. But even if you're not a student (hell, even if you *hate* students), the long, winding streets dominated by three- and four-story half-timbered houses are still enticing. Much of the Altstadt is a cobbled pedestrians-only zone, and modern sculptures are sprinkled throughout the town. The city walkways are lined with *Imbisses* (food stands), specialty shops, and student hangouts.

BASICS

BUCKET SHOPS **Reiseladen Zentralmensa** (central cafeteria on the main campus) has a helpful staff that offers package deals. **Reiseladen Kloppmann** (Jüdenstr., tel. 0551/496040) has good deals on plane fares.

The Little Goose Girl

Göttingen's symbol is the fountain of Gänseliesel, the "little goose girl" in the Grimms' collection of fairy tales. Traditionally, graduates of the university kiss this cold hunk of metal on the lips when they receive their diplomas. Since her completion in 1907, she's become the most kissed girl in Germany, despite a 1926 resolution by the Göttingen city council banning this practice. Students still throw caution to the winds to get a little action from the bronze babe.

LAUNDRY Dump your clothes in the **Waschcentrum** on Ritterplan and then slip into the Städtisches Museum (*see* Worth Seeing, *below*) across the street. Don't get so engrossed in the museum's wonders that you forget your clothes, though, because *Penner* (homeless people) may make off with them.

MAIL AND PHONES The **Hauptpost,** just outside the train station, provides the usual post office and telephone functions. *Burgstr., tel. 0551/49860. Open weekdays 6 AM–10 PM, Sat. 8–5, Sun. 9–noon.*

VISITOR INFORMATION **Tourist Office am Bahnhof** (tel. 0551/56000), at the Hauptbahnhof, is open weekdays 10–1 and 2–6 and Saturday 10–1. However, you may want to walk to the center of town to check out the better-equipped **Fremdenverkehrsverein Altes Rathaus** (tel. 0551/54000), in the Old Town Hall on the Marktplatz. This office also sells youth hostel passes; it's open weekdays 9–6 and weekends 10–4.

While you're at the tourist office on Marktplatz, check out the myriad attractions of the Rathaus, including the great murals and coats of arms of Hanseatic towns which line the main lobby walls. The unassuming lion doorknocker is the oldest of its kind, dating from 1300.

You can track down all kinds of alternative organizations through the university's Zentralmensa (*see* Food, *below*). Check out the lesbian scene through the **Frauen-Lesben-Zentrum** (Women and Lesbian Center, Düstere Str. 21, tel. 0551/46910). In addition, gays and lesbians can find out what's going on by calling 0551/43438 on Monday 8 PM–10 PM.

COMING AND GOING

BY TRAIN Trains leave Göttingen's Hauptbahnhof, located just west of the city center, for Braunschweig (eight per day, one hour, DM 26), Goslar (1 per hour, 1½ hours, DM 19), Hannover (two–three per hour, 1½ hours, DM 25), Hannoversch–Münden (one per hour, 40 minutes, DM 10.80), and Hildesheim (one per hour, 1½ hours, DM 21).

BY MITFAHRZENTRALE Göttingen has two ride-sharing organizations. **Citynetz** (Burgstr. 7, tel. 0551/19444) has a computer network that is linked with many other major German cities. **Cheltenham House** (Friedrichstr. 1, tel. 0551/485988) charges a few marks less for some trips, so you may want to try them first. The commission for a trip to Berlin is DM 8 at Cheltenham House and DM 11 at Citynetz; gas runs about DM 20 unless the driver prorates the cost according to the number of passengers. At Citynetz, a ride to Amsterdam costs a total of about DM 48, to Barcelona DM 99, and to Athens DM 222. To avoid paying a commission, use the ride shares posted on boards by the Zentralmensa in the main part of campus.

BY TAXI If you get stuck somewhere, the cheapest taxi service is **Mini-Car** (tel. 0551/44872). At night, cheap taxi service for women is available through **Hallo Taxi** (tel. 0551/34034).

WHERE TO SLEEP

Hotel-Restaurant Onkel Toms Hütte. This hotel is charming and clean, with a nice outdoor garden. Ten of the doubles go for DM 85, and the other 20 doubles are DM 110. Breakfast is included. *Am Gewende 10 and 11, tel. 0551/72036. From Hauptbahnhof, take Bus 4 to Am Markt, then Bus 5 or 6 to last stop, Reinhäuser Landstr. 50 rooms with bath. Latest check-in 2 AM.*

Hotel zum Schwan. In a modern building on a big, ugly street, this is a relatively clean place to sleep. In fact, some of the rooms smell *too* clean, like those revolting air fresheners. It's a 15-minute walk from here to the center of town, 20 minutes to the Hauptbahnhof. Doubles cost DM 65 and DM 79 with bath. Showers on each floor cost an extra DM 3. Breakfast is included. *Weender Landstr. 23, tel. 0551/144863. From Hauptbahnhof, walk through town on Weender Str., which becomes Weender Landstr. 24 rooms, some with bath. Check in until 10 PM, reservations accepted all day except Sat. 2–7 and Sun. after 2.*

Landgasthaus Lokeman. Locals descend on this friendly, country-style hotel in a suburb of Göttingen for the hotel restaurant's good German cooking. Small, light, airy rooms have unfinished furniture for that rustic look. You share a bathtub with hand shower with your neighbors on each floor. Ask for one of the 10 singles that go for DM 35 or one of the 10 doubles at DM 55, breakfast included. It takes about 25 minutes to get here from the center of Göttingen. Check out the map of walking trails that start at the nearby bus stop. *Im Beeke 1, tel. 0551/21582. Bus 10 from Kornmarkt in center of Göttingen toward Herbenhausen, get off at last stop and follow large sign. Check in until 10 or 11 PM, desk closed Mon. afternoon.*

HOSTEL **Jugendherberge.** This large, modern hostel has a few doubles and singles; the rest are six-bed dorm rooms. Upper rooms have skylights, and there is a common room for smokers. You can get three meals a day, including a vegetarian lunch on request. Bicycles cost DM 8 per day, DM 5 a day if you rent for more than three days. You can make and receive calls from an international phone in the lobby. Those under 27 pay DM 17.50 per night; over 26 pay DM 21.50; breakfast included. Bedding costs DM 5. *Habichtsweg 2, tel. 0551/157622. From Hauptbahnhof, walk past tourist information and turn right on Berliner Str.; turn left on Groner Tor Str. and take Bus 6 at next stop on right side of st. to Jugendherberge stop. 150 beds. Check-in and reservations 1–10 PM, checkout 9 AM, last entry 11:30 PM.*

CAMPGROUND Sadly, the nearest **campground** (Hoher Hagen, tel. 05502/2147) cowers 12 kilometers (7 miles) west of Göttingen, in the town of Dransfeld. Bus 2554 goes there every hour; once in Dransfeld, walk south and ask for directions. A spot costs DM 6 for one person, DM 10.50 for two, DM 14.50 for three.

FOOD

Göttingen's pedestrian walkways are full of eateries. Students tend to frequent cheaper international food restaurants, such as Italian, Greek, and Turkish. Student *Mensen*, or cafeterias, are located all over town; they sell soup for DM 1.50 and a full meal for DM 4.50 to anyone with a student ID, although you'll rarely get carded. The **Mensa Italia** (Roedererstr.) has made-to-order salads. The **Zentralmensa,** in the Blauer Turm on the main campus, has a bulletin board as well as cheap meals. Other mensas include **Nordmensa,** on the northern campus near the Chemistry department, and **Alte Mensa,** on Wilhelmsplatz in the Aldstadt (Old Town).

Cron und Lanz. This is the fanciest, tastiest bakery in town, with gorgeous chocolate cakes for DM 3 and fresh fruit cakes for DM 4. A cup of coffee is DM 2.50, and a *Kännchen* (little pot) is DM 5. The chocolate marzipan reproduction of the Gänseliesel is not just a decorative gimmick—it's some of the best chocolate you'll get in Germany. *Weender Str. 25, tel. 0551/56022.*

Nudelhaus. This woody, efficient restaurant serves *Auflauf* (soufflés), *Grüne Bandnudeln* (spinach linguine), and exotic combinations like the Monaco (DM 9.80), which features pineapple, kiwi, and cream sauce. Prices average DM 8–DM 11 per dish. *Rotestr. 13, tel. 0551/44263.*

Pfannkuchenhaus. More than 20 different kinds of thin German pancakes stuffed with savory or sweet fillings are served at long tables in dark, timbered rooms. Favorites with students and other customers are No. 24 (fresh mushrooms and cream sauce garnished with salad) for DM 8.50, No. 19 (vanilla ice cream, hot cherries, and *Kirschwasser*) for DM 10, No. 26 (with cheese, bacon and *Lauch,* or leek) for DM 10, No. 11 (*Teufelspfannkuchen*—Devil's Pancake—with kidney beans, onions, corn, and a spicy sauce) for DM 8.50, or the traditional No. 2 (with pieces of apple) for DM 6.

Speckstr. 10, tel. 0551/41870. From Rathaus walk up Barfüsserstr. through Wilhelmspl., turn left on Burg Str. and left on Speckstr.

WORTH SEEING

Don't come here for traditional tourist sights; Göttingen's real charm lies in its nightlife and other student activities. Considering how influential the university is in German cultural and scientific life, the city has surprisingly little in the way of major museums or collections.

STADTISCHES MUSEUM In Germany's town museums, you're guaranteed to find a motley collection of antiques and oddities gathering dust. In this one you'll discover the history of early civilizations, Jewish history, toys, religious art, and an old apothecary as well. *Ritterplan 7–8, tel. 0551/40028. From information bureau, walk up Weender Str., turn right on Jüden Str. and left on Ritterplan. Admission free. Open Tues.–Fri. 10–5, weekends 10–1.*

VOLKERKUNDLICHE SAMMLUNG DER UNIVERSITAT GOTTINGEN This museum of ethnography has more than 16,000 specimens—tools, cult objects, artwork, clothing, and ornaments from so-called primitive cultures. The most famous exhibitions are the Cook/Forster collection from the Pacific Ocean and an 18th-century collection from Northern Asia and the northwestern United States. You have to wonder whether the original owners parted willingly with these objets d'art, especially the religious ones. *Theaterplatz 15, tel. 0551/39–7892. From Rathaus, walk up Weender Str., turn right on Theaterstr. to Theaterpl. Open Sun. 10–1.*

CHEAP THRILLS

At the tourist office pick up a copy of *Aktuell in Göttingen*, a monthly guide to local happenings, including regular free concerts.

As in many medieval towns, Göttingen's Altstadt is encircled by an earth-and-brick wall, originally meant to ward off marauders. A wide walkway, crunchy with leaves in the fall and winter and lined with lilacs in the warmer months, runs along the top of the wall and makes for perfect strolls with a loved one. Be sure not to miss the **Bismarckhaus,** a small stone cottage that sits just outside the wall at the southern end of town. After the teenage Otto Von Bismarck was booted out of the city for feeling his oats, he lived here in exile. Nowadays the house is open April–September Wednesday–Saturday 10–5:30; at other times of the year it's open only until dusk.

Göttingen is famous for the woods that surround the city walls. Weekend *Spaziergänge* (walks) in the woods sometimes resemble a day in New York's Central Park, with everyone and his or her brother out on bikes, rollerskates, and skateboards. To get away from it all, pick up a map of Göttingen and walk south of town through the forest until you reach the **Kehr,** a large clearing at the top of the woods. Here you'll find outdoor pens of wild pigs and deer. On chilly days, stop off at the café for a rich and warming *heiße Kakao* (hot chocolate).

Row, row, row your boat on the **Kiessee,** a large park-encircled lake south of town. A small hut near the Sandweg stop (Bus 19) rents out two-person kayaks for DM 6 per hour, and rowboats for DM 8 per hour. For less conventional watersports, take Bus 2580 from the station to Barterode, then ask directions to the **Baggersee.** This deep quarry, now filled with extremely cold water, is used as a nude bathing hole by the younger generation.

FESTIVALS Göttingen's **Altstadtfest,** held around the last weekend in August, is billed as the biggest outdoor party in Lower Saxony. The festivities dominate the Fußgängerzone (pedestrian mall) and include alcohol, and live music, as well as the usual array of culinary delights.

At the end of May or early June, Göttingen hosts the **Handelfest,** during which international groups play the composer's music all over town for several days.

AFTER DARK

The free *Kultur in Göttingen* magazine, available at the information desk in the Altes Rathaus, has schedules of music as well as theater.

BARS AND CLUBS **Blue Note.** About once a week during the school year (Oct.–June), this Keller bar specializes in live jazz and blues; the cover charge for live music runs DM 8–DM 10. Wednesday is always salsa-merengue-lambada night; Friday is "Tropical Dance Night," with African, Carribean, and reggae music; every second Monday is Arabian-music night. Juices run DM 2–DM 3, beers DM 3–DM 5. *Wilhelmspl. 3, tel. 0551/46907. From Rathaus walk up Weender Str., turn right on Barfüßerstr., right on Wilhelmpl. Closed Sun.*

Irish Pub. If you're dying to order a drink in English, this is the place to go. Most of the staff are British and like to talk about the sports back home. Beer specialties include Guinness and Irish Kilkenny on tap for DM 2–DM 3. You can catch live musicians, usually doing their very own personalized versions of the Beatles' greatest hits, for no extra charge! *Mühlenstr. 4A, tel. 0551/45664. From Hauptbahnhof, walk up Goetheallee, turn left on Am Leinekanal, right on Mühlenstr.*

KAZ. All of Göttingen gathers here on warm summer nights to suck down beers. The quintessential *Bierzelt* (atmosphere) prevails outdoors. On winter nights, folks mingle with the theater crowd in the main dining area or downstairs in the *Keller* (cellar) with black-clad anarchist types. A plate of the house specialty, *pommes rotes/weißes* (fries with ketchup and mayonnaise), will help prepare you for the wide variety of *Flaschenbier* (bottled beer) available here. Salads are DM 6.50–DM 9.50, spaghetti dishes DM 8–DM 10. Breakfast is served 11–2 for DM 6.80. *Hospitalstr. 6, tel. 0551/53062. From Rathaus, walk down Kurze Str. and turn left.*

Sonderbar. Not only does this place stay open later than any other bar in town (till 5 AM), but it acts as a backdrop for the city's leftist, hip types to pose and have conversations on deconstructionism. Ice-cream-parlor decor dominates the inside, but, in summer, tables outside are great for people-watching. Beers start at DM 3.75, juice is DM 2.50–DM 5. Music ranges from hip hop to punk to soul. *Kurze Str. 9, tel. 0551/43143. From tourist information office, walk up Rote Str., turn right on Kurze Str.*

Tangente. Some claim this is a biker, teenybopper, heavy-metal disco; others say it's the only place to escape the chic disco crowd. Dancing starts after 11 PM and goes until about 3 AM. *Goetheallee 8A, no tel. Up the st. from Hauptbahnhof after underpass. Closed Sun., Mon.*

Trou. This bar is housed in an old wine cellar that's all that remains of a 15th-century cloister. Thick stone walls and ceilings, candles, and the smell of *Glühwein* (mulled wine) make you feel like not much has changed in the last 300 years. Try a slug of Wienbrand Otto, a mild brandy delivered in bulk containers, for DM 1.50. Beer on tap starts at DM 1.90, juice is DM 2.50, and wines start at DM 3. *Burgstr. 20, no tel. From Weender Str. walk up Theaterstr., turn left on Burgstr.*

Near Göttingen

Göttingen lies midway between the towns of Hannoversch–Münden, to the southwest, and Duderstadt, to the east. Of the two, Hannoversch–Münden, a quick train ride away, is the more impressive and accessible.

HANNOVERSCH-MUNDEN

Always referred to simply as "Hann–Münden," this city is jam-packed with more than 700 half-timbered houses. Many streets here haven't seen a new building in 300 years, and the occasional 18th-century residences in the Altstadt look jarringly modern. The town's medieval towers, bereft of their connecting ramparts since 1802, mark the edges of Germany's most concentrated collection of Weser Renaissance buildings.

The town, surrounded by thickly wooded hills, sits at the confluence of the Fulda and Werra rivers, which merge to form the Weser, once a commercially important waterway. Major sights in town include the 14th-century stone **Rathaus;** the half-timbered home of **Johann Andreas Eisenbart** (34 Lange Str.), a famous 18th-century doctor; and the **Welfenschloß,** a Renaissance palace looking out over the Werra River. A small **museum** in the Welfenschloß displays some mediocre art and an exhibit on half-timber construction methods; it's free and open Tuesday–Friday 10–noon and 2:30–5 (weekend hours are shorter). On Wednesday and Saturday mornings, a **market** is held in Marktplatz, next to the Rathaus.

The ride of all rides has got to be the Weser Radweg, a path that follows the Weser all the way from Hannoversch-Münden to the river's mouth at Bremerhaven. A durable booklet called the Weser-Radweg, *sold in bookstores and tourist offices the length of the river, has topo maps and brief notes on sight-seeing wonders.*

The **tourist information office,** open weekdays 8–5 and Saturday 8:30–12:30, is tucked away on one side of the Rathaus; they charge DM 2 to book rooms. When they're closed, the **Auskunftschalter** (open Mon.–Sat. 8–8), in the same building, has some of the same info.

COMING AND GOING Your best bet is to travel here by rail; a train from Göttingen (40 min., DM 10.80) stops here every hour on its way to Kassel. From the station, follow the INNENSTADT sign down Bahnhofstraße, hook a right on Burgstraße, and then a left on Marktstraße to the Rathaus and tourist information.

Rent bikes at **Fahrzeuge Wieland** (Aegidienpl. 4, tel. 05541/4872), in front of St. Aegidien, for DM 10 per day. The **youth hostel** (*see below*) has bikes as well for DM 6 per day or DM 3 per half day. You can rent rowboats and canoes in front of the campground at **Weserbootsverleih** (tel. 05574/818).

WHERE TO SLEEP AND EAT The cheapest hotels in town are **Gasthaus im Anker** (Bremer Schlagd 18, tel. 05541/4923), which offers beds for DM 30–DM 35 per person, and **Gasthaus zur Hafenbahn** (Blume 54, tel. 05541/4094), which has rooms for DM 27–DM 40 per person. The **Jugendherberge Hann. Münden** (Prof.-Oelkers-Str. 10, tel. 05541/8853) sits by the banks of the Weser, a 40-minute walk from the town center. Guests under 27 pay DM 16.50, otherwise it's DM 20, breakfast included. To get here from the station, go down Beethoven-Straße, turn left on Wallstraße, cross the bridge, then turn right on Veckerhäger Straße and look to the right; otherwise, take the infrequent Bus 5203 from the station (1 per hour). The crowded but scenic **Campingplatz Münden** (Oberer Tanzwerder, tel. 05541/12257), on an island in the Fulda, charges DM 7 per person, DM 3 per car, and DM 3 for a tent site. Take Tanzwerderstraße west and cross the bridge.

DUDERSTADT

Thirty kilometers (19 miles) east of Göttingen, Duderstadt stands on the old border separating East and West Germany. The town's 500 half-timbered buildings, though not as numerous as Hannoversch-Münden's, possess a style and life at least as impressive. The carved facades of the houses often have prayers and sayings chiseled into the beams. **Apothekenstraße** and **Hinterstraße** have the best buildings, but be sure to check out the great supporting figures on the building that faces the Gothic St. Cyriakus church on Marktstraße. The **Westerturm,** built in 1424 without a stabilizing beam in its steep witch's-hat roof, has since twisted a good 75° on its axis. A fun walk is the 3.5-kilometer (2-mile) **wooded trail** that follows the route of the old walls around Duderstadt; the walls are now nothing more than an earthen mound. A big booklet in the tourist office has the scuttlebutt on this and other longer walks. The office, called the **Fremdenverkehrsamt** (Marktstr. 66, tel. 05527/841200), resides in the basement of the split-level medieval-Renaissance **Rathaus**; it's open weekdays 9–4:30 and weekends 9:30–12:30.

From Göttingen, Duderstadt is accessible only by bus. Several buses make the trip, but only Bus 2480 (six–eight per day, one hour, DM 7.80) stops on the way at **Ebergötzen.** This sleepy hamlet is home to the **Wilhelm-Busch Mühle,** where Busch, creator of the twisted "Max and Moritz" cartoons, spent his childhood and later years with his lover Ernst Bachmann. *Admission: DM 4, DM 2 students. Open Mon., Tues., Wed., Fri. 9–1 and 2–5; Sun. 10–1, 2–5.*

WHERE TO SLEEP AND EAT The cheapest place to stay is in a private home. The tourist office has a list of rooms to let, starting in the DM 15–DM 20 range. The brand-new, 110-bed **Jugendgästehaus Duderstadt** (Mühlhauserstr. 27, tel. 05527/73001) charges DM 21 for a bed (DM 25 for guests over 26), breakfast included. Guests share a communal kitchen. To get here, walk east along Marktstraße, which turns into Obertorstraße and then Nordhäser Straße, and then follow the sign to the right; it's about a 15-minute walk.

Facing the drab church St. Servatius, **Italia Ristorante-Pizzeria** serves DM 10–DM 13 pizzas and DM 11 *gnocchi* (tiny pasta dumplings) with ham and cream. An à-la-carte meal at the **Chinese Restaurant Pacific** (Spiegelbrücke 10), just up the street, costs at least DM 17, but at lunch you can chow on pork in peanut sauce and the soup of the day for DM 8. After dark, **Pub Memory** (Marktstr. 20), sequestered away inside Die Tanne, is about as lively as nightlife gets in Duderstadt. Draft beer starts at DM 2.50.

Harz Mountains

The Harz Mountains are a densely forested and relatively gentle range beloved by the sort of Germans who like to hike 17 kilometers (10 miles) before breakfast. Winter in the Harz range brings temperatures in the low teens and lots of snow, so budget travelers must be prepared for haphazard transit schedules and winter price-gouging—many of the resorts are geared toward big spenders. Come spring, however, backpackers and families take advantage of the region's extensive network of hiking trails, and a string of thoughtfully placed youth hostels makes longer hikes through the hills a snap.

Serious hikers have even more options since reunification: No longer do barbed wire and watchtowers present an obstacle to the appreciation of nature. Square one for any expedition is the knowledgeable **Harzer Verkehrsverband** in Goslar (Marktstr. 45, tel. 05321/20031), open weekdays 8–5, with stacks of pamphlets on sights, hotels, and campgrounds. The **Harz hot line** (tel. 05321/20024) rattles off the latest weather forecast in German; knowing what the heavens are up to is important, given the mercurial and occasionally violent local weather.

If you prefer short walks or just hanging out, you're better off focusing on towns that are well served by public transport. In the northeast, the principal towns are Wernigerode and Bad Harzburg. Each has its own distinct personality—Wernigerode feels like a Baroque market town, Bad Harzburg like an upper-class resort—and both are well connected by train to Hamburg, Hannover, and Erfurt. The same goes for Herzberg and Osterode, two mid-size towns on the southern fringe of the Harz region. Otherwise, the Harz Mountains are not conducive to casual exploration—you need a serious sense of purpose (and humor) and at least a week. Many of the area's best destinations, particularly the remote villages near Altenau and the famous Brocken Mountain (3,768 feet), are isolated and difficult to reach. And because of the region's poorly structured bus system, one village often serves as a necessary stepping-stone to the next. Even Braunlage, a popular and comparatively accessible resort town, requires a half day of travel from Wernigerode, which in turn requires a full day of travel from Hannover or Erfurt. Sadly, the shortcomings of public transport have not kept tourism to a minimum. The majority of Harz Mountains visitors—a group that yearly increases in size—have their own cars and can thus hop at will from one village to the next. Budget travelers, on the other hand, must rely on buses, their wits, and their ability to befriend people with big cars.

Goslar

Embraced by the northern arms of the Harz range, Goslar grew wealthy on silver mining, and the resultingly rich Altstadt boasts some incredibly lovely timber-framed houses. In World War II, Allied bombers mercifully spared the town and its architectural treasures. The mines have only recently run dry, though memories of the silver age live on in various museums. Today, Goslar serves as the best jumping-off point for hikers heading into the Harz Mountains.

VISITOR INFORMATION **Tourist Information,** across the Marktplatz from the *Rathaus,* is often swamped, but for DM 3 they'll find you a room. *Markt 7, tel. 05321/42111. Open May–Oct., weekdays 9–6, Sat. 9–2; Nov.–Apr., weekdays 9–5, Sat. 9–1.*

Harzer Verkehrsverband (Marktstr. 45, tel. 05321/20031) brims with information on the Harz Mountains, though English brochures and speakers are nearly nonexistent.

COMING AND GOING **Trains** travel to Goslar from Braunschweig (one–two per hour, 1¼ hours, DM 12.60), Göttingen (one per hour, 1½ hours, DM 19), Hannover (one per hour, 1¼ hours, DM 19), and Hildesheim (one per hour, 45 minutes, DM 12.60). You can rent small DM 2 and larger DM 4 lockers in a corner of the Hauptbahnhof. The train station lies north of the Altstadt; walk about 10 minutes down Rosentorstraße to reach Marktplatz.

Buses leave from the train station and are invaluable for forays into the railless Harz Mountains. Consult the destination table outside the train station to find the appropriate carrier.

WHERE TO SLEEP **Gästehaus Noack.** If you're desperate, resort to this decrepit joint on the other side of a ferocious hill southeast of town. Two cranky old women rent out aging rooms in their home for DM 30 per person, regardless of whether you're alone or a couple. *Rosenberg 26, tel. 05321/22585.*

Hotel Goldener Stern. Close to the Altstadt, this hotel has clean and comfy singles for DM 30, DM 50 doubles without shower, and DM 60 doubles with shower. Call ahead. *Bäringer Str. 6, tel. 05321/23390.*

Pension Aschler. Run by the delightful Frau Aschler, this hotel is about a 15-minute walk from the station. Rooms, painted in broad beige tones, cost DM 35 for a single and DM 60 for a double. Televisions, phones, showers, and cloudlike comforters are standard, and a large buffet-style breakfast is included. Call ahead. *Klosterstr. 9A, tel. 05321/22574.*

➢ **HOSTEL • Jugendherberge Goslar.** This hostel perches on a hilltop far from town. A bed costs DM 16.50 (DM 20 for guests over 26) including breakfast, and sheets are DM 5. Reception is open 8:30–10 AM, 4–7, and 9:30–10. *Rammelsbergerstr. 25, tel. 05321/22240. Bus C (one per hr) to Theresienhof, or Bus A to Rammelsbergerstr.; look for signs and head uphill for 10–15 min.*

➢ **CAMPGROUND • Campingplatz Sennhütte.** Ten minutes out of town by bus, this is a nasty but cheap campground right on the edge of the B241 freeway. Sites are DM 4, plus DM 5 per person. *Clausthalerstr. 28, tel. 05321/22498. Bus toward Bockswiese to Sennhütte.*

FOOD You'll find the best deals not on the big tourist thoroughfares but one or two streets away; for example, check out the wide variety of reasonably priced restaurants on Worthstraße and Abzuchtstraße, just down the canal from the throngs of Hoher Weg. In the cozy hunting-cabin interior at **Horrido** (Breite Str. 96), hung with tiny antlers from unidentifiable critters, various wursts generally cost DM 10.50 or below; curry wurst and fries are DM 8. Down the street, **Percy's Pub** (Breite Str. 79) offers a multitude of DM 9.90 schnitzels, including a broccoli schnitzel with hollandaise sauce. **Prost Malzeit** (Fleischscharren at Marktplatz) spoons out cheap stand-up meals—curry wurst with bread is DM 4. On Tueday and Friday, the Marktplatz is home to a morning **market** that sells equally cheap, more nutritious food.

Catch up on your postcard writing amid the coffee scents of **Cafe Klatsch,** at the corner of Marktstraße and Bulkenstraße. At night, locals congregate in the dark and wacky recesses of **Das Total Verrückte Kneipen Cafe** (Fischemäker Str. 12), open nightly till 2.

WORTH SEEING All the major sites lie close to one another. It'll take only a day or two to tour the town on foot, but you ought to plan your attack in advance; a lot of places are open for short or eccentric hours.

➢ **ALTSTADT** • The 16th-century **Brusttuch** house (Hoher Weg behind the Marktkirche) is probably the best known of Goslar's old homes and adorns many a postcard. The wood-beam carvings depicting randy women, come-hither maidens, and naughty Cupids are products of the tremendous horniness that affected artisans' work during the German Renaissance. In general, though, Goslar's timber-frame buildings are more notable for aesthetic grace than inventiveness of detail. A handful of gorgeous buildings cluster near the corner of **Bergstraße** and **Schrieberstraße,** where vibrantly painted half-timbered houses contrast with **Siemenshaus,** the large brick-and-black-wood edifice at the intersection.

➢ **KAISERPFALZ** • The stern facade of this 12th-century imperial palace is about as interesting as this overrated building gets. Its imposing bulk and Roman windows look great from the outside, but the yawn-inspiring murals in the main hall and the diminutive **St.-Ulrichskapelle** hardly justify the DM 3.50 entrance fee (students DM 2). *Southern end of Altstadt. Open Apr.–Oct., daily 10–5; Nov.–Mar. daily 10–4.*

Goslar's cathedral used to stand at the bottom of the Kaiserpfalz's front yard. Destroyed in 1822, it's been replaced by a parking lot for tourist buses, but the preserved antechamber still stands. Inside, you can goggle at the 11th-century bronze imperial throne. Admission is free, and it's open the same hours as the palace.

➢ **MARKTPLATZ** • Several old edifices line this lovely little square; the sober **Rathaus** and a delicately crafted light gray-and-slate-hued building on the south offset the jovial red facade of the **Kaiserworth Hotel** and the central fountain's silly-looking imperial eagle. The **"Goslarer Elle"** rod, a medieval measurement specific to this city, hangs from a post in front of the Rathaus. A **Glockenspiel** depicts Goslar's mining history at 9, noon, 3, and 6.

The **Huldigungssaal** (Hall of Honor) in the Rathaus is painted with splendid but fragile 16th-century murals; at press time the town was agonizing about whether to close the deteriorating room. Until they decide, it's open June–September daily from 10 to 5, October–May from 10 to 4. The mandatory tours leave every half hour and cost DM 3 (DM 1.50 students).

Behind the Rathaus stands the **Marktkirche,** with its exquisitely detailed baptismal font depicting biblical scenes. Also note the frothy wooden altar and ornate, rainbow-hued pulpit, supported by bearded entities with breasts. *Open Tues.–Thurs., Sat. 10:30–3:30; Fri. 10:30–2; Sun. noon–3:30.*

➢ **MUSEUMS** • The **Mönchehaus,** a fantastic modern art museum, hangs cannily chosen exhibits in the old wood-beamed rooms of a 16th-century artisan's house. The contrast works wonders. Don't miss the yard and out-buildings in back. *Mönchestr. 3 at Jakobistr., tel. 05321/4948. Admission: DM 3.50, DM 2 students. Open Tues.–Sat. 10–1, 3–5; Sun. 10–1.*

The **Musikinstrumente und Puppenmuseum** is worth a visit more for its extensive musical collection than its attic display of Nordic-looking dolls. Instruments include a Brazilian *xarango*, with an aardvark for a sounding board, and an obese, three-string, four-foot-wide Russian balalaika. *Hoher Weg, tel. 05321/26945. Admission: DM 3.50. Open daily 11–5.*

For a fascinating glimpse of the town's mining heritage and a chance to put on miner's duds and explore the geological strata under the watchful eye of a tour guide, visit the **Rammelsberger Bergbaumuseum.** Try to find some silver to help you pay the stiff DM 6 entrance fee (DM 3.50 for those under 17). For a fun mouth game, repeat the museum's title endlessly. *Bergtal 19, tel. 05321/2891. Bus C to Hoher Weg/Amstgericht. Open daily 9:30–5.*

Bad Harzburg

Bad Harzburg has the look and feel of an expensive resort town. Despite its semi-isolated location, the city has gone overboard with its mountainside condominiums and expensive shopping avenues. The **Bummelallee,** Bad Harzburg's version of a smart Parisian-style street, is crowded with jewelers and smarmy clothing stores, and the adjacent Herzog-Wilhelm Straße brims with tourist shops and outrageously priced restaurants. Needless to say, Bad Harzburg is popular with an older, wealthier crowd and has little to offer the budget traveler. Unfortunately, Bad Harzburg is also the region's principal rail hub. If you're traveling by train, odds are you'll spend at least one night here waiting for a connection to Erfurt, Hannover, or Hamburg.

One of the few cheap things to do here is to ride the 1-kilometer-long (⅔-mile-long) **Bergbahn** (DM 3). This gondola connects the Kurpark lodge (from the tourist office, turn left on Am Stadtpark and follow the signs) with the undemanding peak of **Groß Burgberg** (1,590 feet), which is the trailhead for a dozen easy trails (ski slopes in winter). For information on winter ski rentals and lift tickets (DM 70), contact the main lodge, the **Harzburger Hof** (opposite the Kurpark, tel. 05322/3044), or the tourist office. Otherwise, there's good summer hiking to the south and west of Bad Harzburg, and in the forest that abuts the ski resort's main lodge.

BASICS The **tourist office** is 1 kilometer (½ mile) south of the train station; you'll see signs leading to it from the Bummelallee (turn right past the post office). *Kurverwaltung, tel. 05332/75300. Open weekdays 9–5, Sat. 9–1.*

The **post office** offers the usual services, as well as an international phone desk. *Herzog-Wilhelm Str. 80 at Bummelallee, tel. 05332/7870. Open Mon.–Sat. 9–4:30.*

For currency exchange, head to the **Harzburger Volksbank** (Herzog-Wilhelm Str. 84, tel. 05332/75390).

COMING AND GOING The **Bahnhof** (Am Bahnhof Platz, tel. 05332/4360) is 1 kilometer (½ mile) north of Bad Harzburg's small city center; head straight out of the station and walk to the end of Herzog-Wilhelm Straße. Inside the depot, you'll find timetables and an information desk (open weekdays 9–5), generally staffed by German-speakers only. From Bad Harzburg, five trains go daily to Hannover (DM 21) and

Göttingen, where you must transfer to reach Erfurt. Three trains run daily to nearby Goslar (DM 3), where you can catch a connecting train to Osterode (DM 10.80), Nordhausen (DM 20), and Hamburg (DM 65).

Most **buses** bound for the Harz Mountains leave from the Bahnhof, but only the tourist office has an English-speaking staff to help with timetable and route questions. Bus destinations from the Bahnhof include Wernigerode (2 daily, DM 9), Braunlage (6 daily, DM 8), Torfhaus (6 daily, DM 6.80), and Osterode (3 daily, DM 10.40).

WHERE TO SLEEP AND EAT The youth hostel **Braunschweiger Haus** (Waldstr. 5, tel. 05322/4582) has beds for DM 20; reception is open from 3:30 PM. The hostel lies 2 kilometers (1 mile) from the train station; to get there, walk straight out of the depot to the end of Herzog-Wilhelm Straße, then to the end of the pedestrians-only Bummelallee. Turn left on Papenbergstraße, and then right on Waldstraße.

According to legend, the world's witches gather on the summit of Brocken on Walpurgisnacht (April 30) to brew up some mischief. A version of this appears in Goethe's Faust; *Goethe himself was an avid walker who spent many summers in the area.*

Restaurants in Bad Harzburg include the excellent but expensive **China Haus** (Herzog-Wilhelm Str. 11A, tel. 05322/50814), and the more reasonably priced **Mythos** (Herzog-Wilhelm Str. 48, tel. 05332/50364), a popular Greek eatery. For cheaper meals try any of the wurst stands in the city center; for outstanding coffee try **Cafe Rosé** (Papenbergstr. 3–5, tel. 05332/2377).

NEAR BAD HARZBURG

West of Bad Harzburg, the Harz Mountains become steep and dramatic, dotted with lakes and covered with thick forests. For serious hikers the villages of Altenau and Torfhaus are a must, for both their quiet isolation and their proximity to the area's best hiking trails. Of particular note is the Brocken (3,768 feet), the tallest peak in the Harz range.

Beautiful as these villages are, the hassle of reaching them may outweigh their limited offerings. A more urban option is Braunlage, a more accessible burg that has struck a happy balance between its beerhalls and gift shops and its stunning mountain setting. Either way, the only way into the region is by bus from Bad Harzburg; service between Bad Harzburg, Torfhaus, and Braunlage is the most frequent. Less frequent, especially during winter, are buses for Altenau.

BRAUNLAGE Braunlage, 26 kilometers (16 miles) south of Bad Harzburg, is a good place to come for a healthy dose of the Harz Mountains without straying too far from urban comforts. As one of the region's principal tourist resorts, it has all the amenities of a large town—budget pensions, beerhalls, restaurants, and gift shops—happily mixed with first-rate scenery and convenient access to alpine trails. Braunlage is no secret, though, so prepare yourself for large crowds and inflated prices, especially during the ski season. The ski slopes are too gentle and undemanding, but they're still exceedingly popular with wealthy German families, who find them ideal for showing off their new skiwear. Braunlage's three ski areas are carved out of the **Wurmberg** (3,204 feet), one of the region's tallest peaks. A lift leads to some novice slopes behind the Rathaus on Albrecht Straße; otherwise, ride the **Wurmberg Seilbahn** cable car to the top for DM 10. You'll find signs leading to both in front of the **tourist office** (Elbingeröder Str. 17, tel. 05520/1054).

After the spring thaw, Braunlage also makes an excellent base for hiking. The village is split by the lazy Warme Bode river; if you follow this south for 7 kilometers (4 miles) you'll end up in the remote, picture-perfect village of **Tanne.** Another good extended hike is to **St. Andreasberg,** 5 kilometers (3 miles) west. Stop by the tourist office for detailed maps and suggestions. A good option for a short day hike is the **Wurmberg summit** itself: You can take the cable car to the mountaintop Bergstation and return to

Braunlage via one of a dozen well-marked trails. The most scenic trail is the 3-kilometer (2-mile) **Bärenbrücke**; the most demanding is the 13-kilometer (8-mile) **Dreieckiger Pfahl,** which offers good views of the nearby Brocken.

➢ **COMING AND GOING** • The **Busbahnhof** (Bahnhofstr., tel. 05520/2241) is ½ kilometer (⅓ mile) south of the village center. Turn right from the station and walk down Bahnhofstraße, which quickly turns into Herzog-Wilhelm Straße. Destinations from Braunlage include Bad Harzburg (four per day, DM 5), St. Andreasberg (two per day, DM 3.20), Torfhaus (four per day, DM 3.80), and Weringerode (two per day, DM 13).

➢ **WHERE TO SLEEP AND EAT** • Braunlage's **Jugendherberge** (Von-Lagen Str. 63, off Herzog-Wilhelm Str., tel. 05520/2238) is tucked in the woods on the fringe of town; DM 19.50 will get you a bed, and the reception opens at 3 PM. For a few extra marks you can get a well-equipped private room at the **Hotel Parkblick** (Elbingeröder Str. 13, tel. 05520/1237), two doors down from the tourist office; rates run DM 25 per person including breakfast. Another good bet is the intimate, family-run **Haus Irene** (Herzog-Wilhelm Str. 15, tel. 05520/1302), with rooms for DM 24 per person with breakfast; it closes in November and December. Braunlage's only **campground** (Rte. B27, tel. 05520/413) is 1.5 kilometers (1 mile) west of the bus station. From the depot, turn right onto Bahnhofstraße, left on Wiesen Straße, and then left again on Lauterberger Straße; walk under the B4/Bad Harzburg overpass and veer left at the sign 100 yards ahead. Sites run DM 11; the campground is closed February–March.

Harzburger Straße and Herzog-Wilhelm Straße boast the highest concentration of beerhalls and restaurants. **Wienerwald** (Herzog-Wilhelm Str. 30, tel. 05520/1410) does traditional German meals for under DM 25. If you're sick of wieners and beer, try **Rhodos** (Elbingeröder Str. 30, tel. 05520/2223), a popular Greek restaurant that also serves excellent pizza (DM 10).

ALTENAU AND TORFHAUS Despite its isolation, the village of **Altenau** is equipped with dozens of beerhalls and pensions, and its well-groomed streets teem with German families in summer. For hikers its most important feature is its location, at the foot of three very challenging trails. The first is the 28-kilometer (17-mile) **Bruchberg,** which winds its way through dense forest before cresting on the Bruchberg Summit (3,033 feet), after which it's an easy descent into Torfhaus. Another good trail is the **Polsterberger,** a moderately difficult 15-kilometer (9-mile) hike that skirts dozens of teardrop lakes before reaching the village of Clausthal-Zellerfeld. Finally, there's the **St. Andreasberg** trail, a 19-kilometer (12-mile) journey that leads to the remote village of St. Andreasberg; unfortunately, you also have to hike back or try your luck at hitching. Before heading out on any of these hikes, pick up a detailed elevation map from Altenau's **tourist office** (Kurverwaltung, Schultal Str., tel. 05328/8020), located 150 yards east of the bus depot on the Torfhaus/Bad Harzburg road.

There's a **Jugendherberge** (Auf der Rose 11, tel. 05328/361) on the south side of the village, with beds for DM 19.50 per person. To get here, turn left as you exit the bus depot, go left again on Marktstraße, and then continue south; the road changes its name four times—to Breite Straße, Große Oker, Schatzkammerstraße, and finally Auf der Rose. More comfortable is **Haus Sachsenross** (Kleine Oker 46, tel. 05328/201), a family-owned pension off Breite Straße, with rooms for DM 34 per person. Slightly cheaper are **Anneliese Günther's** private rooms (Breite Str. 33, tel. 05328/608), which cost only DM 16 per person. As for food, the **Hotel Deutsches Haus** (Marktstr. 17, tel. 05328/350) serves traditional German fare—wurst, sauerkraut, and beer—for under DM 18 per person, from 9 AM until 10 PM. **Cafe Meier** (Breite Str. 32, tel. 05328/354), open 11–11, is similarly priced and has a large selection of regional beers.

Torfhaus, 4 kilometers (2½ miles) east of Altenau, consists of just a few hotels and a **Jugendherberge** (Torfhaus Str. 3, tel. 05320/242, DM 21 per night). If you end up here, though, you probably didn't come for the amenities, but to hike. Head in any direction from this puny mountaintop burg and you'll lose yourself in a maze of pristine forest and uninhabited valleys. The area immediately surrounding Torfhaus is laced with cross-country ski trails that also make excellent summer day hikes. Or try the marked **Bruchberg** trek (*see* Altenau, *above*), connecting Torfhaus with Altenau; there's a sign for the trailhead by the Torfhaus youth hostel.

Four daily buses connect Bad Harzburg and Braunlage with Torfhaus. One-way fare from either town costs under DM 5. Torfhaus's bus stop is on the B4 highway, near the large parking lot. From here you can also catch the bus to Altenau (DM 3), which leaves once daily at 10:40 AM in summer (Mon.–Sat.), and weekdays at 11 AM in winter.

Wernigerode

Wernigerode was first established in 1230, yet it wasn't until the early 1900s that its stunning Mühlental Valley location was exploited by tourists in search of a pastoral hideaway. Today, there are a few ruthlessly modern shops and hotels in the city center, but much of historic Wernigerode looks as it always has—a dense jumble of half-timbered houses and cobbled plazas. To get a good sense of this, spend some time exploring **Am Markt,** its central marketplace, and the maze of streets that fan out from it. Besides the street sellers who gather here most afternoons, Am Markt's main attraction is the 13th-century **Rathaus** (Am Markt 1, tel. 0927/33904), which houses an expensively atmospheric beerhall, open daily 11–11. More interesting is the **Oberfarrkirchof,** a shaded 13th-century square directly behind the Rathaus. Across from here is the **Schloß Wernigerode Harzmuseum** (Am Klint 10, tel. 0927/3700), with a good exhibit on the town's history; admission is DM 4. One block east is the 18th-century **Kochstraße House** (Kochstr. 43, closed to public), Wernigerode's smallest dwelling. Only 10 feet wide and 14 feet tall, this privately owned timber house has just one room and a Hobbit-size door. One block north on Breite Straße, look for **No. 72** and **No. 95.** No. 72, an intricately carved timber house, was built in 1674 and is considered Wernigerode's best example of Baroque styling. No. 95 was built in 1678; the sculpted horsehead indicates its role as the town's smithy.

Famed for its Baroque architecture and colorful open-air bazaars, Wernigerode offers a refreshing example of a village that has escaped the worst effects of tourism and resort-building, albeit at a rather extreme cost—45 years of communist rule.

Wernigerode occupies a flat expanse in the Mühlental Valley, a semiforested plateau cut in half by the Holtemme and Zillierbach rivers. You need to go deeper into the Harz Mountains for serious hiking, but for a good short walk, head to **Wernigerode Schloß,** the city's brick-and-timber castle. Built in 1202 and greatly reinforced in the late 17th century, it now contains a small folk museum, immaculately restored rooms, and beautiful examples of Renaissance carving and carpets. But the views are the main reason to make the steep, 30-minute climb from the city center. From Am Markt, walk south down Marktstraße, turn left on Bach Straße, right on Thälmann Straße, left on Bohlweg, then right on Am Schloß. *Am Schloß, tel. 0927/3245. Open daily 10–5.*

BASICS Wernigerode's **tourist office** is one block east of Am Markt and the Rathaus. It has no brochures in English, but it does have city maps and information on private rooms. *Breite Str. 12, tel. 0927/33035. Open Mon.–Sat. 9–5.*

Near the tourist office is **Ratsapotheke,** the local pharmacy. *Breite Str. 22, tel. 0927/32439. Open weekdays 9–5.*

The **post office** is one block south of Am Markt. Inside is an international telephone annex for collect and direct-dial calls, but be prepared to wait upwards of an hour for connections to the States. *Marktstr., tel. 0927/32178. Open Mon.–Sat. 8–6.*

To change money head to any of the banks huddled near Am Markt, or try the **Volksbank.** *Breite Str., across from tourist office, tel. 0927/32185. Open Sun.–Wed., Fri., Sat. 8–4, Thurs. 8–5.*

COMING AND GOING Wernigerode's principal train depot, the **Bahnhof** (Bahnhofstr., tel. 0927/36331), is 2 kilometers (1 mile) north of the city center. Turn right from the station, left on Albert-Bartels-Straße, then right on Breite Straße; the tourist office is 50 yards ahead on your left. From Wernigerode, the only destination of note is Nordhausen (three per day, DM 15 single), from where there are daily connections to Erfurt, Bad Harzburg, Eisenach, Weimar, and Hannover. If you're headed deeper into the Harz Mountains, consider going by bus. Buses leave the **bus depot** (tel. 0927/21150), adjacent to the Bahnhof, for Bad Harzburg (two per day, DM 9), Braunlage (two per day, DM 13), and Osterode (1 daily, DM 22).

WHERE TO SLEEP AND EAT Wernigerode has two youth hostels. The first **Jugendherberge** (Friedrichstr. 53, tel. 0927/32061) is 2 kilometers (1 mile) west of the city center. From Am Markt, walk west on Westernstraße, turn right on Bach Straße, then left onto Friedrich Straße. A bed here will cost you DM 19, and the reception desk is open from 3 to 8 PM. The second **Jugendherberge** (Am Großen Bleek 27, tel. 0927/32059) is smaller and closer to town; beds cost DM 18, and the reception desk is open from 3 to 11 PM. To get here from Am Markt, walk south on Marktstraße and cross the river; turn right on Hilleborchstraße, left on Lindenbergstraße, and then right onto Am Großen Bleek. Otherwise, there's a handful of pensions near the Bahnhof; try **Günther Koch** (Bahnhofstr. 10, no tel.), DM 25 per person.

Dozens of cafés and beer halls cluster around Am Markt. Streetside foodstands sell the cheapest grub—wurst and fries—or try **Zur Post** (Marktstr. 17, tel. 0927/32436) for traditional dinners between DM 15 and DM 20.

Lüneburger Heide

Anchored by the towns of Lüneburg to the north and Celle to the south, the Lüneburger Heide encompasses several large and beautiful nature parks, famous for their heaths (*Heiden*). The heather, kept knee high by the nibblings of ridiculous-looking sheep, blooms gloriously into seas of vibrant purple in August and early September; the frequently foggy weather during those months is the only reminder that you're not in Provence. If you miss the blooming heather or you've left behind your purple Insta-Bloom Goggles, don't fret; the wild fields and forests are lovely year-round. The rolling countryside ranges from dense stands of fir to scattered birch and brush. Scattered throughout the area are myriad backwater hamlets that will acquaint you with small-town German life. The region rewards the bold and intrepid; the farther out you go, the better you'll grasp the allure of its tiny towns and unspoiled natural beauty. Though small, the towns of Lüneburg and Celle are lively refuges; Celle holds more than one attraction up its sleeve, and Lüneburg offers a sparky nightlife.

BASICS

VISITOR INFORMATION By far the richest source of information, **Fremdenverkehrsverband Lüneburg Heide** in Lüneburg overflows with pamphlets on the whole region. None of the staff speaks English, but they stock thick *Urlaubs-Magazins,* in which you'll find hotel listings, bike rentals, riding stables, and swimming spots. If you can summon up the German, ask them to set you up for the night in a bed-and-breakfast farmhouse. *Am Sande 5, tel. 04131/42006. Open Mon.–Thurs. 7:30–5.*

COMING AND GOING The rail line between Hamburg and Hannover runs through Lüneburg and Celle; if you're coming from Bremen, though, you need to change trains in Harburg. Trains will take you to the big towns, but only buses run to the small towns and parks on the heath. Whatever your destination, ask at the station; infrequent train service is often supplemented by bus service. Happily, cars are forbidden within the nature parks; instead, you can ride in a horse-drawn carriage, rent bikes, or walk along the fenced-off trails. The regional tourist office in Lüneburg (*see above*) has addresses of bike-rental places, plus maps of good local biking roads. They also pass out *Reiten*, a guide to horsey pleasures around the heath.

WHERE TO SLEEP The area's hotels can be hopelessly jammed from June through early September; always call ahead to find out if there are any rooms available. *Heu-Hotels*, farmhouses that give you a stack of comfy hay and a big breakfast for about DM 15, dot the area, including one in Celle, one in Bispingen on the eastern edge of the *Naturpark*, and a handful southeast of Lüneburg. Ask the regional tourist office in Lüneburg (*see above*) for a list. The regional office also stocks the *Lüneburg Heide Gastgeberverzeichnis*, a guide to accommodations throughout the entire region.

FOOD *Heide* specialties include anything made from the meat of the *Heidschnucken*, the long-horned, straggly haired sheep that graze the heath. Industrious heath bees produce loads of delicious honey.

Lüneburg

The calm brick facades of centuries-old houses line Lüneburg's sedate Altstadt; harmonious and unassuming, many are minor architectural wonders. They were built on the wealth of the large salt mines deep below the city, which supplied all of Denmark and Northern Germany back in the days when salt was as good as gold. The salt mines closed forever in 1980, but you can get a taste of what it was all about in the *Salzmuseum* (Salt Museum). Lüneburg has an extraordinary nightlife for a town its size; the bars on Stintmarkt nightly see throngs of happily hammered college students.

BASICS Dial 04131/1091 for the **Lüneburg police,** 04131/31878 for an **ambulance,** and 04131/7171 for the town **hospital.** Lüneburg's main **post office** (Bahnhofstr. 3, tel. 04131/707402) is visible from the train station.

The **tourist office** sits in the yellow Rathaus on Marktplatz; the unsympathetic staff doesn't speak English and charges DM 5 to find rooms. *Am Markt, tel. 04131/309593. Open weekdays 9–1, 2–6; Sat. 9–1; May–Sept. also Sun. 9–1.*

COMING AND GOING Lüneburg has two train stations, facing one another across Bahnhofsplatz. If you come from Hamburg (one–three per hour, 45 minutes, DM 10.80), Hannover (one–two trains per hour, 50 minutes, DM 30), or Lübeck (one–two per hour, 1 hour, DM 16.80), you arrive at the **Bahnhof Ost.** From here, go right, down a short hill, turn left on Lünertorstraße, and then left on Bardowicker Straße to find the Marktplatz. **Bahnhof West** only serves small nearby destinations.

WHERE TO SLEEP Lüneburg's surprisingly expensive hotels fill to the bursting point in August. **Hotel Lübecker Hof** (Lünertorstr. 12, tel. 04131/51420) has fine rooms and a distinguished entryway close to the station. Singles are DM 38–DM 52, depending on amenities, and doubles are DM 65–DM 98. Call at least a week in advance, if possible. **Hotel "Stadt Hamburg"** (Am Sande 25, tel. 04131/44438) has an even grander entryway and an even longer waiting list; singles are DM 35–DM 45, and doubles run DM 60–DM 80.

The **Jugendherberge** (Soltauer Str. 133, tel. 04131/41864) is often full, especially in summer. The affable but firm owner sometimes puts up desperate hostellers on mattresses in the basement. The reception desk is open between 4 and 7 PM and from 9:45 to 10 PM. Beds are DM 16.50 (DM 20 for guests over 26), and sheets an extra DM 5. Unfortunately, the 10 PM curfew is for real. To get here from Am Sande, head down Rote Straße, bear right onto Lindenstraße, then cut left on Solltauer Straße; if you want to avoid the 40-minute walk, take Bus 1 (DM 2) to Scharnhorstraße.

Camping Rote Schleuze (tel. 04131/791500) lies an hour's walk south of town, on the left off the B4; take the bus toward Deutschevern. Sites are DM 3 (DM 7.50 for a tent and car spot), plus DM 5 per person.

If you can't find a place to stay in Lüneburg, **Uelzen**'s youth hostel (Fischerhof 1, tel. 0581/5312) can probably bail you out. The problem is that Uelzen is 35 kilometers (21 miles) south of Lüneburg, or 20 minutes away by train (DM 8.40).

FOOD University students hang out and bullshit in the hip brick-and-wood interior of **Camus** (Am Sande 30, at the bottom of the square), where pizzas runs about DM 11, although you can get a cheese-on-a-crust version for DM 6.80. There are also a dozen "vegetarian" choices, but read the ingredients carefully—many are just *mostly* vegetarian. The blander **Tolstefanz** (Am Berge 26), just down the street, also attracts a student crowd with its varied menu: spinach pasta with cheese, ham, and a salad runs DM 10; baguette sandwiches are DM 6–DM 7. **Gärtnerhof Neuland** (Rosenstr. 50) serves as the local hippie provisions store, and whips up some impressive carrot soup (DM 5) and bean-sprout sandwiches (DM 2.50). **Lüneburg Nudelkontor** (Auf dem Kauf 1) doles out generous portions of delicious tortellini, lasagna, and spaghetti, all for around DM 7. The cheapest-eats-in-town award goes to the cafeteria-style **Sandkrug,** at the bottom of Am Sande, where the mostly elderly diners munch three-course meals for DM 5.50–DM 9.50 (open daily 8 to 6). **Markets** appear in front of the Rathaus on Wednesday and Saturday mornings.

WORTH SEEING Don't miss the brick beauties lining Lüneburg's streets; grab the *Walk through Lüneburg* brochure at the tourist office for an intelligently planned tour. The area down by the old crane and the Abbot's Water Tower is especially picturesque.

Two kilometers (1 mile) north of town stands the **Kloster Lüne** (Domanehöf, over the Lünetor Bridge), a 15th-century monastery with an assortment of idyllic brick and half-timbered houses. *Tour: DM 4. Tours Apr.–Oct. 15, Mon.–Sat. 9–11:30, 2:30–5.*

Delve into the saline secrets of the town's biggest cash cow at the **Salzmuseum,** an excellent attempt to explain all aspects of the salt industry. Everything's in German, though. *Sulfmeisterstr. 1, tel. 04131/45065. Admission: DM 4, DM 3 students. Open weekdays 9–5, weekends 10–5.*

The interior of the medieval **Rathaus,** on the west side of the Marktplatz, is probably one of the most impressive in Germany. The 14th-century main hall features intricate stained-glass windows and fancy ceiling and wall decorations. Tour guides shuttle you through for a stiff DM 5 (students DM 3.50); tours leave hourly 10–4 from Tuesday through Sunday. On Am Sande looms the brick bulk of **St. Johanniskirche.** Parts of the church date back to the 14th century, but the building is probably most famous for its massive pipe organ, cobbled together with parts dating from the 16th to 18th century. The Gothic **Michaeliskirche,** on J.S.-Bach-Platz in the western part of the town, was built of brick on sinking ground; as a result, the steeple now leans drunkenly to one side; stand in the nave and look back to get the gist.

Talk to the tourist office about tours to the enormous **Scharnebeck ship factory,** 8 kilometers (5 miles) northeast of town. Alternatively, rent a bike at **Laden 25** (Am Werder 25, tel. 04131/37960) for DM 12 a day, and ride there yourself. Bus 1 goes there from Am Sande, too; before you board, make sure it stops at the Schiffshebewerk; not all buses do.

AFTER DARK Students frolic, beer in hand, on Stintmarkt, down by the river across from the old crane. Indistinguishable but great bars tirelessly hand out brews for DM 2 a glass, DM 4 per mug. **Pit's Bierbar** (9 Obere Schrangenstr.), Lüneburg's gay bar, opens nightly at 6 PM. **Copntra** (Auf der Altstadt 8), an alternative dance club and café, presents films and a wide variety of live music, as well as monthly lesbian and gay nights. The monthly ***21zwanzig*** periodical covers the music and theater scene in Lüneburg and nearby Uelzen.

NEAR LUNEBURG

NATURSCHUTZGEBIET LUNEBURGER HEIDE Dozens of parks are scattered across the entire region from Celle to Lüneburg, but the best spots—and the most visited—lie west of Lüneburg in the Naturschutzgebiet Lüneburger Heide. Here, large fields bloom on low hills freckled with sparse pine and birch, and sandy paths cut through the area. Seven herds of *Heidschnucken*, an odd brand of sheep with the long hair and curved horns of goats, roam the heath, keeping the heather low by eating it. Climb the 557-foot **Wilseder Berg** to look out over the heaths, then visit the gorgeous, juniper-strewn **Totengrund Valley,** both half-hour walks from the hamlet of **Wilsede** (population 40).

Though not technically on the heath, **Undeloh** (population 850) is the best base for further forays, for three reasons. First, Bus 1910 travels here every other hour from Lüneburg, and Bus 1901 does the same from Hamburg. Second, it has an embarrassment of cheap lodgings; five pensions have beds for under DM 26. Ask the **Verkehrsverein** (Zur Dorfeiche, tel. 04189/333) or the tourist office in Lüneburg for the list. There's also a **Jugendherberge** (Heimbucherstr. 2, tel. 04189/279) with beds for DM 15 (over 26, DM 18). Third, you can rent bikes here: **Seume-Haus** (Wilseder Str. 23, tel. 04189/294) rents bikes for DM 2.50 per hour, DM 8 per day; **Homann** (Wilseder Str. 7, tel. 04189/234) rents bikes for DM 2.50 per hour, DM 9 per day; and **Hotel Heiderose** (Wilseder Str. 13, tel. 04189/311) rents bikes for DM 3 per hour, DM 10 per day. You can also hire a horse-drawn carriage (around DM 10 per person) for a 2½-hour ride through the heath; just look for the parked carriages downtown.

Another good base is **Bispingen,** which has a youth hostel (Töpinger Str. 42, tel. 05194/2375) with beds for DM 16 per night (over 26, DM 19.50), a Heu-Hotel (Greyenhof 6, tel. 05194/1294) with piles of fresh hay for DM 14.14, and bike rentals. Buses run to and from Lüneburg. **Egestorf,** on the same bus line as Undeloh, has the nearest Campingplatz (Landesieger, tel. 04175/661).

Celle

Celle has a tourist problem. Like bees to flowers, visitors swarm around the town's 480 colorfully painted timber-framed houses. Even if you think you might barf if you see one more half-timbered house, Celle does have some refreshingly different attractions that merit a day trip: A rare prewar synagogue, a bee institute, and a magnificent stud farm lie scattered on the town's southern fringe; what's more, they're all free. Far more sobering is a visit to the monument on the site of the Bergen-Belsen concentration camp, an hour's bus ride out of town.

BASICS Dial 05141/2771 for **police,** 05141/6034 for an **ambulance,** and 05141/3081 for the **hospital.** Celle's central **post office** is at Schloßplatz 8 (tel. 05141/170), across from the castle.

The sleekly modern **Tourist-Information** sits across the street from the elaborately painted *Rathaus*, and will book rooms for free. *Markt 6, tel. 05141/1212. Open May–Oct. 15, weekdays 9–6, Sat. 9–1 and 2–5, Sun. 10–12; Nov.–Apr., weekdays 9–5, Sat. 10–noon.*

COMING AND GOING Celle lies on the big Hannover–Hamburg rail line; three–four trains head to Hannover each hour (45 minutes, DM 10.80), and one goes hourly to Hamburg (1½ hours, DM 32) by way of Lüneburg (45 minutes, DM 19). To get to town from the station, take Bus 2, 3, or 4 to the castle (DM 2), or walk down Bahnhofstraße and head left when you see the cobblestones of the pedestrian zone.

WHERE TO SLEEP Celle's cheapest lodging lies far from the center; expect to pay DM 50 minimum for a hotel in town. By far the most adventurous sleeping option is Celle's own **Heu-Hotel** (Lachtehäuser Str. 28, tel. 05141/34002), where an exuberantly friendly family will give you, as a bed, a big pile of fresh hay in a large barn, plus a monstrous and delicious breakfast, all for DM 14.14. Warning: You and your sleeping bag (you need your own) will smell strongly of hay. To get here, take Bus 2 or 5 to Langenhangen, 4 kilometers (2½ miles) away. Of course, the big black **Jugendherberge** (Weghausstr. 2, tel. 05141/53208) has its own inescapable smell, situated as it is in the middle of horse pastures a half-hour walk north of town. DM 16.50 (over 26, DM 21) gets you a bed and breakfast. Reception stays open between 5 and 7 PM; doors close at 10. To reach the hostel, go left out of the station, following the tracks, turn left on Bremer Weg, and then right at the sign on Petersburgstraße; otherwise, take Bus 3 to Dorfstraße. **Raststätte Davy** (Celler Str. 43, tel. 05141/51765) has an Englishman for an owner; small but pretty rooms go for DM 40 (singles) and DM 70 (doubles). Take Bus 11 (direction Hustedt) from the Schloß to Lange Straße, a 4-kilometer (2½-mile) trip.

FOOD The Französischer Garten and the park around the Schloß are great for picnics. To get all the fixin's, head for the morning market held on Wednesday and Saturday at Brandplatz and around the Rathaus; in addition, the **Ronitz** bakery on Großer Plan has big 500g loaves of pesto bread for DM 3.80. **Pizzeria Vulcano** on Großer Plan at Poststraße has late hours and DM 3.50 slices of pizza, though the tuna-and-onion one is not recommended.

WORTH SEEING The standard walking tour, indicated on the tourist office's map, assures you of seeing almost all of the town's *Fachwerk* (half-timbered) houses, though it's better to hit the biggies quickly, then sneak off to the smaller, less frequented side streets where the houses aren't obscured by seas of video cameras and trinket hawkers. If you're short on time, forget the **Schloß.** The unbelievably boring tour, in German only, goes into coma-inducing detail about all its past owners; even the opulent chapel at the end isn't reward enough. Tours begin hourly between 10 and 4 (except at noon) and cost DM 2.

Among the more interesting buildings in town are the **Hoppener Haus** (Rundestr. at Poststr.), a half-timbered house built in 1526; the **Löwenapothek,** a 16th-century pharmacy on Stechbahn; and the Weser Renaissance-style **Rathaus,** with its 14th-century pub. At Im Kreise 24 stands one of Germany's oldest surviving **synagogues,** though it was so energetically restored in the '70s that it hardly shows its 250 years. All decoration was destroyed during Kristallnacht, but the building escaped being burned, and the rabbi saved the torah (ask to see it). The synagogue is open only Tuesday–Friday 3–5; yarmulkes (traditional skullcaps) are provided for men.

From there, walk down Wehlstraße to the **Bieneninstitut** (Bee Institute) and its gardens (open weekdays 9–noon and 2–4). Wade through clouds of bees near hive entrances, and open the side panels of the thin yellow hive boxes. Behind the institute lies the **Französischer Garden,** green, manicured, and very French.

From the south side of the Schloß, walk down Hannoversche Straße and turn right on Spörckenstraße to the **Niedersächsisches Landgestüt** (Stud Farm), where 200 superb stallions live to propagate their oh-so-expensive genes. The studs are truly magnificent. In late September and October, the horses are put through their paces at the popular **Hengstparade** (Stallion Parade); unfortunately, you have to buy tickets months in advance. *Stables open to public mid-July–mid-Feb., weekdays 8:30–11:30, 3–4:30.*

NEAR CELLE

WIENHAUSEN Ten kilometers (6 miles) southeast of Celle and accessible by both bus and train, this half-timbered village is remarkable for its soul-soothing **Kloster,** a 13th-century nunnery composed of several impressive brick buildings that are still in operation today. The nuns themselves give tours of the interior and the delicate, luminously painted chancel. The nunnery's famous tapestries go on show annually for 11 days around Pentecost, in mid-June. *Tours: DM 5, DM 3 students. Tours Mon.–Sat. hourly 10–11 and 2–5, Sun. 11:30 and hourly 1–5; Nov.–Mar., last tour at 4.*

BERGEN-BELSEN Though British troops burned down the barracks in May 1945, an obelisk, memorial wall, document room, and mass graves mark the site of what was the Bergen-Belsen concentration camp. Around 50,000 Jews, mostly women, and 30,000–50,000 Russian, French, and Belgian soldiers died here. Most died from the extreme overcrowding in the last months before Liberation. Go, and give yourself some time. Bus 104 makes the one-hour journey from Celle's *Bahnhof* at 11:55, 1:40 (the ideal time), and 3:45; the only bus back leaves at 4:54. No buses run on weekends.

Bremen

In the fairy tale by the Brothers Grimm, the Bremen town musicians never actually make it to Bremen; the donkey, dog, cat, and rooster scare a band of thieves from their forest hideout with their raucous music, and decide to stay there instead. Don't make the same mistake. Bremen has enough great neighborhoods—perfect for lazy exploration and long café schmoozes—to avoid the Rathaus–Museum–Schloß rut altogether (besides, there is no Schloß).

You would never know that Bremen is Germany's second-largest port. Not only is it many kilometers from the sea (ships travel up the Weser River to the North Sea), but it doesn't suffer from the industrial disease so common in major port cities. For example, the Schnoor quarter's medieval roofs shelter artisans' shops and excellent restaurants; on Bötcherstraße, shops peep out from art nouveau brick whimsies; and Ostertorsteinweg is as close as a German street gets to Haight-Ashbury. Bremen, along with its deep-water harbor at Bremerhaven, makes up the smallest Land in Germany; its government, one of the most leftist in Germany, is responsible for the freewheeling, alternative atmosphere at Bremen's university.

BASICS

AMERICAN EXPRESS Friendly AmEx flunkies greet you at their office up the hill from Herdentorsteinweg; they change money and cash traveler's checks for no charge, hold mail for clients, run an efficient travel service, and even give advice on discothèques. *Am Wall 138, tel. 0421/14171. Open weekdays 9–5:30, Sat. 9–noon.*

BUCKET SHOPS The **Hapag-Lloyd Reisebüro** is a good bet for last-minute flights as well as student fares and special train tickets. *Bahnhofspl. 17, beside Hauptbahnhof, tel. 0421/350065. Open weekdays 9–6, Sat. 9:30–12:30.*

LAUNDRY **Wasch-O-Center,** the laundromat closest to the town center, washes 7 kilograms for DM 6; dryers cost DM 1 for 15 minutes. *Vor dem Steintor 75. Open daily 7 AM–10 PM.*

MAIL AND PHONES The clean **post office,** to the left as you walk out of the train station, has a do-it-yourself fax, plenty of phones, *poste restante* service (address Hauptpostamt Bremen, 2800 Bremen 5), and a currency exchange desk that offers decent rates and a DM 3 commission on traveler's checks. *An der Weide at Löningstr. Open daily, 7 AM–10 PM.*

VISITOR INFORMATION **Tourist-Information,** though large, suffers from a paucity of English-speakers and a complete lack of acceptable maps. However, they will let you pore through their *Bremen* magazine for free. Pay DM 3 and a DM 10 deposit for the room-finding service. *Hillmannpl. 6, across Bahnhofpl. from Hauptbahnhof, tel. 0421/308000. Open weekdays 9:30–6:30, Thurs. 9:30–8:30, Sat. 9:30–2, Sun. 9:30–3:30.*

COMING AND GOING

BY TRAIN Bremen's neoclassical **Hauptbahnhof** lies near the tourist office, just north of the city center. Trains arrive here from Berlin (one per hour, 6 hours, DM 78), Göttingen (two per hour, 2½ hours, DM 54), Hamburg (two per hour, 1¼ hours, DM 28), and Hannover (two per hour, 1½ hours, DM 29). The station info office is open daily 5:50 AM–10 PM. You can rent a small locker for DM 2, a larger one for DM 4. **Buses** to nearby attractions like Worpswede and the industrial port of Vegesack leave from in front of the Bahnhof.

HITCHING The distant autobahns are a pain in the ass to reach; don't even try to walk to them. The A27 runs north to Bremerhaven and south through Hannover; to get to it, take Tram 5 to Kulenkampfallee, then Bus 21 to W.-V.-Siemens-Straße. The A1 runs northeast to Hamburg and southwest to Düsseldorf; to get to it, ride Tram 1 south to Kattenturm-Mitte, then Bus 51 to Arster Landstraße.

The **Mitfahrbüro** (Körnerwall 1, off Sielwall between Ostertorsteineweg and Osterdeich, tel. 0421/72022) finds travelers long-distance rides with drivers for nominal fees; it also manages a student-oriented travel agency.

BY FERRY Daily **Schreiber Reederei** ferries (Schlachte 2, tel. 0421/321229) leave from the dock at the end of Bötcherstraße for the ports of Vegesack (DM 10, round-trip DM 14) and Bremerhaven (DM 19, round-trip DM 30); ferry prices are competitive with train prices. Harbor tours are also available.

GETTING AROUND

Bremen centers on the Weser, with all the interesting stuff lying north of the river. A confusing tangle of tram and bus lines serve stations up to 25 kilometers (15 miles) from the town center; most routes, though, pass by the Bahnhof or the **Domsheide,** a plaza situated between the cathedral and the river. You can buy DM 2 tickets from the driver or a DM 6 **Bremen Kärtchen,** good for all-day travel until midnight, at the booth outside the Bahnhof. **Night buses** leave the Domsheide Friday and Saturday nights at 1 and 2:30 AM. If you miss the bus, call 0421/14141 or 0421/14014 for one of those pale yellow Mercedeses that pass as **taxis** in Germany.

Fahrrad Station, to the left as you leave the Bahnhof, rents bikes for DM 13 per day plus a DM 50 deposit; you can upgrade to a three-speed for an extra DM 1. *Open Mon., Wed.–Fri. 9:30–1, 2:30–5, weekends 9:30–noon.*

WHERE TO SLEEP

Chilly welcomes, few vacancies, and steep prices mark the Bremen hotel scene; even the hostel shakes you down for a bundle. If you're stuck, try the hostel in Worpswede, an hour's bus ride north. Unless you're incredibly tired when you arrive or incredibly rich, avoid the hotels around the Hauptbahnhof—you probably won't find anything around there for less than DM 50 per person. The most fun scene is the Ostertor District, full of funky stores and cafés and *the* happening scene at night. Single women should be careful off the main streets, though. Another option is to stay on the south side of the River Weser. Although most of the sites and the action lie on the north bank, you can at least find a decent, *affordable* place on the south bank.

OSTERTOR DISTRICT **Hotel-Pension Weidmann.** This place only has five rooms and they are frequently full. Small but clean rooms, all with their own TV and towels, go for DM 45 per person, but if you stay longer than one night, it's DM 40 per person. Bring earplugs because the tram rattles by right under the windows. Ask about the solarium. *Am Schwarzen Meer 35, tel. 0421/494055. Tram 2, 3, or 4 to St-Jürgen-Str., backtrack a few paces and turn right on Lüneburger Str., then right on Am Schwarzen Meer. Breakfast included, showers in the hall.*

Pension Kosch. On a quiet side street near the Ostertor area and the river, this pension is often full, so call ahead. A harried but unusually hospitable Hausfrau offers handsome wood-panelled rooms. Two singles run DM 45; five doubles go for DM 75–DM 95. *Celler Str. 4, tel. 0421/447101. Take Tram 2, 3 or 10 to St-Jürgen-Str., walk down Lüneburger Str. toward water, turn left on Celler Str. 7 rooms. Breakfast included, shower and toilets in hall.*

SOUTH OF THE WESER **Gästehaus Walter.** An unfriendly staff officiously manages this frequently full hotel. Rooms are clean, unremarkable, and relatively cheap. Basic singles and doubles cost DM 40 and DM 68; for DM 65 or DM 98 you get a larger pad with TV, phone, shower, and toilet. *Buntentorsteinweg 86, tel. 0421/558027. Cross Wilhelm-Kaisen bridge and turn left on Buntentorsteinweg, or Tram 1 to Rotes-Kreuz Krankenhaus. 12 rooms. Breakfast included, toilets and showers in hall. Reservations strongly advised.*

Hotel Enzenspenger. Small lace-curtained rooms, usually full of travelers who reserved in advance, perch above a restaurant near (but not within sight of) the river. Singles are DM 42, DM 47 with shower, and doubles go for DM 68, DM 78 with shower. The owner mans the desk in the early morning and late afternoon. *Brautstr. 9, tel. 0421/503224. Cross Weser on Wilhelm-Kaisen bridge, turn right on Osterstr. and right on Brautstr. 10 rooms. Breakfast included, toilets and showers in hall. Reservations strongly advised.*

Hotel-Pension Haus Neustadt. You've probably got as good a chance of securing a spot in this out-of-the-way hotel as at any other. Cramped, spotless, and very white rooms run DM 45 for singles, DM 59 with shower; doubles are DM 75, DM 89 with shower. Clean bathrooms are in the corridor. The hotel is a 25-minute walk from the station. *Graudenzer Str. 33, tel. 0421/551749. Cross Wilhelm-Kaisen bridge, turn left on Kornstr., right on Graudenzer Str.; or Bus 26 to Meyerstraße and continue to Graudenzer Str. 12 rooms. Closed Sun. noon–8 PM, breakfast included. Reservations advised.*

HOSTELS **Jugendgästehaus Bremen.** First, the bad news: The mercenary staff charges DM 22.50 a night (DM 26.50 if you're over 26), breakfast lasts only a half hour, and a 9–noon lockout quells any thoughts of sleeping in. The flip side: Beds are clean and comfy, breakfast includes an all-you-can-eat muesli bowl, and curfew doesn't start till 1 AM. Some rooms look out over the Weser. The walk from the station takes about 20 minutes. *Kalkstr. 6, tel. 0421/171369. From Hauptbahnhof, follow rails down Bahnhofstr. to Herdentorsteinweg, turn right on Am Wall, left on Bürgermeister-Schmidt-Str., right along banks of river; or Tram 6 or Bus 26 to Am Brille, and follow riverbank to right. 160 beds. Reception open noon–10 PM, breakfast and sheets included.*

Jugendherberge Bremen-Blumenthal. Only the really desperate will be able to stomach the 1½-hour odyssey to this tiny hostel, 20 kilometers (12 miles) downstream along the banks of the Weser. Beds in spartan octuples are DM 15, DM 18 if you're over 26. Call ahead, because it's beloved by school groups. *Bürgermeister-Dehnkamp-Str. 22, tel. 0421/601005. Tram 10 to Gröpelingen terminus, then Bus 70 or 71 for 45 min. to Kreinsloger; cross park, walk down to st. along banks, turn right. 54 beds. Reception open 5–8 PM.*

CAMPGROUNDS **Campingplatz Bremen.** This distant, RV-filled campground snuggles into a bend of a canal. Prices run DM 6 per person and DM 8 per tent. *Tram 5 to Kulenkampfallee, then Bus 22 or 23 2 stops to Munte, continue down Kuhgrabenweg and turn left on Hochschulring. Closed Nov.–Easter.*

FOOD

Cheap Middle Eastern stand-up eateries dot Ostertorsteinweg. For even cheaper fare, bring your student card to the **Mensa** cafeteria at the university (take Tram 5 to its Kulenkampfallee terminus, then board Bus 21 or 23 to Universität/Zentralbereich). **Markets** brighten up the cathedral area on Tuesday and Saturday mornings; take your picnic supplies to the grassy river bank off Osterdeich and watch the boats go by. If you're willing to shell out DM 50 for a fantastic meal in an intensely romantic and atmospheric restaurant, stroll through the Schnoor quarter at night, and pick a likely spot. If you schnoored too long last night, you can have breakfast till 3 PM at **Ambiente** café (Osterdeich at Lüneburger Str.), with a glorious view of the Weser from the ivied terrace. Breakfast here runs DM 6–DM 18, but it's only DM 3 for the "Schwarzes Frühstuck," an espresso and a cigarette.

➢ **UNDER DM 10 • Gasthof Kaiser Friedrich.** Amble into one of the town's best and coziest pubs, on the edge of the Schnoor. In the casual interior, old black-and-white photos of sailing ships look down on boisterous reunions. The menu runs from DM 6.50 for a bowl of carrot soup to DM 14.50 for schnitzel, onions, and noodles. Salads go for DM 5, and one-third liters of draft beer for DM 3.60. *Am Landherrnamt 12 at Kolpingstr.*

Tandour. This popular nook's aromatic, wood-paneled interior smells of both curry and oregano—that's because the kitchen dishes out quick pizzas as well as Indian treats. Half a snack-size pepperoni pizza runs DM 4; DM 8 buys you a large vegetarian stuffed pita. The list of drinks is as long as your arm. *Am Sielwall 5, s. of Ostertorsteinweg.*

➢ **UNDER DM 20 • Engel.** This "in" café-restaurant-bar looks out over a buzzing, active square in the heart of Ostertor. The patrons have a tendency to pose rather than just sit. An ever-changing menu encompasses various dainty dishes in the DM 13–DM 19 range. Nothing's a deal, but remember you're paying for matchless people-watching. In summer, only nerds sit inside. A tomato salad with mozzarella costs DM 9.50, coffee DM 3. *Ostertorsteinweg 32, tel. 0421/76615.*

Kleiner Ratskeller. Moderate portions of good food are served amid subdued lights, dark green tables, and the hubbub of old friends catching up on all the news. Photos of unknown human beings crowd the walls. The traditional German menu changes daily, but bratwurst and beef goulash are guaranteed to be there. Most dishes cost DM 9.50–DM 15. *Hinter Dem Schütting 11, up st. from Bötcherstr. entrance, tel. 0421/326168.*

COFFEEHOUSES **Cafe Knigge** (44 Sögestr.) purveys a mind-boggling quantity of packaged chocolate and cream confections, plus generous slices of various pies, for around DM 3.50. **Cafe Fölke** (Am Landherrnamt 1, in the Schnoor district), elegant in a down-at-the-heels sort of way, serves up DM 2.30 coffees and the formidable Peppermint Love (DM 8.50), a chocolate drink guaranteed to transcend your wildest desires. Cognac and coffee is only one of the 17 caffeinated concoctions at the **Wall Cafe** (Am Wall 164, tel. 0421/324878), an artsy hangout perched above an artsy bookstore.

WORTH SEEING

Touring Bremen is largely a matter of soaking up the atmosphere of various neighborhoods and involves very little indoors work. It's possible to see the lot in one day if you hustle. The tourist office gives two-hour tours in English for DM 7.50, but for that kind of money you could almost afford a Peppermint Love at **Cafe Fölke** (*see* Food, *above*).

BOTCHERSTRAßE Ludwig Roselius, local coffee nabob, transformed this short alley south of Marktplatz, originally a barrelmakers' street, into his own artistic vision. The 1920s Worpswede artist colony, and Bernhard Hoetger especially, rallied to his call, creating a jumbled passageway of playful brick constructions, now occupied by shops and galleries. The "Bringer of Light" relief over the entrance is Hoetger's. The 14th-century edifice at No. 6, renamed the **Roselius Haus,** holds a small museum of art; the DM 2.50 entrance fee (students DM 1.50) includes entrance to the exhibition of works next door by Worpswede artist Paula Modersohn-Becker. Both galleries are open Monday–Thursday 10–4, and weekends 11–4.

MARKTPLATZ This is one of the most impressive market squares in Europe, bordered by the Rathaus, an imposing 900-year-old cathedral, a 16th-century guild hall, and a modern glass and steel parliament building. On the square itself stands the famous stone **statue of the knight Roland,** erected in 1400. Three times larger than life, the statue serves as Bremen's shrine, good-luck piece, and symbol of freedom and independence.

The ancient **Rathaus** is a Gothic building that acquired a Renaissance facade in the early 17th century. Its opulent interior proves just as interesting as the exterior; various artists, including Worpswede bigshot Heinrich Vogeler, have worked on it intermittently since the 15th century. You can take free tours of the Rathaus on weekdays at 10, 11, and noon (Mar.–Oct., weekends at 11 and noon as well). At the northwest corner of the Rathaus stands Gerhard Marck's bronze statue of the **Bremen Town Musicians,** based on the fairy tale about the rooster, cat, dog, and donkey who set off for Bremen to make their fortunes. You can also snag a free tour (weekdays at 10 and 2:15) of the intelligently designed **Haus der Bürgerschaft,** the controversial state parliament building erected in the '60s.

Goggle at the great doors before entering the ocher-, sandstone-, and slate-colored interior of **St. Petri Dom.** A museum (admission DM 2) exhibits flotsam and jetsam from its past. The blackened but well-preserved corpses of several workers who slipped from the roof during the cathedral's construction are morbidly displayed in the Bleikeller in the southeast corner (DM 2 entry; closed Sun.). Pick up the Kirchenmusik brochure at the tourist office for listings of roof-rattling pipe organ concerts in the cathedral. *Dom open May–Oct., weekdays 10–5, Sat. 10–noon, Sun. 2–5; Nov.–Apr., weekdays 1–5, Sat. 10–noon, Sun. 2–5.*

MUSEUMS The best of Bremen's museums is the **Kunsthalle,** with changing modern exhibits, plus paintings by Monet, Van Gogh, and Dürer. Decide if you want to make the trip to nearby Worpswede by studying the large collection of works by Worpswede painter Paula Modersohn-Becker. *Am Wall 207, tel. 0421/329080. Admission: DM 6, DM 3 students. Open Tues. 10–9, Wed.–Sun. 10–5.*

The **Ubersee Museum** has lively exhibits on Oceania, East Asia, and the Americas. *Bahnhofspl. 13, tel. 0421/397–8357. Admission: DM 2, DM 1 students. Open Tues.–Sun. 10–6.*

OSTERTORVIERTEL This wacky street, refuge of punks and poets, wails a distinctly alternative tune to the Altstadt's more sedate melodies. Litter-filled sidewalks lead past innumerable cafés, cheap student snack places, and clothing stores specializing in leather. Browse through the bookstore across from Engel (*see* Food, *above*) for the best selection of gay literature. This neighborhood really lights up at night, though the side streets can get a bit dicey.

SCHNOORVIERTEL Between the cathedral and the river lies the Schnoor quarter, a cobblestoned patchwork of cramped lanes and steep-roofed medieval dwellings. Most of the houses have been too thoroughly restored to be striking, but the wealth of enticing restaurants and artisan shops makes for fun (and labyrinthine) strolls. The area was originally the haunt of fishermen and tradespeople.

AFTER DARK

A free monthly publication, ***Mix,*** has exhaustive lists of all theater, film, music, and literary events in town, though it rarely gives addresses. The monthly periodical ***Bremen,*** available for DM 3.50 at newsstands, has lists of events *and* addresses; consult the tourist office's copy for free. You can buy tickets to most concerts and events at the tourist office, too. If you don't have any money, you can always loaf around Marktplatz and listen to the street musicians.

Bremen locals approach life a bit more casually than most other Germans; that, plus the considerable student population, adds up to a lively nightlife.

Local breweries Beck's and Haake Beck's churn out Bremen's favorite thirst-quenchers. Crowds sit out on the Marktplatz all day and long into the night at the **Haus am Markt,** industriously downing big mugs of Beck's for DM 4.90 apiece. A younger crowd doesn't get going till late at **Achims Becks Haus** (Carl-Ronning-Str. at Sögestr., tel. 0421/15555), but when it does get going, it's unstoppable. Buy in bulk and save at the **Schüttinger Brauerei** (Hinter dem Schütting 13, near Bötcherstr. entrance); their 10-liter kegs and low, arched drinking room are perfect for long, albeit sodden, confabs. The immensely popular **Delight** (Liebfrauenkirchhof, tel. 0421/328622) pumps out funk and soul Friday and Saturday from 9 PM on. Thankfully, the disco ball spinning above the entrance is the club's only one. On Friday and Saturday nights, you can hear traditional jazz at the **Jazzclub Bremen** (Bahnhofspl. 29, tel. 0421/327977).

Near Bremen

Bremerhaven and Worpswede are classic examples of the one-attraction town, but they do it with style: The former's strong suit is all things maritime, while the latter's is art. Both lie north of Bremen, in what was once a desolate, marshy stretch of treacherous peat bogs. Nineteenth-century dikes and engineering miracles have made the land dry and habitable, but it retains a disconcerting flatness.

BREMERHAVEN

Built as Bremen's deep-water harbor when the Weser started to silt up in the 19th century, Bremerhaven's industrial docks handle mammoth tankers and cargo ships from around the world. The large **Deutsches Schiffartsmuseum** (German Maritime Museum), jammed with innumerable models and figureheads, explores every possible facet of humanity's relationship with the sea. Without a doubt, the best part is the pool full of drive-it-yourself model ships. The DM 5 entrance fee (students DM 2.50) includes access to several real ships moored outside. The black *Seute Dern* sailing ship has a restaurant on board; you can poke around the upper decks for free. *Von-Renzelen-Str., tel. 0471/482070. Open Tues.–Sun. 10–6.*

Also moored nearby is the claustrophobic **U-Boot Wilhelm-Bauer**, a WWII sub. If you thought youth hostel dorms were cramped, check out the berths here; these are actually quite roomy compared to those on earlier U-boats. *Admission: DM 2.50, DM 1.50 students. Open daily 10–6.*

The **Zoo am Meer,** in the building marked *Strandhalle*, displays our fishy brothers in a big aquarium. *Across parking lot to right of museum. Admission: DM 3.*

VISITOR INFORMATION The **Tourist-Information** occupies an office in a big shopping center close to the Ship Museum. *Van-Ronzelen-Str., tel. 0471/42095. Open weekdays 10–6, Sat. 10–1.*

COMING AND GOING Bremerhaven lies 48 kilometers (30 miles) up the Weser from Bremen. **Trains** make the one-hour journey 1–3 times an hour (DM 14.80). To get to the tourist office and Ship Museum from Bremerhaven's train station, take Bus 2, 5, 6, or 8 to the Th.-Heuss-Platz stop. Otherwise, walk 25 minutes down Friedrich Ebert Straße as it curves to the left and over a bridge; make for the huge blue-and-white eyesore high rises.

WHERE TO SLEEP AND EAT Take Bus 6 from the train station to Eckernfeldstraße and the town's **Jugendgästehaus** (Gaußstr. 54–56 at Eckernfeldstr., tel. 0471/590–2533), a big place with beds for DM 29.60. **City Hotel** (Schillerstr. 8, tel. 0471/20332) has its own restaurant and singles from DM 38, doubles from DM 65.

Relive high school: Get instant acne from the deep-fried, unbelievably greasy *Backfisch* sold by several stands outside the Ship Museum; it comes on a roll, with potato salad. **PizzAmore,** right outside the station, sells cheap pizza and DM 3.90 salads. Day-long **markets** enliven Bürgermeister-Schmidt Straße on Tuesday, Thursday, and Saturday.

WORPSWEDE

Tiny Worpswede has been a big artists' colony for over a 100 years; every other house is a gallery, and even drugstores know enough to border their advertisements with art nouveau–style curlicues. An extraordinary group of late-19th-century artists kicked off the tradition, coming here to paint powerful, reflective landscapes and peasant portraits, often realistic in a blowsy, free way, and sometimes deeply symbolic. Heinrich Vogeler and Otto Modersohn dominated the scene; Modersohn's wife Paula Modersohn-Becker wasn't acknowledged as the group's real genius until after her death. Somehow, the colony just kept going; some of the original group's offspring still paint here, alongside many other genuinely good artists.

The **Kunstschau-Graphotek** houses two small rooms of Modersohn-Becker's portraits of peasants and local girls, as well as a bunch of Vogeler's stuff and an archaeology adjunct. Don't miss the sculpture garden outside. *Lindenallee 1–3, tel. 04792/1302. Admission: DM 5, DM 3 students. Open daily 10–6.*

Just down the street, the **Kunsthalle** displays more of Paula, more of Heinrich, and some of Otto. Most breathtaking of all is the postcard counter, over 300 cards strong. *Bergstr. 17, tel. 04792/1277. Admission: DM 4, DM 2 students. Open daily 10–6.*

Amble past farmhouses with thatched roofs and sun-dappled folds of forest to neat and beautiful **Barkenhof,** Heinrich's house, hung with his own works. Poet Rainer Maria Rilke, who hung out with the Worpswede group, visited here often. *Ostendorfer Str. 10, tel. 04792/3968. Admission: DM 3, DM 2 students. Open daily 10–6.*

Heinrich's wife Martha lived in the brick-and-timber **Haus im Schluh** after their divorce. This house, too, is hung with his creations, plus a joyful *Lovelife in Nature,* painted by the entire original group. Martha's daughter lives here now. *Off Im Schluh, tel. 04792/7160. Admission: DM 3, DM 1.50 students. Open daily 2–6.*

VISITOR INFORMATION The **Verkehrsamt** tourist office has excellent English brochures with cursory histories of Worpswede. *Bergstr. 13, tel. 04792/1477. Open weekdays 9:30–12:30 and 2:30–5; Apr.–Oct., also Sat. 10–2.*

COMING AND GOING Worspwede lies 25 kilometers (15 miles) north of Bremen. Bus 140 leaves every other hour from Bremen's Bahnhof (45 mins, DM 4.30, rail passes not valid); tell the driver whether you're going to the Jugendherberge or the town proper.

WHERE TO SLEEP AND EAT Get off the bus at the Jugendherberge stop for (surprise!) the **Jugendherberge** (Hammeweg 2, tel. 04792/1360), a big sloped-roof affair set amid seas of corn. The rambunctious, eccentric owner opens the reception desk sporadically between 8 and 12:30, 3 and 4:45, and then again from 9:45 to 10, when curfew begins. Beds are DM 17 apiece (over 26, DM 21), breakfast included.

Tourist cafés abound in Worpswede. The **Cafe Central** (Bergstr. 11) has a reputation as the local youth-and-artist watering hole, though it's pretty quiet on weekdays. DM 6 garners you coffee and your choice of pie. A stubbornly unartistic **Spar** supermarket (Osterweder Str. at Sophie-Bötjer-Weg) has picnic supplies.

Friesland and East Frisian Islands

Jutting out into the North Sea near Holland, Friesland is a wet, windy peninsula of interminable flatness and dreary gray weather. An immense, 150-kilometer (92-mile) dike and a network of canals have only lately drained what was once swampy, unpassable bog; now farms cover the mildly fertile land, their sweeping flatness broken only by dikes and sturdy windmills. Of course, the "unusable" bog had been a tremendously rich ecological niche; it's now almost extinct. Thousands of bird species, clams, grasses, and other wetland organisms still live here, though.

The Frisians have managed to hold on to their own culture, which includes a strong maritime bent and the whispery *Plattdeutsch*, a dialect similar to Dutch. Open all conversations with a cheerful "*Moin!*," the ubiquitous Plattdeutsch greeting. East Frisians also delight in their idiosyncratic and massive tea consumption; local blends, brewed strong, are poured over *Klöntjes*, big sugar crystals, and drunk unstirred. Anytime is teatime.

Wet, gray weather and ferocious, tooth-rattling winds are the norm for much of the year on the East Frisian islands. From May through August the sun breaks through, but the wind rarely lets up. This is not the French Riviera.

In summer, lemminglike throngs of German vacationers crowd the string of sandy islands off the coast. The islands see the sun only briefly, but they're fine for brooding communions with the wind and gray sea. If it is sunny, the endless beaches are hard to beat, and with a little work you can find as much isolation as you want.

Long sandy beaches line every island's north coast; most have *Frei-Körper* (nudist beaches) tucked in somewhere. The southern coasts, and much of the mainland's coast, bog down in gluey *Watten* (mud flats); these can be extremely dangerous, and occasionally adventurous souls never come back from their explorations. A better solution is to go with pathfinding *Wattführer*, who lead groups on tours, giving detailed lessons on the clams, worms, and other fauna that inhabit the mud.

BASICS

VISITOR INFORMATION Most tourist offices in the region stock ferry schedules to nearby islands, but little else. The helpful folks at Norddeich's **Kurverwaltung** (Dörper Weg 22, tel. 04931/17202), however, dispense thick pamphlets to each and every island for DM 1 apiece; these include hotel lists, useful addresses and information, and lots of pretty pictures.

WHEN TO GO Mainland, noncoastal towns see few tourists no matter what the season, and they look just as good in winter mists as in summer sunshine. Norddeich and the islands sink under floods of German tourists from May through November, when empty beds become very scarce. This is, of course, the best time to visit; the key is to phone ahead and to put a lot of distance between you and the more popular islands.

All the island youth hostels close from November through February, except Helgoland's, which is closed in November and December only.

COMING AND GOING Rail lines run up the east and west coasts of the peninsula, but no trains serve the northern coastal towns in between. Some of the grimiest, most unloved trains in all of Germany chug laboriously from Leer north through Emden to Norden and Norddeich, and from Oldenburg up to Wilhelmshaven or Esens. For other towns on the north coast, however, you'll have to take buses.

Ferries cruise over to the islands from the mainland. Most offer one-day excursion passes (*Tagesrückfahrkarten*) that are cheaper than regular round-trip tickets; unfortunately, rail passes will get you nothing in the way of discounts or perks. There is no official island-to-island transport, but the charming, moneyed, or persistent can sometimes get rides from fishing boats and the like down at the harbor. **Frisia-Luftverkehr** (tel. 04931/4377) flies tiny prop planes to all the islands from its Norddeich airfield; prices range from DM 45 to DM 120, or DM 90–DM 190 round-trip.

Emden and Environs

On the west coast of the peninsula, the quiet port town of Emden offers little besides connections to Borkum and Greetsiel—the city was flattened by bombing raids during the war. While you wait for your train or ferry, you can float around the waterways on 50-minute **harbor tours.** Tours leave daily on the hour from 10 to 4 (except noon) from the canal in front of the Rathaus, and cost DM 5 (students DM 2.50). In the same canal, inside an old fire ship, is the **tourist office** (tel. 04921/29904). To get here from the station, walk down Abdenastraße, just to the right of the watertower, and turn right on Neutorstraße.

Emden has its own **Jugendherberge** (An der Kesselschleuse 5, tel. 04921/23797), a long walk to the east; beds are DM 15 apiece, and there's space outside for tents.

BORKUM **Ag Ems** ferries (tel. 04921/42057) run three–four times per day from Emden to Borkum, a large and overcrowded island with all the usual resort attractions, including a nude beach, a casino, and a marina; you can probably do better on another island. Borkum is the most westerly of the East Frisian islands—the islands you see to the west belong to Holland. Good luck finding a space at the huge but often booked **Jugendherberge** (Jann-Berghaus-Str. 63, tel. 04922/579). Ferries cost DM 44 round-trip, DM 22 for a one-day excursion, and leave from the **Borkumkai docks,** a long walk south of Emden's Bahnhof.

KRUMMHORN The Krummhörn, an area of reclaimed land, forms a bulge in the peninsula just west of Emden. Canals crisscross the area's flat, soggy farmland, connecting a score of tiny villages to each other and the sea. Avoid drab Pewsum in favor of the admittedly touristy town of **Greetsiel** (pronounced "Great-seal"). It's easy to see why this old shrimping town attracts so much attention: Cobblestone streets, picturesque docks, and windmills are all guaranteed to incite a tourist feeding-frenzy. The **tourist office** here (Zur Havener Hodge 15, tel. 04926/1331) cheerfully passes out regional info, and you can rent bikes and boats in town for unusually low rates. Take a gander at the two great **windmills** on Mühlenstraße; the green one houses a café, and you can walk around the inside of the red one for DM 1.50.

Greetsiel's friendly **Jugendherberge** (Kleinbahnstr. 15, tel. 04926/550) puts travelers in two big dorm rooms for DM 15 apiece (over 26, DM 18). Reception opens at 5, and the hostel closes from November through March. Sip East Frisian tea and watch the husky fish butchers at the **Hafenkiefer** restaurant-café, right down on the docks. Between two and four buses run daily to Greetsiel from Emden (one hour) and Norden's Marktplatz (½ hour).

Western Islands

The islands at the western end of the string of East Frisian islands are the most easily accessible from the mainland. As a result, they see the most sun worshippers toting beach chairs and waiting for the wind to let up. Of these islands, Juist offers the best chance for a little solitude and more natural surroundings, while Norderney features one of the oldest German health resorts and an incredible array of attractions for everyone from gamblers to sunbathers and swimmers. Baltrum, on the other hand, is just plain tiny.

To get an idea of how different Juist and Norderney are, look out across the sea from Norddeich: Juist is the green and sandy one to the left, and Norderney's the built-up one with the huge high rises on the right.

NORDEN Along with Norddeich, serene Norden is one of the best jumping-off points for many of the islands. The town lies more than 5 kilometers (3 miles) from the ocean, though, so don't come here expecting to board a ferry. For many of the more distant islands, it's much cheaper to take a bus from Norden to the tiny harbors along the north coast that serve the individual islands.

At the heart of Norden lies a grand **Marktplatz,** half cobblestone and half park. On one side rises the brick **Ludgerikirche** and its colorful midnave pipe organ; on the other side stands the **Fremden Verkehrsbüro** (tel. 04931/172201), a nice but ineffectual tourist office with bus and ferry schedules but not much else. To get to the Marktplatz from the train station, turn right down Bahnhofstraße, go straight for a long time, and then turn left up Osterstraße; it should take about 25 minutes. The best place to stay in town is the pretty **Hotel zur Post** (Am Markt 3, down from the post office, tel. 04931/2787), with beds for DM 30–DM 39 per person.

NORDDEICH Norddeich, right behind the coastal dikes, has few charms, but its island ferry connections make it a likely stopover. The unusually helpful **Kurverwaltung** (Dörper Weg 22, tel. 04931/17202) has stacks of facts about all the islands, and can help with accommodations and transportation schedules. To get here from the train station, head west along the dike on Badestraße, and turn left on Dörper Weg. The small and friendly **Jugendherberge** (Sandstr. 1, tel. 04931/8064) has beds for DM 16.60 (over 26, DM 20.10), and tent spots out back for DM 12.50. Head west from the station on Badestraße and look to your left for Sandstraße. The reception's open from 5 to 8.

Ferries chug out of Norddeich's harbor for Juist, Norderney, Helgoland, and even the Netherlands; the harbor's train stop, Norddeich Mole, lies a few hundred yards past Norddeich's main stop.

JUIST Juist (pronounced "yoost") is occasionally overcrowded, but its ban on cars and its large nature preserves give it more of a natural, isolated feel than its cosmopolitan eastern neighbor. The north coast is one uninterrupted 17-kilometer (10-mile) beach, with space enough for everybody. Instead of staying in the bland town in the middle, escape to the low, wind-raked preserves, famous for their birds, at the west end of the island. The **Kurverwaltung** (Friesenstr. at Warmbad Str., tel. 04935/809222) can find rooms in pensions for DM 30 and up, or try for a room at the immense, 350-bed **Jugendherberge** (Loogster Pad 20, tel. 04935/1049). The obligatory full-board deal costs DM 22.60. To get to the hostel from the harbor, walk inland and then to the left along Billstraße, at the northern foot of the dike; it's a half-hour trek. Bike-rental places dot the town, and you can rent Windsurfers at the harbor.

Reederei Norden-Frisia (tel. 04931/180224) sends one–two ferries daily from Norddeich. Check the schedules carefully, since the DM 25 one-day excursion sometimes only gives you four hours on the island. A four-day round-trip ticket costs DM 36, an open-ended round-trip DM 38, and bikes are DM 8.

NORDERNEY This glitzy resort, by far the most popular of the islands, packs several casinos, a sizable shopping district, and a handful of discothèques into its limited space. The eastern nature areas sparkle with soda cans, tires, beer bottles, and other litter from the happy crowds. Cars are permitted and numerous, and buses connect the harbor to town and points east. The **Kurverwaltung** (Weststrandstr. at Am Weststrand, tel. 04932/8910) charges DM 3.80 for island maps and DM 5 to find rooms.

➢ **COMING AND GOING** • **Reederei Norden-Frisia** (tel. 04931/180224) controls the ferry cartel here as well. Round-trip tickets are DM 20, one-day excursions DM 17.50. Ferries leave hourly between 7 AM and 6 PM from Norddeich.

Fahrrad Verleih (tel. 04932/1326), 300 yards up Hafenstraße from the harbor, rents bikes for DM 10 per day, DM 6 for a half day. In town, **Fahrrad Verleih Grönsfeld** (Langestr. 15, tel. 04932/1610) charges DM 8 for a day, DM 5 for a half day.

➢ **WHERE TO SLEEP** • To reach the first **Jugendherberge** (Südstr. 1, tel. 04932/2451), go left out of the ferry terminal, take the first right onto Deichstraße, then cut back on Südstraße; it's about a 20-minute walk. You pay DM 22.20 (over 26, DM 25.70) for the first night; after that the price goes up to DM 31.90 (over 26, DM 35.40) for mandatory full-board fare. The office opens daily from 5:15 to 7 PM.

Take Karl-Rieger-Weg east, or the bus from town, to the other **Jugendherberge** (Am Dünensender 3, tel. 04932/2574), a low building entirely hidden by wind-sculpted brush. It charges the same prices as the other hostel, but is slightly larger and has tent spots for DM 5. **Campingplatz Booken** (Waldweg 2 at Kiefernweg, tel. 04932/448) has nasty cramped tent spots for DM 8, plus DM 10 per person.

BALTRUM This is the smallest of the islands. Not only are cars forbidden, but visitors are strongly urged not even to bother with bikes. Baltrum's beaches and fine nature preserve make a great day trip, but it gets boring pretty quickly—you can walk all the way around the island in three hours. There's no youth hostel, and you must get permission from the **Kurverwaltung** (tel. 04939/800) before heading to the campground.

Synchronized relays of buses and ferries take you from Norden's *Bahnhof* to Neßmersiel, then across the waves to Baltrum; call 04939/235 for information. Round-trip tickets cost DM 36, but one-day excursions are only DM 22.

Eastern Islands

It's more of a hassle getting to the eastern islands than to their western brethren, but you're rewarded for your efforts with smaller crowds and unspoiled nature. Besides, what's an island if it isn't a lot of trouble to get to? With the exception of the hypertouristed cliffs of Helgoland, differences are minimal between these hideouts; all are long and low, center on one bland, car-free town, have superb beaches, and are plenty isolated. All things considered, Wangerooge may be slightly more interesting: It's got the pick of the youth hostels, unbeatable dunes and marshlands, and its own miniature train.

LANGEOOG Eight ferries travel daily (Oct.–May, three per day) to Langeoog from Bensersiel; tickets are DM 34 round-trip, DM 25 for a one-day excursion. To get to Bensersiel, you first have to take a bus to Esens from Norden (two per day) or a train from Oldenburg; from Esens, another bus runs you to nearby Bensersiel harbor (DM 3.50). The **tourist information** office (Hauptstr., tel. 04972/6930) on Langeoog is more or less useless. At the **Jugendherberge** (Domäne Melkhörn, tel. 04972/276), obligatory full room-and-board jacks up the daily price tag to DM 27.30, although you can always brave the wind in the campground outside. The hostel is open mid-April–October.

SPIEKEROOG Spiekeroog, the least developed of the islands, flaunts its isolation and considerable backwardness. As with Langeoog (*see above*), you first have to get yourself to Esens (*see* Langeoog, *above*), where you then catch a bus to Neuharlingersiel's harbor and the ferry. Ferries leave 2–4 times daily, and tickets cost DM 35 round-trip, DM 26 for a one-day excursion. Once in Spiekeroog, drop by **tourist information** (Noorderpad 25, tel. 04976/170) if you have questions. Spiekeroog's itty-bitty **Jugendherberge** (Bid' Utkiek, tel. 04976/329) lies near the town center. Mandatory room-and-board costs DM 32.50 a day.

WANGEROOGE Little Wangerooge adds a small train and a lighthouse museum to the traditional island goodies of endless grassy dunes, scads of birds and other animals, and a nude beach. The **tourist information** (tel. 04469/375) kicks back on Strandpromenade. The *Westturm,* an old stone tower, houses the remarkable **Jugendherberge** (tel. 04469/439), open May–September. Full room-and-board runs DM 27, but you can pay DM 16 for just bed and breakfast. The views from the hostel tower are great, but can't compare with those from the nearby **lighthouse.** A small train chugs ferry passengers into town from the harbor, but the hostel is closer to the harbor than town.

Take a bus from Norden to Harlesiel, where you catch the ferry to Wangerooge. Ferries run two–three times daily, and round-trip tickets cost about DM 45.

HELGOLAND A bizarre plateau of deep red cliffs way out in the North Sea, miniscule Helgoland attracts way too many gawking tourists for comfort. If those serrated precipices draw you anyway, try getting a bed in the **hostel** (tel. 04725/341). Ferries for Helgoland leave from Bremerhaven, Wilhelmshaven, and several ports in Schleswig-Holstein. Round-trip from Wilhelmshaven runs DM 46, DM 40 for a day trip. From Bremerhaven, the ferry costs DM 68 round-trip and DM 55 for a day trip, but youth hostel card-carriers can get a round-trip for DM 50 and a day trip for DM 27.

SCHLESWIG-HOLSTEIN AND MECKLENBURG-VORPOMMERN

13

By Geraldine Poon

Schleswig-Holstein and Mecklenburg-Vorpommern are the two *Länder* (provinces) that form the bulk of the northern coast. Taken together they encompass an incredible range of sights—white sandy beaches, chalky cliffs, medieval churches, Baroque half-timbered houses, ancient ports, and remote fishing villages where time is best measured by the stormy moods of the sea. Life in Schleswig-Holstein, which joins Germany with Denmark, has always been dominated by the ocean, but, because ownership of the region has shifted between Germany and Denmark throughout history, there's also a strong Danish influence—mostly in the opulent merchant homes that line many city squares. These are reminders of Schleswig-Holstein's membership in the long-lived Hanseatic League, the powerful merchant bloc that dominated trade on the Baltic from the 13th to 17th centuries.

Mecklenburg-Vorpommern, endowed with its own ancient port towns and half-timbered merchant homes, owes a similar debt to Hanseatic League traders. But this legacy is sometimes lost in the shuffle of more recent history. Prior to 1989 Mecklenburg-Vorpommern was part of the now-defunct German Democratic Republic (GDR). In a scenario repeated throughout East Germany, the region was partly industrialized and partly left to rot. In some towns you'll find once-elegant squares lined with a jarring mix of cement high rises and dilapidated 14th-century churches. Since Mecklenburg-Vorpommern was the only GDR Land that offered access to the sea, many towns were built up with sprawling dock complexes that now lie unused and listless, contributing to the overall economic malaise that plagues the region.

When you look at a railroad map you'll realize how few trains actually brave the coast's remoter reaches. This isn't a serious problem for most backpackers because all the major stadts and burgs (and even a few dorfs) are served by train with reasonable regularity. Yet hikers and anyone intent on a long commune with nature should consider renting a bike long-term or investing in some sort of rail pass, since many buses in Schleswig-Holstein and Mecklenburg-Vorpommern accept Deutsche Bundesbahn train passes. Another thing to remember is that the weather can be a nasty and unpredictable beast. Summer is generally sunny and warmish with the occasional bout of windy rain. During winter, however, when many hostels and restaurants have abbreviated hours, the weather is bone-chillingly cold and wet, wet, wet.

Schleswig-Holstein

Locals joke that the land here is so flat they can see someone approaching on Monday who won't arrive till Friday. Schleswig-Holstein—that stubby strip of land that connects Germany with Denmark and splits the Baltic from the North Sea—is in fact an amazingly bland Land, at least once you leave the coast. The interior, which stretches from Hamburg in the south to the Danish border in the north, is little more than a repetitive expanse of farmland and swampy marsh. And it's no coincidence that a Holstein is a type of cow or that this Land is famous throughout Germany for its dairy products (the sure signs of a rural hickland).

The coast is a completely different story. For centuries Schleswig-Holstein's port towns dominated trade on the Baltic, first as independent city-states and then, when pirating became common, as partners in the powerful Hanseatic League. Nearly every coastal town in Schleswig-Holstein has a historic core dominated by a smart-looking marketplace, and every square is lined with opulent merchant houses. These ancient relics give Schleswig-Holstein much of its modern appeal and are reminders of the fact that this region is still tied to the sea. You won't find towering cliffs or mountainside fishing villages in Schleswig-Holstein, only peaceful (okay, and flat) coastal settlements where time and custom seem to stand still. This is less true of a town like Lübeck, the Land's largest and probably best-preserved Hanseatic-era port. But on one of the North Frisian islands—those sandy bumps in the water off the west coast—prepare for limitless horizons, the constant rush of the sea, and a tough seafaring population who for centuries have eked a living from the storm-battered Baltic.

German novelist Thomas Mann unjustly slammed Schleswig-Holstein cuisine when he said, "No one could eat it, unless he grew up with it as a child." Local specialties you'll want to try are Rote Grütze *(a berry dessert);* Pharisäer *(coffee and rum topped with cream); and* Birnen, Bohnen, und Speck *(pears with beans and bacon).*

Most every town has a tourist-information office, called *Kurverwaltung, Fremdenverkehrsamt,* or *Stadt-information.* These offer an ocean of brochures, maps, accommodations listings, and advice. If you want a flood of material before breaching the borders write **Fremdenverkehrsverband Schleswig-Holstein e.V.** (Niemannsweg 31, 2300 Kiel, tel. 0431/561061).

That Ain't German

After spending some time on the northern coast you'll notice that not everyone speaks the same High German you learned in school. That's because **Plattdeutsch** ***(Low German, literally "stale" or "dull" German), a dialect common in Schleswig-Holstein, Hamburg, and Mecklenburg-Vorpommern, is still spoken in small villages, especially by the older generation. Recently, there's even been a movement to preserve Platt in local schools, much to the chagrin of southerners who view Platt as the language of farmers and country bumpkins. Some common words that have found their way from Platt into High German are*** **Moin** ***(hi),*** **Tschüß** ***(bye), and*** **so ein Scheit** ***(shitty).***

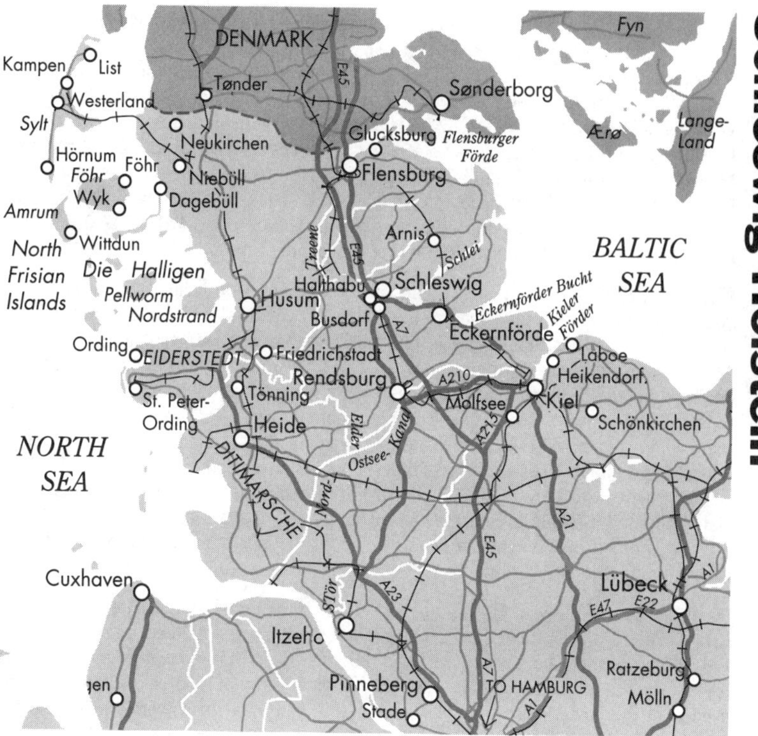

Lübeck

With more historical monuments (more than 1,000) than any other German city, the small port of Lübeck is a museum in itself. The ancient core of Lübeck, the area surrounding its impressive Marktplatz (marketplace), was founded by Henry the Lion in 1173; nowadays, Lübeck's Altstadt is protected by UNESCO as a World Heritage Site, placing it in the same league as the Great Wall of China, the Acropolis, and Venice. Needless to say, you'll want a couple of days to explore the Altstadt's myriad historical sights—its medieval lanes, Gothic and Baroque churches, cobblestone courtyards, centuries-old canals, and waterside promenades.

BASICS At the main **post office** (Am Markt, tel. 0451/488–1342), across from the Rathaus, you can buy stamps and send a fax (DM 22 per page) or telegram anywhere around the world. The **Wasch-Center** (An der Mauer and Hüxterdamm, open daily 6 AM–11 PM) charges DM 6 per load (including soap) and DM 2 for 15 minutes of dryer time. The **Touristinformation Hauptbahnhof** (tel. 0451/72300; open Mon.–Sat. 9–1, 3–7), located in the train station, stocks city maps and books rooms for a DM 5 fee. It also has a competitive bureau de change. Other tourist offices include **Touristbüro am Markt** (Am Markt, tel. 0451/122–8106), **Touristbüro Beckergrube** (Beckergrube 95, tel. 0451/122–8109), and **Touristbüro Breitestraße** (Breitestr. 75, tel. 0451/ 72339). All are open Monday–Saturday 9–1 and 3–7. Pick up the useful "Hanseatic City of Lübeck: A City of Cultural Treasures and the Sea" (DM 1) at any tourist office. Lübeck's sights are all within walking distance of one another, but you can rent bikes at **Leihcycle** (Schwartauer Allee 39, tel. 0451/42660) for DM 5 per day.

COMING AND GOING From the **Hauptbahnhof** (Am Bahnhof, tel. 0451/19419) walk toward the Holstentor and into the Altstadt. The train station features a tourist-information office, a bureau de change, luggage storage (DM 2 for small locker, DM 4 for large locker), and a grocery store. Train destinations from Lübeck include Hamburg (every 30 minutes, DM 16), Kiel (six trains per day, DM 19), and Schwerin (eight trains per day, DM 14.80). From the Lübeck suburb of Travemünde, accessible by frequent train service, the following ferry companies offer year-round service: **Vogelfluglinie (DB/PSB)** (tel. 04371/2168) to Rodby and Puttgarden, Denmark; **TT-Line** (tel. 04502/8010) to Trelleborg, Sweden; **Nordoe Link** (tel. 04502/80550) to Malmö, Sweden; **Finnjet-Silja-Line** (tel. 04502/4077) to Helsinki; and **Poseidonschiffahrt OHG** (tel. 0451/150741) to Poland. Lübeck has two ride-share offices, the established **Mitfahrzentrale Einsteiger** (Fischergrube 45, tel. 0451/71074) and the newer **Mitfahrzentrale** (Kanalstr. 70, in Werkhof center, tel. 0451/77825).

WHERE TO SLEEP Any tourist office can provide you with a hotel list and/or book you a room for a DM 5 fee. Head to the Altstadt if you'd rather find your own budget pension. Another good bet is the **Hotel Rucksack** (Kanalstr. 70, tel. 0451/706892). This *umweltfreundlich* (environmentally friendly) hotel has an efficient gas system for heating, electricity, and hot water. It also has a gadget that collects rainwater for the toilets. The Rucksack is part of the Werkhof community, a P.C. cultural center complete with a *Mitfahrzentrale* (ride-share office), a recycled-goods store, a weavery, and a veggie restaurant. Beds in its comfortable four- to six-person rooms cost DM 18–DM 33 per night. The only drawback: It's a definite bus ride from Lübeck. From the Hauptbahnhof take Bus 1, 3, or 12 toward Burgfeld and alight at Koberg or the Beckergrube Theater; in a pinch, the driver will probably understand if you look confused and mumble, "Hotel Rucksack."

➢ **HOSTELS** • Only a 10-minute walk from the Hauptbahnhof, the **CVJM-Haus** (Große Petersgrube 11, tel. 0451/78982) has doubles and 10-bed dorm rooms for DM 14 per person. The hostel stays open until 12:15 AM during summer for late-night trains. The friendly international staff will automatically let solo women travelers in even after the hostel closes. Tough luck, guys. If you want rooms with loud, clanking metal doors, take Bus 1 or 12 from the train station to the **Jugendherberge** (Am Gertrudenkirchhof 4, tel. 0451/33433), which lies outside the Altstadt. Rooms in this Spartan complex fetch DM 16 (26 and under) and DM 19.50 (over 26). More convenient and centrally located is the **Jugendgästehaus** (Mengstr. 33, tel. 0451/70399), located on the same street as the Mann family's Buddenbrookhaus. The DM 23 price includes a buffet breakfast. The reception desk is closed noon–1 and 6–7.

➢ **CAMPGROUNDS** • Equipped with washing machines, hot and cold water, and cooking facilities, **Campingplatz Lübeck-Schönböcken** (Steinrader Damm 12, tel. 0451/893090 or 0451/892287) charges DM 8 per tent and DM 6 per person per night. From the Hauptbahnhof take Bus 7 or 8 to Dornbreite.

FOOD The Altstadt is jam-packed with *Imbisse* (food stands) that offer sausages and pizza for less than DM 5. It's also infested with semi-elegant restaurants that nourish hordes of local students: At **Tipasa** (Schlumacherstr. 14, tel. 0451/74811), **Hieronymus** (Fleischhauerstr. 81, tel. 0451/151117), and **Schmidts** (Dr. Julius Str. 60–62, tel. 0451/76182), you'll find local students nursing beers and munching on freshly made gourmet pizzas (about DM 8). At **Schweinske** (An der Unterfraue 90, tel. 0451/151677), part of a northern German chain, you can pig out in every sense of the word. The restaurant prepares their specialty, pork, in about a dozen ways (most for less than DM 10). If you're looking for a pub, head for **Engelsgrube Straße** (from Holstentor turn left on An der Untertrave and right on Engelsgrube). The street is crammed with pubs and grimy dive bars. Locals chug the popular beer *Zwickelbier*, in the combination bar-microbrewery at **Brauberger** (Engelsgrube 45A), which produces some 1,100 gallons a week for local consumption.

WORTH SEEING A striking feature of Lübeck is its skyline, formed by tile roofs, smokestacks, and seven imposing church towers. By far the most impressive church is **Marienkirche** (Marienkirchhof), set atop a hill at the spiritual (if not exact geographic) heart of the city. The nave and aisles, carefully rebuilt after they were badly damaged by Allied bombers on March 29, 1942, show almost no sign of damage. The only reminders of the raid are the church bells embedded in the floor, left exactly where they fell in 1942.

Get a good view of town from the top of nearby **Petrikirche** (Schmiedestr., admission DM 1), another of Lübeck's Gothic landmarks. It's just behind (and built in the same redbrick style as) the Holstentor gate. More inspiring is the **Dom** (Domkirchhof), an imposing Gothic creation that took more than 150 years to complete. The cornerstone of the redbrick cathedral was laid in 1173 by the town's founding father, Henry the Lion, making the Dom the oldest standing structure in Lübeck. A similar sense of history infuses the town's arcaded **Marktplatz,** a short walk from the churches. Lübeck's Marktplatz is one of Europe's most evocative medieval squares. Its most notable feature is the green-glazed **Rathaus** (town hall), dating from 1240 and built in a mishmash of styles that has left it with Romanesque arches, Gothic windows, and a Renaissance roof. Tours of the Rathaus (DM 3, DM 1 students) are given weekdays at 11, noon, and 3. Inside you'll see an old courtroom with two elaborately carved wood doors, one very big, the other very small. In the old days, those the court found guilty had to slink out through the small door, while the innocent held their heads high and exited through the larger one.

On your way from the train station to the Altstadt it's impossible to miss the Holstentor, a mammoth redbrick gate built in 1464. Prior to German reunification the gate was pictured on the DM 50 note.

Marktplatz's other historic buildings are almost always closed to the public, so head instead down Breitestraße from the square. Along the way you'll pass **Jakobikirche** (Breitestr. 45, open Mon.–Sat. 9–6, Sun. noon–5), dedicated to Lübeck's lost seamen. Inside check out Jakobikirche's celebrated pews—they're adorned with laughing faces carved *underneath* the pew for God knows what reason. A bit farther along, Breitestraße is intersected by Mengstraße, home to **Buddenbrookhaus** (Mengstr. 4). This 18th-century Baroque structure belonged to the Mann family from 1841 to 1891 and was featured in Thomas Mann's novel *Buddenbrooks*. The house, now privately owned, is slated to become a museum in the near future. Continue along Breitestraße to Koberg; turn right and you'll stumble into the **Heiligen-Geist-Hospital** (Am Koberg, tel. 0451/222040), a 13th-century hospice that's been converted into a sprawling retirement community. Okay, it sounds more than a little dull, but this city within a city is honest-to-God stunning; the small lanes and courtyards have a definite medieval feel, and walking along some of the better-preserved streets it's easy to forget what century you're in. Especially evocative are the following houses (all closed to the public): **Flütlingshof** (Glockengießerstr. 23), **Glandorps Gang und Glandorps Hof** (Glockengießerstr. 39–53), and **Hellgrüner Gang** (Engelswisch 28).

NEAR LUBECK

RATZEBURG Ratzeburg, a tiny town 25 kilometers (16 miles) south of Lübeck, sits on an island linked to the mainland by three marsh-enveloped causeways. Although it's small (population 12,200), Ratzeburg has an overwhelming number of sights. Foremost is its **Dom.** It dates from 1220 and is the oldest Romanesque brick church in northern Germany. In the Dom's courtyard look for Ernst Barlach's bronze statue ***Bettler auf Krücken*** (*Beggar on Crutches*). For more Barlach go to the **Ernst-Barlach-Museum-Altes Vaterhaus** (Barlachpl. 3, tel. 04541/3789). The museum curator, Dr. Horst O. Müller, is fluent in English and happy to explain things in detail. Also don't miss the **A. Paul Weber-Haus** (Domhof 5, tel. 04541/12326), which exhibits lithographs, drawings, and oil paintings by Weber—stinging satires on politics, pollution, and militarism that got Weber in trouble with the Nazis. To culture yourself silly, purchase the **Ratzeburg Museum Gemeinschaftskarte** (DM 5, DM 2.50 students). It grants free access to the Barlach Museum, the Weber Museum, the local-history **Kreis Museum** (Domhof, tel. 04541/12325), and **Haus Mecklenburg** (Domhof 41, tel.

04541/83668), which exhibits typical regional furnishings and clothing. You can purchase the pass at any of the four museums.

Ratzeburg's tourist office, **Fremdenverkehrsamt** (Am Markt 9, tel. 04541/800081, open weekdays 9–1 and 2–5, Sat. 9–1) sells brochures and town maps, and, for a DM 4 fee, can book you a room. Ratzeburg doesn't draw many overnight visitors, but you can sleep cheaply in the local **Jugendherberge** (Am Küchensee, tel. 04541/3707). It has 150 beds that cost DM 13 (26 and under) or DM 15.50 (over 26) each. To reach Ratzeburg take Bus 1806 from Lübeck's train-and-bus depot. The trip takes 40 minutes and costs DM 6 each way.

Kiel

Some locals call Kiel a *Landeshauptdorf* (capital village) because they don't think it's exciting enough to be called the capital *city* of the Schleswig-Holstein state. Yet Kiel does have a couple of claims to fame. First, it lies at the convergence of **Kieler Förde** (Kieler Fjord) and the **Nord-Ostsee Kanal** (Kiel Canal). The latter is the busiest artificial waterway in the world. Sadly, that's not saying much; watching the ships go by is about as thrilling as watching your toenails grow. A better bet is the free ferry that takes foot passengers from the canal observation platform, through the locks, and finally to a free museum that documents the canal's building. Kiel is also home to **Holstenstraße,** Germany's first pedestrian-only zone. After 80% of Kiel was destroyed in World War II, Holstenstraße and much of Kiel's city center were rebuilt with multistory department stores and a slew of shopping malls. Don't be put off—a few sights are interspersed among the seemingly endless line of shops. And even if you quickly grow sick of Kiel's number-one activity—leisurely promenades along the water—the city does make a good base for exploring nearby Molfsee and Eckerförde (*see* Near Kiel, *below*), two small oceanfront villages about 10 kilometers (6 miles) north.

Most of Kiel's attractions are in the town center, on the west side of its craggy fjord and south of the canal. Kiel's smooth bike paths are ideal for biking to the sights. Ask at the tourist-information office about bike rentals. On Kiel's dully modern Alter Markt, a stone's throw from the water, stands the **Rathaus** and its surrounding troop of cafés and food stands. For DM 1 you can ascend the Rathaus's 350-foot-tall tower and treat yourself to a good view of the city. The cluster of spires and crosses visible in the distance marks **St.-Nikolai-Kirche** (open daily 10–5). Outside this 17th-century cathedral is an Ernst Barlach sculpture, the *Geistkämpfer* (roughly, in English, *Fighter for the Spirit*). Nearby is the **Kunsthalle** (Düsternbrooker Weg 1–3, tel. 0431/3756 or 0431/3751, admission DM 3, open Tues.–Sun. 10–5), which has a mighty collection of 19th- and 20th-century German and international art. The **Aquarium des Instituts für Meereskunde** (Düsternbrooker Weg 20, tel. 0431/597–3857, admission DM 3.50, open Tues.–Sun. 10–5:30) has 31 aquariums filled with Baltic Sea creatures, and an enclosed pool that's home to some playful seals.

The only time Kiel gets really hoppin' is during late June's **Kieler Woche,** the biggest sailing regatta in the world. This festival not only attracts 4,000 yachts of all shapes and sizes but also tourists who grab every available hotel room and take over the Spiellinie, a lively promenade along the water. The regatta is great to watch, but some people make reservations more than a year in advance. If you're traveling anytime between June 15 and July 1, get the heck outta here if you don't like boats. Contact a tourist office for more information on the regatta, including a free listing of regatta-related events.

BASICS The **Hauptpostamt** changes money and has poste restante services. Kiel's postal code is 2300. You can make international phone calls from here. *Stresemannpl., near Hauptbahnhof, tel. 0431/9860. Mailing address: Kiel Postamt 1, Stresemannpl., 2300 Kiel. Open weekdays 8–6, Sat. 8–1.*

For an **ambulance** call 0431/19222, for **emergency medical** service call 0431/19292. The **Wasch-Center** (Kirchhofallee 54, tel. 0431/672787), about a 10-minute walk from the Hauptbahnhof, lets you wash 15 pounds of your grimy clothes for DM 6 (including soap); dryers are DM 1 per 15 minutes. It's open 6 AM–11 PM. Across the street from the Hauptbahnhof is **Tourist Information Kiel e.V.** (Sophienblatt 30, tel. 0431/679100), which equips visitors with an English-language "Town Guide" (DM .50) and reserves rooms for a DM 3.50 fee. The **Mitwohnzentrale** (Knooperweg 90, tel. 0431/51436) can also set you up in a private house or apartment for about DM 20 per person.

COMING AND GOING Frequent trains leave the **Hauptbahnhof** (Sophienblatt 32, s. end of fjord, tel. 0431/6011) for Lübeck (1¼ hours, DM 19) and Hamburg (1¼ hours, DM 25). Directly across from the Hauptbahnhof is the main bus station, **ZOB** (tel. 0431/6661), which offers service to Copenhagen (DM 30), Berlin (DM 38), and Hamburg's airport (DM 17.50). Dozens of ferries set sail from docks near the Hauptbahnhof: **Color Line** (tel. 0431/974090) sails daily to Oslo; **Stena Line** (tel. 0431/9090) sails daily at 7 PM to Göteborg, Sweden; **Langeland-Kiel Linien** (tel. 0431/91652) sails three times daily to the Danish island of Langeland; and **Baltic Express Line** (tel. 0431/982000) goes to St. Petersburg every Saturday. Kiel also has two ride-share offices, or **Mitfahrzentrale** (Knooperweg 90, tel. 0431/51431; Sophienblatt 54, tel. 0431/671772).

Kiel's sights are easy to conquer on foot, but if the weather is bad and/or you're planning a trip to nearby Molfsee (*see* Near Kiel, *below*), consider investing in a *Kieler Karte*. This travel pass can be purchased at the train station in one-day (DM 10), three-day (DM 15), and seven-day (DM 25) increments. It's valid on all intercity buses and trams, including the bus that goes to Molfsee's Freilichtmuseum.

WHERE TO SLEEP Most hotels in Kiel cater to rich businesspeople with expense accounts. Budget travelers looking for a double under DM 100 may have to hit the suburbs. If you're lucky enough to get a room at the friendly **Touristhotel Schweriner Hof** (Königsweg 13, tel. 0431/61416) near the Hauptbahnhof, you'll pay DM 80–DM 105 for a double. **Hotel Runger,** on the other side of the fjord (Elisabethstr. 16, tel. 0431/731992), charges DM 86–DM 115 per double. Another option is **Hotel Rendsburger Hof** (Rendsburger Landstr. 363, tel. 0431/690131), where clean and simple doubles start at DM 75—the cheapest hotel room in town. From the train station, ride 11 stops on Bus 15 to Rutkamp.

The difference between the newly renovated rooms and the crappy old ones in the **Jugendherberge** (Johannesstr. 1, tel. 0431/731488) is astonishing: grime and peeling plaster versus new fixtures and comfy beds. You should obviously ask for a renovated room, especially since the cost is the same: DM 15 (26 and under) or DM 18 (over 26). From the train depot take Bus 4, 24, 34, or 64 to Kiel Straße, walk back a block in the direction you came from, and turn left on Johannesstraße. If you want to camp, take Bus 44, 64, or 71 to Grüner Berg and its nearby **Campingplatz Falckenstein** (Palisadenweg 171, tel. 0431/392078, closed Nov.–Mar.). Not much to scream about, just cheap tent spaces (DM 8) and friendly families on holiday.

Kiel's local specialty is Kieler Sprats, *smoked and salted herring that you eat by chopping off the head and tail and then devouring the body whole.*

FOOD **Klosterbrauerei** (Alter Markt 9, tel. 0431/92524) is your typically robust German beer hall—a place where you'll pay about DM 10 (depending on the weight of your plate) for a buffet-style meal of wieners, things cabbagey, and dumplings. If you're not hungry try the house specialty for DM 2.50—pilsner beer brewed on site. **Schöne Aussichten** (Düsternbrooker Weg 16, tel. 0431/566107), which translates as "beautiful view," serves freshly prepared seafood in the DM 15–DM 20 range. From the dining room there's also a nice—not really beautiful—view of Kiel. For the cheapest eats explore the university's environs, especially Knooper Weg and Holtenauer Straße. **Forstbaumschule** (Düvelsbeker Weg 46, tel. 0431/333496) is popular for its antiquity (circa 1905) and its outdoor beer garden. Try one of the green salads or meat-filled gyros for less than DM 10.

NEAR KIEL

Ferry across the Kieler Förde to **Laboe,** a popular beach resort and home to the **Marine-Ehrenmal** (Ostseebad Laboe, tel. 04943/8755). This navy memorial honors sailors lost in the world wars. From the top of the 280-foot-high monument you'll get a good view of the fjord and the city. Another favorite Kieler beach resort, this time on the Kiel side of the fjord, is **Heikendorf-Möltenort.** Its claim to fame is its submarine memorial, the only one in the world. Take a free ferry (any labeled HEIKENDORF) from Kiel's waterfront, or hop on Bus 50 from the train station.

ECKERNFORDE Eckernförde's beaches have been attracting tourists for more than 160 years. In addition to clear shallow waters and sand strands, this resort features a small port and shopping promenades. When the weather is grim there's no reason to come. But on any warm day the beach is packed with eager sunbathers and lots of friendly teenage types. Water-sports enthusiasts should call **Tauchsport Heese** (Am Exer 28, tel. 04351/2567), which rents scuba gear to experienced divers (certification required) and offers lessons (DM 68 per half-day) for the uninitiated. If you're really bored, stop at Eckernförde's Rathaus, which houses the **Heimatmuseum Eckernförde,** detailing the town's history. The only other reason to visit is to catch a ferry; contact **Reederei Cassen Eils** (Eckernförde Außenmole, tel. 04351/5531) for information about its daily service to Denmark. The **Kurverwaltung** tourist office (Im Meerwasserwellenbad, Preußerstr. 1, tel. 04351/90520) stocks city maps and books rooms. The **Jugendherberge** (Sehestedter Str. 27, tel. 04351/2154), at the south end of town, has dorm-room beds for DM 14 (26 and under) and DM 16.50 (over 26). To reach Eckernförde, catch one of 15 daily trains from Kiel (DM 4) or a bus (DM 7.50) from Rendsburg (*see below*).

MOLFSEE No time to tour all of Schleswig-Holstein? No problem. Visit Molfsee's **Freilichtmuseum** (tel. 0431/65555; admission DM 7, DM 3 students; open Tues.–Sun. 10:15–7), which displays full-scale replicas of traditional Schleswig-Holstein homes. The 148-acre museum contains farmhouses from the 16th to 19th centuries, barns, smithies, and windmills. Sometimes employees dress up as bakers, potters, basket weavers, and milkers to perform demonstrations. This isn't the kind of place to waste a whole day on. But considering it's only a short bus ride from Kiel, the museum is an amusing stop on the way somewhere else. From Kiel's ZOB station there are four buses daily to Molfsee's ZOB depot; the trip takes 30 minutes and costs DM 6 each way. From Molfsee's ZOB station take the Autokraft bus to the museum (DM 2.50). If you have a Kieler Karte, the bus ride and admission to the museum are free.

Schleswig

Schleswig is a medium-size town perched at the tip of the Schlei, an arm of the Baltic Sea that reaches some 40 kilometers (25 miles) inland. Schleswig's seafront location, and the fact that it provides access to the rural heart of Schleswig-Holstein, has long made Schleswig a strategic trading township. Sometime in the early 8th century, the Vikings established a settlement here, called Haithabu. Under the Vikings, Schleswig became a major trading center for sea-roving pirates—a fact the Schleswig tourist board will not let visitors forget. Thor and Odin no longer welcome you to Viking land, but you can learn about their kin, take a peek at ancient runic stones, and marvel at a Viking ship in the fascinating **Wikinger Museum Haithabu** (An der B76, s. side of Schlei; tel. 04621/813300; admission DM 4, DM 2 students), housed in a structure that looks like an upside-down longboat. The museum is a bit of a trek from town (from the train station take any bus marked HAITHABU and ask the driver for directions, or hike/bike south on Route B76 toward Kiel). During summer the boats *Astrid* and *Johannes* (tel. 04621/8010) will shuttle you from Schleswig harbor (just south of the Dom, at the foot of Am Hafen) across the Schlei to Haddeby. From there it's a 20-minute walk south to the museum (follow the signs).

Schleswig itself is rather spread out. The town has grown in the shape of a big "C," curving around the Schlei. In the northeast corner are the Altstadt and Dom (and ferry connections to the south side of town); in the middle there's Schloß Gottorf and the harbor complex; and in the south there's the train station. Confine yourself to the Altstadt and nearby waterfront promenades to avoid the city's look-alike residential quarters. The Altstadt has a **central market** (Am Markt) and the inevitable **Rathaus,** but these are both overshadowed by the impressive 12th-century **St.-Petri-Dom** (Süderdomstr. 13), three blocks west of the Markt. The Dom houses the awesomely intricate **Bordesholm Altar,** one of Europe's most celebrated pieces of wood carving. This 42-foot-high work in oak was created by Hans Brüggemann in 1521 and is decorated with the delicately carved figures of some 390 discernible, very lifelike people. According to legend, poor Hans Brüggemann was blinded by his greedy patron, the selfish duke of Gottort, so Brüggemann could never create anything else as beautiful as this altar. Follow the water west from the Dom, and you can't help but see Schleswig's premier attraction, the 16th-century **Schloß Gottorf** (tel. 04621/83211), built in the style of a grand château and with a pleasant view of the Schlei. This former residence of the dukes of Schleswig-Holstein houses the not-to-be-missed **Schleswig-Holsteinisches Landesmuseum** and the **Archäologisches Landesmuseum** (both open Apr.–Oct., daily 10–6; Nov.–Mar., Tues.–Sun. 10–4). Inside you'll find the *Nydam,* a 1,600-year-old rowboat; a collection of *Moorleichen*, the eerie corpses of hapless people who, despite their 2,000-year sojourn in a peat bog, are preserved shockingly well; and a solid collection of German expressionist art by the likes of Emil Nolde and Ernst Barlach. You've got to go, at least to see the boat and the peat people.

BASICS The **post office** (Stadtweg 53, tel. 04621/8530, open Mon.–Sat. 9–5) is just north of the Altstadt on the pedestrianized Stadtweg. It exchanges currency (no fee) and traveler's checks (DM 3 per check) at competitive rates and has an international phone annex. The English-speaking staff at the **Städtische Touristinformation** (Plessenstr. 7, tel. 04621/814226 or 04621/814227) has plenty of brochures, city maps, and accommodations options; for a DM 5 fee they'll also make you a room reservation. Wash your clothes at **Bio Wasch** (Stadtweg 70, tel. 04621/25202) for DM 6 per load and DM 1 per 15 minutes of drying time. **Luggage lockers** at the train station cost DM 2 per day.

COMING AND GOING The **train station** (Bahnhofstr., tel. 04621/23342) is 2 kilometers (1¼ miles) south of Schloß Gottorf and a long, long way from the Altstadt. To get there from the train depot take Bus 1 or 2 to the main bus station, **Zentral Omnibus** (Königstr. 1), which is at the end of the line in the heart of the downtown area. Train destinations from Schleswig include Flensburg (DM 11), Kiel (DM 10.80), and Husum (DM 8.40).

Holm, Sweet Home

From Am Markt it's only a short walk east to Holm, a tiny fishing village that is Schleswig's oldest settled quarter. In Holm, narrow lanes and quiet walkways meander through a maze of short half-timbered houses adorned with flowers. Explore Holm's white, Lilliputian chapel and adjacent cemetery. The ocean has traditionally given Holm its livelihood and flavor, and nearby on the waterfront old men still gather to spin yarns about the big one that got away.

The sights in Schleswig are spread out, so you can't rely on ped power to get you everywhere. You're going to have to catch a bus (DM 1.60 per ride) or, better yet, rent a bike at the train station for DM 8 per day; from **Aral-Tankstelle** (Königstr. 20, tel. 04621/24279) for DM 9 per day; or from **Splettstößer** (Bismarckstr. 13, tel. 04621/24102).

WHERE TO SLEEP The tourist office distributes two helpful leaflets: "*Hotels, Speiselokale, Cafés*" lists hotels and restaurants, and "*Unterkunftsverzeichnis*" lists private rooms that cost DM 20–DM 25 per person. Doubles start at DM 80 at **Pension Schleiblick** (Hafengang 4, tel. 04621/23468 or 04621/25987), a spacious house with clean private rooms and a smart-looking spiral staircase. Ask for a room with a view of the Schlei. The cramped, noisy rooms at the local **Jugendherberge** (Spielkoppel 1, tel. 04621/23893) are not unlike renovated jail cells—claustrophobes stay away. Beds fetch DM 14.50 (26 and under) and DM 17.50 (over 26). From the train station take Bus 1 or 2 to the Stadttheater on Lollfuß.

Camp out from March through October near the Wikinger Museum, at **Camping Haddeby** (2381 Haddeby/Schleswig, tel. 04621/32450), 3½ kilometers (2 miles) from the train station and about 8 kilometers (5 miles) from the Altstadt. It's an overcrowded campground (because it's the only one) that's operated by a crabby old man. Sites cost DM 8 plus DM 5 per person. Take any bus marked HAITHABU from the train station.

FOOD The best street for cheap student dives and alternative-type bars is Lollfuß. It runs parallel to the Schlei between Schloß Gottorf and Schleswig's northside residential areas. One of the best places to eat is the unusual **Lolly-Pub** (Lollfuß 79, tel. 04621/26072), a funky restaurant that specializes in inventing new German dishes (DM 6–DM 9) with far-out, untranslatable names. Older locals frequent **Bier & Speeldeel** (Lollfuß 98A, tel. 04621/21008), where you can shoot a game of pool while waiting for a meal; the soups (DM 4) and sandwiches (DM 2) get rave reviews. **Patio** (Lollfuß 3, tel. 04621/29999) is a cozy two-story restaurant specializing in hot, simple meals—sandwiches, pasta, and pizza—for about DM 10. **Maske** (Theaterstr., near youth hostel, tel. 04621/28999) serves excellent Spanish *tapas* (hors d'oeuvres, DM 8–DM 10), or try a hearty combination plate for about DM 15.

Flensburg

Flensburg, Germany's northernmost city, perches on the border with Denmark, so its Danish flavor—Danish flags and the occasional Danish street sign, Danish butter cookies and cheeses—is authentic. Yet Flensburg is not a mere extension of Denmark. At the very least, Flensburg is famous among Germans as the hometown of Beate Uhse, proprietor of one of the country's largest sex-shop chains (you'll find a Beate Uhse sex shop in any respectable German city). Flensburg is also known as the home of the wacky cartoon character Werner, infamous for his once-incessant guzzling of the town's other famous product, Flensburger Pils beer. Unfortunately, the brewery owner didn't appreciate the publicity, so Werner now drinks Bölkstoff. Speaking of potables, Flensburg also produces its own brand of rum, a drink as popular in northern Germany as on any Caribbean beach.

Most people come to Flensburg only on their way to Denmark, but the city does have a few worthwhile sights. Be sure to bring along the creatively named "6: Flensburg, English," an invaluable brochure that distinguishes the courtyards, lanes, and churches in the city center. It's available at the **tourist office** (Norderstr. 6, tel. 0461/23090 or 0461/25901, open Mon.–Sat. 9–5). It's hard to miss Flensburg's pair of "historic olde avenues"—**Rote Straße**, with its cutesy houses, and **Kompagniestraße,** also noted for its stoically weathered, Baroque-era facades. Kompagniestraße is a short walk from the tourist office and from **Kompagnietor,** the former sailors' guildhall, where there's a small exhibit of sea-oriented material—mainly sailors' outfits, ship riggings, and fishnets. The three biggest churches in Flensburg are **St. Johannis** (Johanniskirchhof 22), also the oldest; **St. Nikolai** (Südermarkt 16), by far the most beautiful; and **St. Marien** (Marienkirchhof 4–5), with its stunning stained-glass windows.

Visitors often take advantage of Flensburg's location to sail across the Danish border, usually to Sønderborg (which has a groovy medieval castle). Special visas are not required for U.S. and U.K. citizens. Docked in Flensburg's harbor, at the end of Flensburger Förde, are ferries that make the trek dozens of times daily for as little as DM 25 round-trip.

A good half-day jaunt from Flensburg is **Glücksburg,** a spa-resort that lies 8 kilometers (5 miles) northeast. Besides the usual beach activities—sunbathing when the weather's good, drinking beer or tea inside when it's grim—you can also explore the late Renaissance **Glücksburg Schloß** (Schloßhof, tel. 04631/2243, open Tues.–Sun. 10–5), a creamy-white castle that juts out of the surrounding artificial lake. Admission is DM 6 (DM 3 for students) and includes a cheap thrill: Don those fuzzy gray slippers they give you and have fun sliding away on the polished wood floors. It's not really encouraged by the castle staff, but it's almost as fun as in-line skating. Buses leave daily from ZOB's Platform 11 for Glücksburg; the trip takes 20 minutes and costs DM 6 round-trip.

COMING AND GOING The Flensburg **Bahnhof** (Am Bundesbahnhof, tel. 0461/861301) offers daily connections to Hamburg (two hours, DM 34), Kiel (70 minutes, DM 16.80), and Schleswig (40 minutes, DM 8.40). If you arrive by train, avoid the 20-minute walk downtown by presenting your train ticket at any ticket window to purchase the **DB Tagesrückfahrkarte** (DM 2). This gives you two hours of free bus rides. To reach the city center from the train station, hop on any bus marked ZENTRUM. Intercity buses depart from **ZOB** (Süderhofenden 1, tel. 0461/22700) for Hamburg (DM 26) and Kiel (DM 11), as well as most minor hubs in Schleswig-Holstein. Flensburg's **Mitfahrzentrale** (St. Jürgen-Pl., tel. 0461/23305) is near the tourist office.

WHERE TO SLEEP Try the convenient and fairly priced **Pension Annegret Ziesemer** (Wilhelmstr. 2, tel. 0461/25164; Augustastr. 8, tel. 0461/23770). The pension, housed in two buildings behind the ZOB bus station and run by a friendly older couple, has doubles for DM 65. Around the corner, **Hotel Handwerkerhaus** (Augustastr. 2, tel. 0461/144800) offers slightly older and more expensive doubles for DM 75. For cheaper sleeps take Bus 3, 5, or 7 to Stadion for the **Jugendherberge** (Fichtestr. 16, tel. 0461/37742), which rents standard dorm beds for DM 14.50 (26 and under) and DM 17.50 (over 26).

Niebüll

Niebüll, which lies 16 kilometers (10 miles) west of Flensburg and only 11 kilometers (7 miles) south of the Danish border, is a small town of 7,000 noted for its beautifully tended streets. But the real reason it's in this guidebook is strictly practical: Niebüll lies on the main Hamburg–Sylt rail line, and if you're on your way to Westerland on nearby Sylt Island (*see below*), you've got no choice but to pass through Niebüll. Consider a brief stopover and check out its two museums. The **Richard-Haizmann-Museum,** in the Rathaus (Rathauspl., tel. 04661/60175), displays works by the local painter-sculptor. Haizmann was labeled a degenerate by the Nazis in the early 1930s, and in 1934 the expressionist was exiled to what the Nazis considered the most remote spot in Germany—Niebüll. The museum's collection consists mostly of works Haizmann finished while living in town, although there are a few pieces that date from his days in Berlin. The **Friesiches Museum Niebüll-Deezbüll** (Osterweg 76, tel. 04661/3656) has rooms that introduce you to the pre-flush toilet and pre-microwave living standards of the 17th and 18th centuries; it's open only by appointment.

Find out about other attractions and events—and about local private rooms—at **Tourist-Information** (tel. 04661/69190), in the Rathaus. The best pension in town is Enke Greve's Pension **"Haus Enke"** (Deezbüller Str. 12, tel. 04661/6550). Colorful double rooms cost DM 60 and include a free buffet breakfast, free laundry, and free pickup from the train station. The **Jugendherberge** (Deezbülldeich 2, tel. 04661/8762) is set in a century-old thatched-roof house with 38 beds (DM 14). Check out Hauptstraße for grocery stores, cafés, and restaurants. Niebüll's **Bahnhof** (Bahnhofstr., tel. 04661/4233) is only a short walk down Rathausstraße from the tourist office and town center. Destinations include Sylt Island's Westerland (DM 8.50), Schleswig (DM 7), Dagebüll (DM 4.20), and Husum (DM 8.50). The central bus station, or ZOB (Marktstr., tel. 04661/8775), handles bus connections for Flensburg; Dagebüll; and Tønder, Denmark.

North Frisian Islands

Just off the west coast you can sometimes see the flat outline of the North Frisian Islands—a scattered group of sandy, mostly flat islands that seem in danger of being submerged whenever the weather gets rough. Sylt, the largest, is not really an island but rather a T-shape sand spit (trains exploit the passage, making Sylt super easy for budget travelers to explore). The other islands in the group—Amrum, Föhr, and Pellworm—are honest-to-goodness islands, which means they're accessible only by ferry. Ferries leave throughout the year (less often in winter) from Dagebüll, a small port town with frequent bus and rail connections to Niebüll, 10 kilometers (6 miles) to the northeast. Ferries to Pellworm leave only from Nordstrand, a short train or bus ride from Husum. Prices vary according to the season, but a round-trip ferry ride generally costs DM 25–DM 35 in summer, about DM 10 less in winter.

AMRUM AND FOHR

On windswept and storm-battered Amrum and Föhr you get a sense of how generations of North Sea fishermen have managed to eke a living from the ocean. Unspoiled and with lots of sandy beach, Amrum and Föhr are ideal for bike rides, hikes across sand dunes and through small forests, swimming, and surf fishing but not much else. If you're searching for peace and quiet and magnificent ocean views, look no farther.

Wyk is the largest village on Föhr. It attracts the bulk—okay, the small handful—of island day-trippers because of its few shops and eateries. On the edge of Wyk, near a private airfield, is the youth hostel **Jugendherberge Wyk** (Fehrsteig 41, tel. 04681/2355, closed Feb.), which has 186 beds and costs DM 15.20 (26 and under) and DM 18.70 (over 26), including breakfast. The hostel is a 45-minute walk from the

Next Stop, Denmark

Frequent buses leave Niebüll and hop across the border to Tønder, Denmark. The trip takes 45 minutes and costs DM 15. In Tønder, Denmark's oldest city, elaborate gabled houses surround the ornate Kristikirk (Christ Church), itself a stunning contrast of white walls and dark wood pews. The Tønder Museum (Kongevej 55, tel. 74/722657) displays a unique collection of furniture and **Klöppelspitzen** ***(fine hand-made lace). In the same building, the Sondeerjyllands Kunstmuseum exhibits contemporary works by Danish artists. Stop by the impossible-to-miss tourist office, located smack in the center of Tønder's walkable old town, for city maps and lodging guides.***

ferry port along a clearly marked path. In town, **Fremdenverkehrsgemeinschaft Föhr** (2270 Süderende, tel. 04681/444) provides tourist information and can book private rooms in the DM 20–DM 30 range. In **Wittdün,** the largest village on Amrum, is a 212-bed **Jugendherberge** (Mittelstr. 1, tel. 04682/2010, closed Dec.). Located off Badestrand, about 300 yards from the ferry port, the hostel charges DM 15.20 (26 and under) and DM 18.70 (over 26), including breakfast. Ferries connect both islands with Dagebüll twice or so daily during summer, three times a week in winter, weather permitting. A round-trip ticket generally costs DM 30.

PELLWORM

The island of Pellworm is noted for its untroubled pastureland and lazy farm villages—quite the antithesis of Sylt. Bike riding, walking, musing on the horizon, and surf combing (there aren't any proper beaches on Pellworm, only grassy strands that buffer the sea) are the norm here. Don't expect any nightlife because there isn't any—only a few lonely restaurants where old men drink and tell stories to keep warm. This serene environment attracts an older, low-key crowd. If you happen to visit on a rainy day, duck inside one of Pellworm's two churches, the **Alte Kirche** (Old Church), whose original cornerstone was laid in 1095, and the not-so-new **Neue Kirche** (New Church), built in 1528. Ferries run between Pellworm and Nordstrand, near Husum, three to five times daily. Tourist information is available at the **Kurverwaltung Pellworm** (tel. 04844/544).

SYLT

The long (40 kilometers, or 25 miles) and skinny (3 kilometers, or 2 miles) island of Sylt is the playground of Germany's wealthy. On Sylt every other car is an out-of-town Mercedes, BMW, or Porsche, and come nightfall the island's swank restaurants are filled with loaded yuppies having a good but expensive time. Windsurfers, too, flock to Sylt in summer, when the island's population surges from 20,000 to 110,000. In September the island hosts the **Wind Surfing World Cup,** an internationally televised event that sees Sylt's population swell to almost unbearable proportions. Crowds are less of a problem in **Hörnum,** the southernmost town on Sylt, but there's not a lot to do there. A better bet is **Westerland,** Sylt's largest town. It's located smack dab in the middle of the island and is where the bulk of restaurants, bars, and tourist shops are found. **Kampen,** north of Westerland, is where the rich—and those who like to think they're rich—have summer homes. It's considered the noble town on Sylt, where the self-appointed VIPs hang out. The rest of the island is less developed and more suited to long bike rides, hikes over tall desertlike sand dunes, and windsurfing.

Numerous tourist facilities and the ease of getting here make Sylt a good first choice if you're bound for a North Frisian island. Trains from Dagebüll (DM 10.80), Niebüll (DM 8.50), and Husum (DM 17) stop at Westerland. Just outside the station is the **tourist-information office** (tel. 04651/24001), which can set you up with lists of bicycle-rental shops, pensions, and other information offices on the island. Sylt has two remote **Jugendherbergen,** one (which used to be a Nazi barracks) way up north in the small village of List (Mövenberg, tel. 04652/397) and one in Hörnum (Friesenpl. 2, tel. 04841/2714), at the southern tip.

Husum

German author Theodore Storm (1817–1888) once called Husum, his adopted home town, "*die graue Stadt am Meer*" ("the gray town by the sea"). Husum may be battered by fierce gales during the suffocatingly long winter, but it's a bit more appealing than Storm suggests—especially in April when millions of irises bloom and cast a light purple haze around the emphatically ungray Husum. Spring's effulgence is particularly noticeable in the **Schloßpark** (Schloß vor Husum, tel. 04841/67588), a former monastic site that now contains acres of lush gardens. When the flowers aren't in bloom the most memorable thing about Husum may be its harbor. Because of the tides Husum's harbor is navigable only six hours each day, but this hasn't hindered the centuries-old fishing industry. Take a peek at the **Schiffbrücke** marina, near the central Markt, for a good cross section of modern trawlers and rough-hewn fishing skiffs.

Am Markt, the typically smart-looking central marketplace, is surrounded by a stoic collection of half-timbered and Baroque facades and a bunch of shops and pleasant cafés. (Pick up the English-language pamphlet "Husum: A Stroll Through the Town" at the tourist office, located in the Markt's Rathaus.) Husum's high-culture attractions include the **Nissenhaus** (Herzog-Adolf-Str. 25, tel. 04841/2545), which has a large collection documenting the northern Friesian landscape and the area's culture and history. Also worthwhile is the **Storm-Haus** (Wasserreihe 31, tel. 04841/666270), where Storm lived and wrote from 1866 to 1880. Ask for the English pamphlet with Storm's biography and a description of the house. Kitsch lovers shouldn't miss the awkwardly named **Tabak-und-Kinder Museum,** or Tobacco and Children's Museum (Wasserreihe 52, tel. 04841/61276). This small two-story complex is packed with dolls, toys, ashtrays, and cigar boxes—just about anything that could conceivably be linked with children or smoking, which is a lot. In the middle of May, Husum hosts the **Amerikanische Woche,** a festival dedicated to Frieslanders who emigrated to America.

BASICS If you're down to the last pair of whatever you've been wearing, nuke the grungies for DM 6 per load at the **Wasch-Center** (Norderstr. 12, tel. 04841/3110). The **tourist office** (Rathaus, tel. 04841/66991) has the usual city maps, brochures, and listings of local accommodations. **Zweirad Clausen** (Osterende 94, tel. 04841/72975) and **Service Center** (Schulstr. 4, tel. 04841/4465) rent bikes for DM 7 per day.

COMING AND GOING The **Hauptbahnhof** (Poggenburgstr., tel. 04841/4074), less than a 10-minute walk from the town center, is your best bet if you're heading to St. Peter-Ording (DM 15), Sylt's Westerland (DM 17), Nordstrand (DM 12), or Hamburg (DM 27). **Autokraft GmbH** (Ringstr. 3–9, tel. 04841/3634) is a long-distance bus network you can use in the unlikely event the train doesn't go in your direction. The cost to travel by **Mitfahrzentrale** (Stadtweg 46, tel. 04841/6012) is about DM 1 per kilometer (⅝ mile).

WHERE TO SLEEP Stop by the tourist office for listings of hotels, most priced at about DM 70 per person, and private rooms, which generally fetch DM 30 per person. **Rödekrog** (Wilhelm Str. 10, tel. 04841/3771), with a sunny patio, breakfast buffet, and convenient location near the train station, is a steal at DM 65 per double. Hostel seekers should take Bus 3 (DM 2) or make the 30-minute walk to **Theodore Storm Jugendherberge** (Schobüller Str. 34, tel. 04841/2714), a spacious, clean, dorm-style hostel that charges DM 14 (26 and under) and DM 16 (over 26) per person. The closest **campground** is near the beach at Dockkoog (tel. 04841/61911).

FOOD Sample the local specialty, *Krabben Brötchen* (small shrimp sandwiches) for about DM 5 at one of the zillion Imbisse along the harbor. **Café Kö** (Schiffbrücke 5, tel. 04841/2050) quickly serves pizza (DM 8–DM 15), pasta (DM 7–DM 11.50), and salads (DM 4.50–DM 11.50). Locals line up for DM 9 helpings of *Bauernfrühstück mit Schinken* (farmer's breakfast with ham) in the always-packed **Gastätte "Treffpunkt Am Zob"** (Süderstr. 2, tel. 04841/477). Wash it all down with a beer at the longest bar in Schleswig-Holstein, the **Husum Pub** (Hafenstr. 6, tel. 04841/62788). When you're craving a decent hot meal for less than DM 10, make a beeline for **Bier u. Weincomptoir** (Poggenburgstr. 11A, tel. 04841/2810), a hole-in-the-wall eatery across from the train station.

NEAR HUSUM

ST. PETER-ORDING St. Peter-Ording is a semi-upscale resort town on the Eiderstedt peninsula, 41 kilometers (25 miles) southwest of Husum. The most notable thing about St. Peter-Ording is its beach—a 12-kilometer-long (7½-mile-long) strip of plush sand that looks out over the North Sea. St. Peter-Ording attracts sun-loving vacationers throughout summer and, even during winter, a few adventurous sorts intent on experiencing the favorite local pastime, *Strandsegeln* (beach sailing). This involves a sporty go-cart supplemented by a sail, a strong wind, and a love of plowing face-first into a sandbank after a crosscurrent blows you out of control. All in all, gosh darn fun. To learn beach sailing or rent gear, contact Doris Lindemann (tel. 04863/5463) between 4 and 7. Annoyingly, if you just want to lounge on the beach, be warned that money-grubbing officials charge a *Kurtaxe* (visitor's tax) of DM 4 (DM 2 students) in summer, half that in winter.

If you're headed for Denmark, the prominent Danish retailers **Fr. Einsmann & Sohn** (tel. 04863/3014) shuttle visitors daily on their private buses. At DM 5 each way, it's cheaper than a bus or ferry from Flensburg or Niebüll. Trains connect St. Peter-Ording and Husum hourly; the 50-minute trip costs DM 8.40.

Mecklenburg-Vorpommern

Reunification has taken its toll on Mecklenburg-Vorpommern—the docks at Rostock, the former GDR's largest port, now lie largely idle, and unemployment is high. Still, you won't find the same level of decaying industry here as you will in other eastern German Länder, although in some towns you will have to navigate a gruesome *Neustadt* (New City) before escaping into the historic and good-looking old town. But you don't come to Mecklenburg-Vorpommern for its cities. The former GDR's least populated and poorest state offers spectacular natural beauty. Of Germany's nine national parks, three are found in the region: Nationalpark Jasmund, Nationalpark Müritz, and Nationalpark Vorpommische Boddenlandschaft. These half-forgotten wonders, as unfamiliar to "unified" Germans as they are to foreigners, are complemented by more than 1,100 kilometers (680 miles) of rugged coastline and sandy beach, ancient ports and fishing villages.

Sixty-five percent of the region is devoted to agriculture, and another 22% is blanketed by forest—mainly tight-clustered beech forest that stretches for miles along the coast. With the exception of Mecklenburg-Vorpommern's 10 or so bigger cities, most towns in the region have populations of fewer than 20,000. Mecklenburg-Vorpommern is a lazy, subdued place, attuned to people who aren't bored by kilometer-wide views over burnt-yellow fields.

Despite being neglected during the communist era, Germany's northern coast is again becoming the holiday destination of choice for many Germans. Summer in the larger resorts brings families with children and the occasional young German couple. During summer and school holidays don't expect to waltz in and get a room with a snap of your fingers (on Rügen Island some people reserve a year in advance). In winter divide the crowds by 10 and add 40 years to the average age; on the coast, winter is the time for *Omas* and *Opas* (grandmas and grandpas) to stroll the beachfront and reminisce about the good old days.

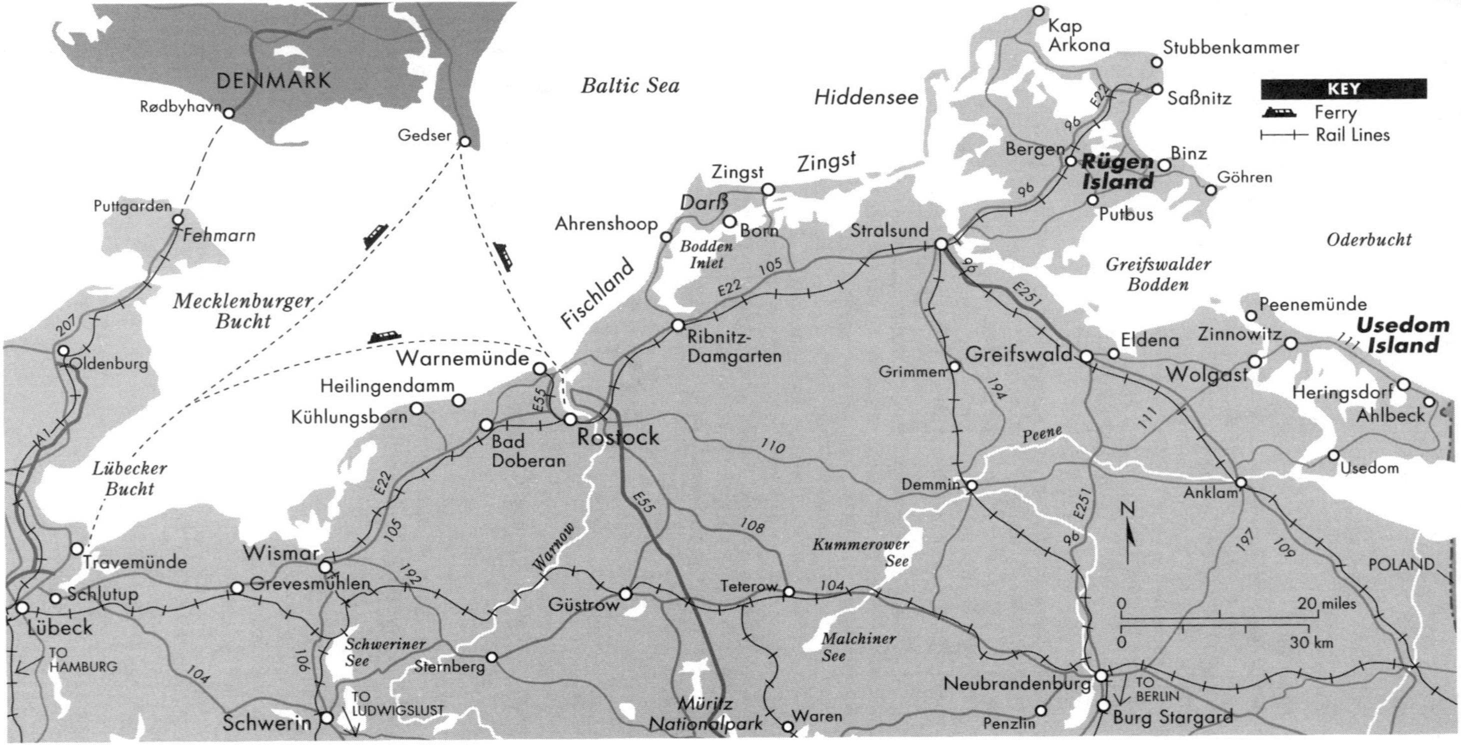

Mecklenburg-Vorpommern

KEY
Ferry
Rail Lines

Baltic Sea
DENMARK
Rødbyhavn
Gedser
Puttgarden
Fehmarn
Oldenburg
Mecklenburger Bucht
Lübecker Bucht
Travemünde
Schlutup
Lübeck
TO HAMBURG
Wismar
Grevesmühlen
Schwerin
Schweriner See
TO LUDWIGSLUST
Kühlungsborn
Heiligendamm
Warnemünde
Bad Doberan
Rostock
Warnow
Sternberg
Güstrow
Müritz Nationalpark
Waren
Fischland
Ahrenshoop
Darß
Bodden Inlet
Born
Zingst
Zingst
Ribnitz-Damgarten
Teterow
Malchiner See
Kummerower See
Hiddensee
Stralsund
Grimmen
Demmin
Greifswald
Neubrandenburg
Penzlin
Burg Stargard
TO BERLIN
Peene
Kap Arkona
Bergen
Rügen Island
Putbus
Binz
Saßnitz
Stubbenkammer
Göhren
Greifswalder Bodden
Eldena
Wolgast
Zinnowitz
Peenemünde
Usedom Island
Oderbucht
Heringsdorf
Ahlbeck
Usedom
Anklam
POLAND
N
0 20 miles
0 30 km
A1 207 104 106 105 E22 192 E55 108 110 194 96 E251 111 197 109

Schwerin

Schwerin, the modern capital of Mecklenburg-Vorpommern, is a very un-Baltic sort of town. It's nearly 35 kilometers (22 miles) from the coast and was mostly ignored by Hanseatic League merchants. As a result, Schwerin never developed a core of elegant merchant dwellings on the scale you find elsewhere on the Baltic Coast. Schwerin does have a few historic sights, but it wasn't until the 19th century that it was transformed into a posh lakeside retreat. Schwerin's largest lake, the **Schweriner See,** is a stone's throw from the historic old town. Meandering through the Altstadt's cobblestone streets it's not uncommon to dead-end right at the shore—pretty neat. And even though Schwerin blossomed late in life, its riverside promenades and stunning castle draw tourists from near and far.

You've missed the highlight of the Baltic region if you're near Schwerin and don't make the effort to come here.

COMING AND GOING Schwerin's train station, located to the west of Pfaffenteich Lake, has daily connections to Berlin (via Wittenberge, 10 per day, DM 31), Halle (DM 55), Hamburg (five per day, DM 29), Köthen (DM 47), Leipzig (DM 64), Lübeck (via Bad Kleinen, eight per day, DM 14.80), Magdeburg (DM 36), and Rostock (11 per day, DM 19). To reach the old town from the train station, follow Herbert-Warnke-Straße to Pfaffenteich Lake, turn right and go straight. The bus station is in the old town by the Schloß.

WHERE TO SLEEP AND EAT Imbiß stands are everywhere in the old town for the cheapest in cheap eating. Or try **Ritter Stube** (Ritterstr. 3, tel. 0385/865725), an informal restaurant cum beer hall with traditional Mecklenburger dishes (cabbage, wursts, smoked goose, salted fish) for as little as DM 13. **Waldburg** (Schloßgartenallee 70, tel. 0385/812552), on the banks of the Schwerin See, is a cozy restaurant specializing in game, mostly goose. Expect to pay at least DM 20 per person for dinner.

Inexpensive accommodations are so hard to come by that the mosquito-infested **Jugendherberge** (Waldschulenweg 3, tel. 0385/213005) is the unfortunate first choice. The management's advice about the coed and communal basement shower room is "Be careful!" Spaces in this 93-bed complex fetch DM 13.50 (26 and under) and DM 16 (over 26), including breakfast. From the train station take Bus 15 to the last stop. Otherwise, stop by the tourist office for their woefully short list of budget accommodations in town. Failing that, the ever-cranky **Frau Mars** (Körnerstr. 18) runs a room-renting service.

WORTH SEEING Standing on the shore of Schweriner See you get an unbeatable view of the famous **Schloß Schwerin** (Lennestr., admission DM 3, open Tues.–Sun. 10–5). This opulent fairy-tale castle was built by the Mecklenburg royal family in 1857 in a mishmash of Renaissance, Baroque, and Gothic styles. It stands alone on a

Fish, Fish, Beer, and Fish

In a region with a 1,100-kilometer-long (680-mile-long) coastline, you'd better like fish. Try **Matjes** ***(white herring), prepared in at least 10 ways. Other good bets are*** **Mecklenburger Fischsuppe** ***(fish soup with veggies, tomatoes, and sour cream), and*** **Pannfische,** ***a sort of McFishwich-looking patty lavished with cabbage. Fish aside, try*** **Mecklenburger Griebenroller** ***(potato, egg, and bacon casserole) and, to wash it down,*** **Eierbier** ***(egg beer). Although it's less common nowadays, you may still come across*** **Soljanka,** ***a Russian meat-and-vegetable soup.***

small island on the edge of the Schwerin See, adorned with 15 turrets and surrounded by a lush expanse of well-kept gardens. The Communists did a good job keeping this eclectic-looking castle in prime condition. Inside its 80 rooms you'll find pristine antiques, silk tapestries, carved wood floors, and ornately decorated, plaster-inlaid walls. The Throne Room is magnificently posh. On the second and third floors also look for the **Technisches Landesmuseum Schwerin** and the **Archäologisches Landesmuseum,** two tiny museums that do a reasonable job of explaining (in German) the history of Mecklenburg-Vorpommern. The adjacent chapel dates from 1560 and is the only reminder of an earlier Renaissance castle that once stood on the site. What makes the chapel so memorable are the surrounding Schloßgarten, Burggarten, and Grüngarten, three picture-perfect parks that were laid out in the 18th century. For a great view, hop on one of the boats docked in front of the castle; an hour's putt-putt across the lake costs about DM 10. Similar excursions are offered by **Weiße Flotte** (tel. 0385/861464 or 0385/581–1595). Stop by the palace's second-floor coffee shop, the Schloßcafé, for outstanding pastries and homemade ice cream. Free concerts are sometimes held here on summer afternoons.

The **Alter Garten,** Schwerin's impressive central square, is opposite the Schloß. The majestic **Staatstheater** on the square offers a hodgepodge of opera, classical music, and mostly German-language drama. Stop by the **tourist office** (Am Markt 11, tel. 0385/812314) or check the notice board at the theater for current performance schedules; cheap student tickets are available for most shows. The **Staatliches Museum Schwerin** (tel. 0385/57581, admission free, open Tues.–Sun. 9–4), the building with all the steps next to the theater, houses a solid collection of Flemish and Dutch masters. Also on display are works by 19th-century German artists like Max Liebermann and Lovis Corinth. A short walk from here is Schwerin's Gothic cathedral, or **Dom** (Buschstr.). The cathedral's bronze baptismal font dates from the 14th century, the altar from 1440. More impressive is the adjoining 320-foot-high church tower (open Mon.–Sat. 11–noon and 2:30–4:30, Sun. 2:30–4:30). Huff and puff your way up its 219 steps for sweeping views of Schwerin and its seven lakes.

A good day-trip from Schwerin is to the nearby town of **Ludwigslust,** a 20-minute train ride away. Ludwigslust (its local nickname is "Lulu") was the residence of the dukes of Mecklenburg from 1756 to 1837. The main attraction here is an 18th-century **Schloß,** a typical late Baroque creation that dominates Lulu's old quarter. The castle is accessible only by tour, daily at 11, 2, and 3. Many of the castle's elaborate vases and other ornaments are made of papier-mâché. Wander around the **Schloßpark,** and you might stumble across some old ruins that aren't really that old—the castle caretakers constructed them to give the park an ancient feel.

Wismar

Although not known as a big tourist attraction, Wismar, governed by Sweden until 1903, has heaps of ancient buildings. This is partly due to Wismar's association with the long-defunct Hanseatic League. In the 13th century, when pirates ruled the Baltic, the port towns of Wismar, Lübeck, and Rostock banded together in a mutual-defense pact. This dealt effectively with the pirate problem and helped regional trade blossom. Clever enough to recognize a good thing when they saw it, the leaders of these three cities formed the powerful and prosperous bloc that went on to dominate the Baltic region for centuries—you guessed it, the Hanseatic League. The Thirty Years War crippled the league, and Wismar started its slow but sure decline. Sweden eventually took control of the city and then, short on cash, mortgaged it to a Mecklenburg duke in 1803 on a 100-year lease. When this expired, Wismar was legally reconnected to Germany.

Despite the league's decline, the wealth generated by Hanseatic merchants can still be seen in Wismar, particularly in the ornate, gabled houses that front the **Marktplatz,** the biggest in northern Germany. Dominating the square are the **Rathaus**; the 16th-century Dutch Renaissance **Wasserkunst,** an ornate pumping station that supplied the town's water until 1897; and the **Alte Schwede,** Wismar's oldest town house (now an expensive tourist restaurant). Look up at the skyline for a glimpse of the 250-foot tower of the ruined **Marienkirche,** just behind Marktplatz. The church was bombed during World War II, but the tower still houses a bevy of bells, played daily at noon, 3, and 5. The 16th-century **Fürstenhof,** next door, is the former home of the dukes of Mecklenburg. Its facade is covered with ornate friezes depicting scenes from the Trojan War. Also next door is the **Georgenkirche,** another ruined cathedral—reportedly the largest religious ruin in Europe. Head back through Marktplatz, then along Krämerstraße, and you'll soon stumble upon **Nikolaikirche** (Schweinsbrücke). This late Gothic church houses religious treasures salvaged from the wreckage of Georgenkirche and Marienkirche, most notably the former's 17th-century altar.

Walk along the harbor and look for the colorful **Schweden Köpfe** (Swedish heads)—souvenirs from Wismar's Swedish years—in front of the Baumhaus (tree house). With its jetties and quays, the port is a pleasant place to hang out on a sunny afternoon. Grab coffee and a pastry at one of the waterfront cafés, or hop on one of **Weiße Flotte**'s harbor cruises. These generally cost about DM 10 per person and last 45 minutes; contact the tourist office for current schedules.

VISITOR INFORMATION The **tourist office** (Stadthaus am Markt, tel. 03841/2958; open weekdays 9–5, Sat. 10–3) is opposite the Alte Schwede on Marktplatz. It sells minimaps with all the sights labeled and can also book you into a private room (DM 20–DM 30) or pension.

COMING AND GOING Wismar's **Hauptbahnhof** (Bahnhofstr., tel. 03841/622892) is a 10-minute walk from the city center; make a left on Bahnhofstraße, turn right on Mühlengrube, then left on ABC-Straße. You can go by train from here to Bad Doberan (five per day, DM 8.40), Rostock (eight per day, DM 12.60), and Schwerin (eight per day, DM 6.40). The **bus station,** a five-minute walk to the right of the train station, has an information booth and a posted listing of bus destinations—notably Schwerin (DM 5) and Rostock (DM 9.50). Frau Flom runs a small ride-share service, the **Mitfahrzentrale** (Claus-Jesup-Str. 47, tel. 03841/611227), where you'll end up paying an outrageous DM 1 per kilometer (⅔ mile).

WHERE TO SLEEP The tourist office arranges private rooms in the DM 20–DM 30 (per person) range—the only real budget option, considering that Wismar doesn't have a hostel. If all the private rooms are booked, try **Mecklenburg Hof** (Gerberstr. 16, tel. 03841/2706), a tidy pension only a few minutes' walk from Marktplatz. Doubles—some with bath—cost less than DM 70. Outside the city, **Hotel Bertromshof** has shoe-box-size doubles for DM 95; take Bus D or E to the Sporthalle. If you have the urge to camp, head for **Campingplatz Leuchtturm** (Westküste, tel. 03841/216 or 03841/224) on the island of Poel. Weiße Flotte operates daily ferries from Wismar's harbor to Poel for about DM 12 round-trip; contact the tourist office for current schedules.

FOOD Lübschestraße and Krämerstraße, the main pedestrian drags, are littered with department stores, bakeries, and small cafés. Eat simple, reasonably priced meals among locals and tourists at **Zum Hirsch** (Lübschestr. 35, tel. 03841/3205). A few doors down is **Zum Weinberg** (Lübschestr. 31, tel. 03841/3550, closed Sun. and Mon.), a wood-beamed wine tavern that's been in business since 1575. Meals fetch DM 15–DM 20 per person, and there's a substantial wine list. Cheaper still is **Gastmahl des Meeres** (Altböterstr. 6, tel. 03841/2134), popular with locals for its Mecklenburg Fischsuppe and Pannfisch—both priced less than DM 15.

Rostock

Rostock, the largest city in Mecklenburg-Vorpommern, has had a turbulent history. Once a thriving member of the powerful Hanseatic League, Rostock fell into decline following the dissolution of the Hanseatic Pact in 1669. For the next few centuries Rostock continued to eke its living from the sea, but it wasn't until the late 1940s that the city regained some of its ancient glory. Recognizing the need for a port city on the Baltic, the GDR spent millions of deutsche marks improving Rostock's harbor facilities. Shipbuilding once again became a major industry, and this helped transform Rostock into a well-to-do and reasonably cosmopolitan town—the "Gateway to the World," if you believe the former GDR's propaganda. Reunification, however, has not dealt kindly with Rostock. Nowadays companies can import goods into eastern Germany more cheaply by rail and truck than by boat, so Rostock's harbor is nearly stagnant. Since reunification, neo-Nazi skinheads and unemployed riffraff also have made a habit of ruthlessly beating Jews and immigrant foreigners—mostly Turks and Africans—in a show of Aryan "supremacy." Many Rostockians feel nothing but contempt for the neo-Nazi movement, but many others have expressed quiet support for the beatings and the burning of several foreign-worker hostels. The bottom line: Visitors should be prepared for the occasional outburst of racial violence. Jews and people of color should not be deterred from visiting, but avoid working-class quarters, and don't walk after dark.

Rostock is known for its excellent university, the oldest in northern Europe. Students carrying loads of books can be seen everywhere, and a slew of student bars and cafés contribute to the city's bacchanalian nightlife. Universitätsplatz, halfway down Kröpelinerstraße, is a popular hangout with students and tourists alike.

Rostock proper covers a 15-kilometer (9-mile) stretch of coast, yet the historic city center, at least, still seems compact. Don't be surprised to see the same student, businessman, or tourist twice while walking along **Kröpelinerstraße,** the main pedestrian-only zone, sometimes called simply the Kröpe. Rostock was severely damaged during World War II, but the core of the old town has been rebuilt, including portions of the medieval town wall and a number of Hanseatic League–era facades. If you start at **Kröpeliner Tor,** one of four remaining medieval gates (there were originally 22), and head down Kröpelinerstraße you'll pass dozens of smart half-timbered houses before reaching Rostock's central marketplace, **Am Markt.** Anchoring the square is the 13th-century **Rathaus,** topped by seven slender towers and surrounded by a photo-worthy collection of gabled Baroque facades. Look for the stone snake on the Rathaus's second column from the left. No one is sure why it's there, but people speculate that it was used as a test of Rostockian citizenship: The story goes that, in lieu of a passport, residents could mention the snake on the Rathaus to prove they came from Rostock.

From Am Markt, head north on Langestraße, and you'll soon stumble upon the stunning 12th-century **Marienkirche** (St. Mary's Church). It's home to a 40-foot-tall astronomical clock that dates from 1472. The clock tells you everything about time (except the future) and is set to run until Easter of 2017. If you're in the neighborhood around noon, check out the clock's *Spiel*: Apostles prance out, greet Jesus, get blessed, and pass through the heavenly gates (which, incidentally, slam in Judas's face). At the rear of Marienkirche is Rostock's former mint, the **Münze.** Between 1361 and 1864 the city coined its own money; depicted on the outdoor stone relief are Rostockian coin makers going about their work.

Rostock is full of lesser-known attractions that are worth a quick look. Touted as the only floating shopping center in the world, the **Portcenter,** on the Unterwar, is popular with old women who like to pick through the bargain displays. Tucked in the back of the **Alter Friedhof** (Lindenpark) is a small, peaceful Jewish cemetery and monument. The tallest building on August-Bebel-Straße—and the surrounding complex of buildings—used to be the local **Stasi headquarters.** Some believe that you can still spot "former" members of the secret police hanging about suspiciously. And if ships really turn you on, don't miss the nearby **Schiffahrtsmuseum der Hansestadt Rostock** (August-Bebel-Str. 1, tel. 0381/22697; admission DM 1.50). It traces the history of Baltic shipping and has a display of ships throughout the ages.

BASICS The **Deutsche Bank** (Kröpelinerstr. 84, tel. 0381/45650, open weekdays 10–4) charges a 3% commission for exchanging traveler's checks, no commission for cash transactions. Other banks with bureaux de change include **Commerzbank** (Universitätspl., tel. 0381/455834) and **Sparkasse Rostock** (Lange Str. 7–8, tel. 0381/45620). To send telegrams, make long-distance and collect calls, and buy handy telephone cards (good for international use), go to the central **post office** (Am Markt, Hauptpost Rostock, 0–2500 Rostock; tel. 0381/456–8319) in a gabled building across from the Rathaus. You can also receive mail here, but make sure the sender writes *Postlagernd* on the envelope, along with your name.

Rostock's main **tourist-information office** (Schnickmaster 13–14; tel. 0381/25260, 0381/34602, or 0381/22619) stocks city maps and can book private rooms for DM 5 (save the DM 5 fee by booking over the phone at least one day in advance). A second tourist office (tel. 0381/454026) is located in the train station and offers similar services. Both can book a boat tour of Rostock harbor with Weiße Flotte. The 90-minute harbor cruise costs about DM 15 per person.

COMING AND GOING From Rostock's **Hauptbahnhof** (Goethestr., tel. 0381/34454), just south of downtown, there's frequent daily service to Berlin (DM 31), Halle (DM 54), Leipzig (DM 60), Neustrelitz (DM 25), Schwerin (DM 12), Stralsund (DM 14.80), Waren (DM 14.80), and Wismar (DM 12.60). There's an S-Bahn stop at the train station for the 24-minute trip to Warnemünde (DM 1.20). The **bus station** (Pl. der Freundschaft, tel. 0381/818444) is behind the train depot; destinations include Greifswald (DM 12), Schwerin (DM 11.20), and Wismar (DM 7.40). From Rostock harbor, ferries leave year-round for Trelleborg, Sweden, and Gedser, Denmark; inquire at the tourist office for schedules.

Rostock students run a free **ride-matching service** (August-Bebel-Str. 28, tel. 0381/379–2481). Tell them when and where you're going, and they'll provide you a name and phone number whenever possible. You're responsible for arranging payment with the driver, so if you don't speak a little German you may have a problem.

WHERE TO SLEEP Most hotels in Rostock have recently been renovated and have doubled their prices. Student housing (*see* box, *below*) is the way to go, but if it's already packed, **Zimmerbörse** (Lange Str. 19, tel. 0381/22386) arranges private rooms starting at DM 25 per person. The **Hotel an der Stadthalle** (Pl. der Freundschaft, tel. 0381/440–0170), usually booked by businesspeople, has doubles for DM 65.

Sleeping for Really Cheap

Rostock's student-housing scene is a budget traveler's dream come true. For DM 4 (students) or DM 10 (nonstudents) you can hang with university students who may show you Rostock's real nightlife. The unbelievably low price also gets you an old but comfortable dorm room with bunk beds and kitchen and laundry access. The only hitch is trying to reach someone at the office, Studentenwerk Rostock (Am Vögenteich 13–15, tel. 0381/369613; Marksplanckstr. 1, tel. 0381/440–5443). Most dorms are within walking distance of downtown.

There are two youth hostels in and around Rostock. The **Jugendgästeschiff Rostock-Schmarl** (tel. 0381/716202 or 0381/716224) is on board a ship that doubles as a museum. It sounds strange, but the facilities are excellent, and you're only a short crawl from the beach. Space in one of the 85 beds costs DM 24.50 (26 and under) and DM 30.50 (over 26), including breakfast. Take the S-Bahn to Lütten Klein, and walk 20 minutes toward the water. In nearby Warnemünde, **Jugendherberge Rostock-Warnemünde** (Parkstr. 31, tel. 0381/52303) is cheaper (DM 13–DM 15.50), smaller (69 beds), and also within minutes of the beach. Take the S-Bahn to Warnemünde, and follow the signs toward the water; it's 25 minutes on foot. The nearest **campground** (tel. 0381/54841), overlooking the water in the small village of Markgrafenheide, is a long trek from Rostock. During summer, Bus 41 connects the campground with Rostock's train depot; otherwise you'll have to hitch or hike. Space in one of the oceanside sites costs DM 6 plus DM 2.50 per person.

FOOD Cruise Kröpelinerstraße and Breite Straße for small, low-price cafés and bakeries with yummy bread and pastries; **Die Brezelbäckerei,** at the end of Breite Straße, is highly recommended. Also try **Taverne** (Kröpelinerstr.), which serves Italian and Greek dishes for less than DM 15 amid nautical decorations. **Gastätte Krohn** (Alter Markt) is a small restaurant frequented by older locals where you can eat for less than DM 15. Pig out on fresh fish (less than DM 15) while sitting under life preservers and model ships that dangle from the ceiling at **Zur Kogge** (Wokrenterstr. 27). Enjoy a cup of coffee among students at the **Studentenkeller** (Universitätspl., through green doors and on left). There are two grocery stores on the main pedestrian drag: **Spar** (Kröpelinerstr.) and the super-cheap **Netto,** behind the Hauptbahnhof.

AFTER DARK You'll find lots of nautical pubs between Lange Straße and Ufer Am Strande—the sorts of places popular with aging, leathery men. Rostock's gay scene revolves around the club **Rat & Tat** (Am Strande 14, tel. 0381/27805; closed Mon., Tues., Thurs.). The adjoining café is popular with gays and straights alike, mostly because it's fairly priced. The straight and under-25 scene parties in Rostock's hundreds of student clubs. Club life is organized, and most clubs are sponsored by educational departments. They're at their best on weeknights (when students should be working) and rather quiet on weekends (when many students go home to Mom and Dad). A visit to a student club generally entails plentiful, cheap beer; listening to American heavy metal; and chatting with people looking to practice their English. Rostock's student clubs have notoriously short life spans, so check a newspaper or the monthly magazines *Rostocker* and *Das Stadtblatt*, available at the tourist office and most newsstands, for listings. Some current favorites are **Meli-Club** and **LT-Club,** both on Tierfelder Straße, and **ST-Club** (Albert-Einstein-Str.).

NEAR ROSTOCK

BAD DOBERAN AND ENVIRONS Bad Doberan, 11 kilometers (7 miles) west of Rostock, is famous for two things. The first is **Doberaner Münster** (Doberan Minster, admission DM 2), a redbrick cloister built by Cistercian monks between 1294 and 1368. Inside there's a 14th-century altarpiece and a whopping 45-foot-tall crucifix. The real reason for a visit, however, is to take a ride on ***Molli,*** a famous narrow-gauge train that runs 13 times daily between Bad Doberan and Kühlungsborn, 18 kilometers (11 miles) north. The first train leaves at 5 AM and the last returns at 10 PM; a round-trip ticket costs DM 4.50. *Molli* whizzes along Bad Doberan's cobbled main drag at a brisk 10 kilometers (6 miles) per hour, barely missing parked cars, then strikes out for the coast, passing some top-rate countryside on the way. *Molli* departs from a small depot opposite the main train station, which is a short walk from the **Jugendherberge** (Tempelberg, tel. 038203/2439). Bad Doberan's **tourist office** (Goethestr. 1, tel. 038203/3001) is at *Molli*'s first stop, Goethestraße.

Continue with *Molli* to the health resort of **Heiligendamm,** Germany's oldest seaside town. Exploring the "*Weiße Stadt am Meer*" ("White Town on the Sea") will take you an hour at most, if you crawl. Meander through the woods on the beach, and admire the stately white buildings. *Molli*'s last stops are in Kühlungsborn, a long town with a forest in the middle. Get off at Kühlungsborn Ost for the **Jugendherberge** (Dünenstr. 4, tel. 038293/270), whose reception desk opens at 3 PM, and at Kühlungsborn West for the **tourist-information center** (Poststr. 20, tel. 038293/620) and the campground, **Campingpark Kühlungsborn** (Waldstr., tel. 038293/7195).

GUSTROW Modern Güstrow, 33 kilometers (20 miles) south of Rostock, is a rich repository of German culture. In Güstrow's glory days, the rich and famous hobnobbed at its elegant palace, home to the mighty dukes of Mecklenburg-Güstrow. The **Renaissanceschloß,** undeniably the most impressive Renaissance building in Germany, is now one of the Baltic Coast's most popular tourist stops, especially with western German families. The complex was opened to the public in 1974, and its dazzling rooms have since been meticulously restored. Of special note is the Festivity Hall, where musicians once entertained royalty from the Trumpeter's Chair—built in an elevated cubbyhole so the musicians couldn't observe the heady intrigues of the courtiers below. Occupying two floors of the castle is the **Schloßmuseum** (admission DM 2, DM 1 students). The intertwined letters "U" and "E," decorating the entrance chamber's ceiling, are the initials of the duke of Mecklenburg, Ulrich, and his wife, Elisabeth. Don't miss the museum's 1618 globe, with its wacky vision of North America and Australia.

Güstrow was also home to Ernst Barlach, one of Germany's most renowned modern sculptors. Barlach and his work fell victim to the Nazis' aesthetic revisionism: Short on ammunition, they melted down his most famous creation, *Der Schwebende Engel* (*The Hovering Angel*) and cast it into bullets. After World War II a plaster copy of the angel was found in Köln and recast; now the angel once again stands in Güstrow's Gothic **Dom** (cathedral). The **Gertrudenkapelle** (between Gertruden Str. and Kapellenstr.), a small brick chapel in the middle of a romantic-looking cemetery, houses many of Barlach's other pieces. If the works move you, make the 30-minute trek to Barlach's **Atelierhaus** (studio, Heidberg 15), where some minor and unfinished pieces are kept in his old studio.

Güstrow Information (Gleviner Str. 33, tel. 03843/61023) distributes maps, brochures, and souvenirs; it also books accommodations. Because there's no youth hostel in town, lodging fills up quickly, so try to arrive as early as possible. The nearest campgrounds, **Campingplatz Lohmen,** 20 kilometers (12 miles) southwest of Güstrow, and **Campingplatz Krakow am See,** 23 kilometers (14 miles) south of Güstrow, are accessible by bus. Güstrow has convenient daily train connections to Neubrandenburg (DM 19), Rostock (DM 6.40), and Schwerin (DM 12.60).

Stralsund

The port town of Stralsund is the last stop before Rügen Island (*see below*), but it's more than just a convenient place to pick up supplies. Stralsund is a historic port associated with the Hanseatic League, which explains the number of Dutch Renaissance merchant homes in the town center. During its time within the GDR, Stralsund was infested with cement apartment towers and unsightly industrial complexes, but to judge by the number of buildings under construction it's only a matter of time before the town purges itself of the communist era's worst excesses. A number of its medieval and Renaissance buildings have already been restored, and the old town has benefited from a major rebuilding campaign.

In medieval times Stralsund played a dominant role in the Hanseatic League, and it is still Germany's main producer of fishing boats. In 1249 Stralsund was attacked by a fleet from Lübeck. In response a brawny defensive wall was erected around the present-day old town (fragments of the wall are still visible) to protect the impressive **Alter Markt.** It's flanked by dozens of Baroque and Renaissance merchant homes, most notably the **Wulflamhaus,** with its ornate, steeply stepped gables. The 13th-century **Rathaus,** which houses the tourist office (tel. 03831/59728 or 03831/ 59215), is the highlight of the square. This Gothic redbrick building is considered one of the finest examples of secular Gothic architecture in northern Germany and is adorned by Stralsund's coat of arms. Also facing the square is **Nikolaikirche,** with 56 altars, a 15-foot-tall cross, and one of the world's oldest astronomical clocks. If you head down the adjacent **Ossenreyerstraße,** the main pedestrian and commercial zone, you'll pass through the quieter **Appollonienmarkt** before butting into **Katherinenkloster,** a former cloister, on Mönchstraße. The **Meeremuseum,** inside the cloister, has displays on anything and everything to do with the sea, except maybe Aquaman.

In early June, Stralsund hosts its annual sailing festival, the Stralsunde Segelwoche. Head to the port for a bird's-eye view of hundreds of sailboats parading and racing. Frankenteich and Strelasund, two waterfront promenades, are also good viewing points. For a listing of events stop by the tourist office, but note that lodging in June is pretty scarce, so book early.

The rest of Stralsund is not very memorable, but if you want a taste of Rügen Island without too much hassle you can hop on one of Weiße Flotte's (tel. 03831/692473) daily ferries. These leave Stralsund harbor every few hours for Saßnitz and Hiddensee (round-trip fare, DM 15 and up). You can take in a few of Rügen's sights, spend time walking the shore, have some lunch, then return to Stralsund by nightfall.

COMING AND GOING Stralsund's **Hauptbahnhof** is southwest of the city, by Tribseer Damm. It has direct connections to Neubrandenburg (six per day, DM 16.80) and Rostock (hourly, DM 14.80), and to Binz (eight per day, DM 12), Bergen (12 per day, DM 6.40), and Saßnitz (12 per day, DM 10.80), on Rügen Island. The central **Busbahnhof** is a few minutes south of the Marienkirche, but you can catch intercity and long-distance buses outside the train station.

WHERE TO SLEEP Pretend you're a soldier defending your city while staying in the **Jugendherberge Stralsund** (Am Kütertor 1, tel. 03831/292160), housed in a city gate dating to 1293. Climb a maze of staircases to reach your dorm room (DM 13.50–DM 16). The staff at the reception desk (open 3–11) is notorious for saying the hostel is full when it isn't, so be pesky. Either way, they will direct you to other budget options. These generally include the **Jugendherberge Stralsund-Devin** (Sandstr. 21, tel. 03831/5258, closed Dec. 12–Jan. 31). Take Bus 3 from the train station to Devin, a 20-minute journey. Call ahead, as they, too, are often booked. The **Zentrale Zimmerbörse** (Ossenreyerstr. 23, tel. 03831/293894) books private rooms in the DM 25–DM 30 range. It's open weekdays 9–6 and Saturday 10–noon.

FOOD Walk in any direction on Ossenreyerstraße, and you're sure to find cheap eats in one of its many bakeries, cafés, Imbisse, and grocery stores. **Wulflamstuben** (Alter Markt 5, tel. 03831/291533), in a late Gothic gabled house dating from 1370, prepares traditional German food in the DM 10–DM 15 range. Slightly more expensive is **Scheelhaus** (Fährstr. 23, tel. 03831/2987), an old-fashioned restaurant fronted with elegant 10-foot-tall windows. Try the onion soup, the pork and peaches, or *Kartoffelbällchen* (potato dumplings filled with almonds, apples, and cinnamon), all priced less than DM 20.

Rügen Island

Among veteran travelers Rügen Island is a don't-miss attraction—the sort of destination you plan your Baltic Coast trip around. Rügen wasn't developed until the mid-19th century, when railroads first encouraged tourism in the northernmost point in Germany. During the 1920s and '30s Rügen's main towns—Bergen, Saßnitz, and Putbus—became popular holiday resorts, and Rügen continues to balance its natural wonders with the less wonderful creations of modern society (tourist shops, bars, and even a few stern communist-era hotels). Yet people don't come here for the architecture or nightlife but for the incredible mix of sights. There are the famous chalk cliffs around Stubbenkammer; fields of barley and wheat in the interior; lighthouses at Kap Arkona and Hiddensee; scattered thatch-roofed cottages; exclusive bathing resorts; Stone Age megalithic graves; and endless sandy beaches. Rügen's coast is nearly 600 kilometers (372 miles) long, and on the weather-beaten cliffs and beaches you'll encounter some sights that will stick with you forever.

Your best bet here is to find one place to settle down and then take day-trips to explore the nooks and crannies. The fact that Bergen, Saßnitz, and Binz are well connected to the mainland by train makes it easy to explore Rügen from Stralsund. But make the extra effort to stay on Rügen itself. There are 18 campgrounds on Rügen and a slew of private houses that rent space for DM 20–DM 30 per person. Lists of campgrounds and private rentals are available in the tourist-information offices spread around the island. Rügen's extensive bus network will get you almost anywhere you want to go, but you'll enjoy the countryside more if you rent a bike and pedal between the sights. In southeast Rügen the steam engine ***Rasender Roland*** chugs along at 30 kilometers (19 miles) per hour between Putbus, Binz, Granitz, and Göhren. Your trip here is not complete without a ride on this romantic, narrow-gauge train. If you're coming from Rostock, the best train for day-trips is the 9 AM Rostock–Rügen run; it reaches Bergen by 11 and Saßnitz by 11:25.

If you're really adventurous consider an excursion to nearby **Hiddensee,** a 17-kilometer-long (11-mile-long) island that lies off the west coast of Rügen. Hiddensee is known as "*dat söte Lännpken*" ("the Sweet Little Island"), but in reality it's a wild and remote place that allows no cars. Around the turn of the century Hiddensee prospered as a bathing and resort town popular with the likes of Albert Einstein, Thomas Mann, and Sigmund Freud. Nowadays Hiddensee is the place to rediscover the languid rhythms of nature—a place where animals lazily graze; where nature and stillness surround you. Contact **Zimmervermittlung und Information** (Rathaus, Vitte, tel. 038300/242) for tourist and room information. Ferries operated by **Weiße Flotte** (tel. 03831/692371) run daily from Stralsund on the mainland and Schaprode on Rügen to three villages on Hiddensee: Kloster, Vitte, and Neuendorf.

BERGEN Centrally located and connected to the mainland by frequent trains, Bergen—the island's nominal capital—is *the* launching pad for excursions. From the train station and adjacent bus depot you can catch buses to nearly every block-long village on Rügen. The tourist office, **Stadtinformation Bergen** (Marktpl. 12, tel. 03838/21129), on Bergen's central square, organizes guided day tours in the DM 20–DM 30 range. These generally last three to four hours and cover the main coastal sights, from Göhren in the south to the intense Kap Arkona in the extreme north. Also consider renting a bike at the train station (DM 8 per day) and striking out on your own. Head northeast on quiet Route 96, and you'll soon skirt the edge of Grosser Jasmunder Bodden, a giant sea inlet, before stumbling onto the village of Saßnitz. (If you'd rather take the train to Grosser Jasmunder Bodden, ride one stop north from Bergen to Lietzow). Another option is to head southeast toward Göhren, a small village surrounded by a sandy beach and cliffs.

Bergen has a few worthwhile sights, so save a couple of hours to explore its walkable city center. Start on Marktplatz, by the tourist office, and meander toward Kirchplatz, the town's other main square. On one side of the square is the redbrick **Marienkirche,** dating from the late 14th century. Faded frescoes adorning the walls and ceilings were painted with a strange mixture of pigment and sour milk. Particularly interesting are those on either side of the altar, showing heaven (left) and hell (right). At the back of the church stands the **Toten Uhr** (Death Clock), which has not ticked for 100 years (ever since, rumor has it, a woman died of fright after looking at it. You see, the skeleton above the clock formerly beckoned to onlookers at every hour of every day of every year—kind of morbid, ain't it?). Bergen doesn't have a DJH hostel, only the privately owned **Thomas Müntzer** (Thomas-Müntzer-Weg 9, tel. 03838/320), a 70-bed hostel with plain dorm-style rooms and a DM 20 price tag. For DM 70 per double try the more pleasant **Mecklenburger Hof** (Bahnhofstr. 67, tel. 03838/263), a simple guest house near the train station. From the station you can catch hourly trains to Binz (DM 6.40), Lietzow (DM 3), Sagard (DM 4.20), Saßnitz (DM 5), and Stralsund (DM 6.40).

BINZ Binz, on the east coast of Rügen and home to the island's largest bathing resort, has little to offer except location. Take a quick look at the town's principal sight—the 3½-kilometer-long (2-mile-long) beachfront boardwalk—then head to the nearby **Jagdschloß Granitz,** which looks like a perfectly formed sand castle with symmetric round towers. For DM 4 (DM 2 students) you can take a gander at the elaborate ceilings of the castle's lavishly restored rooms. On the way out climb 125 steps to the top of the adjacent watchtower for a staggering view of the coast. A popular half-day excursion from Binz is **Vilm,** a small island that on clear days is visible offshore. (Vilm is also known as Honecker Island because the former GDR president once had a summer home here). Vilm is a wildlife sanctuary, so little disturbs the peace and quiet except flocks of chattering birds. A boat leaves Binz Harbor daily at 1 for Vilm. The town itself is a bit dull, but when the weather's good the boat trip offers great views of Rügen. Round-trip tickets cost roughly DM 12; call 038393/251 for information and reservations.

Trains from Binz run daily to Bergen (DM 6.40) and Saßnitz (DM 2). Buses, which depart from a stop down the street from the train depot, leave throughout the day for Putbus (DM 4) and Göhren (DM 4). The local youth hostel, **Jugendherberge Binz** (Strandpromenade 35, tel. 038393/2423, closed Dec. 15–Jan. 2), is a five-minute walk down the beachfront promenade from either station. The hostel has 108 beds that cost DM 14–DM 17, breakfast included. Try for a room overlooking the sea. To book a private room or stock up on city maps, head to one of Binz's two tourist offices, **Fremdenverkehrsverein e.V.** (Wylichstr. and Schillerstr., tel. 038393/2215) and **Binz Information** (Haupstr. 9, tel. 038393/2302).

PUTBUS South of Bergen and Binz is the tiny village of Putbus, best known for its classical architecture. Books say that its castle, the former residence of the princes of Putbus, was torn down in 1962 to rid the town of a "decadent stigma," but locals will tell you the Schloß went kaput due to a lack of funds. Console yourself with the **Circus,** Putbus's unique central square. It's dominated by odd geometric designs and adjacent, orderly white plazas. Nearby **August-Bebel-Straße** contains the best examples of Putbus's small, one-story merchant houses, and **Park Zu Putbus,** with almost 75 varieties of exotic trees, makes for a cool walk. The **Orangerie,** on the edge of the park, houses the **Kurverwaltung Putbus** (tel. 038301/431), which sells city and park maps. Putbus also marks the starting point for ***Rasender Rolander*** (*Racing Roland*), the narrow-gauge train that puffs daily between Putbus and Göhren, 25 kilometers (16 miles) south. The hour-long journey costs about DM 6 and is highly recommended. Call 038301/27172 for *Rolander* timetables.

SAßNITZ Like Binz, the best thing about Saßnitz is its location, perched on the northern tip of Rügen, within easy reach of some incredible sights. Foremost is its proximity to the chalk cliffs of **Stubbenkammer,** an incredible outcropping of bone-white shale that form an eerie contrast with the murky greens and blues of the Baltic Sea. Obviously, it's difficult to study the cliffs from land, so consider one of **Weiße Flotte's** (tel. 03831/22267) many daily boat trips from Saßnitz to Stubbenkammer. These generally last 60–90 minutes, cost DM 10 round-trip, and are greatly recommended when the weather isn't all gloom and doom. You can take Bus A/419 from Saßnitz to Stubbenkammer or, even better, make the 3½-hour trek through the **Nationalpark Jasmund.** This seaside nature reserve contains six clearly marked trails, each running along beach and cliff. Also consider the short path from Saßnitz to **Wissower Klinken,** a group of rugged chalk cliffs made famous by German artist Caspar

David Friedrich. Farther north is the equally famous cliff **Königstuhl** (King's Chair), towering 393 feet above the sea. It got its name (so goes the legend) from a footrace held each year by the Ranen, an ancient race of Slavs: The first runner to reach the cliff top was crowned king for a year. Nowadays DM 2 (DM .50 students) buy admission to the crowded platform atop Königstuhl. Hike down (10 minutes) to Victoriasicht for an awesome view of the cliffs themselves.

The Saßnitz tourist office, **Fremdenverkehrsverein** (Hauptstr. 70, tel. 038392/32037) has accommodations information, maps, and brochures. Trains connect Saßnitz daily with Bergen (DM 5), Lietzow (DM 4.20), and Stralsund (DM 10.80). From Saßnitz's train depot buses depart daily for Kap Arkona (DM 7) and Stubbenkammer (DM 3). From Saßnitz's harbor, ferries leave for Bornholm, Denmark (daily at 9 AM), and Trelleborg, Sweden (daily at 3 PM). For more information contact Deutsche Reichsbahn (Trelleborger Str., tel. 038392/22267). As for food try **Gastmahl des Meeres** (Strandpromenade 2, tel. 038392/22320, closed Mon.), a popular fish restaurant located on Saßnitz's boardwalk. A full meal costs about DM 20; try the house specialty, *Zander* (perch cooked in an herb cream sauce). The only youth hostel in town is the privately owned **Wilhelm Thews** (Stubbenkammerstr. 2, tel. 038392/22693 or 038392/32090), a 75-bed dormitory within walking distance of the sea. Beds fetch DM 15–DM 20 per person, including breakfast.

Greifswald

Greifswald has two things going for it. First—like so many Baltic Coast port towns—Greifswald is well stocked with Hanseatic merchant homes and medieval relics. Consider the **Rathaus.** It has an impressive carved and gabled facade and sits on the expansive **Platz der Freundschaft,** the town's central marketplace and site of a daily produce fair. Complementing the Rathaus (and dominating the skyline) are Greifswald's three medieval churches: the 13th-century **Dom St. Nikolai,** at the foot of Martin-Luther-Straße, with a 300-foot-tall tower that affords good views of the town below; the 14th-century **Marienkirche** (Brügstr. and Friedrich-Loeffer-Str.), noted for its impressive arches and adjoining tower; and the 13th-century **St. Jakob's,** another brawny medieval creation. This is a respectable catalog of sights, but Greifswald is perhaps best known for its university and for its association with native son and German Romantic painter, Caspar David Friedrich. Now the bad news: An 18th-century fire destroyed many of the original medieval university buildings. And, despite the fact

Kap Arkona

Kap Arkona, perched on the storm-battered tip of Rügen Island, is the northernmost point in Germany. The cape is best known for its rugged cliffs, its sweeping view of the horizon, and its two lighthouses. This area used to be jealously guarded by the GDR's army because of its proximity to Sweden, 77 kilometers (48 miles) away. Nowadays there are few people here and even fewer distractions. Vitt, a small fishing village 1 kilometer (⅔ mile) from the cape, consists of 45 thatched houses preserved in their original condition and protected as a World Heritage Site by UNESCO. Sing your heart out in the dead center of the small, white, octagonal church—the acoustics are amazing. If you walk from the cape you'll pass it on the outskirts of town. To reach the cape, hop on a bus from Saßnitz or, if you're adventurous, make the 20-kilometer (12-mile) hike along a luscious stretch of coast..

that little Caspar spent his college years wandering the streets of Greifswald, there's only one exhibit of his work—**Das Museum der Stadt Greifswald** (Pylstr. 1–2, tel 03834/3998), which has a meager permanent display of two Friedrich paintings. You're better off hopping on Bus 30, 40, or 41 and alighting at Makarenkostraße for the **Botanischer Garten** (Botanical Garden, Mündter Str. 2), where you can take a relaxing stroll through many, many trees.

Greifswald was one of the few towns in Germany left unscathed by World War II. The reason: A local army commander, Colonel Rudolf Petershagen, loved Greifswald and its people enough to risk humiliation by voluntarily surrendering to Soviet troops in 1945. Unfortunately, his sacrifice was made partly in vain, for years of neglect under the GDR has left many of Greifswald's historic buildings in need of a good fixin'.

Although you can't see many Caspar David Friedrich canvases in the town where he was born and raised, you can at least experience firsthand a ruin that became famous through his work. In some form or another **Klosterruine Eldena** appears in a handful of Caspar canvases, which has probably saved the ruined monastery from further demolition. If you're not a die-hard fan of brick ruins or C. D. Friedrich, you may not feel like taking the 40-minute walk from town (follow the signs). Instead, hop on Bus H at the train station and take it to the end of the line. There's another quick excursion (a 35-minute walk) to the nearby village of **Wieck.** Wieck's claim to fame is its 100-year-old wood drawbridge. The bridge, protected by UNESCO, is among the last of its kind in operation. Residents of Wieck have a pass allowing them auto access to the bridge; all other drivers pay DM 5.

BASICS The **Informationsbüro** (Str. der Freundschaft 102, tel. 03834/2378) arranges private accommodations—there's no youth hostel in town—and stocks the usual city maps. For a hearty meal under DM 5, plus a lively student atmosphere, head to the **Mensa am Wall** (Schutzenstr., tel. 03834/5021). The eclectic **Café Amberland** (Bachstr. 22, tel. 03834/3202) serves drinks and snacks for less than DM 7 in a funky room furnished with arty chairs and crude wood sculptures. If you can't hear the live music drifting from this student hangout, ask someone to point you in the right direction—at press time the place did not have a sign. For listings of student clubs and discos grab a copy of *"Aktuellen Greifswald"* at the tourist office or from most newsdealers. Greifswald is less than 30 minutes from Stralsund (DM 6.40) and 40 minutes from Wolgast (DM 6) by train. The bus station, across from the rail depot, serves a bevy of smaller towns in the area.

Usedom

Locals say that no matter where you are on this skinny, 40-kilometer-long (25-mile-long) island, you can always hear waves crashing on the shore. More than 85% of Usedom is designated a protected nature area, and the whole island may eventually be

Polish up Your Polish

After inspecting Ahlbeck, add another passport stamp to your collecion by taking a short trip to Świnoujście, Poland. Cars are not allowed across the border, so either ride the bus (there's only one) or walk across. After flashing your passport to an uninterested border guard, mosey down the main street and check out the maze of vendors (Germans come to Swinoujście to buy duty-free cigarettes). In about 20 minutes you'll hit downtown, which is nondescript and looks more like a busy suburban street than a bustling city center.

turned into a national park. This means Usedom has few reminders of the communist era—no cement-and-steel high rises and no gruesome factories belching toxic muck—only miles of sand, the sea, and an endless horizon. Stay in the small resort towns of Wolgast, Ahlbeck, or Heringsdorf, and then strike out into the natural wonderland of Usedom by day. Most of the island belongs to Germany, but the eastern part has been Polish territory since 1945.

BASICS The island's regional tourist office, **Fremdenverkehrsverband Insel Usedom** (Dünenstr. 11, Ahlbeck, tel. 039775/2884) has two useful pamphlets, *"Camping Führer,"* which lists all nine campgrounds on Usedom, and *"Wander Führer,"* detailing the island's hiking trails. Down the street is Ahlbeck's **tourist office** (Dünenstr. 45, tel. 039775/8228), which stocks city maps and can help you book a private room (DM 20–DM 30). It also rents bicycles for DM 10 per day. Trains connect Wolgast with Stralsund (DM 12.40) and Greifswald (DM 6). From Wolgast there is local train service to Heringsdorf (DM 6.40), Peenemünde (DM 5), and Zinnowitz (DM 3).

WHERE TO SLEEP Zinnowitz, the largest resort on Usedom, has a shockingly small and shabby youth hostel, **Jugendherberge Zinnowitz** (J.-Morsche-Str. 24, tel. 038377/2227, reservations required Oct.–Mar.). This 50-bed place charges DM 11.50–DM 13.50 and is a long, long walk from the train station; turn right out of the depot and walk straight until the road forks, then veer left. A better bet is the youth hostel in Heringsdorf, **Jugendherberge Heringsdorf** (Puschkinstr. 7–9, tel. 038378/2325, closed Dec. 15–Jan. 1); after you leave the station, cross Route F11 and walk toward the beach for 300 yards. This 104-bed hostel, in a lovely old building on the beachfront, charges DM 13–DM 15.50, including breakfast. **Hotel Ostseestrand** (Kurstr., tel. 038378/8381) has simple doubles for DM 60.

WORTH SEEING **Wolgast** is not technically a part of Usedom. It is on the German mainland, overlooking Usedom from across the Peenestrom, an arm of the Baltic Sea. Wolgast has a few worthwhile sights and is the main jumping-off point for island-bound travelers. First is the old town square, **Karl-Liebknecht-Platz,** where the elegant Baroque **Rathaus** sits. The **Kreismuseum** (Karl-Liebknecht-Pl. 6, tel. 038372/3041; admission free), opposite the Rathaus, is a don't-miss for the display on V-1 and V-2 rockets—those nasty doodlebugs that bombarded London throughout World War II.

V-1 and V-2 rockets, incidentally, were developed in nearby **Peenemünde,** at the northern tip of Usedom Island. Neil Armstrong probably wouldn't have made it to the moon if it hadn't been for Peenemunde and its world-famous scientist Wernher von Braun (Wernher built the first-ever jet rocket, then went on to develop the American space program). The **Historisch-technisches Informations Zentrum Peenemünde-Geburtsort der Raumfahrt** (Bahnhofstr. 28, tel. Peenemünde 225) documents the history of space flight and of secret-enshrouded Peenemünde (which was off-limits to visitors until recently). You can request a short tour in English or view an English-language video. The museum is a five-minute walk from the Peenemünde train station.

Ahlbeck, on the island's eastern side, is a hop, skip, and a jump from Poland's border. It is famous for its wood pier adorned with four towers—the only one of its kind in Germany. At the end of the pier is the popular Seebrücke restaurant, in business since 1898. Now under lease for 25 years to the first American investor in the ex-GDR, it is rapidly gaining popularity for its food, decor, and service. The nearby beachfront promenade is lined with turn-of-the-century villas whose rooms are sometimes rented to visitors; look for ZIMMER FREI signs and haggle away. Just west of Ahlbeck you'll stumble into **Heringsdorf,** the oldest resort on the island. Kaiser Wilhelm II built a villa here, and Russian playwright Maxim Gorky spent the summer of 1922 strolling the promenade.

HAMBURG

14

By Geraldine Poon

When travelers learn that Hamburg is Germany's largest port they conjure up images of heavy industry, cranes, oil-soaked waters, and sleazy bars. They're right about the sleazy bars, but most visitors are surprised by how green and elegant large parts of this city are. Nearly half the city is parkland or open space, and lakes and canals further break up the urban landscape. That's not to say that Hamburg is gemütlich, because it's not. If you want cozy, go to Bavaria—Hamburg is too busy making money to bother with such niceties. The city isn't too picky about how it makes its money, either. A lot of gray-suited commerce types earn money the old-fashioned way, but another segment of the population makes its moola in even older fashion. Prostitution, pornography, and sex shows have given Hamburg a reputation (not altogether deserved) as a sort of Teutonic Sodom. But Hamburg offers more traditional tourist attractions as well, including some beautiful (and wealthy) neighborhoods, excellent museums, a lively university district, and a happening nightlife. It's easy to while away a few days in this pleasant city, even if you never let your libido out of its cage.

Germany's second-largest city has been an autonomous city-state since the Middle Ages. Although much of it burned in the Great Fire of 1842, and bombing raids almost entirely destroyed it between 1940 and 1944, it has been beautifully restored. The city's classic red structures, beautiful expanses of green, and innumerable canals form an odd contrast to its fast-paced and thoroughly modern inhabitants and its exclusive consumer culture.

Water in every form still dominates the "Venice of the North," which has more than 2,400 bridges—more than London, Amsterdam, and Venice combined. The River Elbe runs into Hamburg, and the city center is graced with the Binnen- and Aussenalster, two artificial lakes. Around the lakes are elegant villas; the magnificent Rathaus, the Renaissance-style town hall; and many department stores. Water also dominates the city in a meteorological sense: Baltic rains permeate Hamburg life for much of the year, so people take advantage of any sunny days to stroll, bike, or bare their pallid bodies in the city's parks.

Okay, okay, you're saying, that's all well and good, but what was that about the modern Sodom? Yup, Hamburg's Reeperbahn has the dubious distinction of being one of the most famous sex streets in the world, and it continues to entice, titillate, and gross out tourists from all over. Even grosser or more titillating, depending on your particular tastes, is the Herbertstraße. Closed off to women and to children under 18, this is where the best of the world's oldest professionals sit behind glass windows. Come to window-shop and stay for the sheer pleasantness of the city, or vice versa: Any way you take it, Hamburg is a very well-rounded city.

Basics

AMERICAN EXPRESS **The American Express *Reisebüro,*** directly across from the Rathaus, refunds lost or stolen traveler's checks and cards; holds mail; sells traveler's checks; and books hotel, airplane, and train tickets. The office's bureau de change cashes all traveler's checks and changes cash for no commission. *Rathausmarkt 5, tel. 040/331141. Open weekdays 9–5:30, Sat. 9–noon.*

BUCKET SHOPS **Rainbow Tours** (Johanniswall 4C, tel. 040/323551) arranges bus tours all over Europe that are geared to young people who want to have cheap fun. Consider buying a day trip to another city (Prague, DM 88; Amsterdam, DM 48), then stay as long as you like on your own. Both **Akzent-touristik** (Grindelallee 28, tel. 040/443061) and **RDS** (Rentzelstr. 16, tel. 040/442863) specialize in student trips and cheap last-minute flights, and they also sell International Student I.D. cards (DM 10). You'll find a slew of companies offering last-minute flights and trips in **Terminal 1** at Hamburg airport. Many of these companies sell discounted trips (30%–50% off), which you can purchase one to two weeks before departure.

BUREAUX DE CHANGE **Deutsche Verkehrs-Kredit-Bank AG,** in the Hauptbahnhof (tel. 040/308–00475 or 040/308–00480) and Hamburg-Altona train stations (tel. 040/390–3770), charges DM 1 for cash exchanges and DM 3 for traveler's checks. The German banks in the downtown area offer pretty uniform rates and don't charge a commission on cash. The **American Express** office (*see above*) cashes traveler's checks for free, and **MARWEX** (Kirchenallee 19, tel. 040/302–96202) offers good rates. For late-night emergencies, try the machines in the Hauptbahnhof, which give cash advances on your Visa or MasterCard, or use the Visa machine at **Citibank** (Rathausstr. 2, tel. 040/302– 96202). Exchange offices proliferate in and around the Hauptbahnhof (Kirchenallee side) and the Reeperbahn, but read the fine print first—some places charge up to an 8% commission.

CONSULATES Hamburg has more consulates (84) than any other city in the world except New York.

United States. Colloquially known as the "little White House," the American Consulate General overlooks the Alster. *Alsterufer 27–28, tel. 040/411710. Open weekdays 8–noon.*

Traveling Hamburgers Have Their Own Mors Code

You can always recognize Hamburgers by their license plates, marked with the letters HH. Whenever Hamburgers see each other away from Hamburg, one greets the other with* "Hummel, Hummel," *and the other answers back* "Mors, Mors" *in Plattdeutsch (Low German). The origins of this tradition go back hundreds of years, to when Hamburg's water was supplied by individual water carriers, who hauled around buckets on their shoulders. There was one especially unfriendly water carrier, whom the city kids taunted by calling out his name,* "Hummel, Hummel." *The man regularly responded with* "Mors, Mors," *which, roughly translated, means "Lick my ass!"

United Kingdom. *Harvestehuderweg 8A, tel. 040/446071. Open weekdays 9–noon and 2–4.*

EMERGENCIES **Police:** tel. 110. **Fire:** tel. 112. **Ambulance:** tel. 19218. **Medical assistance:** tel. 228022. **Foreigner Legal Service:** Cremon 11, tel. 040/366534. **Pharmacies** (*Apotheken*) take turns staying open late; most pharmacies put a note in the window indicating whose turn it is. All hospitals and even the emergency telephone operators speak English.

ENGLISH BOOKS AND NEWSPAPERS Most major department stores and newsstands sell English periodicals. **Frensche-International** (Spitalerstr. 26E, tel. 040/327585) has an extensive selection of English books ranging from romances to politics and current affairs. **Thalia Bücher** (Spitalerstr. 8, tel. 040/302–07201) has a good choice of fiction. The **Amerika Haus** (Tesdorpfstr. 1, tel. 040/411–71270) and the **British Council** (Rothenbaumchaussee 34, tel. 040/446057) have reading libraries open to the public. The **International Bookshop** (Eppendorfer Weg 1, tel. 040/439–8041), "the place for English books," offers an array of used books at secondhand prices.

LAUNDRY The **Münzwaschsalon,** on a side street off the Reeperbahn, has instructions in English. Bring change for the washing machines (DM 7, including soap), dryers (DM 1 for 10 minutes), and pinball machines. *Hein-Hoyer-Str. 12, no tel. Open Mon.–Sat. 7 AM–10 PM, Sun. 10–10.*

Wasch-Center, a chain that charges DM 6 per wash with soap and DM 1 for the dryer (15 minutes), has several locations in the downtown area. The most convenient to hotels and pensions around the Reeperbahn is at Nobistor 34.

LUGGAGE STORAGE The **Hauptbahnhof** and **Hamburg-Altona** train stations, as well as many S-Bahn (suburban-train) stations, have lockers that cost DM 1–DM 4, depending on their size. The Hauptbahnhof also has a luggage-check service, open daily 8 AM–11 PM, that charges DM 2 per piece per day.

MAIL Called the *Hühnerposten* (translation: the Chicken Coop) by locals, the **Hauptpost** is across from the Hauptbahnhof, near the ZOB (*see* Coming and Going by Bus, *below*). The large building is divided into sections dealing with mail and telephones. Unlike most post offices, this one does not exchange money. *Hühnerposten 12, tel. 040/23950. Open weekdays 8–6, Sat. 8–noon.*

The post office in the **Hauptbahnhof** (Hachmannpl. 13, Kirchenallee exit, tel. 040/23950) offers the usual services downstairs, and upstairs you'll find a number of telephones, including a credit- card phone that accepts Visa, American Express, and MasterCard.

PHONES Hamburg has the standard yellow German phones and also some nifty wheelchair-accessible phone booths. You can use coins, but if you're making a long-distance call (they're expensive) your best bet is to buy a DM 12 or DM 50 (worth DM 60) phone card from a post office. Not only is a phone card convenient, but you can actually see the money ticking away on the phone's display. The telephone center in the Hauptbahnhof post office is open daily 6:15 AM–10 PM. Hamburg's area code is 040.

VISITOR INFORMATION With five tourist offices scattered throughout the city, Hamburg is well prepared for visitors. All offices offer identical services, including an English-speaking staff, ticket sales, maps, brochures, guides, and a room-booking service (DM 6). The offices also sell the **Hamburg-CARD,** which gives you access to public transport, entrance to 11 museums, and up to a 30% discount on city tours. A one-day card costs DM 9.50 (group card, good for up to four adults plus three children, DM 19.50); a three-day card is DM 17.50 (group card, DM 29.50). Be sure to pick up "Where to Go in Hamburg," a monthly pamphlet with important addresses and calendars, and "The Hamburger," which has similar tourist-oriented information. To get a grip on the nightclub, disco, and bar scene and on local concerts and musical events, buy *Prinz* (DM 4) or *Szene* (DM 4.50) from any bookstore or kiosk. You'll find tourist offices at the following locations:

Bieberhaus, *Hachmannpl., tel. 040/300–51244. Open weekdays 7:30–6, Sat. 8–3.*

Hauptbahnhof, *Kirchenallee exit, tel. 040/300–51230. Open daily 7 AM–11 PM.*

Hause-Viertel, *Poststr. entrance, tel. 040/300–51220. Open weekdays 10–6:30, Sat. 10–3, Sun. 11–3.*

Airport, *Terminal 3, tel. 040/300–51240. Open daily 8 AM–11 PM.*

Harbor, *St. Pauli Landungsbrücken, between bridges 4 and 5, tel. 040/300–51200. Open Mar.–Oct., daily 9–6; Nov.–Feb., daily 10–3.*

COMING AND GOING

BY PLANE Hamburg's international airport, **Flughafen Fuhlsbüttel** (Paul-Bäumer-Pl., tel. 040/50750), is about 10 kilometers (6 miles) north of downtown. Airlines serving the city include **United, Delta,** and **Lufthansa**. It's a small airport with just three terminals, but construction is under way, so expect major changes. At present, last-minute ticket counters line the edges of Terminal 1. The Deutsche Bank (Terminal 2) cashes traveler's checks and exchanges money, but the post office (Terminal 2) gives slightly better rates for cash and cashes traveler's checks (DM 3). The bottom floor of Terminal 3 contains an American Express money machine and the tourist-information office (tel. 040/300– 51240). You can store your luggage for DM 3 per piece per day at the *Gepäckaufbewahrung* (luggage check), open 6 AM–11 PM.

➢ **AIRPORT TRANSPORT** • The fastest and most convenient way to travel between the airport and downtown Hamburg is aboard the **Airport–City Bus,** which makes the 30-minute trip (DM 8) from the Hauptbahnhof every 20 minutes from 6 AM until about 10 PM. The free **HVV Airport Express** Bus 110 runs every 10 minutes from the airport to the Ohlsdorf S-Bahn stop; from there take S-Bahn line 1 (S1) to the Hauptbahnhof for DM 3.40, or DM 11.50 for a group of four. Depending on traffic, a taxi to the Hauptbahnhof from the airport costs about DM 30.

BY TRAIN All trains, except for those heading north to destinations such as the island of Sylt, stop at the **Hauptbahnhof** (tel. 040/19419) in central Hamburg. Trains run frequently from here to Lübeck (DM 14.80) and Friedrichstadt (DM 34), among other destinations. You can easily get to the station using the S-Bahn (suburban train) or U-Bahn (subway). The station itself sits between the grimy, drug-infested neighborhood of St. Georg and the elegant shopping promenades on Mönckebergstraße and Spitalerstraße. The tourist-information office is located near the Kirchenallee exit, which is also the best exit to take to reach the St. Georg district and many of the cheap hotels. The **Altona** station (Max-Brauer-Allee, tel. 040/39181), west of downtown, handles trains heading north. The S-Bahn connects Hauptbahnhof with Altona, which has a DVK money-exchange office and a post office.

BY FERRY The **MS *Hamburg,*** operated by Scandinavian Seaways (Jessenstr. 4, tel. 040/389–03117), sails to Harwich, England, every other day. Prices range from DM 92 to DM 490, depending on day, season, and cabin. Students and passengers under 26 get a 25% discount. From Harwich there's a direct train connection to London. All ferries sail from **St. Pauli Landungsbrücken,** at the harbor (U-Bahn stop St. Pauli Landungsbrücken).

BY BUS **ZOB,** across from the Hauptbahnhof, is the central station for a bunch of bus companies that offer service all over Germany and Europe. To find the best deal, take a trip to the ZOB and visit the various travel agencies. **Continentbus** (tel. 040/247106 or 040/245310) handles **Euro-Lines,** the extensive international bus network; they'll sell you a ticket to cities like Barcelona (DM 249), Paris (DM 99), and

Amsterdam (DM 55). Students under 26 get a 10% discount. The station has lockers for DM 2. *Adenauerallee 78, tel. 040/247576. Open daily 5 AM–9 PM.*

If you don't find anything at ZOB, try **Berbig** (Lange Reihe 36, tel. 040/280–3464), which offers reasonably priced bus trips to cities like Berlin (DM 23) and Potsdam (DM 30).

HITCHHIKING The only way to get anywhere with your thumb is to first escape the downtown area. If you're heading for Berlin or Lübeck, take U-Bahn line 3 (U3) to Horner Rennbahn, then Bus 261 two stops to the traffic circle known as Horner Kreisel, on Sievekingsallee. If you want to get to Kiel or the North Sea, take the U2 to Hagenbecks Tierpark and then Bus 190 or 281 two stops to Kilerstrasse. If you're heading south, take the U-Bahn or S-Bahn to Berliner Tor and go to Heidenkampsweg.

The University of Hamburg (S-Bahn stop Dammtor) has a ride board near the cafeteria that's plastered with notices by people offering and asking for rides.

MITFAHRZENTRALE Hamburg has a bevy of *Mitfahrzentrale* (ride shares), none of which is really superior to another. Rates vary drastically depending on how many people are in the car and where the car is heading. You'll probably have to call more than one agency to find the right ride going in the right direction at the right time. Among the different agencies are **Karl Mai** (Rutschbahn 3, tel. 040/414–02611); **Frauen-Mitfahrzentrale,** for women only (Rutschbahn 3, tel. 040/457800); **Citynetz Mitfahr-Zentrale** (Gotenstr. 19, tel. 040/19444); and **Altona-Mitfahr-Zentrale** (Altona train station, Lobuschstr. 22, tel. 040/391721).

GETTING AROUND

Hamburg is a sprawling metropolis, but most of the major sights and interesting neighborhoods are sandwiched in the walkable area between the River Elbe and the two lakes, the Binnenalster and Aussenalster. Here, you'll find Jungfernstieg and Mönckebergstraße, the two main shopping streets, which lead to the **Rathaus** (Town Hall), the central point in the downtown area. The **St. Pauli/Reeperbahn** area, including Hamburg's famous red-light district, is west of downtown, near the harbor. A smaller red-light district, St. Georg, is behind the Hauptbahnhof, near Lake Aussenalster. The University district sits north of the city center and west of the Aussenalster.

Even though everything is centrally located, it'll take you a long time to see it all on foot. **HVV,** Hamburg's public-transportation system, operates an extensive network of buses, as well as the U-Bahn and S-Bahn. A Tageskarte, an all-day pass that costs DM 6.50, is good for all forms of public transit except night buses and first class on the S-Bahn. A **Familienkarte** (DM 11.50) works just like the Tageskarte but is good for four adults. Consider buying the **Hamburg-CARD** (*see* Visitor Information, *above*), a really good deal that includes unlimited use of mass transit. If you just want a one-way ticket (DM 2.20–DM 3.40) valid on the U-Bahn, S-Bahn, and buses, you can buy one at the orange ticket-dispensing machines located in U-Bahn and S-Bahn stations and at most bus stops; check the price tables on the machines for the exact price.

BY SUBWAY/RAIL The **U-Bahn** and **S-Bahn** can be used interchangeably to get around the city, although the S-Bahn will take you farther into the suburbs. Trains run every 5, 10, or 20 minutes until about 12:30 AM. Color-coded maps of the system are posted in stations. InterRail and Eurail are valid in second class on the S-Bahn. Because there is no regular ticket control, many people *schwarzfahren* (ride without a ticket). You fahre schwarz, you gamble, because if inspectors do check tickets you're out DM 60. Bikes are allowed on the U-Bahn and S-Bahn except during weekday rush hours. The **A-Bahn,** another kind of suburban train that heads farther into the suburbs, caters mostly to commuters; tourists rarely ride it unless they're lost.

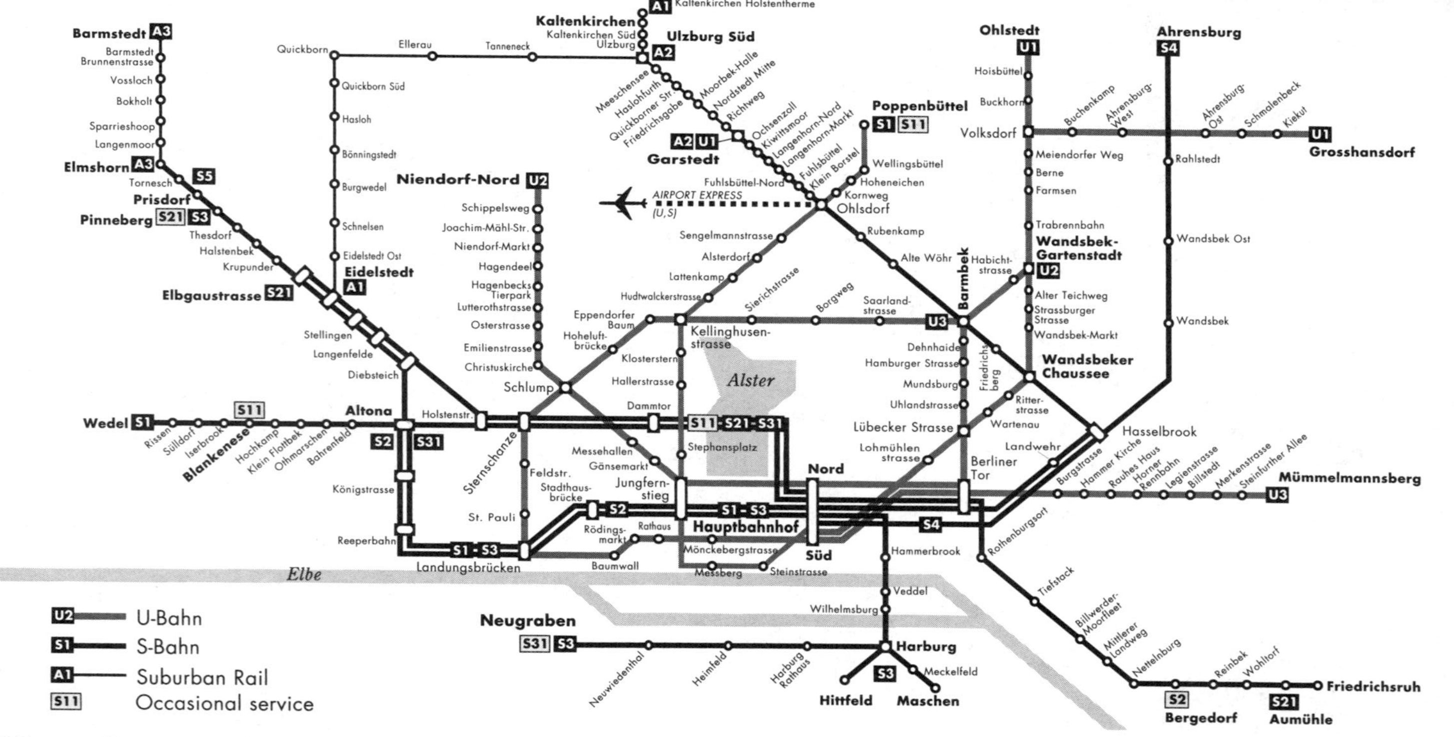

Hamburg Public Transit System

BY BUS You probably won't need to use the somewhat complicated bus system unless you're traveling to the outskirts: The rail system is generally easier and more efficient, and the maps are much more comprehensible. Lawless types often board buses from the rear entrance so they don't have to pay, although at night everyone has to board in front and show the driver his or her ticket. **Night buses 600–640** serve the downtown area after the subway closes, at 12:30, and are a perfect place to meet wasted partyers going home after a night on the Reeperbahn. Buses leave the Rathausmarkt and the Hauptbahnhof every hour all night long for limited destinations; maps at the stops outline the routes. For more bus information call the Hamburg Passenger Transport Board (tel. 040/322911).

BY TAXI Taxis come in handy at night or when you're with a big group of people. You can always find a couple of cream-color Mercedes taxis at taxi stands near the train stations. The meter starts at DM 3.60; every additional kilometer (about ⅔ mile) costs DM 2.20. If you order a taxi by phone (tel. 040/211211 or 040/611061), expect an extra fee of DM 1. A tip of about 10% is normal.

BY BIKE Excellent paved bike paths circle the Binnenalster and Aussenalster. Unless it rains, it's fun to explore the different neighborhoods by bike. Rent one at the tourist office in the **Bieberhaus** (Hachmannplatz) for DM 10 per day.

Where to Sleep

Hamburg has lots of great hotels, like the Vier Jahreszeiten (Four Seasons), the Atlantic Hotel, and the Marriott. Unfortunately, a double in any of these costs up to DM 500—a wee bit beyond the average shoestring budget. Cheaper hotels, with double rooms for DM 80–DM 100, are in the red-light districts of St. Pauli and St. Georg. Some dubious hotels, known as *Stundenhotels,* rent rooms for about DM 20 per hour. You can find cheap rooms here and there in dark, run-of-the-mill hotels, or you can have the tourist office find you a slightly more expensive room for a DM 6 fee. Other budget lodging options in Hamburg include private rooms, campgrounds, and hostels.

REEPERBAHN

Your mom probably wouldn't be very happy to know you're spending nights on the Reeperbahn, a.k.a. "the world's most sinful mile," but it's just not that bad. Here you'll find some of Hamburg's cheapest accommodations, and the area frequented by tourists is fairly safe. If you venture off into the side streets you'll encounter more houses of ill repute. Many hotels here are booked up by the government for asylum seekers and people on welfare. A room right on the Reeperbahn is perfect for late-night partyers because you can just stumble into your nearby bed. Don't expect a peaceful night's sleep, though—after all, this is the Reeperbahn, where sex, nightclubs, and sex are the raisons d'être. To reach the Reeperbahn take U3 to St. Pauli or S1 or S3 to Reeperbahn.

In the past seven years, long-term guests have occupied more and more budget-hotel rooms; the government books these rooms for the needy and Hamburg's many asylum-seekers.

UNDER DM 85 **Auto-Hotel "Am Hafen."** The name is misleading. It's not a hotel for autos, and it isn't on the *Hafen* (harbor). If no one's at the reception desk when you arrive, mosey into the bar nextdoor: You'll probably find the managers tending bar for a bunch of locals who appear permanently rooted to their bar stools. Like all places on the Reeperbahn, this hotel can get loud at night. Doubles start at an astonishing DM 60 per night. *Spielbudenpl. 11, next to gas station, tel. 040/316631. U3 to St. Pauli. 21 rooms, some with bath.*

Hamburg Lodging

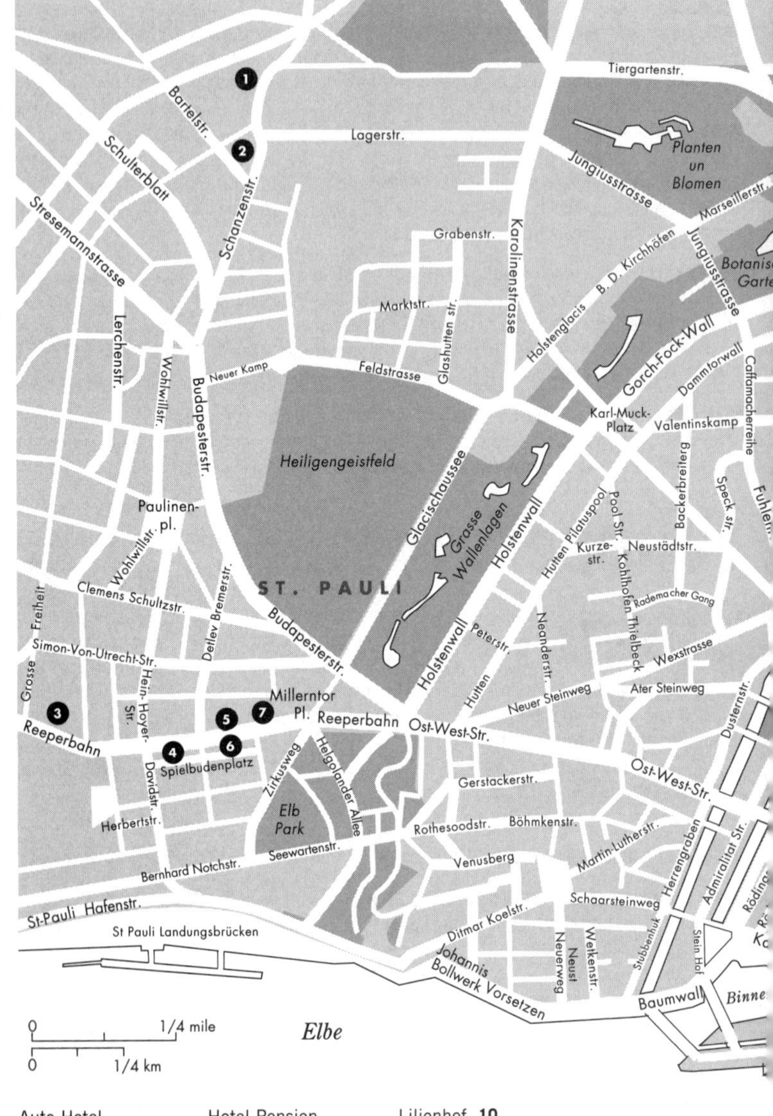

Auto-Hotel "Am Hafen", **6**
Gästehaus, **15**
Hamburg "Auf dem Stintfang", **8**
Hotel Alt Nürnberg, **20**
Hotel Bremer Hof, **18**
Hotel Florida, **4**
Hotel Hanseat, **7**
Hotel Inter-Rast, **3**
Hotel-Pension Köhler, **13**
Hotel-Pension "Nord", **19**
Hotel-Pension Remstal, **21**
Hotel-Pension Riedinger, **12**
Hotel Sternschanze, **1**
Jugendgästehaus Hamburg "Horner Rennbahn", **23**
Kieler Hof, **17**
Kunstlerpension Sarah Petersen, **16**
Lilienhof, **10**
Pension Helga Schmidt, **9**
St Georg, **11**
Schanzenstern, **2**
Terminus, **22**
Wedina, **14**
Weller's Hotel, **5**

Hamburg Lodging

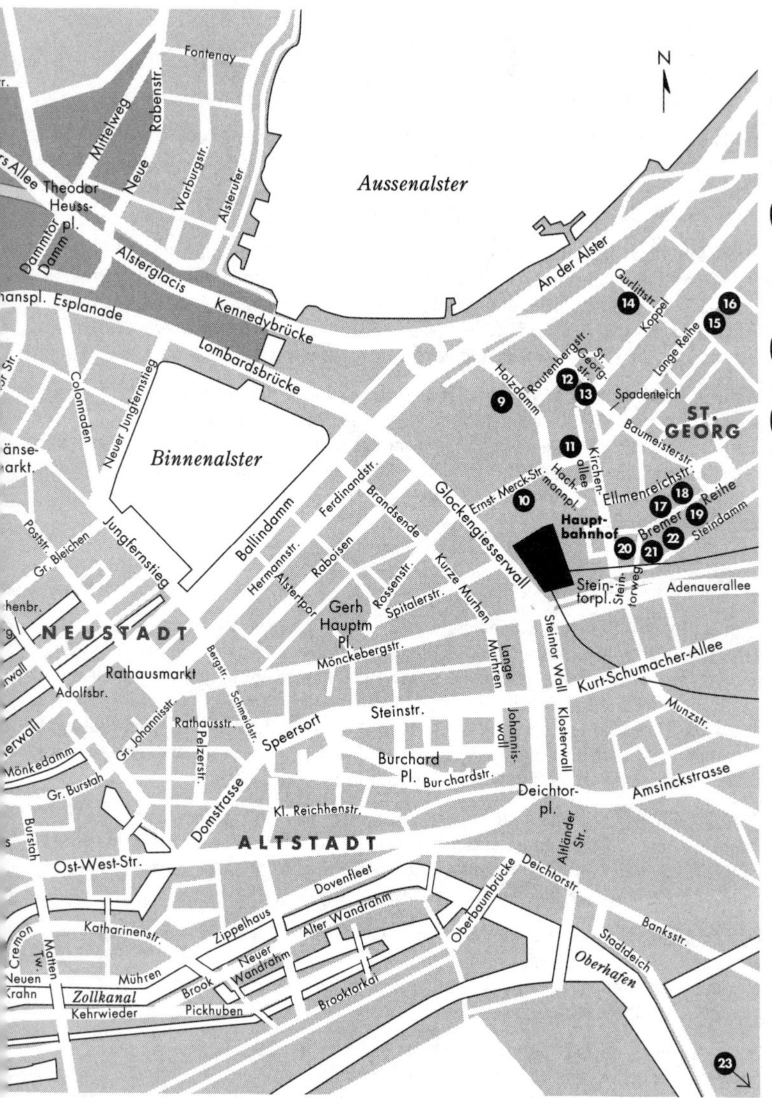

Hotel Florida. Even the most respectable hotels, like this one, have condom machines conveniently located right outside your door, in the hallway. Clean, airy doubles cost DM 85, with breakfast. *Spielbudenpl. 22, tel. 040/314393. U3 to St. Pauli. 14 rooms, none with bath.*

Hotel Hanseat. From the outside this hotel looks like a dark little hole-in-the-wall. Climb the dark narrow stairway, and you'll realize it *is* a dark little hole-in-the-wall. The small cramped rooms, reminiscent of college dorms, go for just DM 60. *Reeperbahn 15, tel. 040/312982. U3 to St. Pauli.*

Hotel Inter-Rast. Popular with groups, this gigantic 420-bed hotel sits at the end of the Reeperbahn, near Große Freiheit. It's basically like a youth hostel but with a little more quality. Doubles, including breakfast but not showers, start at DM 76. *Reeperbahn 154–166, tel. 040/311591. Near S-Bahn station Reeperbahn. 208 rooms, some with bath. Limited wheelchair access, luggage storage.*

Weller's Hotel. Run by an extremely friendly man who's used to having lots of foreign guests (especially Americans), this hotel beckons bed-seekers with its bright yellow sign. Go up the creaky old stairs to the living room–like reception area, and then go up even more stairs to get to the standard, clean rooms. Doubles go for DM 79, not including breakfast. *Reeperbahn 36, tel. 040/314838. U-Bahn to St. Pauli or S-Bahn to Reeperbahn. 28 beds.*

ST. GEORG

This is probably the most convenient area in which to spend the night because of its proximity to the Hauptbahnhof and ZOB. St. Georg has a fairly prominent drug scene, and you see plenty of prostitutes and shady men hanging out on the streets. Needless to say, it's not the best neighborhood, but it's relatively safe—if you keep your wits about you, look like you have a purpose, and don't get offended if someone asks you how much you cost for an hour. Adopting an "I eat men like you for breakfast" look never hurts. The street **Bremer Reihe** is loaded with budget lodgings.

UNDER DM 60 **Gästehaus.** Run by a crabby old man, this skanky place is usually filled to capacity with asylum-seekers, but you can't beat the price—a double costs only DM 60. Call ahead: Rumor has it the place may close soon. *Lange Reihe, tel. 040/243121. Luggage storage, no breakfast.*

UNDER DM 85 **Hotel Alt Nürnberg.** This cheap, neat hotel has a beautiful reception area, and you'll find clean, if worn, rooms upstairs. Doubles start at DM 80, with breakfast. *Steintorweg 15, tel. 040/246–02324. 16 rooms, some with bath. Luggage storage. Closed Christmas–New Year's.*

Hotel-Pension Remstal. The rooms here are big, a bit smelly, and have a colorful, ratty decorative scheme. The reception is super friendly and the hotel attracts a young crowd. Remstal is situated on a quiet street near the Hauptbahnhof. Doubles with breakfast cost DM 85. *Steintorweg 2, tel. 040/244560. 40 rooms, none with bath. Showers DM 1, luggage storage.*

Kieler Hof. The rooms here are very tidy, with wood beds and fresh white linen; what's more, the bathrooms have a powerful lemony smell. Some people say the Kieler Hof's owners supplement their income by renting their rooms at an hourly rate, but the management vehemently denies it. Dim doubles with shower/toilet in the hall go for DM 85; breakfast is included. *Bremer Reihe 15, tel. 040/243024. 28 rooms, some with bath. Luggage storage.*

Kunstlerpension Sarah Petersen. This small pension is listed in almost every travel book, so the rooms are always booked. Call the eccentric artist/owner Sarah Petersen ahead of time to ensure that you get one of the six comfy rooms. The state may fund a historical renovation of this 200-year-old house. Doubles go for DM 84, with breakfast. *Lange Reihe 50, tel. 040/249826. 6 rooms, none with bath. Laundry facilities.*

Terminus. This is a true backpacker's hotel, and you're likely to encounter a lot of Americans here. The hotel usually has a free room, but consider calling a couple of days in advance. The management is about to change, but the hotel is supposedly going to stay the way it is. The DM 55 singles are miniscule, but DM 80 doubles are a good deal; breakfast isn't included. *Steindamm 5, tel. 040/280–3144. 20 rooms, none with bath. Showers DM 1, luggage storage. Closed Christmas–mid-Jan.*

UNDER DM 100 **Hotel Bremer Hof.** A typical hotel with standard, clean rooms. In other words, it's nothing spectacular, but the prices are reasonable. Doubles start at DM 90. *Bremer Reihe 21, tel. 040/245312. 30 rooms, some with bath. Showers DM 5, limited wheelchair access, luggage storage, breakfast DM 8.50.*

Hotel-Pension Köhler. The roly-poly manager of this quiet, homey hotel proffers a famous guest list, real Oriental carpets, and a cabinet full of gifts from satisfied guests. Doubles with breakfast go for DM 88, but if you stay three nights the price falls to DM 80. The price includes one "normal"-length shower per day. Call ahead for reservations. *St.-Georg-Str. 6, tel. 040/249065 or 040/280–3425. 5 rooms, none with bath.*

Hotel-Pension "Nord." The friendly guy who runs this place insists that "Nord" marks the border where Bremer Reihe turns into a sleaze hole. He says the hotels toward the Hauptbahnhof are okay, but everything the other way is a bit questionable. Border or no border, it's still tough to tell which hotels are for tourists and which cater to a seedier clientele. Nord falls into the safe category, but its doubles are dreary, dark, and DM 90 without breakfast. *Bremer Reihe 22, tel. 040/244693.*

Hotel-Pension Riedinger. Riedinger, next to Köhler (*see above*), offers well-kept, airy doubles for DM 98. *St.-Georg-Str. 8, tel. 040/247463. 12 rooms, none with bath. Luggage storage.*

Pension Helga Schmidt. This small pension isn't quite as nice as the Atlantic, across the street, but a room here costs only about a third of what the Atlantic charges. Rooms are comfortable and clean, with fluffy down comforters. Doubles start at DM 92. It's ideally located, just a couple of minutes from the Alster. Reservations are strongly advised. *Holzdamm 14, tel. 040/280–2119 or 040/280–3078. 17 rooms, some with bath. Luggage storage, kitchen facilities, breakfast DM 10.*

Wedina. A friendly Swiss man runs this ultramodern hotel. He's also in charge of the *Gästehaus* (guest house) across the street, which has brand-new rooms and bathrooms; doubles start at DM 95. It doesn't get any cleaner or better than this. *Gurlittstr. 23, off Lange Reihe, tel. 040/243011. Luggage storage, breakfast included.*

UNDER DM 110 **Lilienhof.** An English-speaking husband-and-wife team runs this hotel, with doubles starting at DM 108, without breakfast. The rooms are simple and clean, and many have TVs. *Ernst-Merck-Str. 4, behind Hauptbahnhof, tel. 040/241087. 21 rooms, some with bath. Luggage storage.*

St. Georg. Every room in this hotel is unique. The owner runs the place as a hobby and changes the decor whenever he feels like it. Try to get a room with a fantastic landscape mural over the bed. The bathrooms even have nifty rotating plastic seat covers to ensure that you're a sani-sitter. Since each room is special, the management tries to match the traveler's personality with a particular room. Doubles with breakfast cost DM 105. Reservations are recommended. *Kirchenallee 23, behind Hauptbahnhof, tel. 040/241141. 26 rooms, some with bath. Luggage storage.*

SCHANZENVIERTEL

The Schanzenviertel, north of St. Pauli, has a reputation for being somewhat alternative; it attracts a lot of students and foreigners and offers plenty of secondhand shops, ethnic grocery stores, and lively pubs to keep you from becoming too mainstream while in Hamburg. The centrally located neighborhood lies within walking distance of St. Pauli and downtown. To reach it, take the S-Bahn or U-Bahn to Sternschanze.

UNDER DM 80 **Hotel Sternschanze.** Once you squeeze out of the narrow hallways and into your clean, bright room you can relax in a relatively quiet atmosphere, unless the traffic outside your window is particularly heavy. A friendly Korean man runs this place. Doubles without breakfast will run you only DM 75. *Schanzenstr. 101, tel. 040/433389. Opposite S-Bahn station Sternschanze. Luggage storage, reception open daily 10–10.*

Schanzenstern. Located in a former Mont-Blanc pen factory, this alternative hotel is run by a group of five: Perhaps that's why it took three years to plan it. The one-, two-, and four-bed rooms are decorated with natural-wood furniture and nontoxic paints. The hotel shares the building with a movie theater, a school, a drug-counseling center, and the Schanzenstern Restaurant Cafe, which offers meals for about DM 8.50. Doubles are DM 80, with breakfast. *Bartelsstr. 12, tel. 040/439–8441. U-Bahn or S-Bahn to Sternschanze, then 10-min. walk. 50 beds, some with bath. Wheelchair access, luggage storage. Closed Dec. 24–Jan. 2.*

HOSTELS

Hamburg has two IYHF-affiliated hostels, both enormous and very, very popular and by far the city's cheapest lodging options.

Hamburg "Auf dem Stintfang." Overlooking Hamburg's lively harbor, this 350-bed youth hostel is almost always full. Call ahead or come before 6 PM if you expect to get a bed. The hostel is in a great spot, within spitting distance of the harbor and the Reeperbahn. The 1 AM curfew, though, puts a damper on the possibility of exploring Hamburg's dirty nightlife, since things only really start happening at about 12:30 AM. The hostel offers discounts of up to 50% on harbor tours. Guests who are 26 or younger pay DM 16.50, and those older pay DM 20.50. *Alfred-Wegener-Weg 5, tel. 040/313488. 350 beds. U3 to St. Pauli Landungsbrücken. Information boards.*

Jugendgästehaus Hamburg "Horner Rennbahn." A bit removed from downtown but quickly accessible on public transportation, the hostel offers high-quality modern rooms for a correspondingly high price of DM 24 (26 or under) and DM 28 (over 26), including bed linen and breakfast. The rooms are locked up from 9 AM to 1 PM for cleaning, and the reception desk starts accepting new guests at 1 PM. Try calling ahead or come early to ensure a bed. *Rennbahnstr. 100, tel. 040/651–1671. U3 toward Mümmelmannsberg to Horner Rennbahn, then 10-min. walk. 277 beds. 1 AM curfew, wheelchair access, swimming pool. Reception open Mar.–Jan., daily 7:30 AM–9 AM and 1 PM–1 AM. Closed Feb.*

STUDENT HOUSING

Hamburg is a big university town experiencing a housing crunch, like most of Germany. Most student dorms have three or four *Gästezimmer* (guest rooms), which are reserved throughout the year for temporary renters. Unfortunately, the burly *Hausmeister* (people who run the dorms) don't look kindly upon guests who want to stay for one or two nights; they prefer renting the rooms for two to four weeks for DM 270–DM 370. Even these rooms are hard to come by, though. During the summer vacation, students often lease their rooms by the month, but it's almost not worth the hassle to try to get one of these rooms, which cost DM 15–DM 25 per night. Call the **Studentenwerk** (tel. 040/412–2263) for general info (although they'll probably just say "no go"), or try contacting the **Paul-Sudeck-Haus** (Barmbeker Str. 64 and Wiesendamm 135, tel. 040/279–0050).

CAMPGROUNDS

Campingplatz Buchholz. With just 75 sites, Buchholz is a small campground, right off Kieler Straße. Although your tent will sit on cool green grass, it's tough to ignore the traffic streaming by. Make reservations a week in advance during the crowded summer months. Tents cost DM 10.50–DM 16.50 plus DM 5.50 per person. *Kieler Str. 374, tel. 040/540–4532. U-Bahn or S-Bahn to Sternschanze, then Bus 182. 75 sites. Showers DM 1, wheelchair access. Reception open daily 7:30 AM–10 AM and 4 PM–10 PM.*

City Camp Tourist. Four times as big as Buchholz, City Camp Tourist also lies just off Kieler Straße, so don't expect to hear birds singing. Lots of backpackers frequent this high-security, highly organized campground, which charges DM 7 per person and DM 10–DM 20 per tent. *Kieler Str. 650, tel. 040/570–4498. U2 to Osterstr., then Bus 182 toward Eidelstedt to Reichsbahnstr. 150 sites. Laundry, free showers, wheelchair access, small grocery store.*

Zeltdorf. From May to the end of August, five- and eight-bed tents unfold in the 370-acre Volkspark of Hamburg, making for a nice green escape from the hectic pace of the downtown area. Campers can play table tennis, volleyball, or badminton or go swimming in northern Germany's biggest pool. Although lots of large groups descend on the place, there's usually room for one or two lone travelers. Bring your sleeping bag, because it costs DM 10 to rent a blanket. Beds are DM 17.50 per night, including breakfast. *Sylvesterallee 3, tel. 040/831–9939 or 040/831–7966. S3 or S21 to Eidelstedt or Stellingen from downtown, then walk 15 min. 500 sites. Showers, food stands, limited wheelchair access.*

ROUGHING IT

Life sucks if you're stuck in Hamburg with no money and nowhere to sleep. If you're willing to face the cold—and, more often than not, wet—weather, try one of Hamburg's many parks. The **Stadtpark** is so big you're unlikely to be bothered, let alone found. The train stations, however, have become a less viable option, since the police recently began to crack down on the drug dealers, pushers, and homeless who camp out there. The **Bahnhofs Mission–Hauptbahnhof** (Steintorwall 20, tel. 040/326869 or 040/326068), a Christian organization, offers beds (DM 15) for the truly needy and helpless. (In other words, don't take advantage of the low prices just because you're a cheapskate and don't feel like dishing out a couple of bucks.)

MITWOHNZENTRALE

Hamburg has a whole slew of **Mitwohnzentrale** agencies that find travelers rooms (DM 30 and up) in private houses and apartments. The Mitwohnzentrale at Schulterblatt 112 (tel. 040/19445) charges a DM 8 commission (per person per night) to find you a room: Just tell them your price range and the area of town you prefer. Check the telephone book for further listings of Mitwohnzentrale.

Food

With more than 4,000 restaurants, bars, and cafés, Hamburg serves everything from exotic, expensive cuisine to standard fast food but specializes in fish in all forms. For the most economical seafood, check out any of the small restaurants in the port area. The most celebrated dish is probably *Aalsuppe* (eel soup), a tangy concoction not unlike Marseille's famous bouillabaisse. A must in summer is *Aalsuppe grün* (green eel soup), seasoned with dozens of herbs. Smoked eel, called *Räucheraal,* is a particularly fatty Hamburg specialty. Other specialties to try are *Birnen, Bohnen, und Speck* (pears, beans, and bacon) and the sailor's favorite, *Labskaus,* a stew made from pickled meat, potatoes, and (sometimes) herring, garnished with a fried egg, sour pickles, and lots of beets. Finish off your meal with the sweet dessert *Rote Grütze,* a red berry concoction traditionally served with vanilla sauce. Wash it all down with the local drink, *Alsterwasser,* a mix of beer and clear lemon soda. The ubiquitous German sausage costs just a couple of deutsche marks at street-corner stands. If it's picnic weather, buy a carton of potato salad, a few slices of locally cured ham, and a *Rundstück* (Hamburg's name for rolls) from the food department of any chain store on Mönckebergstraße, and make for the banks of the Alster to enjoy a low-cost alfresco lunch. Around the Schanzenviertel and on the Reeperbahn you'll find a hefty number of ethnic restaurants (especially Turkish, Greek, and Italian) offering delicious, if not downright cheap, meals.

INNENSTADT

This refers to the main part of town, which lies within the area originally enclosed by the city walls. Here you'll find most of the main tourist attractions, the train station, and very few affordable restaurants.

UNDER DM 10 **bon appetit.** This busy stand-up café behind Mönckebergstraße serves area businesspeople who know a good lunch when they eat one. Don't be put off by the incredibly long lunch lines—they move quickly. Standard meat-and-potatoes dishes cost less than DM 10. Both the DM 7.90 *Bauernfrühstück* (farmer's breakfast) and the salad bar are good deals. *Rathausstr. 4, tel. 040/324570. Limited wheelchair access. No dinner.*

Daniel Wischer. Conveniently located on pedestrians-only Spitalerstraße, Daniel Wischer is always jam-packed during lunch. Take a table inside (expect to share), or sit outside and people-watch while you chow down some old-fashioned, greasy fish and chips. Try the *Seelachsfilet* (salmon fillet) with potato salad or fries for DM 7.90. Salads start at a bargain DM 3.95. *Spitalerstr. 12, tel. 040/382343. Wheelchair access. Closes at 7:30.*

UNDER DM 15 **Gestern & Heute Treff.** Open 24 hours a day (a true abnormality in Germany), this restaurant is a favorite with Hamburgers. Among the cheap, decent menu items: scampi (DM 11.10), rump steak (DM 10.80–DM 16.80), and pizza (DM 9.10). *Kaiser-Wilhelm-Str. 55, tel. 040/344998.*

Kartoffelkeller. The waitresses are dressed in old potato sacks, and the red candles support about a pound of dried dripped wax in this unique restaurant on historic Deichstraße. All dishes—even the dessert—are made with spuds. They're a little expensive, but you should be able to find something for under DM 15. *Deichstr. 21, tel. 040/365585. No lunch.*

Old Spaghetti Factory. This tastefully decorated restaurant features stained glass, whimsical tassled lamps, wood paneling, tall wood chairs, and old-fashioned ambience. There's an old streetcar in the restaurant and a sign asking you to wait to be seated, something you don't see often in Germany. The standard pasta dishes and salads will run you DM 10–DM 18. *Poststr. 20, tel. 040/343401.*

REEPERBAHN/ST. PAULI

UNDER DM 15 **Billard-Salon.** Lit only by beautiful old-fashioned light globes, this atmospheric restaurant serves cola (DM 2.50), beer (DM 3.50–DM 5), and *Rahmgulasch,* a cream-base goulash (DM 12.50). The place fills up at about 7 PM *with people grabbing a bite before seeing a play or a show. Upstairs there are more than 20 pool tables. Spielbudenpl. 27, tel. 040/315815.*

Medusa. This modern, family-run Italian restaurant features lasagna, tortellini, or fettuccine for a bargain DM 12 or broccoli *überbacken* (baked with cheese on top) for DM 7.50. Through a small window that opens onto the kitchen you can watch your meal being made. *Spielbudenpl. 21, tel. 040/313503. No lunch.*

ST. GEORG

UNDER DM 10 **Cafe Benito.** Benito does everything himself. He serves the drinks, buses the tables, and concocts tasty Italian dishes (DM 6–DM 8). Although the menu constantly changes, it features consistently yummy fare. *Lange Reihe 111, tel. 040/246165. No lunch. Closed Sat.–Tues.*

Cafe Gnosa. This is the place to go to check out the gay scene and get some fantastic meals. Daily dishes start at a mere DM 9.50. Try the vegetarian *Auflauf* (DM 9.50), a casserole of zucchini, cauliflower, carrots, and cheese. The waiters serve a mean piece of homemade cake. *Lange Reihe 93, tel. 040/243034.*

Max & Consorten. Conversation buzzes over the low music and through the smoky air as local students and the occasional tourist gather here for a quick beer (DM 4) or a cheap meal. The DM 8 Bauernfrühstück fills you up any time of day. *Spadenteich 7, tel. 040/245617.*

SCHANZENVIERTEL

This area just north of St. Pauli and west of the university doesn't appear on maps, although everybody knows where it is and what it refers to. Its fairly large immigrant and student population has created, among other things, a wide variety of reasonably priced cuisines, including Greek, Chinese, and Turkish, as well as many alternative bars, cafés, and secondhand clothing shops. Wander down **Schulterblatt** to find something you fancy. To reach the area, take the U-Bahn or S-Bahn to Sternschanze.

UNDER DM 10 **noodle's & mehr.** Newly redecorated, noodle's is a modern, clean restaurant serving noodles and pasta. Not many tourists have discovered this great find, where most dishes cost DM 9. Try the tortellini in a rich cream sauce with broccoli and mushrooms. *Schanzenstr. 2–4, tel. 040/439–2840. Limited wheelchair access.*

Taverna Olympisches Feuer. "Kitschy" is the only word to describe this Greek restaurant in the heart of the Schanzenviertel. Ignore the plastic-and-paper decor and concentrate on the food. The portions are good size, and the taste is even better. *Kalamares* (squid) cost DM 9. *Schulterblatt 63, tel. 040/435597.*

UNIVERSITY QUARTER

The streets around the university will see you right when it comes to cheap eats. Wander down Grindelallee to find a good restaurant or bar or to get a gander at students doing the same thing. Take the S-Bahn to Dammtor, then walk up E-Siemers-Allee to Grindelallee.

UNDER DM 6 **Mensa Studenthaus.** Hamburg's biggest student cafeteria seats 1,060 hungry and unselective people. Dishes range from DM 1.70 to DM 5.20. Remember to put your tray away when you're done. *Schlüterstr. 7.*

UNDER DM 15 **Dwaraka.** This restaurant features excellent Indian food in an elegant setting. The bar beckons drinkers with about 50 bottles stacked up like a pyramid. Try the *palak paneer,* a rice plate with small portions of different things (DM 12). *Rentzelstr. 38, tel. 040/453237.*

Limerick. Students take advantage of this restaurant's reasonably priced dishes and its proximity to the university and the Dammtor train station. Colorful posters, music, and dark wood set the scene. The 18 varieties of pizza average about DM 10. Also try the fresh salads (DM 4.90–DM 10.60) or the pasta (DM 6.80–DM 12.80). *Grindelallee 18, tel. 040/447836.*

Exploring Hamburg

All of Hamburg's main sights and attractions are accessible either via the city's public transportation system or on foot. It will take you at least a couple days to familiarize yourself with the diverse corners of this city on your own; if you're in a hurry, consider taking one of the many sightseeing tours that give you a quick, if superficial, overview of the city. The tourist office (tel. 040/300–51245) organizes bus tours of the city, in English, that last one to 1½ hours and cost DM 22–DM 28. All tours start at the **Kirchenallee,** near the Hauptbahnhof. The tourist office also offers city tours on the schlocky ***Hummelbahn,*** converted railroad wagons pulled by a tractor. The hourly tours, accompanied by static-filled commentary, cost DM 18 (DM 13 students); tours can be combined with a harbor tour for DM 8–DM 10 extra. A number of alternative city tours cover the history of Nazism in Hamburg and include the concentration camp Neuengamme. Ask at the tourist-information office for details. One of the most enjoyable ways to get to know Hamburg is on a trip around its massive harbor; in summer **HAPAG excursion boats** (tel. 040/311–7070) leave every half hour from the *Landungsbrücken* (piers) for 90-minute tours of the harbor (DM 14). Departures in winter are less frequent; if you happen to be in town during some subzero weather, take the tour anyway, if only for the unusual experience of being aboard as the boat cracks the ice. Boat tours around the Alster lakes and through the canals leave every half hour 10–6 from Jungfernstieg, in the center of the city. The daily tours cost DM 10 and last about 50 minutes. For information on other tours call 040/341141.

WORTH SEEING

ALTONA (OTTENSEN) Altona, west of Hamburg, was an autonomous city for almost 300 years, until the Nazis decided to make it part of Hamburg. In the last couple of years this district has acquired a mix of young people, students, foreigners, retirees, small theaters, and restaurants. Altona's **Elbchaußee,** packed with elegant mansions hidden by tall, grand trees, is perfect for a stroll. To get to Altona take the S-Bahn to the Altona station.

BINNENALSTER AND AUSSENALSTER Once an insignificant waterway, the Alster was dammed during the 18th century to form an artificial lake. Divided by a pair of graceful bridges, the **Lombardsbrücke** and **Kennedybrücke,** the Alster now consists of the Binnenalster (Inner Alster) and the much larger Aussenalster (Outer Alster). Stately hotels, department stores, fine shops, and cafés line the Binnenalster, and the Aussenalster is framed by spacious parks and set against a background of private mansions. From late spring into fall you'll see sailboats and Windsurfers skimming across the surface of the Aussenalster, narrowly missing passenger steamships that zip back and forth.

In winter the Alster lakes sometimes freeze over, and the pure white stretches of snow-covered ice are dotted with residents in vibrantly colored snowsuits, mittens, and caps.

BLANKENESE Although this waterside village 15 kilometers (9 miles) west of Hamburg is now one of the city's wealthiest neighborhoods, it still manages to preserve some of its fishing-village ambience. Dotted with villas, the 58 lanes that wind through town are built for exploring. Many people compare Blankenese to towns on the French and

Italian rivieras, although the smell of Bain de Soleil is hardly in evidence. To get back into town, lots of people do the fairly easy 13-kilometer (8-mile) walk along the Elbe or take the ferry. To get to Blankenese, take a ferry from Landungsbrücken, or the S1 to Blankenese.

DEICHSTRAßE For the last 600-plus years, people have lived on Deichstraße, a genuinely charming and peaceful residential street that runs along one of Hamburg's oldest canals. Although many of the street's oldest residences were destroyed in the Great Fire of 1842, a number of homes date from the 17th to 19th centuries, and many others have been restored, giving the street a pleasant uniformity of style. Among the oldest structures are No. 27, a warehouse dating from 1780, and No. 39, whose Baroque facade dates to 1700. You should definitely spend some time on this street to get a dose of old Hamburg; better yet, follow one of the small alleys that lead off the main drag to catch a glimpse of the houses' uneven backsides, where merchandise was unloaded in the olden days.

EPPENDORF Northwest of the Alster lies Eppendorf. Its beautiful streets are lined with stucco peach, silver gray, and apricot villas, which provide a pleasant backdrop for the trendy student life that has sprung up here of late. You could easily spend a couple of hours wandering the streets, admiring the houses, and looking in the small boutiques that sell candles, tea, jewelry, and other knickknacks. The two main shopping streets are **Eppendorfer Baum** and **Eppendorfer Landstraße.** To get here, take U3 to Eppendorfer Baum.

FISCHMARKT Every Sunday morning, crazy early morning risers and late-night party-goers congregate at the Fischmarkt, Hamburg's most famous market, which opens at 5 AM (7 AM in winter) and runs until 10 AM. If you can manage to get up you can get fresh fish, rabbits, birds, cheap fruit, flowers, veggies, knickknacks, and souvenirs and even listen to free jazz in the **Fischauktionshalle.** Prices go down at about 9:30, when the market begins to wind down. Try very, very hard not to miss this superlative Hamburg experience, even if it means forcing yourself to stay up all night. Prepare to contend with massive crowds. To get here, take the U3, S1, S2, or S3 to Landungsbrücken.

HAFEN Hamburg's Hafen (harbor), one of the largest and most efficient in the world, will send ship aficionados into raptures; the rest of us may not be able to generate quite so much excitement. But consider this: 33 individual docks and 500 berths,

Squatting on the Hafenstraße

"These houses are occupied." With this pronouncement in 1981, students and other young people, frustrated with the city's increasingly difficult housing situation, took over the decrepit buildings on Hafenstraße and proceeded to set up house. Not surprisingly, the city didn't take too kindly to this, and when police claimed that members of the Red Army Faction (RAF) were using the buildings as a base for a pirate radio channel, the shit really hit the fan: In an effort to hold off some 6,000 police officers the squatters erected barricades and barbed wire. Before the tension could lead to a riot the mayor stepped in, suggesting that the squatters might be allowed to stay if they removed the barricades and wire. Since then squatters have had several violent run-ins with police attempting to evict them, but they still live here. Stop by and see for yourself—maybe you'll end up living here one day.

Hamburg

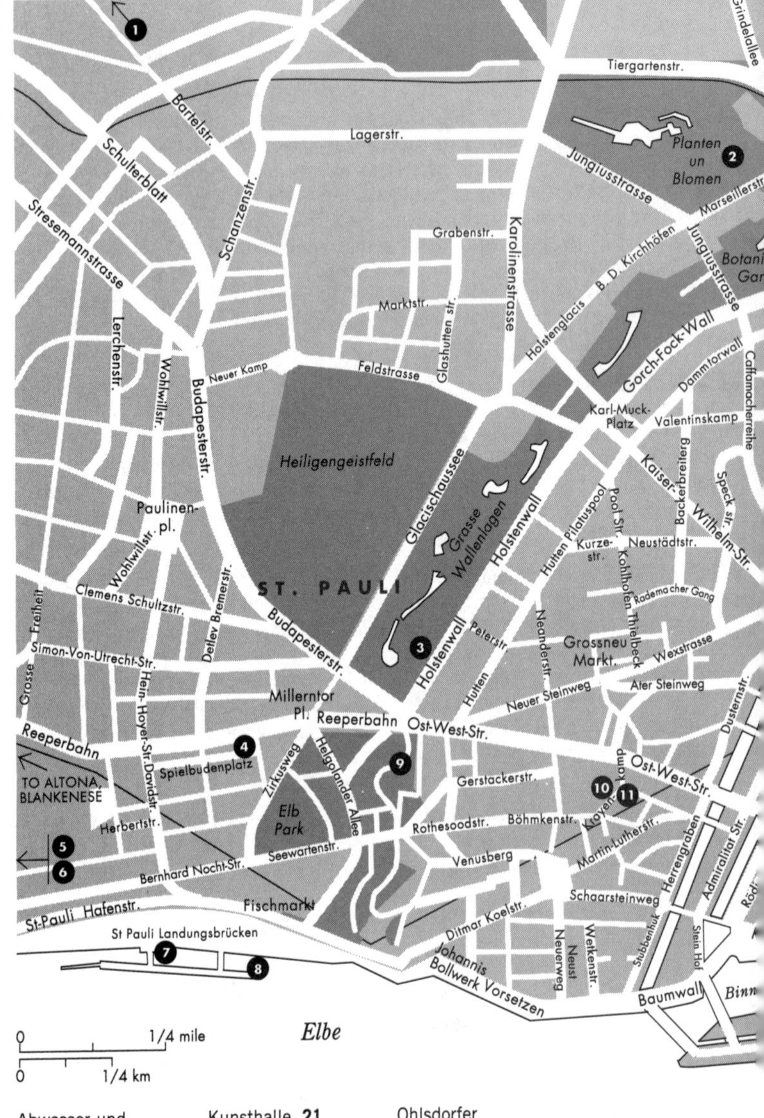

Abwasser-und Sielmuseum, **7**

Bismarck-Denkmal, **9**

Deichtorhallen, **26**

Electrum: Museum der Elektrizität, **24**

Ernst-Barlach-Haus, **5**

Iman Ali Moschee, **22**

Jakobikirche, **20**

Katharinenkirche, **17**

Krameramts-wohnungen, **11**

Kunsthalle, **21**

Michaeliskirche, **10**

Museum für Hamburgische Geschichte, **3**

Museum Für Kunst und Gewerbe, **25**

Museum für Völkerkunde, **13**

Museumschiff *Rickmer Rickmers*, **8**

Museumshafen Övelgönne, **6**

Nikolaikirche, **16**

Ohlsdorfer Friedhof, **23**

Panoptikum, **4**

Petrikirche, **19**

Planten un Blomen, **2**

Rathaus, **15**

Russisch-Orthodoxe Kirche St. Prokopius, **1**

Speicherstadt, **18**

Stadtpark, **14**

War monument, **12**

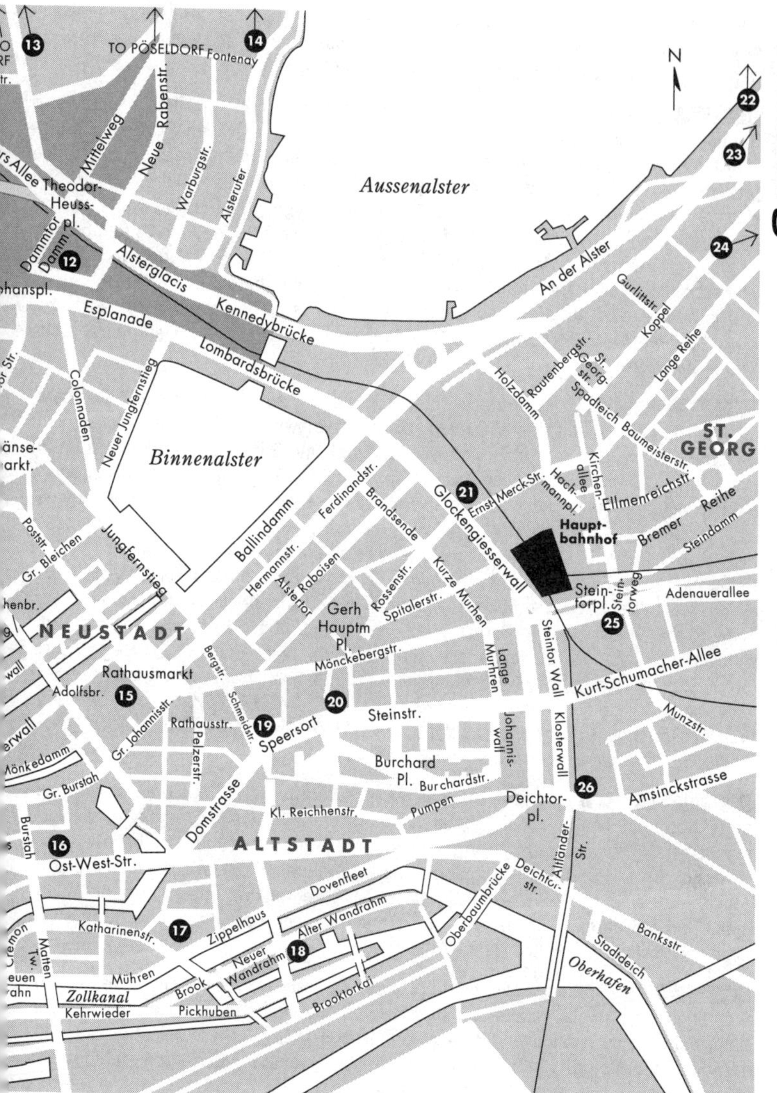
Hamburg
N
TO PÖSELDORF
Fontenay
Aussenalster
Mittelweg
Neue Rabenstr.
Warburgstr.
Alsterufer
Theodor-Heuss-pl.
Dammtor Damm
Alsterglacis
Esplanade
Kennedybrücke
Lombardsbrücke
An der Alster
Gurlittstr.
Koppel
Lange Reihe
Holzdamm
Rautenbergstr.
St. Georg str.
Spadteich
Baumeisterstr.
ST. GEORG
Colonnaden
Neuer Jungfernstieg
Binnenalster
Ballindamm
Ferdinandstr.
Brandsende
Glockengiesserwall
Ernst-Merck-Str.
Hachmannpl.
Kirchenallee
Ellmenreichstr.
Hauptbahnhof
Bremer Reihe
Steindamm
Steintorpl.
Steintorweg
Adenauerallee
Poststr.
Gr. Bleichen
Jungfernstieg
Hermannstr.
Alstertor
Raboisen
Rossenstr.
Kurze Murhen
Spitalerstr.
Gerh Hauptm Pl.
NEUSTADT
Rathausmarkt
Adolfsbr.
Mönckebergstr.
Bergstr.
Schmiedstr.
Lange Murhen
Steintor Wall
Kurt-Schumacher-Allee
Gr. Johannisstr.
Rathausstr.
Pelzerstr.
Speersort
Steinstr.
Johanniswall
Klosterwall
Munzstr.
Mönkedamm
Gr. Burstah
Domstrasse
Burchard Pl.
Burchardstr.
Pumpen
Deichtorpl.
Amsinckstrasse
Kl. Reichhenstr.
Burstah
ALTSTADT
Ost-West-Str.
Dovenfleet
Oberbaumbrücke
Deichtorstr.
Altländer-Str.
Katharinenstr.
Zippelhaus
Alter Wandrahm
Neuer Wandrahm
Banksstr.
Stadtdeich
Oberhafen
Matten Tw.
Mühren
Brook
Brooktorkai
Zollkanal
Kehrwieder
Pickhuben
12
13
14
15
16
17
18
19
20
21
22
23
24
25
26

a huge amount of merchandise entering and exiting every year, a case study in modernity and efficiency. Still not enraptured? Try a harbor tour, and remember to dress warmly. Take the U3, S1, S2, or S3 to Landungsbrücken.

KUNSTHALLE The Kunsthalle houses one of the most important art collections in Germany. The 3,000 paintings, 400 sculptures, and coin and medal collections present a remarkably diverse picture of European artistic life from the 14th century to the present. Those into the hit-and-run method of art appreciation might pick up "An Hour in the Hamburg Kunsthalle" (DM 1.50), which highlights the museum's masterpieces, ranging from the German Romantic greats Runge and Friedrich to Rembrandt, German impressionist Max Liebermann, expressionist Edvard Munch, and French impressionists Manet and Monet. The Kunsthalle is going through some reconstruction and is adding new buildings, so expect some changes. *Glockengieserwall Str. near Hauptbahnhof, tel. 040/248–62612. Admission: DM 3, DM .70 students. Open Tues.–Sun. 10–6.*

MICHAELISKIRCHE Hamburg's most famous and best-loved landmark, Michaeliskirche (St. Michael's Church, popularly known as "Michel"), stands guard over the city, attracting tourists and worshipers of fine Baroque architecture from all over. Not only does its copper-covered spire make a distinct mark on Hamburg's already stately skyline, but the restored interior is elegant enough to make you reconsider converting to Krishnaism. In the vault you can see a presentation on the church's history (DM 2.50, DM 1.50 students), as well as the grave of J. S. Bach's son Carl Philipp Emanuel Bach, who was Hamburg's church musical director for 20 years. As if all this weren't enough, the Michael's distinctive 433-foot brick-and-iron tower is also home to the largest clock in Germany. At press time (fall 1993) the viewing platform, with its magnificent vista, was under reconstruction. Twice daily, at 10 AM and 9 PM (on Sunday at noon only), a watchman plays a trumpet solo from the tower platform. It ain't Dizzy Gillespie, though. *Krayenkamp 4C, tel. 040/371727. S1, S2, or S3 to Stadthausbrücke. Organ-concert admission: DM 6. Open Mon.–Sat. 9–5:30, Sun. 11:30–5:30. Organ concerts in summer, Sat. 4 PM.*

POSELDORF For a long time this neighborhood on the Alster was popular with students from the nearby music school and university. Nowadays, though, everyone around here looks as though they graduated and earn a lot of money. The small passageways of the Pöseldorf now feature lots of pretentious cafés and expensive boutiques, including Hamburg's own **Jil Sanders.** Good walking streets include **Milchstraße** and **Mittelweg,** both of which have been spruced up with colorful murals. To reach the Pöseldorf, take the U1 to Hallerstraße.

RATHAUS The Rathaus (town hall) presides impressively over the city-state of Hamburg, sheltering legislators and tourists alike in its neo-Renaissance, Nordic hugeness. When neither city council nor state government is in session (both institutions convene in the building) you can tour the Rathaus's innards. Especially opulent and rather tragic is the intricately carved **Orphan's Room,** where 80 orphan carvers between the ages of 8 and 14 worked to achieve the fine aesthetic quality you see today. Construction of the sandstone structure began in 1866, when 4,000 oak trunks were sunk into the moist soil to provide stability for its mighty bulk. *Rathausmarkt, tel. 040/368–12470. U3 to Rathaus or S-Bahn or U-Bahn to Jungfernstieg. Tour fee: DM 1. Tours Mon.–Thurs. hourly 10:15 –3:15, Fri.–Sun. hourly 10:15–1:15.*

REEPERBAHN/ST. PAULI To create an image of energy and health, Wheaties boxes show the faces of famous athletes; on its labels, St. Pauli beer shows a buxom prostitute toting frothing mugs of beer. And that about sums up the popular image of St. Pauli. In truth, most of St. Pauli is residential, but it's the Reeperbahn and its seamy side streets that everyone remembers. Extending west from the St. Pauli U-Bahn stop, the Reeperbahn beckons all those who are prepared to pay to get laid, to watch somebody else get laid, or watch somebody else pretend to get laid. However, an increasing number of more staid activities are now being offered in St. Pauli, so don't write off the neighborhood unseen. Even on the Reeperbahn, discos, theaters, and alternative cafés are helping balance the sleaze factor. Although it's known as the "wickedest mile in the world," the Reeperbahn itself is really pretty tame. It's the side streets like **Große Freiheit** (or Great Freedom, and they ain't kidding) and **Herbertstraße** —off-limits to women, children, and autos—that you gotta either avoid or look for, depending on whether you read the *Hite Report* or Henry Miller. Behind the walls lining the Herbertstraße sit some of Hamburg's finest prostitutes, who charge DM 50 for a simple hand job. Große Freiheit is home to some explicit sex shows, including the **Safari.** The most explicit of them all, though, is the **Salambo,** which encourages audience participation in the entertainment. Also in the same area, on Große Freiheit 36, sits the **Kaiserkeller,** formerly called the Star Club, where the Beatles performed in the early days. Don't bother coming during the day, when the streets are empty; things don't get exciting until well after midnight. To get here, take the S1, S2, or S3 to Reeperbahn or the U3 to St. Pauli.

Women who aren't prostitutes are not welcome on Herbertstraße and should be prepared to have a glass of water tossed in their faces by one of the street guards if they try to venture in.

SPEICHERSTADT This collection of warehouses for the port of Hamburg dates from the 19th century. Warehouses generally don't elicit oohs and aahs for their architecture, but you have to admit these are mighty fine storage sheds. The enormous, Gothic-influenced brick structures are loaded with carpets and bags of coffee, as well as less exotic wares like rivets and oats; you may be requested to fill out a customs declaration before you leave to ensure that you're not trying to smuggle out a cross beam under your shirt. To prevent this type of activity, the warehouses themselves are closed, but you can wander the grounds all day long. To get here, take the U2 to Meßberg.

HOUSES OF WORSHIP

Every other month the **Amt für Kirchenmusik** (Unlandstr. 49) publishes a free calendar, available in churches and tourist-information offices, that lists all free organ concerts. **Michaeliskirche,** Hamburg's most famous church and one of its major landmarks, is so well loved that the citizens have given it its own nickname (*see* Worth Seeing, *above*).

IMAN ALI MOSCHEE Built in 1961, this modern, shiny mosque overlooks the Aussenalster and serves the needs of the city's large Muslim population. You can tour it every Saturday between 10 AM and noon. *Schöne Aussicht 36, tel. 040/221220 or 040/221240. From Hauptbahnhof, Bus 108 toward Borgweg to Zimmerstr.*

JACOBIKIRCHE This 13th-century church was rebuilt after being severely damaged during World War II. The reconstruction of the interior is rather uninspiring and plain, but some of the church's treasures— including three Gothic altars and a unique 1693 Baroque organ upon which Johann Sebastian Bach supposedly played—remain intact. *Jacobikirchhof 22, tel. 040/327744. U3 to Mönckebergstr. or U1 to Steinstr. Open weekdays 10–5, Sat. 10–1.*

KATHARINENKIRCHE This restored Baroque church overlooking the harbor is dedicated to the martyred 4th-century Princess Catherine of Alexandria. For DM 5 you can see the 40-minute show "Under the Spires of the City," which chronicles Hamburg's history in 1,300 slides on a large panoramic screen. *Katharinenhof 1, tel. 040/336275. U1 to Meßberg or S1/S11 to Ingfennstieg. Open Oct.–Apr., daily 9–4; May–Sept., daily 9–6.*

NIKOLAIKIRCHE All that remains of this 19th-century neo-Gothic church destroyed in World War II is the 485-foot tower (Hamburg's tallest) and the outside walls. The church ruins are a monument to those killed and persecuted during the war. *Ost-West-Str./Hopfenmarkt. U3 to Rödingsmarkt.*

PETRIKIRCHE Considered the oldest church in Hamburg, this early 13th-century building fell victim to the Great Fire of 1842 and was rebuilt shortly afterward. It has a tall copper-covered spire and contains a number of attractions, including a Gothic pulpit and various votive panels. *Speersort 10, tel. 040/324438. U3 to Rathaus or S1, S2, S3, U1, or U2 to Jungfernstieg. Open weekdays 9–6, Sat. 9–5, Sun. 9–noon and 1–10.*

RUSSISCH-ORTHODOXE KIRCHE ST. PROKOPIUS With green roofs and blue onion domes, this elegant white Russian Orthodox church is patterned after the medieval church of Novgorod. Inside you're overwhelmed by strong incense and colorful, vibrant wall murals. The church is open only by appointment, so call ahead. *Hagenbeckstr. 10, n. of downtown, tel. 040/405560. U2 to Lutterothstr.*

MUSEUMS AND GALLERIES

In addition to its fabulous Kunsthalle (*see* Worth Seeing, *above*), Hamburg has more than 30 museums, ranging from the ridiculous to the highbrow, and more than 100 art galleries. Pick up *The Museums* (DM 1), a good description of the Hamburg museum scene complete with a helpful map, at a tourist-information office. The **Hamburg-CARD** (*see* Visitor Information in Basics, *above*) includes free entrance to 11 museums. Otherwise, consider investing in a museum pass (DM 15), which is good at all of Hamburg's museums for one week. Ask at a tourist-information office about these passes.

ABWASSER UND SIELMUSEUM Built in the form of a real sewer, the one-room Abwasser und Sielmuseum (Sewage Museum) is home to a variety of collectibles that were found in the 5,000-kilometer (3,100-mile) sewage network and 6,841 sewers of Hamburg. Call ahead, or stop by and ask for Mr. Rees, to get a look at the museum's unbelievable collection of lingerie, gold credit cards, a birth certificate, glasses, bicycles, and false teeth—supposedly from people who got friendly with the porcelain princess after drinking a little too much. The workers here take pride in their small museum; they'll ask you to sign their guest book and might even take you on a personal tour of the massive, putrid sewer system. *St. Pauli Landungsbrücken 49, near Bridge 9, tel. 040/380–73341. U3, S1, or S3 to Landungsbrücken.*

DEICHTORHALLEN This large, old building near the Hauptbahnhof used to be a vegetable-and-flower market, but it now displays changing modern- art exhibitions in its airy rooms. Don't mistake the simple sculpture outside the entrance for archaic remains or garbage—it's a work by artist Richard Serra. *Altländer Str., near Hauptbahnhof, tel. 040/323735. Admission price varies with exhibition. Open Tues.–Sun. 11 AM–6 PM.*

ELECTRUM: MUSEUM DER ELECTRIZITAT Sponsored by the Hamburgische Electricitäts-Werke AG (a.k.a. the electric company), this museum lets you press lots of different buttons that start up gadgets like light bulbs and phonographs. This is definitely a museum for technology freaks: You can see primitive toasters, and hair dryers and curlers that resemble futuristic octopi. Take a break in the small café, where Cokes cost an unbelievable DM .50 and warm cake just DM .80. *Klinikweg 23, tel. 040/639–63641. U2 to Hamburger Str. Admission free. Open Tues.–Sun. 9–5.*

ERNST-BARLACH-HAUS The Ernst-Barlach-Haus contains a mighty collection of the artist's works, including 116 sculptures and more than 300 drawings, prints, and documents on his works and life. Barlach was born in nearby Wedel and, like many other modern artists, was declared degenerate by the Nazis in the 1930s. *Baron-Voght-Str. 50A, in Jenisch-Park, tel. 040/826085. Admission: DM 3.50, DM 1.50 students. Open Tues.–Sun. 11–5.*

KRAMERAMTSWOHNUNGEN This cluster of courtyard houses in the shadow of the Michel dates from the 1620s, when they were built to house shopkeepers' widows. Nowadays the tiny old structures—a real rarity in bombed-to-hell Hamburg—mostly house galleries and other tourist-oriented businesses, as well as a museum that replicates the setup of a typical house, minus the widow. *Krayenkamp 10–11, tel. 040/350–4236. S1, S2, or S3 to Stadthausbrücke. Admission to museum: DM 1.50, DM .50 students. Open Tues.–Sun. 10–5.*

MUSEUM FUR HAMBURGISCHE GESCHICHTE The Museum for Hamburg History traces the history of Hamburg from its origins in the 9th century to the present day. Americans who are desperate for the past will enjoy perusing the museum's record of German immigrants to the United States, between 1850 and 1914. The Historic Emigration Office's microfilm lists the names of almost 5 million people who left the port of Hamburg for the promise of a better life in the New World. The first-floor office will research individual cases for visitors and provide information and documents. Allow an hour for this service, and expect to pay a fee of DM 50–DM 100. *Holstenwall 24, tel. 040/350–42360. U3 to St. Pauli. Admission: DM 3, DM .70 students. Open Tues.–Sun. 10–5.*

MUSEUM FUR KUNST UND GEWERBE Built in 1876 as a museum and school combined, the Arts and Crafts Museum now contains an impressive collection of handicrafts from all over the world. Included in the extensive collection are works from ancient Egypt, Greece, Japan, and China, as well as applied European arts from the last several centuries. The museum also houses a range of 15th- to 18th-century scientific instruments. *Steintorpl. 1, near Hauptbahnhof, tel. 040/248–62630. Admission: DM 3, DM 1 students. Open Tues.–Sun. 10–5.*

MUSEUM FUR VOLKERKUNDE One of the largest museums of ethnology in Germany, this museum has particularly extensive and well-presented displays on Africa and South America. *Rothenbaumchausee 64, tel. 040/441–95524. U1 to Hallerstr. Admission: DM 3, DM .70 students. Open Tues.–Sun. 10–5.*

MUSEUMSCHIFF RICKMER RICKMERS This beautiful 19th-century East Indies windjammer is docked on the harbor and open to visitors. *By St. Pauli Landungsbrücken, Brücke 1, tel. 040/356–93119. Admission: DM 4, DM 3 students. Open daily 10–6.*

MUSEUMSHAFEN OVELGONNE The aim of the privately owned Harbor Museum is to maintain and restore ships for occasional outings and public display. Most of the restored ships are seaworthy, and the collection features steam tugs, wood cutters, and fire-fighting ships. *Anleger Neumühlen, tel. 040/390–0070. From Altona, Bus 183 to Neumühlen. Admission free.*

PANOPTIKUM Just what you came to Germany to do, gaze at poor wax replicas of Elvis and J.F.K. Homesick Americans will love the sheer inanity of the place. *Spielbudenpl. 3, on Reeperbahn, tel. 040/310317. Admission: DM 5. Open weekdays 11–9, Sat. 11 AM–midnight, Sun. 10–9.*

PARKS AND GARDENS

Tourist brochures herald Hamburg as "the world's greenest city," a debatable but not implausible claim: Almost half the city is covered by parks (more than 120 of them), green areas, nature reserves, lakes, and canals. There's even a law that forbids you to chop down a tree of a certain width without authorization. Hamburgers take advantage of their parks and often go for long *Spaziergänge* (walks). Weather permitting, they sunbathe.

"Ohlsdorf Cemetery is twice the size of Monaco but not quite as lively."

OHLSDORFER FRIEDHOF Patterned after English landscape gardens, Ohlsdorf Cemetery was opened on July 1, 1877, and is now the largest in the world—it's twice the size of Monaco but not quite as lively. More than 1.3 million souls rest in peace here, and there are more than 2,800 benches from which the living can keep an eye on them. Hamburgers come here to commune with the dead, walk, make out, and have picnics. Two city buses, 170 and 270, run right through the cemetery. *Fuhlsbüttler Str. 756, tel. 040/591051. Entrance outside U- and S-Bahn station Ohlsdorf. Open daily at 8.*

PLANTEN UN BLOMEN Although "Planten un Blomen" technically refers to one garden within the larger Alter Botanischer Garten, everyone just refers to the whole thing as Planten un Blomen, or Plants and Blooms. That pretty much sums up this park smack in the middle of the city. Besides the ubiquitous flower-surrounded pathways and green expanses, the park offers playgrounds for children (or you), an open-air stage where free summer concerts are held, a small lake, and a **greenhouse** where you can see tropical plants. At 10 PM from May to September, crowds gather to watch a free water-and-light concert accompanied by classical music. The nearby **TV Tower** (Lagerstr. 2, tel. 040/438024) affords a great view of the city for DM 6. *U-Bahn to Stephanspl. or S-Bahn to Dammtor.*

STADTPARK This popular spot north of the Aussenalster is Hamburg's biggest park. Hamburgers jog, walk, sunbathe, play football, picnic, and do just about everything else here; there's even a small lake for swimming. "Open Air Stadtpark" concerts attract music lovers to the open-air stage in summer. *S1 to Alte Wöhr or U3 to Borgweg.*

MONUMENTS

People have written entire books about Hamburg's numerous *Kunst im öffentlichen Raum* (open-air statues and sculptures). By far the most interesting is the **war monument** near Stephansplatz and Dammtor. Originally intended to commemorate World War I, it was built during the Nazi years and turned out to be a monument to Nazi ideology. Accompanying a relief of a column of identical-looking soldiers, an inscription states: *"Deutschland muß leben auch wenn wir sterben müßen"* ("Germany must live, even if we have to die"). In recent history the monument has been the site of a lot of controversy, including massive demonstrations that often leave it covered with red paint. On the other side of the story is a group that hopes to keep the monument paint-free by guarding and cleaning it, the rationale being that the monument should stay as a reminder of the danger of Nazism. Next to the monument is a half-finished sculpture testifying to the horrors of war, by artist Alfred Hrdlicka. He began the work in the mid-1980s with a government grant of DM 862,500; when his later request for another million to complete the work was denied, he quit altogether. Now it sits, half-finished and disconcerting, in the shadow of the bigger war monument.

Hamburg's biggest monument is the 113-foot-high **Bismarck-Denkmal** near Landungsbrücken, by the port. Otto von Bismarck, the former chancellor, impressed citizens with his devotion to a reunited Germany; now he impresses visitors with his giant, 17-foot head.

The plain slab of concrete near the Rathaus, an Ernst Barlach work, depicts a sorrowful mother hugging a child. The Nazis didn't agree with the artwork's message and replaced it with an eagle, which was supposed to represent Germany's strength and power. After the war the Barlach work was reconstructed as a warning against war.

CHEAP THRILLS

Hamburg can drain your wallet, precipitating the need for some free or very cheap fun. Exploring the downtown area and people-watching always make for good cheap thrills; **Spitalerstraße,** the pedestrian zone near the Hauptbahnhof, usually has a mix of musicians, from Peruvian folk musicians to rockers to violinists to accordion players. Head over to **Jungfernstieg** for some people-watching and window-shopping for items you won't be able to afford. Around the **Alsterhaus** department store you can usually find an unusual street performer—he's the guy painted silver. The **Aussenalster** is usually dotted with colorful sailboats and sailboarders, and sunbathers line the banks in summer. It's legal to go topless in Hamburg.

You can rent boats all around the Alster from April through October; pedal- and rowboats usually go for less than DM 15 per hour for two people. **Alfred Seebeck** (tel. 040/247652) and **Hans Pieper** (tel. 040/247578), just outside the Hotel Atlantic, rent boats. There are at least nine other rental places in Hamburg. Ask at a tourist-information office for further details.

Around the **Binnenalster** and **Aussenalster** in winter, entrepreneurial types erect stands selling mulled wine, candy, and corn on the cob. If you are lucky enough to be here during subzero weather, don your mittens and scarf with everybody else in town and head out on the Alster, where you'll see folks with sleds and other wintery paraphernalia. Loads of fun, but requiring extraordinary amounts of balance, is *Glitschen* (sliding): You clear the snow off a 30-foot strip of ice, take a running start, and slide across it.

Although the city doesn't lie on the coast, it has one popular **beach** on the River Elbe where people picnic, drink, and just have a good time when the sun manages to peek through. A small kiosk sells snacks and drinks, but a lot of people bring their own beer. Don't be fooled into thinking you can actually swim in the water. Most Hamburgers wouldn't stick their pinky in the polluted waters of the Elbe. *Am Schulberg, tel. 040/880–1112. From Reeperbahn, Bus 36 toward Blankenese to Liebermann Str. Open Apr.–Sept., daily 1–11.*

Hamburg is also ideal terrain for **biking,** as long as the weather cooperates; you can rent bikes from the tourist-information office in Bieberhaus, outside the main train station. Prices range from DM 2 per hour to DM 20 for the weekend. For more information call 040/300–51245.

The **Freiluft Kino auf dem Rathausmarkt** shows movies on a big screen in front of the Rathaus at night. Admission is free, and there are usually a couple of movies in English with German subtitles. The movies are shown on weekends in July and August.

FESTIVALS

➢ **MARCH** • Every year from late March to late April thousands of fun seekers visit the **Frühlingsdom** (Spring Dom) at the Heiligengeistfeld, near the Reeperbahn. The Dom, Germany's biggest fun fair, traces its history to the 10th century, when tradesmen and craftsmen, as well as the odd artist or wacko, took refuge from the elements in the Dom (St. Mary's Cathedral). This didn't sit well with Archbishop Burchard of Bremen, the spiritual lord of the cathedral, who kicked everyone out. This didn't sit well with the citizens of Hamburg, who tried their best to get the craftsmen to go back in the cathedral. The bishop broke down and allowed the lively market to settle there until 1804, when the building was demolished. In 1833 the market settled on the Heiligengeistfeld. The modern version features a giant amusement park, complete with dizzying and expensive rides; roller coasters; food booths selling candy, wurst, and ice cream; beer tents; stuffed animals; and the world's biggest transportable Ferris wheel. The rides are expensive (DM 3–DM 10), but prices go down every Wednesday (family day). There's a free fireworks show Friday. *U2 to Messehallen or U3 to St. Pauli or Feldstr. Open Mon.–Thurs. and Sun. 3–11, Fri. and Sat. 3–midnight.*

➢ **MAY** • Every year around May 7, Hamburg's 800-year-old harbor comes alive, when hordes of people gather to celebrate the **Hafengeburtstag** (Harbor Birthday). Back in 1189, Kaiser Friedrich Barbarossa signed a charter declaring Hamburg a duty-free state. The celebration has evolved into a spectacle of historic ships, food booths, and loud music.

➢ **JUNE** • The **Schleswig-Holstein Musik Festival** is a series of summer-long classical concerts featuring international musicians performing throughout Schleswig-Holstein. Founded by acclaimed pianist Justus Frantz, the festival makes a regular stop at Hamburg. Tickets are available at major ticket outlets. Try the **Theaterkasse Central** (Gerhart-Hauptmann-Pl. 48, tel. 040/324312), in the Landesbank-Galerie, a covered mall.

➢ **JULY–AUGUST** • The summer Dom (*see* March, *above*), known as the **Hummelfest,** takes place at the Heiligengeistfeld, near the Reeperbahn.

➢ **SEPTEMBER** • Street theaters, vendors, food booths, musicians, and herds of people crowd the streets around the Alster during the **Alstervergnügen** (Alster Enjoyment). Fireworks and music also highlight this festival, held on different dates in September every year.

➢ **NOVEMBER–DECEMBER** • Around the end of November and the beginning of December, Hamburg celebrates the holiday season with a **Weihnachtsmarkt,** or Christmas market. Don your mittens and earmuffs, and browse through the booths lining the streets for the perfect Christmas gift. You can get hot cider and *Glühwein* (hot wine) to warm your spirits. The **Winterdom** (*see* March, *above*) is held at the Heiligengeistfeld, near the Reeperbahn.

Shopping

Shopping isn't just a pastime in Hamburg—it's an institution. For budget travelers, though, it's more of a spectator sport. On the main shopping streets, **Mönckebergstraße** and **Jungfernstieg,** you'll find a long stretch of expensive, glass-covered shopping arcades. **Karstadt** (Mönckebergstr. 16, tel. 040/30940) is a monster eight-story department store that has brochures in various languages to help you find your way around. The more famous **Alsterhaus** department store (Jungfernstieg 16–20, tel. 040/359010) has been graced by such blissfully wedded celebrities as Prince Chuck and Lady Di. The Alsterhaus also houses **WOM** (tel. 040/351511), which has the best selection of music in town, as well as headsets on which you can listen to new releases. Hamburgers like to boast about their 15 modern glass-enclosed shopping galleries, the most elegant and expensive of which is the **Hanse-Viertel,** near Jungfernstieg. Check out **Marktstraße** and **Schanzenviertel** for good secondhand shops. You can buy typical blue-and-white sailor shirts or the Hamburg favorite, *Buddelschiff* (ship in a bottle), around the port on **Landungsbrücken.** All souvenir shops stock Hamburg **Hummel figurines.**

SPECIALTY STORES **Condomerie.** At some point during your carousals on the Reeperbahn you might just wonder, "Where the hell is a condom store when I need one?" Look no more; here you can choose from scented ones, flavored ones, textured ones, musical ones, and even very, very big ones—more than 100,000 condoms in all. The condom that causes the most titillation and idle speculation is a custom-made, 5-inch-wide superrubber; any man who can fill this puppy up wins DM 100; on-site proof required. The manager says two men have already succeeded and he even has photos to prove it. Unfortunately, no amount of cajoling will get you access to these photos. *Spielbudenpl. 18, tel. 040/319–3100. Open until midnight.*

Harry's Hamburger Hafenbasar. This amazing 2,400-square-yard bazaar occupies a total of five houses. It's owned by the bearded Harry Rosenburg, a collector of anything and everything for the last 36 years. Most of the collections here come from his personal stock or are original gifts from seamen. The collections focus on African and Asian art and include more than 2,000 carved masks. It's like a museum, but you can touch, pick up, and buy everything. The highlight of the collection is a young girl's shrunken head; found in Brazil, it's about the size of a very small apple. Rosenberg charges DM 2.50 for a view of it. The last head he sold went for a cool DM 12,000. *Bernhard-Nocht-Str. 63, near harbor, tel. 040/312482. Admission: DM 4, but admis-*

sion price is subtracted from purchases of more than DM 10; free entrance on birthday. Open daily 10–6.

Isemarkt. The Isemarkt, near the Hoheluftbrücke, is considered the most beautiful and best market in the city; it has about 300 stalls selling produce, fish, clothing, and toys. Under the U-Bahn tracks in a residential district, the market is held Tuesday and Friday 8:30–2. Unlike the touristy Fischmarkt, this is a real Hamburger market, primarily for locals.

After Dark

As you might imagine, Hamburg's nightlife is totally *galvanized,* spanning the spectrum from live sex shows to performances of John Neumeier's renowned ballet company. Pick up tickets to the city's theater and music productions at most tourist-information offices. Try getting same-day tickets at **Last-Minute im Hanse-Viertel** (Ecke Poststr. Groß Bleichen, tel. 040/353565) or at the particular theater's *Abendkasse* (box office). For a totally different scene check out some of the city's many pubs and discos, which are clustered around St. Pauli and the Reeperbahn (what the locals call *Kiez*), Gänsemarkt downtown, and Groß Neumarkt near S-Bahn station Stadthausbrücke; also take a look around Altona and the Schanzenviertel. Young Hamburgers usually have a couple of beers in a pub until 11:30 PM or midnight, then head to the disco til dawn. Expect the full night to run you at least DM 20. Buy either *Prinz* (DM 4) or *Szene* (DM 4.50) for good listings of pubs and discos. *Gay Express* covers the gay scene.

KNEIPEN (PUBS)

Havanna Bar. This is one of Hamburg's most famous bars, serving cocktails (about DM 10) in a Caribbean setting. *St. Pauli Fischmarkt 4–6, tel. 040/310713.*

Kölsch und Altbierhaus am Gänsemarkt. In this dark, unassuming *Bierlokal,* you can order beer by the meter—a 1-meter (3½-foot) tray covered with 15 beers (DM 33). *Valentinskamp 89–90, tel. 040/352387.*

Rock Café. This Hard Rock Café wanna-be features the standard array of classic rock memorabilia on its walls. *Große Freiheit 39, tel. 040/319–1234.*

Schramme. Peanut shells litter the floor of this small pub in Eppendorf, where the crowd comes for the gemütlich (pleasant, cozy) atmosphere and the free peanuts. *Schrammsweg 10, tel. 040/477828.*

September. A truly mixed crowd gathers here for a truly mixed program of music and gemütlich surroundings. *Feldstr. 60, tel. 040/437611.*

Shamrock. An international crowd, including lots of English-speaking international students, meets in Hamburg's only true Irish pub, complete with Irish music and Guinness. *Feldstr. 40, tel. 040/439–7678.*

DISCOS

Café Keese. It's ladies' choice here, and the men *can't* say no. More than 200,000 people have found the love of their life here. *Reeperbahn 19, tel. 040/310805.*

Fabrik. This old converted factory is now a cultural center, presenting offbeat performers, musicians, and dancers. Some of the most interesting performances in Hamburg are staged here. *Barnerstr. 36, tel. 040/391070.*

Kaiserkeller. This dark, cavernous disco underneath Große Freiheit 36, is always a hit. *Große Freiheit 36, tel. 040/319– 3649.*

Knust. This club specializes in *Engtanzfeten,* which translates literally as "tight dance parties." That's right, they play only slow music, perfect for getting close and friendly with that special someone. *Brandstwiete 2, tel. 040/324933. Cover: DM 5.*

Madhouse. In a recent poll of disco-goers, Madhouse was voted number 1. It's always crowded, thanks to the variety of supreme music. Prince rented it twice for after-concert celebrations. *Valentinskamp 46A, tel. 040/344193. Cover: DM 6–DM 12, women enter free.*

Trinity. This is where the beautiful people go, because there's "face control" at the door. International photo models dance away to funk and house, or sit at the V.I.P. bar. *Eimsbütteler Chaussee 5, tel. 040/439–8095. Cover: about DM 10.*

MOVIE THEATERS Going to see a flick in Hamburg can be pretty expensive, running about DM 10. Prices sink a bit for matinees and on "movie days" (usually Tuesday or Wednesday) and are sometimes cheaper for those with a student ID. When you're looking at the movie listings, check for the notations *OF* and *OmU,* which refer to "original language" and "original language with subtitles," respectively. The **Abaton,** near the university, is an enormously popular alternative cinema; even if you can't understand the film, the café-restaurant one level up will keep you entertained. The **Metropolis** (Dammtorstr. 30, tel. 040/342353) showcases plenty of foreign classics and offbeat movies, often in English. **The British Film Club** (Rothenbaumchaussee 34, tel. 040/446057) shows films in English. Many movie theaters sporadically show popular American films in English, but you can *always* count on **Streits** (Jungfernstieg 38, tel. 040/346051) to show one or two American films per week, late Wednesday night and/or early Sunday morning. **City-Kino** (Steindamm 9, tel. 040/244463), near the Hauptbahnhof, always has at least one popular hit in English and is a good place to meet English-speaking foreigners and Germans.

MUSIC

➢ **CLASSICAL** • Hamburg's three symphony orchestras, the **Philharmonische Staatsorchester,** the **Sinfonieorchester des Norddeutschen Rundfunks (NDR),** and the **Hamburger Symphoniker,** and a variety of guest musicians perform regularly in Hamburg's most important concert hall, the neo-Baroque **Musikhalle** (Karl-Muck-Pl., tel. 040/346920). The **Hamburgische Staatsoper** (Dammtorstr. 28, tel. 040/351721) is one of the most beautiful theaters in the country and the leading north German venue for top-notch opera and ballet. The **Operettenhaus** (Spielbudenpl. 1, tel. 040/270–75270) puts on light opera and musicals.

The Gay Scene in Hamburg

Hamburg has good gay and lesbian nightlife, including cafés, bars, and discos; for general information or in case of crisis contact the Gay Switchboard (Gurlittstr. 47, tel. 040/240333; weekdays 4–10). Popular bars and discos include:

- ***Adagio. Lesbian café.*** **Max-Brauer-Allee 114, tel. 040/382409.**
- ***Café Gnosa. This gay-run café has excellent food, and anyone's welcome*** **(see *St. Georg in Food,* above). Lange Reihe 93, tel. 040/243034.**
- ***Camelot. This is one of the few gay discos for both men and women.*** **Hamburger Berg 12. Cover: DM 6.**
- ***Front. Gay disco.*** **Heidenkampsweg 32, tel. 040/232523. Cover: DM 10.**
- ***Spurdloch. Hamburg's oldest homosexual disco.*** **Paulinenstr. 19, tel. 040/310798.**
- ***Tom's Saloon. Leather predominates at this all-men's pub.*** **Pulverteich 17.**
- ***Toom Peerstall. Gay pub.*** **Clemens-Schultz-Str. 44, tel. 040/319–3523.**

➢ **JAZZ** • Although Hamburg isn't necessarily the first place you'd look for jazz, it has a large and diverse jazz scene. More than 100 venues feature everything from Dixieland to bebop to fusion. For consistently good jazz, check out **Cotton-Club** (Alter Steinweg 10, tel. 040/34378), Hamburg's oldest jazz club; **Birdland** (Gärtnerstr. 122, tel. 040/405277), featuring everything from traditional New Orleans sounds to avant-garde electronic jazz; and **Mojo Club** (Reeperbahn 1, tel. 040/405584), a former bowling alley with jazz music. Early Sunday morning you can enjoy smoke-free jazz concerts in the **Fischauktionshalle** (Fischmarkt, Groß Elbestr. 9) while consuming fresh waffles and coffee.

THEATER Hamburg has a good variety of year-round theater productions, most of which, of course, are staged in German. The **Deutsche Schauspielhaus** (Kirchenallee 39, tel. 040/248713), in all its restored 19th-century opulence, is now the most important venue in Hamburg for classical and modern theater, including American musicals. **Thalia-Theater** (Alstertor, tel. 040/322666) presents a varied program of plays old and new, and **Ohnsorg-Theater** (Groß Bleichen 23, tel. 040/350–8030) presents works in the local dialect, Plattdeutsch. **The English Theater** (Lerchenfeld 14, tel. 040/227–7089) has reasonably priced tickets (usually about DM 10) for funny, whimsical productions in English. Hit the **Schmidt und Schmidts Tivoli** (Spielbudenpl. 24–27, tel. 040/311231) for cabaret shows and variety numbers that you should be able to understand regardless of linguistic ability—slipping on a banana peel is international. Some theaters take a summer break.

Near Hamburg

ALTES LAND **The Altes** Land, a fertile fruit-growing region, extends 30 kilometers (19 miles) west from Hamburg along the south bank of the Elbe, making for some blissful wanderings. Take a day hike, or picnic among the canals, half-timbered farmhouses, and fruit trees. May, when the apple and cherry trees bloom pink and white, is especially beautiful. Some of the prettiest walks take you along the dikes running next to the Rivers Este and Lühe. You can buy fresh fruit from local farmers for dessert. *S1, S2, or S3 to Landungsbrücken, then HAPAG lines ship from Brücke 3 to Altes Land (Cranz or Lühe).*

NEUENGAMME It's frightening to stand on this peaceful overgrown land, realizing that half a century ago more than 55,000 prisoners died here. The concentration camp in Neuengamme, in operation between 1938 and 1945, saw the internment of more than 100,000 victims of the National Socialists. Today a museum chronicles the horrors that occurred here, with reconstructions of daily life in a concentration camp, accompanied by documents and photographs. *Jean-Dolidier-Weg 39, Neuengamme, tel. 040/723–1031. S2 or S21 toward Bergedorf to last station, then Bus 227 toward Neuengamme to Jean-Dolidier-Weg. Admission free. Open Oct.–Mar., Tues.–Sun. 10–5; Apr.–Sept., weekends 10–6.*

SCHLOß AHRENSBURG Fans of the Renaissance will enjoy strolling around the romantic, 16th-century Ahrensburg Castle, a white-brick edifice, surrounded by lush parkland, on the banks of the Hunnau. Don't miss the moat or the nearby lake and tranquil grounds, perfect for restoring your sanity after the madness of the Reeperbahn. You can see the opulent interior only on a guided tour, but first you have to don some protective gray fuzzy slippers. The castle has a huge collection of ancient housewares, including paintings, fine porcelain, and exquisite furniture. *Lübecker Str. 1, Ahrensburg, tel. 041/024-2510. S4 to Ahrensburg, then 15-min. walk. Admission: DM 5, DM 3 students. Open Tues.–Sun. 10–12:30 and 1:30–dusk.*

BONN, KÖLN, AND DÜSSELDORF 15

By Adam Ruderman

Don't just jet into the northwestern region of Germany, take a picture, and head east for the more historic plazas of Berlin or go south to the more fabled streets of Munich. If you do, you won't have a complete picture of Germany. This region is to tourism what research is to writing, what practice is to playing, and what brewing is to drinking; it gets none of the fame and holds all of the secrets and innuendos of Germany's culture, Germany's success, and Germany's geography.

The rolling Teutoburger Wald (Teutoburg Forest), filling the void between Hannover and Münster with seemingly endless woods, is one of those places you can penetrate deeply enough that you don't know what century it is. Not that much has changed here since Germans first stood against Romans centuries ago. *They* charged through the forest on the winding footpaths; *you* charge through the forests on the winding footpaths. After a hard day *they* drank wine; after any day of any type *you* drink wine (or beer or whatever).

About 100 kilometers (62 miles) southwest of the Teutoburger Wald is the Ruhrgebiet (Ruhr River district). Unlike its wooded neighbor, this region has changed radically since Germany's late-19th-century industrial revolution and is in the midst of a change to a postindustrial state. What was once mostly green and mellow was ripped open by grimy industrial towns and more than a hundred coal mines and steel mills. Essen, Duisburg, and Dortmund carried Germany's industry into two wars and back to economic prominence again during the "economic miracle," the period of economic reconstruction after World War II. The cities here have plenty of bruises to prove it: Witness the charmless neo-Bauhaus architecture that replaced the traditional buildings destroyed in World War II.

Where for so long the fires of Germany's steel and coal industry burned, today there are but embers. The Ruhrgebiet's a mere shadow of its former self. The more coal they dug up, the deeper they needed to dig, and the more costly it got. Now fewer than 20 mines are operating in the region. Left behind are the unemployed and unemployable, not the least of whom are the many old, retired coal miners with sooty fingernails and bad lungs. Enter the sprawlingly vague "service professions," which are training and channeling many Ruhrgebieters into white-collar environments. It'll be a while, though, before the new lush-and-green-and-smart-and-clean image that the Ruhrgebiet towns are pushing really takes hold.

Strung out along the Rhine River winding south from the Ruhrgebiet is the region's trio of cities—Düsseldorf, Köln, and Bonn. They have little in common besides the famous vein of Rhine water that links them, and their collective status as the three largest towns along the Rhine. Düsseldorfers are a handsome and cocky lot. For years Düsseldorf reaped the benefits of the Ruhrgebiet's toil and sweat and simply counted the money as it flooded in. Currently there is little panic or concern in this financial and commercial center regarding the fate of the Ruhrgebiet, but there should and will be.

Köln is a different story altogether. A *New York Times Magazine* cover story (September 6, 1992) entitled "The Cologne Challenge," by Deborah Solomon, posed the question "Is New York's Art Monopoly kaput?" The answer, quite simply, is "yes." Köln's numerous museums and galleries have catapulted the million-person Rhineside metropolis to preeminence in the art world. Köln ushered in something called neo-expressionism in the 1980s and retains an aggressive check-it-out attitude for its art seekers. Beyond art, Köln issues a serious challenge to Munich's already debatable monopoly on hedonism and Berlin's monopoly on cultural history; bars are as common as revelers on the streets at 3 AM or as ancient ruins. Köln's got that Seattle-Portland feel but with medieval ruins—it's happening.

Bonn is basically boring but dependable. Receiving the mantle of "Capital of West Germany" after World War II, in 1949, and the flood of bureaucrats that went with it, only made the formerly quiet town quieter. Ironically, soon after the Bundestag voted to move the capital back to Berlin in 1991, Bonn opened its two outrageous modern-art museums, the first feeling of in-your-face the town has seen.

Bonn

Every Thursday night at 8 about 200 people gather in the Marktplatz in front of the Rathaus to protest the switching of the capital of Germany from Bonn back to Berlin. The decision was made in 1991, but the move will take at least 10 years because a zillion bureaucrats, along with their families and files, need to be transplanted. If the protesters continue to rally throughout the next decade, they'll probably do so in the same subdued manner as they did in the summer of 1992. In fact, locals do everything—work, play, study—in a subdued manner. Bonn's equanimity made it the ideal place to move the West German capital after the end of World War II. The government couldn't move to a powerhouse city like Frankfurt or Hamburg because it would be overshadowed by commerce and industry; naturally the politicians wanted to be the center of attention. Besides, chancellor-guru Konrad Adenauer lived nearby and didn't want to have to commute so far. With none of the excitement, culture, and metropolitan flair of capital cities worldwide, Bonn plodded along for 43 years. Buildings were constructed, embassies moved in, and statues were hastily erected in places that were supposed to be important. Bonn went from being a mellow university town full of retirees from Köln and Düsseldorf to a mellow university and governmental town with retirees from Köln and Düsseldorf. Today Bonn's biggest tourist attraction is still the birthplace of Beethoven.

BASICS

BUREAUX DE CHANGE The **Deutsche Verkehrs Bank** in the Hauptbahnhof will exchange money and traveler's checks and give cash advances on credit cards if you've got a passport. To change money in the evenings, go to the post office (*see* Mail and Phones, *below*). *Im Hauptbahnhof, tel. 0228/632958. Open weekdays 7:30–noon, 12:30–6:30; weekends 9–3:30.*

CONSULATES The **American Consulate** (Deichmanns Aue 29, tel. 0228/339–2053) and the **Australian Consulate** (Godesbergeralle 107, tel. 0228/81030) are open weekday mornings, and the **Canadian Consulate** (Godesbergerallee 119, tel.

Bonn

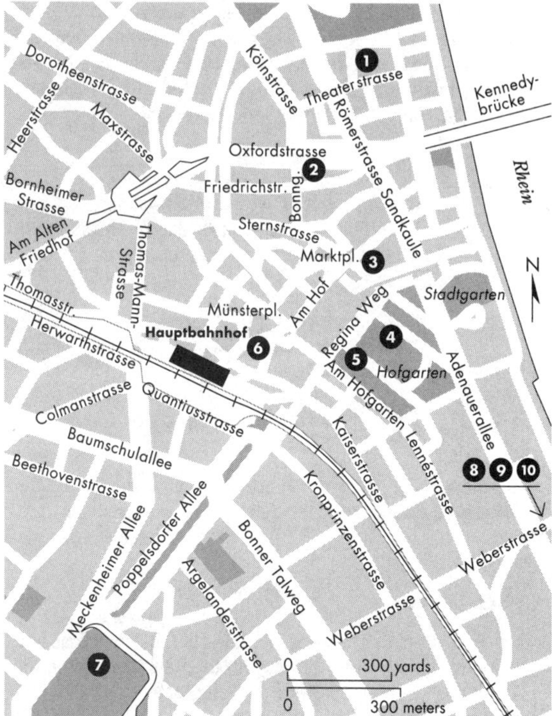

Beethoven Geburtshaus, **2**
Beethovenhalle, **1**
Bundeskanzler Adenauer Haus, **9**
Friedrich Wilhelms Universität, **4**
Government Buildings, **8**
Kurfürstliches Schloß, **5**
Münster, **6**
Museum Mile, **10**
Poppelsdorfer Schloß, **7**
Rathaus, **3**

0228/281–0060) is open weekdays 8–4. Great Britain's consulate is in Düsseldorf (*see* Basics in Düsseldorf, *below*).

LAUNDRY At **Münz wasch-o-center,** you can wash a small load (DM 6) and dry it (DM 1 for 10 minutes). *Wilhelmstr. and Kölnstr. on Wilhelmspl. Open Mon.–Sat. 7 AM–11 PM.*

LUGGAGE STORAGE You can store your luggage at the **Hauptbahnhof** for DM 4 or DM 2, depending on the locker size.

MAIL AND PHONES The **main post office** (Münsterpl. 17, 5300 Bonn) has poste restante services and a night window (open until midnight) for money exchange and traveler's checks. Both this post office and a small one in the Hauptbahnhof have metered, card-, and coin-operated phones. Both are open weekdays 8–6 and Saturday 8–1.

VISITOR INFORMATION You won't find crowded counters at the **tourist office,** just orderly lines. The English-speaking staff will pass you brochures through slots in their windows or book a room for you for DM 3. They also offer a bus tour in German and English (the woman repeats everything she says in both languages) for DM 8, if you're into that kind of thing. Tours leave from the office at 10 and 2. *Münsterstr. 20, tel. 0228/773466. Follow* STADTMITTE *signs from Hauptbahnhof onto Poststr., then turn left on Münsterstr.; look for blue "i" signs. Open Apr.–Oct., Mon.–Sat. 8 AM–9 PM, Sun. 9:30–12:30; Nov.–Mar., Mon.–Sat. 8–7, Sun. 9:30–12:30.*

COMING AND GOING

BY TRAIN AND SUBWAY Traveling between Bonn and Köln is easy. From downstairs at both Hauptbahnhofs (follow the blue "U" signs), take U-Bahn 16 or 18. If you want to use your Eurailpass, you have to ride **Deutsche Bundesbahn,** the national train service, which also makes the Köln–Bonn run a few times every hour. By train the trip takes only 20 minutes (about half the subway-ride time). Bonn is also the northernmost stop on the Mainz–Bonn train route that runs along the Rhine. Any major city that has direct connections to Köln is usually connected to Bonn as well, including Frankfurt, Munich, Berlin, Paris, and Amsterdam. Call 0228/7151 for information.

BY CAR AND HITCHHIKING Autobahn 57 runs north to Köln, Autobahn 61 via 57 goes south toward Heidelberg, and Autobahn 4 goes west toward Aachen and east toward Route 45, which connects Dortmund in the north and Offenbach in the south. If you're hitching, just head for the on ramp you need, and hold up a sign with your destination on it.

BY MITFAHRZENTRALE **Citynetz Mitfahr-Zentrale,** a ride-share agency, needs two days to secure you a ride to Munich (DM 48) or Berlin (DM 51), one day if you're lucky. They don't deal with short distances (like to Köln), since trains cost the same or less. *Herwarthstr. 11, tel. 0228/19444. Exit rear of Hauptbahnhof toward Quantiusstr., turn right on Quantiusstr., right on Meckenheimer Allee, left on Herwarthstr. Open weekdays 9–6:30, Sat. 9–2, Sun. 11–2.*

BY PLANE Bus and train shuttles run from the Hauptbahnhof to the **Köln-Bonn Flughafen** (airport); go to Köln for a train to the Frankfurt Flughafen. For flight information, call 02203/404001.

GETTING AROUND

Compared to Köln's, Bonn's subway system is a breeze to figure out, mostly because it has fewer lines. One line (61) runs directly north–south, with the Hauptbahnhof in the middle; two other lines (18 and 66) form an "X" with the Hauptbahnhof in the middle. These lines are not only the core of Bonn's public-transit system but are also the southernmost lines of Köln's massive subway system, since the two systems are interconnected and require the same tickets. Hence the ticket-buying procedure and rules are the same (*see* Getting Around in Köln, *below*). Bonn also has an extensive series of bus lines. The Busbahnhof is outside the Hauptbahnhof and to the right as you exit. Each of the more than 20 *Bussteig* (bus platforms), which are numbered, have schedules posted. Bonn is an easy city to walk, however, so don't fret if you're bus-phobic. Most major tourist sights (except for the two new museums and the government center) and all the restaurants, bars, and hotels are reachable by foot. If you need a taxi call 0228/555555 from anywhere in Bonn.

BY SUBWAY The subway (U-Bahn) system is the same here as it is in Köln (*see* Getting Around in Köln, *below*). Familiarize yourself with U63 because to see the city you're going to have to get on it (or take a *long* walk). To find it, follow the blue "U" signs to the basement of the Hauptbahnhof; before you go down one more level to the tracks, look for the metal signs with black writing that say RHEINALLEE/BAD GODESBERG to make sure you go to the right platform.

BY BUS The Busbahnhof is directly outside the Hauptbahnhof, to the right as you exit. You'll need a bus to get to the youth hostel, but you won't need it in the inner city because the U-Bahn is cheap and convenient. The platforms and bus numbers are well marked, so you shouldn't have a problem finding what you need.

WHERE TO SLEEP

Bonn gets more than its fair share of tourists, but it's never sold out, and the many diplomatic visitors won't be looking for budget accommodations. During major German holidays or summer breaks you don't have to worry—Germans don't vacation here. Bonn also has the friendliest hotel owners and operators in the Rhineland, perhaps because the stream of guests flows in a lot more slowly than it does in Köln and Düsseldorf.

➢ **UNDER DM 70 • Damaskus.** Across the Rhine in the little town of Beuel, this is the cheapest hotel around. The train runs out to Beuel until 12:30 AM, so you can get a little night action in Bonn before you have to head back. The walk would take about an hour. The rooms are sparse and dark—in short, they're cheap digs. Singles are DM 30, DM 45 with shower, and doubles are DM 65, DM 75 with shower. You can't make reservations here. *Goetheallee 9, tel. 0228/468771. U62 from Hauptbahnhof toward Beuel to Beuel Bahnhof, turn left, then take 1st right on ill-posted Goetheallee. 42 rooms.*

Virneburg. Often a hotel's lobby will be shabby and poorly decorated, but the rooms themselves pleasantly surprising. Not in this case. Verging on dump, and painted about the worst off-peach imaginable, this place has a nice owner and nice prices. Singles are DM 35, DM 55 with shower, and doubles are DM 65, DM 85 with shower. *Sandkaule 3A, tel. 0228/636366. Take U62, U64, or U66 toward Bad Honnef, Obertassel, or Siegburg to Bertha-von-Stuttner Pl.; turn left on Sandkaule. 27 rooms. Breakfast included.*

➢ **UNDER DM 90 • Hotel Eschweiler.** The stairs up to the first-floor reception desk are rickety, and the carpets have that worn-down-the-middle look, but this place is clean and has an unbeatable location right above the Chicago Pizza Pie Factory (*see* Food, *below*), some 20 yards from the Marktplatz. Remember that Bonn is mellow, so even though you'll be in the city center you don't have to worry about being kept up by all-night parties. Singles are DM 54, DM 74 with shower, and doubles are DM 85, DM 105 with shower. *Bonngasse 7, tel. 0228/631760. Exit Hauptbahnhof toward Stadtmitte and follow Poststr. to Münsterpl., then cross plaza to right, turn left on Remiquisstr. until you come to Marktpl., turn left, then quick right on Bonngasse. 46 rooms. Breakfast included.*

Savoy. In this family-run place about a 15-minute walk from the train station, the bellhops (the proprietors' kids) will lead you to the smallest elevator imaginable and up to your room. The rooms are extraordinarily large, and the floor-to-ceiling windows make them feel even larger. Singles are DM 48, DM 75 with shower, and doubles are DM 85, DM 95 with shower. *Berliner Freiheit 17, tel. 0228/651356. Take U62, U64, or U66 toward Bad Honnef, Obertassel, or Siegburg to Bertha-von-Stuttner Pl. and walk in train's direction on Berliner Freiheit. 46 rooms. Breakfast included.*

➢ **UNDER DM 150 • Beethoven.** This is a large, dull, corporate-type hotel, but gigantic hotels like this often have advantages: efficiency, cleanliness (or rather, spotlessness), and always a room free. It's also close enough to the Rhine that you could throw your ice cubes in; the walk from the train station takes about 20 minutes. Singles cost DM 55, DM 85 with shower, and doubles are DM 145, all with showers. *Rheingasse 26, tel. 0228/631411. Follow STADTMITTE signs out of Hauptbahnhof onto Poststr., straight through Münsterpl., then follow Acherstr. as it curves, turn left on Rathausgasse, which becomes Rheingasse. 102 rooms. Breakfast included.*

Hotel Weiland. Located in the rambling Altstadt, amid the hippest night spots in town, this hotel usually caters to the younger set. It's run by friendly folk and has a basic, boring, bright lobby that is similar to the rooms. Singles are DM 50, DM 85 with showers. Doubles with showers are DM 135, and triples with showers are DM 165. *Breite Str. 98A, tel. 0228/655057. U62, U64, or U66 from Hauptbahnhof toward Bad Godesberg, Oberkassel, or Siegburg to Stadthaus; turn right on Berliner Pl., left on Maxstr., then quick right on Breite Str. 33 rooms. Breakfast included.*

HOSTELS **Jugendgästehaus Bonn–Bad Godesberg.** All the superlatives applied to this sharply dressed, entirely sterile youth hostel before its comrade (*see below*) got a face-lift in 1991. This is still your second-greatest option. Beds are DM 26.20 per night. *Horionstr. 60, tel. 0228/317516. U63 to Bad Godesberg Hauptbahnhof, then Bus 615 to Jugendherberge. 90 beds. 1 AM curfew, sheets and breakfast included.*

Jugendgästehaus Bonn-Venusberg. This place, fronted by the youth-hostel flag and the Bonn city flag, should be the poster child for *Better Youth Hostels and Gardens.* The rooms are two- or four-bedders and usually two to four rooms share sinks and showers. Breakfast is free, and they offer a multiple-option small (DM 7.50) or huge (DM 10.50) lunch and dinner. The small bistro, Come Together, in the lobby is burdened with a terrible Marilyn Monroe replica that collects dust in the corner and watches the pizza and beer flow. Another perk is that this place is poised on the edge of the lush Kottenforst (*see* Near Bonn, *below*) and is a great place to access hours of footpaths. Beds are DM 26.20 per night. *Haager Weg 42, tel. 0228/281200. Bus 621 from Platform B1 to Jugendherberge; trip takes about 15 min. 257 beds. 1 AM curfew, laundry facilities.*

CAMPGROUNDS **Campingplatz Genienau.** The closest campground to Bonn is a half-hour to 45-minute trek from town. You can try to call to reserve a place, but the managers are delinquent phone-answerers. Located in a suburban area along the Rhine, it's filled with more tents than car campers. Slots are DM 8 per person. *Tel. 0228/344949. U63 or U16 to Bad Godesberg, then Bus 613 toward Wehlem Süd to last stop.*

FOOD

The streets of Bonn are punctuated by lots of plazas. Not all are as big as **Münsterplatz** or **Marktplatz,** but all share something with their sprawling cousins: cafés. Most of these have outdoor seating when the weather's good. At Marktplatz you'll find a sea of umbrella-topped fruit, vegetable, cheese, and meat stands open weekdays till 6. You've never heard such competitive fruit-bartering, either—these people are constantly trying to undersell one another, and you reap the benefits. You can also hit the supermarket in the basement of the massive department store **Hertie** on Poststraße, 100 yards from the Hauptbahnhof.

➢ **UNDER DM 8** • **University Mensa.** Located in the student union, this cafeteria serves lunch and dinner, each for less than DM 3. Check the large chalkboard in the entrance hall for the day's selections (usually about five options), or go to the pay-by-weight salad bar (DM 5 per kilogram [about 2 pounds]). Underneath the cafeteria (which is one floor up) is a café-bar where students stop to take a breather and have a smoke, a beer, or some juice. It has the same hours as the cafeteria. *Nassestr. 11. Exit Hauptbahnhof toward Stadtmitte and walk 10 min. down Maximilianstr. (which becomes Kaiserstr.), turn left on Nassestr. No Sat. dinner. Closed Sun.*

➢ **UNDER DM 15** • **Chicago Pizza Pie Factory.** The pizza here (about DM 20 for two people, DM 10 for an individual portion) is thick and delicious. The best thing about this place is the Monday special: half-price pizza for students with I.D.s. *Bongasse 7, tel. 0228/635836.*

Hähnchen. It looks as though this place has occupied the corner of Münsterplatz forever. Come here if you're looking for a local crowd and local eats. The long list of piled-high German grub includes meaty *Goulaschsuppe* (goulash soup, DM 6); *Schweineschnitzel* (pork cutlet, DM 15), which comes with fries and salad; and *Bockwurst* (sausage) with potatoes (DM 6.50). *Münsterpl. 11, tel. 0228/652039.*

Miebach. At this refined café you can drink espresso out of beautiful china for not-so-refined prices: espresso costs DM 3.50, cappuccino DM 4. They also have a wide selection of salads; the chicken salad (DM 15) is your best bet. The Mexican tacos (DM 9.50) are not so Mexican, but they're good anyway. *Marktpl. 8, tel. 0228/692500.*

Pfänchen. This café's chairs flood the Marktplatz, especially on weekends, when the fruit and vegetable stands are gone. The salads (DM 7–DM 14.50) vary in size and content, the macaroni (DM 10) is a safe bet, and the pizzas are large. The real treat, though, is the huge Krystall beers, served with a twist (DM 5.50). *Marktpl. 7, tel. 0228/696999.*

Zur Kerze Künstkeller. This is not only a late-night eatery but a happening bar, as well. The eclectically decorated cellar-restaurant—replete with indoor tree branches, fishnets, and portraits of humans who bear a faint resemblance to everybody you've ever sat next to on the bus—is a catacomb of small booths, none of which is very well lit. But by the time they stop serving food, at 5 AM, you'll be too lit to care about the lighting. Try the spaghetti (DM 8), salads (about DM 6), or taco platter (DM 12). *Königstr. 25. Exit Hauptbahnhof toward Stadtmitte, turn right on Maximilianstr. (which becomes Kaiser Str.), then right on Königstr. Closed Sun.*

WORTH SEEING

The sights in the center of town, such as the **Münster** (cathedral), the **Rathaus** (town hall), and Beethoven's birthplace, can easily be covered on foot. However, you'll need to take the subway to get to the university, government center, and the new Museum Mile: Take U16 or U63 south toward Rheinallee/Bad Godesberg and get off at Heussalle/Bundeshaus. Most of these sights lie on or around Adenauerallee (which becomes Friedrich-Ebert-Allee), parallel to the Rhine.

BEETHOVEN GEBURTSHAUS Your first stop on the Beethoven tour should be Münsterplatz, which is centered around a stoic, powerful statue of the composer looking angry as ever but holding his composer's pen in an utterly delicate manner. Next you should visit **Beethoven Geburtshaus** (Beethoven's birthplace). The tour is tough on the non–German speaker, but the limited English material is enough to give you an idea of the raw intensity with which Ludwig lived his life. If you're looking for a bust, don't go for the cheap plastic ones in the Geburtshaus; get a plaster mini-model at one of the stores on Oxford Straße. *Bonngasse 20, tel. 0228/635188.*

Speaking of busts, Bonn has one of the best and worst you'll ever see. An 8-foot Beethoven's head sits on the grass in front of the **Beethovenhalle,** north of Theaterstraße along the Rhine. It's important to approach the work from the back, so walk up Theaterstraße from the river. As you walk, keep looking to your right. Once you get to Welschnonnenstraße you'll realize that the gray-black ball of spaghetti you've been staring at is actually an intricate portrait of Beethoven with his hair at its wildest.

BUNDESKANZLER ADENAUER HAUS The famed first chancellor of West Germany, Konrad Adenauer, was treated pretty shabbily by the sculptor who created his hollow-looking, emaciated, 9-foot iron bust, one of the country's least flattering memorials. The head sits on Bundeskanzlerplatz in front of the Bundeskanzler Adenauer Haus, where exhibits explain the import of the most famous German politician since Hitler. *Konrad-Adenauer-Str. 8C, tel. 02224/6731.*

FRIEDRICH WILHEMS UNIVERSITAT If you follow Stockenstraße out of Marktplatz to Regina Weg, you'll arrive at the **Kurfürstliches Schloß,** an old castle turned university administration building. This building is far too nice to be a bureaucratic hot spot. Behind the Schloß are the **Hofgarten** and **Stadtgarten,** two parks filled with students, sunbathers, punks, bums, and lots of trash. Continuing down Regina Weg past the Schloß will take you onto the sandy paths that line Poppelsdorfer Allee. The grass patch running along the middle is a prelude to the Botanical Gardens lying behind the 18th-century **Poppelsdorfer Schloß,** another building too nice to contain university offices.

GOVERNMENT BUILDINGS Just because it isn't a bustling capital doesn't mean Bonn has nothing of political interest. From the Heussallee/Bundeshaus station walk to the Rhine, and you'll find the **Bundeshaus,** Germany's state senate, and the **Bun-**

destag, the parliament building (both on Görresstrasse). The best time to visit is when they're in session (check with the tourist office), even if you can't understand what they're saying. Tours begin every hour at Hermann-Ehlers-Str. 29. Bring a passport. *Open mid-Mar.–Dec., weekdays 9–4, weekends 10–4; Jan.–early Mar., weekdays 9–4.*

MUSEUM MILE It's ironic that months after the decision was made to move the country's capital to Berlin, Bonn opened two of the most spectacular modern-art museums (if not *the* most spectacular) in Germany. You can't walk through the **Kunstmuseum** and the **Kunst und Ausstellungshalle der Bundesrepublik Deutschland** without experiencing some kind of emotion. Some exhibits in the Kunst und Ausstellungshalle are aggressively modern, like Alexander Calder's *The White Frame,* which seems broken, it makes so much noise. Established modernists, including Americans Jackson Pollock and Sam Francis, dominate the bottom floor. Although not as varied or strange as its neighbor, the Kunstmuseum Bonn still goes off on some strange but enjoyable modern-art tangents. Georg Baselitz's portraits are bright, fun, and upside-down. His "*rote nose*" features a strange-looking figure with a nose that looks like Burt's on "Sesame Street," and is that odd shape in "Die Riesin" a vagina or a redwood tree? Just try to figure out Cy Twombly's untitled work that looks like a chalkboard attacked by some angry eight-year-olds. *Kunst und Ausstellungshalle, Friedrich-Ebert-Allee 4, tel. 0228/917–1200. Kunstmuseum Bonn, Friedrich-Ebert-Allee 2, tel. 0228/776262. Admission to both: DM 10, DM 5 students. Admission to either: DM 5, DM 3 students. Both open Tues.–Sun. 10–7.*

The **Zoologisches Forschungsinstitut** is a fine natural-history museum noted for its annual collections, particularly its birds. *Adenauerallee 160, tel. 0228/91220. Admission: DM 4, DM 2 students. Open Tues.–Fri. 9–5, Sat. 9–12:30, Sun. 9:30–5.*

The new **Haus der Geschichte der Bundesrepublik Deutschland,** a museum of contemporary history, addresses the shadows of the nation's recent past. *Adenauerallee 242, tel. 0228/260990. Admission and hrs not available at press time.*

AFTER DARK

You may wonder: If this town is so mellow, where do the 40,000 university students go at night? They go out to bars and cafés, same as everywhere. Maybe the crowds are smaller and not as boisterous as they are in Köln, but you can still have a good time here. And you don't *have* to be mellow. To find out what's going on in terms of bands, concerts, and films (occasionally in English), find a copy of the monthly *Schnüss* at a café or bar, or ask at the tourist office.

Bonn's Altstadt (north of Berliner Platz and east of Kölnstraße) has a string of dark little bars that attract university students who lean toward the offbeat. If you ask for something to eat at the **Pawlow** (Heerstr. 64, tel. 0228/653606), they'll offer you a box of nuts. That's it. The motif here is "broken things," exemplified by the shattered mirror on the wall and shattered glass under the bar. The employees are trying to switch the motif to "different-color things," and have splotched some different hues on the back wall, as well as on their heads. You can't miss **Gekko** (Wolfstr. 3, tel. 0228/693387), because the wall outside is crawling with paintings of lizards. The place should be called "chameleon" because of its nightly metamorphosis from a quiet little dive bar to a noisy little dive bar. Teenyboppers inhabit **Das Bonn-Bons** (Heerstr. 145, tel. 0228/658781) till about 10, but it's safe to go in after that. The music is loud, and every band sounds like an AC-DC/Rush fusion. Don't tell the barkeeps that the picture on the wall isn't Tom Petty—they'll be crushed—and don't stare as they masterfully stroke beer out of the temperamental spigot. **Duck** (Heerstr. 132, tel. 0228/653359), the only place in Bonn with mostly black patrons, is a small, plain bar that plays some reggae and has a few posters of Bob Marley.

At **Bla Bla** (Bornheimer Str. 20–22, tel. 0228/637041), as the name suggests, the staff just doesn't give a damn. Try to make small talk, and you may get one of those pregnant glares that translates into, "How can you make small talk when I am so angry about everything?" The patrons likewise don't give a damn; neither, apparently, did the interior decorators, judging by the concrete floors, scuffed furniture, and walls plastered with fliers for such unabashedly subcultural bands as Shock Therapy, Justice Just a Disease, and My Lai. Burp noisily if you need to.

Near Bonn

ADDENDORF This is a peaceful way to spend the day—but it'll be a whole day, so don't even start if you're in a rush. Take U16 or U63 to Bad Godesberg, then Bus 857 to Addendorf Church. You'll be in the middle of the tiniest of villages southwest of Bonn. Addendorf is a pottery village; you'll find pottery shops scattered all along the main street (if you can call it that).

KOTTENFORST Bonn has one huge advantage over Köln and Düsseldorf: the Kottenforst, a huge forest that lies a half-hour walk southwest of Bonn. You can take beautiful hikes on the well-marked trails or tour the region by bike. Choose from a variety of bikes at **Autovermietung Kurscheid** (Römerstr. 4, tel. 0228/631433), which rents for DM 10–DM 15 per day. Before you set out, head to Bonn's tourist office and pick up a free "*Fahrradroutenplan Bonn*," which clearly marks the major trails and their access routes from town. If you want a bigger, more detailed map, you can buy one at a bookstore.

Köln

Summarizing a city is difficult, especially when it's a city as large, diverse, and intricate as Köln, but the key is usually in the people. The residents of Köln are united. They may not like one another all the time, they may disagree, they may even hate one another. But there's something they identify with beyond personalities: their town. Before being Europeans, Germans, or Rhinelanders, they are Kölners. Somehow you can sense this in the way they joke and laugh together. Many locals hypothesize that the legacy of Italian blood and culture in Köln, the most heavily colonized Roman city in the Germanic territories more than 1,500 years ago, makes it a little more jovial and lighthearted. Kölners' characteristic joviality even extends to visitors. You might expect that a town with so much municipal pride would frown on tourists, but this one doesn't. Instead, everyone wants to show you why the place is so great.

Some think the city's greatness lies in the wealth of art museums and galleries that make Köln the art center of Germany. Some think it lies in the town's history, evident in its churches, Roman ruins, and monstrous Dom (cathedral). But some say it's because Köln is fun: Kölners hit the bars every night, and some will even tell you that Köln has more bars than any other German city. Don't be shy about asking a Kölner for a suggestion about where to go, what to eat, or where to drink; everyone in this place is a tour guide.

BASICS

AMERICAN EXPRESS This place is so dinky it seems even more packed with Americans than it is. You can change money and traveler's checks and pick up mail. You can only get a cash advance on your American Express card if you know your personal identification number (PIN). *Burgmauerstr. 14, across from Dom, tel. 0221/235613. Open weekdays 9–5:30, Sat. 9–noon.*

MEDICAL AID The **Universitätsklinik** (University Clinic, Joseph Stelzmann Str. 9, tel. 0221/4780) can give you advice in English, over the phone or in person. The pharmacy closest to the Hauptbahnhof is **Dom Apotheke** (Komödienstr. 5, tel.

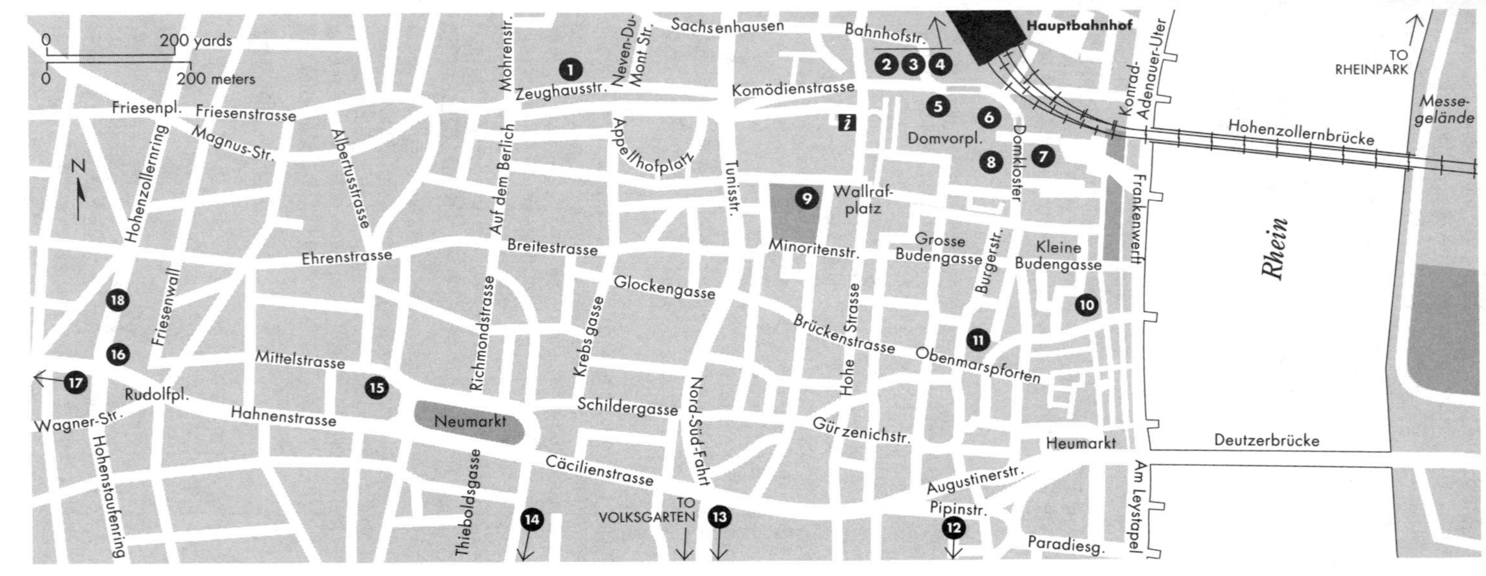

Dom, **6**
Eiglesteintor, **3**
Groß St. Martin, **10**
Hahnentor, **16**
Kölnisches Stadtmuseum, **1**
Medieval City Wall, **18**
Museum für Angewandte Kunst, **9**
Museum für Ostasiatische Kunst, **17**
Rathaus, **11**
Roman North Gate, **5**
Römisch-Germanisches Museum, **8**
St. Aposteln, **15**
St. Maria Himmelfahrt, **4**
St. Maria im Kapitol, **12**
St. Pantaleon, **14**
St. Ursula, **2**
Severinstor, **13**
Wallraf-Richartz-Museum/Ludwig Museum, **7**

Köln

0221/215807), around the corner from the tourist office (*see* Visitor Information, *below*).

LUGGAGE STORAGE There are large lockers (DM 4) and small lockers (DM 2) at the **Hauptbahnhof** and at the **Neumarkt U-Bahn station.**

MAIL AND PHONES The **Post** in the Hauptbahnhof is fronted by a bunch of coin- and card-operated phones. Inside there are metered phones—ask the representative in the far right window for a **Kabine** (a little booth). The office also sends and receives faxes. Köln's zip code is 5000. The post office is open weekdays 7 AM–10 PM, Saturday 11–8, and Sunday 10–8.

VISITOR INFORMATION The **Verkehrsamt** (tourist office) is across the street from the Dom (*see* Worth Seeing, *below*). The place is well staffed, and everybody speaks English. City maps are free, but other brochures will cost you, so check out the display copies at the far end of the counter. You can book a room here (DM 3) and sometimes get a bargain. *Unter Fettenhennen 19, tel. 0221/221-3345. Open Apr.–Oct., Mon.–Sat. 8 AM–10:30 PM, Sun. 9 AM–10:30 PM; Nov.–Mar., Mon.–Sat. 8 AM–9 PM, Sun. 9:30–7.*

COMING AND GOING

BY TRAIN More than 1,000 trains per day pass under the huge metal-and-plastic canopy covering the platforms in Köln's **Hauptbahnhof.** The trip to Düsseldorf takes about 30 minutes, and trains leave about every 15 minutes; direct connections are available to Berlin (DM 119), Paris (DM 94), Amsterdam (DM 56.80), and just about anyplace else. For train information call 0221/1411.

BY BUS The **Busbahnhof** is behind and to the right of the Hauptbahnhof. All the *Bussteig* (platforms) are confusing, so check with the bus-information office (tel. 0221/547–3333 for buses around Köln, 0221/124412 for long-distance routes). Buses go to and from Düsseldorf and from the ends of the subway lines to the residential areas around Köln. But if you're going far you're better off taking the train, because the buses have to sit in Köln's heavy traffic.

BY BOAT Köln is the northernmost point on the Rhine for the **Köln-Düsseldorfer,** a fleet of passenger liners that go as far south (upstream) as Mainz. Eurailpasses will get you free passage; otherwise, the trip costs DM 72 from Köln to Koblenz and another DM 72 from Koblenz to Mainz. Call 0221/208–8318 for information, or pick up a pamphlet at the tourist office.

BY MITFAHRZENTRALE Yet another harried, understaffed public-service office, the **Mitfahr Büro** can get you to any major city in Germany with about a day's notice, although two days' is better. *Saarstr. 22, tel. 0221/219991. From U-Bahn Eifelpl. walk n. on Am Duffenbach, turn left on Saarstr. Open Mon.–Sat. 9–7.*

BY PLANE The **Köln-Bonn airport** (a 20-minute drive southeast of Köln) isn't as big as Frankfurt's or Düsseldorf's, but it's growing and already has direct service to the United States, Paris, London, Munich, and Berlin. From the Hauptbahnhof you can get a train or bus to the Köln-Bonn airport.

GETTING AROUND

To see Köln properly, you're going to have to ride some public transportation, because many of the best spots are far from the Hauptbahnhof. Only the Altstadt, the museums and sights directly around the Dom, and the major *Fußgängerzonen* (pedestrian zones) Hohe Straße and Schildergasse are accessible by foot. Luckily Köln has an incredibly extensive subway-streetcar system that will get you to within a few blocks of anywhere you want to go.

Almost all of the **subway** lines, which become streetcar lines outside the city center, pass underneath the **Dom Hauptbahnhof** (follow the blue-and-white "U" signs). Pick up a public-transit map at the tourist office or from the ticket window downstairs in the Hauptbahnhof. Buying a fare card is easy; go to one of the large red ticket machines located at some *Haltestellen* (stops) and on all buses and subway cars. There you'll find a list of every destination with a price code next to it (a letter such as "K"). Press the appropriate letter to find out how many deutsche marks you need to feed the machine for a ticket to your destination. The **buses** run on the same fare plan. If you transfer from one subway line to another or to a bus, restamp your ticket in the red, shoebox–size machine on the bus or subway car you've transferred to. If you don't buy a ticket or stamp it correctly, you could be slapped with a DM 60 fine and prosecution.

At the Very Bottom

After World War II, West Germany got a huge influx of Eastern Europeans who provided labor during the so-called economic miracle of the 1950s. In the 1960s Germany was again experiencing an economic boom, so workers were imported from the poorer nations of southern Europe. The West German government made agreements with the governments of Turkey, Yugoslavia, Greece, and Italy for workers to come to Germany for a few years to fill the labor gap. These men were called **Gastarbeiter** ***(guest workers). It seemed to be a great deal all around; Germany got its requisite work force, the Gastarbeiter got better wages and social benefits than were possible at home, and their home countries were relieved of the social burden of more than a million citizens.***

However, when recession hit in the 1970s, things went awry. Most Gastarbeiter didn't return home as planned, but remained in Germany and brought their wives and children to live with them. Major cities all over Germany began to develop ghettos, occupied primarily by foreign workers who did jobs most Germans felt were beneath them. Today there are more than 4 million citizens from southern Europe living in Germany, and the situation is growing increasingly tense. Köln, for example, has a large Turkish population that has based itself in the neighborhoods of Nippes and Chorweiler. Kölners occasionally call Streetcar 9 the Istanbul Express, since its northern terminal is Chorweiler, almost half of whose residents are Turkish. Towns with intense pride such as Köln find it difficult to cope with the Turks, whose cultural and religious practices seem so foreign. As a result, Turks experience discrimination in the street and workplace, don't get the same social benefits, and can't vote. In 1986, in his book **Ganz Unten (At the Very Bottom)**, ***a German journalist described his experiences disguised as a Turkish worker. The discrimination, terrible living conditions, and poor pay shocked many Germans, brought the issue into the open, and started what has turned into a major debate.***

For a **taxi** call 0221/2882 and tell the dispatcher your street corner or the nearest public-transit Haltestelle. The dispatcher can usually derive your location from the number code on the public telephone you call from.

WHERE TO SLEEP

Next to the Köln Hauptbahnhof hang green KOLN-MESSE (Köln Convention) signs. Throughout the year the city is flooded with fashion-industry representatives, who flock to the huge convention center in Deutz, on the west side of the Rhine. Needless to say, Köln's hotels are often packed. Fortunately, these Messe goers usually stay in the inner city, so if you're willing to stay in a youth hostel or pension, you'll be OK. If not, come when the tides are low or call *way* ahead. Almost all hotels have showers on the same floors as the rooms, but ask, just to make sure. If none of the hotels listed below can accommodate you, try one of the many cheap hotels on Brandenburger Straße: the **Berlin** (tel. 0221/123051), the **Brandenburgerhof** (tel. 0221/122889), the **Thielen** (tel. 0221/123333), the **Ludwig** (tel. 0221/160510), and the **Müller** (tel. 0221/124318).

NEAR THE HAUPTBAHNHOF

➢ **UNDER DM 80 • Hotel Berg.** The hotel gods threw up all along Brandenburger Straße; about the only thing that distinguishes the various establishments they left behind is the color of their signs. Not even the owner can explain how the Berg is different, but it's usually the last to fill up. The breakfast is bland, and the room decorations are poised on the edge of style—the "going out of" edge. The best thing about this place is that it's less than a five-minute walk from the train station. Singles are DM 50, DM 80 with shower. Doubles are DM 80, DM 130 with shower. *Brandenburger Str. 6, tel. 0221/121124. Exit rear of Hauptbahnhof, walk on Johannisstr. (parallel to Rhine), turn left on Brandenburger Str. 20 rooms, some with bath.*

Hotel Garni. If you miss "The Waltons," you'll love this hotel about a 15-minute walk from the Hauptbahnhof. A spiral staircase leads right to the kitchen, where all the guests breakfast together. An added perk is the elegant fountains, reflecting ponds, and flowers lining Kaiser-Wilhelm-Ring, one block west. Singles are DM 48, DM 65 with shower. Doubles are DM 75, DM 105 with shower. *Probsteigasse 6, tel. 0221/135338. Exit front of Hauptbahnhof and follow Dompropst-Ketzer-Str. until it becomes Gereonsstr. and then Christophstr., turn right on Probsteigasse. 13 rooms, some with bath. Breakfast included.*

➢ **UNDER DM 90 • Hotel Einig.** The only reason this place doesn't belong on Brandenburger Straße with the other dull hotels is that for an extra DM 5 you get a television, a phone, and, if you're lucky, a VCR. But all this stuff doesn't alleviate the blandness. Singles are DM 55, DM 85 with shower. Doubles are DM 85, DM 105 with shower. *Johannisstr. 71, tel. 0221/122128. Walk in opposite direction from DOM and REISEZENTRUM signs in Hauptbahnhof, exit rear of station, cross st. and follow Johannisstr. 22 rooms, some with bath. Breakfast included.*

➢ **UNDER DM 100 • Hotel Buchholz.** This is a great option if you're looking for some affordable luxury. Velvet curtains, chandeliers, and fancy rugs adorn the lobby, and the rooms are large and have high ceilings. The triples seem like suites because they have alcoves with foldout couches and mirrored, dark-wood wardrobes. These rooms can sleep three comfortably and six easily (although the proprietors might not agree—so stick with three). Singles are DM 55–DM 85, triples DM 85–DM 150. *Kunibertsgasse 5, tel. 0221/121824. Exit Hauptbahnhof at rear and walk along Johannisstr., turn right on Machabäerstr., then left on Kunibertsgasse. 17 rooms. Breakfast and TV included.*

OUTSIDE CITY CENTER

➢ **UNDER DM 80 • Tagungs und Gästehaus St. Georg.** This place strikes a nice balance between hostel and hotel. Run by Köln's Boy Scouts, the Gästehaus occupies two buildings and was recently refurbished. You won't complain about a curfew or lack of privacy, as you might in a youth hostel, but you will meet a lot of youngish people, especially in the café, **Bipi's,** across from the reception area. This tiny café named after Baden-Powell, the English founder of the European Scouts' Association, has outdoor tables with umbrellas; a limited selection of soups, chilies, and pastas for less than DM 10; and beer until 1 AM. All this and clean sheets, too. The trip from the center of town takes about 20 minutes. Singles are DM 42, DM 62 with bath; doubles are DM 79, DM 110 with bath. *Rolandstr. 61, tel. 0221/383046. U16 toward Neumarkt to Chlodwigpl., turn right on Merowingerstr., left on Maria Hilfstr., then cross Rolandstr. 31 rooms, some with bath.*

➢ **UNDER DM 90 • Pension Jansen** and **Pension Kirchener.** Because these two pensions are great bargains, they sell out quickly—so call ahead. Both are located in the same building, above an apartment, and you'll get a key to come and go as you please. The rooms are comfortable, beige, and small. At the Kirchener, singles are DM 25–DM 50, and doubles are DM 60–DM 80; at the Jansen, singles are DM 35–DM 45, and doubles are DM 70–DM 90. *Richard-Wagner-Str. 18, Jansen tel. 0221/251875, Kirchener tel. 221/252977. U9, U12, U16, or U18 from Dom to Neumarkt, then Streetcar 1 toward Junkersdorf to Moltkestr., then double back down Richard-Wagner-Str. 34 rooms, none with bath. Breakfast included.*

HOSTELS **Jugendgästehaus Köln-Riehl.** This monstrosity—the biggest youth hostel in Germany—is a serious factory. It takes in travelers, feeds them, bathes them, sleeps them, and churns 'em out. Even the ping-pong tables downstairs, with their solid wood nets, seem kinda cold and industrial. But hey—it's clean, functional, and efficient, like any good production-line factory, and it's all within 15 minutes of the train station. To break the monotony, rap with the workers, most of whom are here doing their social service. They know the city well and are probably right around your age. Bed, breakfast, and sheets are included in the DM 26.50 fee, and for an extra DM 7.50 you can get a three-course dinner, as well. Rooms have either four or six beds. *An der Schanz 14, tel. 0221/767081. U16 or U18 from Hauptbahnhof toward Ebertpl. to Boltensternstr., then walk 100 yds in same direction as train. 400 beds.*

Jugendherberge Köln-Deutz. Not to be outdone by its production-line competition across the Rhine, this hostel has introduced lunch and dinner buffets for DM 8.50, featuring five choices of main course, plus soup and salad. They'll even blast MTV for you while you eat. A little smaller and a little cheaper (DM 23 per night), it's also a little dirtier and a little louder than its counterpart. But it does offer a laundry room for guests; detergent costs DM .50. *Siegesstr. 5A, tel. 0221/814711. U9 from Hauptbahnhof toward Neumarkt to Deutz-Kalker Str., turn 180° and head down Deutzer Freiheit, turn right on tiny Neuhöfferstr. and left on Siegesstr. 374 beds.*

CAMPGROUNDS **Campingplatz Poll.** This manicured field next to the Rhine is easy to get to, but it's not for nature lovers. In Köln the banks of the Rhine are industrial, and car campers predominate here. Slots cost DM 8 per tent, DM 7 per person. *Marienburg, tel. 0221/831966. From Hauptbahnhof U16 toward Neumarkt to Marienburg, then cross Rodenkirchener Bridge.*

FOOD

You won't find a lot of typical pig-and-potato German fare in Köln, but you will find zillions of southern European restaurants, especially Greek, Turkish, and Italian. The best places to go for German food are the breweries. The *Doner Kebabs* (Turkish gyros) served at virtually every Turkish *Schnell-Imbiß* (fast-food restaurant) are cheap and filling but not that healthy. If you're just looking for some bread, cheese, and vegetables, a stroll along **Hohe Straße** and **Schildergasse** will provide everything at cut-rate prices. Another place to create your own meal is at any **Aldi** supermarket in town (look for the black letters surrounded by orange and blue stripes) or in the markets in the basement of **Kaufhof** department stores (they're huge—you can't miss 'em). Cafés and bars are also good places to eat. If you do only one thing in town besides see the Dom, sample some **Kölsch beer.** Brewed by more than 40 different houses, it's served in every restaurant, bar, café, and disco for about DM 2 a pop. Kölsch sometimes smells a little funny, but don't let it bother you. That's what happens when a beer has no preservatives. You won't find this fresh stuff in bottles on supermarket shelves.

➢ **UNDER DM 8 • Osho's.** If you admit here that you haven't heard of Osho the Bagwan from Oregon, no one will believe you. Apparently the spiritual cult is thriving not only in the United States' Pacific Northwest; Osho's disciples live in Köln and own and operate a little complex of entertainment spots here. This tiny eatery with stand-up tables sells great food at very low prices—all vegetarian and all fresh. It's not exactly gourmet, but the enchiladas (DM 6), pizzas (DM 3.50), and sandwiches (DM 4) are served fast and hot. If you want to eat and run, however, don't tempt any of the employees with open-ended questions like "What does Osho believe?" or "I don't get it." If you do, it'll be a long night. But that's OK, because this place serves food till 5 AM, the **café** 10 feet away serves coffee at least that late, and the **Petit Prince** downstairs features live music to complement the **One World** disco upstairs. Same owners all around—the Bagwan guys and gals. Both music spots have covers, but they're never more than DM 8 and are usually more like DM 5. The Prince's musical theme changes nightly: salsa on Thursday, Brazilian on Saturday, jazz on Monday—check the schedule. On Tuesday night One World becomes the **Pink Triangle** (*see* box, *below*), a gay-and-lesbian disco. *Hohenzollernring 90, north of Friesenpl., tel. 0221/574–9725. U5 from Hauptbahnhof toward Neu Ehrenfeld to Friesenpl.*

➢ **UNDER DM 15 • Alcazar.** This place is constantly packed with university students and casual yuppies. Crowds form at about four o'clock for beer and coffee, grow bigger for dinner, and remain large throughout the night. The quality of the food is outstanding and healthy (they have tons of salad), and the prices (DM 12–DM 15 for a meal and drink) are fair. *Bismarckstr. 39, tel. 0221/515733. U5 to Friesenpl., walk on Venloer Str., and turn left on Bismarckstr. No weekend lunch.*

Pacifico's Cafe Especial. Here you'll find the best Mexican food in Köln—although that's like pointing out the lushest spot in the Sahara or the most intelligent thing Ronald Reagan ever said. Well, maybe that's too harsh, because the food here isn't bad. The plates are highly organized in an oh-so-German manner, rather than in a typical Mexican mishmash: beans in this quarter, rice 37° away . . . but it's all there. You can get a good burrito for about DM 13, but the Mexican beer will kill your budget. *Neuhöfferstr. 32, around corner from Köln-Deutz youth hostel, tel. 0221/814755. U9 from Hauptbahnhof toward Neumarkt to Deutz-Kalker-Str., turn 180° and walk down Deutzer Freiheit, then turn right on Neuhöfferstr. No Mon. lunch.*

Sansome. This restaurant has arguably the best pasta in town. Don't be scared off by the napkins folded into little cones or the multiple forks, for although this place is definitely elegant, the pasta dishes are surprisingly affordable. You can eat for DM 12.50–DM 16.50, but stay away from the meat, fish, and lobster, or you're looking at another DM 10–DM 15. Naturally the clientele is refined, or at least well pressed. Many of them walk over from the massive Holiday Inn across the street, but you'll pass in jeans and a T, even in shorts. *Händelstr. 47, behind Holiday Inn on Rudolfpl., tel. 0221/252949. Streetcar 1 toward Junkersdorf from street level at Neumarkt Junkersdorf to Rudolfspl. Closed Sun.*

BREWERIES AND BEER GARDENS **Früh am Dom.** Don't come here for the crowd—it's all tourists and businesspeople. But if you have only a short time in the city, and you want a quick Kölsch or five before your train, the location is unbeatable. This place is immense, with high ceilings, traditional German porcelain ovens, and gruff waiters with blue aprons carrying the round trays that breweries have used since . . . a long time ago. Früh is just one type of Kölsch, but it's a good one. If you're ready for some serious eating, the meals here are fairly expensive (DM 15–DM 20), but the portions are monstrous—strict meat-and-potato fare. Order a salad, get a funny look. *Am Hof 12–14, tel. 0221/212621. Turn left from front door of Dom.*

Päffgen. This is the youngest of three breweries with the same name (there's one in the Altstadt and another on the other side of the Rhine), and also attracts a younger crowd. It manages, however, to retain what's most important for a Köln brewhouse: good beer, loud waiters, and lots of pig on the menu. Don't mind the dark wood and the old decor; you should be concentrating on your beer, anyway. *Friesenstr. 44–46, tel. 0221/135461. U5 toward Neu Ehrenfeld to Friesenpl.*

Stadtgarten. This place has everything. In warm weather the rows of picnic-style tables in the huge outside seating area get packed with as many as 500 rowdy drinkers. There's no sign at the door barring anyone, but most of those under 20 and over 30 seem to know not to hang out here; the oddballs who do, do it in a casual, chic, jovial manner. Inside, the atmosphere is entirely different; the people are the same, but the setting switches from gravel and benches to dark wood, Formica, and the latest in German lighting. If you want something more substantial than pizza (DM 4–DM 7), served outside until 10:30, try the moderately priced meals at the restaurant inside (DM 12–DM 20). If you don't want to eat, and you don't want to drink, and you don't want to look at the avant-garde art on the walls, check to see if there's a concert going on in the small theater behind the bar. Three or four nights each week a band rolls through and plays. Check the Stadtgarden's program, along with the programs for other small music theaters in Köln, in the rack just inside the door. *Venloer Str. 40, tel. 0221/516039. U5 from Hauptbahnhof toward Neu Ehrenfeld to Friesenpl.*

Remember that when Kölners toast, they butt glass bottoms—not tops.

WORTH SEEING

Studying a map of Köln will show you that the Rhine and Hohenzollernring, part of a curving street that connects Rudolfplatz and Friesenplatz and changes its name about 10 times, form something resembling a half moon. The curving street, or "Ring Road" (the west side of the moon), runs along what was the medieval fortification wall, completed in about 1200. Even then Köln was a large city; walking in a straight line from Ebertplatz to Chlodwigplatz, the northern and southern ends of Hohenzollernring, takes at least an hour. A walk from the Dom to Friesenplatz or Rudolfplatz, whether on a sightseeing or a beer-drinking tour, is a good way to explore the inner city, and it won't take too long. If you want to tour Köln's museums—it'll be a marathon if you're truly determined—buy a three-day **Museumpaß** (DM 8) at one of the museums or at the tourist-information office (*see* Visitor Information, *above*). By the way, if you smell something moldy when you're walking around the city (around Gereonskirche, for instance), don't get angry at whomever you're with—that's the smell of Kölsch brewing.

DOM Even if you hate the whole idea of churchgoing and get sick of trudging through holy place after holy place, this House of God should be able to inspire some awe. If you really dig churches, set aside a day. Construction began more than seven centuries ago on this granddaddy that looks like a huge drip-sand castle, and now maintenance is continual. Repairing and refurbishing the Dom, what with all the bombs that hit it in World War II and all the acid-rain droplets that have scarred it since, is a permanent endeavor. The old blackish-gray cathedral, although sturdy, seems sad and weary. The interior of the Dom is no less monstrous but much less despoiled. Five intricate 15th-century stained-glass windows flank the slender main nave, which leads up to the huge 104-seat choir. Sculptured pillars depicting Jesus, Mary, and the 12 Apostles watch over the choir stalls. Behind the pillars are the 56-

foot-high stained-glass windows depicting the 48 kings, and farther back behind the altar is the 13th-century shrine of the Three Magi, which looks like the Ark of the Covenant from *Raiders of the Lost Ark.*

Climb the 509 steps of the **Südturm** (south tower) for a great view of the Rhine. More spectacular, however, is the **Glockenstube** (400 steps up), where the Dom's nine bells are housed, including the Petriglocke—the world's heaviest working bell. To see the cathedral's pious treasures, go to the **Domschatzkammer** (Cathedral Treasury) and **Diozesan Museum** (across the plaza), which house art and rings and scepters and funny hats and everything else you might expect. In front of the Dom, on the **Domvorplatz,** you'll find a hopelessly eclectic gathering of tourists, musicians, kids, drunks, transients, punks, and sidewalk artists with chalk in hand, drawing huge scenes from that all-time bestseller, the Bible, or reproducing famous works of art. Directly out the Dom's front door and to the left you'll find a series of strung-up note cards featuring quotations from visitors from all over the world. If you can think of something short, trite, and/or heartfelt enough (examples include "You can't hug a child with nuclear arms" and "Let's have a moment of peace forever"), grab a card, and hang your entry.

MEDIEVAL CITY WALL What was the original city wall during the dark and often violent Middle Ages is now a major throughway, the Ring Road. Three large fortified gates still remain, however, marking the northern, western, and southern buttresses of the old wall. The fourth, or eastern, border of the old medieval city was the Rhine. To cover the entire Ring Road on foot would take a couple of hours (more if you include beer stops). You can take U9, U12, U16, or U18 from the Hauptbahnhof to Ebertplatz to check out the **Eiglesteintor,** the gate that protected the city's northern border. Take Streetcar 1 from Neumarkt (or walk from the Dom or Neumarkt) to Rudolfplatz, and check out the western gate, **Hahnentor.** To reach the southern gate, **Severinstor,** from the Hauptbahnhof, take U16 toward Neumarkt to Chlodwigplatz.

ROMAN CITY WALL Long before the Middle Ages, Köln was a Roman-occupied city—and the Romans had their wall, too. You can check out the ruins of this fortification at a number of places. Start at the Domvorplatz and you'll notice a rickety old stone archway. This is part of the original **Roman North Gate.** Continue west from the Domvorplatz down Komödienstraße (diagonally to the right from Dom's front door) to Tunisstraße to see sections of the wall from the 1st century AD (restored, naturally). For more Roman ruins, head to the basement of the new **Rathaus**, where you'll find traces of Roman civilization from the 1st through 4th centuries, including some of the **Regia** (imperial palace).

ROMANESQUE CHURCHES They'll all look the same after a while unless you have a keen eye, but Köln's garland of 12 Romanesque churches, all located within the former walls of the medieval city, is unique. The oldest church, commissioned by the archbishop Bruno, is **St. Pantaleon** (Waisenhausgasse and Martinsfeld), consecrated in 980. Perhaps even more impressive than the original architecture of the churches was their amazing reconstruction after World War II, when 90% of the city was damaged or destroyed. **St. Maria Himmelfahrt**'s (north of Dom) Baroque architecture might be the finest example of reconstruction—check out the before and after pictures on the inside for proof. The unique golden chamber of **St. Ursula** (Ursulapl., northwest of Hauptbahnhof) is a tribute to the virgin who, legend has it, was killed by Huns, along with 11,000 virgin consorts. Their bones are said to lie buried underneath the building. Each church has its highlights, from the intricate wood doors of **St. Maria im Kapitol** (north of Marienpl.) to the blend of old and new at **St. Aposteln** (Apostelnstr. and Mittelstr.), built in 1230, to the castlelike **Groß St. Martin** (west of Rheingarten).

MUSEUMS **Kölnisches Stadtmuseum.** Housed in what was the armory for the free city of Köln during the 16th century, this museum picks up the city's history where the **Römisch-Germanisches** (*see below*) leaves off (about AD 750) and traces Köln's development to the present. There are many photographs of the Dom, knights' and horses' armor from the 16th century, displays related to Köln's carnival, and a curt chapter on the Nazi era. On the first floor stands a model of a Ford limousine built in Köln in 1937 and named after the city; on the ground floor the 1913 city model gives you a good idea of what Köln was like before World War I. Zeughausstr. 1–3, tel. 0221/221–2398. *From Domvorpl. follow Komödienstr. to Zeughausstr. Admission: DM 2, DM 1 students. Open Tues.–Wed., Fri.–Sun. 10–5, Thurs. 10–8.*

Römisch-Germanisches Museum. A tribute to and a documentation of Roman life, this museum has a very, very old preserved mosaic floor (AD 220) and a resurrected tomb of the Roman soldier Poblicius (AD 40). After a while all the artifacts blend together, but they still manage to convey the former power of the Roman world. *Roncallipl. 4, behind Dom, tel. 0221/221–2304. Admission: DM 5, DM 2.50 students. Open Tues., Fri.–Sun. 10–5, Wed.–Thurs. 10–8.*

Wallraf-Richartz-Museum and **Museum Ludwig.** Located in the same building right behind the Dom, these two museums form the core of Köln's art scene. The Wallraf's basement, dominated by a huge collection of medieval paintings, houses art from the Middle Ages through the Renaissance. On the floors above is the **Ludwig**'s massive collection of 20th-century art. Some of the hypermodern stuff on display may evoke that troubling question: "Is this *really* art?" But much of the collection is thoughtful and provocative, like Dwayne Kienhulz's *The Portable War Memorial,* a critique of American patriotism complete with "God Bless America" rasping out from underneath an overturned trash can. Don't leave without seeing Gerhard Richter's 48 portraits of European artists and philosophers. Check with the women at the information desk for a roster. *Bischofsgartenstr. 1, Wallraf-Richartz, tel. 0221/221–2372; Ludwig, tel. 0221/221–2370. Admission: DM 8, DM 4 students. Open Tues.–Thurs. 10–8, Fri.–Sun. 10–6.*

Besides the aforementioned big guns, Köln has a smattering of smaller museums. The **Museum für Angewandte Kunst** (An der Rechtschule, tel. 0221/221–3860), about 200 yards from the Domvorplatz, features applied arts from around Europe, including jewelry, furniture, glass, and weapons. In the Ludwig, the **AGFA Foto Historama** (Bischofsgartenstr. 1, tel. 0221/221–2411) presents a photographic look at the last 150 years in Köln.

Take Streetcar 1 from Neumarkt toward Junkersdorf, and get off at Universitätstraße to get to the **Museum für Ostasiatische Kunst** (Universitätstr. 100, tel. 0221/405038). Focusing primarily on Chinese, Japanese, and Korean sculptures, paintings, and ceramics, it's surrounded by a serene Japanese garden and reflecting pool. If you haven't tired of museum hopping yet, pick up the pamphlet "Cologne: City of Museums" from the tourist office (*see* Visitor Information, *above*).

CHEAP THRILLS

If the sun is shining, head for one of the grassy spots where Kölners flock to sunbathe. The **Volksgarten** in the *Neustadt-Süd* (Southern New City) is packed mostly with students and young people having a beer or smoking some odd-smelling cigarettes. To get here from the Hauptbahnhof take U16 toward Neumarkt to Ulrepforte, and walk south on Vorgebirg Straße or Kleingedankstraße. Another option is the long lawn running along Universitätstraße between Aachener Straße and Luxemburger Straße. From the street level at Neumarkt, take Streetcar 1 toward Junkersdorf or Streetcar 7 toward Sülz, and get off at Universitätstraße. This area is also a good place to catch a late-afternoon or weekend pickup soccer game.

The hangouts along the east side of the Rhine are frequented by people of all ages and are not as crowded as those on the west side. Topless sunbathers are common here. To get to the **Rheinpark,** south of the Zoobrücke, take U16 or U18 from the Hauptbahnhof toward Ebertplatz to Zoo/Flora, and cross the bridge—you'll see the big grassy lawn on your right. Farther south, below Severinsbrücke, near the Köln-Deutz youth hostel (*see* Where to Sleep, *above*), is another popular strip of grass. From the

Hauptbahnhof take U9 toward Neumarkt. As the train crosses the Rhine you'll see the grass on the far bank to your right. Get off at the first stop past the river (Suvenstraße) and backtrack.

Finally, check out the **Autobahn.** Seriously. Köln is a great place to see this monster of German civil engineering because the expressways come pretty close to the city. Take U9 from the Hauptbahnhof toward Neumarkt out to Porzer Straße, turn right when you come out of the station, and you're directly above an Autobahn. At night the effect of the cars whizzing out of the Königsforst (*see* Outdoor Activities, *below*) is shocking, even breathtaking. Take along a few beers and a friend, and ponder questions like "Is it morally reprehensible to appreciate an accomplishment like this Autobahn despite the fact that it's a product of the Third Reich?" or more practical questions like "If they drive so fast, what happens when it gets foggy?" Answer Number 1 is debatable. Answer Number 2: 200- to 400-car accidents at one time, which pile up for hours or even days.

AFTER DARK

This is a party town, but not in the wild, mayhem sense. Every night masses flock to the bars, *Kneipen* (pubs), cafés, and discos, but partyers are seldom unruly or hyper; in fact, they're pretty subdued. Köln doesn't party in waves and flashes—its action doesn't peak on a certain night or at a certain time. Köln parties every night, very late, day after day. Even if people aren't drinking beer, they're out drinking something else: coffee, wine, or tequila.

CAFES AND BARS **Biermuseum.** Young Kölners avoid the Altstadt because it's usually filled with tourists and older Kölners. But if you want to head down there, try this place. It's always crowded, and the drinking is pretty serious. Hang out upstairs, and watch people in the pit below or on the street. *Buttermarkt 39, along Rhine s. of Dom near Fischmarkt, tel. 0221/240–1579.*

Halmuckenrenthur. Lots of clubs shun the cheesy art deco of the late '60s and early '70s, but this place embraces it. Most of the decorations, including lava lamps and TVs that look like space helmets, belong in Greg Brady's attic room. But the trippy decor is kinda funky, and the strictly student crowd tries to dress appropriately. *Brüsseler Pl. 9, tel. 0221/517970. From Hauptbahnhof take U5 toward Neu Ehrenfeld (or walk) to Friesenpl., follow Hohenzollernring s. toward Rudolfpl., and turn right on Maastrich Str. to Brüsseler Pl.*

A Carnal Carnival

An overwhelming number of Kölners celebrate their birthdays late in November. It makes sense, because nine months prior to the end of November is the end of February, and the end of February is when Köln's carnival is most intense. Officially the carnival starts at the 11th minute of the 11th day of the 11th month. But the real debauchees arrive with Rose Monday (the last Monday before Lent), when the parades and processions march down Köln's streets, and the costumed revelers scream, dance, kiss, and drink with passion. The November-birthday trend will probably fade; average 40- to 70-year-old Kölners may have let loose only around carnival, but their sons and daughters let loose a lot more often.

Hotelux. Once you set foot in this place you'll probably get an irresistible urge to order a vodka (DM 4). It seems like this bar was decorated by a surrealist trying to portray Russia. The black curtain in the doorway lets you into a crowded little room with red stars and hard metal tables. Luckily the crowd isn't as glum as the decor, but they dress the part. *Rathenaupl. 21, tel. 0221/241136. From Neumarkt station's street level take Streetcar 7 toward Sülz (or walk) to Zülpicher Str., turn right on Roon Str., then left on Rathenaupl.*

Linus New Pub. Come to this pub to experience the nightlife in the Südstadt (southern part of the city) around Chlodwigplatz, home to many students and young 'uns. This place blasts some hard music and is pretty dark and gray—even the paint splotches on the wall are dull-hued. The crowd, however, is bright and stands out against the drab background. *Ubierring 22, tel. 0221/328720. From Hauptbahnhof take U16 toward Neumarkt to Chlodwigpl., turn left on Ubierring.*

Spitz. Named after the prissy little dog encased in glass above the main entrance, this place is frequented by Köln yuppies who come to strut their clothes and attitudes—both of which are elegant but not overdone. The food here is excellent; you can get a salad or some pasta for DM 8–DM 10. *Ehrenstr. 43, tel. 0221/246163.*

MUSIC AND DANCING If you're looking for some "real" music, ask the Köln **ticket office** behind the Dom, next to the Römisch-Germanisches museum, for **Köln Philharmonie** tickets. They're expensive (DM 8–DM 10) unless you can get a student discount, which is not offered for all performances. You can also inquire here about other concerts—rock, pop, whatever. If you want to dance, tons of discos await you. The in

Gay Nightlife

Outside that of Berlin and Munich, Köln's gay nightlife is probably the most thriving in Germany. Many bars, discos, and some saunas cater mostly or exclusively to homosexuals. The Gloria (Apostelnstr. 11, tel. 0221/254433), a café and disco based in an old movie theater, is loaded with well-dressed dancers and drinkers, mostly men. Yocoto (Kaiser-Wilhelm-Ring 30–32, tel. 0221/132262), north of Friesenplatz, proclaims itself the home of the "young, elegant crowd." Friday through Sunday it's open until 4:30. Some activities in the smaller alcove rooms get pretty steamy and illicit. You can party at Corner (Schaafenstr. 57–59, tel. 0221/249061), which also offers a hearty Sunday brunch (starting at noon). One of the oldest gay meeting spots in Köln is Treff am Gürzenich (Gürzenichstr. 28, tel. 0221/237739). On Tuesday night the disco at Osho's (see Food, above) becomes the Pink Triangle, a lesbian-and-gay disco. A few of the city's many saunas also cater to the gay community, such as the Badehaus am Römerturm (Friesenstr. 23–25, near Friesenpl., tel. 0221/230353). Köln is a liberal-minded city, so many homosexuals feel comfortable here. In fact, heterosexual Kölners are usually more accepting of the varying sexual preferences of homosexuals than of the religious and cultural practices of the Turks. This may be due to the docile nature of Köln's gay community, which is neither as flamboyant nor as politically active as its counterparts in cities such as New York and San Francisco.

disco is always changing, but all of them are so packed (especially on weekends) that it won't matter if one or another has lost its happenin' title.

Das Ding. Much smaller but no less packed than the E-Werk (*see below*), this place lets you swap sweat with Germans on the crowded dance floor or around the long bar. *Hohenstaufenring 30–32, near Zulpicher Str. streetcar stop, tel. 0221/246348. Cover: DM 5. Closed Tues.*

E-Werk. In an industrial sector outside the city on the east side of the Rhine, this gigantic warehouse has two floors, multiple bars, and a quieter café to cool off in. Hundreds of young Germans, drably dressed, move to the pumpy-jumpy technobeat. Weekdays you can sometimes catch live music here; days and quality vary. *Schanzen Str. 28, tel. 0221/621091. From Dom take U16 or U18 toward Ebertpl. to Wienerpl., then follow Clevischer Ring or Genovevastr., turn right on Keupstr., left on Schanzenstr. Cover: DM 15, including 2 drinks. Closed Sun.–Thurs. except for occasional live performances.*

Luxor. Dark and dirty, this place is a near dive, but the random local bands that play here are wonderfully odd. Some nights, entrance is free, but the bands occasionally command a cover charge of about DM 6. *Luxemburger Str. 40, tel. 0221/219503. From Hauptbahnhof take U16 toward Neumarkt to Barbarossapl., then follow train's direction down Luxemburger Str. Cover: DM 12 Fri.–Sat., free–DM 6 weeknights.*

Near Köln

AACHEN This town also goes by the names Bad Aachen, because of its supposedly rejuvenating hot springs (*Bad* means "baths"), and Aix-la-Chapelle, because of the 8th-century, 16-sided chapel that now supports the rest of the city's **Dom**. It's also called "Rome North" because Holy Roman emperor Charlemagne really dug this town. His ailing father, Pippin, had dragged the family here for the healing waters, and the emperor-to-be got hooked. Charlemagne made the trek down to Rome to be crowned emperor but then returned to his Frankish roots up north, and it was here, in Aachen's Dom, that the next 32 emperors were crowned. The golden shrine in the cathedral—which looks like a big dollhouse with the windows and doors filled in—contains Charlemagne's remains. One wonders how he would feel if he knew that a piece of his own skull was used in the bust (by Karl IV, a prince from Bohemia). The bust is still on display in the **Domschatzkammer** (Cathedral Treasury), acclaimed as the richest in Europe.

Across from the Dom, on the **Katsch Hof** plaza (which has a fruit-and-vegetable market daily until 1 PM), stands the **Rathaus**. It's so regal you'd think it was Charlemagne's; it does, in fact, stand on the spot where the former emperor's palace once stood. Built early in the 14th century, the building was pulverized during World War II but has since been renovated. Along the north wall of the building stand 50 statues of Holy Roman emperors, many of whom received their titles in Aachen. Charlemagne's disappointingly flaccid bronzed likeness stands atop the **Kaiserbrunnen** fountain in the Marktplatz, dwarfed by McDonald's golden arches.

The hot springs drew the Romans here, so when you're in Rome North, do as the Romans did—take a bath. The entire area south of the Hauptbahnhof is filled with natural springs appropriately called **Kurgebiet** (Cure Territory), but the more affordable spas are farther uptown. At the **Kurbad Quellenhof** (Monheimsallee 52, tel. 0241/180–2922) you can take a two-hour hot-spring bath for DM 15. It's not as cheap as it was for Charlemagne, but no one ever said that being emperor of the West didn't have its advantages.

There are two affordable hotels within walking distance of the Hauptbahnhof. The **Hotel Rösener** (Theaterstr. 62, tel. 0241/407215), only a few blocks away, has singles for DM 52 and doubles for DM 80. The **Hotel Weiss** (Adalbertsteinweg 67, tel.

0241/505007) is a little farther away, but the rooms are a few DM cheaper. The **Jugendherberge** (Maria-Theresia-Allee 260, tel. 0241/71101) is easy to get to. Exit the Hauptbahnhof, turn left on Lagerhausstraße, go past the tiny gate-tower **Marschiertor,** and pick up Bus 2 at the corner of Lagerhausstraße and Karmeliterstraße; ride two stops, to Ronheide. Trains from Köln leave for Aachen (50-minute trip) twice an hour.

BRUHL For Americans, who come from a land without old, extravagant castles, Brühl's **Schloß Augustusberg** is pretty spectacular. You can tour these ritzy digs, built in the 18th century by the archbishop of Köln, for DM 3 (DM 1.50 students) daily 9–noon and 3:30–4. But you don't need to go inside to get the majestic gist. Just go around back to the **Schloßpark** (open until 9) and wander along the footpaths, among the fountains and reflecting pools, and marvel at the manicured hedges.

The **Phantasialand amusement park** in Brühl was Europe's best stab at a fun park before the phenomenon of Euro-Disney, which may have permanently reduced it to the status of a dinosaur. The place makes no pretenses about campiness—you'll undertand when you see the Hacienda de Mexico—but the log ride's a splash, the white-tiger show is pretty cool, and the Grand Canyon roller coaster holds its own. Unfortunately, the price is steep (DM 25), and students don't get a discount. *Open Apr.–Sept., daily 9–6.*

The easiest way to get to Brühl is by subway from Köln's Dom; the trip takes about a half hour. Take U18 toward Bonn, and get off at Brühl Mitte. Follow the ZENTRUM/SCHLOß signs to the city center; you will also see signs leading to the Schloß Augustusburg and the Jüden Friedhof (*see* box, *above*). Bus 706 goes from Brühl Mitte to Phantasialand.

Düsseldorf

In Düsseldorf you'll see some beautiful, stylishly dressed women with set jaws and prominent cheekbones, and some handsome, short-haired men wearing tortoiseshell glasses and driving BMWs—but they probably won't see you. Düsseldorfers try really hard to look good, and try even harder to look like they're not trying to. Wrapped up in what they're doing, they're neither rude nor friendly to newcomers—simply uninterested. Maybe this is because of all of the money around town—the annual income of Düsseldorfers is 25% higher than that of the average German. The second-largest financial center in Germany—behind Frankfurt—Düsseldorf is sort of the front office for the **Ruhrgebiet** (*see* Near Düsseldorf, *below*), the big industrial area north of the city. The major firms have their offices here, the head honchos live here, and the money comes here. It's not surprising that Düsseldorf is Japan's largest German colony, with 6,000 Japanese residents and 400 Japanese companies.

This is not a very popular town among Germans because of its double-edge reputation. On the one hand, Düsseldorfers are considered snobby because of their wealth; on the other hand, the city is written off as a dumping ground for partying blue-collar workers from the Ruhrgebiet. Perhaps the most critical are the city's southern neighbors in Köln, who take it for granted that the vapid *Dorf* (village) to the north pales in comparison to their own culture-and-fashion mecca. But Düsseldorf has nothing to be ashamed of. It contains a preserved medieval village and a ruined fort, excellent modern-art museums, a wealth of bars and nightclubs, and a renovated castle, to boot.

BASICS

AMERICAN EXPRESS This office holds mail for cardholders, takes phone messages, and cashes traveler's checks. For a cash advance on your card, you need to know your home bank-account number, have a personal check, and show identification. In halting English the folks at the front desk will recommend a restaurant, find you a flight, or help you plan a trip. *Heinrich-Heine-Allee 14, across from Opera, s. of Grabbepl., tel. 0211/80222. Open weekdays 9–5:30, Sat. 9–noon.*

CONSULATES Most foreign consulates are in Bonn; **Great Britain**'s (tel. 0211/94480) is here, at Yorckstraße 19.

MEDICAL AID The closest hospital to the Hauptbahnhof and city center is **Marien Krankenhaus** (Rochusstr. 2, tel. 0211/44000), which has English-speaking doctors. For emergency **dental service** call 0211/666291. The pharmacy **Apotheke im Hauptbahnhof** (tel. 0211/365626) is near the front entrance of the train station and is open weekdays 8–6:30 and Saturday 8:30–1.

LAUNDRY **SB Waschsalon** may seem like the normal, boring Laundromat, but the occasional "wash-party," with live music, lets you dance, fold, and meet Düsseldorfers over underwear rather than beer. Washing a large load costs DM 12, and drying it costs DM 1.50 every 10 minutes. *Ackerstr. and Hermannstr. Turn right out of Hauptbahnhof, follow Worringer Str. to Worringer Pl., turn right on Ackerstr. to Hermannstr. Open daily 6 AM–11 PM, last wash 10 PM.*

MAIL AND PHONES You can change traveler's checks and make phone calls at the **Post** near the rear of the Hauptbahnhof, which has longer hours than the main post office on Konrad-Adenauer-Platz. You can use coins, phone cards (which you can buy at the counter), or metered phones. Ask one of the employees for the latter; you pay when you're finished with your call. The postal code is 4000. *Daytime customer service, tel. 0211/163–1310; evening, tel. 0211/163–1857. Open weekdays 7 AM–8 PM, weekends noon–8.*

VISITOR INFORMATION The **Verkehrsverein** (tourist agency) is surely one of the best-staffed in Europe, and all the employees speak English. They're happy to make hotel reservations (DM 3), tell you how to get somewhere, or tell you what special events are going on. However, since the office is always busy, the staff is prone to answer questions with brochures rather than words. *Konrad-Adenauer-Pl. 12, across from Hauptbahnhof and to right, tel. 0211/350505. Open weekdays 8:30–6, Sat. 9–12:30. Rooms reserved Mon.–Sat. 9 AM–10 PM, Sun. 4–10.*

COMING AND GOING

BY TRAIN The **Düsseldorf Hauptbahnhof** is like a small, self-contained city in which you can get money, have a coffee or a beer, buy anything from an apricot to a condom, then store or mail either. Rail connections leave four times hourly for Köln (with a break between 1:30 AM and 5 AM) and hourly for Frankfurt, Hannover, and Amsterdam. Call the **Deutsche Bundesbahn** (tel. 0211/19419) for information. Many S-Bahn lines originate at the Hauptbahnhof and serve almost every major city within an hour of Düsseldorf, including Recklinghausen, Solingen, and Wuppertal. S-Bahn tickets for these shorter trips are cheaper than DB (Deutsche Bundesbahn) tickets, but you can't use your Eurailpass. To get to the S-Bahn platforms follow the green "S" signs.

HITCHHIKING Düsseldorf is hooked up to almost every German city by Autobahn. When hitching, simply stand near an on ramp and hold a sign—look for the Autobahn 57 south to Köln, Autobahn 3 south to Frankfurt, or Autobahn 46 east to Hannover or Hamburg.

BY MITFAHRZENTRALE **Citynetz Mitfahr-Zentrale** is a hectic little office, but the English-speaking operators, whose movements seem to scream "overworked and underpaid," can usually get you where you need to go with as little as 24 hours' notice. Rides to Munich (DM 52) and Berlin (DM 50) are frequent. *Kurfürstenstr. 30, tel. 0211/19444. From Hauptbahnhof turn right on Worringer Str., left on Kurfürstenstr. Open weekdays 9–6, Sat. 10–2.*

BY PLANE **Düsseldorf International Airport** is connected to the Hauptbahnhof by the S-Bahn (20-minute ride) three times an hour, and Lufthansa has a free shuttle for ticket holders. The airport serves Munich, Berlin, London, and Paris hourly and has two daily nonstops to New York. Call 0211/421–2223 between 6 AM and midnight for information.

GETTING AROUND

Getting around in Düsseldorf might seem intimidating—there are a lot of options, a lot of symbols, and a lot of numbers—but you can walk to most major tourist sights from the Hauptbahnhof in less than 25 minutes. Most of the Altstadt (Old Town) is bordered by Königsallee on the east, the Rhine on the west, Hofgarten on the north, and Haroldstraße on the south. For a **taxi**, call 0211/33333.

Düsseldorf's **U-Bahn** leaves from the Hauptbahnhof's lower level; streetcars and buses leave from in front of the station. The good news is that, no matter how you travel, you can use the same tickets and fare plans. Every stop has a fare list; simply find the place you want to go, and match it to the listed price. **Bus** riders can buy individual tickets from the driver, but streetcar and subway riders must purchase tickets from a machine or office beforehand. With a "go-as-you-please" ticket (DM 8.50) you can use any of Düsseldorf's people-movers for a whole day. If you're traveling with another adult and up to three children under 14, they can accompany you at no extra charge. You can buy these day tickets from ticket machines or bus drivers. The subway-streetcar-bus map has a shocking array of colors, numbers, and names, but it's actually very complete and helpful once you get used to it. Pick one up from the tourist office and give it a chance.

Düsseldorf, like many other German cities, has taken steps to alleviate fare evasion by switching to undercover enforcement officials. It is no longer possible to abandon ship as they board. Don't be surprised if Granny in the seat next to you puts down her knitting and says, *"Ihr Fahrausweis, bitte"* ("Fare card, please").

WHERE TO SLEEP

When you get off the train in Düsseldorf you'll probably notice that next to the large DÜSSELDORF HAUPTBAHNHOF signs hang equally large (and considerably more ominous) signs that read IHRE MESSESTADT (YOUR CONVENTION CITY). Conventions bring droves that fill hotels and raise the prices of rooms by DM 20–DM 40. Call the tourist office to find out when something is happening (or not happening). Don't turn the page yet—there's a bright side. When there's no Messe, the prices become reasonable, and you'll find cheap lodging within a 5- or 10-minute walk of the train station.

➢ **UNDER DM 80 • Christlicher Verein Junger Menschen.** CVJM is the German YMCA. Although the setting is not overly pious, religious reading material is available for guests, and most rooms include a picture of the Lord at no extra cost. Because this place has no curfew, young people cruise in and out at all times. Sneaking an extra person into your room isn't that difficult, especially if the stowaway isn't sporting a backpack or suitcase. Singles are DM 48, doubles DM 78, and there are showers on every floor. *Graf-Adolf-Str. 102, tel. 0211/360764. From Hauptbahnhof turn left on Graf-Adolf-Str. 27 rooms, none with bath. Breakfast included.*

Diana. Forget about this place during Messe, but, when available, the small rooms with adjoining bathrooms (as opposed to the frequent shower stall in a corner of the room) are comfortable, although somberly furnished. The Altstadt is a 10-minute walk away. Singles cost DM 55, doubles DM 75 (DM 70 and DM 85 with shower). *Jahnstr. 31, tel. 0211/375071. From Hauptbahnhof turn left on Graf-Adolf-Str., left on Pionierstr., right on Luisenstr., left on Jahnstr. 20 rooms, some with bath. Breakfast included.*

Domo. It's not much of a looker, but this hotel is adequate and a mere two blocks from the Hauptbahnhof. They'll even put a TV in your room free of charge so you can practice your German or just generate some white noise. Singles are DM 59, and doubles are DM 79 (DM 69 and DM 109 with shower). *Scheurenstr. 4, tel. 0211/374001. From Hauptbahnhof turn left on Graf-Adolf-Str., left on Scheurenstr. 20 rooms, some with bath. Breakfast included.*

➢ **UNDER DM 90 • Tal.** This hotel has two things going for it: price and convenience (it's a three-minute walk to Königsallee, a 15-minute walk to the Hauptbahnhof). The rooms smell slightly stale, and the decorator seems to have had his or her mind on other things, but you can probably handle both drawbacks. Besides, Tal's atmosphere scares off the more refined hotel-seeking competition, so you may have a better chance of finding a room here when everything else is booked. Singles are DM 60, doubles DM 85, and triples DM 115. Prices are higher for showers in your room and/or breakfast. *Talstr. 36, tel. 0211/370051. From Hauptbahnhof turn left on Graf-Adolf-Str., then left on Königsallee, which becomes Talstr. 26 rooms, some with bath.*

➢ **UNDER DM 100 • Komet.** This is probably your best bet. Rooms are competitively priced, the location can't be beat, and the huge windows make the rooms comfortable and airy. Singles are DM 60, doubles DM 95 without shower (DM 75 and DM 105 with). *Bismarckstr. 93, tel. 0211/357917. Turn left out of Hauptbahnhof, then quick right on Bismarckstr. 18 rooms, some with bath. Breakfast included.*

➢ **UNDER DM 110 • Haus Hillesheim.** This place is modestly decorated and modestly priced. However, the four thin pieces of plastic fitted together in the corner of your room are not what you'd call an ideal private shower. Singles are DM 65, doubles DM 90 (DM 75 and DM 100 with shower). They'll move a roll-away bed into your room for an extra DM 20. *Jahnstr. 19, tel. 0211/371940. From Hauptbahnhof turn left on Graf-Adolf-Str., left on Pionierstr., right on Luisenstr., left on Jahnstr. 17 rooms, some with bath. Breakfast included.*

Hotel Amsterdam. Once you get past the mundane blue-tile facade, the comforting, motherly proprietor Frau Schimanski will take you into her superclean rooms replete with little soaps on the sinks. The reception desk closes at about 1 AM, but ask for a front-door key and you can come in as late as you want. Singles are about DM 55, doubles DM 100 (with shower, DM 70 and DM 125). *Stresemannstr. 20, tel. 0211/84058. From Hauptbahnhof turn left on Graf-Adolf-Str., right on Stresemannstr. 17 rooms, some with bath. Breakfast included.*

HOSTELS **Jugendherberge und Jugendgästehaus Düsseldorf (IYHF).** Unhappy, usually a little drunk, and looking somewhat like Jack Nicholson in *The Shining*, the guests gather on the front steps waiting to be let in after the 1 AM curfew. Luckily they only have to wait an hour, for one of the hapless receptionists gets up every hour to let latecomers in. Once in, the guests head for their crowded, bunk-filled rooms to pass out in hammocklike beds. This youth hostel (DM 18.50 per night) is packed and run down but alive and bustling. The lobby is a great place to meet fellow travelers; sit down and whip out a map or guidebook, and you're inviting conversation. The rooms in the adjacent **Jugendgästehaus** (DM 26.50) are newer and quieter. You can ask for a single, but they're the first to go. The hostel is a 15-minute trip from the train station. *Düsseldorf Str. 1, tel. 0211/557310. Bus 835 from Platform 10 of Hauptbahnhof to Jugendherberge. 280 beds. Laundry facilities, luggage storage, breakfast included, lunch and dinner available (DM 7.50), bike rental (DM 7 per day). Reception closed daily 9:30–12:30, 2–4, 5:30–6, and after 9:30. Closed 2 wks around Christmas.*

CAMPGROUNDS **Campingplatz Lörick.** When camping on the Rhine be prepared to wake up to the sight of coal barges churning through the murky waters. You'll be sharing this "scenic" spot with car campers. It's a half-hour trip from the train station, and spots cost DM 8 per person, DM 12 per tent. *Niederkasseler Deich 305, tel. 0211/591401. U717 or U705 from Hauptbahnhof toward Hoterheide or Neuß to Belsenpl., then Bus 828 to Straudab Lörick. Bathrooms, showers. Closed Oct.–Mar.*

Campingplatz Unterbacher See. Quiet and peaceful, nestled in the tiny Stadtwald Düsseldorf (City Forest), this campground is farther from the city (the trip takes about an hour) and a little nicer than Lörick. Spots cost DM 12 per person, DM 22 for three-person tent. *Unterbacher See, tel. 0211/899–2038. S7 to Eller (not Eller Süd), then Bus 735 to See Weg. Bathrooms, showers. Closed late Sept.–early Apr.*

FOOD

If the Altstadt is the heart of Düsseldorf, pumping all day and beating furiously at night, then *Alt Bier* is the blood that courses through the sector's veins—and taps. The rich, sweet brew is available everywhere—just ask for an Alt. The traditional breweries strewn about the Altstadt are great places to eat as well as drink. The Altstadt and Königsallee are also lined with cafés, many of which have outdoor seating. To put your own meal together, head for the open-air market on Karlsplatz, open weekdays 8–6 and Saturday 8–2. Otherwise, try the **Indischer Schnell-Imbiß** (Indian fast-food stands), which serve hearty portions of spicy chicken curry (DM 8) and rice and vegetables (DM 5.80). For candy bars and other snacks hit the **Pink Kiosk** (Neubrück Str. 14, tel. 0211/327302) before 9 PM. Also known as **Bier Paradies,** it specializes in international beers (150 types). The rough, black bottle of the aptly named "skull" beer (DM 9), with its higher alcohol percentage, will do what it says—get you skulled.

➢ **UNDER DM 10 • Bambus Garden.** The chicken with rice or noodles (DM 6.50) is fantastic here, especially if it's past 1:30 AM and you've been drinking. The friendly Chinese woman behind the counter speaks horrible German, but it's a lot better than her English. Just point and groan, and she'll know what you want—she manages to get all her drunk customers fed. *Liefergasse 3, off Ratinger Str., tel. 0211/324298.*

➢ **UNDER DM 15 • Hausbrauerei zum Schlussel.** The Schlussel offers a large kettle brimming with brew in the back and a similarly large selection of traditional delicacies (DM 9–DM 15). *Bolkerstr. 43, tel. 0211/326155. From n. end of Königsallee walk w. on Elberfelder, which turns into Bolkerstr.*

Neu Liebe. If you want to escape the Altstadt, try this peaceful, bright little café west of town. The happy-go-lucky management has kindly provided chalkboards in the bathrooms for graffiti, and the patrons seem to return the favor by keeping their language clean. Try the hearty slab of lasagna (DM 12) or the salad buffet (DM 12). *Grafenberger Allee 119, tel. 0211/663410. From Hauptbahnhof take Bus 746 or 781 (Platform 16) or Bus 736 (Platform 9) to Lindemannstr. and backtrack 100 yds.*

Zur Uel. Offering an entirely different experience from that of the traditional brew houses, the Uel (owl) teems with university-age eaters and drinkers who seem a little frayed and a little on edge. Although the clientele is not mainstream, the food—mostly salads, soups, and pastas (DM 9–DM 14)—is basic, and the portions are generous. Every cultural and political event in the city is advertised on at least one of the posters in the entry hall. *Ratinger Str. 16, tel. 0211/325369.*

➢ **UNDER DM 20 • Atlantico Café.** The Mexican food here is good, relative to Mexican food in Germany. The decor in the restaurant and bar upstairs is campy Mexican; the pseudo-adobe walls, piñatas, and woven chairs are hardly for real. The burritos, although pricey (DM 15–DM 18), are your best bet; nachos are good and a little more affordable (DM 10.50). As you walk downstairs to the bar you'll see fewer south-of-the-border decorations and hear loud music. The partying and dancing go until 5 AM on Friday and Saturday. Feel free to write on the walls—everybody else does. *Mertensgasse 2, off Bolker Str., tel. 0211/323190. No lunch. Closed Mon.*

Goldener Kessel. Tradition in Düsseldorf mandates that you drink plenty of Alt while standing around the long tables outside this place or sitting around the long tables inside, that you take plenty of flak from the blue-apron-clad waiters, and that you eat plenty of pork. If you really want to brave the local cuisine, try the aggressively anti-diet meat specialty *Rheinischer* sauerbraten (DM 18). *Bolkerstr. 44, tel. 0211/326007. From n. end of Königsallee walk w. on Elberfelder, which turns into Bolkerstr.*

Mövenpick. This huge Swiss chain is getting a foothold in Germany, having opened restaurants in Stuttgart, Hannover, Hamburg, and Düsseldorf. Don't be put off by the word "chain"—Mövenpick's a welcome sight. On the *Untergeschoß* (lower level) of the posh Kö Gallerie on Königsallee, you can dine in style at a full-service Mövenpick that serves huge salads (DM 15) and pastas (DM 10–DM 16). Or walk across the plaza to the small stand **Mövenpick Markt,** which specializes in fish salads: Try the shrimp-apple-celery salad if it's available (DM 5.50). The pride of Mövenpick and a haven for budget eaters, however, is the restaurant **Marché,** also downstairs. This buffet-style bonanza has pastas, salads, juices, fruit, ice cream, beer, and daily specials, all for less than DM 10. If you're a vegetarian, the veggie buffet (DM 3.20–DM 8.50) is culinary heaven. *Königsallee 60, in Kö gallerie, tel. 0211/320681.*

WORTH SEEING

Düsseldorf is easy to explore because many of the city's sights are in the Altstadt. Bordered by the serene Hofgarten park to the north and east and by the Rhine to the west, this maze of small streets and alleys is home to more than 200 bars and restaurants. If you forget the next day where you were the previous night, go to the top of the 770-foot **Rheinturm** (Stromstr. 20), and glance down at the sprawling city of 600,000; along the Rhine you'll see rows of houses that were reconstructed in the old style after 80% of Düsseldorf's buildings were destroyed in the war. The Altstadt is only about 12 blocks long and 5 blocks wide; pick up a walking map from the tourist office, and be prepared to press your nose to it as you wind your way around the curving streets. More historic sights, easily accessible by public transport, are located in neighboring towns.

HOFGARTEN The Hofgarten's grassy knolls, trees, sandy walking paths, and lake form the northern and upper-eastern borders of the Altstadt. Düsseldorfers come here to stroll, sunbathe, bike, or just have a beer on a bench; thousands of geese, ducks, and pigeons come here, too, and mingle on the lake's shores. There are no pooper-scooper laws in the Hofgarten, but there *are* plenty of dogs. Watch your step.

KAISERPFALZ Weeds and vines blanket the ruins of Kaiserpfalz, a fort north of the present town of Kaiserwerth. The grounds of the fort, which was built in 1184 by Holy Roman Emperor Frederick Barbarossa, are now just a park, but you can still tell that this was a strategic location for controlling the Rhine. Next door the **Wintergarten** beer garden (Burgallee 1, behind Burghof restaurant, tel. 0211/401423) is loaded with bodies, especially on sunny late afternoons. *U79 from under Hauptbahnhof (Richtung Duisburg) to Klemenspl., cross tracks, follow Klemenspl. to Kaiserwerther Markt, turn left at Rhine (45-min. walk). Park open sunrise–7.*

KONIGSALLEE Here's a prime example of a tourist attraction that simply doesn't live up to all the press it gets. Dubbed "the essence of Düsseldorf," the Königsallee is just a nice shop-lined street with a canal next to it. But the street is not without charm; the streetlamps and telephone booths are beautiful and as art-nouveauish as these things get.

LOBBECKE MUSEUM AND AQUAZOO The display text in this ultramodern aquarium is in German, but whatever language you speak you can enjoy the seals, penguins, sharks, turtles, and alligators, and some of the hugest catfish possible. Watch the alligators' nostrils; if they move you know they aren't dead. *Kaiserwerther Str. 380, tel. 0211/899–6150. U78 or U79 from Hauptbahnhof to Nordpark/Aquazoo. Admission: DM 8, DM 4 students. Open daily 10–6.*

SCHLOß BENRATH The brochure calls this 80-room castle a "complete work of art," in which architecture, sculpture, painting, and garden are interwoven. You might call it "gaudy." The best parts are the benches, flowers, tree-canopied footpaths, and reflecting pools behind the Schloß. The park, open 24 hours, is a great place to relax or take a stroll. The **Naturkundliches Heimatmuseum Benrath,** in the front of the Schloß, supposedly the natural-history museum for the lower Rhine basin, seems more like a taxidermy exhibit. *Benrather Schloßallee 102–104, tel. 0211/899–7271 (Schloß), or 0211/899–7219 (museum). From Hauptbahnhof take U717 (Richtung Benrath) to Schloß Benrath. Admission: DM 3, DM 1.50 students. Tours of Schloß every ½ hr. Tues.–Fri. 11–4, weekends 10–4.*

OTHER MUSEUMS The curators of the dark and shiny modern-art museum **Kunstsammlung Nordrhein-Westfalen** seem to have an inferiority complex—perhaps they feel overshadowed by the art epicenter of Köln, a few kilometers south. They acknowledge "large gaps" in their representation of certain art movements, and the museum brochure is quick to point out that the exhibits make no pretense of "completeness." But the museum does focus on individual artists—and the curators should be proud of their fine collection, which includes not only works by Pablo Picasso and Marc Chagall, but one of the finest Paul Klee exhibits anywhere. *Grabbepl. 5, tel. 0211/133961. Admission: DM 8, DM 5 students. Open Tues.–Sun. 10–6.*

Across the street are the **Städtische Kunsthalle** (Grabbepl. 4, tel. 0211/131469) and **Kunstverein für die Rheinlande und Westfalen** (Grabbepl. 4, tel. 0211/327023), both sharing the same building and featuring modern art, photography, and sculpture. The eclectic **Kunstmuseum** up the road (Ehrenhof 5, tel. 0211/899–2460) features sculpture, glasswork, furniture, and six centuries' worth of paintings and drawings. The modern-art exhibit focuses on local painters commissioned by the academy at Düsseldorf after World War II. The **Heinrich-Heine-Institut** (Bilker Str. 12–14, tel. 0211/899–5571) won't do much for you if you don't read German; seeing the man's opera glasses, his library, and his desk doesn't evoke the brave, radical thinker whose criticism of Prussian militarism and social inequality got him exiled. A similar fate awaits the non-German reader at the **Goethe Museum** (Jacobistr. 2, tel. 0211/899–6262), housed in the posh, gilded **Schloß Tägerhof.** Literary types may have a better time at the **Schiffahrt Museum** (Burgpl. 30, tel. 0211/899–4195), where you don't have to read anything to understand the models and pictures tracing the history of shipping on the Rhine.

ZONS For a peaceful little jaunt, follow the footpath from behind Schloß Benrath to the Rhine, and board the ferry bound for Zons, a tiny, preserved medieval village complete with a castle wall and tower. The small boat has deck seating on sunny days and a gruff old salt for a captain. The ferry costs DM 5 round-trip and leaves twice each hour for the 10-minute trip. Don't miss the last boat, which leaves Zons at 6:30—it's a nice afternoon trip, but you don't want to be stuck here all night. For ferry information call **Zonser Personen-Schiffahrt** (tel. 0211/42149).

AFTER DARK

Some Düsseldorfers don't like the weekend-warrior partyers who flock here from the Ruhrgebiet. But that doesn't stop the locals from shedding their glossy facades and joining the crowd in the bars that cram the Altstadt. There are also plenty of dance clubs in the Altstadt, including the **Atlantico Café** (*see* Food, *above*). For technofunk go to the **Ratinger Hof** (Ratinger Str. 14, DM 10 cover), whose industrial-looking exterior matches the solemn faces of its black-clad patrons. For an entirely different type of crowd and music, try the grungy **Purple Haze** (Lieferstr. 7), with black-and-whites of Jimi Hendrix and Pete Townsend on the walls inside, and graffiti extolling the virtues of bands such as Motorhead, Slayer, and the Ramones on the outside. The message is clear—this place is hard, loud, and rocky. The two latter spots are closed Sunday–Tuesday.

Near Düsseldorf

The Ruhrgebiet, named for the river that flows into the Rhine at Duisburg, used to be one of the most polluted areas in the world. The northern Ruhrgebiet, including Recklinghausen and the River Emscher, is still extremely industrial. This district outside Düsseldorf was Germany's coal- and steel-production center following the industrial revolution. By the 1960s the coal had become too deep and too costly to mine, so production levels were halved, and the region began to revert to the green lushness that distinguished it a century ago.

ARCHAEOLOGICAL PARK IN XANTEN When the Romans were taking over this part of Europe 1,800 years ago, they established a town called Colonia Ulpia Traiana. But they were so busy enlarging their empire that they forgot all about this little place—so it never developed. Traiana is now a sprawling park that reveals the layout of the original town with the help of full-size building facsimiles. The park demonstrates early Roman architecture (amphitheater and temple), technology (building crane and mills), and advanced feats of civil engineering (streets, drainage channels, and water conduits). Even if you're not a history buff you'll love this glimpse of ancient culture. The park is a 15- to 20-minute walk from the Xanten Hauptbahnhof—follow the signs. The best way to get to Xanten by train is via Duisburg, which has trains to Düsseldorf, Essen, and Dortmund several times each hour.

DORTMUND Like most Ruhrgebiet cities, this one is eager to shed its industrial image. The brochures and tourist reps boast of the city's natural allure and suggest you take the "49% walk," a route named for the percentage of Dortmund covered in greenery. But the city's real calling card is beer, which has been brewed here since the 15th century. Second only to "Meel-vo-kay" (Milwaukee) in beer production, at least according to the **tourist office** (Königswall 18, tel. 0231/542–22174), Dortmund brews more than 600 million liters and 25 different varieties of beer each year. If you don't like beer, don't bother visiting.

To get a taste—literally and figuratively—of beer in Dortmund, head for the **Brewery Museum** (Märkische Str. 85, tel. 0231/542–24856), then find the real thing in any of the bars and Kneipen in the inner city, directly out of the Hauptbahnhof and up the stairs. Dortmund's other museums make it easy to save money for beer—they're all free. The **Museum am Ostwall** (Ostwall 7, tel. 0231/23247) is packed with examples of German expressionism, much of which was suppressed during the Third Reich. The museum now stands on what was the oldest part of Dortmund. Be sure to check out the **Police Museum** (Markgrafenstr. 102, tel. 0231/132–4055), which opened in September 1992.

ESSEN AND BOCHUM Alfred Krupp didn't just produce coffeemakers and alarm clocks; he was also the most powerful influence in creating the industrial Ruhr and making Essen the biggest, baddest coal-mining town in Europe. Essen's coal legacy ended when the last mine closed in 1986, but Krupp has left his mark. Although his morals and economics were questionable and confusing—he treated his workers far better than was fashionable at the time, providing great benefits, housing, and pay, but he collaborated openly with the Nazis and received armaments contracts and slave labor in return. His own taste in accommodations is clear: He liked 'em big. The **Villa Hügel** (Auf dem Hügel, tel. 0201/188–4848), where he and his family resided until 1950, is monstrous. So monstrous, in fact, that you could put a museum in it, as the city did: It chronicles Krupp's achievements and family history. Krupp's villa is not the only architectural attraction in Essen, however. The pale-green dome of the **Alte Synagogue** (Steeler Str. 29, tel. 0201/884643) was destroyed twice, once during Kristallnacht, in 1938, and once by bombs during the war. It's disturbing, to say the least, that the city council was so reluctant to turn the synagogue into a postwar memorial, as the city's Jews requested; scarier still was the text on the stone coffin that stood outside the synagogue from 1949 through 1981 (when the text was finally removed), explaining how Jewish victims of the Nazi genocide "had to lose their lives." When you roam around the memorial (a sparse collection of documents and photographs) today, it's frightening to imagine what the onlookers were thinking as they watched the synagogue burn during 1938's pogrom—a moment captured on film.

What Essen's other major sights lack in emotion, they make up for in age and tradition. The **Münster** on Burgplatz was around when it took only three digits to write the year, and the statue in the courtyard of the Virgin Mary, ***Goldene Madonna,*** is the oldest in western Europe. For an industrial town, Essen has a pretty hip troika of museums, as well. The list of 19th- and 20th-century German and French painters represented at the **Museum Folkwang** (Im Museumzentrum, Goethestr. 41, tel. 0201/888484) reads like the starting lineup for the modern-art all-stars. The Museumzentrum's **Fotographische Sammlung** contains 20,000 photographs covering the history and development of artistic, documentary, and journalistic photography. In the town center, the posters in the **Deutsches Plakat Museum** (Rathenaustr. 2, Theaterpassage, tel. 0201/884114) come from all over Europe—Poland to England—and show that even mainstream ads (like circus announcements) can be artistic. For information about other attractions in Essen go to the **tourist office** (tel. 0201/235427) in the Hauptbahnhof near the south entrance.

Fifteen kilometers (9 miles) east of the town of Bochum you'll see cleaner streets, better-dressed students, and fewer drug deals than in Essen (where deals are made in plain sight right across from the Hauptbahnhof). Bochum has two attractions that seem to symbolize the changing economics and identity of the region. The **Deutsches Bergbau Museum** (Am Bergbaumuseum 28, tel. 0234/51881) offers a look into the history of mining and takes visitors down into a working "demonstration pit." With the changes in the Ruhr, however, this hands-on exhibit is more of a memorial to an industry in its death throes. More symbolic, but no less a testament to the struggle between past and present, is the ***Starlight Express*** (tel. 0234/13031). This musical performed on roller skates by singers costumed as trains is a modern tortoise-and-the-hare story featuring the stronger, faster, modern diesel; the ancient coal engine; and everything in between. Throw in a little Romeo-and-Juliet love story between locomotives of different eras, and you've got one of the weirdest stage shows imaginable. You can get tickets at Bochum's **tourist office** (Im Hauptbahnhof, tel. 0234/13031).

Essen and Bochum are easily accessible from Köln and Düsseldorf by trains that run four or five times each hour. The 20-minute ride between the two Ruhrgebiet cities is even more frequent. Essen's tourist office will make room reservations for you, but, if you want a reasonably close, cheap room, call the blandly functional **Hermannseck** (Eltingstr. 30, tel. 0201/314937), which has singles for DM 30 and doubles for DM 60. The same adjectives apply to the **Hotel Nordstern** (Stoppenberger Str. 20, tel. 0201/31721), where rooms go for DM 40–DM 55 (single) and DM 78–DM 81 (double). The hostel closest to Essen is in the neighboring town of Werden. To get there take S6 to Bahnhof Werden, cross the Rhine, and follow signs to the **Jugendherberge** (Pastoratsberg 2, tel. 0201/491163). It's tricky to find, so call 'em if you have trouble.

WUPPERTAL AND SOLINGEN Here's a partial list of analogies that have been used to describe Wuppertal's world-famous (?) suspension railway, the **Schwebebahn**: the slithering gray millipede, the meandering metal dragon, the floating iron snake, the strong city's steel backbone, and the big zipper. Suffice it to say this thing puts the fun back into mass transit. Unfortunately, the thrill of traveling 50 feet above the rambling Wupper River and having to time your disembarkation as the huge suspension cars sway back and forth in the stations is lost on local riders. You can't really blame them, though, since the monorail's been trundling along its 13-kilometer (8-mile) course for more than 80 years and today carries as many as 50,000 commuters each day. For you, though, the levitating petrified worm is a must ride.

Best seats are near the front, where you can pester the driver with questions about safety records and watch the full panorama of the Wupper Valley unfold. Pick up the Schwebebahn at its westernmost terminus, the Hauptbahnhof in Wuppertal, and ride it to Vohwintel (the end of the line). From here, ride Bus 683 all the way to the end, to **Schloß Burg** in Solingen. Cross the street and begin the 300-foot ascent on foot, or ride the **Seilbahn** (chair lift) for DM 3.50 and a nice view. This mighty castle, of the corner-piece-on-a-chess-set variety, was the home of Engelbert, the count of Berg, the archbishop of Köln, the duke of Westphalia—a man with a lot of titles. Unfortunately, power was his game, and he was minced by his cousin at the age of 40, in 1225. His crushed bones rest in Köln's cathedral to this day. His stained, acid-rained likeness, mounted on his similarly stained but trusty steed, stands gallantly before the gates of his former fortress. You can see the castle's old defense system in the huge battery tower, the walkways that line the walls, and the dungeon below.

Once down the hill again, you should check out the **Müngsten Brücke,** a 30-minute walk from the bus stop; just cross the river and turn left on Münstener Straße. Sixteen hundred feet long and 350 feet high (the highest in Europe), this railway bridge looks like the evil older brother of the hapless bridge over the River Kwai. With luck it will reach its centennial in 1997. The Nazis and the Allies wanted the bridge destroyed during World War II. Nazi plans to bomb the bridge were thwarted by business interests in the towns of Solingen and Remscheid on either side of it, and the Allies' plans were thwarted by bad aim. Hundreds of years of daggers and swords pack the **Deutsches Klingen Museum** (Klosterhof 4, tel. 0212/290–59822), appropriately located in central Solingen, a city once renowned for its sword-making prowess. The post–World War I Treaty of Versailles prohibited Germans from making any more weapons, so Solingen simply turned to making world-famous scissors and cutlery.

Wuppertal and Solingen are connected to other towns in the Ruhrgebiet by S-Bahn and to Köln and Düsseldorf by Deutsche Bundesbahn trains, which run three times an hour.

Münster

If you don't get hit by a cyclist, you'll cer-tainly have a close call while walking the winding streets of Münster. Contrary to what you might think, kids, teens, and university students don't corner the market on reckless speeding—your assailant could be a suited businessperson, a 70-year-old, or a nun. The stressful, sometimes hostile encounters on street corners among cyclists, pedestrians, and cars give you an idea of what Münster's residents are like: tense and hyperactive.

Differences of opinion in Münster go beyond questions of who has the right-of-way. As often happens in university cities, the young liberals pit themselves against the middle-aged conservatives. Home to the immense Wilhelms Universität (the third largest in Germany), Münster is teeming with mostly left-leaning students, whose presence and energy pervade protests, rallies, and the mass of bars and cafés in the Kuhviertel (*see* After Dark, *below*). If you don't read German, look for the word *gegen,* featured on most posted announcements; it means "against" and is a crucial part of the Münster student's vocabulary.

Ironically, liberalism runs rampant in a town steeped in tradition and conservatism. In addition to students, the university has brought well-bred, well-educated, neo-aristocratic professors and administrators to Münster. They join with old-guard Münsteren—those who were around to experience the city's massive destruction during World War II and equally massive postwar reconstruction—to give Münster a decidedly conservative element. The combination and clash of very conservative and very liberal does not drown Münsteren in anger and resentment but forces the two sides to acknowledge each other. The nose-ringed, leather-clad student coming out of the **Cuba-Kneipe** (Achtermann Str. 20, tel. 0251/58217) after taking in a film about lesbians, and the suit-and-tie businessman emerging from an old-style café after an espresso and some marzipan cannot ignore each other as they pass. At least not every day.

Although it was almost totally demolished in the war, Münster has recovered quite nicely; you'll find it attractive, walkable, and very well reconstructed. To get a good feel for the city, take a walk from the Hauptbahnhof to the university; in between you'll pass along a series of pedestrian-only streets and bike paths, then through the Altstadt, most of which isn't so old anymore.

BASICS

BUREAUX DE CHANGE **Deutsche Verkehrs Kredit Bank.** The friendly employees help you change money, change traveler's checks, or get a cash advance on your Visa card. *Bahnhofstr. 9, outside Hauptbahnhof, tel. 0251/58068. Open Mon.–Thurs. 8–noon and 12:45–3:45; Fri. 8–noon and 12:45–2:45.*

LAUNDRY **Wasch-Zentrum.** You can get all your wash done for DM 6. *Wolbecker Str. 26, tel. 0251/65092. Turn right on Bahnhofstr., then right on Wolbecker Str. Open Mon.–Sat. 8–8.*

MAIL AND PHONES The post office directly to the left of the Hauptbahnhof has metered phones for direct local calls and outside phones from which you can make collect and credit-card calls. For international calls dial 013–00010 for the AT&T operator. You get your DM .30 back after the call. The area code for Münster is 0251. *Berliner Pl. 37. Open weekdays 8–6, Sat. 8–1, Sun. and holidays 9–10.*

VISITOR INFORMATION The **Stadtwerbung und Touristik** (tourist office) can book rooms, provide maps and English guidebooks, and counsel you on the intricacies of the Münsterland (the farmland around the city). The office is well staffed and seldom overcrowded. *Berliner Pl. 22, across from Hauptbahnhof, tel. 0251/51018. Open weekdays 9–7, Sat. 9–1, Sun. and holidays 10:30–12:30.*

Jugend Information und Beratung. Affectionately known as the "JIB," this youth center is staffed by social workers. Susana and her colleagues will do everything they can to let you know about events, protests, rallies, and concerts in Münster but probably not with the same energy with which they counsel young runaways who seek refuge in this run-down brick building. Don't expect any colorful pamphlets. *Hafenstr. 34, at Von-Steuben-Str., tel. 0251/532760. From Hauptbahnhof turn left on Von-Steuben-Str. Open weekdays 3–6.*

COMING AND GOING

Münster is in northwestern Germany, about 50 kilometers (31 miles) from the border of the Netherlands. Trains run southwest to Köln (every hour), southwest to Düsseldorf, northeast to Bremen (every hour), and northeast to Hannover. The **Münster/Osnabrück airport** serves Berlin, Frankfurt, and Munich daily; London, Sunday through Friday; and Paris on weekdays. Train shuttles run from the airport to Münster's Hauptbahnhof. Münster offers a zillion buses to anywhere in or near the city. The little **bus-information hut** (tel. 0251/694732) in the parking lot in front of the Hauptbahnhof can give you information, but no one speaks English very well. If you're not getting anywhere, go to the main office (Syndikatgasse 9, tel. 0251/694716). Since cycling is the most popular means of travel in Münster, you won't have any problem finding a rental shop. at the "Vermietung" counter across from International Press in the Hauptbahnhof, has lots of rickety bikes that add some excitement to your rides. Make sure the gruff bike renter adjusts the seat for you—otherwise your back will never be the same. Rentals cost DM 6–DM 10, depending on bike speeds, and the counter is open daily 7 AM–10 PM. Remember: Bike bells are not kiddie toys in Münster. Use yours. Also, make sure you ride with traffic, or you could get pulled over by a police officer (this town takes cycling *very* seriously).

WHERE TO SLEEP

Finding a hotel in Münster is easy—there are plenty near the Hauptbahnhof. Finding a cheap one is next to impossible. The **Bockhorn** (Bremer Str. 24, tel. 0251/65510) is the cheapest near the station. It hasn't been redecorated, it seems, since its opening in 1956, but, hey, style is often retroactive. Call ahead to reserve a single for DM 45 or a double for DM 85. Breakfast is included. The other option that won't break you is the **Haus vom Guten Hirten** (Mauritz-Lindeweg 61, tel. 0251/36048), about a 20-minute walk from the train station. Turn right out of the station, right on Wolbecker Straße, left on Hohenzollern-Ring, right on Manfred-von-Richthofen Straße, then left on Andreas-Hofer Straße. The church group that runs the House of the Good Shepherd has kindly put *die Bibel* on every table and a Gothic picture of the Lord on every wall. Makes you think twice before doing anything sinful. Singles cost DM 44 and doubles DM 80. The price includes breakfast.

Camping in the area is possible, but the closest campsites are a half hour away by bus. Let the tourist office call around for you before you venture into the Münsterland.

FOOD

It's possible to go cheap and eat healthy in Münster but not all the time. If it's Wednesday or Saturday, head toward the Domplatz for the **farmer's market.** The produce is fresh, the prices are cheap, and the air reeks of true German cuisine—*Fleisch* (meat). Between Tuesday and Friday the **Mensa** (Bismarckallee 11) at the university offers hearty lunches and vegetarian meals (DM 3–DM 5). **Maac-Bio** (Berliner Pl. 23, tel. 0251/518972), a trendy new health-food chain-to-be, serves buffet-style pastas and salads (DM 6–DM 10) and some great homemade juices. The decorator of **Cadagues** (Ludger Str. 62, tel. 0251/43028) had a somewhat loose grip on the would-be Mediterranean theme, but the cook makes excellent paella (DM 10.50), which is a challenge for one person to finish. They also serve salads and a huge selection of pasta dishes until 1 AM. If you're looking for a mellow outdoor café, try the **Diesel** (Harsewinkelgasse 1–4, tel. 0251/57967), where you can eat, drink, and play pool into the night.

WORTH SEEING

To get an idea of just how long a night it was in the **Altstadt** when the bombs fell on Münster in 1943, check out the sobering photographs in the entryway of the 13th-century **Dom St. Paulus** (St. Paulus Cathedral). Head to the **Friedenssaal** (Prinzipalmarkt, tel. 0251/832580) to see a more peaceful time in Münster's history. Carvings and relics of Westphalia's past are housed here, where the treaty ending the Thirty Years War was signed in 1648. The entrance to and main administrative center of the university is the majestic **Schloß**—far too nice a building for bureaucracy. Behind it lie the **Botanic Gardens,** which have a lot more roses than you could possibly smell.

Don't leave Münster without glancing up at the three cages hanging from the front of **St. Lambert's** church, off the Prinzipalmarkt. In the 16th century the bishop's troops left three Anabaptist protesters in the cages to rot. Whether the bishop saved the town from evil or the troops zealously squelched a peaceful protest depends on who's telling the story. Either way, the three cages are displayed in the **Stadtmuseum** (Salz Str. 28, tel. 0251/492–2945). On a Sunday visit the **Museum of Leprosy** (Kinderhaus 15, tel. 0251/211044). Admission won't cost you an arm and a leg—it's free. Contact the tourist office (*see* Visitor Information in Basics, *above*) for the names and addresses of Münster's other museums.

AFTER DARK

Münster's multifaceted nightlife never wavers. The cafés around the **Kuhviertel** (old student quarter) are always crowded at night. Many bars in the area are expensive, but you can get a good beer in a relaxed atmosphere at **DeStille** (Kuhstr. 10, tel. 0251/43726), surrounded by photos of German and Polish jazz musicians, and listen to some of them play on the stage. **Der Bunte Vogel** (Alter Steinweg 41, tel. 0251/56524) is a different experience altogether. This classy pre-yuppie bar has outside seating until 11 and plays classic American rock at a reasonable noise level. **Gleis 22** (Hafenstr. 34, tel. 0251/532760), a café affiliated with the JIB (*see* Visitor Information in Basics, *above*) and located next door, has pool and Ping-Pong tables and one of the highest tattoo-and-nose-ring ratios per capita west of Berlin. Catch live music Wednesday at 10 (DM 5) and a different vegetarian meal every weekday for lunch (DM 4). For DM 6 you can dance at the **Jovel** (Grevener Str. 91, tel. 0251/201080), where the decor is either very esoteric or very random. Half of a car hangs over one of the bars, palm trees are illuminated by neon lights, and there's a painting of the Statue of Liberty—upside down. If mainstream music isn't your style, go to **Odeon** (Frauenstr. 51, tel. 0251/43447) to hear hard-core indie bands (cover, DM 3). The club, according to the manager, is better during the week than it is on Saturday night, when all the "kiddies" come. To find out everything about nightlife, pick up a copy of *Na Dann*, an alternative magazine passed out in cafés and bars all over town. It comes out Wednesday and is so popular that it's usually gone by Thursday morning.

Bielefeld and the Teutoburger Wald

Bielefeld is the best city to start from if you're exploring the Teutoburger Wald, whose beech and spruce trees cover most of northwestern Germany. There aren't many tall mountains or steep hills in the forest, so hikers, backpackers, and cyclists can get around easily. It's also a piece of cake to get from town to town in the forest, because they're all connected by rail.

Besides the fact that their city is the largest city (population 300,000) at the heart of the Teutoburg Forest, most Bielefeld residents think their hometown is boring. It's not overly political, and it's not inundated with historical architecture. It's solid and clean, and it's got a medium-size university. In other words, Bielefeld is average. But the city's mediocrity provides a good reason to visit: to interact with Germans in a real German city that's not crawling with hordes of tacky tourists. By default, Bielefeld can be a good city for touring.

BASICS

LAUNDRY At **SB Waschsalon,** you can wash a small load for DM 6. Dryers cost DM 1.50 for 20 minutes. *Friedrich Str. and Arndt Str. Open daily 6 AM–11 PM.*

MAIL AND PHONES You can make collect or credit-card calls from the Hauptbahnhof (dial 013–00010 for an AT&T operator) and local calls from the metered phones in the **post office.** *Herforder Str. 14, at Friedrich-Ebert Str. Open weekdays 8:30–6.*

VISITOR INFORMATION The unusually helpful staff at the **tourist office** can book rooms and provide information on all outdoor activities in Bielefeld and the Teutoburg Forest. *Am Bahnhof 6, tel. 0521/178844. From Hauptbahnhof veer right and cross st. Open weekdays 9–5:30, Sat. 9–1.*

COMING AND GOING

Trains from Bielefeld to Hannover (55 kilometers [32 miles] northeast) and to Köln and Düsseldorf (100 kilometers [62 miles] southwest) leave every hour. Bielefeld's limited **subway system** has only two lines but works well when supplemented by the extensive bus system. Get a public-transportation map from the tourist office (*see* Visitor Information in Basics, *above*). The **Mitfahrzentrale** (Siegfried Str. 46, tel. 0521/130088) office can get you a ride to almost any major city in continental Europe if you give the staff a day or two to arrange it. They speak good English, so don't hesitate to leave a message on the answering machine if the office is closed. Prices vary with distance and number of passengers; rides to Berlin and Munich cost about DM 13 and DM 17, respectively. Bielefeld is a manageable city, so you'll be able to see most everything on foot. Simply turn right out of the Hauptbahnhof, and you'll enter the pedestrian zone that cuts through town.

WHERE TO SLEEP AND EAT

The only affordable hotel within walking distance of the Hauptbahnhof is small and characterless, but at DM 32 for a single and DM 65 for a double, who cares? Call the **Hotel Kaiser** (Schildescher Str. 47, tel. 0521/61984) to see if any of their well-kept rooms is available. If you're willing to pay a little more, ask for a hotel list at the tourist office (*see* Visitor Information in Basics, *above*). The front porch of the **Jugendherberge** (Oetzer Weg 25, tel. 0521/22227) overlooks the rolling hills of the Teutoburg Forest. The facility itself is nothing special, but it provides easy access to the Hermannsweg (*see* Outdoor Activities, *below*) and other hiking paths in the vicinity. Two campgrounds are accessible by bus from the Hauptbahnhof: **Campingplatz Quelle** (Vogelweide 9, tel. 0521/450336) and **Campingplatz Schröttinghausen** (Beckendorfstr., tel. 05203/3146). Call before showing up; these places are quite far from town.

Bielefeld's Bahnhof-straße and the other pedestrian streets around it are laden with produce stands, bakeries, and delicatessens. You can pick and choose and put together a big meal for DM 5–DM 10. For the only vegetarian restaurant in town (so boasts the owner), head down August-Bebel Straße to **Zapata** (August-Bebel Str. 16–18, tel. 0521/63816). The burritos (DM 9.50) are unique, and the crowd is earthy. On the hipper side is the **Casablanca** (Karl-Eilers Str. 12, tel. 0521/179702), a café-bar that stays crowded all day and keeps the crepes and salads coming (DM 6–DM 10). You won't lack reading material here; fliers describe concerts and protests around the city, and graffiti in the bathroom claim "Reality Sucks" in at least three languages.

WORTH SEEING

Bielefeld's most exciting sight is the **Sparrenburg** (open Apr.–Oct., daily 10–6), a fortress with a tower that makes you want to run out and play a game of chess. But seriously, if you're in the right mood, the Sparrenburg can be a moving experience. The rickety wood stairs leading to the tower are not as rickety as the *very* rickety metal spiral staircase that takes you to the top. When you get there, stop and take a look. Behind you (to the southwest) is a forest that has stood almost as long as time; under your feet is a structure that defended its inhabitants more than 700 years ago; in front of you are two churches, the **Neustädter Marienkirche** and the **Altstädter Nicolaitkirche,** which have graced Bielefeld since 1400 and 1340; near the city center is the towering central post-office building; and farther still is a modern smokestack. Somehow it all makes you want to join Rodin's *The Thinker,* poised pensively in front of the city's **Kunsthalle** (Arthur-Ladebeck Str. 5, tel. 0521/512479).

OUTDOOR ACTIVITIES

The **Hermannsweg** is a major hiking path that leads from the small town of Rheine, at the northwestern end of the Teutoburg Forest, through Tecklenburg and Bielefeld to Detmold (*see* Near Bielefeld, *below*). It's easy to pick up the trail in Bielefeld since it goes right through the town. For information about Hermannsweg, hiking, and backpacking go to the **Herausgaben von Teutoburger Wald** (August-Bebel Str. 162, tel. 0521/63019), an office with camping and hiking information. Another way to see the town or the forest is by bicycle. The **Flottweg** (Bahnhofstr. 2, tel. 0521/178817) rents bikes for about DM 7 per day and DM 35 per week. You can get maps of bike trails at the **Allgemeiner Deutscher Fahrrad Club** (Bielsteinstr. 34A, tel. 0521/64221). If bikes and hiking boots make you feel restricted, inquire about hot-air ballooning at **Air-Taxi-Service-Bielefeld** (Osningstr. 1, tel. 05204/2042) or gliding at **Betriebsbüro Windelsbleiche** (Am Flugpl. 1, tel. 0521/49051).

Near Bielefeld

DETMOLD Traveling to and within Detmold is a cinch, and staying here is relatively cheap. There are some interesting attractions in and near the city, which might draw packs of tourists someday; but for now the place is quiet and self-contained. At the center of town stands the **Detmolder Residenzschloß** (tel. 05231/22507). Most of the tour guides can muster up enough English to answer your questions; if they can't, refer to the English tour book you get when you pay for admission. Gilded mirrors, ruby lamps, and porcelain figures adorn the lavish *Rot Saal* (Red Hall), and another room contains four centuries' worth of fox-hunting weapons. Even if you're bored with the tour, the oversize wool slippers they make you slip over your shoes so you don't scuff the floor are worth the money. The **Westfälisches Freilicht Museum** (Westphalian Open-Air Museum, tel. 05231/706105), a huge outdoor area with more than 100 preserved buildings, tools, and traditional crafts, some gathered in villages, lets you sample a smattering of the surroundings, kind of like the *Reader's Digest* version of the Westphalian landscape. Spend an hour in the museum and you don't need to travel throughout Westphalia in search of landscape, culture, and history.

➢ **COMING AND GOING** • Train connections to Detmold are through Herford. From Herford trains run to Köln every three hours, to Bielefeld every hour, and to Hannover every hour. Detmold's bus system is simple; all routes start at the Hauptbahnhof. Destination signs are posted, but if you have questions see the jovial, pot-bellied worker at **Bus Verhker Ostwestfalen GmbH** (Geshäfstelle Detmold, Bahnhofstr. 8, tel. 05231/23866), the bus-information booth. He knows every stop, every bus, and every platform.

➢ **WHERE TO SLEEP** • Directly across from the Hauptbahnhof are two cheap, clean hotels. **Hotel Brechmann** (Bahnhofstr. 9, tel. 05231/25655) charges DM 50 for singles and DM 100 for doubles. The price includes a spiffy room with stylized furniture, an in-room shower, and breakfast. About 20 yards away is the **Hotel Meier** (Bahnhofstr. 9A, tel. 05231/33007), which costs less because the showers are in the halls. The rooms are compact but clean, and the breakfast is even a little better than the one served next door. Singles cost DM 35, doubles DM 70. The **Jungegästehaus** (Bahnhofstr. 9A, tel. 05231/33007) is often packed with kids on weekend trips with their classes. Everything is clean and looks newly repaired, but boys will be boys, and boys will miss: Don't be surprised if the bathroom smells. The cost of DM 15.50 includes sheets and breakfast. For camping, check with the **Stadt Verkehrsamt** (Rathaus 1, tel. 05231/977328).

➢ **FOOD** • Cafés in Detmold are quiet but in a laid-back rather than reserved way. **AGWA** (Meier Str. 23, tel. 05321/25361) has a mellow atmosphere and a large selection of beer and wine. Similar in feel but a little bigger and more brightly lighted is the **Café Treibsard** (Lauger Str. 83, tel. 05231/33575).

THE RHINE AND MOSEL VALLEYS 16

By Adam Ruderman

Germany is crisscrossed by mighty rivers—the Elbe, the Danube, the Oder, and the Main, to name a few—but the Rhine is the undisputed king. Often referred to as "Vater Rhein" (Father Rhine) by Germans, the river runs 1,355 kilometers (840 miles) from Switzerland, through Germany, and into Holland. It would take weeks to follow the entire course of the Rhine, and your enjoyment would probably be hit-or-miss—parts of the river are heavily industrial and polluted. This chapter focuses on the most glorious stretch of the river, between Worms and Koblenz, and its beautiful tributary, the Mosel. Together they rank among the country's most popular tourist attractions.

This region has one of the richest histories of any area of Germany. The city of Trier, on the Mosel, was capital of Constantine's Western Empire and boasts some of the finest Roman ruins in Germany. Along with Worms and Mainz (both on the Rhine), Trier was also a major seat of the Holy Roman Empire, a legacy evident in the many elaborate palaces and cathedrals that survive in all three cities.

But for many travelers here, history takes a back seat to sheer romance. The landscape, after all, is stunning: Around every river bend, it seems, a castle hangs over the water, vineyards cling to steep river slopes, and tiny hamlets peddle their fabulous wines. To best appreciate the Rhine, you must take a boat ride, be it a long journey on the KD Rhine Line (free for Eurail- and Deutsche Bundesbahn pass-holders) or a simple ferry crossing from St. Goar to Goarhausen.

The only thing that might turn you off is the sheer scale of the tourism. Too many faux-happy tour guides and self-consciously cute towns threaten to turn a national treasure into a staged event. To avoid the worst, try to visit outside the main summer months, or, if you can't manage that, get your act together before tour buses start disgorging their loads, around midmorning. If you're short of time, it's not worth exploring both the Rhine and Mosel valleys—they both have their share of castles, half-timbered buildings, and vineyards. Choose one and you'll get the gist.

Not surprisingly, lodging along both rivers is very expensive. If you're strapped for moolah, try to get a room in a private home. Although hostels cost about the same amount, a private home will give you a taste of everyday German life. Most small towns have a few residents who rent rooms—check with local tourist offices. If you're looking for cheap hotels, stick to smaller towns, and avoid Trier, Mainz, and Worms.

The Rhine and Mosel Valleys

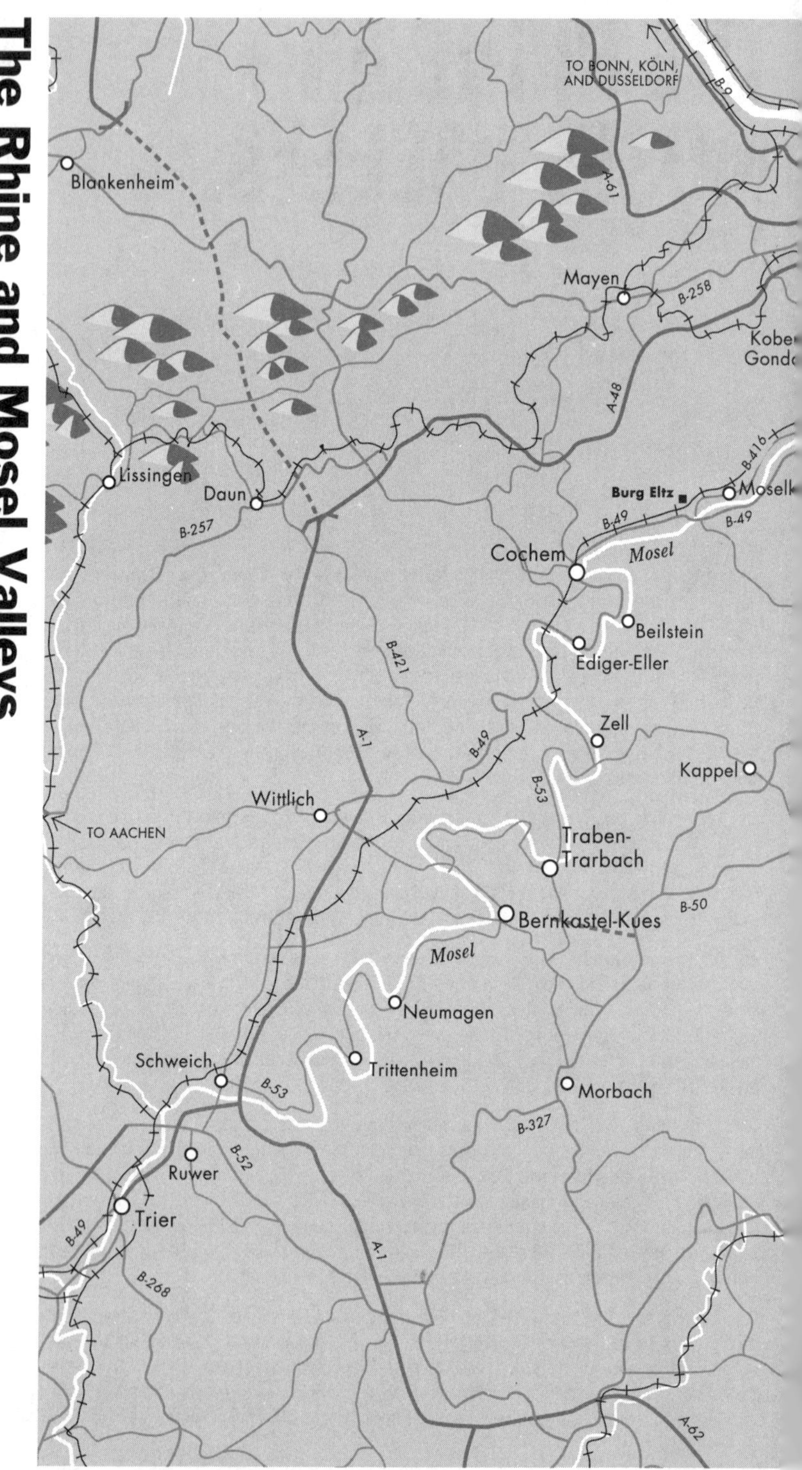

The Rhine and Mosel Valleys

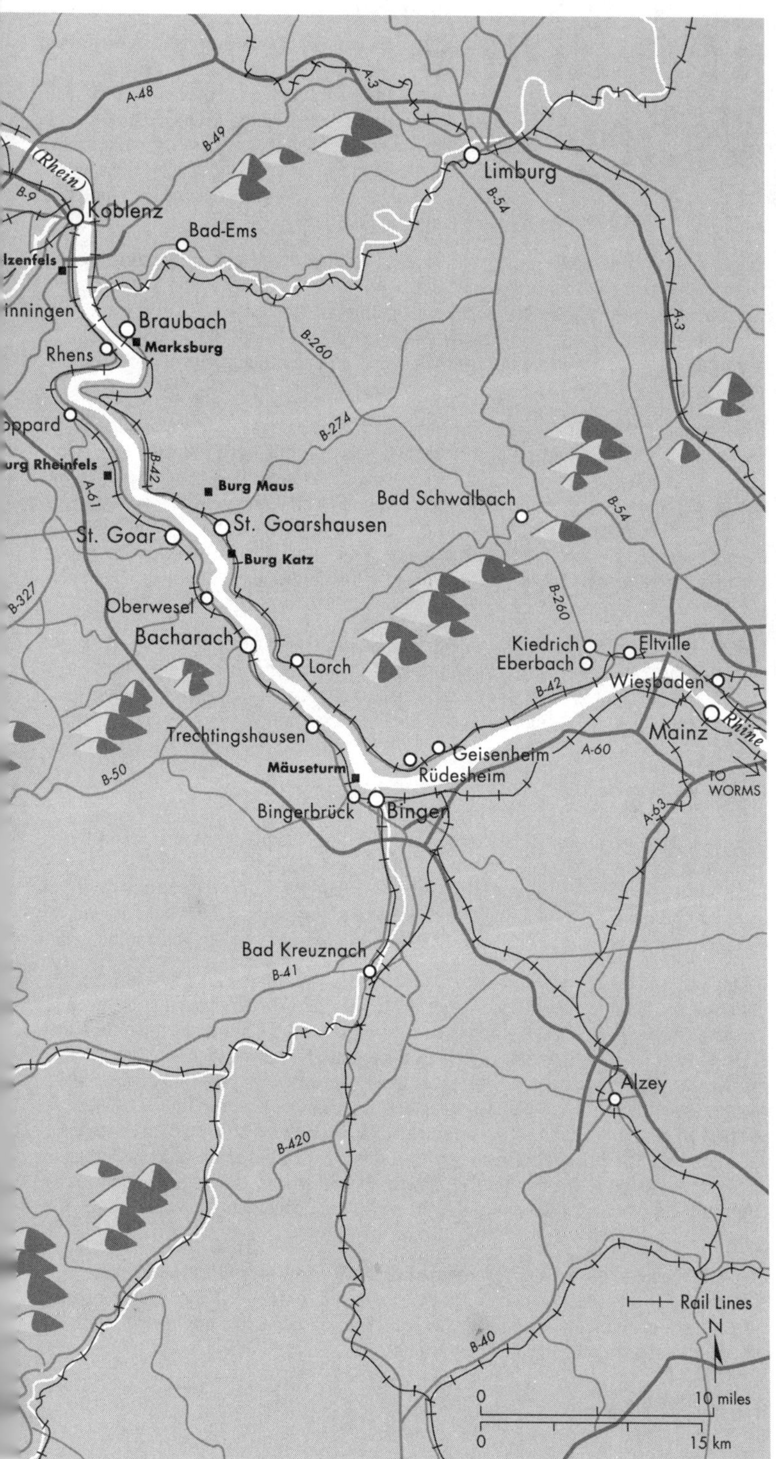

The Rhine Valley

Since the 18th and 19th centuries, when aristocratic Englishmen first sailed the Rhine and romanticized its lush beauty, blush wines, and plush estates, European-culture and history buffs have made pilgrimages here. Nowadays, visitors flock to the winding river on tour boats, following the procession of barges along the Rhine Gorge, the fabulous, castle-laden stretch of river between Mainz and Koblenz.

Before a central authority was established in Germany, unscrupulous robber barons erected castles along this 80-kilometer (50-mile) stretch of the Rhine to extract tolls from passing boats and barges. Frequent fighting erupted between barons, who were all essentially competing for the same blackmail buck. The result is plenty of castles and castle ruins rising above the riverbanks and an entertaining mix of myth, history, and legend.

The highlights of the Rhine Gorge are very much the river, the scenery, and the area's famous wine, but it would be a mistake to bypass the principal cities of the region, especially if you can hack the high cost of lodging. Worms, Mainz, and Koblenz witnessed some of the watershed events in German and European history. It was in Worms in 1521, for example, that Martin Luther outraged the Catholic church with his heretical views on religion, and it was in Mainz that Gutenberg developed his revolutionary printing press. (For information about cities farther upstream, like Mannheim, *see* Chapter 3.)

The danger of a visit to the Rhine Valley is cultural overload. Don't even try to see every castle; that would be like seeing every Catholic church in Germany. In the end you'd be bored shitless and utterly densensitized. Pick a few, enjoy 'em, and don't force it. The Rhine is a region to wander in, not power through.

Worms

Despite being one of Germany's most ancient cities, Worms is overshadowed by its larger, more populous northern neighbors, Mainz and Koblenz. The Dom (cathedral) is large but not quite as large as Mainz's. The Altstadt (Old City) is charming, but not quite as charming as Koblenz's. The surrounding areas along the Rhine are worthwhile, but not quite as interesting as those near Mainz and Koblenz. You get the idea.

Worms was settled by the Romans, but the town's salad days came and went in the 16th century, when it served as a major center for the Holy Roman Empire. In 1521 Emperor Charles V and the Imperial Diet (royal assembly) heard the then-heretical views of Martin Luther here. In trying to reform the Roman Catholic church, Luther sparked the Reformation, which brought about Protestantism. Martin wouldn't heed demands that he renounce his evil ideas and was summarily kicked out of Germany, creating an eternal conflict between Protestantism and Catholicism. Worms was home not only to Christians but also to one of the earliest and largest Jewish communities in Germany. Although the *Judenfriedhof* (Jewish cemetery) and synagogue remain, their caretakers are practically the only Jews left here—the population was wiped out by the Nazis.

Worms probably won't be your favorite part of the Rhine Valley, unless, of course, you lose yourself in the great golden wines that make the town one of the most important wine centers of Germany. The town is a solid starting point, though, and it will help highlight the more glamorous northern region.

Worms

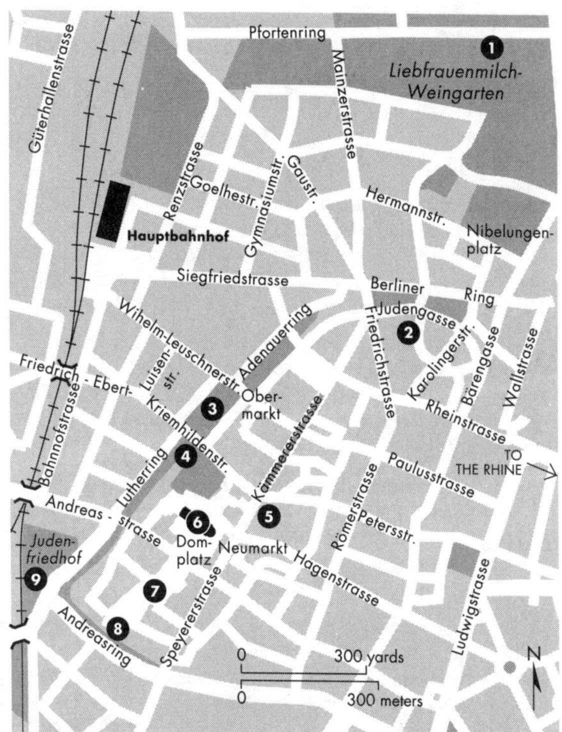

Dom St. Peter, **6**
Dreifaltigkeits-kirche, **5**
Judenfriedhof, **9**
Kunsthaus Heylshof, **4**
Liebfrauenkirche, **1**
Lutherdenkmal, **3**
Magnuskirche, **7**
Museum der Stadt Worms, **8**
Synagogue, **2**

BASICS

➢ **BUREAUX DE CHANGE** • Don't hang around the Hauptbahnhof looking to change money—you'll get much better rates at Neumarkt, near the Dom St. Peter, where you'll find **Wormser Volksbank** (Marktpl. 19, tel. 06241/8410). Here you can change money and get a cash advance on your credit card. After business hours go to the **Dom Hotel** (Obermarkt 10, tel. 06241/6913), whose *Geldwechsel* (exchange office) is open 24 hours. The hotel charges a larger commission (DM 6.50 per DM 50) than the banks do, but that's the price you pay for convenience.

➢ **PHONES AND MAIL** • The **Hauptpost** (main post office) on Ludwigsplatz exchanges money and traveler's checks. You can make local and long-distance calls from the office's metered phones; remember to pay the phone clerk after you finish your call. *Kämmererstr. 44, tel. 06241/850820. From Hauptbahnhof follow Wilhelm-Leuschner-Str., which becomes Hardtgasse; turn left on Kämmererstr. Open Mon.–Wed. and Fri.–Sat. 8–6, Thurs. 8–7:30.*

➢ **VISITOR INFORMATION** • A rotund, jovial Wormser with a unique command of English runs the **Verkehrsverein Worms** (tourist office) on Neumarkt near the Dom. After business hours you can get a city map for DM .50 from the machine in front of the building. *Neumarkt 14, tel. 06241/25045. Open weekdays 9–noon and 2–5, Sat. 9–noon.*

COMING AND GOING Trains run between Mainz and Worms about every half hour, and buses make the 50-kilometer (31-mile) journey every two hours. The train takes 45 minutes, the bus two hours. Trains also connect Mainz to Frankfurt's airport. If you've got wheels you can drive to Worms on the windy but scenic Route 9 along the Rhine. Once you get there, walk. Everything worth seeing is within a 20-minute radius, and the Altstadt is only minutes from the Hauptbahnhof down Wilhelm-Leuschner-

Straße. Wilhelm-Leuschner-Straße (which turns into Hardtgasse and Am Römischen Kaiser) and Kämmererstraße are the major *Fußgängerzonen* (pedestrian zones).

WHERE TO SLEEP You might expect Worms to have really cheap hotels since it isn't a tourist haven. It doesn't. Still, lodging here is cheaper than in Mainz and Koblenz. You'll find 14 hotels within walking distance of the Hauptbahnhof, the most inexpensive of which charge DM 35–DM 50 for singles.

Hotel Boos. A tall glass of cold orange juice in the morning and televisions in all the rooms set this hotel apart from its cheaper neighbors. The carpets are a little worn, but the bathrooms are clean. If you have a travel partner, come here to take advantage of the firm, queen-size beds. Singles are DM 40, doubles DM 80. *Mainzer Str. 5, tel. 06241/4763. 10-min. walk from Hauptbahnhof up Siegfriedstr., turn left on Mainzer Str. 25 rooms. Breakfast included.*

Hotel City. This place is a serious dive, but it's cheap and very close to the Hauptbahnhof. Some guests look as musty and downtrodden as the stairs and rooms. Singles are DM 30, doubles DM 60. *Siegfriedstr. 29, tel. 06241/6284. Less than 50 yds from Hauptbahnhof. 11 rooms. Breakfast included.*

Hotel Hüttl. Although it's nothing spectacular, this place is cheap and centrally located and has lots of rooms. Singles are DM 40, and doubles are DM 62. *Petersstr. 5–7, tel. 06241/87874. From Hauptbahnhof follow Wilhelm-Leuschner-Str., turn right on Kämmererstr., left on Petersstr. 30 rooms. Breakfast included.*

Weinhaus Weis. With its good prices, good location (a 15-minute walk from the Hauptbahnhof), and clean rooms, this hotel is your best budget bet. It does have a few drawbacks, though: It's small, it sells out fast, and the managers have been known to take extended vacations in late July. If you call in summer don't be surprised if the phone just rings and rings. Singles are DM 28, and doubles are DM 45. *Färbergasse 19, tel. 06241/23500. From Hauptbahnhof walk on Wilhelm-Leuschner-Str., which becomes Hardtgasse; turn right on Kämmererstr., left on Petersstr., and left on Färbergasse. 8 rooms. Breakfast included.*

➢ **HOSTEL** • **Jugendherberge Worms.** Sandwiched between tiny Magnuskirche and enormous Dom St. Peter in the middle of town, this hostel shares the pious, dead-quiet atmosphere of its neighbors after hours. It also has a musty, hamster-cage smell, but it's clean, cheap, and rarely full. Beds cost DM 13.50. *Dechaneigasse 1, tel. 06241/25780. 20-min. walk from Hauptbahnhof down Wilhelm-Leuschner-Str., right on Lutherring, left on Andreasstr., right on Dechaneigasse. 138 beds. Breakfast included.*

FOOD Worms is far from being a culinary mecca—you won't even find good German food here. For cheap eats grab a *Döner Kebab* (like a gyro) from one of the Turkish fast-food stands along the pedestrian streets Wilhelm-Leuschner-Straße and Kämmererstraße. If you want a more substantial meal and are sick of pigs and potatoes, try some pasta at **La Carbonara Ristorante** (Adenauerring 4, tel. 06241/28220), where you can sit outdoors on warm days. Choose from a wide selection of pastas and pizzas (DM 7–DM 10); the four-cheese tortellini (DM 9) won't disappoint. Worms makes up for its dearth of good food with some of the best ice cream in Europe. The café **Venezia** (Kämmererstr. and Petersstr.), in the kiosk on Marktplatz, has outstanding lickables, especially the strawberry and the German favorite, *Himbeere* (raspberry).

WORTH SEEING

➢ **CHURCHES** • The 11th-century **Dom St. Peter** is a huge, solid cathedral. Like Köln's Dom (*see* Chapter 15), its exterior is plagued with telltale signs of pollution and acid rain, which give it a burned look. Although it's categorized as Gothic because of its pointed arches inside, the Dom has incorporated some Baroque architecture—specifically the glitzy, gilded columns and gold crowns above the altar. As for the sign at the front door requesting that dogs, chewing gum, and slovenly dress be left outside, disregard it—all the Germans do. Don't miss the grim tombs of religious dudes downstairs, a special treat for DM .20. *Dompl. From Hauptbahnhof walk on Wilhelm-Leuschner-Str., turn right on Lutherring, left on Andreasstr. to Dompl. Open daily 8–5:45.*

Once you've seen the Dom, Worms's other churches pale in comparison, at least architecturally. The **Magnuskirche,** the oldest Protestant church in Germany, lies only a few hundred yards from the Dom but is worlds away in terms of appearance. The church is plain and simple, in line with the Protestant work ethic. The Lutheran **Dreifaltigkeitskirche** (Church of the Holy Trinity) is also modest, but it's a good place to ponder Martin Luther. If you want to honor him or anyone else with a toast, buy a cheap bottle of Liebfraumilch (Blue Nun), once Germany's most renowned export wine, at the vineyard next to the **Liebfrauenkirche** (Church of Our Lady). To get to Liebfrauenkirche from the Hauptbahnhof walk east on Siegfriedstraße, turn left on Mainzer Straße, then right on Pfortenring. It'll take you about 20 minutes.

➢ **JUDENFRIEDHOF** • Stained, dilapidated headstones stand among overgrown vines and weeds at the 900-year-old Jewish cemetery. You might wonder why some of the gravestones stand only inches from one another. That's because the cemetery got so crowded over the years that grave diggers had to stack the coffins on top of one another, but obviously they couldn't do the same with the stones. The Judenfriedhof, surprisingly, escaped the violence of the Nazi era, and looks like it hasn't been disturbed in centuries—unlike the Judengasse (Jewish Lane) and synagogue (*see* Synagogue and Raschihaus, *below*). Andreasring, *10-min. walk from Hauptbahnhof. Walk s. on Bahnhofstr., turn left on Andreasstr. and right on Andreasring.*

➢ **LUTHERDENKMAL** • The Luther monument, built in 1868, features the man himself standing boldly with documents in hand, almost begging you to imagine the courage he showed in front of the Imperial Diet in 1521. Surrounding the monument are fountains, small flower gardens, and statues of some of Luther's friends and supporters who helped bring about the Reformation. Luther's buddies were once victims of the wrath of the Catholics; now their likenesses are victims of pollution and pigeons. *Lutherpl. From Hauptbahnhof walk on Wilhelm-Leuschner-Str. and turn right on Lutherring.*

Religion in Germany Is a Taxing Business

Germany's piety, like that of most other postindustrial nations, has declined since the days when Luther stood before the Imperial Diet, and today only about 30% of Catholics and 10% of Protestants in the country attend church. Despite poor attendance, however, many churches are rich and influential, levying taxes that can eat up 8%–9% of each member's annual income taxes. Although some of the money goes toward convalescent homes, hospitals, and child-care facilities, much of it goes toward new churches and (some say) into the pockets of church officials. Citizens have grumbled about the tax lately, but neither sect will lower it, claiming that to do so would make them as poor as the Catholic church in France. The only way to avoid the tax is to actively break with the church, and this means losing church privileges: no church marriage, no funeral service, no nothin'.

➢ **MUSEUMS** • Martin Luther is honored throughout Worms, but the dry, boring Luther room in the **Museum der Stadt Worms** doesn't do him justice. The museum, in the Romanesque Andreasstift (St. Andrews Church) chronicles Worms's history from Roman times to the present, but it intentionally leaves out the Weimar and Nazi periods. *Weckerlingpl. From Judenfriedhof walk s. on Andreasring, which curves left, to Weckerlingpl. Admission: DM 2, DM 1 students. Open Tues.–Sun. 10–noon, 2–5.*

The only serious art you'll find in Worms is at the **Kunsthaus Heylshof,** in the tiny, manicured **Heylshofgarten.** It was on this site, in the long-destroyed imperial palace, that Luther, after nailing his 95 religious theses to the door of the Castle Church in Wittenburg, declared before the Imperial Diet: "Here I stand. I can do no different. God help me. Amen." The museum houses a dark and dank collection of depressing Gothic and Renaissance art, including Peter Paul Rubens's *Madonna with Child* and a collection of porcelain, ceramics, stained glass, and graphic art. *Im Heylshofgarten, n. of Dom St. Peter. From Hauptbahnhof, walk on Wilhelm-Leuschner-Str., turn right on Lutherring, left on Kriemhildenstr. Admission: DM 2, DM 1 students. Open Tues.–Sat. 10–5.*

➢ **SYNAGOGUE AND RASCHIHAUS** • "Jewish Worms" isn't some Semitic delicacy but the title of the cheesy video shown in German and English at the Raschihaus Museum. The narrator discusses the rise and fall of Worms's Jewish community while twangy harps play in the background. The museum's displays are few, but they manage to convey the dramatic drop in the number of Jews living here. Next to the museum stands the dull but meaningful 11th-century **synagogue,** the oldest in Germany. This poor old building has been clobbered time and again, especially on *Kristallnacht,* in 1938, when German citizens led by the Nazis burned synagogues all over the country. The synagogue's most recent reconstruction, in 1961, incorporated as much of the original material as possible. Running perpendicular to Kämmererstraße and leading up to the synagogue is **Judengasse** (Jewish Lane), which features replicas of the original buildings of the old Jewish quarter. *From Hauptbahnhof walk e. on Siegfriedstr., turn right on Martinspforte and left on Judengasse; synagogue and museum on right. Museum admission: DM 1. Synagogue admission free. Both open Tues.–Sun. 10–noon, 2–5.*

CHEAP THRILLS One of the few out-of-the-ordinary cheap thrills you'll find in Worms is the strange **Backfischfest** (Baked-Fish Festival), held in late August and early September. Locals drink wine, eat baked fish, and even engage in *Fischerstechen* (drunken jousts) by the riverside.

NEAR WORMS

The stretch of the Rhine that flows northward from Worms to Mainz is neither as dirty nor as industrialized as the areas near Düsseldorf, but it's no pristine stream, either. The entire 50 kilometers (31 miles) is fairly dull, save for a few minor attractions.

OPPENHEIM AND NIERSTEIN Wine, wine, and more wine. Oppenheim and Nierstein are two of the most famous wine towns in Germany. Both are small, well preserved, filled with middle-age German tourists, and crammed with wine shops and cafés. Trains from Worms leave every two hours for Oppenheim. Nierstein, 1½ kilometers (1 mile) north of Oppenheim, is always the next stop. You won't find a whole lot to do in these tiny towns except sample the wines (as Charlemagne did), stroll around Oppenheim's old market square, with its half-timbered houses, and climb the tiring staircase to **Katharinenkirche,** where you'll get a view of—you guessed it—vineyards. You can get a map of the town and a hotel list at Oppenheim's tourist-information office (Merianstr. 2, in Rathaus, tel. 06133/2444).

Mainz

Mainz is the business center of Germany's lower Rhine and the capital of Rhineland-Palatinate. Although the city was bombed heavily during the war, the town center has been rebuilt in its old medieval style; it's now a pedestrian shopping zone graced with plazas and fountains. The city's most important role, perhaps, is as gateway to the most spectacular, castle-studded stretch of the Rhine, between Mainz and Koblenz (*see* the Rhine Gorge, *below*). Travelers, politicians, and poets romanticized the Rhine north of Mainz even before Mainz's most famous son, Johannes Gutenberg (1390–1468), invented movable type. Life in Mainz moves as swiftly as the river itself, and to experience it you have to jump in and go with the current. You'll probably wind up at Augustiner Straße at night, along with hordes of college-age locals and tourists. This street, loaded with cafés, bars, and restaurants, is *the* party spot in the city. Coming in second is Schillerplatz, where Mainz's fledgling transient community parties it up on benches around the carnival fountain.

BASICS

➢ **BUREAUX DE CHANGE** • The **Deutsche Verkehrs Bank,** in the Hauptbahnhof information room, exchanges money and traveler's checks. *Im Hauptbahnhof, tel. 06131/238616. Open Mon.–Sat. 7:30–noon and 12:45–6:45, Sun. 9–3:30.*

➢ **PHONES AND MAIL** • The **Hauptpost** performs standard postal services and has a room full of coin-operated, card-operated, and metered phones. To use a metered phone, ask the counter clerk to direct you to one of the numbered booths; pay when you're finished. Make sure you get the city or country code you need before you try your call. You can also exchange money and traveler's checks here. *Bahnhofstr. 2, tel. 06131/01188. Post office open Mon.–Sat. 8–6; money exchange, phones open daily 7 AM–8 PM.*

➢ **VISITOR INFORMATION** • You can't ask for a clearer sign than the one right outside the Hauptbahnhof pointing toward the right and announcing TOURIST INFORMATION in big red and white letters. The staff speaks English and charges DM 5 for hotel reservations. *Bahnhofstr. 15, tel. 06131/286210. Open weekdays 9–6, Sat. 9–1.*

COMING AND GOING

➢ **BY TRAIN** • Mainz is the main town on the Rhine south of Köln. Trains leave hourly for the 1½-hour trip to Köln, twice an hour for Koblenz, and hourly for Worms, 50 kilometers (31 miles) south. Intercity trains make the 20-minute trip to Frankfurt every hour; regular **Deutsche Bundesbahn** (German Railroad) service to Frankfurt takes 45 minutes. The **Hauptbahnhof** (Bahnhofstr.) lies just northwest of the town center.

➢ **BY BUS** • **Europabuses** leave twice daily from Frankfurt's Hauptbahnhof for Mainz (two-hour trip, DM 12); call 069/790–3240 for information. Every few hours regional buses connect Mainz with Koblenz or Worms, but the long and winding ride is sweltering in summer.

➢ **BY BOAT** • As the gateway to the most beautiful part of the Rhine, Mainz is an excellent place to start a boat tour. The **Deutsche Rheinschiffahrt KD** (tel. 0221/208–8318) has 22 ships that sail between Mainz and Köln, and several operators offer short "castle tours." KD boats leave from the docks in front of the Rathaus (Rheinstr.). For more information about Rhine boat trips, *see* the Rhine Gorge, *below.*

GETTING AROUND Mainz's Altstadt, leveled in World War II but later restored, has almost everything a visitor needs—food, wine, and sights. It forms a compact triangle that's easy to explore on foot. **Kaiserstraße,** lined by small manicured parks filled with benches and flowers, runs northeast from the Hauptbahnhof to the Rhine and forms one side of the triangle. **Bahnhofstraße,** which turns into **Schillerstraße,** acts as the second side of the triangle, and the Rhine forms the final side. Within the triangle are pedestrian zones, restored buildings, and a wealth of attractions.

Public transportation in Mainz consists of buses and streetcars. Most lines terminate or make stops at platforms on Bahnhofsplatz, in front of the Hauptbahnhof. Be careful—crossing the plaza outside the station is shockingly treacherous because the pedestrian walkways are hard to find, and the bus and streetcar drivers are aggressive. A streetcar or bus ride within the city center costs DM 2; you can pick up a transit map at the tourist office.

WHERE TO SLEEP Finding a cheap hotel room within walking distance of Mainz's city center is virtually impossible. Even the hotels in the surrounding districts are not cheap enough to be worth the trek. The best option in Mainz is the youth hostel, which is a sad statement. The budget traveler—or even the prudent traveler—will have better luck staying in a private home in Bingen (*see* the Rhine Gorge, *below*), a few kilometers north of Mainz. If you're bent on sleeping in Mainz, try the **Terminus Hotel** (Alicestr. 4, tel. 06131/229876) or **Pfeil Continental** (Bahnhofstr. 15, tel. 06131/232179), which have decent singles without showers for DM 65 and doubles for DM 90–DM 100. Otherwise, check with the tourist office for the hotel list, and brace yourself.

➢ **HOSTEL** • **Jugendgästehaus.** If the light bulbs aren't burned out in the bathrooms, you'll be able to see the swarms of bugs as they dive-bomb you from the ceiling. You can't pick them off with crumpled toilet paper because you probably won't find any; the interesting graffiti on the walls will at least distract you from the insects. It won't, however, be interesting enough to distract you from the urine stench. 'Nuff said? This place is a shit-hole. The curfew is at midnight; stay out as long as possible. Rooms are DM 14–DM 30, depending on their size. *Am Fort Weisenau, tel. 06131/85332. From Bahnhofspl. take Bus 1 toward Laubenheim to Jugendherberge, follow signs to left. 172 beds. Breakfast included.*

➢ **CAMPGROUND** • **Campingplatz Maaraue.** Located on a boring grass splotch on the east bank of the Rhine, the site is plain but adequate. At least you *expect* bugs here. Spots are DM 5.50 per person, DM 4.50 per tent, and DM 4 per car. *Tel. 06134/4383. Bus 13 from Bahnhofspl. to Brückenkopf Kastel (about 25 min.; bus stops running at 11:30 PM on weekends). Reception desk open daily 8:30–1, 3–8:30.*

FOOD Mainzers aren't preoccupied with cuisine. The city has plenty of places to eat but not a lot of distinguished restaurants. If you're under 25 and casually dressed, the staffs at the few fancy establishments may greet you with a sneer if you try to get in without a reservation. For a budget meal, head for the pedestrian streets, where you'll find a variety of decent sit-down restaurants, some with outdoor seating. In particular, try **Augustiner Straße.** For some of the best pizza in Germany, go to **Pepe's** (Augustiner Str. 21, tel. 06131/229986). This place is always packed—and for good reason. You can get anything here, from a cheese pizza to a pizza topped with tuna and egg. The pizza calzone looks like a big, white, semideflated football but is filled with goodies—no air. Pepe's also serves good pastas, but the selection is more limited. If you get the late-night munchies you can grub at Pepe's till 1 AM on Friday and 2 AM on Saturday. The **Markthalle,** a collection of specialty food stands in the cellar of the huge **Kaufhof** department store (Schuster Str. and Stadthaus Str.), is another good budget option. You can eat sitting down, or sample the goods as you walk around. In one pass you can get some bratwurst, a salad, carrot juice, a glass of wine, an espresso, a mussel, a croissant, some jelly bears. . . . You get the point. You can eat and drink a lot for DM 10. If you spend DM 20 you're eating like a horse, so take a rest. The Markthalle shares the Kaufhof's hours: Monday–Wednesday and Friday 9–4:30, Thursday 9–6:30, and Saturday 10–2.

WORTH SEEING

➢ **GUTENBERG MUSEUM** • Mainz's most popular museum, dominated by displays about the town's local hero, has also crowned itself the International Museum of the Art of Printing. The museum is housed in the Renaissance **Haus zum Römischen Kaiser,** which lends itself to the antique feel of the exhibits. Woodcuts, lithographs, early presses, and a fairly tacky replica of the Mainz master's early workshop do their best to glamorize the potentially boring history of publishing. Don't leave without looking at the 550-year-old Gutenberg Bible, the first book printed using movable type. *Liebfrauenpl. 5, in center of Altstadt, tel. 06131/122640. From Hauptbahnhof follow Bahnhofstr. to Schillerstr., turn left on Ludwigsstr., and pass Dom; Liebfrauenpl. is on right. Admission free. Open Tues.–Sat. 10–6, Sun. 10–1.*

➢ **LANDESMUSEUM** • You won't find any live horses in this museum in the former imperial stables, but you will be greeted by a stiff, forever-rearing stallion on the roof. The spacious, no-nonsense Landesmuseum features art and history exhibits that cover centuries but focus on Germany's imperial days. A smattering of Roman ruins is thrown in for good measure, and a small annex holds a new regional modern-art gallery and municipal-history museum. *Große Bleiche 49–51, tel. 06131/232955. From Hauptbahnhof follow Bahnhofstr. and turn left on Große Bleiche. Admission free. Open Tues.–Thurs., weekends 10–5; Fri. 10–4.*

Geniuses always seem to be destitute. By all accounts, Gutenberg's invention of the movable-type printing press should have made him a wealthy man. However, creditors seized his new creation as payment for old debts, and Gutenberg became just another impoverished publishing type.

➢ **MARTINSDOM** • Dominating the Marktplatz in the center of the Altstadt, this mammoth cathedral with six towers looks like it was crunched together by heavenly hands. Amazingly, the Dom has kept its pale rosy color despite the ravages of weather and pollution. Like so many of its siblings, this Dom is something of a bastard, having been built, rebuilt, and altered constantly since construction began in the 10th century. It was supposed to be Romanesque, but Baroque, Gothic, and bombing influences have taken their toll. On sunny days the massive stained-glass windows (not part of the original design) fill the interior with colored light; they didn't survive Allied redecorating but were later reconstructed. The **Dom und Diözesan Museum** (Cathedral and Treasury Museum) houses glitzy ecclesiastical objects and some remnants of the Holy Roman Empire. *Museum: Domstr. 3, off Marktpl., tel. 06131/253344. From Hauptbahnhof follow Bahnhofstr., which becomes Schillerstr., left on Ludwigsstr. Admission free. Cathedral and museum open weekdays 9–6:30, Sat. 9–4, Sun. 1–5.*

➢ **NATURAL HISTORY MUSEUM** • You might find this natural-history museum skanky and dilapidated, especially when you see the stuffed tiger on the stair landing, worn to the skin from being touched too much. On the other hand, the museum's eccentricity is refreshing, and some of the displays are simultaneously fascinating and sickening. You probably never knew beetles and moths could get so big! Every hour the monstrous hourglass out front takes a methodical 180° turn, which fits in well with the slow pace of the museum. *Reichklarastr. 1, at Mitternacht, tel. 06131/122646. From Hauptbahnhof follow Bahnhofstr., turn left on Große Bleiche and right on Mitternacht. Admission free. Open Tues.–Wed., Fri.–Sun. 10–5; Thurs. 10–8.*

➢ **ROMISCH-GERMANISCHES MUSEUM** • This hard-core museum chronicles the history of the region from Roman times. Because it's primarily a research institution, its exhibits are stark and professional: no cutesy captions, no displays you can touch, basically nothing to guide you through what one visitor described as a "spruced-up artifact warehouse with Sani-clean toilets." The curators figure the sheer age of something like an engraved candelabra from 500 BC speaks for itself. Part of the attraction here is the setting; the museum is housed in the regal **Kurfürstliches Schloß,** the former digs of the archbishop. *Große Bleiche, tel. 06131/232231. From Hauptbahnhof follow Schott Str. to Kaiserstr., turn right on Greiffenklaustr. and left on Diether-von-Isenburg-Str. Admission free. Open Tues.–Sun. 10–6.*

➢ **STEPHANSKIRCHE** • In 1973 Father Klaus Meyer asked the famous Jewish surrealist Marc Chagall to design the watery-blue stained-glass windows that dominate the front of this otherwise ordinary church. Chagall juxtaposed select biblical events to show that Jews and Christians should unite and live together in peace. He died in 1988, at the age of 98, shortly before the unveiling. *Stefansstr. From Hauptbahnhof* *follow Bahnhofstr. to Schillerstr., walk through Schillerpl. past carnival fountain, turn right on Gaustr. and left on Stefansberg. Open daily 10–noon, 2–5.*

The Rhine Gorge

Your relatives will look at you funny if you go all the way to Germany and don't visit the Rhine Gorge. It's that big a deal. You already know what it looks like—the gorge's castles, clinging to vine-covered hillsides over the Rhine, have been spattered across every German tourist brochure since Gutenberg cranked up his press. You must also know that every tourist from Passaic to Kathmandu is going to be there right beside you, especially if you go in the peak summer season. Such is life.

The Rhine Gorge stretches 80 kilometers (50 miles) from Mainz to Bonn, but it's at its finest between Bingen, just north of Mainz, and Koblenz, at the confluence of the Rhine and Mosel rivers. With its spectacular castles, hillside wineries, and river scenes, the gorge has enthralled poets, painters, and artists for centuries. Goethe couldn't forget the place; William Turner painted sunsets here; and even the crusty old Baedecker guides got their start here in 1834.

Unless you're prepared to stay in private homes or in hostels (and reserve ahead), try to avoid staying in the towns along the way—hotel prices are high. It's easy enough to come for the day from Frankfurt—it's only a 20-minute train ride from Mainz—and save your money to buy some of the great wines that are made here.

Rail lines run up both sides of the river, but the views from the west side are better. No bridges cross the river between Mainz and Koblenz, but you can always hop on a ferry if you want to visit a town on the other side. Buses also run every few hours between Mainz and Koblenz, but the train is a better bet (cooler, too, in summer). The proper way to see the Rhine Gorge, though, is by boat. It's expensive, but you would be cheating yourself if you didn't take at least a short run on the Rhine. The major operator is the **Köln-Düsseldorfer Deutsche Rheinschiffahrt** (tel. 0221/208–8318), known as the KD Rhine Line. The trip from Mainz to Köln costs DM 143 (one-way); the trip from Mainz to Koblenz costs DM 72.60 (one-way). The best thing about KD service is that you can use your Eurailpass or Deutsche Bundesbahn pass. If you don't have a pass, check out KD's combined river-rail tickets, which allow you to break your river trip at any place the boats stop and continue by train. Pick up a schedule at the tourst office.

Two shipping companies in Koblenz organize short "castle cruises" from Easter through September. Two boats, the *Undine* and the *Marksburg,* ply the Rhine between Koblenz and Boppard, passing 10 castles during the 75-minute, one-way voyage. Contact **Personenschiffahrt Merkelbach** (Emserstr. 87, tel. 0261/76810) or **Personenschiffahrt Wolfgang Vomfell** (Koblenzerstr. 64, tel. 02628/2431). Another Koblenz operator, **Rhein und Moselschiffahrt Gerhard Collee-Holzenbein** (Rheinzollstr. 4, tel. 0261/37744), runs day cruises as far as Rüdesheim.

BINGEN

Bingen and its northern neighbor, Bingerbrück (a 10-minute walk), straddle the **Nahe,** a Rhine tributary that winds westward a few kilometers north of Mainz. If you're exploring Mainz consider making either town your home base; both are close to the city, and rooms are DM 10–DM 15 cheaper here than in Mainz. Trains run between Mainz and Bingen every hour, but the last train returns to Bingen at about 11 PM on Friday and 11:30 PM on Saturday, severely curtailing your social life. The towns share a **tourist-information office** (Rheinkai 21, tel. 06721/184205), about 200 yards upriver from Bingen's Hauptbahnhof. For a DM 2 charge the English-speaking staff can book you a room in a hotel, but you're better off staying in one of the 15 private rooming houses nearby (ask the staff about this option). It'll cost you about DM 25–DM 30 per night, and you'll get to chat it up with the friendly owners.

Make sure you check out **Burg Klopp,** nicknamed "Burg Klopp the Invincible." The castle's owners, the Cathedral Chapter of Mainz, repaired the damage inflicted on the "Invincible" by Louis XIV and his French soldiers way back in 1689, only to destroy the castle themselves in 1875 to prevent its use as an enemy base in later wars. The town bought the castle in 1897, restored it, redug the 172-foot-deep castle well that was first dug in Roman times, and moved the town hall and folk museum into the brick château. Burg Klopp is open to visitors April 1–September 15.

Just north of Bingen is Burg Sooneck, which was the most feared stronghold in the Rhineland in the 12th century, and Burg Reichenstein, a castle that's now a luxury hotel. Follow the path from the hotel through the vineyards to Siebenburgblick (Seven-Castle View), one of the most spectacular vantage points in the Rhineland.

From the shore where the Nahe meets the Rhine at Bingen and Bingerbrück, you can see the **Mäuseturm** (Mice Tower), a 13th-century building on a tiny offshore island. Legend has it that a greedy old bishop constructed the tower to levy taxes against river users. The townspeople hated the place and despised its avaricious caretaker so much that they wouldn't let him come to shore safely. Stuck in his creation, he was devoured by mice. The Mäuseturm is not open to visitors.

Across the river is the incredibly touristy but beautiful town of Rüdesheim, famous for its wines (*see* Chapter 2). A ferry shuttles back and forth between the two towns (DM 650).

BACHARACH

A few kilometers from Bingen, Bacharach is named for the Roman god Bacchus, not because the townspeople hold bacchanalian festivals but because they grow and sell rivers of wine. The small town is wedged between the Rhine and steep, grapevine-covered hills, and the clustered medieval dwellings and cobblestone streets within the 14th-century defensive wall make Bacharach seem even smaller. You'll be amazed that it contains 12 wineries, where you can sample the local blends. Wine-drinking here won't kill your budget, either. You can get a bottle of local vino for as little as DM 6.50 at **Weingut Toni Jost** (Oberstr. 14, tel. 06743/1216). Better yet, hit the **Spar Markt** (Koblenzer Str. 66) for a bottle as cheap as DM 3. For a list of wineries, head to the **tourist-information office** (Oberstr. 1, in the Rathaus, tel. 06743/1297) near the Hauptbahnhof. The staff can also set you up with a room (tourist offices must book rooms in private homes for you) for as little as DM 25 (DM 45 for a double).

When you've had enough wine, walk over to the **Burg Stahleck.** Since 1925 the former 12th-century fortress has served as a youth hostel. Surely the most bitchin' hostel in Germany, the **Jugendburg Stahleck** (tel. 06743/1266) provides a perfect combo; you can experience German history and crash in a clean place at the same time. Although the hike up there is a pain (from the Hauptbahnhof turn right on Mainzer Straße, then left on Blücherstraße, and follow signs marked BURG CASTLE, then climb the steep stair-switchbacks), the view and majestic setting are worthwhile, especially if you take some of Bacharach's finest vintage along for the hike.

The town of **Oberwesel** lies 8 kilometers (5 miles) north of Bacharach. Sixteen of the original 21 medieval towers that lined the town walls still stand. Towering above the town are the remains of the 1,000-year-old **Burg Schönburg,** which was destroyed by French troops in 1689.

ST. GOARSHAUSEN AND ST. GOAR

St. Goarshausen and St. Goar, a little more than halfway between Mainz and Koblenz, sit on opposite sides of the Rhine. The character of the river changes here, as it narrows, deepens, and quickens around treacherous rock outcroppings. One of the most famous Rhine legends concerns the craggy **Loreleiberg,** commonly known as the Lorelei, which towers over a bend in the river a few kilometers south of St. Goarshausen. Legend has it that a beautiful maiden (or a spirit, or a group of maidens, depending on who's spinning the tale) sat upon the Lorelei rock entrancing sailors with her killer golden locks, looks, and voice. When the breeze wafted her sweet melodies toward passing sailors they would immediately take leave of their senses and their helms and dash their ships against the treacherous rocks. You can climb up to the Lorelei for a great view of the surroundings, and if you take a ride on one of the touristy ferries you'll hear the Lorelei song—a Heinrich Heine poem set to music.

To get to the top of the Lorelei from St. Goarshausen's Hauptbahnhof, walk south on Rheinstraße for about 3 kilometers (2 miles), then climb the steep staircase. On the way, check out the **Lorelei statue,** a seductively posed iron woman sitting on a rock near the shore. Stop by the **Verkehrsamt,** the tourist office (Bahnhofstr. 8, tel. 06771/427), near the Hauptbahnhof, to find out more about the Lorelei and to pick up the all-important, blue *Stadtplan* (city map). The map lists the town's hotels and shows the routes to the Loreleiberg and **Jugendherberge St. Goarshausen** (Auf der Lorelei, tel. 06771/2619), your basic youth hostel with beds for DM 15. You can make your own hotel reservations or let the lady at the tourist office make them for you for free. The cheapest rooms run about DM 25 per person.

You'll notice two castles on either side of St. Goarshausen, on the same bank of the Rhine. Slightly upstream (to the south) is **Burg Katz,** built in 1371 by Count Wilhelm II von Katzenelnbogen, whose name means "cats' elbow." The competition for Rhine tolls and duties was so intense between Wilhelm II and his rival in the castle to the north, that the downstream neighbor was dubbed **Burg Maus** (Mouse Castle). Neither castle is open to the public, but you can get a good look at Burg Katz during the tiring ascent to the Loreleiberg. On the grounds of Burg Maus is the **Adler und Falkenhof** (a kind of bird zoo, tel. 06771/7669), with eagles and falcons galore, some of which take to the air daily at 11, 2:30, and 4:30. To get to Burg Maus, turn right outside the Hauptbahnhof, then right on Nastätterstraße for about 350 yards, and climb the path to the left.

Ferries (DM 2.50 round-trip) for St. Goar leave from in front of St. Goarhausen's tourist office. Unfortunately, St. Goar is a kitschy tourist town. It's lost much of the excitement and all of the danger that came with its centuries of military involvement. The **Stiftskirche** (Collegiate Church) was the site of a legendary shot by a marksman named Kretsch, who pegged a French general and demoralized his shipbound troops, ending their siege during the Thirty Years War. The **Rhein in Flammen** (Rhine in Flames) fireworks festival, on the third Saturday every September, has nothing to do with military history but simply celebrates life on the Rhine in the two towns.

Before you leave St. Goar, hike up to the ruins of **Burg Rheinfels,** yet another medieval castle, a few kilometers north of town. The hike is nice, especially if you're staying just below the castle at the adequate hostel **Jugendherberge St. Goar** (Bismarckweg 17, tel. 06741/388), which offers serene Rhine views for DM 16 per night. Trains run through St. Goar from Mainz and Koblenz and through St. Goarshausen from Koblenz and Wiesbaden (*see* Chapter 2).

BRAUBACH

Braubach is home to **Marksburg,** the last castle along the river as you travel north from Mainz to Koblenz. Classic in its impenetrable defensive position and layout, it's the only fortress on the Rhine that has remained untouched—no one ever blew it up, ripped it down, or captured it. It's even got some quirky legends (*see box*).

The castle tour is in German, but you can read along with the free English leaflet and ask the guide questions if you catch him or her between stops. If you think life is cruel today, take a look at the brattice, a wide chute from which the castle's defenders poured hot tar and oil on attackers; an armory showing the development of weapons between 600 BC and AD 1500; and, grimmest of all, a stable full of torture devices. They wouldn't have to change a thing to film a new version of Robin Hood at this place. To reach Braubach, take the Wiesbaden–Koblenz rail line or any train on the Rhine's east bank. Once in Braubach, exit the Hauptbahnhof on the *Stadt* (city) side, turn right, and pick up the green-and-yellow tram MARKSBURG EXPRESS (DM 5 round-trip) across from the Post, in front of the Rhine-Klause restaurant. If you'd rather walk, exit the Hauptbahnhof and continue straight up the hill; follow signs for the 40-minute ascent to Marksburg. Tours leave every hour and cost DM 5.50 (DM 4.50 for students).

Koblenz

You can learn a lot about Koblenz from the Schängelbrunnen (Scalawag Fountain), a basic bronze fountain with a statue of a young boy. Every three minutes or so the young hooligan spits water on the path in front of him and whoever happens to be on it. Then he's quiet again. Koblenz locals, especially those in their twenties, are like the young rascal. Usually they're mellow, but occasionally they let their darker sides show—as they drink and litter cavalierly, as they ride their loud motorcycles, sporting ripped jeans and ponytails. Koblenz isn't crowded, but its location, at the confluence of the Rhine and its most important tributary, the Mosel, means that endless processions of boats and barges plug along beneath the city's bridges. When the Romans founded this town, in AD 9, they named it *Castrum ad Confluentes* (Camp at the Confluences). The name evolved to *Koblenz,* and the town became powerful because of its strategic location. The Allies were well aware of this and promptly pulverized 85% of Koblenz in World War II. Most of the city has been carefully restored and is best explored slowly on foot. Koblenz has plenty to see, but you'll miss some of the best parts if you nose-dive into a map-driven tour. Worse yet, you might get spat on.

The Jealous Husband

Marksburg was once ruled by Ludwig the Cruel, lord of Braubach. Ludwig was harshly abusive to his beautiful but tragically stupid wife, Maria. Maria was smart enough to know she deserved better, though, and began a liaison with Henry, one of her evil husband's stewards, but she accidentally sent one of her illicit love letters to Ludwig instead of Henry. Whoops. Ludwig the Cruel promptly threw his wife, Henry, the maid who acted as courier, and a few bystanders off the 500-foot cliff on which the fortress stands. When he cooled down, Ludwig felt such remorse that he later opened a nunnery and honored his wife by naming it after her.

Koblenz

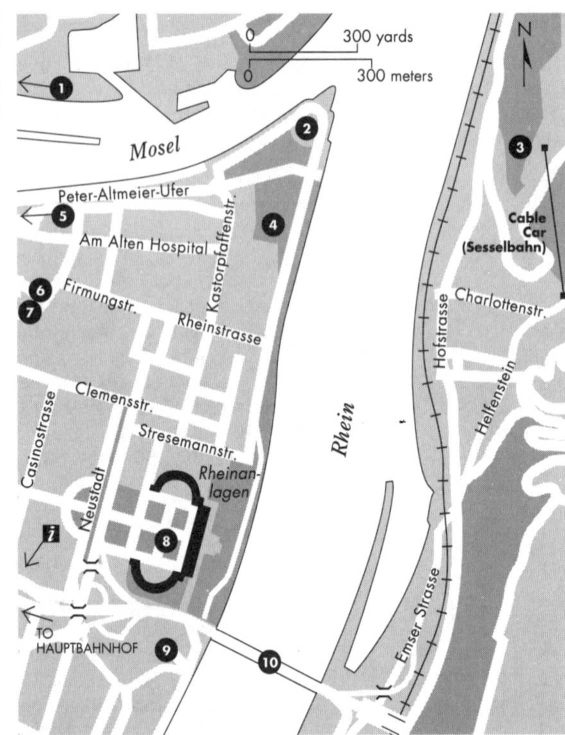

Deutches Eck, **2**
Festung Ehrenbreitstein, **3**
Liebfrauenkirche, **6**
Mittelrhein Museum, **5**
Pfaffendorfer Brücke, **10**
Residenzschloß, **8**
St. Kastor Kirche, **4**
Schängelbrunnen, **7**
Wehrtechnische Studiensammlung, **1**
Weindorf, **9**

BASICS

➢ **PHONES AND MAIL** • The **Hauptpost** (main post office) is not only the best place to go for the usual mail errands and phone calls but also for **exchanging money** or traveler's checks. Rows of coin- and card-operated and metered phones are at your beck and call. *Postamt Koblenz, tel. 0261/1280. Near Hauptbahnhof. Open weekdays 8–6, Sat. 8–noon.*

➢ **VISITOR INFORMATION** • The **Koblenz Verkehrsamt** (tourist office) is across the street from the Hauptbahnhof. The office provides hotel listings, makes reservations, recommends restaurants, and distributes and explains boat schedules and city maps—all in decent English. *Postfach 2080, tel. 0261/31304. Open Mon.–Sat. 8:30 AM–8:15 PM, Sun. 2–7.*

COMING AND GOING Trains are the best way to get here. Trains run twice hourly to Koblenz from both Köln (one hour) and Mainz (one hour). Hourly trains also arrive from Trier. Buses run between Koblenz and Mainz; they're fine for short trips among neighboring towns, but stick with trains when going the full distance, especially when it's hot. Koblenz is a good walking town. From the Hauptbahnhof, as you face the plaza, the Rhine is six blocks in front of you (although you can't see it yet) and the Mosel is on your left (you can't see that, either). Everything worth seeing lies within the area between the station and the two rivers, unless you find German suburbia particularly fascinating. You may need to take a few bus rides, but finding your way around is a piece of cake, since the Busbahnhof, a series of open-air platforms, is across the street from the Hauptbahnhof, and the tourist office is nearby. Taking a bus will cost you the standard DM 2.

WHERE TO SLEEP Koblenz's location makes it a convenient place to spend the night, but it's pricey and not terribly exciting. The smaller cities on the Rhine between here and Mainz are easier on your wallet.

Gasthaus Christ. If you stay in Koblenz, do your best to get a room here. The rooms are large for the price, and the two sisters who run the hotel are ultra-nice. You might even feel guilty paying so little (doubles DM 60, singles DM 30), considering the service, cleanliness, and family atmosphere. Prices go down for stays of more than three nights. Breakfast is included in the price; if you want an egg, ask. Call ahead; this place may close. *Schützenstr. 32, tel. 0261/37702. 10-min. walk from Hauptbahnhof; turn right in front of Hauptbahnhof onto Chlodwigstr., turn right under train tracks and left on Schützenstr. 10 rooms, none with bath.*

Hotel Jan van Werth. It doesn't have half the homeyness or class of Gasthaus Christ, but it has the all-important advantage of incredible convenience—a five-minute walk from the train station. Singles are DM 35, doubles DM 70. Breakfast is included in the price. *Van Werth Str. 9, tel. 0261/36500. Turn left on Bahnhofstr., then right on Van Werth Str.; hotel is 1 block after Rizzastr. 17 rooms, none with bath.*

➢ **HOSTEL** • **Jugendherberge.** The youth hostel is in a shockingly prime location, in the castle across the Rhine. Beds cost DM 15.50 for those under 27, DM 20.50 if you're over 26. *Im Festung, tel. 0261/73737. Take ferry (DM 2.40 round-trip) from docks on Rhine (at Rheinstr.) to bottom of hill, then take Sesselbahn (chair lift) or make 25-min. climb.*

FOOD It's difficult to tell where the **beer garden** (Königin-Augustus-Anlage 20, tel. 0261/33147) in and around Rheinanlagen, a promenade by the river, begins and ends, due to the many beer trailers that stretch out on either side. Outside, the huge elevated patio is cluttered with cheap plastic tables and a fountain that looks like a surrealist baseball. The 50 yards between the beer garden and its restaurant are taken up by picnic tables, a trailer of Königsbacher Pils, and a sprawling array of shoddily dressed, bottle-guzzling street rats. Bikes and motorcycles line the path as the Rhine flows calmly alongside, yet this is a mellow environment for a mellow evening. Liter beers are only DM 4, so take your shoes off and join the sprawlers on the grass. Sauerbraten (DM 19.50) is a Rhenish delicacy worth the splurge. The restaurant serves cheaper meals, too—mostly meaty stuff. Walk from the Hauptbahnhof straight down

Baby-Doomers

If you're at the Rheinanlagen (see Food, above) having a beer and chilling with Koblenz's youth, take a good look—this is the future of Germany. You'd never know it here, but since 1974 western Germany has had the lowest birthrate in the world; for every seven people who died, six were born. The rate of 1.3 children per marriage is much lower than the 2.2 necessary to sustain the region's present population of 80 million. Theories on the baby deficit are endless and complex. Many attribute it to culture-wide skepticism among today's youth, triggered by economic hardship and some dark chapters in recent German history. Although maternity-leave laws are generous in Germany, there are no laws that insure against housing discrimination, and those with children often lose out. Other reasons are floated, from a so-called selfish preoccupation with material goods, to the legalization of abortion in 1974. Perhaps the darkest theory is that many Germans simply don't like kids. Whatever the cause, the German government remains concerned. In 1984 Bonn began an incentive program appealing to German patriotism. Have more kids, they pleaded, at least 200,000 more a year, but so far the birthrate remains flat.

Johannes-Müller-Straße (or any other street) till you hit the Rhine, and turn left; or start at the Deutsches Eck (*see* Worth Seeing, *below*) and walk along the Rhine.

WORTH SEEING The **Deutsches Eck** (corner of Germany) is a pointed, cobbled protrusion that juts into the water where the Mosel joins the Rhine. In 1897 a 46-foot-tall equestrian statue of Kaiser Wilhelm I, the first emperor of the newly united Germany, was erected on the Deutsches Eck, but only the sturdy base remained after the statue was bombed in World War II. Replacing it is the **monument to German unity,** a big podium with nothing on it. The Deutsches Eck is a great place to begin a Mosel or Rhine stroll. Behind the monument is **St. Kastor Kirche,** a drab Romanesque church built in 836 that's been remodeled more times than the White House. In 843 the Treaty of Verdun was signed here, officially making France and Germany separate entities. The two countries met again on this spot in 1812, when Napoleon constructed the **St. Kastor Fountain** outside the church in honor of what he was sure would be a victorious Russian campaign. He was wrong, and soon the Russians kicked him all the way across Europe. When his Russian enemies got to Koblenz, they ironically inscribed words meaning "seen and approved" in the base of the fountain—an amazing show of humor during wartime.

You can't miss the huge castle **Festung Ehrenbreitstein,** with its 390-foot-high tower, as you glance across the Rhine from the Deutsches Eck. A frequent ferry carries you (DM 2.40 round-trip) from the docks (at the corner of Rheinstraße) to the base of the Festung. From here, take the Sesselbahn or make the 25-minute climb. Another option is Bus 9 to Ehrenbreitstein from the Busbahnhof, behind the tourist office. From the top it's clear why the rulers of Trier built a fortress here in the 16th century; with such a commanding view of the Rhine and Mosel, any ruler could rule with a firm hand. Indeed the fortress withstood multiple sieges by the French between 1794 and 1799 and fell only when the people were starved out and the walls blown away by 30,000 tons of dynamite. In 1817 the castle finally found peace in the hands of Prussia and was rebuilt. New to the fortress are several museums, including the interesting **Staatliche Sammlung Technischer Kulturdenkmäler Museum** that houses, among other cultural trinkets, the rickety Vogel Greif cannon the French stole in 1794. The cannon switched hands two more times before President Mitterand returned it graciously in 1984. Also in the fortress are the **Rheinmuseum** of Rhineland history and the **Museum für Vorgeschichte und Volkskunde** (Museum of Prehistory and Ethnography). *Fortress and museums admission free. Open Easter–Oct., daily 9–5.*

The **Mittelrhein Museum,** housed in a carefully reconstructed house on the Mosel, may put you to sleep, but it's free. Dropped in among the collection of German art and antiques is a string of paintings by German Baroque artist Januarius Zick. *Florinsmarkt 15–17. Open Tues.–Sun. 10–4:30.*

The **Wehrtechnische Studiensammlung** houses a collection of military equipment including small arms, mortars, clothing, and panzers (tanks). Erwin Rommel, the World War II field marshal and tank commander, would be proud of this place. Take Bus 5 across the Europabrücke and get off at Mayener Straße, or trek 30 minutes over the Mosel. *Mayener Str. 85–87, tel. 0261/400799.*

Spending a few hours walking around the **Altstadt** is definitely worthwhile in Koblenz. Down near the Rhine, under the **Pfaffendorfer Brücke** (bridge), is the **Weindorf,** a self-contained "wine village," one of the city's major tourist attractions. Across the bridge, toward the Deutsches Eck, is the **Residenzschloß,** built in 1786, once the palace of the prince elector (a sort of noble) and today home to the city government. Continue downstream (northward) to the Deutsches Eck (*see above*) and follow the Mosel to the Mittelrhein Museum (*see above*), then turn left and head into the cramped shopping-and-eating streets surrounding the **Liebfrauenkirche** (Church of Our Lady) and **Marktplatz.** Particularly old and picture-worthy are the tiny Gemüsegasse (Vegetable Lane), Mehlgasse, and Florinspfeffengasse, all running parallel to one another between

Liebfrauenkircheplatz and the Mosel. Next to the church is the **Schängelbrunnen** fountain (*see above*).

OUTDOOR ACTIVITIES No trip to this region is complete without a stroll along the Rhine and Mosel. If you don't want to walk the full 10-kilometer (6-mile) path stretching south from the Deutsches Eck, the short journey (15 minutes by foot) from the **Pfaffendorfer Brücke** to the Eck will do. Bring a bottle of wine and sit on a bench. If you want to bike (or spend a whole weekend biking along the Rhine), go to the **Pro Ju** (Hohenzollern Str. 127, tel. 0261/911–6015) rental shop, where you can get high-quality sport bikes for DM 15 a day, DM 28 for a weekend. Biking to another town and catching the train back with the bike is *kein Problem* (no problem).

The Mosel Valley

The Rhine's most famous tributary has its source in the Vosges Mountains of France, but more than half of its 545 kilometers (338 miles) run through Germany before it meets the Rhine at Koblenz. Like its sister river, the Mosel is lined with castles, fortresses, and vineyards and is rich in legend. Perhaps the biggest difference between the two river valleys is that the Mosel has no cities larger than tiny Trier, with a population of about 100,000. Because the Mosel's hamlets are so small, the huge numbers of tourists are that much more noticeable. They're everywhere. Most of the towns, as a result, are littered with trinket shops peddling kitsch and tawdry drinking souvenirs. Many are overpriced, too.

In the Mosel Valley, buses are probably a better bet than trains. Although trains run between Trier and Koblenz at least twice hourly (DM 23 one-way), you won't see much from the windows—the line keeps cutting inland from the river. Express service between Trier and Koblenz takes only 90 minutes, but you have to take local trains if you want to get off at smaller towns like Cochem and Kobern-Gondorf. Traveling by bus is very slow—the road consists of sharp bends and switchbacks—but the views are great. If you have a Eurailpass or a Deutsche Bundesbahn pass, the train-bus argument is moot—you can take a **Köln-Düsseldorfer Deutsche Rheinschiffahrt** (tel. 0221/208–8288) ferry between Koblenz and Cochem for free. **Mosel-Personenschiffahrt Bernkastel-Kues** (Goldbachstr. 52, Bernkastel-Kues, tel. 06531/8222) is one of many other companies offering sailings on the Rhine.

For about DM 10 a day (or half that with a train ticket or rail pass), you can rent a bike at a train station and cruise over the bike lanes lining most stretches of the Mosel on a barely adequate one-speed clunker. Send your luggage ahead, take your bike with you on the train for part of the journey, and return the bike at any train station—no backtracking necessary. Consult any tourist office for the lowdown. Rental shops charge more and don't offer the same convenience, although their bikes are usually of better quality.

Burg Eltz

The Mosel's banks, like the Rhine's, are lined with castles. But no castle on either river has the grandeur of this monstrous château. Eltz is to castles what the Eiffel is to towers and what Fenway is to ballparks. The castle has sat undisturbed on a crag above the tiny town of Moselkern for 800 years. The arduous 3-kilometer (2-mile) trek up to the fortress from the train station at Moselkern takes you through a forest. The setting is remote, serene, and evocative of the past. If you don't want to walk, take one of the **Moselland-Busreisen Knieper** (Endertstr. 30, tel. 02671/40812) buses that run Thursday and Saturday at 9 AM from Cochem to the castle for DM 13. The bus back leaves when the castle closes. The castle is open for tours and inspection of old weapons April–October, daily 8:30–5:30. Admission is DM 6.50 (DM 4.50 for students).

Cochem

You have to sidestep the caravan of black-windowed tour buses parked along the river to get a glimpse of the Mosel once you leave the train, and the Mosel's not even the main attraction here. Cochem is known for its wine and for the **Reichsburg,** a 1,000-year-old castle on a vineyard-covered hill above the town. As you dodge countless middle-age German tourists, you can almost see Louis XIV's French hordes scrambling up the windy paths to capture the castle in 1689. Luckily for Cochem, a Berlin merchant bought the place in 1868 and compulsively fixed it up. Now the city is in charge of the castle's keep, and they're doing a fine job; all they need to do is throw some arrows around and film *Henry V* here. The tour of the interior is worthwhile and the wood furnishings are as delicate as the torture devices are gruesome. The Nazis ravaged half the castle's rooms and sold off the goods, but enough remains to keep the place interesting. The castle is easy to find but a pain to get to—especially on a blistering-hot midsummer day. From the Hauptbahnhof, walk south along the river on the Moselpromenade and turn right on Schloßstraße. *Tour cost: DM 4, DM 3.50 students. Open daily 9–5; tours leave hourly.*

VISITOR INFORMATION Although it's packed with people, the **tourist office** can be a big help, once you get to the front of the line. When you're within shouting distance, you can holler for a map and book a room without paying a service charge. *Am Endertpl., tel. 02671/3971. From Hauptbahnhof turn right at Rhine and right onto Endertpl., before 1st bridge. Open June–Oct., weekdays 9–1 and 2–5, Sat. 10–3; Nov.–May, weekdays 9–1, 2–5.*

WHERE TO SLEEP Cochem is a good town to crash in because it has an abundance of private rooms that the tourist office will book without a service charge. You can usually find single rooms for DM 30–DM 40, although double rooms are a better bargain at DM 45–DM 55. Most hotels are clean and easily accessible, but prices tend to be randomly set; call ahead to reserve the cheapest. The **Hotel Alte Thorscheake** (Brückenstr. 3, tel. 02671/7059) offers single rooms for DM 28 and doubles for DM 55, but those sell out fast. **Hotel Zum Landskuecht** (Moselpromenade 28, tel. 02671/7030) is on the river and offers more rooms at similar prices. If these are filled, cross the Moselbrücke (the bridge south of the Hauptbahnhof) to the east bank, where the hotels are just as cheap and often less full. If you're willing to walk 20–30 minutes call **Hotel Gute Quelle** (Talstr. 6, tel. 02671/7485, singles DM 28–DM 32, doubles DM 56–DM 80) or **Haus Sonnschein** (Uferstr. and Kerwerstr., tel. 02671/7134, singles DM 30–DM 35, doubles DM 60–DM 100).

Traben-Trarbach

About midway between Trier and Koblenz on the Mosel is Traben-Trarbach. The towns of Traben and Trarbach are on opposite sides of the river, and telling them apart is not easy. Even the ruins perched above them don't help you distinguish which one is which. As with so many fortresses close to the river, only about half of the original walls of **Schloß Grevenburg,** on the west bank above Trarbach is still standing. However, this Schloß seems to have fared better over the years than **Mont Royal,** its bigger neighbor across the river. The two castles competed for river taxes centuries ago. Mont Royal, a massive fortress built in 1687 by Louis XIV of France, served as the base from which his forces slaughtered the people of Cochem (*see above*), who still hold a faint grudge against the French. A bridge with a twin-towered guardhouse at the south end called the **Brückentor** connects the two towns. The half-timbered houses of Trarbach are the subject of many postcards and seem slightly crooked during the momentous **Weinfest** in the second weekend of July, a must-see, must-fest event.

VISITOR INORMATION The **Verkehrsamt** (tourist office) provides lodging listings and a useful map of area highlights. *Bahnhofstr. 22, 3 blocks from Hauptbahnhof, tel. 06541/9011. Open weekdays 8–noon, 2–5; Sat. 10–noon.*

WHERE TO SLEEP The **Jugendherberge** (Am Letzten Hirtenpfad, tel. 06541/9278), on the same side of the river as the train station (a 15-minute walk), offers beds for DM 20.20, including breakfast. The **Gasthaus Germania** (Kirchstr. 101, tel. 06541/9398) charges DM 25 per person. You can camp at **Rißbacher Straße 165** (tel. 06541/6352) for DM 5 per head.

Bernkastel-Kues

About 27 kilometers (16 miles) south of Traben-Trarbach is Bernkastel-Kues. It doesn't look very different from other Mosel towns, but it's a true find, in that its remote location allows you to avoid brushing sweaty shoulders with too many visitors. Bernkastel-Kues is on one side of a large "U" in the Mosel, and Traben-Trarbach is on the other. It's a relatively long trip between towns by boat or car, but a footpath allows you to cut across the peninsula in an hour. On the north bank is Bernkastel, centered around the **Marktplatz.** No matter how many cobblestone market squares you've seen, this one should still evoke some feeling. A closer look at the buildings, many more than 400 years old, reveals intricate carvings that provide a glimpse into the aesthetics of Germany's pre-imperial past. **Michaelsbrunnen** (Michael's Fountain) in the town square used to spout wine on special occasions, but you'll have to use your imagination now, even if you arrive during the **Weinfest** (most towns have one), in the first week of September. It's a 20-minute ascent to **Burg Landshut,** an evil-looking castle that has loomed over the town since the 13th century. The castle has seen better times, like when the archbishops of Trier hung out here in summer, before a fire destroyed it in 1693. Today flowers grow among its ruins (visit anytime), and a café serves overpriced food. The view from the castle, however, is probably as majestic as it was 500 years ago. One redeeming quality of the castle's café is that it serves Bernkasteler Doktor, the town's famous brand of wine. This potent drink reputedly saved the life of one of Trier's prince-bishops when all medicinal remedies had flopped. Across the river in **Kues,** the outshined half of the duo, lies the town's other attraction, the **St. Nikolaus Hospital** (Cusanusstr. 2). Also known as the Cusanusstift, this home for the aged and downtrodden owes its beginnings to Cardinal Nikolaus Cusanus. This German humanist also oversaw the decoration of the elaborate chapel on the grounds. Cusanus even had the foresight to install in front of the hospital a vineyard that still thrives; you can taste free samples of its wine daily at 3. In the area around the hospital you'll find the largest collection of Gothic buildings on the Mosel, including a few ornate mansions and the **Moselweinmuseum,** which honors the region's sweet fluids; you can honor them yourself at any market or café.

VISITOR INFORMATION The **tourist office** distributes maps and locates rooms for free. *Am Gestude 5, across from Zentral Omnibus and docks, tel. 06531/4023. Open weekdays 8–noon, 2–5.*

WHERE TO SLEEP Situated on top of a hill above Burg Landshut, the **Jugendherberge** (Jugendherbergstr. 1, tel. 06531/2395) provides beds for kiddies and the poverty-stricken for DM 16.50. Or try **Pension Esslinger** in Bernkastel (Kirchhof 8, tel. 06531/6617), for DM 22 per person. Camp at **Campingplatz Kueser Werth** (Am Hafen 2, tel. 06531/8200) for DM 6.

Trier

At the **Hauptmarkt** in Trier stands a red house bearing the inscription ANTE ROMAM TREVERIS STETIT ANNIS MILLE TRECENTIS PERSTET ET AETERNA PACE FRUATUR, which means "Trier existed 1,300 years before Rome. May it continue to exist and to enjoy an eter-

Trier

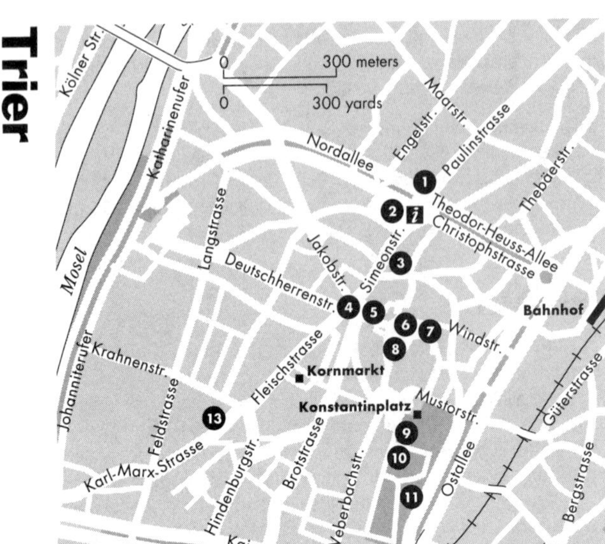

Bischöfliches Museum, **7**
Dom, **6**
Dreikönigshaus, **3**
Hauptmarkt, **4**
Kaiserthermen, **12**
Karl-Marx-Haus, **13**
Kurfürstliches Palais, **10**
Liebfrauenkirche, **8**
Petrusbrunnen, **5**
Porta Nigra, **1**
Rheinisches Landesmuseum, **11**
Römische Palastaula, **9**
Städtisches Museum Simeonstift, **2**

nal peace." Well, the peace hasn't been eternal, considering the destruction heaped on the city at the end of both world wars. Bombs fell and enemies focused on Trier in 1916 and 1943 for the same reason that a visionary Celtic prince named Trebeta established a settlement here in 2000 BC and named it Treberis, after himself—its strategic location. In the 1st century BC, Julius Caesar's troops came through town and began the transformation of Trier into Roma Secunda, a second Rome north of the Alps. Many Roman all-stars, including Augustus and Claudius, hung out in Trier, but it was during the early 4th century, when Constantine lived here, that the town experienced its greatest fame, serving as capital of the western empire. Such an honor brought civic adornments to Trier, including baths, palaces, barracks, an amphitheater, and plenty of churches. After Rome fell, Trier was able to change with the times, prospering as a center for Christianity and as a trade center through the Renaissance and Baroque periods; in the last century it has concentrated on pleasing tourists. Now the town seems like a theme park of Roman architecture and culture because its relics are close enough together that you can see them all easily on foot. At the tourist office (*see* Visitor Information, *below*) you can get a ticket good at all of the Roman sights for DM 6, a significant discount. The tourist office also leads two-hour bus tours in English (DM 12) that leave the Porta Nigra at 10:30 and 2:30 daily and walking tours (DM 6) that leave the Porta Nigra daily at 2; both are conducted May–October.

The logical first stop in Trier is the **Porta Nigra** (Black Gate), which formed part of the mighty 2nd-century Roman city wall that encircled the city. The four towers attest to the prominence of the gate as a defensive centerpiece. For extra strength, couplings made of iron and lead, not mortar, join the huge stones. If you look closely at the seams of the blocks, you'll notice many scars from pillaging Franks who scraped them for precious metals. The gate's name comes from centuries of soot that have turned it dark gray (maybe it'll be black in a few more centuries). *In front of tourist office, 10-min. walk down Theodor-Heuss-Allee from Hauptbahnhof. Admission: DM 2, DM 1* *students. Open Jan.–Mar., Tues.–Sun. 9–1 and 2–5; Apr.–Oct., daily 9–1 and 2–5; Nov. and Dec., daily 10–4.*

Next to the Porta stands the Romanesque Simeonskirche, which now houses the **Städtisches Museum Simeonstift,** named after a Greek from Syracuse who locked himself in the Porta to protect it from pillagers. Philistines will find the art pretty dull, but there are a few gems. *Admission: DM 2, DM 1 students. Open Tues.–Fri. 9–5, Sat. 9:30–3:30.*

Walk a few hundred yards through the arches and down Simeonstraße to the **Hauptmarkt** (main market). Most of the buildings surrounding the square have stood for hundreds of years. If you continue through the Hauptmarkt, you'll notice two pedestrian zones: One trails diagonally to the left down Brotstraße, the other to the right down Fleischstraße. Since 1595 the angelic **Petrusbrunnen** (St. Peter's Fountain) has stood at the southeast corner of the square. One of Trier's famous Renaissance architects, Ruprecht Hoffman, designed it with four allegorical statues of the main virtues: *Justitia* (justice), *Fortitudo* (fortitude), *Temperentia* (temperance), and *Prudentia* (prudence). The inscription on the pedestal reads: "Out of these virtues pour continuously, like the water from its source, salvation for the people and all good things for the city." On your way down Simeonstraße to the Hauptmarkt, check out the **Dreikönigshaus** (House of the Three Magi), named by a pious owner. You'll notice that the front door is on the second floor. People have speculated that the owner was so disliked that he would pull his entrance ladder up whenever angry citizens gathered.

If you turn left down Stirnstraße from the Hauptmarkt you'll head toward Trier's beautiful, marble-adorned **Dom** (cathedral). Its airiness and natural illumination are a happy alternative to the usual gloom and stale stench of most other old churches. Constantine began construction in AD 326, at about the same time as St. Peter's in Rome and the Church of the Holy Sepulcher in Jerusalem were built. Since then the Dom has picked up odds and ends from just about every era. Behind its front altar you can peek through locked doors at the eerily encased **Tunica Christ** (Holy Robe of Christ), supposedly the garment worn by Him at His trial by Pontius Pilate. Legend has it that Helen of Constantine brought the robe to Trier. It is so highly valued and delicate that Dom bigwigs bring it out for public display only every 30 years. Next viewing: 2019. Other, less sacred religious artifacts are housed in the Dom's **Schatzkammer** (treasury). *Admission: DM 1. Cathedral open Apr.–Oct., daily 6–6; Nov.–Mar., 6–noon and 2–5:30. Treasury open Mon.–Sat. 10–noon and 2–5, Sun. 2–5.*

Although the people of Köln would say otherwise, Trier's cathedral is the most magnificent in Germany.

Stop by the Dom's next-door neighbor, **Liebfrauenkirche** (Church of Our Lady), one of the oldest purely Gothic churches in Germany. It won't blow you away, and it'll make the Dom seem even more impressive. Behind the cathedral is the dull **Bischöfliches Museum** (Windstr. 6–8), which houses artifacts unearthed during excavations around the museum. Its main claim to fame is a 4th-century ceiling mural said to have adorned the emperor Constantine's palace. *Museum open Mon.–Sat. 9–1 and 2–5, Sun. 1–5.*

South of the Dom, down Konstantinstraße, is the **Römische Palastaula** (Roman Basilica), built by Constantine in about AD 300 as an imperial throne room and now enjoying a reincarnation as Trier's major Protestant church. At 293 feet long, 93 feet wide, and 108 feet high, it resembles a warehouse more than a place of worship, but if you squint you can envision the splendid decoration Constantine must have heaped around his throne.

Next door and seemingly attached to the basilica is the **Kurfürstliches Palais,** former residence of the archbishop electors of Trier that now houses bureaucrats. Paths lead through the regal **Palastgarten** (Palace Garden) to the **Rheinisches Landesmuseum** (Rhineland Archaeological Museum) on the eastern edge. The museum houses the largest collection of Roman antiquities in Germany, including hundreds of podiums, busts, and stone reliefs. Don't miss the Egyptian casket and mummy. *Museum: Ostallee 44. Admission free. Open Mon. 10–4, Tues.–Fri. 9:30–4, Sat. 9:30–1, Sun. 9–1.*

From the museum, follow the garden paths to the **Kaiserthermen** (Imperial Baths), once the Roman Empire's third largest and probably as big as three football fields. *Open Jan.–Mar. and Nov., Tues.–Sun. 9–1, 2–5; Apr.–Sept., daily 9–1, 2–6; Oct., daily 9–1, 2–5.*

The decidedly un-Roman **Karl Marx Haus,** devoted to the famous native son, is on Karl-Marx-Straße. Born here in 1818, Marx is commemorated by one of the most dull, drab, and unimaginative museums imaginable, basically a set of big, empty rooms with cryptic documentation on the walls. You'd have to be a serious Marx fan to get a kick out of this. *Admission: DM 2, DM 1 students. Open Apr.–Oct., Tues.–Sun. 10–6, Mon. 1–6; Nov.–Mar., Tues.–Sun. 10–1 and 3–6, Mon. 3–6.*

VISITOR INFORMATION Some of the harried staff at the **tourist office** seem unhappy, but don't let them put you off. They offer maps, lodging listings, and English-speaking tours (DM 7). *Porta Nigra, tel. 0651/48071. Open Apr.–Oct., Mon.–Sat. 9–6:45, Sun. 9–3:30; Nov.–Mar., Mon.–Sat. 9–6, Sun. 9–1.*

WHERE TO SLEEP Although Trier is a big tourist town, it usually attracts only those with money. The best budget accommodation is the **Jugendhotel Kolpinghaus und Hotel Kolpinghaus** (Dietrichstr. 42, tel. 0651/75131), a hotel-hostel around a tiny plaza one block from the Hauptmarkt. The hotel offers singles and doubles for about DM 25 per person; the hostel has mostly four-bed rooms for about DM 17 per bed per night. Often the hostel is so empty you can get your own room by asking the friendly staff not to book anyone else in your room if possible. Neither place has showers in the rooms, and the only difference between them is that the hotel is as clean as a new hospital and the hostel is as clean as an old hospital. Nine blocks from the Hauptmarkt, down Brotstraße, is the decent, clean, relatively inexpensive **Hotel Saarbrücker Hof** (Saarstr. 45, tel. 0651/75161), where you can get a single for DM 35 or a double for DM 60. The equally plain **Hotel in der Olk** (In der Olk 33, tel. 0651/41227) has the same prices and the same indifferent decor as does Saarbrücker but is a little closer to the Hauptmarkt.

Trier's **Jugendherberge** burdens you with all the basic hostel inconveniences like a midnight curfew and a 9:30 AM–1 PM lockout, but it's adequate and is without the sterile feel of many of its hostel brethren. Prices per night are DM 15.50 for those under 27, DM 18.50 for those 27 and over. *Maarstr. 156, tel. 0651/29292. 30-min. walk from Hauptbahnhof down Theodor-Heuss-Allee, right on Paulihustr., then left on Maarstr. Wheelchair access. Breakfast included.*

German Glossary

German is not an easy language. We are, after all, talking about a language that declines the definite article and forms megacompounds that can take days to decipher. To make things even tougher, German is extremely guttural—Germans all sound as if they have a throat disease or a nasty postnasal drip. Nevertheless, you should try to master at least a few phrases. You may never need them—many Germans speak English—but it's arrogant to *expect* them to switch to English for you. Below are a few phrases and words to help you out. In addition, consider buying some basic language tapes and/or phrase books before you go. Living Language™ cassettes, CDs, phrase books, and dictionaries make it easy to learn the essentials. If you can't find them at your local bookstore, call 800/733–3000.

English	*German*	*Pronunciation*
Basics		
Yes/no	Ja/nein	yah/nine
Please	Bitte	**bit**-uh
Thank you (very much)	Danke (vielen dank)	**dahn**-kuh (**fee**-lun dahnk)
Excuse me.	Entshuldigen Sie.	ent-**shool**-de-gen-zee
I'm sorry.	Es tut mir leid.	es toot meer lite
Good day	Guten Tag	**goo**-ten tahk
Mr./Mrs.	Herr/Frau	hair/frow
Pleased to meet you.	Sehr erfreut.	zair air-**froit**
How are you?	Wie geht es Ihnen?	vee **gate** es **ee**-nen
Very well, thanks.	Sehr gut, danke.	zair goot **dahn**-kuh
And you?	Und Ihnen?	oont **ee**-nen
Do you speak English?	Sprechen Sie Englisch?	**shprek**-hun zee **eng**-lish?
I don't speak German.	Ich spreche kein Deutsch.	ikh **shprek**-uh kine doych
Please speak slowly.	Bitte sprechen Sie langsam.	**bit**-uh **shprek**-en zee **lahng**-zahm
I am American/British.	Ich bin Amerikaner(in)/ Engläder(in).	ikh bin a-mer-i-**kahn**-er(in)/**eng**-glahn-der(in)
My name is . . .	Ich heiße . . .	ikh **hi**-suh
Where are the rest rooms?	Wo ist die Toilette?	vo ist dee twah-**let**-uh
Left/right	Links/rechts	links/rekhts
Open/closed	Offen/geschlossen	**o**-fen/geh-**shloss**-en
Where is . . .	Wo ist . . .	**vo** ist
the train station?	der Bahnhof?	dare **bahn**-hof
the bus stop?	die Busthaltestelle?	dee **booss**-hahlt-uh-**shtel**-uh
the subway?	die U-Bahn-Station?	dee **oo**-bahn-**staht**-sion
the airport?	der Flugplatz?	dare **floog**-plahts
the post office?	die Post?	dee **pohst**
the bank?	die Bank?	dee **bahnk**
I'd like to have . . .	Ich hätte gerne . . .	ikh **het**-uh-gairn
How much is it?	Wieviel kostet das?	**vee**-feel **cost**-et dahs
I need . . .	Ich brauch . . .	ikh **brow**-khuh

Numbers

One	Eins	eints
Two	Zwei	tsvai
Three	Drei	dry
Four	Vier	fear
Five	Fünf	fumph
Six	Sechs	zex
Seven	Sieben	**zee**-ben
Eight	Acht	ahkt
Nine	Neun	noyn
Ten	Zehn	tzane

Days of the Week

Sunday	Sonntag	**zon**-tahk
Monday	Montag	**mon**-tahk
Tuesday	Dienstag	**deens**-tahk
Wednesday	Mittwoch	**mitt**-vokh
Thursday	Donnerstag	**don**-ners-tahk
Friday	Freitag	**fry**-tahk
Saturday	Samstag	**zahm**-stahk

Where to Sleep

Youth hostel	Jugendherberge	**you**-gint-**hair**-bear-geh
A room	ein Zimmer	ein **tsim**-er
The key	den Schlüssel	den **shluh**-sul
A bed	ein Bett	ine bet
With/without	Mit/ohne	mit/**own**-ah
Bath	Bad	baht
Breakfast	Frühstück	**froys**-took

Food

A bottle of . . .	eine Flasche . . .	i-nuh **flash**-uh
A cup of . . .	eine Tasse . . .	i-nuh **tahs**-uh
A glass of . . .	eine Glas . . .	i-nuh glahss
Bill/check	die Rechnung	dee **rekh**-nung
I'd like to order . . .	Ich möchte bestellen . . .	ikh **mugh**-te-buh-shtel-en
I am a vegetarian.	Ich bin Vegetarier.	ikh bin ve-guh-**tah**-re-er
The menu	die Speisekarte	dee **spy**-zeh-car-tuh
Bread	Brot	broht
Rolls	Brötchen	**broht**-shen
Milk	Milch	mill-gh
Eggs	Eier	**a**-yer
Ham	Schinken	**shin**-kin
Veal	Kalb	cahlp
Lamb	Lamm	lahm
Beef	Rind(er)	**rint**-(er)
Pork	Schwein(e)	shvine
Fish	Fisch	fish
Cheese	Käse	**kay**-zuh
Onions	Zwiebeln	**tzvee**-bulln
Potato(es)	Kartoffel(n)	cart-**off**-ell(n)
Apple	Apfel	**ahp**-full

Index

Notes

Notes

Notes

Notes

Reader's Survey

Your Name ______________________________
Address ______________________________
______________________________ Zip ______________

Where did you buy this book? City ______________ State ______________

How long before your trip did you buy this book? ______________

Which Berkeley guide(s) did you buy? ______________

Which other guides, if any, did you purchase for this trip? ______________

Which other guidebooks, if any, have you used before? (Please circle)
Fodor's Let's Go Real Guide Frommer's Birnbaum Lonely Planet
Other ______________________________

Why did you choose Berkeley? (Please circle as many as apply)
Budget Information More maps Emphasis on outdoors/off-the-beaten-track
Design Attitude Other ______________________________
____

If you're employed, occupation? ______________

If you're a student: Name of school ______________ City & State ______________

Age ______________ Male ______________ Female ______________

What magazines or newspapers do you read regularly? ______________
____

How many weeks was your trip? (Please circle) 1 2 3 4 5 6 7 8 More than 8 weeks

After you arrived on your trip, how did you get around? (Please circle one or more)
Rental car Personal car Plane Bus Train Hiking Biking Hitching
Other ______________________________

When did you travel? ______________________________
Month(s)

Where did you travel? ______________________________
____

Did you have a planned itinerary? Yes ______________ No ______________

The features/sections I used most were (Please circle as many as apply):
Basics Where to Sleep Food Coming and Going Worth Seeing Other

The information was (circle one):
Usually accurate Sometimes accurate Seldom accurate

I would ____ would not ____ buy another Berkeley guide.

These books are brand new and we'd really appreciate some feedback on how to improve them. Please also tell us about your latest find, a new scam, a budget deal, whatever—we want to hear about it.

For your comments:

____

____

Send complete questionnaire to The Berkeley Guides, 505 Eshleman Hall, University of California, Berkeley, CA 94720.

COMPLETE OFFICIAL RULES

THE BERKELEY GUIDES

"You Can't See the Forest If There Aren't Any Trees" Contest

"YOU CAN'T SEE THE FOREST IF THERE AREN'T ANY TREES"

Win a Grand Prize trip for two to the rainforest...

or a Berkeley "You Can't See the Forest If There Aren't Any Trees" T-shirt... and help the environment at the same time!

HOW TO ENTER:

First, think of an idea that will help the Rainforest Action Network promote rainforest awareness and activism. Then present your idea in the medium of your choice, e.g., artwork, fund-raising plans, slogans, an essay, or music.

Complete the official entry form found on the opposite page or hand print your name, complete address, and telephone number on a piece of paper and securely attach it to your entry. Mail your entry to: The Berkeley Guides Rainforest Contest, PMI Station, Box 3532, Southbury, CT 06488-3532 U.S.A. You may enter as often as you wish, but each entry should be different. Entries must be received by January 15, 1995.

Your ideas will judged by the Rainforest Action Network and a panel of independent judges on the basis of originality and relevance to the mission of the Rainforest Action Network. Our Grand Prize Winners will receive a fabulous trip for two featuring a guided tour of the rainforest, and First Prize winners will receive a hip Berkeley T-Shirt with a recycling message.

PRIZES: Two (2) Grand Prizes, a trip for two to a rainforest, will be awarded – one to the highest-scoring entry from the United States and Canada and one to the highest-scoring entry from the United Kingdom and the Republic of Ireland. Each Grand Prize consists of round-trip coach air travel from the major commercial airport closest to the winner's residence; double-room accommodations for 9 days/8 nights; guided tours of several rainforests and national parks; ground transportation; and $500 spending money. The value of the trip will be determined by the winner's geographic location and seasonal rates but is approximately $8,000. All other expenses are the winner's responsibility. Winners must give 45 days advance notice of travel plans, and trips must be completed by February 15, 1996. Travel and accommodations are subject to availability and certain restrictions. Valid passport and visa required.

Five hundred (500) First Prizes: A Berkeley "You Can't See the Forest If There Aren't Any Trees" T-shirt. Approximate retail value: $20. (250) T-shirts will be awarded to entrants from the United States and Canada and (250) T-shirts will be awarded to entrants from the United Kingdom and the Republic of Ireland.

This promotion is open to legal residents of the United States, Canada (except Quebec), the United Kingdom, and the Republic of Ireland who are 18 years of age or older. Employees of Random House, Inc.; the Rainforest Action Network; their subsidiaries, agencies, affiliates, participating retailers and distributors, and members of their families living in the same household are not eligible to enter. Void where prohibited.

Winners will be selected from the highest-scoring entries. In the event of a tie, the winner will be determined by the highest originality score. Winners will be notified by mail on or about February 15, 1995.

JUDGING: Entries from the United States and Canada will be judged separately from those received from the United Kingdom and the Republic of Ireland. In each contest, entries will be judged equally on the basis of originality, relevance to the mission of the Rainforest Action Network, presentation of the idea, and clarity of expression. Judging will be conducted jointly by a panel of independent judges and members of the Rainforest Action Network under the supervision of Promotion Mechanics, Inc.

GENERAL: Taxes on prizes are the sole responsibility of winners. By participating, entrants agree to these rules and to the decisions of the judges, which are final in all respects. Entries become the property of the sponsors, and entrant grants to sponsors all rights of ownership, reproduction, and use for any purpose whatsoever. Further, each winner agrees to the use of his/her name and/or photograph for advertising and publicity purposes without additional compensation (except where prohibited by law). No correspondence about entries will be entered into, nor will entries be acknowledged or returned. Sponsors are not responsible for late, lost, incomplete, or misdirected entries. Grand Prize winners will be required to execute an affidavit of eligibility and liability/publicity release which must be returned within 14 days, or an alternate winner may be selected. Travel companions must be timely in executing the liability release. No prize transfer or substitution except by sponsors due to unavailabilty. One prize per person.

WINNERS LIST: For a list of winners, send a self-addressed, stamped envelope to be received by February 15, 1995, to: The Berkeley Guides Rainforest Winners, PMI Station, Box 750, Southbury, CT 06488-0750, U.S.A.

Random House, Inc., 201 East 50th St., New York, NY 10022

Securely attach this Offical Entry Form to your entry and mail to:
Berkeley Rainforest Contest/ PMI Station/ Box 3532/ Southbury, CT/ 06488-3532/ U.S.A.

Name ____________________

Address ____________________

____

Country ____________________

Telephone ____________________

I bought this Berkeley Guide at the following store:

____

Youth, a soft seat and 50,000 lbs. of thrust.

Call us the new kids on the tarmac. We're BALAIR, a Swiss airline with a brand new fleet of jets.

And each week we crisscross the Atlantic, connecting the U.S. with Zurich, one of Europe's most central gateways.

We offer Swiss service along with something that might be new to you. It's called "Relax Class". It's our version of business class, yet it costs less than many airlines' coach fares.

For more information call us at:
1-800-322 5247

Switzerland's more colorful airline.

Balair